Contemporary Writers Series

D1271738

CONTEMPORARY
SOUTHERN
WRITERS

CONTEMPORARY SOUTHERN WRITERS

GUEST FOREWORD BY
THOMAS M. CARLSON

EDITOR
ROGER MATUZ

St. James Press

AN IMPRINT OF GALE

DETROIT • LONDON

Roger Matuz, *Editor*

Margaret Mazurkiewicz, *Project Coordinator*

Laura Standley Berger, Joann Cerrito, David Collins, Nicolet V. Elert,
Miranda H. Ferrara, Kristin Hart, Michael J. Tyrkus, *Contributing Editors*
Peter M. Gareffa, *Managing Editor, St. James Press*

Mary Beth Trimper, *Production Director*
Deborah Milliken, *Production Assistant*
Cynthia Baldwin, *Art Director*
Pamela A. E. Galbreath, *Senior Art Director*

The paper used in this publication meets the minimum
requirements of American National Standard for Information Sciences—
Permanence Paper for Printed Library Materials, ANSI Z39.48-1984.

This book is printed on recycled paper that meets Environmental Protection Agency Standards.

R
810.9
975
Cont

Contemporary Southern Writers / guest foreword by Thomas M. Carlson : editor, Roger Matuz.
    p.   cm.
    Includes bibliographical references and index.
    ISBN 1-55862-370-1 (alk. paper)
    1. American literature--Southern States--Bio-bibliography--Dictionaries.   2. American literature--20th century--Bio-bibliography--Dictionaries.   3. Authors, American--Southern States--Biography--Dictionaries. 4. Authors, American--20th century--Biography--Dictionaries. 5. American literature--Southern States--Dictionaries. 6. American literature--20th century--Dictionaries. 7. Southern States--In literature--Bibliography. I. Matuz, Roger.
PS261.C569   1998
810.9'975'03--dc21
[B]
                                                                                                        98-35875
                                                                                                        CIP

Printed in the United States of America
Published simultaneously in the United Kingdom

St. James Press is an imprint of Gale

10 9 8 7 6 5 4 3 2 1

CONTENTS

GUEST FOREWORD

Early in this century the Baltimore writer H. L. Mencken dismissed the South as a cultural wasteland, "the Sahara of the Bozart," to which the Nashville Agrarian, Andrew Lytle, responded: "this is like the thief who robs the house the second time and complains that the owners do not eat with silver." Lytle was referring to the destruction of the Civil War and the debilitating effects of radical reconstruction in the South, both vividly described to him by a grandmother who as a child in 1863 was shot by a Yankee sniper and wore a black scarf around her neck the rest of her life to cover the wound.

Until his death in 1995 Lytle continued to ponder the consequences of "The War of Northern Aggression" and to inveigh against the triumph of industrialism over traditional Southern agricultural life. Cleanth Brooks, Walker Percy, Peter Taylor, and James Dickey also died within the last decade. All are included in this collection of entries on contemporary Southern authors, a list which ranges from such literary icons as Lytle, Brooks, and Eudora Welty who grew up before World War I and participated in the Southern Literary Renascence, to writers born after the Vietnam conflict. Many authors included in this collection were profoundly affected by the wars through which they lived, from William Styron's contemplation of the Nazi Holocaust to Robert Olen Butler's somber preoccupation with Vietnam. As we near the end of this violent and bloody century, a resurgence of interest in the most destructive war in American history has inspired several Civil War narratives, most recently Charles Frazier's *Cold Mountain* and Madison Jones's *Nashville 1864*. Even our finest Southern satirists cannot escape its shadow: "The Wawer! The Wawer!" Simons declaims in Padgett Powell's *Edisto Revisited*. "I do not want to be remembered as a soldier" but "a momma's boy" who "went AWOL."

While several writers continue to shoulder what C. Vann Woodward calls "the burden of Southern history," other contemporary authors, such as Richard Ford, have fled from their Southern roots as swiftly as the Fugitive poets in the early 1920s fled from the mannered sentimentality of the old South. However, most of those Fugitives returned to the South to become Agrarians in the late 1920s, providing the "backward glance" that the Fugitive/Agrarian poet Allen Tate argues gave us the Southern Renascence, "a literature conscious of the past in the present."

The Vanderbilt Agrarians attempted to rescue Southern culture from both Mencken's ridicule and the myth of the old South. Although they attacked forces that threatened the Southern community, most Agrarians did not want to resurrect the old order. Allen Tate conceded that he preferred an indoor commode "so long as he didn't have to kneel down and worship it before using it." Arguing that the main function of literature was to probe the deficiencies of a tradition, exploring a history distorted by nostalgia and regret, the Agrarians, along with William Faulkner and Thomas Wolfe, found a Southern version of the fall of man, not the Arcadian myth promulgated by plantation novels before the war and the local-color fiction that came after it. Many writers gave a backward glance to Thomas Jefferson's defense of the yeoman farmer—"Those who labor in the earth are the chosen people of God"—as well as Jefferson's attack on slavery in *Notes on the State of Virginia*. Those two issues became obsessive concerns for Southern writers over the next 200 years.

Two distinctive forms of Southern literature began to emerge in the first half of the nineteenth century: plantation novels that defended slavery and antebellum Southern culture, and Southwest or backwoods humor that provided a corrective to plantation sentimentality by shifting the class perspective to life on the Southern frontier. The continued appeal of the antebellum romance can be seen in Margaret Mitchell's *Gone with the Wind*, while the anti-genteel bite of backwoods humor can be found in Faulkner's Snopes clan, Flannery O'Connor's bible salesman, and other grotesques in twentieth-century literature.

Edgar Allen Poe's gothic tale, "The Fall of the House of Usher," written in the 1840s, reduced the antebellum plantation to a barren wasteland cut off from the human community and from nature. The Southern gothic genre with roots in Poe's *Tales of the Grotesque and Arabesque* continues to flourish in the fiction of O'Connor and more recently Harry Crews, Barry Hannah, and Mark Richard.

Mark Twain, the most influential nineteenth-century Southern writer, inherited both the pastoral and backwoods traditions, briefly sustaining the Arcadian vision in Tom Sawyer before obliterating it along with the Grangerford clan in *The Adventures of Huckleberry Finn*. In a world contaminated by greed and racial bigotry, Huck, like the hero of backwoods humor, survives by his wits before heading West, disillusioned and alone. Cormac McCarthy recently followed suit, moving from Tennessee to West Texas. In his *Border Trilogy* he finds the romantic myth of the American West to be as compelling and dangerously illusory as the myth of the old South.

At the end of the nineteenth century, Joel Chandler Harris's nostalgic tales of Uncle Remus helped to preserve the vanishing dialect and stories of Southern blacks. Combining local color dialect with social criticism, Charles Chesnutt created Uncle Julius, a subversive Uncle Remus, whose tall-tales have influenced many twentieth-century black authors, including Ernest Gaines.

As William Faulkner's novels demonstrate, a consideration of Southern history created the possibility of tragedy, but that tragic sense has obviously declined in recent years. Madison Jones's *A Cry of Absence* may be the last pure tragedy written by a Southerner. Much has been said and written about the present historical discontinuity and increasing homogenization of a South more defined by Wal-Marts and trailer parks than by Agrarian values and folk customs. Many contemporary Southern writers have used settings outside the South and most are suspicious of regional labels. Flannery O'Connor asserted that being called a Georgia author is "on the same order as, for a pig, being a Talmadge ham.... A pig is a pig, no matter who puts him up." Richard Ford goes further, arguing that "there is no such thing as Southern writing or Southern literature or Southern ethos." The critic Fred Hobson disagrees, describing Frank Bascombe in Ford's novel *The Sportswriter* as a disguised Quentin Compson who protests, "I am not interested in the South. I'm not. I'm not!" "What's he running from?" Hobson asks. Perhaps Fred Chappell puts it best: "You've got to come from somewhere. Not everyone can be born in the Museum of Modern Art."

Certainly for writers like Chappell and Wendell Berry, Agrarian values are not dead as they continue the critique of the philosophy of progress with occasional apocalyptic warnings. Other authors, wary of Southern conservatism, have fewer misgivings, pointing out that John Crowe Ransom's prediction in the Agrarian manifesto, *I'll Take My Stand*, that "neither the creation nor the understanding of works of art is possible in an industrial age" has proven to be untrue.

Further attempts to categorize the writers in this collection except in terms of genre, geography, and time would be to ignore the great variety and diversity of contemporary Southern literature. However, one trait shared by many writers in this volume should not be overlooked. Flannery O'Connor's imperative that "it takes a story to make a story" recognizes an oral and a written tradition that continue to exist side by side in much of the South. Described by Robert Penn Warren as "the perfect listener to tales because he was the perfect teller of tales," Andrew Lytle embodied the best of both traditions. A child of one century, a father and grandfather in another, he sums up the peculiar power of contemporary Southern literature in this time of change: "In a materialistic and secular world, language and literature, and the richness of language is literature, seems to me as the best if not the only way to rescue us from the rapid advance of a confusion of tongues." Lytle's conclusion could serve as a fitting epigraph for this entire project: "Life is melodrama. Only art is real."

—Thomas M. Carlson
University of the South

EDITOR'S NOTE

As a region the American South is larger in size than most nations of the world and has diverse topographical features—mountain ranges, tidewater basins, wiregrass, tropics, deltas and bayous, and arid plains—stretching from Appalachia to Key West, Chesapeake Bay to the Rio Grande. Within the vastness the people of the region developed distinctive cultural traits, as surveyed in *The Encyclopedia of Southern Culture* (1989) and numerous other historical and cultural documents. Certain literary styles, themes, and idioms, for example, can be considered uniquely Southern.

The literary riches of the region are as diverse as its topography. Many scholarly works have helped identify Southern literary movements and trends, but such insights can also be used carelessly to generalize about and pigeonhole writers from the South. The contemporary, Pulitzer Prize-winning historian C. Vann Woodward wrote of "the burden of history" on the South; the region's rich literary history can seem similarly burdensome, when once it was liberating. The grand achievement of a William Faulkner can become a burden of Southern literary history on subsequent authors, a circumstance that led the fine young writer Padgett Powell to exclaim, "I discovered Faulkner at a late age—thank God." A refreshing debate has ensued over the last decade about what we mean when we say "Southern writer" and what expectations we bring to the table, so to speak: do we expect to be served grits or peach cobbler, mint juleps or corn whiskey?

Richard Ford addressed the issue in a *Harper's* magazine essay. "What is Southern Literature?" he asks: "Writing just by Southerners? Or just writing about the South? Could we also mean writing by people born in the South but living elsewhere? Or writing by people not born in the South but living there? Would writing by Southerners on non-Southern subjects also qualify?"

The Advisory Board of *Contemporary Southern Writers* considered those qualifications and identified Southern writers for this publication as an author born and raised in the South or a writer born elsewhere who lived and worked in the region for a significant period of their life. Those parameters allowed for generous coverage of the contemporary literary scene while also providing a clear criteria for inclusion: authors must have more than a casual acquaintance with the region and its people.

Some of the authors included in this book have lived in the South their entire lives; some left and made a permanent residence elsewhere; some came to the region later in life; some left and never looked back, while others left and retained a special connection—"I go back to the South, physically and in my memories, to remind myself who I am, for the South keeps me going," said Mississippi-born Willie Morris, who first made his national reputation by traveling north to edit and reinvigorate *Harper's*. The shared distinction of the writers covered in this reference source, then, is their experience living in the South—regardless of what the individual author has chosen to do with that experience in artistic terms. That choice, of course, is theirs to make, and ours to read.

One of many ways to sample the diversity in this book (and the region) is through a literary cuisine: crabcakes in Baltimore remind James Allan McPherson to celebrate the simple things in life; grits, to Harry Crews, symbolize a toughness and simplicity needed to survive in an often harsh world; learning to pick peaches and to use them in recipes are ways of connecting people from different backgrounds in the fiction of Dori Sanders; a recipe for pickled cantaloupe is among the Southern "exotic" treats found in Michael Lee West's *She Flew the Coop: A Novel Concerning Life, Death, Sex and Recipes in Limoges, Louisiana;* and Tex-Mex fare fuels the last cowboys in Larry McMurtry's *Lonesome Dove* and in Cormac McCarthy's *Border Trilogy,* where the cowboys always roll a last tortilla into a wad they use to sop up the remaining gravy, just as in their lives they sop up what remains of a vanishing frontier.

That frontier was once untamed, stretching from Appalachia, where Davy Crockett was born, to the Alamo, where he died. Remnants of the frontier spirit have faded as well in contemporary times—through urbanization since the 1960s and 1970s, for example, or, some might argue, in the emergence of the New South. New voices—Lee Smith, Bobbie Ann Mason, and Jill McCorkle among them—have explored the impact. There is, in fact, such a wealth of themes and writers exploring them in all the literary genres that contemporary Southern writers—as defined above—continue to make as great a contribution to the world's literary scene as had their forbearers, who included contributors to the early formation of the United States, tellers of the distinctly American tall tale, and giants of the Southern Renascence.

This source explores contemporary achievements in fiction, poetry, drama, criticism, and nonfiction. The Advisory Board has defined "contemporary" for this publication as those writers living in the late 1990s and those recently deceased who published new works into the 1990s. Many recent authors not often covered in reference sources of this kind will gain proper exposure through this definition of contemporary, while more established authors are represented as well with up-to-date information and from new perspectives.

All entries in *Contemporary Southern Writers* are organized in the following manner:

Biographical data: Listing, if known, of the author's place and date of birth, education, family, career, awards, agent, and contact information.

Bibliography: Listing of titles, location, publisher, and original publication date of the authors' works, arranged by genre; some entries provide information on media adaptations, manuscript collections, and a list of interviews and critical studies.

Personal statement: When provided, authors speak of their purposes and approaches or of influences on their writing.

Critical essay: An essay on the author's works and career, written by an established critic or literary specialist, concludes each entry; the views presented in each essay are wholly those of the essayist and should not be viewed as those of St. James Press and the editor of this publication. Each essay ends with the writers' byline.

Additional features include:

A **Guest Preface** by Thomas M. Carlson, University of the South.

An expansive **Timeline of Southern Literary History**, compiled by Roger Matuz, Thomas M. Carlson, and John Grammer. The timeline is arranged to feature many notable authors by the date of a major publication or their winning a major literary award. In order to accommodate great breadth in a user-friendly format, almost all authors are mentioned only once with a brief career summary.

Title Index

Notes on Advisors and Contributors

Acknowledgments

Contemporary Southern Writers exists because of the efforts of many people. Advisory Board members Doris Betts, Thomas M. Carlson, David K. Jeffrey, Donald S. Noble, and Shannon Ravenel were very generous with their time and experience. Close to 100 contributing essayists and editors, many of whom made significant suggestions to help improve the book, brought the project into reality. Thanks also to Allison Jones and Kathy Dauphinais for their various forms of support. George Core and John Grammer of the University of the South provided astute commentary and advice. Margaret Mazurkiewicz at St. James Press was very patient and expertly guided the large undertaking.

The editorial staffs of Manitou Wordworks, Inc.—freelance print and website developers—and St. James Press hope that *Contemporary Southern Writers* is a useful reference tool. Comments and suggestions are welcome: please address them to, The Editor, *Contemporary Southern Writers,* St. James Press, 27500 Drake Rd., Farmington Hills, MI 48331-3535.

—Roger Matuz
Editor

TIMELINE OF SOUTHERN LITERARY HISTORY

Pre-17th Century
Among the earliest, non-indigenous writers/explorers of the South were Álvar Nú ez Cabeza de Vaca of Spain (*Relacion*, 1542), René Goulaine de Laudonnière of France (*L'histoire notable de la Floride*, 1586), and Thomas Harriot of England (*Briefe and True Report of the New Found Land of Virginia*, 1588).

1600-09
John Smith (1580-1631) was among the first Southern settlers to report on America. He helped found the first permanent settlement in Jamestown, Virginia, and wrote six books about his experiences in America, including *A True Relation* (1608), *A Map of Virginia* (1612), and *The Generall Historie of Virginia, New England* (1631). The books promoted American settlement, showed Smith as a hero, and related the Pocahontas story, among other tales and facts.

1607
George Percy's recording of his first impressions of Virginia during the founding of the Jamestown colony can be considered the first work of Southern literature.

1610-29
Virginia is championed in literary tracts by Robert Johnson (1609 and 1612), Lord De La Warr (1611), William Strachey (1612), and, later, Edward Waterhouse (1622); in poems by Richard Rich (1610) and Christopher Brook (1622); and in the anonymous ballads *The Last Newes from Virginia* (1611, no copy known) and *Good News from Virginia* (1624).

1633
The first Maryland colonization tract, *A Declaration of the Lord Baltimore's Plantation in Mary-land* (1633), was written by Andrew White (1579-1656) and promised two thousand acres of land to immigrants who brought over good equipment and at least five servants. George Calvert, Lord Baltimore, had created a feudal Catholic colony on the northern Chesapeake Bay and enlisted the aid of Jesuits, including his friend White, an English Jesuit, former professor of theology, and prefect of studies at various seminaries, who volunteered to spread Catholicism among American Indians.

1649
William Bullock's *Virginia Impartially Examined* is published.

1656
John Hammond publishes the promotional tract *Leah and Rachel; or, The Two Fruitfull Sisters, Virginia and Maryland*.

1662
A Song of Sion, an outstanding example of meditative religious poetry prominent in the colonies, is published by John Grave.

1664
William Hilton's *A Relation of a Discovery Lately Made on the Coast of Florida*, the first important Carolina promotion tract, features a detailed description of the Cape Fear area of North Carolina.

The anonymous pamphlet *A Brief Description of the Province of Carolina*, probably written by Robert Horne, promises 100 acres of land to every person who pays for his own transportation to reach the province.

1666
George Alsop's promotion tract, *A Character of the Province of Mary-Land*, is published.

1682
Thomas Ash's *Carolina* features the first reference to corn whiskey.

Robert Ferguson's *Present State of Carolina* includes important details on the Indians of the Carolinas.

Samuel Wilson's *Account of the Province of Carolina* praises the easy life offered by the warm Carolina climate.

1683
John Crafford's *New and Most Exact Account* (1683) argues that Indians were descended from the Israelites.

1684
Carolina Described (anonymous) reprints excerpts from previous descriptions and offers new enticements for immigrants.

1705
Robert Beverley (1673-1722) journeys to London and publishes *The History and Present State of Virginia*, an account of the colony's history, natural resources and products derived from them, and reports on local Indians and living conditions.

1708
Ebenezer Cook's *The Sot-Weed Factor* presents the uproarious adventures of an Englishman who journeys to Maryland to seek his fortune. The wild country and astute settlers prove too formidable, and the poem's speaker returns to England with only a grudge.

1726
The *Maryland Gazette*, established by William Parks at Annapolis, is the first Southern newspaper.

1728
William Byrd II (1674-1744) begins journal notes for *The History of the Dividing Line*, which includes elements of history, nature study, a promotional tract on Virginia, and satirical sketches of backwoods people (the "dividing line" of the title refers to differences between civilized, aristocratic farmers, and backwoods poor people). The manuscript wasn't published until 1841, almost a century after Byrd's death, when it is hailed as one of the first examples of distinctly American literature.

1731
Newspapers begin serving as important publishing houses: for example, a new edition of Ebenezer Cook's *The Sot-Weed Factor* is printed through the *Maryland Muse*.

1736

William Parks's *Virginia Gazette* prints original essays and promotes books, including William Dawson's *Poems on Several Occasions*.

1751

The first newspaper in North Carolina is established.

1763

The first newspaper in Georgia is established.

1770-79

Two comic dramas by Robert Munford, *The Candidates* and *The Patriots*, entertain audiences in the Virginia-North Carolina region. The plays, written in the 1770s but not published until 1798, take place in recently settled Southside Virginia (near the North Carolina border) and present local character-types and conflicts.

1776

Thomas Jefferson (1743-1826) pens *The Declaration of Independence*. Jefferson wrote several essays but only one book, *Notes on Virginia* (first published in France in 1785 and then in Jefferson's approved version in 1787), was published during his lifetime. His letters, state papers, speeches, and essays cover a wide range of topics, including politics, farming, literature, Virginia's geography, natural resources, and people, government, and religion.

1800

Mason Locke Weems publishes his popular biography of George Washington.

1803

William Wirt's (1772-1834) *The Letters of the British Spy* is published serially in Richmond's *Virginian Argus* in 1803 and proves so popular that it goes through ten book editions during Wirt's life. Wirt's later book, *Sketches of the Life and Character of Patrick Henry* (1817), a biography, is his most important contribution to Southern and American letters. Also a copious essayist, Wirt wrote three series essays in the Addisononian manner.

1809

Edgar Allan Poe is born in Boston. He spends parts of his life in Massachusetts, England, New York, Pennsylvania, Maryland, and mostly in Virginia, the state which he associated himself most closely. Some critics, including Lewis P. Simpson, have argued that several Poe works fit in with Southern literary traditions: "The Fall of the House of Usher" (1839), for example, has been viewed as a decadent cousin of the Plantation Novel and one of several Poe works that influenced the Southern Gothic tradition.

1820-29

The Plantation Novel, a staple of Southern fiction, is established with George Tucker's *The Valley of the Shenandoah* (1824), which recounts the "tale of the ruin of a once prosperous and respected family."

1824

Charleston's William Gilmore Simms (1806-70), a champion of national and Southern literature, publishes his first of over 80 books of history, poetry, fiction, drama, sketches, criticism, biography, and polemics.

1829

The earliest-known published black Southern poet, George Moses Horton, who lived in Chatham and Orange counties in North Carolina, has his first volume, *The Hope of Liberty*, printed.

1830-39

The advent of the Southwest humorists, important and dynamic contributors to a distinctly Southern as well as a national literature. Their work begins appearing in such sources as the *Southern Literary Messenger*, *Spirit of the Times* (a New York sporting journal), and in local Southern newspapers. The writers most often identified among the Southwest humorists are Augustus Baldwin Longstreet, William Tappan Thompson, Johnson Jones Hooper, Thomas Bangs Thorpe, and George Washington Harris.

1832

John Pendleton Kennedy's (1795-1870) *Swallow Barn*, the most influential novel of plantation life, is published. Equally popular are Kennedy's later historical romances, *Horse-Shoe Robinson* (1835), set during the Revolution, and *Rob of the Bowl* (1838), set in colonial Maryland.

1834

Among the early literary magazines is the *Southern Literary Messenger* (1834-64).

1835

Longstreet's *Georgia Scenes*, the earliest book of Southwest stories to capture national attention (eleven editions printed in the nineteenth century), featured two gentlemen, Hall and Baldwin, reporting on back country customs and speech.

1836

Davy Crockett is among those who die defending the Alamo. In addition to being a frontier adventurer, Crockett was a storyteller of backwoods humor and tales and served Tennessee as a representative in Congress.

1842

Southern Quarterly Review (1842-57) is established.

1843

William Tappan Thompson's *Major Jones's Courtship*, featuring the adventures of Major Joseph Jones of Pineville, Georgia, is published.

1845

Frederick Douglass (1818-95) publishes *Narrative of the Life of Frederick Douglass, an American Slave*, one of the most widely read books of the era, documenting the evils of slavery and championing liberty.

William Alexander Carruthers publishes *The Knights of the Golden Horseshoe*, a notable historical novel and celebration of Southern character.

Johnson Jones Hooper's (1815-62) *Some Adventures of Captain Simon Suggs*, another of the important Southwest humor works, is published.

1846

Thomas Bangs Thorpe publishes a quintessential work of Southwest humor, "The Big Bear of Arkansas," in *The Mysteries of the Backwoods*. That same year, William Elliott of South Carolina publishes *Carolina Sports*; both books, concerning the Southern passion for hunting, may be said to prefigure William Faulkner's "The Bear."

1847

Another great slave narrative—*Narrative of William W. Brown, a Fugitive Slave*—by an author of travel books, essays, and histories, is published. William Wells Brown's (1814-84) later work, *Clotel; or, The President's Daughter* (1853), is the first novel written by an African-American.

1853

Flush Times of Alabama and Mississippi, by Joseph Glover Baldwin, recounts the boom-and-bust era of the Southwest frontier.

1854

John Esten Cooke (1830-86) publishes two popular, antebellum romances, *Leather Stocking and Silk* and *The Virginian Comedians*. Postbellum novels by Cooke, who served with the Confederate Army, pay tribute to Stonewall Jackson (*Surry of Eagle's Nest*, 1866) and J. E. B. Stuart and Robert E. Lee (*Mohun*, 1869), and *The Heir of Gaymount* (1870) concerns a man's struggle to maintain his estate during Reconstruction.

1860-69

Mary Boykin Chesnut (1823-86) writes an "inside narrative" approach to the Civil War. Chesnut's manuscript was originally published as *A Diary from Dixie* in 1905 and again in 1949. The definitive version, *Mary Chesnut's Civil War*, was edited and introduced by C. Vann Woodward in 1981, and Woodward won the Pulitzer Prize in history for his efforts.

1860

George William Bagby publishes *Mozis Addums' New Letters* (1860), which along with *The Letters of Mozis Addums to Billy Ivvins* (1862) offers humorous stories of rural Virginia.

1861-62

Henry Timrod (1828-67), called the "Poet Laureate of the South," writes several Civil War poems, including "Ethnogenesis," "The Cotton Boll," "A Cry to Arms," and "Charleston."

1863

Augusta Jane Evans Wilson (1835-1909), perhaps the most widely read Southern author just after the Civil War, publishes *Macaria; or Altars of Sacrifice* in Richmond and the manuscript is smuggled to New York for a Northern edition in 1864. Wilson had published two novels before the war (*Inez: A Tale of the Alamo*, 1855, and *Beulah*, 1859), but she became popular with her Civil War novel that counters Harriet Beecher Stowe's views of the South in *Uncle Tom's Cabin*. Wilson, an ardent secessionist, later authored *St. Elmo* (1866), a bestseller said to have been read by over one million people within four months of its publication.

1864

Richard Malcolm Johnston (1822-98), who publishes under the pseudonym of Philmon Perch, releases *Georgia Sketches*; he would later earn recognition for his *Dukesborough Tales* (1871, 1874, 1883, 1892) that focus on white, middle-class characters in a town modeled on Powelton, Georgia.

1866

Northern Georgia is the setting of *Bill Arp, So Called* and four sequels by Charles Henry Smith.

1867

Using the frame story characteristic of the Southwest humorists and featuring highly vernacular prose, George Washington Harris introduces the irascible Sut Lovingood in *Sut Lovingood: Yarns Spun by a "Nat'ral Born Durn'd Fool."*

1870s

Beginnings of what literary historians have called the "local color" movement in American letters, which will run through the end of the century.

Irwin Russell (1853-79) of Mississippi became well known for his dialect verse of the late 1870s and 1880s. He experimented with black dialects and hoped to write a "Negro novel." His contributions to journals, never collected during his lifetime, were posthumously published in *Christmas Night in the Quarters* (1913, 1917).

1872

Paul Hamilton Hayne is lauded as laureate of the South for his verse in *Legends and Lyrics*, followed by *The Mountain of the Lovers* (1875), and *Poems* (1882); love for his homeland, family, and nature permeate his poems, and several address the theme of death.

1874

Mark Twain's "A True Story" is published, one of many works set in the South. Born in Missouri, then a slave state, and briefly a Confederate volunteer during the war, Twain explored Southern life in such tales as *Adventures of Tom Sawyer* (1876), *Life on the Mississippi* (1883), *Pudd'nhead Wilson* (1894), and, of course, *Adventures of Huckleberry Finn* (1885).

1877

Sidney Lanier's (1842-81) innovative *Poems*, featuring experiments with sound and music, makes him nationally-known. The posthumously published *Poems of Sidney Lanier* (1884) added to his renown as one of the most beloved writers of his time.

Albery Allson Whitman (1851-1901), a black poet-preacher, writes the five thousand-line, *Not a Man Yet a Man*. His other major work is *Twasinta's Seminoles, or The Rape of Florida* (1884).

Joel Chandler Harris (1848-1908) begins contributing Uncle Remus sketches to the *Atlanta Constitution* in 1877, developing the characters and setting showcased in *Uncle Remus: His Songs and His Sayings* (1880), which sold 10,000 copies within four months of publication.

1879

George Washington Cable (1844-1925), who was wounded while serving with the Confederate cavalry, publishes his first book, *Old*

Creole Days, which contains six New Orleans tales and sketches (including "Sieur George," "Posson Jone'," "Jean-ah Poquelin," and "Belles Demoiselles Planation") he composed earlier in the 1870s; the tales reveal conflicts and richness in the diverse cultures of his native city. His best-known work, the novel *The Grandissimes*, appeared in 1880.

The Southern Student Hand-Book of Selections for Reading and Oratory, edited by John G. James, superintendent of the Texas Military Institute in Austin, is published and contains 220 speeches, essays, excerpts, and poems on Southern topics designed to champion the antebellum South as an ideal society and a center of classical culture.

1884

Thomas Nelson Page (1853-1922) uses Old Virginia and the plantation as his setting for "Marse Chan," his first and most popular story, which is published in *Century*. The story features a former slave named Sam narrating in dialect the colorful and tragic life of the title character in the Civil War. Page later became known for his novels, most notably *Red Rock* (1898) and *Gordon Keith* (1903), celebrating the life and the values of the older plantation South.

Mary Noailles Murfree (1850-1922) enjoys acclaim for her works of local color, beginning with her first story collection, *In the Tennessee Mountains*.

1887

Charles W. Chesnutt (1858-1932), who focused much of his work on the lives of black Americans in the postbellum South, publishes "The Goophered Grapevine" in the *Atlantic Monthly* in August. Chesnutt was born in the North and spent the years just after the war in Fayetteville, North Carolina. Chesnutt's tales of Uncle Julius McAdoo appear in *The Conjure Woman* (1899), followed by his trilogy—*The House Behind the Cedars* (1900), *The Marrow of Tradition* (1901), and *The Colonel's Dream* (1905)—which deal, respectively, with black characters who pass for white, with the 1898 race riots in Wilmington, North Carolina, and with a white, ex-Confederate officer who tries to bring economic recovery and racial enlightenment to his hometown after the war.

1888

Amelie Louise Rives' (1863-1945) romantic tales set in Virginia are published in *Brother to Dragons and Other Old Time Tales*.

1892

Sewanee Review founded.

1895

Louise Manly's textbook, *Southern Literature from 1579-1895*, provides a thorough selection of works from eighty-nine authors arranged in four chronological sections with an additional list of thirty-nine recommended writers and a comprehensive appendix of about fourteen hundred other writers of merit.

1896

Kentucky local colorist John Fox, Jr. (1863?-1919), publishes his first collection, *A Cumberland Vendetta and Other Stories*.

1897

Ellen Glasgow (1873-1945) enjoys critical and popular success with her first novel, *The Descendant*, which offers a more critical and realistic view of her native Virginia than works of the Plantation tradition. Glasgow's long and illustrious career culminated with *In This Our Life* (1941), for which she was awarded the Pulitzer Prize.

1899

Kate Chopin (1851-1904), considered a Southern local colorist during her time but more recently championed as an early feminist, publishes *The Awakening*. Condemned by some critics as immoral, the seminal novel develops an independent, passionate woman bolder than the stereotypical Southern lady.

1900

Popular writer Mary Johnston (1870-1936) publishes her best-known historical novel, *To Have and To Hold*, about the early Jamestown settlement.

1901

Booker T. Washington (1856-1915), who spent much of his energy nurturing the Tuskegee Institute and writing prolifically about the education, history, and social issues concerning blacks, publishes *Up from Slavery* (1901), first serialized in *Outlook* and then published in book form to critical acclaim. One of several of his autobiographical books, *Up from Slavery* became an immediate bestseller.

1904

Prolific Virginia author James Branch Cabell (1879-1958) has his first novel, *The Eagle's Shadow*, published. *Jurgen* (1919) and *Something about Eve* (1927) are among his best-known works.

1912

James Weldon Johnson (1871-1938) publishes *The Autobiography of an Ex-Colored Man*, the most important literary work by the activist, poet, and novelist.

1916

New Orleans-native Elizabeth King (1852-1932) publishes *The Pleasant Ways of St. Medard*, the best example of her sympathetic approach to her native city.

1917

Maryland writer H. L. Mencken (1880-1956) roundly condemns the South for its lack of culture in his famous essay, "The Sahara of the Bozart" (the title puns *beaux arts*). First published in the *New York Evening Mail* and expanded for his collection, *Prejudices: Second Series* (1920), the essay chastises the region for lapsing into sentimentality after having been a significant contributor to "the finest civilization the Western Hemisphere had seen"— the early days of the United States. The essay infuriated many Southerners and also served as a wake-up call.

1919

John Crowe Ransom publishes his first book of verse, *Poems about God*. Ransom would become a key figure in Southern literary history, as a poet, as a member of the Fugitives and the Agrarians, and as a leading proponent of The New Criticism.

1920s

Beginning of the Southern Renascence, a remarkable flowering of writing by Southern authors that dominates literary activity in America for thirty years. Three of the most significant literary groups in twentieth-century America were centered in the South—the Fugitives, the Agrarians, and the New Critics—and some of the nation's most enduring writers reached prominence during this period.

1922

T. S. Stribling's (1881-1965) *Birthright* (1922) begins a series of didactic novels on bigotry and materialism in small-town life in the mid-South. *Teeftallow* (1926) and *Bright Metal* (1928) are set in Tennessee, *Backwater* (1930) in Arkansas; these were followed by a trilogy, *The Forge* (1931), *The Store* (1932), and *The Unfinished Cathedral* (1934).

A group of young poets—Ransom, Donald Davidson, Allen Tate, and Robert Penn Warren—based at Vanderbilt University produce a significant poetry journal, *The Fugitive,* that lasted until 1925; their formal association was completed with *Fugitives: An Anthology of Verse* in 1928. Their collective name came from their desire to flee "the high-caste Brahmins of the Old South."

1925

Virginia Quarterly Review founded.

The Scopes Evolution Trial, in which science teacher John Thomas Scopes is tried for teaching scientific evolution in a public school—against Tennessee law—begins in Dayton, Tennessee in July. In highlighting differences between provincial beliefs and modern, scientific approaches, the trial is used by some, including H. L. Mencken, to show the "backwardness" of Southern culture. Members of the Fugitive group share their outrage at the way in which their region is flippantly mocked by society embracing modernist ideals and industrialization. By the end of the decade, the four Fugitive poets banded with eight other Southern writers to champion traditional agrarian values that had been nurtured in Southern society—of the value of life lived in harmony with the natural world.

1926

Frances Neuman, an Atlanta librarian, publishes her iconoclastic novel *The Hard-Boiled Virgin.*

Paul Green's (1894-1981) folk play, *In Abraham's Bosom: The Biography of a Negro*, is a surprise hit on Broadway and wins the Pulitzer Prize. After two more successes, *The Field God* (1927) and *The House of Connelly* (1928), Green returned to the South and became a significant force in Southern regional drama.

Elizabeth Maddox Roberts (1881-1941), of Perryville, Kentucky, emerges on the literary scene with her novel *The Time of Man.* *The Great Meadow* (1930) brought her international acclaim.

1927

Julia Peterkin (1880-1961) publishes *Green Thursday*, a collection of twelve stories, followed by her novels *Black April* (1927) and *Scarlet Sister Mary* (1928), for which Peterkin won the Pulitzer Prize.

Publication of *The Tall Men*, a nine-part poem by Donald Davidson, one of the leaders of the Fugitive and Agrarian movements; later works in verse and prose include *Lee in the Mountains and Other Poems* and *The Attack on Leviathan* (both 1938).

1928

Allen Tate introduces an early version of his major poem, "Ode to the Confederate Dead," which he completed in 1937. Associated with the Fugitives and the Agrarians, Tate rallied behind the South by writing powerful biographies, essays, and poetry following criticism of the region during the Scopes Evolution Trial. He would later become as well known as a critic, embracing the tenets of the New Criticism.

1929

The first two novels of William Faulkner's (1897-1962) Yoknapatawpha series—*Sartoris* and *The Sound and the Fury*—are published and initiate a remarkable string of works published during a seven-year period, including *As I Lay Dying* (1930), *Light in August* (1932), and *Absalom, Absalom!* (1936).

Evelyn Scott's (1893-1963) *The Wave*, one of her several modernist novels, draws more enthusiastic attention than *The Sound and the Fury.*

Thomas Wolfe's (1900-38) *Look Homeward, Angel* is published to astonishing praise, beginning the spectacular rise of Wolfe's reputation that would wane by the time of his early death from pneumonia and tuberculosis in 1938. Remarkably talented yet highly unstructured, Wolfe's writings fell in popularity, beginning with *Of Time and the River* in 1935. Neither *The Web and the Rock* (1939), *You Can't Go Home Again* (1940), or *The Hills Beyond* (1941), matched the acclaim of *Look Homeward, Angel.*

1930

Ransom, Davidson, Tate, Warren and eight other Southerners, most with Vanderbilt ties, produce *I'll Take My Stand*, in which they proclaim their strong preference for a traditional agrarian way of life in opposition to the "progress" of industrialization. Ransom concludes the manifesto's "Introduction: A Statement of Principles" with "this much is clear: If a community, or a race, or an age, is groaning under industrialism, and well aware that it is an evil dispensation, it must find the way to throw it off. To think that this cannot be done is pusillanimous. And if the whole community, section, race, or age thinks it cannot be done, then it has simply lost its political genius and doomed itself to impotence."

Katherine Anne Porter (1890-1980) begins a remarkable career with *Flowering Judas and Other Stories*; her *Collected Stories* (1966) won both the National Book Award and the Pulitzer Prize.

1931

Arna Bontemps (1902-73), born in Alexandria, Louisiana, but raised and educated in California, traveled to New York at the height of the Harlem Renaissance and made a lasting contribution with his 1931 novel, *God Sends Sunday.* Bontemps later returned to the South and was for many years the librarian at Fisk University.

Sterling A. Brown publishes *Southern Road,* a highly-regarded collection of poems that recreate black dialects and blend in other idioms. Brown would not publish more original work for decades, but his work collecting and promoting dialectical poetry and lyrics as well as his essays on folklore are invaluable contributions to a field were authentic recreation often proves elusive or simplified.

1932

Erskine Caldwell publishes *Tobacco Road* (1932), followed by *God's Little Acre* (1933).

1934

Stark Young (1881-1963), one of the contributors to *I'll Take My Stand*, publishes his most significant novel, *So Red the Rose*. A native of Mississippi who went to New York in his early forties after almost twenty years of teaching, Young became a leading drama critic and had two plays produced on Broadway.

Caroline Gordon (1895-1981) publishes her most significant novel, *Aleck Maury, Sportsman*.

Jesse Stuart (1907-84), a native of eastern Kentucky, publishes *Man with a Bull-tongue Plow*, a collection of 703 sonnets. A collection of stories, *Head o'W-Hollow* (1936), an autobiography, *Beyond Dark Hills* (1938), and a novel, *Trees of Heaven* (1940) are his other best-known works.

1935

Southern Review (1935-42, 1965—) founded.

1936

Harriette Simpson Arnow (1908-86) of Wayne County, Kentucky, publishes the first of her Appalachian novels, *Mountain Path*. Her second novel, *Hunter's Horn*, appeared in 1949 followed by her masterpiece, *The Dollmaker*, in 1951.

Margaret Mitchell (1900-49) finally finds a publisher for a manuscript she wrote during the late 1920s. *Gone with the Wind* becomes a best-seller and is adapted three years later into a film that remained the highest-grossing motion picture for decades.

Cleanth Brooks and Robert Penn Warren publish *An Approach to Literature: A Collection of Prose and Verse*, followed in 1938 by *Understanding Poetry*, among their instructive texts that became standard sources in university English courses.

Andrew Lytle (1902-95), one of the Agrarians, publishes his first novel, *The Long Night*. As an editor, scholar, and writer, Lytle made enormous contributions to American letters, including his best-known novel *The Velvet Horn* (1957).

1937

Zora Neale Hurston (1891-1960) publishes *Their Eyes Were Watching God* (1937), a work that has had a great influence on contemporary African American literature.

1938

Richard Wright (1908-60), a native son of Mississippi who moved to Chicago in his late teens, publishes his collection of stories of southern racial conflicts, *Uncle Tom's Children*. His American classic, *Native Son*, follows in 1940, and his autobiography, *Black Boy*, in 1945.

John Gould Fletcher's *Selected Poems* wins the Pulitzer Prize. A native of Arkansas, Fletcher had a remarkable career that included contributions to the development of Imagism in London and associations with the Fugitive and the Agrarians.

Marjorie Kinnan Rawlings (1896-1953) publishes *The Yearling*, set in the Florida backwoods. The following year she wins the Pulitzer Prize for the novel and is elected to the National Academy of Arts and Letters.

1939

Lillian Hellman's (1905-84) most popular Broadway play, *The Little Foxes* (1939), set in small-town Alabama of 1900, enjoys a long run. She later won a National Book Award for her first of four books of memoirs, *An Unfinished Woman* (1969).

1940

Carson McCullers (1917-67) begins her remarkable string of acclaimed works that explore spiritual isolation with *The Heart Is a Lonely Hunter*, followed by *The Ballad of the Sad Cafe* and *Reflections in a Golden Eye* (both 1941) and *A Member of the Wedding* (1946).

1941

James Agee's (1909-55) *Let Us Now Praise Famous Men*, is published; Agee would later win the Pulitzer Prize posthumously for *A Death in the Family* in 1958.

Eudora Welty's (born 1909) long and fruitful career begins with the first of three early short story collections, *A Curtain of Green* (1941), followed by *The Wide Net* (1943), and *The Golden Apples* (1949).

W. J. Cash's *The Mind of the South* traces the character of the white, male Protestant Southerner.

1944

Tennessee Williams' (1911-83) *The Glass Menagerie*, focusing on a young girl based on his sister Rose, opens successfully in Chicago and moves to New York in 1945, where it wins the Drama Critics Circle Award. *A Streetcar Named Desire* follows in 1947 and wins the Pulitzer Prize. *Cat on a Hot Tin Roof* (1955) wins a Pulitzer Prize and the Drama Critics Circle Award, which was also awarded to his *Night of the Iguana* (1961).

1945

Randall Jarrell (1914-65) publishes one of his most famous poems, "The Death of the Ball Turret Gunner." A major figure in twentieth-century literature for his poetry, essays, and reviews, Jarrell associated with Fugitive poets and was among the most prominent poets to incorporate the influences of W. H. Auden and T. S. Eliot. Jarrell was struck by a car and died at age 51, cutting short his remarkable contribution to American letters.

1946

Robert Penn Warren (1905-89) publishes *All the King's Men*, which wins the Pulitzer Prize. As a poet, critic, novelist, consultant to the Library of Congress, and the nation's first poet laureate, Warren was among the twentieth-century's most distinguished man of letters.

1947

Georgia Review founded.

1948

Mississippi Quarterly founded.

Peter Taylor (1917-94) wins critical recognition with *A Long Fourth and Other Stories.* His first novel, *A Woman of Means,* follows in 1950. His distinguished career spanned to 1985's *The Old Forest and Other Stories,* which received the PEN/Faulkner Award, and his second novel, *A Summons to Memphis* (1986), which won the Pulitzer Prize.

Truman Capote's (1923-84) largely autobiographical first novel, *Other Voices, Other Rooms,* appears. *A Tree of Night and Other Stories* (1949), *The Grass Harp* (1951), *A Christmas Memory* (1956), and *Breakfast at Tiffany's* (1958), add to his renown, as does *In Cold Blood* (1965) and his later prominence on the celebrity circuit.

1949

Shelby Foote's (born 1916) *Tournament* is published, followed in 1952 by *Shiloh,* then his epical *The Civil War: A Narrative* (Vol. I: *Fort Sumter to Perryville,* 1958; Vol. II: *Fredericksburg to Meridian,* 1963; Vol. III: *Red River to Appomattox,* 1974), which took him nearly twenty years to complete.

1952

Ralph Ellison (1914-94) publishes *Invisible Man,* an immediate popular and critical success and winner of the National Book Award.

Randall Stewart and others publish *The Literature of the South,* which in its many editions became perhaps the most influential Southern literature anthology.

1954

North Carolina writer Doris Betts (born 1932) publishes her first collection of stories, *The Gentle Insurrection.*

1955

John Barth (born 1930) publishes *The Floating Opera* (1955), followed by *The End of the Road* (1958) and *The Sot-Weed Factor* (1960), none of which gain much popular attention yet all remain staples on college reading lists.

1957

Madison Jones publishes *The Innocent,* his first novel. A student of Donald Davidson and Andrew Lytle, Jones would publish several more novels, the most notable of which was *A Cry of Absence* (1971), one of the most powerful fictional treatments of Southern race relations.

1960

Harper Lee's (born 1926) Pulitzer Prize-winning *To Kill a Mockingbird,* set in her native Monroeville, Alabama, captures national attention as a novel and later as a film, with the screenplay adapted by Horton Foote. In the 1990s *To Kill a Mockingbird* remains the single most-often studied work in American high school English classes.

1961

Walker Percy (1916-90), at age forty-five, publishes his first novel, *The Moviegoer,* which wins the National Book Award for fiction.

Southern Studies founded.

Louis D. Rubin (born 1923) publishes *South: Modern Southern Literature in Its Cultural Settings* (with R. D. Jacobs), among the many works of Southern literary history he edits and helps compile; others include *A Biographical Guide to the Study of Southern Literature* (1969); *The Writer in the South* (1972); *Southern Writers: A Biographical Dictionary* (with Robert Bain and Joseph N. Flora; 1979); *The History of Southern Literature* (with Blyden Jackson, Rayburn S. Moore, Lewis P. Simpson, and Thomas Daniel Young; 1985); and *The Edge of the Swamp: A Study in the Literature and Society of the Old South* (1989).

1962

Southern Quarterly founded.

Mississippian Ellen Douglas (born 1921) publishes her first novel, *A Family's Affairs.*

North Carolinian Reynolds Price (born 1933) publishes his first novel, *A Long and Happy Life.*

1963

Martin Luther King, Jr. delivers his famous "I Have a Dream" speech in Washington, D.C. In addition to being a powerful orator, the Nobel Peace Prize recipient authored such widely-studied pieces as "Nonviolent Resistance" and "Letter from Birmingham Jail."

1964

Flannery O'Connor (born 1925) dies at age thirty-nine. Her two novels and two collections of stories remain major influences—some argue the most important influences on contemporary Southern writers.

1965

Shirley Ann Grau (born 1929) of New Orleans wins the Pulitzer Prize for her third novel, *The Keepers of the House.*

James Dickey (1923-97) caps his steadily-growing reputation as a poet with *Buckdancer's Choice,* which wins the National Book Award. In addition to being a noted scholar and serving as a consultant in poetry at the Library of Congress, Dickey won wide recognition for his 1970 novel *Deliverance,* which was adapted for film in 1972. The Georgian recited a poem at the 1977 inauguration of fellow Georgian, President Jimmy Carter.

Cormac McCarthy (born 1933) publishes his first novel, *The Orchard Keeper* (1965), the first of several novels set in his native South for which he won much critical recognition but little popular renown. That would change in the 1990s with his immensely respected and popular *The Border Trilogy,* completed with *Cities on the Plain* (1998).

Wendell Berry (born 1934) buys a small farm, Lanes Landing, at Port Royal in his native Henry County, Kentucky, initially as a summer retreat, but then as a working farm and lives by tenets similar to those championed by the Agrarians more than three decades earlier. His early novels, *Nathan Coulter* (1960) and *A Place on Earth* (1967), emphasize the importance of place, a theme of his essays collected in *A Continuous Harmony: Essays Cultural and Agricultural* (1972), *The Unsettling of America: Culture and Agriculture* (1977), and *The Gift of Good Land: Further Essays Cultural and Agricultural* (1981).

1966

Margaret Walker's (born 1915) historical novel, *Jubilee*, is published to international acclaim, capping a literary career that began with her 1942 collection, *For My People,* which won the prestigious Yale Series of Younger Poets competition.

1967

William Styron's (born 1925) *The Confessions of Nat Turner*—a controversial novel during the racially divisive 1960s—wins the Pulitzer Prize. Styron would later win the National Book Award for *Sophie's Choice.*

1968

Harry Crews (born 1935) publishes his first novel, *The Gospel Singer,* initiating his concern for the vanishing rural South.

Southern Literary Journal founded.

Founding of The Society for the Study of Southern Literature (SSSL), an organization of scholars that provides programs for major professional conventions and supports a development of bibliographic and reference works.

Virginian Lee Smith's *The Last Day the Dogbushes Bloomed* initiates her focus on Appalachia.

1969

John Kennedy Toole (1937-69) commits suicide before much of his work is published. His New Orleans-based novel *A Confederacy of Dunces* is published in 1980 through the efforts of his mother and the support of Walker Percy. A humorous and melancholy satire of modern life in New Orleans, the novel won the Pulitzer Prize.

1970

Maya Angelou's (born 1928) autobiographical *I Know Why the Caged Bird Sings* brings national attention she would sustain with diverse works of poetry, autobiography, and fiction. She was invited to prepare and read a poem for the inauguration of President Bill Clinton, a fellow Arkansas-native, in 1993.

1971

Ernest Gaines's *The Autobiography of Miss Jane Pittman* connects the inequities of slavery and segregation through the long life of one woman.

George Garrett (born 1929), already with a strong reputation as a writer and scholar, publishes the surprising *Death of a Fox*, an experimental historical novel that becomes a critical and popular success. He publishes two later Elizabethan-period novels, *The Succession: A Novel of Elizabeth and James* (1985) and *Entered from the Sun* (1991).

1973

A. R. Ammons (born 1926) wins his first of two National Book Awards with *Collected Poems, 1951-1971*; he would later win for 1983's *Lake Effect Country.*

1976

Alex Haley's (1921-92) resoundingly popular *Roots*, which traces the author's ancestry back to Africa, becomes a bestseller; the following year it is adapted for television and becomes the most widely-viewed miniseries in television history.

The journal *Callaloo* is founded at Southern University in Baton Rouge.

New Orleans native Anne Rice begins her highly popular *Vampire Chronicles* series with *Interview with the Vampire.*

1978

Mary Lee Settle's (born 1918) *Blood Tie* wins the National Book Award.

1980

Donald Justice wins the Pulitzer Prize for his *Selected Poems.*

1981

North Carolina poet and novelist Fred Chappell (born 1936) publishes *Midquest* (1981), a single, long, midlife poem comprised of four earlier volumes, *River* (1975), *Bloodfire* (1978), *Wind Mountain* (1979), and *Earthsleep* (1980).

Mississippian Beth Henley wins the Pulitzer Prize for drama for *Crimes of the Heart.*

1982

Anne Tyler (born 1935) emerges as a major writer with such novels as *Dinner at the Homesick Restaurant* and *The Accidental Tourist* (1985); her 1989 novel *Breathing Lessons* was awarded the Pulitzer Prize.

Alice Walker's (born 1944) National Book Award- and Pulitzer Prize-winning epistolary novel, *The Color Purple* is published, following her earlier works, *The Third Life of George Copeland* (1970) and *Meridian* (1976).

Kentuckian Bobbie Ann Mason (born 1940) debuts with *Shiloh and Other Stories.*

1984

Virginia poet Henry Taylor (born 1942) publishes *The Flying Change: Poems*, receiving the Witter Bynner Prize for poetry and the Pulitzer Prize.

Ellen Gilchrist's (born 1935) novel *Victory Over Japan* wins the National Book Award.

North Carolina novelist Jill McCorkle's (born 1958) *The Cheer Leader* and *July 7th* are published simultaneously, introducing the author among several popular and acclaimed writers examining the New South.

1985

Larry McMurtry's *Lonesome Dove*, a sweeping epic of the old west, is a bestseller and wins the Pulitzer Prize. The novel is among his several notable works based in Texas in which he explores the mythology of the west.

Texas-born, Alabama-raised poet Andrew Hudgins publishes his first book, *Saints and Strangers*, which is nominated for the Pulitzer Prize. Later volumes would include *After the Lost War* (1988) and *The Glass Hammer: A Southern Childhood* (1994). Many of his poems concern Southern themes and settings.

1986

South Carolina writer Pat Conroy (born 1945), who drew attention earlier with *The Great Santini* (1976), publishes a bestseller, *Prince of Tides* (1986).

1987

West Virginia native Henry Louis Gates, Jr., emerges as a leading contemporary critical theorist with *Figures in Black: Words, Signs, and the Racial Self* followed in 1988 by *The Signifying Monkey: Towards a Theory of Afro-American Literary Criticism*.

The Pulitzer Prize is awarded to Rita Dove for *Thomas and Beulah*. Dove would later become the nation's poet laureate.

North Carolinian Kaye Gibbons (born 1960) enjoys an auspicious debut with *Ellen Foster*.

1988

Native Atlantan Alfred Uhry wins the Pulitzer Prize for his popular play, *Driving Miss Daisy*; he would also win an Academy Award for his screenplay adaptation of the play.

1989

The massive *Encyclopedia of Southern Culture*, compiled and edited by William R. Ferris and Charles Reagan Wilson, is published.

1990

South Carolinian farmer Dori Sanders publishes her first novel, *Clover*, as she nears sixty and becomes a much sought after speaker.

1991

Mississippian John Grisham's (born 1955) *The Firm* begins his annual string of bestselling novels set in the world of law.

1994

Louisiana-born poet and editor Yusef Komunyakaa wins the Pulitzer Prize for *Neon Venacular: New and Selected Poems*.

1995

Horton Foote's *The Young Man from Atlanta* wins the Pulitzer Prize, capping the career of the dramatist whose first play was produced fifty years earlier, and whose credits include fiction, teleplays, and Academy Award-winning screenplays for *To Kill a Mockingbird* and *Tender Mercies*.

1996

Richard Ford (born 1944) wins the Pulitzer Prize for *Independence Day*.

1997

North Carolinian Charles Frazier publishes his Civil War novel *Cold Mountain*, which becomes a bestseller and wins the National Book Award.

1998

W. W. Norton & Company publishes *The Literature of the American South*, edited by William L. Andrews and others. It is the first acknowledgment of Southern literature by the most influential purveyor of literature anthologies.

ADVISERS

Doris Betts
Thomas M. Carlson
David K. Jeffrey

Donald S. Noble
Shannon Ravenel

CONTRIBUTORS

Fleur Adcock
Kathleen Aguero
Daniel Anderson
Alvin Aubert
Frances E. Badgett
Janes S. Bakerman
William C. Bamberger
Perry Bear
K. Wesley Berry
Anne Boyd
M. E. Bradford
Tammy J. Bronson
Jackie Buxton
Thomas M. Carlson
Michael M. Cass
Paul Christensen
William E. Clarkson
Emma Cobb
Rae M. Carlton Colley
Jennifer Coman
George Core
Richard Damashek
George DeMan
R. H. W. Dillard
Paul A. Doyle
Don Keck DuPree
Gayle Edwards
Elizabeth Evans
Norman Friedman
Barry W. Gardner
Greg Garrett
Lois Gordon
John Grammar
Benjamin Griffith
Pat Borden Gubbins
Janet V. Haedicke
Catherine D. Halley
Kristin Hart
Mary Hess
Hillary Holladay
Janis Butler Holm
Jennifer Hubbard
Theodore R. Hudson
Elaine W. Hughes
Dot Jackson
David K. Jeffrey
Jeanine Johnson

Paul Christian Jones
Sue Laslie Kimball
Jerome Klinkowitz
Judson Knight
Judith C. Kohl
Mel Koler
Norbert Krapf
Jay Lamar
Canidis LaPrade
Janice Milner Lasseter
Chris Leigh
Mary Lystad
Tom Mack
Tod Marshall
Robert McDowell
Martin McGovern
Ian McMechan
Howard McNaughton
Kev P. McVeigh
Deborah T. Meem
Preston Merchant
Christopher Metress
David Middleton
Tyrus Miller
Joseph R. Millichap
Robert Miola
Jason P. Mitchell
Charmaine Allmon Mosby
Elizabeth Mulligan
Donald R. Nobel
Jeanne R. Nostrandt
Kristin Palm
Jay Parini
Leigh Tillman Partington
Eric Patterson
Annette Petrusso
Frank T. Phipps
Shannon Ravenel
John M. Reilly
Rosemary M. Canfield Reisman
John Herbert Roper
Hugh Ruppersburg
William J. Schaffer
Andy Solomon
Carol Simpson Stern
Keith Stiles
Christopher C. Swann

David Y. Todd
Dennis Vannatta
Alphonse Vinh
Bruce Walker
Elinor Ann Walker
Michelle L. Wallace
Mary Warner

Virginia Watkins
Denise Wiloch
J. J. Wilson
Gary K. Wolfe
Harold Woodell
Jon Woodson
Dawn Gilchrist Young

CONTEMPORARY SOUTHERN WRITERS

LIST OF ENTRANTS

Alice Adams
Betty Adcock
Dorothy Allison
Lisa Alther
A. R. Ammons
Claudia Emerson Andrews
Maya Angelou
Tina McElroy Ansa
Gloria Anzaldúa
James Applewhite
Alvin Aubert
Marilou Awiakta

William Baldwin
Dave Barry
Frederick Barthelme
Steven Barthelme
Rick Bass
Richard Bausch
Madison Smartt Bell
Gregory Benford
Lerone Bennett, Jr.
Wendell Berry
Doris Betts
Sallie Bingham
Diann Blakely
Jerry Bledsoe
Roy Blount
Cindy Bonner
Sheila Bosworth
David Bottoms
Edgar Bowers
John Ed Bradley
Cleanth Brooks
Dee Brown
Larry Brown
Linda Beatrice Brown
Rita Mae Brown
Sandra Brown
Jimmy Buffett
James Lee Burke
Franklin Burroughs
Jack Butler
Robert Olen Butler

Will Campbell
Turner Cassity
Fred Chappell
Mark Childress
Lucille Clifton
William Cobb
Judith Ortiz Cofer
Pat Conroy
Stephen Coonts
George Core

Alfred Corn
Patricia Daniels Cornwell
Vicki Covington
Harry Crews
Moira Crone

Janice Daugharty
Guy Davenport
Angela Davis
Ossie Davis
Elizabeth Dewberry
James Dickey
R. H. W. Dillard
David Dooley
Ellen Douglas
Rita Dove
Andre Dubus
John Dufresne
Pam Durban

Tony Earley
Charles East
Charles Edward Eaton
Clyde Edgerton
John Ehle
Ralph Ellison
Percival Everett

William R. Ferris
John Finlay
Fannie Flagg
Horton Foote
Shelby Foote
Jesse Hill Ford
Richard Ford
Connie May Fowler
William Price Fox, Jr.
John Hope Franklin
Charles Frazier
Robert Fulghum

Ernest J. Gaines
George Garrett
Henry Louis Gates, Jr.
Tim Gautreaux
Kaye Gibbons
Margaret Gibson
Ellen Gilchrist
Nikki Giovanni
Gail Godwin
Sue Grafton
Shirley Ann Grau
Melissa Fay Greene
Jim Grimsley
John Grisham

Lewis Grizzard
Winston Groom
Allan Gurganus

Alyson Hagy
John Haines
Alex Haley
James Baker Hall
Barry Hannah
Elizabeth Hardwick
Thomas Harris
Shelby Hearon
Beth Henley
Carl Hiaasen
William Hoffman
Mary Hood
Andrew Hudgins
T. R. Hummer
William Humphrey
Josephine Humphreys

Molly Ivins

John Jakes
Mark Jarman
David Jauss
Edward P. Jones
Gayl Jones
Madison Jones
Patricia Spears Jones
Rodney Jones
Donald Justice

Terry Kay
Randall Kenan
James Kilgo
Nanci Kincaid
Florence King
Barbara Kingsolver
Peter Klappert
Yusef Komunyakaa
Charles Kuralt

Patricia Lear
Harper Lee
Romulus Linney
Bret Lott
Beverly Lowry
George Ella Lyon
Andrew Lytle

David Madden
Haki R. Madhubuti
Clarence Major
Bobbie Ann Mason
Cormac McCarthy
Ed McClanahan
Jill McCorkle
Sharyn McCrumb
Tim McLaurin
Larry McMurtry
James Alan McPherson

Vassar Miller
Joseph Mitchell
Marion Montgomery
Elizabeth Seydel Morgan
Robert Morgan
Willie Morris
Albert Murray

Lewis Nordan
Marsha Norman
Helen Norris
Naomi Shihab Nye

Chris Offutt

Linda Pastan
David Payne
T. R. Pearson
Walker Percy
Dale Ray Phillips
Jayne Anne Phillips
Sam Pickering
Daniel Manus Pinkwater
Padgett Powell
Minnie Bruce Pratt
Eugenia Price
Reynolds Price
Wyatt Prunty

Ishmael Reed
John Shelton Reed
Sheri Reynolds
Anne Rice
Adrienne Rich
Mark Richard
Tom Robbins
Louis D. Rubin, Jr.

James Sallis
Ferrol Sams
Sonia Sanchez
Dori Sanders
Valerie Sayers
James Seay
Mary Lee Settle
Eve Shelnutt
Anne Rivers Siddons
Margaret Skinner
Dave Smith
Julie Smith
Lee Smith
William Jay Smith
Elizabeth Spencer
Max Steele
James Still
Leon Stokesbury
Ruth Stone
Dabney Stuart
William Styron

Henry Taylor
Mildred Taylor

Peter Taylor
Hunter S. Thompson
Christopher Tilghman
Richard Tillinghast
Anne Tyler

Alfred Uhry

Ellen Bryant Voigt

Howard Waldrop
Alice Walker
Margaret Walker
Brad Watson
Eudora Welty
Michael Lee West

Bailey White
Greg Williamson
James Wilcox
Sylvia Wilkinson
Joan Williams
John A. Williams
Miller Williams
Calder Willingham
Charles Reagan Wilson
Chris Wiltz
Tom Wolfe
Tobias Wolff
C. Vann Woodward
C. D. Wright

Shay Youngblood

A

ADAMS, Alice

Born: Fredericksburg, Virginia, 14 August 1926. **Education**: Radcliffe College, Cambridge, Massachusetts, A.B. 1946. **Family**: Married in 1946 (divorced 1958); one son. **Career**: Has worked as secretary, clerk, and bookkeeper; writes full-time. Currently lives in San Francisco. **Awards**: O. Henry Awards, Doubleday & Co., 1971-82 and 1984-96; National Book Critics Circle Award nomination, 1975, for *Families and Survivors*; National Endowment for the Arts grant, 1976; Guggenheim fellowship, 1978; O. Henry Special Award for Continuing Achievement, 1982; Best American Short Stories Awards, 1992 and 1996. **Address**: c/o Knopf Inc., 201 East 50th Street, New York, New York 10022.

PUBLICATIONS

Novels

Careless Love. New York, New American Library, 1966; as *The Fall of Daisy Duke*, London, Constable, 1967.
Families and Survivors. New York, Knopf, 1975; London, Constable, 1976.
Listening to Billie. New York, Knopf, and London, Constable, 1978.
Rich Rewards. New York, Knopf, 1980.
Superior Women. New York, Knopf, 1984; London, Heinemann, 1985.
Second Chances. New York, Knopf, and London, Methuen, 1988.
Caroline's Daughters. New York, Knopf, 1991.
Almost Perfect. New York, Knopf, 1993.
A Southern Exposure. New York, Knopf, 1995.

Short Story Collections

Beautiful Girl. New York, Knopf, 1979.
To See You Again. New York, Knopf, 1982.
Molly's Dog. Concord, New Hampshire, Ewert, 1983.
Return Trips. New York, Knopf, 1985; London, Heinemann, 1986.
After You've Gone. New York, Knopf, 1989.

Uncollected Short Stories

"Earthquake Damage," in *New Yorker*, 7 May 1990.
"The Last Lovely City," in *New Yorker*, 11 March 1991.

Other

Roses, Rhododendron: Two Flowers, Two Friends. Minneapolis, Redpath Press, 1987.
Mexico: Some Travels and Travelers There. New York and London, Prentice Hall, 1990.

*   *   *

Alice Adams is noted for her character studies of women in which she focuses on specific, defining incidents in their lives, particularly during transitional periods as they pursue happiness and independence. Her fiction can be rich in detail of settings, interpersonal relationships, and activities relating to her protagonists' professions—which include interior design and writing—while spanning many years. Adams draws heavily on her own background for the geography of her characters, both literally and figuratively. Like Adams herself, many of her characters were raised in the South, went to college in Boston, and end up in San Francisco. Her repeated exploration of personal change can relate to a larger social context—the post World War II era when more women pursued self-realization, for example, and more casual discussion of personal sexual experiences.

While the experiences of Daisy Duke in *Careless Love* (1966), Adams's first novel, are typical of many of Adams' heroines in her detail-laden novels, this work has a more sentimental tone than those that followed. Duke renounces her husband as too inadequate and a lover as too ordinary before finding happiness with another lover as dashing as Rudolph Valentino. Adams next two works define her maturity as a novelist. The narrative of *Families and Survivors* spans three decades in the life of Louisa Calloway, a woman who grew up privileged in the South. Calloway's social circle includes a professor of English who is an unsuccessful novelist, a psychiatrist of Jewish extraction, and many women confidantes. *Families and Survivors* also introduces the kind of narrative pacing typical in Adams's work: the action can slow to describe in detail a few moments in Calloway's life—a description of a social function, or meeting a new love interest—while years can be condensed in a few sentences.

Listening to Billie (1978) has two main characters, Eliza Hamilton Quareles and her half-sister, Daria, though Eliza predominates. Daria has a successful marriage while Eliza is widowed when her husband dies young, as husbands often do in Adams' novels, though Eliza's husband, unlike others, commits suicide. Eliza then has a series of affairs and a relatively successful life. The title, *Listening to Billie*, refers to performances and songs by jazz singer Billie Holiday that Eliza remembers and which form a backdrop to her story. Middle-aged Daphne Matthiessen, a native of Wisconsin, is the heroine of *Rich Rewards* (1980). While visiting Europe with her husband, Matthiessen has a brief tryst with a Frenchman, Jean-Paul. After returning to the United States, she leaves her husband and starts a career as an interior decorator. Her life is a series of love affairs until she resumes her relationship with Jean-Paul twenty years later.

Superior Women (1984), one of her most acclaimed works, is often compared to Mary McCarthy's novel, *The Group*, as Adams follows the lives of four very different friends from their schooldays at Radcliffe, beginning in the 1940s. The four have strong ties to each other, their lovers, and their own life histories. However, like many other Adams heroines, they measure themselves by the men they have loved and engage in Freudian analysis of there experiences. Larger social concerns become more prominent in *Second Chances* (1988). As in all her works, Adams focuses on the interpersonal relationships of her characters, but in *Second Chances* they are the concerns of people in their sixties and facing the problems of aging and death. In *Almost Perfect* (1993), Adams presents the rise and fall of the relationship between journalist Stella Blake and artist Richard Fallon. The details are recorded minutely and described from many characters points of view. Adams' 1995 novel, *A Southern Exposure*, features a couple from New England, Cynthia and Harry Baird, and a familiar circle of frustrated friends. The couple's move from New England to North Carolina results in new perspectives on their lives.

The transitions women undergo in their search for happiness and independence central to Adams's novels is also a key element of her short stories. While Adams is usually compassionate in her portrayal of her female characters, she can also explore the ironies in their lives. But as illustrated in the deftly emotional short stories found in her four collections *Beautiful Girl* (1979), *To See You Again* (1982), *Return Trips* (1985), and *After You've Gone* (1989)—many of her female characters find a sense of financial freedom through inheritance. With that money, the women are free to live as they like—redecorating their home, or, more often than not, replacing their husband with a new love. In other stories, the female protagonist holds a steady job and cares for a child.

In Adams' world of the wealthy, women move forward to find a new love, or step back to contemplate their old relationships. Indeed, lovers are more valued than husbands. The end of a marriage is less painful than the loss of a lover. In her novels, especially, Adams' women gauge their sufferings by the men in their lives. Though her female characters are learned, they chose a loose interpretation of Freud as their primary cerebral wellspring. A number of her heroines discover deep emotional ties to their father or an adversarial relationship with their mother as a source of their present troubles. Beyond these generalities, each of Adams' novels has no unexpected twists, though they are replete with much action.

—Annette Petrusso

ADCOCK, Betty

Born: Elizabeth Sharp in Fort Worth, Texas, 16 September 1938. **Education:** Texas Tech University, 1956-57; North Carolina State University, 1965-66; Goddard College, 1966-68. **Family:** Married Donald B. Adcock (an associate director of music, North Carolina State University), June 1957; one child. **Career:** Copywriter and producer, Ralph Johnson Associates, 1969-73; freelance advertising copywriter, since 1973; instructor, Poets-in-the-Schools programs in North Carolina and Virginia; visiting writer in residence, Kalamazoo College; instructor in creative writing, Duke University; Kenan Writer in Residence, Meredith College, Raleigh; served as an editor of *Southern Poetry Review*; member of women's committee, Cooperative of Small Magazine Editors and Publishers. **Awards:** Poetry selected for inclusion in Borestone Mountain Poetry Awards, Best Poems of 1966, 1967; North Carolina Award for Literature, 1996, for dedication to writing and teaching.

PUBLICATIONS

Poetry Collections

Walking Out. Baton Rouge, Louisiana State University Press, 1975.
Nettles. Baton Rouge, Louisiana State University Press, 1983.
Beholdings. Baton Rouge, Louisiana State University Press, 1988.
The Difficult Wheel: Poems. Baton Rouge, Louisiana State University Press, 1995.

Others

Contributor, *New Southern Poets.* University of North Carolina Press, 1975.
Contributor, *I Have Been Hungry All The Years.* Solo Press, 1975.

*

Critical Studies: "Coming Home to Texas: The Poetry of R.G. Vliet and Betty Adcock" by Dave Oliphant, *Pawn Review*, Spring 1984; "Betty Adcock" by Tom Hawkins, *Southern Poetry Review*, Spring 1989.

* * *

There is something about the South that is inescapably ironic, and Betty Adcock knows it. Much of the past is lost, but that loss is ever-present. We have to look back to move forward. Life is beautiful, and it hurts. Poems reside in small things, but from these small things arise grand ideas.

Poetry, Adcock affirms, is a type of knowledge, a way of perceiving and understanding. But hers is no romantic vision of the world, as *Walking Out*, her first collection (1975) attests. Adcock is a realist but not a pessimist, a world view she further embraces in her second book, *Nettles* (1983). In "Traveling, 1950," a poem dedicated to William Stafford, a fellow realist, Adcock merges vision and theme. The speaker, like Adcock, accepts, from the beginning, dark realities, but the image rolls on, snagging itself on a sliver of light: "It is winter. We can just glimpse the moon / passing where the trees are gone." The speaker rides with her father through farm land, and just as she begins to drift into the darkness of sleep, they "pass a house so near the road / we're touched with small, sudden light / from the windows, bolts of dim yellow / flung like silk across a broken porch." Perhaps all of Adcock's poetry strives to drape light over blackness and decay; therefore, this image is particularly illuminating. The truth of the experience, the grand idea of it, concludes the poem:

Some things are just so simple they are seen
exactly true just once, and then forever
the pieces of the mind come back
not fitting anywhere,

clear only then
in poor houselight that clouds our car
as if we are the mirror passed
across a face for evidence,
across a sleeping country where some war
has just commenced.

I say it's nothing. I don't speak of it.
My breath on the dark glass leaves a dripping print.

When Adcock says it's nothing, we know, of course, it's something. Even if it is merely breath on dark glass, it is a smudge of hope, evidence of life.

Redemption is found not only in the content of Adcock's work, but also in the process of poetry itself, in taking an experience and turning it into language. "The Case for Gravity," from *Beholdings* (1988), captures the complexity of her technique, as well as that characteristic Southern irony. The literal situation of the poem is the speaker's recalling a moment when she was five years old and toppled from the porch into a bed of hydrangeas, but observe how Adcock takes the seeds of this experience and nourishes them into full-fledged religious celebration:

I flopped hard, like a trout,
on a world gone bust, blue bits of it
floating sweetly down the pewter air
as I stood up baptized with mud . . .

After the first fall, there are the others:
vertigo's possibilities, the love
like a dropped cup, all hope
spilled so out of reach the world lets go
to bluest distance.

Always the ground
reels me in to its cruel flowers, nothing ideal,
blue taste of beauty on the bitten tongue.
Say this time too I'll stand
mud-colored, abloom with bruises, vivid with news.

Say these are sheaves of fishes in my hands.

Adcock explores the idea that if there had been no original fall, there would be no grace. She plays on the concept of gravity, the alternate meanings of the word, as well as the fact that gravity always follows the same path. It is fair to say that in this poem, the speaker and poet are one, and therefore the speaker, in becoming the fish, also becomes the poem. So the poem itself, through the process of being written and through its eventually permanent form, transubstantiates into spiritual food.

Adcock heralds the meaning of form in poetry—its ability to balance life, to rotate it on its axis and to bring it into light. Her work is exceedingly careful, a life's work, a treasure chest of over a quarter-century of writing. And she is still going strong. Since her last book, *The Difficult Wheel: Poems* (1995), she has been honored as one of five finalists for the William Carlos Williams Paterson Prize and has received, for her lifetime of dedication, the 1996 North Carolina Award for Literature. She has helped edit an anthology of poems celebrating the 50th anniversary of the North Carolina Museum of Art, and she is currently compiling a collection of new and selected poems.

Adcock is a lasting poet, in part because she revisits the same themes and ironies much in the way we revisit our own lives, but also because she teaches us to trust that although we are inextricably linked to our pasts, our environments, and our pains and fears, poetry—this otherworldly knowledge—is a thing, a most beautiful thing, that comforts us.

—Jennifer Hubbard

ALLISON, Dorothy

Born: Greenville, South Carolina, 11 April 1949. **Education:** Florida Presbyterian College, St. Petersburg, B.A. 1971; New School of Social Research, M.A. in anthropology. **Family:** Companion of Alix Layman since 1987; one son. **Awards:** Lambda Literary awards, 1988, for *Trash;* National Book Award nomination and Bay Area Book Reviewers Association Prize for Fiction, both 1992 for *Bastard out of Carolina.* **Agent:** Frances Goldin, 305 East 11th Street, New York, New York 10003.

PUBLICATIONS

Poetry

The Women Who Hate Me. Brooklyn, New York, Long Haul Press, 1983; as *The Women Who Hate Me: Poetry, 1980-1990,* Ithaca, New York, Firebrand Books, 1991.

Short Story Collection

Trash. Ithaca, New York, Firebrand Books, 1988.

Novels

Bastard out of Carolina. New York and London, Flamingo, 1993.
Cavedweller. New York, Dutton, 1998.

Essay Collection

Skin: Talking about Sex, Class, and Literature. Ithaca, New York, Firebrand Books, 1994.

Uncollected Essays

"I Am Working on My Charm," in *Conditions: Six*, 1980.
"The Billie Jean King Thing," in *New York Native*, 18(31), May 1981.
"Confrontation: Black/White," in *Building Feminist Theory: Essays from "Quest"* edited by Charlotte Bunch and others. New York, Longman, 1981.

Autobiography

Two or Three Things I Know for Sure. New York, Dutton, 1995.

*

Media Adaptations: *Bastard out of Carolina* (audiocassette), New York, Penguin/HighBridge, 1993; *Bastard out of Carolina* has been optioned for film.

Critical Studies: "White Trash in Your Face: The Literary Descent of Dorothy Allison" by David Reynolds, *Appalachian Jour-*

nal, 1993; "Dorothy Allison" by Lisa Moore, *Contemporary Lesbian Writers of the United States: A Bio-Bibliographical Critical Sourcebook* edited by Sandra Pollack and Denise Knight, Westport, Connecticut, Greenwood Press, 1993; "The Roseanne of Literature" by Alexis Jetter, in *New York Times Magazine,* December 17, 1995.

*   *   *

The life and writing of Dorothy Allison illustrate her firm commitment to the two "outlaw" cultures with which she identifies: her "white trash" South Carolina family, and her sexually daring (and non-PC) lesbian activist associates. Allison's poetry, essays, and fiction explore the terrible violence and beauty of both these cultures; indeed, she says, "writing is the only way I know to make sure of my ongoing decision to live."

Born in 1949, Allison grew up in Greenville, South Carolina, in a hardscrabble "trash" family where the women died of cancer and the men of knife wounds or cirrhosis long before they were old enough to qualify for Social Security. Her stepfather abused her sexually from the time she was five until she was eleven years old. The memory of this abuse, and of her mother's inability to protect her from it, represent the core of much of Allison's writing. Several of the stories in her 1988 collection *Trash* attempt to make sense of her painful and impoverished childhood.

In 1992 Allison's first full-length novel, *Bastard out of Carolina,* introduced Bone, a semi-autobiographical title character. Bone's life—from her illegitimate birth through young adulthood—is described in raw detail and with painful love. *Bastard out of Carolina* was a finalist for the National Book Award; Allison had transformed her vision of her painful roots into a nationwide bestseller. She would follow up this success with a nonfiction meditation on her family, entitled *Two or Three Things I Know for Sure* (1995). In this memoir Allison includes stories, personal memories, and photographs of family members who would otherwise be forgotten; "The bottom line," she says, "is I'm writing to save the dead."

Allison's other writings focus on her life as a lesbian activist. Here again she writes from the margins, describing not only her involvement in lesbian-feminist communal life in the early 1970s, but also her status as a sexual outlaw during the so-called "Lesbian Sex Wars" of the 1980s. Allison's 1983 poetry collection, *The Women Who Hate Me,* outraged mainstream feminists by praising sexual promiscuity, sadomasochism, and butch-femme lesbian roles. Some of the stories in *Trash* also push the PC envelope, as does Allison's 1994 essay collection *Skin: Talking about Sex, Class, and Literature.* Allison says, on the one hand, that her involvement in "vanilla-sex" feminism "saved my life." At night, however, she would "sneak out of the collective to date a butch woman my house mates thought retrograde and sexist." Even in the aggressively countercultural world of lesbian feminism, Allison was a maverick.

For Allison, writing is a dramatic, life-affirming act in a world which consistently threatens death. A storyteller since childhood, Allison chronicles her discovery how telling even her most terrible stories out loud confines them to the realm of the "ironic and playful," but writing them down gives her power over the experiences she describes. "Putting those stories down on paper," she writes, enables her "to shape my life outside my terrors and helplessness, to make it visible and real in a tangible way." Rather than whitewashing unpleasant experience, Allison's writing opens the way into healthy truth-telling. Herein lies the connection between her writing and her lesbian identity and politics. For Allison, telling the truth about growing up "trash" is part of a politics of disclosure: "It is only as the child of my class and my unique family background that I have been able to . . . regain a sense of why I believe in activism, why self-revelation is so important for lesbians." Her queer writing seeks to portray the world as "a place where the truth would be hallowed, not held on contempt, where silence would be impossible." In short, in a world where Silence = Death, Allison insists on the counter-equation Self-revelation = Life = Survival.

This philosophy plays itself out repeatedly in her writing. A frequent theme is how a female character journeys from an oral to a "literate" culture, a journey which leads the young woman away from silence towards voice, from lies towards truth, from death towards life. In *Bastard out of Carolina,* for instance, Bone learns that both her orality-based "trash" culture and academic "book-learning" are helpless to prevent the violence that threatens to engulf her—poverty, sickness, beatings, rape, death. Sensing that survival is linked to telling stories, Bone learns to lie. With engaging bravado she enthralls neighbor children with her tales, and dreams of spinning spellbinding sermons in revival tents. But behind the dreams lay only silence where the truth should have been. Only after Bone breaks the conspiracy of silence surrounding her stepfather's abuse can the healing begin. Similarly, author Allison's books emerge from her desire "to be real in the world, without lies or evasions or sweet-talking nonsense." For her, books represent a kind of reality that "real" experience lacks. She uses literature to communicate the "dreams I dare not speak" but can write. Such written dreams form part of a literary, cultural, and political project that Allison sees as "vital to organizing your own survival."

Cavedweller, her 1998 novel, reaffirms these values, with the "organizing of survival" occurring as her protagonist begins to take a greater sense of personal responsibility for herself and others. Delia Bird left behind a troubled past that included abuse for an adventurous life with a rock star; she also abandoned two daughters and is remembered in her small Georgia hometown as "the bitch" who ran off and left her babies. When her partner dies in a motorcycle accident, Delia undertakes a journey home with her young daughter, Cissy, to confront her past. Allison has said that the abuse she endured stole away her childhood and her literary endeavors are an act of reclamation. So, too, in *Cavedwellers*, Delia's return is an act of reclamation, symbolized in Cissy's preoccupation with exploring a cave. When her ex-husband dies from cancer—Delia's caring for him is another act of reclamation—the four females—mother and daughters—begin a new life together to reclaim their stolen worlds.

—Deborah T. Meem and Mel Koler

ALTHER, Lisa

Born: Lisa Reed in Kingsport, Tennessee, 23 July 1944. **Education:** Wellesley College, 1962-66, B.A. 1966. **Family:** Married

Richard Alther, 1966; one daughter. **Career:** Editorial assistant, Atheneum Publishers, New York, 1966; staff writer, Garden Way Publishers, Charlotte, Vermont, 1969-72; visiting lecturer, St. Michael's College, Winooski, Vermont, 1980. **Address:** c/o Watkins-Loomis Inc., 133 E. 35th St., No.1, New York, New York 10016.

PUBLICATIONS

Novels

Kinflicks. New York, Knopf, 1976.
Original Sins. New York, Knopf, 1981.
Other Women. New York, Knopf, 1984.
Bedrock. New York, Knopf, 1990.
Five Minutes in Heaven. New York, Dutton, 1995.

Uncollected and Anthologized Short Stories

"Encounter," in *McCall's,* August 1976.
"The Art of Dying Well." In *A Collection of Classic Southern Humor,* edited by George William Koon, Atlanta, Peachtree, 1984.
"Termites." In *Homewords,* edited by Douglas Paschall, Knoxville, University of Tennessee Press, 1986.
"The Politics of Paradise." In *Louder than Words,* edited by William Shore, New York, Vintage, 1989.

Other

Non-Chemical Pest and Disease Control for the Home Orchard. Charlotte, Vermont, Garden Way, 1973.
Author of introduction, *Tess of the D'Urbervilles: A Pure Woman* by Thomas Hardy. New York, Signet Classic, 1999.

*

Critical Studies: "Condemned to Survival: The Comic Unsuccessful Suicide" by Marilynn J. Smith in *Comparative Literature Studies,* March 1980; "Alther and Dillard: The Appalachian Universe" by Frederick G. Waase in *Appalachia/America: The Proceedings of the 1980 Appalachian Studies Conference,* edited by Wilson Somerville, Johnson City, Tennessee, Appalachian Consortium Press, 1981.

Lisa Alther comments:
Amazon.com: How did you begin writing? Did you intend to become an author, or do you have a specific reason or reasons for writing each book?

Lisa Alther: In the fourth-grade play I was Miss Noun, who was married by the preacher to Mr. Verb. But in the tenth grade I read Faulkner's *The Sound and the Fury* and was delighted to discover that in stream-of-consciousness writing, you didn't always have to have a noun and a verb in every sentence. I thought this was really cool, so I wrote a stream-of-consciousness story for my high school newspaper. It was set in the head of Nathan Hale, the American patriot, on the morning he was to be hanged by the British for spying. As the soldiers appeared to take him away, he watched an autumn leaf fall to the ground and get trampled by their boots: "Spiraling down. Red and green and gold . . . etc."

I thought it was really profound and moving, but when it appeared in the paper, it had been rewritten. I raced into the faculty advisor's classroom and demanded to know who had wrecked my story. The advisor, an English teacher who was the wife of the local sheriff, said, "I bet you thought that story was pretty good?" I said , "I didn't think it was so bad that it needed to be completely redone." She said, "Well, let me tell you something, little lady: That story wasn't even written in complete sentences." I said if she was going to rewrite it , then she should put her own name on it. She said if I was going to speak to her in that tone of voice, I should just march myself right down to the principal's office and see what he had to say about it. He suggested that I sit home for a couple of days and consider the wisdom of being rude to my superiors.

This was my first experience with editors, and its lessons have come in handy ever since.

*   *   *

Lisa Alther comments with shrewdness, insight, and a hefty measure of irony upon American types, their trendy habits, and their dreams. Typical though they be, Alther's protagonists are, nevertheless, fully realized individuals who are sometimes despairing, prickly, dense, or self-destructive, but who are also unfailingly interesting folk, often surprisingly courageous survivors. These factors, along with Alther's keen sense of place, her clever manipulation of point of view, and her exploitation of various levels of comedy are the chief strengths of her five novels.

Alther's manipulation of point of view contributes to the sprawling effect of her bulky novels even as it helps control them. The picaresque *Kinflicks* alternates between third-person narration of the present moment as Ginny Babcock Bliss keeps vigil at her mother's deathbed, and first-person flashbacks which hilariously and satirically recount Ginny's penchant for redesigning herself to suit those who successively dominate her affections—parents, gum-chewing football hero, motorcycle hood, lesbian reformer, snow-mobile salesman, disturbed Viet vet, baby daughter. Ultimately, alone but rather more determined, she sets out to suit herself. The distancing effect of Ginny's memories facilitates the bald, raucous humor of the book for, in effect, Ginny is laughing at herself *with* her readers; the detachment of the third-person narrator in the alternate chapters legislates against melodrama or shallow sentimentality.

Though *Original Sins* is told in the third person, major sections allow readers to share the consciousness of five protagonists. Members of a huge extended family, sisters Emily and Sally Prince, brothers Jed and Raymond Tatro, and Donny Tatro are inseparable as children, but are later driven apart by circumstances of sex, social class, personal ambition, and race (Donny is black).

A *Bildungsroman, Original Sins* depicts youngsters who believe they can do anything, becoming adults who often wonder if anything worthwhile can be done—but who don't stop trying. *Other Women,* a "delayed *Bildungsroman,*" also uses the third person throughout and shifts between the consciousness of its protagonists, Carolyn Kelley, a single mother whose lesbian relationship is dissolving, and her therapist, Hannah Burke. As Hannah counsels Carolyn toward acceptance of herself, adulthood, and responsibility, some of her own very old, deep wounds begin to heal, and the novel concludes with a note of genuine hope symbolized by the women's developing friendship.

In *Other Women* and *Original Sins,* the availability of each protagonist's thought processes lends immediacy and realism as it arouses empathy. Readers may not fully endorse the protagonists' decisions, but they remain involved and concerned with the characters because their motivations are so clearly drawn. Suitably, the humor in these novels is quieter, developing more from quirks of personality and wry social comment than from the slapstick situations of *Kinflicks.*

Because both *Kinflicks* and *Original Sins* are set primarily in Tennessee, her home state, Alther has been dubbed a regionalist. She recognizes the influence of fellow southerner Flannery O'Connor upon her literary sensibilities and freely acknowledges the usefulness and attraction of the "ready-made social context" available to southerners writing about their area (see her article "Will the South Rise Again?" in *New York Times Book Review,* 16 December 1979).

It is equally important, however, to note that Alther's settings range across the eastern United States. Her assessment of college life on a New York City campus, her stringent portrayal of the power struggles among supposedly egalitarian Northern civil rights workers (*Original Sins*), her lovingly drawn Vermont landscapes in *Other Women*—as well as her acknowledgment that conducting a private life privately is just as difficult in any closed Northern community as it is in a southern one (*Kinflicks*)—attest to her understanding of several locales and make explicit the wide scope of her social commentary. In this way, Alther differs a bit from regionalists who imply rather than dramatize the larger applications of their social comment.

Considered by many to be a feminist writer, Alther focuses primarily upon contemporary American women, giving great attention to the limitations thrust upon them, but she also details their self-imposed restrictions and stresses the need for each to assume responsibility for her own life. In an interview with Andrew Feinberg (*Horizon,* May 1981), she comments, "People are assigned roles because of their external characteristics and then are forced to play them out . . . unless they are lucky enough to figure out what is going on and get out."

The process of getting out, always painful, sometimes unsuccessful, is the motivational force in Alther's plots and functions as effectively for several male characters as it does for females. Alther's awareness that despite the deep social divisions which exist between many contemporary women and men, there are also shared problems—such as the constrictions of traditionalism, the desire to escape from parents' demands, the difficulties of assimilation into another cultural-geographic region—demonstrates the universality of feminist fiction just as her humor reveals that feminist writers can treat serious subjects without being deadly dull. By modifying critical categories, Alther produces novels incorporating strong plots and intriguing characterizations with effective social commentary.

Bedrock and *Five Minutes in Heaven* continue Alther's portrayal of characters in the process of self-discovery and "getting out" with her typical blend of humor and insight. In *Bedrock* Alther

draws on the twenty-year friendship between Virginia Woolf and Vita Sackville-West in the tale of two contemporary women who are emotional opposites and eventually come to express their love. Alther has said that the two women—Clea, a vibrant and sometimes shallow photographer, and Elke, a German-immigrant sculptor who is more profound and more susceptible to depression—can be viewed as different modes of a single personality. Clea has lived an adventurous life of travel, domesticity (she was married and mothered a child), and sexual experiences, but an escape trip to Vermont with Elke exposes her deeper feelings of anomie and Elke's more sober view of life—each finding a better personal balance through their relationship. Their different temperaments, as well as the easy flow of Alther's prose and the humor always present in Alther's work, are apparent in the moment they acknowledge sexual attraction for each other:

> "What are we going to do about this?" asked Elke.
> "About what?" asked Clea, swallowing with difficulty.
> "Don't be coy." Putting her hands on Clea's shoulders, she studied Clea at arms' length until Clea dropped her eyes and nodded. "After all, isn't this why we're here?"
> Clea said nothing. She had wanted Elke to herself, but there was a reason Elke had so studiously avoided this—and here it was. With all their innocent talk of joint studios, they had both watched the locomotive approach, bound firmly to the tracks by desire. She took one of Elke's hands from her shoulder and held the wrist to her lips. Elke's pulse pounded against her lower lip.
> "Yes, I guess so," replied Clea, poised somewhere between terror and elation.

Alther's easy humor is evident again in a preceding passage, as Clea clandestinely photographs Elke as she sleeps:

> Raising her camera and adjusting the focus, Clea studied Elke through her zoom lens—the silver hair and high cheekbones, the sharp chin and slightly parted lips. Slowly she pressed the shutter release. The click resounded in the hot, still afternoon like a gunshot. Wishing she had a silencer, she continued shooting.

Five Minutes in Heaven concerns Jude, who undergoes a comic series of adventures in pursuit of love, the personal-quest story that Alther has come to master, full of wry humor, sexual adventurousness, and an acknowledgment of deeper concerns through which characters begin to see through their own illusions and temporal pleasures. Pursuing an erotic dancer in Paris sets the stage for a mesmerizing journey where Jude's comic detachment will not suffice in acknowledging the external forces and events that have influenced her life. The events include several deaths—her young mother, her friend Molly killed in a car crash, her friend Sandy, liberated sexually then consumed by AIDS. As in each of Alther's works, we are drawn into her protagonists' pursuits of pleasure, the comic views of life, the spirited lifestyles and uneasy adventures, then begin to face the more difficult and darker realities sometimes submerged—the personal quest motif applied to contemporary times and values.

—Jane S. Bakerman and Mel Koler

AMMONS, A. R.

Born: Archie Randolph Ammons in Whiteville, North Carolina, 18 February 1926. **Education:** Wake Forest College, B.S. 1949; University of California, Berkeley, 1951-52. **Military Service:** U.S. Naval Reserve, 1944-46. **Family:** Married Phyllis Plumbo in 1949, one son. **Career:** Principal, Hatteras Elementary School, Hatteras, North Carolina, 1949-50; executive vice-president, Freidrich and Dimmock, Inc. (glass manufacturers), Millville, New Jersey, 1952-61; poetry editor, *Nation*, 1963; professor of English, since 1964, Goldwin Smith Professor of Poetry, since 1973, Cornell University, Ithaca, New York; visiting professor of English, 1974-75, and visiting distinguished professor of poetry, 1997-98, Wake Forest University. **Awards:** Bread Loaf Writers Conference scholarship, 1961; Guggenheim fellowship, 1966; American Academy of Arts and Letters traveling fellowship, 1967, and award, 1977; Levinson Prize, 1970; National Book Award, 1973 and 1994; Bollingen Prize, 1973-74; MacArthur fellowship, 1981; National Book Critics Circle Award, 1981; Lannan Foundation Award, 1992; Poetry Society of America Robert Frost Medal, 1993; D.Litt. from Wake Forest University, 1972, and University of North Carolina, Chapel Hill, 1973. **Member:** American Academy of Arts and Sciences; Institute of Arts and Letters and Fellowship of Southern Writers.

PUBLICATIONS

Poetry

Tape for the Turn of the Year. New York, Norton, 1965; reprinted 1994.
Northfield Poems. Ithaca, New York, Cornell University Press, 1966.
Selected Poems. Ithaca, New York, Cornell University Press, 1968.
Uplands. New York, Norton, 1970.
Briefings: Poems Small and Easy. New York, Norton, 1971.
Collected Poems, 1951-1971. New York, Norton, 1973.
Sphere: The Form of a Motion. New York, Norton, 1974.
Diversifications. New York, Norton, 1975.
The Snow Poems. New York, Norton, 1977.
The Selected Poems, 1951-1977. New York, Norton, 1977.
Highgate Road. Ithaca, New York, Inkling Press, 1977.
Selected Longer Poems. New York, Norton, 1980.
A Coast of Trees. New York, Norton, 1981.
Wordly Hopes. New York, Norton, 1982.
Lake Effect Country. New York, Norton, 1983.
The Selected Poems: Expanded Edition. New York, Norton, 1986.
Sumerian Vistas. New York, Norton, 1987.
The Really Short Poems of A. R. Ammons. New York, Norton, 1990.
Garbage. New York, Norton, 1993.
Rarities. Brooktondale, New York, Larch Tree Press, 1994.
Stand-in. Brooktondale, New York, Larch Tree Press, 1994.
Brink Road. New York, Norton, 1996.
Glare. New York, Norton, 1997.

Other

Set in Motion: Essays, Interviews, and Dialogues edited by Zofia Burr. Ann Arbor, University of Michigan Press, 1996.

Author of introduction, *North Carolina's 400 Years : Signs Along the Way: An Anthology of Poems by North Carolina Poets to Celebrate America's 400th Anniversary* edited by Ronald H. Bayes. Durham, Acorn Press, 1986.

Audio recordings: *Selections, 1984,* Kansas City, New Letters, 1984; *Poets in Person,* by Gary Soto with Joseph Parisi, Chicago, Modern Poetry Association, 1991.

Adaptations: *Passages: For Soprano and Instrumental Ensemble* (based on poems by A. R. Ammons) by Ellen Taaffe Zwilich, Newton Centre, Massachusetts, Margun Music, 1981; *Four Poems of A. R. Ammons: For Baritone and Six Instruments* by Steven Stucky, Bryn Mawr, Merion Music, 1992.

*

Bibliography: *Ammons: A Bibliography, 1954-1979* by Stuart Wright, Winston-Salem, Wake Forest University, 1980.

Critical Studies: "Ammons Issue" of *Diacritics*, 1973; *A. R. Ammons* by Alan Holder, Boston, Twayne Publishers, 1978; *A. R. Ammons* edited by Harold Bloom, New York, Chelsea House Publishers, 1986; "The Work of A. R. Ammons," special issue of *Pembroke Magazine*, 1986; *A. R. Ammons and the Poetics of Widening Scope* by Steven P. Schneider, Rutherford, New Jersey, Fairleigh Dickinson University Press, 1994; *Critical Essays on A.R. Ammons* edited by Robert Kirschten, New York, G. K. Hall, 1997; *Approaching Prayer: Ritual and the Shape of Myth in A. R. Ammons and James Dickey* by Robert Kirschten, Baton Rouge, Louisiana State University Press, 1998.

*   *   *

The span of A. R. Ammons' talents is aptly symbolized by the first and last poems of his collection, *Brink Road* (1996). The volume begins with "A Sense of Now," an eighteen-line lyric that evokes H.D. and Williams with its crisp, poised, third-person couplets. It ends with "Summer Place," a poem of over one thousand lines whose tercets, scope, and first-person narrative recall Dante and the epic tradition. In between these ends of the formal and thematic spectrum are poems that exhibit his interest in the natural world, his tendencies toward scientific precision, and his belief in the importance of explicitly reflecting on poetic processes. For the most part, the themes, forms, and voices in *Brink Road* are not new: Ammons' career has followed a kind of spiraled course, a continuous and self-perpetuating investigation into the unified multiplicity that is the universe.

The long poem *Garbage* (1993) is another indicator of—and provides another metaphor for—the ways that Ammons' poetics have progressed by curling back in on themselves. He composed *Garbage* on a roll of adding machine paper, returning to the same unusual technique of his much earlier volume, *Tape for the Turn of the Year* (1965). Ammons engages this thoroughly inorganic restriction of form in both poems to mock the arbitrariness of such constraints, but also to confirm the role of artifice in composing poetry. At the beginning of *Tape for the Turn of the Year*, Ammons simultaneously ridicules and reinscribes the conventional invocation of a poetic muse. He then cautiously proceeds, remarking that "two weeks / have gone by, and / the Muse hasn't / rejected it, / seems caught up in the / serious novelty."

Novelty is perhaps the poem's greatest virtue, yet it is more than a self-indulgent exercise for Ammons. It is necessary for him to display and interrogate the ways that poems come to be, to reveal his own explorations into the procedures by which many words become—however tenuously and arbitrarily—a single work of art.

Ammons' second adding tape composition is more accomplished and is the work of a poet long convinced of the value of poetic self-reflection. The extraordinary accretion of images in *Garbage* is delivered by an accumulation of unrhymed couplets. The poet attests that "garbage has to be the poem of our time because / garbage is spiritual, believable enough // to get our attention, getting in the way, piling / up, stinking . . ." The casual, direct address and the predilection to explain himself are typical of Ammons' style. Willard Spiegelman declares that "as an explainer, A. R. Ammons is without peer. He constantly tells where he is going, taking retrospective glances when necessary at where he has been."

Ammons guides us on his search through the concept (and the literal evidence) of disposal. Garbage summons us as the most tangible and durable documentation of the fact that we have been alive. Throughout the poem, Ammons plays with the trope of decomposition, a much more powerful force than poetic creation: "words are a way of fending in the // world: whole languages, like species, can / disappear without dropping a gram of earth's // weight, and symbolic systems to a fare you well / can be added without filling a ditch or thimble." Garbage gets in the way and piles up, but poetry has no such material extension: it is not a thing in itself but a record of relationships between objects and ideas.

With *Garbage*, Ammons has reproduced another earlier feat: it won the National Book Award in 1994, as had his *Collected Poems, 1951-1971*, in 1973. A prolific and much-honored writer, Ammons has published over two dozen poetry collections to date and has received, among many other awards, the National Book Critics Circle Award, the Bollingen Prize, and a MacArthur fellowship. *The Selected Poems: Expanded Edition* (1986) provides the best introduction to Ammons. It contains many of his well-known works, such as "Corsons Inlet," "One: Many," "The City Limits," and "Easter Morning."

Ammons was born and raised in North Carolina and attended Wake Forest College (now University). Since then, for nearly fifty years, Ammons has lived and worked almost exclusively in the North. However, he has never fully freed himself as a poet from the influence of his upbringing, marked by what he calls the "religious saturation" of "a rural and defeated South."

Rustic scenes and his explorations of belief perhaps most clearly reveal a Southern inflection in his work, but he is not a regional writer. Ammons acknowledges his role as a Southern poet and admits that he has always felt like something of an exile in the North. In a 1978 interview, he affirmed, "I identify very deeply with the South emotionally and historically." Nevertheless, he adds that "the South has never welcomed my poetry particularly, or encouraged it at all. But the North has."

If Ammons has been pulled in two directions, it has proved beneficial to his work. The extended final image of the splendid poem "Easter Morning" offers a lesson on the benefits of having divided interests. In the poem, Ammons recalls returning to his hometown and visiting the cemetery in which many of his relatives are buried. After reflecting on "life nearest to life which is / life lost," he describes two birds heading northward. They interrupt their flight momentarily to circle back southward, "possibly / rising—at least, clearly resting," and then continue north. The poet exults in this "sight of bountiful / majesty and integrity: the having / patterns and routes, breaking / from them to explore other patterns or / better ways to routes, and then the return." Like these birds, Ammons has established patterns only to break them. Eventually, though, he circles back to his original starting point, his poem and his person having changed and improved for the experience.

—Jeannine Johnson

ANDREWS, Claudia Emerson

Born: Claudia Emersonin Chatham, Virginia, 13 January 1957. **Education:** University of Virginia, B.A. in English; University of North Carolina at Greensboro, M.F.A. in creative writing 1991. **Family:** Married Jesse Andrews. **Career:** Academic dean of Chatham Hall (a girls' boarding school), Chatham, Virginia, 1996-98; assistant professor of creative writing, Mary Washington College, Fredericksburg, Virginia, since 1998. **Awards:** Individual Artist fellowship, National Endowment for the Arts, 1994; Individual Artist Fellowship, Virginia Commission for the Arts, 1995; Associated Writing Programs Intro Award, 1997; Academy of American Poets Prize, 1997; nominated for the Pulitzer Prize, 1997, for *Pharaoh, Pharaoh*.

PUBLICATION

Poetry Collection

Pharaoh, Pharaoh. Baton Rouge, Louisiana State University Press, 1997.

*

Claudia Emerson Andrews comments:
    I've lived all my life in the same rural town (Chatham, Virginia); this is what I know. I, like other Southern writers, have a lot of respect for the generations that came before me. Up until my father's generation, my family has lived on and worked the land since the 1600s. My father gave it all up to run a store in town, and even though I've never owned an inch of land in my life, I feel very much tied to it.

*   *   *

    Claudia Emerson Andrews laughs as she traces the beginnings of her poetic vision to tenth-grade English, when her teacher asked the class to personify something. "I personified a storm," Andrews recalls, "and my teacher praised and read what I had written in front of the class." But having begun the M.F.A. program at Universtiy of North Carolina atGreensboro at age 32, Andrews feels as if she has come to poetry relatively late in life, and however true that feeling may be, a mere nine years later, in 1997, Andrews' first collection, *Pharaoh, Pharaoh*, was nominated for the Pulitzer Prize.

Pharaoh, Pharaoh explores the irony of loss, a theme Andrews identifies as particularly Southern. Andrews feels a familial relationship to other Southern writers: to William Faulkner and his indulgence of language; to Betty Adcock, a poet whom she classifies as "a very important person" in her life, noting that their friendship was forged after reading and admiring each others' work; and to Ellen Bryant Voight, who also is from Chatham and whose mother was Andrews' fourth-grade teacher.

Andrews believes that all Southern writers share a relationship with the landscape, from which she gathers most of her metaphors. "Cleaning the Graves," a poem Andrews notes as the most personal of the ones in *Pharaoh, Pharaoh*, exemplifies this relationship: "The once a year we come here is as close / as my mother comes to mourning. These graves / are all she has left of land she hated / losing. And I am descended from this / loss . . ." This idea of rebirth emerges as a major theme as Andrews pieces together the wreckage of her speakers' lives, which, she notes with a laugh, she finds much more interesting than her own.

Andrews is a pleasant person and a generous writer, politely pointing her readers toward what she plans to reveal. Her epigraph—"Everything we cannot see is here"—establishes *Pharaoh, Pharaoh* as a tribute to poet Robert Watson, one of her mentors, and lays the thematic groundwork. Thus, the reader begins his journey, observing in the first poem, "Searching the Title," that the speaker is given, just as Andrews gives to the reader, a map that "unscrolls to an old, forgotten dimension" with a legend revealing that a "changeless place, / unchartered, lies beneath these fields—a cave / whose mouth is lost." Knowing that the "way back is lost to dream," the speaker—and the reader—is prepared to excavate this darkness by returning "to the point and place of beginning." With this last phrase of the poem, Andrews sparks the reader's own search for light.

When she and her editor, Dave Smith, were deciding upon the organization of *Pharaoh, Pharaoh*, Andrews knew that she wanted "Inheritance" to be the final poem. Her logic is clear: "Inheritance" returns to the place of origin, to the irony revealed in the epigraph and to the irony of loss, through a narrative but spiritual account of a visit the speaker makes to her great-aunts, who, as they offer her "cider in their darkened parlor," tell her of her grandmother:

> With the butt of her knife, she cracked the baked hen's skull
> like an egg, dug out of the delicate brain, this above
> the clutter of tattered bones—back, wind, and thigh.
>
> The wild meat darker, leaner—gamey. She
> could close her eyes and taste the sassafras leaves,
> the apples hard and cidery, the evening dew.
> If she could hold the night on her tongue, it would taste

> like this doe who had swung as a suicide swings,
> suspended above the rest of us, her belly
> opened and divested of all that had defined her:
> lung, hunger, heart, desire, the slow compulsion
> of blood. She did dream night, gutted, tasted
> like this—at once—dead, and so deliciously wild.

Through this excerpt, one can see how Andrews creates tension between the line and the sentence and, thus, tension in the speaker and the reader. The idea of night being simultaneously dead and alive parallels the central paradox of *Pharaoh, Pharaoh*—being bound by something absent. The poem concludes

> And to her, I owe this terrible desire
> for lightness, a dark longing to wake to crow-
> black wings, to hold in my mouth not some sweet
> insistent lyric—but the one raucous thought that bears
> repeating, to carry between my lips the wild
> plum—round as a vowel—become perfect, singular
> in its loss of the world, to steal away from here
> the vain details I love—a thing bright and shiny
> that bears its saving: a thimble, a ring, a needle—
> its only eye worn wide, diminishing.

This eye, of course, becomes a metaphor for the speaker's eye, which recalls the epigraph and the opening poem's map, from which a "a murder of crow rises from a broken field / as though from violent seed," and, suddenly, one is overwhelmed by how meaningfully Andrews communicates with her readers, how she is able, so delicately, to illuminate their own stormy beginnings.

—Jennifer Hubbard

ANGELOU, Maya

Nationality: American. **Born:** Marguerite Johnson in St. Louis, Missouri, 4 April 1928. **Education:** Studied music privately and dance with Martha Graham, Pearl Primus, and Ann Halprin; studied drama with Frank Silvera and Gene Frankel. **Family:** Married Tosh Angelos (divorced); married Paul de Feu in 1973 (divorced); one son, Guy. **Career:** Actress and singer; Northern coordinator, Southern Christian Leadership Conference, 1959-60; associate editor, *Arab Observer*, Cairo, 1961-62; assistant administrator, School of Music and Drama, University of Ghana Institute of African Studies, Legon and Accra, 1963-66; freelance writer for *Ghanaian Times* and Ghanaian Broadcasting Corporation, both Accra, 1963-65; feature editor, *African Review*, Accra, 1964-66; lecturer, University of California, Los Angeles, 1966; writer-in-residence or visiting professor, University of Kansas, 1970, Wake Forest University, 1974, Wichita State University, 1974, and California State University, 1974; since 1981 Reynolds Professor, Wake Forest University; also composer, television host and interviewer. **Awards:** Yale University fellowship, 1970; Rockefeller grant, 1975; *Ladies Home Journal* Woman of the Year in Communications, 1976; North Carolina Award in Literature, 1987; Langston Hughes award, City College of New York, 1991; recipient, Horatio Alger award, 1992; *Essence* magazine Woman of the Year, 1992; named Distinguished Woman of North Carolina, 1992; Inaugural poet for President Bill Clinton, 1993; Grammy, for Best Spoken Word Album, 1994; honorary degrees from Smith College, Northampton, Massachusetts, 1975, Mills College, Oakland, California, 1975, Lawrence University, Appleton, Wisconsin, 1976, Wake Forest University, Winston-Salem, North Carolina, 1977. **Member:** American Revolution Bicentennial Council, 1975-76; board of trustees, American Film Institute, 1975; board of trustees, American Federation of Radio and Television Artists; advisory board, Women's Prison Association, Harlem Writer's Guild, National Commission on the Observance of International Women's Year, Directors' Guild. **Agent:** Lordly and Dame Inc., 51 Church Street, Boston, Massachusetts 02116-5493.

PUBLICATIONS

Plays

Cabaret for Freedom, with Godfrey Cambridge. Produced in New York, 1960.
The Least of These. Produced in Los Angeles, 1966.
Ajax (from the play by Sophocles). Produced in Los Angeles, 1974.
Encounters. Produced in Los Angeles, Mark Taper Forum, 1974.
And Still I Rise (also director; produced Oakland, California, 1976). New York, Random House, 1978.
King (lyrics with Alistair Beaton; book by Lonne Elder III, music by Richard Blackford). Produced in London, 1990.

Non-Fiction

I Know Why the Caged Bird Sings. New York, Random House, 1970.
Gather Together in My Name. New York, Random House, 1974.
Singin' and Swingin' and Gettin' Merry Like Christmas. New York, Random House, 1976.
The Heart of a Woman. New York, Random House, 1981.
All God's Children Need Traveling Shoes. New York, Random House, 1986.
Conversations with Maya Angelou, edited by Jeffrey M. Elliot. Oxford, University of Mississippi Press, 1989.
Wouldn't Take Nothing for My Journey Now. New York, Random House, 1993.
Lessons in Living. New York, Random House, 1993.
Even the Stars Look Lonesome. New York, Random House, 1997.

Poetry Collections

Just Give Me a Cool Drink of Water 'fore I Diiie. New York, Random House, 1971.
Oh Pray My Wings Are Gonna Fit Me Well. New York, Random House, 1975.
Poems. New York, Bantam, 1986.
Shaker, Why Don't You Sing?. New York, Random House, 1983.
Now Sheba Sings the Song. New York, Dial Press, 1987.
I Shall Not Be Moved. New York, Random House, 1991.
On the Pulse of the Morning. New York, Random House, 1993.
Complete Collected Poems of Maya Angelou. New York, Random House, 1994.
A Brave & Startling Truth. New York, Random House, 1995.
Phenomenal Woman: Four Poems Celebrating Women. New York, Random House, 1995.

Children's Books

Mrs. Flowers: A Moment of Friendship. Minneapolis, Redpath Press, 1986.
Life Doesn't Frighten Me. New York, Stewart, Tabori, and Chang, 1993.
Soul Looks Back in Wonder. New York, Dial, 1993.
My Painted House, My Friendly Chicken, and Me. New York, Crown, 1994.
Kofi and his Magic. New York, Clarkson Potter, 1996.

Other

Caribbean and African Cooking, with Rosamund Grant. New York, Interlink Publishing Group, 1997.

Editor with Joyntyle Theresa Robinson, *Bearing Witness: Contemporary Works by African American Women Artists.* New York, Rizzoli International Publications, 1996.

Recordings: *Miss Calypso*, Liberty, 1957; *The Poetry of Maya Angelou*, GWP, 1969; *Women in Business*, University of Wisconsin, 1981; *Black Pearls: The Poetry of Maya Angelou*, audio cassette, Rhinos Press, 1998.

Screenplays: *Georgia, Georgia*, 1972; *All Day Long*, 1974.

Television Plays: *Sisters, Sisters*, with John Berry, 1982.

Television Documentaries: *Black, Blues, Black*, 1968; *Assignment America*, 1975; *The Legacy*, 1976; *The Inheritors*, 1976; *I Know Why the Caged Bird Sings*, 1979; *Sister, Sister*, 1982; *Trying to Make It Home* (Byline series), 1988; *Maya Angelou's America: A Journey of the Heart* (also host); *Brewster Place*, 1990; *Who Cares About Kids, Kindred Spirits, Maya Angelou: Rainbow in the Clouds*, and *To the Contrary* (all Public Broadcasting Service productions).

*

Manuscript Collection: Wake Forest University, Winston-Salem, North Carolina.

Theatrical Activities: Director—Plays: *And Still I Rise*, Oakland, California, 1976, *Moon on a Rainbow Shawl*, London, 1988. Film: *All Day Long*, 1974. **Actress**—Plays: *Porgy and Bess*, tour, 1954-55; *Calypso Heatwave*, New York, 1957; *The Blacks*, New York, 1960; *Cabaret for Freedom*, New York, 1960; *Mother Courage*, Accra, Ghana, 1964; *Medea*, Hollywood, 1966; *Look Away*, New York, 1973. Television: *Roots*, 1977.

Critical Studies: *Maya Angelou: Woman of Words, Deeds, and Dreams*, by Stuart A. Kallen, Edina, Minnesota, Abdo & Daughters, 1993; *Maya Angelou*, by Miles Shapiro, New York, Chelsea House, 1994; *Maya Angelou: Greeting the Morning*, by Sarah E. King, Brookfield, Connecticut, Millbrook Press, 1994.

*   *   *

"Everything about Maya Angelou is transcendental in its outreach," commented Robert Fulghum in *Washington Post Book*

World, "from the resources of a specific life, specific gender, color, social place, landscape and vocation, she writes of elemental human experiences, concerns, and values." In her highly acclaimed four-volume autobiographical series, Angelou (born Marguerite Johnson) has chronicled not only the specific events of her life over a span of forty years, but also has recounted with characteristic candor and intimacy the details of her own geographical, literary, and—above all—psychological journey from her early childhood in Stamps, Arkansas, through her troubled adolescence as a single mother, to her combined literary production and political activism as an adult.

By all accounts, Angelou's autobiographical collection provides more than an extended chronology of an (admittedly fascinating) life, and reveals more than her own creative and lyrical authorial voice. Rather, Angelou's autobiographies expose her didactic impulse, her intent not only to disseminate her own stories, but also to impart their accompanying lessons, which, as many critics have noted, maintain a universal appeal and application. Perhaps by virtue of this very didactic character, then, Angelou has proffered her own spiritual peregrination as somehow paradigmatic. As Lynn Z. Bloom, has suggested in the *Dictionary of Literary Biography*:

It is clear from [this series of autobiographies] that Angelou is in the process of becoming a self-created Everywoman. In a literature and a culture where there are many fewer exemplary lives of women than of men, black or white, Angelou's autobiographical self, as it matures through successive volumes, is gradually assuming that exemplary stature.

The first of Angelou's autobiographies, *I Know Why the Caged Bird Sings* (1970), has garnered lavish praise from critical and commercial audiences alike, and is generally considered the best of the four volumes. The story, while articulated by the adult Angelou, is projected though the narrative focalizer of the young Marguerite Johnson, and concentrates primarily on three main geographical stages of her life though age sixteen.

In the first volume, she struggles to comprehend and, eventually, to reconcile herself to the oppressive, racially polarized environment surrounding the otherwise safe haven of her grandmother's dry goods store in Stamps. In the second—and to many readers, most distressing—phase, Angelou describes her move from Stamps to St. Louis, where she is raped at the age of eight by her mother's boyfriend, thereby causing Marguerite both to retreat further into the world of literature and also to adopt a self-imposed vow of silence. The third phase of the narrative describes, among other things, Marguerite's gradual psychological recovery, as well as her relocation to San Francisco, where she acquires a variety of jobs (including streetcar conductor) and, at age sixteen, gives birth to a son, Guy. While the narrative of *I Know Why the Caged Bird Sings* remains fraught with painful episodes and demoralizing circumstances, Angelou's language and style reveal the story as ultimately one of tenacity and transcendence, of endurance and the will to prevail.

Sidonie Ann Smith explains in *Southern Humanities Review* the relevance of Angelou's own graceful (and often humorous) narrative voice to the text's transcendent character:

That [the author] chooses to recreate the past in its own sounds suggests to the reader that she accepts the past and recognizes its beauty and its ugliness, its assets and its liabilities, its strengths and its weaknesses . . . Ultimately Maya Angelou's style testifies to her reaffirmation of self-acceptance, [which] she achieves within the pattern of the autobiography.

The second volume of Angelou's autobiography, *Gather Together in My Name* (1974), proved less successful, both commercially and critically speaking, than did its predecessor. Some critics have speculated that the very content of the text remains comparatively less palatable than that of *Caged Bird*. As Bloom suggested, "Angelou is less admirable as a central character than she was in *I Know Why the Caged Bird Sings*."

In *Gather Together in My Name*, Angelou recounts with unapologetic candor her struggle both to wrest herself from the sanctuary of her mother's home, and to carve out for herself and her infant son an entirely independent identity. This impulse for autonomy leads the still-adolescent Marguerite (now fashionably abbreviated to "Rita") southward to Sacramento and later to San Diego, where she experiments with a number of occupations of waning integrity, including Creole cook, professional dancer, cocktail waitress, madam, and eventually, prostitute. *Gather Together in My Name* initially threatens to function only as a confessional, steeped in bathos and apologia. However, the juxtaposition of the young Angelou's swaggering bravura to the narrator Angelou's graceful language yields a delicate equilibrium, counterpointing innocence and experience, blustering bravado and eloquent regret. Bloom comments: "The wit and panache with which she narrates the picaresque tale prevent it from being a confessional; the writing of this volume itself may be the final exorcism of the flaws."

The third volume, *Singin' and Swingin' and Gettin' Merry Like Christmas* (1976), focuses on Angelou as a young adult in the mid-1950s, recounting in particular her (failed) marriage to a white ex-sailor, Tosh Angelos, as well as her subsequent career as a dancer in a local (and predominantly white) bar. Her terpsichorean talents lead her Europe, where she participates as a member of the touring cast of *Porgy and Bess*, a passionate and celebratory venture that she describes as "more like a party than a chore." Prompted by a sudden and renewed sense of parental obligation, Angelou returns to the United States and to a more sobering (and to Angelou, rather tedious) bourgeois existence.

In The Heart of a Woman (1981), the fourth and reportedly final installment of her autobiographical series, Angelou not only concentrates on her own personal—more specifically, romantic—developments, but also traces the dual trajectories of her career as both a writer and a social activist. Her involvement in the Harlem Writers Guild both hones her then latent literary inclinations and introduces her to an influential and established group of African-American writers that includes Paule Marshall and James Baldwin. Encouraged by this energetic group of young black intellectuals, Angelou becomes increasingly involved in the civil rights movement, and later is appointed the northern coordinator of Dr. Martin Luther King Jr.'s Southern Christian Leadership Conference. Her eventual (and again, doomed) engagement to a South African revolutionary, Vusumzi Make, leads her on a whirlwind journey to Egypt, where she acquires a position as associate editor of an

English language newspaper, *Arab Observer*, and discovers the sexism so deeply entrenched within African culture at large.

—L. Michelle Wallace

ANSA, Tina McElroy

Born: Tina McElroy in Macon, Georgia, 18 November 1949. **Education:** Spelman College, B.A. 1971. **Family:** Married Jonée Ansa, 1 May 1978. **Career:** Writer and editor for the *Atlanta Constitution* and *Charlotte Observer*; instructor in mass media, Clark College, Atlanta; writer-in-residence and writing workshop supervisor, Spelman College; contributor of video "postcards" to *Sunday Morning,* CBS Television. **Member:** Authors Guild. **Awards:** *New York Times* Notable Book of the Year and American Library Association Best Book for Young Adults, both 1989 for *Baby of the Family;* Georgia Authors Series Award, 1989 and 1996.

Publications

Nonfiction

Not Soon Forgotten: Cotton Planters and Plantations of the Golden Isles of Georgia. Coastal Georgia Historical Society, 1987.

Novels

Baby of the Family. San Diego, Harcourt Brace Jovanovich, 1989.
Ugly Ways. New York, Harcourt Brace & Co., 1993.
The Hand I Fan With. New York, Doubleday, 1996.

*   *   *

Tina Ansa's three published novels place her squarely in the tradition of Southern writers such as Eudora Welty, Flannery O'Connor, and Ansa's role model, Zora Neale Hurston. Among her clearly Southern themes is the interrelatedness of past and present: her characters and their present actions are seen to be shaped by the ghosts, literal and figurative, which seem to envelop them. Shared family ties, which often are the strongest bonds molding and sustaining the characters, form one link with this past; in two of the three novels, the extended family plays an essential role, and in *Ugly Ways* the Lovejoy sisters finally reproach their mother for having cut them off from just such relationships. Extended families usually involve a common attachment to place, and Ansa also shares her predecessors' emphasis upon the importance of roots in a specific, limited geographical area. All of her novels so far are set in the small town of Mulberry, Georgia, her microcosm. As she has observed, "for me a small town is a manageable complex universe. You know you can get to know the people. But I've found even when writers write about a big city, they invariably write about a small community whether it's just a household or the whole of Brooklyn."

Equally Southern are Ansa's characters, most of whom are delineated with humor in the tradition of Southern literature. The citizens of Mulberry may be selfish, petty, and even disagreeable at times, but the novelist describes them with an amused tolerance that makes them seem comically eccentric, and more than

slightly familiar; in fact, the comments of readers at book signings suggest that in attempting to portray black women realistically, Ansa has actually created prototypal American females. Even more Southern is the emphasis these female characters place on interaction with their larger community. The McPhersons and the Lovejoys, for example, are acutely aware of their roles in Mulberry's social framework and are particularly sensitive to their fellow citizens' attitudes toward them.

As important as the characters' relationship to their community is their sense of their role in the larger universe. Whether protagonists like Lena McPherson and the Lovejoy women, or supporting characters like Grandmama McPherson and the nuns at Blessed Martin de Porres School, Ansa's characters understand their relationship to a world in which their presence is only temporary, while the natural world and the world of souls and spirits will last long after these mere mortals have passed from the scene. Thus, Ansa differs from earlier generations of Southern writers for whom time seemed to represent inimical forces of change; in her novels, time becomes a continuing flow whose force, properly savored, can lead to revitalizing self-knowledge.

On a literal level, *Baby of the Family* follows the pattern of a relatively traditional initiation novel, tracing the life of its protagonist from her exceptional birth through a series of life-altering encounters and rejections and Lena McPherson's first experience with the death of a close relative; however, Ansa also uses Lena's story to develop the conflict between reason and faith. All the other characters consider Lena special. To Nurse Bloom, Grandmama McPherson, Dr. Williams, and most of the Mulberry community, she is special because she was born with a caul over her face. They believe she will always be lucky, and they gossip that she can communicate with ghosts and spirits. In contrast, Lena's mother Nellie prides herself on being too modern and rational to engage in old-fashioned "superstitions." Thus, when Nurse Bloom gives her the carefully preserved caul and a bottle of caul tea for Lena to drink, Nellie burns the caul and pours the tea into a vase of flowers. Only after Lena is grown does Nellie realize the mistake she has made. Still, Lena is special to Nellie, not only because she is the baby of the family, but because she is the daughter her mother has always wanted.

From her early childhood memory of nearly being drawn into the portrait of her dead aunt, to her teenage experiences of sleepwalking and being ridden by witches, Lena fights to maintain a rational facade, while cringing each time she walks down the hall and sees the spirits who inhabit her house. With her mother's encouragement, she convinces herself that she can best deal with these spirits by ignoring them and denying their existence. Unwilling to believe in her gift/curse, she seeks a substitute in religious faith, but her attempts to deny her own identity lead only to emotional upheaval. Because neither she nor her parents will admit to knowing about her sleepwalking, this secret diminishes their faith in each other and Lena's faith in her own sanity.

On the other hand, Lena and her family come to believe in the power of her touch to correct all kinds of mechanical malfunctions, but she learns that this touch cannot disperse the hovering spirits or heal broken relationships. Though she is loved by her family's adult friends and associates, she longs for the acceptance of her classmates. Nevertheless, her efforts to fit in inevitably fail, and the people she cares about disappear from her life. For example, her friendship with Sarah, her neighbor and first playmate, ends when Sarah's mother discovers the two girls engaging in play which imitates sexual intercourse. Despite Sarah's protests that she initiated the game, her mother blames Lena and soon moves her family to the other side of town; as a result, Lena never sees Sarah again. A few years later, the situation is repeated when one of the spirits takes possession of Lena's voice and blurts out the name of the parent who insulted one of the teaching nuns. Although Lena has been very popular with the girls at her school, all of them turn against her, and for the rest of her school years, Gwen is her only friend.

Throughout the novel, Lena learns from a series of adult mentors. Among these are the ghost Rachel, who teaches her about personal courage and choice; the hairdresser Mamie, who encourages her to be curious; and handyman Frank Petersen, who shows her the power of imagination and the importance of holding steadfastly to one's dreams. The most important influences, however, were her parents and her grandmother. By her example, Nellie instills in Lena not only the basics of style, charm, and manners, of course, but also a woman's potential for managerial skill and the affluent woman's social responsibility. From her father, Jonah, Lena learns the power of money and the importance of developing a network of friends. Grandmama McPherson provides Lena's link with her ancestral past; she knows and accepts the lore that Nellie rejects and that Jonah believes his money will allow him to ignore. Because Grandmama believes in spirits, she understands the battle Lena is fighting, and she can provide comfort for her granddaughter. Her death at the novel's ends leaves Lena isolated and fearful, as well as grief-stricken.

The Lovejoy women in *Ugly Ways* are equally isolated, though it is the eccentric behavior of their mother (Mudear) that has cut them off from their community, and even from themselves. To them, their fate seems to have been sealed when Mudear "changed." From that time on, they were never able to invite anyone into their home, and few of their childhood friends returned to play after being told they would have to go home if they wanted a drink of water or need to use the bathroom. The sisters know that Mudear also alienated all of her friends by refusing to talk with them on the telephone, and all three are convinced that the townspeople of Mulberry expect them to become as "crazy" as their mother. Attempting to escape their past, Annie Ruth has fled to Los Angeles, which she hates, and Emily has moved to Atlanta, though she returns each Saturday for Betty to do her hair. Ansa further suggests the inescapable connection of past and present by allowing Mudear's spirit to comment upon the stories told by her daughters (Chapters 4, 9, 11, 13, 17, 20, 27, 31, 33); in fact, appropriately enough, Mudear is given the last word, concluding the novel with the warning that none of her "girls ever gonna be free of her" and the promise that she will be "hovering over" her granddaughter.

The eldest daughter, Betty, is the only one with clear memories of their family life before Mudear "changed." In those days, their father, Ernest, seemed to dominate his wife, Esther, completely: she cooked the food he liked, and she manicured his nails daily to remove chalk residue from the kaolin mines. Threatened by her intense sexuality, he maintained tight control over every aspect of the household and family life. Eventually, though, his pride led

him to overextend himself financially; and when Esther used her meager savings to pay the essential bills, control in the Lovejoy family abruptly shifted. Spending her days sleeping or watching television, Esther delegated the household tasks to her daughters, Betty, Emily, and Annie Ruth, the youngest of whom was just barely out of diapers. From that point on, she insisted upon being called Mudear (a contraction of Mother Dear), and she never left the house again, except to work in her garden almost every night. Ansa describes her as a monster, commenting that "unfortunately many of us turn into the tyrants we overthrow."

Ugly Ways carefully explores the dynamics of the Lovejoy family. As the novel opens, Mudear has died and her family must plan her funeral and resolve their feelings toward her. Each of the daughters are successful but carry the psychological wounds. In fact, as teenagers, the three of them swore they would never become mothers because they feared they would repeat Mudear's pattern. So far, all of them are single and childless. Betty, who has continued to live in Mulberry, has parlayed her talent as a hair stylist into a successful business, but her personal life has revolved around her responsibility to maintain the family home, meet the emotional and financial needs of her sisters, and always be at Mudear's beck and call. Though she is involved in a long-term relationship with a man her own age and an affair with an attractive young boy, she has remained emotionally detached from everyone but her sisters. The sister most bound by society's expectations, Betty is also the least likely to voice her complaints; nevertheless, she still resents Mudear's refusal to send her to college, but she has struck back at her mother by sending both of her sisters through college, and eventually she reveals that she has also destroyed Mudear's favorite bed jacket out of spite.

Emily, the middle daughter, is professionally successful, but her personal life has sustained greater damage than Betty's, perhaps because only rarely has she accepted responsibility for anyone beyond herself. After years of psychotherapy, an abortion, several financial crises, a divorce, and a series of failed relationships, Emily frequently considers suicide. Finally forced to express her grievances against Mudear, she plaintively sobs, "I just always wanted a mama," and she eventually tells her mother's corpse, "When I was nine or ten, Mudear, I used to pray that you would die so we would get a new mama."

Initially the youngest sister appears to be the weakest of the three. When Annie Ruth calls Betty and Emily to pick her up at the airport, she is near collapse. Ruth, as she is known professionally, has a troubled psychological history. A television news anchor, she has already suffered an on-air nervous breakdown, which in turn led to a period of hospitalization; she hallucinates repeatedly, always seeing menacing cats between her and whatever door she wants to enter; and she seems incapable of dealing with either her mother's death or her father's attempt to apologize for tolerating Mudear's behavior. Surprisingly, though, Annie Ruth summons the strength to break the family pattern of maternal neglect. Despite Emily's opposition and Betty's attempt to evade the issue, she announces that she is pregnant and she does not know who the father is, but she intends to keep her baby. Annie Ruth believes she can become the mother she wishes she had had, but she insists that she and her sisters cannot put the past behind them until they go to the funeral home and tell Mudear precisely what they think.

The sisters' denunciation of their mother takes place in a highly comic scene very much in the Southern humor tradition. First, Annie Ruth disrupts two funeral services, bursting in with the explanation that she is looking for her mother. When one of the funeral directors attempts to stop and console her, she claws at his face until he backs off. At last she finds Mudear in a white oak casket resting upon a collapsible gurney. Betty and Emily's attempts to restrain Annie Ruth cause all three of them to fall, and in the process, the gurney collapses and Mudear's body pops out of the casket. With all four of the Lovejoy women sprawled on the floor, the sisters are no longer intimidated by their mother, and each tells Mudear how she truly feels. Meanwhile, a crowd has gathered at the door of the chapel, and clearly this incident will be discussed in Mulberry for a long time.

The Hand I Fan With, the most controversial and arguably the best of Ansa's novels to date, chronicles a year in the life of Lena McPherson. Now in her mid-forties, she has indeed become the hand that all of Mulberry fans with. To "her people," she is not only a special person, but a kind of superwoman. Constantly aware of her role and her responsibility in the community, she rescues individuals from financial ruin, reconciles divided families, consoles those in physical or emotional pain, helps them bury their dead, and in many instances settles their estates after years of managing most of their business. Yet—though "her people" regularly show up at the door of her river retreat and keep her supplied with more food than she can possibly eat—she is essentially isolated. Her parents and brothers are dead and she lives alone on an estate maintained, almost anonymously, by loyal, long-time friend/employees. Micro-management of her businesses and her responsibilities to "her people" have eaten away the time she can spend in personal pleasures, such as swimming, horseback riding, or simply observing nature on her hundred acres of land.

The frequent flashbacks interspersed among the accounts of Lena's current activities fill in the story of Lena's life since *Baby of the Family* and show how, in her efforts to be "normal," she has failed to know or accept her own true nature. Attempting to escape the terrifying spirits through religious devotion and service to others, she has made the townspeople dependent upon her, and though she has always been lucky, her presence and her support generally are taken for granted. Only her college classmate and best friend, Sister, really worries about Lena's emotional welfare. Knowing that her year-long sabbatical research project will put her out of Lena's reach, she insists that the two of them conjure up a lover to take care of Lena. Fueled by potent Caribbean alcohol, marijuana, and Lena's half-belief, the conjuring ceremony has taken place about a week before the novel opens. Although she does not yet know the cause, Lena realizes that there is literally a change in the air, and the breeze playing down her back makes her happy.

Ansa prepares carefully for the first appearance of Herman in Chapter 12. Having been dead for more than one hundred years, Herman is delighted to be in human form again so that he can enjoy his favorite physical activities, eating and sex. He remains with Lena precisely one year, and in that times he gradually teaches her to get in touch with her own spirit, to observe nature around her, to set priorities that allow her time for both personal renewal and the projects she really wants to pursue, and to have the courage to disregard the criticisms of her people. Thus, Lena's

year with Herman parallels Thoreau's similar period of personal growth at Walden Pond; and like Thoreau, at the end of that cycle Lena moves on to what Thoreau calls other lives. Because she now knows that Herman's protective presence has been one of those spirits surrounding her throughout her life, and because she believe he will always be nearby to help her, Lena at last is strong enough to live her life fully and to accept her relationship with the spirit world; her home is filled with the happy ghosts of her relatives and friends. As she converses with the shades of people who died long before she was born, Lena acknowledges the inter-relationship of past and present. The novel ends with her comment, "Well, Lord," as she realizes that her menses stopped two months earlier and she is about to set off on a new adventure.

In this novel Ansa has gambled that readers will see beyond the highly erotic descriptions in the love scenes to the novelist's deeply spiritual intent. Lena has always believed that she must have her own man and her own children before she can experience joy, but Herman tells her she doesn't have a clue as to what is really important. Only when she realizes that she cannot and should not replace God in her people's lives can she learn what *The Hand I Fan With* repeatedly affirms: that time must be carefully used and not wasted, that human actions directly affect the natural world, and that love is the only force capable of transcending time and space. Thus, after Herman has faded away, she divests herself of the possessions she no longer wants or needs, dedicates herself to the shelter for runaways she has established in her parents' deserted home, and refuses to be concerned when she reads in the townspeople's thoughts that "the change" has made her crazy. Her family ghosts reassure her: Nellie tells her, "If you don't let yourself be crazy sometimes, baby, then you go mad," and Grandmama admits, "When I was 'live, I thought I knew a thing or two. Knew how things oughta be. Thought I knew 'bout life and death, too. But, Lena, I didn't have a clue." Through Herman's tutelage, Lena has acquired this knowledge while she is still alive and can pass it on to the runaway teenagers who have become her true spiritual children.

While Tina Ansa has used language and imagery that might have made her Southern predecessors uncomfortable, in her novels she has followed their example in capturing the diction and rhythms of contemporary speech. Believable characters express both traditional values and contemporary issues in an idiom that might be heard today in The Place or in many other conversations. Most important, though, Ansa celebrates individuals' uniqueness, personal dignity, and the resilient strength of women—precisely the qualities celebrated by generations of Southern women writers. She summarized her attitude in a Doubleday interview: "As we move into another century, I think all of our citizens, but particularly black folks, have to claim what's ours. We've got to acknowledge who we are as a people, what and where we came from, what we believe in, what got us to where we are today. We've got to stop jettisoning things that are important."

—Charmaine Allmon Mosby

ANZALDÚA, Gloria

Born: In Jesus Maria of the Valley, Texas, 26 September 1942.
Education: Pan-American University, Edinburg, Texas, B.A. 1969;

University of Texas at Austin, M.A. 1973; studied at University of California at Santa Cruz. **Career:** English instructor in high school, migrant, adult, and bilingual programs in Texas; teacher of creative writing, women's studies, and Chicano studies at University of Texas at Austin, Vermont College of Norwich University, and San Francisco State University; writer-in-residence, the Loft, Minneapolis; artist-in-residence, Pomona College; contributing editor, *Sinister Wisdom*; participant in lectures, panels, and workshops throughout the United States, Canada, and Mexico. **Awards:** MacDowell Colony fellowship, 1982; National Endowment of the Arts award for fiction, 1991; Astraea National Lesbian Action Foundation Lesbian Writers Fund Sappho Award, 1992. **Address:** c/o Literature Board, University of Santa Cruz, Santa Cruz, California 95064.

PUBLICATIONS

Poetry

Borderlands/La Frontera: The New Mestiza. San Francisco, Spinsters/Aunt Lute, 1987.

Children's Literature

Prietita Has a Friend/Prietita tiene un Amigo. San Francisco, Children's Book Press, 1991.
Friends from the Other Side/Amigos del otra lado. San Francisco, Children's Book Press, 1993.
Prietita and the Ghost Woman/Prietita y La Llorona. San Francisco, children's Book Press, 1996.

Novels

La Prieta. San Francisco, Aunt Lute, 1997.

Other

Lloronas, Women Who Howl: Autohistorias—Torias and the Production of Writing, Knowledge, and Identity. San Francisco, Aunt Lute, 1996.

Editor with Cherrie Moraga, *This Bridge Called My Back: Writings by Radical Women of Color.* Watertown, Massachusetts, Persephone Press, 1981.
Editor and contributor, *Making Face, Making Soul/Haciendo Caras: Creative and Critical Perspectives by Women of Color.* San Francisco, Aunt Lute, 1990.

*

Critical Studies: "Dare to Write: Virginia Woolf, Tillie Olsen, Gloria Anzaldúa" by Carolyn Woodward, in *Changing Our Power: An Introduction to Women's Studies,* Dubuque, Kendall/Hunt, 1988; interview with Elizabeth Baldwin, *Matrix,* May 1988; "Living on the Borderland: The Poetic Prose of Gloria Anzaldúa and Susan Griffin" by Diane P. Freedman, *Women and Language,* Spring 1989; "Experience, Writing, Theory: The Dialects of *Mestizaje* in Gloria Anzaldúa'a *Borderlands/La Frontera*" by Hector A. Torres, *Cultural and Cross-Cultural Studies and the Teaching of Literature,* 1991; "On *Borderlands/La Frontera:* An Interpretive Essay" by Maria Lugones, *Hypatia,* Fall 1992.

Media Adaptations: *This Bridge Called My Back: Writings by Women of Color* (sound recording), 1983.

*   *   *

A versatile author who has published poetry, stories and children's books—and edited two collections of works by women of color—Gloria Anzaldúa expresses a Chicane/lesbian politics in all of her writing. She has also postulated a new type of literature for Third World women that would tear down distinctions of all kinds and foster the emergence of multiple-voiced spokespersons.

Anzaldúa's first published work appears in the anthology *This Bridge Called My Back: Writings by Radical Women of Color,* which she edited with Cherrie Moraga. *This Bridge* features writings by a variety of women, including several essays written by Anzaldúa herself that help clarify her own stance as a writer and activist. In the essay "Speaking in Tongues: A Letter to 3rd World Women Writers," Anzaldúa argues for a new theory of writing that mixes fact and theory in a more individual way to counter abstract and distanced writing of academia. In practice, this approach is highly subjective. As Hector A. Torres writes in the *Dictionary of Literary Biography,* "for Anzaldúa, in the construction of a theoretical framework that would articulate the experience of the minority writer, anything is allowed."

In her poetry collection, *Borderlands/La Frontera: The New Mestiza,* Anzaldúa mixes genres in an idiosyncratic manner meant to open new literary terrain and allow a multitudinous voice to express itself. Combining poetry and prose, English and Spanish, and the real with the imaginary, *Borderlands* speaks in a myriad of voices to create a kind of creative autobiography. The collection begins with an extended essay, "Atravesando Fronteras/Crossing Borders," in which Anzaldúa explores various aspects of living on a border, particularly the movement of people over the Texas/Mexico border. She references historical instances of migration in the region, suggests similar borders existing between scholarly writing and the writing of immigrants, and finally proposes that humanity is on the verge of a disintegration of borders of all kinds, resulting in a "radical, ideological, cultural and biological cross-polinization" that will break down all existing formations and lead to a new and hybridized humankind.

The collection's second section is a gathering of Anzaldúa's poems dealing with lesbian feminism, religion, migrant workers, and her own personal history. The character of the undocumented woman appears in several pieces; this character straddles such borders as those between rich and poor, between people with different religious and political beliefs, and between those with differing sexual preferences. "This is her home/this thin edge of/ barbwire," Anzaldúa explains in one poem.

Anzaldúa has more recently turned to writing children's fiction. *Prietita and the Ghost Woman* is based on a traditional Mexican folktale about a young girl seeking aid for her sick mother from a ghost woman with strange powers. In *Friends from the Other Side,* Anzaldúa spins another tale of Prietita, a Mexican-American girl who befriends a Mexican boy.

—Denise Wiloch

APPLEWHITE, James

Born: James William Applewhite in Stantonsburg, North Carolina, 8 August 1935. **Education:** Duke University, A.B. 1958; M.A. 1960; Ph.D. 1969. **Family:** Married Janis Forrest, 28 January 1956; three children. **Career:** Professor of English and former director of Institute of the Arts, Duke University. **Awards:** Emily Clark Balch Prize from *Virginia Quarterly Review*, 1966, for *The Journey*; National Endowment for the Arts grant, 1974; Borestone Mountain Poetry Awards, 1975, for *Roadside Notes* and 1977, for *William Blackburn, Riding Westward*; Guggenheim fellow, 1976; Associated Writing Programs Contemporary Poetry Series Award, 1979; North Carolina Literary and Historical Association poetry award, 1981, 1986; recipient of prize in International Poetry Review competition, 1982; North Carolina Poetry Society award, 1990; American Academy and Institute of Arts and Letters, Jean Stein Award in Poetry, 1992; *Shenandoah* magazine, James Boatwright III Prize for Poetry, 1992; North Carolina Department of Cultural Resources, North Carolina Award in Literature, 1993. **Address:** Department of English, 308 Allen Building, Duke University, Durham, North Carolina 27706.

PUBLICATIONS

Poetry Collections

War Summer: Poems. Poquoson, Virginia, Back Door, 1972.
Statues of the Grass. Athens, University of Georgia Press, 1975.
Following Gravity. Charlottesville, University Press of Virginia, 1980.
Forseeing the Journey. Baton Rouge, Louisiana State University Press, 1983.
Ode to the Chinaberry Tree and Other Poems. Baton Rouge, Louisiana State University Press, 1986.
River Writing: An Eno Journal. Princeton, Princeton University Press, 1988.
Lessons in Soaring. Baton Rouge, Louisiana State University Press, 1989.
A History of the River: Poems. Baton Rouge, Louisiana State University Press, 1993.
Daytime and Starlight. Baton Rouge, Louisiana State University Press, 1997.

Other

Seas and Inland Journeys: Landscape and Consciousness from Wordsworth to Roethke. Athens, University of Georgia Press, 1985.

Editor with Anne Lloyd and Fred Chappell, *Brown Bag*. Greensboro, 1971.
Editor, *Voices from Earth*, Greensboro, 1971.

Uncollected Essays

"Children in Contemporary Poetry," in *South Carolina Review*, Spring 1985.
"Modernism and the Imagination of Ugliness," in *Sewanee Review*, Summer 1986.
"Building Confidence in Yourself as a Poet," in *Writer*, August 1988.

"Postmodernist Allegory and the Denial of Nature," in *Kenyon Review*, Winter 1989.

*   *   *

In his poetry, James Applewhite weaves together family, memory, nature, and the complications of growing up Southern. He explores the tension between pleasant and painful memories, and the clash of childhood memory with adult reality. Applewhite's deeply personal poetry recalls his most vivid memories.

As a child, Applewhite was struck by rheumatic fever, and he writes of this illness from one of his first volumes of poetry, *Statues of the Grass*, to his most recent, *Daytime and Starlight*. He also remembers vividly his father rescuing him from a speedboat accident and his father moving a tanker away from a lumberyard fire, saving the family gas station and the lives of Applewhite and his mother. Instead of being washed out by repetition, these images become more powerful as he returns to them, letting them play like echoes off the walls of memory and childhood.

Statues of the Grass establishes the themes he continues to explore today. Applewhite opens with "Driving hrough a Country that Is Vanishing," which laments the disappearance of simpler times. Set in the quiet of winter, the poem opens with the clashes between past and present. "It begins to snow in a country / Between the past and what I see." In "Looking for a Home in the South," he describes his fear of over-development and encroaching modernization. "This particular spring day, over which we are constructing despair / with materials of depression and concrete, the land we have missed, lying hidden, / Trickles and glistens in the dark, radiant to roots." In "The Man," Applewhite wistfully describes the decline of small-town life. "The land dreamed in color of old summer, /Heard long-drawn mourning dove's distresses / Consoling with sadness. Rivers turned over / In slumber, oil-slick ripples boiling up / From thought's turmoil underneath." Without rage or sentimentality, Applewhite communicates a palatable sense of loss, a requiem for the plowed-over field or the parking lot-paved meadow.

In *Statues of the Grass*, Applewhite also grapples with the memory of his grandfather, whose death becomes the subject of many subsequent poems. In "My Grandfather's Funeral," the grandfather, W. H. Applewhite, is described, "Generous, a tyrant to his family / Who kept bright jars of mineral water / On his screened, appled backporch, who prayed / With white hair wispy in the moving air, / Who kept the old way in changing times." Applewhite often describes his grandfather as lost in prayer and detached. In "A Vigil," Applewhite recalls a Thanksgiving memory: "I sat on the porch beside him, spell-bound by columns. / Horizon woven to softening by orbits of swallows. / It's been eighty-six years and it seems like a day." These words resonate with Applewhite, who incorporates them in future poems. The jars of mineral water, the porch where Applewhite recovered from rheumatic fever, the general store William Applewhite owned, and the tobacco fields he farmed, all return as flashes of memory.

Forseeing the Journey is set against the frame of a transatlantic flight. Applewhite further develops his established themes, exploring in detail his childhood illness, his heroic but distant father, his uneasiness with his family's Civil War legacy, and his father's Esso station. Recovering from his illness, he watches his father mow the lawn, an image is burned into many of Applewhite's poems. His father, who has saved him from drowning, a serious fire and an explosion, is now saving him from illness. He writes, "The shape of his strength / Would save me from fever, by mowing forever." His father looms throughout his poetry as heroic, yet unattainable. In "Iron Age Flying," Applewhite writes, "Riding the river in the speedboat with father, / I didn't feel fearful. I wasn't so personal." He continues, "the red fire jumping as if speaking in tongues. He drove away the tanker for our lives, through / The gasoline sea of her fear." In "Morning Prayer" Applewhite puts himself in his father's place as he becomes the hero, saving his son from the Agreen shadows of algae."

Forseeing the Journey ends with an examination of the stages of life, woven through images of nature, that is a fitting end to a collection of poems that revisit memories and compress time into distilled images of childhood, nature, and a long, ponderous airplane flight.

In *Ode to the Chinaberry Tree and Other Poems,* Applewhite continues to examine his childhood memories, but they darken and become nightmarish. "A Shoreline Consciousness" chronicles a nightmare in which Applewhite imagines himself drowning. "Submerged, Inarticulate, I couldn't get / my head up for air." In "A Dream of War" Applewhite weaves his recurring nightmares about World War II, and a plane crash in the woods behind his grandparents' house. In poems like "Barbecue Service" and "Collards," Applewhite explores the role traditional Southern food plays in gathering people at picnics and dinners. In "Barbecue Service," he writes: "I want to see all the old home folks, / Ones who may not last another year. / We will rock on porches like chapels / and not say anything." He also includes "How to Cook a Pig (as told by Dee Grimes)," a poem that reaches into the oral historical tradition, as if tape-recorded for posterity. The speaker begins, "Take a piece of tin that's / Blowed off a barn in a storm." Through these poems, Applewhite celebrates the South through food and the congregations and families who gather at long tables.

In "For W. H. Applewhite," Applewhite remembers his grandfather with granular detail, from the glass in the windows of his house to the furrows of his garden. He conjures the image of his grandfather as a dedicated farmer, sowing rows of tobacco and vegetables. He writes with warmth: "William Henry, you were the one true / Father, the Bible-carrying walker-on-water / Of a time that escapes us." In the descriptions of his grandfather's life, Applewhite demonstrates a genuine affection for W. H. Applewhite.

In *A History of the River: Poems,* Applewhite examines primarily the history of the South, as both a lesson and an example. In "Among Names of My Fathers," he writes, "I read you initials, scriptures, the year / of your births, death. But the distance between us / seems unbridgeable, you lie in deeds I can't approve." But the lifestyles of the men buried in that cemetery—and the self-sufficiency of the small family farms they ran—captivate Applewhite. In "Making Tobacco Money," Applewhite's love poem to the old ways, he describes the routines on a nineteenth-century farm in detail. He writes, "These folk identified themselves not by wealth on paper but / by visible achievements of their hands: the farmhouse white in its trees, the fields around engraved with rows, / the corn uniformly flourishing."

Applewhite also examines the life of a farmer who stands stoically against the changing world around him. In "A Change of Sky," he describes this farmer at a church picnic, distanced from everything around him. "He looked beyond the temporary / gathering to see the mules still waiting in their pastures." Applewhite explores the isolation of farmers, like the one in "A Change of Sky," as well as the isolation they feel being the last farmers left practicing the "old ways." In "A Wilson County Farmer" he describes the tobacco farmer's inability to adapt to the change in farming techniques, "With the quotas, the declining / prices, every day more news about cancer, this man / who learned tobacco from his father, who himself couldn't write / feels his station in this place lit by blue light and T.V. as odd and as lonely." Applewhite effectively captures the loneliness of these "old ones" and praises their unchanging practices, which he sees as a kind of salvation from the burdens of modernism.

In *Daytime and Starlight,* Applewhite further refines his poetry borne of memory and family. His message of memory, loss, and history expands to include observations about his travels to Rome. "In the Capitoline Museum" muses: "Perhaps the past isn't. These ideas in stone surrounded by gazes only / look more naked and honest." In "Coming Home to the Villa Aurelia," Applewhite creates a montage of sunset images, of people making love in Fiats, the endless landscape of dome-upon-dome, the Pantheon piercing through the coming dusk. His response to this crash and blend of images is, fittingly, "We're all in this together."

Haunted by the devastating loss of the "old ways," Applewhite has explored this theme with the grace and deep feeling throughout his career. In his angry poem, "The Absence of New Graves in Fields," Applewhite lashes out at the mobile homes and ranch houses that dot the once-pristine landscape near his home town: "ranch-style homes, azalea blooms, production-line rooms / as in a train. The hardship of a homemade beauty / has been voted away by money." Applewhite tells more wistfully of loss in "Father and Son," "Furrows settle in on themselves with the relic / harrow, its seat rusting as well as the discs, / while honeysuckle mixes with the iron briars / to create a final harmony in abandonment." In "Circling the Time Line," Applewhite combines this profound sense of loss for a simpler life, his reverence for nature, his fatherhood, and a sense of hope for the future, all bound into a canoe trip with his son. Instead of the loss of simplicity in life, he finds, "succession lending / itself to the heart." In the poem "Daytime and Starlight," he sees the patterns of life as corroded by pollution, scarred by power lines, gouged by quarries, but, finally, beautiful, as night descends, "A log barn leans into history, / our mirror sensing behind us a blackness where starlight / impinges on houses, ruthlessly kind in time to their dreamers, / asleep in the fabulous geometries of chimneys and gables."

James Applewhite's poetry of memory, childhood, family, and the quiet farms of his neighbors and forebears digs deep into the rich tradition of the personal narrative. Although his poems are deeply personal, he manages to explore larger themes, as in the preservation of nature, or the quilt of family history. Applewhite, like all great poets, is a miniaturist and a universalist.

—Frances E. Badgett

AUBERT, Alvin

Born: Alvin Bernard Aubert in Lutcher, Louisiana, 12 March 1930.
Education: Southern University, Baton Rouge, Louisiana, B.A. in English 1959; University of Michigan, Ann Arbor (Woodrow Wilson fellow), A.M. 1960; University of Illinois, Urbana, 1963-64, 1966-67. **Family:** Married Olga Alexis in 1948 (divorced), one daughter; married Bernadine Tenant in 1960, two daughters. **Career:** Instructor, 1960-62, assistant professor, 1962-65, and associate professor of English, 1965-1970, Southern University; visiting professor of English, University of Oregon, summer 1970; associate professor, 1970-74, and professor of English, 1974-79, State University of New York, Fredonia; professor of English, 1980-92, and since 1992 professor emeritus, Wayne State University, Detroit, Michigan; member of board of directors, Coordinating Council of Literary Magazines, 1982-86; advisory editor, *Drama and Theatre*, 1973-75, *Black Box*, 1974-79, *Gumbo*, 1976-78, and *Callaloo*, 1977-83; founder and editor, *Obsidian* magazine, Fredonia, New York, and Detroit, 1975-85; since 1985 senior editorial consultant, *Obsidian II*, Raleigh, North Carolina. **Awards:** Bread Loaf Writers Conference scholarship, 1968; National Endowment for the Arts grant, 1973, 1981; Coordinating Council of Literary Magazines grant, 1979; Annual *Callaloo* award, 1989. **Address:** English Department, Wayne State University, Detroit, Michigan 48202.

PUBLICATIONS

Poetry

Against the Blues. Detroit, Broadside Press, 1972.
Feeling Through. Greenfield Center, New York, Greenfield Review Press, 1975.
South Louisiana: New and Selected Poems. Grosse Pointe Farms, Michigan, Lunchroom Press, 1985.
If Winter Came: Collected Poems, 1967-1992. Pittsburgh, Carnegie Mellon Press, 1994.
Harlem Wrestler. East Lansing, Michigan, Michigan State University Press, 1995.

Play

Home from Harlem, adaptation of *The Sport of the Gods* by Paul Laurence Dunbar (produced Detroit 1986). Detroit, Obsidian Press, 1986.

*

Bibliography: "Alvin Aubert: A Primary Bibliography," in *Black American Literature Forum* (Terre Haute, Indiana), Fall 1989.

Critical Studies: Herbert W. Martin, in *Three Rivers Poetry Journal,* November 1978; Herbert W. Martin, in *Black American Literature Forum,* Fall 1987; Tom Dent, in *Black American Literature Forum,* Spring 1988; by Jerry W. Ward, in *Black American Literature Forum,* Fall 1989.

Alvin Aubert comments:
    A poem is a verification of experience in thought and feeling, but mostly the latter, for feeling is the means by which essential experience is received and transmitted. If the feeling is right, the intellectual content is also, which is to say that in the poem that works there takes place a mutual verification of thought by feeling, feeling by thought. I am African American and conscious of my roots in South Louisiana with its confluence of African, Native American, and European (French and Spanish) cultural influences. My sensitivity is of course African American, thus leaving no doubt as to the source of the experiences that verify my poems as well as find verification in them. My thematic concerns are as universal as they are particular. The themes identified by James Shokoff—"death, the shapes of the past, the terror of existence, and the pain of endurance"—are all there, and then some. Their particularity is perhaps best identified in Tom Dent's observations about my South Louisiana origin.

*   *   *

The title of Alvin Aubert's first book of poetry, *Against the Blues,* directs us to read his verse against a background of recalled popular sources. For example, "Whispers in a County Church" simulates an exchange of worldly gossip among the, no doubt, pious; "De Profundis" relates the practical plea of a drinker for some sign, less miraculous than a burning bush, to move him to sobriety. These stock comic figures are matched in a pair of poems, opening the book, that invoke Bessie Smith in an allusion to the muse and announce the news of the dispensation of the blues. None of the poems is long. All have the apparent simplicity of direct statement. Except for the references to Bessie Smith and, in another poem, Nat Turner, the immediate subjects are personal experiences. Just like the blues! The singer-poet presents first-person experiences in ways that will make them typical.

As both singer and poet know, it is not so much the experience itself, though that is surely familiar, as the form in which it is rendered that makes the song and poem typical. Thus, Aubert typifies his poems through the patterns of language. The characters of Zenobia in "Photo Album" or "Uncle Bill" and "Granny Dean" are familiar not only because we may know people like them but because the poet's lines about his characters approximate the habits of speech. Often a use of negatives or identical rhymes echoes the oral games of black English. Sometimes, as in "Garden Scene," the verse nearly assumes the form of anecdotal exemplum. Of course, it is not to imitate, even the patterns of spoken language, that Aubert writes. The typicality provided by linguistic patterns acknowledged by poet and reader serves as subject for creative imagination.

Aubert opens his second book of poetry, *Feeling Through,* with "Black Aesthetic," a poem that proposes to reverse Duchamp's *Nude Descending a Staircase* so that it would portray a black man going up, not down. And out. "Feeling Through," the title poem, illustrates Aubert's point, pulling experience up into reflective consciousness and setting it out as the new experience of a poem. With a characteristic syntactic economy, now become almost elliptical, Aubert establishes a situation. He, or his persona, sits on a porch swing, looking through a window at the reflection in a mirror of a carnival photograph. A partial dialogue is overheard but quickly displaced, so that wonder about the old photograph is transformed into a soliloquy on the problem of recapturing the past. The scene and events of "Feeling Through" are the material of a family story. Narrative, however, remains inchoate as the poetic voice plays feelings held in the foreground of mind over the background of anecdote. The poem is, thus, both a gloss on the latent tale of the photograph and the expression of a newly defined experience.

Aubert increasingly attaches subjective significance to his imagery. In poems such as "Economics" from the first volume, or "The Opposite of Green" from the second, details explain the mundane appearance of racism, but "Nightmare" and "Levitation," both in the second book, have highly personal references. Still, the tactics of language are consistent throughout Aubert's work. The texts of his poems maintain a continuity with Afro-American tradition by simulation and innovation that become a commentary on the richness of his sources and evidence of authentic re-creation.

—John M. Reilly

AWIAKTA, Marilou

Born: Marilou Awiakta Bonham in Knoxville, Tennessee, 24 January 1936. **Education:** University of Tennessee, B.A.(magna cum laude) in English and French 1958. **Family:** Married Paul Thompson in 1957; two daughters and one son. **Career:** Poet and author active in environmental, Native American, and women's issues; lecturer at various institutions, including Brandeis University, Tufts University, and University of New Mexico; civilian liaison officer and interpreter for U.S. Air Force, Laon Air Force Base, France, 1964-67; consultant for film *The Good Mind*, 1982, and Aaron Copeland Film Festival; cofounder, 1982, ambassador-at-large, 1986-90, Far-away Cherokee Association (now Native American Inter-Tribal Association); member of literary panel, 1982-89, chair, 1987-89, Tennessee Arts Commission; commissioner, Mayor's International Heritage Commission, Memphis, 1987-89; contributor to periodicals, including *Callaloo, Greenfield Review, Ms., Parabola, Southern Exposure, Southern Style, Who Cares?* and *Women of Power.* **Awards:** Nashville "Homecoming '86" Literary Festival honor, 1986; Woman of Vision Award, Women of Achievement, 1988; Distinguished Tennessee Writer Award, Smokey Mountain Writers' Conference, 1989; Appalachian Writers Association Award, 1991; Women's Rights Leadership Award, National Conference of Christians and Jews; Person of Quality Award, National Organization for Women; Grammy Award nomination, 1995, for audio version of *Selu: Seeking the Corn Mother's Wisdom.* **Member:** National Conference of Christians and Jews (board member, 1984-90), Network of Girl Scouts of America, Leadership Memphis, Women's Foundation of Greater Memphis (board member, beginning 1995). **Address:** c/o Fulcrum Publishing, 350 Indiana St., Suite 350, Golden, Colorado 80401.

PUBLICATIONS

Poetry

Abiding Appalachia: Where Mountain and Atom Meet. Memphis, St. Luke's Press, 1978.

For Children

Rising Fawn and the Fire Mystery: A Story of Heritage, Family, and Courage, 1833, illustrated by Beverly Pringle. Memphis, St. Luke's Press, 1983.
Selu: Seeking the Corn-Mother's Wisdom, illustrated by Mary Adair, foreword by Wilma Mankiller. Golden, Colorado, Fulcrum, 1993.

Uncollected Essays

"Seed Corn Must Not Be Ground." In *Confessing Conscience: Churched Women on Abortion* edited by Phyllis Tickle, Nashville, Abingdon Press, 1990.
"A Bridge is a Gift to the People." In *Keepers of Life* by Michael J. Caduto and Joseph Bruchac, Golden, Colorado, Fulcrum, 1994.
"Grandmothers." In *Oxford Companion to Women's Writing in the United States* edited by Cathy N. Davidson and Linda Wagner-Martin, New York, Oxford University Press, 1995.
"Southern Women" and "Southwestern Indian Women." In *The Reader's Companion to U.S. Women's History* edited by Wilma Mankiller, Gwendolyn Mink, Marysa Navarro, Barbara Smith, and Gloria Steinem, Boston, Houghton Mifflin, 1996.

*

Recordings: Audio—*Selu: Seeking the Corn-Mother's Wisdom* (music by Jo Harjo and Poetic Justice), Audio Literature, 1995. **Video**—*Focus on Conservation* (conservation education package), Lexington, Kentucky Educational Television, 1991.

Teleplays: "Telling Tale," "Little Deer and Mother Earth," and "Rising Fawn and the Fire Mystery," in *Focus on Conservation,* PBS, 1991.

Interviews: "A Woman of Substance" by Marilyn Sadler, *Memphis,* September 1994;

Critical Studies: "Nuclear Visions" by Jane Caputi, *American Quarterly,* March 1995; "Marilou Awiakta" by Giney Carney, *Journal of Appalachian Studies,* No. 7, 1995; "Selu" by Jerold Savory, *Southern Humanities Review,* Spring 1995; "Selu" by M. Rupert Cutler, *Now & Then,* Spring 1995; *Women Reshaping Human Rights* by Marguerite Bouvard, Wilmington, Delaware, Scholarly Resources, 1996.

Marilou Awiakta comments:
   In my life and work, I take up the ancient "Song of the Grandmothers," sing it in the key of my own voice and times, and pass it on. This is the song:

   I am Cherokee.
   My people believe in the Spirit that unites all things.
   I am woman. I am life force. My word has great value.

The Beloved Woman is one of our principle chiefs. Through her the Spirit often speaks to the people. In the Great Council at the capital, she is a powerful voice. Concerning the fate of hostages, her word is absolute.

Women share in all of life. We lead sacred dances. In the Council we debate freely with men until an agreement is reached. When the nation considers war, we have a say, for we bear the warriors.

Sometimes I go into battle. I also plant and harvest.

I carry my own name and the name of my clan. If I accept a mate, he and our children take the name of my clan. If there is deep trouble between us, I am as free to tell him to go as he is to leave. Our children and our dwelling stay with me. As long as I am treated with dignity, I am steadfast.

> I love to work and sing.
> I listen to the spirit.
> In all things I speak my mind.
> I walk without fear.
> I am Cherokee.

This song is from "Amazons in Appalachia" in *Selu.*

*   *   *

The story of Awiakta's names suggests the outlines of her rich heritage: Bonham from her Scottish ancestors who settled in the mountains of East Tennessee seven generations ago, and Awiakta, meaning "eye of the deer" in Cherokee. The Cherokee and Appalachian "component cultures"—*not* sub-cultures, as Awiakta is quick to remind us—combine in her very veins the indigenous and Celtic traditions of storytelling and spiritual connections to the land.

Awiakta's father worked at Oak Ridge, Tennessee, one of the first nuclear research communities, and Awiakta has always sought the relationship between science and traditional Cherokee philosophy, feeling at home with the language of science and the atom. As if all these languages were not enough (a writer can never have too many), Awiakta lived in France from 1964-67, serving as interpreter and civilian liaison officer at a U.S. Air Force base where her husband was stationed. Rather than being "lost in translation," she has found herself in the confluence of all these cultures. As she tells us in her retrospective and forward-looking book, *Selu:* "Living in France made me think deeply about who I was, about the value of my heritages, and about the necessity of working out harmonies with peoples from different cultures. By the time I returned to America, I knew I was a Cherokee/Appalachian poet. I was determined to sing my song."

This demanding calling brought with it burdens as well as joy during the social strife of the late-1960s. In the aftermath of the civil rights movement, before the women's movement, Awiakta's path was difficult and lonely. But her "song"—her work—gradually attracted supporters such as Phyllis Tickle of St. Luke's Press (who commissioned Awiakta's first book, *Abiding Appalachia: Where Mountain and Atom Meet,* in 1978) and mentors such as Cherokee chief Wilma Mankiller and Joseph Bruchac (an Abenaki), Rene Parks Lanier, and African American writers Alice Walker and the late Etheridge Knight. Paula Gunn Allen and Leslie Silko were also significant literary influences, as was Virginia Woolf.

It was around 1982 that she decided to use her middle name, Awiakta. "Traditionally, it is a Native American custom to have several names during one's lifetime," she say of this decision. "In

childhood and youth, I was called 'Marilou.' When my spirit had deepened and I had reached a new level of understanding and creativity, it was time to move to the name that expressed my more mature state of being." Five years before, while visiting Oak Ridge's Museum of Science and Energy, Awiakta had a profound visionary experience with the white deer sacred to the Cherokee: the story of *Awi Usdi,* or Little Deer, teaches the law of respect. "With my whole being I made a quantum leap and connected Little Deer to the web of my life —at the center . . . . That night, I drew what I'd seen: a white stag leaping at the heart of three atopic orbits." This unique image of so much in her past, present, and future, has become her personal logo. "To me it signifies the hope that if we have respect for everything—down to the atom—we can restore harmony and balance to our world."

Awiakta also identifies with what she terms the "new tribes"— the women's movement and environmental groups, which she hopes will help make modern society more permeable to the Cherokee traditions of women holding leadership positions. In response to critics who claim that women's judgement might be impaired by their menstrual cycles, Awiakta answers with lively feminist wit and impeccable logic: "If that's the case, looking at history and all the wars through the ages, men must have been having a continual period!"

On a more serious note, she recalls the words of her mother: "When I was young and said, 'I want to be a poet,' my mother would always say, 'That's good. And what will you do for the people?'" Awiakta accepts the full consequences of the Cherokee belief that "true art is for Life's sake, as well as for individual expression." She has taken her fusion of science and Cherokee/Appalachian philosophy "wherever people asked me to come": to festivals, schools, conservation conferences, prisons, women's groups, and hospitals. Through her poetry and her presence, Awiakta has inspired countless gatherings, from a tender talk she gave to some young women graduating *cum laude* from their high school to a keynote address at a National Colloquium on Nuclear Waste Disposal.

These many conversations and writings, ranging from matters of public policy to personal philosophy, culminated in what Jane Caputi calls an "extraordinarily beautiful, complex, persuasive meditation on the powers of corn as a sacred tradition." *Selu: Seeking the Corn-Mother's Wisdom,* a ground- and genre-breaking compendium of Awiakta's work, celebrates, at its center, Selu the Corn-Mother (*not* a Goddess, but a living spirit to Native Americans), whose story teaches survival wisdoms of strength, respect, balance, adaptability, and cooperation. Awiakta applies these common-sense teachings to contemporary concerns: the environment, gender issues, cultural diversity, and government. What emerges from this fusion is a transfusion of new-old ideas and images, what Jerold Savory has praised as "required reading for all of us who are ready to be informed, inspired, and shaped by the native roots of our national heritage." Since its publication in 1993 *Selu* has been adopted by universities spanning the United States for courses ranging from sociology and women's studies to literature. It has been compared to such works as Vine Deloria's flagship book on Native spirituality, *God Is Red,* and Rachel Carson's *Silent Spring.*

Important to *Selu's* unique effect is its double-woven basket form. "Reading will be easy if you keep the weaving mode in mind:

Over ... under ... over," writes Awiakta. "A round basket never runs 'straight-on.'" This form reflects the author's perspective, for Native realities are cyclical experiences of interrelationship and renewal.

While *Selu* encompasses such painful issues as the flooding of the historic heartland of the Cherokee in the Tellicoe Dam initiative, it also dares to be humorous, as in "Selu and the Sex Expert." And Awiakta's all-pervasive feminist perspective "busts out" in such poems as "Song of Grandmothers," "When Earth Becomes an 'It'," "Mother Nature Send a Pink Slip," and "On Being a Female Phoenix," where she protests "Not only do I rise/ from my own ashes,/I have to carry them out!" In her longer poem "Anorexia Bulimia Speaks from the Grave" comes the following advice: "Listen young women,/the Grandmothers and Anorexia Bulimia/are talkin' to you—Feed your body./Feed your soul./Feed your dream./BUST OUT!!!"

Also contained in *Selu*'s flexible basket structure are essays that had appeared earlier, such as "Amazons in Appalachia," "Living in the Round: What Maria's Bowl Teaches Me," and "Baring the Atoms' Mother Heart," which Gloria Steinem heralded as a "groundbreaking" piece. "Awiakta is one of the rare writers whose words help readers see the world in a different way," noted Steinem. "Her weaving of essays, stories and poems in *Selu* creates the sense of an ancient knowledge being brought to bear on modern problems. For the majority culture of this country, she brings an inkling of the wisdom it has done its best to destroy, and the generosity of spirit that continues giving that wisdom as gift."

Awiakta is imbued with that same generosity of spirit and will continue giving and developing in her work. The paradoxical terms *continuity* and *growth,* along with Little Deer's leap and balance, may help describe why Awiakta remains such an interesting writer to watch. As Paula Gunn Allen has said, "Thank you Grandmother Corn, Selu, for Awiakta."

—J. J. Wilson

B

BALDWIN, William

Born: McClellanville, South Carolina in 1944. **Education:** Clemson University, B.A. **Family:** Married, wife Lilian. **Career:** Construction (houses and boats), shrimper and oysterman, teacher, historian, novelist. **Awards:** Lillian Smith Award for Fiction, 1993, for *The Hard to Catch Mercy.*

PUBLICATIONS

Novels

The Hard to Catch Mercy. Chapel Hill, Algonquin Books, 1993.
The Fennel Family Papers. Chapel Hill, Algonquin Books, 1996.

Nonfiction

Lowcountry Daytrips: Plantations, Gardens, and a Natural History of the Charleston Region. Charleston, Legacy Publications, 1991.
Mrs. Whaley and Her Charleston Garden, with Emily Whaley. Charleston, Fireside, 1998.

*

William Baldwin comments:
I believe in the perhaps now unfashionable notion of the indomitable and the enduring. I believe that all life is sacred . . . and that skin color, sex, and sexual preference are simply veneers overlaying an equally old-fashioned concept of all-encompassing life force."

*   *   *

William Baldwin's two novels feature sweeping, often manic narratives filled with quirky characters and protagonists who develop from passive to assertive individuals. With passages detailing comic eccentricities and darkly satirizing human vanities, Baldwin's novels encompass elements of history, religion, superstition, and social customs in the Lowcountry area of South Carolina with which he is intimate. Ghosts, demonic and enchanting characters, superstition and magic, mysteries and decadence lend his stories larger-than-life qualities and a kind of colorful existence in which his protagonists learn to live: they confront sinister characters and move outside of their insular worlds to more active participation in family and community life.

The Hard to Catch Mercy, Baldwin's first novel, is essentially a coming-of-age tale about Willie T. Anderson, who has had an insular upbringing in a fishing village. The arrival of two relatives, Jimmy and Lydia, who move in with his family in 1916, prove catalysts for Willie to look outward, beyond his limited experience, to find truth. Lydia, for example, arrives with progressive views on race relations, differing from the strict separatism and suspiciousness preached within Willie's family, which includes a Civil War veteran. Through Jimmy, whose aggressive courtship of

Amy Mercy, a local girl, accidentally leads to tragedy, Willie learns about love and asserting his individuality.

A cast of odd locals includes Amy's brother, the title character so-named for his ability to find lost animals. When the demonic Hard to Catch Mercy absconds with his sister's body during her funeral, the mad pursuit culminates with a confrontation between Willie and Hard to Catch that proves pivotal in Willie's maturation. Baldwin's strength with local color and history are evident in his depiction of the extended Anderson family. Their home was destroyed and dowry lost to the Union army, and as the story begins around fifty years later they are still emerging from the ruins. After the wild series of events through which Willie comes of age, the specter of World War I looms in the end, likely to claim several of the characters just emerging as adults.

The Fennel Family Papers is also a coming-of-age tale, though its protagonist is already an adult with a professional career. Still, Professor Paul Danvers is leading a safe, uneventful life going nowhere in a nondescript position and concerned mostly about his tenure track. When he discovers that one of his students, Ginny Fennel, is related to the historically prominent Fennel family, Danvers seizes his chance for making his name by exploring the family's mysterious past and involvement in significant events. Fennel uses the student (seducing her, perhaps, though his comic ineptness and the general mayhem surrounding the family make it difficult to be certain of the goings-on) to become intimate with the family and gain access to their artifacts and papers.

The eccentric Fennel family includes ghosts, an overzealous nephew, a protective matriarch, and a family servant who practices magic. While the artifacts prove historically useless—the papers are filled with recipes and weather charts—the family is an inexhaustible resource, particularly the servant. Their customs, superstitions, religious practices, dark secrets and memories, involvement in slave running and miscegenation—their survival, in fact—are vital examples of lived experience that Danvers lacks, as Baldwin satirizes academic approaches to history that are divorced from the people and sites of events researched and addressed. Danvers' personal transition occurs in what can be seen as a characteristic Baldwin emphasis on adventurousness and physical experience, as Danvers protects a young woman by fighting off modern-day pirates.

Action-packed adventures and misadventures, carefully captured local color—from comical quirks to darker hints of evil—historical allusions, and sympathetic protagonists who rise to their occasions are the stuff of Baldwin's engaging novels.

—Emma Cobb

BARRY, Dave

Born: Armonk, New York, 3 July 1947. **Education:** Haverford College, B.A. 1969. **Family:** Married 1) Elizabeth Lenox Pyle in

1975 (divorced), one son, Robert; 2) Michelle Kauffman. **Career**: Reporter, *Daily Local News*, West Chester, Pennsylvania, 1971-75, Associated Press, Philadelphia, 1975-76; lecturer on effective writing for businesses, R. S. Burger Associates (consulting firm), 1975-83; free-lance humor columnist, since 1980; syndicated humor columnist, *Miami Herald*since 1983. **Awards**: Distinguished Writing Award, American Society of Newspaper Editors, 1986; Pulitzer prize for commentary, 1988; Best in Business, *Washington Journalism Review*, 1989. **Agent**: Al Hart, Fox Chase Agency, Public Ledger Bldg., Room 930, Independence Sq., Philadelphia, Pennsylvania 19106. **Address**: Miami Herald, 1 Herald Plaza, Miami, Florida 33123-1693.

PUBLICATIONS

The Taming of the Screw: Several Million Homeowners' Problems Sidestepped. Rodale Press, 1983.
Babies and Other Hazards of Sex: How to Make a Tiny Person in Only Nine Months, with Tools You Probably Have around the Home. Rodale Press, 1984.
Bad Habits: A 100% Fact Free Book. Doubleday, 1985.
Stay Fit and Healthy until You're Dead. Rodale Press, 1985.
Claw Your Way to the Top: How to Become the Head of a Major Corporation in Roughly a Week. Rodale Press, 1986.
Dave Barry's Guide to Marriage and/or Sex. Rodale Press, 1987.
Dave Barry's Greatest Hits. Crown, 1988.
Homes and Other Black Holes: The Happy Homeowner's Guide. Fawcett/Columbine, 1988.
Dave Barry Slept Here: A Sort of History of the United States. Random House, 1989.
Dave Barry Turns Forty. Crown, 1990.
Dave Barry Talks Back. Crown, 1991.
Dave Barry's Guide to Life. Crown, 1991.
Dave Barry Does Japan. Random House, 1992.
Dave Barry Is Not Making This Up. Crown, 1994.
Dave Barry's Guide to Guys: A User's Manual. Random House, 1995.
Dave Barry's Bad Lyrics. Andrews & McMeel, 1996.
Dave Barry in Cyberspace. Crown, 1996.

Contributor, *Naked Came the Manatee*, edited by Carl Hiaasen. Fawcett Books, 1997.

*   *   *

Irreverent humorist Dave Barry finds his most insightful material in the everyday lives of Americans—computer use, home ownership, work, family, vacations, and the like. While Barry's home base is a column for the *Miami Herald* newspaper, his comic musings are syndicated to a larger audience of over 150 newspapers. As a newspaper commentator, Barry has won a Pulitzer Prize (1988) and was named the "Best in Business" (1989) by the *Washington Journalism Review*. Barry has also published nearly 20 books featuring his brand of sardonic wit, and several titles have appeared on the *New York Times* bestseller list.

In his columns as well as his books, Barry always manages to find a wacky angle on his chosen topic, whether it is grammar, history, or Pop Tarts. He plays on the irony embedded within daily life to point out the absurdities of modern human existence. Nothing is safe or sacred to Barry: he can both biting and silly on

nearly everything he sets his comic mind to. Even while dealing with mundane and topical subjects, the unexpected is Barry's most potent comic tool, most successfully communicated through his use of non sequiturs.

From explaining the "black holes" involved with home ownership in his first book, *The Taming of the Screw: Several Million Homeowners' Problems Sidestepped* (1983), to parodies of history in 1989's *Dave Barry Slept Here: A Sort of History of the United States*, Barry showed a gift for exposing absurdities in common experiences and developed a large and devoted audience. In *Dave Barry Slept Here*, the author writes his version of American history because, as he points out, most people never learned it in the first place. He parodies the textbooks people didn't read, what was said in classes they slept or daydreamed through, and his own ignorance on the subject. Barry suggests all important historical events, including the Fourth of July, for example, should be celebrated on October 8 (his son's birthday, coincidentally), so students can remember dates more easily. However, Barry deliberately misinterprets and improvises material for a laugh. There are few wars discussed in his book, and not a lot of facts either. One highly amusing passage discusses Cliff, among the first important American novelists and the all-important author of Cliff Notes.

In his 1991 book, *Dave Barry's Guide to Life*, he gives his own version of parental advice, from dating (doing everything you won't do when you're married) to financial matters (making your own credit cards). Barry is not above putting himself at the butt-end of his humor: his next book, *Dave Barry Turns Forty* (1990), describes his own personal take on becoming a middle-aged man. Indeed, "guy humor" is at the core of much of Barry's success, as his 1995 book, *Dave Barry's Guide to Guys: A User's Manual*, attests.

Other topics Barry has explored have included vacation experiences, as in his 1992 book, *Dave Barry Does Japan*, and 1996's *Dave Barry in Cyberspace*, where Barry finds humor that appeals to both the computer literate and the computer illiterate, the inanities of tech support hotlines, and the advent of multi-tasking, which, as he observes, gives computer users the power to waste time more quickly. Barry attempts to explain how computers work, the process of buying a computer, and how to become computer literate (ask a 14-year-old for help), then moves on to the Internet and the World Wide Web. Barry coins terms to explain computers—WGU stands for Whirring Grinding Unit—and gives advice on how to make documents look bigger (dave barry tip:fonts). Some of Barry's best material concerns the always odd world of net etiquette, or netiquette.

Through his range of material, Barry always manages to maintain a certain freshness with each book. His tongue-in-cheek approach has evolved stylistically over the course of his career but remains as youthful and sacrilegious as ever. As Alison Teal noted in a *New York Times Book Review* piece on *Dave Barry's Greatest Hits*, a 1988 compilation of his columns, Barry "has a gift for taking things at face value and rendering them funny on those grounds alone, for squeezing every ounce of humor out of a perfectly ordinary experience."

—Annette Petrusso

BARTHELME, Frederick

Born: Houston, Texas, 10 October 1943. **Education:** Tulane University, New Orleans, 1961-62; University of Houston, 1962-65, 1966-67; Johns Hopkins University, Baltimore (teaching fellow; Coleman Prose award, 1977), 1976-77, M.A. 1977. **Career:** Architectural draftsman, Jerome Oddo and Associates, and Kenneth E. Bentsen Associates, both Houston, 1965-66; exhibition organizer, St. Thomas University, Houston, 1966-67; assistant to director, Kornblee Gallery, New York, 1967-68; creative director, BMA Advertising, Houston, 1971-73; senior writer, GDL & W Advertising, Houston, 1973-76; since 1977 professor of English, director of the Center for Writers, and editor of *Mississippi Review*, University of Southern Mississippi, Hattiesburg; visual artist, with exhibitions at galleries in Houston, Norman, Oklahoma, New York, Seattle, Vancouver, Buenos Aires, and Oberlin, Ohio, 1965-74. **Awards:** National Endowment for the Arts fellowship, 1979; University of Southern Mississippi research grant, 1980.

PUBLICATIONS

Novels

War and War. New York, Doubleday, 1971.
Second Marriage. New York, Simon and Schuster, 1984.
Tracer. New York, Simon and Schuster, 1985.
Two Against One. New York, Weidenfeld and Nicolson, 1988.
Natural Selection. New York, Viking, 1990.
The Brothers. New York, Viking, 1993.
Painted Desert. New York, Viking, 1995.
Bob the Gambler. New York, Houghton Mifflin, 1997.

Short Stories

Rangoon. New York, Winter House, 1970.
Moon Deluxe. New York, Simon and Schuster, 1983.
Chroma and Other Stories. New York, Simon and Schuster, 1987.

Uncollected Short Stories

"Cooker," in *New Yorker*, 10 August 1987.
"Law of Averages," in *New Yorker*, 5 October 1987.
"Shopgirls," in *Esquire* (Japanese edition: Tokyo), August 1988.
"War with Japan," in *New Yorker*, 12 December 1988.
"Driver," in *New American Short Stories 2*, edited by Gloria Norris, New York, New American Library, 1989.
"With Ray and Judy," in *New Yorker*, 24 April 1989.
"Domestic," in *Fiction of the Eighties*, edited by Gibbons and Hahn, Chicago, *TriQuarterly*, 1990.
"The Philosophers," in *Boston Globe Magazine*, 22 July 1990.
"Margaret and Bud," in *New Yorker*, 15 May 1991.
"Jackpot," in *Frank* magazine, 1992.
"Retreat," in *Epoch*, 1993.

*   *   *

In his novels and short stories, Frederick Barthelme captures the more mundane essence of contemporary urban life in an intriguingly obscure, nearly minimalist manner. His fiction thrives on details and buzzwords of consumerism: brand names prolifer-ate, and his settings are often apartment complexes, restaurants, and other recognizable structures in the urban landscape. Though he is specific about what his characters purchase and where they go, almost to the point of cataloging, Barthelme omits other particulars about their lives—where they live, what they do for a living, where they have been. The effect is disconcerting— realistic, but vacant, and a reflective commentary on modern life.

Barthelme published two works of fiction in the early 1970s, a novel, *War and War* (1971) and a collection of short stories, *Rangoon* (1970). They were overly stylized affairs, and Barthelme continued dabbling in his many other talents and interests. The son of an architect, Barthelme was an architectural draftsman during the mid-1960s, and, like his brother, Donald, a famous fiction writer, Frederick Barthelme had an interest in the visual arts— Donald Barthelme wrote art criticism before concentrating on fiction, Frederick was an exhibition organizer as well as a creative visual artist. Barthelme also served as a creative director at an advertising agency during the mid-1970s. After completing his MA at Johns Hopkins University in 1977, Barthelme became a professor of English at the University of Southern Mississippi. He has since served as director of the Center for Writers and editor of the *Mississippi Review*. Barthelme also found his voice and began publishing his distinctive brand of fiction with the short story collection, *Moon Deluxe* (1983).

Barthelme's stories are almost always written in the first or second person from the point of view of a male character. In his early works these male protagonists have many common characteristics. They are usually near 40 in age and live alone, either bachelors or divorced. They are retiring in nature. Barthelme's women characters, on the other hand, are active, taking the lead role in initiating and maintaining relationships. His men maintain an indifference in all matters, including interactions with their female counterparts, divulging next to nothing about their lives, reflected in the distant and uninvolved tone in which the stories are told.

Barthelme's choices in style and substance of his stories suggest a disaffected manner in which contemporary American society operates. But the author is not above seeing the humor in lives that revolve around malls and fast food, and he draws his episodes in his characters' lives appropriately. He also creates artificial drama, implying throughout his stories that an important moment is about to occur, though it rarely does. The stories in *Moon Deluxe* (1983), for example, uses immediacy as each narrative's most successful effect. The stories are postmodern— interestingly drawn gestures, rather than fully crafted pieces. Similarly, the stories in *Chroma and Other Stories* (1987) relay monotony and estrangement in brief narratives.

In his novel *Second Marriage* (1984), Barthelme draws a more full-bodied comedy that finds humor in current mores. At the beginning of the novel, Henry and his wife, Theo, encounter an unusual circumstance when his former wife, Clare, moves in with them. The women get along well, better in fact than either of them does with Henry, and they get him to move out of his own home. The novel then follows his life after his ejection, adrift, waiting for the call to come home. Like many of Barthelme's men, Henry is a nice enough guy but is often perplexed by life around him: he find solace in food, especially at restaurants and usually of the fast food variety. This activity occupies time, giving them a temporary purpose, but fast food, like the lives of Barthelme's men, lacks satisfying nourishment.

Tracer (1985) follows the life of Martin after the dissolution of his marriage with Alex. Martin moves to Florida and lives in a motel-condo owned by Alex's sister, Dominica. Dominica is also separated from her husband, Mel. After Martin and Dominica begin sleeping together, Alex and Mel both appear at the establishment. Barthelme weaves his witty brand of comedy through these complicated ties, relying on unsuccessful contact and dislocation in a novel more engaging than his earlier work. Through dialogue that features somewhat meaningless, though funny, monologues, the author highlights the detached aspect of modern life.

In *Two Against One* (1988), the protagonist Edward turns 40. On his birthday, his wife, Elise, from whom he has been separated for six months, resurfaces and expresses a desire to reunite and to allow her ex-boyfriend, Roscoe, to move into their house as well. Roscoe's wife was killed in a traffic mishap. This situation puts Edward in a typical Barthelme bind: a mature man faces an unconventional living arrangement, but the absence of any real emotional or moral commitment makes the odd situation seem viable and non-threatening.

Natural Selection (1990) marks a turn toward a darker sensibility. Because the central character, Peter Wexler, is unhappy in his marriage to Lily, his second wife, he wanders aimlessly though shopping centers and drives on freeways without a destination. The solution of his ennui comes from an unexpected source: a fatal accident occurs while he is driving with Lily on the freeway late one night, and the resulting sense of anguish usually unstated in Barthelme's work receives an unexpectedly strong voice.

Barthelme's 1997 novel, *Bob the Gambler*, features Raymond Kaiser, an architect in Mississippi. He is married to Jewel, and they live with her teenaged daughter, RV, from a previous marriage. Raymond and Jewel are increasingly lured to the offshore gambling world as Raymond's architectural work becomes less lucrative, which results in increasing debt, trouble with RV, who is left alone as Raymond and Jewel gamble each night, and later crisis caused by the death of Raymond's father. After piling up insurmountable debts and quitting the architect business, Raymond and the family move in with Ray's mother and each finds personal forms of satisfaction. Like Barthelme's previous books, *Bob the Gambler* is replete with the seemingly insignificant details of modern life, but the characters have a sense of loyalty that was a mere undercurrent, if noticeable at all, in his earlier books.

—Emma Cobb

BARTHELME, Steven

Born: Houston, Texas, 7 July 1947. **Education:** Boston College, 1965-66; University of Texas at Austin, B.A. 1972; John Hopkins University, M.A. 1984. **Career:** Review editor, *Texas Observer*, Austin, 1972-73; copywriter for advertising agencies in Austin and Houston, 1973-83; instructor, Northeast Louisiana University, Monroe, 1984-86; associate professor of English, Univer-

sity of Southern Mississippi, Hattiesburg, since 1986; writer. **Awards:** *Transatlantic Review* Award for Fiction, 1984; honors from P.E.N. Syndicated Fiction Project, 1985, 1986, 1987; Short Story Award, Texas Institute of Letters, 1988, for "Zorro"; Hemingway Short Story Award, 1990. **Agent:** Andrew Wylie, 250 West 57th St., Suite 2106, New York, New York 10107. **Address:** Department of English, University of Southern Mississippi, Southern Station, Box 5144, Hattiesburg, Missouri 39406.

PUBLICATIONS

Short Stories

And He Tells the Little Horse the Whole Story. Johns Hopkins University Press, 1987.

Uncollected Short Stories

"Telephone," in *North American Review*, June 1996.
"Interview," in *Yale Review*, April 1997.

*   *   *

Steve Barthelme published his first book of short fiction, *And He Tells the Little Horse the Whole Story*, in 1987. In these seventeen stories, many of which appeared in respected journals and won awards, Barthelme's gifts as a resourceful writer with a dark sense of humor are evident. He uses a choppy style of writing with spare sentences, minimal and to the point. Indeed none of the stories are long and most could best be described as sketches. This style's effectiveness reinforces the kind of characters Barthelme creates. His stories feature such oddities as a fake therapist who feels compelled to murder a dull patient ("Samaritan"), a professional market analyst who fakes being a professional football player, and a house cat with powers of perception into the lives of humans ("Chat").

Indeed, with such characters and blunt stylistic considerations, Barthelme is often compared to Raymond Carver. Comparisons to his brothers, Donald and Frederick, both of whom favor a postmodern, minimalistic style, are also inevitable: Donald's munificence of experimentation and Frederick's spareness notwithstanding, Steve Barthelme carves his own unique identity as an author. The kinds of subtle twists in his stories and their intention is perhaps best indicated in the collection's title, which is from "Lament" by the Russian playwright/short story author Anton Chekhov. In Chekhov's story, a destitute cabdriver has no one to talk to but a horse after his son's death. The characters in Barthelme suffer from communication problems, hobbling through the stories and unable or simply not interested in understanding those whom they encounter.

This lack of communication sometimes forms more than the core of the stories, some of which take place in cars and several of which are conversations between strangers. The primary characters are usually white, middle-class males in their 30s. Many of them have reached a crossroads in their amorous relationships, but even if the characters in the stories are strangers, communicating with others, especially members of the opposite sex, are most revealing. For example, in "Failing All Else," a young man tries to communicate with a young woman in a cafe by reading a book to her. In the "The Friend," the main character, a male driver, goes one step farther, picking up a younger woman while on the road and proceeds to rant about proper folks, schooling, and "big words," then he rapes the woman.

Other stories are specifically about people involved in relationships and adultery. In "Pick," a husband takes his wife to a restaurant to meet his lover. Some of the couples are dealing with separation, on their way to divorce, as in "Zach," where a pet is returned to a husband separated from his wife. In "Problematical Species," a couple already separated takes a camping trip together. These basic situations, as momentous and yet as unresolvable as the situation in "Lament" concerning the grieving man with no one to share his feelings, present opportunities for delving beyond superficialities, but the moment passes and a larger monotony prevails. Indeed, "Stoner's Lament" concerns a son long gone as recollected by his father. The silences and the lack of meaningful communication become the essence conveyed.

—Emma Cobb

BASS, Rick

Born: Fort Worth, Texas, 7 March 1958. **Education:** Utah State University, B.S. 1979. **Family:** Married Elizabeth Hughes; daughters Mary Katherine, Lowry. **Career:** Petroleum Geologist, 1979-87; contributor to periodicals, including *Paris Review, Esquire, GQ,* and *Quarterly,* and anthologies, including *Best American Short Stories, New Stories from the South,* and *The O. Henry Awards.* **Awards:** General Electric Younger Writers Award, 1987; PEN/Nelson Algren Award Special Citation, 1988, for *The Watch.*

PUBLICATIONS

Short Story Collections

The Watch. New York City, Norton, 1988.
Platte River. Boston, Houghton, 1994.
In the Loyal Mountains. Boston, Houghton, 1995.
The Sky, The Stars, The Wilderness. Boston, Houghton-Mifflin, 1997.

Nonfiction

The Deer Pasture. College Station, Texas A&M University Press, 1985.
Wild to the Heart. Harrisburg, Stackpole, 1987.
Oil Notes. Boston, Houghton, 1989, reprinted Dallas, Southern Methodist University Press, 1995.
Winter: Notes from Montana. Boston, Houghton, 1991.
The Ninemile Wolves: An Essay. Livingston, Montana, Clark City Press, 1992.
The Lost Grizzlies: A Search for Survivors in the Wilderness of Colorado. Boston, Houghton, 1995.
The Book of Yaak. Boston, Houghton, 1997.

*   *   *

When Rick Bass won the PEN/Nelson Algren Award Special Citation in 1988, the judges mentioned his ability to "write a tale that is larger than life." The tale is central to Bass's work, both fiction and non-fiction. His characters are storytellers, sometimes failed storytellers, and everything depends on getting a story right, telling it true.

One of Bass's strengths is his own story-telling voice, his ability to cut away the superfluous so that the reader can judge the heart of both story and character. This voice tells a story true, strong and intimate; the details of his language are lush and pure, providing just the right amount of landscape or inner turmoil. Above all, his stories are about precarious balances: between men and women, children and adults, friends, lovers, and between humans and the natural world. His language reflects that balance. Like Eudora Welty, to whom he is often compared, Bass pays close attention to inner and outer surfaces, watching where and how they meet, and he captures those meeting places on the page.

The poetry of Bass's language can lull you into forgetting the physicality of his writing. He has also been compared to Hemingway for his tight, muscular prose. His characters, in fiction and non-fiction, are passionate and, above all, physical. They think, wonder, love, and doubt, but they also make love, lift weights, hike, hunt, drive, break things, garden, swim, drink, and play with the same intensity. Sex is part of the human relationship with the natural world, it connects us to wildness, as does any strenuous activity, and Bass never forgets that, no matter what his subject. Bass also knows the importance of a sense of place; like Welty, he believes that "it is by knowing where you stand that you grow able to judge where you are."

Bass's non-fiction provides the reader with a continuous narrative of his thoughts and his maturation as a man and as a writer. The boyish exuberance of *The Deer Pasture* becomes the lyricism of *Winter,* which meshes with anger in *The Book of Yaak.* The characters Bass describes are himself, his family, his friends, various environmental activists and politicians; the landscapes he details are those which he loves. The act of writing is a continuous theme: Bass distinguishes between telling the facts and telling the truth and discusses the responsibilities of telling any story well. But particularly in his latest three non-fiction works,

The Ninemile Wolves: An Essay, The Lost Grizzlies: A Search for Survivors in the Wilderness of Colorado, and *The Book of Yaak,* Bass tackles moral issues of environmental stewardship: how we, as humans, live upon the earth. He offers both sides of arguments, but he always argues the side of responsibility over greed, care over carelessness.

The Deer Pasture (1985) tells a continuous story, in short essay-sketches, of a family's connection to the hill-country of Texas through the yearly ritual of deer hunting. The distinctive Bass voice is in evidence, although not yet strong and smooth. The important themes are in place: the beauty of nature and the responsibility that beauty implies, family (including dogs), and the various ways that wildness manifests itself in our hearts and lives. This volume sets a pattern for Bass's non-fiction works in its attention to story-telling, the connections between family and land, and the traditions that bind us together yet inevitably alter from generation to generation.

Wild to the Heart (1987) continues the description of a young man coming to terms with himself and his relationship to nature, providing lovingly-crafted descriptions of eccentric characters and places and the connections between food, place, and family. Bass explores wild places in Mississippi, Alabama, Georgia, North Carolina, Utah, and Wyoming, and in his own heart.

Oil Notes (1989) describes Bass's days as a petroleum geologist with the lyric attention to detail the writer had, by then, perfected. In describing how one finds oil, he interweaves two equally important narratives about subterranean processes, one of falling in love and one of becoming a writer.

Winter: Notes from Montana (1991) documents, in journal form, his move from Mississippi to Montana, from petroleum geologist to writer and environmentalist. Bass celebrates the Yaak valley, his new home, by telling its stories; he details its people, its weather, and its history. The major theme is surviving a first winter without most of the amenities he has grown up with, including electricity and a telephone. In this community of people who prefer to live far from cities, Bass finds the place he has been writing about in fiction and non-fiction, a place of wildness. But like *Oil Notes, Winter* is also about falling in love, committing to a life, a person, and a place.

The Ninemile Wolves (1992) is the most journalistic of Bass's work. A carefully crafted narrative blend of facts, interviews, and biology, this book-length essay explores the reintroduction of wolves into the American West and the precariously balanced relationship between humans and the environment. While government agencies and citizens' rights groups debate the fate of the wolf, nature moves ahead of human planning; families of wolves appear in various "unsanctioned" places in Montana, most notably in the Ninemile valley outside of Missoula. Bass tracks their progress and the human struggle to find a place in our lives for predators.

The Lost Grizzlies (1995) relates more than its ostensible theme, the quest to prove that grizzlies still live south of Yellowstone. As in *The Ninemile Wolves*, Bass combines facts with other important details: descriptions of the people involved, the largeness and wildness of their hearts, the passions that both the beauty and the misuse of nature inspire. As the search for bears unfolds, Bass uncovers truths about writing, about being a father, and, above all, the importance of wild spaces to the human soul.

The Book of Yaak (1997) contains the most direct of Bass's calls to action. He blends statistics and lyrical language in a description of a beleaguered wilderness, the Yaak valley, a place where the Pacific Northwest forests meet the Northern Rockies ecosystem, creating a uniquely diverse wilderness unlike any other in the lower 48 states. It also provides a crucial connector between the wilds of Canada, Waterton-Glacier International Park and the Yellowstone-Grand Teton National Parks. This deepest wildness is Bass's home, and it is unprotected against logging and other devastating exploitation. Whereas *Winter* celebrates the Yaak valley, *The Book of Yaak* is a roar of anger that such a place could be in danger of vanishing. The essays describe Bass's attempts to save his valley and serve as a continuous meditation about the relationship between art and activism.

Bass's fiction, like his non-fiction, celebrates wildness, both in people and places. Being wild at heart requires living with inten-

sity, and Bass's characters live fully immersed in their lives even if they think that they have failed at living in some way. They feel the pressure of time, the pressure of loyalty, and the pressure of living in a world that does not always seem to notice them. His characters crave connection, but not the shallow social connections with which most make do. They long for one person, one fish, one place, one action in which they can invest all of their intensity. Great fiction is not about clear answers, Welty once wrote. There are no clear answers in Bass's fiction, but he captures the joy, the wonder, and the despair that accompany the big questions. His characters continue to seek answers, despite their shortcomings.

The Watch (1988) contains short stories about wildness at heart, about dreams that don't quite work out, love that doesn't quite last. Bass's fiction, like Welty's, reaches comfortably into the tall tale zone, with characters and events that seem a little larger than life. Most of these stories revolve around variations of escape: from love, family ties, society, even from one's self.

Platte River (1994), comprising three novellas, takes on the idea of escape, but also explores ways of finding a place in the world where one belongs. Through interaction with each other and the environment, characters learn how they fit together, physically and spiritually, with each other and the natural world. The title story tells of a disintegrating love affair and a man's mid-life questions about the nature of love, friendship, and life. In "Mahatma Joe," the central character is a failed evangelist who transforms his vision of paradise into an earthly garden; Bass interweaves the stories of the two women who come to share Joe's vision. "Field Events" describes two brothers obsessed with discus-throwing, the stranger who changes the very structure of their family, and the freedom that strength, both emotional and physical, can provide.

In the Loyal Mountains (1995) is a collection of short stories about human relationships—about passion and ordinary lives and the way lives can go astray, sometimes so badly that they cannot be repaired. Bass writes about characters who deal with the disappointments and small triumphs of adulthood while never losing the ability to experience wonder at the path they have taken.

The Sky, The Stars, The Wilderness (1997) tackles the big questions: why are we here, what does it mean to be happy, to love, to die? These three novellas explore how the system—the world, individuals, the spirit—are interrelated, how we are sometimes prey, sometimes predator, sometimes loved, sometimes lost. In the title story, a woman tells of her life as she sees it inscribed on the landscape of her family's Texas ranch. The "Myth of Bears" describes a man who literally tracks his lover through the Canadian wilderness in winter, as they trade roles of prey and predator. "Where the Sea Used to Be" unfolds both above and below the land's surface, as a young petroleum geologist maps oil wells and his future on the Mississippi landscape and races to find oil before his rivals at a large oil company. Bass seems to conclude that "the heart of it all is mystery," which is the closest thing to an answer he is willing to provide.

—Leigh Tillman Partington

BAUSCH, Richard

Born: Fort Benning, Georgia, 18 April 1945. **Education**: George Mason University, B.A. 1974; University of Iowa, M.F.A. 1975. **Family**: Married Karen Miller (a photographer); five children. **Military Service**: U.S. Air Force, 1965-69. **Career**: Worked as a singer-songwriter with the rock band, Luv'd Ones; Professor of English, George Mason University, since 1980. **Awards**: PEN/Faulkner Award nominations, 1982, for *Take Me Back*, and 1988, for *Spirits*; Guggenheim fellowship, 1984. **Address**: Department of English, George Mason University, 4400 University Dr., Fairfax, Virginia 22030.

PUBLICATIONS

Novels

The Real Presence. New York, Dial, 1980.
Take Me Back. New York, Dial, 1981.
The Last Good Time. New York, Dial, 1984.
Mr. Field's Daughter. New York, Linden Press/Simon & Schuster, 1989.
Violence. New York, Houghton Mifflin/Seymour Lawrence, 1992.
Rebel Powers. New York, Houghton Mifflin/Seymour Lawrence, 1993.
Good Evening Mr. & Mrs. America, and All the Ships at Sea: A Novel. New York, HarperCollins, 1996.
In the Night Season. New York, HarperCollins, 1998.

Short Story Collections

Spirits and Other Stories. New York, Linden Press/Simon & Schuster, 1987.
The Fireman's Wife and Other Stories. New York, Linden Press, 1990.
Rare & Endangered Species: A Novella & Stories. New York, Houghton Mifflin Co, 1994.

* * *

Born to a family of storytellers, which includes his identical twin brother and fellow novelist, Robert Bausch, Richard Bausch writes compelling narratives related to family, loves, and fears—things that can be lost and longed for. The actions of characters attempting to deal with their shortcomings and to overcome inner turmoil are surprising, even drastic, occurring as sudden twists in narratives of growing desperation. Interior thoughts and feelings, hopes and expectations, conflicts, unhappiness, desires, and other struggles surface into dramatic action by means of a catalyst—another character, a situation, even a subtle and mundane change in a character's life, unraveling uneasy bonds of spirituality, family, or friendship.

In his first novel, *Real Presence*, Bausch draws on his Roman Catholic background to explore themes of spirituality through his protagonist, a rancorous older priest. Monsignor Vincent Shepherd has recently suffered a heart attack and has distanced himself from the world. Newly assigned to a parish in West Virginia, Shepherd faces additional problems than his inner sufferings because of the parish's love for the charismatic priest he is replacing. Shepherd emerges from his own musings when an impover-

ished family, the Bexleys, come to town. The father, Duck, is a terminally ill vet and ex-con, and the mother, Elizabeth, is pregnant with the couple's sixth child. Elizabeth stirs something in Shepherd, and after her husband dies and she delivers her child, Shepherd proclaims that he must leave the priesthood and become the family's father. As is typical of Bausch's work, this novel has a well-developed story with subtle plot twists enhanced by narrative elements that enrich his tales: the symbolic importance of the priest's name, for example, suggests thematic questions concerning the role of priests and differences between spiritual guidance and direct action.

Alternating points of view in the narrative of Bausch's second novel, *Take Me Back*, relate the effects of deep turmoil within a family consisting of Gordon Brinhart, a failed insurance salesman who is also an alcoholic, his wife, Katherine, an ex-musician, and her son, Alex, born out of wedlock with another man. A neighboring family is also significant, especially the 13-year-old daughter, Amy, who is dying of leukemia, a physical ailment over which she has no control that contrasts with behavioral degradations of other characters. Brinhart drinks himself to near oblivion, gets fired from his job, and has sex with a teenaged neighbor girl, and Katherine responds to her husband's actions by attempting to kill herself. These tragedies are wrought within the relative peace and mendacity of a contemporary urban landscape.

Character studies are central to the novels *The Last Good Time* and *Mr. Field's Daughter*. In the former, Bausch delves into friendship and personal needs in presenting the relationship between Edward Cakes, 75, and Arthur Hagood, 89. Their friendship and mutual support is strained when a young woman, Mary Virginia Bellini, 24, comes into their lives and has sex with Edward as a means of emotional and financial support. Arthur, confined to a hospital bed, learns of the affair through Edward's visits. Mary Virginia eventually leaves, and Edward becomes involved with an elderly woman who lives above him. Similarly, the drama in *Mr. Field's Daughter* occurs through Bausch's development of characters—their thoughts, activities, and motivations that might not be apparent to other characters, or even themselves. This work concerns an extended family: James Field, a widower in his 60s, works as a loan officer and is head of a household that includes his widowed sister, Ellen, his daughter, Annie, and Annie's daughter, Linda. Their odd but rather peaceful domestic situation is thrown into confusion by Linda's father, Cole Gilbertson, who brings violence, drugs, and familial conflict to the scene.

Familial relationships are focused in Bausch's later novels, from different angles. As in his previous work, events set in recognizable contemporary American settings among people living unremarkable lives profoundly illuminate a central theme, which can be suggested in a title, like *Violence,* which explores violence in public and private forms. The novel delineates a chain of related emotional crises of Charlie Connally, living a life of quiet desperation suddenly overturned when he happens upon a robbery in progress in a convenience store and saves a woman's life. Though he is treated as a hero in the press, the event and its aftermath end up greatly disturbing Connally's life: he becomes depressed, drops his pursuits for self-improvement, and strains his marriage.

Rebel Powers (1993) and *Good Evening Mr. & Mrs. America, And All Ships At Sea: A Novel* (1996) occur during the 1960s and

1970s and concern young men coming of age in turbulent times. *Rebel Powers'* main character, Thomas Boudreaux, writes a memoir of his youth from the perspective of middle age. In that year, his father was dishonorably discharged from the Air Force for stealing and put in civilian prison. During his years of incarceration, his family moves from Virginia back to Wyoming while caught up in larger historical and social circumstances. *Good Evening Mr. & Mrs. America* is a bittersweet comedy about idealistic, 19-year-old Walter Marshall trying to find his way during the years of the Kennedy administration, when many youths shared a sense of optimism about the country and their future. Marshall's misadventures, among them becoming simultaneously engaged to two women and basing his career choices on the occupations of his idols—are amusingly hapless and made poignant against forthcoming events that make his idealism seem endearing.

Bausch is accomplished as well as a short story writer, where his penchant for presenting sudden incidents that cause ruptures in the guarded feelings of his characters become more intensely focused. In his first collection, *Spirits and Other Stories* (1987), Bausch explores the inner being of characters, the pressures of following one's own inclinations and living with others, of being assertive and forgiving. "Spirits," the final and longest of the stories, unites themes relating to spirit that had been probed in the other stories, which concern spirits of evil, murder, and erotic fantasy, among others. The unnamed narrator of "Spirits," for example, has fantasies that violate a woman's privacy and reveal the darkness in his soul. Reflecting back after his discovery that another character is a rapist and murderer, he recalls similarities between himself and the now-imprisoned man and ways in which he had simulated the other man's identity. The narrator is also a violator, living his own version of passionless violence—his story, written years later, is his confession.

In his second collection, *The Fireman's Wife and Other Stories* (1990), Bausch continues to traverse tension between the darker side of life and the desire for illumination and redemption. For example, in "Equity," three sisters weigh the emotional and moral cost of caring for their helpless mother, who suffers from Alzheimer's disease. Relationships are central, as they are in all of Bausch's works, with possible forms of redemption occurring through understanding, as he deals realistically with the troubles of ordinary Americans.

—Emma Cobb

BELL, Madison Smartt

Born: Williamson County, Tennessee, 1 August 1957. **Education:** Princeton University, New Jersey, A.B. (summa cum laude) in English 1979; Hollins College, Virginia, M.A. 1981. **Family:** Married Elizabeth Spires in 1985; one daughter. **Career:** Writer-in-residence, Goucher College, Towson, Maryland, 1984-86, since 1988; lecturer, YMHA Poetry Center, New York, 1984-86; visiting lecturer, University of Iowa Writers Workshop, Iowa City, 1987-88; lecturer, 1989-91, visiting associate professor, 1989-93, Johns Hopkins University Writing Seminars, Baltimore, Maryland, 1989-91. **Awards:** Lillian Smith award, 1989; Guggenheim fellowship, 1991; Maryland State Arts Council award, 1991;

Howard Foundation fellowship, 1991; Robert Penn Warren Award for the Fellowship of Southern Writers, 1995. **Agent:** Vivienne Schuster, John Farquharson Ltd., 162-168 Regent Street, London W1R 5TB, England; Jane Gelfman, John Farquharson Ltd., 250 West 57th Street, New York, New York 10107. **Address:** Department of English, Goucher College, Towson, Maryland 21204.

PUBLICATIONS

Novels

The Washington Square Ensemble. New York, Viking Press, 1983.
Waiting for the End of the World. New York, Ticknor and Fields, 1985.
Straight Cut. New York, Ticknor and Fields, 1986.
The Year of Silence. New York, Ticknor and Fields, 1987.
Soldier's Joy. New York, Ticknor and Fields, 1989.
Doctor Sleep. San Diego, Harcourt Brace, 1991.
Save Me, Joe Louis. San Diego, Harcourt Brace, 1993.
All Souls' Rising. New York, Pantheon, 1995.
Ten Indians. N.p., 1996.

Short Stories

Zero DB and Other Stories. New York, Ticknor and Fields, 1987.
Barking Man and Other Stories. New York, Ticknor and Fields, 1990.

Other

The History of the Owen Graduate School of Management. Nashville, Tennessee, Vanderbilt University, 1988.

*   *   *

Madison Smartt Bell's special province is the sensuousness of desperation, the aesthetic hideaways in which the disenchanted, disenfranchised, and dysfunctional seek refuge from storms raging in their own minds. That has been clear from his first novel, *The Washington Square Ensemble,* whose tangle of first-person narratives follows a gang of urban heroin dealers through a jungle of violence and sin.

The violence and frantic edge-running of Bell's novels invite comparison with the early novels of Robert Stone. Both writers probe the grimy underbelly of life and characters balanced precariously between suicide and murder. But as dark as Bell's tales may be, rays of affirmation seep in, unlike Stone's. For Stone's characters, the darkening world offers little chance to wrench from it a life. But for Bell's, the moral condition of the world is either static or cyclic rather than entropic. There are dusks, but there are also dawns. In that way, Bell's world may be truer than Stone's, and less soul-deadening.

Bell's characters are in quest of redemption and rebirth. They'll blow bullet holes in traditional moral tablets, as do Stone's, but they seem more eager to pick up a pen and write new ones than to cling to the pistol.

This quest appears in Bell's 1985 novel, *Waiting for the End of the World,* the story of a plot to detonate a nuclear device under

New York. Larkin, an associate member of a cell led by the profoundly maladjusted psychiatrist Simon Rohnstock, has the unenviable position of human trigger for the weapon—a kind of guerrilla Valhalla entirely appropriate to Bell's message, for the author seems to suggest that only gestures of immense proportion can have any lasting impact in an age of mass lassitude.

Ultimately, collective will disintegrates as Rohnstock decides that this venture might be just the vehicle to propel him to parapolitical supremacy, and Larkin begins to doubt his own purpose. By this stage however, the focus has shifted towards the novel's other themes: Larkin has "adopted" Tommy, the child victim of vicious ritualistic abuse, and is being pursued by the boy's demented father—a dark avenging angel. Descending into the detritus of New York society, Bell unifies several quasi-religious subtexts, blending a spate of spontaneous combustions, elements of Russian Orthodoxy, and a liberal dose of Satanism. The subsequent action takes on mystic overtones—Tommy's real name is revealed to be Gabriel, and he, previously mute, manifests visionary powers and a voice suitable to their expression. Larkin's own spectacular fate is just one of many impressive flashes of invention that litter a script which is both a convincing study of personal motivation and an accomplished semi-allegorical interpretation of late 20th-century malaise.

Straight Cut reveals a clear movement towards order. Bell follows the rivalry between Tracy Bateman and Kevin Carter, former friends and colleagues in an independent film-making company that has been their cover for drug smuggling. Kevin and Tracy represent two sides of the same nature, one scheming and manipulative, the other intuitive and unambiguous; platonically in love with each other and both in love with Tracy's estranged wife Lauren. The real interest of the book lies not in the high-tension plot twists, but in the duel between intellect and instinct, a tussle kept alive brilliantly by Bell's rapid scene shifting and neat line in tough-guy backchat.

The Year of Silence fuses multiple narrative perspectives, offering a series of individual reactions to Marian's death from an overdose. Friends, lovers, and nodding acquaintances are all struggling desperately to come to terms with a world bereft of her presence. In truth, only Gwen, Marian's cousin, has by the end of the book reached a compromise, and we leave her in the sanctuary of a white clapboard holiday home, preparing to restart her life. The loss of a "flair for transforming the tacky into something transcendent" is to be mourned, but whether it quite merits the indulgence of a whole book is questionable. Depending on your preference, Bell either offers a stunning essay on the idolization of vacuousness or fails to evoke sufficient sympathy for Marian for us to feel much moved by the bleatings of the bereaved.

If *The Year of Silence* lacks completeness, almost all of the pieces in *Zero db* are the finished article: polished, absorbing, and of a consistently high standard. This is Bell in virtuoso form, producing an utterly compelling range of voice and concern, and throwing off the shades of Faulkner and Poe which have coloured his previous technical and imaginative achievements. "Today Is a Good Day to Die" is a memorable highlight, and, happily, in "Triptych I" and "Triptych II" we are at last afforded a real insight, from an insider, into life on a Tennessee hog farm.

In *Soldier's Joy*, Thomas Laidlaw returns from Vietnam to his family's now-deserted farm outside Nashville. A loner, Laidlaw wants little more than peace, freedom to roam the landscape, and time to hone his considerable talents as a bluegrass banjo player. He's been half a world away dispensing and avoiding death.

Tennessee seems the ideal place to heal from a disorienting war. Bell's minutely observed description make Laidlaw's deliberate actions feel like Nick Adams returning to the Big Two-Hearted River, his farm an arcadian balm to his senses. Then comes Laidlaw's reunion with his black childhood friend and Vietnam comrade Rodney Redmon, and Laidlaw learns he has simply left one war zone for another. *Soldier's Joy* is a tale of life lived close to the bone. Once again Bell tenses his muscular grip on the feel and meaning of violence, wrenching a piece of literary art from a plot whose outline could sound like that of a television movie.

In *Doctor Sleep*, Bell weaves an arresting if uneven tapestry. Its several threads unfurl from three closely observed days and nights in the life of Adrian Strother. Four years earlier, Adrian had sworn off both heroin and New York City and moved to London. Now he works as a hypnotist, "a sort of psychological repairman," whose most interesting client, Eleanor Peavy, suffers multiple personalities: prim Miss Peavey by day, prostitute Nell by night.

She is the least of Adrian's problems. Wracked by insomnia, he walks London's streets where a serial killer brutally murders little girls. Mistaken for his friend Stuart (a born-again former addict now forming a heroin self-help center), Adrian is stalked by thugs and abducted by London's chief heroin distributor. When drug traffickers are not hunting him, he's hunting them under pressure from Scotland Yard. On free nights, he moonlights as a stage hypnotist at a burlesque club or works out at a tae kwon do studio and spars with his West Indian friend Terence after class in the dark.

Back in Adrian's flat, his pet boa constrictor is losing color and won't eat, and Adrian's neglected girlfriend Clara has left him for the fourth time. Nicole—the dazzling former call-girl Stuart battered and Adrian secretly married—is in London, maybe to pick up with Adrian again or maybe to ask him for a divorce. All the while, Adrian reflects obsessively on the Hermetic mysticism of Renaissance philosopher Giorano Bruno. Little wonder Adrian cannot sleep.

As far removed from the Tennessee hills, glacial pacing, and third-person restraint of *Soldier's Joy* as *Doctor Sleep* is, the two books feel strongly linked. Like returning soldier Thomas Laidlaw, Adrian seldom eats and never sleeps, has thematically important attachments to both his male friends and his animals, and is painfully reticent about his feelings. Most importantly, like Laidlaw just back from Vietnam, Adrian is a solitary figure in need of healing.

There is nothing new about that. Since his first novel, *The Washington Square Ensemble,* with its cluster of heroin dealers, Bell has always written with conspicuous sympathy for the alienated and the bruised. He searches for characters beaten down by a combination of life and poor choices, whose hearts (to paraphrase a line of Spires's) are a bit off-center, yet who desire affirmation. At some point, a moment flickers where new choice is possible, and they choose to move toward grace, often amid religious symbolism.

As the elements of *Doctor Sleep* bond artfully together—as Eleanor Peavey's pathology links to the vicious child murders which tie to the London drug lord who bears on Adrian's work with Scotland Yard and Adrian's need to face the truth which joins him in spirit to Eleanor Peavey—perhaps the most important element turns out to be Adrian's fasting snake. Adrian feels a Jungian connection to it and keeps it "in honor and acknowledgment of the snake in" himself. The boa constrictor will not eat for the same reason Adrian cannot sleep: he is undergoing a dramatic metamorphosis.

Bell may not always hid the symbolic seams where plot and philosophy join, he can oversensationalize an ending, and his fascination for characters from society's dingiest creases does put off some readers. But in *Doctor Sleep* he once again artfully blends perceptiveness, a deadpan mastery of the grotesque, and a startling profundity of mind.

Though Bell meanders between the beatific Appalachian rurality of his childhood, the decaying gothic grandeur of the New York that nursed from him his first novel, and foggy London, he is, in fact, a regional writer. His region is the misty border buffering purgatory from hell in the sootiest creases of contemporary society. In *Save Me, Joe Louis,* 23-year-old Macrae walks that border. He is AWOL from the army and living in New York's Hell's Kitchen. He hasn't enjoyed much of anything since his teen years in Tennessee when he was in love, without knowing it, with a spirited photographer named Lacy.

Petulant and lost, Macrae often takes "a wring fork in the crisscross trails of conversation" and blindly strews mines along his own path. He forms unfortunate attachments, one to a prostitute whose pimp decides to blow half her head off. Macrae's most dangerous alliance is with his increasingly unstable partner-in-crime Charlie, whose rationale—"Ain't nobody cares that much what you do"—faintly recalls Flannery O'Connor's Misfit. After they've made New York too hot for their comfort by forcing people to withdraw and turn over money from their ATMs, they head south to Baltimore where they add a third partner, a benign young black man named Porter, fresh off a jail term for a bar fight that turned inadvertently gory. The three hold up an armored bank truck, but police arrive, bullets fly, and the trio heads full speed for Macrae's father's farm outside of Nashville.

Were trigger-happy Charlie not with him, Macrae might at last feel he's returned from far east of Eden. There's the potential for a wholesome life in Tennessee. Adjacent to Macrae's land is the farm of Thomas Laidlaw, the hero of *Soldier's Joy.* Not only is Laidlaw there, still playing banjo with his bluegrass band and still with Adrienne Wells, but the beautiful Lacy has returned home from art school in Philadelphia. That she still loves Macrae is clear to everyone but him, who keeps stumbling aimlessly in restless confusion. After a robbery attempt which they botch even worse than the Baltimore fiasco, Macrae, Charlie, and Porter flee to the South Carolina coast. There it grows obvious that Macrae may have outlived his usefulness to Charlie, and that the book's final page won't be big enough to hold both of them.

In *Save Me, Joe Louis,* Bell once again invites us to care about characters who offer scarcely an inch of ground to build affection on. Yet once again, by combining subtle technique and native com-

passion, he succeeds, walking sympathetically among contemporary thieves and moral lepers with a charity that either converts or shames his readers.

—Ian McMechan, updated by Andy Solomon

BENFORD, Gregory

Pseudonym: Sterling Blake. **Born:** Gregory Albert Benford in Mobile, Alabama, 30 January 1941. **Education:** University of Oklahoma, Norman, B.S. in physics 1963; University of California, San Diego, M.S. 1965, Ph.D. 1967. **Family:** Married Joan Abbe in 1967; one daughter and one son. **Career:** Fellow, 1967-69, and research physicist, 1969-71, Lawrence Radiation Laboratory, Livermore, California; assistant professor, 1971-73, associate professor, 1973-79, and since 1979 professor of physics, University of California, Irvine; visiting professor, Cambridge University, 1976, Torino University, 1979, Florence Observatory, 1982, M.I.T., 1993. **Awards:** Nebula award, 1974, 1981; John W. Campbell Memorial award, 1981; United Nations medal in literature, 1990; Lord Foundation award (for achievement in science), 1995. **Agent:** Ralph Vicinanza, 111 8th Ave., New York, New York 10011. **Address:** Department of Physics, University of California, Irvine, California 92717. **Online Address:** gbenford@uci.edu.

PUBLICATIONS

Novels

Deeper Than the Darkness. New York, Ace, 1970; revised edition, as *The Stars in Shroud,* New York, Berkley, 1978.
Jupiter Project. Nashville, Nelson, 1975; revised as *The Jupiter Project,* New York, Berkley, 1980.
If the Stars Are Gods, with Gordon Eklund. New York, Berkley, 1977; revised, New York, Bantam, 1989.
In the Ocean of Night. New York, Dial Press, 1977.
Find the Changeling, with Gordon Eklund. New York, Dell, 1980.
Timescape. New York, Simon and Schuster, 1980.
Shiva Descending, with William Rotsler. New York, Avon, 1980.
Against Infinity. New York, Simon and Schuster, 1983.
Across the Sea of Suns. New York, Simon and Schuster, 1984; revised, Bantam, 1987.
Artifact. New York, Tor, 1985.
Heart of the Comet, with David Brin. New York, Bantam, 1986.
Great Sky River. New York, Bantam, 1987.
Tides of Light. New York, Bantam, 1989.
Beyond the Fall of Night, with *Against the Fall of Night,* by Arthur C. Clarke. New York, Ace, 1990.
Chiller (as Sterling Blake). New York, Bantam, 1993.
Furious Gulf. New York, Bantam, 1994.
Sailing Bright Eternity. New York, Bantam, 1995.
Foundation's Fear. New York, New York, HarperPrism, 1997.
COSM. New York, Avon Eos, 1998.

Short Story Collections

Time's Rub. New Castle, Virginia, Cheap Street, 1984.
Of Space/Time and the River. New Castle, Virginia, Cheap Street, 1985.

In Alien Flesh. New York, Tor, 1986.
We Could Do Worse. Laguna Beach, California, Abbenford, 1988.
Iceborn, with Paul A. Carter, published with *The Saturn Game* by Poul Anderson. New York, Tor, 1989.
Centigrade 233. New Castle, Virginia, Cheap Street, 1990.
Matter's End. New York, Bantam, 1995; expanded edition, Bantam, 1995.

Other

Editor, with Martin H. Greenberg, *Hitler Victorious: Eleven Stories of the German Victory in World War II.* New York, Garland, 1986.
Editor, with Martin H. Greenberg, *Nuclear War.* New York, Ace, 1988.
Editor, with Martin H. Greenberg, *What Might Have Been? I: Alternate Empires [II: Alternate Heros] [III: Alternate Wars] [IV: Alternate Americas].* New York, Bantam, 4 vols., 1989-92.
Editor, *Far Futures.* New York, Tor, 1995.

*

Manuscript Collection: Eaton College, University of California, Riverside.

Gregory Benford comments:

I am a resolutely amateur writer, preferring to follow my own interests rather than try to produce fiction for a living. And anyway, I'm a scientist by first choice and shall remain so. I began writing from the simple desire to tell a story (a motivation SF writers seem to forget as they age, and thus turn into earnest moralizers). It's taken me a long time to learn how. I've been labeled a "hard SF" writer from the first, but in fact I think the job of SF is to do it *all*—the scientific landscape, peopled with real persons, with "style" and meaning ingrained. I've slowly worked toward that goal, with many dead ends along the way. From this comes my habit of rewriting my older books and expanding early short stories into longer works (sometimes novels). Ideas come to me in a lapidary way, layering over the years. Yet, it's not the stirring moral message that moves me.

I think writers are interesting when they juxtapose images or events, letting life come out of the stuff of the narrative. They get boring when they preach. To some extent, my novels reflect my learning various subcategories of SF—*Deeper Than the Darkness* was the galactic empire motif; *Jupiter Project* the juvenile; *If the Stars Are Gods* and *In the Ocean of Night* both the cosmic space novel, etc. *Timescape* is rather different, and reflects my using my own experiences as a scientist. Yet short stories, where I labored so long, seem to me just as interesting as novels. I learned to write there.

Nowadays, my novels begin as relatively brisk plot lines and then gather philosophical moss as they roll. If all this sounds vague and intuitive, it is: that's the way I work. So I cannot say precisely why I undertake certain themes. I like Graham Greene's division of novels into "serious" and "entertainment," though I suspect the author himself cannot say with certainty which of his own is which.

It seems to me my major concerns are the vast landscape of science, and the philosophical implications of that landscape on mortal, sensual human beings. What genuinely interests me is the strange, the undiscovered, but in the end it is how *people* see this that matters most.

*   *   *

Drawing in various measures on his Southern boyhood, his background as a youthful science fiction fan, his interest in literary tradition, and his training as a professional physicist, Gregory Benford has pioneered a mode of science fiction that can best be described as literary hard SF. Historically, hard SF has privileged technology and philosophy over character and style, awesome effects over detailed observations, but Benford's best work achieves a remarkable and richly textured balance among all these qualities. His literary antecedents range from the visionary fiction of Olaf Stapledon and Arthur C. Clarke (with whom he has "collaborated" by writing a sequel to the latter's *Against the Fall of Night*) to his fellow Southerner William Faulkner (some of whose works he has reimagined in science fiction terms) to the introspective fiction of John Updike and the realistic novels of scientists at work of C.P. Snow (whose notion of the "two cultures" of science and the humanities has often been addressed by Benford). At the same time, he has defined a territory of hard science fiction uniquely his own, while occasionally branching out into literary experiments and even international thrillers.

Benford began publishing short stories in 1965, and his first novel, *Deeper Than the Darkness,* appeared in 1970. Revised as *The Stars in Shroud* in 1978, it introduced what would become a familiar theme in Benford's work: contact with mysterious aliens, and the unexpected effect this contact has on humans—in this case, a plague of agoraphobia which turns out to be the aliens' chief weapon. *Jupiter Project* (1975) was a competent Heinlein-style juvenile which introduced a character who would later play a major role in *Against Infinity* (1983).

Benford's first major novel, *In the Ocean of Night* (1978), introduced a complex and ambivalent hero in British astronaut Nigel Walmsley and combined its first-contact theme with a sophisticated portrayal of messianic movements on Earth and even the legend of Bigfoot. (Part of this novel appeared as early as 1969, and by the time the series concludes with *Sailing Bright Eternity* in 1995, it begins to take on the aspect of a life's work.)

Walmsley appeared again in *Across the Sea of Suns* (1984), some 57 years older but not greatly aged due to rejuvenation treatments and time spent in cold sleep aboard an interstellar craft trying to track the sources of mysterious radio signals. Alienation is a central theme in the novel; Walmsley is already alienated from the rest of humanity through his earlier transforming experience in *In the Ocean of Night,* and now faces an internal battle with his own cancer as well as edgy relationships with the two women in his life. Meanwhile, another narrative set on Earth involves a castaway whose ship has apparently been sunk by aliens, who have appeared in the oceans. It gradually becomes apparent that the very survival of organic life in the universe is threatened by an ancient machine civilization located somewhere near the center of the galaxy—a notion more fully explored in the later connected series of novels which begins with *Great Sky River* (a 1987 reprint of *Across the Sea of Suns* adds a new final chapter to make the connections between series more clear).

Before returning to this theme, however, Benford turned to the near future and the near past in what many still regard as his finest single work, *Timescape* (1980). Set alternately in a 1963 California and a 1988 Cambridge, it details the efforts of future scientists to use tachyons to warn the past of an impending ecological catastrophe. As a portrayal of the politics, anxieties, and methods of working scientists, the novel is unsurpassed in science fiction; as a sophisticated treatment of a kind of scientifically rationalized "time travel" (or at least cross-time communication) and an exploration of the alternate-world theme, it achieves a haunting poignancy almost equally rare. *Against Infinity* (1983) returns to a more colorful hard SF setting—the Jovian moon Ganymede—but continues Benford's exploration into literary fiction by transposing William Faulkner's 1942 novella "The Bear" into a tale of a young man's search for a mysterious alien machine called the Aleph. (Benford similarly "adapted" Faulkner's *As I Lay Dying* in his 1985 post-catastrophe novella "To the Storming Gulf.")

Artifact (1985), on the other hand, frankly reaches for the headlong suspense of the international espionage thriller, as scientists and Greek government officials vie for possession of a strange archaeological artifact which seems to contain a miniature black hole. (Benford again returned to the thriller mode with his 1993 novel *Chiller,* published under the name of "Sterling Blake" concerning a serial killer targeting scientists working on the cryonic suspension of life.) Benford has also collaborated with other novelists on occasion. *Shiva Descending* (1980), with William Rotsler, is a fairly familiar tale of a huge meteor threatening the Earth; *Heart of the Comet* (1986), with David Brin, is a more successful Vernian novel concerning a group of scientists exploring Halley's Comet.

Benford's most ambitious sustained work to date is the four-novel sequence beginning with *Great Sky River* (1987), which returns to the machine-organic struggle introduced in the Nigel Walmsley novels, but raises it to genuinely epic and cosmological proportions. On Snowglade, a desolate planet near the core of the galaxy, a small band of human survivors led by Killeen of the Family Bishop struggle to escape extermination by the immensely powerful machine intelligences who seek to dominate the universe, and who have destroyed their last remaining Citadel. Each human survivor carries "Aspects" which contain the minds of dead ancestors, and many are themselves enhanced with technological devices. Hounding them is the bizarre "mech" being known as the Mantis, from whose point of view we learn about the mech view of the Universe and its controlling intelligences.

In *Tides of Light* (1989), the Family Bishop escape Snowglade to a planet orbiting Abraham's Star, only to find that yet another form of life—cyborgs—share the struggle for supremacy, and are acting out their own mythical destiny as well. This involves, among other things, using a cosmic string to disassemble the planet and begin the process of capturing all the energy of the star—and eventually of the whole galaxy—for their use. They hope to join an even more mysterious alien race, the Starswarmers, and become part of the "Summation" that represents a kind of Teilhardian Omega point for intelligence in the universe. *Furious Gulf* (1994) shifts the action to Killeen's son Toby. Again the family has found a kind of redoubt, and again the mechs pursue relentlessly—this time hoping to capture Killeen and Toby for some nefarious purpose. Toby's chief ally is the cyborg Quath, who befriended his father in the previous novel, and one of his chief opponents turns

out to be the Mantis from *Great Sky River.* By recapitulating themes and figures from earlier novels in the series, *Furious Gulf* also sets the stage for the return of Nigel Walmsley.

Both this series and the earlier Nigel Walmsley series reach their culmination in the 1995 novel *Sailing Bright Eternity.* Here, Benford achieves a true cosmic perspective, in the tradition of Olaf Stapledon, within the rigorous context of hard SF. Taken as a unified work (which required some revision of the earlier novels in later editions) the Galactic Center series raises so many questions about the nature and problems of SF that it has to be regarded as one of the major accomplishments in the recent history of the field. It suggests the grand theme of SF, as revealed by Benford out of Stapledon (with Clarke as intermediary), is nothing less than the relationship of mind and nature. This theme not only haunts the work of all three writers, but subsumes nearly every favorite subtheme of the genre, from space travel to alien intelligence to technology—all of which are important to Benford's series as well. In taking up such a vast theme, Benford devises several strategies to get his characters meaningfully involved in such questions as the one Walmsley himself asks at the end of *Sailing Bright Eternity,* "Does human action have any meaning?"

From its opening prose poem on black holes, "photovores," and "metallovores" to the strange space-time continuum or "esty" in which much of the action takes place, the novel demands a great deal more of readers than the series' first novel, *In the Ocean of Night;* in fact, the entire six-volume sequence might almost be read as a course in how to understand hard science fiction. One of the classic problems of such science fiction is combining a rhetoric of action and human drama with a rhetoric of science and philosophy in a way that must be made to appear seamless. Benford (as he puts it) plays with the net up—and not only the net of scientific consistency, but the net of believable character relationships as well. Nigel Walmsley, whose interstellar voyage began in *Across the Sea of Suns,* arrives near the galaxy's core some 30,000 years in the future and meets the survivors of the Family Bishop. Somewhat protected by an artificial "esty" constructed by higher intelligences and consisting of different "lanes" and time lines, they brace for a final confrontation and eventually discover an unlikely key to defeating the mechs.

Throughout the Galactic Center series, Benford's basic strategy is to focus on small groups of individuals acting against spectacular backdrops, while introducing his epic themes through a variety of dramatic devices—conversations with mechs or cyborgs, occasional trips into the far future, flat-out narrative exposition. The result is that his Stapledonian perspective emerges only as a function of the ways in which he has constructed the novels themselves—the novels control our perspective, not the other way round as it was with Stapledon. This has to be counted as a major achievement in realizing the potential of hard SF not only as speculation, but as literature, and it suggests that *Sailing Bright Eternity,* even though it might have some problems as a stand-alone novel (which it clearly isn't intended as), is Benford's most important single work to date, and the series as a whole is his masterpiece.

If anything, Benford's short fiction, partly collected in *In Alien Flesh* (1986) and *Matter's End* (1995), show more versatility and variety than his novels. Some of the most memorable stories, like

Timescape, depict the lives of working scientists; "Exposures" (1981) uses the metaphor of photographic plates to explore the strange ways the universe reveals itself to us, from evidence of alien life discovered by the astronomer narrator to the cancer of his son's teacher, while the physicist narrator of "Mozart on Morphine" (1993) speculates on how remote his research seems from daily life as he undergoes an appendectomy (very similar to Benford's own). Other stories, like "Nooncoming" (1978) or "Snatching the Bot" (1977) are experiments in recasting the closely observed detail of the contemporary literary short story in science fiction terms. Still others engage in direct dialogue with earlier science fiction stories: "Matter's End" (1993) and "Centigrade 233" (1993) address issues raised in particular stories by Arthur C. Clarke and Ray Bradbury. Humor is also a continuing theme in Benford's short fiction. "Doing Lennon" (1975) is a celebration of Beatles-era culture, "Freezeframe" (1993) a realization of every working parent's childcare fantasy, "Time Guide" (1979) a satirical portrait of our own culture from the point of view of a time travel tourist brochure. In general, Benford's short fiction, collected in *In Alien Flesh* (1986) and *Matter's End* (1995) is highly eclectic, ranging from traditional science fiction adventures to his most ambitious literary experiments.

Benford easily earns the mantle of the most important American writer of hard science fiction to emerge since the 1960s, and his considerable ambition—not only in his science fiction works, but in his thrillers and his various efforts to popularize science both on television and in essays (he began writing the monthly science column for *The Magazine of Fantasy and Science Fiction* following the death of Isaac Asimov)—make it hazardous to venture any predictions as to where he might move next. His major works, *Timescape* and the six Galactic Center novels, have already altered the landscape of science fiction in profound ways, bringing a new dimension of literary style to hard science fiction and a new dimension of speculative science to mainstream fictions. Of all current science fiction writers, he may stand the best chance to finally dissolve the arbitrary barrier between the "two cultures" of science and literature.

—Gary K. Wolfe

BENNETT, Lerone, Jr.

Born: Clarksdale, Mississippi, 17 or 19 October 1928. **Education:** Morehouse College, A.B. 1949; Atlanta University, graduate study, 1949. **Family:** Married Gloria Sylvester, 21 July 1956; four children. **Career:** Atlanta *Daily World,* reporter, 1949-1952, city editor, 1952-53; *Jet* magazine, Chicago, associate editor, 1953; *Ebony* magazine, Chicago, associate editor, 1954-57, senior editor, 1958-87, executive editor, since 1987; visiting professor of history, Northwestern University, 1968-69; senior fellow, 1969 and member of board of directors, Institute of the Black World, 1969; member of board of directors, Chicago Public Library; member of board of trustees, Martin Luther King Memorial Center, Chicago Historical Society, Morehouse College, and Columbia College. **Awards:** Book of the Year Award, Capital Press Club, 1963; Patron Saints Award, Society of Midland Authors, 1965, for *What Manner of Man*; Academy Institute Literary Award, American Academy of Arts and Letters, 1978; Humanitarian of the Year,

United Negro College Fund, 1991; D.L. from Morehouse College, 1965; D.Hum. from Wilberforce University, 1977; D.Litt. from Marquette University, 1979, Voorhees College, 1981, and Morgan State University, 1981; L.H.D. from University of Illinois, Lincoln College, and Dillard University, all 1980; honorary doctor of letters, Morris Brown University, 1985, South Carolina University, 1986, and Boston University, 1987. **Address:** *Ebony,* 820 South Michigan Ave., Chicago, Illinois 60605.

PUBLICATIONS

Nonfiction

Before the Mayflower: A History of the Negro in America, 1619-1966. Chicago, Johnson Publishing Co., 1962; fifth edition, 1982.
The Negro Mood, and Other Essays. Chicago, Johnson Publishing Co., 1964.
What Manner of Man: A Biography of Martin Luther King, Jr., 1929-1968. Chicago, Johnson Publishing Co., 1964; fourth revised edition, 1976.
Confrontation: Black and White. Chicago, Johnson Publishing Co., 1965.
Black Power U.S.A.: The Human Side of Reconstruction, 1867-1877. Chicago, Johnson Publishing Co., 1967.
Pioneers in Protest. Chicago, Johnson Publishing Co., 1968.
The Challenge of Blackness. Chicago, Johnson Publishing Co., 1972.
The Shaping of Black America. Chicago, Johnson Publishing Co., 1975.
Wade in the Water: Great Moments in Black History. Chicago, Johnson Publishing Co., 1979.
Succeeding Against the Odds, with John H. Johnson. New York, Warner Books, 1989; as *Succeeding Against the Odds: The Inspiring Autobiography of One of America's Wealthiest Entrepreneurs*, New York, Amistad, 1993.
The Shaping of Black America, with illustrations by Charles White. New York, Penguin Books, 1993.

Other

Contributor, *The Day They Marched.* Chicago, Johnson Publishing Co., 1963.
Contributor, *New Negro Poets: U.S.A.*, Bloomington, Indiana University Press, 1964.
Contributor, *The White Problem in America.* Chicago, Johnson Publishing Co., 1966.

Author of introduction, *In the Shadow of the Great White Way: Images from the Black Theatre.* New York, Thunder's Mouth Press, 1989.

*   *   *

Employing a journalistic approach honed by years of experience as a newspaper reporter and as an editor for *Ebony* magazine, Lerone Bennett, Jr. writes highly objective, non-rhetorical accounts of African-American history. Four of his books, written during the height of the civil rights movement, educated many Americans about the ongoing black struggle.

Bennett's first major work, *Before the Mayflower: A History of the Negro in America, 1619-1966,* traced the odyssey of blacks from the origins of the slave trade through the civil rights movement while celebrating the achievements of great leaders like Frederick Douglass and W. E. B. DuBois and highlighting the black soldiers who fought with valor during this country's major wars while facing the same discrimination in the Army that they faced at home. Bennett presented facts squarely and left it to the reader to form opinions, but he also appealed to reader's emotions, as well as their intellects. For example, Bennett not only used numbers to describe the lynchings that took place in 1918 and 1919, but also used an appalling anecdote of a woman who was lynched even though she was pregnant. *Before the Mayflower* is a significant contribution to American history and, particularly, the important role blacks have played in shaping this country's history.

What Manner of Man: A Biography of Martin Luther King, Jr. shed light upon this famed black leader while the civil rights movement was at its height (and while King was still alive). In a straightforward manner, Bennett presented the facts of King's life and described the influences upon his character—his solid upbringing, his Christian background, and his experiences of racial discrimination. Bennett posed the question, "What manner of man is this?" To indicate the extent of King's influence as a significant shaper and symbolic leader Bennett wrote an eloquent summary: "'Tracked down' and 'chosen' by the times, King transcended the occasion, changing the times and transforming a diffuse uprising into a mass movement with passion and purpose."

By the time Bennett wrote *Confrontation: Black and White,* so many books had already been written about the Negro "problem" that all new efforts appeared redundant. But Bennett's book was different, presenting a thorough account that followed the American black's struggle starting from the 1600s. Bennett wrote that by the mid-1960s, blacks and whites lived in "shattered community," where "Negro and white Americans do not belong to the same social body" or share "that body of consensus or common feeling that usually binds together people sharing a common land."

Without resorting to polemics, but obviously impassioned as the passage show, Bennett called for blacks to come together within a mass, united movement. At the same time, he was not afraid to question certain philosophies and players of the ongoing civil rights movement. For example, Bennett criticized the N.A.A.C.P. and the Urban League for being distant from the masses, and questioned whether blacks should surrender their right to self-defense to Martin Luther King's philosophy non-violence.

In a *New York Times Book Review* piece, Nat Hentoff summarized the benefits of *Confrontation: Black and White*: "The book is a provocative primer for the vast numbers of whites ignorant of black American history and could be of particular value if it were assigned for high school and college classes in American history and social sciences. "*Black Power U.S.A.: The Human Side of Reconstruction, 1867-1877* is Bennett's narrative of the post-Civil War period. Despite the Reconstruction era's vast confusions and contradictions, Bennett saw this first emergence of black power as a dream unfulfilled: in his view, the black man entered a "desperate and bloody struggle for political survival, flanked by two white allies, one Southern-born, the other Northern-born. To gain power, the black man had to help preserve the coalition. But to preserve the coalition he had to make fatal concessions on radical reform."

Like a good journalist, Bennett documented not only the defeats, but the triumphs: for example, Bennett wrote that a larger percentage of students attended integrated schools in New Orleans between 1868 and 1877 than in New York and Chicago in the late-1960s. Moreover, Bennett looked at the performance of all players, black and white, within the context of background and environment. Better understanding of Reconstruction proved important, for by the 1967 publication of *Black Power, U.S.A.*, this country was witnessing the dawn of a new era of reconstruction.

—Eric Patterson

BERRY, Wendell

Born: Wendell Erdman Berry in Henry County, Kentucky, 5 August 1934. **Education:** University of Kentucky, Lexington, A.B. 1956, M.A. 1957; Stanford University, California (Stegner Fellow), 1958-59. **Family:** Married Tanya Amyx in 1957; one daughter and one son. **Career:** Taught at Stanford University, 1959-60, and New York University, 1961-64; from 1964 to 1977 and since 1987, member of the English Department, University of Kentucky; since 1977, consultant, Rodale Press, Emmaus, Pennsylvania. **Awards:** Guggenheim fellowship, 1951; Rockefeller fellowship, 1965; Bess Hokin prize, *Poetry,* 1967; National Endowment for the Arts grant, 1969.

PUBLICATIONS

Novels

Nathan Coulter. Boston, Houghton Mifflin, 1960; revised edition, San Francisco, North Point Press, 1985.
A Place on Earth. New York, Harcourt Brace, 1967; revised edition, San Francisco, North Point Press, 1983.
The Memory of Old Jack. New York, Harcourt Brace, 1974.
Remembering. San Francisco, North Point Press, 1988.
A World Lost. Washington, D.C., Counterpoint, 1996.

Poetry Collections

November Twenty-Six, Nineteen Hundred Sixty-Three. New York, Braziller, 1964.
The Broken Ground. New York, Harcourt Brace, 1964.
Openings. New York, Harcourt Brace, 1968.
Findings. Iowa City, Prairie Press, 1969.
Farming: A Hand Book. New York, Harcourt Brace, 1970.
The Country of Marriage. New York, Harcourt Brace, 1973.
An Eastward Look. Berkeley, Sand Dollar, 1974.
Falling Asleep. Austin, Texas, Cold Mountain Press, 1974.
To What Listens. Crete, Nebraska, Best Cellar Press, 1975.
Horses. Monterrey, Kentucky, Larkspur Press, 1975.
Sayings and Doings. Lexington, Kentucky, Gnomon, 1975.
The Kentucky River. Monterrey, Kentucky, Larkspur Press, 1976.
There Is Singing Around Me. Austin, Cold Mountain Press, 1976.
Three Memorial Poems. Berkeley, Sand Dollar, 1977.
Clearing. New York, Harcourt Brace, 1977.
The Gift of Gravity. Deerfield, Massachusetts, Deerfield Press, 1979.
A Part. San Francisco, North Point Press, 1980.

The Salad. San Francisco, North Point Press, 1980.

The Nativity. Great Barrington, Massachusetts, Penamen Press, 1981.

The Wheel. San Francisco, North Point Press, 1982.

Collected Poems 1957-1982. San Francisco, North Point Press, 1985.

Sabbaths. San Francisco, North Point Press, 1987.

Some Differences. Lewiston, Idaho, Confluence Press, 1987.

Traveling at Home (includes essay). San Francisco, North Point Press, 1989.

A Consent. Monterey, Kentucky, Larkspur Press, 1993.

Entries: Poems. New York, Pantheon Books, 1994.

A Timbered Choir: The Sabbath Poems 1979-1997. Washington, D.C., Counterpoint, 1997.

Nonfiction

The Rise. N.p., Graves Press, 1968.

The Long-Legged House. New York, Harcourt Brace, 1969.

The Hidden Wound. Boston, Houghton Mifflin, 1970.

The Unforeseen Wilderness: An Essay on Kentucky's Red River Gorge, photographs by Eugene Meatyard. Lexington, University Press of Kentucky, 1971.

A Continuous Harmony: Essays Cultural and Agricultural. New York, Harcourt Brace, 1972.

The Unsettling of America: Culture and Agriculture. San Francisco, Sierra Club, 1977.

Recollected Essays 1965-1980. San Francisco, North Point Press, 1981.

The Gift of Good Land: Further Essays Cultural and Agricultural. San Francisco, North Point Press, 1981.

Standing by Words: Essays. San Francisco, North Point Press, 1983.

(Editor, with Wes Jackson and Bruce Coleman) *Meeting the Expectations of the Land: Essays in Sustainable Agriculture and Stewardship.* San Francisco, North Point Press, 1984.

The Landscape of Harmony: Preserving Wildness and Does Community Have a Value? (lectures). Shenmore, Hereford, Five Seasons, 1987.

Home Economics. San Francisco, North Point Press, 1987.

The Work of Local Culture. Iowa City, Iowa Humanities Board, 1988.

The Hidden Wound. San Francisco, North Point Press, 1989.

Harlan Hubbard: Life and Work. Lexington, University Press of Kentucky, 1990.

What Are People For?. San Francisco, North Point Press, 1990.

Standing on Earth: Selected Essays. Ipswich, England, Golgonooza, 1991.

Sex, Economy, Freedom, & Community: Eight Essays. New York, Pantheon Books, 1993.

Another Turn of the Crank. Washington, D.C., Counterpoint, 1995.

Play

The Cool of the Day. Produced in Louisville, Kentucky, 1984.

Short Story Collections

The Wild Birds: Six Stories of the Port William Membership. San Francisco, North Point Press, 1986.

Fidelity: Five Stories. New York, Pantheon Books, 1992.

Watch with Me: And Six Other Stories of the Yet-Remembered Ptolemy Proudfoot (1872-1943) and His Wife, Miss Minnie, née Quinch (1874-1953). New York, Pantheon Books, 1994.

The Discovery of Kentucky. Frankfort, Gnomon Press, 1991.

Two More Stories of the Port William Membership. Frankfort, Kentucky, Gnomon Press, 1997.

*

Critical Studies: *Wendell Berry* (American Authors Series) edited by Paul Merchant, Lewiston, Idaho, Confluence Press, 1991; *Seeking Awareness in American Nature Writing* by Scott Slovic, Salt Lake City, University of Utah Press, 1992; *Wendell Berry* by Andrew J. Angyal, New York, Twayne, 1995.

*   *   *

Wendell Erdman Berry was born on August 5, 1934, in Henry County, Kentucky. He attended the University of Kentucky at Lexington and in 1956 graduated with a B.A. in English. The following year he received from the University of Kentucky a master's degree in English and married Tanya Amyx. They have two children, Mary Dee and Pryor Clifford. In 1958, Berry moved with his family to the West Coast, where for the next two years he studied, wrote, and taught in the creative writing program at Stanford University. *Nathan Coulter*, Berry's first novel, was published in 1960. Berry taught at New York University for two years before returning to his native state in 1964 to teach at the University of Kentucky.

In 1965 Berry returned to his Henry County roots after buying the Lanes Landing property, a hillside farm overlooking the Kentucky River, near Port Royal. Berry continued to teach at the university until he resigned his professorship in 1977. Since moving back to the area of his family's history, Berry has committed himself to farming and writing.

The northern Kentucky hill country serves as the setting for Berry's fictional Port William and provides the inspiration for his poetry and collections of cultural criticism. Berry has lived in this land for all but a few years of his life, and his literary work expresses deep affection for his native soil and the human and non-human inhabitants who dwell there. He advocates that every person find a place, put down roots, and care for that place as if he or she would live there forever.

Wendell Berry speaks out against the mainstream. In the face of the global economy, where financial and political power is concentrated in the hands of multinational corporations, Berry speaks in defense of the small farmer and the independent merchant. He writes under the assumption that one feels more affection for a place when it is one's settled home, and that long-term inhabitation is necessary to know the intricacies of a place.

Berry believes corporate production is damaging the health of the planet, because corporations operate under a system of absenteeism: they extract the raw materials for production from areas in which they do not live, and thus treat the land destructively. Berry is a staunch critic of agribusiness, government, and the universities that support the technological invention that allows more land to be farmed by fewer people.

Berry criticizes American culture for its dependency on fossil fuels and other nonsustainable resources. We decrease our freedom, he says, when our livelihood depends on fuel imported from abroad. A healthier alternative to current agribusiness food production, which is dependent upon imported fossil fuels and the heavy use of chemical fertilizers and pesticides, is to purchase food and other necessities locally. When a community supports itself with food, textiles, and other necessities of living, it reduces its dependency on the destructive absentee economy of big business.

The eight essays in *Sex, Economy, Freedom and Community* (1993) are unified by this theme of "sales resistance." Local economic entities—households, farms, factories, banks, consumers, suppliers—should cooperate to return economic self-determination to the people. Berry advocates "a quiet secession by which people find the practical means and the strength of spirit to remove themselves from an economy that is exploiting them and destroying their homeland."

Berry is the author of eleven volumes of nonfiction. Most of these are collections of essays centered around his critique of American "culture and agriculture." In *Another Turn of the Crank* (1995), Berry turns once more to issues he believes are important to the health of our land and bodies: the fostering of small-scale agricultural communities and sustainable local economies, and the "affectionate" use of the land by farmers and foresters and others making a profit from natural resources. He says neighbors should work together for the well-being of their community and always put the health of the community—including the plant and animal members—ahead of profit.

A strong religious sensibility runs throughout Berry's nonfiction. Berry believes our ecological crisis—the diminishing natural habitats, pollution, and extinctions plaguing the earth—is brought about by the failure of people to live religiously.

Berry draws from his inherited religion, Christianity, to support his arguments, but also owes a debt to Buddhism and Native American creation myths. His primary religious stance is a belief in the mystery of the universe and the importance of all life. In *The Unsettling of America*, a book that received national attention when published in 1977 by the Sierra Club, Berry argues the necessity of a holistic religion that respects "Creation"—every living creature—and understands that humans are only a small part this complex mystery.

In *Home Economics* (1987), Berry refers to the conception of life's interconnectedness as the "Kingdom of God" or "The Great Economy." Berry endorses an ecologically sensitive religious practice that cultivates "a continuous harmony" between human beings and the environments in which we exist. In living religiously, he says, a person should care for the health of the body and the earth, for both are intimately connected.

Berry's poetry establishes the same concerns as his nonfiction: the "marriage" or essential relationships between farming, family, and community. Religious faith also surfaces in his poetry, particularly in *A Part* (1980), *The Wheel* (1982), and most recently in *A Timbered Choir: The Sabbath Poems 1979-1997*, a collection inspired by solitary Sunday walks Berry has taken on his farm and surrounding countryside during the last twenty years. In *Sex,*

Economy, Freedom and Community, Berry calls the Bible a "hypaethral book," "a book open to the sky" that is best read and understood outdoors. Likewise, outdoors is perhaps the best place to read Berry's Sabbath poems, since they were composed under the ceiling of the sky.

Another of Berry's primary poetic subjects is death—how one can approach death as complementary to life, as a means of forming a holistic conception of one's place on earth. Berry's poems are often elegies acknowledging the wound opened in a close-knit community when a member leaves it. When a senior member dies, stories and wisdom about the land and people may be lost to succeeding generations. Mourning is in part a recognition of this lost ancestral wisdom.

Berry's fiction is likewise elegiac. *The Memory of Old Jack* (1974) is a tribute to Jack Beechum, a pillar of the Port William community. The narrative follows the history of Jack's long life within the community, including the hardships he experiences in marriage and farming. Jack's "failure" was that "he had not united farm and household and marriage bed." Lacking the love a woman, Jack devotes himself to his farm. Jack was a "true husband" of his land; he knew it well, and poured years of history and work into it. When Jack dies near the novel's end, the community feels the loss, particularly the men who have been influenced by Jack's agricultural knowledge and generosity.

A Place on Earth (1967; revised 1985) is structured by a similar pattern of loss, work, and healing. Mat Feltner, a key character, learns early in the novel that his son, Virgil, is missing in action in World War II. He copes with the loss by turning to the work of the farm. Mat's "healing" involves his acceptance of life's uncertainty and mutability. He learns that one must work well, even though the objects of the work will, like fleeting human life, pass away.

Berry continues to write and farm at Lane's Landing, standing in word and deed as a counter-friction to the violence, speed, and abstractions of contemporary life. His history there serves as a model of the long-term "fidelity" to a place he advocates. In the Foreword to *Another Turn of the Crank*, Berry praises the "hundreds of organizations actively at work all over our country on behalf of local health, conservation, and economy." He says these people have given him "hope." Berry's fidelity to his land and his prolific literary output stand a testaments to this steadfast hope for a sustainable future.

—K. Wesley Berry

BETTS, Doris

Born: Doris June Waugh in Statesville, North Carolina, 4 June 1932. **Education:** Woman's College, University of North Carolina, Phi Beta Kappa, 1950-53; University of North Carolina at Chapel Hill, 1954. **Family:** Married Lowry M. Betts (an attorney and judge), 5 July 1952; three children; three grandchildren. **Career:** Worked for *Statesville Daily Record*, 1946-50, and stringer for UPI and various North Carolina newspapers, including *Chapel Hill Weekly,* 1953-54, and later through 1957; taught typing for the North Carolina Highway Patrol, 1954; office manager and sec-retary-treasurer, Simplified Farm Record Book Company, Chapel Hill, 1955-57; full-time feature writer and daily columnist, *Sanford Daily Herald,* 1957-58, and full-time editor, *Sanford News Leader,* 1960; lecturer in the Department of English, 1966-74, director of Freshman/Sophomore English, 1972-78, associate professor, 1974-78, professor, since 1978, chair of Committee on Athletics and the University, 1988-89, University of North Carolina, Chapel Hill; visiting lecturer in creative writing, Duke University, 1971; directed North Carolina Fellows Program, 1975-76; named to Na-tional Humanities Faculty, 1978, served on literature panel for Na-tional Endowment for the Arts, 1978-80, and chair, 1979-80; board of governors, University of North Carolina Press, 1981-84, and elected chair of the faculty, UNC-Chapel Hill, 1982-85; judge for the PEN-Faulkner Awards, 1984; consultant to Southern Growth Policies Board, 1986, and to Florida Forestry Commission, 1988; faculty director, UNC Publishing Institute and member of the board of trustees, Union Theological Seminary, Richmond, Virginia, 1992; member of board of trustees, National Humanities Center, 1992.

Awards: *Mademoiselle* College Fiction Contest Winner, 1953, for "Mr. Shawn and Father Scott" (story included in *Best Short Sto-ries of 1953*); G.P. Putnam-U.N.C. Booklength Manuscript Prize, 1954, for *The Gentle Insurrection and Other Stories*; Sir Walter Raleigh Best Fiction by Carolinian Award, 1958, 1965, 1973; Guggenheim fellowship, 1958; Tanner Award for Distinguished Undergraduate Teaching, 1973; North Carolina Medal, 1975, for literature; named alumni distinguished professor, Catherine Carmichael Award for teaching, and Golden Fleece, UNC-Chapel Hill induction, all 1980; Academy Award, Best Short Feature, and Special Grand Jury Award, Huston Film Festival, both for *Violet,* a film version of her story "The Ugliest Pilgrim," 1981; Parker award, 1982-85, for literary achievement; John dos Passos award, 1983; Celebrated Teacher Title, Modern Language Association, 1986; Doris Betts Teaching Award established, UNC-Chapel Hill, 1986; Medal of Merit in the Short Story, American Academy and Institute of Arts and Letters, 1989; Salem Award for Literary Achievement, 1989; "The 'Home Truths' of Doris Betts" Sym-posium held at Methodist College, 1989; R. Hunt Parker Memo-rial Award, North Carolina Literary and Historical Association, literary achievement, 1991; Alumni Award for distinguished teach-ing, UNC-Chapel Hill, 1991; John Tyler Caldwell Award, North Carolina Humanities Committee, 1992; Fellowship of Southern Writers Selection, 1992; Southern Book Award, Southern Book Critics Circle, 1995; Inauguration Speaker, North Carolina Gover-nor, James B. Hunt, January 11, 1997; Presbyterian Writer of the Year, 1998; honorary member, South Atlantic Modern Language Association, 1998; Honorary D.Litt. from Greensboro College, 1987, and University of North Carolina, 1990; D. Litt. from UNC-Greensboro, 1989, University of the South, 1998, and D.H.L. from Erskine College, 1994. **Member:** National Humanities Center, 1993. **Agent:** Russell and Volkening, 50 West 29th Street, New York, New York 1001. **Address:** English Department, CB# 3520, Univer-sity of North Carolina, Chapel Hill, North Carolina 27599-3520.

Publications

Novels

Tall Houses in Winter. New York, Putnam, 1954.
The Scarlet Thread. New York, Harper, 1964.

The River to Pickle Beach. New York, Harper, 1972.
Heading West. New York, Knopf, 1981.
Souls Raised from the Dead. New York, Knopf, 1994.
The Sharp Teeth of Love. New York: Knopf, 1997.

Short Story Collections

The Gentle Insurrection. New York, Putnam, 1954.
The Astronomer and Other Stories. New York, Harper, 1966.
Beasts of the Southern Wild & Other Stories. New York, Harper, 1973.

Other

Creative Writing: The Short Story. Chapel Hill, UNC-Extension Division, 1970.

Uncollected Writings

"Brief Prose, Long Subjects," in *South Atlantic Quarterly*, Vol. 72, 1965.
"My Grandfather Haunts This Farm," in *Saturday Evening Post*, January/February, 1977.
"For[e]ward," in *New Southern Writing* edited by Moira Crone. Baltimore, Numen, 1980.
"The Fiction of Anne Tyler," in *Southern Quarterly,* Vol. 21, no. 4, 1983.
"Undergraduate Creative Writing Courses," in *ADE Bulletin*, Win-ter 1984.
"The Fingerprints of Style," in *Voicelust: Eight Contemporary Fic-tion Writers on Style,* edited by Allen Wier and Don Hendrie, Jr., Lincoln, University of Nebraska Press, 1985.
"Kitty Carmichael," in *The University Report,* "UNC Women Speak Out." (Symposium to honor Katherine K. Carmichael, former Dean of Students, UNC-CH), January 1988.
"The Arts in Red and Gold," in *Nine from North Carolina: An Exhibition of Women Artists.* Washington, D.C., National Mu-seum of Women in the Arts, 1989.
"The First 'Good Ole Girl,'" in *Life,* March 1990.
Introduction to *Southern Women Writers: The New Generation* edited by Tonette Bond Inge. Tuscaloosa, University of Ala-bama Press, 1990.
"Tyler's Marriages of Opposites," in *The Fiction of Anne Tyler* edited by C. Ralph Stephens, Jackson. University Press of Mississippi, 1990.
"Daughters, Southerners, and Daisy," in *The Female Tradition in Southern Literature* edited by Carol S. Manning. Urbana, Uni-versity of Illinois Press, 1993.
"Whispering Hope," in *Image: A Journal of the Arts and Reli-gion*, Fall 1994.
"Doing Lunch," in *New Harmony Journal*, 28 August 1995.
"Keeping All the Options Open: The Christian Vocation in the Secular Academy," in *Image: A Journal of the Arts and Reli-gion,* Vol. 11, 1995.
"Lost in Translation," in *Brightleaf,* September/October 1997.
"The Goal of a Realist," in *The Store of Joys,* edited by Huston Paschal. Winston-Salem, John F. Blair, 1997.
"Whose Child Is This?" (Reading at Gov. James B. Hunt's Inau-guration, 11 January 1997). http://www.unc.edu/news/gaz/ar-chives/97jan15/file.4.html

*

Film Adaptation: *Violet,* adaptation from her own short story "The Ugliest Pilgrim."

Manuscript Collection: Boston University, Boston.

Interviews: With George Wolfe, *Conversations with Twelve Southern Writers* edited by John Carr, Baton Rouge, Louisiana State University Press, 1972; with Laura Alderson, *Poets and Writers,* Vol. 20, no. 1, 1992; with William J. Walsh, *Speak So I Shall Know Thee: Interviews with Southern Writers,* Asheboro, Down Home Press, 1993; with Dannye Romine Powell, *Parting the Curtains: Interviews with Southern Writers,* Winston-Salem: John F. Blair, 1994; with A. G. Harmon, *Image: A Journal of the Arts and Religion,* Vol. 11, 1995; with Dale Brown, *Southern Quarterly,* Vol. 34, no. 2, 1996.

Critical Studies: "Superstition in Doris Betts's New Novel" by Ruth Moose, *North Carolina Folklore Journal,* Vol. 21, 1973; "Doris Betts: Making a Difference in Many Lives" by Mark William Scandling, *Carolina Quarterly,* Vol. 32, no. 2, 1980; "Faith and the Unanswerable Questions: The Fiction of Doris Betts" by David Marion Holman, *Southern Literary Journal,* Vol. 15, no. 1, 1982; "Doris Betts's Nancy Finch: A Heroine for the 1980s" by Dorothy M. Scura, *Southern Quarterly,* Vol. 22, no. 1, 1983; *The Home Truth of Doris Betts,* proceedings of 8th annual Southern Writers Symposium (includes a bibliography), edited by Sue Laslie Kimball and Lynn Veach Sadler, Fayetteville, Methodist College Press, 1992; "Doris Betts: Resting on the Bedrock of Original Sin" by Susan Ketchin, *The Christ-Haunted Landscape: Faith and Doubt in Southern Literature,* Jackson, University Press of Mississippi, 1994; *Doris Betts* by Elizabeth Evans, New York, Twayne, 1997.

*   *   *

Accomplished in fiction as both a short story writer and a novelist, Doris Betts is equally at ease with scholarship, criticism, social and religious comment in writing and in speaking. Her words shoot straight to the heart of the matter in a no-nonsense, penetrating delivery. While not as violent, her rhetoric is reminiscent of the fiery preachers in fundamentalist religions that dot the South. Her strongest fictional influence, in fact, is Biblical scripture and religious teachings.

Betts' themes involve the eternal truths of love and its absence, joy and pain, morality and history, living and dying. Like the writers of scripture, she creates characters who face the problem of evil in a modern world. Her plots are adventure stories, leading readers to the next event as she instills a moral and psychological lesson in their minds. Her sense of place involves piedmont North Carolina—its sense of family and community, religion and values, language and expression. The scene, however, moves from rural North Carolina to the beach and into the western states as her fiction evolves. The geography and its cultural values serve only as frame for the psychological explorations essential in her stories.

Her three short story collections and uncollected stories illustrate Betts' development in the genre. Her first short story collection, *The Gentle Insurrection,* which contains twelve stories, focuses on a personal "insurrection" in a character's life. The themes of death and love that mark her fiction are evident in this collection as is the humor underlying even the most solemn events. For example, "A Sense of Humor," in which children's curiosity leads them to tread on traditionally sacred territory, shows both Betts' humor and the children's awakened understanding of practical joking. Scripture from Isaiah, "and a little child shall lead them," takes an ironic and humorous twist in this story, illustrating Betts' depth of scriptural understanding and its skillful application to everyday life.

The Astronomer and Other Stories, her second collection, includes seven stories and a novella. Adding to themes of the first collection, Betts includes autobiographical, first-person narrations and enlarges on humorous aspects of life. Two of the most comic stories are "The Dead Mule," about the foibles of a bootlegger, and "Careful, Sharp Eggs Underfoot," about an annual egg fry on hot pavement festival in a small town. The latter story holds comic allusions to the Old Testament vengeful God and His turning Lot's wife into a pillar of salt. The emerging comedy of the stories illustrates Betts' sense of humor and quick wit. As her fiction develops, her humor becomes more apparent and her uses of different kinds of comedy more skilled. The moral implications of the human comedy, to Betts, is as applicable in the twentieth century as in Lot's day.

The third collection is *Beasts of the Southern Wild & Other Stories.* Outstanding in this group of seven stories is "The Ugliest Pilgrim," a story made into an Academy Award-winning short film and into a musical, both named *Violet.* Violet, the protagonist, goes on a quest journey, but, like the medieval searcher, misses the original object of her search only to gain a better reward. Her initiation into life through sex brings both a deeper understanding of herself and love. Betts often uses the sensual and sexual experience to awaken depths in characters and to explore their dark corners. The story, as do others, examines the mysterious ways in which God moves. The collection is an indication of Betts' move toward using female protagonists for her psychological explorations; all these stories revolve around women's consciousness.

Betts' six novels expand her characters' lives onto a broader canvas, experiences she has distilled in the more concentrated short story form. *Tall Houses in Winter* is an apprentice novel that, according to most reviewers, fails to create characters who communicate as well as did her short story people. The novel evokes a story within a story through the introspection of a middle-aged academic. Betts begins creating characters who move out of their environment and, at the same time, stretch their consciousness. *The Scarlet Thread,* a turn of the century historical novel, uses a larger cast and spreads the tale over a longer period of time. This novel is more adept than the previous one at revealing character and in examining family relationships. Using techniques she refined in the short story, Betts concentrates on multiple levels of the novel, but her structure suffers from disjointedness. In *The River to Pickle Beach,* Betts takes her scene to the beach from North Carolina rural towns, and, thereby, moves her own point of view. The story's central action involves a senseless act of violence, a theme of the time—late 1960s and early 1970s in American culture—according to some critics. Larger than a reflection of the time, however, the story examines values in human experience and the reality of evil. The violent person and the cultural mores out of which they emerge interests Betts.

In *Heading West,* Betts reworks her short story portraits and concentrated questions onto a wider scene, a longer journey and a more clearly articulated introspection. Nancy Finch, kidnaped from a family outing, becomes the mover rather than the victim in the story; through her journey west, she attains independence and maturity. In this psychological thriller, Betts expands the quest journey motif from that of Violet in "The Ugliest Pilgrim"; here she creates a protagonist who takes control of the event. Betts learned by early reading of Zane Grey books about the attractions of adventure stories, and her trip down the white water of the Colorado River through the Grand Canyon revealed to her aspects of nature she had not realized. The open spaces and geological signs of pre-history offered her new territory for characters' development.

The inner, unexplored spaces for Betts' characters give way to the bright light of comprehension and self-discovery when they face crises. Often, they uncover desires and longings they did not even imagine. In *Heading West,* Betts uses a female protagonist for the first time in her novels, and she continues to do so in the subsequent two novels. Awakenings of hidden desires and yearnings for answers to philosophical questions is a human dilemma Betts sees in people of all ages. *Souls Raised from the Dead*, for instance, deals with a dying 13-year-old girl who serves as the center around which family and community (extended family) revolve. In the process, both the girl and the family learn about faith and about death and dying, but also about life and living and loving. Shifting points of view take the reader inside the minds of those involved in the crisis while subtle humor alleviates details of illness and death. Death gives life definition in Betts' fiction; when faced as a reality, her characters attain direction.

The Sharp Teeth of Love, takes the protagonist into the wilderness to escape life and its problems. What she finds there is not only a family, but a renewal, a resurrected self through love that filled an emptiness she barely sensed. Betts' favorite characters, in fact, are those who find fulfillment after having only a vague sense of emptiness. She explores qualities of ordinary people and their eccentricities—those traits that differentiate them from others. Each finds her completion in another—loving is caring for and meeting another's needs only after finding one's own strengths. Her contemporary people face the same moral dilemmas ancient people faced. Betts' own hard-won faith permeates her stories, her observation of family and personal relationships structure them, and her ear for the music of speech infuse their language. She is a regional writer in the best sense of that expression; her cultural and moral values extend into the human scene.

—Jeanne R. Nostrandt

BINGHAM, Sallie

Born: Louisville, Kentucky, 22 January 1937. **Education:** Radcliffe College, B.A. (magna cum laude), 1958. **Family**: Married 1) A. Whitney Ellsworth, 1958 (divorced, 1963); 3) Tim Peters (a construction company owner), 1983; three children. **Career:** Instructor of English and creative writing, University of Louisville; founder, Kentucky Foundation for Women, The Ameri-

can Voice, and Santa Fe Stages; writer. **Awards:** MacDowell Colony fellowship, 1979; Yaddo Colony fellowship, 1980.

PUBLICATIONS

Novels

After Such Knowledge. Boston, Houghton, 1960.
Small Victories: A Novel. Cambridge, Zoland, 1992.
Upstate: A Novel. Sag Harbor, New York, Permanent Press, 1993.
Matron of Honor. Cambridge, Zoland, 1994.
Straight Man: A Novel. Cambridge, Zoland, 1996.

Short Story Collections

The Touching Hand, and Six Short Stories. Boston, Houghton, 1967.
The Way It Is Now: Stories. New York, Viking, 1972.

Contributor, *Solo: Women on Women Alone*. New York, Delacorte, 1977.
Contributor, *From Mt. San Angelo: Stories, Poems, and Essays*. Associated University Presses, 1984.

Plays

Milk of Paradise. Produced in New York at American Place Theatre, 1980.
Paducah. Produced in New York at American Place Theatre, 1985.

Other

Passion and Prejudice: A Family Memoir. New York, Knopf, 1989; with introduction by Bingham, New York, Applause Books, 1991.

*

Critical Studies: *New York Times Book Review*, 18 June 1967; *New York Review of Books,* 9 November 1967; *New York Times Book Review*, 2 April 1972; *Times Literary Supplement*, 23 November 1972; *New York Times*, 4 March 1980; *New York Times*, 22 April 1985; *Belles Lettres*, Summer 1992; *New York Times Book Review*, 27 September 1992; *Washington Post Book World*, 24 May 1994.

*   *   *

While Sallie Bingham's fiction is not completely autobiographical, her life experiences have determined the thematic nature of her fiction. Born into a prosperous publishing family in Kentucky, Bingham had a privileged upbringing. In her adulthood, however, the darker side of wealth became apparent as Bingham became involved in a rancorous inner-family conflict over control of her father's extensive business holdings. Thematically, the emotional pain of such conflicts is vital in Bingham's fiction, as are relationships in general, presented with a satiric edge.

Bingham's early work, written before the turmoil surrounding family business, is replete with emotional concerns. She published her first novel, *After Such Knowledge* (1960), at age 21. The protagonist, a wealthy but sheltered woman, lives a desperately lonely life she finds not worth continuing. Bingham's next publications were two collections of short stories, *The Touching Hand* (1967) and *The Way It Is Now* (1972). These works show her mastery of the short story form through precisely constructed episodes that can be compared to works by Katherine Mansfield and Eudora Welty. Within these well-structured stories, which generally reflect on emotionally unsatisfying lives of well-off, young women, Bingham exhibits a careful eye for detail, especially in capturing nuances of character and an unsentimental vision of their emotional distress.

In the 1990s, after her family feud had been settled, Bingham's fiction addressed ruthlessness within families. 1992's *Small Victories: A Novel*, for example, is a family drama set near the end of the 1950s in Kentucky and North Carolina, with scenes also in Cambridge, Massachusetts. The characters are sharply drawn with her knowing eye, particularly Bingham's heroine, 45-year-old Louise Macelvens, who lives a quiet, unmarried life, her pleasure coming from small triumphs most people do not discern. Some of these victories come while caring for her mentally retarded sister, Shelby. Such accomplishments as getting Shelby to eat her breakfast give Louise a meaningful existence. Most of her relatives do not view Louise's relationship with Shelby as healthy, and their cousin, a state senator in Kentucky, arranges for the disabled woman to be put in a mental hospital. Louise tries to free Shelby and eventually succeeds on her own; she had expected help from her cousin, Tom, a 19-year-old college student in Cambridge, but he has problems of his own, including loneliness, guilt, and sexual immaturity, all of which result in his loss of a girlfriend. Tom's parents, including the state senator known as "Big" Tom, maintain distance and expect a similar detachment from Tom. Petty and inexorably discordant family relations form the core of the story, showing Bingham's masterful creations of these kind of situations and enhanced by individualized character personalities: Big Tom is a humorous character despite his dominant bearing.

Bingham's next novel, *Matron of Honor* (1996), occurs in the early 1970s and revolves around the upcoming nuptials of Apple Mason, a rich girl, and Billy Long, a young man who works for her father and is looking to climb socially through this marriage. The lives of young women from well-off families of the time are especially well-drawn. The relationship between Apple and her sister, Cory, for example, reflect tensions between sisters wanting some measure of control over their lives while also trying to maintain traditions and meeting the expectations of their family, who subscribe to the mores of patriarchal families and society at large.

In *Straight Man: A Novel* (1996), Bingham's preoccupation with family is less prevalent, as her title character, Colby Winn, is a man straight to his own fate. Colby is a professor ostracized from the eastern academic establishment—he taught at Harvard and Columbia—who returns to Kentucky to teach at a state university. At home he must face his past, the catalyst occuring when he picks up a hitchhiker, a young aspiring actress named Ann Lee. Their tumultuous relationship results in revelations about their turbulent family relationships. Bingham draws these characters with empathy but shows them engaging

in unappealing behaviors as well, often bringing in surprising plot twists.

—Annette Petrusso

BLAKELY, Diann

Pseudonym: Diann Blakely Shoaf. **Born:** Harriet Diann Blakely in Anniston, Alabama, 1 June 1957. **Education:** University of the South, B.A. 1979; Vanderbilt University, M.A. 1980; Vermont College, M.F.A. 1990. **Career:** Teaching assistant and junior tutor, Harvard University, 1986-87; faculty, Harpeth Hall School, Nashville, 1988-97; adjunct lecturer, Belmont College, Nashville, 1989-90; Walter E. Dakin Fellow, Sewanee Writers' Conference, 1993; Robert Frost Fellow, Bread Loaf Writers' Conference, 1994; assistant poetry editor, *Antioch Review*, since 1995; faculty, Sewanee Young Writers' Conference, University of the South, since 1996; poet-in-residence, Harpeth Hall School, Nashville, since 1997. **Awards:** Harold Stirling Vanderbilt Fellowship, Vanderbilt University, 1979-80; Pushcart Prize, 1994 and 1995; Roundtable Award, Peabody College of Education, Vanderbilt University, 1997.

PUBLICATIONS

Poetry Collections

Hurricane Walk (as Diann Blakely Shoaf). Brockport, New York, BOA Editions, Ltd., 1992.
Farewell, My Lovelies. Brownsville, Oregon, Story Line Press, 1999.

Poems in Anthologies

Lights, Camera, Poetry: American Poets Write about the Movies edited by Jason Shinder. New York, Harvest Books, 1996.
Homeworks: An Anthology of Tennessee Writers edited by Phyllis Tickle. Knoxville, Tennessee, 1996.

*

Diann Blakely comments:

. . . The last time I fell in love
I played Beethoven
so loud
that pictures trembled and china rattled

its shelves, "Chorale" strings and winds and horns confirming
        that joy—freude, freude—
is what we all desire, that while deep-kindled by the scent
 of hair, or the brief feathery touch of a hand,
        or the sight of a parted mouth,
desire arrows its way into the brain till flesh and mind
become as one, singing
our unrequitable ache to drown in sweetness.

—from "Chorale" in *Farewell, My Lovelies.*

*   *   *

In "Unfinished Sketch of an American Woman," from *Hurricane Walk*, Diann Blakely's first collection of poems, the speaker asks British painter John Singer Sargent, "are you fond of raw landscape? Or are ladies like me—done to life-scale—enough?" Blakely's poems explore that "life-scale" in physical and psychological landscapes. Her speakers struggle to discern protection from confinement, as the boundary between the external and the internal is blurred. The short lyrics here survey the raw terrain of human relationships but move quietly and with precision.

In "The Attempt," when the weather is so bad that "most rapists stayed home," a woman in the kitchen hears a scream so loud she drops the glass she is washing. Her husband rushes outside to assist, and she calls the police. The woman outside is fine: "no newspaper harm had been done," but the speaker is wary. When her husband removes a shard of glass from her finger, she says, "You have always been clumsy / with small things, though meaning / no harm. I avoided the park—unreasoning, fearful— / would not let you touch me for days." Events like these, in and out of the house, force her beyond logic, where she is small and abstracted, wishing comfort from no one but herself.

For the women in her poems, interior space—kitchens, bedrooms, doctors' offices—provides little psychological or emotional cover, despite its apparent safety, nor is the out-of-doors particularly liberating. In the book's opening poem, "The Sculpture Garden," the speaker ventures out "Sweaty, disheveled / from the fierce heat of August" only to feel like one of the statues: "If I stay very still, no one will know." She knows she is not like the mythical Galatea, the statue by Pygmalion that was brought to life by Aphrodite, the goddess of love.

Blakely's speaker is Galatea in reverse. Not a work of art but of flesh, with "troublesome" blood in her veins, she notes, "people will wonder / what holds me in thrall." An answer comes later, in the poem "Circe": "There's adventure in home life, / though none of them saw it," says the witch who turned Odysseus' men into swine. "Yet such spaces oppressed them," so they wander without direction. Circe repays them when they come to her wanting "mindlessness, limits": "I saw usual cravings, and blessed them with snouts." In other words, they are given exactly what they need. These lines resonate with the end of "For My Mother," where the speaker says, "I've carved away greed, / prefer love in small measures."

Drawn more obviously from her own experience and with a single consciousness governing, Blakely's second book, *Farewell, My Lovelies*, ranges farther afield, from Nashville, Birmingham, and Charleston to Mexico and New York, as travel refines her sense of ritual, ultimately "pointing the cold way home." For the poet, modern rituals—trick-or-treating, college reunions, cookouts, and family gatherings—mask brutal terror but also penetrate the veneer of our daily negotiations. There is a religious sensibility here, but "what chaotic gods / the heart has always worshiped," she declares in "Descant."

In "Delta Funeral," the poet recalls the dead woman's wayward son, who as a child "for sheer meanness" stripped the wisteria from her backyard trellis, "their wing-shaped petals / like the shadows she saw on walls at midnight / and whispered to or prayed against, we couldn't tell." The boy's cruelty reinforces the idea

that beauty and terror are often of a piece, especially within the confines of a family. The nature of the shadows and the petals hinges on a gesture, one left unresolved in the collection of family rituals called a funeral. Likewise in "Yucatan, November," when a shopkeeper pulls her through a door, she asks, "Am I being kidnaped, punished for not bringing / loved ones along with me? Here family's a religion, / worshiped even past El Dia de Muertos." For Blakely, family is the most chaotic god of all.

History is another quarrelsome deity in *Farewell, My Lovelies*. In "Jehovah Jiveh," the poet remembers the duck-and-cover drill: "Was it first grade when we rehearsed / for Armageddon, our dog tags clanking toward the basement / where we'd watched Kennedy's funeral?" One disaster in the poem, the destruction of a church by storm in which six children are killed during the Easter pageant (another ubiquitous childhood ritual), is juxtaposed with another, the death of the poet's "strayed angel and heart's friend." Begun at Christ's empty tomb, history is a cycle of funerals, a series of rituals to which the artist must respond. She asks, "does it last beyond the grave, this ravening passion / to drown God's mighty thunder with our own scavenged hymns?"

In her scavenging, Diann Blakely leaves no region—physical, psychological, or formal—unexamined. Her work displays a great restless energy (*Farewell, My Lovelies* contains sonnets, a villanelle, and a sestina, as well as syllabic verse and forms of her own devising) that banishes stasis and forces her to probe deeply for her treasures. As in "Chorale," whose lines comprise the Author's Statement above, when she finds sweetness, she will drown in it.

—Preston Merchant

BLEDSOE, Jerry

Born: Danville, Virginia, 14 July 1941. **Family:** Married Linda Boyd on 11 July 1964; son Erik. **Career:** Reporter and columnist, *Greensboro News & Record*, 1966-77 and 1981-89; feature writer, *Louiville Times*, 1971; contributing editor, *Esquire*, 1972-76; columnist, *Charlotte Observer*, 1977-81; publisher and editor, Down Home Press, Asheboro, North Carolina, since 1989. **Military Service:** U.S. Army, 1960-63. **Awards:** Twice winner of the Ernie Pyle Award for the human qualities in his news writing and commentary. **Agent:** Michael Congdon, Don Congdon Associates, 156 Fifth Ave., Suite 625, New York, New York 10010. **Address:** Down Home Press, P.O. Box 4126, Asheboro, North Carolina 10022.

PUBLICATIONS

True Crime Books

Bitter Blood: A True Story of Southern Family Pride, Madness, and Multiple Murder. New York, Dutton, 1988.
Blood Games. New York, Dutton, 1991.
Before He Wakes: A True Story of Money, Marriage, Sex, and Murder. New York, Dutton, 1994.
Death Sentence: The True Story of Velma Barfield's Life, Crimes and Execution. New York, Dutton, 1998.

General Nonfiction

The World's Number One, Flat-Out, All-Time Great, Stock Car Racing Book. Garden City, New York, Doubleday, 1975.

You Can't Live on Radishes: Some Funny Things Happened on the Way Back to the Land. Greensboro, North Carolina, Grape Hill Press, 1976.

Just Folks: Visitin' with Carolina People. Charlotte, North Carolina, East Woods Press, 1980.

Carolina Curiosities: Jerry Bledsoe's Outlandish Guide to the Dadblamedest Things to See and Do in North Carolina. Charlotte, North Carolina, East Woods Press, 1984.

From Whalebone to Hot House: A Journey Along North Carolina's Longest Highway, U.S. 64. Charlotte, North Carolina, East Woods Press, 1986.

Country Cured: Reflections from the Heart. Atlanta, Longstreet Press, 1989.

The Bare-Bottomed Skier and Other Unlikely Tales. Asheboro, North Carolina, Down Home Press, 1990.

Blue Horizons: Faces and Places from a Bicycle Journey Along the Blue Ridge Parkway. Asheboro, North Carolina, Down Home Press, 1993.

The Angel Doll: A Christmas Story. Asheboro, North Carolina, Down Home Press, 1996.

*

Media Adaptations: *In the Best of Families* (adapted from *Bitter Blood: A True Story of Southern Family Pride, Madness, and Multiple Murder*), CBS Television, 1989.

*   *   *

Though Jerry Bledsoe is most widely known for his true-crime books and their resulting films, the diversity of his work defies any attempt to bind this North Carolina/Virginia writer in any genre. Bledsoe is one of the premier journalists recording bloodlust in America, and conversely one whose parallel strengths are humor and a gift for warmth and pathos. Most lately, he is the spinner of a semi-fictional yarn called *The Angel Book,* a small, heart-breakingly tender book from childhood. A sequel is in progress.

Twice winner of the Ernie Pyle Award for the human qualities in his news writing and commentary, Bledsoe first got into print as a teenager in the U.S. Army at Okinawa, drawing propaganda cartoons on flyers to be dropped on Vietnam. His Thomasville, North Carolina, high school record had won him no gold stars beyond a summer-school diploma; the Army would be his only school of journalism. A kid whose boyhood was spent working at any gritty job he could find to help his family, he never had time to go to college. It may be just as well; every wild hare experience was grist for a literary mill that turned out some of the South's best-read and best-remembered newspaper columns and books of homey essays. And he who detested high school English was by nature an almost flawless grammarian and good editor.

Uproariously disgusted with the glass-office power games of modern newspapers, Bledsoe moved back and forth between the South's larger and more prestigious newsrooms, including the *Greensboro Daily News, Louisville Courier-Journal,* and *Char-*

lotte Observer. The number of fans he made carried weight when economics would send him back to a job he may have once cast off in rowdy indignation.

Bledsoe was not long out of the army and running a Biff-Burger stand when he got his first civilian newspaper job at the *Daily Independent* in Kannapolis, North Carolina. The hamburger business had rewards: he had hired a waitress named Linda Boyd and they were soon married (he was 23, she was 17). The Biff-Burger became the setting of his first novel, a book he seems to have made no attempt to publish. At the risk of telling too much about this epic, it involved a heist in which the villains hooked the hamburger wagon to their getaway car and sped off with the Biff-Burger careening through the streets, patties flying.

Bledsoe was a contributing editor at *Esquire* in 1975 when Doubleday published his first book, *The World's Number One, Flat-Out, All-Time Great, Stock Car Racing Book.* Critically it was pronounced a fine effort, but then, as it turned out, stock car racing fans, as a group, were not avid readers.

Bledsoe began to self-publish in 1976 with a comically woeful, personal back-to-the-land memoir called *You Can't Live on Radishes: Some Funny Things Happened on the Way Back to the Land.* Following came *Just Folks: Visitin' with Carolina People, Country Cured: Reflections from the Heart, The Bare-Bottomed Skier and Other Unlikely Tales,* and several others, all light-hearted. He lugged boxes of books everywhere, to fairs and tractor pulls and hotdog suppers. Sometimes they sold well. Even so, he lamented, book-peddling was "one big pain in the ass."

Always a careful reporter, Bledsoe found truth, in meticulous detail and especially about murder, far more gripping and hair-raising than anything a writer could make up. The first major case in point was a mid-1980s series of ghastly killings that struck down two connected, well-to-do families, one in Winston-Salem, North Carolina, and the other in Louisville, Kentucky. The finale of this blood bath came in a funereal, low-speed "chase" in which deranged cousins Fritz Klenner and Susie Lynch died in a car explosion in view of pursuing police. The bodies of Mrs. Lynch's two little boys were also found in the wreckage; both had been poisoned and then shot.

Bledsoe was then at the *Greensboro Daily News* and was assigned to the case. For a week, his stories of the cousins' bizarre vendetta against their family and Mrs. Lynch's former in-laws commanded two or more news pages daily. Reporters in distant newsrooms begged Greensboro colleagues for copies, passed them desk to desk, pinned them to bulletin boards. Researched and written in about six weeks, it was, fellow newsfolk agreed, a stellar piece of journalism. A book version was published by Dutton as *Bitter Blood,* a detail-packed narrative paced with maddening precision toward that inevitable, slow-motion climax—a masterpiece of horror. It made the *New York Times* bestseller list for 26 weeks and was later made into a CBS movie, *In the Best of Families.*

After *Bitter Blood* and hard-pressed to equal its drama came *Blood Games,* an account of a murder plot by three college students who planned to share an inheritance one of them expected, if they could only help his family "pass away." *Blood Games* also became a made-for-TV movie and was followed by another chiller, *Before He Wakes,* the story of a self-styled model wife and mother and her quest for an insurance-sweetened widowhood. Two husbands later (each managed to shoot themselves accidentally in their sleep) the woman was found guilty of murder and sent to prison. 1998's *Death Sentence,* Bledsoe's rendering of the life and works of a Bible-toting North Carolina grandma named Vera Barfield, whose generosity with ant-poison tea and sympathy led to several deaths and ultimately to her own execution.

Soon after the publication of *Bitter Blood* Bledsoe founded Down Home Press, a regional publishing house, to publish books by his friends and others whose work he thought deserved an audience. In its first decade Down Home Press has built a hefty catalog, with a few less succesful volumes boxed up in a barn. Due to the hateful load of paperwork and taxes and the egos of some would-be authors, it has not been all fun, but Down Home Press is still afloat and follows the Bledsoe philosophy about writing and publishing: "Why the hell would anybody do this when they could be selling hamburgers? We made a good hamburger. Sold lots of 'em. I think about that."

—Dorothy Jackson

BLOUNT, Roy

Born: Roy Alton Blount, Jr., Indianapolis, Indiana, 4 October 1941. **Education:** Vanderbilt University, B.A. (magna cum laude), 1963; Harvard University, M.A. 1964. **Military Service:** U.S. Army, 1964-66; became first lieutenant. **Family:** Married Ellen Pearson, 6 September 1964 (divorced March 1973), three children; married Joan Ackerman, 1976. **Career:** Reporter and sports columnist, *Decatur-DeKalb News,* Decatur, Georgia, 1958-59, *Morning Telegraph,* New York City, summer, 1961, *New Orleans Times-Picayune,* summer, 1963; reporter, editorial writer, and columnist, *Atlanta Journal,* 1966-68; instructor, Georgia State College, 1967-68; staff writer, 1968-74, associate editor, 1974-75, and free-lance writer since 1975, *Sports Illustrated*; occasional performer for American Humorists' Series, American Place Theatre, 1986, and 1988, and *The Prairie Home Companion*; member of usage panel, *American Heritage Dictionary*; lecturer.

PUBLICATIONS

Nonfiction

About Three Bricks Shy of a Load. Boston, Little, Brown, 1974; as *About Three Bricks Shy—and the Load Filled Up: The Story of the Greatest Football Team Every,* New York, Ballantine, 1989.
Crackers: This Whole Many-Sided Thing of Jimmy, More Carters, Ominous Little Animals, Sad-Singing Women, My Daddy and Me. New York, Knopf, 1980.
One Fell Soup; or, I'm Just a Bug on the Windshield of Life. Boston, Little, Brown, 1983.
What Men Don't Tell Women. Boston, Atlantic/Little, Brown, 1984.
Not Exactly What I Had in Mind. Boston, Atlantic Monthly Press, 1985.

It Grows on You: A Hair-Raising Survey of Human Plumage. Garden City, New York, Doubleday, 1986.
Now, Where Were We? New York, Villard, 1989.
Camels Are Easy, Comedy's Hard. New York, Willard Books, 1991.
Roy Blount's Book of Southern Humor. New York, Norton, 1994.
Be Sweet. New York, Knopf, 1998.

Novel

First Hubby. New York, Villard, 1990.

Other

Roy Blount's Happy Hour and a Half (one-man show). Produced Off-Broadway at American Place Theatre, 1986.
Soupsongs/Webster's Ark (double book of verse). New York, Houghton, 1987.

Contributor, *The Baseball Hall of Fame 50th Anniversary Book.* New York, Prentice Hall Press, 1988.

*

Audio recordings: *Roy Blount Reads Excerpts from Crackers,* Columbia, Missouri, American Audio Prose Library, 1983; *Roy Blount Interview,* Columbia, Missouri, American Audio Prose Library, 1983; *Now, Where Were We?,* Holmes, Pennsylvania, Sound Editions, 1989; *Not Exactly What I Had in Mind,* Albuquerque, New Mexico, Newman, 1994.

Critical Studies: *Roy Blount, Jr.* by Jerry Elijah Brown, Boston, Twayne, 1990.

Roy Blount comments:

Raised in South by Southern parents. Couldn't play third base well enough so became college journalist. Ridiculed cultural enemies. Boosted integration. Decided to write, teach. Went to Harvard Graduate School. Didn't like it. Went back to journalism. Liked it. Got a column. Ridiculed cultural enemies. Wrote limericks. Boosted integration. Wanted to write for magazines. Took writing job at *Sports Illustrated.* Have seen country, met all kinds of people, heard all different kinds of talk. Like it. Ready now to write a novel that sums it all up.

*   *   *

Roy Blount's writing reflects a deep and restless imagination approaching a wide variety of topics with droll humor, wild ideas, and engaging wordplay. His essays typically begin with a humorous observation on a recognizable aspect of human behavior, a topical event, a daily life encounter, or a more specific subject—gardening, God, food, genius grants, hair—whatever bothers him enough to activate his imagination; the subject is explored from various perspectives while the sagacity of the curmudgeon's wit leads the reader on in a conversational style that repeatedly lampoons targets in a cumulative pattern that builds into an enjoyable essay. His breadth of topics is remarkable, and his style blends casual observations with learned details.

Magazine journalism proved a perfect outlet for such fecund wit: an observation is explored in depth and shortly exhausted, but not before Blount has had a chance to level off presumptions, expose folly, and get in a good deal of humorous play with language. Songs, limericks, and short stints in comedy forums, such as *The Prairie Home Companion,* are other outlets he has used more for pure fun, as in his hilarious food songs, like "Hymm to Ham" and "Song Against Broccoli"—

> The neighborhood stores are all out of broccoli,
> Loccoli.

Blount has been writing columns since he was fifteen, he explained to Jean Ross in *Contemporary Authors:* "The first time I wrote for publication was in high school, and I was satirizing my school. Whenever we'd have to write a theme on some topic like "What I Did Last Summer," I would hate that sort of straightforward assignment, so I'd write about something odd. I had several English teachers who encouraged me, but one in particular, Ann Lewis, in my sophomore year, gave me Perelman and Benchley and Thurber and E. B. White and Wolcott Gibbs to read. They were inspirations to me, and influences. But I'd always read lots of funny writers. I was a big enthusiast of Pogo and read Mark Twain and Booth Tarkington—Penrod, Penrod and Sam, all that stuff. I tended to like funny stuff. I could get all analytical about what humor does, at least for me. I think it's a way of resolving contradictions and tensions in a way that people can enjoy. But that's a boring thing to say." After college Blount worked primarily for newspapers—the *Decatur-DeKalb News, Morning Telegraph, New Orleans Times-Picayune,* and *Atlanta Journal*—before becoming a regular contributor to *Sports Illustrated* from 1968 to 1975.

Blount's first book, *About Three Bricks Shy of a Load,* follows the Pittsburgh Steelers football team, exploring the thrills of competition, the brutality of football, and the lives of players. Since 1975 he has contributed to a wide variety of journals, and his columns have been collected in several books, some with a particular approach, as in *Crackers: This Whole Many-Sided Thing of Jimmy, More Carters, Ominous Little Animals, Sad-Singing Women, My Daddy and Me,* which examines Jimmy Carter's administration and the late 1970s in general from a Good Ol' Boy perspective, where honesty and straightforwardness are valued over finesse and political correctness. This misanthropic viewpoint allows Blount to celebrate common values and to poke fun at those who attempt to manipulate appearances to gain social or political acceptance.

Blount's more free-ranging pieces are collected in *One Fell Soup; or, I'm Just a Bug on the Windshield of Life,* where several pieces consider food, *What Men Don't Tell Women, It Grows on You: A Hair-Raising Survey of Human Plumage,* basically an historical exploration of attitudes about hair that shows Blount's knack for blending factual detail with imaginative ruminations, and *Camels Are Easy, Comedy's Hard.* Camels includes book reviews and original poetry, travel writing (dog-sledding in Vermont, an African safari, a surrealistic journey up the Amazon) and character studies, one of which recounts how his Mama became a famous storyteller. Typical is a piece on coon-dog hunting that proves informative and rollicking.

1998's *Be Sweet: A Conditional Love Story* is somewhat of a departure for Blount by focusing more on his past and delving

into painful experiences, but his characteristic humor and conversational style remain. His frequent use of irony is displayed as well, as in the title—a phrase his mother used to say to him to calm his mischievousness; the book explores his sense of mischief and humor. Related through a series of interconnected pieces that weave back and forth in time, the essays in *Be Sweet* address such familiar topics as travel, including a trip to China, and observations on common things—the war between the sexes, the pressures a boy faces when being named "junior" (as Blount himself was), food (including an inspired bit on peppers)—but consistently turn back to Blount's boyhood experiences and development as a humorist, with self-loathing as a surprising catalyst. Blount's mother's inconsistent behavior—sometimes overly nurturing, at other times cold, distant, and suspicious, caused him deep feelings of anguish. At the same time, she instilled in him a love of language and storytelling that obviously had a positive influence on his life.

At 55, Blount takes stock and tries to make sense of his life, as he has with the weird goings-on in late-twentieth century America and life in general. "I tell stories," he writes in the memoir, "and mine, for reasons that we may or may not get to the bottom of, are generally humorous. Which means I have left things out." This time, he adds, "I'm putting everything in." The result is not too different than what Blount has always offered—barbs to deflate pomposity, engaging extended monologues on seemingly odd or shallow topics, playful use of language, and downright playing for laughs—with a more serious and self-conscious investigation of the speaker, resulting in comic observations that lose nothing in gaining a greater sense of poignancy. In a *New York Times Book Review* piece, Josephine Humphreys noted as much: "*Be Sweet: A Conditional Love Story* is a wild tell-all, a raucous, unflinching memoir as funny as anything he's ever written, and that's saying a lot, since Blount's one of America's wittiest writers. Like his 14 previous books, *Be Sweet* is both literary and down-home, a thinking man's thigh slapper, crammed with the verbal dazzle we've come to expect from him—puns, allusions, jokes, outrageous anecdotes, eye-opening commentary. But this book's different, because it's also a serious heartbreaker." Blount had cautioned in the mid-1980s interview with Ross: "I could get all analytical about what humor does, at least for me. I think it's a way of resolving contradictions and tensions in a way that people can enjoy. But that's a boring thing to say." In *Be Sweet,* he has found a funny way of saying it.

—Mel Koler

BONNER, Cindy

Born: Cynthia Rayburn in Corpus Christi, Texas, 14 June 1953. **Education:** University of Southern Mississippi, 1971-73; San Antonio College, 1979. **Family:** Married Tommy D. Sutton, 3 October 1970 (divorced, March 1972); married Charles Randolph Bonner, 19 August 1972; two children. **Career:** Has worked variously as a yoga instructor, computer operator, real estate manager, blues/rock band manager, clerk in a western wear store, a co-owner of a wholesale nursery, and a nursery stock seller for large growers; started writing seriously in 1982; volunteer worker in school library.

PUBLICATIONS

Novels

Lily. Chapel Hill, Algonquin Books, 1992.
Looking After Lily. Algonquin Books, Chapel Hill, 1994.
The Passion of Dellie O'Barr. Chapel Hill, Algonquin Books 1996.

* * *

Cindy Bonner's McDade Cycle—three novels set on the Texas frontier late in the nineteenth century—recreates the struggles of farmers, ranchers, and small town inhabitants while exploring the passions of individuals who challenge social expectations and limited opportunities. Her heroines grow to be tough, independent young women drawn to men living outside the ascribed bounds of propriety, as Bonner uses love stories, conventions of the Western, and historical detail to explore intriguing questions about corruption in individuals and communities. The title character of *Lily* and *Looking After Lily,* the first two books, is a hard-working, self-reliant farm girl who falls in love with a handsome young man from a family with a bad reputation. Lily's younger sister, Dellie O'Barr, the focus of the third book, becomes infatuated with a political radical of the Populist movement. Brought alive through Bonner's descriptive powers and wealth of historical detail, the tough landscape and strict social codes of the region prove equally formidable challenges for these characters.

Lily introduces the title character as a fifteen-year-old motherless girl with an endless string of chores and a domineering father. She becomes physically attracted and sympathetic to Marion Beatty, a young man from a disliked family of outlaws. When a violent crime occurs for which Beatty is blamed, he becomes a fugitive. Lily's father and the townspeople form a vigilante squad to bring him to justice. Although Beatty is not as violent and criminal as his reputation, he is not an innocent either, and Bonner's countering the strict code of the townspeople with such less clearly ordered things as human passion is among the conflicts enriching the novel. Right and wrong become blurred in the rapid and indiscriminate form of vigilante justice meted out by the seemingly most upstanding townspeople, for example, and Lily in her commitment to Beatty crosses beyond innocence, forsaking community values. The reader is left to ponder which of the crimes and sins are most dangerous.

Looking After Lily addresses another situation where bounds of propriety are obscured by the passions and disorder of life, when questions of right and wrong become blurred. In this work, Marion and Lily are married and expecting, but Marion is jailed for two years and pleads to his brother, Haywood, to help care for Lily. Haywood, just released from prison, had planned to resume his life of boozing, gambling, and chasing women, but a series of misfortunes and the difficult birth of the baby gradually makes him more responsible and attentive to Lily. As Haywood matures he falls in love with Lily, and another seemingly unassailable moral code is addressed as the two confront the situation.

Strict codes of conduct and the more wild, frontier spirit again clash in Bonner's third novel, *The Passion of Dellie O'Barr,* which centers on Lily's younger sister, Dellie, who has lived an extremely conventional life under her domineering father and reaped the reward of marrying a wealthy farmer/lawyer, Daniel O'Barr. His frequent absences and general dullness contribute to Dellie's increasing restlessness, and she becomes invigorated at a picnic for Confederate veterans when she meets Andy Ashland, who gives an impassioned speech for the Populist political cause. With the death of her father a few days later, Dellie experiences a sense of personal liberation, and she begins pursuing Andy, himself married (his wife has psychological problems and is hospitalized at an asylum) and father of two. A series of missed trysts and impulsive acts on Dellie's part—she sets fire to the store owned by a man Andy is in debt to—leads her to become a fugitive and then to return to McDade to face retribution for her actions.

The novel explores passion that passes understanding and larger individual, family, and community issues that influence individual actions. Each of the works of the McDade Cycle blur distinctions between right and wrong, good and evil, as settling the frontier proves as volatile as the metaphorical frontier of life choices faced by spirited individuals. Along with rich plot twists and descriptions of settings, Bonner interweaves historical information. The blend of fact into fiction is most apparent in *The Passion of Dellie O'Barr,* where the ideas and enthusiasm of the Populist movement—a vibrant, if short-lived, challenge to American political orthodoxy—are recreated, but all of the works have authentic details of buildings, landscape, dress, and equipment. As Dellie grows from submissive young lady to bold suffragette, from attentive wife to arsonist, her husband becomes equally energized into becoming a better companion, all of which reveal the complications of life even as people attempt to tame the frontier.

—Mel Koler

BOSWORTH, Sheila

Born: New Orleans, Louisiana, 1950. **Education:** Sophie Newcomb College, Tulane University, B.A. **Family:** Married; two daughters. **Career:** Homemaker and writer.

PUBLICATIONS

Novels

Almost Innocent. New York, Simon and Schuster, 1984.
Slow Poison. New York, Knopf, 1992.

Nonfiction

Contributor, *A World Unsuspected: Portraits of Southern Childhood,* edited by Alex Harris. Chapel Hill, University of North Carolina Press, 1987.

* * *

Sheila Bosworth's novels are as distinctive as the people and the place she writes about. Set in Bosworth's native New Orleans and in Covington, just across Lake Pontchartrain, *Almost Innocent* (1984; new edition published by Louisiana State University Press in 1996) and *Slow Poison* (1992) create a world so enchanting that it is all the more heartbreaking when things go dreadfully wrong.

As a Southerner, a Catholic, and a woman, Bosworth is fully conscious of the paradoxes in her highly-structured world. Though the Christian faith is supposedly based on love, at their Catholic schools her narrators learn to fear priests, nuns, and God. Heaven seems unattainable, Hell inevitable. In *Almost Innocent*, on the morning of her first communion, young Clay-Lee Calvert unthinkingly takes a sip of water, thus breaking her fast. Terrified of the nun her father calls "Sister Torquemada," Clay-Lee makes her communion, though she is convinced that thereby she will lose her immortal soul. In *Slow Poison*, Rory Cade thinks that she caused her grandmother's death by failing to make a novena for her. The cure for such guilt is not the confessional and a kindly priest, but a visit to the hired help—blacks in the kitchen, whose role in both novels seems to be as the voice of common sense.

The fact that they are Southern also helps to explain why Bosworth's characters feel and act as they do. In *Slow Poison*, an obtuse young man from New York realizes that New Orleans society is governed by a set of "rules" he does not know. Weeping, he complains to Eamon Cade that around Southern girls he feels that he is in the dark. Even though his guest's drunken soliloquy was prompted by the New Yorker's love for his own future bride, Eamon Cade listens politely until, finally realizing that he is speaking to his rival, the Yankee calls Eamon an "old mick bastard." That affront to honor results in the New Yorker's being thrown out of the house. A few years earlier, he would not have escaped so easily.

What happens to outsiders in a closed society is one of Bosworth's major themes. Given some family credentials and impeccable manners, even a Yankee may be accepted in time. However, when the daughter of a working-class immigrant marries into an aristocratic family, they are bound to display their displeasure. With the satirical wit that makes her books such a delight, Bosworth lists some of the ways the Cades reminded Timothy Cade's wife Patricia of her inferiority, buying her "cheap" Christmas presents, misspelling her name on place cards, somehow omitting her name from guest list for a luncheon. In all fairness, Bosworth also notes that after Timothy died, Patricia's relatives descended upon her with "suitcases in hand," and within seven years had picked the estate quite clean, just as the Cades undoubtedly predicted.

When one knows an individual's background, one has some idea of what to expect. In *Almost Innocent*, Judge Alexander warns his daughter Constance that though the Calverts are a "fine old family," they have "gone to seed," as proven by the fact that her suitor, Rand Calvert, is an artist and a liberal. When Constance elopes with him, the Judge pins his hopes for his little girl's future on good blood and Rand's being a Southern gentleman.

Because this male-dominated society holds to the notion that a lady is so delicate she must depend for protection on a gentleman, girls expect the same treatment from their husbands that they received from their fathers. If, like Constance, they were doted upon in childhood, they are certain to be disappointed as adults. In *Almost Innocent*, Constance is shocked when she has to take on a nighttime intruder herself because Clay is still asleep. When she realizes that Clay is not likely even to provide for her the kind of life she wants, Constance turns to an older, wealthy man, Clay's notorious uncle, wrecking the marriage and her life. It is no wonder that so many of Bosworth's men drink, drive fast cars,

gamble away their property, and commit suicide. Eamon Cade is typical; for all his talent and his charm, he is unable to take care of himself or of anyone else and finally sinks into hopeless alcoholism. Bosworth's women, too, are damaged by this myth of gender roles. Because they do not think themselves capable of facing their problems, they escape by plunging into feverish gaiety, taking drugs, or, like Jane Ann Cade, going crazy.

However, Bosworth does not think of her books as tragedies. Like the Old Fashioneds consumed in *Slow Poison*, her characters' memories are both bitter and sweet. Rory recalls mornings when her father telephoned friends to get help with her homework, afternoons when she came home from school to the heavenly scent of red beans, rice, and hot sausage. Later, there were steamy evenings in Johnny Killelea's Corvette convertible, which smelled of Dixie beer, "dirty rain," and cigarette smoke. In *Almost Innocent*, Clay-Lee describes a Mardi Gras open house that lasted twelve hours, with everyone in costume, a jazz quartet, servants circulating with champagne, and the Rex parade just below the balcony. Bosworth captures the spirit of this society as well in dialogue as she does in description, the seeming aimlessness of their conversations, the comic exaggerations, the self-parodies, the pervasive wit.

Bosworth's brilliance in handling particulars should not cause one to miss her profound concern with universal issues. Both of her novels begin in the present, then proceed into the past, where the protagonist-narrators hope to find some explanation of the tragedies they have observed and experienced. In the process, they consider society, sin, and, most important of all, the nature of God. The author is much too honest to suggest any easy answers. However, each of these truly remarkable novels concludes with the protagonists' having attained a degree of understanding and arriving at some hope of redemption.

—Rosemary M. Canfield Reisman

BOTTOMS, David

Born: Canton, Georgia, 11 September 1949. **Education:** Mercer University, 1968-71, B.A.; West Georgia College, 1971-73, M.A.; Florida State University, 1979-82, Ph.D. **Family:** Margaret Lynn Bensel, 2 February 1972 (divorced 1987); married Kelly Jean Beard, 3 July 1989. **Career:** High school teacher of English, Douglasville, Georgia, 1974-78; assistant professor of English, beginning 1982, associate professor, beginning 1987, Georgia State University; poet-in-residence, University of Montana, 1986. **Member:** International PEN, Poetry Society of America, Associated Writing Programs. **Awards:** Walt Whitman Award, Academy of American Poets, 1979, for *Shooting Rats at the Bibb County Dump*; Book of the Year in Poetry, Dixie Council of Authors and Journalists, 1983, for *In a U-Haul North of Damascus*, 1987 for *Under the Vulture-Tree*; Levinson Prize, *Poetry* magazine, 1985; fellowship in creative writing, National Endowment for the Arts, Ingram Merrill Foundation Award, and award in literature, American Academy and Institute of Arts and Letters, all 1988. **Agent:** Maria Carvainis Agency, 235 West End Ave., New York, New York 10023. **Address:** Department of English, Georgia State University, Atlanta, Georgia 30303.

PUBLICATIONS

Poetry Collections

Jamming with the Band at the VFW. Austell, Georgia, Burnt Hickory Press, 1978.
Shooting Rats at the Bibb County Dump. New York, W. Morrow, 1980.
In a U-Haul North of Damascus. New York, W. Morrow, 1983.
Under the Vulture-Tree. New York, Morrow, 1987.
Armored Hearts: Selected and New Poems. Port Townsend, Washington, Copper Canyon Press, 1995.

Novels

Any Cold Jordan. Atlanta, Peachtree Publishers, 1987.
Easter Weekend. Boston, Houghton Mifflin, 1990.

Other

Editor, with Dave Smith, *The Morrow Anthology of Younger American Poets.* New York, Quill, 1985.

*   *   *

In 1979 Robert Penn Warren discovered a young poet named David Bottoms and selected his manuscript, *Shooting Rats at the Bibb County Dump*, for the Academy of American Poets' Walt Whitman Award. Warren wrote: "David Bottoms is a strong poet, and much of his strength emerges from the fact that he is temperamentally a realist. In his vision the actual world is not transformed but illuminated." Critics continue to find in his narrative poems those figurative overtones that tough archetypal patters and uncover profound meaning. He writes his own distinctive tone, about which James Dickey commented: "One cannot read him without being nerve-touched by his sardonic yet compassionate countryman's voice." Critic Ron Rash finds his poems both accessible and complex, obvious and mysterious, and comments that this "difficult fusion" is the "defining characteristic" of his work. Until 1986, when he spent a year as poet-in-residence at the University of Montana, Bottoms' poems were set almost exclusively in the South.

Set in venues far from the poetic mainstream—carnivals, cockfights, beer joints, vandalized graveyards—*Shooting Rats at the Bibb County Dump* (1980) is made up of poems dealing with death, religion, and discoveries of human links to animals and the primordial. In the title poem, carloads of drunken teenagers ply their bizarre blood sport of shooting rats, transfixed by headlights, at the city dump. The poem ends with lines typical of this poet's use of irony and his ability to superimpose meaning,

> It's the light they believe kills.
> We drink and load again, let them crawl
> for all they're worth into the darkness we're headed for.

His wide range of characters includes honky-tonk angels, gang-raping farmers, faith healers, truck drivers, and country musicians.

Bottoms continues to refine and develop such themes as the relationship between beauty and danger, as well as internalized conflicts between human and animal nature, in his volume, *In a U-Haul North of Damascus* (1983); however, he also begins to focus more on human relationships, the nature of love and suffering, and the redemptive powers of love. In the title poem, a husband, unable to cope with his wife's miscarriage, packs his few possessions in a U-Haul and drives toward Florida. At dawn he is stricken with guilt, asking, "Could I just be another sinner who needs to be blinded / before I can see?" With precise language, he transmutes sights and sounds into memorable metaphors: the shadow of bats "zipping across the grass like black snakes," "the sea oats wash back and forth in a gold froth," and the frogs' "bass-throb belching in the starless night." Other poems explore mysteries in nature, many involving water. The rambunctious *carpe diem* of the first volume continues as drunken hunters vandalize a church and burn hymnals for warmth, suburban neighbors practice throwing knives at plywood animal targets, and good old buddies drink beer and engage in a duel with rifles.

In *Under the Vulture Tree* (1987) Bottoms' art reaches more deeply personal levels as he pays tribute to his father and lays bare the subtle estrangements of husband and wife. He delineates the desperation of a poet trapped in suburban sameness, retreating into nature, searching for "something small and changing." The rat-shooter reappears as risk-taking teenager and as a boy who burglarizes a school to steal a desk with his father's initials and speeds to a tryst with a rural prostitute. Bottoms' recurring interest in country music—dating from the chapbook *Jamming with the Band at the VFW* (1978)—enlivens several poems. The title poem is extraordinary for its elevation of a powerful image—hundreds of vultures perched on a dead oak tree—to the level of religious experience. The poet calls the vultures "dwarfed transfiguring angels, / who flock to the side of the poisoned fox, the mud turtle / crushed on the shoulder of the road, who pray over the leaf-graves of the anonymous lost, / with mercy enough to consume us all and give us wings."

His latest volume, *Armored Hearts* (1995) includes poems selected from previous collections as well as important new poems that are somewhat darker in tone, emotionally cooler, and more overtly religious than the earlier poems. Many of these are set in Montana, where nature is redder in tooth and claw than on Southern fishing lakes, and where the epiphanies from the animal world to the human are eerily mysterious. There is also a new level of immediate revelation. Bottoms once told a reviewer: "Ironically, the seeds of creativity are mixed into what Jung calls the 'slime from the depth,' that psychic slime, the ugliest and most animalistic aspect of our personality." In "Altoona Evening," the poet, despondent after the ending of his first marriage and the seeming demise of his literary career as his books go out of print, hears a message from the crickets and tree frogs as he fishes:

> lay it down, they say, your ambition,
> which is only anger,
> which sated could bring you to no better place.

Among a group of fine religious poems, "Free Grace at Rose Hill" and "Hard Easter, Northwest Montana" may prove to be the most lasting and profoundly moving.

Although his poetry has received more critical acclaim, Bottoms also authored two novels, *Any Cold Jordan* (1987) and *Eas-*

ter Weekend (1990). In the first, Billy Parker, the best flat-pick guitarist in Tallahassee, Florida, leads an idyllic life, fishing and playing his music. But his marriage turns sour, and Jack Giddens, a Vietnam veteran, turns up to lead him into a dangerous interception of drug money on a Florida backroad. Bottoms brings the atmosphere of the countryside, the music, and the fishing boat vividly to life.

In *Easter Weekend,* Carl leads his brother Connie, a gullible ex-boxer, into a plot to kidnap a rich college boy. When some local mobsters move in, headed by a maniacal murderer named Tommy, the suspenseful plot moves to a showdown in a cemetery. This novel has been compared to the works of James M. Cain, author of several *film noir* classics.

Critic Vernon Shetley finds that Bottoms' poems "inhabit two contiguous landscapes, one the small-town and rural South, the other a realm of elemental nature often found lurking just beyond the zone of human habitation."

—Benjamin Griffith

BOWERS, Edgar

Born: Rome, Georgia, 2 March 1924. **Education:** University of North Carolina, Chapel Hill, B.A. 1947; Stanford University, California, M.A. 1949, Ph.D. 1953. **Military Service:** U.S. Army, 1943-46. **Career:** Instructor, Duke University, Durham, North Carolina, 1952-55; assistant professor, Harpur College, Binghamton, New York, 1955-58; Since 1958 member of the English department, and currently professor of English, University of California, Santa Barbara. **Awards:** Fulbright fellowship, 1950; Swallow Press New Poetry Series award, 1955, for *The Form of Loss*; Guggenheim fellowship, 1958, 1969; *Sewanee Review* fellowship; Edward F. Jones Foundation fellowship; Poetry Silver Medal, Commonwealth Club of California, 1973; University of Carolina Institute of Creative Arts fellowship Merrill award, 1974; Brandeis University Creative Arts Medal, 1978; Bollingen Prize, 1989, and Harriet Monroe prize, *Poetry*, 1989, both for *For Louis Pasteur*.

Publications

Poetry

The Form of Loss. Denver, Shallow, 1956.
Five American Poets, with others, edited by Ted Hughes and Thom Gunn. London, Faber, 1963.
The Astronomers. Denver, Swallow, 1965.
Living Together: New and Selected Poems. Boston, Godine, 1973.
Thirteen Views of Santa Barbara. Woodside, California, Occasional Works, 1987.
Walking the Line. Florence, Kentucky, R.L. Barth, 1988.
Chaco Canyon. Los Angels, Symposium Press, 1988.
For Louis Pasteur. Princeton, New Jersey, Princeton University Press, 1988.
How We Came from Paris to Blois. El Cerrito, California, Jacaranda, 1990.
Collected Poems. New York, Knopf, 1997.

*

Bibliography: *The Published Works of Edgar Bowers, 1948-1988* edited by Jeffrey Akard and Joshua Odell, Florence, Kentucky, R.L. Barth, 1988.

Critical Studies: *Forms of Discovery* by Yvor Winters, Denver, Swallow, 1967; *Alone with America* by Richard Howard, New York, Atheneum, 1969, revised edition, Atheneum, 1980; "The Theme of Loss in the Earlier Poems of Catherine Davis and Edgar Bowers," in *Southern Review*, Summer 1973, and "Contexts for 'Being,' 'Divinity,' and 'Self' in Valéry and Edgar Bowers," in *Southern Review,* Winter 1977, both by Helen A. Trimpi.

*   *   *

· Edgar Bowers has neither sought publicity nor achieved notoriety. He has not written in the modish confessional manner of some of his contemporaries. He has simply written some of the great poems of the latter half of the twentieth century. Bowers's work deserves a slow and careful reading; his poems are worth taking the time to understand.

Bowers's powerful treatment of themes of deception and honesty, of shadow and lucidity, of loss and form can be found in his earliest poems; but his depth and range have grown—with no diminution of his prosodic mastery. A chief characteristic of his poems, as Yvor Winters pointed out, is that "sensory perception and its significance are simultaneous." This is especially true of "Autumn Shade," a sequence of ten poems that ends the 1965 collection *The Astronomers.* The sequence begins with a sense of destiny that amounts almost to predestination, a sense that appears in other poems by Bowers,

> Now, toward his destined passion there, the strong,
> Vivid young man, reluctant, may return
> From suffering in his own experience
> To lie down in the darkness.

The young man wakes, he works, he sleeps again; but the first poem ends with a chilling image, "The snake / Does as it must, and sinks into the cold." In another poem the young man lights a fire as the night grows cold:

> Gently
> A dead soprano sings Mozart and Bach.
> I drink bourbon, then go to bed, and sleep
> In the Promethean heat of summer's essence.

This is pentameter so subtle in modulation that the casual reader may miss a good deal of its technical virtuosity. So much is packed into the subdued, suggestive style that one may overlook the complexity of life and of emotional response to sensations being presented. The young man is aware that the things "I have desired / Evade me, and the lucid majesty / That warmed the dull barbarian to life. / So I lie here, left with self-consciousness." Within the sequence, the young man's books, his old neighbor who drives through rain and snow, the recollection of Hercules and of his own father, and his view out the window of a Cherokee trail ("I see it, when I look up from the page") all indicate the reality of the external world. The density of reference suggests the presence of the past and the complexity of perception. The young man is trying in this dark night, during these seasons of the soul, to understand his own past and thus his present. His old neighbor's driving in snow prompts him to remember his own driving in war,

> Was this our wisdom, simply, in a chance
> In danger, to be mastered by a task,
> Like groping round a chair, through a door, to bed?

Not many poets in the language could have written those lines. The verbal precision evokes deep resonance of response. Bowers's firm control and stylistic brilliance permit him a potentially dangerous ending for the sequence: it would be trite after this night of darkness and cold to have the sunlight transform the room, so even shadows become "substantial light." But like all masters, Bowers takes the potentially trite and makes it hugely moving. The man of the sequence survives: "I stay / Almost as I have been, intact, aware, / Alive, though proud and cautious, even afraid." This ending is indicative of one of Bowers's strengths as a man and as a poet: his refusal to be deceived, his almost desperate honesty.

The dramatic monologue "The Prince" is a major examination of what has been termed "German war guilt"; in it, familial relations serve as the vehicle for a poetic rendering of moral relations:

> My son, who was the heir
> To every hope and trust, grew out of caring
> Into the form of loss as I had done,
> And then betrayed me who betrayed him first.

Likewise, in another fine poem, "From J. Haydn to Constanze Mozart (1791)," a verse letter expressing grief becomes a meditation on the rare fusion of mind and body, sense and reason, that Mozart's music embodies: "Aslant at his clavier, with careful ease, / To bring one last enigma to the norm,/Intelligence perfecting the mute keys." These poems, along with "Amor vincit omnia" (the greatest poem on the theme of the Magi since Yeats's), "The Mountain Cemetery," and "The Astronomers of Mont Blanc" are part of the enduring body of work that distinguishes Bowers's books. In Bowers we have a poet at once exact and exciting in his use of language. The word always fits the sense, and the sense never exceeds what language is capable of doing, "Whereof we cannot speak, thereof we must be silent."

—James Korges

BRADLEY, John Ed

Born: Opelousas, Louisiana, 12 August 1958. **Education:** Louisiana State University, B.A. 1980. **Career:** Staff writer, 1983-87, contributing writer, 1988-89, *Washington Post;* contributing editor, *Esquire,* since 1991; contributing writer, *Sports Illustrated,* 1993. **Agent:** Esther Newberg, International Creative Management, 40 West 57th St., New York, New York 10019.

PUBLICATIONS

Novels

Tupelo Nights. New York, Atlantic Monthly Press, 1988.
The Best There Ever Was. New York, Atlantic Monthly Press, 1990.
Love and Obits. New York, Holt, 1992.
Smoke. New York, Holt, 1994.

*   *   *

John Ed Bradley's first novel established his niche in the tradition of southern Gothic writers. Emphasis on the grotesque, the macabre, and the excessive pull of environment is predominant. Much of the setting in *Tupelo Nights* features the local cemetery, where the hero's best friend is a gravedigger and where he meets Emma Groves, the love of his life. Emma goes every night to pray at the grave of her infant son. The cemetery motif is constant. John Girlie, the novel's antihero, works the graveyard shift at a pipeline company, and images of death haunt the book.

Girlie had been an all-America football player at Louisiana State University and had a promising offer to play professional football. Under his domineering mother's influence, however, he returns to his hometown and cannot until late in the novel extricate himself from his oedipal situation. At times Bradley's plot flirts with melodrama, but this is more than overcome by his keen gift for dialogue and vivid descriptions that are often poetically lyrical. Bradley captures the atmosphere of time and place with persuasive authenticity, totally immersing the reader in the stifling environment and grimness of Girlie's small Louisiana town.

Harold Gravely, the main figure in *The Best There Ever Was,* is a college football coach in his sixties. Almost thirty years before his team won the national championship. Since then, Gravely's teams have had mostly losing seasons, and the students, alumni, and college officials want him to resign. Learning that he has lung cancer, Gravely decides to forego treatment in the hope that the situation generated by his condition will force the college administration to renew his contract so that he can coach one final year.

The figure of Coach Gravely is drawn with believable and persuasive strokes perfectly conveying his loud, egotistical, and overbearing temperament. As the Old Man, a term he favors, he is a memorable if unpleasant character. Bradley also uses comedy to cleverly satirize the coach and emphasize the grotesque aspects of the situation.

Joseph Burke, in *Love and Obits,* is a newspaper reporter who has been demoted to writing obituaries. Divorced, Burke lives with his wheelchair-bound father. Although he and his father are on good terms, Joseph is presented as one of the melancholy, lonely men who walk about the city at night looking for something they never had or for something they have lost and will never find again. Burke's father, Woody, takes on more cheerfulness and hope when he falls in love with his day care nurse; Burke himself becomes more positive when he attracts the attention of widow Laura Vannoy. Burke had written the obituary article about her prominent husband, so even love is entwined with death. At the book's end, Woody, in an epiphany of love, performs a Christ-like action of feeding his fisherman's catch to the poor.

Smoke is both a continuation of previous characteristics of Bradley's work and a worrisome development, which was present on occasion in the earlier books. Smoke is a small town in Louisiana where Jay Carnihan's goal is to kidnap Monster Mart's founder, billionaire Rayford Holly, and require him to apologize for forcing so many downtown stores in America out of business.

Kidnapped on one of his nationwide inspection trips, Holly proves to be an exceedingly lovable, down-to-earth individual who even pitches in as a short order cook at the lunch counter of Carnihan's small store. Again, Bradley demonstrates his gifted talent for recording dialogue and lively characterization, but the narrative becomes too far-fetched, and melodrama and sentimentality predominate. Even the theme of love over death, which was so effectively presented in *Love and Obits*, becomes mawkish and cloying in *Smoke*. Bradley is a considerable talent in handling dialogue and characterization, but he must temper plot excesses and a tendency to overelaborate a narrative.

—Paul A. Doyle

BROOKS, Cleanth

Born: Murray, Kentucky, 16 October 1906. **Education:** Vanderbilt University, B.A. 1928; Tulane University, M.A. 1929; Oxford University, Rhodes Scholar, 1929-32, B.A. (with honors) 1931, B.Litt. 1932. **Family:** Married Edith Amy Blanchard, 12 September 1934 (died 1 October 1986). **Career:** Lecturer, 1932-47, and visiting professor, 1970 and 1974, Louisiana State University; professor of English, 1947-60, Gray Professor of Rhetoric, 1960-75, professor emeritus, beginning 1975, Yale University; visiting professor of English, University of Texas, summer, 1941, University of Michigan, summer, 1942, University of Chicago, 1945-46, Kenyon School of English, summer, 1948 (fellow, beginning 1948), University of Southern California, summer, 1953, Breadloaf School of English, summer, 1963, University of South Carolina, 1975, Tulane University, 1976, University of North Carolina, 1977 and 1979, and University of Tennessee, 1978 and 1980; research professor with Bostick Foundation, 1975; Lamar Lecturer, 1984, Jefferson Lecturer, 1985; co-managing editor, *Southern Review*, 1932-41, co-editor, 1941-42; member of advisory committee for Boswell Papers, beginning 1950; Library of Congress, fellow, 1953-63, member of council of scholars, 1984-87; cultural attache, American Embassy, London, England, 1964-66; senior fellow, National Humanities Center, 1980-81. **Awards:** Guggenheim fellowship, 1953 and 1960; senior fellowship, National Endowment for the Humanities, 1975; Explicator Award, for *William Faulkner: Toward Yoknapatawpha and Beyond*; honorary B.A., 1931, and B.Litt., 1932 from Oxford University; D.Litt. from Upsala College, 1963, University of Kentucky, 1963, University of Exeter, 1966, Washington and Lee University, 1968, Tulane University, 1969, University of the South, 1975, Newberry College, 1979, and Indiana State University, 1992; L.H.D. from University of St. Louis, 1968, Centenary College, 1972, Oglethorpe University, 1976, St. Peter's College, 1978, Lehigh University, 1980, Millsaps College, 1983, University of New Haven, 1984, University of South Carolina, 1984, and Adelphi University, 1992. **Died:** New Haven, Connecticut, 10 May 1994.

PUBLICATIONS

Critical Theory

Understanding Poetry, with Robert Penn Warren. New York, Holt, 1938; third edition, 1961, contains a transcript of tape recording, *Conversations on the Craft of Poetry: Cleanth Brooks and Robert Penn Warren, with Robert Frost, John Crowe Ransom, Robert Lowell, and Theodore Roethke.*

Understanding Fiction, with Robert Penn Warren. New York, Appleton-Century-Crofts, 1943; published as *The Scope of Fiction*, Appleton-Century-Crofts, 1960.
Modern Rhetoric, with Robert Penn Warren. New York, Harcourt, 1949.
An Approach to Literature: A Collection of Prose and Verse with Analyses and Discussions, with John Thibaut Purser and Robert Penn Warren. New York, Appleton-Century-Crofts, 1964.

Critical Studies

Modern Poetry and the Tradition. Chapel Hill, University of North Carolina Press, 1939.
The Hidden God: Studies in Hemingway, Faulkner, Yeats, Eliot and Warren. New Haven, Yale University Press, 1963.
William Faulkner: The Yoknapatawpha Country. Baton Rouge, Louisiana State University Press, 1963.
Milton: Poems, the 1645 Edition, with Essays in Analysis by Cleanth Brooks and John Edward Hardy. New York, Gordian Press, 1968.
William Faulkner: Toward Yoknapatawpha and Beyond. New Haven, Yale University Press, 1963.
William Faulkner: First Encounters. New Haven, Yale University Press, 1983.
On the Prejudices, Predilections, and Firm Beliefs of William Faulkner: Essays. Baton Rouge, Louisiana State University Press, 1987.
Community, Religion, and Literature: Essays. Columbia, University of Missouri Press, 1995.

Editor

The Percy Letters, with David Nichol Smith. Baton Rouge, Louisiana State University Press, 1944.
Understanding Drama: Twelve Plays, with Robert B. Heilman. New York, H. Holt, 1945.
The Well Wrought Urn. New York, Reynal & Hitchcock, 1947.
An Anthology of Stories from the "Southern Review," with Robert Penn Warren. Baton Rouge, Louisiana State University Press, 1953.
Tragic Themes in Western Literature: Seven Essays. New Haven, Yale University Press, 1955.
An Approach to Literature, with John Thibaut Purser and Robert Penn Warren. Englewood Cliffs, New Jersey, Prentice-Hall, 1975.

Other

The Relation of the Alabama-Georgia Dialect to the Provincial Dialects of Great Britain. Baton Rouge, Louisiana State University Press, 1935.
Fundamentals of Good Writing, with Robert Penn Warren. New York, Harcourt, 1950.
Literary Criticism: A Short History, with William K. Wimsatt. New York, Knopf, 1957.
A Shaping Joy: Studies in the Writer's Craft. New York, Harcourt, 1972.
American Literature: The Makers and the Making, compilee with R. W. B. Lewis and Robert Penn Warren. New York, St. Martin's Press, 1973.
The Language of the American South. Athens, University of Georgia Press, 1985.

Historical Evidence and the Reading of Seventeenth-Century Poetry. Columbia, University of Missouri Press, 1991.

Contributor, *Eudora Welty: A Form of Thanks,* edited by Louis D. Dollarhide and Ann J. Abadie. Jackson, University Press of Mississippi, 1979.

Correspondence

Cleanth Brooks and Robert Penn Warren: A Literary Correspondence edited by James A. Grimshaw, Jr. Columbia, University of Missouri Press, 1998.
Cleanth Brooks and Allen Tate: Collected Letters, 1933-1976 edited by Alphonse Vinh. Columbia, University of Missouri Press, 1998.

*

Manuscript Collections: Brooks's papers are collected at the University of Kentucky; Beinecke Rare Book and Manuscript Library, Yale University; Newberry Library, Chicago; and Joint University Libraries at the University of Tennessee.

Bibliography: *Cleanth Brooks: An Annotated Bibliography* by John Michael Walsh, New York, Garland Publishers, 1990.

Critical Studies: "The Critical Monism of Cleanth Brooks" by R. S. Crane, *Critics and Criticism: Ancient and Modern* edited by Crane, et al., Chicago, University of Chicago Press, 1952; *The Southern Critics: An Introduction to the Criticism of John Crowe Ransom, Allen Tate, Donald Davidson, Robert Penn Warren, Cleanth Brooks, and Andrew Lytle* by Louise Cowan, Irving, University of Dallas Press, 1971; *The Possibilities of Order: Cleanth Brooks and His Work* edited by Lewis P. Simpson, Baton Rouge, Louisiana State University Press, 1976; *Cleanth Brooks at the United States Air Force Academy, April 11-12, 1978* edited by James A. Grimshaw, Jr., Colorado Springs, Department of English, U.S. Air Force Academy, 1980; *Cleanth Brooks, An Assessment* by D. A. Shankar, Bangalore, IBH Prakashana, 1981; *American Literature and the Academy: The Roots, Growth, and Maturity of a Profession* by Kermit Vanderbilt, Philadelphia, University of Pennsylvania Press, 1986; *Cleanth Brooks Came to Millsaps: A Remembrance* by Frances Broeckman, Jackson, Mississippi, F. Broeckman, 1996; *Cleanth Brooks and the Rise of Modern Criticism* by Mark Royden Winchell, Charlottesville, University Press of Virginia, 1996.

*   *   *

At the time of his death in 1994, Cleanth Brooks was considered to have had a greater influence than any other critic on the ways that Americans relate to literature. Although Brooks was one of the most highly regarded scholars of William Faulkner, he is best known for his advocacy of the "New Criticism," a critical theory that pays special attention to the internal tensions and ironies in works of literature in order to allow them to be examined as works of art apart from historical, religious, and personal circumstances. The New Criticism's emphasis on judging literature by esthetic qualities, rather than the older categories of period, genre, and author, as well as its method of close reading, have characterized most classroom literary study for over fifty years.

This has remained true despite much opposition, early and late, most prominently (and loudly) accusations of blindness to historic and social context. As Claude Rawson, a colleague of Brooks's, explains, the New Criticism "did not, contrary to the views of some contemporaries and some latter-day ideologues, exclude history and biography from the study of literature, though it sought to establish some demarcations in critical practice. These demarcations, thoughtfully and delicately conceived, required a certain discipline of intellect as well as a feeling for words—commodities not always in large supply in academic departments of literature."

Brooks was born to a Methodist clergyman in rural Kentucky and was educated first at the McTyeire School, a small academy with a rigorous classical curriculum. Students there studied three years of Greek and four of Latin, and, as Brooks recalled: "they were thoroughly taught. They were not taught primarily in what I would call a literary way, but we did have to give close attention to the language: what it said, how it said it, the means by which it said it. I'm sure that was all to the good for me."

After his graduation from McTyeire School, Brooks entered Vanderbilt University in 1924, when it was the home of the Fugitives, a literary movement that included such eminent writers as John Crowe Ransom, Donald Davidson, Allan Tate, and Robert Penn Warren. Their discussions of modern literature, very different from the prevailing classroom mode, which generally stressed studying literary works from such perspectives as "the author's life," helped to build the theoretical foundations of the New Criticism. While Brooks had planned to be a lawyer, his exposure to the Fugitives led him to make a career of literary study. He said, "The thing that I got most out of Vanderbilt was to discover suddenly that literature was not a dead thing to be looked at through the glass of a museum case, but was very much alive."

In 1928 Brooks was graduated from Vanderbilt, and he continued his education at Tulane University. On receiving his M.A. in 1929, he was nominated for a Rhodes Scholarship, and studied at Exeter College, Oxford, earning a second B.A. with honors and then a graduate degree in 1932. In that same year, after returning to the United States, he accepted a position at Louisiana State University, where he was once again working with Robert Penn Warren. Their professional collaboration lasted until Warren's death nearly sixty years later. Both Brooks and Warren eventually made their way to Yale, where both served for many years. Among their early achievements was the founding of the *Southern Review* in 1939. It remains one of the most highly regarded critical journals in the world.

It was his experience in the classroom, however, that led to Brooks's most influential project. Along with Warren, he was greatly disappointed in the textbooks of his day, and so the two of them created their own, editing, over the succeeding years, *An Approach to Literature: A Collection of Prose and Verse with Analyses and Discussions, Understanding Poetry,* and *Understanding Fiction.* Their approach was quite novel; since they felt that the central problem of teaching literature was getting students to read literary works closely, they included not only questions to help the student to analyze works, but even model analyses, a number of which are still considered classics.

Brooks's textbooks were also very controversial, inspiring the familiar accusation that Brooks and Warren ignored matters of biographical and cultural history. In his defense, Brooks argued that he was merely advocating closer attention to the text, so that common readers could appreciate literature. As he observed near the end of his life, "I have always thought that the great use of the critic was to be a humble servant of the Muses, to help open up poems and novels and dramas to the reader . . . . I think that's an important job."

This same concern for making literature accessible carried over into his books on Faulkner, leading prominent critic Jonathan Yardley to describe his *William Faulkner: First Encounters* (1983) as "the key to the kingdom" for the general and student audience. Yardley opined that while *First Encounters* "can be read with profit by the scholar . . . the reader who will value it most is the daunted but determined one who wants to gain admission to one of the great bodies of work in the English language." Brooks' first study of Faulkner, *William Faulkner: The Yoknapatawpha Country*, considers the author as a product of the South and carefully examines the major themes and characters of the Yoknapatawpha novels. Also highly regarded is 1963's *William Faulkner: Toward Yoknapatawpha and Beyond*, which takes a longer view of Faulkner's artistic development and further examines the novels not set in Yoknapatawpha. These books, like *First Encounters*, are considered essential for the beginning student of Faulkner.

—Jason Mitchell

BROWN, Dee

Born: Dee Alexander Brown in Alberta, Louisiana, 28 February 1908. **Education:** Arkansas State Teachers College (now University of Central Arkansas); George Washington University, B.L.S. 1937; University of Illinois, M.S. 1952. **Military Service:** U.S. Army, 1942-45. **Family:** Married Sara Baird Stroud, 1934; two children. **Career:** Library assistant, U.S. Department of Agriculture, Washington, D.C., 1934-39; librarian, Beltsville Research Center, Beltsville, Maryland,1940-42; technical librarian, U.S. War Department, Aberdeen Proving Ground, Aberdeen, Maryland, 1945-48; librarian of agriculture, University of Illinois at Urbana-Champaign, 1948-72, professor of library science, 1962-75. **Awards:** Clarence Day Award, American Library Association, 1971, for *The Year of the Century: 1876*; Christopher Award, 1971; Buffalo Award, New York Westerners, 1971, for *Bury My Heart at Wounded Knee*; named Illinoisan of the Year by Illinois News Broadcasters Association, 1972; Best Western for Young People Award, Western Writers of America, 1981, for *Hear That Lonesome Whistle Blow: Railroads in the West*; Saddleman Award, Western Writers of America, 1984. **Member:** Authors Guild, Western Writers of America, Society of American Historians.

PUBLICATIONS

Novels

Wave High the Banner. Macrae Smith, 1942.
Yellowhorse. New York, Houghton, 1956.
Cavalry Scout. New York, Permabooks, 1958.

They Went Thataway. New York, Putnam, 1960; as *Pardon My Pandemonium,* August House, 1984.
The Girl from Fort Wicked. New York, Doubleday, 1964.
Creek Mary's Blood. New York, Holt, 1980.
Killdeer Mountain. New York, Holt, 1983.
Conspiracy of Knaves. New York, Holt, 1986.

Nonfiction

Fighting Indians of the West, with Martin F. Schmitt. New York, C. Scribner's Sons, 1948.
Trail Driving Days, with Schmitt. New York, Scribner, 1952.
Grierson's Raid. Urbana, University of Illinois Press, 1954.
The Settlers' West, with Schmitt. New York, Scribner, 1955.
The Gentle Tamers: Women of the Old Wild West. New York, Putnam, 1958.
The Bold Cavaliers: Morgan's Second Kentucky Cavalry Raiders. New York, Lippincott, 1959.
Fort Phil Kearny: An American Saga. New York, Putnam, 1962; as *The Fetterman Massacre,* Barrie & Jenkins, 1972.
The Galvanized Yankees. Urbana, University of Illinois Press, 1963.
The Year of the Century: 1876. New York, Scribner, 1966.
Action at Beecher Island. New York, Doubleday, 1967.
Bury My Heart at Wounded Knee: An Indian History of the American West. New York, Holt, 1970.
Andrew Jackson and the Battle of New Orleans. New York, Putnam, 1972.
Tales of the Warrior Ants. New York, Putnam, 1973.
The Westerners. New York, Holt, 1974.
Hear That Lonesome Whistle Blow: Railroads in the West. New York, Holt, 1977.
American Spa: Hot Springs, Arkansas. Little Rock, Rose Publishing, 1982.
Wondrous Times on the Frontier. Little Rock, August House, 1991.
When the Century Was Young: A Writer's Notebook. Little Rock, August House, 1993.
The American West. New York, Scribner, 1994.

Children's Books

Showdown at Little Big Horn. New York, Putnam, 1964.
Teepee Tales of the American Indians. New York, Holt, 1979; as *Dee Brown's Folktales of the Native American, Retold for Our Times,* illustrated by Louis Mofsie, Owl Books, 1993.

Other

Images of the Old West, paintings of Mort Künstler, text of Dee Brown. New York, Park Lane Press, 1996.
Dee Brown's Civil War Anthology, edited by Stan Banash. Santa Fe, Clear Light Publishers, 1998.

*

Sound Recordings: *Dee Brown,* Kansas City, New Letters, 1986.

Critical Studies: *Dee Brown* by Lyman B. Hagen, Boise, Idaho, Boise State University, 1990.

*   *   *

Dee Brown's interest in Native American history stems from, his childhood in rural Arkansas, where contact with the large local Indian population forced him to question his conventional notions about the history of the American West. While pursuing a lifelong career as a librarian for the U.S. government and the University of Illinois, Brown began writing western novels in the 1940s and produced his first nonfictional history in the mid-1950s. All of his works reflect Brown's painstaking research and skillful use of source material, highly readable and sometimes gripping prose, and scholarly thoroughness that is nevertheless addressed to the popular reader.

His first novel, *Wave High the Banner* (1942), dramatized the life of American pioneer Davy Crockett in a tale that *Saturday Review* found unimaginatively "straightforward" but the *New York Times* lauded as "exceptionally shrewd and just." Brown followed it with several traditional westerns, from *Yellowhorse* (1956) and *Cavalry Scout* (1958) to *The Girl from Fort Wicked* (1964). In his more recent western, *Creek Mary's Blood* (1980), Brown chronicles the life of a Creek Indian woman and her two sons as they endure the cruel "manifest destiny" of westward-pushing American settlers. In *Killdeer Mountain* (1983), Brown narrated the tale of 19th-century newspaperman Sam Morrison's efforts to learn the ambiguous truth about a U.S. Army major soon to have a fort named after him. *Library Journal* praised the novel as "an intriguing and exciting tale," and *Newsweek* described it as "compelling."

Brown's novel *Conspiracy of Knaves* (1986) is a fictionalized account of the so-called Northwest Conspiracy by Confederate-sympathizing Copperheads during the Civil War; in that conspiracy, a "second Confederacy" of midwestern sympathizers was to be established in Indiana, Illinois, and Ohio. The reviewer for the *New York Times* criticized Brown for narrating the story from the point of view of a purely mercenary double agent and for casting the Copperheads in a wholly negative light; the *Chicago Tribune,* however, described *Conspiracy* as an "energetic, engaging narrative" with a "powerfully lifelike" denouement.

Despite his many novels, Brown's literary reputation is based primarily on his nonfiction and in particular on *Bury My Heart at Wounded Knee,* his highly regarded study of the destruction of Native American civilization in the American West between 1860 and 1890. Relying on original documents from Indian treaty councils and the clear-eyed reminiscences of such Indian leaders as Chief Joseph and Geronimo, Brown painted a grim portrait of the U.S. government's war to drive the Indians from their lands. Critical reception was enthusiastic: *Atlantic* described *Bury My Heart* as "painfully eloquent"; *Best Sellers* called it "an angry book [that] deserves the attention of Americans"; the *New York Times* praised it as "compelling" and "carefully documented"; and the *New Statesman* found it "startling" and "tragic."

Although *Bury My Heart* was Brown's only true bestseller, he is the author of no less than 16 other historical works. In his early histories he explored such subjects as cattle-driving in the American West of the late 1800s (*Trail Driving Days,* 1952); a successful Union cavalry campaign of the Civil War (*Grierson's Raid,* 1954); a history of women's role in the "Wild West" (*The Gentle Tamers,* 1958); a narrative of a highly effective Kentucky cavalry troop during the Civil War (*The Bold Cavaliers,* 1959); a history of the Fetterman Massacre of 1866 in which 80 U.S. soldiers were killed by Native Americans in Wyoming (*Fort Phil*

Kearny, 1962); and an account of the Confederate prisoners of war who were enlisted into the Union army to fight Indians on the frontier (*The Galvanized Yankees,* 1963).

Brown's later nonfictional work has included a chronicle of America's first centennial (*The Year of the Century: 1876,* 1966); an introductory popular history of the American West (*The Westerners,* 1974); a narrative account of transcontinental railroad construction before 1900 (*Hear That Lonesome Whistle Blow,* 1977); a collection of humorous frontier anecdotes that dispel myths about the Old West (*Wondrous Times on the Frontier,* 1991); and a general history of the American frontier between 1838 and 1914 (*The American West,* 1994).

In addition to his many novels and histories, Brown has written numerous historical articles, three children's books (including *Showdown at Little Big Horn,* 1964, and *Teepee Tales of the American Indians,* 1979), and an autobiographical work (*When the Century Was Young,* 1993). He will in all likelihood be remembered primarily as the author of *Bury My Heart at Wounded Knee,* a work that compellingly conveyed the Indians' contemporary perception of their culture's eradication.

—Paul S. Bodine

BROWN, Larry

Born: Oxford, Mississippi, 9 July 1951. **Education:** Attended University of Mississippi, 1982. **Military Service:** U.S. Marine Corps, 1970-72. **Family:** Married Mary Annie Coleman (a secretary), August 17, 1974; two sons, one daughter. **Career:** Firefighter, Oxford Fire Department, Oxford, Mississippi, 1973-90, captain, 1986-90; full-time writer, since 1990. **Awards:** Award for Literature, Mississippi Institute of Arts and Letters, 1990, for *Facing the Music;* Southern Book Critic's Circle Award for fiction, 1992.

PUBLICATIONS

Short Story Collections

Facing the Music. Chapel Hill, Algonquin Books, 1988.
Big Bad Love. Chapel Hill, Algonquin Books, 1990.

Novels

Dirty Work. Chapel Hill, Algonquin Books, 1989.
Joe. Chapel Hill, Algonquin Books, 1991.
Father and Son. Chapel Hill, Algonquin Books, 1996.

Nonfiction

On Fire. Chapel Hill, Algonquin Books, 1994.

*

Works Adapted for Other Media: *Dirty Work,* with Richard Corley, for stage, 1994.

*   *   *

Larry Brown is a soft-spoken, laid-back writer living in Yocona, Mississippi, whose works portray the harshness of life in a rural South where people struggle daily to survive. Critics acclaim his writings as raw, rough, violent; a native good old boy simply says, after reading Brown's novel *Joe,* "he's been there." Brown writes with an authentic voice of beer-drinking, pick-up truck-driving county workers, pulpwooders, and mechanics; of roadside honky-tonks and jukeboxes filled with Tom T. Hall songs; of waitresses and would-be whores; of sad, sullen men and dulled, lonely women. Their tales of hardships depict struggles with poverty, alcoholism, abuse, lost love and lost dreams.

A critic in the *Chicago Tribune* describes Brown as a contradiction, "Firefighter, ex-Marine, the sharecropper's son who flunked high school English, the next William Faulkner." Self-taught, Brown spent nine years writing during his idle hours at the Oxford fire station and, after numerous rejection slips, finally succeeded in getting the attention of Shannon Ravenel, senior editor at Algonquin Books. Publication in 1988 of his first collection of short stories, *Facing the Music,* brought immediate acclaim from critics for his honest, gut-wrenching portrayal of the daily dilemmas that plague people and their frequent inability to deal with them. The title story reveals the inner anguish and denial of a man whose wife has just had a mastectomy and needs his love and affection. Critics noted Brown's varying approaches to his subjects, his experimentation with narrative techniques, and his near perfect ear for language.

In his second book, the novel *Dirty Work,* Brown focuses on the effects of war on people's lives, a subject he understands because of his father's battle with the scars of his World War II experiences. Set in a VA hospital, the story introduces two Vietnam veterans from Mississippi, one black and one white, who discuss their plights. The black quadriplegic lies hopelessly waiting to die; the white man struggles to escape the torments of his head wound. Their shared grief and their longing for hope transcend all barriers of race and background. Though painful to read, the work was lauded by critics for its gripping, honest portrayal of war and its consequences.

Brown's next two works explore the darker side of humans and their relationships. *Big Bad Love,* a collection of nine short stories and one novella, portrays ways that love can go wrong. Brown's male characters never seem to give up trying to find it, just as they never give up on drinking more beer or traveling another road in their pick-ups. Two of the stories, "Discipline" and "92 Days," depict the plight of the struggling artist searching for hope in piles of rejection slips. In the novel *Joe,* Brown presents a world of violence and depravity, peopled with characters who are evil and crude, who participate in the destruction of life as easily as the destruction of the landscape. Joe Ransom, a middle-aged loser, becomes the archetypal guide in leading Gary, a fifteen-year-old illiterate, to his own maturity and identity, to his overthrow of his degenerate father, Wade Jones.

On Fire, a collection of essays on his experiences as a firefighter, demonstrates Brown's powerful command of language, as well as his darkly comic view of life's hazards. He writes in the same sardonic tone of driving to a near disaster a loaded pumper truck with no brakes as he does of removing a woman trapped in an overturned truck or teaching his dog how to make puppies. His lyrical prose makes the terrifying seem almost beautiful:

The fire is running across the ceiling. It's almost like water the way it flows, every board and nailhead in the room consumed and living in bright orange fire. We get on our knees and the heat comes down to welcome us into its inner reaches.

Published in 1996, Brown's novel *Father and Son* continues his themes of violence and depravity in small-town rural settings. Four days of terror develop as released convict Glen Davis returns to set right some of his sins and omissions from the past. A complex interweaving of psychological dramas, the novel presents characters who seem destined to accept that burden of the sins of their fathers. Brown shifts narratives as each of the characters examines his or her role in shaping the tragedy that envelops them.

Larry Brown is a contemporary voice who has emerged "howling" from the dark throes of a Southern culture still seeking its twentieth century identity. His gripping, realistic portrayal of ordinary people caught up in their version of the universal problems of mankind has been compared to that of William Faulkner and Flannery O'Connor, who also wrote of what they know best—their respective worlds.

—Elaine W. Hughes

BROWN, Linda Beatrice

Born: Akron, Ohio, 14 March 1939. **Education:** Bennett College, B.A.; Case Wester Reserve University, M.A.; Union Graduate School, Ph.D. **Family:** Married Harold E. Bragg (divorced, 1962); married Vandorn Ninnant; two children (first marriage). **Career:** Instructor in English, University of North Carolina at Greensboro, 1970-86; assistant professor, Guilford College, Greensboro, 1986-92; since 1992 distinguished professor of humanities, Bennett College, Greensboro; Consultant in anti-racism training. **Awards:** First Prize, North Carolina Coalition for the Arts, 1984, for *Rainbow 'Roun Mah Shoulder.* **Agent:** Marie Brown, Marie Brown Associates, 625 Broadway, New York, New York 10012. **Address**: Bennett College, 900 East Washington Street, Greensboro, North Carolina 27401.

PUBLICATIONS

Novels

Rainbow Roun Mah Shoulder. Chapel Hill, Carolina Wren Press, 1984.
Crossing Over Jordan. New York, Ballantine Books, 1995.

Poetry Collections

A Love Song to Black Men. Detroit, Broadside Press, 1974.

Other

Contributor, *A Living Culture in Durham, Carolina.* Chapel Hill, Carolina Wren Press, 1987.
Contributor, *Forget-Me-Not: The Art & Mystery of Memory Jugs.* Winston-Salem, Winston-Salem State University, 1996.

*   *   *

Linda Beatrice Brown has described herself as an African-American storyteller whose narratives are intended to inspire and empower later generations. Although her first book-length publication was a volume of poetry, *A Love Song to Black Men*, Brown is best known as the author of two compelling novels. By the time the first of them, *Rainbow Roun Mah Shoulder*, appeared in 1984, she had been married twice, brought up her children, and taught on the college level for two decades. Brown's maturity and her knowledge of life are evident in her novels, as is her passionate concern for African-American women, who have to contend both with prejudice against their race and with long-standing assumptions about the female gender.

The epigraph of *Rainbow Roun Mah Shoulder* is the long passage from St. Paul's "First Epistle to the Corinthians" that ends, "now abideth faith, hope, charity, these three; but the greatest of these is charity." If we correctly define "charity" in this usage as active intervention on behalf of the most unfortunate members of society, then it is hard to believe that a woman who, like protagonist Rebecca Florice Letenielle, is called to devote her life to so noble a task would encounter any opposition. However, it is difficult for any woman to reject her assigned role. Though Rebecca is certain God has told her "to heal folks and give my life for God," her husband Mac scoffs at the idea that anyone might have the gift of healing, least of all his wife, then accuses her of having an adulterous relationship with her priest, and finally walks out. When Rebecca does use her power to heal, she always insists on a promise of secrecy. There are always those who believe she is a witch. In fact, in Greensboro, North Carolina, one of the other members of her church, who has heard rumors about Rebecca's healing hands, accuses her of doing "the devil's work."

If there is any abiding sin in Rebecca's heart it is her desire for forbidden men. In New Orleans, she is weak with desire for a Catholic priest, and it is his will, not hers, that prevents their friendship from becoming something more. In Greensboro, Rebecca and a married preacher, Robert Brown, fall in love at first sight. After their affair has gone on for some time, he has himself transferred rather than risking the loss of his vocation, his wife, and his family. Devastated, Rebecca resorts to a voodoo ritual that will kill her, but after being saved by a woman friend, she realizes that she must go on with her work.

At one point in the novel, Rebecca thinks about all that she has lost by loving "all and nothing, no one and yet everyone all at the same time." Certainly, her vocation has cost her a great deal, but her accomplishments are impressive. She has healed more than physical ills; she has rescued Robert from his own cowardice, supported Alice and Harriet through pregnancy and into motherhood, and provided a foster child, if only briefly, with the only real home he will ever know.

In *Rainbow Roun Mah Shoulder*, every now and then there is a reference to the process by which caterpillars become butterflies. Rebecca's transformation takes thirty-nine years, but there is finally a moment when she is fully aware of a "Light around her shoulders." She has fulfilled her mission.

Brown's second novel, *Crossing over Jordan*, is a much more complex work than her first. It covers a longer time period, a hundred and thirty-nine years, and instead of representing only the protagonist's viewpoint, as *Rainbow Roun Mah Shoulder* does, it is told from a number of different perspectives. As Brown switches from one point of view to another, she presents her readers with various versions of the truth, leaving them to arrive at their own interpretation of events. This technique directs us to one of the major themes of the book: that what a human being considers the truth is actually just one part of the whole picture.

Crossing over Jordan also emphasizes the complexity of mother-daughter relationships. Though the novel moves back and forth through time with a frequency that some critics find confusing, it actually consists of four stories, each of them about a woman and her daughter. The first is that of the slave Georgia McCloud, as related by her daughter Sadie, who is one of three half-white children that Georgia had "'fore Massa McCloud leave her alone." At fourteen, seeking independence, Sadie moves to the Cook plantation, but soon she is pregnant. Georgia's placid acceptance of Sadie's departure and then of her precipitous marriage to Jacob Temple is hardly surprising. Having never had the freedom to make her own decisions, Georgia knows only how to be passive.

Like her mother, Sadie has to survive however she can. After her first pregnancy ends in a miscarriage, she is raped at knifepoint by the Cooks' fifteen-year-old son. Sadie's husband reacts by abusing Sadie and, later, their older daughter, Story. As a preacher he can think of himself as doing God's will, suppressing the evil impulses that he believes are inherent in womanhood. Sadie remains in the marriage only because she is ill-equipped to support herself. However, Story despises her mother for what she sees as weakness, and she resolves never to make herself vulnerable by loving anyone. As a result, when Story accidentally happens into motherhood, she can provide only for her daughter's physical needs. She will not even admit that she is Hermine's mother, but rears her as an orphaned niece. Ironically, Story is as rigid and essentially as abusive, in a non-physical way, as Jacob was. It is also ironic that in her old age Story has to ask Hermine to take care of her. However, their living together proves to be providential, for it forces both women to become storytellers.

Brown concludes both of her thought-provoking novels on an optimistic note. As Hermine says, even if a woman cannot fully fulfill her destiny, just the effort "gives a bottom to the river and a refuge in the storm." It is the attempt, Hermine tells her dead mother, that "brings us to the journey's end" and "lets us cross over Jordan."

—Rosemary M. Canfield Reisman

BROWN, Rita Mae

Born: Hanover, Pennsylvania, 28 November 1944. **Education:** University of Florida, Gainesville; New York University, B.A. 1968; New York School of Visual Arts, cinematography certificate, 1968; Institute for Policy Studies, Washington, D.C., Ph.D. 1976. **Career:** Photo editor, Sterling Publishing Company, New York, 1969-70; lecturer in sociology, Federal City College, Washington, D.C., 1970-71; founding member, Redstockings radical feminist group, New York, 1970s; visiting member, faculty of feminist studies, Goddard College, Plainfield, Vermont, since 1973.

Awards: New York Public Library Literary Lion award, 1986.
Agents: Julian Bach Literary Agency, 747 Third Avenue, New York, New York 10017; American Artists Inc., P.O. Box 4671, Charlottesville, Virginia 22905.

PUBLICATIONS

Novels

Rubyfruit Jungle. Plainfield, Vermont, Daughters, 1973.
In Her Day. Plainfield, Vermont, Daughters, 1976.
Six of One. New York, Harper, 1978.
Southern Discomfort. New York, Harper, 1982.
Sudden Death. New York, Bantam, 1983.
High Hearts. New York, 1987.
Bingo. New York, Bantam, 1988.
Wish You Were Here, with Sneaky Pie Brown. New York, Bantam, 1990.
Rest in Pieces, with Sneaky Pie Brown. New York, Bantam, 1992.
Venus Envy. New York, Bantam, 1993.
Dolley: A Novel of Dolley Madison in Love and War. New York, Bantam, 1994.
Murder at Monticello; or, Old Sins, with Sneaky Pie Brown. New York, Bantam, 1994.
Pay Dirt. New York, Bantam, 1995.
Riding Shotgun. New York, Bantam, 1996.
Murder She Meowed: Or Death at Montpelier: A Mrs. Murphy Mystery. New York, Bantam, 1997.

Plays

Television and film scripts: *I Love Liberty*, with others, 1982; *The Long Hot Summer*, 1985; *My Two Loves*, 1986; *The Alice Marble Story*, 1986; *Sweet Surrender*, 1986; *The Mists of Avalone*, 1987; *Table Dancing*, 1987; *The Girls of Summer*, 1989; *Selma, Lord, Selma*, 1989; *Rich Men, Single Women*, 1989; *The Thirty Nine Year Itch*, 1989.

Poetry

The Hand that Cradles the Rock. New York, New York University Press, 1971.
Songs to a Handsome Woman. Baltimore, Diana Press, 1973.
Poems. Freedom, California, Crossing Press, 1987.

Memoirs

Rita Will: Memoir of a Literary Rabble Rouser. New York, Bantam Books, 1997.

Other

A Plain Brown Rapper (essays). Baltimore, Diana Press, 1976.
Starting from Scratch: A Different Kind of Writers Manual. New York, Bantam, 1988.

*

Critical Study: *Rita Mae Brown* by Carol M. Ward, New York, Twayne, 1993.

*   *   *

Many of Brown's novels feature strong and appealing female protaginists who find humor in the odd situations and characters they encounter. Her stories are generally set in small towns and rurals areas of the South, which Brown knew in her youth. Her thematic focus on the struggles of individuals to find their place in society is usually explored through the adventures of lesbian-feminist protagonists, and she occasionally experiments with narrative structure to highlight their travails and triumphs. In all of her work, which includes essays, memoirs, scripts, and poetry, as well as fiction, Brown emphasizes tolerance for diversity as a means for promoting essential human decency and love.

Brown's first novel, *Rubyfruit Jungle* (1973), reflects these concerns. The narrative follows Molly Bolt, a Huck Finn-like character, on an adventure of self-discovery. Bolt wants to transcend her working class background without renouncing her roots, to use her sagacity against pretense, and to be accepted on her own terms—processes Brown herself underwent and which she draws on throughout her work. During the course of the novel, Bolt grows from an enterprising girl in Florida to a rebellious woman living in New York City, suffering many hardships along the way, but ending up successful. *Rubyfruit Jungle* remains the work for which Brown is best known.

In Her Day (1976), Brown's second novel, concerns the affair between a young radical lesbian and a worldly college professor, both of whom discover ways for giving positive service to the woman's movement, which is also viewed as the thinly-veiled motivation for the book, robbing it of much of the humor and drama of *Rubyfruit Jungle*. *Six of One* (1978) is more effective as a novel. Nikel (Nichole), the contemporary narrator of this work and its sequel, *Bingo* (1988), tells the story of her family from 1909 until her present. The works offer an alternative view of traditional, male-centered historical versions of that time period, with *Bingo* continuing this approach to history up to contemporary times through its focus on Nikel.

Other novels use historical incidents and approaches to present characters breaking barriers of gender, race, and class to free themselves from compliance and to establish their individual identities. *Southern Discomfort* (1982) explores early 20th century morality and hypocrisy among the various classes in Montgomery, Alabama, while *High Hearts* (1986) emphasizes socially liberating aspects of the Civil War period. The heroine of this novel goes to battle in a Confederate uniform and undergoes a process of self-discovery and realization.

In *Dolley: A Novel of Dolley Madison in Love and War* (1994) Brown offers historical fiction treatment in diary form to the life of the wife of the fourth president of the United States. *Riding Shotgun* (1997) employs a back-in-time experience, as a 20th century widow, Pryor Deyhle "Cig" Blackwood, learns lessons from her experiences in 17th-century Virginia about love and marriage that help her deal with her own circumstances. The humor that balanced so well with earnest intent as displayed in *Rubyfruit Jungle* is less evident in these works, leaving them more sober and less engaging, and a reader's response to a work by Brown may well depend on which is more valued.

Extremes of those positions are perhaps best represented in the novels *Venus Envy* (1993) and *Sudden Death* (1983). In the former, a young woman mistakenly told that she is dying mails letters to her family members informing them of her true sexual orientation, only to learn the doctor mixed her results with those of another patient's. The subsequent effects of this error are comic, but the mistake becomes a catalyst for self-realization. *Sudden Death* is more of an expose, exploring sexism and homophobia in the women's professional tennis circuit. Loosely veiled novel as a novel, *Sudden Death* (1983) is based on experiences Brown witnessed and learned while associating with famous tennis star Martina Navratilova.

With *Wish You Were Here* in 1990, Brown began a series of mystery books allegedly "written" with her cat, Sneaky Pie Brown. The protaginist of the books is a cat detective named Mrs. Murphy who helps solve cases while teaching the value and power of interaction between animals and humans. Other titles in the Kitty Crime series include *Rest in Pieces* (1992) and *Murder She Meowed: Or Death at Montpelier: A Mrs. Murphy Mystery* (1996). Brown has also made succesful forays into nonfiction. In 1988, she published *Starting from Scratch: A Different Kind of Writer's Manual*, a how-to book for creative writing that features her wit while exploring techniques for creative writing. In 1997, she published an autobiography, *Rita Will: Memoir of a Literary Rabble Rouser*. As in her best fiction, the writing is witty and sassy and engages with larger than life experiences, while candid opinions of actual people, including her family and some of her former lovers, lead to questions of motivations for her writing and our reading.

—Emma Cobb

BROWN, Sandra

Pseudonyms: Laura Jordan, Rachel Ryan, Erin St. Claire. **Born:** Waco, Texas, 12 June 1948. **Education:** Attended Texas Christian University, Oklahoma State University, and University of Texas at Arlington. **Family:** Married Michael Brown in 1968; one daughter, one son. **Career:** Manager, Merle Norman Cosmetics Studios, Tyler, Texas, 1971-73; weather reporter, WLTV-TV, Tyler, 1972-75, WFAA-TV, Dallas, 1976-79; model, Dallas Apparel Mart, 1976-87; writer.

PUBLICATIONS

Novels

Breakfast in Bed. New York, Bantam, 1983.
Heaven's Price. New York, Bantam, 1983.
Relentless Desire. New York, Berkley/Jove, 1983.
Tempest in Eden. New York, Berkley/Jove, 1983.
Temptation's Kiss. New York, Berkley/Jove, 1983.
Tomorrow's Promise. New York, Harlequin, 1983.
In a Class by Itself. New York, Bantam, 1984.
Send No Flowers. New York, Bantam, 1984.
Bittersweet Rain. New York, Silhouette, 1984.
Sunset Embrace. New York, Bantam, 1984.
Riley in the Morning. New York, Bantam, 1985.
Thursday's Child. New York, Bantam, 1985.
Another Dawn. New York, Bantam, 1985.
22 Indigo Place. New York, Bantam, 1986.

The Rana Look. New York, Bantam, 1986.
Demon Rumm. New York, Bantam, 1987.
Fanta C. New York, Bantam, 1987.
Sunny Chandler's Return. New York, Bantam, 1987.
Adam's Fall. New York, Bantam, 1988.
Hawk O'Toole's Hostage. New York, Bantam, 1988.
Slow Heat in Heaven. New York, Warner, 1988.
Tidings of Great Joy. New York, Bantam, 1988.
Long Time Coming. New York, Doubleday, 1989.
Temperatures Rising. New York, Doubleday, 1989.
Best Kept Secrets. New York, Warner, 1989.
A Whole New Light. New York, Doubleday, 1989.
Another Dawn. New York, Warner, 1991.
Breath of Scandal. New York, Warner, 1991.
Mirror Image. New York, Severn, 1991.
French Silk. New York, Warner, 1992.
Honor Bound. New York, Harlequin, 1992.
A Secret Splendor. New York, Harlequin, 1992.
Shadows of Yesterday. New York, Warner, 1992.
Texas! Trilogy. New York, Doubleday, 1992.
    Texas! Lucky. 1990.
    Texas! Chase. 1991.
    Texas! Saga. 1992.
Where There's Smoke. New York, Warner, 1993.
Charade. New York, Warner, 1994.
The Witness. New York, Warner, 1995.
Exclusive. New York, Warner, 1996.
Hawk O'Toole's Hostage. New York, Bantam Books, 1997.
Fat Tuesday. New York, Warner Books, 1997.
Unspeakable. New York, Warner Books, 1998.
Love's Encore. New York, Bantam, 1998.

Novels as Laura Jordan

Hidden Fires. Richard Gallen, 1982.
The Silken Web. Richard Gallen, 1982; as Sandra Brown, Warner, 1992.

Novels as Rachel Ryan

Love beyond Reason. New York, Dell, 1981.
Love's Encore. New York, Dell, 1981.
Eloquent Silence. New York, Dell, 1982.
A Treasure Worth Seeking. New York, Dell, 1982.
Prime Time. New York, Dell, 1983.

Novels as Erin St. Claire

Not Even for Love. New York, Harlequin, 1982.
A Kiss Remembered. New York, Harlequin, 1983.
A Secret Splendor. New York, Harlequin, 1983.
Seduction by Design. New York, Harlequin, 1983.
Led Astray. New York, Harlequin, 1985.
A Sweet Anger. New York, Harlequin, 1985.
Tiger Prince. New York, Harlequin, 1985.
Above and Beyond. New York, Harlequin, 1986.
Honor Bound. New York, Harlequin, 1986.
The Devil's Own. New York, Harlequin, 1987.
Two Alone. New York, Harlequin, 1987.
Thrill of Victory. New York, Harlequin, 1989.

*   *   *

After being fired from her job as a television weatherperson in 1979, Sandra Brown bought a dozen Harlequin romances and several how-to writing guides and began to school herself in the romance novel trade. She proved to be a fast study. Before the year was out Dell Books had purchased her first manuscript (*Love's Encore*), and Brown was launched on an unusually prolific and profitable career as one of America's most bankable romantic suspense novelists.

Writing under the pseudonyms Laura Jordan, Rachel Ryan, and Erin St. Claire (as well as her own name), Brown became adept at generating the "category romances" most often associated with the Harlequin Romance publishing imprint. By 1986 she had published a staggering 27 titles with such genre-determined titles as *Heaven's Price* (1983), *Tempest in Eden* (1983), *A Secret Splendor* (1983), and *Tomorrow's Promise* (1983). In 1990 and 1991, after only a decade in the business, Brown finally reached the *New York Times* bestseller's list with *Mirror Image* (1991) and *Breath of Scandal* (1991), and in the summer of 1992 three of her novels assaulted the *New York Times* bestseller list simultaneously—a feat previously achieved only by Tom Clancy, Stephen King, and Danielle Steel. By the mid-1990s, 40 million Sandra Brown books were in print worldwide, and Warner Books had signed the "Queen of Texas melodrama" to a new three-book contract reported to be worth "well into the multi-millions."

In 1990, Brown embarked on a series of romances for Doubleday Books titled "Texas!" that focused on the exploits of a literary version of television's *Dallas* family, here named the Tylers. The first installment, *Texas! Lucky* (1990), focused on the romantic adventures of Lucky Tyler, one of the two handsome and virile brothers upon whom the continued wealth of the oil-drilling Tylers depends. In the series' second installment, *Texas! Chase* (1991), the younger brother, Chase, loses his wife in a car accident and Brown's heroine swoops in to rescue him from grief-stricken disintegration and, naturally, take his deceased wife's place.

In the trilogy's conclusion, *Texas! Sage* (1992), Brown tells the story of the Tyler brothers' younger sister, Sage, a smart and virginal M.B.A. who finds herself the object of the flirtatious attention of a drifter recently hired by Tyler Drilling. The two eventually find themselves teamed together on a company sales trip, and, after numerous steamy bedroom interludes, Sage learns her suitor is "loaded with a capital L," and Tyler Drilling is saved. *Publishers Weekly* described Chase as a "slick contemporary romance" and Sage as "fluff" with a "factory-made happy ending," while *Kirkus Reviews* dismissed the trilogy as a whole as "lowbrow."

In *French Silk* (1992), later made into a television movie, Brown tells the story of a New Orleans D.A. who, while investigating the murder of an antismut evangelist, finds he is sexually attracted to the crime's principal suspect, the sultry owner of a lingerie company named French Silk. Brown's 1993 novel, *Where There's Smoke,* returned to the Texas oil fields of her *Texas!* trilogy in the tale of comely physician Lara Mallory, who arrives in East Texas to take over a medical practice willed to her by Congressman Clark Tackett before his unexplained drowning death. While she tries to persuade Clark's brother to help her return to the Third World country where her husband and daughter were killed, several subplots move the reader closer to the truth behind Clark's death and Mallory's central role in the sex scandal that preceded it. In *Cha-*

rade (1994), soap opera star Cat Delaney gets a heart transplant and a new boyfriend only to learn that a psycho is killing everyone who might have received his former girlfriend's heart, including, perhaps, Cat herself. Brown published her 57th novel, a legal thriller titled *The Witness,* in 1995 and followed it in 1996 with *Exclusive.* Of her fortuitous choice of careers, Brown has said: "I can't fathom an occupation from which I could derive so much satisfaction as that of writing. It's simply something I must do. Being paid to do it is icing on the cake."

—Paul S. Bodine

BUFFETT, Jimmy

Born: Pascogoula, Mississippi, 25 December 1946. **Education:** Auburn University, 1964; University of Southern Mississippi, B.S. 1969. **Family:** Married second wife, Jane Slagsvol, in 1977; two daughters. **Career:** Songwriter and performer, since 1960s; writer, Billboard Publications, Nashville, 1971-73. **Member:** Greenpeace Foundation (honorary director), Cousteau Society, Save the Manatee Commission of Florida (chair). **Agent:** Morton Janklow, 598 Madison Ave., New York, New York 10022. **Address:** Margaritaville Records, 54 Music Sq. E., Suite 303, Nashville, Tennessee 37203; and 1880 Century Park E., Suite 900, Los Angeles, California 90067.

PUBLICATIONS

Novel

Where Is Joe Merchant? A Novel Tale. New York, Harcourt, Brace, Jovanovich, 1992.

Fiction for Children

The Jolly Mon, with daughter Savannah Jane Buffett, illustrated by Lambert Davis. San Diego, Harcourt, Brace, Jovanovich, 1988.
Trouble Dolls, with Savannah Jane Buffett. San Diego, Harcourt, Brace, Jovanovich, 1991.

Other

Tales from Margaritaville: Fictional Facts and Factual Fictions. San Diego, Harcourt, Brace, Jovanovich, 1989.
Daybreak on the Equator. New York, Random House, 1997.
A Pirate Looks at Fifty: A Journal. New York, Random House, 1998.

*

Recordings: *Down to Earth,* Barnaby, 1972; *A White Sport Coat and a Pink Crustacean,* Dunhill, 1973; *Living and Dying in 3/4 Time,* Dunhill, 1974; *A-1-A,* Dunhill, 1974; *Rancho Deluxe* (soundtrack), United Artists, 1975; *High Cumberland Jamboree,* Barnaby, 1976; *Havana Daydreamin',* ABC, 1976; *Changes in Latitudes, Changes in Attitudes,* ABC, 1977; *Son of a Son of a Sailor,* ABC, 1978; *Jimmy Buffett Live, You Had to Be There,* MCA, 1978; *Volcano,* MCA, 1979; *Somewhere over China,* MCA,

1981; *Coconut Telegraph*, MCA, 1981; *One Particular Harbor*, MCA, 1983; *Riddles in the Sand*, MCA, 1984; *Last Mango in Paris*, MCA, 1985; *Songs You Know by Heart: Jimmy Buffett's Greatest Hits*, MCA, 1986; *Floridays*, MCA, 1986; *Hot Water*, MCA, 1988; *Off to See the Lizard*, MCA, 1989; *Boats, Beaches, Bars, and Ballads*, MCA, 1992; *Before the Beach* (reissue of *Down to Earth* and *High Cumberland Jamboree*), Margaritaville Records, 1993; *More Songs for Sleepless* Nights, Epic Soundtrax, 1993.

*

Biographical Studies: *Jimmy Buffett: The Man from Margaritaville Revealed* by Steve Eng, New York, St. Martin's Press, 1996; *The Parrothead Companion: The Insider's Guide to Jimmy Buffett* by Thomas Ryan, Secaucus, New Jersey, Carol Publishing Group, 1998.

*   *   *

Jimmy Buffett has always been a writer. For years he was best-known as a writer of songs, many of them ballads rich with literary ambition and allusions. However, at the height of his musical career he branched out and became a prose writer as well.

Crossing boundaries is not surprising in an artist whose work has always defied genres and definitions. Buffett's music is both rock and country, or a fusion of the two, together with reggae and Caribbean influences. He has recorded over 20 albums since his 1973 debut, *A White Sport Coat and a Pink Crustacean*. Although his music is not often played on the radio and many people are familiar only with *Margaritaville,* his concerts are legendary for their party atmosphere, and his fans, known as "Parrot-heads," are renowned for their loyalty to the entertainer.

In the mid-1980s Buffett began to deemphasize the allusions to drinking and rowdiness that had occasionally peppered his songs. He began to present a more mature and responsible persona, but without losing his sense of humor. Meanwhile, he decided to try fiction writing as a way to expand the stories embodied in his songs onto a larger canvas. His songs and his books are mainly set in and full of the ambience of the South, especially coastal places like Mobile, Alabama, and Key West, Florida.

Buffett's writing shows respect and affection for many great American authors, especially Mark Twain, to whom he often alludes, and Pat Conroy, with whom he shares the theme of growing up Catholic. The world Buffett creates through his lyrics and his fiction is a world of the senses; the reader can see, hear, feel, and even smell what the author describes. There is magic in Buffett's world, and there is drama, but it is still the real world, so there are also bizarre relatives and memorable fishing trips. Buffett's writing is for people who understand the wisdom of occasionally stepping back from the serious tedium of everyday life in order to better appreciate the beauty and spontaneity that make it worthwhile.

Buffett co-wrote his first book, *The Jolly Mon* (1988), with his daughter Savannah Jane. Father and daughter also collaborated on *Trouble Dolls,* released in 1991. Both are children's books using Buffett's favorite settings—from Florida to the Caribbean—to frame youthful adventures flavored with folklore and fantasy. Both

books are beautifully illustrated by Lambert Davis with whimsical seaside scenes that complement the text. They are ideal for families to read together.

In 1989 Buffett published *Tales from Margaritaville,* a collection of short stories gathered from his many travels. Several of the stories, such as "Son of a Son of a Sailor" and "Off to See the Lizard," are familiar, since they spring from his songs, while others, including "The Swamp Creature Let One In" and "A Gift for the Buccaneer" are completely new.

In 1992 Buffett published *Where is Joe Merchant?* the story of swashbuckling pilot Frank Bama and his quest to find a long-lost legendary guitarist. It is a light-hearted adventure with liberal doses of intrigue and comic relief. The tone of the book shows the influence of another of Buffett's favorite authors, John D. McDonald (who wrote the Travis McGee mysteries), but with Buffett's unmistakable penchant for boyhood delights like the desire to be a pirate.

Both of Buffett's adult books reached best-seller status. Although they did not receive a great deal of critical attention, most of the reviews they did get were favorable. *Publishers Weekly* and *New York Times Book Review* agreed that Buffett's work is enjoyable to read. The critics also agree on this: Buffett's books are not Great Literature—he is in no danger of going down in history with William Faulkner or Ernest Hemingway. Yet he is a great storyteller, and his stories, whether printed or sung, allow the audience to have wonderful adventures with colorful friends. Buffett's writings contain few big words or burning social issues, but they do have an unmistakable rhythm that can only be described as the rhythm of life, or at least the kind of rhythm life ought to have. Sometimes it dances and sometimes it skips, but it's always a pleasant motion. Ultimately, Buffett's books are like his music, irresistible and contagious because of their joyful spirit.

—Bruce Guy Chabot

BURKE, James Lee

Born: Houston, Texas, 5 December 1936. **Education:** University of Southeastern Louisiana, Lafayette, 1955-57; University of Missouri, Columbia, B.A. in English 1959, M.A. in English 1960. **Family:** Married Pearl Pai in 1960; four children. **Career:** English instructor, University of Southwestern Louisiana, Lafayette, University of Montana, Missoula, and Miami-Dade Community College, Florida; social worker, Los Angeles, 1962-64; reporter, Lafayette, 1964; worked for the U.S. Forest Service, Kentucky, 1965-66. **Awards:** National Endowment grant, 1977; John Simon Guggenheim fellowship, 1989; Mystery Writers of America Edgar Allan Poe award, 1989. **Address:** Philip Spitzer, 788 Ninth Avenue, New York, New York 10019.

PUBLICATIONS

Novels ("Dave Robicheaux" series)

The Neon Rain. New York, Holt, 1987.
Heaven's Prisoners. New York, Holt, 1988.
Black Cherry Blues. Boston, Little Brown, 1989.

A Morning for Flamingoes. Boston, Little Brown, 1990.
A Stained White Radiance. New York, Hyperion, 1992.
In the Electric Mist with Confederate Dead. New York, 1993.
Dixie City Jam. New York, Hyperion, 1994.
Burning Angel. New York, Hyperion, 1995.
Cadillac Jukebox. New York, Hyperion, 1996.

Other Novels

Half of Paradise. Boston, Houghton Mifflin, 1965.
To the Bright and Shining Sun. New York, Scribner, 1970.
Lay Down My Sword and Shield. New York, Crowell, 1971.
Two for Texas. New York, Pocket Books, 1983.
The Lost Get-Back Boogie. Baton Rouge, Louisiana State University Press, 1986.

Short Story Collection

The Convict. Baton Rogue, Louisiana State University Press, 1985.

*

James Lee Burke comments:

I try to write everyday and in some way make the world a better place through my art. I believe that whatever degree of talent I possess is a gift and must be treated as such. To misuse one's talent, to be cavalier about it, to set it aside because of fear or sloth is unpardonable. In my view good and evil are very real elements in the world, and the forces which represent each are in constant struggle against one another.

As William Faulkner and George Orwell both suggested, the artist has an obligation to give voice to those people who have none, and ultimately the artist must tell the truth about the period in which he lives and expose those who would exploit their fellowmen and make the earth an intolerable place. I take great happiness in being part of that struggle. I hope that my work will be remembered because it details the lives of people who possess both courage and compassion. It is those two virtues, I feel, that enable us to make art greater than the creation of one individual.

*   *   *

James Lee Burke is the author of a crime series set in New Orleans and Southern Louisiana's bayou country. Burke's protagonist in the series is Dave Robicheaux, a Cajun and a recovering alcoholic, who resigns from the New Orleans Police Department at the end of *The Neon Rain* and investigates crimes in which he becomes inadvertently involved in *Heaven's Prisoners* and *Black Cherry Blues.* Burke is a writer of extraordinary talent and power, a writer whose novels reveal interests both Southern and international; the novels convey Burke's affection for Cajun country, customs, people, and speech, while they also reveal his disdain for America's political misadventures (in Vietnam and Central America, for example). At the same time, the novels are well-plotted, suspenseful, and action-packed: their characters are complicated and psychologically real, their violence shocks and horrifies.

In *The Neon Rain* Burke introduces many of the characters who will figure in the series. Burke's protagonist, Dave Robicheaux, is a graduate of the University of Southwestern Louisiana with a

degree in English, a Vietnam veteran haunted by memories of the war, an alcoholic recovering from his past bad behavior and failed marriage, and a 14-year veteran of the New Orleans Police Department. His partner is Cletus Purcel, a loutish, heavy-drinking redneck—corrupt, tough, and wildly funny. Robicheaux's brother, Jimmie, owns a New Orleans bar/restaurant and has connections with organized crime. During the course of the novel, Robicheaux meets and falls in love with Annie Ballard, a cellist and social worker. Burke's villains here (some of whom recur as types if not as individuals) include a Mafia don, a Nicaraguan drug lord, a retired general involved in arms smuggling and right-wing causes, four sociopathic hitmen, and an assortment of sleazy lowlifes connected to the New Orleans rackets. Aware that America's political alliances in the past several years have been what might charitably be called tangled, Robicheaux also suspects the involvement of agents of the federal government in his case.

That case, the most complicated of the series, opens when Robicheaux discovers the drowned body of a Negro prostitute in a bayou while he is fly-fishing, an invasion of violence into an Edenic environment that is a characteristic Burke opening. Robicheaux's concern with the murder leads him to Didoni Giaconi, Julio Segura, and General Abshire, and also to his brutalization at the hands of three hitmen, the murder of a federal agent, the attempted murder of Robicheaux's brother, Robicheaux's shooting of Segura and one of the hitmen and his arrest of another, and to Purcel's flight to Guatemala after he murders another of the hitman for money.

Burke's treatment of violence shocks because he handles it as a matter of fact. His humanistic Robicheaux, who retains ethical and religious ideals despite his experiences on the street and in Vietnam, contrasts with the cynical Purcel, who believes that criminals are "human garbage" to be humiliated and exterminated. Neither view seems viable, and at the novel's conclusion Robicheaux resigns from the department and returns to the bayou country in which he was raised, while Purcel flees one step ahead of the law. The novel was a strong debut.

Heaven's Prisoners is an even better novel, its plot more tightly focused, its violence truly stunning, and its concentration on Robicheaux's attempts to cope with his losses poignant and moving. The novel begins with Robicheaux, now the owner of a bait and boat-rental business near New Iberia, Louisiana, trawling for shrimp in the Gulf of Mexico with Annie, now his wife. When a small plane crashes near them and Robicheaux rescues a child from the wreck, he and Annie unofficially adopt the girl, whom Robicheaux names Alafair, after his mother. His report of the incident, however, arouses the interest of Immigration officials and agents of the DEA. His own interest in the incident leads to his brutal humiliation by two sociopathic hitmen and, eventually, to Annie's murder. Liquor assuages his grief only temporarily; indeed, because he is an alcoholic, liquor only creates other problems. Drying out, working out, wrestling with his desire for another drink, and exacting revenge and some measure of justice in the last half of the book, Robicheaux is a deeply tormented character, by turns pitiful and pitiable, sensitive yet strong. Burke's ear for dialogue is acute; his rendering of Cajun and black dialects is never condescending. *Heaven's Prisoners* is an exceptional novel, one which other critics have accurately claimed expands the genre.

In *Black Cherry Blues* Robicheaux continues to wrestle with his grief; both Annie and his father, an oilrigger killed years before, visit him in his sleep and in waking dreams. Trouble finds him in the person of his college roommate, Dixie Lee Pugh, a former rhythm and blues singer battered by his predilection for drugs and alcohol and now working as an oil leaseman in Montana for Star Drilling, the company on whose rig Robicheaux's father was killed. Pugh asks for advice after he overhears two other leasemen discussing murder, and Robicheaux gradually becomes more and more enmeshed until his own troubles outweigh Pugh's. Accused of murdering one of the two leasemen after he receives a mailed threat against Alafair, Robicheaux and the girl follow the other, a sociopath named Mapes, to Montana. There Robicheaux discovers that Pugh's oil leasing involves Sally Dio, a Mafioso with whom Pugh had done time in a Texas prison. Dio employs as head of security Cletus Purcel, back from Guatemala, the murder charge against him dropped. Burke's handling of Robicheaux's gradual reconciliation with Purcel, of their partnership and mutual respect, is one of a fine novel's finest points. Still loud, crude, and mean, Purcel also has a rough sensitivity and outrageous humor that make him a fascinating original. Purcel's vengeful "justice" on Sally Dio forms as satisfactory a conclusion to that aspect of the plot as Robicheaux's extrication from his own legal difficulties involving Mapes.

A Morning for Flamingoes opens with Robicheaux, now a detective in the New Iberia Sheriff's Department, transporting two men to electrocution in Louisiana's Angola prison. The men escape after one, Jimmie Lee Boggs, wounds Robicheaux and kills his partner, and Robicheaux spends much of the rest of the novel wrestling with his sense of his own inadequacy, his fear, and his mortality. Agreeing to work undercover in New Orleans for the DEA, he establishes a contact with a Mafia don, Tony Cardo, and, surprisingly, finds Cardo as tortured and human as he himself. Like Robicheaux, Cardo has returned from the nightmare of Vietnam unable to forget his experiences or to forgive himself; like Robicheaux, Cardo is an anxious and loving father. The conclusion of the novel, in which Robicheaux gains his revenge against Boggs and allows Cardo and his son to flee to Mexico, is powerful—tense and exciting. Burke's portrayals of the complicated relationships between Robicheaux and Cardo, Cardo and his son, and Robicheaux and his first love, Bootsie, whom he marries at the novel's end, are particularly fine.

Burke continues to explore the complexities of family relationships, as well as the vagaries of Louisiana politics, in *A Stained White Radiance.* Here, the Mafia don, Joey Gouza, and his hitmen are psychopathic losers whom Robicheaux either captures, kills, or frames entertainingly. Burke's portrayal of Bootsie's attacks of lupus, his gradual discovery of the incestuous relations among the three Sonnier children, his childhood friends, and his account of racial relations in Louisiana—sorely tested by a David Duke-like politician Robicheaux would very much like to implicate in Gouza's rackets—all figure more importantly in the novel than the crimes on which it opens.

Burke takes amazing chances in his next novel, *In the Electric Mist with Confederate Dead,* which has a complicated, multilayered plots that resist summary. At the heart of the novel are Robicheaux's conversations—during an LSD trip, a coma, and acid-induced flashbacks—with Confederate General John Bell Hood

about differences between concepts of justice, law, and honor, then and now. Events in New Iberia provide constant proof of the differences: the local businessmen have welcomed into their community a Hollywood movie crew whose leading man—Elrod Sykes—converses with the general regularly during alcoholic blackouts and whose principal backer is one of Robicheaux's childhood friends—Julie "Baby Feet" Balboni (now a mobster); Sykes has discovered, during the shooting of the film the skeleton of a black man whose murder Robicheaux witnessed in 1957; Robicheaux, aided by FBI Agent Rosie Gomez, begins seeking a serial killer when the bodies of two women, murdered and savagely mutilated, are discovered in New Iberia and a nearby parish; during the investigation, a Lafayette police detective, Lieutenant Lou Girard, is murdered, and someone also tries to set Robicheaux up as the murderer of one of Girard's informants. Robicheaux eventually uncovers and eliminates the killer and establishes the links among many of these seemingly separate plots. The ghostly Confederate presences—startling in a crime novel—provide thematic point and purpose, and Burke proves here, among other things, that he is not afraid to take great risks with the mystery novel.

In *Dixie City Jam,* one of the best of the Robicheaux series, Burke creates Robicheaux's most powerful antagonist, Will Buchalter, an incestuous, bisexual, psychopathic fascist who, with his sister, repeatedly invades Robicheaux's home and violates, terrorizes, and tortures both him and Bootsie. Buchalter is a truly frightening portrayal of evil. By contrast, Burke's other villains here—mobsters Max and Bobo Calucci, New Orleans police lieutenant Nate Baxter, who is on their payroll, Channel Irish mobster Tommy Lonighan, and Manuel Ruiz, Tommy's factotum whom the Caluccis have been using to scare black drug lords out of the trade in housing projects—seem nearly tame by comparison. Among many notable achievements in the novel are Baxter's horrifyingly casual racism and power over two black colleagues in the NOPD, Sgts. Lucinda Bergeron and Ben Motley; his eventual humiliation; Bergeron's difficult relationship with her teenaged son, Zoot; Hippo Bimstine, the Jewish businessman who offers Robicheaux thousands of dollars to find a U-boat sunk off Louisiana's Gulf coast; and Clete Purcel's blunt presence.

Burning Angel is also a complex novel, one which again reveals Burke's concern with Louisiana's complicated racial history, its politicians' corruption and greed, and the impact avarice and vice have had on the state's environment. Among the mysteries of the novel: whether the powerful lawyer Moleen Bertrand or his wife Julia was driving a car that killed a black child years ago; whether Moleen will leave his wife for the woman of mixed races he loves; what Moleen and the Giacono mob have begun to build on his plantation; and the extent of his involvement with the mercenaries who have come to New Iberia and who fought in Central America. At the center of the novel is Sonny Boy Marsallus, who had fled to Central America to avoid the Giaconos but has returned with a diary that, fearing his death, he gives to Robicheaux; the diary chronicles his involvement in the horrors of the political wars there, and Robicheaux's reading of the diary triggers his memories of the horrors of Vietnam. Like Faulkner, whose prose style he echoes in some of the novel's most beautifully lyrical passages, Burke demonstrates how powerful an impact this country's racial and political past has on the present, how powerfully present is the past.

Burke began his career as a writer of "serious" novels, but he has found a wide audience and popular success as a writer of "series" novels that have revealed the serious possibilities of the hard-boiled crime genre. The Robicheaux series reveals Burke's lyrical/poetic eye for setting, psychological realism, strong plotting, political concern, and traditional, humane values. Burke is in the process of redefining the crime genre, and it is as exciting to witness this process as it is to read his novels.

—David K. Jeffrey

BURROUGHS, Franklin

Born: Franklin Gorham Burroughs, Jr., in Conway, South Carolina, 7 March 1942. **Education:** University of the South, Sewanee, Tennessee, B.A. 1964; Harvard University, Cambridge, Massachusetts, A.M. 1965, Ph.D. 1970. **Family:** Married Susan Hay; three daughters. **Career:** Professor of English, since 1968, and Harrison King McCann Professor of the English Language, Bowdoin College, Bowdoin, Maine, since 1968.

PUBLICATIONS

Nonfiction

Billy Watson's Croker Sack. New York, W. W. Norton, 1991; new edition, University of Georgia Press, Athens, 1998.
Horry and the Waccamaw. New York, W. W. Norton, 1992; new edition published as *The River Home: A Return to the Carolina Low Country*, University of Georgia Press, Athens, 1998.

*

Franklin Burroughs comments:

The primary things always seem elusive, indistinct, shadowy—more like the arrowy shapes that come whistling out of the dark before shooting time than like the solid, ponderable bird—drake or hen, wood duck, teal, black, or mallard—that you can take from the good dog's mouth, admire for a moment, and put into your coat. I have an idea that many of the things we do may be like that—more important in their incidental details and accidental associations than at the center, and most important at the remotest boundaries, where your conscious, finite purpose draws its nourishment from unrealized or half-realized impulses and memories.

—From "Dawn's Early Light," in *Billy Watson's Croker Sack.*

* * *

A writer of non-fiction, Franklin Burroughs has been haunted by what he describes as "that strange Wordsworthian hunger for landscape" that grows "out of an individual and cultural maturity, is complexly regressive, and involves much attempted calling back of things that probably exist only in the echo of the caller's voice." But despite his affinity for regions at the periphery of memory, he does not romanticize them. For him, clear-minded prose allows local history—in the mouths of its denizens, in the rust of a fishhook, in the bricks of a crumbling church—to speak for itself. Storied river towns have provided a distinctly American fiction;

Burroughs is drawn to places where nothing of great import has occurred, places "now indistinguishable within the vast influx of the present."

The River Home: A Return to the Carolina Low Country is Burroughs' account of his 1985 canoe journey down part of the Waccamaw River, beginning in southern North Carolina and passing through his home town of Conway, South Carolina. Burroughs sought to retrace the route of Nathaniel Holmes Bishop, who chronicled a series of trips in *The Voyage of the Paper Canoe*, which was published in 1878 and not reprinted. The obscurity and whimsy of it—Bishop navigated the Waccamaw and its swamps in a prototype canoe—appealed to Burroughs, who set out in "an unadventurous boat, of retrospective design, and well suited to my purposes." *The River Home* is both a literary-minded travel narrative and a meditation on the nature of historical consciousness.

"For most of our history," he writes, "topography has been destiny." In Horry County, South Carolina, a few inches of elevation determine the tidal range of the rivers and delineate where rice may be grown and where pine woods thrive. Before the Civil War, the region's paddies and mills prospered quietly. Later, as the demand for cotton supplanted that of rice, Horry County vanished from history—a fact reinforced today by the extensive draining of the swamps for golf courses and shopping malls. In a region without battlefields or ruins, the "undramatic landscape . . . was its chief monument." Burroughs knows that history will be los,: "The accumulated memory is disappearing with the landscape, and people can no longer assume that, simply by being born in the country, they have its history by heart, and need not think further about it."

The River Home is thus a personal journey and a voyage into "a past that now seems as remote as the one that was wept for by the waters of Babylon." Burroughs visits places where he fished and hunted as a boy, the old cabin where he listened to his father and his friends tell stories about World War II, the sloughs and freshets where the river's course is unclear, abandoned plantations, fish camps, and roadside stores. Nathaniel Bishop is his river guide; Burroughs' own memories juxtaposed with the meager historical record of the Horry District, with its genealogies and statistical data, are his touchstones. "Sentimental memory," he writes, "is a form of amnesia."

Burroughs' earlier book, *Billy Watson's Croker Sack*, is a collection of personal essays set in South Carolina and Maine, where he has spent most of his adult life. These are the musings of an English professor in the out-of-doors, and Burroughs might admit that the writer, like the fly fisherman, is one who "seeks to progressively rarefy the quality of his failure." As an essayist, Burroughs is circumspect without losing the sense of narrative or argument. His prose is confident and clear.

Such directness is essential as Burroughs sifts through his memories and the landscapes of Conway and Bowdoinham, where local color could readily distract. In "A Snapping Turtle in June," two figures—the ancient, bellicose turtle and Billy Watson, a "river rat" and woodsman who worked for one of Burroughs' cousins—are the focus of a meditation on the "law of tooth and nail." In a roadside store, where the locals have caught a snapper the size of a washtub, a drunk accuses Billy of being a game warden, grabs a pistol from behind the counter, hauls the turtle up by the tail, takes it outside, and shoots it. "That's what I'd do to that goddamned McNair," he says. Billy is unfazed, having been merely the catalyst in the inevitable drama where the gun must go off. Burroughs calls animals "the secondary ecology of human thinking," as they serve to focus thought and embody human desires and impulses. Billy, the turtle, and the drunk remind Burroughs that the daily routines of Conway, South Carolina, offer a glance into the primordial—the almost comic but still lethal scene would not have occurred without the presence of the ancient, ungainly snapping turtle.

The source of things is Burroughs' delight. The book concludes with a postscript, a letter to one of his colleagues who wanted to know what exactly a croker sack is. The etymology, it turns out, is unclear: Croker "has nothing do with 'croaker,' a fish, or 'crocus,' an old term for jasmine, whose dealers were called crokers." Other theories are dead ends. Of the sturdy, utilitarian, large cloth sacks, commonplace on the southern coast, Burroughs writes, "Their abnormality, their peculiarity, is the small aperture through which our normality gets a peek at the deeper structure of things, and learns to see beyond its own conventions and assumptions." Billy's sack is an emblem for Conway, Burroughs' youth, and the characters he has met along the rivers of Maine and South Carolina. It "quietly sits there, not exactly inviting inquiry, but refusing to be reduced by explanation, filed away, forgotten."

—Preston Merchant

BUTLER, Jack

Born: Alligator, Mississippi, 8 May 1944. **Education**: Central Missouri State College (now University), B.S. 1966, B.A. 1966; University of Arkansas, Fayetteville, M.F.A. 1979. **Family**: Married twice, second wife, Jayme Thomas Tull (a purchasing manager), 20 February 1983; two children (first marriage); two stepchildren. **Career**: Joint Educational Consortium, Arkadelphia, Arkansas, writer in residence, 1974-77; University of Arkansas, Fayetteville, instructor in English, 1977-79; Cancer Cooperative Group of Northwest Arkansas, Fayetteville, science writer and director of public relations, 1979-80; Blue Cross/Blue Shield of Arkansas, Little Rock, actuarial analyst, beginning 1980; Hendrix College, Conway, Arkansas, assistant dean; actuarial consultant to Arkansas State Employees Insurance Commission. **Awards**: Boatwright Literary Festival, 1971, for *Voices*; first prize for fiction, *Black Warrior Review*, 1978, for *Without Any Ears*, and 1981, for *A Country Girl*. **Agent**: Ted Parkhurst, 1010 West Third, Little Rock, Arkansas 72201.

PUBLICATIONS

Novels

Jujitsu for Christ. Little Rock, August House, 1986.
Nightshade. New York, Atlantic Monthly Press, 1989.
Living in Little Rock with Miss Little Rock. New York, Knopf, 1993.
Dreamers. New York, Knopf, 1998.

Short Story Collection

Hawk Gumbo and Other Stories. Little Rock, August House, 1983.

Poetry Collection

West of Hollywood: Poems from a Hermitage. Little Rock, August House, 1980.

Other

The Kid Who Wanted to Be a Space Man. Little Rock, August House, 1984.
Jack's Skillet: Plain Talk and Some Recipes from a Guy in the Kitchen. Chapel Hill, Algonquin Books, 1997.

*   *   *

In his fiction, Butler employs various traditional and innovative literary techniques to present intensely detailed portraits of his Southern protagonists, capturing nuances with accurate and deftly rendered colloquial expressions, accents, and distinct voices. These elements are embellished them through his use of such literary devices as interior monologues, omniscient and metaphysical narrators, and narrative intrusion by the author, who often offers comments as a minor character. For example, *Living in Little Rock with Miss Little Rock* features narration by the Holy Ghost and flow charts of characters's conversations. Butler stated that he writes most of his stories from inside a character: "We estimate each other very largely from voice: we listen for character in the ways people talk—richnesses, inconsistencies, secrets, fears, honesty, eagerness, confidence, humor. We may not all be story writers, but we are all judges of character. I like for my readers to discover my characters and their worlds in just the way I discovered them."

Butler first gained literary recognition as a poet. Early in his career he had works anthologized in *Best Poems of 1976*, edited by Joyce Carol Oates, and he published his first volume of poems, *West of Hollywood: Poems from a Hermitage*, in 1980. Since then, Butler has published poems in various national magazines and literary reviews, including *New Yorker, Atlantic Monthly, Poetry, Poetry Northwest, Cavalier, Southern Poetry Review, Mississippi Review*, and New Orleans Review. Butler's second publication was a short story collection, *Hawk Gumbo and Other Stories*, where his adept handling of Arkansas rural accents and idiomatic speech is already apparent. In his first novel, *Jujitsu for Christ*, Butler satirizes Southern political life in Little Rock, a topic he revisited with more surety in *Living in Little Rock with Miss Little Rock* (1993). Before the success of the latter novel, however, Butler published a science-fiction novel, *Nightshade*.

Living in Little Rock with Miss Little Rock garnered Butler critical praise and public popularity. Set in the early 1980s in the Arkansas state capital, the novel blends elements of humor, suspense, and metaphysics. The novel's liberal lawyer protagonist, Charles Morrison, married to the former beauty queen of the title, campaigns against proposed state legislation politically validating Creationism. Morrison's political stance jeopardizes his marriage and political aspirations to be governor of Arkansas, which are complicated further when his political opponents spread rumors that Morrison has been unfaithful to his wife and, later, kidnap her. Butler employs a fictional Holy Ghost as narrator, and also includes God as one of the novel's characters. This inventiveness and moments of poignant satire made the novel popular, helped further by the timing of its publication: the setting mirrors President William Clinton's political origins, and detailed descriptions of Little Rock landmarks, customs, and social life evokes the local color.

Butler's subsequent novel, *Dreamers*, adapts elements from espionage thrillers to relate the story of a dream researcher for a pharmaceutical company who becomes involved in an adversarial relationship with the CIA and the agency's competing spies. Unlike his previous fiction set in Arkansas, *Dreamers* takes place in Santa Fe, New Mexico, whose inhabitants's predilection for New Age and other alternative systems of beliefs are satirized by Butler with the same verve as his approach to Arkansas politics. The research of the novel's protagonist leads her to examine sources outside traditional empirical scientific truths, including Indian shamans, New Age mystics, and a shape-shifting vampire that materializes from the protagonist's own dreams. A CIA agent takes interest in her work for purposes of artificial intelligence, seeking to abscond with her findings before his competitors within the agency stop him. Extended dream passages, which feature writing of highly charged eroticism, reflect Butler's penchant for flights of fancy while direct hit satire grounds his works in the follies of contemporary times.

—Bruce Walker

BUTLER, Robert Olen

Born: Robert Olen Butler, Jr., in Granite City, Illinois, 20 January 1945. **Education:** Northwestern University, B.S. (summa cum laude) in oral interpretation 1967; University of Iowa, M.A. in playwriting 1969; postgraduate study at the New School for Social Research, 1979-81. **Military Service:** U.S. Army, Military Intelligence, 1969-72, served in Vietnam, became sergeant. **Family:** Married Carol Supplee, 1968 (divorced, 1972); married Marilyn Geller (a poet), 1 July 1972 (divorced, 1987); married Maureen Donlan, 7 August 1987 (divorced, 1995); married Elizabeth Dewberry, 23 April 1995; one child (second marriage). **Career:** High school teacher in Granite City, Illinois, 1973-74; Electronic News, New York, New York, editor/reporter, 1972-73; reporter, Chicago, Illinois, 1974-75; editor-in-chief, *Energy User News*, New York City, 1975-85; member of faculty at various writers' conferences, since 1988; assistant professor, 1985-93, and professor of fiction writing, since 1993, McNeese State University, Lake Charles, Louisiana. **Awards:** TuDo Chinh Kien Award for Outstanding Contributions to American Culture by a Vietnam Vet, Vietnam Veterans of America, 1987; Emily Clark Balch Award 1990, and *Virginia Quarterly Review* award, 1991, for Best Work of Fiction; Pulitzer Prize for Fiction in 1993, Richard and Hilda Rosenthal Foundation Award from the American Academy of Arts and Letters, nominee for the PEN/Faulkner award, and 1993 Notable Book Award from the American Library Association, all for *A Good Scent from a Strange Mountain*; Guggenheim fellow, 1993; National Endowment for the Arts fellow, and L.H.D., McNeese

State University, 1994. **Agent**: Candida Donadio, Candida Donadio & Associates, Inc., 111 West 57th St., New York, New York 10019. **Address:** Department of English, McNeese State University, 4100 Ryan Street, Lake Charles, Louisiana 70609.

PUBLICATIONS

Novels

The Alleys of Eden. New York, Horizon Press, 1981.
Sun Dogs. New York, Horizon Press, 1982.
Countrymen of Bones. New York, Horizon Press, 1983.
On Distant Ground. New York, Knopf, 1985.
Wabash: A Novel. New York, Holt, 1987.
The Deuce. New York, Holt, 1989.
They Whisper. New York, Holt, 1994.
Fragments. New York, Holt, 1997.
The Deep Green Sea. New York, Holt, 1998.

Short Story Collections

The Deuce. New York, Holt, 1989.
A Good Scent from a Strange Mountain: Stories. New York, Viking Penguin, 1992.
Tabloid Dreams. New York, Holt, 1996.

*

Critical Studies: *Re-Writing America: Vietnam Authors in Their Generation* by Philip Beidler, 1991; "Suffering and Desire" by Pat C. Hoy II, *Sewanee Review,* Fall, 1992.

*   *   *

Like the modern English novelist Ford Maddox Ford, Robert Olen Butler uses sudden shifts in mood and in affiliation to indicate his characters' removal from their surroundings. His characters simply concentrate on coping with the hardships and burdens inherent in everyday life. Butler's consistent focus on the results of the Vietnam War gives these portrayals resonance.

In his first novel, *The Alleys of Eden* (1981), Butler tells the story of Cliff, an American Army deserter who lives in Saigon, with a Vietnamese prostitute, Lanh, during the final years of the war. After Saigon falls, Cliff brings Lanh to the U.S., where their cultural differences are exposed. In *Sun Dogs* (1982) Butler takes a secondary character from *The Alleys of Eden* and gives him center stage. Wilson Hand, formerly a prisoner of war, is now a private investigator; his ultimate search is to understand both the war and his wife's suicide. Butler's stylistic mastery emerges in this novel, which has been compared to the works of both Raymond Chandler and Dashiell Hammett.

His next novel, *Countrymen of Bones* (1983), leaves the terrain of Vietnam, but remains within the arena of war. It is set in the New Mexico desert around the end of World War II and focuses on an archaeologist's work on a burial site that will soon be destroyed by the first testing of the atomic bomb. Butler maintains realism in his characters, even as the characters actualize his theme of violence. *On Distant Ground* (1985) returns to the Vietnam

War through intelligence officer David Fleming, a man who lives by strictly defined moral codes, necessary because of his work and made interesting because of the ways in which the codes inform other parts of his life. His job involves getting information from the enemy; however, upon reading a scrawled message from a prisoner, Fleming's obsession shifts to freeing him. The ensuing events, all results of his own actions, bring Fleming's code to question on every level.

Wabash (1987), Butler's fifth novel, is a real departure from his intense examination of war and its effects. This novel focuses on a depression-era Illinois couple's attempts to recover after the death of their daughter. Both parents, Deborah and Jeremy Cole, take off in inexplicable directions in their grief. Deborah writes letters to rodents, while Jeremy plots to kill his boss. In the end, Deborah repairs their relationship by impeding Jeremy's attempt at an assassination. Working within this strange plot, Butler's prose remains as strong as ever.

In *The Deuce* (1989) Butler again returns to themes relating to the Vietnam War in a postwar narrative that follows sixteen-year-old Tony, the son of a Vietnamese mother and an American father. When the boy tires of his life in the suburbs, he runs away to New York City. This novel is Butler's ambitious attempt at portraying the danger and grit of a child's life on the streets and was effective in its drama.

Butler himself made a dramatic literary turn, from writing novels to publishing short stories. His first collection, *A Good Scent From a Strange Mountain,* was awarded the Pulitzer Prize for fiction in 1993. The fifteen stories in the collection are set in southern Louisiana, where Butler moved after writing *The Deuce.* They feature Vietnamese-American characters attempting to adjust to life in the U. S. through bizarre and sometimes enchanted means. Following the success of *A Good Scent From a Strange Mountain,* Butler's novel, *They Whisper* (1994) was praised for its daring and its fascinating exploration of sexuality. Since the narrative revolves around the sexual escapades of Ira Holloway, the 35 year old protagonist, a number of women characters emerge to be examined. Some critics called them generic, without strong voices or distinguishable characteristics.

Tabloid Dreams (1996) was Butler's second short story collection and, for it, he departed the avenues of war and entertained the headlines of supermarket tabloids. Butler was commended once again for his mastery of the short story form and for telling the heartbreaking and poignant tales of people whose stories are rarely told. His obvious amusement at the headlines is juxtaposed against his exploration of exile and loss and every person's search for self. That mixture creates a quintessentially American collection, often funny and always real.

In the novel, *Fragments* (1997), Butler returns to his study of Vietnam and its effects, with the story of Jack Fuller. A former correspondent for *Stars and Stripes*, now a Pulitzer Prize-winning editorial writer and publisher, Fuller navigates the fiery nature of love and friendship. Again, Butler was praised for his ability to represent the effects of the Vietnam War with authenticity and empathy for his characters.

Butler's most recent novel, *The Deep Green Sea* (1998) is perhaps his least well-received. It tells the story of Ben, a Vietnam veteran who returns to the country in order to regain the stirring that he has not felt since the war. However, his return is unsatisfactory, and rather than getting what he hoped to find, Ben falls in love with a woman named Tien. When he begins to take more interest in her pursuits, rather than following his own, the tragedy begins to dissipate. Butler says that his urge to tell what he saw emerged on the streets of Saigon. It was there that he realized that fiction must be the means by which he related what he knew to be true. In each of Butler's stories, there is the sense that he, too, has experienced loss and yearned for the unattainable. He writes about the loss and remembrance of places or people and then conveys the despair over having that memory fade with time as accurately as one who has felt it all himself.

—Virginia Watkins

C

CAMPBELL, Will

Pseudonym: David Brett. **Born:** William Davis Campbell in Liberty, Mississippi, 18 July 1924. **Education:** Attended Louisiana College, 1941-43; Wake Forest College (now University), A.B. 1948; Tulane University, graduate study, 1948-49; Yale University, B.D. 1952. **Military Service:** U.S. Army, World War II. **Family:** Married Brenda Fisher, January 16, 1946; three children. **Career:** Pastor of Baptist church in Taylor, Louisiana, 1952-54; director of religious life, University of Mississippi, 1954-56; consultant in race relations, National Council of Churches, New York City, 1956-63; preacher-at-large, Committee of Southern Churchmen, Nashville, 1963-72; contributor to magazines, Columnist, *Christianity and Crisis*, former publisher of *Katallagete*; civil rights activist, itinerant social worker, farmer, and tour bus cook for Waylon Jennings; contributor of stories to National Public Radio, CNN and other media; farmer; commentator, Odyssey Channel News. **Awards:** Lillian Smith Prize, Christopher Award, and National Book Award nomination, all for *Brother to a Dragonfly*; first place award for fiction, Friends of American Writers, 1982, for *The Glad River*; Lyndhurst Prize; Alex Haley Award for distinguished Tennessee writers; Richard Wright Prize, Natchez Literary Celebration, for *Providence*; First Prize for Nonfiction, Mississippi Institute of Arts and Letters, for *And Also With You*.

PUBLICATIONS

Nonfiction

Race and the Renewal of the Church. Louisville, Westminster, 1962.
Brother to a Dragonfly (memoir). New York, Seabury, 1977.
God on Earth: The Lord's Prayer for Our Time, text by Will Campbel; photographs by Will McBride; poetry by Bonnie Campbell). New York, Crossroads, 1983.
Forty Acres and a Goat (memoir). Atlanta, Peachtree Publishers, 1986.
Covenant: Faces, Voices, Places, photographs by Al Clayton. Atlanta, Peachtree Publishers, 1989.
Providence. Atlanta Longstreet, 1992.
The Stem of Jesse: The Costs of Community at a 1960s Southern School. Macon, Georgia, Mercer University Press, 1995.
And Also With You: Duncan Gray and the American Dilemma. Franklin, Tennessee, Hillsboro Press, 1997.

Editor with James Y. Holloway, *Up to our Steeples in Politics*. New York, Paulist Press, 1970.
Editor with James Y. Holloway, *The Failure and the Hope: Essays of Southern Churchmen*. Grand Rapids, Michigan, Eerdmans, 1972.
Editor with James Y. Holloway, *. . . And the Criminals with Him: Luke 23:33; A First-Person Book About Prisons*. New York, Paulist Press, 1973.
Editor with James Y. Holloway, *Callings!* New York, Paulist Press, 1975.

Contributor, *Mississippi Writers: Reflections of Childhood and Youth*. Oxford, University Press of Mississippi, 1986.

Novels

The Glad River. New York, Holt, 1982.
Cecelia's Sin. Macon, Georgia, Mercer University Press, 1983.

Books for Children

Chester and Chun Ling. Nashville, Abingdon, 1989.
The Pear Tree That Bloomed in the Fall. Franklin, Tennessee, Providence House Publishers, 1996.

*

Critical Studies: *Saints & Sinners: Walker Railey, Jimmy Swaggert, Madalyn Murray O'Hair, Anton LaVey, Will Campbell, Matthew Fox* by Lawrence Wright, New York, Knopf, 1993.

*   *   *

The Reverend Will Davis Campbell, a Mississippian residing in Nashville, Tennessee, is a Southern Baptist preacher whose central and persistent message is custom-made to bring the wrath of the self-righteous down upon their heads. Campbell writes and preaches in his parables a simple Gospel. It is a stern message that is only occasionally overtly theological, often cloaked in drama or humor, sometimes earthy, and rarely if ever tempered so as not to offend. His chosen text is "Love one another," and it sits poorly in a world of material values and particularly, the comfortably pious.

Campbell knows the province of the poor, the sinner, the prisoner, and something about how a lot of them got there. He experienced first-hand the trials of the underdog he loves to champion. Though a product of Wake Forest College and the Yale Divinity School, he did not come into the world on Easy Street. Born in 1924, on a declining farm in Amite County, Mississippi, he was a baby when farmers across the South began hitting the economic rock bottom that would not collapse Wall Street until 1929. The Depression hit these rural people twice: first with failure of the farms, and then with the nation-wide dearth of non-farm jobs to turn to. However provident were Campbell's parents, Lee Webb and Hancie Parker Campbell, however wise and tenacious the two sets of grandparents who contributed so much to his raising and his internal balance and security, all the hard work in the world was not going to save his family from privation and serious affronts to their innate dignity.

Early in *Brother to a Dragonfly*, his 1977 memoir of brotherly love and tragedy that was a finalist for the National Book Award, Campbell recalls the demoralizing effect of newfound poverty and the expectations of a culture totally foreign to the self-ruled agrarianism of his folks:

> Daddy had accepted a W.P.A. job but the rigidity and
> the discipline of it was more than he could take. He had

never had someone to tell him when to pick a shovel up before, when to put it down, which rock to move, when to begin, when to quit. When the rural poor, like the reservation Indians before them, were poured into a mold not of their own doing, one which made no sense except to the foreman and timekeeper, they failed—and were known thereafter as lazy, shiftless, no-initiative 'rednecks.' For whatever reason, Daddy failed, quit or was fired.

That left no alternative but ... welfare.... He was a proud man, a man who was no stranger to hard work, and had never been without resources before.

A sympathy and a particular bent was born in Will Campbell, perhaps right then. His father's kind was legion, and the bewildered and oppressed in every walk deserved a friend. They found one in Campbell, whose sympathies tend to lie wherever the shadow of the bully is falling. Famously, the bully loomed over the Civil Rights campaigners of the 1960s. Time to time, the oppressed even included people like the Ku Klux Klan, who had certain rights, however feeble, to wear their sheets out on the sidewalks and look foolish, even if most people did not like them.

Over the years the sage in his long black frock coat and slouchy old broad-brimmed parson hat has turned up in freedom marches and on university rostrums and in the prison halls of death; by his own description, he has been "a soldier in World War II, a university chaplain, civil rights activist, itinerant social worker, farmer and tour bus cook for Waylon Jennings." When a Jennings band member died in the spring of 1998, Campbell was called to preach the funeral. As the multitude of his friends and fellow-travelers ages, "I'm getting a lot of this," he says. He has also written 16 books, a list as diverse and yet of-a-piece as the rest of his life: *God on Earth* (1983) is his sumptuous and engrossing take on the Lord's Prayer; *Chester and Chun Ling* one of his two books for children, is a love affair, as he says, of "a great big guitar and a beautiful, lady-like violin"; his World War II novel, *The Glad River,* (1982) which won the Friends of American Writers first prize for fiction, once again pursues the theme is love, this time the mutual devotion of three Southern soldiers who meet in the homesick misery of basic training and bond for life, and after, in a hellish outpost in the South Pacific. In this work, the enemy that brings these young men to the worst grief is not Japanese; indeed, a salutary lesson of the spirit comes to the principal character, Doops Momber, through a dying Japanese prisoner he tries to save. The ugliest injury is a product of the bigotry of "true believers" that awaits the three back home.

Plainly, Campbell was at home in the Bible-reading, deep-thinking Anabaptist Doops Momber's skin. Was *The Glad River* as autobiographical as it seemed? He declares it is fiction. Except, "I WAS in the South Pacific," he says; "I was a medic. And the part about the [Japanese soldier] did happen."

Meanness on the home front seems also to have ample roots in truth. Campbell's love-thy-neighbor message was not popular in the time of civil rights troubles; "neighbor" in his text was too all-inclusive. "Tacky and sorry" is the way he describes his home state during that time, and thus his visits home were rare and cautious. "There was a (unpreacherly word) contract on my life," he says.

In 1956 Campbell and his wife Brenda settled on a farm in Mt. Juliet, near Nashville, Tennessee. Their three children were raised there, along with crops that Will's genes declared must be planted, and still do. "Am I farming? Of COURSE I am," he says. "I grow anything you can eat. Anything that'll grow in central Tennessee. 'Cept 'backer. I'm not growing any 'backer now because I quit chawing." At 74 he remains prodigiously active. His 1992 book, *Providence*, a collection of his stories for National Public Radio, CNN and other media, won the Richard Wright Prize of the Natchez Literary Celebration. *The Stem of Jesse*, published in 1995, focused on community and the schools, and *And Also With You* (1997), an exploration of the human rights work of Episcopal bishop Duncan Gray, won first prize for non-fiction from the Mississippi Institute of Arts and letters.

Campbell does wry commentary on Odyssey Channel News; he is also working on a manuscript about recent political leaders who have led Mississippi in profound economic and social gains. Though Will and Brenda, married now 56 years, remain in Tennessee, he loves Mississippi, and all the South; there is not a shred of duplicity in embracing the sinner while flailing without mercy at the sin. This is more than just a tenet of the faith. It is quintessentially Southern.

—Dot Jackson

CASSITY, Turner

Born: Allen Turner Cassity in Jackson, Mississippi, 12 January 1929. **Education:** Millsaps College, B.A. 1951; Stanford University, M.A. 1952; Columbia University, M.S. 1956. **Military Service:** U.S. Army, 1952-54. **Career:** Assistant librarian, Jackson Municipal Library, Jackson, Mississippi, 1957-58; assistant librarian, Transvaal Provincial Library, Pretoria, South Africa, 1959-61; chief of serials and binding department, Emory University Library, Atlanta, since 1962. **Awards:** Blumenthal-Leviton-Blonder Prize for poetry, 1966.

PUBLICATIONS

Watchboy, What of the Night? Middletown, Wesleyan University Press, 1966.
Steeplejacks in Babel. Boston, Godine, 1973.
Silver Out of Shanghai: A Scenario for Josef von Sternberg, Featuring Wicked Nobles, a Depraved Religious Wayfoong, Princess Ida, the China Clipper, and Resurrection Lily, with a Supporting Cast of Old Hands, Merchant Seamen, Sikhs, Imperial Marines, and Persons in Blue. Atlanta, Planet Mongo Press, 1973.
Yellow for Peril, Black for Beautiful: Poems and a Play. New York, Braziller, 1975.
The Defense of the Sugar Islands. Los Angeles, Symposium Press, 1979.
Keys to Mayerling (chapbook). Florence, Kentucky, Barth, 1983.
The Book of Alna: A Narrative of the Mormon Wars. Florence, Barth, 1985.
Hurricane Lamp. Chicago, University of Chicago Press, 1986.
Lessons. Para, 1987.
Between the Chains. Chicago, University of Chicago Press, 1991.

The Destructive Element: New and Selected Poems. Athens, Ohio University Press, 1998.

*

Critical Studies: *Sewanee Review* review by Paul Ramsey, Spring, 1974; *Poetry* by Jerome J. McGann, October, 1974; "Turner Cassity" preface by Richard Howard, to *Yellow for Peril, Black for Beautiful*, New York: Braziller, 1975; "On Turner Cassity" by Donald Davie, *Chicago Review,* Summer 1983; "Turner Cassity: Particulars and Generals" by Charles Gullans, *Southern Review,* Spring 1975; *American Poetry and Culture 1945-1980* by Robert von Hallberg, Cambridge, Harvard University Press, 1985.

* * *

Turner Cassity's second volume of poetry, *Steeplejacks in Babel*, contains the poem "In Sydney by the Bridge," one of his most frequently discussed works and one which several commentators—Richard Howard and Donald Davie among them—view as his *ars poetica.* Looking out over a harbor, the voice in the poem juxtaposes cruise ships ("Cruise ships are, for the young, all of that which varies") with ferries ("Always it is middle age that sees the ferries"), the excitement of traveling the wide ocean with panache compared to the regular routes and scenes of ferries ("where what occurs, Occurs."). What occurs in Cassity's verse amid the regularly metered lines, frequently in couplets (heroic, tetrameter, dimeter), and terse, unadorned forms are observations suggesting a moralist's stance, using irony, satire, and occasional dark images and humor to probe human ambition. His lyrics and narratives are written in a plain style reminiscent of the English Renaissance, and settings range from South Africa, to the Caribbean, to North America, to China. This poet rides the ferry, observing a scene and slowly working up a description, from long narratives that recount historical incidents, to lyrics with playful rhymes, puns, and satire, to verse with more pronounced rhetoric and grotesque extremes.

Many of Cassity's short and long narrative poems have British colonial or post-colonial settings, particularly South Africa, where Cassity spent time as a civil servant in the late 1950s and early 1960s. Previous to that, Cassity studied at Millsaps College and Stanford University, where he was tutored by his mentor, Yvor Winters. Like Winters, Cassity's verse features a plain style, convention meter, and couplets, with which Cassity plays variations for heightened rhetorical qualities. Following his graduation with an M.A. from Stanford in 1952, Cassity served in the U.S. Army for two years and was stationed in the Caribbean, another frequent setting of his poems. He returned to his native Georgia in the 1960s, continuing to work as a librarian while pursuing his literary career.

Cassity's first book, *Watchboy, What of the Night?* (1966), introduces his varying settings and moralist's stance. The poems are grouped into four sections—life in the tropics, South Africa, the Caribbean, and the United States (mostly for middle-class farce or satire of Hollywood). While generally adhering to tight forms and displaying careful balance and repetitions, the poems occasionally become more engaged: sentimentalism can creep in, and so can outrage, both somewhat muted but lending a greater sense of passion to usually sober verse. "In the Western Province," for example, rises nearly to bard-like prophecy in expounding on evils of apartheid. "Calvin in the Casino" is more of a philosophical and playful meditation in rhymed couplets.

During the latter half of the 1960s, Cassity turned to writing lengthy narrative poems in blank verse, including "The Airship Boys in Africa," spanning 44 pages and first published in a 1970 edition of *Poetry,* and *Silver Out of Shanghai* (1973), a book-length poem. The latter again touches on Hollywood—on the title page Cassity calls it "A Scenario for Josef von Sternberg"—with Cassity recreating the filmmaker's expressionistic techniques while presenting a colonial scenario with not a few elements of farce. Von Sternberg had directed *Shanghai Express,* and Cassity with cinematic development focuses on an elaborate gold-smuggling scheme in colonial China with a cast of decadent characters, evoking a sordid imperialist atmosphere and addressing human folly. Similarly, folly in the form of extreme faith in technology (a dirigible is described in terms that suggest the image of a god) is addressed in "The Airship Boys in Africa," which details a failed German effort during World War I to rescue soldiers trapped in an isolated fort in German Southwest Africa.

In 1973, Cassity published a second work of shorter poems, *Steeplejacks in Babel,* which includes lyrics in traditional meter with occasional variations. The verse resembles his work and the layout of *Watchboy, What of the Night?*, as he groups poems into sections where landscapes and political ambitions are metaphorically linked, as suggested by the section titles —"Bundles for Fascists," "The Thoughtful Islands and the Just Republics," and "Mapping the Lost Continent." The poem "In the land of great aunts" draws on Cassity's Southern experience, presenting as rituals such activities as picking fruit, making jelly, churchgoing, and visiting a family graveyard.

Yellow for Peril, Black for Beautiful (1975), contains a verse drama, "Men of the Great Man," which takes place around the deathbed of imperialist Cecil Rhodes, whose vast holdings of gold and diamonds helped finance the establishment of South Africa and whose imperialistic views on nature and natives helped perpetuate great suffering. The price of ambition, a recurring theme in Cassity's work, is played to great effect here: details of Rhodes' often bizarre imperialistic views, the strategic placement of black South Africans in background and supporting roles, and images of gold dust on the landscape are among elements that lend richness to this work. *The Defense of the Sugar Islands* (1979), a poetic sequence featuring a narrative about a Korean War-era soldier stationed in Puerto Rico, is similarly ambitious. Requiring a familiarity of colonial histories as well as techniques of cinema and opera in addition to verse, Cassity's poetry in this work is more intellectually demanding but rarely perplexing because of the regular syntax.

Keys to Mayerling (1983) is a more surreal chapbook, featuring the peculiar sequence, "Mayerling," named for the location of a 19th-century double suicide, which involved Rudolf, the Austrian Archduke and Crown Prince as one of the victims. Broad in satirical reach, *Keys to Mayerling* picks easy targets—Hollywood, Walt Disney World—and makes allusive connections with the Mayerling historical incident that had great dramatic fodder. *Hurricane Lamp* (1986), on the other hand, reflects more maturity and a growing pithiness, balancing moral tones and playfulness.

As in his earlier publications, Cassity's poems are polished while adding hints of melancholy and self-reflexive elements new to his verse. The more recent poems in *The Destructive Element: New and Selected Poems* (1998), while ranging widely in subject matter, continue in this manner but are generally lighter in tone, with satire played more overtly for humor. Such is the case in his advertising poems, "Knowledge Is Power, But Only If You Misuse It," "Do Not Judge by Appearances. Or Do.," and "Some People Have No Small Talk," which revive his interest in poking fun at materialism; this trend harkens back to *Steeplejacks in Babel*, which had a piece called "Allegory with Lay Figures" that modernized T.S. Eliot's "The Love Song of J. Alfred Prufock" (the lines "In dark blue suits intently go/The brisk young men of Tokyo," for example). "Meaner than a Junkyard Dog, or, Turner's Evil Twin" and "Vegetarian Mary and the Venus Flytrap" are other examples of lightness in tone that increasingly characterize Cassity's later verse, still incisive in its view of human folly.

—Emma Cobb and Mel Koler

CHAPPELL, Fred

Born: Born Frederick Davis Chappell in Canton, North Carolina, 28 May 1936. **Education:** Duke University, B.A. 1961, M.A. 1964. **Family:** Married Susan Nicholls; one son. **Career:** Since 1964 professor of English, University of North Carolina, Greensboro. **Awards:** Sir Walter Raleigh prize, 1972; North Carolina Award for Literature, 1980; Bollingen prize, 1985; World Fantasy awards, 1992, 1994; T.S. Eliot prize, 1993; Max Gardner Award (faculty honor of the University of North Carolina); named North Carolina's poet laureate in 1997. **Agent:** Rhoda Weyr, 151 Bergen Street, New York, New York 14416.

PUBLICATIONS

Novels

It Is Time, Lord. New York, Athenaeum, 1963.
The Inkling. New York, Harcourt Brace, 1965.
Dagon. New York, Harcourt Brace, 1968.
The Gaudy Place. New York, Harcourt Brace, 1972.
I Am One of You Forever. Baton Rouge, Louisiana State University Press, 1985.
Brighten the Corner Where You Are. New York, St. Martin's Press, 1989.
More Shapes Than One. New York, St. Martin's Press, 1991.
Farewell, I'm Bound to Leave You. New York, Picador USA, 1996.

Poetry

The World Between the Eyes. Baton Rouge, Louisiana State University Press, 1971.
River. Baton Rouge, Louisiana State University Press, 1975.
The Man Twice Married to Fire. Greensboro, North Carolina, Unicorn Press, 1977.
Bloodfire. Baton Rouge, Louisiana State University Press, 1978.
Awakening to Music. Davidson, North Carolina, Briarpatch Press, 1979.

Wind Mountain. Baton Rouge, Louisiana State University Press, 1979.
Earthsleep. Baton Rouge, Louisiana State University Press, 1980.
Driftlake: A Lieder Cycle. Emory, Virginia, Iron Mountain Press, 1981.
Midquest. Baton Rouge, Louisiana State University Press, 1981.
Castle Tzingal. Baton Rouge, Louisiana State University Press, 1985.
Source. Baton Rouge, Louisiana State University Press, 1985.
First and Last Words. Baton Rouge, Louisiana State University Press, 1988.
C. Baton Rouge, Louisiana State University Press, 1993.
Spring Garden: New and Selected Poems. Baton Rouge, Louisiana State University Press, 1995.

Short Story Collection

Moments of Light. Los Angeles, New South, 1980.

Other

The Fred Chappell Reader. New York, St. Martin's Press, 1987.
Plow Naked: Selected Writings on Poetry. Ann Arbor, University Michigan Press, 1993.
A Way of Happening: Observations of Contemporary Poetry. New York, Picador USA, 1998.

*

Manuscript Collection: Duke University, Durham, North Carolina.

Critical Studies: *Dream Garden: The Poetic Vision of Fred Chappell* edited by Patrick Bizzaro, Baton Rouge, Louisiana State University Press, 1997.

Fred Chappell comments:
    To be serious but not ponderous, or to be light but not frivolous: these are the qualities I strive for. They require clarity, and this is my strongest ambition.

*   *   *

    When he was named North Carolina's poet laureate in 1997, Fred Chappell remarked, "I'm just trying to get through today without disgracing myself." This is a typical statement of the modest poet, novelist, critic, and teacher who has won the Bollingen prize for poetry and the North Carolina Award for Literature, as well as the Sir Walter Raleigh prize for fiction and the Max Gardner Award, the highest honor the University of North Carolina bestows on a faculty member.

    As Chappell has said, "Any genuine literature takes place somewhere," and his is indeed genuine, its locale most often the mountains of his native state, North Carolina. He was once the guest celebrity poet for a Collard Festival at East Carolina University, and he was the editor of a poetry collection called *Brown Bag Verses*. While he purports to be an "aw shucks," down-home mountaineer who goes by the name of "Ole Fred," he is well acquainted with and makes liberal use of Dante, of all of the arts, of

Rimbaud and Baudelaire, of the Bible, of Virgil and Horace, of scientists and of composers.

Moments of Light (1980) is a collection of eleven stories that had appeared in literary reviews. They appear in "moral chronological order" and they "narrate the history of man," says Annie Dillard in the foreword. In these tales about such varied characters as Stovebolt Johnson, Judas, Mrs. Benjamin Franklin, Franz Joseph Haydn, and Rosemary McKay, we see humans seeking order and binding it together with music.

Early novels include *It Is Time, Lord* (1963), the first of his North Carolina family farm novels; this work is considered Faulknerian because it utilizes time-shifting and a tale-within-a tale technique. *The Inkling* (1965) is an allegorical story about a boy who represents pure will and his sister, who represents appetite. Chappell believes that these two forces cause all human conflicts. *Dagon* (1968) is currently being published in paperback and placed by booksellers in their science fiction section. Chappell has said of it that the sermon is the core. Peter Leland, the protagonist, is a Methodist minister who preaches on Dagon, a maimed god from the book of Samuel. Dagon represents the fault of men who "act without reflecting," says Chappell. *The Gaudy Place* (1972) has multiple narrators.

Books of poetry include *The World Between the Eyes* (1971), *River* (1975), *The Man Twice Married to Fire* (1977), *Bloodfire* (1978), *Awakening to Music* (1979), *Wind Mountain* (1979), *Earthsleep* (1980), *Driftlake: A Lieder Cycle* (1981), *Midquest* (1981), and *Castle Tzingal* (1984). Dabney Stuart, in his introduction to *The Fred Chappell Reader* (1987), describes the medieval *Castle Tzingal* as "a verse-novel in voices, almost a play without stage directions," in which a deranged king decapitates a traveling minstrel whose head continues to sing. *Source* (1985) culminates in an atomic vision. *Midquest* is actually four books of eleven poems each, in which, notes Chappell, the first poem is mirrored by the last, the second poem by the penultimate poem. The sixth poem is each group has no counterpart and is concerned with the garrulous Virgil Campbell, who runs a general store. The four books represent earth, air, fire, and water, respectively. Several family poems are narrated by Old Fred.

In *Spring Garden: New & Selected Poems,* Chappell has set up a structure like that of a formal garden. The poem-flowers are well-tended, placed for contrast, and ornamental, as are the plants in Chappell's wife's (Susan) garden. He weaves reflections about his and Susan's life and love with meanings of the herbs and flowers, and the result is a thematic, unified whole. Even so, the poet himself calls this concoction a "salade composee."

On May 28, 1971, his thirty-fifth birthday, Chappell decided that he would write four volumes of poetry and four short novels that would paint the self-portrait of an artist as a young man. The first of this series of novels, *I Am One of You Forever* (1985), is about a farm family and the eccentric uncles who visit. From them young Jess learns to confront life and its disappointments, nature and its destructive power, as well as the loss of a friend who was like a brother to him. The second is *Brighten the Corner Where You Are. Farewell, I'm Bound to Leave You* (1996), the third of the proposed quartet, was actually a collection of sketches that accomplishes Chappell's mission to celebrate the

hardships and the joys of life. Sometimes accused of sentimentality, "Ole Fred" (his name for himself) claims that he not only risks sentimentality but steps over the line. In a near-fairy-tale setting Chappell places some strong women, most of them based on his relatives and childhood neighbors. The protagonist is young Jess Kirkman, who will grow up to be the writer Fred Chappell, and the general store proprietor is Virgil Campbell.

In every genre, Chappell proves to be erudite, and he is ruthless as a reviewer. He has corrected John Updike's grammar, called the Beat writers "self-advertisers," and dared to describe Maya Angelou as awkward and "a weak poet." Some of these essays appear in *Plow Naked* (1993). *A Way of Happening: Observations on Contemporary Poetry* (1998) is a collection of essay reviews of contemporary poetry that he has written and published within the last few years. A review of the reviews reveals that Chappell has chosen to discuss not-so-well-known poets who have merited his favor, leaving the Nobel Prize winners to other critics.

In his essay, "A Pact with Faustus," which concludes *The Fred Chappell Reader*, Chappell declares that Mann's Dr. Faustus has been his favorite twentieth-century fiction since boyhood because it is a story about a modern artist and what an artist's life is like. From the protagonist, Adrian Leverkuhn, Chappell has derived his own artistic goals. With his typical modesty, Chappell says that in his case "adventurous experiment with form" may have led to "overintellectualization." He has tried to achieve in his writing "something of Mann's richness combined with the economy and brilliance of lyric poetry." Unable to achieve this effect, he has decided to draw up the intellectual structure of a novel and then abandon it except as a large system of reference. Theme will "seep" into the novel, and the result will be unity, which Chappell desires above all.

A meticulous, caring poet-novelist-essayist, Chappell sometimes writes in his two allotted hours a day only ten or twelve lines, listening for tone and voice. "On a good day," he smiles, "I may erase all of these and start over."

—Sue Laslie Kimball

CHILDRESS, Mark

Born: Monroeville, Alabama, 1957. **Education:** Attended Louisiana State University in Shreveport, 1974-75; attended University of Alabama, 1974-78. **Career:** *Birmingham News*, Birmingham, Alabama, writer, 1977-80; *Southern Living*, Birmingham, Alabama, features editor, 1980-84; *Atlanta Journal-Constitution*, Atlanta, Georgia, regional editor, 1984-85; fiction writer and book reviewer (including the *New York Times Book Review, Los Angeles Times, San Francisco Chronicle, Philadelphia Inquirer*, and *London Times* since the mid-1980s. **Agent:** Frederick Hill Associates, 1842 Union St., San Francisco, California 94123.

PUBLICATIONS

Novels

A World Made of Fire. New York, Knopf, 1984.
V for Victor. New York, Knopf, 1988.

Tender. New York, Harmony Books, 1990.
Crazy in Alabama. New York, A. A. Knopf, 1993.
Gone for Good. New York, A. A. Knopf, 1998.

Children's Books

Joshua and Bigtooth. Boston, Little, Brown, 1992
Henry Bobbity Is Missing: And It Is All Billy Bobbity's Fault!. Boston, Little, Brown, 1996
Joshua and the Big Bad Blue Cross. Boston, Little, Brown, 1996

*   *   *

Mark Childress's fiction approaches the tall tale, as humorous and fantastic events happen to recognizable and exaggerated character-types, who can include adolescents coming-of-age, women asserting their independence, and successful musicians searching for something more than adulation and material wealth. He carefully crafts detailed and realistic settings, evoking various time periods of the twentieth century in Southern locales. Into these ordinary scenes, characters rise from humble beginnings to experience extraordinary circumstances, enlivened by Childress's deft use of first-person narratives as well as extended metaphor and superstition.

That his novels feature meaningful flights of fancy is not surprising for an author who has also penned children's books in which his young protagonists encounter mobs of crabs and sympathetic alligators. Still, the authentic realism and extended metaphors of his work offer vital insights into such eras in Alabama as the years just prior to World War I, the homefront during World War II, the turbulent 1960s, and more contemporary times.

Born in Monroeville, Alabama, Childress was raised in a family that moved to several different states before finally settling again in the South. Southern life and landscapes have remained prominent in Childress's novels. He attended Louisiana State University and the University of Alabama through the late 1970s, served as features editor for the journal *Southern Living* in between stints with the *Birmingham News* and the *Atlanta Journal-Constitution,* and turned to creative writing full time in the mid 1980s.

Childress's first novel, *A World Made of Fire*, is set in the pre-World War I years of Alabama in an isolated area where superstitions reign. Enhanced by many Gothic elements, the narrative concerns the only two impoverished survivors of a house fire, Stella and Jacko. Jacko's paralysis is blamed by superstitious townspeople for an epidemic crippling local children, which makes him the victim of the townspeople's cruelty, and Stella contends alone with the physical and mental changes of her puberty and adolescence. In order to find their place in life, the orphaned siblings initiate a search for their biological father, who was their mother's adulterous lover. Their quest, enriched by period details and a colorful cast of characters, leads to a series of violent and comic events as the two experience fears, confusion and tenderness, which Childress underscores with recurring references to fire that take on symbolic meanings related variously to desire, destruction, warmth, and other associations.

The protagonist of Childress's second novel, *V for Victor*, is a sixteen-year-old boy left in charge of his grandmother when his older brother enlists during World War II. Set on Mobile Bay, the novel recounts Victor's coming of age on the homefront, far from what he presumes are the exciting events of far off battles. The realistic narrative focusing on the adolescent psyche is complemented by fantastic elements and unusual coincidences of plot. Victor awakes one night to find his boat being burned, finds a decomposing corpse, and observes an enemy submarine surfacing. Suddenly thrust into peril, Victor begins a series of fabulous adventures to defend the homeland.

Two of Childress's novels, *Tender* and *Gone for Good*, study stardom from the perspectives of music stars. Closely paralleling the life of Elvis Presley, *Tender*'s Leroy Kirby is born in a shack in Tupelo, Mississippi, moments after his stillborn twin brother. Like Presley, Kirby is a surviving twin raised in poverty and develops a close relationship with his mother. Kirby, in fact, emulates Presley openly by adopting his hairstyle and taste in clothing. An early rock 'n' roll recording made in a small studio becomes a hit, spurring Kirby to stardom, fan adoration, and enormous wealth. Like Presley's, however, Kirby's fame is tempered by the death of his mother and the reality of the draft board, which inducts him into the Army. Kirby returns from service to stardom, becoming increasingly isolated as a result of his popularity, but his feelings of loneliness are eased through visits by the voice of his dead twin.

In *Gone for Good*, Ben "Superman" Willis is a 1970s folk-rock singer who resents the burdens of his own enormous success. He escapes through flights of fancy, literally. At the height of his popularity and while flying solo, Willis's personal aircraft is blown off-course, crash landing on a Pacific island populated by other celebrities who have disappeared from public view. Meanwhile, Willis's son and wife, a former Louisiana beauty queen, stage an all-star memorial concert for Willis at the Hollywood Bowl, before his son begins a search for his father. Again Childress weaves fabulous incidents and more mundane events, symbolism and metaphor, exploring personal and material success through magic, humor, and various views of what makes for a good life, particularly discrepancies between ideals of popular culture and individual needs.

The fabulous elements in *Gone for Good* contribute to an *Odyssey* like adventure, but the novel that preceded it, *Crazy in Alabama*, is Childress's most ambitious blend of bizarre elements and social realism. *Crazy in Alabama* is an off-beat depiction of two young boys's coming-of-age during the racial turmoil of the mid-1960s. Orphan brothers Peejoe and Wiley are taken to live with their mortician uncle, who sides with the town's African-Americans over desegregating the town's public swimming pool. Parallel to this young, eye-witness account of social friction and violence in the summer of 1965 is the story of one woman's personal liberation from male dominance, as the boys's Aunt Lucille arrives on the scene. A widow who fed her husband rat poisoning and preserved his head in a plastic food container that she carries with her, Aunt Lucille is larger-than-life in her determination to assert her identity and live with the unbound independence of which she has always dreamed. Her wilds adventures are paralleled with Childress's recreation of actual events, from Alabama's Governor George Wallace standing in a doorway at the University of Alabama to block the registration of black students, to the famous Selma marches, among others, all recast in the town of Industry, Alabama.

The re-setting is of great importance, bringing large, historical events to a smaller stage in order to reflect myriad reactions as well as subtleties that humanize the most outrageous characters and provide insight to the most egregious actions.

Crazy in Alabama is a significant work, exploring, as its title suggests, manic characters and confusing events, where questions of right and wrong, heroism and cowardice, are never neatly resolved. Fantastical elements contribute to ambiguities and ironies that are more true to life than simple beliefs about black and white, good and evil. *Crazy in Alabama* takes on the semblance of magic realism, the Latin American post-World War II literary trend (of which several writers, including Gabriel Garcia-Marquez, have acknowledged influences of writers of the American South) where fabulous events and social realism intertwine to represent a richly meaningful place and time defying simplification in its brutalities, acts of benevolence, eccentricities, and myriad influences.

Such fabulous elements are evident in Childress's stories for children. In *Joshua and the Big Bad Blue Crabs,* for example, a mob of blue crabs steal a huckleberry pie Joshua is delivering to his grandmother. No one believes this story, so Joshua undertakes a battle of wits with the crabs leading to increasingly humorous and dangerous incidents until a truce is established. Joshua returns in *Joshua and Bigtooth,* a lighthearted fantasy where he catches a baby alligator, cares for him, then attempts to conceal and keep the growing alligator. The eventual return of the alligator to his kind occurs only after a telling encounter between humans and beasts, the kind of poignant and humorous intrusion of fantasy into the realities of daily life that makes all of Childress's work so engaging and meaningful.

—Mel Koler

CLIFTON, Lucille

Born: Thelma Lucille Saylesin Depew in New York, New York, 27 June 1936. **Education:** Howard University, Washington, D.C., 1953-55; Fredonia State Teachers College, New York, 1955. **Family:** Married Fred J. Clifton in 1958 (died 1984); four daughters and two sons. **Career:** Claims clerk, New York State Division of Employment, Buffalo, 1958-60; literature assistant, U.S. Office of Education, Washington, D.C., 1969-71; professor of literature and creative writing, University of California, Santa Cruz, 1985-89; Visiting writer, Columbia University School of the Arts; poet-in-residence, Coppin State College, Baltimore, 1972-76; visiting writer, George Washington University, Washington, D.C. 1982-83; poet laureate for the State of Maryland, 1976-85; distinguished professor of humanities, St. Mary's College of Maryland, since 1989. **Awards:** YM-YWHA Poetry Center Discovery award, 1969; National Endowment for the Arts grant, 1970, 1972; Juniper Prize, 1980; American Library Association Coretta Scott King Award, 1984; National Book Award and *Los Angeles Times* Book Award finalist, both 1996; Lannan Award, 1996. **Agent:** Marilyn Marlow, Curtis Brown, 10 Astor Place, New York, New York 10003.

PUBLICATIONS

Poetry

Good Times. New York, Random House, 1969.
Good News about the Earth. New York, Random House, 1972.
An Ordinary Woman. New York, Random House, 1974.
Two-Headed Woman. Amherst, University of Massachusetts Press, 1980.
Good Woman: Poems and a Memoir, 1969-1980. Brockport, New York, BOA, 1987.
Next. Brockport, New York, BOA, 1987.
Ten Oxherding Pictures. Santa Cruz, California, Moving Parts Press, 1989.
Quilting: Poems, 1987-1990. Brockport, New York, BOA, 1991.
The Book of Light. Port Townsend, Washington, Copper Canyon Press, 1993.
The Terrible Stories. Brockport, New York, BOA, 1996.

Books for Children

The Black BC's. New York, Dutton, 1970.
Some of the Days of Everett Anderson. New York, Holt Rinehart, 1970.
Everett Anderson's Christmas Coming (Year, Friend, 1-2-3, Nine Month Long, Goodbye). New York, Holt Rinehart, 6 vols., 1971-83.
Good, Says Jerome. New York, Dutton, 1973.
All Us Come Cross the Water. New York, Holt Rinehart, 1973.
Don't You Remember. New York, Dutton, 1973.
The Boy Who Didn't Believe in Spring. New York, Dutton, 1973.
The Times They Used to Be. New York, Holt Rinehart, 1974.
My Brother Fine with Me. New York, Holt Rinehart, 1975.
Three Wishes. New York, Viking Press, 1976.
Amifika. New York, Dutton, 1977.
The Lucky Stone. New York, Delacorte Press, 1979.
My Friend Jacob. New York, Dutton, 1980.
Sonora Beautiful. New York, Dutton, 1981.

Other

Generations. New York, Random House, 1976.

Audio and Video Recordings: *The Place for Keeping* (audiocassette), Watershed, 1977; *Lucille Clifton* (video), reading and interview with Lewis MacAdams, the Lannan Foundation in association with Metro Pictures and EZTV, 1989; "Where the Soul Lives," from *The Power of the Word* (video) with Bill Moyers, Public Affairs TV and David Grubin, 1989; *The Language of Life* (video) with Bill Moyers, Public Affairs TV, 1994; *Lucille Clifton* (video), reading and interview with Quincy Troupe, the Lannan Foundation, 1996.

*

Lucille Clifton comments:
I am a black woman poet, and I sound like one.

*   *   *

Although widely known as the good-humored African-American woman behind poems such as "homage to my hips" and "wishes for sons," Lucille Clifton is also a highly ethereal poet preoccupied with injustice and the specter of mortality. Sorrow and suffering, along with hope and wit, find their way into each of her volumes. In these respects, her connection to Walt Whitman is profound, and Clifton openly acknowledges the kinship by sprinkling quotes from "Song of Myself" throughout her family memoir, *Generations*. Like Whitman, Clifton champions the resilient spirit; in a 1996 poem, "come celebrate with me," she writes, "come celebrate with me that everyday / something has tried to kill me / and has failed."

A seemingly autobiographical persona appears often in her poetry: some poems emphasize her gender, others, her race, still others, her unique identity as "Lucille Clifton." The changing emphasis helps create a social context and suggests that the various aspects of one's identity do not have fixed boundaries. That is, the poems about womanhood overlap with those about being black, and those that appear quite personal inevitably address the poet's race and gender. As for those readers who are not black or female, her poems ask us to inhabit an identity that is at once physical, cultural, racial, and familial.

Clifton is typically categorized by race and gender rather than geographic dominion, but there are reasons to look at this New York State native in relation to Southern literature. Her father came from Bedford, Virginia, and her mother from Rome, Georgia, and Clifton herself has lived much of her adult life in Maryland. Among other Southern subjects, she has written about her African slave ancestor brought to Virginia as a young child ("ca'line's prayer" in *Good Times*), her father's Virginia hometown ("I went to the valley" in *An Ordinary Woman*), and antebellum plantations ("at the cemetery, walnut grove plantation, maryland, 1989" and "slave cabin, sotterly plantation, maryland, 1989," both in *Next*). Although Clifton has said, "I don't think that I particularly feel a geographical identity," her family's Southern roots and the history of slavery in the South are integral to her verse.

Beginning with *Good Times*, Clifton's verse has achieved a unique blend of irony and earnestness. Reflecting the widespread social unrest of the Civil Rights era, *Good Times* and *Good News About the Earth* recount the travails of black family life and racial injustice. Though not as optimistic as their titles indicate, Clifton's vision of good times and good news is far from cynical. In both volumes, as in all her work, hope and defiance are twin beacons in the night. The Biblical overtones of *Good News* reflect the long view that Clifton takes of social mores and individual morality.

Her next three volumes, *An Ordinary Woman*, *Two-Headed Woman*, and *Good Woman: Poems and a Memoir 1969-1980*, insist on a female perspective while modifying that perspective in intriguing ways. An "ordinary" woman sounds anonymous and unexceptional, yet the title implies that such a life deserves recognition. By contrast, a "two-headed" woman is at best a mythological emblem and at worse a freak and, hence, the ordinary woman's polar opposite. Yet Clifton's multi-faceted portrayal of womanhood implies that the ordinary woman and the two-headed one are complementary aspects of a single self. *Good Woman*, the title of the book collecting her first four volumes and her memoir, embraces and subsumes the identities of *An Ordinary Woman* and *Two-Headed Woman* while harking back to *Good Times* and *Good News About the Earth*. Because her poetry consistently demon-

strates a wry humor, a willful rejection of the white patriarchy, and a frank interest in sex, the pious-sounding *Good Woman* seems ironic. Her abiding interests in family and religion, however, would suit an archetypal "good woman." The title, like much of her writing, thus manages to be both ironic and true.

Seeking to define her role in the historical continuums of gender, race, and family, Clifton's poems repeatedly ask how, and to what purpose, we survive so much loss and suffering. In the enigmatically titled *Next*, published the same year as *Good Woman*, she grapples with death, in particular her husband's death at age 49. Given the book's often bleak subject matter, the title implies that all living people are "next" in line to die. Yet the volume's epigraph from a Galway Kinnell poem, "A December Day in Honolulu," concerns the "next" singer who fills in for the one who has vanished; *Next* likewise promises continuation and regeneration.

In *Quilting* (1991), the title's unifying conceit symbolizes the importance of women's friendships and communal action. The section titles come from traditional quilting designs, such as "catalpa flower" and "eight-pointed star," and these groupings suggest that artistic patterns evolve naturally from human experience and observation. Then, in the Biblically inspired *The Book of Light* (1993), Clifton deftly links the name "Lucille" with "light" and "Lucifer," all three sharing the Latin root "luc." This masterful book demonstrates supreme technical control, especially in the concluding sequence, "brothers," where Clifton responds to Genesis and Milton's *Paradise Lost*.

The Terrible Stories (1996), like *Next*, is a book about the horror and nearness of mortality, but this time it is the poet's own. Recounting Clifton's battle with cancer, the book is a bracing companion to *The Book of Light*. In "1994," she writes:

> i was leaving my fifty-eighth year
> when I woke into the winter
> of a cold and mortal body
>
> thin icicles hanging off
> the one mad nipple weeping
>
> have we not been good children
> did we not inherit the earth
>
> but you must know all about this
> from your own shivering life

That she survived breast cancer and kept writing suggests that her poetic "stories" are not just terrible; they are awe-inspiring. For Clifton, poems and stories help us to connect with one another and see the enduring value of our lives.

—Hilary Holladay

COBB, William (Sledge)

Born: Eutaw, Alabama, 20 October 1937. **Education:** Livingston State College, 1957-61, B.A. in English 1961; Vanderbilt University, 1961-63, M.A. in English 1963; Breadloaf School of English, Middlebury College, 1967-68. **Family:** Married Loretta Douglas in 1965; one daughter. **Career:** Professor of English, 1963-89, and since 1989, writer-in-residence, University of Montevallo, Alabama. **Awards:** *Story Magazine*'s story of the year award, 1964; National Endowment for the Arts fellowship, 1978, for creative writing; Atlantic Center for the Arts grant, 1985, for playwriting; Alabama State Council on the Arts grant, 1985, for playwriting, and 1995, for fiction writing. **Agent:** Albert Zuckerman, Writers House, 21 West 26th St., New York, New York 10011. **Address:** 200 Shady Hill Drive, Montevallo, Alabama 35115.

PUBLICATIONS

Plays

The Vine and the Olive. Produced in Livingston, 1961.
Brighthope. Produced in Montevallo, 1985.
Recovery Room. Produced in New Orleans, 1986.
Sunday's Child. Produced in Montevallo, 1986; produced in New York, 1987.
A Place of Spring. Produced in New York, 1987.
Early Rains. Produced in New York, 1988.

Uncollected Short Stories

"The Year of Judson's Carnival," in *The Sucarnochee Review,* 1961.
"A Single Precious Day," in *Livingston Life,* 1961.
"The Time of the Leaves," in *Granta,* 1963.
"The Stone Soldier," in *Story,* Spring 1964.
"'Suffer Little Children . . . ,'" in *Comment,* Spring 1967.
"The Iron Gates," in *Comment,* Winter 1968.
"The Hunted," in *The Arlington Quarterly,* Summer 1968.
"A Very Proper Resting Place," in *Comment,* Autumn 1969.
"An Encounter with a Friend," in *Inlet,* Spring 1973.
"Walk the Fertile Fields of My Mind," in *Region,* November 1976.
"Somewhere in All This Green." In *Anthology of Bennington Writers,* edited by John Gardner, Delbanco, 1978.
"The Night of the Yellow Butterflies," in *Arete,* Spring 1984.
"Old Wars and New Sorrow," in *The Sucarnochee Review,* Spring 1984.
"Faithful Steward of Thy Bounty." N.p., n.d.
"The Queen of the Silver Dollar," in *Amaryllis,* Spring 1995.

Novels

Coming of Age at the Y. Columbia, Maryland, Portals Press, 1984.
The Hermit King. Columbia, Maryland, Portals Press, 1987.
A Walk Through Fire. New York, Morrow, 1992.
Harry Reunited. Montgomery, Alabama, Black Belt Press, 1995.

Short Stories

Somewhere in All This Green: New and Selected Stories. N.p., 1998.

Other

Plato's Sophist. N.p., 1990.

*

Manuscript Collection: Vanderbilt University Library, Nashville, Tennessee.

William Cobb comments:

A strong influence, perhaps the strongest, on the structure of *Harry Reunited* is Robert Altman's wonderfully funny film *Nashville,* which I saw years ago when it was first released and have since watched countless times on video. I wanted to write a novel about a disparate group of people whose only real connection is something ephemeral—in this case a vague and distant past—whose lives touch others' lives in various ways as they pass through a sequence of events, and who are finally brought together and at the same time separated by one apocalyptic event. I did not, of course, want to retell *Nashville.* It had to be my own story.

Since I had not attended my own high school class'es 25th reunion (I was somehow left off the invitation list; I'm still not sure what that says about me!), I was able to pose a hypothetical question to myself: What happens when a man goes back home, into an artificially created environment that attempts to mirror, even recreate, a period in his past, and he has to confront all the demons from that past? As I began to work on the novel all sorts of other nuances and themes began to appear, among them the inevitable facing of middle age, that middle passage in which we invariably begin to look both backward and forward with varying emotional consequences. And as a Southern writer, I've always been fascinated with the presence of the past, of our histories both individually and collectively, and with the notion of the abiding importance of "place," and as I wrote I found those themes emerging as well.

And I quickly fell in love with Bud Squires. Even though it's Harry's book, it is Bud's book, too, because it is he who provides the counterpoint to Harry's semi-comfortable life. It is Bud who is the avenging angel, and I was able, in a way, through my creation of Bud, to exorcise some of the guilt I suspect I still carried around with me for the cruel things I must have done in my own adolescence and which I have conveniently forgotten or blacked out. Bud became a wonderful comic character for me, a man who awakens, in varying degrees and in various startling ways, all the people in the book—and gives a kind of new life to them.

Finally, it was the comic mode that most drove me as I created this book. I very consciously wished to return to the comedy of my first novel, *Coming of Age at the Y,* and I wanted to paint this story with broad strokes. It is full of the kind of humor that I love, subtle and sly and almost slapstick at the same time. A humor of character. I *love* all these characters—Bernie Crease, as ineffectual as he is; Marie, as innocently slutty as she is; the foul-mouthed adolescents in the Sacristy before the Sunday morning service; the little black kid in the fish-net shirt; the three women at the yard sale; Cholly Polly, poor, poor Cholly Polly; Vera Babbs, the "message artist," and on and on; I love them all! That is the gift that comic writing like this gives back to the writer. I got the richest, warmest laughs of all. And I, too,—even though I was not invited—was finally reunited!

*   *   *

William Cobb studied with the last of the Fugitives at Vanderbilt University, and his fiction is deeply rooted in the southern soil that the Agrarians revered; however, his political views have not always been in keeping with the conservative views of his mentors. Throughout his work there runs a deep respect for spirituality, the importance of family, and the necessity of maintaining a sense of place. Many readers feel that Cobb is at his best as a comic writer (his flair for the profane is certainly apparent); however, his more serious civil-rights novel, *A Walk Through Fire,* brought Cobb national acclaim. Cobb's body of work includes an impressive number of short stories, four novels, and six plays, including three plays that were produced in New York.

Cobb's first national recognition came in 1964 when his story "The Stone Soldier" won the prestigious *Story Magazine*'s story of the year award and was the title story in that year's collection. "The Stone Soldier" has since been anthologized a number of times. Cobb's flair for the vulgar was apparent in his vivid description of Lyman Sparks, a scalawag who preys on the families of Civil War soldiers. His "sausage legs" and "squiggly eyes" are indelibly printed in the reader's mind.

Another short piece of fiction was recognized as an outstanding contribution in the premier edition of *Arete: A Journal of Sport Literature,* published at San Diego State University. In "The Night of the Yellow Butterflies" the main characters are a minor league baseball coach and his star player, Luke Easter—who may or may not be an apparition. The theme of baseball, with its hopes and dreams—often lost ones—is recurrent in Cobb's work. This particular story weaves the real and the supernatural in a mysterious manner that is quite convincing.

There was some negative response to the bawdy nature of Cobb's satirical novel *Coming of Age at the Y.* Certainly, he took some chances writing a satirical coming-of-age story with a female protagonist (not always considered politically correct as early as the 1970s). However, it is hard to see how any reader could miss the tone of the book from its title. Though some readers felt that his heroine, Delores Lovelady, was a bit passive, most felt that it was a fine attack on sexism—loaded with irony. Lucille Weary, the "worldly" traveler on the Greyhound with Delores, is a wonderfully funny echo of *The Wife of Bath* cramped in a century full of the New South and Shoney's Big Boys.

Cobb's second novel, *The Hermit King,* is a more traditional coming-of-age novel. The main story line here is between two runaway adolescents and an old black man who has lived a hermit's life much like Thoreau's a century earlier in quiet protest to the setting tradition offers him. Cobb's descriptive power is clear.

Cobb also has an ear for dialogue that seemed to lead him inevitably to write for the stage. Horton Foote, who admired his work, suggested that he send a trilogy to H.B. Playwright's Studio in New York. All three plays were done there over a two-year period. Herbert Berghoff said that Cobb's plays are like Foote's plays in that they are domestic plays that deal with quiet human conflicts.

Cobb's third novel, *A Walk Through Fire,* was well received. Both *Library Journal* and *Publisher's Weekly* gave the book a strong endorsement in 1992, its year of publication, and the *West Coast Review of Books* declared it one of the most important books of the year. Caught up in an interracial triangle, the three main char-

acters spin a story filled with passion and strength. The reader can see clearly Cobb's firm sense of place in the following scene, where O. B. Brewster, a white farm implement dealer (and former baseball player), offers to help an old black farmer plow his field:

> The black earth turned smoothly on each side of the shiny blade. *I am not too far removed from this soil that I can't feel its message again, in my legs and in my heart.* The loamy earth was damp, and it smelled fecund and rich, fertile as life itself. Tears misted his eyes, one droplet spilling down his cheek, but he could not wipe his face because he held to the handles of the plow.

Reviewers have said that Cobb has undoubtedly had his turn at the plow in that soil. His description of the violence and pain of our collective history during those years is seared into the minds of his readers through the fire imagery that permeates the book. Most importantly, we are reminded that those with intense faith can walk through fire.

Many of Cobb's central characters have a quiet strength that comes from life lived close to the earth. The setting is almost always southern, but the struggles of the human heart transcend the regional boundaries and make valuable commentary on life in the last half of the 20th century in the United States.

—Chris Leigh

COFER, Judith Ortiz

Born: Judith Ortiz in Hormigueros, Puerto Rico, 24 February 1952. **Education:** Augusta College, B.A. 1974; Florida Atlantic University, M.A. 1977; attended Oxford University, 1977. **Family:** Married Charles John Cofer in 1971; one daughter, Tanya. **Career:** Bilingual teacher, Palm Beach County, Florida, public schools, 1974-75; scholar of English Speaking Union at Oxford University, 1977; adjunct instructor in English, Broward Community College, Fort Lauderdale, Florida, 1978-80, instructor in Spanish, 1979; lecturer in English, University of Miami, Coral Gables, Florida; adjunct instructor, Palm Beach Junior College, 1978-80; fellow of Fine Arts Council of Florida, 1980; Bread Loaf Writers' Conference, scholar, 1981; instructor in English, University of Georgia, Athens, Georgia, since 1984. **Member:** Poetry Society of America, Poets and Writers, Associated Writing Programs. **Awards:** John Atherton Scholar in Poetry, 1982; O. Henry Award for "Nada," published in 1994 edition of *O. Henry Prize Stories* collection; "Silent Dancing" selected by Joyce Carol Oates for *The Best American Essays,* 1991; *The Line of the Sun* and *Silent Dancing* selected by the New York Public Library as outstanding books of the year, the latter also winning a PEN American/Albrand Special Citation; Riverstone Press International Poetry Competition, 1985, for *Peregrina;* received fellowships from National Endowment for the Arts, Witter Bynner Foundation for Poetry, and Georgia Council for the Arts. **Agent:** Berenice Hoffman Literary Agency, 215 West 75th Street, New York, New York 10023. **Address:** Department of English, University of Georgia, Athens, Georgia 30602.

PUBLICATIONS

Poetry Collections

Latin Women Pray. Florida Arts Gazette Press, 1980.
The Native Dancer. Pteranodon Press, 1981.
Among the Ancestors. Louisville News Press, 1981.
Reaching for the Mainland. Tempe, Bilingual Review Press, 1984.
Peregrina. Golden. Colorado, Riverstone Press, 1985.
Terms of Survival. Houston, Arte Público Press, 1987.

Novel

The Line of the Sun. Athens, University of Georgia Press, 1989.

Plays

Latin Women Pray. First produced at Georgia State University, Atlanta, June, 1984.
The Wedding March and *!El Apagon!* (one-act plays). Produced at Teatro Pregones, South Bronx, New York, 1993.

Nonfiction

Silent Dancing: A Partial Remembrance of a Puerto Rican Childhood. Houston, Arte Público Press, 1990.

Prose and Poetry Collections

The Latin Deli: Prose and Poetry. Athens, University of Georgia Press, 1993.
The Year of Our Revolution: Selected and New Stories and Poems. Houston, Piñata Books, 1998.

Short Story Collection

An Island Like You: Stories of the Barrio. New York, Puffin Books, 1996.

*

Interviews: "A *MELUS* Interview: Judith Ortiz Cofer," Edna Acosta-Belen, *MELUS,* Fall 1993; "The Art of Not Forgetting: An Interview with Judith Ortiz Cofer," by Marilyn Kallet, *Prairie Schooner,* Winter 1994; "The Infinite Variety of the Puerto Rican Reality: An Interview with Judith Ortiz Cofer," by Rafael Ocasio, *Callaloo,* Summer 1994; "An Interview with Judith Ortiz Cofer" by Jocelyn Bartkevicius, *Speaking of the Short Story: Interviews with Contemporary Writers,* edited by Farhat Iftekharuddin, Mary Rohrberger, and Maurice Lee, Jackson, University Press of Mississippi, 1997.

Critical Studies: "Judith Ortiz Cofer's Rituals of Movement" by Juan Bruce-Novoa in *The Americas Review: A Review of Hispanic Literature and Art of the USA,* Winter 1991; "Liminality, In-Betweeness and Indeterminacy: Notes toward an Anthropological Reading of Judith Cofer's The Line of the Sun" by Genevieve Fabre, in *Acraa* 18, 1993; "The Puerto Rican 'Rainbow': Distortions vs. Complexities" by Lucille H. Gregory, in *Children's Literature Association Quarterly,* Spring 1993; "Books from Parallel Cultures: Growing Up Is Hard to Do" by Rudine

Sims Bishop, in *Horn Book,* September 1995; "Narratives of National (Be)longing: Citizenship, Race, and the Creation of Latinas' Ethnicities in Exile in the United States" by Suzanne Oboler, in *Social Politics,* Summer 1996.

Judith Ortiz Cofer comments:
Maybe [the tree] is the metaphor for the artist, that we're always under that tree waiting for the fruit to come down, and it does, and you eat, but it's not enough, it's not enough. You keep waiting for that which will fill you. Fulfill you maybe. My father was an absence in my life, an absence that I loved, I loved him very much, but he was always gone. And when he was there he was just authority. And so the women filled the void with words and with their physical presence for me.

—Cofer to Jocelyn Bartkevicius in *Speaking of the Short Story: Interviews with Contemporary Writers,* 1997.

*   *   *

At first glance, Judith Ortiz Cofer would seem to be an unlikely candidate for an anthology of Southern writers. After all, she was born in Hormigueros, Puerto Rico, in 1952, and when her family did emigrate to the United States, they settled in Paterson, New Jersey, in 1956. However, Cofer, who has lived in the South since 1968, writes about some of the region's most enduring themes, including the trials of growing up, the intricacies of family life, and the process of change, assimilation, and transformation.

Like many writers, Cofer mines her own biography for inspiration, but unlike most writers she is equally proficient in almost any genre. Her oeuvre includes six collections of poetry, two books of nonfiction essays, three plays, a book of short stories, and a novel, *The Line of the Sun,* favorably reviewed by the *New York Times,* among other sources. Cofer names her literary inspirations as James Joyce, Virginia Woolf, and, particularly, the Southern writers Eudora Welty and Flannery O'Connor.

Readers can easily identify Woolf's influence in Cofer's essays along with Welty's feel for character and O'Connor's sense of religion and place. Cofer has written so often and so well of growing up that her books are frequently shelved in the young adult sections of bookstores. Her stories and memoirs of a bicultural childhood resonate with many readers in a fragmented and transitory world.

Cofer seems to have a particularly close personal connection to her poetry. The titles of the collections give away their themes: *Among the Ancestors, Reaching for the Mainland, Terms of Survival, Peregrina.* Each book reveals Cofer's desire to retain a connection with her Puerto Rican ancestors while embracing the possibilities offered by her adopted country.

Terms of Survival, for example, features a technique often used by Cofer: dividing the book into sections according to subject matter, the first half representative of Puerto Rico, the second of the United States. In *Terms of Survival* (which contains many of the poems from her two earlier chapbooks, *Peregrina* and *The Native Dancer*), the first section is called "Palabras" with each of the poems titled in Spanish. The epigraph (the use of which is another favorite technique of Cofer's) comes from *Hamlet*, where Polonius asks, "What do you read my lord?," and Hamlet responds, "Words, words, words" (II, ii).

Cofer's poetry, almost always narrative in form, reveals a sweetly lyrical voice that belies the poems' serious subject matter. The opening poem of the collection, "Quinceañera" describes the unexpected sense of shame experienced by a fifteen-year-old girl at the onset of her menstrual cycle. Cofer's young, first-person narrator compares her own blood to "the blood of saints and men in battle" and wonders why hers is considered shameful and unclean. The poem, although a vivid glimpse at Puerto Rican culture, addresses the universal travails of growing up female, even as it celebrates the Latin culture that so confuses the quinceañera. The need to stay faithful to tradition is a strong theme in Cofer's work. Indeed, the last poem in this section, "El Olvido" (forgetfulness), warns the reader that it "is a dangerous thing / to forget the climate of your birthplace . . . dangerous / to disdain the plaster saints / before which your mother kneels / praying with embarrassing fervor."

The second section of *Terms of Survival* evokes the merging of Cofer's two cultures. Titled "Common Ground," the section takes as epigraph a quotation from Tennessee Williams's *The Glass Menagerie*, "For time is the longest distance between two places" (scene vii). The group of poems is a paean to Cofer's Puerto Rican relatives both in the U.S. and in their native land. Cofer has offered a telling statement on her use of familial materials: "My family is one of the main topics of my poetry; the ones left behind on the island of Puerto Rico, and the ones who came to the United States. In tracing their lives, I discover more about mine. The place of birth itself becomes a metaphor for the things we all must leave behind; the assimilation of a new culture is the coming into maturity by accepting the terms necessary for survival. My poetry is a study of this process of change, assimilation and transformation" (*Contemporary Authors*, Vol. 115).

One of the last poems in this section (and, indeed, the book) is "Holly," a poem dedicated to Cofer's then-eleven-year-old daughter, Tanya. The poem uses holly as a symbol of the differences between Puerto Rico and America and between the young and old. The implication is that just as Cofer has learned the importance of her Latin heritage and of maintaining a connection to her distant relatives, so too must her daughter. Cofer's description of the voyage of discovery that parents and children take together echoes the familial values of the South that the poet immortalizes in "Holly" and her other work.

Cofer's two collections of nonfiction essays, *Silent Dancing* (1990) and *The Latin Deli* (1993), have received enthusiastic if scant critical attention, although *Silent Dancing* received a PEN American/Albrand Special Citation. The organization of *The Latin Deli* made reviewers wary, uncertain if they were reading a collection of short stories, essays, or poetry. Cofer bemoans that need to compartmentalize literature into a certain genre in an interview with Jocelyn Bartkevicius: "Very few people are daring to review [*The Latin Deli*], which I find sad, because to me, writing is writing. I go from a story to a poem easily in that I'm covering the same material. One of the epigraphs from *The Latin Deli* is the line from Emily Dickinson, 'Tell all the truth but tell it slant.' I see writing essays, poems, and short stories as seeing the same

material with different illumination. But it is a specialized society; it's very hard to write a book in three genres and have people pay it attention because they specialize in only one genre."

The book is divided into two sections, stories and poems and personal narratives and poems, and Cofer frequently uses first-person narrators, and her characters live in the author's Paterson, New Jersey. A reviewer's confusion is understandable, as it's often difficult to tell the stories from the personal narratives. Her point, however, is that the assignment of a literary genre is unnecessary and trivial. Her blurring of traditional genres helps to explain both the realistic detail in her fiction and the interwoven plots and finely developed characters in her essays.

Another recurring theme in Cofer's work is the blurring of categories, not merely genres but also genders. The paradox in much of Cofer's writing is that although she offers a window on Latin culture, particularly that of Puerto Rico, she also depicts her life experiences as universal, easily accessible not just to Latina girls but to men and women of any age, class, or ethnicity. For example, her poem "The Changeling" describes a young girl who dresses as a boy and is prohibited by her mother from coming to the dinner table. The girl's dilemma lies in the fact that only as a "boy" can she win the interest of her father; once she returns to her female self, she becomes invisible to him. Cofer has called the poem an exploration of how we respond to one another according to which mantle we wear. Cofer states, "I am not naïve enough to think that just changing clothes changes you but I think changing attitudes changes you . . . . I think that eventually I'm going to be wise enough to make the statement that I want to make—I'm not wise enough yet-which is, what if we stop thinking in terms of strict categories and just allow people to grow up exposed to similar things, not just boys with baseball and girls with stories" (Bartkevicius).

Readers of Cofer's prose might disagree with her opinion on her lack of readiness. A disdain for traditional categories permeates her writing, from poetry to essays to novel. In *The Latin Deli*, Cofer's essay "The Paterson Public Library" describes her encounter as a young girl with an African-American schoolmate, Lorraine, who terrorizes the smaller, more bookish Judith Ortiz. Cofer characterizes this incident not as a unique racial encounter between black and Puerto Rican cultures but as a universal description of the uneasy, often violent, relationship between "teacher's pets" and students prejudged as "problem children." In this case, Cofer blurs the lines of race, gender, and class so that her readers can identify with the struggles faced by both young girls: dismissed by teachers as unteachable, chosen last for school athletic teams, cast out by other students because of superior grades, shunned because of any "difference," real or perceived. Cofer brings all of these ritual childhood humiliations into startling focus.

A similar obfuscation of categories occurs in Cofer's novel, *The Line of the Sun*. As Cofer herself has stated, one of her primary themes is an exploration of the process of assimilation. Using a Scheherazade motif that is a hallmark of Cofer's work, where a storyteller inspires a storyteller who relates the tale, we meet Guzmán, whose colorful past inspires his niece Marisol to tell his story. In the first part of the novel, a third-person narrator (whom the reader later learns is Marisol) follows a young Guzmán through the village of Salud, as his restless spirit and rowdy behavior continually court trouble. Fearing a negative influence on their own families, the women of the village intervene. However, Guzmán woos the spiritist that they hire to tame him and is cast out of the village. He disappears to America and surfaces much later as the black-sheep uncle of Marisol, whose family lives in El Building, a Paterson apartment building dominated by Puerto Rican immigrants. Gradually Guzmán and Marisol become confidants and the stories of his wild youth ease her tensions over assimilation. As political and cultural tensions threaten to overwhelm El Building, Guzmán becomes wounded in a deadly fire, scarring his body yet reaffirming his status as a hero to Marisol. The ultimate message of both Guzmán and Cofer may be found in the novel's final paragraph, as Marisol winds down her uncle's story: "In the years that followed I concluded that the only way to understand a life is to write it as a story, to fill in the blanks left by circumstance, lapses of memory, and failed communication." Marisol's project seems to dovetail Cofer's own. In "Advanced Biology," a personal narrative from *The Latin Deli*, Cofer writes of her need to "rest myself from the exhausting enterprise of leading the examined life." However, her exhaustion yields a precious reward for readers, for Cofer's examination of her life history teaches readers much to cherish about their own.

—Rae M. Carlton Colley

CONROY, Pat

Born: 26 October 1945, in Atlanta, Georgia. **Education:** The Citadel, B.A. 1967. **Family:** Married Barbara Bolling, 1969 (divorced, 1977); one daughter; two step-daughters, Jessica, Melissa; married Lenore Gurgewitz, 1981, divorced; married Susannah; two stepchildren. **Career:** High school teacher, Beaufort, South Carolina, 1967-69; elementary school teacher in Daufuski, South Carolina, 1969; began writing full-time in 1970. **Awards:** Leadership Development grant, Ford Foundation, 1971; Anisfield-Wolf award, Cleveland Foundation, 1972, for *The Water Is Wide,* National Endowment for the Arts award for achievement in education, 1974; Georgia Governor's Award for Arts, 1978; Lillian Smith Award for fiction, Southern Regional Council, 1981; inducted into the South Carolina Hall of Fame, Academy of Authors, 1988; Thomas Cooper Society Literary Award, Thomas Cooper Library, University of South Carolina, 1995; South Carolina Governor's Award in the Humanities for Distinguished Achievement, South Carolina Humanities Council, 1996; Humanitarian Award, Georgia Commission on the Holocaust, 1996; Lotos Medal of Merit in Recognition of Outstanding Literary Achievement, 1996. **Agent:** Julian Bach Literary Agency, 747 Third Ave., New York, New York 10017.

PUBLICATIONS

The Boo. Charleston, McClure, 1970.
The Water Is Wide. New York, Houghton, 1972.
The Great Santini. New York, Houghton, 1976.
The Lords of Discipline. New York, Houghton, 1980.
The Prince of Tides. New York, Houghton, 1986.
Beach Music. New York, Doubleday, 1995.

*

Media Adaptations: Films—*Conrack,* adapted from his novel *The Water Is Wide,* 1974; *The Great Santini,* 1979; *The Lords of Discipline,* 1983; *The Prince of Tides,* 1991.

*   *   *

Pat Conroy's work is distinguished by its focus on characters coping with and attempting to rise above often bitter conflicts within families and relationships and by his loving recreation of Southern settings and culture. "I am a child of the marshes and the tides," he told William W. Starr in 1997's *Southern Writers,* a statement referring to his youth and later return to South Carolina's Lowcountry and reflecting the kind of metaphor that frequently enriches his ironic, humorous, and disturbing views of relationships among families and friends. Whether the conflicts are more overt and active, as in *The Great Santini,* or slowly revealed and psychological, as in *The Prince of Tides,* Conroy's work is repeatedly peopled with stern and demanding, sometimes abusive father figures and characters attempting to transcend such harshness to establish a more life-embracing identity.

Conroy's six works can be paired into three kinds. *The Boo* (1970) and *The Water Is Wide* (1972), his first two books, are thinly fictionalized accounts of his experiences, respectively, at The Citadel, from which he earned his B.A. in 1967, and at an elementary school on Daufuskie Island, near Beaufort, South Carolina, where he taught for one year. *The Great Santini* (1976) and *The Lords of Discipline* (1980) have young men undergoing rites-of-passage within militaristic environments, the former based on Conroy's upbringing by a gruff, career soldier, the latter set at Carolina Military Institute, which is modeled on The Citadel. *The Prince of Tides* (1986) and *Beach Music* (1995) have adult protagonists coming to terms with their broken lives and trying to understand and free themselves from the influence of past miseries.

Neither *The Boo* nor *The Water Is Wide* are great literary achievements but their treatments of heavily autobiographical content offer insights into Conroy's personal and literary development and concerns.

The Boo is an insider's view of the Citadel through a portrait of the Assistant Commandant of Cadets, a tough, demanding leader who becomes a symbol for the military academy itself. Common elements of Conroy's style are noticeable in this work: individuals precariously balance opposing influences—in this case iconoclastic behavior and respect for authority—and quirky, wryly humorous events are blended with sober concerns for order and purpose.

The Water Is Wide is based on Conroy's experience as an elementary school teacher in an impoverished and isolated black community on Daufuskie Island. The children had little previous schooling and no experiences with the world outside, and the community is threatened by encroaching pollution and development. Conroy took the position with well-meaning intentions, in many ways symbolic of 1960s idealism for social improvement. The book relates his attempts to break through the differences between himself and the children and his use of non-traditional teaching methods that led to clashes with authorities. Conroy's fictional treatment is sensitive to the local environment (which becomes the fictional Yamacraw Island) and with presenting well-rounded characters, traits that show in his later work and lend depth to contentious situations among sympathetic and unsympathetic characters. The river separating the island from the mainland is a metaphor for separation of the different worlds as well as a potential crossing of social borders.

The Great Santini explores the effects an explosive and infallible military man has on his family, particularly the eldest son, Ben Meecham. Ben is likeable and a star basketball player but is continually challenged by his father, Bull, who makes no differentiation in the way he acts as colonel or as father. As Ben attempts to distinguish between myth and reality, strict codes of conduct and admissions of vulnerability and wider experience, his relationship with his profane and violent father comes to a resolution, which occurs as they compete in a game of basketball. Bull's personality is reflected in the fact that he never lost a game of any kind—from dominoes to basketball—against any of his family members, and Ben's passage into manhood depends upon asserting his individual identity. Even with this clear conflict, the novel offers no easy resolutions, as symbolic acts—Bull's presenting a cherished flight jacket to his son, for example, and his later flying accident—are among perplexing mysteries Ben probes as part of his emotional and intellectual development.

The Lords of Discipline also addresses the effects of a Spartan, militaristic life. Set in the mid-1960s at the fictional Carolina Military Institute, which strongly resembles The Citadel, this work focuses on senior cadet Will McLean through his relationship with three roommates, his commander, and a secret group that maintains traditions of the Institute. Will is given the assignment of helping the Institute's first black recruit, particularly as the recruit undergoes an initiation ritual called The Taming, the equivalent of hazing. Will faces dilemmas concerning group loyalty so vital to the Institute versus personal responsibility, as he learns about the existence of the legendary cadet group—Ten—whose insistence on maintaining traditions includes enforcing the white-only history of the Institute.

The lasting influence of family is central to *The Prince of Tides*, a hugely popular novel, and *Beach Music*, a sprawling, much-anticipated work published almost a decade later. Adult males dealing with family demons of the past and their own unfulfilled lives are the focus of these works.

In *The Prince of Tides*, Tom Wingo travels to New York following the attempted suicide of his twin sister, Savannah, a famous poet. His discussions with her psychiatrist, Susan Lowenstein, become as vital to his personal growth as they are in helping the psychiatrist treat Savannah. By acknowledging the past, which comes through his difficult reminiscences to Lowenstein, Tom begins to find balance in a life of broken commitments, lost love, and violence. The changing tides—the flotsam and jetsam of life experiences—are effectively used as metaphors throughout the work, and Conroy's strong character development—Tom can be both brutish and sensitive—gradually reveal various angles on the Wingo family, which includes an abusive father and a materialistic and ambitious mother.

In *Beach Music* Conroy continues to weave in metaphors connecting the natural world and the situations of his characters—the

ruins of Rome, for example, and physical and moral decay in the contemporary South—while making use of modern historical events, an aspect not often present in his work that makes this novel his most ambitious undertaking. The Holocaust and the Vietnam War are among the historical events significant in this work, the influence of the latter manifested in the different life paths characters take—some join the military, others become antiwar protestors, and all are affected in some way by the War. In this work, Jack McCall moves with his daughter to Rome following his wife's suicide. He returns to South Carolina to be with his mother, who is dying of leukemia, and undergoes a journey of discovery about family and larger social betrayals—the painful process of acknowledging duplicities, abuse, and coming to terms with death that all Conroy protagonists experience.

—Mel Koler

COONTS, Stephen (Paul)

Born: Morgantown, West Virginia, 19 July 1946. **Education:** West Virginia University, A.B. 1968; University of Colorado, J.D. 1979. **Military Service:** U.S. Navy, 1968-77, served as aviator in Vietnam, 1971-73; became lieutenant; received Distinguished Flying Cross. **Family:** Married Nancy Quereau, 1971 (divorced, 1984); three children. **Career:** Cab driver and police officer, 1977-81; in-house counsel, Petro-Lewis Corporation (oil and gas company), Denver, Colorado, 1981-86; full-time writer, since 1986. **Awards:** Author award of merit, U.S. Naval Institute, 1986, for *Flight of the Intruder*. **Agent:** Robert Gottlieb, William Morris Agency, 1350 Avenue of the Americas, New York, New York 10019.

PUBLICATIONS

Novels

Flight of the Intruder. U.S. Naval Institute Press, 1986.
Final Flight. Doubleday, 1988.
The Minotaur. Doubleday, 1989.
Under Siege. Pocket Books, 1990.
The Red Horseman. Pocket Books, 1993.
The Intruders. Pocket Books, 1994.
Fortunes of War. Pocket Books, 1998.

Nonfiction

The Cannibal Queen: An Aerial Odyssey across America. Pocket Books, 1992.
War in the Air: True-Life Accounts of the 20th Century's Most Dramatic Air Battles. Pocket Books, 1996.

*

Film Adaptations: *Flight of the Intruder*, 1991; *Under Seige*, 1994.

*   *   *

Former Navy flyer and bestselling novelist Stephen Coonts relies heavily on his career experiences for the subject matter in his books. Despite mixed reviews, he has amassed a considerable and loyal following since the publication of his first book, *Flight of the Intruder,* in 1986. *Flight,* as well as Coonts' *Under Siege* (1990), were adapted to the screen. Coonts has also penned a nonfiction book, *The Cannibal Queen: An Aerial Odyssey across America* (1992).

In *Flight of the Intruder,* Coonts details events in the life of A-6 Intruder pilot Jake Grafton, who flies a bomber past enemy flak and surface-to-air missiles in North Vietnam. He then must maneuver the plane at night onto the small deck of an aircraft carrier. He becomes disillusioned after countless raids on seemingly meaningless targets. After his best friend is killed by a random bullet, Grafton plans an unauthorized, solo raid on the Communist Party Headquarters in downtown Hanoi. Critics praised Coonts' excellent depiction of the nerve-wracking aspects of modern air raids. On the ground, however, Coonts seems to be out of his element. M. S. Kaplan nevertheless described the book as a "thrill-a-minute joy ride."

The second installment, *Final Flight* (1988), finds Jake commanding the air wing of a carrier after his failing eyesight precludes any night flying. In Naples, an Arab plot, masterminded by one Colonel Qazi, is detailed which consists of trying to steal the ship's nuclear weapons. Coonts was once again lauded for his well-detailed lives of Navy pilots. The dialogue may be stilted at times, but the plot is riveting.

Jake Grafton returns in *The Minotaur* (1989). This time he is in charge of developing a new tactical aircraft, the Minotaur, which depends on a variation of Stealth technology. He also must track down an information leak at the highest levels of the Defense Department. The book is especially compelling when Coonts looks into the inefficiency and thievery of government military contracts and the pork barrel philosophy of United States senators. The only place this techno-thriller gets bogged down is when Coonts moves into the domestic realm.

Better received was *Under Siege* (1990). The setting is modern-day Washington, D.C., where a Colombian drug lord brought there for trial sends killer squads to terrorize the city with a series of mass murders. In addition, a shadowy assassin is running around stalking top officials. The reader is offered a well-drawn, if stereotypical, cast that includes George Bush and Dan Quayle. Jake Grafton is joined in this sprawling plot by journalist Jack Yocke and undercover narcotics officer Harrison Ronald Ford. Coonts may see his world in absolutes, but his gripping portrait of the United States' vulnerability to corruption demands attention.

Coonts' adventure fiction continues with *The Red Horseman* (1993). Jake Grafton is now a rear admiral and deputy director of the Defense Intelligence Agency (DIA). Jake learns that Jewish media big wheel Nigel Keren was poisoned by the CIA. Grafton and sidekick "Toad" Tarkington are threatened with similar fates after discovering, right before a mission to Moscow to oversee the dismantling of their nuclear arsenal, that the DIA offices are bugged. The action, staged on three continents, was heralded by one critic as "one of the most compelling post-glasnost thrillers to date."

More recently, *The Intruders* (1994) picks up Jake Grafton in 1973, right after *Flight of the Intruder.* It has been widely criticized as the weakest in the series. The novel seems to be made up of a hodgepodge of flight scenes which Coonts wasn't able to fit into any of his previous novels.

—Jennifer G. Coman

CORE, George

Born: Lexington, Kentucky. **Education:** Transylvania College; Vanderbilt University, B.A. and M.A.; University of North Carolina, Ph.D. **Military Service:** U.S. Marine Corps, 1960-64; officer. **Family:** Married Susan Darnell; four children. **Career:** Editor, University of Georgia Press, 1967-73; editor, *Sewanee Review* and adjunct professor of English at the University of the South, since 1973; contributing essayist and reviewer, including *Hudson Review, Virginia Quarterly Review, New York Times Book Review,* and *New Republic*; since 1973, consultant to the National Endowment for the Humanities, serving on various panels to evaluate fellowship proposals; jurist, Pulitzer Prize committee (three times); evaluates manuscripts for various university presses, including University of Illinois, Louisiana State University, and University of Missouri; instructor of English at the University of Georgia, Davidson College, and Vanderbilt University; visiting professor, Emory University, summer 1976. **Awards:** Fellowship, National Endowment for the Humanities.

PUBLICATIONS

Editor

Regionalism and Beyond: Essays of Randall Stewart. Nashville, Vanderbilt University Press, 1968.
The Southern Tradition at Bay: A History of Postbellum Thought, with M. E. Bradford. New Rochelle, Arlington House, 1968.
Southern Fiction Today: Renascence and Beyond. Athens, University of Georgia Press, 1969.
Katherine Anne Porter: A Critical Symposium, with Lodwick Hartley. Athens, University of Georgia Press, 1969.
Selected Letters of John Crowe Ransom, with Thomas Daniel Young. Baton Rouge, Louisiana State University Press, 1985.
Revelation and Other Fiction from the Sewanee Review: A Centennial Anthology. Louisville, Harmony House Publishers, 1992.
The Critics Who Made Us: Essays from Sewanee Review. Columbia, University of Missouri Press, 1993.
Sallies of the Mind, with John McCormick; by Francis Fergusson. New Brunswick, New Jersey, Transaction, 1998.

* * *

The devotee of light summer reading, the browser among popular novels and the best-seller lists, probably will never encounter editor George Core straight-on; his name is not apt to appear in copper letters bigger than the title on the book jacket. But where there is serious literary quality, the author's work may have at some point passed through Core's respectful hands and received his thoughtful encouragement, for the thirty-some years of Core's professional life have been spent fostering fine writing. For over 25 of those years he has been editor of the *Sewanee Review,* a literary magazine with a long history of nudging along writers and poets of real promise and keeping them in the fold, continuing to print their mature work. Robert Penn Warren, Allen Tate, Flannery O'Connor and a Who's Who of celebrated Southern writers have been contributors.

Literary magazines are not known as the deep pockets of publishing, but a few are prestigious enough to draw submissions from the writerly elite even though the money is in a different league from the big slick magazines and publishing houses. (One of the sad truths is that few of the big slickies are in the market for literature, at all.) Thus, the *Sewanee Review* has continued to publish such poets and writers as Fred Chappell, Seamus Heaney, Wendell Berry, Reynolds Price, Shelby Foote, Louis Rubin, Elizabeth Spencer, George Garrett, Donald Hall, Hayden Carruth and a string of others who, along with whatever other reasons, simply enjoy working with George Core. One thing that gets a rise out of the *Review*'s thoughtful and soft-spoken editor is when someone tags his publication "a little magazine." "Monroe Spears wrote about 'Little Magazines' as chiefly poetry and fiction without a critical program," Core notes. Such a program is the base of a serious literary magazine.

Core has long taken deep notice of literary trends in the South, as in all the literary world. In one of his occasional essays of criticism, this one called "The Best Residuum of Truth" and published in the Fall, 1966 issue of the *Georgia Review,* he writes: "We have lost the great colossus of Faulkner and his genius of the old generation, and the brightest star of the new, Flannery O'Connor, but there is still a remarkable amount of good writing being done in the South today." The greatest living writer of short fiction at that time, Core wrote, was Katherine Anne Porter. "She has avoided the trap which has caught so many American authors—Bret Harte, Mark Twain, O. Henry, Faulkner, William Styron, Robert Penn Warren." That trap, he wrote, was to surrender one's fiction to "the demands of the mass audience, the popular magazine and the book club." The surrender, Core added, took on "a peculiar form in recent times, and more and more authors are turning to it—journalism. It may be thinly veiled as social and political commentary, in the manner of Norman Mailer, but it is still journalism. Truman Capote's current 'documentary' *In Cold Blood* is a case in point and its author has pretentiously called it a 'non-fiction novel.' The new generation of Southern writers seems to be turning toward this literary Gomorrah."

Core also writes about the use of language, "The ideal literary language is what Wordsworth calls, 'The very language of men.'" The writer who does it well "does it so gracefully that we are unaware of style—it reveals meaning through precision, economy and directness."

Whatever bent the writers are taking today, the flow is not diminished. "Some days we get 18 or 20 submissions," Core says. "We probably get a thousand stories a year." These are screened in a two-person office, although sometimes there is a little student help. Core knows within the first two or three pages whether he's got a winner, or whether there's hope. "I'm looking for first-rate work," he says. "I want a conflict and I want a resolution; a strong narrative pulse and characters to generate action. And I like poetry the same way." He added, "I have a selfish point of view—if I can't read something four or five times, I'm not going to expect our readers to read it once."

Of course, not all possibilities come in wearing blue ribbons and ripe for the press. "I can usually see where a story goes off the track," Core says. "The trick is to get the writer to see it and make it work." Which may not be easy. Writers are not the least-defensive people on the globe. But, Core responds to a certain common plaint: "We can't publish something just because a writer worked a long time on it. And a lot of writers don't do their homework," he adds. He has also learned not to send out proofs of work that has been edited and is about to be published. "Writers often revise on the proof," which makes the process never-ending.

Core's background includes attaining his B.A. and M.A. from Vanderbilt University, and his Ph.D. from the University of North Carolina, as well as service as an officer in the U.S. Marine Corps. He served as an editor at the University of Georgia Press, 1967-73, while establishing himself as an essayist and reviewer; he has also written many forewords and introductions for a variety of critical, fiction, and nonfiction works. During his earlier period, which spans his honorable discharge from the Marines and his association with the University of Georgia Press, Core edited several books, including *Regionalism and Beyond: Essays of Randall Stewart* (1968), *The Southern Tradition at Bay: A History of Postbellum Thought* (with M. E. Bradford, 1968), *Southern Fiction Today: Renascence and Beyond* 1969), and *Katherine Anne Porter: A Critical Symposium* (with Lodwick Hartley, (1969). Then, in the summer of 1973, the opening came at the *Sewanee Review*, at the University of the South, in Sewanee, Tennessee. It was a match.

There is no estimating how many he has inspired and led along in the love and, as George says, the precision of good writing. It is not an easy road. Witness this assessment Core wrote in a *Georgia Review* piece in 1970:

> There is a new urgency which the critic must feel. The signs of the times are generally bad: the artist in and out of the South is bereft, probably for the first time in history, of almost any vestige of shared belief. Ours is very nearly a post-Christian age: chaos looms at every hand; anarchy is celebrated throughout the land; order in society and in art have never had a lower valuation; the forces of darkness seem to be getting the upper hand....

> This progressive decay of modern culture has by now overtaken the country as a whole, and with it, finally, the South.... The decadence of our society is truly reflected in the decadence of our art.

> The critic must be free of the commercial pressures which are the very pulse of our economy and often of our lives.

—Dot Jackson

CORN, Alfred

Born: Alfred Dewitt Corn in Bainbridge, Georgia, 14 August 1943.
Education: Emory University, Atlanta, 1961-65, B.A. in French 1965; Columbia University, New York (Woodrow Wilson fellow;

faculty fellow), 1965-67, M.A. 1967; Fulbright fellow, Paris, 1967-68. **Family:** Married Ann Jones in 1967 (divorced 1971). **Career:** Preceptor, Columbia University, 1968-70; associate editor, *University Review,* New York, 1970; staff writer, DaCapo Press, New York, 1971-72; visiting lectureships or associate professorships at various colleges, including Yale University, 1977-79, Connecticut College, 1978-81, Columbia University, 1983, City University of New York, 1983-84, Columbia School of Arts, writing division, 1985 and 1987, and Silliman College, Yale University, 1986; Elliston Professor of Poetry, University of Cincinnati, Ohio, 1989; visiting professor, University of California, Los Angeles, and Ohio State University, 1990; resident, Thurber House, Columbus, Ohio, 1990; instructor, graduate writing division, Columbia University, 1991-95; Bell Professor, University of Tulsa, 1992; Hurst Resident in Poetry, Washington University, 1994; **Awards:** Ingram Merrill Foundation fellowship, 1974; George Dillon prize, 1975; Oscar Blumenthal prize, 1977; National Endowment for the Arts fellowship, 1980, 1991; Levinson prize, *Poetry,* 1982; Davidson prize, 1982; American Academy Of Arts and Letters Award, 1983; Academy of American Poets fellowship, 1987; Guggenheim Foundation Fellowship, 1986-87; Lamont Poetry Prizes, 1987, 1988, and 1989, Roethke Prize, 1989, and John Masefield Poetry Prize, 1992.

PUBLICATIONS

Poetry Collections

All Roads at Once. New York, Viking Press, 1976.
A Call in the Midst of the Crowd. New York, Viking Press, 1978.
The Various Light. New York, Viking Press, 1980.
Notes from a Child of Paradise. New York, Viking Press, 1984.
An Xmas Murder. New York, Sea Cliff Press, 1987.
The West Door. New York, Viking, 1988.
Autobiographies. New York, Viking, 1992.
Present. Washington, D.C., Counterpoint, 1997.

Novel

Part of His Story. Minneapolis, Mid-List Press, 1997.

Other

The Metamorphoses of Metaphor: Essays in Poetry and Fiction. New York, Viking 1987.
"Part of His Story" (novel excerpt) in *Kenyon Review,* Summer 1991.
The Poem's Heartbeat: A Manual of Prosody. Brownsville, Oregon, Story Line Press, 1997.

Editor, *Incarnation: Contemporary Writers on the New Testament.* New York, Viking, 1990.

Translator, *L'Indifferent,* by Marcel Proust. New York, Sea Cliff, 1992.

*

Sound Recordings: *Daniel Halpern and Alfred Corn Reading Their Poems in the Montpelier Room,* Library of Congress, March 6, 1997, Washington, D.C., Library of Congress, 1997.

Critical Studies: "Alfred Corn's Speaking Gift" by George Kearns, *Canto* (Andover, Massachusetts), Fall 1978; "In the Place of Time" by G.E. Murray, *Parnassus* (New York), Spring-Summer 1983; "The Traveler: On the Poetry of Alfred Corn," Richard Abowitz, in *The Kenyon Review,* Fall 1993.

Alfred Corn comments:

(1990) Observers have noted that books of mine have an upward or downward direction. If *Notes from a Child of Paradise* was in the mode of ascent, then *The West Door* is in the mode of descent, many of the poems concerned with incarnational themes. To go out of the west door of the sanctuary is an entry into a world of physicality, of suffering and death. The book is dedicated to David Kalstone, critic and teacher, who died of AIDS in 1986. The collection's longest poem is "An Xmas Murder," a narrative and dramatic poem set in Vermont, recounting a crime and its aftermath in the life of one of the characters. There are two extended sequences in the book, "Tongues on Trees," a pastoral exploration of nature and language, and "After Ireland," a series of Irish subject. "New Year," the volume's concluding lyric, is in the tradition of sunset poems such as Baudelaire's "Recueillement."

(1995) *Autobiographies* is in two parts, an opening section of metered lyrics and medium-length poems, including "My Neighbor, the Distinguished Count," a characterized monologue in the voice of a young woman initiated into vampirism by Dracula; and "Contemporary Culture and the Letter K," a comic survey of recent history ending with a serious reflection concerning the AIDS epidemic. "La Madeleine" is a poetic sequence around the theme of Mary Magdalene and Proust's "petite madeleine," in which loss is balanced by the redemptive powers of memory and faith. "The Jaunt" is a twilight meditation on a boat trip not taken, to be understood as an allegory for the surprising directions imposed by the poet's private sense of calling.

The volume concludes with "1992," a long autobiographical sequence in 20 sections with dates for their titles, the earliest 1949, the latest, 1992. Each section juxtaposes an incident from the narrator's life with an incident from the life of a series of fictional characters in different parts of America. In fact, every state of the Union is mentioned during the course of the poem. The sequence provides something like a portrait of the United States in the latter half of the twentieth century, concluding with the quincentennial year of the Columbian voyage.

* * *

Although Alfred Corn was born and reared in Bainbridge, Georgia, he later came to view New York City as his real home. However, Corn abhors limitations. Like Walt Whitman, to whom he is often compared, Corn embraces the world and the people who inhabit it. Like Dante, whom he admires and on occasion imitates, Corn ranges through time to assemble the real and fictitious characters who can illustrate his transcendent vision. In reading Corn, one cannot help thinking of Dante's beloved teacher, Brunetto Latini, a good man whom the poet had to place in Hell because of his homosexuality. As a twentieth-century gay who is profoundly religious, Corn rejects such judgements as limiting the ways in which love can be expressed. However, he is also aware that now, because of AIDS, acts which he believes can be a kind of incarnation may well result in a horrible death.

The title of Corn's first book of poems, *All Roads at Once*, indicates the importance of incorporating as much as possible into one's experience. Like Hart Crane, the subject of "The Bridge, Palm Sunday, 1973," Corn tries to fix images while at the same time using them to inspire his meditations. "Measuring a Rooftop in the Cast-Iron District" illustrates this approach. The images presented—heat, tar, garbage thrown into a dumpster—seem unlikely to inspire anyone, but Corn suggests that this "American randomness" does have a deeper significance, though it may take some effort to unriddle it. Even viewed superficially, however, these poems reflect the poet's delight in the moment, in love, nature, and art, whether the setting is Paris or Oregon, a forest, a seashore, or a room in New York's Metropolitan Museum where Chinese porcelains are displayed.

Always more traditional than romantic, Corn eschews confessional poetry. However, like Dante, he does make autobiographical references as he attempts to find his way out of his own "Dark Wood" and come to an understanding of God's master plan. Corn's first book, *A Call in the Midst of the Crowd*, is dedicated to his ex-wife, Ann Jones, and includes recollections of his travels with her, as well as a poem to a male lover. However, though in the long title poem of the volume he does examine human relationships, the poet's primary purpose is to define New York City and to voice his own ambivalent feelings about it. As he was often to do in later works, Corn here broadens the scope of his poetic study of the city by inserting within the text relevant quotations from other writers, as well as from newspapers and magazines, a guidebook, and an encyclopedia.

Though it is not considered his best work, *The Various Light* does contain a fine poem about Corn's Southern childhood. Somewhat in the manner of William Wordsworth's *Prelude*, "The Outdoor Amphitheater" traces the poet's development by recapturing his thoughts and feelings, in this case, as he viewed or participated in the various public events that were the high points of small town life. It is also notable that where earlier Corn had been fairly free in meter and form, in *The Various Light* Corn seems to be moving toward the more traditional approach to poetic composition termed New Formalism.

Critics were enthusiastic about Corn's fourth volume, *Notes from a Child of Paradise*. Like Dante's *Divine Comedy*, on which it is modelled, the long poem is made up of one hundred cantos, grouped into three sections, and culminates in a vision of divine harmony. However, this narrative is set very much in this world. Part of the action takes place during a cross-country trip, and there are other segments in such centers of 1960s student activism as Columbia, Berkeley, the Haight, and Paris. Like Dante, Corn enriches his account with plentiful allusions, many of them to another trip westward, the Lewis and Clark expedition. However, though Corn ends his poem by presenting his lady as his spiritual and artistic guide, unlike Dante he makes the story of their love the basis of his plot. As the poem progresses, Alfred and Ann meet, break up, reconcile, and marry. With Alfred increasingly uncertain about his sexual orientation, the marriage founders, and there is a divorce. Only then does Ann fully assume her role as Corn's Beatrice.

With *An Xmas Murder*, first published separately and then as part of *The West Door*, Corn took still another step toward New

Formalism. *An Xmas Murder* is a gloomy story, related as a blank-verse monologue much like those of Robert Browning and Robert Frost. Corn also uses the dramatic monologue form for the equally dark poem in *Autobiographies*, "My Neighbor, the Distinguished Count," where the speaker is one of Dracula's victims. Quite different in form and tone is the primary work in *Autobiographies*, the long, realistic poem "1992," which combines travelogue, autobiography, fiction, and conjecture in a mesmerizing account of a year spent wandering through America.

The breadth of Corn's interests is reflected in several volumes of prose, including essays on literature, a prosody manual, and his edited work *Incarnation: Contemporary Writers on the New Testament*. His increasing focus on the spiritual is evident in his novel *Part of His Story*, about a playwright who, having lost his lover to AIDS, is wary of becoming emotional involved with anyone else. However, when a relationship begun as a casual indulgence develops into selfless love, it is suggested that this new commitment may well bring the unbelieving protagonist into the community of believers. Selflessness and religious faith are also the primary themes in *Present*. Thus, "Stepson Elegy" describes the "work / And housework" of Corn's stepmother as a gift (present) to others, while "A Goya Reproduction" refers both to God's gift of talent and to the recipient's selfless offerings in art. Another definition of "present" is explored in "A Marriage in the Nineties." Though an AIDS patient "just out of intensive care" is certain only of the present moment, from a Christian perspective every moment is linked to the eternal. The kind of love "where we make a present of ourselves / to stranger and neighbor" can lead to the union of body and soul, sense and spirit, which transcends time and death. Alfred Corn's spiritual depth, combined with his panoramic view of the world and his impressive artistry, warrant his being ranked vary high among contemporary poets.

—Rosemary M. Canfield Reisman

CORNWELL, Patricia Daniels

Born: Portland, Maine, 9 June 1956. **Education:** Davidson College, B.A. 1979. **Family:** Married Charles Cornwell, 1980 (divorced 1990). **Career:** Police reporter, *Charlotte Observer*, Charlotte, North Carolina, 1979-81; computer analyst, Office of the Chief Medical Examiner, Richmond, Virginia, since 1985; volunteer police officer. **Awards:** Investigative reporting award, North Carolina Press Association, 1980, for a series on prostitution; Gold Medallion Book award for biography, 1985, for *A Time for Remembering*, from Evangelical Christian Publishers Association, 1985; John Greasy award, British Crime Writers Association, Edgar award, Mystery Writers of America, Anthony award, Boucheron, World Mystery Convention, and Macvity award, Mystery Readers International, all in 1990, for best first crime novel *Postmortem*; British Crime Writers Gold Dagger award, 1994; French Prix du Roman d'Adventure. **Member:** Authors Guild, International Crime Writers Association, Mystery Writers of America, National Association of Medical Examiners, Virginia Writers Club, International Assocation of Chiefs of Police, International Association of Identification. **Agent:** International Creative Management, 40 W. 57th St., New York, New York 10019. **Address:** Cornwell Enterprises, P.O. Box 35686, Richmond, Virginia 23235.

PUBLICATIONS

Novels

Postmortem. New York, Scribner, 1990.
Body of Evidence. New York, Scribner, 1991.
All that Remains. New York, Scribner, 1992.
Cruel & Unusual. New York, Scribner, 1993.
The Body Farm. New York, Scribner, 1994.
From Potter's Field. New York, Simon & Schuster, 1995.
Cause of Death. New York, Putnam, 1996.
Hornet's Nest. New York, Putnam, 1997.
Unnatural Exposure. New York, Putnam, 1997.

Nonfiction

A Time for Remembering (with Charles Cornwell). New York, Harper, 1983.

*   *   *

Before Patricia Cornwell became a crime fiction writer, she spent many years having work experiences that would later shape the content of her stories. After a stint with the *Charlotte Observer* as an award-winning crime reporter from 1979 through 1981, Cornwell was employed in the chief medical examiner's office, first as a voluntary police officer and then as technical writer and computer analyst before becoming a consultant to the chief medical examiner of Richmond, Virginia. In 1983, Cornwell published a biography, *A Time for Remembering*, with her then husband, Charles Cornwell, of Ruth Bell Graham, wife of evangelist Billy Graham.

The main character in Cornwell's crime novel series is Kay Scarpetta, a Richmond chief medical examiner. Richmond had among the highest per capita crime rates in the United States during the 1980s and 1990s. Drawing on her observations from her real-world work, Cornwell's Scarpetta and her associates seem very authentic because of the carefully employed details used by the author; the works recreate medical autopsies and other methods related to criminal investigations. Scarpetta also reflects Cornwell's background as a forty-something divorced woman using forensic medicine and computer programming to enhance her investigations. Scarpetta's clues come from the dead, and the only way they can "speak" is through their chemical and biological testimonies, such as discoloration, rigor mortis, and entry wounds.

Postmortem (1990), the first crime novel to feature Scarpetta, became the only novel to win five prestigious mystery awards in one year (The Edgar award, the Creasey award, the Anthony award, the Macavity award, and the French Prix du Roman d'Adventure). In *Postmortem*, Scarpetta accomplishes two goals: she tracks down a serial rapist/killer and proves herself a skilled professional, strong enough to handle "a man's job." This theme of Scarpetta's sometimes-tense relationship with her mostly male colleagues runs throughout the series. In the beginning, Scarpetta is the subject of humor from male police personnel who are uneasy and suspicious of a woman medical examiner. Through time, these men come to respect and admire her because of her obvious abilities, courage, and perceptive insights into cases. This aspect of the series is exemplified by Scarpetta's relationship with detective Pete Marino, with whom she works in each novel. Their relationship grows from his doubting of her to his exasperating tendency to overprotect her.

FBI agent Mark James, another key male figure in Cornwell's books, is introduced in her second novel, *Body of Evidence* (1991), when he becomes involved in that novel's investigation with Scarpetta. In *All That Remains* (1992), for example, a subplot involves James's conflict between his personal life and career, while Scarpetta deals with minimal clues—jack of hearts playing cards, bones, and bits of clothing—in a series of difficult cases. 1993's *Cruel and Unusual* exhibits the bewildering nature of Scarpetta's cases: after a convicted murderer is executed, another murder occurs in the exact same method of operation. While Scarpetta investigates obtuse bits of evidence, such as a specific kinds of duct tape, mysterious marks and odors, DNA evidence, and strands of fiber, she must also face the loss of James, who was killed by a terrorist bomb.

Scarpetta confronts her feelings about James's death in *The Body Farm* (1994), while in *From Potter's Field* (1995) she has promise of new love. In the latter, she tracks a serial killer named Temple Gault, who was first introduced in *Cruel and Unusual*. Though set in New York City, *From Potter's Field* again reflects the extensive research and local ambience Cornwell evokes into her novels.

The character of Scarpetta is a duality. As a medical examiner, she has the training and professionalism to keep an objective distance that lets her rely on keen intellect to give insight into the many murders she encounters. Though she can distance herself from the aftermath of violence at a crime scene, Scarpetta's emotional and intellectual sensitivity to the human element (as opposed to being coldly clinical or hardened) and her personal revulsion at the desecrations associated with murder make the crimes that much more abominable, and real. Through Scarpetta's struggles, Cornwell has stated, she better understands that as a medical examiner grows more proficient in taking apart death, she comprehends it much less.

The life Cornwell constructs for Scarpetta resembles parts of her own. Like Cornwell, Scarpetta is divorced, has no children, has origins in Miami, a Windsor Farms home, and is fascinated with Malibu. Scarpetta and Cornwell share an insatiably curious intellect as well as an unstoppable determination. In addition to exhibiting proficiencies with technical and procedural matters of investigative work, Cornwell's novels are carefully plotted and in Scarpetta, a personable, knowledgeable female detective character, offer an uncommon perspective on murder cases.

—Annette Petrusso

COVINGTON, Vicki

Born: Victoria Marsh in 22 October 1952, in Birmingham, Alabama. **Education:** University of Alabama, B.A. 1974, and M.S.W. 1976. **Family:** Married Dennis Covington (a writer), 24 December 1977; two daughters. **Career:** Social worker in substance abuse programs, University of Alabama in Birmingham, 1978-88; writer, since 1988. **Awards:** Fellow of National Endowment for the Arts,

1988. **Agent:** Amanda Urban, ICM, 40 West 57th Street, New York, New York 10019.

PUBLICATIONS

Novels

Gathering Home. New York, Simon and Schuster, 1988.
Bird of Paradise. New York, Simon and Schuster, 1990.
Night Ride Home. New York, Simon and Schuster, 1992.
The Last Hotel for Women. New York, Simon and Schuster, 1996.

Uncollected Short Stories

"September Saint," in *Southern Humanities Review,* Vol. 18, no. 1, 1984.
"Magnolia," in *The New Yorker,* 24 March 1986.
"Duty," in *The New Yorker,* 18 August 1986.
"Affairs," in *Southern Magazine,* April 1988.
"The Natural Order of Things," in *Shenandoah,* Vol. 38., no. 2, 1988.
"Simple Things," in *Southern Humanities Review,* Vol. 26, no. 1, 1992.

Uncollected Essays

"Telling the Story," in *Southern Living,* February, 1990.
"The House Within," in *Southern Humanities Review,* Vol. 26, no. 1, 1992.

Works Adapted to Other Media: *The Last Hotel for Women,* adapted for stage, 1997.

*   *   *

Vicki Covington exemplifies the contemporary Southern writer who grapples with the social and political issues of her world, the late twentieth century in a South beset by its search for a new identity. One of Alabama's best-known contemporary writers, Covington depicts family life in the South in a period of tumultuous change and characters longing for lost traditions and values of an earlier time.

In *Gathering Home,* her first novel, Covington attacks head-on one of the most sensitive issues of Southern religion—the conflicts in the Southern Baptist Convention between conservatives and liberals and their widely-disparate views on race, women's rights, homosexuality, and the inerrancy of the Bible. Her young narrator, Whitney Gaines, reveals the perplexity she faces as she attempts to understand the hostility of church members and political opponents to the liberal ministry of her adoptive parents. Covington's novel is filled with optimism for the capabilities of the South's youth in finding its way through this threatening maze of political upheaval—in government, in the church, in families—with renewed faith and greater understanding.

Covington's second novel, *Bird of Paradise,* exhibits her skill at characterization in the memorable Honey Shugart, who has had more than her share of hardships in life but has endured with dignity. An Alabama waitress who has suffered financial hardships and life with an alcoholic husband, Honey's fortunes change dra-

matically with a family inheritance and an urban development proposal. These opportunities, however, have costs, and reliance on her rural upbringing helps to show Honey the way through these painful decisions.

Covington continues this exploration of the intricate relationships of place and family in her third novel, *Night Ride Home,* which depicts the harsh realities of life in the small mining camps of Alabama. Set in 1940, during the heyday of the coal industry near Birmingham, the novel gives an intimate view of the threatening daily existence of the miners and their families, who have lived with strikes and explosions, with danger and death, long before the intrusion of Pearl Harbor and World War on their lives. The young protagonist, Keller Hayes, and his bride-to-be face not only the perils of a new marriage but also the pending birth of his illegitimate child and the unknown fate of his father in a mining disaster. Covington portrays a world where love, faith, and spirituality prevail in the midst of hardships and seeming contradictions, a world whose inhabitants believe, "if you give a black newborn kid to somebody you love, it will bring good luck."

Her 1996 novel, *The Last Hotel for Women,* depicts one of the most painful periods of Alabama history—the tumultuous 1960s and the battle over civil rights. In her delicate, probing portrayal, Covington reveals the humanness beneath the headlines, individuals caught up in an issue far greater than their perception and deeply troubling. As in her other novels, Covington succeeds in presenting this world and its inhabitants with realism and sensitivity, in her protagonist Dinah Fraley and in her portrayal of the infamous "Bull" Connor. Dinah endures the friendship of Connor and his visits to their now-reputable hotel because of his earlier relationship with her mother when the hotel was a brothel. Covington succeeds in showing the complex nature of these characters and their emotions, as Dinah and her brother become involved with one of the injured Freedom Riders and encounter the expected wrath of Connor. The novelist accomplishes the difficult task of making the arch-segregationist Connor and his unpopular views understandable, at least in the context of an embattled South where traditional mores and customs are no longer acceptable.

Covington's realism and her sparse style, her use of historic events and characters, are disarmingly deceptive. Her succinct prose says little but suggests much, as seen in her sensuous descriptions of Sweetgum Flat in *Night Ride Home*: "There in Spring, fields would begin to bear traces of green corn seedlings, and the smell of manure mixed with sweetshrub gave off a natural, sordid blending of something terribly alluring." Though sometimes dealing with sordid situations, Vicki Covington succeeds in blending a realistic depiction of her society while filling her characters with optimism and hope and her pages with an affirmation of the human spirit's ability to prevail in this troubling world.

—Elaine W. Hughes

CREWS, Harry

Born: Harold Eugene Crews in Alma, Georgia, 6 June 1935. **Education:** University of Florida, B.A. 1960, M.S.Ed. 1962. **Mili-**

tary Service: U.S. Marine Corps, 1953-56; sergeant. **Family:** Married Sally Thornton Ellis, 1960 (divorced); two sons (one deceased). **Career:** English instructor, Broward Junior College, Ft. Lauderdale, Florida, 1962-68; associate professor, 1968-74, professor of English, University of Florida, Gainesville, since 1974. **Awards:** American Academy of Arts and Sciences Award, 1972; National Endowment for the Arts grant, 1974.

PUBLICATIONS

Novels

The Gospel Singer. New York, Morrow, 1968.
Naked in Garden Hills. New York, Morrow, 1969.
This Thing Don't Lead to Heaven. New York, Morrow, 1970.
Karate Is a Thing of the Spirit. New York, Morrow, 1971.
Car. New York, Morrow, 1972.
The Hawk Is Dying. New York, Knopf, 1973.
The Gypsy's Curse. New York, Knopf, 1974.
A Feast of Snakes. New York, Atheneum, 1976.
All We Need of Hell. New York, Harper, 1987.
The Knockout Artist. New York, Harper, 1988.
Body. New York, Poseidon, 1990.
Scar Lover. New York, Simon & Schuster, 1992.
The Mulching of America. New York, Simon & Schuster, 1995.
Celebration. New York, Simon & Schuster, 1998.

Short Stories

The Enthusiast. Palaemon Press, 1981.
Two. Northridge, California, Lord John, 1984.

Other

A Childhood: The Biography of a Place. New York, Harper, 1978.
Blood and Grits. New York, Harper, 1979.

Collections

Florida Frenzy. Gainesville, University Press of Florida, 1982.
Classic Crews: A Harry Crews Reader. New York, Poseidon, 1993.

*

Bibliography: *Harry Crews: A Bibliography* by Michael Hargraves, Westport, Connecticut, Meckler, 1986.

Interviews: Print—*Writing in the Southern Tradition: Interviews with Five Contemporary Authors* edited by A. S. Crowder, Atlanta, Rodopi, 1990. **Audio Recording**— *Interview: Harry Crews.* Columbia, Missouri, American Audio Prose Library, 1982.

Critical Studies: "Matters of Life and Death: The Novels of Harry Crews" by Allen Shepherd, *Critique,* Vol. 20, no. 1, 1978; "Georgia Boys: The Redclay Satyrs of Erskine Caldwell and Harry Crews" by John Seelye, *Virginia Quarterly Review,* Vol.12, 1980; *A Grit's Triumph: Essays on the Works of Harry Crews* edited by David K. Jeffrey, Port Washington, Associated Faculty Press, 1983; "Murder and Mayhem in Crews's *A Feast of Snakes*" by David K. Jeffrey, *Critique* Vol. 28, 1986; "Harry Crews After *A*

Childhood" by Frank Shelton, *The Southern Literary Journal,* Vol. 24, no. 2, 1992; "The Violent Bear It As Best They Can: Cultural Conflict in the Novels of Harry Crews" by Robert C. Covel, *Studies in the Literary Imagination,* Vol. 27, no. 2, 1994.

Harry Crews comments:

I've always thought a writer has an obligation to show the skull. This is not original with me. I think Flannery O'Connor may have said it—that if you don't show the skull behind the smile, then you haven't shown it all . . . . When I'm writing, I want the novel to be terrifying and beautiful and joyful and full of anguish and laughter at the same time, so that you're thinking, "My God, my God, what are we in here?" Now, why do I want to do that? I don't know. It's just part of who I am. I can't explain it to you. It's just the way it comes out.

*   *   *

Harry Crews, the author of twenty books, is in some ways a quintessentially "Southern" writer in his concern for the vanishing rural South; in his thematic use of grotesques; in his fascination with man's relationship with God and with the effects of a Protestant upbringing; and in his recognition that the "modern" South—the South of Faulkner, O'Connor, Caldwell, and Welty, a South of traditional values—has been lost.

His characters—alienated, bemused, angry, often violent—seek meaning in a variety of sometimes traditional and sometimes bizarre pursuits or places, and, at their best, Crews' novels are funny and startling works.

The works at the middle of Crews' career are his strongest, including at least two powerful and important novels (*The Gypsy's Curse* and *A Feast of Snakes*), a collection of fascinating essays (*Blood and Grits*), and one of the best autobiographies in American literature (*A Childhood: The Biography of a Place*), one which deserves to be read alongside Franklin's *Autobiography* and *The Education of Henry Adams*.

Crews was born in 1935 and raised in Bacon County, Georgia, the son of a sharecropper who died shortly after Harry was born. Harry's mother married her brother-in-law, Harry's uncle, a drunken, violent man; violence was a part of the household and a part of his daily life: during his first five years, before his uncle/stepfather tried to kill Harry's mother with a shotgun, prompting her to escape to Jacksonville, Florida, Harry fell into a vat of boiling water at a hog-scalding and watched his flesh fall off; he'd also suffered—either from polio or from an hysterical reaction to the violence in his home—the pain and indignity of having his legs contract at the knees, so that his heels touched his buttocks, a sight that drew first relatives and then total strangers to his home to view him, as one might view a monster (an experience that goes far to explain Crews' fascination with the freaks and grotesques that populate his novels).

Indeed, freaks appear as important characters in Crews' first three novels—a circumstance that led Crews' puzzled wife to ask at the time, "You don't intend to make a career out of midgets, do you?"—and in many of the later ones. Crews believes that his grotesques function importantly in his novels because they so obviously lack the "disguises" that keep contemporary man from self-knowledge; they exhibit the values Crews admires—courage, honesty, and strength among them; and they reflect the real condition of man in a postlapsarian world. Freaks are thus paradoxically normative characters in Crews' works.

In his first novel, *The Gospel Singer*, the titular protagonist eventually learns from Foot (a midget with a 27" foot) and the members of his Freak Fair the truth about corrupt and fallen human nature, but when he announces that truth, and the truth of his own corruption, to his startled congregation, they lynch him. In *Naked in Garden Hills* Crews chronicles the transfer of power in a Floridian Eden (a phosphate pit where 36 families now live) from Fat Man, a 600-pound Metrecal addict whose father originally owned the land, to Dolly, a former beauty queen who has transformed the phosphate plant into a discotheque. The novel comments satirically on the absence of religious value and purpose in contemporary life, on the power of Mammon to corrupt, and on the triumph of modern barbarism. *This Thing Don't Lead to Heaven* deals with a confusing array of characters, including a midget masseur, a dying 80-year-old man, a voodoo priestess, a preacher who denies the reality of death, a burial salesman, a postal sorter/aspiring writer, and the owner of an old people's home; satirizing America's preoccupation with and horror of death—Evelyn Waugh and Jessica Mitford by way of Erskine Caldwell—this is Crews' least successful early novel.

In *Karate Is a Thing of the Spirit, Car*, and *The Hawk Is Dying* Crews continues his satiric commentary on contemporary ways, particularly on our fascination with material things and with power and with our confusion of either for religious, spiritual, or ethical value. In *Karate* John Kaimon finds a measure of peace in the self-discipline of karate and eventually of happiness in his love of the beauty queen, Brown Belt, an American ideal who combines the potential for sex and death; however, he also comes to recognize that he lacks the ability to believe that karate or heroes or gods avail and might affirm or transform anything. In *Car* Herman Mack loves cars so much he wants to consume one, to do as Fat Man in the earlier novel had done—put everything outside himself inside himself. The novel amusingly chronicles the public Florida spectacle that surrounds his attempt. *Hawk* chronicles George Gattling's quest for meaning in the traditional pursuit of falconry, a response to the mundanity of his own life as the owner of a car upholstery business and to the death of his retarded nephew, who has drowned in his waterbed, the only person for whom George has ever felt love. All three novels comment in their ways on man's various dualities—spirit and body, illusions and realities, for example, suggesting as well how seldom love prevails.

Crews published what are in my view his best works between the years 1974 and 1979. *The Gypsy's Curse* takes as its protagonist Marvin Molar, a deaf-mute strongman without functional legs, and tells the story from his point of view; miraculously, the novel works. Marvin allows Hester Maile, the object of his hopeless love, to disrupt the family of peaceful punch drunks and gym rats with whom he lives, to cuckold him, and effectually to murder his surrogate father before he kills her. The novel is a powerful portrayal of the desperation and hopelessness involved with love. Both horrifying and funny, *A Feast of Snakes*, Crews' best novel, follows Joe Lon Mackey, a 20-year-old illiterate redneck and former high school football hero, during the four-day course

of a rattlesnake rodeo in his hometown of Mystic, Georgia. Now the husband of a ruined wife, Elfie, with two sons, a psychotic sister, and a violent father who trains fighting dogs, Joe Lon despairs of his life even as the novel and the festival of the rodeo opens. In the course of the action, he finds meaning neither in his family nor friends nor community; only in violence and murder does he eventually find release from his pain and anguish.

A Childhood: The Biography of a Place is in the opinion of most critics Crews' best work. Beautifully written and crafted, the book is an amazing and touching account of the first five savage and brutal years of Crews' life and of life in the rural South during the late 1930s. Like *A Feast of Snakes* in the horrific black humor of some of the events it chronicles, *Childhood* also describes poignantly and without sentimentality the hardscrabble life of farmers near the edge of ruin. *Blood and Grits* contains some of the essays Crews wrote during his stint as an *Esquire* columnist; many of them, "Climbing the Tower" and "Carny," for example, offer straightforward statements about violence and about freaks and, thus, important insights into his novels.

Crews has said that although he had hoped it would be "cathartic," writing *A Childhood* "took a lot out of me" ("An Interview with Harry Crews," *AWP Chronicle*, vol. 24, #4, 1992, p.4), and there is an 8-year gap before the publication of *All We Need of Hell*, his first novel in eleven years. The work recycles one of the relatively minor characters from *Feast,* Duffy Deeter, and although interesting and amusing for a few chapters (chapters which originally appeared six years earlier as *The Enthusiast*) it collapses into sentimentality and narrative chaos in the latter half. *The Knockout Artist* and *Body* are both better novels. The former uses the extraordinary capacity of its protagonist, a glass-jawed boxer, to knock himself out as a metaphor of man's willingness to punish and corrupt himself; only his relationship with an innocent Cajun fighter he agrees to manage redeems him and earns him back his self-respect. The latter recycles a relatively minor character from *The Gypsy's Curse,* Russell "Muscle" Morgan, here the bodybuilding coach of Shereel Dupont, nee Dorothy Turnipseed. The latter satirizes the desire of contemporary men and women to remake themselves in a corrupt urban world and calculates the painful expense of their attempts and their ultimate failures.

Scar Lover has its critical fans, particularly Robert C. Covel, who believes the novel a "radical departure from Crews's earlier novels because, he suggests, for the first time, the possibility of a catharsis that moves beyond violence and toward more constructive human interrelationships." This "catharsis" involves the acceptance of one's own literal and metaphorical scars and those of others, no matter how repugnant they may appear; this seems to me a view that Crews has stated less sentimentally in earlier novels and in the essay "Carny." *The Mulching of America* is an embarrassing work, a largely unfunny satire of America's desire for material success, while Crews' most recent novel, *Celebration*, chronicles the effect of a beautiful blonde, Too Much, on a Florida trailer-park filled with the dying aged; while the book returns to the subject of *This Thing Don't Lead to Heaven*, man's fear of and consequent despair about the fact that he must die, it is less fragmented than that work.

Crews said earlier in his career that "I always wanted twenty titles because I thought if you did . . . , if you wrote as well as you could and as honestly as you could and with as much concentration, focus, diligence . . . as you could, well, then, out of twenty you might get a good one" (*A Grit's Triumph*). He now has those twenty titles and at least four "good ones" by my count. His works are powerful tales of a world by turns violent and brutal, dangerous and darkly comic, filled with characters who are literally or metaphorically grotesque yet for whose despair and pain and need and desire the reader often feels a poignant sympathy.

—David K. Jeffrey

CRONE, Moira

Born: Goldsboro, North Carolina, 10 August 1952. **Education:** Smith College, Northhampton, Massachusetts, B.A. (high honors) 1970-74; Johns Hopkins University, M.A. 1976-77. **Family:** Married Rodger Kamenetz; two daughters. **Career:** Visiting professor, Johns Hopkins University, 1977-81; visiting professor, Goucher University, 1977-81; co-editor, *City Lit*, 1980; assistant, associate, and full professor of English, Louisiana State University, since 1981; editor and founder, *The New Delta Review*, 1983-86. **Awards:** Elliott Coleman award for fiction, 1977; Pirates Alley Faulkner Society Collin C. Diboll award for short story, 1993; Bunting Institute fellowship, Radcliffe College of Harvard University, 1987-88; National Endowment for the Arts Humanities Summer Institute fellowship, University of North Carolina at Chapel Hill, 1989; National Endowment for the Arts fellowship in fiction, 1990; fellowship to the Ragdale Foundation, 1995. **Address:** Louisiana State University, English Department, Allen Hall, Baton Rouge, Louisiana 70808.

PUBLICATIONS

Novels

The Life of Lucy Fern, Part One. New York, Cambridge, Adult Fiction, 1983.
The Life of Lucy Fern, Part Two. New York, Cambridge, Adult Fiction, 1983.
A Period of Confinement. New York, Putnam, 1986.

Collections

The Winnebago Mysteries and Other Stories. New York, Fiction Collective, 1982.
Dream States: Stories. University of Mississippi Press, 1995.

Uncollected or Anthologized Short Stories

"Easter," in the *Greycourt Review*, Spring 1973.
"Death and the Pastime Diner," in the *Greycourt Review*, Winter 1974.
"Defining Affairs," in *The Falcon*, Fall 1977.
"During a Night in the Winter," in *Gallimaufry 12: These Women*, 1978.
"Having Always Confused My Body with Hers," in *The Washington Review of the Arts*, Summer Fiction Issue, 1978.
"The Brooklyn Lie," in *The Falcon*, Winter 1979.

"Cleanliness," in *The City Paper* (Baltimore), 10 August 1979.
"Crocheting," in *Washington Review of the Arts*, Summer Fiction Issue, 1980.
"Kudzu," in the *Ohio Review*, Summer 1980.
"Aphasia," in the *Western Humanities Review*, Winter 1983.
"Oslo," in the *New Yorker* (New York), 28 May 1984.
"Paris Leaves Me Cold," in *Mademoiselle*, January 1985.
"German," in *American Voice*, Spring 1988.
"Just Outside the B.T.," in the *Southern Review*, Spring 1989.
"Plans," in the *Boston Sunday Globe Magazine*, 15 October 1989.
"Recovery," in *New Stories by Southern Women* edited by Mary Ellis Gibson. Columbia, University of South Carolina Press, 1989.
"Just Outside the B.T.," in *New Stories from the South: The Year's Best, 1990* edited by Shannon Ravenel. New York, Algonquin Books of Chapel Hill, 1990.
"Fever," in *Missouri Review*, Winter 1993.
"There Is a River in New Orleans," in *Negative Capability*, August 1994.
"Dream State," in *Gettysburg Review*, January 1995.
"Gaugin," in *North American Review*, Winter 1995.

*   *   *

Moira Crone explores separation and relationships among families, especially between mothers and their children, most often their daughters. Her women often are finding their way in the world, away from their homes and families, penetrating emotions surrounding individual identity amid the complexity of motherhood. Human relationships are fragile in her work, with characters concerned about difference and individuation and often fearing the hardships of failure more than trusting in support and lasting bonds.

Crone's first published book, *The Winnebago Mystery and Other Stories* (1982), includes the title novella and six additional short stories. "The Winnebago Mystery" centers on 19-year-old Ruth Stark, a college dropout who sets out hitchhiking instead of going home and facing her parents. Stark is picked up by Clack Clark in his Winnebago. Like Ruth, Clark has chosen to have no permanent address, opting to live in his camper and drive around the country.

Part of the narrative of "The Winnebago Mystery" is comprised of letters Ruth writes to her parents and their replies, which remain unmailed since she can give them no return address. The relationship between Ruth and her mother, Gloria Stark, to whom most of her letters are written, is illuminated in these passages. The unmailed letters reveal the strain in Gloria's marriage to Ruth's father, George, as well as Gloria's contradictory personality. Gloria is a difficult woman, a perfectionist with unbelievable demands for her family, and an essentially unhappy woman. Despite their conflicts, the family members cannot live without each other: where there is conflict, there is bond, and where there is rancor, there is need and dependency. Gloria leaves George to try to find Ruth, and, in turn, George leaves their home to find both Gloria and Ruth. Gloria's search parallels that of Ruth's, and she eventually finds her daughter. But when they meet, their unresolved conflicts are manifested in a hair-pulling fight. Indeed, such symbolic action pervades the end of the novella: Ruth abandons Clark, pilfers the camper, and after the fight with her mother, Ruth crashes the Winnebago into a tree, paralleling the broken home of her family—wrecked but not beyond at least a temporary fix.

Similar themes pervade Crone's novel, *A Period of Confinement* (1986), whose protagonist, Alma Taylor, is a painter and instructor. Her father, an alcoholic, abandoned Alma and her mother many years ago but has never been totally absent from their lives. Alma's mother continues an antagonistic relationship with her former husband yet still feels ties to him. For example, she salvages him from far off bars when he phones her, obviously drunk and always without money.

During the course of the novel, the father falls in love with a much younger woman who is involved with another woman. Alma's relationships with her parents, her friends, and her lover are equally complicated. Her circle includes a friend who has undergone a sex change and now lives with another female friend and a woman who left her husband for another woman; Alma is intimately involved with a man who marries and has a child with another woman, and she is rebuffed when trying to become close to his family.

Throughout the text of *A Period of Confinement*, Crone underscores the idea that many people fear relationships with others because things often go wrong. Both parents and their children—who learn this behavior from them—make mistakes. Crone emphasizes in the undercurrent of her narrative that people are invariably disconnected from each other, and they can feel most isolated when it seems that they are together. Crone's vibrant expression of this basic human contradiction gives her writing a deeply felt edge.

—Annette Petrusso

D

DAUGHARTY, Janice

Born: Janice Elaine Staten in Lowndes County, Georgia, 24 October 1944. **Education:** Attended Valdosta State University, 1985-90. **Family:** Married Seward Daugharty (a contractor), 25 December 1963; three children. **Career:** Homemaker; librarian, 1991-92; writer in residence, Valdosta State University, since 1996. **Agent**: Ginger Barbe, 101 Fifth Avenue, New York, New York 10003. **Address:** Valdosta State University, Department of English, Valdosta, Georgia 31698.

PUBLICATIONS

Novels

Dark of the Moon. Dallas, Baskerville, 1994.
Necessary Lies. New York, HarperCollins, 1995.
Pawpaw Patch. New York, HarperCollins, 1996.
Earl in the Yellow Shirt. New York, HarperCollins, 1997.
Whistle. New York, HarperCollins, 1998.

Short Story Collections

Going through the Change. Princeton, New Jersey, Ontario Review Press, 1994.

* * *

In a sense, Janice Daugharty spent the first five decades of her life preparing for a literary career. She was born and reared in rural Georgia, married after high school, had three children, and did not begin to write until she was thirty-nine, did not publish her first work until ten years later. If that first novel, *Dark of the Moon*, does not seem like the work of a novice, surely the reason is that the author had spent years experiencing life, observing her surroundings, and speculating about the meaning of it all.

Daugharty's fiction is set in the sparsely-populated section of Georgia that lies near the Florida border, a region of sandy soil, scrub timber, and a reputation for poverty, ignorance, violence, and bigotry. Daugharty is not a sentimentalist. Indeed, she recognizes the fact that many of her characters cannot afford to be law-abiding citizens. In *Earl in the Yellow Shirt*, which was nominated for the Pulitzer Prize, the Scurvy boys cannot think of any way but bootlegging to raise money for their mother's funeral. Hank Lee, the moonshiner in *Dark of the Moon*, has no qualms about beating his sons or getting rid of revenuers; if he has never laid a hand on his wife, it is only because she is more useful undamaged. Violence comes naturally to most of the men in Daugharty's fiction. In *Necessary Lies*, after Pappy Ocain Flowers is saved, he shoots off his trigger finger so that he cannot kill again. One of the short stories in *Going through the Change* is about attempted rape, while others involve child neglect and kidnaping. Bigotry flourishes among the good Christian fundamentalists in Daugharty's fiction, as Chanell Foster discovers in *Pawpaw Patch*. After someone starts a rumor that she has African-American blood, she very nearly has to leave town.

In this male-dominated society, it is not easy for women to survive, let alone to flourish. They are worked like mules and bred like cattle. The men take no responsibility for their wives' pregnancies. After his wife Louella dies in childbirth, the shiftless head of the Scurvy clan blames her for producing a child he "hain't even ordered, " complaining, "Every time I paid that woman a little attention, she'd come up in the family way." Pregnancy can put an end to any hope a woman might have of escaping from her fate. In *Necessary Lies*, the brightest of Pappy Ocain's children, Cliffie Flowers, knows that pregnancy means an end to her schooling. Even if Roy Harris Weeks marries her and takes her to Fort Bragg with him, she will never fulfill her potential.

However, Daugharty's heroines are strong women who accept hardship and have a tremendous capacity for love. After she learns that Roy Harris is her half-brother, Cliffie will not get rid of her unborn child. Even if it is defective, she knows that she will love it. It is impossible for these women to desert their children. In *Dark of the Moon*, Merdie Lee has put up with Hank for years, rather than leave her sons to be corrupted by him. Her sense of duty prevails both over her desire for fame as a country singer and her yearning for real love. One of Daugharty's most moving scenes is in *Earl in the Yellow Shirt*, when sixteen-year-old Loujean Scurvy, who can "outread and outfigger evry one in my class," sits down in the rocker where her mother nursed so many children and cuddles the newborn baby, weeping for her dead mama, her little sister, and her own future.

One might dismiss Daugharty's characters as merely pitiable, like Loujean and Cliffie, or despicable, like the totally worthless Old Man Scurvy, or evil, like the appalling Roy Harris Weeks. However, almost all of them have some admirable qualities, which shine more brightly because there is so much darkness in their lives. Even Hank Lee lives by a code of conduct. He is not a killer; moreover, though he sees nothing wrong with moonshine, he does not want his sons in the more lucrative drug trade. Family still means something to these people. The Scurvy boys risk their lives to give their mother a decent burial. In *Necessary Lies*, her parents see that Cliffie is cleared of murder charges, even though it takes perjury to solve the problem. There is also a strong sense of community among these people and old rituals for times of crisis. As soon as people hear about Louella Scurvy's death, as if by magic the kitchen is scrubbed and the table covered with bowls of food, the front room and the porch filled with people talking or just sitting, to help the bereaved get through the difficult hours that follow any death. Even when the community turns on one, as in *Pawpaw Patch*, in time there can be reconciliations and even apologies, though one can hardly blame Chanell for making it difficult for some of her nastiest critics to get a hair appointment.

However she chooses to tell a story, through a first person narrator, as in *Dark of the Moon*, or through several narrators, as in

Earl in the Yellow Shirt, or in the narrowly focused third person, as in *Necessary Lies* and *Pawpaw Patch*, Daugharty has the power to draw her readers into her world. Part of her secret is language, her authentic idioms, for example: her characters speak of "plunder" or a "chester drawers," or say that someone "belonged to sing." Part of it is the exactness of even the most trivial descriptions, as when Chanell's former sister-in-law Bell puts "her great Aigner bag on a small, wobbly table." Daugharty's comic scenes are almost unbearably funny: for instance, the account of Chanell's spitefully painting her house purple and sowing garbage around it "like fertilizer," or Old Man Scurvy's running narrative of his wild ride in a stolen car, which ends with him so shaken he has to admit to the notorious Sonia Lee that he is too old for her. Though some have placed her in the Southern Gothic tradition or suggested a kinship to Flannery O'Connor, Janice Daugharty has a narrative voice unlike that of any other Southern writer. It is as unique as the rapidly vanishing way of life so magnificently re-created in her fiction.

—Rosemary M. Canfield Reisman

DAVENPORT, Guy

Born: Guy Mattison Davenport, Jr., in Anderson, South Carolina, 23 November 1927. **Education:** Duke University, B.A. 1948; Merton College, Oxford (as a Rhodes scholar), B.Litt. 1950; Harvard University, Ph.D. 1961. **Military Service:** U.S. Army Airborne Corps, 1950-51. **Career:** Instructor, Washington University, St. Louis, 1952-55; assistant professor, Haverford College, 1961-63; professor, University of Kentucky, 1963-91; writer, book reviewer for literary, political, and popular journals. **Address:** 601 Sayre Avenue, Lexington, Kentucky 40508.

Publications

Poetry

Flowers and Leaves: Poema vel Sonata, Carmina Autumni Primaeque Veris Transformationum. Highlands, North Carolina, Williams, 1966.
Thasos and Ohio: Poems and Translations, 1950-1980. Manchester, United Kingdom, Carcanet, 1985; San Francisco, North Point, 1986.

Short Story Collections

Tatlin! New York, Scribners, 1974.
Da Vinci's Bicycle: Ten Stories. Baltimore, Johns Hopkins University Press, 1979.
Eclogues: Eight Stories. San Francisco, North Point, 1981.
Apples and Pears and Other Stories. San Francisco, North Point, 1984.
The Jules Verne Steam Balloon: Nine Stories. San Francisco, North Point, 1987.
The Drummer of the Eleventh North Devonshire Fusiliers. San Francisco, North Point, 1990.
A Table of Green Fields: Ten Stories. New York, New Directions, 1993.

The Cardiff Team: Ten Stories. New York, New Directions, 1996.
12 Stories. Washington, D.C., Counterpoint, 1997.

Essay Collections

The Geography of the Imagination: Forty Essays. San Francisco, North Point, 1981.
Every Force Evolves a Form: Twenty Essays. San Francisco, North Point, 1987.

Visual Arts Books

Trois Caprices. Louisville, Pace Trust, 1981.
Goldfinch Thistle Star. New York, Red Ozier, 1983.
The Art of Lafcadio Hearn, with Clifton Waller Bennet. Charlottesville, University of Virginia Library, 1983.
A Balthus Notebook. New York, Ecco, 1989.
The Drawings of Paul Cadmus. New York, Rizzoli, 1990.
Art of the Forties. New York, Museum of Modern Art, 1991.
Charles Burchfield's Seasons. San Francisco, Pomegranate, 1994.
The Balance of Quinces: The Paintings and Drawings of Guy Davenport, edited by Eric Anderson Reece. New York, New Directions, 1996.
The Hunter Gracchus and Other Papers on Literature and Art. Washington, D.C., Counterpoint, 1996.

Criticism

Cities on Hills: A Study of IXXX of Ezra Pound's Cantos. Ann Arbor, UMI Research, 1983.

Novellas

The Bicycle Rider. New York, Red Ozier, 1985.
Jonah. New York, Nadja, 1986.

Translations

Carmina Archilochi: The Fragments of Archilochos. Berkeley, University of California Press, 1964.
Sappho: Poems and Fragments. Ann Arbor, University of Michigan Press, 1965.
Archilochos, Sappho, Alkman: Three Lyric Poets of the Late Greek Bronze Age. Berkeley, University of California Press, 1980.
Herakleitos and Diogenes. Bolinas, California, Grey Fox, 1980.
The Mimes of Herondas. Berkeley, Grey Fox, 1981.
Boris de Rachewiltz, Maxims of the Ancient Egyptians. Louisville, Pace Trust, 1983.
Seven Greeks. New York, New Directions, 1995.
The Logia of Yeshua: The Sayings of Jesus, edited by Benjamin Urruitia. Washington, D.C., Counterpoint, 1996.

Other

Pennant Key-Indexed Study Guide to Homer's Iliad. Philadelphia, Educational Research Associates, 1967.
Pennant Key-Indexed Study Guide to Homer's Odyssey. Philadelphia, Educational Research Associates, 1967.

Editor, *The Intelligence of Louis Agassiz: A Specimen Book of Scientific Writings.* Boston, Beacon, 1963.

Illustrator, *The Lug of Days to Come: New and Selected Poems and Translations*, with Daniel Haberman et al. John Daniel & Co., 1996.

*

Bibliographies: "Guy Davenport: A Bibliographical Checklist," *American Book Collector*, March/April 1984; *Guy Davenport: A Descriptive Bibliography, 1947-1995* by Joan St. C. Crane, Haverford, Pennsylvania, Green Shade, 1996.

Interview: "An Interview with Guy Davenport," with Barry Alpert, *Vort*, Vol. 3, no. 3, 1976.

Critical Studies: "Invention in Guy Davenport's Da Vinci's Bicycle" by Robert Morace, *Critique,* Vol. 22, no. 3 , 1981; "Rare Bird" by George Steiner, *New Yorker,* November 30, 1981; "Erotic Ear, Amoral Eye" by Alain Arias-Misson, *Chicago Review,* Spring 1986; "A Guydebook to the Last Modernist: Davenport on Davenport and *Da Vinci's Bicycle*" by Lance Olsen, *Journal of Narrative Technique,* Spring 1986; "Apples and Pears and Other Stories" by Jerome Klinkowitz, *The Review of Contemporary Fiction,* Spring 1986.

*   *   *

In his essay "The Symbol of the Archaic," Guy Davenport proposes that a revival of interest in the pre-Industrial past can reenergize creative impulses and lead to a course different than that offered in modern times—a course where imagination and instinct are more greatly valued and where humanity lives more in harmony with nature. This process of rediscovery—of "awakening an archaic sense of the world" as he states in the essay—is reflected in the artists, writers, architects, and engineers whose works he explores in his essays and whose views he incorporates in his fiction. In the Modernist tradition of James Joyce and Ezra Pound, Davenport creates mythopoeic works that draw on and reveal the perpetuity of myths, ideals, and invention—what he terms "Daedalian art." His fiction displays immense erudition and includes a series of pieces in which Davenport explores the reanimating of instinctual urges based on the ideals of Charles Fourier, who wrote a dozen books outlining how a happy society might evolve.

Davenport is Modernist in method, assembling historical references, facts, and allusions in stories and critical discourse, crafting verse-like prose to create literary collages: his pieces develop through recurring structural patterns, juxtapositions, and parataxis—mirroring the discovery and associative processes in which they form (as suggested in the title, *Every Force Evolves a Form,* of one of his essay collections). Linear development and other evidence of rationalism are absent. Instead, in his prose we view the imagination as it reacts with reality and draws on a wealth of historical, often archaic knowledge—whatever is appropriate for recasting essential truths and for enlightening through extended associations, forming an account of inquiries in the geography of imagination that stretches through time and place from the ancient Mediterranean world to contemporary America.

Thus, a Davenport essay on Grant Wood's famous painting *American Gothic* yields insight on the history of spectacles (worn by the farmer) and the sunscreen on the porch in the background, relates such information to Wood's maturing as an artist, and imaginatively speculates on the images presented. In other essays he traces allusions to the Orpheus myth in stories by Edgar Allan Poe and Eudora Welty, of the Persephone myth in a story by O. Henry, and elucidates referential power in phrases by Poe that were seemingly used for aural, rhetorical effects ("Nicean barks of yore" and "perfumed sea" in "To Helen" Davenport associates, respectively, with ancient shipyards at Nice and wafting aromas from orchards along the shoreline courses sailed by ancient mariners). There is a constant foraging for information by Davenport that expands the implications of his studies, and he careful situates bits of esoteric knowledge in his prose. Picasso, for whom he expresses admiration as an artist who foisted off the rationalizing elements of civilization to regain a childlike innocence, scoured scrap heaps for materials he assembled into works of art, and Davenport, too, searches among a vast body of discarded culture to make new and enrich his writings.

A rare personal reference occurs in his essay "Finding" from the collection *The Geography of the Imagination,* where Davenport recalls spending many Sundays of his youth with his family looking for Indian arrows and other artifacts in the area around his native Anderson, South Carolina—a precise metaphor for his own scholarly pursuits. His two collections of essays, *The Geography of the Imagination* (1981) and *Every Force Evolves a Form* (1987), range far in their discussions of history, literature, and art, consistently favoring writers and artists whose works display an inclusiveness of historical referents—Pound, Poe, Joyce, Picasso, for example. He can ground discussion in scholarly attention to standard topics and details (tracing Joyce's indebtedness to Homer, for example), while pursuing arcane allusions. Consistent with this method is his championing of contemporaries like Charles Olson and Louis Zukofsky over Confessional poets such as Robert Lowell. Less debatable are his lucid and penetrating analyses of works by Welty and Marianne Moore that display his characteristic wealth of discovery and explication.

Davenport's erudition and collage compositional method are in evidence in his stories, which he has referred to as "assemblages of history and necessary fiction." "The Aeroplanes at Brescia" (*Tatlin!,* 1974), for example, recreates the famous 1909 air show in Paris that was attended by Franz Kafka (who wrote a newspaper article about the event), Giacomo Puccini, and Gabriele D'Annunzio, among others, and Davenport includes linguistic philosopher Ludwig Wittgenstein, whom Kafka believes he spotted in the crowd, among the characters. Their impressions of the historically significant event creates a lively fictional account offering several perspectives. In other stories, people are seen interacting within and outside of their actual historical time periods, as Davenport imagines discussions, impressions, and relationships in important events, from Gertrude Stein in Paris, to Alexander the Great meeting Diogenes, to Nixon in China. As Davenport wrote in a postscript to *12 Stories* (1997):

> When I rolled up my sleeves, took a deep breath, and began to try my hand at fiction back in the 1970s, my hope was to make a few imaginative structures about various people and events in the fabric of history that were, at the time, unfamiliar enough to be interesting and consequential enough to be known—the Russian genius

Vladimir Tatlin, the discovery of the prehistoric painted cave at Lasceaux, the traveler Pausanias walking around Greece in the second century of our half of time. I tried to be as inventive as I could, obeying the injunction "in letters of gold on T'ang's bathtub" to "yet again make it new" that Thoreau quotes in *Walden* and Ezra Pound used as a battle cry.

The titles of Davenport's collections are significant in understanding his recurring themes. *Tatlin!* (1974), for example, refers to the humanistic artist and engineer who was demeaned by Stalin, symbolic of the mechanistic, Industrial Age crushing creative, humanistic impulses. *Da Vinci's Bicycle* (1979) points to sketches in the master artist's notebooks and references the grand imagination Davenport champions; it also provides the kind of jumping-off point in which Davenport revels—Da Vinci imagined flying machines, but it was the Wright Brothers, themselves bicycle mechanics, who made the successful leap from ground to air vehicle, and the flight motif itself (kites, gliders, planes) recurs as a symbol of freedom in Davenport's stories. The title of *Eclogues* (1981) alludes to a pastoral literary form used by classical Greek and Roman poets and reflects Davenport's ongoing idylls on ideal life conditions for happiness. *Apples and Pears* (1984) suggests fall and redemption (through rediscovery of pre-lapsarian values), the apple representing the loss of Eden, the pear symbolizing recovery.

Several stories develop ideal life conditions posited by Charles Fourier through the ongoing adventures of Adriaan von Hovendaal, a fictional Dutch philosopher of physical and intellectual strength and beauty, to establish a pastoral utopia. Small social units, usually comprised of teenagers and most often emphasizing male physical beauty, are organized by von Hovendaal to pursue instinctual pleasures of the mind and body in bucolic settings. Rendered through the notebook and diaristic observations of von Hovendaal, the stories evoke the vision of Fournier in liberating the imagination and passions. Increasingly, the stories develop into indulgent sexual escapades, usually homoerotic, presented with inexhaustible tenderness. The absence of sexual tension realizes the vision of Fourier's New Harmonium: humanity is intrinsically good and sexual impulse is a most natural form of expression.

This theme is continued in *The Jules Verne Steam Balloon* (1987), with new settings and symbols, but most significant is the intrusion of tension and evil, meditated on by Tvemunding, a theological student and budding artist, and exemplified in the character Bicycle Rider, a drug user. Davenport implies that drug use is an example of practices that turn the mind inward for visions and pleasure, eventually leading to chaos and madness as opposed to communal harmony and happiness. This outlook also suggests why, in his essays on contemporary poets, Davenport derides Confessionalism, with its inward nature, as a dead end. "The Dawn of Erewhon" (*Tatlin!*), which draws on Samuel Butler's visionary writings, and "Apples and Pears," where the four-part form corresponds roughly to the stages set by Fourier, are Davenport's most extended explorations of Fourier's vision while brimming with mythic allusions, puns, and linguistic intricacies.

12 Stories collects pieces from three previous short story volumes and provides an excellent sampler of Davenport's fiction. The aforementioned "The Aeroplanes at Brescia" and "Robot," based on the discovery of prehistoric drawings in the Lascaux caves, feature his fictional recreation of historically significant mo-

ments. Kafka returns in "The Chair" accompanied by the rebbe of Belz: the two tour Paris, visit a spa, and contemplate the theme of artifice and nature while considering a decorative chair (significantly embroidered with apple and pear leaves). Allusions to Wallace Stevens, on whom Davenport has written insightful criticism, are rife in "The Chair" (where the object is approached in the manner of Stevens' "Anecdote of the Jar") and in "Fifty-Seven Views of Fujiyama" (which recalls Stevens' "Thirteen Ways of Looking at a Blackbird"). The latter story interweaves allusions to Basho's mountain journey with the story of a couple vacationing in the mountains of New Hampshire. "The Bowmen of Shu" reconstructs the battlefield diaries of sculptor Henri Gaudier-Brzeka, and "Badger" is comprised of numerous brief sections, some only a sentence long, developing through juxtaposition and parataxis a Davenport collage, where high classicism mixes with Modernism and eclectic learning blends with dense phrasing in assemblages of history and necessary fiction.

—Perry Bear

DAVIS, Angela (Yvonne)

Born: Birmingham, Alabama, 26 January 1944. **Education:** Brandeis University, B.A. (honors) in philosophy c. 1965; studied at Institut für Sozialforschung, Frankfurt; University of California, San Diego, M.A. 1968. **Family:** Married Hilton Braithwaite. **Career:** Lecturer in philosophy, University of California, Los Angeles; joined Communist Party, 1968; travelled to Cuba, 1969; active in Soledad Brothers Defense Committee; acquitted of charges of murder, kidnapping, and conspiracy, 1972; ran for vice-president on the Communist Party ticket, 1980, 1984; lecturer at colleges and universities, including University of California, Berkeley, University of California, Santa Cruz, and San Francisco University. Contributor of articles to periodicals, including *Ebony*. **Awards:** Honorary Ph.D., Lenin University. **Member:** National Committee of the Communist Party, National Alliance against Racist and Political Repression, National Black Women's Health Project.

PUBLICATIONS

Autobiography

Angela Davis: An Autobiography. New York, Random House, 1974.

Political/Social Theory

Women, Race, and Class. New York, Random House, 1981.
Violence against Women and the Ongiong Challenge to Racism. N.p., 1987.
Women, Culture, and Politics. New York, Random House, 1989.
Resisting State Violence: Radicalicism, Gender, and Race in U.S. Culture. N.p., 1996.
Blues Legacies and Black Feminism: Gertrude 'Ma' Rainey, Bessie Smith, and Billie Holiday. N.p., 1998.

Uncollected Essays

"Reflections on the Black Woman's Role in the Community of Slaves," in *Black Scholar*, 3(4), December 1971.

Other

Editor with others, *If They Come in the Morning.* N.p., Third Press, 1971.

Recording: *Angela Davis Speaks,* Folkways, 1971.

*

Critical Studies: *The People vs. Angela Davis* by Charles R. Ashman, Pinnacle, 1972; *From Where I Sat* by Nelda J. Smith, New York, Vantage, 1973; *Black Macho and the Myth of the Superwoman* by Michele Wallace, New York, Dial Press, 1978.

*   *   *

In a decade of activism, Angela Davis stands out as a radical activist and as an author of tremendous influence. She is certainly one of the best-known black women in America—a charismatic, brilliant educator who continues to infuriate the academic and political establishment and has been a consistent critic of America's racism, sexism, and imperialism for over 30 years. A writer of uncommon power, Davis has been one of the best chroniclers of the anti-war and Black Power movements as well as one of the first scholars to write extensively on the history of black women. Her seminal essay, "Reflections on the Black Woman's Role in the Community of Slaves," written while Davis was in jail charged with murder, kidnapping, and conspiracy to commit both, has been cited as an early call—which few heeded—to consider the unique role of slave women. Davis wrote: "We, the black women of today, must accept the full weight of a legacy wrought in blood by our mothers in chains.... As heirs to a tradition of supreme perseverance and heroic resistance, we must hasten to take our place wherever our people are forging on towards freedom."

Born 26 January 1944, in Birmingham, Alabama, Davis is the daughter of middle-class professionals who fostered their talented child's ambition to learn. Her mother, Sallye E., and her father, B. Frank Davis were schoolteachers, although Davis's father later started his own gas station to better support his family. Her mother and grandmother instructed Angela in African American history, and the child's keen awareness of the social inequities of her surroundings grew as she participated in civil rights actions with her mother. Her education molded the radical woman she became, from the Elizabeth Irwin High School she attended in New York on scholarship (where Davis became a Marxist-Leninist) to Brandeis University, where she studied French literature.

Davis spent a watershed year at the Sorbonne in Paris, deepening her commitment to helping the oppressed as she learned of the struggle in Algeria against the French. When the infamous church bombing in Birmingham in 1963 killed four little girls Davis knew, she was ready to advance politically, and found the mentor she sought in the philosopher Herbert Marcuse. As Marcuse's student, Davis became a philosopher and studied in Germany with Theodore Adorno and Oskar Negt. She earned her masters in philosophy in 1969 from the University of California at San Diego and moved swiftly to complete her Ph.D. requirements other than her dissertation. During these years, her campus activism led her to the Student Non-violent Coordinating Committee and Franklin and Kendra Alexander, who became her close friends and advi-

sors. Franklin was active in the Black Panthers and the Communist Party, and Davis herself joined the Party in 1968.

This action would have tremendous repercussions on Davis's academic life, as she lost her faculty position in philosophy at the University of California at Los Angeles at the behest of the then-governor, Ronald Reagan, in 1969. She was reinstated, but not rehired the next year on the pretext of her radical activity and citing her lack of a doctorate. At this time she became involved with the effort to free the "Soledad Brothers," three Black inmates charged with the murder of a white prison guard. Davis threw herself into giving speeches on their behalf and, through a correspondence with George Jackson, one of the Soledad Brothers, she became personally involved. Despite the fact that the charges against him had been dropped, Jackson remained in prison and was killed by guards in an alleged escape attempt; his brother Jonathan attempted a rescue of another inmate from San Quentin and was killed along with two prisoners and the judge. Angela's guns had been used in the hostage-taking, and even though she had obtained them legally and had purchased them for her protection, she was forced into hiding when the FBI placed her on its "Ten Most Wanted" list in 1970. She was found in New York and placed in jail in California without bail.

Davis's celebrity peaked with the "Free Angela" movement of the early 1970s, which made her the focus of a groundswell of popular opinion demanding her release, and in 1972, she was acquired of all charges. Despite Ronald Reagan's and the Board of Regents' mandate that she would never again teach in a California university, Davis has taught at San Francisco State and the University of California at Santa Cruz and remains politically active as a speaker and a writer. She travels extensively and lectures throughout the world. Her work on black women is provocative and challenges easy assumptions—increasingly her focus has been on health issues, and she has been on the board of the National Black Women's Health Project since 1986.

Her best-known books are her 1988 autobiography, and *If They Come in the Morning* (1971). She is as direct and fearless as ever: in an essay entitled "Rape, Race and the Myth of the Black Racist," her aim is not only to eviscerate this persistent myth but to take to task two respected feminist writers, Susan Brownmiller and Shulamith Firestone (among others) for their being deceived by it. Two essay collections, *Women, Race, and Class* (1981) and *Women, Culture, and Politics* (1989), best represent the maturation of Angela Davis as an activist and an intellectual. She has said she is surprised and gratified that young people continue to be interested in her and her ideas. With characteristic modesty, Davis wrote, "My own work over the last two decades will have been wonderfully worthwhile if it has indeed assisted in some small measure to awaken and encourage this new activism."

—Mary A. Hess

DAVIS, Ossie

Born: Cogdell, Georgia, 18 December 1917. **Education:** Attended Howard University, 1935-39, and Columbia University, 1948. **Family:** Married Ruby Ann Wallace (an actress and writer under name Ruby Dee), 9 December 1948; three children. **Military Service:** U.S. Army, World War II. **Career:** Janitor, shipping clerk, and stock clerk, New York City, 1938-41; actor for stage, film, and television, since 1941; motion picture director, since 1981; chair of the board, Institute for New Cinema Artists; founder with Ruby Dee of Emmalyn II Productions; performer on recordings for Caedmon and Folkways Records. **Awards:** Antoinette Perry (Tony) Award nomination, best musical, 1970, for *Purlie*; Coretta Scott King Book Award from American Library Association, and Jane Addams Children's Book Award, both 1979, for *Escape to Freedom: A Play about Young Frederick Douglass*. **Agent:** Emmalyn II Productions, PO Box 1318, New Rochelle, New York 10802.

PUBLICATIONS

Plays

Goldbrickers of 1944. 1944.
Alice in Wonder. 1952.
Purlie Victorious. 1961.
Curtain Call, Mr. Aldridge, Sir. 1968.
Purlie (an adaptation of *Purlie Victorious*, with Philip Rose, Peter Udell and Gary Geld). 1970.
Escape to Freedom: A Play about Young Frederick Douglass. 1976.
Langston: A Play. 1982.
Bingo (musical adaptation of *The Bingo Long Traveling All-Stars and Motor Kings* with Hy Gilbert). 1994.

Novels

Just Like Martin. New York, Simon & Schuster, 1992.

Screenplays and Teleplays

Gone Are the Days (film adaptation of *Purlie Victorious*). 1963.
Cotton Comes to Harlem, with Arnold Perl, based on a novel by Chester Himes. 1970.
Kongi's Harvest (adapted from work by Wole Soyinka). 1970.
Today Is Ours. CBS-TV, 1974.
Countdown at Kusini, with Ladi Ladebo and Al Freeman, Jr., based on a story by John Storm Roberts. 1976.

*   *   *

Ossie Davis has artistic accomplishments as an actor, director, producer, and writer, the latter in screenplays, teleplays, and stage plays, as well as fiction and music. The common thread that draws the disparate facets of his career together is Davis's desire to relate the story of African Americans and their experiences in the United States. His commitment extends beyond cultural expression and into social activism and community leadership. He shares this involvement with his wife, Ruby Dee, a similarly diverse artist and activist.

Davis began writing seriously while serving in the Army during World War II. After a stint as a medical technician stationed in Liberia, Davis transferred to the Army's Special Services division, where he began to write and produce stage plays and similar entertainments for soldiers. After the war ended, Davis continued to work as a playwright while his acting career in theater was established.

Davis's first play, *Alice in Wonder* (1953), draws on the suspicious social and political environment of the McCarthy era in its depiction of a singer who gradually compromises his artistic and individual integrity: he abandons his singing career to work in public relations position for a broadcasting firm, then helps undermine black activism as a means for keeping his job. The straightforward treatment of the effects of the highly-charged and controversial period of the McCarthy House Un-American Activities hearings lack dramatic engagement but helped Davis's career as a playwright, particularly in expressing his concern for the black experience in the context of American society at large.

Davis's 1961 comedy, *Purlie Victorious*, proved popular with critics and audiences, and, with Davis's input, was adapted into a motion picture and a musical. The title character is a preacher, and the play concerns his efforts to open an integrated church in an old barn that once served as a church for African Americans. Victorious, an eloquent man, has tired of his itinerant ways and returns to his native Georgia to purchase the barn as a permanent spiritual home. To buy the barn, however, Victorious has to acquire a $500 inheritance from his dead aunt, a former slave, whose daughter has also recently died. The death of Victorious's cousin is unknown to the holder of the inheritance, Captain Cotchipee, an unsympathetic white plantation owner. Victorious schemes to have a comely young woman pose as his cousin and obtain the money from the Captain. The comical schemes of Victorious and his family, as well as Charlie Cotchipee, the Captain's liberal son, to outsmart the antagonist form the heart of the action. Through the play's characters, Davis presents a spectrum of different ways African Americans have responded to poverty and oppression. The characters are meant to be caricatures and stereotypes, forming a kind of mythic treatment that exposes dangers of typecasting individuals even as it plays them for satiric humor.

While critics praised the play, audiences were predominantly black and their support was not enough to turn a profit for Davis or his producer in conventional dramatic venues of the time. The importance of *Purlie Victorious,* however, cannot be overshadowed by its initial box office disappointments. Davis's satiric "Southern fable" offers a brilliant exploration of how archetypes and stereotypes can be overstated to the point of absurdity, and the play probes ways in which idealistic beliefs in justice can run counter to concepts of law and order. The cinema version of *Purlie Victorious*, a Davis-penned adaptation titled *Gone Are the Days*, was relatively inauspicious and lacked cinematic sweep, but the musical stage version, *Purlie* (1970) proved far more grand in its presentation and reach. Also in 1970, Davis published *Curtain Call, Mr. Aldridge, Sir*, a reading for five actors that presents a condensed biography of Ira Aldridge, a famous black Shakespearian actor of the 19th-century.

Davis's commitment for preserving the integrity of art and making it a more relevant means for exploring social and racial issues is reflected in several activities: he founded the Institute of Cinema Artists in 1973 to train young black artists for media careers, Davis and Ruby Dee have been popular in lectured and readings tours, and they produced a Public television anthology, *With Ossie and Ruby* in 1981. Davis has also written works directed primarily at young adults. His 1976 play, *Escape to Freedom,* recounts early experiences of Frederick Douglass, ending with his escape from slavery.

Davis's young adult novel, *Just Like Martin* (1992), is set in 1963 at the height of the Civil Rights movement and concerns the complicated relationship between young teenager Issac Stone and his father, Ike. Young Isaac, an all-A student in Alabama, admires the work and non-violent methods of Martin Luther King, Jr., and wants to be a preacher, following King's lead. He intends to show his support for King and his causes by attending a civil rights march in Washington, D.C., with a church youth group. His father is opposed to his participation for a number of reasons: Ike does not share his son's belief in non-violence, and he finds his son's admiration of King worthy of belittlement. The matter is further complicated by the fact that Stone's mother has recently died, and Ike fears his son will be harmed if he goes to Washington. Eventually, after two of Stone's friends are killed and another seriously injured because of the bombing of a church, he coordinates a children's march. As the novel unfolds, young Stone must come to terms with his belief in nonviolence after getting into a fist fight in the church.

The evolving father-son relationship is particularly compelling, as Davis presents them as characters with depth, rather than as mouthpieces for conflicting viewpoints, and as people caught in an historically-important moment, trying to find their way, but not always sure of exactly what that means. Davis is realistic in his depiction of Stone's inner struggle to follow King's passive resistance methodology, a conflict that has tested many through time. Davis's own experiences in the Civil Rights Movement and his continued commitments to the larger community no doubt contributing to the profound resonance of this work.

—Annette Petrusso

DEWBERRY, Elizabeth

Pseudonyms: Elizabeth Dewey; Elizabeth Dewberry Vaughn. **Born**: Birmingham, Alabama, 7 September 1962. **Education:** Vanderbilt University, B.S. 1983; Emory University, Ph.D. 1989. **Family:** Married Robert Olin Butler, 23 April 1995. **Career:** Instructor of English, 1987-88, visiting assistant professor of English, Emnory University, 1989-90; Samford University, adjunct assistant professor of English, 1991-92; assistant professor of English, Ohio State University, 1992-94; teaching fellow, Wesleyan Writers' Conference,1993; visiting lecturer of creative writing, University of Southern California, 1993; faculty member, Sewanee Writers' Conference, 1994 and Bread Loaf Writers' Conference, 1994; Tennessee Williams fellow, University of the South, 1995. **Member:** PEN. **Awards**: Artist-Initiated Project Grant, Georgia Council for the Arts, 1989-90; Walter E. Dakin Fellowship, Sewanee Writers' Conference, University of the South, 1991; Alabama Arts Council Individual Artist Grant, 1992-93; Bread Loaf Fellowship in Fiction, Bread Loaf Writers' Conference, 1993; Teaching fellowship, Wesleyan Writers' Conference, 1993; Tennessee Williams Fellowship, University of the South, 1995. **Agents:** (fiction) Elaine Markson, Elaine Markson Literary Agency, 44 Greenwich Ave., New York, New York 10011; (drama) Joyce Ketay, Joyce Ketay Agency, 1501 Broadway, Suite 1910, New York, New York 10036.

PUBLICATIONS AND PRODUCTIONS

Novels

Many Things Have Happened Since He Died and Here Are the Highlights, as Elizabeth Dewberry. New York, Doubleday, 1990.
Break the Heart of Me, as Elizabeth Dewberry Vaughn. New York, Vantage, 1994.

Plays

Many Things Have Happened Since He Died, with Tom Key (adapted from Dewberry's novel). Produced at Alliance Theatre, Atlanta, Georgia, 1993.
Head On. Produced at the Humana Festival of New Plays, Actors Theatre of Louisville, 1995.
Flesh and Blood. Produced at the Humana Festival of New Plays, Actors Theatre of Louisville, 1996.

Uncollected Essays

"'Truer Than Anything True': *In Our Time* and Journalism," in *The Hemingway Review,* Vol. 11, no. 2, 1992.
"*In Our Time* and Picasso," in *Hemingway Repossessed* edited by Kenneth Rosen, Westport, Connecticut, 1994.
"Hemingway's Journalism and the Realist Dilemma." In *The Cambridge Companion to Ernest Hemingway* edited by Scott Donaldson, Cambridge, Cambridge University Press, 1996.
"Praying for a Home: Some Thoughts on Writing and God," in *Image: A Journal of the Arts and Religion,* Vol. 15, 1997.

*

Interviews: "'In the Beginning Was the Word,'" with William Walsh, *High Plains Literary Review,* Vol. 8, no. 3, 1993; "It's a Risk," in *Fighting Words: Words on Writing from 21 of the Heart of Dixie: Best Contemporary Authors* edited by Bill Caton, Montgomery, Black Belt Press, 1995; "500 Words A Day," in *Of Fiction and Faith: Twelve American Writers Talk About Their Vision and Work* edited by W. Dale Brown, Grand Rapids, Eerdmans, 1997.

Critical Studies: "*Many Things Have Happened Since He Died and Here Are the Highlights*" by Bettina Berch, *Belles Lettres: A Review of Books by Women*, No. 8., 1992; "Paper Chase" by Katherine Dieckman, *Village Voice Literary Supplement*, April 1992; "Fundamentalist Views and Feminist Dilemmas" by Gloria Cronin, in *Traditions, Voices, and Dreams: The American Novel Since the 1960s* edited by Marvin J. Friedman and Ben Siegel, Newark, University of Delaware Press, 1995.

* * *

Elizabeth Dewberry's work is best described as tragicomedy. Her novels and plays are replete with black humor, wrong-headed faith, and psychic threat brought on by abuse followed finally by self-realization in her female protagonists. Dewberry's greatest strength as an artist is the rendering of a distinctively authentic voice. The speakers in both of her novels, *Many Things Have Happened Since He Died* and *Break the Heart of Me*, is alarmingly naive and alternately engaged in self-flagellation and self-congratulation, telling her story in a teetering, thrashing, surviving and emerging, confident voice.

For Dewberry, a writer but also teacher and scholar, the writing craft is essentially redemptive. She explains in an essay in *Image: A Journal of the Arts and Religion* that her stories "use language to celebrate the presence of divine mystery in everyday life, to transform pain into beauty and chaos into meaning" ("Praying for a Home"). The action of grace that Flannery O'Connor claims integral to her work is also a strain in Dewberry's stories as well. The depictions of hypocrisy resound in Dewberry's fiction, as they do in O'Connor's and in those of her artistic forbearer, Nathaniel Hawthorne.

Hawthorne's concern with the past, which exorcises shameful familial guilt, also permeates Dewberry's novels. All three writers, Hawthorne, O'Connor, and Dewberry, are troubled by the practice of a faith distinguished by harsh judgement with its consequent alienation of individuals from themselves, their families, and communities. The past, with its unresolved religious tensions enacted in individuals caught up in Manicheanism as their way of practicing Christianity, creates a fiction which might be defined as a theodicy. Evil masked in robes of righteousness, especially as it has to do with love, guilt, and family, is plumbed in Dewberry's work.

Her first novel, *Many Things Have Happened Since He Died and Here are the Highlights*, is essentially stream-of-consciousness, told by an unnamed narrator who details her father's suicide, her fundamentalist husband (Malone)'s abuse of his wife and himself (through drugs), an unwanted pregnancy, and her own ambition to be a renowned writer. Because her fundamentalist faith requires she be a submissive wife, she tries valiantly to adopt the view of her mother as someone who is keeping her father's inheritance from her, the view held by Malone and his mother. When she happens upon Malone and three men engaged in sexual acts in her bed, she turns on herself rather than Malone. The self-punishment she inflicts on herself pushes her toward hysteria in the form of religious babble and psychic collapse until, finally, when Malone dies from a drug overdose she gives away all of Malone that remains—his body parts to organ banks and the baby she is carrying to adoption. She plans to turn the notes she has been making of her life into an autobiography that will "illustrate the strength of modern woman against tribulation and the loss of God in modern society and be a best seller."

Dewberry's second book, *Break the Heart of Me*, is the story of Sylvia Grace Mullins, who tells her story alternately as an adult and a child. Raised by her grandparents (her mother died and her father is in a bad marriage), Sylvia undergoes a tumultuous life—her grandmother dies during Sylvia's childhood, she is educated in a fundamentally Christian school, has ambitious to be a country-western singer, is abused sexually by her grandfather, marries an older man, has an affair with a rising country star—while struggling to reconcile her life situation with the ideals of evangelical Christianity. The title, *Break the Heart of Me*, is taken from a Langston Hughes poem that speaks of love "as a shadow on a gnarled and naked tree." Dewberry's white female narrator experiences "love" in a similarly perverted fashion.

Dewberry, like her protagonists, comes from a fundamentalist Christian upbringing. In her essay "Praying for Home" (in *Image:*

A Journal of the Arts and Religion), Dewberry reveals that the emotional core, not the plot, of this second novel—"the anger and the abuse and the healing from it . . . which has something to do with grace"—is similar to her own. This novel helped her to understand her own memories of being sexually molested by her grandfather and then of revealing abuse by the man who was her first husband. She ended her relationships with both men. Her subsequent marriage to novelist Robert Olin Butler and the healing that has followed have taught her, she says, "something about redemption." Revelations of the abuse have resulted in broken relationships in her immediate family, and this has had something to do with the play *Flesh and Blood,* about two sisters who view their shared past so differently that they can't connect in the present and one ends up stabbing the other in the back, literally: says Dewberry," You can guess where that came from."

For this young artist, "art is a prayer for a home in God's universe . . . For me and for my characters, finding God's grace has something to do with finding the right words and creating something good and lasting and true out of them."

—Janice Milner Lasseter

DICKEY, James

Born: James Lafayette Dickey in Atlanta, Georgia, 2 February 1923. **Education:** Clemson College, 1942; Vanderbilt University, B.A. (magna cum laude) 1949, M.A. 1950. **Military Service:** Pilot in the U.S. Army Air Force during World War II and as a training officer in the Air Force during the Korean War. **Family:** Married Maxine Syerson, 1948 (died 1976), two sons; married Deborah Dodson, 1976, one daughter. **Career:** Instructor, Rice University, 1950, 1952-54, and University of Florida, 1955-56; poet-in-residence, Reed College, Portland, Oregon, 1962-64, San Fernando Valley State College, Northridge, California, 1964-66, and University of Wisconsin, 1966; consultant in poetry, Library of Congress, Washington, D.C., 1966-68; beginning in 1969, professor of English and writer-in-residence, University of South Carolina; Yale Younger Poets contest, judge, 1989-94; read poem "The Strength of Fields" at Inauguration of U.S. President Jimmy Carter, 1977, and read poem "For a Time and Place" at second inauguration of Richard Riley, governor of South Carolina, 1983. **Awards:** *Sewanee Review* poetry fellowship, 1954-55; *Poetry* magazine, Union League Civic and Arts Foundation Prize, 1958, Vachel Lindsay Prize, 1959; Longview Foundation award, 1960; Guggenheim fellowship, 1961; National Book Award, the Poetry Society of America's Melville Crane Award and National Institute of Arts and Letters Award, all in 1966 for *Buckdancer's Choice*; Medicis Prize (France), for Best Foreign Novel, 1971, for *Deliverance*; New York Quarterly Poetry Day Award, 1977; Levinson prize, 1981; inductee, South Carolina Academy of Authors, 1986. **Died:** In 19 January 1997.

PUBLICATIONS

Poetry

Into the Stone and Other Poems. New York, Scribner, 1960.
Drowning with Others. Middletown, Connecticut, Wesleyan University Press, 1962.

Helmets. Middletown, Connecticut, Wesleyan University Press, 1964.

Two Poems of the Air. Portland, Oregon, Centicore Press, 1964.

Buckdancer's Choice. Middletown, Connecticut, Wesleyan University Press, 1965.

Poems 1957-1967. Middletown, Connecticut, Wesleyan University Press, 1967.

The Achievement of James Dickey: A Comprehensive Selection of His Poems, with a Critical Introduction, edited by Laurence Lieberman. Chicago, Scott Foresman, 1968.

The Eye-Beaters, Blood, Victory, Madness, Buckhead and Mercy. New York, Doubleday, 1970.

The Zodiac. Bloomfield Hills, Michigan, Bruccoli Clark, 1976; revised edition, New York, Doubleday, 1976.

The Strength of Fields. Bloomfield Hills, Michigan, Bruccoli Clark, 1977; revised edition, New York, Doubleday, 1979.

Veteran Birth: The Gadfly Poems 1947-1949. Winston-Salem, Palaemon Press, 1978.

Head-Deep in Strange Sounds: Free-Flight Improvisations from the UnEnglish. Winston-Salem, Palaemon Press, 1979.

Falling, May Day Sermon, and Other Poems. Middletown, Connecticut, Wesleyan University Press, 1981.

The Early Motion. Middletown, Connecticut, Wesleyan University Press, 1981.

Puella. New York, Doubleday, 1982.

Värmland. Winston-Salem, Palaemon Press, 1982.

The Central Motion: Poems 1968-1979. Middletown, Connecticut, Wesleyan University Press, 1983.

False Youth: Four Seasons. Dallas, Pressworks, 1983.

For a Time and Place. Columbia, South Carolina, Bruccoli Clark, 1983.

Intervisions, photographs by Sharon Anglin Kuhne. Penland, North Carolina, Visualternatives, 1983.

The Eagle's Mile. Middletown, Connecticut, Wesleyan University Press, 1990.

The Whole Motion: Collected Poems 1949-1992. Middletown, Connecticut, Wesleyan University Press, 1992.

James Dickey: The Selected Poems. Hanover, New Hampshire, University Press of New England, 1998.

Nonfiction

The Suspect in Poetry. Madison, Minnesota, Sixties Press, 1964.

A Private Brinksmanship (address). Claremont, California, Pitzer College, 1965.

Spinning the Crystal Ball: Some Guesses at the Future of American Poetry. Washington, D.C., Library of Congress, 1967.

Metaphor as Pure Adventure (lecture). Washington, D.C., Library of Congress, 1968.

Babel to Byzantium: Poets and Poetry Now. New York, Farrar Straus, 1968.

Self-Interviews, edited by Barbara and James Reiss. New York, Doubleday, 1970.

Sorties (essays). New York, Doubleday, 1971.

Exchanges...: Being in the Form of a Dialogue with Joseph Trumbull Stickney. Bloomfield Hills, Michigan, Bruccoli Clark, 1971.

Jericho: The South Beheld, paintings by Hubert Shuptrine. Birmingham, Alabama, Oxmoor House, 1974.

God's Images: The Bible: A New Vision, illustrated by Marvin Hayes. Birmingham, Alabama, Oxmoor House, 1977.

The Enemy from Eden. Northridge, California, Lord John Press, 1978.

In Pursuit of the Grey Soul (on fishing). Columbia, South Carolina, Bruccoli Clark, 1979.

The Water-Bug's Mittens: Ezra Pound, What We Can Use (lecture). Moscow, University of Idaho, 1979.

The Starry Place Between the Antlers: Why I Live in South Carolina. Columbia, South Carolina, Bruccoli Clark, 1981.

The Eagle's Mile. Columbia, South Carolina, Bruccoli Clark, 1981.

The Poet Turns on Himself. Portree, Isle of Skye, Aquila, 1982.

Night Hurdling: Poems, Essays, Conversations, Commencements, and Afterwords. Columbia, South Carolina, Bruccoli Clark, 1983.

Wayfarer: A Voice from the Southern Mountains, photographs by William A. Bake. Birmingham, Alabama, Oxmoor House, 1988.

The Voiced Connections of James Dickey: Interviews and Conversations, edited by Ronald Baughman. Columbia, University of South Carolina Press, 1989.

Striking In: The Early Notebooks of James Dickey. Columbia, University of South Carolina Press, 1996.

Translator, with others, *Stolen Apples* by Yevgeny Yevtushenko. New York, Doubleday, 1971.

Editor, *From the Green Horseshoe: Poems by James Dickey's Students.* Columbia, University of South Carolina Press, 1987.

Novels

Deliverance. Boston, Houghton Mifflin, 1970.

Alnilam. New York, Doubleday, 1987.

To the White Sea. Houghton, 1993.

Books for Children

Tucky the Hunter (for children). New York, Crown, 1978.

Bronwen, The Traw, and the Shape-Shifter: A Poem in Four Parts (for children). San Diego, Harcourt Brace, 1986.

*

Recordings: *Poems,* Spoken Arts, 1967; *James Dickey Reads His Poetry,* Caedmon, 1971.

Screenplays: Film—*Deliverance,* produced and directed by John Boorman, Warner Bros., 1972. **Television**—*The Call of the Wild,* from the novel by Jack London, 1976.

Bibliographies: *James Dickey: A Bibliography 1947-1974* by Jim Elledge, Metuchen, New Jersey, Scarecrow Press, 1979; *James Dickey: A Bibliography* by Stuart Wright, Dallas, Pressworks, 1982; *James Dickey: A Descriptive Bibliography* by Matthew J. Bruccoli, Pittsburgh, University of Pittsburgh Press, 1990.

Manuscript Collection: Olin Library, Washington University, St. Louis.

Critical Studies: *James Dickey: The Expansive Imagination: A Collection of Critical Essays* edited by Richard J. Calhoun, Deland, Florida, Everett Edwards, 1973; *James Dickey* by Richard J. Calhoun and Robert W. Hill, Boston, Twayne, 1983; "James Dickey Issue," *South Carolina Review,* April 1978; *James Dickey:*

Splintered Sunlight edited by Patricia De La Fuente, Edinburgh, Texas, Pan American University School of Humanities, 1979; *The Imagination as Glory: Essays on the Poetry of James Dickey* edited by Bruce Weigl and T.R. Hummer, Urbana, University of Illinois Press, 1984; *Understanding James Dickey* by Ronald Baughman, Columbia, University of South Carolina Press, 1985; *James Dickey: The Poet as Pitchman* by Neal Bowers, Columbia, University of Missouri Press, 1985; *James Dickey* edited by Harold Bloom, New York, Chelsea House, 1987; *Outbelieving Existence: The Measured Motion of Dickey* by Gordon Van Ness, Columbia, University of South Carolina Press, 1992; *James Dickey and the Politics of Canon: Assessing the Savage Ideal* by Ernest Suarez, Columbia, University of Missouri Press, 1993; *Critical Essays of James Dickey* edited by Robert Kirschten, New York, G. K. Hall, 1994; *Struggling for Wings: The Art of James Dickey* edited by Robert Kirschten, Columbia, University of South Carolina Press, 1997; *Approaching Prayer: Ritual and the Shape of Myth in A. R. Ammons and James Dickey,* by Robert Kirschten, Baton Rouge, Louisiana State University Press, 1998.

Theatrical Activities: Actor, Film—*Deliverance,* 1972.

James Dickey commented:

The only way in which I am a Southern writer is that I am simply a writer who happens to come from the South. I don't have any doctrinaire feelings about this at all. I surely couldn't be considered as a regionalist or an agrarian. I don't have any particular ax to grind.

On the other hand, it is inevitable that a good deal of my outlook would be colored by the fact that I *am* a Southerner and that I was raised here and was raised according to a certain way of life and a certain outlook and a certain set of values that are peculiar to this region. All this inevitably gets into the writing in some way—in ways that are so subtle that I don't even know what they are.

—from an interview with John Logue, *Southern Living,* February 1971.

* * *

James Lafayette Dickey, poet, novelist, critic, teacher, lived most of his life in the South. He was born the second of three sons to Maibelle Swift and Eugene Dickey in the Buckhead section of Atlanta, and died in Columbia, where he had been poet-in-residence at the University of South Carolina since 1969. Dickey's South—landscape, diction, emotion, mind-set, is evident throughout his oeuvre. His upbringing by his mother and grandmother, both invalids, and a cock-fighting attorney father from the North Georgia mountains supplied material; his German grandmother lent impetus with her repeated dictum, "Do it right!" He obeyed her, becoming a superb athlete at track, football, archery and canoeing; he taught and inspired many future writers, picked the guitar and left a wealth of memorable words.

Dickey honored his home cities, Atlanta and Columbia, one in poetry, "Looking for the Buckhead Boys," and the other in an April, 1981 essay, "The Starry Place Between the Antlers," for *Esquire.* In the essay, he also wrote about Charleston and Savannah:

No Hollywood dream of antebellum Southernism could be as beautiful as these heavy-aired, muffled towns, or the gardens in and around them. The softness of all things there is slowly and inexorably overwhelming: a kind of delicate blur . . . creatively out-of-focus, a heartbreaking and heartening unclearness: a triumph of the creative nearsightedness of God on the third day of Creation, when he was still trying things out, and liking some of them.

Dickey first left the South when, after playing football one semester for Clemson College (1942), he enlisted in the U.S. Army Air Corps. As a member of the 418th Night Fighter Squadron, he flew nearly a hundred missions in the South Pacific in 1943-45.

After World War II he entered Vanderbilt University, where he majored in English and philosophy and minored in astronomy. He earned his B.A. (1949) and M.A. (1950) degrees there, mentored by his freshman English teacher William Hunter and then Donald Davidson and Monroe Spears, who remained Dickey's friend for life. Spears died just one year after the death of his famous student; Dickey had praised his mentor with a glowing tribute when Spears was inducted into the South Carolina Academy of Authors. Dickey himself had been the Academy's first living inductee, in 1986.

While a student Dickey had poems accepted by the Vanderbilt literary magazine *Gadfly* and the *Sewannee Review.* His first teaching job, at Rice Institute, was interrupted by his return to service during the Korean War. He left Rice again in 1954 to accept a fellowship from the *Sewannee Review,* which funded his first visit to Europe. A later Guggenheim fellowship took him back to Positano, Italy, in 1961. After Dickey's first trip abroad, Andrew Lytle helped him get a job at the University of Florida, where he taught one year. Then he worked in advertising for about five years, first in New York and then Atlanta. He was good at it, but would later describe this venture as "selling my soul to the devil by day and buying it back by night by writing poetry." During the 1950s and 60s, he published about 60 poems in literary magazines; in 1960 Scribner's published his first book of poetry, *Into the Stone,* and other volumes followed. His early narrative poetry is characterized by a strong anapestic beat, while his later lyric poetry would become more open and open-ended.

The year in Italy permitted him to devote all his time to writing. When he returned to America he spent a series of years as poet-in-residence at several colleges, including Reed College, San Fernando Valley State, The University of Wisconsin at Madison and Milwaukee, George Washington University and Georgia Tech. He was on his way to Hollins when he was appointed poetry consultant to the Library of Congress, 1966-68. All this moving around made him feel "like a poetical bum," he said.

Still, he was coming into his own. *Buckdancer's Choice* won the National Book Award, the Poetry Society of America's Melville Crane Award and National Institute of Arts and Letters Award, all in 1966. He was situated for life at the University of South Carolina when his novel of adventure and death on a mountain river, *Deliverance* (1970) and his subsequent screenplay and the movie (1972) brought him fame where poetic tastes were rare.

Primitive nature, war, sex, love, death, myth, rebirth and renewal permeate his poetry and his novels, *Deliverance, Alnilam*

(1987), and *To the White Sea* (1993). Throughout his career he experimented with language, subject matter, theme and technique. Two of his books were for children, *Tucky the Hunter* (1978) for his grandson and *Bronwen, The Traw and the Shape-Shifter* (1986) for his daughter. The latter he considered among his best works. He also published a dozen non-fiction books, among them volumes of criticism, of which he wrote, "If I have made any contribution to literary criticism, it is that I have reintroduced sensibility and emotion back into it" (from Sorties). Hundreds of biographical and critical studies have been published about James Dickey and his works. Ronald Baughman's scholarship is notable. One of Dickey's two sons, Christopher Swift, European division head of *Newsweek*, has written a memoir of his father, *Summer of Deliverance* (1998).

A Hemingwayesque character, Dickey often went to extremes, especially with alcohol. Yet nothing diminished his brilliance. He declared imagination and lucidity his drugs of choice.

A long period of physical but not intellectual decline ended with Dickey's death on January 19, 1997. He and Maxine are buried in what he called "the mild wilderness" of All Saints Churchyard, Pawley's Island.

—Gayle Edwards

DILLARD, R. H. W.

Born: Richard Henry Wilde Dillard in Roanoke, Virginia, 11 October 1937. **Education:** Roanoke College, Salem, Virginia, 1955-58, B.A. 1958 (Phi Beta Kappa); University of Virginia, Charlottesville (Woodrow Wilson Fellow, 1958-59; DuPont Fellow, 1959-61), M.A. 1959, Ph.D. 1965. **Family:** Married Annie Doak in 1965 (divorced 1975); married Cathy Hankla in 1979. **Career:** Instructor in English, Roanoke College, summer 1961, and University of Virginia, 1961-64; assistant professor, 1964-68, associate professor, 1968-74, since 1971 chair of the graduate program in contemporary literature and creative writing, and since 1974 professor of English, Hollins College, Virginia; vice-president, *Film Journal,* New York, since 1973; contributing Editor, *Hollins Critic,* Hollins College, Virginia, 1966-77; editor-in-chief, *Children's Literature,* since 1992; member of literary board, Virginia Center of the Creative Arts, and editorial advisory board, *New Virginia Review;* member, Roanoke County Democratic Committee and delegate to state political conventions. **Awards:** Academy of American Poets prize, 1961; Ford grant, 1972; O.B. Hardison, Jr. Poetry Award, Folger Shakespeare Library, 1994. **Agent:** Blanche C. Gregory, 2 Tudor City Place, New York, New York 10017. **Address:** Box 9671, Hollins College, Virginia 24020.

PUBLICATIONS

Poetry Collections

The Day I Stopped Dreaming about Barbara Steele and Other Poems. Chapel Hill, University of North Carolina Press, 1966.
News of the Nile. Chapel Hill, University of North Carolina Press, 1971.

After Borges. Baton Rouge, Louisiana State University Press, 1972.
The Greeting: New and Selected Poems. Salt Lake City, University of Utah Press, 1981.
Just Here, Just Now. Baton Rouge, Louisiana, Louisiana State University Press, 1994.

Novels

The Book of Changes. New York, Doubleday, 1974.
The First Man on the Sun. Baton Rouge, Louisiana State University Press, 1983.

Short Story Collections

Omniphobia. Baton Rouge, Louisiana, Louisiana State University Press, 1995.

Other

Horror Films. New York, Monarch Press, 1976.
Understanding George Garrett. Columbia, University of South Carolina Press, 1988.

Editor, with Louis D. Rubin, Jr., *The Experience of America: A Book of Readings.* New York, Macmillan, and London, Collier Macmillan, 1969.
Editor, with George Garrett and John Rees Moore, *The Sounder Few: Essays from "The Hollins Critic."* Athens, University of Georgia Press, 1971.

*

R. H. W. Dillard comments:
   Although I have thought a good deal about what I am doing in my poems, I don't know that I really am able to express the results of that thinking very clearly, except (I hope) in the poems themselves. Allow me, then, to offer in place of an introductory statement about my poetry, excerpts from three poems which might do the job.

   The first, from the poem "News of the Nile," is just a description of the source of my poems experience in the broadest sense: "All these things I have read and remembered,/Witnessed, imagined, thought and written down...."

   The second, from the poem "Construction," may be a bit more helpful, for it is as close as I've come to an explicit esthetic statement, and it also makes explicit my central concern with the vital involvement of seeing and saying, of action and belief:

   To say as you see. To see as by stop-action,
   Clouds coil overhead, the passage of days,

   Trees bend by the side of the road
   Like tires on a curve, plants uncurl,

   How the world dissolves in the water of the eye:
   The illusion speed produces. The reality of speed.

   A result: to see as you say,
   As gravity may bend a ray of light.

To say the earth's center is of fire:
Life leaps from the soil like sun flares.

To see the world made true,
An art of rocks and stones and trees,

Real materials in real space,
L'esthétique de la vitesse.

The third, from the long poem *January: A Screenplay,* is a prayer which states briefly the faith and the humility which I hope is at the heart of everything I do:

For my sorrow in this depth of joy,
Gift beyond reward, I'm sorry.
For the joy I feel in this broken world,
This sorrow, this woe, I thank you,
I thank you.

* * *

Taking work from his first three books, R. H. W. Dillard's *The Greeting: New and Selected Poems* (1981) established him as an unusual and important contemporary poet. The earliest of the three volumes, *The Day I Stopped Dreaming about Barbara Steele and Other Poems* (1966), is a highly sophisticated and humorous collection. Also his most traditionally formal, it is impressive in its sardonic rendering of a wide range of experiences; however, sometimes, in labored attempts to charge the ephemeral with beauty and significance, Dillard comes across as an overly witty aesthete, thus compromising some of the emotional qualities of the poems.

News of the Nile (1971) develops Dillard's voice in a different, interesting direction. The witty, stylized, intellectual voice of the first volume becomes more autobiographical and personal, even troubled. Influenced by his study of horror movies, Dillard examines the perverse side of human nature—blood lust, cannibalism, the macabre. Such poems as "Night of the Living Dead," "Event: A Gathering; Vastation," and "Act of Detection" revel in the horrific. Not all the poems in the volume deal with such subjects; others give poignant accounts of a more personal nature.

Dillard's third book, *After Borges* (1972), represents a mature achievement, arising out of a profound experience with the Argentine writer's work. Returning to the wit which fueled his first volume, such poems as "Round Ruby," "What Can You Say to Shoes," "Sweet Strawberries," and "Wings" express joy and pathos at life's absurdities and trivialities, as well as its beauties. The series of poems that purport to be "after the Spanish of Jorge Luis Borges"—"Limits," "The Other Tiger," "Argumentum Ornithologicum," and "Epilogue"— are more introspective, serious, and complex. "Epilogue," for instance, gives an introspective account of the poet setting "out to shape a world"; the poem ends in self-confrontation at a "face, wearing/And worn, warm as worn stone./A face you know: your own." It is not surprising that Dillard is attracted to the intellectual labyrinths of Borges; what makes this book interesting is how Dillard's poems appropriate Borges's musings and reshape them into a felt, personal response to the Argentine's work.

In *The Greetings: New and Selected Poems* Dillard shows the versatility of his published work, as well as the direction of his later poems. Indeed, the collection brings together much of the best work from his earlier books. One of its most interesting achievements is a sixty-page screenplay in verse. Called "January," it tells a story of two lovers who are forced to carry on a long-distance relationship across the Atlantic. Adopting a style reminiscent of Yeats's dreamy dramas of the romantic Irish past and of Robbe Grillet's film *Last Year at Marienbad,* Dillard depicts a hazy, rose-colored world of vague emotions, shifting settings, and constant longing. Although the conclusion (emphasizing the message "The only knowledge is love") is somewhat banal and some of the language is flat, the parameters of the project are ambitious. This screenplay illustrates not only Dillard's devotion to film but his interest in expanding the genre confines of poetry. It is worth noting that he attempts such expansion again in his novel *The First Man on the Sun* (1983) by including a long section of poetry by one of the characters.

In *Just Here, Just Now* (1994) Dillard combines several of the qualities of his earlier books. Returning to the techniques of his second volume, where he used a great many references to horror films, and of his third, where he appropriates Borges, *Just Here, Just Now* relies heavily upon allusions to film, culture, and art for its success. Although there are places where Dillard's strong personal voice shines through, the reliance on allusion can seem overly cerebral:

And my case, in fact, will seem
Quite insecure if I depend
Only on the *Tractacus*
Or make Whitehead and Russell
My solid ground, my fact . . .

Besides these, there are allusions to Hart Crane, E. A. Poe, H. Rousseau, Frankenstein, Lawrence Becker, and George Garrett— all in the first seventeen pages. Even so, Dillard at his best can be found in this rather brief book, especially in the epistolary poems "Autumn Letter to London," "Winter Letter to Bluefield," and "Spring Letter to Paradise," which successfully combine his erudition with a strong, emotional voice.

—Richard Damashek and Tod Marshall

DOOLEY, David (Allen)

Born: Knoxville, Tennessee, 3 November 1947. **Education:** University of Tennessee, 1964-67, and in the late 1970s, M.A. in English; Johns Hopkins University, 1967-68, B.A. 1968. **Career:** Since 1982 paralegal, Matthews and Branscomb, San Antonio. **Awards:** Nicholas Roerich prize, 1988, for *The Volcano Inside.*

PUBLICATIONS

Poetry

The Volcano Inside. Brownsville, Oregon, Story Line Press, 1988.
The Revenge by Love. Brownsville, Oregon, Story Line Press, 1995.

* * *

David Dooley's extraordinary debut volume, *The Volcano Inside,* won the inaugural Nicholas Roerich Poetry prize. Published in 1988, it inspired the critic Helen Vendler to declare on National Public Radio that its author was one of the most exciting new poets she had come across in years. Poet-critic Allen Hoey claimed that the poems "...cut out a territory for themselves foreign to most people writing poems today—to say that they are the product of an individual voice would not reduce [Dooley's] accomplishment to a platitude but would belie the multiplicity of voices he has mastered in the volume." This last comment is particularly accurate, for to quote any one segment from *The Volcano Inside* is to risk overlooking the poet's exuberant versatility:

> So I'd give her the kind of fucking she was meant for
> and afterwards sometimes I'd go to the typewriter buck
>   naked
> and start writing till she bitched about the noise
> though more than once she fell asleep and honked like a
>   flight of geese
> but she'd bitch so I'd open a notebook and while she
>   slept,
> on summer nights the windows open and she lay there
>   naked asleep
> the covers tangled down at her knees till I wouldn't know
> if I were writing with my pen or my cock, I'd use
> whatever tool I needed. There were no answers
> because there were never any questions. If you write,
> You need books and paper and food and cunt and drink
> and that's it. By daybreak there'd be pages of Olga in the
>   typewriter,
> pages of Olga in the notebook, and squirming in the bed
> she'd be rubbing the yellow muck out of her big cow eyes.

These lines from "How I Wrote It" are part of an earthy older writer's monologue. Part confession, part harangue, the comments are directed at a younger person, presumably an aspiring writer. The speaker's point of view is refreshingly uncomplicated yet avoids the shallow simplicity from which so much current opinion bubbles to the surface. His vision is also essentially compassionate, a key point that may be overlooked as a result of his consistent vulgarity. But careful reading reveals the compassion in his genuine affection for his inspiration-whore-companion and in his love of writing and the things of the common world: "I knew how to live with the grime, you see./The grime on a tenement is as beautiful as the sunrise."

This writer, and the poet who created him, descends from George Crabbe and Robert Browning and, later, from our tradition of Frost and Jeffers. Literary schools and theories hold little interest for them, but real life, lived by real people, contains the stuff of poetry. Donald Hall recognized this in the *Harvard Book Review* when he declared, "David Dooley's poetry is not like anybody else's: It is energetic, often long-lined and propulsive, with a headlong compelling rhythm.... Dooley uses justly-observed speech to fix character." In long lines that drive through subjects with the haunting echo of classic blank verse or in clipped, short-lined stanzas, Dooley gives eloquent voice to lovers, parents, and loners, to mind readers, movie makers, joggers, country-and-western singers, and so many overlooked "others" who make up our world, the people we see when we look in the mirror.

Dooley's second volume, *The Revenge by Love* (1995), features a compelling eleven-poem sequence about the great American painter Georgia O'Keeffe and her mentor, lover, and eventual husband, the photographer Alfred Stieglitz. In other poems an emotionally devastated Saint-Saëns spends a winter in Egypt, a wealthy gay man chooses a life of hedonism over a political career, a woman's attitudes towards love and marriage are revealed in her relationship with food, a young writer begins to understand the implications of sleeping with his best friend's girl. This dramatic, narrative verse, exploring the depths of human relationships, is unusually accessible. It satisfies even more with repeated reading:

> Far out in the dark are hills which turn angry red
> when a cloud passes. Oh, but in other lights
> they are pink as flesh. What will tomorrow's first colors
>   be?
> Coral? Peach? Pale yellow? Opalescent blue?
> And then the sun will rise.

—Robert McDowell

DOUGLAS, Ellen

Born: Josephine Ayeres in Natchez, Mississippi, 7 December 1921. **Education:** University of Mississippi, B.A. 1942. **Family:** Married Kenneth Haxton in 1945 (divorced); three sons. **Career:** Writer-in-residence, Northeast Louisiana University, 1978-82, and University of Mississippi, since 1982; visiting professor, University of Virginia, 1984; Welty Professor, Millsaps College, 1988. **Awards:** Houghton Mifflin fellowship, 1961; Mississippi Institute of Arts and Letters award, 1979; Fellowship of Southern Writers award, 1989. **Agent:** R.L.R. Associates, 7 West 51st Street, New York, New York 10020.

<small>PUBLICATIONS</small>

Novels

A Family's Affairs. Boston, Houghton Mifflin, 1961.
Where the Dreams Cross. Boston, Houghton Mifflin, 1968.
Apostles of Light. Boston, Hougton Mifflin, 1973.
The Rock Cried Out. New York, Harcourt Brace, 1979.
A Lifetime Burning. New York, Random House, 1982.
Can't Quit You, Baby. New York, Atheneum, 1988.

Short Stories

Black Cloud, White Cloud. Boston, Houghton Mifflin, 1963.

Uncollected Short Story

"On the Lake," in *Prize Stories 1963* edited by Richard Poirier. New York, Doubleday, 1963.

Other

The Magic Carpet and Other Tales. Jackson, University Press of Mississippi, 1987.

*

Manuscript Collection: University of Mississippi Library, Jackson.

*   *   *

Ellen Douglas's novels, written over a period of 30 years, have consistently dealt with the South, with relationships between the individual and family, between men and women, and between blacks and whites. Never adopting a programmatic feminist stance, Douglas has nonetheless consistently made clear the difficulties faced by women in the world of Southern gentlemen and rednecks. Never adopting a stance of political activism, Douglas has also consistently stressed the close, complex, and ambiguous relationships between black and white Southern women. Throughout works notable for strong and sensitive characterizations, Douglas has created plots that test such humanistic values as love, responsibility, and respect for tradition against impersonality, arrogant individualism, and materialism in the contemporary New South.

Her first novel, *A Family's Affairs,* won a Houghton Mifflin fellowship and was named one of the *New York Times* best novels of 1962. The story focuses on the Anderson family during the years 1917-48, when Kate, the family matriarch, dies at the age of 85. At the novel's center are five women: Kate, her three daughters, and a granddaughter. Through Anna's eyes we experience the family crises that make up the novel's plot—crises which usually result from the feckless behavior of the daughters' husbands and Kate's son. Their egocentric individualism contrasts with the women's sense of responsibility to the family and with what Anna calls at the end of the novel "the habit of moral consciousness."

Anna figures in one of the two novels and both of the short stories collected in *Black Cloud, White Cloud,* Douglas's second book. Here Douglas concentrates on the responsibilities of Southern whites to their black servants; the works attest to the complicated relationships between the races, acknowledging the guilt whites feel for their oppression of blacks and the difficulty of redeeming their relationships despite shared pasts.

Where the Dreams Cross is Douglas's weakest novel, attacking in obvious and easy ways the bigotry and greedy materialism of the New South's politicians and the empty-headed frivolity of Old and New Southern belles by contrasting those vices with the virtues of the beautiful but hard-drinking, scandalous but morally responsible heroine. *Apostles of Light,* however, deservedly won a nomination for the National Book award. Douglas here sensitively portrays the plight of the elderly, revealing the frustrations of her heroine, Martha, as, first, her mind and body begin to betray her, then as her relatives begin to betray her as well. Torn between their sense of responsibility for Martha and their fear that she will become a financial burden to them, her relatives convert the old family mansion into a profitable nursing home, the ironically named Golden Age Acres. Douglas's powerful and contrasting characterizations of Martha with the home's villainous manager, who treated the elderly residents as prisoners, provide the novel's tension.

The Rock Cried Out won praise in the popular press for its portrayal of a young man's loss of innocence and for Douglas's original handling of elements of the Southern Gothic tradition. The novel chronicles the return of Alan McLaurin to Mississippi af-

ter years in Boston and his discovery that the car wreck that caused the death of his first love, Phoebe, was the result of a Ku Klux Klansman's bullet. The Klansman's confession of his crime during a 25-page monologue on the CB in his truck (which McLaurin overhears) marks a flaw in Douglas's narrative technique and strains the reader's credulity. However, McLaurin's maturation (his youthful idealism is gradually replaced by a worldly cynicism) is handled well, and Douglas portrays vividly the tensions in the South between both races and classes during the civil rights era. Here, too, Douglas reveals her angry belief that technology and materialism have replaced traditional values in the New South.

A Lifetime Burning takes the form of the diary of a 62-year-old English professor, Corinne, who discovers her husband George's infidelities and who writes in order to understand her own blindness, to make sense of what she had thought a "good" life with him, and to leave a record for their grown children. In the course of the six months during which Corinne keeps her diary, she first writes an absurdly comic (and perhaps false) account of George's affair with "The Toad," worries that his distaste for her aging body has motivated that affair, and eventually writes of George's affair with "The Musk-Rat," a male intern at the hospital where George practices. As critic Carol S. Minning noted, Corinne's diary entry for the first affair makes it easier for her to accept the second, the comic anticipates the more shocking, the false anticipates the true. Throughout the novel invention anticipates confession; in dream begins reality. In Douglas's novel, as in the epistolary novels of the 18th century, Corinne writes so that she may find an order to the chaotic facts her life lacks; in her diary she seeks to illuminate the truth of human mystery, her own, her husband's, and her family's.

Douglas followed a collection of classic fairy tales, *The Magic Carpet and Other Tales,* with her best novel, *Can't Quit You, Baby.* It tells the stories of two middle-aged women, Cornelia—sheltered, privileged, white, and deaf—and her black servant, Julia, or Tweet—experienced, vital, and enduring. As the women work at common household tasks in Cornelia's house, Julia's stories of her violent and poverty-ridden past awaken Cornelia's memories of crises in her own past. Julia's courage eventually helps Cornelia to survive the death of her husband, to endure her own grief, to live, and to help Julia sustain herself during a subsequent crisis. The novel also assesses the difficulties of story-telling: given the "deafness" of listeners such as Cornelia (or of the reader), how is a narrator such as Julia (or Douglas) to be heard? Intelligent, comic, and poignant, the novel validates the early claim of the *New York Times Book Review* that Douglas is "one of the best . . . American novelists."

—David K. Jeffrey

DOVE, Rita

Born: Rita Frances Dove in Akron, Ohio, 28 August 1952. **Education:** Miami University, Oxford, Ohio, B.A. (summa cum laude) 1973; University of Tubingen, West Germany, 1974-75; University of Iowa, Iowa City, M.F.A. 1977. **Family:** Married Fred Viebahn in 1979; one daughter. **Career:** Research assistant, 1975, and teaching assistant, 1976-77, University of Iowa; assistant professor of creative writing, 1981-84, associate professor, 1984-87, professor of English, Arizona State University, Tempe, 1987-89; since 1989 professor of English, and since 1993 Commonwealth Professor of English, University of Virginia, Charlottesville; International Working Period for Authors Fellow, North-Rhine-Westphalia Ministry of Culture and Univeristat Bielefeld, 1980; writer-in-residence, Tuskegee Institute, Alabama, 1982; chair, poetry grants panel, National Endowment for the Arts, 1985; Rockefeller Foundation residency, Bellagio, Italy, 1988; member of editorial board, *National Forum*, 1984-89; associate editor, *Callaloo*, since 1986; advisory editor, *Gettysburg Review*, since 1987, *Triquarterly*, since 1988, *Ploughshares*, since 1990, *The Georgia Review*, since 1994, and *Bellingham Review* since 1996; member of advisory board, *Iris*, since 1989 and *Civilization*, since 1994; Commissioner, Schomburg Center for Research in Black Culture, New York Public Library, since 1987; member of board of directors, Associated Writing Programs, 1985-88 (president 1986-87); member of advisory board, North Carolina Writers' Network since 1991, and U.S. Civil War Center, since 1995; since 1994, member, Council of Scholars, Library of Congress, and Awards Council, American Academy of Achievement; final judge, Walt Whitman award, 1990, and Brittingham & Pollak prizes, 1997; juror, Ruth Lilly prize, National Book award for poetry, and Pulitzer Prize in poetry, 1991, Anisfield-Wolf Book awards since 1992, Newman's Own/First Amendment award, PEN American Center, 1994, and Shelley Memorial award, Amy Lowell travelling fellowship, 1997; chair, poetry jury, Pulitzer Prize, 1997; consultant, *Woman to Woman,* Lifetime TV; member, Afro-American Studies Visiting Committee, Harvard Univresity, Council of Scholars, Library of Congress, National Launch Commitee, Americorps; senator, Phi Beta Kappa.

Awards: Fulbright fellowship, 1974-75; National Endowment for the Arts grant, 1978, fellowship, 1982, 1989; Ohio Arts Council grant, 1979; Guggenheim fellowship, 1983; Lavan Younger Poets award, 1986; Pulitzer Prize, 1987, for *Thomas and Beulah;* Mellon fellowship, 1988-89; Ohioana awards for *Grace Notes,* 1990, for *Selected Poems,* 1994; named New York Public Library "Literary Lion," 1991; Harvard University Phi Beta Kappa poet, 1993; Virginia College Stores Association Book award, 1993, for *Through the Ivory Gate; Glamour* magazine Women of the Year Award, 1993; NAACP Great American Artist Award, 1993; Folger Shakespeare Library Renaissance Forum award for leadership in the literary arts, 1994; American Academy of Achievement Golden Plate Award, 1994; International Platform Association Carl Sandburg Award, 1994; W. Alton Jones Foundation grant, 1994; Kennedy Center Fund for New American Plays award, 1995, for *The Darker Face of the Earth;* Heinz Award in the Arts and Humanities, 1996; The White House/National Endowment for the Humanities Charles Frankel Prize, 1996; U.S. Poet Laureate/Consultant in Poetry, Library of Congress, 1993-95; H.D.L. from Miami University, 1988; Knox College, 1989; Tuskegee University, University of Miami, Florida, Washington University, St. Louis, Missouri, Case Western Reserve University, and University of Akron, all 1994; Arizona State University, Boston College, and Dartmouth College, all 1995; Spelman College, and University of Pennsylvania, both 1996; University of North Carolina at Chapel Hill and University of Notre Dame, both 1997. **Address:** Department of English, 219 Bryan Hall, University of Virginia, Charlottesville, Virginia 22903.

PUBLICATIONS

Poetry Collections

Ten Poems. Lisbon, Iowa, Penumbra Press, 1977.
The Only Dark Spot in the Sky. Tempe, Inland Porch, 1980.
The Yellow House on the Corner. Pittsburgh, Carnegie-Mellon University Press, 1980.
Mandolin. Athens, Ohio Review, 1982.
Museum. Pittsburgh, Carnegie-Mellon University Press, 1983.
Thomas and Beulah. Pittsburgh, Carnegie-Mellon University Press, 1986.
The Other Side of the House. Tempe, Pyracantha Press, 1988.
Grace Notes. New York, Norton, 1989.
Selected Poems. New York, Pantheon, 1993.
Lady Freedom among Us. West Burke, Vermont, Janus Press, 1994.
Mother Love. New York, Norton, 1995.

Short Story Collection

Fifth Sunday. Lexington, University of Kentucky Press, 1985.

Plays

The Siberian Village. In *Callaloo* (Charlottesville, Virginia), vol. 14, no. 2, 1991.
The Darker Face of the Earth (verse drama; produced Oregon Shakespeare Festival, 1996). Brownsville, Oregon, Story Line Press, 1994; completely revised second edition, 1996.

Novel

Through the Ivory Gate. New York, Pantheon, 1992.

Essay Collection

The Poet's World. Washington, D.C., Library of Congress, 1995.

On-Line Projects

Lady Freedom Among Us. htttp://www.lib.virginia.edu/etext/fourmill.html

Musical Collaborations: *Between Sisters,* with composer Alvin Singleton, 1990; *Rita Dove Tryptich,* with composer Sabin Pautza, 1994; *Sing'n Sepia,* with composer Tania Leon, 1996; *Umoja—Each One of Us Counts,* with composer Alvin Singleton, 1996; *Grace Notes,* with composer Bruce Adolphe, 1997; *Seven for Luck,* with composer John Williams, 1997.

*

Recordings: Video—"Our Voices," Black Entertainment TV, 1992; "A Conversation with Poet Laureate Rita Dove," Library of Congress, 1993; "Who's Afraid of Poetry?," National Press Club, C-Span and NPR, 1994; "Shine Up Your Words: A Morning with Rita Dove," Virginia Center for the Book, 1994; "Poet Laureate Rita Dove," *Bill Moyers' Journal,* Public Affairs Television, Inc., 1994. **Audio**—*Poets in Person: Rita Dove with Helen Vendler,* Chicago, Modern Poetry Association, 1991.

Critical Studies: "A Conversation with Rita Dove" by Stan Rubin and Earl Ingersoll, in *Black American Literature Forum* (Terre Haute, Indiana), vol. 20, no.6, Fall 1986; "The Assembling Vision of Rita Dove" by Robert McDowell, in *Callaloo* (Charlottesville, Virginia), vol. 9, no. 1, 1986; "The Poems of Rita Dove" by Arnold Rampersand, in *Callaloo,* vol. 9, no. 1, 1986; "Scars and Wings: Rita Dove's *Grace Notes"* by Bonnie Costello, in *Callaloo,* vol. 14, no. 2, 1991; "Rita Dove: Crossing Boundaries" by Ekaterini Gorgoudaki, in *Callaloo,* vol. 14, no. 2, 1991; "Rita Dove's *Mother Love:* A Discussion," edited by Mark Edmundson, Mark, *Callaloo: A Journal of African American and African Arts and Letters*, Winter l996.

*   *   *

In *The Poet's World* (1995), a collection of essays written during her l993-95 term as the United States' seventh Poet Laureate, Rita Dove makes a surprising declaration, "My pleasures are taken in the intimate details of life, the miracles of the ordinary." Dove's artistic range seems boundless, fed by her knowledge of world history and literature. But a generous spirit guides her intellectual curiosity: she does not want to learn facts or to observe art and artifacts; she wants to engage with the world and its people.

Whether writing about herself, her grandparents, an ancient Chinese princess, a German woman widowed during World War II, mythological characters, the blues singer Bessie Smith, or even a fossilized fish, Dove brings readers closer to ourselves, our world, and each other. She has read widely and travelled extensively, but she also grounds her work in her own intimate, ordinary experiences as a daughter, granddaughter, wife, mother, African American, woman and teacher. As she observed in a l991 interview published in *Callaloo*, "significant events in the private sphere are rarely written up in history books, although they make up the life-sustaining fabric of humanity." This same fabric gives life, warmth, texture, and color to Dove's poetry, fiction, essays, and drama.

Born in Akron, Ohio in l952, Dove only recently became a "Southerner": In l993 she took the position of Commonwealth Profesor of English at the University of Virginia and now lives near Charlottesville, Virginia, with her husband, the German novelist Fred Viebahn, and their daughter, Aviva. Although a Midwesterner by birth, Dove can trace some of her personal as well as her artistic heritage back to the South.

Like many contemporary Southern writers, her works often convey the importance of recognizing one's connection to a particular place and the need to remember the past, even—or especially—when that past evokes painful memories. Her grandparents, on whose lives she loosely based the sequence of poems *Thomas and Beulah*, were among the many African Americans who left the south for the north during the Great Migration that occurred during the early twentieth century. According to Ekaterini Georgoudaki, Thomas's mandolin playing "preserves and conveys to the next generation of blacks their rich cultural heritage and the communal values which many of them lost when they migrated from the rural south to the industrial north. The poet inherits both her grandmother's transforming imagination and her grandfather's storytelling ability." Dove earned the l987 Pulitzer Prize for *Thomas and Beulah*, a tribute to her, her grandparents, and to the vitality of the southern African American folk tradition.

As a poet, Dove is an iconoclast and a traditionalist, both in terms of subject and technique. She admires the Western tradition's heroes and heroines, its saints and its artists, but when speculating on the private moments of these individuals, she focuses on their quirks as well as their accomplishments, their sexuality as well as their spirituality.

In the poem "Robert Schumann, Or: Musical Genius Begins with Afflictions," she imagines the composer driven by lust and music while engaged in an encounter with a prostitute; in "Catherine of Alexandria" she explores the sexual connection that may have existed between this saint and her God:

Deprived of learning and
the chance to travel,
no wonder Sainthood
came as a voice in your bed—
and what went on
each night was fit for nobody's ears.

On occasion, Dove also writes against the grain of the African American literary tradition. "Upon Meeting Don L. Lee, In a Dream" offers an irreverent, even caustic look at one of the most significant writers of the Black Arts Movement of the l960s. The speaker, presumably Dove, sees "caviar / Imbedded like buckshot between his teeth. / His hair falls out in clumps of burned-out wire." But while this dream version of Lee disintegrates, "The music grows like branches in the wind" and the the speaker lie down, "chuckling as the grass curls around me."

Well-versed in the craft of poetry, sensitive to the nuances of language, rhythm and meter, Dove often revises traditional poetic forms. For example, her experiments with the villanelle and the sestina allowed her to write "Parsley." This poem explores the mind and motives of the genocidal Dominican dictator Rafael Trujillo who, on October 2, 1957, had 20,000 Black Haitians executed, allegedly because they could not pronounce the letter "r."

In her most recent collection of poems, *Mother Love* (1995), she uses a series of sonnets based on the myth of Demeter and Persephone to grapple with mother-daughter relationships. Aware that she does not always strictly adhere to the conventions of the Shakespearean and Petrarchan sonnet, Dove contends: "Much has been said about the many ways to 'violate' the sonnet in the service of American speech or modern love or whatever; I will simply say that I like how the sonnet comforts even while its prim borders (but what a pretty fence!) are stultifying; one is constantly bumping against Order" ("An Intact World," preface to *Mother Love*).

Although in *Mother Love* Dove does take liberties with the sonnet form, a transgression she stops just short of confessing, she implies that she retains the sonnet's essence: the ability to create order and to exist as a world unto itself.

When addressing the issues of race and gender, Dove also asserts her artistic independence. "In my poems, and in my stories, too, I try very hard to create characters who are seen as individuals—not only as Blacks or as women, or whatever, but as a Black woman with her own particular problems, or one White bum struggling in a specific predicament—as persons who have their very individual lives, and whose histories make them react to the world in different ways," (1991 *Callaloo* interview). "One could argue that insisting upon that individuality is ultimately a political act, and to my mind, this is one of the fundamental principles a writer has to uphold, along with a warning: don't be swallowed up. Don't be swallowed up."

Dove does not shy away from addressing the effects of race and gender on individual identity. In fact, she often approaches the question of being black and female from an intensely personal perspective. In her autobiographical poems about her daughter, who has the physical characteristics of both her black mother and her white father, Dove reflects on, questions, and celebrates her own experiences as an African American and as a woman. In "Genetic Expedition," Dove observes: "My child has / her father's hips, his hair / like the miller's daughter, combed gold. / Though her lips are mine, housewives / stare when we cross the parking lot because of that ghostly profusion." The poem "After Reading *Mickey in the Night Kitchen* for the Third Time Before Bed" suggests that the mother-daughter bond transcends race: "Every month she wants / to know where it hurts / and what the wrinkled string means / between my legs. This is good blood / I say, but that's wrong, too. / How to tell her that it's what makes us— / black mother, cream child. / That we're in the pink / and the pink's in us." Given Dove's inclusive vision, readers might also interpret us to mean all people in addition to the poet and her daughter.

There are no easy answers to questions of racial and gender identity, as Dove reveals in numerous works. Based on a little known historical incident, "The Transport of Slaves From Maryland to Mississippi" focuses on an enslaved woman's decision to help a black wagon driver wounded during a violent slave revolt. The speaker helps this individual because "I am no brute. I got feelings. / He might have been a friend of mind." As a result of her assistance, this man rides for help and the slaves are recaptured. Dove relates this woman's story from a detached perspective, leaving questions of morality, betrayal, loyalty, and salvation up to the reader. This poem is one of the many in which Dove gives voice to her interest in "the underside of the story" not in "big historical events." Like many African American writers, Dove treats history with suspicion; she knows that the official records record time, not moments, and only moments provide the real source of truth.

Though she is best known for her poetry, Dove has also written fiction and drama. When asked in an 1986 interview if her foray into fiction was a sidestep, she replied: "Just as it's tragic to pigeonhole individuals according to stereotypes, there's no reason to subscribe authors to particular genres, either. I'm a writer, and I write in the form that most suits what I want to say." Her novel, *Through the Ivory Gate* (1992), tells the story of a young black woman's coming of age. The protagonist, Virginia Evans, is a musician and an aspiring actress. Dove skillfully blends the story of this young woman's quest for personal knowledge and fulfillment with numerous observations about the magic of art. The advice Virginia receives from one of her college professors, Nathan Mannheim, seems to echo Dove's own *ars poetica*: "Don't be afraid of the space around you . . . . Take it in your hands. Shape it. Make it come to life."

Fifth Sunday (1985), a collection of eight short stories, also reflects the author's virtuosity, including her use of alternating first-person narrators in one of the stories, "Damon and Vandalia," and recreating her experiences in Germany in "The Spray Paint King."

Her only full-length play, *The Darker Face of the Earth*, written in 1994 and revised for a second edition published in 1996, tackles a rarely discussed aspect of slavery: sexual relationships between white mistresses and their male slaves and the offspring such unions often produced. Dove weaves the story of Oedipus into her account of a white woman, Amalia, her African American lover, Hector, and their offspring, Augustus. The mingling of Greek tragedy and American history effectively shows not only the tragic consequences of slavery but also the suffering that stems from jealousy, pride, and deception, no matter where or when stories take place or lives are lived.

Since her first book, *The Yellow House on the Corner* (1980), Dove has taken her readers on extraordinary journeys into what she describes as "her poetic consciousness of occupied space — of the space we inhabit, of the shape and pressure of absence" (*The Poet's World*). According to Dove, to inhabit "space with thought is analogous to the notion that language is a house we inhabit—a poet explores those spaces of sensual apprehension made inhabitable by vocabulary and syntax" (*The Poet's World*).

Dove listens to and recreates sounds others seem not to hear. Her fiction, poetry, drama, and essays are standing invitations to enter her linguistic house, an intimate, homey yet also extraordinary space. While there we can explore life, death, love and loss; we can hear voices history has not recorded and understand the need for compassion and forgiveness because of the cost bigotry has exacted from us all. Most importantly, her works, because they dwell in the timeless world of art and the imagination, have the power to unite individuals, cultures, as well as the past, present and future. Perhaps more than any other contemporary writer, Rita Dove understands the true value of multiculturalism because she has found her place.

—Candis LaPrade

DUBUS, Andre

Born: Lake Charles, Louisiana, 11 August 1936. **Education:** McNeese State College (now University), Lake Charles, B.A. 1958; University of Iowa, Iowa City, M.F.A. 1966. **Military Service:** U.S. Marine Corps 1958-64; captain. **Family:** Married Patricia Lowe in 1958 (divorced 1970), four children; married Tommie Gail Cotter in 1975 (divorced 1977); married Peggy Rambach in 1979 (divorced 1989), two daughters. **Career:** Creative writing teacher, Bradford College, Massachusetts, 1966-84; since 1984 visiting teacher, University of Alabama, Birmingham, and Boston University. **Awards:** National Endowment for the Arts fellowship, 1985; MacArthur Foundation award, 1988-93. **Agent:** Philip G. Spitzer, 50 Tulmage Farm Lane, East Hampton, New York 11937.

PUBLICATIONS

Novel

The Lieutenant. New York, Dial Press, 1967.

Short Story Collections

Separate Flights. Boston, Godine, 1975.
Adultery and Other Choices. Boston, Godine, 1977.
Finding a Girl in America: Ten Stories and a Novella. Boston, Godine, 1980.
The Times Are Never So Bad: A Novella and Eight Short Stories. Boston, Godine, 1983.
We Don't Live Here Anymore. New York, Crown, Pan, 1984.
Land Where My Fathers Died (single story). Winston-Salem, Wright, 1984.
Voices from the Moon and Other Stories, with David Godine. Boston, Godine, 1984.
The Last Worthless Evening: Four Novellas and Two Short Stories. Boston, Godine, 1986.
Blessings (single story). Elmwood, Connecticut, Raven Editions, 1987.
Selected Stories. Boston, Godine, 1988.
Into the Silence. Cambridge, Massachusetts, Green Street Press, 1988.
The Cage Keeper and Other Stories. New York, E. P. Dutton, 1989.
Bluesman. Boston, Faber and Faber, 1993.
Dancing After Hours. New York, A. A. Knopf, 1996.

Essay Collections

Broken Vessels. Boston, Godine, 1991.
Meditations from a Moveable Chair. New York, Knopf, 1998.

*

Critical Studies: *Andre Dubus: A Study of the Short Fiction* by Thomas E. Kennedy, Boston, Twayne Publishers, 1988.

*   *   *

Often compared to Ernest Hemingway and Raymond Carver, Andre Dubus is known for his realistic fiction about the small, everyday wars fought between men and women. He is a Southern writer who seldom sets his stories in the South. His characters are disillusioned by today's world and sometimes confused about their places within it. As a result, they tend to live first and think second. Dubus' compassion for his characters, especially the females, is particularly in evidence in his work.

Dubus' only novel, *The Lieutenant* (1967), is usually overlooked in references to his principal works. Not considered one of his finest works, it nevertheless opens up his lifelong focus on truth and sincerity. In 1970, his story "If They Knew Yvonne" appeared in *Best American Short Stories,* and in 1975, the collection, *Separate Flights,* presented readers with seven stories and one novella, "We Don't Live Here Anymore," portraying couples' lives in late 20th Century America. The collection *Adultery and Other Choices* (1977) included nine of Dubus' short stories and the novella, "Adultery." Again, his stories resonated with their honest portrayal of relationships between men and women. That same year, he received a Guggenheim fellowship.

The pieces in his 1980 collection, *Finding a Girl in America,* are most effective in stories about revenge and the effects of troubled marriages on children. *The Times Are Never So Bad* (1983) included eight stories and the novella, "The Pretty Girl," all of which feature Dubus' unique voice and his use of singular details in presenting unusual characters. His belief that characters must be complete but not necessarily sympathetic is evident in this collection. *Voices from the Moon* (1984) is a novella told from the point of view of Richie Stowe, a twelve-year old who lives with his divorced father. While his father agonizes over decisions about his love life, Richie exhibits his level head and uses his Catholic faith and the attentions of a thirteen year old girl to keep steady. In the end, Dubus puts forth the belief that love can be achieved in small doses, by those patient enough to wait.

"We Don't Live Here Anymore" was one of three novellas, including "Adultery" and "Finding a Girl in America," collected in 1984's *We Don't Live Here Anymore.* The three novellas feature Terry and Jack Linhart and Edith and Hank Allison and follow the trials and small crises that make up their relationships. As in the past, Dubus was again lauded for the gritty realism of his stories, and for presenting his female characters with strength and respect.

The Last Worthless Evening (1986), a collection of stories, appeared to favorable reviews just prior to Dubus' receipt of a second Guggenheim Fellowship. In stories about race relations, failure, and murder, Dubus again reveals his own compassion for his characters and their situations. In the end, he gives them credit for having been a success at something and allows them to leave their failures behind.

In 1986, Dubus was injured and lost a leg while trying to help a driver stranded on the side of a road. This accident informs his later works, including new pieces in *Selected Stories* (1988) that focus on parental bereavement, loneliness, and the unlimited love of a parent for a child. All are told in Dubus' lyric and direct voice, with precision and generosity, and display Dubus' consistent understanding of, and moral responsibility for, his characters. Dubus' recent collection of stories, *Dancing After Hours* (1996), was again praised for its lyric quality, for his characteristic understatement, and for the absolute aptness of his details. The collection features characters being tested physically and spiritually. That same year, Dubus received the Rea Award for the short story in recognition of his career achievement. Many of the characters in this collection are lonely, emotionally empty, and lost. Not fooled by their situations, they nevertheless settle for whatever they can get. Placing them in small cities slowly crumbling into disrepair, Dubus reveals their need for institutions like the military or the church to replace the frameworks once afforded by family and work.

Broken Vessels (1991), a collection of essays on subjects ranging from his accident and resultant physical struggle to the end of his marriage, are written within the context of his own faith and moral code, endowed with the resonance of his own truth. A second essay collection, *Meditations from a Moveable Chair* (1998), includes pieces on his sister's prayers for the man who raped her, Dubus' own childhood, his time in the Marines, his first marriage, a recent meeting with a woman who witnessed his accident, and the experience of having grandsons, all sifted through the power of his faith. Though he has been criticized for being emotionally self-indulgent and for searching too hard for irretrievable experiences, Dubus' moral sensitivity and compassion give his writing its resonance and power.

—Virginia Watkins

DUFRESNE, John

Born: Worcester, Massachusetts, 30 January 1948. **Education:** Worcester State College, B.A. 1970; University of Arkansas, M.F.A. 1984; attended State University of New York at Binghamton, 1987-88. **Family:** Married Marilyn Virbasius in 1971 (divorced, 1978); married Cindy Chinelly in 1985; one son, Tristan Jude. **Career:** Social worker, crisis intervention counselor, 1970-82; English instructor, Northeast Louisiana University, 1984-87, Augusta College, 1988-89; English professor, Florida International University, since 1989. **Awards**: *Transatlantic Review* Award, 1983; PEN Syndicated Fiction Award, 1984; *Yankee* Magazine Fiction Award, 1988; Florida State Arts Council grant, 1992. **Agent:** Richard P. McDonough, P.O. Box 1950, Boston, Massachusetts 02130. **Address**: Department of English, Florida International University, North Miami, Florida 33181.

Publications

The Way that Water Enters Stone. New York, W. W. Norton, 1991.
Louisiana Power & Light. New York, W. W. Norton, 1994.
Naked Came the Manatee, with other Florida writers. New York, Putnam, 1996.
Love Warps the Mind a Little. New York, W. W. Norton, 1997.

*

John Dufresne comments:

Sometimes you tell a story for its own sake, keep it alive so it will grow, mature, you hope, consider its own being and its place in a grander scheme of things, perhaps even wander onto some fundamental truth or other. Your story, after all, is a consciousness that, like the rest of us, given time and tenacity, can begin to find out what it means. As you tell the story, you trust it will not be one of those tales that refuses to look below the surface of its own behavior, examine its values and motives, ask, "Why?" Possibly, said story discerns that the cause of our apprehension and its own misfortune is the enfeebled and transient condition we share. When we afford mortality all of our attention, no benevolence, tenderness, or beauty can console us.

—from *Louisiana Power & Light.*

*   *   *

A native of Worcester, Massachusetts, John Dufresne is a contemporary Southern writer because of his birth date (1948), because of his current residence in Florida, because of his choice of subject matter and setting in five wonderful stories in his first book, and by virtue of his stunning first novel, *Louisiana Power & Light.* (The remaining eight stories in *The Way That Water Enters Stone* and his second novel, *Love Warps the Mind a Little*, are set in New England, usually in Worcester. Dufresne contributed a chapter to *Naked Came the Manatee,* a serial novel published over

13 weeks in the *Miami Herald*; the 12 other contributors included Dave Barry, Elmore Leonard, and Carl Hiaasen.)

The five Southern stories in *The Way that Water Enters Stone* are postmodern versions of Faulkner and Caldwell and Welty and O'Connor, in that Dufresne deconstructs the myths and stereotypes about the South and about low- and lower-middle class Southerners that the earlier authors helped to invent. Thus, in "The Freezer Jesus" a brother and sister in Holly Ridge, Louisiana, are visited by a miracle—the appearance of the face of Jesus on their Amana appliance—but the story performs its own miracle-of making the brother/narrator's stupefaction and religious belief at once believable and sympathetic.

In "Must I Be Carried to the Sky on Flowered Beds of Ease" the narrator/protagonist is a 57-year-old cotton farmer, a hard man, abandoned by his wife and older son; the story recounts his willing acceptance of his youngest son, an AIDS victim, who has returned to the farm to die. The narrator's acceptance of his son, of his love for his son, and of his own desire to see his wife again, as well as Dufresne's masterful control of tone, make this an especially powerful story. "What Follows in the Wake of Love," set in Florida in 1955, follows the history of a county sheriff as he considers his marriage, his parents' marriage, the murderous relationship between a harlot and two of her lovers, and the relationship of the largest landowner in the county with his migrant workers. Dufresne allows us to make connections among these relationships, connections the sheriff himself nearly sees.

"My Love, My Dove, My Undefiled" is a wonderfully comic story; its narrator, a pharmacist in Flandreau, Louisiana, worries throughout both over the love of a teenaged boy, Adlai Birdsong, for the narrator's daughter, Anniece Pate, and over the nature of love itself. "The Fontana Gene" recounts the story of the last of Monroe, Louisiana's cursed Fontanas, Billy Wayne, of his relationship with his two wives, Earleane and Tami Lynne, and of his death and the deaths of his sons Duane and Moon Pie. All of Dufresne's characters in these five stories are caught in the grip of love and thrash with its mysteries. If the protagonists of four of them are more or less grotesque—indeed, rednecks and trailer trash—they are neither stereotypical nor laughable but rather poignantly sympathetic figures. Furthermore, because the five Southern stories are collected with eight stories set in New England that also feature characters of similar class similarly puzzled by life and love, it seems clear that Dufresne's vision is neither sneering nor regionalistic. The volume demonstrates as well Dufresne's love and control of language, which he is able here to make sing in new and surprising ways.

Dufresne's first novel, *Louisiana Power & Light*, takes as its starting point the last and longest story of his earlier collection, "The Fontana Gene," and does not merely expand but reconstructs it, teasing out of it new themes and new meanings. The story ponders such topics as God, faith, heredity, fate, love, life, class, politics, friendship, and story-telling, among other things, and it does so in intelligent, even wise, new ways. Dufresne examines at length and with compassion the relationships among Billy Wayne and his wives, his children, his friends, and the Monroe community, represented by several characters and the narrator's voice.

The novel is remarkable for many things—the leisurely pace and seemingly tangential nature of the plot, a wonderfully diverse and original cast of characters, the rich textures of Dufresne's language, the sensitive compassion of his comedy, and his willingness to collapse fiction and real life (since I know many of the characters to be alive and relatively well in Monroe).   Whether Dufresne chooses to continue writing about Louisiana or New England or sets his next work in Florida (where he now lives), he is an immensely talented writer, well worth reading.

—David K. Jeffrey

DURBAN, Pam

Born: Rosa Pamela Durban in Aiken, South Carolina, 4 March 1947. **Education:** University of North Carolina, Greensboro, B.A. 1969; University of Iowa, M.F.A. 1979. **Family:** Married Frank H. Hunter, 18 June 1983. **Career:** Editor and writer, *Atlanta Gazette*, 1974-75; visiting assistant professor of creative writing, State University of New York at Geneseo, 1979-80; assistant professor of creative writing, 1980-81, Murray State University; associate professor of creative writing, Ohio University, 1981-86. **Awards:** Fiction Award, *Crazyhorse*, 1982, for "In Darkness"; James Michener Fellowship, University of Iowa, 1982-83; Rinehart Award in fiction, Rinehart Foundation, 1984, for collected work; fellowships from Ohio Arts Council, 1983-84 and 1986-87; National Endowment for the Arts creative writing fellowship, 1998. **Agent:** Gail Hochman, Brandt & Brandt Literary Agents, Inc., 1501 Broadway, New York, New York 10036. **Address:** Department of English, Georgia State University, Atlanta, Georgia 30303.

PUBLICATIONS

Short Story Collection

All Set About with Fever Trees and Other Stories. David Godine, 1985.

Novel

The Laughing Place. New York, Scribner's 1993.

Other

Editor, *Cabbagetown Families, Cabbagetown Food*. Atlanta, Patch Publications, 1976.

*

Pam Durban comments:
   I began writing fiction after working for a year or so in an urban textile mill community in Atlanta, Georgia, interviewing people who lived there. Their voices stuck in my mind and I continued to think about their lives for years afterward. One of my first published stories, "This Heat," came out of that experience, and I believe that the time I spent in that place also helped me see that I was most interested in who people are and how they got to be that way, and what makes them or allows them to go on living in the face of everything that happens to them.

   I don't consider myself a Southern writer in the sense that my subject is Southernness or that I deal with people in my work as representatives of any region. In fact, the whole issue has gotten so tiresome to me that I prefer not to talk about it at all. Why doesn't anyone get asked if he or she is a New England writer or a Great Plains writer or a Northwestern writer?

*   *   *

   Although Pam Durban grew up in South Carolina, she does not consider herself a "Southern writer in the sense that my writing is Southerness."   Nevertheless, most of her stories, as well as her first novel, are set in the South and bear the traditional characteristics of attention to setting and family relationships. As she remarks, her fiction explores "who people are and how they got to be that way, and what makes them or allows them to go on living in the face of everything that happens to them."   Characteristically her characters search for answers to universal questions; family, pride, love and religious faith allow them to endure.

   Durban's character explorations begin in her early story "This Heat" (*Georgia Review*, 1982), collected with six others in *All Set About with Fever Trees* (1985). Based on Durban's interviews with cotton mill workers in Atlanta, Georgia, the story captures their language as it recounts Ruby Clinton's reaction to the sudden, but not entirely unexpected, death of her sixteen year old son, Beau Clinton. Born with a heart defect, Beau brought sorrow to Ruby from the beginning; her husband Charles leaves, and an angry adolescent Beau sees himself as only "a Nelson from the cotton patch and a Clinton straight from hell." The day of Beau's funeral, Ruby searches her memories, wishing for one more chance to explain to Beau that one person's love, in this case hers, is redemption enough.

   Mark, the seventh grader of "World of Women" (*Epoch*, 1980) struggles for importance in the eyes of Sara, his private swimming instructor from Mobile, Alabama, attending the college in Wisconsin where Mark's parents work. The story captures his confusion and acute awareness of his body and Sara's touch as she coaches him through his terror of water and swimming; he spends time comparing Sara to his mother. At the end of his lessons, Sara rewards Mark with a hike; in an emotional turmoil, Marc silently questions Sara, in reality himself, "Where are you going?" His fantasy collapses with Sara's troubled rejection of him, but he takes a step into adulthood. "In Darkness" (*Crazyhorse*, 1982) again features the point of view of a confused, questioning child. Jennifer is sent to spend two months with her Quaker grandparents in Hamilton, New York, while her mother "goes away" for two months. After her father tells her that "Love changes, but it doesn't go away," Jennifer searches for explanations for the disquieting changes in her life; she puzzles over the meaning of love and happiness; she wonders why her father has removed his wedding ring. When her mother returns, Jennifer tries to reestablish her "perfect" family image through "acting out" and playing familiar family games.

   As critics point out, Durban develops the theme of death versus survival, especially in "Notes Toward an Understanding of My Father's Novel" (*Ohio Review*, 1983). Here, Annie searches to understand her Papa and his need to repeat the accounts of his survival of long marches in the Asian Pacific campaign of World

War II, primarily of crossing the River Tor in New Guinea. Years after the war, diagnosed with degenerative arthritis in his hips but unable to acknowledge any perceived weakness, Papa curtly denies the pain. Usually unable to communicate with his children, Papa bewilders Annie with a heretofore untold story of how once, crossing the Tor, he offered a comforting touch to a dying boy and, then, "ran like hell." His revelation begins Annie's insight into her father's burden of his own mortality.

Two additional stories highlight the theme of loss. In "Made to Last" (originally published in *Tri Quarterly*, 1981, as "Let Me Not to the Marriage"), Annie, against her better judgment, visits her estranged husband Stephen so that he can reread the divorce papers which both of them have already signed. "A Long Time Coming, A Long Time Gone" opens with Alice Dyer's short tempered observations of her mother's annual spring garden preparation. Alice, a less than famous country singer, is ready for something to satisfy her hunger to know why she's alive. After a botched recording session in Knoxville, she still waits—for the imagined return of her long dead father and for whatever "it" is. In the collection's title story, "All Set About with Fever Trees" (*Georgia Review*, 1984), Annie Vess recollects her lifelong search for her destiny beginning with her trust in her grandmother, Mariah Palmer, a famous religious teacher who at sixty leaves Macon, Georgia, to teach in the Belgian Congo. Eight-year old Annie needs to know what called her grandmother to Africa, because she has had "glimmerings" that some kind of destiny is waiting for her. Annie feels betrayed when her grandmother returns changed only by now being fat, but her grandmother's stories give the twelve year old something to ponder. At sixteen, Annie, still searching for her destiny, attends a Palmer family reunion in the mountain home of Great-aunt Martha, a clairvoyant who replaces grand-

mother as more likely to tell her about "clear calls, souls, destinies." Annie picks up two pieces of information at the reunion: Grandmother Mariah's birth was special and her mother's sister Louise is an alcoholic. Mariah fiercely believes that her daughter Louise's salvation is a fall foliage tour to Vermont, which she implements with disastrous results. After a hiatus, Annie and her mother visit the dying Mariah; four years later, Annie, now married and a mother, returns to care for her ailing mother. Her visit to a recovered Louise as they look at Mariah's Africa photo album triggers this story's recollection and Annie's appreciation of her destiny.

Annie Vess reappears in Durban's highly praised first novel, *The Laughing Place* (1993), in which she fuses realism with romantic southern gothic. Recently widowed, Annie returns to the ancestral home in Timmons, South Carolina, a quintessential southern town steeped in tradition, to console her suddenly widowed mother, Louise. Timmons is no longer Annie's childhood town. Particularly, her mother has become a born again Christian, her cousin is engaged to a shrewd real estate developer, and the family land lies under a man-made lake, against which her father had fought so valiantly, or so she believed. A love affair with the photographer/ecologist Legree Black and revelations about her father's duplicity in fighting the lake project bring the brooding, depressed Annie into a new life in a new South. In recognition of her eloquent storytelling using rich language and portraying sensible characters coping in their changing worlds, Durban was awarded a 1998 National Endowment for the Arts creative writing fellowship.

—Judith C. Kohl

E

EARLEY, Tony

Born: Tony Lee Earley in San Antonio, Texas, 15 June, 1961. **Education:** Warren Wilson College, B.A. 1983; University of Alabama, M.F.A. 1992. **Family:** Married Sarah Bell in 1993. **Career:** Instructor, University of the South, Carnegie-Mellon University, University of Alabama; columnist and sports editor, *Daily Courier,* Forest City, North Carolina; Professsor, Vanderbilt University. **Awards:** PEN Syndicated Fiction Award, 1991; National Magazine Award for Fiction, 1994; Walter E. Dakin Fellowship, Sewanee Writers' Conference, 1995; named one of *Granta* magazine's "Best Young American Novelists," 1996; John Gardner Fellowship, Breadloaf Writers' Conference, 1997. **Agent:** Gordon Kato, 133 West 75th Street, Suite 1-A, New York, New York 10023.

PUBLICATIONS

Short Story Collection

Here We Are in Paradise. Boston, Little, Brown and Company, 1994.

Novel

Jim the Boy. Boston, Brown and Company, 1999.

*   *   *

Though the author, so far, of only one book of short stories, a forthcoming novel, and a good deal of journalism, Tony Earley is widely considered one of the most promising southern fiction writers of his generation. His work has been praised highly by such oracles as Lee Smith and Louise Erdrich, and he was named, along with nineteen of his contemporaries, as one of the "Best Young American Novelists" by the influential British quarterly *Granta.* His work is notable for its humor, its deep sympathy for its characters, and its shrewd recognitions of human nature, as well as for its perceptive renderings of contemporary southern life.

Though Earley was born in Texas, where his father was serving in the Air Force, his imagination is closely tied to the western North Carolina mountains where his parents were born and to which they returned with him as soon as possible. He grew up in Rutherfordton, a small town near Asheville, and the belt of territory between there and Charlotte is his "postage stamp of native soil," the setting for most of his fiction. In this sense and several others he is a self-consciously southern writer and thus the heir of a literary tradition whose very excellence has overwhelmed some good writers, turning them into imitators or unwitting parodists of their elders. But Earley, so far, has gone his own way, seeing the region for himself rather than through the lens provided by Faulkner, Welty, or any other predecessor. He is not unaware of that tradition; his story "Gettysburg," for example, seems concerned in part with establishing his own relationship to a body of writing characterized by its deep sense of history. Tully, the pro-

tagonist of that story, travels from North Carolina to the famous Pennsylvania battlefield, hoping among other things to learn the fate of a Confederate ancestor who disappeared during the fighting. But as he peers out at the field from Little Round Top, waiting for "some ancestral voice" to speak, he is able to manage nothing more than "a real estate broker's generic appreciation of the view."

The burden of southern history is less important, for Tully as for his creator, than the immediate concerns of love, family, and community. Though departing from a significant part of the regional literary tradition, Earley is anything but indifferent to the region itself. His depictions of life in the contemporary South are simultaneously funny, sad, and photographically accurate. His best work in this vein may be found in two stories, "The Prophet from Jupiter" and "Charlotte." The former is narrated by the damkeeper on a North Carolina reservoir who placidly spends his days gazing out at tourists, water skiers, and sunbathers while obeying the directive to "maintain constant pond level." The nearby Town of Lake Glenn is happy and prosperous, having grown rich from tourism and real estate. But beneath the waters of the lake is the old town of Uree, inundated in 1927, whose ghosts are occasionally perceived along the banks. Wandering the streets of town is Junie Wilson, a harmless but alarming lunatic whom everyone knows to be the son of the Mayor and a black prostitute.

Behind the impassive narrative voice of the damkeeper are deep grief and rage over his wife's adultery. Lake Glenn and its dam are of course metaphors for the concealment and repression that are necessary to maintain the illusions of sunbelt contentment, and the monstrous catfish for which the damkeeper fishes, late at night with deep sea tackle, symbolize the latent savagery and mystery of the human heart, always threatening to break the surface. "Charlotte," which is a kind of signature piece of Earley's and a crowd-pleaser on the reading circuit, at a glance seems very different. The story is set at the mock-epochal moment when the Southeastern Wrestling Alliance, with stars like the Sheik of the East, Comrade Yerkov the Russian Assassin, and Yee-Hah O'Reilly the Cherokee Chief, decamped from Charlotte, North Carolina, to be replaced by a hapless NBA franchise. Earley has enormous fun describing the last night of pro wrestling in Charlotte, with its Apache Death Match, its Texas Chain-Link Massacre, its deviously wielded folding chairs and purblind referees. But the story, oddly enough, is really about love, for which the narrator hopelessly yearns and which his girlfriend—who "like many people in Charlotte, has given up on love"—denies him, and which is defended in a "Final Battle for Love" by the paisley-clad wrestler Lord Poetry. When the beautiful Darling Donnis, the Sweetheart of the SWA, abandons Lord Poetry for his nemesis Bob Noxious, not just the narrator but Charlotte itself seems to lose its illusions for good. The triumph of the story is that Earley manages to attach a real pathos to the narrator's hilarious lament, "Gone is Lord Poetry, and all that he stood for."

Among the best of Earley's stories are three related pieces, "Aliceville," "Story of Pictures," and "My Father's Heart," all of which concern Jim Glass, a North Carolina boy being raised in the 1930's by his widowed mother and her three brothers. These stories were the genesis of Earley's forthcoming novel, *Jim the Boy*. In the best of them, the beautifully wrought "My Father's Heart," Jim Glass grows up to be a railroad fireman and a disappointment to his mother, who has told herself that the son of her dead husband must grow up to do something important. But telling his own stories as an old man teaches Jim that "we are more than who we are inside ourselves, that we also inhabit the stories that others tell about us, and the stories never go away." This conclusion could serve as the epigraph for Earley's work as a whole, which rests on a faith that even ordinary lives, because they are made of stories, matter very much indeed.

—John Gramma

EAST, Charles

Born: Shelby, Mississippi, 11 December 1924. **Education:** Louisiana State University, B.A. 1948, M.A. 1962. **Family:** Married Sarah Simmons, one son, Charles East, Jr. **Career:** Editorial assistant, *Collier's* magazine, New York, 1948-49; reporter, later Sunday magazine editor, *Morning Advocate,* Baton Rouge, 1949-55; assistant city editor, *State Times,* Baton Rouge, 1955-62; editor, later associate director, Louisiana State University Press, 1962-70, and director, Louisiana State University Press, 1970-75; freelance writer, 1975-80; assistant director and Editor, University of Georgia Press, 1980-83; editor since 1981 of the Flannery O'Connor Award Series, University of Georgia Press. **Awards:** Bellaman Award, 1965, for the collection *Where the Music Was.*

PUBLICATIONS

Short Story Collections

Where the Music Was. New York, Harcourt Brace, 1965.
Distant Friends and Intimate Strangers. Urbana, University of Illinois Press, 1996.

Editor

The New Writers of the South: A Fiction Anthology. Athens, University of Georgia Press, 1987.
The Civil War Diary of Sarah Morgan. Athens, University of Georgia Press, 1991.
The Flannery O'Connor Award: Selected Stories. Athens, University of Georgia Press, 1992.
Listening to the Voices: Stories from the Flannery O'Connor Award. Athens, University of Georgia Press, 1998.

*   *   *

In his two collections of precise and honest short stories, Charles East often deals with regret, surfaces and manners. His lonely characters often reflect quietly on a past they cannot reclaim, or make their way in a dreary present far from the hopes and romantic notions with which they started. In his first short-story collection, *Where the Music Was*, East writes of the South in the

1930s and 1940s, when Southern society was more or less in traditional balance, and characters who are alienated, unable to make or maintain any significant attachments in life. In "Where the Music Was," for example, Ben Hadley yearns to be in Chicago because that is where the action is, and from the radio he knows that Chicago is "where the music was." Yet after traveling there and spending several months he barely knows anyone: his three closest acquaintances are as lost as he is and he barely knows anything about his lover. In "Stopover," the young hobo Gar asks his older companion Lou, "What's a good place?" Lou replies, "I never found any . . . . I kept looking, but I never found any." Along with alienated characters are those mired in self-deception, as in "Night Watch," where two Mississippi policemen pretend to hate Negroes by extolling the familiar view of keeping "niggers and their place." In reality, each holds a secret connection to blacks, but they carry on their act because they fear each other.

Other stories show characters motivated more by their quest for personal integrity. In "Four Minutes to the Bridge," an elderly woman tries to prevent her house from being torn down to make room for a new access road to a bridge. Similarly, in "A Sunday Drive," Miss Odell, a nursing home resident, is taken by relatives to visit her old home. She becomes so thrilled that she can claim a home that she risks great loss to remain there.

It was 31 years before East produced his second short-story collection, *Distant Friends and Intimate Strangers*. East's stories here do not have the same sense of place as in *Where the Music Was*. In the 1990s, once-alluring Southern locations such as Memphis and New Orleans have been rendered quite ordinary by a national economy and suburbanization. East revisits themes of alienation, loneliness, and lost dreams.

In "Crazy Heart," Ernie reflects upon his failed marriage, "Where did all those good dreams go bad?" Without any willful action, he falls into a love affair with a 20-year-old girl. "Mr. Allello" depicts a long life's end—but it is an end lacking warmth, meaning, or dignity. A son remembers his father in the "Brain Surgeon") as a man lacking in knowledge about affairs of the heart. And in "Days of Our Lives," a soap opera-addicted widow reduces her late, philandering husband to one simple phrase, "Oh, Emmett started out like a lion."

While it may seem a shame that readers had to wait so long between East's short-story collections, East made significant contributions to literature as an editor, particularly of the short stories deserving of the Flannery O'Connor Award. East also did a superb job of editing *The Civil War Diary of Sarah Morgan*, a journal by a young Baton Rouge woman forced to seek refuge from Union forces in both the Louisiana countryside and in New Orleans. East restored nearly half of the original diary's passages, which had been cut by Sarah Morgan's son for the diary's first published edition. East also wrote an introduction to the diary, where he noted, "It is a life's lesson learned in the most terrible way—compressed into the span of a war instead of a lifetime." A similar outlook befalls East's characters, whose destinies are reflected in the smaller scenes of failure they encounter.

—Eric Patterson

EATON, Charles Edward

Born: Winston-Salem, North Carolina, 25 June 1916. **Education:** Duke University, Durham, North Carolina, 1932-33; University of North Carolina, Chapel Hill, 1933-36, B.A. 1936 (Phi Beta Kappa); Princeton University, New Jersey, 1936-37; Harvard University Cambridge, Massachusetts, 1938-40, M.A. in English 1940. **Family:** Married Isabel Patterson in 1950. **Career:** Instructor, Ruiz Gandia School, Poncé, Puerto Rico, 1937-38; instructor in creative writing, University of Missouri, Columbia, 1940-42; vice consul, American Embassy, Rio de Janeiro, Brazil, 1942-46; professor of creative writing, University of North Carolina, 1946-52; art critic and organizer of art shows. **Awards:** Robert Frost Fellowship, Bread Loaf Writers Conference, 1941; Writers Conference Fellowship, Boulder, Colorado, 1942; Ridgely Torrence Memorial Award, 1951; Gertrude Boatwright Harris Award, 1955; *Arizona Quarterly* Award, 1956, 1975, 1977, 1979, 1982; Roanoke-Chowan Award, 1970, 1987, 1991; Oscar Arnold Young Award, 1971; Golden Rose, New England Poetry Club 1972; O. Henry Award for fiction, 1972; Alice Fay di Castagnola Award, 1974; Arvon Foundation Award, 1980; *Hollins Critic* Award, 1984; Brockman Award, 1984, 1986; *Kansas Quarterly* Award, 1987; North Carolina literature award, 1988; Fortner award, 1993. **Member:** American Academy of Poets.

PUBLICATIONS

Poetry

The Bright Plain. Chapel Hill, University of North Carolina Press, 1942.
The Shadow of the Swimmer. New York, Fine Editions Press, 1951.
The Greenhouse in the Garden. New York, Twayne, 1956.
Countermoves. New York, Abelard Schuman, 1963.
On the Edge of the Knife. New York, Abelard Schuman, 1970.
The Man in the Green Chair. South Brunswick, New Jersey, A.S. Barnes, 1977.
Colophon of the Rover. South Brunswick, New Jersey, 1980.
The Thing King. New York, Cornwall, 1983.
The Work of the Wrench. New York, Cornwall, 1985.
New and Selected Poems 1942-1987. New York, Cornwall, 1987.
A Guest on Mild Evenings. New York, Cornwall, 1991.
The Country of the Blue. New York, Cornwall, 1994.
The Fox and I. New York, Cornwall Books, 1996.

Play

Sea Psalm (produced Chapel Hill, North Carolina, 1933). Published in *North Carolina Drama,* Richmond, Virginia, Garrett and Massie, 1956.

Novel

A Lady of Pleasure. New York, Cornwall, 1993.

Short Story Collections

Write Me from Rio. Winston-Salem, North Carolina, John F. Blair, 1959.
The Girl from Ipanema. Lunenburg, Vermont, North Country, 1972.

The Case of the Missing Photographs. South Brunswick, New Jersey, A.S. Barnes, 1978.
New and Selected Stories, 1959-1989. New York, Cornwall, 1989.

Other

Charles and Isabel Eaton Collection of America Paintings. Chapel Hill, University of North Carolina Art Department, 1970.
Karl Knaths. Washington, Connecticut, Shiver Mountain Press, 1971.
Karl Knaths: Five Decades of Painting. Washington, D.C., International Exhibitions Foundation, 1973.
Robert Broderson: Paintings and Graphics. Washington, Connecticut, Shiver Mountain Press, 1975.

*

Manuscript Collections: (verse) Southern Historical Collection, University of North Carolina, Chapel Hill; (prose) Mugar Memorial Library, Boston University.

Critical Studies: "Charles Edward Eaton" by Louis Untermeyer, *Yale Review,* Winter 1944; "The Poetry of Charles Edward Eaton" by W. W. Davidson, *Georgia Review,* Spring 1953; "Charles Edward Eaton" by May Swenson, *Poetry,* March 1957; "The Greenhouse in the Garden" by William Carlos Williams, *Arizona Quarterly,* Spring 1957; "Betwixt Tradition and Innovation" by Robert D. Spector, *Saturday Review,* 26 December 1970; "The Crisis of Regular Forms" by John T. Irwin, *Sewanee Review,* Winter 1973; "The Shining Figure: Poetry and Prose of Charles Edward Eaton" by Dave Smith, *Meanjin,* Summer 1974; "Charles Edward Eaton" by John Hollander, *Yale Review,* Autumn 1983; "Charles Edward Eaton" by Harold Witt, *The Chariton Review,* Spring 1990 and Fall 1992; "Charles Edward Eaton" by Judy Hogan, *The Arts Journal,* June 1990, and *Paintbrush,* Spring 1992.

Charles Edward Eaton comments:

Though I am resistant in general to definitions of poetry and poets as too limiting, if pressed, I might admit to being a modern formalist, but I should insist on the importance of the qualifying adjective. I compose in a number of verse forms, and write lyrical as well as dramatic poetry, but I do not lean on any poet of the past or present for technical inspiration. I believe that each poet must develop his own organic sense of form and adapt even the most conventional meter to his personal rhythm. For example, a number of my poems are written in triptychs, their long lines rhyming every other line, modulated in an entirely individual way. William Carlos Williams, in a study of my work, called this three-line stanza an Americanization of *terza rima.* Perhaps he felt it was very American in its love of freedom and yet somewhat European in its formal allegiance. There is no doubt that I like poetry that is both vigorous and controlled.

In this respect, I think the best short statement about my work has been made by Robert D. Spector in *The Saturday Review:* "Charles Edward Eaton may not belong at all in the category of unconventional poets, and yet, it seems to me, his use of conventions becomes a very personal thing that removes him from tradition.... If Eaton's poetry, with its use of rhymed stanzas, appears superficially to belong to a formal tradition, his long, free lines and sometimes brutal imagery and diction, pushing his feelings to their limit, suggest otherwise. *On the Edge of the Knife* combines conventional and unconventional in such a way that it is finally the poet's own work. Perhaps, after all, that is the way of poetry. Whether bound to tradition or not, its value rests on the peculiar virtues of the poet."

I am in emphatic accord with any statement about my work which indicates that I believe in working powerfully and freely on one's own terms within the entire range of poetry. I am in no sense a reductionist, but have confidence in the fundamental richness of poetry and the surprise lurking in its possibilities. Form should be an energetic expression of the poet's own psychology, not an artificial imposition, and the poem should convey some sense of the struggle which went into the formal achievement: I have a powerful nature in pursuit of pleasure. / Peace, good will, and I do not share / My time's contempt for passion balanced by strict measure. An extension of what is involved in this position is given at the conclusion of "The Turkey": So the bird I know is like a gaudy catafalque. / If you should carry a secret hump upon your back, / You, too, would have a burdened and uncertain walk. / This is what it is to spread an image in the sun— / This is how we teach thick, precarious balance as if the land moved like a ship / And one set sail heavily, slowly, encumbered with imagination.

As to my subject matter, it is greatly influenced by where I am living and what I am doing at any given time. In this sense, it is always around me, and it moves forward with me as I go along. Almost every poem, hidden though it may be to the reader, has its *donnée* from some aspect of experience. Landscape wherever I have lived (North Carolina, Puerto Rico, Brazil, Connecticut, etc.) comes strongly into my work, but I do not consider myself a nature poet. Animals and flowers are continuous with and contiguous to my interest in human beings, and are a constant motif in my work, but I am not interested in fauna or flora *per se,* and am in no sense a botanical or zoological poet. All of my subjects are finally a way of talking about people in the expanding enclave of interest and experience I have chosen to explore. I have been amused by one magazine editor's recognition of my predilection for "all things, great and small" in welcoming a new submission as another poet from "the Garden of Eaton."

Painting has been another seminal influence, and I have long enjoyed what John Singleton Copley called "the luxury of seeing." This interest is the specific motivation in such poems as "The Gallery," "The Museum," "Homage to the Infanta," and "Nocturne for Douanier Rousseau," among others, but it is a constantly underlying, energizing source. "Five Etudes for the Artist" (*Art International,* November 1972) is an extended statement of this pictorial dedication which has been noted by numerous artists, including the New England painter Karl Knaths who has commented at length on the "vital imaginative reality" of the visual qualities of the poems.

The intellectual content of my poetry and its final outlook and credo has been greatly strengthened by the study of philosophy. Writing in *The New York Times* about *Countermoves,* Wallace Fowlie recognized this influence when he said: "Charles Eaton demonstrates an admirable technical control over the effects he wishes to make, and a clear awareness of at least one major function of poetry. This would be the art of questioning everything, and of questioning in particular the power of poetry."

Fowlie's acknowledgment of the power of sentiment as balancing the intellectual in the poetry is reflected in a line from my long poem, "Robert E. Lee: An Ode": "I believe in the world seen through a temperament." I am certain that it is always the task of the writer to give us his personal vision of reality. This means an uncommon dedication, a determination to keep the fine arts fine, a perpetual sense of renewal and reaffirmation. One must constantly ask oneself in times of discouragement: Who will do my particular kind of writing if I don't? Who will take care of my dreams when I am gone? In our dispersive time, it is not easy to keep a sense of personality and purpose, and, as a consequence, attention to the disciplines of character is equally important with ability. Probably more writers fail through lack of character than of ability. Morale is one of the essential fibers of a meaningful life. Cézanne reminded himself every morning to be *"Sur le motif!"* So must the poet.

*   *   *

The poetry of Charles Edward Eaton ranges from the quiet, reflective, and calmly precise to the colorful, daring, gripping, and raw. The best of his work provides the reader with a delightful though sometimes disturbing experience: he advances confidently, secure in the carefully controlled rhythms, the superbly disciplined energies of syntax, until of a sudden he loses his balance. Upon recovering it the reader discovers that he has been walking on a tightrope, stretched precariously between the world as he usually sees it and the world as it really is.

Eaton is a poet who allows his mind and heart to play upon experience. He sings of ordinary things: the amber light of the sun, the fading fragrance of purple lilacs, the red fire of October, the bodies of swimmers, golden and hard-muscled, a day in spring "like a bell / Rung suddenly in many tones of green, / Sprung full and clear-toned well / Into the rounded air." He sings also of extraordinary things: the Giggler, Voyeur, Centaur, Eunuch, Cowboy, Woman with a Scar, Dagger Thrower's Assistant, and Madame Midget, "Her tiny heart, loaded with feeling close as a plum is to its stone." Repeatedly, through skillful use of conventional form and variations, the poet demonstrates how tenuous and fluctuating is the distinction between the two. For Eaton all experience, the ordinary as well as the extraordinary, the painful as well as the pleasant, is matter for poetry to assimilate and rearrange. "From bee-sting, spider-bite, thorn-prick, hammer-bruise," no less than from "lip-brush" and "hand-grasp," the flesh learns and "grows wise."

On the Edge of the Knife and *The Man in the Green Chair* explore with increasing boldness and vigor the abnormality of the normal. They reveal the bestial power of Eros and descend into the primitive darkness deep within each of us. The verse, like the song of the tree frog, is often "raw with harsh and heartfelt music," a music which reverberates through the intelligent verse paragraphs, the chiseled quatrains, the unorthodox, long-lined triptychs. Such rawness never chafes or offends. Eaton's mastery of form, achieved by years of experience and adapted to the distinctive sound of the poet's individual voice, finally teaches the heart the lesson it learns in "Della Robbia in August," not only to grieve but also to rise "in a brilliant form of care."

—Robert Miola

EDGERTON, Clyde (Carlyle)

Born: Durham, North Carolina, 20 May 1944. **Education:** University of North Carolina at Chapel Hill, B.A. 1966, M.A.T. 1972, Ph.D. 1977. **Military Service:** U.S. Air Force, 1966-71; piloted reconnaissance and forward air control missions in Southeast Asia during Vietnam War; received Distinguished Flying Cross. **Family:** Married Susan Ketchin in 1975; one daughter. **Career:** English teacher, Southern High School, Durham, North Carolina, 1972-73; co-director, English Teaching Institute, Chapel Hill, North Carolina, 1976; associate professor, 1977-81, assistant professor of education and psychology, 1981-85, Campbell University, Buies Creek, North Carolina; associate professor of English and education, St. Andrews Presbyterian College, Laurinburg, North Carolina, 1985-89; writer. Visiting lecturer in English at North Carolina Central University, 1977; writer in residence at Agnes Scott College, 1990; creative writing instructor, Duke University, Durham, North Carolina, 1992; co-chair, Eudora Welty Chair of Southern Studies, Millsaps College, Jackson, Mississippi; lecturer at conferences and workshops. Guest on television and radio programs, including *Today* and National Public Radio's *Sunday Weekend Edition, Morning Edition,* and *Good Evening with Noah Adams.* Musician; member of Tarwater Band. **Awards:** *Publisher's Weekly* named *The Floatplane Notebooks* one of the best books of 1988; Guggenheim fellow, 1989; Lyndhurst fellow, 1991; Fellowship of Southern Writers, 1997; North Carolina Award for fiction, 1997. **Address:** c/o Dusty's Air Taxi, 714 Ninth Street, G-7, Durham, North Carolina 27705.

PUBLICATIONS FOR YOUNG ADULTS

Fiction

Raney. Chapel Hill, North Carolina, Algonquin Books, 1985.
Walking across Egypt. Chapel Hill, North Carolina, Algonquin Books, 1987.
Understanding the Floatplane. Chapel Hill, North Carolina, Mud Puppy Press, 1987.
The Floatplane Notebooks. Chapel Hill, North Carolina, Algonquin Books, 1988.
Cold Black Peas. Chapel Hill, North Carolina, Mud Puppy Press, 1990.
Killer Diller. Chapel Hill, North Carolina, Algonquin Books, 1991.
In Memory of Junior. Chapel Hill, North Carolina, Algonquin Books, 1992.
Redeye. Chapel Hill, North Carolina, Algonquin Books, 1995.
Where Trouble Sleeps. Chapel Hill, North Carolina, Algonquin Books, 1995.

Recordings: *Walking across Egypt: Songs and Readings from the Books "Raney" and "Walking across Egypt,"* music performed by Edgerton and other members of the Tarwater Band, Flying Fish Records, 1987; *Clyde Edgerton Reads "The Floatplane Notebooks,"* Random House Audiobooks, 1989; *The "Killer Diller" Tapes,* Durham, North Carolina, Dusty's Air Taxi, 1991; *The Devil's Dream,* by Lee Smith and the Tarwater Band, Durham, North Carolina, Dusty's Air Taxi, 1993; Edgerton has recorded all his novels for The Freeman Group, Durham, North Carolina.

Other

Contributor, *Weymouth: An Anthology of Poetry,* edited by Sam Ragan. Laurinburg, North Carolina, St. Andrews Press, 1987.
Contributor, *Family Portraits: Remembrances by Twenty Distinguished Writers,* edited by Carolyn Anthony. New York, Doubleday, 1989.
Contributor, *New Stories from the South: The Year's Best, 1990,* edited by Shannon Ravenel. Chapel Hill, North Carolina, Algonquin Books, 1990.

Also contributor, *Best American Short Stories,* 1997, and *On Faith and Fiction,* edited by W. Dale Brown.

*

Media Adaptations: *Walking across Egypt* (play), adapted by John Justice, produced 1989); *Raney* (play), adapted by John Justice, produced in North Carolina 1990; film, Castleway Productions, Atlanta, Georgia; *The Floatplane Notebooks* (play), adapted by Jason Moore and Paul Fitzgerald, produced Chicago 1992.

Critical Studies: Entry in *Contemporary Literary Criticism,* Volume 39, Detroit, Gale, 1986.

Clyde Edgerton comments:

I recently received letters from two eleventh-grade classes in South Carolina. They had just read *The Floatplane Notebooks* and their letters were a response to my story. I was gratified that they found the story interesting and had raised important issues and questions related to the story. I am happy that young adults are able to bring their own lives and experiences to my writing and thus find pleasure and perhaps insights into their own relationships. So far, all my books have had young adults as main characters. I feel about these characters the same way I feel about young readers in general—their youth provides energy, enthusiasm, and fresh insights—and what writer doesn't need readers with these qualities?

*   *   *

Clyde Edgerton is a funny and a profound novelist. In the span of eight years he has published five rollicking stories of small town Southern life. His beat is the Piedmont area of North Carolina. His books are adult novels; individual imperfections and social problems are presented clearly and with humor, and there is no attempt to pass judgment on them. Young adults in their twenties are featured prominently, as are older adults in their seventies, and often the relationships between the two are central to the plot. Edgerton's characters have more faults than most, but they also have considerable virtues, and they are so likable that you want to invite them over for a cup of coffee, a piece of homemade apple pie, and a nice long chat.

Raney is the story of the first two years, two months, and two days in a modern marriage. Set in Listre, North Carolina, it begins just before the wedding, at the K and W Cafeteria, where Raney discovers that her mother-in-law-to-be is a vegetarian. She thought somehow that people were born vegetarians, and she is surprised that Mrs. Shepherd just changed over after some programs on simple living put on by the Episcopalians. Raney herself is Baptist. There are other things Raney learns about, and some adjustments she makes, to life with another family, another approach to class, religion and race, another way of doing the dishes and defining pornography. The need for adjustments continue until the end of the book, when Raney and Charles's first child is born. But throughout, love, and the joys and perplexities of living, are described in detail, with wit and wisdom.

In *Walking Across Egypt* we meet Mattie Rigsbee, a strong-willed senior citizen who at seventy-eight is slowing down, just a bit. Mattie still cooks three meals a day and her house in Listre always smells good from homemade biscuits, fried chicken, pound cake, and apple pie. When a stray dog comes into her yard, she knows she has as much business keeping him as she has Walking across Egypt, which is the title of her favorite hymn. But she warms him up some beef stew and he does not wish to leave. When Wesley Benfield enters her life, or rather when she enters Wesley's life with pieces of cake and pie, he is even less likely a companion than the stray dog. Wesley is a sixteen-year-old delinquent in the Young Men's Rehabilitation Center, there for stealing a car. But in the end Mattie keeps the dog and Wesley, and you can bet with her good spirit and her good cooking, they both will be better off. And maybe Mattie will be better off too. This book is about reaching out, about caring, and about the best southern cooking there is. Edgerton, also a folk musician, has thoughtfully supplied Mattie with the words and music to "Walking across Egypt." It is gratifying to have a new hymn to sing.

The Floatplane Notebooks chronicles the lives of five generations of the Copelands of Listre. There are a fair number of relatives to account for, so the author provides a genealogical chart in the beginning of the book. The time frame is 1956 to 1971, and the book is written from the perspectives of a number of younger family members, a single event being interpreted differently by different individuals. Building a floatplane is the hobby, obsession of the present head of the family, Albert. He writes frequently about its progress in his notebooks. If the plane should crash, he can look through the notebooks to determine why. The notebooks also contain the secrets of family yearning and love. The Copelands enjoy a family isolation until the Vietnam War, and the bonds of love and caring continue after that war, through tragedy and triumph.

In *Killer Diller*, Mattie Rigsbee, somewhat frailer, and Wesley Benfield, somewhat rehabilitated, return. And Edgerton gives us two more songs—"Sour Sweetheart Blues" and "When I Sleep in Class." Listre is a beehive of activity in this book because the Baptist college, Ballard University, has two new programs: Nutrition House, for overweight Christians, and Project Promise, for special education students of the county. Project Promise uses the residents of the rehabilitation halfway house adjacent to the Ballard campus to teach special ed students job-related skills of masonry and plumbing. Wesley is now a halfway house resident and project participant. He teaches bricklaying, while also writing songs for his Baptist band, preaching, and lusting for a certain girl in Nutrition House. Meanwhile Mattie becomes ill and after a hospital stay, ends up in the Shady Grove Nursing Home. Mattie hates the home because she can't cook there. It is Wesley, of course, who finds a way for her to escape to her home.

In *Memory of Junior* is about four generations of the Bales and McCord families. It has a genealogical chart in opening pages, and

it too is written from the perspective of several family members and of other persons, a single event being interpreted differently by different individuals. Grove McCord was Albert Copeland's daddy's sister's boy. Grove was flying his own little plane before Albert started on his floatplane. The improbable plot of this novel focuses on three elderly people, contemplating their final resting places: Laura and Glen Bales and Grove McCord. The families end up with too many graves and too few tombstones. The importance of the grave site to family continuity has come up before in *The Floatplane Notebooks*. In this latter book the importance is explained simply by Uncle Grove, "You're history longer than you are fact." This book too is about day-to-day family life, described with kindhearted humor.

Edgerton, like a number of Southern writers, credits his family with providing him with great family stories, told over and over, for as long as he could remember. His novels about family are full of likable, outrageous, and very human characters. They show love and tenderness, strong feelings of connection, despite death and divorce and desertion. The books are hilarious, touching, wonderful.

—Mary Lystad

EHLE, John

Born: John Marsden Ehle, Jr., in Asheville, North Carolina, 13 December, 1925. **Education:** University of North Carolina, Chapel Hill, A.B. in English 1949, M.A. in dramatic arts 1952. **Family:** Married Gail Oliver, August 30, 1951 (divorced); married Rosemary Harris, 21 October 1967; one daughter. **Military Service:** U.S. Army Infantryman, 1942-46. **Career:** Associate professor in the Communications Center, University of North Carolina, Chapel Hill, 1952-65; visiting associate professor, New York University, 1957-58; special assistant to Governor Terry Sanford of North Carolina, 1962-64, during which Ehle helped to establish "Governor's Schools," the nation's first state-supported high school and college for professional training in the performing arts; Program Officer for the Ford Foundation, 1964-65. **Awards:** Special citation from National Conference of Christians and Jews; two Freedom Foundation Awards; Awards for Best Book by a North Carolinian, 1964, 1967, 1970, 1975, and 1984, and Best Nonfiction Book by a North Carolinian, 1965; Thomas Wolfe Prize, 1984.

PUBLICATIONS

Novels

Move Over, Mountain. New York, Morrow, 1957.
Kingstree Island. New York, Morrow, 1959.
Lion on the Hearth. New York, Harper and Brothers, 1961.
The Land Breakers. New York, Harper and Row, 1964.
The Road. New York, Harper and Row, 1967.
A Time of Drums. New York, Harper and Row, 1970.
The Journey of August King. New York, Harper and Row, 1971.
The Changing of the Guard. New York, Random House, 1974.
The Winter People. New York, Harper and Row, 1982.
Last One Home. New York, Harper and Row, 1984.
The Widow's Trial. New York, Harper and Row, 1989.

Nonfiction

The Survivor: The Story of Eddie Hukov. New York, Holt, 1958.
Shepherd of the Streets: The Story of the Reverend James A. Gusweller and His Crusade on the New York West Side. New York, Sloane, 1960.
The Free Men. New York, Harper and Row, 1965.
The Cheeses and Wines of England and France, with Notes on Irish Whiskey. New York, Harper and Row, 1972.
Trail of Tears: The Rise and Fall of the Cherokee Nation. New York, Doubleday, 1988.
Dr. Frank: Living with Frank Porter Graham. Chapel Hill, Franklin Street Books, 1993.

Uncollected Short Story

"Emergency Call." In *Short Stories from the Old North State* edited by Richard Walser, Chapel Hill, University of North Carolina Press, 1959.

Uncollected Plays

Gabriel: A Play in Three Acts. 1953.
The Road to Orange. Symphonic drama for the bi-centennial pageant of Orange County, North Carolina, 1953.

Essay

"Reflections on Paul Green" in *Paul Green's Celebration of Man, With a Bibliography* edited by Sue Laslie Kimball and Lynn Veach Sadler, Fayetteville, North Carolina, Human Technology Interface, Ink, 1994.

*

Teleplays: Twenty-six plays in the series, *American Adventure*, broadcast by the network of the National Association of Educational Broadcasters, with thirteen repeated by NBC, 1952-53: *Appointment at Fords*; *The Battle*; *Builders on the River*; *The Demagogue*; *Dial Emergency*; *The Eccentric*; *The Federal Lion*; *The Free Man*; *Grandfather Jefferson*; *Grenade*; *Hearthfire*; *Johnny Appleseed*; *The Judas Tree*; *King with Crown*; *Leader of a Dream*; *Man of Iron*; *The Orchid*; *Paint the Big Canvas*; *Pioneer Call*; *The Rat on Lincoln Avenue*; *The Resolute*; *Runaway Justice*; *A Story of a Poet*; *An Unfound Door*; *The Yankee Loves a Lady*; and *The Zenger Trail*.

*   *   *

John Ehle, who grew up in the mountains of North Carolina, has used the mountains and mountain people as place and characters for most of his novels. His narrative techniques and the values they espouse are traditional, and his families, often the Wrights or Kings, exemplify the ties that bind generations of Appalachian pioneers. He has claimed that he has written about more Black characters than have any of his contemporaries, and he has told us a great deal about the human spirit and its determination and honesty. Ehle has also said that the main character in his seven mountain novels is the mountains themselves, which "lord it over my people."

Terry Sanford, the late governor and senator of North Carolina who hired Ehle as his assistant when he himself was governor, had said that if he were writing a book about how to be governor, he would recommend hiring a novelist to be on the staff. The fruits of Ehle's efforts are seen today in the state's "Governor's Schools." Ehle helped to establish the nation's first state-supported high school and college for professional training in the performing arts.

Since Ehle married the English Shakespearean actress Rosemary Harris, he has spent some part of almost every year in England, and some of his books are set in Europe. Harris was nominated for an Academy of Motion Picture Arts (Oscar) Award as Best Supporting Actress in 1996 for the movie *Tom and Viv.* Their daughter Jennifer was nominated for the British equivalent of the Oscar in the same year for her role as Elizabeth Bennett in *Pride and Prejudice.*

Ehle moved a black character from what he thinks is the best short story he ever wrote and built a novel around him. The man had lost his job as a coal deliverer because he had insulted a customer, who complained about him. The novel, *Move Over, Mountain* (1957), tells about the man's efforts to support his wife and two small boys by going into a taxi service business for himself. Ehle believes it is the first serious novel written about Blacks by a white person. Other early works include *Kingstree Mountain* (1959), a dramatic love story set in North Carolina's Outer Banks, and *Lion on the Hearth* (1961), the story of the King family. In the latter, the hardworking mountaineer storekeeper Caleb King is disgusted with people who try to be productive by working only with paper. *The Free Men* (1965) was critical of the University of North Carolina's handling of integration issues. One of the three men whose story it tells is John Dunne, who had rented a room in Ehle's house. All three received two-year prison terms for protesting in civil rights clashes, and Ehle helped to win the eventual parole and pardon of the activists.

The Land Breakers (1964), the first of Ehle's mountain novels, tells about the Wrights, the first white family to come to the mountains to live and found themselves pitted against the wilderness, the snakes, and bears. The protagonist, Mooney Wright, helps a woman whose husband has deserted her and her children, but the husband finally returns. *The Road* (1967) tells about the difficulties of scaling the mountain with a railroad to be built from Old Fort to the Swannanoa Gap in Western North Carolina to open up greater trading opportunities. Intertwined with construction of the railroad is a love story of an educated, sophisticated man, a stranger to the mountains, who falls in love with a beautiful but uneducated mountain lass. She refuses to marry the professor from Chapel Hill, sensing that he sees her as one more example of intriguing oddities of mountain existence. The building of the railroad results in disappointments, accidents, deaths, and, finally, in triumph.

A Time of Drums (1970), a Civil War novel, was adapted as a play by Lee Yopp, director of the Fort Bragg (North Carolina) Theater, and produced there in 1989. In the work, Ehle shows mountain families sometimes divided against themselves, but engaged in questions about slavery and the power of a central government over citizens. Colonel Owen Wright's brother, Woofer, follows him into the Army after making a young widow pregnant. When Owen comes home after being wounded, he falls in love with the widow.

The Journey of August King (1971) tells about the efforts of a white farmer to help a sixteen-year-old slave escape from her abuser. The farmer faces a great deal of peril, but the act helps free himself from feelings of guilt he has had after his wife's suicide. He confronts a mob inflamed by racism and the promise of a Virginia riding horse or two-hundred dollars as reward for capturing the slave girl. August King's journey is physical—fraught with danger—and psychological, and undertaking the journey enables King to examine and know himself. This novel was the source for a movie of the same title produced in 1996.

Ehle wrote *The Cheeses and Wines of England and France* (1972) after spending a great deal of time traveling with his actress-wife to London and Paris. He performed research on French wines, and he and his wife visited many vineyards. He read about English cheeses and ciders in the comfort of the British Museum. When Ms. Harris went to Dublin to rehearse, Ehle studied Irish whiskey in the library there, and he included a commentary on that subject in this book.

The Changing of the Guard (1974), set in France, is surely the most experimental of all of Ehle's books. On one level, it is a modern story about actors and actresses working in a film about the French Revolution; on another it is about those associated with the Revolution, including Marie Antoinette. The actors change to complement the personalities of the historic figures they portray, and their relationships change as a result. *The Winter People* (1982) is the story of a clockmaker who disturbs the mountain peace following his arrival from the East and the young woman who has to choose between her baby and her lover. It tells of two feuding families, the Wrights and the Campbells, and of the bear hunt as a rite of passage for mountain men. The first part of the book is comic, the second half tragic, and at the tale's end, order is reestablished in the community when the two families reach a compromise that unites them. *The Winter People* was adapted to film in 1989 and starred Kurt Russell, Lloyd Bridges, and Kelly McGillis.

Trail of Tears: The Rise and Fall of the Cherokee Nation (1988) is Ehle's study of the removal of Native Americans from the frontier and of a strong Cherokee leader named Ridge, who fought with Andrew Jackson and was frequently invited to the White House. He wanted his tribe left in peace on their lands in North Carolina, but he later accepted the compromise that led to the journey to the west. The Cherokees, always outnumbered by land-hungry whites, received some federal protection, but they were not United States citizens, nor were they a nation with whom treaties could be drawn. When white settlers stole their land, the tribes were helpless. Andrew Jackson pretended to be their friend but refused to obey a Supreme Court ruling in favor of the Cherokees. While Ehle's sympathies are with the tribes, he shows the Cherokees guilty of mismanagement, poor judgment, violence, and thievery. When they were forced to move to Arkansas and Oklahoma, they became a lawless nation that virtually destroyed itself.

The Widow's Trial (1989) is the second of Ehle's books to be set in the present day and the eighth of his mountain novels. It is different in technique, however, because the chapters alternate in point of view among the characters, including a battered wife who kills her husband. As do so most abused wives, Winnette keeps leaving Plover but returning to him, believing she can help him to change. The novel demonstrates Ehle's concern with the modern and the traditional—the introduction of drugs to the mountains and the changing nature of the sexual roles versus the belief in the superiority of the male whose head of the household status is not to be challenged.

The genesis of Ehle's biography, *Dr. Frank: Living with Frank Porter Graham* (1993) occured when the much admired "Dr. Frank" asked Ehle at a reception if he would consider his life as subject for a book. The two had seen each other frequently in New York during the 1950s, when Ehle was there working at the Ford Foundation and Graham was a mediator at the U.N.

A summary of the foregoing list of works reveals John Ehle's versatility, not only in subject matter, but also in genre. He writes about history, foods, biography, and his mountain people; he experiments with form, juggles time and place, at the same time entertaining and informing.

—Sue Laslie Kimball

ELLISON, Ralph

Born: Ralph Waldo Ellison in Oklahoma City, Oklahoma, 1 March 1914. **Education:** Tuskegee Institute, Alabama, 1933-36. **Military Service:** U.S. Merchant Marine, 1943-45. **Family:** Married Fanny McConnell in 1946. **Career:** Writer from 1936; lecturer, Salzburg Seminar in American Studies, 1954; instructor in Russian and American Literature, Bard College, Annandale-on-Hudson, New York, 1958-61; Alexander White Visiting Professor, University of Chicago, 1961; visiting professor of writing, Rutgers University, New Brunswick, New Jersey, 1962-64; Whittall Lecturer, Library of Congress, Washington, D.C., 1964; Ewing Lecturer, University of California, Los Angeles, 1964; Chairman, Literary Grants Committee, American Academy of Arts and Letters, 1964-67; visiting fellow in American studies, Yale University, New Haven, Connecticut, 1966; member, National Council on the Arts, 1965-67; member, Carnegie Commission on Educational Television, 1966-67; member of the editorial board, *American Scholar,* Washington, D.C., 1966-69; honorary consultant in American Letters, Library of Congress, Washington, D.C., 1966-72; Albert Schweitzer Professor in the Humanities, New York University, 1970-79; yrustee, John F. Kennedy Center of the Performing Arts, Washington, D.C., New School for Social Research, New York, Bennington College, Vermont, Educational Broadcasting Corporation, and Colonial Williamsburg Foundation. **Awards:** Rosenwald fellowship, 1945; National Book award, 1953; National Newspaper Publishers Association Russwarm award, 1953; American Academy Rome prize, 1955, 1956; *Invisible Man* selected as the most distinguished postwar American novel and Ellison as the sixth most influential novelist by *New York Herald Tribune Book Week* poll of two hundred authors, editors, and critics, 1965; recipient of award honoring well-known Oklahomans in the arts from governor of Oklahoma, 1966; United States Medal of Freedom, 1969;

Chevalier de l'Ordre des Arts et Lettres (France), 1970; Ralph Ellison Public Library, Oklahoma City, named in his honor, 1975; National Medal of Arts, 1985, for *Invisible Man* and for his teaching at numerous universities; National Medal of Arts, 1985; Coordinating Council of Literary Magazines-General Electric Foundation award, 1988; Ph.D. in Humane Letters, Tuskegee Institute, 1963; Litt.D., Rutgers University, 1966, University of Michigan, 1967, Williams College, 1970, Long Island University, 1971, College of William and Mary, 1972, Wake Forest College, 1974, Harvard University, 1974; L.H.D., Grinnell College, Iowa, 1967, Adelphi University, Garden City, New York, 1971, University of Maryland, College Park, 1974; Commandant, Order of Arts and Letters (France), 1970. **Died**: 1994.

PUBLICATIONS

Novel

Invisible Man. New York, Random House, 1952.

Uncollected Fiction

"The Roof, the Steeple and the People" (excerpts from novel-in-progress). *Quarterly Review of Literature*, 1960.
"And Hickman Arrives" (excerpts from novel-in-progress). *Noble Savage*, March 1960.
"It Always Breaks Out" (excerpts from novel-in-progress). *Partisan Review*, Spring 1963.
"Juneteenth" (excerpts from novel-in-progress). *Quarterly Review of Literature 13*, 1965.
"Night-Talk" (excerpts from novel-in-progress). *Quarterly Review of Literature 16*, 1969.
"Song of Innocence" (excerpts from novel-in-progress). *Iowa Review*, spring 1970.
"Cadillac Flambe" (excerpts from novel-in-progress). *American Review 16*, edited by Theodore Solotaroff, 1973.

Essay Collections

Shadow and Act. New York, Random House, 1964.
Going to the Territory. New York, Random House, 1986.

Other

The Writer's Experience, with Karl Shapiro. Washington, D.C., Library of Congress, 1964.
The City in Crisis, with Whitney M. Young and Herbert Gnas. New York, Randolph Educational Fund, 1968.

Contributor, *The Living Novel: A Symposium* edited by Granville Hicks. London, Macmillan, 1957.
Contributor, *Education of the Deprived and Segregated* New York, Bank Street College of Education, 1965.
Contributor, *Who Speaks for the Negro?* by Robert Penn Warren. New York, Random House, 1965.
Contributor, *To Heal and to Build: The Programs of Lyndon B. Johnson* edited by James MacGregor Burns. New York, McGraw, 1968.
Contributor, *American Law: The Third Century, The Law Bicentennial Volume* edited by Bernard Schwartz. Littleton, Colorado, F.B. Rothman for New York University School of Law, 1976.

Author of introduction, *Invisible Man* (thirtieth anniversary edition). New York, Random House, 1982.

*

Media Adaptations: *Ralph Ellison: An Interview with the Author of 'Invisible Man'* (sound recording), Center for Cassette Studies, 1974; *Is the Novel Dead?: Ellison, Styron and Baldwin on Contemporary Fiction*, with William Styron and James Baldwin (sound recording), Center for Cassette Studies, 1974.

Bibliography: "A Bibliography of Ralph Ellison's Published Writings" by Bernard Benoit and Michel Fabre, in *Studies in Black Literature* (Fredericksburg, Virginia), Autumn 1971; *The Blinking Eye: Ellison and His American, French, German and Italian Critics 1952-1971* by Jacqueline Covo, 1974.

Critical Studies: *The Negro Novel in America*, revised edition by Robert A. Bone, New Haven, Connecticut, Yale University Press, 1958; "The Blues as a Literary Theme" by Gene Bluestein, in *Massachusetts Review* (Amherst), Autumn 1967; "Ellison Issue," *CLA Journal* (Baltimore), March 1970; *Five Black Writers: Essays* by Donald B. Gibson, New York, University Press, 1970; *Twentieth-Century Interpretations of Invisible Man* edited by John M. Reilly, Englewood Cliffs, New Jersey, Prentice Hall, 1970; *The Merrill Studies in Invisible Man* edited by Ronald Gottesman, Columbus, Ohio, Merrill, 1971; *Ralph Ellison: A Collection of Critical Essays* edited by John Hersey, Englewood Cliffs, New Jersey, Prentice Hall, 1973; *Folklore and Myth in Ralph Ellison's Early Works* by Dorothea Fischer-Hornung, Stuttgart, Hochschul, 1979; *The Craft of Ralph Ellison*, Cambridge, Massachusetts, Harvard University Press, 1980; *New Essays on Invisible Man* edited by Robert G. O'Meally, London, Cambridge University Press, 1988; *Ralph Ellison: The Genesis of an Artist* by Rudolf F. Dietze, Nuremberg, Carl, 1982; *Speaking for You: The Vision of Ralph Ellison* edited by Kimberly W. Benston, Washington, D.C., Howard University Press, 1987; *Invisible Criticism: Ralph Ellison and the American Canon* by Alan Nadel, Iowa City, University of Iowa Press, 1988; *Creative Revolt: A Study of Wright, Ellison, and Dostoevsky* by Michael F. Lynch, New York, Lang, 1990.

*   *   *

Although most of his career and canon reflect his life outside the South, Ralph Ellison can be considered a contemporary Southern writer in terms of both his personal origins and his professional concerns. He was born Ralph Waldo Ellison in Oklahoma City in 1914 to ambitious parents who had emigrated only recently from the deep South in search of a better life. Ellison later attended college at the famous Tuskegee Institute in Alabama. His subsequent career and most of his writing were focused in the North, specifically in New York City and Harlem, but Ellison saw himself and his literary personae as products of Southern black life. For Ellison, contemporary African American culture was forged by its Great Migration from South to North, and by dramatizing his own experience he believed he was recreating the consciousness of his race. Therefore, Ellison and his classic novel, *Invisible Man* (1952), are best understood in terms of contemporary Southern writing within the African American tradition.

Despite the fact that he published only a single novel, Ellison remains one of the most important writers in this tradition, comparable only to Richard Wright and James Baldwin in his generation. A discussion of Ellison's work must be centered on *Invisible Man,* but it should not neglect his other writing. Although his single masterpiece seemed to appear from nowhere in 1952, it had a long foreground in Ellison's earlier life and work; likewise, the absence of the long promised second novel does not negate the considerable body of fiction and non-fiction which Ellison completed after *Invisible Man.* His single novel is a prodigious effort as well, considering virtually all of African American culture by combining the epic sweep of traditional narrative with the precise imagery of modern poetry. Before his death in 1994, Ellison's personal and literary achievements were recognized by almost every possible award and honor.

Invisible Man conflates the history of African Americans with Ellison's own story in ways that recall both sides of his divided heritage. Biography and autobiography have been the archetypal forms for the matter of African American life, from the slave narratives to contemporary novels. The romantic individualism of classic white American literature also influenced Ellison—from the works of his namesake, Ralph Waldo Emerson, and his proteges Henry David Thoreau and Walt Whitman, to the darker visions of Herman Melville, Nathaniel Hawthorne, and Edgar Allan Poe—all of whom appear in various guises in the author's work. Perhaps the single most important literary intertext for *Invisible Man* is a book published a century earlier, Melville's classic *Moby Dick* (1851), one of the first works of fiction to face the dislocations of American culture in the early nineteenth century. Like Melville's American classic, Ellison's book is a variation of the *Bildungsroman*, or development novel, where the protagonist engages in a quest for maturity and fulfillment that leads through a series of difficult and dangerous passages.

In Ellison's novel some of these events and themes are recreated from his own life, as well as his earlier writing. His nameless protagonist grows up in the black quarter of a Southern town, attends a patriarchal black college somewhere in the deep South, leaves for job opportunities in New York City, lives in Harlem where he participates in a wide range of cultural upheavals, and withdraws into his personal world when he realizes his invisibility within white America. As in Melville's classic, as well as many black narratives both autobiographical and fictional, Ellison's persona tells his own tale from the perspective of his hard-won maturity; in a sense, he realizes his own story and writes his own narrative.

Ellison's major technical device in this regard is the book's framing envelope: the narrator hibernates in a nineteenth century subcellar beneath the streets of Harlem, allowing the author to introduce his themes in a surrealistic mode counterpointing with the realism of his central narrative.

In another regard, Ellison works through not only his own life experiences but his earlier artistic efforts as well. Although he was always fascinated by literature, the younger Ellison trained as a musician at Tuskegee and studied sculpture in New York City before he began to write under the influence of social realism in the 1930s and 1940s. His most important mentor was Richard Wright, and Ellison's early prose echoed Wright's efforts in both fiction and non-fiction. Like the works of his mentor, Ellison's

first stories depicted young blacks emigrating from the South, symbolic of the traditional agrarian past, to the North, the image of an uneasy technological future. Often the actual transition is dramatized—the journey itself in short stories, or the action before and/or after in longer fictions. For example, several of Ellison's earliest stories, which were published only after his death, present an autobiographical protagonist riding freight trains out of the South in the mode of Depression era social realism which he transcends in *Invisible Man.*

Yet even in his earliest efforts, Ellison is quickly moving beyond his first mentors and models toward an artistic complexity based on the counterpointed rhythms of music and the symbolic shapes of sculpture. Ellison's first writings likewise project the meanings as well as the modes of his later works, since the major theme of *Invisible Man* becomes the protagonist's engagement with the grinding machinery of contemporary American life.

Although modern technology extended into the South, in the form of the railroad, for instance, it pervaded the urban life of the North, where the speeding subway trains and rocketing elevator cars provide the most common symbol in Ellison's narrative. Even more expressionistic examples are discovered as the narrator tries to make his way in the urban environment: in particular, the industrial explosion in the paint factory where he finds work (a surrealistic vision of contemporary American art) and his subsequent trauma by electric shock therapy in the psychiatric hospital (a nightmarish symbol of contemporary social institutions). All of these infernal machines create an image of American history as a self-determined machine, producing the apocalyptic racial discords that precipitate the narrator's retreat.

For all of the protagonist's bitter dilemma in the book's concluding frame, *Invisible Man* is not a pessimistic work. Although Ellison clearly rejects the solutions of the social realists, he does posit a modestly hopeful vision of the future in terms of really understanding the past. The protagonist's hibernation becomes a sort of religious retreat where he learns something of the white other, promising engagement when he does emerge to claim his place in the twentieth century.

In this way, the novel's conclusion prefigures Ellison's later work that tries to realize that glimpse of American possibilities. His major project was another novel, one which projected a protagonist in some sense the most important of the narrator's many doubles in *Invisible Man*, the trickster figure Rinehart. In the projected novel, the protean character of Hickman unites a series of takes on contemporary African American culture, which appeared as short pieces over the remainder of the author's career. Ellison could never bring the novel to the conclusion he wished, though a text is being assembled for publication from his papers by his literary executor. Just as interesting are the two volumes of nonfiction, *Shadow and Act* (1964) and *Going to the Territory* (1986), which collect Ellison's thoughtful criticism of African American culture, literature, music, and art.

Certainly, Ellison left an extensive body of fine work, one which would make him a notable African American writer even without the major achievement of *Invisible Man*, perhaps still the best individual book by a black American. In many ways, Ellison pioneered the continuing Renaissance of contemporary African American letters represented by figures like Alice Walker and Toni Morrison today. Finally, Ellison's career and canon are both rooted in the South, making him one of our most important contemporary Southern writers within the African American tradition.

—Joseph Millichap

EVERETT, Percival

Born: Fort Gordon, Georgia, 22 December 1956. **Education:** University of Miami, A.B. 1977; attended University of Oregon, 1978-80; Brown University, A.M. 1982. **Career:** Employed professionally as a jazz musician, sheep-ranch hand, and high school teacher; associate professor of English and director of the Graduate Creative Writing Program, University of Kentucky, 1985-89; aAssociate professor of English, University of Notre Dame, 1989-92; professor and chair, Creative Writing Program, University of California, Riverside, beginning 1992; associate editor of *Callaloo*. **Awards:** D. H. Lawrence fellowship, University of New Mexico, 1984; Lila Wallace-Reader's Digest fellowship. **Agent:** Candida Donadio, 231 West 22nd Street, New York, New York 10011. **Address**: Department of Creative Writing, University of California, Riverside, California 92521.

PUBLICATIONS

Novels

Suder. New York, Viking Press, 1983.
Walk Me to the Distance. New York, Ticknor & Fields, 1985.
Cutting Lisa. New York, Ticknor & Fields, 1986.
Zulus. Sag Harbor, New York, Permanent Press, 1990.
For Her Dark Skin. Seattle, Owl Creek Press, 1990.
God's Country. Boston, Faber and Faber, 1994.
Watershed. St. Paul, Minnesota, Graywolf Press, 1996.
Frenzy. St. Paul, Minnesota, Graywolf Press, 1997.

Short Story Collections

The Weather and Women Treat Me Fair. Little Rock, August House, 1987.
Big Picture. St. Paul, Minnesota, Graywolf Press, 1996.

Children's Literature

The One that Got Away. New York, Clarion Books, 1992.

Other

Contributor, *From Timberline to Tidepool: Contemporary Fiction from the Northwest*. Seattle, Owl Creek Press, 1989.

*   *   *

Although he was born in Georgia and raised in South Carolina, Percival Everett has been, in his life and work, captivated by the American West. In a May, 1994 interview published in *The State*

(Columbia, South Carolina), Everett commented, "The space and the harshness of the countryside appealed to me. The character of the people, I found, was a lot like Southerners, in their enjoyment of storytelling and their use of language."

Just as his life has been marked by a distinctly westward momentum, Everett's fiction has taken on the semblance of laconic frontier "yarn-spinning." His first and most celebrated novel *Suder* (1983), for example, features the surrealistic adventures of an African-American baseball player in flight from his personal and professional troubles and in quest of some alternate state of transcendence. The narrative, set primarily in the Pacific Northwest, includes flashbacks to the protagonist's childhood in Fayetteville, North Carolina. Through these memories, the author attempts to trace, for the reader, the sources of Craig Suder's propulsive restlessness. Could it be that he has inherited some of his mother's mental instability? Did the residency of a famous jazz pianist in his family home sow the seeds of a personal improvisational approach to life? Whatever the roots of his adult dilemma, Suder's Southern upbringing informs the direction of his later life and provides the impetus for a series of picaresque encounters set against the stern expanses of the Western landscape.

The same bi-regional setting is evident in Everett's second novel, *Walk Me to the Distance* (1985), which chronicles the initially aimless wanderings of a disillusioned Vietnam War veteran named David Larson. Displaced, he thinks, from his settled family life in Savannah, Georgia, by virtue of his life-altering combat experiences, Larson, like Suder, sets out on a journey. It would appear, at least at first, to be motion for motion's sake, but accident deposits him in Wyoming and accident involves him in the lives of the independent-minded people living in and around the fictional town of Slut's Hole.

Everett's first two books most aptly fall into the general category of the literature of discovery. In both, the principal characters set out for strange places, and in exploring the world around them, they find out something about themselves. Suder's quest ends in a celebration of individual idiosyncrasy; Larson finds meaning in his tenuous and perhaps temporary connections to other people. Not all of Everett's fictional works, however, contain these inherent references to the settled South and the protean West. The longer that Everett has himself been a resident of the West, the more exclusively has that part of the country shaped his creative vision.

Most of the stories in both *The Weather and Women Treat Me Fair* (1987) and *Big Picture: Stories* (1996) deal with individuals, especially cowboys, ranchers, and rodeo performers, who face moments of self-determination in a sparsely-populated landscape relatively free of social constraints. Unlike Southern literature, which tends to stress the importance of family and the weight of the past, the literature of the American West most often concentrates on the rugged individualist free to shape his own destiny. Everett appears drawn to this concept. Most of his characters are loners. If they band together at all, it is to satisfy another convention of the Western tale—the posse. In *God's Country*, (1994), for example, Everett constructs a search party made up of a thick-headed white rancher named Curt Marder, a broad-minded black scout named Bubba, and a parentless boy named Jake. The racist, sexist, and ethnocentric Marder does not compare well against his infinitely more humane companions, but this contrast provides the catalyst for most of the dark humor in the book.

In Everett's work, group ties tend to last only so long as the collective enterprise itself. Indeed, the author's natural inclination seems to be singular. Even his one and only children's book *The One that Got Away* (1992) reinforces this contention. It tells the story of three cowboys who, after having round up a whole herd of "ones," quite literally cardinal numbers, spend most of this richly illustrated volume chasing after the "one" that got away. That "one" remains elusive.

This theme of solitariness, either by alienation or self-imposed isolation, or both, can be found even in Everett's creative forays outside fiction of the contemporary West. His science fiction narrative *Zulus* (1990), set in the post-thermonuclear world of the distant future, recounts the frustrated search for sanctuary by the beleaguered three-hundred-pound Alice Achitophel, the only fertile woman left on the planet. Everett's two novels of ancient Greece, *For Her Dark Skin* (1990) and *Frenzy* (1997), also feature characters set apart. *For Her Dark Skin* focuses on Medea, whom the author cuts off from her people by virtue of her dark skin and her black magic. *Frenzy* follows the wanderings of Dionysus, who is separated from others by virtue of his double state of being, half man and half god. To further his anarchic aims, he is forced to use his assistant Vlepo to enter the minds of the people of Thebes. In fact, both novels are told from multiple perspectives, thus further fragmenting any potential unity of vision.

Despite his experimentation with other forms, such as children's literature, science fiction and the reworking of ancient myth, Everett is most comfortable with and best known for his explorations of contemporary mores. With the publication of *Watershed* (1996), for example, critics hailed the author's return to the pattern of his first two novels. Set in Colorado, *Watershed* revolves around an African-American hydrologist who gets involved with a group of Native-American activists after they discover a secret government plot to store chemical weapons on public land, a situation that poses a grave threat to the region's water supply. During the course of the book, the reader comes to understand why Robert Hawkes, a man of no apparent allegiance, is drawn to the Indian struggle through a series of flashbacks to his Southern boyhood and revelations about his grandfather's involvement in the civil rights movement of the 1960s. Thus, in Percival Everett's most characteristic work, South meets West. It is not surprising that as an African-American writer, he should trade in the perceived racial determinism of his native region for the promise of individual self-actualization synonymous with our collective vision of the West.

—Tom Mack

F

FERRIS, William R.

Born: Vicksburg, Mississippi, 5 February 1942. **Education:** Davidson College, B.A. in English literature 1964, M.A. in English literature 1965; University of Pennsylvania, M.A. in folklore 1967, Ph.D. in folklore 1969; Union Theological Seminary, New York, and Trinity College, Dublin. **Family:** Married Marcy Cohen (head of the Museum of the Southern Jewish Experience, Utica, Mississippi). **Career:** Assistant professor of English, Jackson State University, 1970-72; associate professor of Afro-American and American Studies, Yale University, 1972-79; professor of Anthropology, University of Mississippi, 1979-1998; visiting fellow, Stanford Humanities Center, 1989-90; chairman, National Endowment for the Humanities, beginning 1998; director, Center for the Study of Southern Culture. **Awards:** Chevalier, Order of Arts and Letters, 1985; officer, Order of Arts and Letters, 1994.

PUBLICATIONS

Folklore Collections

Mississippi Black Folklore: A Research Bibliography and Discography. Hattiesburg, University and College Press of Mississippi, 1971.
Ray Lum, Mule Trader. Memphis, Center for Southern Folklore, 1977.
Images of the South: Visits with Eudora Welty and Walker Evans. Memphis, Center for Southern Folklore, 1977.
Local Color: A Sense of Place in Folk Art. New York, McGraw-Hill, 1982.
American Folklore Films and Videotapes: An Index. Memphis, Center for Southern Folklore, 1976.
Afro-American Folk Art and Crafts. Boston, G.K. Hall, 1983.
You Live and Learn, Then You Die and Forget It All: Ray Lum's Tales of Horses, Mules, and Men. New York, Anchor Books, 1992.
Mule Trader: Ray Lum's Tales of Horses, Mules and Men. Jackson, University Press of Mississippi, 1998.

Editor, with Mary L. Hart, *Folk Music and Modern Sound.* Jackson, University Press of Mississippi, 1982.

General Nonfiction

Blues from the Delta. Garden City, New York, Anchor Press/Doubleday, 1978.
Encyclopedia of Southern Culture, with Charles Reagan Wilson. Chapel Hill, University of North Carolina Press, 1989.

Recordings Collected

Blues from the Delta. London, Studio Vista, 1970.
Mississippi Folk Voices. Memphis, Southern Culture Records, distributed by Rooster Blues Records, Chicago, 1983.
Fannie Bell Chapman, Gospel Singer. Memphis, Southern Culture Records, distributed by Rooster Blues Records, Chicago, 1983.

Bothered all the Time. Memphis, Southern Culture Records, distributed by Rooster Blues Records, Chicago, 1983.

*

Films: *Mississippi Delta Blues,* 1969; *Black Delta Religion,* 1969; *Delta Blues Singer: James "Sonny Ford" Thomas,* 1970; *Gravel Springs Fife and Drum,* 1972; *Green Valley Grandparents,* 1973; *Ray Lum: Mule Trader,* 1974; *Fanny Bell Chapman: Gospel Singer,* 1974; *Give My Poor Heart Ease,* 1975; *Two Black Churches,* 1975; *I Ain't Lyin',* 1975; *Made in Mississippi,* 1975; *Four Women Artists,* 1977; *Hush Hoggies Hush,* 1978; *Painting in the South,* 1983; *Mississippi Blues,* 1983.

* * *

A native of the Mississippi Delta, Bill Ferris has built his career on the study and interpretation of the culture that surrounded him in his childhood. That career has taken him most recently to the nation's capital, where he presently serves as chairman of the National Endowment for the Humanities.

Like many, particularly those from rural or working-class backgrounds, Ferris found that education can do much to separate one from home. "As I began to go through my education, my feeling was the further you went in your education the less you could go back home," Ferris observed in a recent interview. "I always felt I did not want to lose those ties to my experience in rural Mississippi." This fear lead to his decision to study the culture of his native Delta; as he says, "Folklore was a way as an academic of going back home and going to explore in ways that I didn't growing up."

Treating the art and literature of common people, so-called "low culture," as a subject worthy of serious study still sets Ferris apart from most academics and has given a unique flavor to his work as a scholar and teacher. In his early years at Yale University, Ferris brought bluesman B. B. King to speak to his classes, and played a major role in King's receiving an honorary doctorate from that institution. He also brought legendary mule trader Ray Lum to the campus to auction off an old horse and a bulldog in front of the library. When appearing at the White House in the 1980s, Ferris brought with him James "Son" Thomas, who, wearing a pink leisure suit, serenaded the press corps with "The White House Press Corps Blues."

Ferris's sympathy toward the culture of common people is vividly represented in the Center for the Study of Southern Culture at the University of Mississippi, which he cofounded with historian Charles Reagan Wilson. The Center, the first of its kind in the country, is housed in an antebellum observatory that was slated for demolition when Ferris and Wilson occupied the building and raised funds for its restoration. Now the Center is a model for regional studies, institutes and sponsors a number of popular conferences, including, in a supporting role, the annual Faulkner and Yoknapatawpha Conference, one of the nation's most popular.

Considerable controversy did follow another of the Center's conferences, however, this one on Elvis, which took place in 1995 and 1996. While traditionalists lined up to dismiss Elvis as an unfit subject for scholarly attention, Ferris maintains that "the intellectual and emotional energy that was felt at these sessions was really significant." Unfortunately, however, "there was a sense that Elvis brought an association that the community was not comfortable with. Faulkner scholars were demure pipe-smoking types, whereas the feeling was a conference on Elvis would bring busloads of impersonators."

Rather than the inspiration of "busloads of impersonators," Ferris sees Elvis as the most important figure in American popular culture. As he observes, even Goo Goo Clusters, a beloved Southern candy, can be a significant object of study: "It's not so much the subject as how you do it. Obviously, you can have a cavalier approach to any subject, be it Twain or Goo Goo Clusters. But through food, and in this case a commercially produced candy, you can understand a great deal about the culture of a region."

Ferris promises that a willingness to examine both elite and popular culture will be a hallmark of his administration of the National Endowment, because his vision "includes and embraces the classic canon of literature and history [but] it also includes popular and folk culture." That vision is apparent in Ferris's best known book, *The Encyclopedia of Southern Culture*, which he co-edited with Wilson. This volume of over 1,600 pages includes contributions from over 800 writers on subjects as diverse as iced tea and Eudora Welty. It has sold over 100,000 copies.

Another recent and well-received work of Ferris's is *You Live and Learn, Then You Die and Forget It All: Ray Lum's Tales of Horses, Mules, and Men* (1992), a memoir of Ray Lum, a Mississippi livestock trader whose more than sixty years spent traveling the South gave him an almost unlimited collection of classic folk tales. In vivid language (a cemetery, for example, is a "marble orchard"), Lum recounts such adventures as out-cheating a troupe of gypsies, losing money on his first deal, eating barbecued rattlesnake, barely missing Bonnie and Clyde, and making a deal for wild Texas horses, in a scene straight out of Faulkner.

—Jason Mitchell

FINLAY, John

Born: John Martin Finlay in 24 January 1941, in Ozark, Alabama. **Education:** University of Alabama, Tuscaloosa, B.A. 1964, M.A. 1966; Louisiana State University, Ph.D. 1980. **Career:** Instructor, University of Montevallo, 1966-70, Louisiana State University, intermittently during the 1970s; focused on writing and book reviewing, since 1981. **Died:** 17 February 1991.

P<small>UBLICATIONS</small>

Poetry Collections

The Wide Porch and Other Poems. Florence, Kentucky, R. L. Barth, 1984.

Between the Gulfs. Florence, Kentucky, R. L. Barth, 1986.
A Salt of Exposure. Omaha, The Cunningham Press, 1988.
Mind and Blood: The Collected Poems of John Finlay. Santa Barbara, John Daniel and Company, 1992.

Essay Collection

Hermetic Light: Essays on the Gnostic Spirit in Modern Literature and Thought. Santa Barbara, J. Daniel, 1994.

Other

A Prayer to the Father: Poetry and Prose by John Finlay, edited by David Middleton. Thibodaux, Louisiana, Blue Heron Press, 1992.

Uncollected Writings

"The Unfleshed Eye: A Study of Intellectual Theism in the Poetry and Criticism of Yvor Winters." Ph.D dissertation, Louisiana State University, 1980.
"The Night of Alcibiades," in *Hudson Review,* Spring 1994.
"The Return," in *The Epigrammist,* April 1994.

*

Manuscript Collection: The John Finlay Papers: Archives, Hill Memorial Library, Louisiana State University, Baton Rouge.

Critical Studies: "Featured Poet: John Finlay" by David Middleton, *Poetry Pilot,* January 1990; "Blood and Mind: John Finlay (1941-1991)," *Southern Review* by David Middleton, Summer 1991; "*Mind and Blood: The Collected Poems of John Finlay*" by Guy Davenport, *Louisiana Literature,* Spring 1993; "Testament of a Traditionalist" by William Bedford Clark, *Sewanee Review,* Spring 1993; "'The Sweated Line': The Unclaimed Legacy of John Finlay" by William Bedford Clark, *Explorations,* Vol. 7, 1993.

*   *   *

Both in his poetry and in his essays, John Finlay dramatically combined vivid sensuous details and lucid conceptual thought in a lifelong struggle to affirm the "rational clarities" of Aristotle and Aquinas against the modern fascination with the irrational, the subjective, and the primitive. Firmly traditional in his poetic style and in his philosophical and theological beliefs, Finlay sought in all his works nothing less than "plainest naked truth"—about God, the human intellect, the natural world, and about those threats posed to the intellect by the demonic and the mystical. For over twenty years, Finlay pursued the truth in works that are serious, simple, deep, and almost traumatically revealing of the permanent things in the human condition.

Born in the house of his maternal grandmother in Ozark, Alabama, Finlay grew up on the peanut and dairy farm owned by his parents, Tom Coston Finlay and Jean Sorrell Finlay, just outside the nearby town of Enterprise. Even as a youth Finlay seemed chosen to lead the literary life—reciting Shakespeare to the cows whom he named for Greek goddesses, reading intently while the combine he was driving made its own way across the peanut-fields, and shouting out once in class, "this is such inferior writing" when Longfellow's poetry grated on his nerves. Finlay earned his B.A. (1964) and M.A. (1966) in English at the University of Alabama in Tuscaloosa, then taught for four years at the University of Montevallo before going to Louisiana State University in 1970 to pursue his doctorate. Finlay lived in Baton Rouge during most of the 1970s, though he did spend time on the Greek island of Corfu (1972) and in Paris (1973).

Finlay earned his doctorate at LSU in 1980, the same year in which he converted to Roman Catholicism. From 1981 until his death on 17 February 1991, Finlay lived on the family farm in Alabama, reading widely and writing his essays and poems.

Finlay's poems, all written in measured verse, are of three types: 1) plain-style lyrics in the tradition of Ben Jonson, 2) post-symbolist poems where sensuous details implicitly contain logical thought, and 3) short narrative poems about life in Alabama from the early nineteenth century to the present. Thinking of his own aims as a poet, Finlay once wrote that "the greatest poetry comes, not from fantasy, but from intense, realistic perceptions of the natural and human worlds."

In "Audubon at Oakley," Finlay has Audubon speak of such perceptions as he envisions a painting for his great folio:

I saw my book, taut wings of mockingbirds
In combat with the snake knotted beneath
The nest, its open mouth close to the eggs,
Now held forever in the lean, hard line.

Such intense perceptions also appear in "The Wide Porch," a poem which contains an unforgettable passage on the death of Finlay's grandmother in the old family home:

She who last lived there, finally alone,
Died terrified, flesh holding on to flesh.
No cries came when that agony had ceased.
We closed her eyes, transfixed in nothingness,
Then left her covered in the naked light.

Of Finlay's Christian poems, one of the most impressive is "The Bog Sacrifice." Finlay begins by recalling the ritual murder of a young man in pre-Christian Denmark, a murder meant to appease a savage goddess of the spring. Then, after describing the recovery of the victim's body in modern times, Finlay broods upon this pagan world so far from the atoning sacrifice of Christ:

Before Christ reached this isolated north,
A chthonic goddess, holding iron breasts,
Each year in early spring exacted death.
In winter when the winds blew keen off ice,
Or summer with its rippling swarm of reeds,
The bog seemed never raised above the sea,
But underneath, out of whose depths she came.

In his own last spring, blind and paralyzed, Finlay dictated from his bed the final poem, "A Prayer to the Father," which ends:

O God of love and power, hold still my heart
When death, that ancient, awful fact appears;

Preserve my mind from all deranging fears,
And let me offer up my reason free
And where I thought, there see Thee perfectly.

Of Finlay's verse, Guy Davenport has said that it is "so well written, so firmly made of a literary English that eludes epoch and fashion, that we can predict a future for it . . . a deserved place in American letters.

Finlay has undoubtedly made a permanent contribution to modern literature. In his finest poems he has earned the right to be compared to the best poets the South has yet produced. Of his poem "Salt from the Winter Sea," which tells of south Alabamians going to the Gulf a hundred years ago to gather salt, Ralph Hammond, poet laureate of the state, has written that "never a more accomplished and lasting poem has ever come out of Alabama." The poem concludes:

But the last day, after their work was done,
Those stoics lingered in the cloudless calm,
The warm November sun of their Deep South,
The green Gulf crashing on the golden sand.
They momently then gazed outside themselves,
Struck by the mortal beauty of the waves,
Before they packed the salt and started home.

Sadly, as early as 1981, when news of the terrible disease first broke, Finlay knew he had the virus that causes AIDS. Yet it was during his final decade that Finlay wrote all of his essays and his most mature poetry. The creation of works in both verse and prose of such high quality under such tragic circumstances will someday surely be seen as one of the most courageous acts performed by any writer in contemporary literary history.

—David Middleton

FLAGG, Fannie

Born: Patricia Neal in Birmingham, Alabama, 21 September 1941. **Education:** Attended the University of Alabama; studied at the Pittsburgh Playhouse and the Town and Gown Theatre. **Career:** Actress, including on stage in *Cat on a Hot Tin Roof* and *Just for Openers*, 1966, *Patio/Porch*, 1977, *Come Back to the Five and Dime, Jimmy Dean, Jimmy Dean*, 1979, *The Best Little Whorehouse in Texas*, 1980; performed in films, including *Five Easy Pieces*, 1970, *Some of My Best Friends Are...*, 1971, *Stay Hungry*, 1976, *Grease* and *Rabbit Test*, 1978; and on television; comedienne; producer of *Morning Show*, WBRC-TV, Birmingham, Alabama, 1964-65; speaker on the Equal Rights Amendment. **Awards:** Fashion award, Ad Club, 1965; named outstanding woman of America, Who's Who in American Women in Radio and Television, 1966; two first place awards in fiction, Santa Barbara Writers Conference.

PUBLICATIONS

Novels

Coming Attractions: A Wonderful Novel. Morrow, 1981; as *Daisy Fay and the Miracle Man*, Warner Books, 1992.

Fried Green Tomatoes at the Whistle Stop Cafe. Random House, 1987.

Other

Fannie Flagg's Original Whistle Stop Cafe Cookbook, Fawcett, 1993.

Screenplay: *Fried Green Tomatoes,* with Jon Avnet, adapted from her own novel, 1991.

Sound Recordings: *Rally 'round the Flagg,* RCA Victor, 1967; *My Husband Doesn't Know I'm Making This Phone Call,* Sunflower, 1971.

*   *   *

Fannie Flagg did not begin writing seriously until she was in her thirties, then published two popular novels, *Coming Attractions* (1981) and *Fried Green Tomatoes at the Whistle Stop Cafe* (1988). Both works feature strong female characters in a small Southern community, and her tales reflect the homespun nature of the settings.

Before she was a writer, the personable Flagg was an accomplished actress who appeared on television (*Candid Camera*), film (*Grease*), and stage (*Cat on a Hot Tin Roof*). Flagg's first novel, *Coming Attractions*, is the story of the young girl coming of age in the south in the 1950s. The story is related in the form of a diary kept by protagonist Daisy Flagg Harper beginning on 1 April 1952, when she was 11, and continuing until she was about 17 years old. *Coming Attractions* balances Daisy's humorous exploits and the difficulties of growing up with an alcoholic father, a projectionist at the local movie house who is always looking for a quick buck.

Subtle ironic twists and amusing episodes permeate *Coming Attractions*: Daisy is proud of helping her father do his job and spreading the culture of cinema, only to learn as an adult that nearly all of the movies were "B" pictures—among the turns that keep the novel from being overly sentimental. Many of Daisy's adventures revolve around her father and his get-rich-quick plans, including one where he pulls a Lazarus in an odd mortgage deal. His scheme takes a weird turn during a seance when those who have fallen prey to his deal take the whole thing too seriously and begin speaking in tongues. One woman long dependent on a hearing aid dramatically removes it and believes that she can now hear on her own.

Flagg's second novel, *Fried Green Tomatoes at the Whistle Stop Cafe*, was a bestseller, lauded by the public, critics, and such fellow authors as Harper Lee, Erma Bombeck, and Eudora Welty. The novel is two main stories intertwined: Evelyn Couch and Virginia (Ninny) Threadgoode in modern-day Birmingham, Alabama, and Idgie Threadgoode and Ruth Jamison in Depression-era Whistle Stop, Alabama.

Evelyn Couch is a despondent, middle-aged woman uncertain of her future who is befriended by the elderly Ninny Threadgoode, a resident of the same nursing home as Evelyn's mother-in-law.

It is Ninny's recollections of her free-spirited sister-in-law, Idgie, and Idgie's friend Ruth that helps bring Evelyn out of her depression and find new direction and fulfillment with her life. These flashbacks are supplimented by newspaper articles from the local papers as well as parallel storylines of other characters.

Idgie is the tom-boy younger sister, and devoted shadow, of Buddie, the town darling. Buddy is tragically killed by one of the ever-present trains that run through Whistle Stop. Idgie, up to then barely governable by her family, becomes uncontrollable with grief. It is not until Ruth Jamison comes to stay with her family one summer that she rediscovers her ability to love. Unfortunately, when the summer ends Ruth elects to follow through with her commitment to marry Frank Bennett, who lives in the distant Valdosta, Georgia. Frank is an abusive man and Ruth eventually flees, assisted by Idgie, and with her young son Buddy, back to Whistle Stop. Frank first attempts to frighten Ruth into returning to him, but when he fails he travels to Whistle Stop to abduct Ruth. He is never seen again. It is the mystery of his disappearance that provides suspense and a surprising conclusion. In this shadow Idgie and Ruth, proprietors of the local Whistle Stop Cafe, build their lives together with young Buddy (Stump), surrounded by a colorful group of family and friends.

This narrative has been especially praised for Flagg's portrayal of what would have been in accord with the social mores of the decade. Indeed, the novel presents a careful evocation of the times, including the spread of Hoovervilles and the Klu Klux Klan. Idgie and Ruth's lesbian relationship is dealt with directly and matter-of-factly, without apology or discomfort by the characters. It is Idgie's mother who pushes the relationship in the beginning, after witnessing the calming effect Ruth has on Idgie's "wild animal ways," and from that point everyone else accepts them without condemnation.

Along with the southern small town setting of the novel, *Fried Green Tomatoes at the Whistle Stop Cafe* included a group of recipes at the end for dishes described during the course of the story. The recipes, for typical southern dishes such as fried chicken, pecan pie, and fried green tomatoes, proved so popular that Flagg published a whole cookbook in 1993, *Fannie Flagg's Original Whistle Stop Cafe Cookbook.*

—Kristin Hart

FOOTE, Horton

Born: Wharton, Texas, 14 March, 1916. **Education:** Studied at Pasadena Playhouse School of Theatre, 1933-35, and Tamara Darkahovna School of Theatre, 1937-39. **Family:** Married Lillian Vallish, June 4, 1945; four children. **Career:** Actor in Broadway plays, 1932-42; teacher of playwriting, Productions, Inc., Washington, D.C., 1945-49; writer of teleplays (for programs including Kraft Playhouse and Playhouse 90), stage plays, and screenplays since 1941. **Member:** Writers Guild of America, Authors Guild, Dramatists Guild, Texas Institute of Letters, Fellowship of Southern Writers. **Awards:** Academy Award for best screenplay and Writers Guild of America Screen Award, both 1962 for

To Kill a Mockingbird; Academy Award for best screenplay, 1983, for *Tender Mercies*; Academy Award nomination for best screenplay for *The Trip to Bountiful*, 1985; Evelyn Burkey Award, Writers Guild, 1989; Pulitzer Prize for drama, 1995, for *The Young Man from Atlanta*; honorary degrees from Drew University, Austin College, and American Film Institute. **Agent:** Lucy Kroll, 390 West End Ave., New York, New York 10024.

PUBLICATIONS

Plays

Only the Heart. New York, Dramatists Play Service, 1944.
The Chase. New York, Dramatists Play Service, 1952.
The Trip to Bountiful. New York, Dramatists Play Service, 1953.
A Young Lady of Property (contains *The Dancers, A Young Lady of Property, The Old Beginning, John Turner Davis, Death of the Old Man,* and *The Oil Well*). New York Dramatists Play Service 1954.
The Travelling Lady. New York, Dramatists Play Service 1955.
The Midnight Caller. New York, Dramatists Play Service, 1959.
Harrison, Texas: Eight Television Plays. New York, Harcourt, Brace and Company, 1959.
Three Plays (contains *Roots in a Parched Ground, Old Man,* and *Tomorrow*). New York Harcourt, 1962.
Roots in a Parched Ground. New York, Dramatists Play Service, 1962.
Tomorrow. New York, Dramatists Play Service, 1963.
The Roads to Home. New York, Dramatists Play Service 1982.
Blind Date. New York, Dramatists Play Service, 1986.
On Valentine's Day. New York, Dramatists Play Service, 1987.
1918. New York, Dramatists Play Service, 1987.
Courtships. New York, Dramatists Play Service, 1987.
Courtship; Valentine's Day; 1918: Three Plays from The Orphans' Home Cycle. New York Grove Press, 1987.
Roots in a Parched Ground, Convicts, Lily Dale, The Widow Claire: 4 Plays from the Orphans' Home Cycle. New York, Grove Press, 1988.
Selected One Act Plays of Horton Foote. Dallas, Southern Methodist University Press, 1988.
Cousins; The Death of Papa: Two Plays from The Orphans' Home Cycle. New York, Grove Press, 1989.
Four New Plays (contains *The Habitation of Dragons, Night Seasons, Dividing the Estate, Talking Pictures*). New York, Smith and Kraus, 1993.
The Young Man from Atlanta. New York Dutton, 1995.
Laura Dennis. New York, Dramatists Play Service, 1996.
Taking Pictures. New York, Dramatists Play Service, 1996.
Night Seasons. New York, Dramatists Play Service, 1996.

Novel

The Chase (adapted from the play of the same title). New York, Rhinehart and Company, 1956.

Screenplays

The Screenplay of To Kill a Mockingbird. New York Harcourt, Brace & World, 1964.

Tomorrow & Tomorrow & Tomorrow (contains William Faulkner's short story "Tomorrow," along with Foote's television play and his screenplay based upon it). Jackson, University Press of Mississippi, 1985.
Three Screenplays (contains *The Trip to Bountiful, Tender Mercies, To Kill a Mockingbird*). New York Grove Press, 1989.
Horton Foote's Three Trips to Bountiful (contains Foote's original teleplay, *The Trip to Bountiful,* and his adaptations of it for stage and film). Dallas, Southern Methodist University Press, 1993.

FIRST PRODUCTIONS

Texas Town. Produced in New York City at Weidman Studio, 1941.
Out of My House. Produced in New York City, 1942.
Only the Heart. Produced in New York City at Bijou Theatre, 1944.
Celebration. Produced in New York City at Maxine Elliott Theatre, 1948.
The Chase. Produced on Broadway, 1952.
The Trip to Bountiful. Produced on Broadway, 1953.
The Midnight Caller. Broadcast by NBC, 1953; produced in New York City, 1958.
A Young Lady of Property. Broadcast by NBC, 1954, produced in Los Angeles at Fiesta Hall, 1963.
The Traveling Lady. Produced on Broadway, 1954; broadcast by CBS, 1957.
The Roads to Home. Broadcast by ABC, 1955; produced in New York City at Manhattan Punch Line Theatre, 1982.
Tomorrow (based on a story by William Faulkner). Broadcast by CBS, 1960; Produced Off-Broadway, 1985.
The Road to the Graveyard. Produced in New York City at Ensemble Studio Theatre, 1985.
Blind Date. Produced in New York City at Ensemble Studio Theatre, 1986.
Habitation of Dragons. Produced at Pittsburgh Playhouse, 1988.
Dividing the Estate. Produced in Princeton, New Jersey, at McArthur Theatre, 1989.
Talking Pictures. Produced in Sarasota, Florida, at Asolo Theater, 1990.

Author of the book, *Gone With the Wind* (a musical version of Margaret Mitchell's novel). Produced on the West End, 1972, produced in Los Angeles at Dorothy Chandler Pavilion, 1973.

*

Screenplays: *Storm Fear* (based on novel by Clinton Seeley), United Artists, 1956; *To Kill a Mockingbird* (based on novel by Harper Lee), Universal, 1962; *Baby, the Rain Must Fall* (based on own play, *The Travelling Lady*), Columbia, 1965; *Hurry Sundown* with Thomas Ryan (based on novel by K. B. Glidden), Paramount, 1966; *Tomorrow* (based on story by William Faulkner), Filmgroup, 1971; *Tender Mercies*, Universal, 1983; *1918*, Cinecom International, 1984; *On Valentine's Day*, Angelika Films, 1985; *Spring Moon* (based on novel by Bette Bao Lord), 1987; *The Trip to Bountiful*, Island Pictures, 1985; *Convicts*, M.C.E.G., 1991.

Teleplays: *Ludie Brooks*, CBS, 1951; *The Travelers*, NBC, 1952; *The Old Beginning*, NBC, 1953; *The Oil Well*, NBC, 1953; *The Rocking Chair*, NBC, 1953; *Expectant Relations*, NBC, 1953;

Tears of My Sister, NBC, 1953; *Young Lady of Property*, NBC, 1953; *Death of the Old Man*, NBC, 1953; *Shadow of Willie Greer*, NBC, 1954; *Flight*, NBC, 1956; *Drugstore: Sunday Noon*, ABC, 1956; *Member of the Family*, CBS, 1957; *Old Man* (based on novel by William Faulkner), CBS, 1959; *The Shape of the River*, CBS, 1960; *The Gambling Heart*, NBC, 1964; *The Displaced Person* (based on story by Flannery O'Conner), PBS, 1977; *Barn Burning* (based on story by Faulkner), PBS, 1980; *Keeping On*, PBS, 1983.

Media Adaptations: *The Chase* was adapted to film by Lillian Hellman for Columbia Pictures in 1965.

Critical Study: *You Can Go Home Again: The Focus on Family in the Works of Horton Foote* by Rebecca Luttrell Briley, New York, Peter Lang, 1993.

*　　*　　*

Horton Foote, probably the most important southern playwright since Tennessee Williams, seemed to know what he was doing from the start. His first play, composed when he was in his twenties, was called *Wharton Dance* and concerned the lives of ordinary middle-class Texans living in the town where Foote grew up. Many years later, at age 79, he won the Pulitzer Prize for drama with *The Young Man from Atlanta*, which concerned the lives of ordinary middle-class Texans living in Harrison, a fictional town modeled on Wharton, where Foote still lives in the house built by his grandfather. As theatrical fashions have come and gone, Foote has continued quietly pursuing his themes in his chosen setting. He has done so in spite of the harsh words of some critics, who find him dull, unambitious, and uncritical of the pieties of small-town life. But others—critics, directors, and especially actors—have praised him highly: The respected actress Ellen Burstyn has called him "America's greatest playwright," as he may well be.

Foote seems bland to some because he has chosen to work within what amount to formal constraints. He confines his dialogue to the probable iterations of middle-class, small-town southerners who—even in grief, fury, and terror—speak to each other in grammatically complete sentences from which four-letter words are absent and in which terms like "ma'am," "please" and "thank you" figure prominently. And yet, as Foote has demonstrated over and over, these ordinary lives contain all the passions for which a playwright might wish. Consider his play *1918*, which is set in Harrison during the waning days of World War I and in the midst of a deadly influenza epidemic. Most of Foote's characters, displaying the taste for excitement that also characterizes many of his critics, believe the war to be the more compelling crisis, and news from France occupies their conversations and imaginations. Meanwhile one neighbor after another dies from the flu; gradually we realize that the war, despite its loudly advertised "importance," serves Harrison as a mere diversion from the much deadlier, more inexplicable crisis moving silently through the town. Among the points the play makes is that one need not venture to the extremes of experience—to the battlefields of France, e.g.—in order to find horror, tragedy, courage, and redemptive love; they are all to be found at home.

These themes have been Foote's from the beginning. In his plays and screenplays life, even common, middle-class life, is full of quiet

terror and mystery. The malevolence of escaped convict Bubber Reeves in the early play *The Chase* cannot be explained or mitigated, even by his selflessly devoted mother; the self-destructiveness of Henry Thomas in *The Travelling Lady* proves equally implacable, despite the indefatigable love of his wife Georgette. In a late play, *The One-Armed Man*, a complacent, Babbit-like businessman is confronted in his office by a gun-wielding former employee, now known as "Knub" because of his dismemberment on the job. Knub does not want sympathy, charity, or understanding; what he keeps demanding, up until the moment he kills C. W. Rowe, is his arm back. Behind Knub's personal madness, of course, is the cosmic irrationality of the freak accident that took his arm. There is a terrifying randomness in Foote's world, which beneath its placid surface is not altogether different from the one inhabited by Vladimir and Estragon in *Waiting for Godot*. That randomness may be read in the senseless path of the flu epidemic in *1918*, in the automobile accident which claims the innocent life of Sue Anne, Mac Sledge's daughter in *Tender Mercies*, or even in the advent of "talking pictures" in the play of that name, which threatens to push Myra Tolliver, a piano player at a silent movie house, into destitution.

Against such randomness the bourgeois prudence of C. W. Rowe—who as Knub approaches is lecturing a subordinate on the wisdom of planning ahead—is powerless. What virtues are useful in such a world? Foote speaks as eloquently as Beckett, Faulkner, or Hemingway for simple endurance in the face of seeming hopelessness. But in Foote's world things never are quite hopelessness, for balancing out the world's unpleasant surprises is always the possibility of love, a kind of countervailing, benevolent mystery. See for instance his screenplay for the 1983 movie *Tender Mercies*, which contains some of the best writing Foote has ever done. The protagonist is Mac Sledge, a former country music star who has lost career, marriage, and family to alcoholism. He drifts into the life of Rosa Lee, a war widow raising her child, Sonny, alone. By imperceptible steps, in a series of small scenes in which very little seems to happen, Foote tracks the convergence of hearts that redeems all three lonely people and makes them a family. How does it happen? Mac demands to know in a powerful speech near the movie's end:

> I don't know why I wandered out to this part of Texas drunk and you took me in and pitied me and helped me to straighten out and married me. Why, why did this happen? Is there a reason that happened? And Sonny's daddy killed in the war. My daughter killed in an automobile accident. Why?

Foote provides no answer, but simply sets the mysteries before us: love and grief, side by side.

Home and family, for Foote, are the principal sources of love, though also of much suffering, and so in retrospect it seems inevitable that he would one day write about his own family. He did this in a series of nine related plays which he called *The Orphans' Home Cycle*. The principal characters are Horace Robedaux and Elizabeth Vaughn, who are based on Foote's own parents. The cycle begins with *Roots in a Parched Ground*, in which Horace is a young boy witnessing the death of his father, and it follows his efforts to make a place for himself in the world. At the center of the cycle is a set of three plays— *Courtship, On Valentine's Day,* and *1918*—concerning Horace's courtship and marriage of Elizabeth, who must rebel against her own powerful, overprotective father to make a life with the boy she loves. *1918* captures the central theme of the cycle in its final scenes. Horace, having survived a severe bout with influenza, is in the cemetery visiting the graves of his long-dead father and his newly dead baby daughter, carried away in the epidemic. As he stands among the symbols of his grief his father-in-law approaches to tell Horace that Elizabeth has now given birth to a baby boy. The joy of birth does not precisely compensate for the pain of loss; the two simply exist side by side, each one complicating, as it were, our understanding of the other.

Though *The Orphans' Home Cycle* follows Horace from heartbreak to deep contentment in his marriage and family, it does not offer anything so simple as a happy ending. Rather it describes a true cycle, ending as it began with the death of a father. In *The Death of Papa* it is Elizabeth's father, the formidable Mr. Vaughn, who unexpectedly dies, leaving his seemingly secure family as shaken as Horace was at the cycle's beginning. All of Mr. Vaughn's wealth and prudence have been unable to protect his loved ones, who are cast adrift, forced to take their chances with everyone else in Foote's fallen but redeemable world. The title for the cycle comes from a line by Marianne Moore: "the world's an orphans' home." Loss and loneliness, that is, are eventually everyone's lot. But Foote's orphans do sometimes find one another, and sometimes find real homes, despite the wildness of the world in which they are exiled.

—John Grammar

FOOTE, Shelby

Born: Greenville, Mississippi, 17 November 1916. **Education:** University of North Carolina, Chapel Hill, 1935-37. **Military Service:** United States Army, 1940-44, Marine Corps, 1944-45. **Family:** Married Gwyn Rainer in 1956 (second marriage); two children. **Career:** Held various jobs, including construction worker, radio copywriter, and newspaper reporter, following World War II; full-time writer beginning in the 1950s; Novelist-in-residence, University of Virginia, 1963; playwright-in-residence, Arena Stage, Washington, D.C., 1963-64; writer-in-residence, Hollins College, Virginia, 1968. **Awards:** Guggenheim fellowship, 1955, 1956, 1957; Ford fellowship, for drama, 1963; Fletcher Pratt award, for non-fiction, 1964, 1974; University of North Carolina award, 1975. D.Litt.: University of the South, Sewanee, Tennessee, 1981, Southwestern University, Memphis, Tennessee, 1982, University of North Carolina, Chapel Hill, 1992, University of South Carolina, 1991, University of Notre Dame, South Bend, Indiana, 1994. **Member:** Society of American Historians, 1980; American Academy of Arts and Letters, 1994.

PUBLICATIONS

Novels

Tournament. New York, Dial Press, 1949.
Follow Me Down. New York, Dial Press, 1950.

Love in a Dry Season. New York, Dial Press, 1951.
Shiloh. New York, Dial Press, 1952.
Jordan County: A Landscape in Narrative (includes stories). New York, Dial Press, 1954.
September September. New York, Random House, 1978.

Nonfiction

The Civil War: A Narrative:
    Fort Sumter to Perryville. New York, Random House, 1958.
    Fredericksburg to Meridian. New York, Random House, 1963.
    Red River to Appomattox. New York, Random House, 1974.
The Novelist's View of History. Winston-Salem, North Carolina, Palaemon Press, 1981.
Stars in Their Courses: The Gettysburg Campaign June-July 1863. New York, Modern Library, 1994.
The Beleaguered City: The Vicksburg Campaign December 1862-July 1863. New York, Modern Library, 1995.

Play

Jordan County: A Landscape in the Round. Produced in Washington, D.C., 1964.

Other

The Correspondence of Shelby Foote and Walker Percy edited by Jay Tolson. New York, W.W. Norton & Company, 1996.

Editor, *Chickamauga, and Other Civil War Stories.* New York, Delta Books, 1993.

Contributor, *Gettysburg Multimedia Battle Simular*, CD-ROM. Memphis, Tennessee Iris Press, 1995.

*

Manuscript Collection: Southern Historical Collection, University of North Carolina, Chapel Hill, North Carolina.

Critical Studies: "Shelby Foote Issue" (includes bibliography), *Mississippi Quarterly*, October 1971, and *Delta* (Montpellier, France), 1977; *Shelby Foote* by Helen White and Redding Sugg, Boston, Twayne, 1982; *Conversations with Shelby Foote* edited by William C. Carter, Jackson, University Press of Mississippi, 1989; *Shelby Foote: Novelist and Historian* by Robert L. Phillips, University of Mississippi Press, 1992.

Shelby Foote comments:
    Dates and places are not what history is all about. History is about people and should be studied through the eyes of the people who made it, not through a list of dates.

*   *   *

Shelby Foote is best known for his three-volume history, *The Civil War: A Narrative*, which comprises *Fort Sumter to Perryville* (1958), *Fredericksburg to Meridian* (1963), and *Red River to Appomattox* (1974). *The Civil War: A Narrative* eschews detailing the economic, intellectual, or political causes of the war in favor of a more personal rendering of experiences on the battlefield, reflective of Foote's background as a novelist: he published five novels previous to his Civil War epic. The exhaustive history, which took him twenty years to complete and spans nearly three-thousand pages, earned Foote a National Book Award in 1979.

For the history, Foote used established historical sources and photographs as well as such details as weather and seasonal conditions of each battlefield to depict the war accurately and objectively from both Northern and Southern perspectives. Foote admits to patterning the work on Homer's *Iliad* and Marcel Proust's *A la recherche du temps perdu*. Development of characters, plot, setting, and narrative voice—traits of fiction not traditionally integrated into historical writing—distinguish *The Civil War* as narrative history. Foote's characterizations of such principal figures as Jefferson Davis, Robert E. Lee, and Abraham Lincoln are noted for their historical precision and literary richness. Expansive use of anecdotes offer lively, balanced, and sympathetic portraits of these popularly-known, key figures as well as ordinary soldiers and lesser-known military and political leaders.

Interest in Foote's series was renewed when he appeared as an eloquent commentator in Ken Burns's television documentary *The Civil War*, which aired on PBS in 1991 to wide critical and popular acclaim. The program made Foote an even more sought after speaker, consultant, and writer on the Civil War, reflected in several publications during the mid-1990s. For example, he edited *Chickamauga, and Other Civil War Stories* (1993), an anthology of Civil War stories by such authors as F. Scott Fitzgerald, William Faulkner, Thomas Wolfe, Stephen Crane, Ambrose Bierce, Eudora Welty, and Mark Twain. Previously published as *The Night Before Chancellorsville*, Foote wrote an Introduction and edited the new edition.

Extended passages from *The Civil War: A Narrative* were reworked and published as individual books: *Stars in Their Courses: The Gettysburg Campaign June-July 1863* (1994) concerns the 1863 Gettysburg campaign, while *The Beleaguered City: The Vicksburg Campaign December 1862-July 1863* reports on Grant's siege of the Mississippi port of Vicksburg. Both works maintain the epic scope and literary flavor that make the whole of *The Civil War* so remarkable. Foote was also called on to consult on a CD-ROM, *Gettysburg Multimedia Battle Simular* (1995).

In his fictional works, Foote portrays the effects of economic and social change on his Southern characters. His views on the relationship between literature and history are expressed in his Foreword to the first volume of *The Civil War*: "The novelist and the historian are seeking the same thing: the truth—not a different truth: the same truth—only they reach it, or try to reach it, by different routes." With few exceptions, Foote's fiction is either located in the delta country around fictional Lake Jordan, Mississippi, or contains characters from that area. Lake Jordan is modeled after Washington County, which includes Foote's hometown of Greenville, called Bristol in his fiction. This locale includes two counties (Issawamba and Jordan), Solitaire Plantation, and the town of Bristol on the Mississippi River.

Foote's family roots run deep in the area: his father was a Greenville businessman, his grandfather, Huger Lee Foote, an early planter near Greenville, and his great-grandfather was a cavalry officer at Shiloh. Another ancestor, Isaac Shelby, was governor of Kentucky in its early years and a participant in the Battle of Kings Mountain. Foote was educated through high school in Greenville, where he was influenced by local author William Alexander Percy and was a schoolmate of his Percy's nephew, Walker Percy. Foote had been writing since the age of sixteen, when his poetry was published in the Greenville High School *Pica*. In 1935, he and Percy attended the University of North Carolina at Chapel Hill, where Foote worked for the University of North Carolina literary magazine and published short stories, reviews, and poetry. The friendship of Foote and Percy lasted over sixty years and is represented in *The Correspondence of Shelby Foote & Walker Percy* (1996), edited by Jay Tolson.

Foote joined the Mississippi National Guard in October 1939, and, in 1940, he was mobilized into the U.S. Army as sergeant, rose to captain, but was court martialed and discharged during service in Northern Ireland for leaving to see his girlfriend in Belfast. Foote worked as an Associated Press reporter at the local desk in New York throughout the fall and winter of 1944, then enlisted in the combat intelligence branch of the United States Marine Corps in January 1945, where he served until November that year. After the war he held various jobs, including construction worker, radio copywriter, and newspaper reporter.

Foote completed his first novel before 1940, but its experimental style made it unattractive to publishers. After the war, Foote returned to this novel and rewrote it to remove modernist influences of James Joyce and Thomas Wolfe. The revision of his unpublished novel resulted in his first short story, "Flood Burial," which was published in the *Saturday Evening Post* in 1946. Further portions of the book were reworked for his first published novel, *Tournament* (1949), set against the background of the South's transition from agrarian community to corporate entity. The novel introduces Foote's concerns with human alienation in the face of encroaching industrialization and capitalism, as well as Foote's belief in the arbitrary nature of fate—central themes in all his later fiction.

Follow Me Down (1950) relates eight different first-person narrative reactions to a murder, based on a Delta trial of the 1940s that Foote attended. The central characters of the novel include a tenant farming evangelist at Solitaire Plantation and a young girl whom he seduces and then kills. Foote admits that the structure owes much to Robert Browning's epic narrative poem, *The Ring and the Book*, and displays his attempt to "penetrate to the heart of an event and then emerge, by means of monologues that became increasingly and then decreasingly involved in the story being told. The first and last speakers, for example, are involved by their professions, and both speak in a more or less professional manner. The third and third-from-last are intimates of the principals, and their tone is lyric."

Foote's third novel, *Love in a Dry Season* (1951), is set in Bristol from the 1920s to World War II, a time when the cotton community has become no more than a business-interest owned by a powerful Eastern trust. *Shiloh* (1952) is a historical novel told in a series of first-person monologues. The historical accuracy and immediacy of battle depictions in *Shiloh* earned Foote a publisher's assignment that eventually became *The Civil War: A Narrative*.

After moving to Memphis, Foote published *Jordan County: A Landscape in Narrative* (1953), a collection of thematically ordered short stories that begin in the present and work back in time to the 1700s, a history in reverse, as Foote labeled it. Similar in structure to James Joyce's *Dubliners* and William Faulkner's *Go Down, Moses, Jordan County* can be read and enjoyed for its individual pieces while each story relies on the others to form a whole. *Jordan County* comprises seven tales, or episodes, ranging from 1950 backwards to 1797; each is set in Bristol, Jordan County, Mississippi. Later, while he was playwright-in-residence at Arena Stage in Washington from 1963 to 1964, Foote adapted three sections of *Jordan County* for the stage.

Following the twenty-year period Foote researched, wrote, and published *The Civil War,* he returned to fiction with *September September* (1978), which features characters who are natives of Bristol and have relocated to Memphis. In this novel, Foote incorporates such incidents as the racial integration crisis in Little Rock, Arkansas, and the launching of the U.S.S.R. satellite Sputnik in 1957 to underscore his story about interracial relationships and a kidnaping.

—Bruce Walker

FORD, Jesse Hill

Born: Troy, Alabama, 28 December 1928. **Education:** Vanderbilt University, 1951, B.A. in English (directed by Donald Davidson); University of Florida, 1955, M.A. in creative writing (thesis, *The Thundering Tide*, a novel, directed by Andrew Lytle). **Military Service:** U.S. Navy, 1951-52. **Family:** Sarah Ann (Sally) Davis, 1951 (divorced about 1971-72); married Lillian Pellettiere, 1975; four children. **Career:** Reporter, *The Tennesseean* (Nashville), 1950-51; editorial newswriter, Gainesville, Florida, 1953-55; public relations director, Tennessee Medical Association, 1955-56; assistant for public relations, American Medical Association, 1956-57; freelance professional writer, 1957-96; Fulbright scholar, University of Oslo, 1961; visiting fellow, Wesleyan University Center for Advance Study, 1965; writer-in-residence, Memphis State University, 1969-71; visiting professor, University of Rochester, 1975; writer-in-residence, Vanderbilt University, 1987; regular columns for *USA Today;* scriptwriter for movie producers. **Member:** Overseas Press Club; American-Scandinavian Foundation; St. George's Episcopal Church, Nashville, Tennessee. **Awards:** *Atlantic Monthly* grant, for *Mountains of Gilead*, and "First" Award, for "The Surest Thing in Show Business," both 1959; honorable mention, Columbia Broadcasting System Grant-in-Aid, 1960; O. Henry Awards, 1961 (for "How the Mountains Are"), 1966 (for "The Open Water"), and 1967 (for "The Bitter Bread"); Guggenheim fellowship, 1966; Edgar Award, Mystery Writers of America, 1975, for "The Jail"; honorary D.Litt., Lambuth College (Jackson, Tennessee), 1968. **Died:** Bellevue, Tennessee, 1 June 1996.

PUBLICATIONS

Mountains of Gilead. Boston, Little, Brown, 1961.
The Conversion of Buster Drumwright. Nashville, Vanderbilt University Press, 1964.

The Liberation of Lord Byron Jones. Boston, Little, Brown, 1965.
Fishes, Birds and Sons of Man. Boston, Little, Brown, 1967.
The Feast of Saint Barnabas. Boston, Little, Brown, 1969.
The Raider. Boston, Little, Brown, 1975.

Screenplay

The Liberation of L.B. Jones, with Stirling Silliphant. Los Angeles, Columbia Pictures, 1969.

*

Manuscript Collection: The Ford papers, deposited in the Mississippi Valley Collection at the John Willard Brister Library, University of Memphis, contain typescript fragments of five additional novels, as well as copies of thirty short stories, two poems, and twenty-three articles or reviews.

Recordings: Audio—*Learning to Write the Short Story*, Cincinnati, Writer's Voice, 1972. **Video**—*The Liberation of L. B. Jones*, RCA/Columbia Pictures Home Video, 1984.

Bibliography: *Jesse Hill Ford: An Annotated Check List of His Published Works and of His Papers* by Helen White, Memphis, Memphis State University, 1974.

Biography: *The Life and Letters of Jesse Hill Ford, Southern Writer: With Annotations and Commentary* by Anne Cheney, Lewiston, New York, Edwin Mellen Press, 1996.

Critical Studies: "*The Liberation of Lord Byron Jones*" by Madison Jones, *Mississippi Quarterly*, Winter 1966-67; "What Are You Doing There? What Are You Doing Here? A View of the Jesse Hill Ford Case" by Jack Matthews, *Georgia Review*, Summer 1972.

*   *   *

Like most Southern writers who came of age during the early 1950s, Jesse Hill Ford rebelled against the cavalier tradition and Faulknerian style. Influenced as much by Hemingway and Fitzgerald as by Faulkner and Wolfe, Ford initially developed straightforward plots in a relatively lean prose style that anticipates minimalism. His approach is microcosmic, focusing on personal relationships and individual quandaries that reveal profound social and ethical issues. Thus, his novels should be approached as part of the South's ongoing cultural discourse.

Though in subsequent novels he increasingly adds layers of subplots, with the exception of his last completed work, *The Raider*, Ford does not attempt the sweeping panorama of the epic historical novel; instead, his canvases are rather small, and his emphasis is the search for meaning in the incidents of everyday life. Even though his plots are characterized by extensive action, as Granville Hicks observed, Ford's primary concern is with motives. Thus, his protagonists are seriously flawed, not heroic; many of them suffer a profound angst and cannot articulate their essentially existential dilemmas. Nevertheless, even in his early fiction, where the object of the protagonists' quest remains elusive, Ford's tone is deeply moral as he suggests that spiritual meaning is possible, somewhere just beyond his characters' grasp.

Ford's first published novel, *Mountains of Gilead,* develops the recurring Ford themes of isolation, lack of direction, and a limited redemption through sacrifice combined with grace. The three principal characters find themselves adrift in a world where the values of the past seem no longer applicable and the virtues of their ancestors seem impossible to match. Thus, through most of the novel, Gratt Shafer remains totally self-absorbed, envying his father's dedication to anthropology and his mother's almost obsessive devotion to her only child, but unable to commit himself to anything, even to self-interest. While at times he wishes to break out of his isolation, his inherent passivity leads him first to continue a long and meaningless relationship with Patsy Jo McCutcheon and later to marry Memphis socialite Eleanor Fite, whose personality parallels his own and thus does not threaten him with any emotional demands.

Similarly, Patsy Jo is the stereotypical 1950s woman, a "Sleeping Beauty" figure waiting for marriage and motherhood to define her personality and give meaning to her existence. Assuming that one day Gratt will marry her, she too drifts through life, working in Somerton's "variety store" until the announcement of his engagement makes her an object of pity for the townspeople. The realization that she has been "jilted" awakens her sense of family honor; goading her father into avenging this insult at last provides a direction to her life. A generation removed from these two, Tom McCutcheon can recall echoes of a more heroic past in the person of his grandfather, but his doubts concerning the continued validity of the cavalier tradition have rendered him ineffectual. Adopting the role of his daughter's avenger reluctantly at first, Tom eventually accepts his destiny as he sees a parallel with the Christian allegory of St. George and the dragon. His anguish at killing Eleanor instead of Gratt is tempered by his satisfaction at having finally proved himself capable of decisive action.

Drawn together by their shared sense of moral responsibility for the deaths of Eleanor and Tom, Gratt and Patsy Jo finally marry, and the birth of their son seems to signal Ford's belief that the continuation of the family provides a bulwark against the apparent inconsequence of individual existence. Hence, though the denouement is not precisely positive, Ford does allow hope for redemption.

In contrast, Ford's second novel, *The Conversion of Buster Drumwright*, directly addresses the question of personal redemption. After many years away from his family, Ocie Hedgepath returns to embrace the role of avenger. The man who murdered his sister is in the local jail and is scheduled to be hanged in just a few days, but his own guilt and sense of family honor along with the goading of his brothers require that Ocie kill the murderer (Drumwright) himself. Since the deputy sheriff will allow no visitors to Drumwright's cell, Ocie approaches the jail in the guise of an itinerant preacher who wishes to save Drumwright's soul. Once inside, Ocie discovers to his chagrin that Drumwright is receptive and ultimately repentant. Still plotting revenge, Ocie arranges to return the next day, ostensibly to baptize Drumwright, though actually he plans to drown this man whom he hates bitterly. As he studies the Biblical accounts of St. Paul in order to answer Drumwright's questions, Ocie himself begins to change, almost imperceptibly at first, and the next day he not only baptizes Drumwright, but confesses his original intent and asks his enemy's forgiveness. Though Ocie is killed by one of his brothers and

Drumwright is about to be hanged, Ford clearly intends this novel to be a modern tragedy, complete with tragic insight and cathartic conclusion.

If *The Conversion of Buster Drumwright* is timeless, *The Liberation of Lord Byron Jones* seems in many ways a product of the political and racial turmoil of the 1960s. Again Ford focuses on the dilemmas facing two middle-aged men. Lord Byron Jones, Somerton's African-American mortician, has become wealthy and influential playing by the rules the Caucasian community has set for him. Having unwisely married Emma, a young woman who considers him stodgy and who soon is blatantly unfaithful, Jones decides that his personal honor requires him to divorce her, even though doing so will require him to publicly name the white deputy sheriff who is her lover. Pressured by the white establishment, including his own white lawyer ridiculed by his wife, and threatened by the sheriff and his deputies, Jones must choose between his habitual position of acquiescence and the requirements of his newly aroused sense of personal dignity.

At the same time, Oman Hedgepath, whom Jones has insisted upon hiring to handle the divorce, faces a similar choice between his duty to his client and his lifetime practice of emotional detachment. Unlike Jones, Oman decides to accede to the wishes of his community and give his client only perfunctory representation. Thus, as the novel ends, Oman finds himself facing a life even more isolated and meaningless than before: his law partnership with his nephew Steve has been dissolved, a bitter and disillusioned Steve has also essentially severed all family ties, Oman's one-time fiancee has died, and Oman has only his own death to anticipate. In contrast, Jones' death has energized various elements of the African-American community. Sonny Boy Mosby's pattern of violence at last has some meaning: as he avenges Jones' murder, the African-American community generally respects Jones' courage, and Jones' funeral introduces into that community the Muslim influence, which seems likely to continue in the person of Emma's son and Jones' heir.

Racial conflict likewise serves as the backdrop for *The Feast of Saint Barnabas*, but again Ford's central focus is the individual's search for meaningful values. Assisted by various incomplete "son of consolation" avatars, several major and minor characters struggle with their own flawed identities and their emotional isolation. Each chapter is related through the consciousness of a different character because, Ford said, "I just find that for some stories I can't get the depth of perception, the third dimension, that I like through the mind of any one character. I don't like omniscience, I really don't. So what I do, I try to work in one mind and then another, sort of like playing a bridge game with yourself, trying to win from all sides."

Some of the novel's characters fail in their duty to their community, and so they become increasingly corrupted and emotionally lost. The most notable example is the African-American landlord Purchase Walker, who deliberately provokes the Ormund City riot to gain a business advantage. After the riot he is reputed to engage in voodoo rituals, and he loses the respect of his tenants. In contrast, the riot seems to purify the soul of Father Ned Matthews, the black priest who for sixteen years has served the community's Episcopal mission. Previously too absorbed in his own personal tragedies to give his full attention to his parishioners, he achieves a high level of commitment and sacrifice during the riots, and his closing speech sounds a note of hope as well as a somewhat naive benediction.

Likewise, Boston Humes and Rann Cutler accept the operation of grace and ultimately achieve differing degrees of redemption. Despite lingering doubts concerning its prospects, Humes serves on the Biracial Committee to ease racial tensions in Ormund City. The most profound change, though, is the transformation in Rann's character. Initially a cynical, two-bit hustler willing to betray anyone for his own profit, Rann trusts no one, not even his own family; for years he has been completely isolated, avoiding any type of commitment. Rescued from death through the selfless courage of the Norse sailor Gudliev Lid, Rann realizes that he has also been emotionally rescued by the love and acceptance of Cynthia, a young woman he originally intended simply to use and discard. As the novel ends, he has decided to marry her, to take her to meet his family in Middle Tennessee, and to generally to become a respectable citizen and responsible family man.

In his last published novel, *The Raider*, Ford chronicles the settling of West Tennessee. Elias McCutcheon and his neighbors are typical of those Ford called his people: "Scotch-Irish, English, and African. And they are really interesting to me." Rejecting the myth of cavalier settlement, Ford says of these Southern pioneers, "The people came to this place because they had to, they were pushed. They didn't have anything. That's the reason they jumped off and came here. Yet that shows they are venturesome people, and they are good people, and they won't submit to oppression easily. I like their spirit. They're individualistic people and they're good workers."

Given the author's admiration for this character type, it is not surprising that *The Raider* is his most epical novel and Elias McCutcheon is his most sympathetic protagonist. Elias' adult years span the roughly thirty-year period of transition from frontier to plantation in West Tennessee. The sole survivor of a cholera epidemic in Middle Tennessee, Elias moves west to lose himself in a wild land inhabited only by a few Native American families. Soon, his friendship with Shokotee McNeilly (the head of one of these families) leads to marriage with McNeilly's adopted daughter, Jane Nail. With the help of Jake (a slave McNeilly gives the young couple as a wedding present) and Leota (one of McNeilly's dependents who becomes a kind of housekeeper), Elias and Jane build a plantation and raise two sons, Isaac and Willy. A hard-working farmer and a devoted family man, Elias manages to overcome threats ranging from marauders to rabies and crop failures, but his failures in judgment result in both physical harm and emotional anguish for Jane. One source of pain is his longtime affair with their neighbor, Ellen Ashe. If Jane incorporates the innocence of the frontier, Ellen embodies both the charm and the selfishness of the plantation South. Nevertheless, Elias finds himself repeatedly drawn to her; Jane knows her husband will not leave her, but she is hurt by his divided loyalties.

Most destructive to the McCutcheon family and the entire society, though, is the Civil War. Again loyalties become the central issue. A longtime Unionist, Elias vehemently opposes secession, but he accepts a command in the Confederate army because he considers it a duty he owes his neighbors. Loyalty also figures in similar decisions by Isaac, Jake, and Free Soiler Jasper Coon, all

of whom enlist because they are devoted to Elias. During the war, Jane dies as the result of her loyalty to Elias, and Willy is killed in one of the last skirmishes; after the war, Isaac sets out for a new life in the East, and Ellen spurns Elias for a wealthy carpetbagger. Thus, at the novel's end, Elias seems to have come full circle, but he is not defeated because despite his occasional lapses he has generally managed to maintain his commitments to personal honor and community responsibility.

Generally, critics have treated Ford's short stories more favorably than his novels, perhaps because their themes are wider ranging and less topical. The earliest and arguably the best of these stories are collected in *Fishes, Birds, and Sons of Men*. Here Ford portrays the destructive effects of poverty and racial injustice ("The Bitter Bread" and "Winterkill"), the causes and effects of violent death ("The Highwayman" and "Acts of Self-Defense"), the results of fear and self-delusion (the title story, as well as "How the Mountains Are" and "Look Down, Look Down"), the isolation of the outsider ("Wild Honey" and "Beyond the Sunset"), corrosive family discord ("The Messenger" and "The Rabbit"), death through hubris ("To the Open Water"), a young boy's initiation ("The Cave," "The Trout," and "The Cow"), typical Southern humor ("Surest Thing in Show Business" and "The Britches Thief"), and strange mixture of sexual attraction and personal loathing that develops in a relationship continued only as a matter of habit and convenience ("A Strange Sky" apparently an early exploration of the characters portrayed somewhat more sympathetically in *Mountains of Gilead*). Though Ford continued to publish short stories throughout his career, these later pieces have not yet been collected.

Jesse Hill Ford once declared that writing is "as necessary as religion" because the writer "makes sense out of what is largely senseless and thus provides man's best hope." No doubt for Ford, whom *Tennessean* publisher John Seigenthaler described as "one of the most talented and tortured writers the South has produced," fiction was a way of addressing the fundamental moral questions confronted by twentieth century Southerners, adrift from earlier rural values and attempting to formulate an alternate acceptable in their urban/suburban society. To achieve this goal, Ford created a series of explosive, insensitive, or at least seriously flawed central characters; forced them to confront moral dilemmas resolvable only through commitment to such values as personal honor and loyalty, combined in the later fiction with acceptance of grace and application of Christian ethics; then finally allowed some of these characters to determine a meaning for their lives and, thus, to achieve at least a degree of moral victory. Ford acknowledges man's dual nature, but re-enforces the importance of the human spirit. In fact, his greatest legacy may be his affirmation of hope.

—Charmaine Allen Mosby

FORD, Richard

Born: Jackson, Mississippi, 16 February 1944. **Education:** Michigan State University, B.A. 1966; attended Washington University Law School, 1967-68; University of California, Berkeley, M.F.A.

1970. **Family:** Married Kristina Hensley, 1968. **Career:** Assistant professor of English, Williams College, Williamstown, Massachusetts, 1978-79; lecturer, Princeton University, New Jersey, 1980-81; sportwsriter, *Inside Sports*, New York, 1981; instructor, Harvard University, Cambridge, Massachusetts, 1994; director, William Faulkner Foundation, University of Rennes, Paris, France; Writer-in-Residence, Northwestern University, Evanston, Illinois, spring semesters, 1997-98. **Awards:** Guggenheim fellowship, 1977; National Endowment for the Arts fellowship, 1978, 1983; New York Public Library Literary Lion award, 1989; American Academy award, 1989; Echoing Green Foundation award, 1991; PEN/Faulkner award, 1995, and Pulitzer Prize for Fiction, for *Independence Day*, 1995. **Agent:** Amanda Urban, International Creative Management, 40 West 57th Street, New York, New York 10016.

PUBLICATIONS

Novels

A Piece of My Heart. New York, Harper & Row, 1976.
The Ultimate Good Luck. Boston, Houghton Mifflin, 1981.
The Sportswriter. New York, Vintage, 1986.
Wildlife. New York, Atlantic Monthly Press, 1990.
Independence Day. New York, Knopf, 1995.

Short Story Collections

Rock Springs. New York, Atlantic Monthly Press, 1987.
Women With Men. New York, Knopf, 1997.

Other

Editor with Shannon Ravenel, *The Best American Short Stories 1990*. Boston, Houghton Mifflin, 1990.
Editor, *The Granta Book of the American Short Story*. London, Granta, 1991.

Screenplay: *Bright Angel*, 1991.

Uncollected Non-Fiction

"Walker Percy: Not Just Whistling Dixie," in *National Review*, 13 May 1977.
"My Mother, in Memory," in *Harper's*, August 1977.
"Country Matters," in *Harper's*, July 1981.
"The Three Kings: Hemingway, Faulkner, and Fitzgerald," in *Esquire*, December 1983.
"The Boss Observed," in *Esquire*, December 1985.
"Accommodations," in *Harper's*, June 1988.
"First Things First: One More Writer's Beginnings," in *Harper's*, August 1988.
"Heartbreak Motels," in *Harper's*, August 1989.
"An Urge for Going: Why I Don't Live Where I Used to Live," in *Harper's*, February 1992.
"What We Write, Why We Write It, and Who Cares," in *Michigan Quarterly Review*, Summer 1992.
"A Minors Affair," in *Harper's*, September 1992.
"I Must Be Going: On Moving," in *The Utne Reader*, January 1993.
"Bascombe, In Reality," in *Esquire*, July 1993.

"Bonhomie for a Southern Belletrist," in *The New Yorker*, 19 February 1996.
"Behemoths on Wheels," in *The New York Times*, 20 August 1997.
"In the Face: A Metaphysics of Fisticuffs," in *The New Yorker*, 16 September 1997.

*   *   *

Like Ralph Waldo Emerson, Richard Ford believes that the "lived life" is "its own evidence." Accordingly, his fictional characters never evade the realities that are attendant upon their own choices, their own successes and failures. Somewhat rootless himself, Ford creates many characters who wander and wonder widely, seeking some connection with others but often experiencing their most vivid moments of awareness in utter solitude. Frantic sex, unpredictable violence and sudden death intrude often in Ford's fiction, as if to confirm that human beings make desperate and sometimes unwise attempts to substitute physical contact for intimacy. In settings as diverse as Mississippi, Montana and Paris, among others, Ford situates a variety of characters who struggle to come to terms with their pasts, presents and futures.

In his first novel, *A Piece of My Heart* (1976), Ford uses two characters with differing sensibilities, Robard Hewes and Sam Newel, to govern the narrative structure. Alternating section by section and switching from Hewes's point of view to Newel's, the novel recounts each man's journey to a small island that does not appear on any map but exists on the Mississippi River between Arkansas and Mississippi. The physically grotesque proprietors of the island, Mark and Fidelia Lamb, act as foils for the emotionally hollow men who seek solace there. The Lambs epitomize a kind of intimacy that neither Robard nor Sam seems capable of sustaining. On the run from law school and painful memories of his childhood, Sam goes to the island at the request of his girlfriend, Beebe, the Lambs's granddaughter. Hoping to come to terms with himself, Sam must grapple with nature's unpredictable forces and his own inability to reconcile his father's existence with his own. Robard comes to the island to renew his torrid affair with Beuna, his cousin, leaving behind his wife in California, a decision he will regret. Alternately comic and tragic, the novel draws upon the gothic for its intensity, using imagery of suffocation, entrapment and drowning to reveal that neither Robard's strength nor Sam's intellect can save them from the choices both have made.

Set in Mexico, not Mississippi, Ford's second novel *The Ultimate Good Luck* (1981) tells the story of Harry Quinn, a Vietnam veteran who attempts to free his ex-girlfriend's brother, Sonny, from prison, where he has been incarcerated on counts of drug possession and trafficking. Modernist in its premise— the world is an alien place and human beings are doomed to isolation in it, seeking connection with others but often thwarted in that attempt—the novel is spare in language and style and has reminded many readers of Hemingway's work. Never content simply to emulate, however, Ford subverts the novel's ostensibly modernist theme. Caught in a foreign web of political intrigue and violence, Harry and his ex-girlfriend *do* connect with each other, experiencing a moment of "locatedness," as Ford calls it, an intense and fleeting spot of intimacy that is not dependent on time or place but rather is a kind of spiritual reckoning with self and other.

The Sportswriter (1986) marks a turn in language and style for Ford. Told in the first person from the perspective of Frank Bascombe, this novel chronicles its musing narrator's attempts to come to terms with the recent death of his son from Reye's syndrome and his divorce from the boy's mother, called "X" in the novel because Ford could not figure out an appropriate name for her. The designation remains eerily appropriate, however, since she is Frank's "ex," after all, and Frank remains so enthralled with her that his longing becomes almost nameless. Such longing does not keep Frank single. In the novel's present, he is dating Vicki and preparing to go with her on a trip to Detroit where, as a sportswriter, Frank will interview a crippled professional football player for an "inspirational" story. The story turns out not to be so inspirational, and neither does his later weekend with Vicki's parents, or, for that matter, his return home to grapple with the suicide of his friend, Walter Luckett. Set on Easter weekend, the novel is religious only in the sense that Frank stuggles to make sense out of his life. Despite the rather grim plot elements, *The Sportswriter* is not a gloomy book, mainly because of Ford's deft manipulation of Bascombe's voice, which is at once self-deprecating and solipsistic, wry and poignant.

Set primarily around Great Falls, Montana, *Rock Springs* (1987) includes the stories of men, both young and old, who are divorced, parentless, on the run from the law, or all of the above. Many of the stories are classic rite of passage tales in which a young boy experiences betrayal by a parent or friend, wrestles with sexual desire, or realizes that there are many questions in this life that resist easy answers. Abandonment and familial dissolution are recurrent themes, ones that Ford will also deal with in his next novel, *Wildlife* (1990). Here, the young protagonist Joe must witness his parents' relationship dissolve under both external and internal pressures. His father loses his job and must leave the family to seek work putting out fires; the smoldering of these fires becomes symbolic also of Joe's parents' relationship, doomed yet slow to disappear. Joe witnesses both parents' imperfections: his father's temper and his mother's indiscretions with another man. Told from his adult perspective, the narrative becomes Joe's concession that there is much in life that defies control and human understanding and that one human being can never completely know another.

With the publication of *Independence Day* in 1995, Ford moves away from the violent landscapes of the West and back to crowded eastern suburbia, back into the head of bemused and befuddled Frank Bascombe, now a real estate agent. This time the holiday weekend is July 4th, as the book's title suggests, and the novel deals with the notion of independence—how that privilege, on an individual level, may exclude and isolate even as it imparts freedom. On another journey, this time with his other son to the Baseball Hall of Fame, Frank Bascombe seeks a better understanding of his son and of himself. Coining terms such as the "Existence Period," Bascombe continues in his role as the overly intellectualized narrator whose voice we are forced to trust even as we recognize its penchant for prevarication. The economy of the place—one *is* what one can afford to buy, where one lives—and the changing American landscape are other phenomena that fascinate Bascombe, who regales the reader with his myriad theories about life, the universe and everything. For this novel, Ford won both the Pulitzer Prize for Fiction and the PEN/Faulkner Award, marking the only time one novel has ever received both prestigious recognitions of excellence and securing Ford's own place in literary history.

Ford's most recent work, *Women with Men* (1997), is a collection of three novellas, two of which have been published previously (one in *Granta*, one in *The New Yorker*). Each novella functions as a vignette, capturing a relatively short but critical period in its characters' lives. The themes are familiar: loss, misunderstanding, failed attempts at intimacy, violence, growing up. In "The Womanizer," Martin Austin leaves his wife for a woman he met on a business trip to Paris, only to lose that relationship when he fails to watch the Parisian woman's son closely enough, a mistake that ends in the boy's molestation. Swept along in events, Martin passively succumbs to his own failures, finally acknowledging that he must think through his choices, or at least ponder his past. "Jealous," the middle work on the collection, is the most optimistic of the three, centered around the journey of Larry from Montana to Seattle, where he will visit his mother. A poignant testimony to the strength of his relationship with his father, this narrative demonstrates the frailty of adulthood, the easily pierced veil of "maturity." By contrast, in his youth Larry exhibits remarkable insight, happening upon the truth about intimacy as the adults in his life founder all around him. The final vignette, "Occidentals," tells the story of Charley and Helen and their trip to Paris to celebrate the French translation of a novel that Charley has published previously in the United States to little critical acclaim. The trip proves ultimately disappointing, as trips in Ford's fiction often do, serving to emphasize the emotional distance between Charley and Helen despite their physical intimacy. This story ends in Helen's suicide. Too caught up in his own disappointments, Charley fails to recognize her despair.

Unflinching in characterization and precise in language, Richard Ford forces the reader to determine his characters' triumphs and failures. His fiction has been favorably compared to William Faulkner's, Ernest Hemingway's and, more recently, to the minimalist work of Raymond Carver. Ford insists, however, that he is indebted to more writers than he could possibly name, citing a vast Western literary heritage for inspiration.

—Elinor Ann Walker

FOWLER, Connie May

Born: Raleigh, North Carolina, 1959. **Education:** University of Tampa, B.A. English; University of Kansas, M.A. in English. **Family:** Married Mika Fowler (photographer), 1987. **Career:** Writer. **Awards:** Grant from Florida Division of Cultural Affairs, 1992-93, for *River of Hidden Dreams*. **Agent:** c/o Putnam, 200 Madison Ave., New York, New York 10016.

PUBLICATIONS

Novels

Sugar Cage. New York, Putnam, 1992.
River of Hidden Dreams. New York, Putnam, 1994.
Before Women Had Wings. New York, Putnam, 1996.

*   *   *

For Connie May Fowler, the daughter of a single, alcoholic mother, writing provided salvation from a tumultuous life of near poverty. Drawing upon her experiences, Fowler has written three moving novels all set in Florida—where she has lived most of her life —that lend narrative voice to low-income characters (several of them alcoholic) of varied racial and cultural backgrounds.

Though they live in a sterile present-day world, many of Fowler's characters have a keen sense of the spiritual and the supernatural and live largely mythic lives framed within Florida's remaining natural beauty. As Fowler explained to one interviewer, "We live in a land of myth—of stories and songs and deeds inspired by resilient people living amid rare and diverse ecosystems."

Fowler's debut novel, *Sugar Cage*, is a compelling mix of domestic life and the supernatural, set in drab central Florida with the rise of the civil rights movement providing a social backdrop. We meet Inez Temple, a black maid well-versed in witchcraft, who foretells the future of Rose Looney, a white newlywed. Inez predicts a "sugar cage"—a heartbreaking marriage where "love will eat her up" and Rose will crave the "sweet poison" of Charlie, her philandering husband. Emory, their teenaged son, becomes a sugar cane cutter; he comes of age within the arms of the novel's most vivid character, Soleil Marie Beuauvoir, a part-Seminole, part-Haitian voodoo priestess. In a sometimes heavy-handed manner, Fowler mixes in observations about race: Emory and Soleil Marie are shamed by whites at a carnival, and Inez warns of the coming fall of Martin Luther King, Jr., at Memphis. *Sugar Cage* can prove a difficult read because of Fowler's use of nine different characters to share narrative duties. The effect is muddled, reflecting the blend of routine acts, carnal passions, and magic.

River of Hidden Dreams also has multiple narrators to tell a tale where the mystical weaves its way into the everyday. Sadie, a fortyish woman, lives in the Florida Keys on the small boat that she inherited from her grandmother and her mother. Though Sadie uses pop jargon to analyze herself, she is haunted by the imaginative stories handed down by her forebears. Sadie's grandmother, Mima, was a Plains Indian who was kidnapped by soldiers and raised as a white. Though Mima forgot her native language and beliefs, she could not fit into Southern society and found deep love only with a mulatto boy named Mr. Sammy, who owned a magical chicken. Shortly before the two lovers parted, Sadie's mother was conceived; mother and daughter held an angry silence only until Sadie's grandmother reclaimed her heritage and found self-fulfillment. Sadie, however, is spiritually barren at the novel's start. Between emotional visits from her Cuban-American boyfriend, Carlos, Sadie wonders how much bearing her ancestor's stories have upon the "reality" of her present-day life. She is given chance at redemption by transporting the body of a mummified child up the Intracoastal Waterway to the fort where the soldiers had taken her grandmother.

In *River of Hidden Dreams*, Fowler succeeds in invoking a "vision of an America enriched in spirit by the mingling of cultures," as Judith Paterson noted in the *New York Times Book Review*. Paterson found several similarities between *River of Hidden Dreams* and *Sugar Cage*: "Both novels share a vision of a dry Anglo culture being secretly and magically inspirited by a rich undercurrent of African, Latino, and American Indian influences. Both stories unfold around a group of narrators who are so differ-

ent from one another in outlook and culture that the English they speak hardly seems to be one language."

Fowler's third novel, *Before Women Had Wings*, unlike her previous novels, features only one narrator—nine-year-old Avocet Abigail Jackson, or Bird, for short. Bird and her sister, Phoebe, were given birds' nicknames by their mother in the hope they would fly above the mess in their lives. Bird lives in poverty in an orange grove until her alcoholic father—a wanna-be country music singer prone to drunken rages—commits suicide. Her mother, Glory Marie, takes her children to Tampa, where they live in a weathered trailer—just as Fowler did when she grew up.

Like other heroines in Fowler's novels, Bird meets a woman with strong spiritual presence—Miss Zora, who lives in a cabin near Bird's school. Miss Zora is a healer who teaches Bird and her sister about dignity and forgiveness, which Bird needs when her mother starts to get drunk and abuses her badly. But, with the metaphorical power of a fairy tale, Bird and Phoebe are able to escape and soar to safety with their new-found wings in the kind of blend of realism and fantasy that characterizes Fowler's work. Fowler called *Before Women Had Wings* a "terribly personal book," and her brave honesty resonated with many readers. *Before Women Had Wings* was adapted into a 1997 television movie starring Oprah Winfrey and Ellen Barkin.

—Eric Patterson

FOX, William Price, Jr.

Born: Waukegan, Illinois, 9 April 1926. **Education:** University of South Carolina, B.A. 1950. **Military Service:** U.S Army Air Force, 1943-46. **Career:** Packaging salesman, New York City; instructor, University of Iowa, Writers Workshop, 1968-72, instructor in journalism, 1976-76; writer-in-residence, University of South Carolina, 1976-90s; contributor of numerous non-fiction articles to such magazines as *Harper's* and *Sports Illustrated*; producer, *Writer's Workshop* video series (a production of the University of South Carolina and the South Carolina ETV network), published by the Public Broadcasting System, 1980-82. **Agent:** Lynn Nesbit, International Creative Management, 40 West 57th Street, New York, New York 10019.

PUBLICATIONS

Short Fiction

Southern Fried. Gold Medal Books, New York, 1962.
Southern Fried Plus Six. Philadelphia, Lippincott, 1968.
Dr. Golf. Philadelphia, Lippincott, 1963.
Moonshine Light, Moonshine Bright. Philadelphia, Lippincott, 1967.
Dixiana Moon. New York, Viking, 1981.
Chitlin' Strut and Other Madrigals. Atlanta, Peachtree Press, 1983.

Novel

Ruby Red. Philadelphia, Lippincott, 1971.

Nonfiction

How 'Bout Them Gamecocks!. Columbia, University of South Carolina Press, 1985.
Golfing in the Carolinas. Winston-Salem, J. F. Blair, 1990.
Lunatic Wind: Surviving the Storm of the Century. Chapel Hill, Algonquin, 1992.
South Carolina: Off the Beaten Path. Old Saybrook, Connecticut, Globe Pequot Press, 1996.

*

Screenplays: Episodes of *The Beverly Hillbillies*, CBS Television, 1964-65; *Southern Fried*, 1967; *Off We Go*, 1968; *Cold Turkey*, 1968; *Fast Nerves*, 1969.

Critical Studies: "William Price Fox: The Spirit of Character and the Spirit of Place," by Joan Bobbitt, *South Carolina Review*, Vol. 9, 1976; "William Price Fox," by Matthew J. Bruccoli, *Conversations with Writers I*, Detroit, Bruccoli Clark/Gale Research, 1977; "Fact and Fiction in William Price Fox," by Charles Israel, *Kennesaw Review*, Spring 1988.

William Price Fox comments:

I've had a lot of luck in writing and think much of it has been because I've never tightened up and taken myself too seriously. I guess I find almost anything I deal with slightly funny. And I think students seem to like the way I tell them to relax and write run-on sentences when they get in trouble, or if they can't spell, smudge it.

*   *   *

Although he has written many non-fiction articles for some of the top magazines in America—*Harper's* and *Sports Illustrated*, for example—William Price Fox, Jr., is known as a prose fiction writer in the tradition of the Humorists of the Old Southwest (1830-60). Like Johnson Jones Hooper's *Some Adventures of Captain Simon Suggs* (1845) and George Washington Harris's *Sut Lovingood: Yarns Spun by a "Nat'ral Born Durn'd Fool"* (1867), Fox's short stories and novels are comic tales filled with eccentric characters whose antic behavior sees them entangled in sexual escapades, fundamentalist religion, and borderline legal operations.

Southern writers have long made use of the comic possibilities found in the poor white segment of southern culture. In addition to the Southwest Humorists, writers as diverse as William Byrd (*History of the Dividing Line*, 1728, 1841), William Faulkner ("Spotted Horses," 1931), and Flannery O'Connor ("A Good Man Is Hard to Find," 1953), have exploited characters from the lower socio-economical class in many of their hilarious writings. So it is with Fox, whose fiction is filled with rednecks and small-town hicks.

A high school dropout and son of a moonshiner father, of whom he is especially proud, Fox has done his best writing about blue-collar types in rundown houses and cafes in and around Columbia, South Carolina, where he grew up. Although he treats his characters with raw humor at times, he never shows any contempt or cynicism towards the grifters and losers who find themselves on the razor's edge of survival. In fact, he clearly admires these uneducated outcasts from the good life for their spunk and courage to exert some level of control over their narrow lives.

In *Ruby Red* (1971), for example, the central character, Ruby Jean ("Red") Jamison, is a poor, ignorant girl from Columbia who aspires to become a country-western singer in Nashville. Her only problem is that she has more ambition than talent, yet she finally achieves success of a sort by hosting a 5 a.m. radio talk show in Nashville. Like Moll Flanders in Daniel Defoe's novel, Ruby achieves her goal through hard work, luck, and sex. To make it to the top, Ruby sleeps with Spider Hornsby, the town bootlegger, with Jimmy Lee Rideout, her albino manager-songwriter, and with John Harmon, a fading country singer. However, at no time does Fox portray Ruby as corrupt or as someone who treats people as stepping stones in a rapacious career. Instead, Ruby is shown to care for her men and enjoys pleasing them sexually. Not once does she discard her lovers in a callous manner, even though it is clear that nothing is going to stand in her way to becoming a "star" in the country music business. As Ruby says about herself, "This is one gal that knows how to take care of herself."

Fox's best talent, though, lies in the sketch or short story form with which he began his writing career. His first book-length publication was a 40-cent paperback called *Southern Fried* (1962), still considered his best and most widely read work. Consisting of sixteen sketches and short stories, *Southern Fried* exhibits the best characteristics of Fox's fiction. A master of the vernacular style, he displays a sure ear for southern speech rhythms as, for example, in the title of one sketch, "Have You Ever Rode the Southern?" and in "Lower Mulberry," in which a garbage truck driver reprimands the neighborhood children who love to climb all over his garbage truck with, "All right, you kids, quit messing round that truck."

The stories in this first volume further show Fox's affinity with the Humorists of the Old Southwest in their characterization of lower class whites and African Americans who are uneducated, who work at low paying and low skill jobs, and who are one step away from larceny and violence. But above all, many of the stories in this first volume are based on the contest, a staple of the Humor of the Old Southwest. In this type of story, one person tries to get the better of another character through wit or by a feat of strength. The winner usually demonstrates moral superiority or greater courage while the loser gets his comeuppance and is shown to be a fool. In "Pit Fight," for example, a wildcat destroys dog after dog with its long, razor-like claws in a staged contest until one of the spectators becomes so fed up with seeing so many good dogs killed that he takes a long vacation to train his hound to defeat the wildcat by circling it long enough to grab it by the neck and snap its bones. The crowd that has watched this "sporting" event is ecstatic with the outcome.

Other stories based on the contest motif are "The Ordeal of Lonnie Register," a bragging match between two men, "Razor Fight at the St. Louis Café," in which a small, shy man overcomes a large bully, and "The Hair of the Dog," which shows how a baseball coach wins a game by keeping his star player drunk.

The best example of the contest theme is found in "Southern Fried," the most accomplished story in the volume and one that clearly shows the triumph of virtue over arrogance and pride. Fleetwood Driggers, who has "good soda-fountain hands and a nice smile," lords it over Preacher Watts, an African American who works in the kitchen preparing fried foods at the Holly Yates Café. The antagonism between Fleetwood and Preacher grows until one night, after hours, Fleetwood threatens to beat up Preacher and cut him with his knife. In order to frustrate the ill-tempered Fleetwood, Preacher challenges him to a contest of soda-jerking and beats him by preparing the drinks and banana splits faster than the alleged town master. The victory deflates the spirit of the foolish braggart, leaving him less spiteful than before.

These contest stories show the basic theme that runs through all of Fox's fiction. Poor, uneducated people are worthy of our attention and admiration because they have the wit, courage, and survival instincts necessary to triumph over adversity. Fox's stories applaud dignity and fidelity to principle while mocking proud and self-centered people who try to use other people for their own ends. His sympathetic characters may have stereotypical, comic southern names—Ruby Jean Jamison, Preacher Roebuck Alexander, Spider Harold Hornsby, and Thelma Jean Hooker—but they are good people who win in the end.

—Harold Woodell

FRANKLIN, John Hope

Born: Rentiesville, Oklahoma, 2 January 1915. **Education:** Fisk University, A.B. 1935; Harvard University, A.M. 1936, Ph.D. 1941. **Family:** Married Aurelia E. Whittington, 11 June 1940; one child. **Career:** Professor of history, Fisk University, Nashville, 1936-37, St. Augustine's College, Raleigh, 1938-43; North Carolina College (now North Carolina Central University), Durham, 1943-47, Howard University, Washington, D.C., 1947-56; professor of history and chairman of department, Brooklyn College of the City University of New York, Brooklyn, 1956-64; professor of history, University of Chicago, 1964-82, John Matthews Manly Distinguished Service Professor, 1969-82, chairman of history department, 1967-70; James B. Duke Professor of History, 1982-85, professor emeritus since 1985, Duke University, Durham; visiting professor at University of California, Harvard University, University of Wisconsin, Cornell University, University of Hawaii, Australia National University, Salzburg (Austria) Seminar, and other institutions; Pitt Professor of American History and Institutions, Cambridge University, 1962-63; Board of Foreign Scholarships, member, 1962-69, chairman, 1966-69; member of board of trustees, Fisk University, 1947-84, and De Sable Museum, Chicago; chairman, advisory board to the Presidential Initiative on Race, appointed 1997. **Awards:** Guggenheim fellowships, 1950-51, 1973-74; Jules F. Landry Award, 1975, for *A Southern Odyssey*; Clarence L. Holte Literary Award, 1986, for *George Washington Williams: A Biography*; Presidential Medal of Freedom in 1995; honorary degrees from numerous institutions, including LL.D. from Morgan State University, 1960, Lincoln University, 1961, Virginia State College, 1961, Hamline University, 1965, Lincoln College, 1965, Fisk University, 1965, Columbia University, 1969, University of Notre Dame, 1970, and Harvard Uni-

versity, 1981; A.M. from Cambridge University, 1962; L.H.D. from Long Island University, 1964, University of Massachusetts, 1964, and Yale University, 1977; Litt.D. from Princeton University, 1972.

PUBLICATIONS

Nonfiction

The Free Negro in North Carolina, 1790-1860. Chapel Hill, University of North Carolina Press, 1943.
The Militant South, 1800-1860. Cambridge, Massachusetts, Belknap Press, 1956.
Reconstruction After the Civil War. Chicago, University of Chicago Press, 1962.
The Emancipation Proclamation. New York, Doubleday, 1963.
Racial Equality in America. Chicago, University of Chicago Press, 1976.
A Southern Odyssey: Travelers in the Antebellum North. Baton Rouge, Louisiana State University Press, 1976.
George Washington Williams: A Biography. Chicago, University of Chicago Press, 1985.
Race & History: Selected Essays, 1938-1988. Baton Rouge, Louisiana State University Press, 1990.
Runaway Slaves: Rebels on the Plantation, 1790-1860, with Loren Schweninger. New York, Oxford University Press, 1999.

Editor

The Civil War Diary of J. T. Ayers. Chicago, Illinois State Historical Society, 1947.
From Slavery to Freedom: A History of Negro Americans, with Alfred A. Moss, Jr. New York, Knopf, 1947; published as *From Slavery to Freedom: A History of African Americans*, New York, McGraw-Hill, 1994.
A Fool's Errand. Cambridge, Massachusetts, Belknap Press, 1961.
Army Life in a Black Regiment. Boston, Beacon Press, 1962.
Three Negro Classics. New York, Avon, 1965.
Land of the Free: A History of the United States, with John W. Caughey and Ernest R. May. New York, Benziger, 1965; teacher's edition, 1971.
The Negro in Twentieth Century America: A Reader on the Struggle for Civil Rights, with Isadore Starr. New York, Vintage Books, 1967.
Color and Race. New York, Houghton, 1968.
The Suppression of the African Slave Trade. Baton, Rouge, Louisiana State University Press, 1969.
Reminiscences of an Active Life: The Autobiography of John R. Lynch. Chicago, University of Chicago Press, 1970.
Illustrated History of Black Americans, with the editors of Time-Life Books. New York, Time-Life, 1970.
Black Leaders of the Twentieth Century, with August Meier. Urbana, University of Illinois Press, 1982.
American History Series. Wheeling, Illinois, Harlan Davidson, Inc., 1985.
The Color Line: Legacy for the Twenty-first Century. Columbia, University of Missouri Press, 1993.
African Americans and the Living Constitution, with Genna Rae McNeil. Washington, D.C., Smithsonian Institution Press, 1995.

My Life and an Era: The Autobiography of Buck Colbert Franklin,
with John Whittington Franklin. Baton Rouge, Louisiana State
University Press, 1997.

General editor, *Zenith Book* (series on secondary education). New
York, Doubleday, 1965.
General editor, *Negro American Biographies and Autobiographies*
(series). Chicago, University of Chicago Press, 1969.

Other

Contributor *Problems in American History.* New York Prentice-
Hall, 1952.
Contributor, *The Negro Thirty Years Afterward.* Washington,
D.C., Howard University Press, 1955.
Contributor, *The Americans: Ways of Life and Thought.* New
York, Cohen & West, 1956.
Contributor, *Issues in University Education.* New York, Harper,
1959.
Contributor, *Lincoln for the Ages.* New York, Doubleday, 1960.
Contributor, *The Southerner as American.* Chapel Hill, Univer-
sity of North Carolina Press, 1960.
Contributor, *American History: Recent Interpretations.* New York,
Crowell, 1962.
Contributor, *Soon One Morning.* New York, Knopf, 1963.
Contributor, *The Atlantic Future.* New York, Longmans, Green,
1964.
Contributor, *The South in Continuity and Change.* Durham, Duke
University Press, 1965.
Contributor, *The American Negro Reference Book.* New York,
Prentice-Hall, 1966.
Contributor, *New Frontiers of the American Reconstruction.*
Urnbana, University of Illinois Press, 1966.
Contributor, *The Negro American.* New York, Houghton, 1966.
Contributor, *The American Primer.* Chicago, University of Chi-
cago Press, 1966.
Contributor, *The Comparative Approach to American History.*
New York, Basic Books, 1968.
Contributor, *William Wells Brown: Author and Reformer.* Chi-
cago, University of Chicago Press, 1969.
Contributor, *American Artist.* Chicago, University of Chicago
Press, 1969.
Contributor, *Crusade for Justice: The Autobiography of Ida B.
Wells,* 1970.
Contributor, *Chant of Saints.* Urbana, University of Illinois Press,
1979.
Contributor, *The Voices of Negro Protest in America.* New York,
Greenwood, 1980.
Contributor, *A Melting Pot or a Nation of Minorities.* Austin,
University of Texas Press, 1986.
Contributor, *This Road to Freedom.* Charlotte, Carolina Wren
Press, 1990.
Contributor, *American Studies in Black and White: Selected Es-
says, 1949-1989.* Amherst, University of Massachusetts, 1991.
Contributor, *To Be Free.* New York, Carol Publishing, 1992.

*   *   *

When President Bill Clinton honored John Hope Franklin with
the Presidential Medal of Freedom in 1995, he acclaimed the historian as one who "has both lived and chronicled the history of
race in America." From his birth in the back of a post office in
the all-Black frontier community of Rentiesville, Oklahoma, to his
1997 appointment as the chairman of the Advisory Board to the
President's Initiative on Race, Franklin's life, research and publications bear witness to nearly a century of American race relations and help correct the misrecording of this country's rich heritage.

Inspired at Harvard by Professor Arthur M. Schlesinger, Sr.,
and encouraged by Professor Paul H. Buck, Franklin's dissertation, *The Free Negro In North Carolina, 1790-1860* (1943) examines the "problem" of the free Negro and his status within a larger
pre-Civil War community; Franklin recognized the attitudes of the
larger community as a lingering problem within mid-twentieth century America. The monograph set the standard for the meticulous archival research which Franklin insisted upon throughout
his career. Much of his early research was completed in a separate room in segregated state archives, nor did Franklin's later reputation as a preeminent historian exempt him from the humiliation
of racism, some of which he reveals in "John Hope Franklin: A
Life of Learning," his Charles Homer Haskins Lecture to the American Council of Learned Societies in 1988.

In 1947, Franklin published his influential *From Slavery to Freedom* (6th edition, 1994). In expanded editions reflecting recent scholarship and interests, Franklin, in collaboration with Alfred A. Moss,
traces the history of African Americans beginning in the lands of their
forebearers, such as Ghana and Mali, and describes their way of life
irrevocably changed by the slave trade. He covers the struggle for
freedom in the Western Hemisphere and carries the study into the
twentieth century with chapters that examine the two World Wars,
the Harlem Renaissance, the Depression and the New Deal, the post-
war push for full equality, the Black Revolution of the 1960s, and
new forms of activism in the Reagan years. A classic after more
than forty years, the volume is still considered the authoritative history of African Americans.

During the 1940s, Franklin also began work on a second major
project, *George Washington Williams: A Biography* (1985), a study
that reinstated Williams in the respected circle of Gilded Age historians. Almost a prelude of Franklin's own work, Williams' two-
volumed *The History of the Negro Race in America 1619 to 1890*
is one of the first academic investigations of Blacks in America;
Franklin discovered the volumes while browsing the shelves in
North Carolina College in Durham, where he was teaching. Over
four decades, recounted in the opening chapter "Stalking George
Washington Williams," Franklin gathered the sparse evidence of
the nineteenth century historian's life beginning in Pennsylvania
and covering three continents to his obscure burial in Blackpool,
England. Later, Franklin placed a black granite slab on the grave
commemorating "George Washington Williams, Afro-American
Historian, 1849-1891." (Noting the importance of rescuing the
lives of Afro-American predecessors from obscurity, many critics
point out the similarity of Alice Walker finding and marking the
grave of Zora Neale Hurston in Florida.) Through the continuing
publication of *From Slavery to Freedom* and the Williams biography, Franklin introduced and solidified the academic study of Afro-
American history.

Several of Franklin's other books remain in demand, including
Reconstruction After the Civil War (1962). Here Franklin covers

the controversial period with his typically even-handed analysis of the conduct of local governments and the qualifications of participants on post-war legislatures and conventions. Always committed to professional research, nevertheless, as a moderate social activist, Franklin often uses his intimate knowledge of American history to testify in the courts or to educate an audience. In 1949 he assisted the NAACP in its fight to desegregate the graduate school of the University of Kentucky in *Lyman Johnson v. The University of Kentucky*. Shortly thereafter, he wrote essays for and provided historical context to Thurgood Marshall's team of lawyers in the successful battle to desegregate public schools in the United States in *Brown v. Board of Education*. In 1963, he served as the analyst for the BBC coverage of the "March on Washington," and in 1987 he testified against the appointment of Robert Bork as an associate justice of the Supreme Court. As the Bicentennial Jefferson Lecturer for the National Endowment for the Humanities, he delivered three speeches (published as *Racial Equality in America*, 1976) in three different cities and placed racial inequality within its historical context. Moreover, as an editor, contributor or collaborator, Franklin contributes in print and speeches to the national discussion of the great social issues which "roil about" him.

In 1992, just one day after the Rodney King "not guilty" verdict in Los Angeles, Franklin delivered the Paul Anthony Brick lectures at the University of Missouri, published as *The Color Line: Legacy for the Twenty-first Century* (1993). Here he reflects on the consequences of racism and concludes that opposition to affirmative action by politicians such as Ronald Reagan obstructed race relations in the United States. Many of his lectures and addresses are collected in *Race and History: Selected Essays, 1938-1988* (1989). Several important reference volumes profited from his participation, most notably *Black Leaders of the Twentieth Century* (1982) and the *Encyclopedia of African American Culture* (1996), along with the popular *Illustrated History of Black Americans* (1970). As an editor of autobiographies, Franklin has resurrected other important Afro-American figures. His *Three Negro Classics* (1965) contains editions of Booker T. Washington's *Up From Slavery*, W.E. B. DuBois's *The Souls of Black Folks*, and W. Johnson's *The Autobiography of an Ex Colored Man*. In 1997, in collaboration with his son, Franklin edited *My Life and an Era: The Autobiography of Buck Colbert Franklin*, about his father, a frontier attorney who was admitted to plead before the U.S. Supreme Court.

In 1997 at the age of 82, Franklin accepted what might be his greatest challenge when President Bill Clinton appointed him chairman of the advisory board of the President's Initiative on Race. He accepted the appointment "Because it was an irresistible opportunity to make a contribution to solving our oldest and most intractable problem." Always true to his calling, Franklin sees education as a key component in addressing racism. As he says, "One of the main reasons we are where we are is because of ignorance." He says of both Blacks and Whites, "We don't know our own history." Franklin is responsible for much of what we do know; his work has brought the rich history and contributions of Afro-Americans into the mainstream of American history.

Judith C. Kohl

FRAZIER, Charles

Born: Charles Robinson Frazier in Andrews, North Carolina, 4 November, 1950. **Education:** University of North Carolina, Chapel Hill, B.A. 1973; University of South Carolina, Columbia, Ph.D 1986. **Family:** Married Katherine; daughter Annie. **Career:** Professor of English, University of Colorado, Professor of English, North Carolina State University. **Awards:** National Book Award, 1997, North Carolina Arts Council Artist Fellowship, 1997. **Agent:** Leigh Feldman, 179 Franklin Street, New York, New York 10013.

<small>PUBLICATIONS</small>

Novel

Cold Mountain. New York, Atlantic Monthly Press, 1996.

Other

Adventuring in the Andes: The Sierra Club Guide to Peru, Bolivia, the Amazon Basin, and the Galapagos, with Donald Seacrest. San Francisco, Sierra Club Press, 1985.
Geography and Possibility: Man and the Landscape in Recent Western Fiction. University of South Carolina, Doctoral Thesis.

*   *   *

Charles Frazier's *Cold Mountain* evokes a forgotten lifestyle, a close attachment to nature, disdain for war and violence, and the survival spirit that sustains his characters in adversity. Frazier's novel rejects the romantic Southern myth of heroic soldiers, noble generals, and fainting, delicate Southern belles. Frazier's "belles" are capable, strong, intelligent women, and Frazier's war is bloody, violent, and exhausting.

Frazier brings the battles of the Civil War alive in nightmarish detail, depicting it as a brutal and senseless waste of human life. In an interview with *Newsweek*, Frazier commented, "The kind of romanticizing of the war that Southerners are prone to has always bothered me. So it was important to me to start Cold Mountain when Inman . . . put the war behind him and went home." Inman, the protagonist, not only wants out of the war, he wishes never to look back on it. Frazier asserts, through the casual dialogue of mountain farmers, that the mountain population of the South felt no great sentiment for the "Great Cause" or the "Lost Cause" of the Civil War. Disenfranchised from the politics of the North-South conflict, these people simply wanted to be left alone. Inman embodies this weariness. His spirit is described as "blasted away so that he had become lonesome and estranged from all around him as a sad old heron standing pointless watch in the mudflats of a pond lacking frogs." Thus begins Inman's journey, and the story of *Cold Mountain*.

Inman wants to escape the war as he longs for the comfort of Cold Mountain and the company of his pre-war sweetheart, Ada Monroe. The feeling becomes so strong, he rises from his hospital bed and walks home. Interwoven with Inman's journey is Ada's transformation from a protected and beloved daughter into an independent and capable farmer. As Inman draws closer to Ada, the tension of the story pulls progressively tighter as the reader anticipates their reunion.

Frazier crafted this story as a series of episodes of Inman's trials on the road as an "outlier," or deserter. Throughout his journey, Inman faces attacks by wild animals, severe weather, the ruthless "Home Guard" (soldiers sent to round up outliers), and the people left ravaged and starving from the war, willing to kill for a sturdy pair of boots. Even within the savage conditions of the North Carolina backroads in 1865, Inman finds peace and comfort in a few strangers, mostly war brides and widows, who are purveyors of food and places to rest.

These wise and self-reliant women are the lost story of the Civil War—the women trusted with running society while the men fought and died miles from home. Again, Frazier systematically attacks the myth of the Southern belle, underscoring his conviction through Ruby, a young woman sent to help Ada transform the Monroe homestead into a working farm. Intrepid Ruby, whose self-reliance from childhood makes her the embodiment of survival, is well-schooled in slaughtering, sowing, reaping, gathering, and hunting. She becomes a font of wisdom for Ada, teaching her lessons about the natural world and the superstitions governing that world. Ruby runs the farm according to a lunar calendar: there are the days of the waxing moon for hog killing, the waning moon for cutting wood, and the elusive sheep-killing moon. Ruby forces Ada to attend to the seasons, phases of the moon, and changes in leaves, which Ada views as "an expression of stewardship, a means of taking care, a discipline . . . the signs were a way of being alert." In turn, Ada "educated beyond the point considered wise for females," opens Ruby's eyes to the great stories of literature, and the *Odyssey* in particular.

Frazier created the story of *Cold Mountain* from a story his great-grandfather passed down to him about his great-great grandfather, W.P. Inman, a wayfarer who walked home from the Civil War. In keeping with its genesis as oral history, *Cold Mountain* is an *Odyssey*-inspired epic. Echoes of Homer resonate throughout the story, with our hero Inman as Odysseus and Ada, Inman's pre-war sweetheart, as Penelope. As Inman moves slowly homeward, Ada alters both physically and spiritually from the years apart from him. In a letter to her cousin in Charleston, she writes, "I suspect, were we to meet on Market Street, you would not know me; nor, upon seeing the current want of delicacy in my aspect and costume, would you much care to." Frazier makes direct reference to the Odyssey, as Ada reads to Ruby every night. When the light grows too dim for further reading, Ruby supplies Ada with chapters of her own life story. Ruby had "grown tired impatient with Penelope, but she would sit of a long evening and laugh and laugh at the tribulations of Odysseus, all the stones the gods threw in his passway."

Another epic haunts the story of *Cold Mountain*. Inman carries a tattered edition of *Bartram's Travels*, an account of a man called Flower-Gatherer by the Cherokee for his collection of plants and roots and his attention to "the growth of wild living things." Flower-Gatherer travels through wilderness "describing a world of scarp and crag, ridge after ridge fading off blue into the distance." Inman "had left the book and was simply forming the topography of home in his head." Flower-Gatherer's reverence for nature helps Inman focus through difficult and inhospitable terrain, leading him toward majestic Cold Mountain.

Bartram's Travels is also suggestive of Frazier's previous writing, which includes his doctoral thesis, *Geography and Possibility: Man and the Landscape in Recent Western Fiction*, and a Sierra Club guide to the Andes he co-wrote with Donald Seacrest. Frazier skillfully describes the changing landscapes of Inman's journey, imbuing them with almost human characteristics, revealing the "personalities" of the various features Inman confronts. For example, Inman describes Cape Fear River as "a shit-brown clog to his passage" and the Piedmont of North Carolina as "the place where all that was foul and sorry had flowed downhill and pooled in the low spots." In contrast, Cold Mountain is Inman's trustworthy beacon, his constant in an unstable world, where "all his scattered forces might gather." Perhaps it is also Frazier's experience as a travel writer that lends him the ability to show the deep attachment people felt for the landscape around them.

For Frazier, a large portion of the writing process was the extensive research he conducted. He unearthed outmoded words as if they were artifacts, placing them in a context that keeps them relevant to both the prose and the story. The creation of Ada's farm is so detailed, so steeped in the practices of the time, it stands as a work of historical preservation. Ada asks herself, "Soon: Patch shingles on barn roof; do we have maul and froe?"

His effortless use of these lost words demonstrates Frazier's painstaking research into everything from the exact contents of a wayfarer's haversack to the minutia of a small mountain farm. His affinity for research continues, as his second novel (now in progress) is set in the Grove Park Inn in Asheville at the turn of the century. Frazier told *Newsweek*, "I'm interested in those mountain resorts in the early part of this century. What would it have been like to live at the Grove Park Inn in Asheville all summer long?" If *Cold Mountain* is any indication, Charles Frazier will tell us precisely what it was like, down to the most granular detail.

—Frances E. Badgett

FULGHUM, Robert

Born: 4 June 1937, in Waco, Texas. **Education:** University of Colorado; Baylor University, 1957; Starr King (Unitarian) Seminary; studied at Zen Buddhist monastery, 1972. **Family:** Married Marcia McClellan, 1957 (divorced, 1973); children: Christian, Hunter, Molly Behen; married Lynn Edwards, 1976. **Career:** Ordained a Unitarian minister, 1961; part-time Unitarian minister, Bellingham, Washington, beginning in 1961; part-time minister, 1966-85, minister emeritus, since 1985, Edmonds Unitarian Church, Edmonds, Washington; art teacher, Lakeside School, Seattle, Washington, 1971-88; painter, writer, and lecturer; worked variously as a sales trainee for International Business Machines (IBM), a singing cowboy and amateur rodeo performer at guest ranches in Montana, Colorado, and Texas, a counselor to mental patients and prison inmates, a creator of motel art, a bartender, and a folk music teacher; founder of wilderness camp in Canada. **Member:** Greenpeace, Planned Parenthood, American Civil Liberties Union.

PUBLICATIONS

Nonfiction

All I Really Need to Know I Learned in Kindergarten: Uncommon Thoughts on Common Things. New York, Villard Books, 1988.

It Was on Fire When I Lay Down on It. New York, Villard Books, 1989.

Uh-Oh: Some Observations from Both Sides of the Refrigerator Door. New York, Villard Books, 1991.

Maybe (Maybe Not): Second Thoughts from a Secret Life. New York, Villard Books, 1993.

From Beginning to End: The Rituals of Our Lives. New York, Villard Books, 1995.

True Love: Stories Told To and By Robert Fulghum. New York, HarperCollins Publishers, 1997.

Words I Wish I Wrote: A Collection of Writing that Inspired my Ideas. New York, Cliff Street Books, 1997.

*   *   *

With his greatly successful collections of vignettes and homilies of everyday life, Robert Fulghum has carved out a niche among popular nonfiction writers, emphasizing the beauty and wonder in the ordinary and offering a positive vision of modern existence. Although criticized for his simple style and repetition, Fulghum has struck a chord with readers seeking hopeful messages in today's world.

A Unitarian minister and self-proclaimed philosopher, Fulghum makes no claims to be an intellectual, instead pointing to the importance of basic human values and commonplace rituals that reveal our inherently good natures. His first and best-known collection of what he refers to as "stuff," *All I Really Need to Know I Learned in Kindergarten* (1988), grew out of a list of beliefs from lessons learned in the playground and in kindergarten classrooms; these include such directives as "share everything," "play fair," "don't hit people" and "clean up your own mess."

As Ruth Bayard Smith writes in the *New York Times Book Review,* Fulghum "knows that the appeal of his message lies in its simplicity. He is acknowledging the inner fears and insecurities that are universal." His stories all share the same qualities of being direct and teaching a universal lesson or moral. The topics of are often humorous, ranging from hippie lawyers and the delights of meatloaf to a bride who vomits on her wedding guests during the ceremony.

Fulghum went on to publish more books of a similar nature, including *It Was On Fire When I Lay Down On It* (1989), *Uh-Oh: Some Observations from Both Sides of the Refrigerator Door* (1991), *Maybe (Maybe Not): Second Thoughts from a Secret Life* (1993), and *From Beginning to End: The Rituals of Our Lives* (1995). This repetition of style and substance drew frowns from some critics, including Andrea Cooper, reacting to *Uh-Oh:* "A better editor would have changed that embarrassing title, smoothed the fragmented, ad-copy writing style and encouraged Mr. Fulghum to experiment beyond his predictable format with longer, more substantive reflections." Martin Brady of *Booklist* added, "Not all of [his message] is pithy . . . sometimes Fulghum comes across as Andy Rooney crossed with Richard Bach." However, others find his loosely-connected homilies refreshing. "He's sincere, and his message feels good," writes *People*'s Louisa Ermelino. "Sure, Fulghum is overbearing, oversimplified and saccharine. But he's also touching, practical, and wise." Of his own writing style, Fulghum says, "If you notice phrases, ideas, and anecdotes that closely resemble those that appear elsewhere in my writing, it is not a matter of sloppy editing. I'm repeating myself. I'm reshuffling words in the hope that just once I might say something exactly right."

His readers delight in Fulghum's wisdom and storytelling, finding uncomplicated answers to many problems of daily life. He does not offer much in the way of implementing his solutions, but points out reasonable alternatives to the ways we react to life. While his books are largely indistinguishable from one another, they touch on the importance of the mundane and highlight the fragile connections that keep us attached to our loved ones and the human community at large. By focusing on these fragile connections, Fulghum reveals how much we truly need one another.

—Christopher Swann

G

GAINES, Ernest J.

Born: Ernest James Gaines in Oscar, Louisiana, 15 January 1933.
Education: Vallejo Junior College; San Francisco State College,
B.A. 1955-57; Stanford University, California, 1958-59. **Military Service:** United States Army, 1953-55. **Career:** Writer-in-
residence, Denison University, Granville, Ohio, 1971, Stanford
University, Spring 1981, and Whittier College, California, 1982.
Since 1983, professor of English and writer-in-residence, University of Southwestern Louisiana, Lafayette. **Awards:** Stegner fellow, Stanford University, California, 1958; San Francisco Foundation Joseph Henry Jackson award, 1959; National Endowment
for the Arts grant, 1966; Rockefeller grant, 1970; Guggenheim grant,
1970; Black Academy of Arts and Letters award, 1972; San Francisco Art Commission award, 1983; American Academy award,
1987; National Book Critics Circle award, 1994, and Pulitzer prize,
1994, both for *A Lesson Before Dying*. D.Litt.: Denison University, 1980, Brown University, 1985, Bard College, 1985, Louisiana State University, 1987; D.H.L.: Whittier College, 1986. **Agent**:
JCA Literary Agency, 242 West 27th Street, New York, New York
10001.

PUBLICATIONS

Novels

Catherine Carmier. New York, Atheneum, 1964.
Of Love and Dust. New York, Dial Press, 1967.
The Autobiography of Miss Jane Pittman. New York, Dial Press,
1971.
In My Father's House. New York, Knopf, 1978.
A Gathering of Old Men. New York, Knopf, 1983.
A Lesson Before Dying. New York, Knopf, 1993.

Short Stories

Bloodline. New York, Dial Press, 1968.

Uncollected Short Stories

"The Turtles," in *Transfer,* 1956.
"Boy in the Doublebreasted Suit," in *Transfer,* 1957.
"My Grandpa and the Haint," in *New Mexico Quarterly,* Summer
1966.

Other

A Long Day in November (for children). New York, Dial Press,
1971.
Porch Talk with Ernest Gaines, with Marcia Gaudet and Carl
Wooton. Baton Rouge, Louisiana State University Press, 1990.

*

Manuscript Collection: Dupree Library, University of Southwestern Louisiana, Lafayette.

Critical Studies: "Human Dignity and Pride in the Novels of Ernest
Gaines" by Winifred L. Stoelting, in *CLA Journal* (Baltimore), March
1971; "Ernest J. Gaines: Change, Growth, and History" by Jerry H.
Bryant, in *Southern Review* (Baton Rouge, Louisiana), October 1974;
"Bayonne ou le Yoknapatawpha d'Ernest Gaines" by Michel Fabre
in *Recherches Anglaises et Américaines 9* (Strasbourg), 1976; "To
Make These Bones Live: History and Community in Ernest Gaines's
Fiction" by Jack Hicks, in *Black American Literature Forum* (Terre
Haute, Indiana), Spring 1977; "Ernest Gaines: 'A Long Day in No-
vember'" by Nalenz Puschmann, in *The Black American Short Story
in the 20th Century* edited by Peter Bruck, Amsterdam, Grüner, 1978;
"The Quarters: Ernest J. Gaines and the Sense of Place" by Charles
H. Rowell, in *Southern Review* (Baton Rouge, Louisiana), Summer
1985.

Ernest J. Gaines comments:

I have tried to show you a world of my people—the kind of
world that I came from.

*   *   *

The fictive world of Ernest J. Gaines, as well as certain technical aspects of his works, might be compared to that of William
Faulkner. But useful as such a comparison may be, it should not
be pursued to the point of obscuring Gaines's considerable origi-
nality, which inheres mainly in the fact that he is Afro-American
and very much a spiritual product, if no longer a resident, of the
somewhat unique region about which he writes: south Louisiana,
culturally distinguishable from the state's Anglo-Saxon north, thus
from the nation as a whole, by its French legacy, no small part of
which derives from the comparative ease with which its French
settlers and their descendants formed sexual alliances with blacks.

Gaines's Afro-American perspective enables him to create,
among other notable characters both black and white, a Jane
Pittman (*The Autobiography of Miss Jane Pittman*) whose heroic
perseverance we experience, rather than Faulkner's housekeeping
Dilsey (*The Sound and the Fury*) for whom we have little more
than the narrator's somewhat ambiguous and irrelevant assurance
that "she endured." In general, Gaines's peculiar point of view
generates a more complex social vision than Faulkner's, an advantage Gaines has sustained with dramatic force and artistic integrity. Gaines's fictive society consists of whites, blacks, and Creoles, presumably a traditionally more favored socio-economic class
of African Americans given to fantasies of racial superiority to
those of darker skin, fantasies of the kind the Martinican psychiatrist Frantz Fanon explores in *Black Skin, White Masks*.

The Gainesian counterparts of the Sartorises and Snopeses (the
moribund aristocracy and parvenu "poor white trash" respectively
of Faulkner's mythical Mississippi county) are the south Louisiana plantation owners, mostly of French extraction, and the cajuns,
of French extraction but of lesser "quality." The cajuns are inher-
iting and spoiling the land and displacing the Creoles and blacks,
the former tragically though not irrevocably doomed by a persistent folly, the latter a people of promise who have never really
betrayed their African heritage.

All Gaines's works reflect the inherent socio-economic intricacy of this quadruplex humanity, though we are never allowed to lose sight of its basic element of black and white. In his apprentice first novel, *Catherine Carmier,* for instance, we see the sickly proscribed love of Jackson, who is black, and Catherine, daughter of an infernally proud Creole farmer, as a perverted issue of the miscegenation that resulted from the white male's sexual exploitation of black people. This mode of victimization assumes metaphoric force in Gaines's works, figuring forth in historical perspective the oppression of black people generally. The fictive plantation world, then, is uniquely micro-cosmic. It is south Louisiana, the South, the nation as a whole. This aspect is explored, for example, in the title story of *Bloodline.* Copper, a character of mythopoeic proportion, the militant young son of a now deceased white plantation owner and a black woman field hand, stages a heroic return, presumably from his education in school and in the world at large, to claim his heritage: recognition of kinship by an aristocratic white uncle and his rightful share of the land. In *In My Father's House,* and for the first time, Gaines deals with the black father-son relationship, and explores a neglected aspect of African American life: the perplexities of the public vs. private person relative to individual responsibility. The Reverend Phillip Martin, a grass roots Civil Rights leader in the fictional south Louisiana town of St. Adrienne, is forced to confront his wayward past when his estranged son Etienne, reminiscent of Copper, comes to claim paternal recognition and redress of grievances.

In *A Gathering of Old Men* Gaines extends the thematic concerns of his earlier novels into a new South setting, employing a multiple first-person point of view in the manner of Faulkner's *As I Lay Dying.* The conflict between blacks and cajuns comes to a cinematically stylized, somewhat surrealistic climax and resolution as several old black men gather in mutual militant defense of one of their number who has been accused of killing Cajun farmer Beau Boutan, confronting the local sheriff as well as the slain man's avenging father, "retired" nightrider Fix Boutan. The result is a gripping allegorical tale of race relations in the new South resonant with the Gainesian theme of individual responsibility, this time for holding ground in the wake of the civil rights gains of the 1960s and 1970s.

In Gaines's 1993 novel, *A Lesson Before Dying,* set in 1940, individual responsibility is highlighted again. Wiggins, the novel's narrator, is a young school teacher and one among a number of Gainesian tutelary figures. Wiggins is pressured by his elders into assuming the responsibility of mentoring Jefferson, a young black man-child who awaits execution for having taken part in the murder of a white storekeeper, a crime for which he is apparently unjustly convicted in a racist environment. A National Book Critics Circle award winner and recipient of the Pulitzer Prize for fiction in 1994, *A Lesson* chronicles the young Jefferson's gradual assumption of responsibility, under Wiggins's increasingly committed mentorship, for assimilating the attributes of manhood before he dies in the electric chair. In one of Gaines's characteristic ironies, Wiggins's mentorship of Jefferson contributes to his own edification as well.

—Alvin Aubert

GARRETT, George

Born: George Palmer Garrett, Jr., in Orlando, Florida, 11 June 1929. **Education:** Sewanee Military Academy; The Hill School, graduated 1947; Princeton University, 1947-48, 1949-52, B.A. 1952, M.A. 1956, Ph.D. 1985; Columbia University, New York, 1948-49. **Military Service:** United States Army Field Artillery, 1952-55. **Family:** Married Susan Parrish Jackson in 1952; two sons and one daughter. **Career:** Assistant professor, Wesleyan University, 1957-60; visiting lecturer, Rice University, 1961-62; associate professor, University of Virginia, 1962-67; writer-in-residence, Princeton University, 1964-65; professor of English, Hollins College, 1967-71; professor of English and writer-in-residence, University of South Carolina, Columbia, 1971-73; senior fellow, Council of the Humanities, Princeton University, 1974-77; adjunct professor, Columbia University, 1977-78; writer-in-residence, Bennington College, 1979, and University of Michigan, 1979-84; since 1984, Hoyns Professor of English, University of Virginia; president of Associated Writing Programs, 1971-73; United States poetry editor, *Transatlantic Review,* Rome (later London), 1958-71; Contemporary Poetry Series editor, University of North Carolina Press, Chapel Hill, 1962-68; co-editor, *Hollins Critic,* Virginia, 1965-71; Short Story Series editor, Louisiana State University Press, Baton Rouge, 1966-69; since 1970 contributing editor, *Contempora,* Atlanta; since 1971 assistant editor, *Film Journal,* Hollins College, Virginia; since 1972 co-editor, *Worksheet,* Columbia, South Carolina; since 1981 editor, with Brendan Galvin, *Poultry: A Magazine of Voice,* Truro, Massachusetts; since 1988 fiction editor, *The Texas Review;* contributing editor, *Chronicles,* Rockford, Illinois. Vice-Chancellor, 1987-92, and since 1992 Chancellor, Fellowship of Southern Writers. **Awards:** *Sewanee Review* fellowship, 1958; American Academy in Rome fellowship, 1958; Ford grant, for drama, 1960; National Endowment for the Arts grant, 1967; *Contempora* award, 1971; Guggenheim fellowship, 1974; American Academy of Arts and Letters award, 1985; New York Public Library Literary Lion award, 1988; T. S. Eliot award, 1989; PEN/Malamud award for short fiction, 1990; Cultural Laureate of Virginia, 1986; Hollins College medal, 1992; D. Litt.: University of the South (Sewanee), 1994. **Agent:** Jane Gelfman, John Farquharson Ltd., 250 West 57th Street, New York, New York 10107.

PUBLICATIONS

Poetry

The Reverend Ghost. New York, Scribner, 1957.
The Sleeping Gypsy and Other Poems. Austin, University of Texas Press, 1958.
Abraham's Knife and Other Poems. Chapel Hill, University of North Carolina Press, 1961.
For a Bitter Season: New and Selected Poems. Columbia, University of Missouri Press, 1967.
Welcome to the Medicine Show: Postcards, Flashcards, Snapshots. Winston-Salem, North Carolina, Palaemon Press, 1978.
Luck's Shining Child: A Miscellany of Poems and Verses. Winston-Salem, North Carolina, Palaemon Press, 1981.
The Collected Poems of George Garrett. Fayetteville, University of Arkansas Press, 1984.

Days of Our Lives Lie In Fragments: New and Old Poems, 1957-1997. Baton Rouge, Louisiana State University Press, 1998.

Short Story Collections

King of the Mountain. New York, Scribner, 1958.
In the Briar Patch. Austin, University of Texas Press, 1961.
Cold Ground Was My Bed Last Night. Columbia, University of Missouri Press, 1964.
A Wreath for Garibaldi and Other Stories. London, Hart Davis, 1969.
The Magic Striptease. New York, Doubleday, 1973.
To Recollect a Cloud of Ghosts: Christmas in England. Winston-Salem, Palaemon Press, 1979.
An Evening Performance: New and Selected Short Stories. New York, Doubleday, 1985.

Novels

The Finished Man. New York, Scribner, 1959.
Which Ones Are the Enemy? Boston, Little Brown, 1961.
Do, Lord, Remember Me. New York, Doubleday, 1965.
Death of the Fox. New York, Doubleday, 1971.
The Succession: A Novel of Elizabeth and James. New York, Doubleday, 1983.
Poison Pen. Winston-Salem, Wright, 1986.
Entered from the Sun. New York, Doubleday, 1990.
The Old Army Game (a novel and stories). Dallas, Southern Methodist University Press, 1994.
George Garrett: The Elizabethan Trilogy (*Do, Lord, Remember Me, Death of the Fox, The Succession: A Novel of Elizabeth and James*). Huntsville, Texas Review Press, 1998.

Plays

Sir Slob and the Princess: A Play for Children. New York, French, 1962.
Garden Spot, U.S.A. Produced in Houston, 1962.
Enchanted Ground. York, Maine, Old Gaol Museum Press, 1981.

Other

James Jones (biography). New York, Harcourt Brace, 1984.
Understanding Mary Lee Settle. Columbia, University of South Carolina Press, 1988.
My Silk Purse and Yours: The Publishing Scene and American Literary Art. Columbia, University of Missouri Press, 1992.
The Sorrows of Fat City: A Selection of Literary Essays and Reviews. Columbia, University of South Carolina Press, 1992.
Whistling in the Dark: True Stories and Other Fables. New York, Harcourt Brace, 1992.
Bad Man Blues: A Portable George Garrett. Dallas, Southern Methodist University Press, 1998.

Editor

New Writing from Virginia. Charlottesville, Virginia, New Writing Associates, 1963.
The Girl in the Black Raincoat. New York, Duell, 1966.
Man and the Movies, with W.R. Robinson. Baton Rouge, Louisiana State University Press, 1967.

The Sounder Few: Essays from "The Hollins Critic," with R.H.W. Dillard and John Moore. Athens, University of Georgia Press, 1971.
Film Scripts 1-4, with O.B. Hardison, Jr., and Jane Gelfman. New York, Appleton Century Crofts, 4 vols., 1971-72.
New Writing in South Carolina, with William Peden. Columbia, University of South Carolina Press, 1971.
Craft So Hard to Learn, with John Graham. New York, Morrow, 1972.
The Writer's Voice, with John Graham. New York, Morrow, 1973.
Intro 5, with Walton Beacham. Charlottesville, University Press of Virginia, 1974.
The Botteghe Oscure Reader, with Katherine Garrison Biddle. Middletown, Connecticut, Wesleyan University Press, 1974.
Intro 6: Life As We Know It. New York, Doubleday, 1974.
Intro 7: All of Us and None of You. New York, Doubleday, 1975.
Intro 8: The Liar's Craft. New York, Doubleday, 1977.
Intro 9, with Michael Mewshaw. Austin, Texas, Hendel and Reinke, 1979.
Eric Clapton's Lovers and Other Stories from the Virginia Quarterly Review, with Sheila McMillen. Charlottesville, University Press of Virginia, 1990.
Elvis in Oz: New Stories and Poems from the Hollins Creative Writing Program, with Mary Flinn. Charlottesville, University Press of Virginia, 1992.
The Wedding Cake in the Middle of the Road, with Susan Stamberg. New York, Norton, 1992.
That's What I Like (About the South), with Paul Ruffin. Columbia, University of South Carolina Press, 1993.

Uncollected Short Stories

"The Other Side of the Coin," in *Four Quarters*, Vol. 6, 1957.
"The Rare Unicorn," in *Approach*, Vol. 25, 1957.
"The Only Dragon on the Road," in *Approach,* Vol. 31, 1959.
"3 Fabliaux," in *Transatlantic Review*, Vol. 1, 1959.
"The Snowman," in *New Mexico Quarterly*, Vol. 29, 1959.
"Two Exemplary Letters," in *Latitudes*, Vol. 1, 1967.
"Jane Amor, Space Nurse," in *Fly by Night,* 1970.
"There Are Lions Everywhere," "How Can You Tell What Somebody's Thinking on the Telephone," and "Moon Girl," in *Mill Mountain Review*, Summer 1971.
"Here Comes the Bride," in *Gone Soft*, Vol. 1, 1973.
"Live Now and Pay Later," in *Nassau Literary Magazine*, 1974.
"Little Tune for a Steel String Guitar," in *Sandlapper*, Vol. 9, 1976.
"Soldiers," in *Texas Review*, Vol. 3, 1982.
"Wine Talking," in *Quarterly West*, Vol. 20, 1985.
"Ruthe-Ann," in *Texas Review*, Vol. 6, 1985.
"Genius Baby," in *Chattahoochie Review*, 1986.
"Dixie Dreamland," in *South Carolina Review*, Vol. 19, 1986.
"The Confidence Man." In *Necessary Fictions* edited by Stanley W. Lindberg and Stephen Corey. Athens, University of Georgia Press, 1986.
"Captain Barefoot Tells His Tale," in *Virginia Quarterly Review*, Spring 1990.
"Velleities and Vicissitudes," in *Sewanee Review*, Fall 1990.

*

Screenplays: *The Young Lovers,* 1964; *The Playground,* 1965; *Frankenstein Meets the Space Monster,* with R.H.W. Dillard and John Rodenbeck, 1966.

Teleplays: *Suspense* series, 1958.

Bibliographies: In *Seven Princeton Poets,* Princeton University Library, 1963; "George Garrett: A Checklist of His Writings" by R.H.W. Dillard, in *Mill Mountain Review* (Roanoke, Virginia), Summer 1971; *George Garrett: A Bibliography 1947-1988* by Stuart Wright, Huntsville, Texas Review Press, 1989.

Manuscript Collection: Duke University, Durham, North Carolina.

Critical Studies: By James B. Meriwether, *Princeton University Library Chronicle* (New Jersey), vol. 25, no. 1, 1963; "George Garrett Issue" of *Mill Mountain Review* (Roanoke, Virginia), Summer 1971; "Imagining the Individual: George Garrett's *Death of the Fox*" by W. R. Robinson, in *Hollins Critic* (Hollins College, Virginia), August 1971; "The Reader Becomes Text: Methods of Experimentation in George Garrett's *The Succession*" by Tom Whalen, *Texas Review* (Huntsville), Summer 1983; "George Garrett and the Historical Novel" by Monroe K. Spears, *Virginia Quarterly Review* (Charlottesville), Spring 1985; *To Come Up Grinning: A Tribute to George Garrett* edited by Paul Ruffin and Stuart Wright, Huntsville, Texas Review Press, 1989; *Understanding George Garrett* by R.H.W. Dillard, Columbia, University of South Carolina Press, 1989.

George Garrett comments:

(1972) I feel I am only just beginning, still learning my craft, trying my hand at as many things, as many ways and means of telling as many stories as I'm able to. I hope that this will always be the case, that somehow I'll avoid the slow horror of repeating myself or the blind rigor of an obsession. I can't look back, I'm not ashamed of the work I've done, but it is done. And I am (I hope) moving ahead, growing and changing. Once I've seen something into print I do not re-read it. I have tried always to write out of experience, but that includes imaginative experience which is quite as "real" to me and for me as any other and, indeed, in no way divorces from the outward and visible which we often (and inaccurately) call reality. I only hope to continue to learn and to grow. And to share experience with my imaginary reader. I use the singular because a book is a direct encounter, a conversation between one writer and one reader. Though I couldn't care less how many, in raw numbers, read my work, I have the greatest respect for that one imaginary reader. I hope to manage to please that reader before I'm done, to give as much delight, or some sense of it, as I have received from reading good books by good writers.

(1986) Years and scars, and various and sundry books, later, I would not change much in my earlier statement, innocent as it was. Now that I am in my mid-fifties I would not use the word *hope* so much. Naturally I have less hope for myself; though I insist on maintaining high hopes for the best of the young writers I teach. And I have every intention, with and without hope, to continue working, trying to learn my craft always (never to *master* it), still seeking, sometimes finding my imaginary reader. I know more than a decade's worth of darker, sadder things than I did in 1972. So does the world. So goes the world. Well, I have learned a full deck of new jokes, also, and never ceased to taste good laughter. If some hopes have faded and been abandoned, faith, which is altogether something else, has replaced them. And

the old dog learns new tricks. One: to turn to the light and live on it until it's gone. Another: to be as open as I can until my book is closed.

(1991) In 1989 I was suddenly 60 years old, older than I had planned to be or ever imagined. Not that a whole lot has changed (I was and am still a viable candidate for the American Tomb of the Unknown Writer); but I did finish my Elizabethan trilogy; and now I have a new publisher and have embarked on three related American novels, coming out of our recent history. I am not planning to live forever, but I would like to finish telling these stories and some others on my mind. Meantime I'm a grandfather and have the pleasure of seeing a generation and a half of former students writing and publishing books on their own. And I am sometimes surprised by the kindness of strangers. The world is not (all claims to the contrary) a kinder or gentler place; but, somewhat to my cynical chagrin, I keep discovering worthy and amazing creatures in it.

(1995) Is there anything to add? Years-now I'm 65 and counting. And still working as hard as I can, hoping to get the work done, hoping, from here on, the work will simply speak for itself.

* * *

George Garrett, poet, novelist, screen-writer, teacher, crafter of short stories, has enjoyed a literary career as wide-open and unbounded as the land where he grew up, in central Florida. The world of his childhood, the lake-dotted gentle roll of pasture land, wetland and orange groves under too much bright sky, was nothing like the tourist hive it is today. Pre-Disney Orlando, where Garrett's father practiced law and raised cattle, was a small, liveoak-shaded town where coastal dwellers went to buy oranges and, if threatened by a hurricane, to wait out the winds on the subtle ridgeland far from the beaches with their stinging, wind-whipped sand and surging tides. In populace and demeanor it was Southern to the core, as was the family into which George Garrett was born the middle child, between two sisters, in 1928. Though the Depression was soon upon the nation, and his father's clients might find themselves only able to pay their legal bills in produce (sometimes, literally, in peanuts), the Garretts lived well.

As was expected in such families the son went off to prep at Sewannee Military Academy, then to Columbia University for a year, from whence George transferred to Princeton, where he would take his B.A. and Masters degrees. Like most clans of the South, the Garrett family was extended, and colorful, with grandparents and many cousins on the scene, and a Hollywood uncle who would show up on occasion in a hot new car, and always with a different dishy babe. This uncle was a screenwriter, who may have been a significant influence on a boy making up vivid stories long before he could print his alphabet. The family's Episcopal religion, in which George was firmly grounded (and which he served happily as an acolyte who drank copiously of the left-over communion wine) perhaps had its influence also by way of its formality, subtle drama and a dignified other-worldliness, facets that shine brightly in Garrett's poetry and in his novels of the Elizabethan age. Witness a few lines of his poem "Days of Our Lives Lie in Fragments," written in memory of O.B. Hardison Jr.:

Think how they slip away, one at a time
out of the light of all our ambiguous loves
and into the blaze and bright of another weather.
And soon, soon enough, we shall all cross over
out of the shadowy seasons of sooner and later,
each alone as can be with pain and sorrow.

See how, splendid as geese in flight,
they join hands now to move in a dance
to music we cannot hear, can only guess at.

Somewhere in Garrett's all-observing childhood there must have been a bully with a heart of gold, for such a figure recurs in his work, in such characters as Captain Barfoot, called by a reviewer "the brutal adversary with a tender heart" of *Entered from the Sun*, Garrett's novel on the life and death of Christopher Marlowe. Walter Sullivan, reviewing *Entered from the Sun*, wrote of Garrett's portrayal of the England of Marlowe's time:

A part of his intention and his method has been to compare us to them, them to us, and we are found wanting. Where is our Elizabeth? Who rules so grandly or sets such an example? Where is our Marlowe? No one writes even occasionally as well.

Another kindly bully turns up in a piece that is one of innumerable examples of Garrett's versatility. The influence here, the terse descriptions and action, owe much more to Uncle Oliver the screenwriter, along with Garrett's own spell in Hollywood. Here, in the short story "Cold Ground Was My Bed Last Night," small-town Florida sheriff Jack Riddle is dealing with two prisoners—one a smart-alec outlander and one a jail-house regular, an old man who cherishes his goats and a thirst that keeps him in trouble:

(Sheriff to Goatman) "You think you're still man enough to pull 60 days?"

"No sir," the Goatman says. "The time was when I could do it standing on top of my head. But I just can't no more. It hurts my pride to admit it but that's the God's truth."

The prisoner is still laughing to himself.

"Your pride?"

"Yes, Sir."

Suddenly the Sheriff turns on the laughing prisoner. He moves quick and light-footed, slapping him hard across the face. The prisoner stops laughing. Then the Sheriff returns to the Goatman. "Your pride? What kind of pride have you got?"

"Everybody's got some kind of pride, Sheriff...."

Now Sheriff Riddle goes to his desk. He leans over and begins writing something in the open notebook.

"What are you going to do with me, Sheriff?"

"'I'm going to turn you loose," the Sheriff says. "I don't see why a lot of innocent goats has to suffer because you're no damn good."

Garrett the scriptwriter, though he worked at that trade only briefly, still turns up often in the shorter pieces, as in "Tanks," from the *Sewannee Review*, Winter 1992, a memoir of a horrid Korean War experience written after reading William Styron's *The Long March*:

That's where I wanted to begin—with the sudden, deafening noise of the tank engines and treads, then with the view of the soldiers zipped into their sleeping bags as the cold dark enormous shape of the tank appeared above them and plowed through the little bivouac . . . . Somebody among them must have escaped. Bound to.

I would open with the noise in the misty dark. Then the tank as seen by the soldiers. One of whom, shouting to no purpose against the roaring engine, scrabbles and writhes his way to escape ... Cut away, to us, our outfit, a mile or so away from the scene...We didn't hear or know anything yet. We will hear about it later, at the end of our day. But it will haunt us, shadow us all day long.

Garrett, affable and highly-active in teaching and writing, has seen over thirty of his books published, including the historical novels for which he is perhaps best known: *Death of the Fox*, about the fate of Sir Walter Raleigh; *The Succession: A Novel of Elizabeth and James*, on the relationship of Eliabeth I and her cousin James VI of Scotland; and *Entered from the Sun*.

—Dot Jackson

GATES, Henry Louis, Jr.

Born: Keyser, West Virginia, 16 September 1950. **Education:** Yale University, B.A. (summa cum laude) 1973; Clare College, Cambridge University, M.A. 1974, Ph.D. 1979. **Family:** Married Sharon Lynn Adams, 1 September 1979; two children. **Career:** General anesthetist, Anglican Mission Hospital, Kilimatinde, Tanzania, 1970-71; director of student affairs, 1971, director of research, 1972, John D. Rockefeller gubernatorial campaign, Charleston, West Virginia; staff correspondent, *Time*, London Bureau, England, 1973-75; lecturer, 1976-79, assistant professor, 1979-84, associate professor of English, 1984-85, director of undergraduate Afro-American studies, 1976-79, Yale University; professor of English, comparative literature, and African studies, 1985-88, W.E.B. DuBois Professor of Literature, 1988-90, Cornell University; Richard Wright Lecturer, Center for the Study of Black Literature and Culture, University of Pennsylvania, 1990; John Spencer Bassett Professor of English and Literature, Duke University, since 1990; W. E. B. DuBois Professor of the Humanities, professor of English, chair of Afro-American studies, and director of W.E.B. DuBois Institute for Afro-American Research, Harvard University, since 1991; visiting professor, Virginia Commonwealth University, 1987. Member of committees including National Book Award, PBS Adult Learning Series, Cultural Diversity, Ritz Paris Hemingway Prize Selection Committee, and the Schomburg Commission for the Preservation of Black Culture; member of board of directors, African-American Newspapers and Periodicals: A National Bibliography and Union List, African Labour History, American Council of Learned Societies, Center for the Study of Black Literature and Culture, *Diacritics*, European Institute for Literary and Cultural Studies, Everyman Library, Lincoln Center Theater Project, LIT Literature in Transition, Museum of Afro-American History, Museum of Science, New Museum of Contemporary Arts, Proceedings of the American Antiquarian Society, Studio Museum in Harlem, and UMI Research Press's "Challenging the American Canon" series. Frequent contributor to journals, including the *New Yorker,* 1990s; general editor of *A Dictionary of Cultural and Critical Theory, Middle-Atlantic Writers Association Review*; co-editor of *Transition*; associate editor of *Journal of American Folklore*; member of editorial boards including, *Critical Inquiry, Studies in American Fiction, Black American Literature Forum, PMLA, Stanford Humanities Review,* and *Yale Journal of Law and Liberation.* **Member:** Council on Foreign Relations, American Antiquarian Society, Union of Writers of the African Peoples, Association for Documentary Editing, African Roundtable, African Literature Association, Afro-American Academy, American Studies Association, Trans Africa Forum Scholars Council, Association for the Study of Afro-American Life and History (life), Caribbean Studies Association, College Language Association (life), Modern Language Association, Stone Trust, Zora Neale Hurston Society, Cambridge Scientific Club, American Civil Liberties Union National Advisory Council, German American Studies Association, National Coalition against Censorship, American Philosophical Society, Saturday Club, New England Historic Genealogical Society, Phi Beta Kappa.

Awards: Carnegie Foundation fellowship for Africa, 1970-71; Phelps fellowship, Yale University, 1970-71; Mellon fellowships, Cambridge University, 1973-75, and National Humanities Center, 1989-90; grants from Ford Foundation, 1976-77 and 1984-85, and National Endowment for the Humanities, 1980-86; A. Whitney Griswold fellowship, 1980; Rockefeller Foundation fellowships, 1981 and 1990; MacArthur Prize fellowship, MacArthur Foundation, 1981-86; Yale Afro-American teaching prize, 1983; award from Whitney Humanities Center, 1983-85; Princeton University Council of the Humanities lectureship, 1985; award for creative scholarship, Zora Neale Hurston Society, 1986; associate fellowship from W. E. B. DuBois Institute, Harvard University, 1987-88 and 1988-89; John Hope Franklin Prize honorable mention, American Studies Association, 1988; Woodrow Wilson National Fellow, 1988-89 and 1989-90; Candle Award, Morehouse College, 1989; American Book Award and Anisfield-Wolf Book Award for Race Relations, both for *The Signifying Monkey: Towards a Theory of Afro-American Literary Criticism,* 1989; Potomac State College Alumni Award, 1991; Bellagio Center fellowship, 1992; Clarendon Lecturer, Oxford University, 1992; Best New Journal the Year award (in the humanities and the social sciences), Association of Publishers, 1992; elected to the American Academy of Arts and Sciences, 1993; Plate Achievement Award, 1993; African American Students Faculty Award, 1993; Polk Award for Social Commentary, 1993; Heartland Prize for Nonfiction for People: A Memoir, 1994; Lillian Smith Book Award, 1994; West Virginian of the 1995; Humanities Award, West Virginia Humanities Council, 1995; Ethics Award, (magazine), 1996; Distinguished Editorial Achievement, *Critical Inquiry,* 1996; W.D. Weatherford Award; recipient of honorary degrees from Dartmouth College, 1989, University of West Virginia, 1990, University of Rochester, 1990, Pratt Institute, 1990, University of Bridgeport, 1991 (declined), University of New Hampshire, 1991, Bryant College, 1992, Manhattan Community College, 1992, George Washington University, 1993, University of Massachusetts at Amherst, 1993, Williams College, 1993, Emory University, 1995, Colby College, 1995, Bard College, 1995, Bates College, 1995. **Agent:** Carl Brandt, Brandt & Brandt Literary Agents, Inc., 1501 Broadway, New York, New York 10036. **Addresses:** Department of Afro-American Studies,

Harvard University, 77 Dunster Street, Cambridge, Massachusetts 02138-3810; W. E. B. DuBois Institute, Harvard University, 44 Brattle Street, Cambridge, Massachusetts 02138.

PUBLICATIONS

Criticism

Figures in Black: Words, Signs, and the Racial Self. New York, Oxford University Press, 1987.
The Signifying Monkey: Towards a Theory of Afro-American Literary Criticism. New York, Oxford University Press, 1988.
Loose Canons: Notes on the Culture Wars (essays). New York, Oxford University Press, 1992.

Editor

Black Is the Color of the Cosmos: Charles T. Davis's Essays on Afro-American Literature and Culture, 1942-1981. New York, Garland Publishing, 1982.
Our Nig; or, Sketches from the Life of a Free Black by Harriet E. Adams. New York, Random House, 1983.
Black Literature and Literary Theory. New York, Methuen, 1984.
The Slave's Narrative: Texts and Contexts, with Charles T. Davis. New York, Oxford University Press, 1986.
"Race," Writing, and Difference. Chicago, University of Chicago Press, 1986.
The Classic Slave Narratives. New York, New American Library, 1987.
In the House of Oshugbo: A Collection of Essays on Wole Soyinka. New York, Oxford University Press, 1988.
The Souls of Black Folk. New York, Bantam Books, 1989.
The Autobiography of an Ex-Coloured Man by James Weldon Johnson. Vintage, 1989.
Three Classic African American Novels. Vintage, 1990.
Their Eyes Were Watching God by Zora Neale Huston. New York, Harper, 1990.
Jonah's Gourd Vine. New York, Harper, 1990.
Tell My Horse. New York, Harper, 1990.
Mules and Men. New York, Harper, 1990.
Reading Black, Reading Feminist: A Critical Anthology. New York, Meridian Books, 1990.
Voodoo Gods of Haiti. New York, Harper and Row, 1991.
The Schomburg Library of Nineteenth-Century Black Women Writers (10 volume supplement). New York, Oxford University Press, 1991.
Black Biography, 1790-1950: A Cumulative Index, with Randall K. Burkett and Nancy Hall Burkett. Teaneck, New Jersey, Chadwyck-Healey, 1991.
Mulebone: A Comedy of Negro Life, with George Bass. New York, HarperPerennial, 1991.
Bearing Witness: Selections from African American Autobiography in the Twentieth Century. New York, Pantheon Books, 1991.
Gloria Naylor: Critical Perspectives Past and Present, with Anthony Appiah. New York, Amistad, 1993.
Alice Walker: Critical Perspectives Past and Present, with Anthony Appiah. New York, Amistad. 1993.
Langston Hughes: Critical Perspectives Past and Present, with Anthony Appiah. New York, Amistad, 1993.
Richard Wright: Critical Perspectives Past and Present, with Anthony Appiah. New York, Amistad, 1993.

Toni Morrison: Critical Perspectives Past and Present, with Anthony Appiah. New York, Amistad, 1993.

Zora Neale Hurston: Critical Perspectives Past and Present, with Anthony Appiah. New York, Amistad, 1993.

The Amistad Chronology of African American History from 1445-1990. New York, Amistad, 1993.

Frederick Douglass: Autobiographies. Library of America, 1994.

The Dictionary of Global Culture, with Anthony Appiah. New York, Knopf, 1995.

The Complete Stories of Zora Neale Hurston. New York, Harper Collins, 1995.

Identities, with Anthony Appiah. Chicago, University of Chicago, 1996.

The Future of the Race, with Cornel West. New York, Knopf, 1996.

The Norton Anthology of African American Literature, with N.Y. McKay. New York, Norton and Company, 1996.

The Dictionary of Global Culture, with Kwame Anthony Appiah. New York, Knopf, 1997.

Pioneers of the Black Atlantic: Five Slave Narratives from the Enlightenment, 1772-1815, with William L. Andrews. Washington, D.C., Civitas, 1998.

Black Imagination and the Middle Passage, with Maria Diedrich and Carl Pedersen. New York, Oxford University Press, 1999.

Thirteen Ways of Looking at a Black Man. New York, Random House, 1997.

Series editor, *The Oxford-Schomburg Library of Nineteenth-Century Black Women Writers* (30 volumes). New York, Oxford University Press, 1988.

Other

Colored People: A Memoir. New York, Knopf, 1994.

Compiler with James Gibb and Ketu H. Katrak, *Wole Soyinka: A Bibliography of Primary and Secondary Sources.* New York, Greenwood Press, 1986.

Contributor, *Millenarianism and Messianism in English Literature and Thought, 1650-1800.* Long Island City, E. J. Brill, 1988.

Contributor, *Literature, Language, and Politics.* Athens, University of Georgia, 1988.

Contributor, *Facing History: The Black Image in American Art, 1710-1940.* San Francisco, Bedford Arts, 1990.

Contributor, *Speaking of Race, Speaking of Sex: Hate Speech, Civil Rights, and Civil Liberties,* New York, New York University Press, 1994.

Contributor, *Come Sunday: Photographs by Thomas Roma.* New York, Museum of Modern Art, 1996.

*

Television: Created the series *The Image of the Black in the Western Imagination,* Public Broadcasting Service (PBS), 1982.

Critical Studies: "The Black Cannon: Reconstructing Black American Literary Criticism" by Joyce A. Joyce, *New Literary History,* Winter 1987; "Playing, Not Joking, with Literature" by John Edgar Wideman, *New York Times Book Review,* 14 August 1988; "Henry Louis Gates, Jr., and African-American Literary Dis-

course" by Waheema Lubiano, *New England Quarterly,* December 1989; "The Signifying Monkey: Towards a Theory of Afro-American Literary Criticism" by Kenneth Warren, *Modern Philology,* November 1990; "Two Cheers for Skip Gates" by Sanford Pinsker, *Virginia Quarterly Review,* Summer, 1993; "Loose Canons: Notes on the Culture Wars" by C. Vann Woodward, *Partisan Review,* Vol. 60, No. 3, 1993.

*   *   *

Henry Louis Gates, Jr., is among the most prominent and well-known critics since the early 1980s, with a reputation built on several fronts. As a literary historian, he discovered and in 1983 republished *Our Nig,* a novel penned by Harriet E. Adams and privately printed in 1859, which made it the earliest-known novel by an African-American woman. As a critic and editor, Gates contributed to the broadening discourse on African American literature in the 1980s by editing *Black Is the Color of the Cosmos: Charles T. Davis's Essays on Afro-American Literature and Culture, 1942-1981* (1982) and *Black Literature and Literary Theory* (1984), the latter of which served as a forum for critics to apply various contemporary critical approaches to works by African-American authors. The views Gates had been developing himself are elaborated on in *Figures in Black: Words, Signs, and the Racial Self* (1987) and *The Signifying Monkey: Towards a Theory of Afro-American Literary Criticism* (1988), which offer refreshing critical approaches that consider cultural traditions in African-American literature. His popular renown, based on his writings and the numerous critical texts and republished works he edited, has been enhanced with a memoir, *Colored People* (1994), and through ongoing contributions to journals and periodicals, including the *New Yorker,* where he addresses topical issues. His endeavors in academia, which includes bringing to Harvard such diverse artists as filmmaker Spike Lee and Nobel Laureate Wole Soyinka, are equally commendable, as is his tireless service as an advisor and consultant on a variety of projects.

The manner in which Gates addresses texts as a critic is reflected in his memoir, *Colored People,* an engaging account of growing up in Piedmont, West Virginia, during a time of desegregation. The difficulties encountered, evidences of multicultural assimilation, and a sense of nostalgia for the passing of some unique cultural gatherings show the influence of varying traditions on a community as well as distinctive practices among African-Americans within the community; similarly, Gates promotes a critical approach to literature that embraces traditional modes, contemporary methods, and a more particular understanding of cultural practices shared in many African communities, the Caribbean, and in America that bear influence on African-American works.

While neither ignoring nor separating from Western traditions, Gates has distinguished cultural traits amply in evidence African-American vernacular that must be taken into account in critical discourses of African-American life and art. "From the beginning," noted Waheema Lubiano, "Gates has asserted that he wants to change the perception, held by critics of both Euro-American texts and African-American texts, that African-American texts are transparent reflections of the history, sociology, and psychology of African-Americans. He argues that 'Blackness' as a Western Enlightenment formulation was and is a metaphor for the metaphysical anomaly or non-metaphysicality of African-Americans."

Gates' best expression of this view is set forth in *The Signifying Monkey: Towards a Theory of Afro-American Literary Criticism*, which culminated a decade-long development of ideas he presented in seminars and essays. Those ideas inform his work as editor of *Black Literature and Literary Theory*, a collection of essays in which various contemporary methodologies, including structuralism and post-structuralism, are applied to literary works by African-Americans, and of *Figures in Black: Words, Signs, and the Racial Self*, his semiotic approach to literature. *The Signifying Monkey* elaborates his concept of Signifyin(g); the "g" enclosed in parentheses represents a choice of pronouncing the hard "g" or dropping it, as it is in vernacular speech, which indicates a conscious and active approach to using language. That approach applies as well to the great trope of Afro-American discourse, where signifying is an open-ended process that relies on and plays off of previous expression. In Western traditions, to signify usually means to precisely define something, and when such a practice is applied to literature, Gates argues, it fails to engage in the very approach practiced by the writer. Signifying, as John Wideman wrote in reviewing Gates' work, "is verbal play—serious play that serves as instruction, entertainment, mental exercise, preparation for interacting with friend and foe in the social arena. In black vernacular, Signifying is a sign that words cannot be trusted, that even the most literal utterance allows room for interpretation, that language is both carnival and minefield." Signifyin(g) is "my metaphor for literary history," wrote Gates, and as a critic he participates in the same form of play—an active participant in a tradition in process, helping define that tradition. This understanding helps defamiliarize African-American texts from interpretative models of the past, opening up new possibilities for exegesis through contemporary methods and an approach that contextualizes cultural traditions.

While in Africa on a Carnegie Foundation fellowship and a Phelps fellowship from Yale during 1970-71, Gates traveled widely and became acquainted with various communities and their cultures. He met African writer Wole Soyinka, who became his tutor at Cambridge University, where Gates attained his master's and doctoral degrees. Through his travels, studies, and the mentorship of Soyinka Gates became intimately acquainted with Yoruba mythology and its trickster figure, who mediates between the worlds of gods and people and appears in various forms in several African cultures; in Yoruba the figure is a trickster-god, in other community stories he takes the form of a monkey. These figures serve in their respective traditions, according to Gates, "as points of conscious articulation of language traditions, complete with a history, patterns of development and revision, and internal principles of patterning and organization,"—a heritage sustained in the vernacular of African-American culture.

The theoretical approach Gates develops is then applied in *The Signifying Monkey* to various texts—Zora Neale Hurston's *Their Eyes Were Watching God*, Ishmael Reed's *Mumbo Jumbo*, Alice Walker's *The Color Purple*, for instance. Most liberating is his contention that "blackness" is not something signified to the texts—as to, say, slave narratives, with a slew of expectations and definitions—but rather something that comes to being through signifying within texts. At the same time and reflecting his centrist position, Gates also approaches a work like *The Color Purple* from the perspective of the epistolatory novel tradition. Thus, Gates promotes an approach that transcends what he calls "eth-

nic absolutism," which in discussing a work by an African-American author can be evidenced by strict adherence to Western tenets or, on the other hand, by Afrocentrism. Gates can accommodate both extremes.

The vitality of and openness of a discourse Gates favors is further expostulated in his essays collected in *Loose Canons: Notes on the Culture Wars* (1992), where such topics as gender and multiculturalism are examined within the context of what Gates calls the cultural wars—with extremes on the right staunchly defending the Western Tradition and those on the left seeking radical cultural shifts. Gates, again, takes a more central view, embracing many of the tenets of Western thought (indeed, his writing retains a strong sense of formal, academic style) while arguing for the necessity of diverse and multicultural approaches. This is the important role Gates himself plays: forsaking nothing that promises active and lively engagement in culture and impatient with any form of absolutism.

In his various roles—theorist, periodical contributor, advisor on multicultural projects, academic—Gates is involved in what Wideman called the serious play of Signifyin(g) "that serves as instruction, entertainment, mental exercise, preparation for interacting with friend and foe in the social arena."

—Mel Koler

GAUTREAUX, Tim

Born: Timothy Gautreaux in Morgan City, Louisiana, 1948. **Education:** Nicholls State University, B.A.; University of South Carolina, Ph.D. **Family:** Married Winbourne; two sons. **Career:** Professor of English and director of creative writing Southeastern Louisiana University, since 1972; John and Renee Grisham Visiting Southern Writer-in-Residence, University of Mississippi, 1996. **Awards:** National Endowment for the Arts fellowship; National Magazine Award for fiction, 1998.

PUBLICATIONS

Novels

The Next Step in the Dance. New York, St. Martin's Press, 1998. *Black Bayou*. Unpublished.

Short Story Collections

Same Place, Same Things. New York, St. Martin's Press, 1996.

Uncollected Short Stories

"Welding With Children," in *Atlantic Monthly*, March 1997.

*   *   *

Tim Gautreaux explores the difficulties and values of blue-collar workers in his native Southeastern Louisiana. His hard-working characters often bow under the weight of personal responsibility, nearly destroying their relationships and alienating their families. These characters seek refuge in their work, which provides for them a sense of pride and identity. They are also bound to the values of their culture, Roman Catholic religion, heritage, and upbringing. Confined to the towns of their childhood, they grapple with their own invidious patterns until catastrophe befalls them.

Gautreaux prevents his characters from sliding into irreversible decline, and lets hope dapple their often-dreary lives. Gautreaux paints even the most inimical characters with sympathy and respect, allowing them moments of redemption, and tenderness. The characters often lose their sense of integrity temporarily, only to rediscover it in the fallout of a self-made disaster.

Gautreaux's female characters are dissatisfied with their male counterparts. These women want the impossible: men of unwavering rectitude in a turbulent lifestyle of brawling, drinking, and cheating. His female characters often long for glamorous lives in Las Vegas or Los Angeles. They are tired of negotiating with rough and clueless men and exhausted by monotonous jobs. Out of frustration, these women cut their men with sharp wit and bruising intelligence.

The interaction between the men and women in Gautreaux's collected stories, *Same Place, Same Things,* and his novel, *The Next Step in the Dance,* is often fraught with complexity and intrigue. Caught on an edge of repulsion and sexual tension, they move together and apart, putting up barriers and breaking them down. The women are capable of forgiving the unforgivable, and the men often find their moral backbone, realize their mistakes, and return to their families. In Gautreaux's writing, penance is always rewarded with absolution.

The elderly in Gautreaux's stories are frequently the embodiment of Southeastern Louisiana values and culture. These characters are multi-faceted, sometimes senile and forgetful, sometimes bold, clear-minded, and outspoken; they are frequently the active presence in a story, surpassing their apparent frailties with quick and decisive action. For example, in "Floyd's Girl" (*Same Place, Same Things*), young Lizette is kidnapped by a Texan, setting off a local manhunt. Her uncle T-Jean, her father Floyd, and T-Jean's Grandmère take off in separate cars to rescue her. When they finally catch up, it is Grandmère who pokes out the kidnapper's eye while Floyd and T-jean wallow in the dust, knocked down by the kidnapper's fist. After her attack she declares, "This child belongs with her papa. She got LeBlanc in her, and Cancienne way back, and before that, Thibodeaux." She underscores the importance of familial association to the people in the story.

In *Next Step in the Dance*, Paul's grandfather, Abadie, heads up a search-and-rescue team long after the younger men have given up. He musters his waning strength, pushing his small boat deeper upriver, fueled by the need to find his lost grandson. Merlin LeBlanc ("The Courtship of Merlin LeBlanc") tosses his orphaned infant granddaughter shotgun shells to play with. Exhausted by her demands, he seems bitter and ill-suited for fatherhood. Gradually, he develops feelings for the baby, worries about her, and, finally, accepts her as his own.

The "old ones" are reminders of the long family histories of Southern Louisiana, and the importance those family histories play in the lives of their children and grandchildren. The elderly also show the contrast between the once-isolated culture of their area and the television-era homogenization their culture has experienced. The loss of French from the young people's Cajun, the dwindling role of the Roman Catholic Church in peoples' lives, and the appearance of gumbo and jambalaya on menus all over the country demonstrate a loosening of the tight cultural bonds in the small communities of Southeastern Louisiana. These examples are not specific to Louisiana: they are offered up as examples of how the South itself continues to change, disappear, or spread out to influence other parts of the world. Despite the encroaching influence of television and other factors, Gautreaux's characters manage to maintain much of their heritage. The values of family, the sense of community, and the unique elements of Cajun culture, from language to gumbo, continue to thrive in Gautreaux's stories.

In his collection of stories, *Same Place, Same Things,* Gautreaux again explores the culture of working class Southeast Louisiana. The protagonists are mostly men, with two notable exceptions: Raynelle Bullfinch, a cook on a steam dredge, and Elaine Campbell, a farmer. These folks define themselves by their occupations; they derive satisfaction from hard and dirty work. Gautreaux describes the intricacies of boilers, pumps, and engines, as well as the operation and repair of such mechanisms. These details underscore the important role arduous labor plays in his characters' lives.

The characters in *Same Place, Same Things* range from the dangerously mysterious Ada (the title character of one story), to the bright and funny Raynelle Bullfinch in "Died and Gone to Vegas," to the selfish-cum-generous Bobby Simoneaux in "Deputy Sid's Gift." These characters are consistently vivid and are often transformed, awakened, or renewed in some way. In many cases, Gautreaux's characters lose their perspective and cause major vehicular accidents, wreak havoc through drunken brawls, or destroy relationships. The consequences of their brutality are sometimes far-reaching, as in "Waiting for the Evening News." Jesse McNeil is "running a locomotive while he was drunk . . . charging up the main line at fifty with the chemical train, rattling like a thunderstorm." A major chemical spill ensues, and the once-invisible Jesse, "a man known only by his menopausal wife and his finance company," suddenly becomes the subject of the evening news. While the police form a manhunt, Jesse calls his wife. Her tenderness makes Jesse realize "she had become one of the details of his life that he no longer saw." In the end, a defeated and drunken Jesse succumbs to his fate, "bathed by strobes and headlights and stares, locked in inescapable beams."

In "People on the Empty Road," Wesley "used his recklessness like a tool to get the job done," but ends up crashing into a school bus. Finally aware of the toll his speeding is taking on his life, he looks to the pretty Miz Janie, a kind voice on the radio, to teach him patience and maturity. Gautreaux's messy and willful characters fascinate the reader with their slow shuffle toward tenderness, self-awareness, and redemption.

In an interview with the *Atlantic Monthly,* Gautreaux describes Mark Twain as an early influence on his writing: "Tall tales with their hyperbole and outlandish plots, seem to have had an effect on my writing . . . . I listened to retired tug-boat captains and oil-field workers try to outdo each other in stories. " Nowhere is this more evident than in his story "Returnings," which is set during the Johnson Administration. The story opens with Elaine, a grieving mother who tries to get her tractor started. She takes apart the carburetor, reassembles it, opens the gas valve, fixes a leak, and finally is able to start the tractor. As she resumes work, a helicopter lands on her property. A young Asian pilot emerges with an unreadable map, asking for directions. Elaine obliges to help him, and spends her afternoon flying above the fields and highways of her county. Gautreaux's mastery of detail and vivid characterization makes this "tall tale" utterly plausible. In "Died and Gone to Vegas," the workers on a steam dredge swap legends, each one more outrageous than the last, over a game of bourrèe—another echo of the storytellers of Gautreaux's youth.

The novel *Next Step in the Dance* chronicles the marriage of Paul and Colette Thibodeaux, whose relationship is dismantled and rebuilt throughout the novel, as they approach and retreat from each other like dancers. Paul's pattern of working, drinking, dancing, and fighting exhausts Colette, who longs to be in a place where there are "people who sparkle." In an effort to break away from the stagnancy of Tiger Island, Colette moves to California, the Mecca of sparkle. Like many of Gautreaux's women, Colette's effort to leave her home town and move on is foiled by her familial responsibility and her need for the familiar. Paul follows Colette to California, landing a high-paying job. His skills, common for Louisiana, are peculiar and in high demand in Los Angeles. They both find that the shrimp boats, sawmills, and shacks of Tiger Island are far superior to the vulgarities of L.A., and, separately, they return home. During their absence, Tiger Island transforms from a busy hub of hard work and constant activity into a town sliding into decay. An oil glut dries up jobs and guts the already shaky economy, sending people into other towns and states for work. Paul and Colette end up at the only viable business left in town, an industrial waste processing plant. As Tiger Island comes to resemble a ghost town, Paul and Colette move into and out of each other's lives, unable to abandon each other or their families. When the situation becomes most dire, they hang onto each other with an iron grasp.

At the end of his stories, Tim Gautreaux's characters find themselves redeemed, enlightened, awakened, and transformed. The unforgiving hard work and rows of tin shacks are not enough to keep the people who live in Tiger Island, Pine Oil, or Gumwood from living emotionally productive lives. Full of wisdom and energy, empowered by familial bonds, renewed by the rediscovery of their values, strengthened with tenderness, his characters are often resilient, even when the worst is yet to come. Over games of bourrèe, bowls of gumbo, mornings at Mass, and evenings at the local bar, these characters bond with their community in ways that are rare today. Gautreaux's laborers (and the women they rankle) rise above the drudgery of their lives, find satisfaction with themselves and each other, and atone for their misdeeds. As Gautreaux said in an interview with the *Atlantic Monthly*, "If a story does not deal with a moral question, I don't think it's much of a story."

—Frances E. Badgett

GIBBONS, Kaye

Born: Bertha Kaye Batts Gibbons in Wilson, North Carolina, 5 May 1960. **Education:** North Carolina State University, 1978-

80; University of North Carolina at Chapel Hill, 1985-87. **Family:** Married Michael Gibbons, 12 May 1984 (divorced 1992); three daughters; married Frank P. Ward, 25 September 1993. **Career:** Library assistant while a student at North Carolina State University; various jobs, including waitress and bookstore clerk, 1983; began concentrating on writing, mid-1980s, and has since published novels, poems, essays, and book reviews. **Awards:** Louis D. Rubin, Jr., Prize in Creative Writing, University of North Carolina, Sue Kaufman Prize for First Fiction, American Academy and Institute of Arts and Letters, Ernest Hemingway Foundation, Special Citation, all 1987, all for *Ellen Foster*; National Endowment for the Arts Fellowship, 1989; PEN/Revson Foundation Fiction Fellowship, 1990; Nelson Algren Heartland Award for Fiction, *Chicago Tribune*, 1991; Sir Walter Raleigh Award, 1991, for *A Cure for Dreams; Chevalier de L'Ordre des Arts et des Lettres* (a French Knighthood), for contributions to French literature, 1996.

PUBLICATIONS

Novels

Ellen Foster. Chapel Hill, Algonquin, 1987.
A Virtuous Woman. Chapel Hill, Algonquin, 1989.
A Cure for Dreams. Chapel Hill, Algonquin, 1991.
Charms for the Easy Life. New York, Putnam, 1993.
Sights Unseen. New York, Putnam, 1995.
On the Occasion of My Last Afternoon. New York: Putnam, 1998.

Other

How I Became a Writer: My Mother, Literature, and a Life Split Neatly into Two Halves. Chapel Hill, Algonquin, 1988. (Contents of this pamphlet appeared in the *Raleigh Leader*, November 10, 1988, and in *The Writer on Her Work, Vol II.*, edited by Janet Sternburg, New York, W. W. Norton, 1991.)
Essay, "On Tour: Kaye Gibbons," in *Hungry Mind Review*, available at http://www.bookwire.com/HMR/review/tgibbons.html, 1997.

Uncollected Writings

"The Headache," in *St. Andrews Review,* Spring/Summer, 1987.
"The Proof," in *Quarterly,* Spring 1987.
"Planes of Language and Time: The Surface of the Miranda Stories," in *Kenyon Review*, Winter 1988.
"A Nash Country Girl's Tribute," in *News and Observer,* Raleigh, North Carolina, November 5, 1989.

*

Media Adaptations: *Ellen Foster*, Hallmark Hall of Fame Special, broadcast on CBS, 1997.

Interviews: "Kaye Gibbons, 1960—, Author," in *Broken Silences: Interviews with Black and White Women* edited by Shirley Marie Jordan, New Brunswick, Rutgers University Press, 1993; "Kaye Gibbons," *Parting the Curtains* by Dannye Romine Powell, New York, Doubleday, 1994.

Critical Studies: "Kaye Gibbons's *A Virtuous Woman*: A Bakhtinian/Iserian Analysis of Conspicuous Agreement" by Stephen Souris, *Southern Studies,* Summer 1991; "'The Only Hard Part Was the Food': Recipes for Self-Nurture in Kaye Gibbons's Novels" by Veronica Makowsky, *The Southern Quarterly*, Winter/Spring 1992; "Kaye Gibbons (1960—)" by Julian Mason, *Contemporary Fiction Writers of the South: A Bio-Bibliographical Sourcebook* edited by Joseph M. Flora and Robert Bain, Westport, Connecticut, Greenwood Press, 1993; "Women and 'The Gift for Gab': Revisionary Strategies in *A Cure for Dreams*" by Tonita Branan, *Southern Literary Journal*, Spring 1994; "Simply Talking: Women and Language in Kaye Gibbons' *A Cure for Dreams*" by Kathryn McKee, *The Southern Quarterly*, Summer 1997; "Kaye Gibbons: Her Full-Time Women," *Southern Writers at Century's End* edited by James A. Perkins, et al, Lexington, University Press of Kentucky, 1997.

* * *

In 1987, Kaye Gibbons seemed to burst on the literary scene with her first book, *Ellen Foster.* Actually, Gibbons had been using writing as a personal stabilizing device for years of shifting homes, erratic education, ill-chosen education majors, and bouts of depression. She often tells interviewers that writing is a place she goes, rather than what she does. "It started with my mother, this writing urge," she says. While most writers' first novels depend on experiences from their lives, *Ellen Foster* especially seems to contain events and childhood sensibilities directly out of Gibbons' own memory. In recent interviews, Gibbons acknowledges elements in her work that are autobiographical. The novel, an imaginative re-creation of Gibbons' story, shows Ellen as a character in her own right, however. The eleven-year-old girl displays strength and determination to survive her hostile environment in the directness of first-person narrative. So endearing was she, that *Ellen Foster* enjoyed a popularity unlike that of most writers' first novels. A decade later, this book attained a still larger audience by being selected (along with Gibbons' second novel) by Oprah Winfrey for her "Oprah's Book Club" November 1997, reading. In December, Hallmark Hall of Fame and CBS presented the story adapted for television.

Her second novel, *A Virtuous Woman*, uses two main characters—Ruby and Jack Stokes—who also tell their own stories, though in a different structure. They alternate stories, with Ruby's narration spoken after her death. Gibbons makes the use of first-person narration work by creating characters whose strengths lie in their forthrightness; they are honest and honorable people who command respect and who hold readers' attention. She refines this narrative device to an art and uses it extensively.

In *A Cure for Dreams,* Gibbons's next work, she reveals the story through the consciousness of Betty Davis Randolph, recalling her childhood and her mother's life, and presents characters recognizable in the modern world.

Earlier characters, though masterfully crafted and completely believable, appear as extremes, people who live on the periphery of society. As her novels evolve, Gibbons involves the ordinary scene of her characters and explores the extraordinary realm of their thoughts and dreams. She tells of a teacher who told her she would always write about women's burdens, "I write, in part, to

discover what those burdens are and how a character's load can be lessened, her pain mitigated" ("On Tour"). Her narrative approach, rising from the characters of the people she invents, carries the stories, and each of the first-person presentations is distinctly different. Her interest is in the characters' survival or escape and in their life beyond the brutality.

In her fourth novel, *Charms for the Easy Life*, Gibbons uses multiple levels of three family generations to examine the impact of family and community on the individual psyche. The story spins out of the viewpoint of Margaret, the granddaughter, who looks for escape from heredity. "The women," according to Gibbons, "have to learn to look into their own hearts and minds for comfort and peace."

In *Sights Unseen*, she uses a daughter's narration to tell the story of a marriage in which the mother suffers from manic-depressive disorder. Frederick Barnes, the father, is the most fully-drawn male figure Gibbons has created, a fact she attributes to "having found a relationship with a husband I respect and cherish" ("On Tour"). The revealed thoughts of the children in this family as they react to their mother's moods illustrate Gibbons' use of shifting viewpoints and her concern with family influence. In referring to her own manic-depressive problems and mother-daughter relationship, Gibbons told interviewer Dannye Romine Powell, "That vision of myself through my child's eyes has put me in motion and has helped with the illness more than the twenty-seven pills a day."

On the Occasion of My Last Afternoon, is a retrospective narrative told in 1900 from the viewpoint of Emma Garnet Tate Lowell. The protagonist, born into a mid-nineteenth century, genteel South and a well-to-do family, breaks from her father's control and marries a Boston surgeon of the Lowell family. The story examines the culture of place, the event of the Civil War and subsequent reconstruction, filtered through the memories of Emma. What she suffers is her own civil war, and her narration is her own reconstruction. Emma is as memorable a character as earlier protagonists, but the historical perspective is weak. Twentieth century rural North Carolina and urban Raleigh are places Gibbons knows better; they best provide a sense of place for her fiction as she concentrates on examining the human psyche.

Gibbons is a natural storyteller, gifted in her talent and her craft. Her characters are fully-drawn, complex and emotionally authentic; her place is (usually) detailed and appropriate for those characters' development. Her themes involve the impact of family and community on the psychological development of the impressionable, especially with mother-daughter relationships. The evolution of her novels reveals her maturity as a person and as a writer; since the success of *Ellen Foster*, Gibbons speaks openly about her mother's suicide, her father's alcoholism, and her own illness.

Autobiographical facts serve as impetus and raw material for much of her fiction. If Ellen Foster was the child representing Gibbons in her search for survival and order, the succeeding novels are imaginative projections of life as it might have been. They posit such questions as What if her mother had lived beyond Gibbons' childhood?, and What if her mother (from whom Gibbons suspects she inherited her illness), had the advantages of modern-day treatment? She explained to Powell, "So [by writing] I can pretend that I had a mother who continued to live, and this is my way of knowing her," adding: "This way, I'm working on my father and making him into the man I wanted him to be . . . . He was a brilliant man and he could do anything he set his mind to."

The rhetoric glues together place and character in her novels. Though Gibbons' gift as a teller of stories is innate, she researched for a language that would give her the ambience and stylistic flow needed to make her novels authentic. She found characters and regional expressions in the stories collected in a Works Projects Administration book of interviews—characters surviving the 1930s depression whose lives were impoverished, but whose spirits were strong; their manner of speaking expressed the hardship they endured and gave Gibbons the rhetoric she needed. She has a love of language shared with all Southern writers and an ear for the cadences of music inherent in speech. The talk in her fiction becomes the building blocks of characterization; this is especially evident in *A Cure for Dreams,* where a community of women control the scene and present a new perspective on their daily lives and on history.

Gibbons has converted her manic-depressive illness into a tool for her writing; she has turned an adversity into an asset. Because she remembers the way she observed and reacted to her own mother's illness, she can project her creative perspective into the minds of her children observing her. This imaginatively becomes the stuff of her fiction. Her disorder is also a scheduling device for writing: "I have found that I write best in what is called hypomania, which is halfway between being normal and being full-blown manic . . . . In that in-between state, it's like looking out of a very clear window and seeing the story on the other side. I have a hypersensitivity to language, and my thoughts come easily in an organized, patterned way," she told Powell.

Gibbons' novels are an effective blend of fact and fiction; she rises above adversities in her life and through her fiction. An illness that must have hindered her life in many aspects, she uses as a tool for her craft; her understanding of the abstractions in human endeavor, she hones into an art. Through her novels, she examines her own life and projects an imagined life onto the pages of fiction. The uniqueness of her life—its successes and its failures—has given her a special vision for sights unseen. Gibbons looks directly into the dark corner that most see only peripherally and reveals that vision on the pages of her novels.

—Jeanne R. Nostrandt

GIBSON, Margaret

Born: Philadelphia, Pennsylvania, 17 February 1944. **Education:** Hollins College, B.A. 1966; University of Virginia, M.A. 1967. **Family:** Married Ross Gibson, August 1966 (divorced, May 1974); married David McKain (a poet and teacher), 27 December 1975. **Career:** Instructor of English, Madison College, Harrisonburg, Virginia, 1967-68, Virginia Commonwealth University, 1968-70; professor of English, George Mason University, University of Connecticut, and the Phillips Academy. **Awards:** Woodrow Wilson fellowship, 1967; Lamont Poetry Selection,

Academy of American Poets, 1982, for *Long Walks in the Afternoon*; Melville Crane Awards, Poetry Society of America, 1986, for *Memories of the Future: The Daybooks of Tina Modotti*. **Address:** R.F.D. 1, Matson Rd., Norwich, Connecticut 06360.

PUBLICATIONS

Poetry Collections

Signs. Baton Rouge, Louisiana State University Press, 1979.
Long Walks in the Afternoon. Baton Rouge, Louisiana State University Press, 1982.
Memories of the Future: The Daybooks of Tina Modotti. Baton Rouge, Louisiana State University Press, 1986.
Out in the Open. Baton Rouge, Louisiana State University Press, 1989.
The Vigil: A Poem in Four Voices. Baton Rouge, Louisiana State University Press, 1993.
Earth Energy: New and Selected Poems. Baton Rouge, Louisiana State University Press, 1997.

Other

The Duel (poetry pamphlet). Hollins, Virginia, Tinker, 1966.
Lunes (poetry pamphlet). Washington, D.C., Some of Us Press, 1972.
On the Cutting Edge (poetry pamphlet). Willimantic, Connecticut, Curbstone Press, 1975.

Editor with others, *Landscape and Distance: Contemporary Poets from Virginia.* Charlottesville, University Press of Virginia, 1975.

*

Critical Studies: "Words, Book Words, What Are You?" by Peter Stitt, *Georgia Review,* Summer 1983; "One Man's Music," *Local Assays: On Contemporary American Poetry* by Dave Smith, Urbana, University of Illinois Press, 1985; "Loners Whose Voice Move" by Philip Booth, *Georgia Review,* Spring 1989.

*   *   *

Margaret Gibson's poetry probes the human condition through meditations of personal experience, larger social/political engagement, and through connections with the natural world and spiritual presence. Such varied interests as gardening, political activism, and feminism infuse her work as she considers what makes for a meaningful existence and explores absences, which can include missed possibilities, change, the unknown and unloved, and death. There is a quietness about her work, suggesting a meditative sensibility that carefully considers what is observed, reinforced through recurring allusions to Eastern and Western spiritualism and a reverence for nature. Gibson favors a free-form style, with phrases spilling over lines and insights offered within the expanding flow stretching over several lines. The effect is subtle, not dramatic: significant things occur or are discovered among everyday realities.

Gibson was raised in Virginia, studied at Hollins College and the University of Virginia, and began her literary and academic careers in the state before relocating to Connecticut during the 1970s. Her earliest verse appeared in small press publications beginning in the mid-1960s, but discussions of her poetry properly commence with 1979's *Signs*, which like her next five collections was published by Louisiana State University Press. The poems in *Signs* display her respect for the natural world, observed as vibrant and varied in poems that offer different perspectives and are infused with Christian and Zen spirituality—in metaphysical terms rather than theological constructs.

The four sections of the book correspond roughly to the seasons, and the volume's outstanding theme is indicated in the title poem, "Signs: A Progress of the Soul." These are self-reflective poems observing the passage of time in the natural world and delving into emotional attachments. The speakers in the poems are often engaged in an activity—gardening, for instance—that complements a search for understanding. Such activities, which can range in her work from simple domestic chores to political involvement, are honored, treated by Gibson as crafts requiring skill, commitment, and faith.

Long Walks in the Afternoon, her next collection, has similarly meditative verse, as its title suggests, and includes epigrams from St. Augustine and Kafka that announce a spiritual thematic concern for guiding emotions. The volume is composed of three sections: the first continues the meditative form of *Signs*, the second concerns social and political involvement, and the final section comprises elegies. Poems in the opening section probe consciousness and repeatedly find meaning in such activities as art, social work, and domestic tasks. The poems in the second section are more overtly "meaningful," as even tender moments are invested with larger political realities—death, violence, persecution, and issues of power are never far away, even in moments of physical intimacy. The elegies, a term more descriptive of the poems' pervading tone rather than the traditional use of the term (poems occasioned by death), meditate on absences—things missing; fears are confronted and desire vies with self-control.

Gibson's four later collections can be paired into two categories: in *Memories of the Future: The Daybooks of Tina Modotti (1986)* and *The Vigil: A Poem in Four Voices* (1993) she adopts personas of characters, while she expands on her characteristic, meditative lyrics in *Out in the Open (*1989) and in the new pieces included in *Earth Energy: New and Selected Poems* (1997).

Memories of the Future observes, experiences, and reflects on events from the perspective of Tina Modotti, an actress who appeared in *Greed*, a 1924 film by Erich von Stroheim and who became a political activist, photographer, and nurse during the 1930s in conflicts in Mexico and Spain. Taking the form of a journal, *Memories of the Future* blends feelings with recountings of politically-charged events. Gibson's belief that a sense of identity is attained through work, particularly when work becomes craft and commitment, is evidenced in this collection, as Modotti's activism gives meaning to her life. Modotti also reflects a variety of choices available to women: even as she occasionally broods over not having had children, plenty of other meaningful activities are accessible. Gibson herself was involved in activist causes in Connecticut, working with a group of Puerto Ricans discriminated against ethnically and economically: her local, contemporary work mirrors the larger-scale and historical significance of Modotti's.

The Vigil: A Poem in Four Voices similarly addresses women's choices while undertaking more general issues. This work unfolds stories about the lives of four females spanning three generations of a family. Mysteries are presented in the opening poem and are elaborated on in the subsequent pieces, as the women individually persevere through family hardships. Gathered together at a ceramic firing, the women gradually connect as individuals in spite of familial divisions, their fragile ceramic wares emblematic of solidarity and craft.

Gibson's self-reflective lyrics in *Out in the Open* continue her probing of absences and darker elements of the human condition (called "blind spots" in the title poem) as well as pursuit of meaning, peace, and love. Occasional moments of serene clarity occur, while at other times the poet longs for resolution, even amid beauty and tranquility, even with the calming guidance of Zen and Christian influences.

These varying qualities continue in her subsequent poems collected in *Earth Energy: New and Selected Poems*, with tensions explored in the beauty and changes of nature and human relations. Even as ultimate resolutions prove elusive, quiet revelations occur in scenes of extended observation and contemplation—spiritualism in the everyday communicated within long flowing phrases that express penetrating moments of clarity even as they continue on to other observations, or come to rest. The interplay of natural, human, and spiritual elements and the characteristic Gibson free-form style are displayed in "In the Retreat of the Virgin of Guadeloupe," which speaks of the "inner light" that

can't be contained
within me, that spills
onto adobe pot, fern and fountain, altar cloth,
the hem of my dress . . .

"She intends to derive from the natural world a philosophy of feeling," observed Dave Smith of Gibson's work through 1985, and that continuing pursuit finds connections in natural, human, and spiritual realms in this poem and throughout Gibson's work.

—Perry Bear

GILCHRIST, Ellen

Born: Ellen Louise Gilchrist in Vicksburg, Mississippi, 20 February 1935. **Education:** Vanderbilt University, Nashville; Millsaps College, Jackson, Mississippi, B.A. in philosophy 1967; University of Arkansas, Fayetteville, 1976. **Family:** Three sons. **Career:** Broadcaster on National Public Radio 1984-85; journalist. **Awards:** Mississippi Arts Festival poetry award, 1968; New York Quarterly award for poetry, 1978; National Endowment for the Arts grant, 1979; *Prairie Schooner* award, 1981; Mississippi Academy award, 1982, 1985; Saxifrage Award, 1983; American Book Award, 1985; University of Arkansas Fulbright award, 1985; Mississippi Institute Arts and Letters award, for literature, 1985, 1990, 1991. **Address:** Little Brown, 34 Beacon St., Boston, Massachusetts 02108.

PUBLICATIONS

Poetry

The Land Surveyor's Daughter. Fayetteville, Arkansas, Lost
    Roads, 1979.
Riding Out the Tropical Depression: Selected Poems 1975-1985.
    New Orleans, Faust, 1986.

Novels

The Annunciation. Boston, Little Brown, 1983.
The Anna Papers. Boston, Little Brown, 1988.
Net of Jewels. Boston, Little Brown, 1992.
Anabasis: A Journey to the Interior. Jackson, University of Mis-
    sissippi, 1994.
Starcarbon: A Meditation on Love. Boston, Little Brown, 1994.
Sarah Conley. Boston, Little Brown, 1997.

Short Story Collections

In the Land of Dreamy Dreams. Fayetteville, University of Ar-
    kansas, 1981; Boston, Little Brown, 1985.
Victory over Japan. Boston, Little Brown, 1984.
Drunk with Love. Boston, Little Brown, 1986.
Light Can Be Both Wave and Particle. Boston, Little Brown, 1989.
I Cannot Get You Close Enough: Three Novellas. Boston, Little
    Brown, 1990.
The Blue-Eyed Buddhist and Other Stories. London, Faber, 1990.
The Age of Miracles. Boston, Little Brown, 1995.
Rhoda: A Life in Stories. Boston, Little Brown, 1995.
The Courts of Love. Boston, Little Brown, 1996.

Other

Falling Through Space: The Journals of Ellen Gilchrist. Boston,
    Little Brown, 1987.

*

Critical Studies: *Louisiana Women Writers* by Dorothy Brown
and Barbara Ewell, Baton Rouge, Louisiana State University Press,
1992; *Contemporary Southern Women Fiction Writers: An Annotated Bibliography* by Rosemary Reisman and Christopher
Canfield, Methuen, New Jersey, Scarecrow Press, 1994; *Ellen
Gilchrist* by Mary C. McCay, New York, Twayne Publishers,
1997.

*   *   *

The world Ellen Gilchrist creates in her short stories and novels is a world primarily of women, raised as southern belles and
debutantes by dominant fathers and genteel mothers to be perfect
wives, hostesses, and tennis partners. Gilchrist's heroines—including the feisty Rhoda Manning, the self-reliant Nora Jane
Whittington, and the haunted Anna Hand—resist these stifling expectations of southern women. Their struggles are continual;
throughout Gilchrist's work, these women ceaselessly assert themselves, fighting against a society that threatens to neglect their identities, their desires, and their dreams.

In her first collection of stories, *In the Land of Dreamy Dreams*,
Gilchrist depicts the unhappy lives of a number of such wealthy,
bored women in New Orleans. Among them, young nineteen-year
old "anarchist" Nora Jane robs a bar while dressed as a nun in
order to gain enough money to flee the South and join her felon
lover, Sandy, in California. More memorably, four of these early
stories introduce Rhoda, here seen as a precocious child confronting gender restraints that allow her to be a maid of honor in her
cousin's wedding but deny her a part in a backyard pole-vault
competition. Rhoda also appears as a young mother of two children who comes home to ask her father's assistance in getting an
abortion of a third child so she can finally leave her husband. With
this collection, Gilchrist not only focuses on the archaic social
strictures on women in the South, she also reveals the possibility
of transcendence if women are willing to defy the strong cultural
influence under which they were raised.

Gilchrist's first novel, *The Annunciation*, records this process
in Amanda McCamey, a young Mississippi woman who bears a
child by her cousin Guy, gives the girl up for adoption, and settles
into adult life married to a rich New Orleans business man. She
eventually abandons this posh life of social functions, country
clubs, and drunken malaise to journey to Fayetteville, Arkansas,
to pursue a project translating French poetry. As part of her new
life, she takes a younger lover, gets pregnant, and is reunited with
her lost daughter. The control she finally assumes over her life is
presented in the prayer that closes the novel: "Hallowed be my
name, my kingdom come, my will be done, amen."

In *Victory Over Japan*, Gilchrist returns to Rhoda's life with
stories of her childhood (the title story), adolescence ("Music,"
in which the 14-year-old takes up smoking and loses her virgin-
ity), and marriage ("The Lower Garden District Free Gravity Mule
Blight, or Rhoda, a Fable"). The latter again presents Rhoda as an
unhappy wife, this time pawning her engagement ring, filing a
fraudulent insurance claim, and then seducing the claims adjuster
who investigates her case, all in an effort to gain enough financial
security to establish a new life alone.

Two Nora Jane stories chronicle her arrival in California, where
she finds Sandy involved with another woman and meets a new lover,
bookstore owner Freddy Harwood. In "The Double Happiness Bun,"
she learns of her pregnancy and gains a new sense of independence
as she comforts earthquake victims on a San Francisco bridge.

The final section of stories presents Crystal Manning Weiss,
Rhoda's cousin, and her maid Traceleen, the narrator of these stories. Most notable is "Traceleen, She's Still Talking," in which
Traceleen accompanies Crystal on a trip to Texas to inspect her
spendthrift brother's foolhardy investment, a wild game hunting
camp; by the end of the story, Crystal has destroyed his new car,
set free his antelope, and effectively scuttled the entire venture,
all out of revenge for his squandering their shared inheritance.

This volume also introduces Anna Hand, a character many critics have viewed as Gilchrist's alter-ego. In "Looking Over Jordan," the writer, whose latest novel and previous collection of
stories "based on real-life tragedies in the Crescent City" have
made her the enemy of the cultured New Orleans elite, is unknow-
ingly confronted with her harshest reviewer, who does not have
the integrity to criticize her to her face.

Anna returns in "Anna, Part I" in Gilchrist's next collection, *Drunk with Love*, a meditation on the subject of love through the further adventures of Rhoda, Nora Jane, Crystal, and Traceleen. Anna's tale relates a year-long affair with a married man who refuses to leave his wife, which she transforms into fiction.

Anna appears next in *The Anna Papers*, a novel centered around her suicide, following a diagnosis of cancer, and the legacy she leaves behind for her extended family. Before she dies, she arranges to have her brother's long-lost Native American daughter, Olivia, reunited with the family, and she names her sister Helen, a woman miserable in marriage, as co-executor of her literary estate. While Olivia adapts to her new family, Helen sorts through Anna's papers, is visited by her ghost, and eventually finds the motivation to leave her husband and to begin an affair with a poet, the other executor of the estate. Unlike the individual personal triumphs of Gilchrist's other heroines, Anna Hand's transcendence results in a larger transformation of a community, the other women in her family.

I Cannot Get You Close Enough, a collection of three novellas, continues Gilchrist's treatment of the Hand family. The first novella, *Winter*, chronicles Anna's attempt to save her niece Jessie from her unfit mother. *DeHavilland Hand* recounts the romance and brief marriage of Daniel Hand and Summer Deer, and the early life of their child, Olivia. *A Summer in Maine* follows a group of Hands to a summer house where Anna's papers again occupy their time; Crystal attempts to keep a trunk of Anna's letters from Helen's attention, and Olivia finds them and organizes a literary cult in Anna's honor.

In *Falling Through Space*, Gilchrist bemoaned the difficulty of creating tales about new characters when her old characters, "a Fellini troupe," were "always trying to steal the spotlight." She claimed "it's gotten to the point where it's impossible for me to create new characters because the old ones keep grabbing up all the roles. The minute I think up a new dramatic situation, one of my old characters grabs it up and runs with it." The battle is often won by these old characters, especially in the later works. Rhoda, Nora Jane, Crystal and Traceleen occupy center stage in *Light Can Be Both Wave and Particle*, Rhoda's college years and early marriage are the subject of *Net of Jewels*, and *Starcarbon* returns to the Hand family, focusing on Olivia's return to Oklahoma and Jessie's problematic marriage to Crystal's son. Rhoda, as writer and grandmother, is the subject of most of the stories in *The Age of Miracles*, and Nora Jane and her ten-year-old twins are the focus of *The Courts of Love*.

Despite this group of characters' firm grip on Gilchrist's imagination, she has managed to elude them in a host of stories scattered through her collections and in two of her latest novels. She goes farthest in *Anabasis*, the tale of Auria, a young slave girl in Ancient Greece. However, even in this setting, a long way from the late twentieth-century South, she explores this one woman's quest for art, love, and fulfillment in a society that severely restricts women's freedom. In her recent novel, *Sarah Conley*, Gilchrist returns to more familiar territory, depicting one southern woman from childhood to middle-age, attempting to balance her desire for love and art, a struggle embodied in her choice between a long-lost love and a project adapting a novel to film in France. Both Auria and Sarah Conley share the trials of Nora Jane, Rhoda, Anna, and Crystal, all striving for happiness in a world of men.

The expansive tapestry Gilchrist weaves out of the lives of this group of southern women portrays many different Souths—New Orleans, Charlotte, North Carolina, the Ozark mountains, Oklahoma—and the South that these women carry with them as they leave the region. But readers also see these women's lives change as decades pass. Rhoda develops from precocious child competing with her brother to feisty old writer arguing with her insurance company over coverage, Nora Jane from teenage rebel to patient mother, and Anna Hand from pained mortal to the guardian angel watching over her family. Readers see these women evolve, survive, and triumph.

—Paul Christian Jones

GIOVANNI, Nikki

Born: Yolande Cornelia Giovanni in Knoxville, Tennessee, 7 June 1943. **Education:** Fisk University, 1960-61, 1964-67, B.A. (magna cum laude) in history, 1967; University of Pennsylvania School of Social Work, Philadelphia, 1967; Columbia University, New York, 1968. **Family:** Has one son. **Career:** Edited *Elan*, Fisk University's literary magazine, as a student; assistant professor of Black Studies, Queens College, Flushing, New York, 1968; associate professor of English, Livingston College, Rutgers University, New Brunswick, New Jersey, 1968-72; visiting professor of English, Ohio State University, Columbus, 1984; professor of creative writing, Mt. St. Joseph on the Ohio, then Virginia Polytechnic Institute and State University, since 1985; founder, Niktom Publishers, New York, 1970-74. Editorial consultant, *Encore* magazine, Albuquerque, New Mexico; life member, National Council of Negro Women. **Awards:** Ford Foundation grant, 1968; National Endowment for the Arts grant, 1969. D.H.L.: Wilberforce University, Ohio, 1972; D.Litt.: University of Maryland, Princess Anne, 1974, Ripon University, Wisconsin, 1974, Smith College, Northampton, Massachusetts, 1975, Mt. St. Joseph on the Ohio, 1983. **Address:** Department of English, Virginia Polytechnic Institute and State University, P.O. Box 0112, Blacksburg, Virginia 24063-0001.

PUBLICATIONS

Poetry Collections

Black Feeling, Black Talk. Privately printed, 1968.
Black Judgement. Detroit, Broadside Press, 1968.
Re:Creation. Detroit, Broadside Press, 1970.
Black Feeling, Black Talk / Black Judgment. New York, Morrow, 1970.
Poem of Angela Yvonne Davis. New York, Afro Arts, 1970.
My House. New York, Morrow, 1972.
The Women and the Men. New York, Morrow, 1975.
Cotton Candy on a Rainy Day. New York, Morrow, 1978.
Those Who Ride the Night Winds. New York, Morrow, 1983.
The Selected Poems of Nikki Giovanni. New York, Morrow, 1996.
Love Poems. New York, Morrow, 1997.

Verse for Children

Spin a Soft Black Song: Poems for Children, illustrated by Charles Bible. New York, Hill & Wang, 1971; revised edition, illustrated by George Martins, 1985.

Ego Tripping and Other Poems for Young People. Westport, Connecticut, Lawrence Hill, 1973.

Vacation Time. New York, Morrow, 1980.

Knoxville, Tennessee, illustrated by Larry Johnson. New York, Scholastic, 1994.

The Sun Is So Quiet, illustrated by Ashley Bryan. New York, Holt, 1996.

The Genie in the Jar, illustrated by Chris Raschka. New York, Holt, 1996.

Other

Gemini: An Extended Autobiographical Statement on My First Twenty-five Years of Being a Black Poet. Indianapolis, Bobbs Merrill, 1971.

A Dialogue: James Baldwin and Nikki Giovanni. Philadelphia, Lippincott, 1973.

A Poetic Equation: Conversations between Nikki Giovanni and Margaret Walker. Washington, D.C. Howard University Press, 1974.

Sacred Cows ... and Other Edibles (essays). New York, Morrow, 1988.

Racism 101. New York, Quill, 1994.

Editor, *Night Comes Softly: An Anthology of Black Female Voices.* Newark, New Jersey, Medic Press, 1970.

Editor, with Cathee Dennison, *Appalachian Elders: A Warm Hearth Sampler.* Blacksburg, Virginia, Pocahantas Press, 1991.

Editor, *Grandmothers: Poems, Reminiscences, and Short Stories about the Keepers of Our Traditions.* New York, Holt, 1994.

Editor, *Shimmy, Shimmy, Shimmy Like My Sister Kate: Looking at the Harlem Renaissance through Poems.* New York, Holt, 1996.

*

Manuscript Collection: Mugar Memorial Library, Boston University.

Recordings: Audio—*Truth Is On Its Way,* Right On, 1971; *Like a Ripple on a Pond,* Niktom, 1973; *The Way I Feel: All Poems by Nikki Giovanni,* Niktom, 1975; *Legacies,* Folkways, 1976; *The Reason I Like Chocolate,* Folkways, 1976; *Cotton Candy on a Rainy Day,* Folkways, 1978. **Films**—*Nikki Giovanni,* Verdugo City, California, Pied Piper Productions, 1979; *Spirit to Spirit: Nikki Giovanni, Poets in Performance,* produced by Mirra Bank and Perrin Ireland, Los Angeles, Direct Cinema, 1987.

Interviews: *Conversations with Nikki Giovanni* edited by Virginia C. Fowler, Jackson, University Press of Mississippi, 1992.

Critical Studies: *Nikki Giovanni: From Revolution to Revelation* by Anna T. Robinson, Columbus, State Library of Ohio, 1979; *Race, Gender, and Class Perspectives in the Works of Maya Angelou, Gwendolyn Brooks, Rita Dove, Nikki Giovanni, and*

Audre Lorde by Ekaterini Georgoudaki, Thessaloniki, Greece, Aristotle University of the Thessaloniki, 1991; *Nikki Giovanni* by Virginia C. Fowler. New York, Twayne, 1992; *Imaging the Body in Contemporary Women's Poetry: Helga Novak, Ursula Krechel, Carolyn Forche, Nikki Giovanni* by Amy K. Strawser, New York, P. Lang, 1996.

*   *   *

Over three decades, the signature characteristic of Nikki Giovanni's vision and writing has been change. "You're a fool if you don't change," she warns. Now a poet of introspection and information, she began her career as a poet of revolution and black liberation. Along her changing path she became an immensely popular and highly honored teacher and poet.

An Ayn Rand-Barry Goldwater conservative when she enrolled at Fisk University, Giovanni soon joined the ranks of dissidents and revived the school's defunct Student Nonviolent Coordinating Committee (SNCC). Along with her interest in black power, she also nurtured her writing talents by assisting in John O. KIllen's writers' workshop and editing *Elan,* Fisk's literary magazine. After graduation in 1967, although stunned by the death of her influential maternal grandmother, Giovanni organized Cincinnati's first Black Arts Festival and, thus, established herself as a leader in the black awareness movement. That same year she published her first collection of poetry, *Black Feeling, Black Talk* (1967), dedicated to revolutionary H. Rap Brown, followed by *Black Judgment* (1968), and *Re:Creation* (1970). Steeped in the black power movement and enriched by her own community activism, these angry poems call for black assertiveness; in the militant "The True Import of Present Dialogue, Black vs. Negro," she practically screams, "A nigger can die / We ain't got to prove we can die / We got to prove we can kill." But in the line "Black love is Black wealth" from her favorite poem, "Nikki-Rosa," she laments the effacement of love to the hatred of the revolution. Characteristically, this early poetry bears witness to the social and political events surrounding Giovanni, including Martin Luther King's and Robert Kennedy's assassinations.

Meanwhile, in 1969, Giovanni made a transforming decision. Unmarried, but dedicated to family life, she chose to become a single mother; her focus soon centered on her son, Thomas Watson. Over the next few years, Giovanni traveled, founded NikTom Limited, a publishing cooperative, and edited *Night Comes Softly* (1970), an anthology of black women poets.

Two books signal an important shift in her creative work. Dedicated to her son, *Spin a Soft Black Song: Poems for Children* (1971) recounts the sensibilities of black neighborhood children, beginning an often unknown side of her writing. *Gemini: An Extended Autobiographical Statement on My First Twenty-Five Years of Being a Black Poet* (1971) relates her life's experiences and views about people and current events in a less militant stance while providing warm, loving sketches of her family.

In another modulation, Giovanni recorded the best-selling *Truth Is On Its Way* (1971) on which she reads her poetry against the background of gospel music. Indeed, much of her poetry has a lyrical quality; critics point to its syncopation and repeated refrains, particularly in *My House* (1972). Divided into two sections, these thirty six poems, often monologues, reveal Giovanni's maturing techniques. The softer poems in "The Inside Room" draw on family, older acquaintances and lovers while the modulated militancy in "The Rooms Outside" matches Giovanni's new desire to effect change from within an institution. From 1971 on, Giovanni's popularity steadily grew. A sought after college lecturer and a life member of the National Council of Negro Women, she accepted an honorary doctorate from Wilberforce University, the first of more than a dozen over the next quarter century. Soon she was known as the "Princess of Black Poetry."

Ego Tripping and Other Poems for Young People (1973) opens with the often anthologized title poem, which begins, "I was born in the congo / I walked to the fertile crescent and built / the sphinx." In these poems as in her previous works, Giovanni's purpose is to instill black pride and love through her art. In the early 1970s, two collaborative "conversations" engage Giovanni with other leading black writers. *A Dialogue* (1973), a revised version of the television program *Soul* (1971) features Giovanni in conversation with James Baldwin; their wide ranging discussion includes religion, junkies, black men, literature and writing. The six chapters of *A Poetic Equation: Conversations between Nikki Giovanni and Margaret Walker* (1974) contrast the views of the older, more spiritual Southern woman with the liberal Giovanni. A more introspective poet emerges in the new poems in *The Women and the Men* (1975). Here Giovanni gives full freedom to her talent and perceptions. In "Revolutionary Dreams" her theme shifts from revolution to self realization, a topic that gains emphasis in her future poetry.

Other poems develop issues she discussed with Baldwin and bear the voice of a mellowed revolutionary, a voice continued in *Cotton Candy on a Rainy Day* (1978), where Giovanni casts a mournful eye at the unfinished business of the1960s, but recognizes the changed tenor of the 1970s. Lines such as "I am cotton candy on a rainy day / the unrealized dream of an unborn idea" and "I am a box / on a tight string / subject to pop / without notice" capture the loneliness and fragility of the decade.

Giovanni moved to Cincinnati in 1978 to care for her parents and continued to publish and win awards. While serving on the President's Commission on the International Year of the Child, she published the joyful *Vacation Time* (1980). Reflecting her ever-growing self knowledge, the meditative short paragraphs broken by ellipses of *Those Who Ride the Night Winds* (1983) pay tribute to courageous people who sought change, "who learned to love the stars . . . while crying in the darkness," such as Lorraine Hansberry, Martin Luther King, Jr., Phillis Wheatley and John Lennon. The collection reflects a poet aware of the difficulties and risks involved in speaking out but, nevertheless, continued to do so. Her opposition to the boycott of South Africa led to death threats and blacklisting by TransAfrica, for example.

Giovanni returned to teaching in 1984. Appointed professor of English at Virginia Polytechnic Institute and State University in 1989, her courses include the Harlem Renaissance and The Black Aesthetic. Meanwhile, state, national and international recognition continued. The PBS film *Spirit To Spirit: Nikki Giovanni, Poets in Performance* (1987) received the Oakland Museum Film Festival's Silver Apple Award, and her essays, *Sacred Cows . . . And Other Edibles* (1988) received the Ohioana Library Award.

Giovanni's marvelous books for children continue to instill black pride. In *Grandmothers: Poems, Reminiscences, and Short Stories about the Keepers of Our Traditions* (1994), twenty seven diverse voices including writers, poets, and civil rights leaders celebrate the fundamental role grandmothers play in children's experiences. In *Shimmey, Shimmey, Shimmey Like My Sister Kate* (1996), Giovanni holds a conversation with young adults about black poets. Ranging from Langston Hughes and Countee Cullen to Ishmael Reed and Ntozake Shange, Giovanni places each poet's biography within an Afro-American context and explains the poem's structure and sense. All twenty three sections convey Giovanni's passion for language. The imagery and illustrations of *The Sun Is So Quiet* (1996) capture the cheerful shift of winter into spring, while *The Genie In The Jar* (1996), written as a song for Nina Simone, fosters independence in youngsters by encouraging them to create their own songs.

Throughout her adult *Love Poems* (1997), the poet's soft voice croons a lyric or plays with language. The best introduction to Giovanni's poetry is *The Selected Poems of Nikki Giovanni* (1996). Arranged chronologically beginning with her poetry from 1968 and featuring over 150 poems taken from six previous collections, the poems trace the changing themes and voice of Giovanni's poetry as she bears witness to the social and political issues of her time. The compilation celebrates Giovanni's personal changes and growth from angry revolutionary to loving mother to proud teacher to celebrated poet and, thus, serves as a comprehensive picture of this strong, forthright African American feminist.

—Judith C. Kohl

GODWIN, Gail

Born: Gail Kathleen Godwin in Birmingham, Alabama, 18 June 1937. **Education:** Peace Junior College, Raleigh, North Carolina, 1955-1957; University of North Carolina at Chapel Hill, B.A. in journalism, 1959; University of Iowa, M.A. 1968, Ph.D. in English, 1971. **Family:** Married photographer Douglas Kennedy in 1960 (divorced 1961); married psychiatrist Ian Marshall in 1965 (divorced 1966); long-time partner with musician/composer Robert Starer. **Career:** Reporter, *Miami Herald*, 1959-60; consultant, U.S. Travel Service, London, England, 1961-65; fact-checker, *Saturday Evening Post,* 1966; instructor, English Literature, 1968-71, Writer's Workshop, 1972-73, University of Iowa; fellow, University of Illinois, 1971-72; special lecturer for State Department cultural program in Brazil, U.S. Information Service, spring 1976; lecturer, Vassar College, 1977, Columbia University, since fall 1978; writer and frequent lecturer and visiting scholar at colleges throughout the United States. **Awards**: National Endowment for the Arts grant for creative writing, 1974-75, librettists, 1977-78; National Book Award Nomination for *The Odd Woman*, 1974; Guggenheim fellowship in creative writing, 1975-76; Thomas Wolfe Memorial Award, American Institute and Academy of Arts and Letters, 1981; Lipinsky Endowment, Western North Carolina Historical Association, 1988; Janet Heidinger Kafka Award, University of Rochester, for *A Southern Family,* 1988; Distinguished Alumna, Univeristy of North Carolina at Chapel Hill, 1988; D. Litt., University of the South, University of North Carolina at

Chapel Hill, University of North Carolina at Greensboro, and State University of New York.

PUBLICATIONS

Novels

The Perfectionists. New York, Harper, 1970.
Glass People. New York, Knopf, 1972.
The Odd Woman. New York, Knopf, 1974.
Violet Clay. New York, Knopf, 1978.
Real Life. New York, Doubleday, 1981.
A Mother and Two Daughters. New York, Viking, 1982.
The Finishing School. New York, Viking.
A Southern Family. New York, Morrow, 1987.
Father Melancholy's Daughter. New York, Morrow, 1991.
The Good Husband. New York, Ballantine, 1994.
Evensong. New York, Ballantine, 1999.

Short Story Collections

Dream Children. New York, Knopf, 1976.
Mr. Bedford and the Muses. New York, Viking, 1983.

*

Interviews: "An Interview with Gail Godwin" with Kathleen Welch, *Iowa Journal of Literary Studies*, Vol. 3, 1981; "Gail Godwin" with Katherine Usher Henderson, *A Voice of One's Own: Conversations with America's Writing Women* edited by Katherine Usher Henderson and Mickey Pearlman, Boston, Houghton, 1989; "Gail Godwin," Dannye Romine Powell, *Parting the Curtains,* New York, Doubleday, 1994.

Critical Studies: "More Like An Onion Than A Map" by Doris Betts, *Ms.*, March 1975; "Gail Godwin's *The Odd Woman*: Literature and the Retreat from Life" by Susan E. Lorsch, *Critique: Studies in Modern Fiction,* Vol. 20, 1978; "Gail Godwin: Order and Accommodation" by Anne Z. Mickelson, *Reaching Out: Sensitivity and Order in Recent American Fiction by Women*, Metuchen, New Jersey, Scarecrow Press, 1979; "'Beauty and the Beast' in Gail Godwin's *Glass People*" by Karen C. Gaston, *Critique: Studies in Modern Fiction*, Vol. 21, 1980; "The Role of the South in the Novels of Gail Godwin" by Marilynn J. Smith, *Critique: Studies in Modern Fiction,* Vol. 21, 1980; "Narrating the Self: The Autonomous Heroine in Gail Godwin's *Violet Clay*" by Joanne S. Frye, *Contemporary Literature*, Spring 1983; "Gail Godwin and the Ideal of Southern Womanhood" by Carolyn Rhodes, *Women Writers of the Contemporary South* edited by Peggy Whitman Prenshaw, Jackson, University Press of Mississippi, 1984; "Researching Her Salvation: The Fiction of Gail Godwin" by John Alexander Allen, *Hollins Critic,* April 1988; "Gail Godwin's Evolving Heroine: The Search for Self" by Mary Ann Wimsatt, *Mississippi Quarterly*, Winter 1988-89; "A Hut and Three Houses: Gail Godwin, Carl Jung, and *The Finishing School*" by Anne Cheney, *Southern Literary Journal*, Spring 1989; "A Mother's Story in a Daughter's Life: Gail Godwin's *A Southern Family*" by Kim Lacy Rogers, *Mother Puzzles: Daughters and Mothers in Contemporary American Literature* edited by Mickey Pearlman, Westport, Connecticut, Greenwood Press, 1989; "Ellen

Glasgow and Gail Godwin: Southern Mothers and Daughters" by Kathryn Lee Seidel, *Tulsa Studies in Woman's Literature*, Fall 1991; "Gail Godwin" by Mary Ann Wimsatt, *Contemporary Fiction Writers of the South* edited by Joseph M. Flora and Robert Bain, Westport, Connecticut, Greenwood Press, 1993; *The Evolving Self in the Novels of Gail Godwin* by Lihong Xie, Baton Rouge, Louisiana State University Press, 1995; *Moving On: The Heroines of Shirley Ann Grau, Anne Tyler, and Gail Godwin* by Susan S. Kissel, Bowling Green, Ohio, Bowling Green State University Popular Press, 1996; *Daughters and Fathers in Feminist Novels* by Barbara Sheldon, New York, P. Lang, 1997.

*   *   *

Gail Godwin always knew she wanted to be a writer, composing her first story at age nine. Living with her divorced mother who was a writer and "breadwinner" and a widowed grandmother who was "homemaker," she was an observer at a young age. Godwin grew up in Asheville, North Carolina, where her mother was a teacher and newspaper reporter by day, a romance writer by night. Kathleen Godwin made-up bedtime stories for Gail, "reading" from an address book with blank pages and inspiring creativity in her daughter's fertile imagination. She absorbed the writing process first-hand, its tediousness as well as its rewards, and a perception for examining multi-dimensional values and attitudes in a female three generation home. The forced independence of these women offered Godwin insight into possibilities for characters searching for identities. Her mother, like an older sister, inspired her "when the soft clay of my personality was being sculpted." She tells an interviewer, "As one keeps writing, all characters are parts of oneself."

Her novels, from *The Perfectionists* through *Even Song*, are loosely autobiographical as she reworks experiences out of her own life. The operative word is "reworks": most writers produce works out of what they know; Godwin, however, uses experiences more directly and manipulates them into different possible outcomes, or as outcomes resulting from changed circumstances. *A Southern Family* illustrates such manipulations when she brings members of a family together, connects them through a tragedy, and then sends them on their way. Godwin's personal family tragedy is the springboard from which the drama evolves. By a fictionalized account of a family tragedy, she examines her own psychological turmoil as she examines the reactions to grief through levels of various family and community members.

Each of her novels reflects some episode or segment of her life in fictionalized analysis. Non-personal in that they are not limited to her narrow experience, they mirror crises and dilemmas belonging to human experience. Such broad topics might include family relationships, failed marriages, living in different cultures, education and teaching, careers and professions, awareness of death and dying. Godwin's first three novels—*The Perfectionists, Glass People,* and *The Odd Woman*—for instance, involve female protagonists who find marriage (or lovers) confining and inhibiting of personal and professional growth. Dane Empson (married to a psychotherapist) of *The Perfectionists* and Francesca Bolt of *Glass People* demonstrate such issues involved in working through marriage and career. Jane Clifford of *The Odd Woman* tries to balance a university career and a married lover, but struggles through her dilemma to emerge a stronger, more independent and free individual. Each of these novels, while examining differing viewpoints on the same essential questions, serve as one step to the next, to the third protagonist who evolves into the quintessential female hero Godwin envisions. Unlike fairy tale romances, these novels present a realistic depiction of feminist concerns, struggles and sacrifices encountered in professional and human success.

Violet Clay and *A Mother and Two Daughters* examine women as they grapple with independence and professional choices. Violet Clay, after a failed marriage and an unsatisfying career illustrating romance stories, uses an uncle's bequest to move to a secluded environment and become a serious artist. Her problems involve developing her art rather than dealing with the opposite sex. Nell Strickland and her daughters, Cate and Lydia, of the second novel, present three different viewpoints on female independence and career choices. Nell seeks her selfhood after the unexpected death of her husband ends her successful marriage. Her daughters, caught in a career or a marriage that appeared outwardly successful, shift roles and find an unexpected identity in the process. In this novel, Godwin examines women's struggles from three perspectives and from multiple generational attitudes for the first time.

The Finishing School is a pivotal point in Godwin's fictional evolution. The viewpoints of the two female protagonists develop in a mentor-student relationship; a young Justin Stokes attaches herself to role-model Ursula De Vane. The independent and self-sufficient older woman guides her protegee into a maturity that ultimately brings Justin a successful career. Even though the relationship broke off in earlier years, Justin narrates the story in retrospect to give Ursula credit for her success. Godwin examines the roles played and the inspiration offered and accepted between women of different ages and different family values. Earlier books concentrated on women freeing themselves from traditional restraints in becoming independent; this book, supported by Jungian allusions, examines influences of one independent woman on the developing psyche of an impressionable younger one.

Father Melancholy's Daughter follows the protagonist's psychological development from childhood into her early adult years. Margaret Gower, from age six through her formative years, deals with what seems abandonment by her mother and bouts of depression from her father. Supporting her priest father as traditional hostess and homemaker, she is the dutiful daughter, loyal until his death. In her maturing process, she retraces her mother's path (who left with another woman years earlier), learns about this other woman and her mother's death, and about transformations from traditional roles and duty to independent choices and responsibilities.

In *The Good Husband*, Godwin explores the dying experience, a process of taking stock, setting things in order, examining values and loves. Using multiple viewpoints, again, Godwin presents "dying" as though it were the central character about whom family and community revolve. Precipitated by personal experiences of close deaths, this novel implies that dying, rather than being depressing, is a process worth observing. Magda, the character facing death, no longer struggles for independence and career success, missed pleasures and experiences; Francis, the mild and faithful househusband, knows the pleasures inherent in everyday life;

Hugo, the novelist, by acknowledging aspects of his own blocked life, releases his writer's block; Alice, through her divorce, attains a joy in solitude. Each character orders life differently—loves, pleasures, values—because of the death each faces: Magda's death is a reminder of their own mortality. Death draws from the subconscious of characters aspects of themselves that offer them new directions.

Godwin's short stories collected in *Dream Children* and *Mr. Bedford and the Muses* deal with themes similar to her novels, though they tend to incorporate myth and dreams to a greater degree. Influenced by Jung and such modern religious philosophers as Thomas Merton, Godwin explores her dreams for what they tell her about herself and what they offer for fictional exploration. Her essays, speeches, interviews and published diary sections reveal much about her working and personal life. Life, she indicates, is "an open book, if you just look." The open honesty to which she brings her most successful protagonists is a part of her own life. Godwin takes stock of that life in her writing, a chore that she loves. "I do it [take stock] through my fiction," she told interviewer Dannye Romine Powell (*Parting the Curtains*). "They're like going back and finishing loving people I didn't love well, going back and finishing enjoying things I didn't enjoy well."

—Jeanne R. Nostrandt

GRAFTON, Sue

Born: Louisville, Kentucky, 24 April 1940. **Education:** University of Louisville, B.A. in English 1961. **Family:** Married Steven Frederick Humphrey in 1978; three children from previous marriages. **Career:** Worked as a medical secretary and as a scriptwriter for television before focusing on mystery writing in the 1980s. **Member:** Writers Guild of America, West, Mystery Writers of America (president, 1994-95), Private Eye Writers of America (president, 1989-90), Crime Writers Association of Great Britain. **Awards:** Christopher award, 1979, for teleplay *Walking through the Fire*; Mysterious Stranger award, Cloak and Clue Society, 1982-83, for *"A" Is for Alibi*; Shamus Award for best hardcover private eye novel, Private Eye Writers of America, and Anthony Award for best hardcover mystery, Mystery Readers of America, both 1985, both for *"B" Is for Burglar*; Macavity Award for best short story and Anthony Award, both 1986 for "The Parker Shotgun"; Anthony Award, 1987, for *"C" Is for Corpse;* Doubleday Mystery Guild Award, 1989, for *"E" Is for Evidence;* American Mystery Award, best short story, 1990, for "A Poison That Leaves No Trace"; Falcon Award, best mystery novel, Maltese Falcon Society of Japan, and Doubleday Mystery Guild Award, both 1990 for *"F" Is for Fugitive;* Doubleday Mystery Guild Award, Shamus Award, and Anthony Award, all 1991 for *"G" Is for Gumshoe;* Doubleday Mystery Guild Award and American Mystery Award, both 1992 for *"H" Is for Homicide;* Doubleday Mystery Guild Award, 1993, for *"I" Is for Innocent*, and 1994, for *"J" Is for Judgment;* Shamus Award, 1994, and Doubleday Mystery Guild Award, 1995, both for *"K" Is for Killer*. **Agent:** Molly Friedrich, The Aaron Priest Agency, 122 West 42nd Street, No. 3902, New York, New York 10168.

165

PUBLICATIONS

Novels

Keziah Dane. New York, Macmillan, 1967.
The Lolly-Madonna War. London, Owen, 1969.

Novels: Kinsey Millhone Series

"A" Is for Alibi. New York, Holt, 1982.
"B" Is for Burglar. New York, Holt, 1985.
"C" Is for Corpse. New York, Holt, 1986.
"D" Is for Deadbeat. New York, Holt, 1987.
"E" Is for Evidence. New York, Holt, 1988.
"F" Is for Fugitive. New York, Holt, 1989.
"G" Is for Gumshoe. New York, Holt, 1990.
"H" Is for Homicide. New York, Holt, 1991.
"I" Is for Innocent. New York, Holt, 1992.
"J" Is for Judgment. New York, Holt, 1993.
"K" Is for Killer. New York, Holt, 1994.
"L" Is for Lawless. New York, Holt, 1995.
"M" Is for Malice. New York, Holt, 1996.
"N" Is for Noose. New York, Henry Holt and Co., 1998.

Short Stories

Kinsey and Me. Santa Barbara, Bench Press, 1992.

Editor

Writing Mysteries: A Handbook by the Mystery Writers of America. Cincinnati, Writer's Digest Books, 1992.

*

Screenplay: *Lolly-Madonna XXX,* with Rodney Carr-Smith, 1973.

Television Scripts: "With Friends Like These" (*Rhoda* series), 1975; *Walking through the Fire,* from the book by Laurel Lee, 1979; *Sex and the Single Parent,* from the book by Jane Adams, 1979; *Nurse,* from the book by Peggy Anderson, 1980; *Mark, I Love You,* from the book by Hal Painter, 1980; "Seven Brides for Seven Brothers," "I Love You, Molly McGraw," and "A House Divided," with Steven Humphrey (*Seven Brides for Seven Brothers* series), 1982-83; *A Caribbean Mystery,* with Steven Humphrey, from the novel by Agatha Christie, 1983; *A Killer in the Family,* with Steven Humphrey and Robert Aller, 1983; *Sparkling Cyanide,* with Steven Humphrey and Robert Malcolm Young, from the novel by Agatha Christie, 1983; *Love on the Run,* with Steven Humphrey, 1985; *Tonight's the Night,* with Steven Humphrey, 1987.

Media Adaptation: Film—*Lolly-Madonna XXX,* 1973, from the novel *The Lolly Madonna War.*

Critical Studies: *"G" Is for Grafton: The World of Kinsey Millhone* by Natalie Hevener Kaufman and Carol McGinnis Kay, New York, Henry Holt, 1997.

* * *

The most exciting development in the private-eye novel during the 1980s was the emergence of several creditable female private eyes. One of the best of the lot is Kinsey Millhone, a twice-divorced 32-year-old California private detective created by Sue Grafton.

Tough and brainy, independent and confident of her ability to do what has long been viewed largely as a man's job, Kinsey is more than a Philip Marlowe in skirts. She is both credible as a private detective and fully convincing as a self-reliant contemporary woman—a gritty, modern, cop-turned-detective who jogs, eats junk food, and lives in a converted garage. She is also smart and ironic, and contrasts starkly with the characters one would find in, for example, an Agatha Christie novel. In a Christie novel the body is merely the first clue to a big puzzle. In Grafton's novels, violence hurts, chase scenes are action-packed, and dead bodies are treated as former human beings.

Grafton plans to take Millhone all the way through the alphabet in a detective series starting with *"A" Is for Alibi* (1982), in which Millhone is hired to prove a convicted woman's innocence in the murder of a heartless lawyer. It gets complicated when several people have motives. Millhone tracks down the real killer, earning Grafton praise from Katrine Ames of *Newsweek,* who writes that the plot is "smart, well paced, and very funny." Grafton is, indeed, funny. Yet, in *"B" Is for Burglar* (19845 Grafton's serious consideration of human nature is evident. In that book, Millhone is hired to locate a wealthy woman by the woman's estranged sister so that she might sign a simple legal document. As Millhone scratches the surface of the case, she uncovers a murder. Grafton's philosophy about violence becomes clear. "Mostly what I'm interested in is why we do what we do," Grafton said in an interview with *Modern Maturity.* "Why do we kill each other? Why can't we be happy? I'm looking for answers, looking to figure it out."

In several ways, Grafton's books call to mind Ross Macdonald's Lew Archer series. Kinsey lives and works in Santa Teresa, the fictionalized California coastal town that Macdonald himself used in several of the Archer books. Santa Teresa is modeled on Santa Barbara, home to both Macdonald and Grafton. Like Archer, Kinsey is as much an investigator into other people's lives as she is a crime-solver. Like Archer, she often also forges an emotional bond with her clients; for example in *"C" Is for Corpse,* her commitment to a young crippled client extends beyond his death. Many of the cases she pursues also turn up family secrets hidden deep in the past, another notable characteristic of the Archer series. In *"F" Is for Fugitive,* Kinsey is hired to investigate a murder that occurred 17 years earlier; in *"G" Is for Gumshoe,* she uncovers evidence of several murders that were committed 50 years earlier.

As a character, however, Kinsey is much more developed than Archer ever was. She has an active private life, including some romantic involvements. Sometimes she becomes the focus of the book. In *"E" Is for Evidence* she must become her own client in order to discover who is trying to frame her on a fraud charge; she also has to deal with the unexpected (and unwelcome) return of her ex-husband, whom she has not seen in eight years. In *"G" Is for Gumshoe,* her search for a woman's elderly missing mother is complicated by a threat to her own life, as she must elude a hitman hired to kill her by a man she helped send to prison.

Sassy and irreverent, Kinsey is a very appealing character. She has an engaging sense of humor, an eye alertly poised to expose the phony, and a scathing tongue she isn't afraid to use. She's emotionally tough, yet refreshingly candid about her own vulnerabilities. She isn't often called upon to prove herself in physically threatening situations, but when she does find herself in a tight spot, as for example at the end of *"A" Is for Alibi,* she isn't afraid to use her gun to shoot the man who is stalking her.

Grafton (the daughter of mystery writer C. W. Grafton) writes in a breezy, entertaining style and has a gift for vivid description and sharp characterization. Each of her characters, no matter how secondary to the plot, springs to life on the page. Grafton also understands well how the distinctive voice of first-person narration can be used for more than mere storytelling purposes. Through her colorful descriptions, offhand remarks, and self-deprecating admissions, Kinsey reveals herself to be earthy, unpretentious, and wholly engaging.

As she passes midpoint in the alphabet with 1998's *"N" Is for Noose,* Grafton has endeavored to keep the series fresh and avoid the staleness that often afflicts long-running series by shaking things up. In *"J" Is for Judgment,* for example, Kinsey discovers a long-lost family she never knew she had, while in *"N" Is for Noose* Millhone, by now a two-time divorcee, is on a case given to her by Robert Dietz, a professional and personal colleague who tests her personal and investigative etiquette when she discovers he is living a second life of splendor. Grafton also places her heroine in some unlikely situations, with mixed results. For example, in *"H" Is for Homicide* Kinsey goes undercover in an insurance-fraud case and improbably ends up getting kidnaped and becoming buddy-buddy with the female suspect she has been following. In *"L" Is for Lawless,* her curiosity lands her on a cross-country treasure hunt with a 65-year-old escaped con and his daughter.

On the plus side, Grafton's tinkering with formula also produced one of the strongest entries in the series in *"K" Is for Killer.* An unexpected bout with insomnia thrusts Kinsey into the unfamiliar after-dark hours. Her nocturnal investigation into the murder of a young woman (who worked as a part-time prostitute) results in a compelling case and leads to some difficult moral dilemmas for Kinsey. Also, restricting the action of the novel to the shadowy after hours creates rich atmospheric detail and some of Grafton's finest descriptive prose.

Grafton's inspiration comes from varied sources. For instance, one day she was reading *The Gashlycrumb Tinies,* a children's book of cartoons that deals with the alphabet, and realized that she could base a series of novels on the same idea. "Once I was doing research at a coroner's office and they mentioned that they often have bodies around for years," she said about another idea. "I thought, 'A corpse—what an interesting place to hide something,' and used that in *"C" Is for Corpse* (1986)."

Prior to mystery writing, Grafton wrote in Hollywood, which she now detests. Grafton learned about writing dialogue and action in Hollywood, but turned to mysteries when her plots were criticized, wanting to prove her critics wrong. Grafton says, "My primary lesson, however, was that I'm happy as a solo writer, happiest when I'm making all the executive decisions. I've always been willing to rise or fall on my own merits."

—David Geherin and Liz Mulligan

GRAU, Shirley Ann

Born: New Orleans, Louisiana, 8 July 1930. **Education:** Booth School, Montgomery, Alabama, 1938-45; Ursuline Academy, New Orleans, 1945-46; Sophie Newcomb College, Tulane University, New Orleans, B.A. 1946-50 (Phi Beta Kappa); graduate study, Tulane University, 1950-51. **Family:** Married James Kern Feibleman in 1955; two sons and two daughters. **Career:** Full-time writer since 1950s; creative writing instructor, University of New Orleans, 1966-67. **Awards:** Pulitzer prize, 1965, for *The Keepers of the House;* LL.D.: Rider College, New Jersey; D.Litt.: Spring Hill College, Alabama. **Agent:** Brandt and Brandt, 1501 Broadway, New York, New York 10036.

PUBLICATIONS

Novels

The Hard Blue Sky. New York, Knopf, 1958.
The House on Coliseum Street. New York, Knopf, 1961.
The Keepers of the House. New York, Knopf, 1964.
The Condor Passes. New York, Knopf, 1971.
Evidence of Love. New York, Knopf, 1977.
Roadwalkers. New York, Knopf, 1994.

Short Stories

The Black Prince and Other Stories. New York, Knopf, 1955.
The Wind Shifting West. New York, Knopf, 1973.
Nine Women. New York, Knopf, 1986.

Uncollected Short Stories

"The Things You Keep," in *Carnival,* December 1950.
"The Fragile Age," in *Carnival,* October 1951.
"The First Day of School," in *Saturday Evening Post,* 30 September 1961.
"The Beginning of Summer," in *Story,* November 1961.
"The Empty Night," in *Atlantic,* May 1962.
"The Loveliest Day," in *Saturday Evening Post,* 5 May 1962.
"One Night," in *Gentlemen's Quarterly,* February 1966.
"The Young Men," in *Redbook,* April 1968.

*

Critical Study: *Shirley Ann Grau* by Paul Schlueter, Boston, Twayne, 1981.

*   *   *

Shirley Ann Grau's work is rooted in the South, evoking local color in anthropological detail. She can be described as a novelist of manners, but it is her unsentimental realism that gives her prose its power. Grau's most lauded work, *The Keepers of the House* (1964), won the Pulitzer Prize for fiction. The novel chronicles the lives of Will Howland, a kind, white Southern landowner, and his offspring. When Howland's first wife dies, he brings an African American woman, Margaret, into his household. They are secretly wed and have three children over the course of the novel. The Howland children and grandchildren become mired in racial politics. One of Howland's white granddaughters marries a racist politician, and when one of the children from his second marriage discloses their kinship, the politician is ruined and the Howland estate is attacked. The power of the past and of family traditions as sources of tension as well as continuity of strength predominate thematically in this work, where individual actions, however innocent or praiseworthy, can have explosive consequences.

Grau was born in New Orleans and raised there and in Montgomery, Alabama. She attended elementary school in Montgomery and returned at age fifteen to New Orleans to attend the Ursuline Academy. She continued her college education in New Orleans and began having stories published in local journals; many of these were collected in her first publication, *The Black Prince and Other Stories*. Conflicts among people of different ethnic and racial backgrounds, which permeates her work, are evident in the early stories and in her first novel, *The Hard Blue Sky* (1958), which has a tidier resolution than her third, *The Keepers of the House*, through its ultimate vanquishing of a racist, evil man. Set on Isle aux Chiens in the Gulf of Mexico, *The Hard Blue Sky* explores conflicts between this island's people—of French and Spanish descent—and those of another island, populated by people of Slavic descent. Tension is exacerbated by a romance and marriage of lovers from the different islands. As a fury of emotions engulf the characters, an oncoming hurricane threatens the islands. The metaphorical play of natural phenomena and human events is effectively interwoven through Grau's judicious rendering of local color, which evokes and sustains a strong sense of realism.

Between *The Hard Blue Sky* and *The Keepers of the House*, Grau published *The House on Coliseum Street* (1961), a novel of manners. As in many of her short stories, Grau explores the perversion of ethics in modern society. While her other novels and many of her short stories suggested larger social forces overwhelming individual acts, *The House on Coliseum Street* points to divorce and sexual promiscuousness as contemporary signs of moral decay and the crumbling of aristocracy.

The Black Prince and Other Stories, a well-received debut, contains pieces detailing the struggles of blacks and whites living in the bayous. As in all of her works, local color enriches a hard realism. Her characters are divided between those who live an ordered life that becomes chaotic when individuals transverse subtle bonds and distinctions, and those who live an unstructured, impulsive life of momentary gratification. A lack of depth or probing is sometimes apparent in her straightforward depiction of characters falling easily into these two kinds of existence: those living in the bayous and islands lack a moral code, while those established in urban society experience hardships when passing outside of strict bonds of propriety. That such types are presented without apparent sentiment or irony has caused some to question the depth of Grau's work. Yet, her power for evoking local color is unquestioned. The stories in *The Wind Shifting West*, for example, are rich in descriptions of community and nature.

Grau's story-telling methods evolved over time. In her 1971 novel, *The Condor Passes*, she is in familiar territory—the family drama—but the story is related from the points of view of the five main characters. *Evidence of Love* (1977), which delineates the many forms love can take, from exhileration to hindrances, and the later work *Roadwalkers* (1994) are related through series of short incidents involving a variety of characters. The first part of *Roadwalkers* concerns Baby, a parentless, African American child wandering with her siblings through the South during the Depression, looking for food. Baby is brought to an orphanage, christened Mary Woods, and becomes "civilized." The second half of the novel is told by Mary's daughter, Nanda. Nanda relates Mary's success in life as a dressmaker and how it affected her own life. The novel highlights Grau's strengths with telling character detail. As a white, southern girl who experienced life in landed white society and lived as well in communities with closer interaction among whites and blacks, observing events and individuals, and gradually achieving success in her own right, Nanda can be viewed, perhaps, as a representative for Grau and her experiences, maintaining an anthropologist's detached, or outside, perspective while intimately describing the local color.

—Emma Cobb

GREENE, Melissa Fay

Born: Macon, Georgia, 30 December 1952. **Education:** Oberlin College, B.A. (with high honors) 1975. **Family:** Married Donald Franklin Samuel (an attorney), 15 April 1979; four children. **Career:** Paralegal for General Assistance Legal Services Program, Savannah, Georgia, 1975-79, and Rome, Georgia, 1980-81; nonfiction writer since 1977, with articles appearing in such periodicals and journals as Newsweek, *Life, New York Times, Washington Post, Atlantic, Ms., Chicago Tribune, Los Angeles Times, Parenting,* and *Stagebill*; writer-in-residence and guest speaker. **Awards:** Excellence in Journalism Award, Society of Professional Journalists, 1988, for the article "That Old Lonesome High Hollerin' Tenor"; Robert F. Kennedy Award, Lillian Smith Award, *Chicago Tribune* Heartland Prize, Georgia Author Award, and Lyndhurst Prize Fellowship, all 1992 for *Praying for Sheetrock*; Southern Book Critics Circle Award, Georgia Author of the Year Award, and Georgia Historical Society Book Award, for *The Temple Bombing*. **Agent:** David Block, 220 Fifth Ave., Suite 1400, New York, New York 10001.

PUBLICATIONS

Nonfiction

Praying for Sheetrock. Addison-Wesley, 1991.
The Temple Bombing. Addison-Wesley, 1996.

Other

Contributor, *Writing: The Translation of Memoryy* edited by Eve Shelnutt. New York, Macmillan, 1990.
Contributor, *The Confidence Woman: Twenty-Six Writers at Work,* edited by Eve Shelnutt, Marietta, Georgia, Longstreet Press, 1991.

Adaptation, *Praying for Sheetrock*. Produced at Lifeline Theatre, Chicago, 1997.

*

Melissa Fay Greene comments:

I have tried to combine serious and honorable journalistic and historical research with love of language; to create works of literary richness, pleasing to the senses, gripping to the intellect, yet reliable and true. I believe in the power of words to penetrate deeply and subtly into real past worlds and events; I disdain the use of words to distort, conceal, or rearrange when performed in the name of nonfiction.

*   *   *

Melissa Fay Greene has explored actual incidents of local history in Georgia in her two award-winning books, *Praying for Sheetrock* and *The Temple Bombing*. Events that seem to have particular significance to a small community at a singular point in time take on larger meaning through her storytelling, which blends investigative journalism, historical research, and techniques most commonly associated with fiction. Meticulous development of character and setting, twists of plot, irony, multiple viewpoints, and growing dramatic impact are among the elements that make these nonfiction works read like novels, with Greene's experience as a journalist and paralegal evident in her assemblage of facts and inclusion of historical detail.

Praying for Sheetrock recreates events in a small community of about 1,800 people, half white, half black, in McIntosh County Georgia during the 1970s. Unlike other areas of the South and the nation in general, McIntosh County showed no progress or inclinations toward political balance following the Civil Rights Act of 1965: the area was dominated by a strong-armed white sheriff who manipulated local elections and politics, much like his father before him, and fabricated the appearance of integration to take advantage of civil rights legislation. Through the leadership of Thurnell Alston, an uneducated shop steward, and support of the Assistance Legal Services Program, with which Greene served, the black community began to win political and economic power and to overcome dire conditions of poverty.

The conflict and denouement of these developments are suspensefully drawn, with surprising setbacks, problems, and triumphs, as a host of characters and the local color come alive through Greene's prose, revealing how lives were changed in the fight for representation. The responses to transforming social conditions within the black and white communities as well as the county as a whole, which had been tyrannized by law enforcement officials and an indifferent aristocracy, are especially compelling. Greene's deft storytelling techniques combine the immediacy of journalism with the craft of fiction. Her use of irony, for example, is evidenced in her presentation of the outcomes of Alston, a symbol of the struggle for justice, and the sheriff, a symbol of injustice: a government sting operation ultimately implicated Alston in wrongdoing, while the obviously corrupt sheriff is exonerated on charges of extortion, narcotics trafficking, and counterfeiting.

The Temple Bombing, which centers on the 1958 bombing of an Atlanta synagogue, builds on the increasingly tense social environment stemming from the 1954 *Brown v. Board of Education* Supreme Court ruling that overturned segregation laws, and culminates with the Civil Rights struggle of the 1960s. The story follows Rabbi Jacob Rothschild of Temple, the oldest and most affluent synagogue in Atlanta, who develops from an unremarkable, folksy rabbi to an increasingly outspoken community leader for social justice, a stance that makes some of his congregation weary. The bombing of Temple, allegedly perpetrated by a neo-Nazi group, is directed at his activism.

As with *Praying for Sheetrock*, the basic news story of *The Temple Bombing* is invested with larger significance through Greene's exploration of local communities and their characters. Many liberal-minded people in Atlanta had been priding themselves on examples of progress in race relations, but the existence of neo-Nazis brought them back to a more realistic view of the multifarious factions within a community. Only one of the five men implicated in the bombing is tried, and he is acquitted in a controversial trial where flamboyant lawyers are successful in turning the case into a maze of legal intricacies rather than a judgement of guilt or innocence. Though not pursued in the text, similarities between the bombing and trial of more than a quarter-century ago and events of the 1990s (militia group related bombings, high-profile lawyers, and media-circus trials) have discomfiting relevance.

The Temple Bombing also exhibits Greene's in-depth, journalistic/literary approach in its expansive exploration of forces within communities in the midst of social transformation, revealing uncertainties of how to bring about change and at what speed, presenting the larger historical background, and focusing on particular individuals who become leaders and catalysts for progress. Rabbi Rothschild had experienced a reawakening of his moral responsibility by observing the injustice of segregation, and his activism ultimately helped make a difference. This example of isolated progress within a larger struggle, which Greene also developed in *Waiting for Sheetrock,* is underscored near the end of *The Temple Bombing*, when the local activist rabbi hosts a dinner for Martin Luther King in honor of King's being awarded the Nobel Peace Prize.

—Perry Bear

GRIMSLEY, Jim

Born: Edgecombe County, North Carolina, 21 September 1955. **Education:** University of North Carolina, Chapel Hill, B.A. 1978. **Career:** Member of staff in Radiology Department, Grady Hospital, Atlanta, since 1980; playwright in residence, Seven Stages Theatre, Atlanta, since 1986; instructor, Department of English, Georgia State University, Atlanta, since 1997. **Awards:** Jesse Rehder Prize for Fiction, University of North Carolina, Chapel Hill, 1977; winner, Southeast Playwriting Contest, 1986, and George Oppenheimer Award, *Newsday,* 1988, both for *Mr. Universe*; Bryan Prize for drama, Fellowship of Southern Writers, 1993; Sue Kaufman Prize for first fiction, American Academy of Arts and Letters, 1995; Prix Charles Brisset, French Academy of Physicians, 1995; American Library Association Gay, Lesbian, Bisexual Book Award, 1995, for *Dream Boy*. **Member:** Southeast Playwrights Project, PEN.

PUBLICATIONS

Plays

The Existentialists. Produced Atlanta, 1983.
The Earthlings. Produced Atlanta, 1984.
The Receptionist in Hell. Produced Atlanta, 1985.
Estelle and Otto. Produced Atlanta, 1985.
Dead of Winter. Produced Atlanta, 1986; adapted for radio as *Beam Angel* by Berl Boykin, National Public Radio, 1993).
On the Appearance of a Fire in the West, Produced Atlanta, 1987).
Mr. Universe. Produced Atlanta, 1988.
Math and Aftermath. Produced Atlanta, 1988.
Man with a Gun. Produced Atlanta, 1989.
White People. Produced Atlanta, 1989.
The Lizard of Tarsus. Produced Atlanta, 1990.
The Fall of the House of Usher, Produced Atlanta, 1991.
Belle Ives. Produced Atlanta, 1991.
Aurora Be Mine. Produced Atlanta, 1992.
The Borderland. Produced New York City, 1994.

Performance Pieces

Stop and Think. Performed Los Angeles, 1987.
Anti-Gravity. performed Miami, 1988.
Eating the Green Monkey. Performed Los Angeles, 1989.
Shelter. Performed Atlanta, 1991.
Walk through Birdland. Performed Atlanta, 1992.
The Masturbator. Performed Atlanta, 1992.
Memo to the Assassin. Performed Atlanta, 1992.

Novels

Winter Birds. Berlin, Edition döa, 1993, Algonquin Books of Chapel Hill, 1994.
Comfort and Joy. Berlin, Edition döa, 1993.
Dream Boy. Chapel Hill, Algonquin Books of Chapel Hill, 1995.
My Drowning. Chapel Hill, Algonquin Books of Chapel Hill, 1997.

*

Jim Grimsley comments:

A lot of people have written about poor people, but I don't think the very poorest people have been written about quite the way you really see them. The attitude in literature toward that class of people up until now has been that poor people were just like everybody else, only with fewer things. Nobody dealt with just how animalistic your life can become when you don't have anything.

*   *   *

Jim Grimsley grew up wanting to be a novelist, he has said, and studied creative writing at the University of North Carolina to perfect his craft. But for many years his work, considered too graphic and too bleak in its portraits of life, failed to find a publisher or even an agent. By the time it did, Grimsley had built a strong reputation during the 1980s as a playwright, with numerous productions in Atlanta, Off-Off Broadway, and elsewhere. *Winter Birds* (1993), his first novel, was published in Germany and found an audience there. Word of his talent then crossed the

Atlantic. His German publisher helped him get a contract with Algonquin Books, which happens to be located in the same town where he went to college.

Grimsley's novels have their settings in the South, among people whose poverty is intensified by cruel facts of their existence. Much of the material is taken from Grimsley's own childhood, a far from idyllic world defined by the family's poverty, his hemophilia—which was as financially debilitating to the already beleaguered Grimsleys as it was physically for him—and his one-armed father's own disability. The elder Grimsley had lost the arm in a farm accident and unwittingly signed away his rights to compensation: "He could never stop being just furious," Grimsley later recalled.

Winter Birds (1994) is the story of Danny Crell, an eight-year-old who suffers from hemophilia. Danny, his parents, and his four siblings find themselves constantly on the run from bill collectors, moving from place to place only to be turned out by landlords for failing to pay the rent. These episodes come from Grimsley's childhood, as does the fact that Danny's father has only one arm. Bobjay Crell, like the real-life Jasper Grimsley, can "never stop being just furious," and the novel centers around a Thanksgiving night when his anger leads him on a murderous rampage. Outside the Crell's rented house, snow is falling and the knife-wielding father is on the prowl; inside, the family huddles in fear.

While in school at Chapel Hill in the 1970s, Grimsley began work on *Winter Birds*, and spent years gathering letters from agents and writers who praised his talent but lamented the work's unrelenting darkness. He continued working on it, shifting the point of view and reducing a 600-page manuscript to a lean 200 pages. By 1984, he was finished, but still he had no publisher.

Meanwhile, Grimsley was developing a career as a playwright with such works as the award-winning *Mr. Universe,* and he became writer in residence at Seven Stages Theatre in Atlanta. Del Hamilton, the artistic director of Seven Stages, passed a copy of *Winter Birds* to Frank Heilbert of Edition döa in Berlin, who was amazed that no American publisher wanted the book; by 1992 Grimsley had a publishing contract. Two years later, after Heilbert sold U.S. rights to Algonquin, the American edition saw publication—with a highly enthusiastic response. Craig Seligman of the *New Yorker,* for example, praised *Winter Birds* as a "simple, awful, and very beautiful novel" and compared it to Dorothy Allison's *Bastard Out of Carolina.* Allison herself wrote of Grimsley's novel, "Tell everyone I have rarely read anything so powerful. *Winter Birds* is altogether marvelous, so beautifully written I wanted to steal it and pretend it was mine."

Comfort and Joy, a sequel to *Winter Birds* in which a thirty-year-old Danny brings home a lover, had not seen U.S. publication as of 1998. Grimsley told *Out* magazine in 1994: "Yes, I'm a gay writer and I'm very proud to be." Yet, *Winter Birds* had no explicitly homosexual theme. His next Stateside work, however, 1995's *Dream Boy*, was a gay love story. *Lambda Book Report* called it "Grimsley's 'answer song' to all those novels of the '40s and '50s in which the gay characters have to die." It is the story of Nathan, who falls in love with the boy next door, Roy. Given the abusiveness of Nathan's father, combined with the fact that the two boys are caught in flagrante during a camping trip, that there is plenty of tension developed in the work.

With each story, Grimsley has set himself new challenges. In *Winter Birds* he chose to tell the story in the voice of a second-person narrator, with Danny as a grownup speaking to himself as a child. The use of a third person omniscient viewpoint in *Dream Boy* was not so unusual, but noteworthy are Grimsley's reliance on the present tense and his surprisingly successful use of passive verbs. In *My Drowning*, the challenge came from point of view—that of a female. Grimsley's mother influenced *My Drowning*, which centers on an elderly woman's recurring dream of her mother standing on a flooded riverbank in a rainstorm. As Ellen Tote delves into the meaning of the dream, a deeper mystery is revealed and new questions arise that must be answered.

Grimsley's work has shown an impressively wide range of motifs, all of them employed in the depiction of life among whites at the bottom rungs of Southern society. He has gained accolades from the gay press and the mainstream, from reviewers in New York as well as Atlanta, and has developed a strong following on both sides of the Atlantic. He lives alone just outside of downtown Atlanta, with his two cats; and in defiance of his hemophilia—not to mention the fact that he is HIV-positive—he remains optimistic about the future. "I plan to live to be 100," he told Howorth in her *Reckon* profile. "It makes a lot of difference that I'm happy."

—Judson Knight

GRISHAM, John

Born: Jonesboro, Arkansas, 8 February 1955. **Education:** Mississippi State University, B.S. in accounting 1977; University of Mississippi, LL.D. 1981. **Family:** Married Renee Jones; three children. **Career:** Practiced law, Southaven, Mississippi, 1981-91; legislator, Mississippi House of Representatives, 1984-90; full-time writer since 1990. **Address:** c/o Doubleday, 666 Fifth Avenue, New York, New York 10103.

PUBLICATIONS

Novels

A Time to Kill. New York, Wynwood Press, 1989.
The Firm. New York, Doubleday, 1991.
The Pelican Brief. New York, Doubleday, 1992.
The Client. New York, Doubleday, 1993.
The Chamber. New York, Doubleday, 1994.
The Rainmaker. New York, Doubleday, 1995.
The Runaway Jury. New York, Doubleday, 1996.
The Partner. New York, Doubleday, 1997.
The Street Lawyer. New York, Doubleday, 1998.

*

Media Adaptations: Films—*The Firm,* 1993; *The Pelican Brief,* 1993; *The Client,* 1994; *A Time to Kill,* 1996; *The Rainmaker,* 1997.

Critical Studies: *John Grisham: A Critical Companion,* by Mary Beth Pringle, Westport, Connecticut, Greenwood Press, 1997.

* * *

Among the most popular novelists of the 1990s, with one of his "legal thrillers" routinely topping annual bestseller lists throughout the decade, John Grisham has drawn on his legal and political background to create suspenseful, occasionally formulaic fiction that touches on contemporary social issues within an environment of conspiracy and intrigue.

The Firm (1991), *The Pelican Brief* (1992), and *The Client* (1993) fueled his sales juggernaut and were adapted to popular films, but his virtually unnoticed first book, *A Time to Kill* (1989), and 1994's *The Chamber* may well be his superior literary achievements. In those works, character studies, civil law issues, and carefully delineated settings predominate over more fast-paced, hero/villain clashes of the works that first brought him fame.

Later novels, *The Rainmaker* (1995), *The Runaway Jury* (1996), *The Partner* (1997), and *The Street Lawyer* (1998), continue to feature bright, young professionals discovering grand conspiracies and attempting to bring to justice corrupt and immensely powerful individuals and organizations—a common theme in all of Grisham's work. Grisham's large following is due partly to fiction plotted with action-packed events involving the travails and triumphs of likeable, if unlikely, heroes, as well as for his sophisticated presentation of legal proceedings. Grisham's work often draws on topical issues—homelessness, the clout of the tobacco industry, for instance—to develop recognizable forms of victimization and large-scale corruption against which individuals struggle in a kind of ongoing David *vs* Goliath parable.

Grisham was born in Jonesboro, Arkansas. His father was an itinerant construction worker, and as his father worked at various sites the family moved frequently before settling in Southaven, Mississippi, when Grisham was twelve. Grisham earned a B.S. at Mississippi State University and a law degree at the University of Mississippi.

In 1981, Grisham established a successful practice as a defense attorney in Southaven, first in criminal law and later in civil law, and was elected to the Mississippi House of Representatives in 1984. A Democrat interested in improving Mississippi's educational system, Grisham served six years. Frustrated by his inability to enact changes in the state's education budget and by slow-moving political processes, he resigned half-way through his second term. Following the publication of his first novel, *A Time to Kill*, Grisham left his law practice to write full time.

Grisham's experiences as a lawyer and his frustrations as a crusading politician inform his work. *A Time to Kill*, for example, was inspired by a court scene he witnessed where a preadolescent girl testified against her rapist. "I never felt such emotion and human drama in my life," Grisham told *People* magazine about the incident. "I became obsessed wondering what it would be like if the girl's father killed that rapist and was put on trial. I had to write it down." *A Time to Kill* develops this plot and features a typical Grisham lawyer-hero fighting the case against great odds.

A Time to Kill is enriched by subtle treatment of complex racial issues and careful evocation of a small town, Southern milieu, from the effects of stifling summer heat to local color in such gathering places as coffee shops, where townspeople discuss issues of the day. These same principles are evident in *The Chamber,* where a young lawyer, Adam Hall, becomes an advocate for his grandfather, Samuel Cayhall, who was convicted for a racially motivated murder of two sons of a Jewish civil rights worker. Hall had come to visit his grandfather to learn more about his family history. Crucial to both of these novels, and to Grisham's works in general, are intrigues deep beyond surface evidence as well as individuals battling powerful organizations: the Ku Klux Klan features prominently in both *A Time to Kill* and *The Chamber.*

Powerful and corrupt organizations predominate in Grisham's work: in *The Firm,* a recent Harvard Law School graduate learns that his new law firm is involved with organized crime and risks his life assisting the FBI in uncovering the connections. Similarly young and committed protagonists are thrust into dangerous situations in *The Pelican Brief,* where a Tulane law student hypothesizes on the murder of two United States Supreme Court justices and is subsequently pursued by the killers, and *The Client,* where an eleven-year-old discovers the location of the body of a murdered United States senator and is assisted by a defense attorney to flee corrupt law enforcement officials and crime figures.

Gradual building of suspense, questions of paranoia and truth on the part of characters suspecting conspiracies, and exciting and dangerous situations are among the elements that draw readers into Grisham's works. The simple act of talking about possible conspiracies endangers Grisham's protagonists, who soon find themselves fleeing powerful criminal networks while bravely continuing to uncover clues and communicate their findings.

Grisham described the *modus operandi* of these works to *Entertainment Weekly*: "You throw an innocent person in there and get 'em caught up in a conspiracy and you get 'em out." The novels, then, can be taken unabashedly as entertainments for popular contemporary culture. Thinly drawn characters, occasional whoppers in plot contrivances, and grandiose conspiracies notwithstanding, a Grisham novel is quick to draw the reader into the world of a bright, intelligent, and driven individual whose life is suddenly endangered and swept into a whirlwind of confrontations with powerful adversaries. They are beleaguered heroes, battling corporate lawyers, the mob, the insurance industry, the Klan.

In these parables where the individuals stands out against corrupt giants, Grisham frequently works-in topical issues—capital punishment in *The Chamber,* corporate buyouts and insurance industry fraud in *The Rainmaker,* Big Tobacco (as it is routinely referred to) in *The Runaway Jury,* embezzlement in *The Partner.* In the latter, a law-firm partner fakes his own death and escapes with $90 million, pursued by former partners and a corrupt defense contractor who had planned to help themselves to the money, much of which was collected through a fraudulent claim. The protagonist of *The Partner* is less virtuous than the typical leading character in a Grisham novel, but through him Grisham shows ways in which money can indeed influence events and manipulate the social system.

The individual battling the system theme is continued in *The Street Lawyer,* which pits the homeless against landlords and re-

veals a legal system that favors those with economic clout. The protagonist, Michael Brock, is driven by his desire to become a partner in Washington, D.C.'s, premier law firm, sacrificing his marriage and free time along the way. He is among several lawyers taken hostage by a seedy character in a desperate act that leads to violence, but the event spurs Brock to question his values and to begin using his legal expertise to defend those without power and often without voice in modern America.

—Mel Koler

GRIZZARD, Lewis

Born: Lewis McDonald Grizzard, Jr., in Columbus, Georgia, 20 October 1946. **Education**: University of Georgia, A.B. 1967. **Family:** Married four times, including Dedra Kyle, 16 March 1994. **Career:** Sportswriter and executive sports editor, *Atlanta Journal,* 1968-70s; freelance writer, 1970s; staff reporter, *Atlanta Constitution,* 1970s; sports editor, *Chicago Sun-Times,* 1970s; columnist, *Atlanta Journal and Constitution,* 1979-94; commentator for WSB-TV, 1980; owner of Grizzard Enterprises, Atlanta, 1980-94; lecturer, stand-up comic, and occasional television actor. **Died:** 20 March 1994, in Altanta of complications resulting from heart surgery.

PUBLICATIONS

Humor

Kathy Sue Loudermilk, I Love You. Atlanta, Peachtree Publishers, 1979.
Won't You Come Home, Billy Bob Bailey? Atlanta, Peachtree Publishers, 1980.
Don't Sit Under the Grits Tree with Anyone Else But Me. Atlanta, Peachtree Publishers, 1981.
They Tore Out My Heart and Stomped That Sucker Flat. Atlanta, Peachtree Publishers, 1982.
If Love Were Oil, I'd Be About a Quart Low: Lewis Grizzard on Women. Atlanta, Peachtree Publishers, 1983.
Elvis Is Dead and I Don't Feel So Good Myself. Atlanta, Peachtree Publishers, 1984.
Shoot Low, Boys—They're Ridin' Shetland Ponies: In Search of True Grit. Atlanta, Peachtree Publishers, 1985.
My Daddy Was a Pistol, and I'm a Son of a Gun. New York, Villard Books, 1986.
When My Love Returns From the Ladies Room, Will I Be Too Old to Care?. New York, Villard Books, 1987.
Don't Bend Over in the Garden, Granny, You Know Them Taters Got Eyes. New York, Villard Books, 1988.
Lewis Grizzard's Advice to the Newly Wed; Lewis Grizzard's Advice to the Newly Divorced, illustrated by Mike Lester. Atlanta, Longstreet Press, 1989.
Chili Dawgs Always Bark At Night. New York, Villard Books, 1989.
Lewis Grizzard on Fear of Flying, illustrated by Mike Lester. Atlanta, Longstreet Press, 1989.
Does a Wild Bear Chip in the Woods?: Lewis Grizzard on Golf. Atlanta, Longstreet Press, 1990.

If I Ever Get Back to Georgia, I'm Gonna Nail My Feet to the Ground. New York, Villard Books, 1990.

Don't Forget to Call Your Mama—I Wish I Could Call Mine. Atlanta, Longstreet Press, 1991.

You Can't Put No Boogie-Woogie on the King of Rock and Roll. New York, Villard Books, 1991.

I Haven't Understood Anything Since 1962, and Other Nekkid Truths. New York, Villard Books, 1992.

Pushing Fifty Is Exercise Enough. New York, Random House, 1993.

I Took a Lickin' and Kept on Tickin', and Now I Believe in Miracles. New York, Villard Books, 1993.

Collections

Heapin' Helping of True Grizzard: Down Home Again with Lewis Grizzard. Galahad Books, 1991.

It Wasn't Always Easy, But I Sure Had Fun: The Best of Lewis Grizzard. New York, Villard Books, 1994.

The Last Bus to Albuquerque: A Commemorative Edition Celebrating Lewis Grizzard, edited by Gerrie Ferris. Atlanta, Longstreet Press, 1994.

The Grizzard Sampler: A Collection of the Early Writings of Lewis Grizzard. Atlanta, Peachtree Publishers, 1994.

Grizzardisms: The Wit and Wisdom of Lewis Grizzard. New York, Villard Books, 1995.

The Wit and Wisdom of Lewis Grizzard. Atlanta, Longstreet Press, 1995.

Southern by the Grace of God: Lewis Grizzard on the South, edited by Gerrie Ferris. Atlanta, Longstreet Press, 1996.

Lewis Grizzard: Two Blockbuster Best Sellers. Birmingham, Sweetwater Press, 1997.

Other

Glory! Glory! Georgia's 1980 Championship Season: The Inside Story, with Loran Smith, special photography by Wingate Downs. Atlanta, Peachtree Publishers, 1981.

*

Critical Studies: *How to Tame a Wild Bore and Other Facts of Life with Lewis, the Semi-True Confessions of the Third Mrs. Grizzard* by Kathy Grizzard Schmook, Atlanta, Peachtree Publishers, 1986; *Lewis and Me and Skipper Makes 3* by Ludlow Porch, Atlanta, Longstreet Press, 1991; *Legends in Their Own Time*, New York, Prentice-Hall General Reference, 1994; *Don't Fence Me In: An Anecdotal Biography of Lewis Grizzard by Those Who Knew Him Best* edited by Chuck Perry, Atlanta, Longstreet Press, 1995.

Lewis Grizzard commented:

I'll tell you why I wanted to be a writer. When I was a little boy, I was a big fan of the minor league baseball franchise in Atlanta, the Atlanta Crackers. My mother let me stay up late at night to get the final scores. And my aunt and uncle worked in a cotton mill, a knitting mill, and they'd come home at lunch every day and bring the newspaper. I'd wait there for the paper to see how the games came out. It occurred to me early on in my life that I had no interest in an agricultural future or anything that had to do with manual labor. It occurred to me that they were paying

people to go watch these baseball games and write about them, and I said, "That's for me."

*   *   *

Humorist Lewis Grizzard's early published work consisted mostly of collections from his newspaper column, which he wrote four times a week for the *Atlanta Journal and Constitution* from 1979. The topics were wide-ranging, the focus loose, and humor alone was the unifying factor in his early book publications, such as *Kathy Sue Loudermilk, I Love You* (1979) or *Don't Sit Under the Grits Tree With Anyone Else But Me* (1981). Only later, with *Lewis Grizzard's Advice to the Newly Wed; Lewis Grizzard's Advice to the Newly Divorced* (1989) and *Does a Wild Bear Chip in the Woods?: Lewis Grizzard on Golf* (1990), would he follow a single theme throughout a book. Not long before his death in 1994, according to his widow, Dedra, he had begun to believe that these humor collections had run their course, and was contemplating an extended work, possibly even a novel.

In fact, as Dedra recalled, Grizzard was just about to experience a surge in his career, as Villard Books expanded his nationwide audience far beyond the Southeast. His death in the spring of 1994, from complications as a result of heart surgery, cut short his plans. Yet, despite the many directions of his columns—Grizzard himself would no doubt have admitted a short attention span—a certain unified picture emerged, a world that Lewis Grizzard defined like few others.

Grizzard once claimed that he was the first person to ever put peanuts in a Coke and drink it, and that he pioneered the stylistic touch of wearing docksiders barefoot with khakis and a sport coat. Like many of the tongue-in-cheek assertions he made in his columns, this one is dubious; nonetheless, there is a certain underlying truth. Peanuts in the Coke is the sort of quintessential Southern habit that would make most people from north of the Mason-Dixon Line shake their heads—much the same response that a Lewis Grizzard column might elicit. As for the docksiders and bare feet, it was a virtual uniform in which Grizzard could often be seen at Atlanta hangouts such as Beasley's in Buckhead, drinking a libation he invented, called "the Grizzard"—a screwdriver with a double shot of vodka, resulting from Grizzard's desire to expedite the drinking process.

Contrary to the belief held by many of his fans, Grizzard's bad heart had little to do with his excessive drinking, smoking, and penchant for cholesterol-rich, Southern down-home cooking. His heart condition, about which he wrote in *They Tore Out My Heart and Stomped That Sucker Flat* (1982) and his last book, *I Took a Lickin' and Kept on Tickin', and Now I Believe in Miracles* (1993) was with him from childhood, though his lifestyle certainly exacerbated the problem.

Grizzard's self-destructive habits, his multiple marriages, and the driven quality with which he lived and wrote had their roots in his Moreland, Georgia childhood. He had an intense bond with his mother, Christine, in whose memory he wrote *Don't Forget to Call Your Mama—I Wish I Could Call Mine* (1991). But his bond was every bit as strong with his father and namesake, Lewis Sr., or "The Major" as Lewis Jr. would refer to him later in life. Grizzard's 1986 book, *My Daddy Was a Pistol, and I'm a Son of a Gun*, offered a more lighthearted treatment of his father than *Don't Forget* did his mother, but this may have resulted from the deeper pain associated with his memories of his father. The elder Grizzard fought in the Korean War and came home damaged from his experience. Cursed as much with his ability to charm as with his alcoholism, Lewis Sr. made a living in part by moving from town to town and running scams of various sorts. Like a character in *The Adventures of Huckleberry Finn*, he would go to a church and claim to have put aside his drinking, for which the parishioners would lavish him with hospitality and gifts until he mysteriously disappeared; or he would apply for a job at a high school and obtain a position teaching a subject about which he knew nothing.

Grizzard's parents divorced, and Lewis Sr. later married the mother of future Atlanta radio talk-show host Ludlow Porch. Lewis Jr. attended college at the University of Georgia, whose football team would remain an obsession often reflected in his columns. He attained his degree in journalism, and after a stint with the *Atlanta Journal*, accepted a newspaper job in Chicago. It turned out to be a mistake: Grizzard longed for the South, as he recorded in his 1990 book, *If I Ever Get Back to Georgia, I'm Gonna Nail My Feet to the Ground*. With the help of friend Jim Minter of the *Atlanta Journal and Constitution* he got a job for the Atlanta paper doing what he had wanted to do all along—writing a column—but been prevented from doing because of his demonstrated ability as an editor.

Later Grizzard would tell *Contemporary Authors*, "The best thing about being a columnist is when you ain't got a column to write." It was challenge enough, he said, to come up with four good ideas a year, let alone four a week. But for many years, his columns would entertain readers throughout the Southeast and the rest of the nation, with a steadily growing readership. In his columns and books, Grizzard created a world, that of "the quintessential Southern male"—himself. He was inexorably drawn to women, but confused by them and often involved in a heartbreak, either on the giving or receiving end (*If Love Were Oil, I'd Be About a Quart Low: Lewis Grizzard on Women*, 1983; *When My Love Returns from the Ladies Room, Will I Be Too Old to Care?* 1987.)

Grizzard extolled a traditional, all-American image of manhood (*Shoot Low, Boys—They're Ridin' Shetland Ponies: In Search of True Grit*, 1985), and his heroes were those of the 1950s (*You Can't Put No Boogie-Woogie on the King of Rock and Roll*, 1991). But those old ways had become outmoded, and nobody appreciated the significance of the changes like Grizzard (*Elvis Is Dead and I Don't Feel So Good Myself*, 1984). He made a show of his bewilderment at modern life, yet his confusion only went so far, because he knew he was bewildered (*I Haven't Understood Anything Since 1962, and Other Nekkid Truths*, 1992). In the end, he was philosophical and resigned to change and aging (*Pushing Fifty Is Exercise Enough*, 1993).

In his last year, Grizzard did mellow considerably. The old fire remained, but there was also a new reverence for life, reflected in his last book, *I Took a Lickin' and Kept on Tickin', and Now I Believe in Miracles*. After a lengthy struggle followed closely by his fans in Atlanta and elsewhere, Grizzard died at Emory Hospital on 20 March 1994, just four days after he and Dedra, his longtime companion, were married. Later, Dedra and Grizzard's business manager and close friend, Steve Enoch, fulfilled a last request from Grizzard by scattering his ashes between the goal posts at Sanford Field in Athens, home of his beloved Georgia Bulldogs.

—Judson Knight

GROOM, Winston

Born: Washington, D.C., 23 March 1943. **Education:** University of Alabama, 1965. **Military Service:** U.S. Army, 1965-68; served in Vietnam. **Family:** Married Ruth Noble, 1969 (divorced 1985); married Anne-Clinton Bridges, 1987. **Career:** Edited University of Alabama's campus humor magazine, *The Mahout*, during college; odd jobs, Mobile, Alabama, 1968; reporter, *Washington Star*, 1968-77; full-time writer since 1977. **Awards:** Best Novel Award, Southern Library Association, 1983, Pulitzer Prize nomination, 1984, for *Conversations with the Enemy*.

PUBLICATIONS

Novels

Better Times Than These. Arlington, Texas, Summit, 1978.
As Summers Die. Arlington, Texas, Summit, 1980.
Only. New York, Putnam, 1984.
Forrest Gump. New York, Doubleday, 1986.
Gone the Sun. New York, Doubleday, 1988.
Gump & Co. New York, Pocket Books, 1996.

Nonfiction

Conversations with the Enemy, with Duncan Spencer. New York, Putnam, 1983.
Shrouds of Glory: From Atlanta to Nashville; The Last Great Campaign of the Civil War. New York, Atlantic Monthly Press, 1994.
The Bubba Gump Shrimp Co. Cookbook: Recipes & Reflections from Forrest Gump. Little Rock, Oxmoor House, 1994.
Gumpisms: The Wit and Wisdom of Forrest Gump. New York, Pocket Books, 1994.
Forrest Gump: My Favorite Chocolate Recipes: Mama's Fudge, Cookies, Cakes, and Candies. Little Rock, Leisure Arts, 1995.

*   *   *

While the 1994 film *Forrest Gump* made Winton Groom's name famous, the novel on which it was based was published six years earlier and sold only 30,000 copies in hardcover. It received mixed reviews, with Jonathan Baumbach of the *New York Times* praising the novel's humor yet concluding that it is ultimately "a defanged Candide"—"too ingratiating, too lacking in genuine surprise, too undemanding of itself." *Forrest Gump*, says Baumbach, "tends to fade from memory with surprising dispatch."

Rather than fading from memory, however, *Forrest Gump* went on to inspire a film that grossed over $700 million worldwide, won six Academy Awards, and gave birth to an entire industry of such tie-in products as chocolates, clothing, a small collection of

Gump sayings (1994's *Gumpisms*), and, most recently, a sequel, *Gump & Co*, which examines the relationship between Forrest and his son. This extreme popularity has caused no small worry for a number of cultural critics, who consider it an ominous sign of increasing anti-intellectualism out in the provinces. Typical is *The New Republic*'s Stanley Kauffmann, who fears that "Groom is saying, 'Who needs intelligence?'" The author insists, however, that he intended no such social commentary. As he remarked to Robert Epstein, "I wasn't delivering any messages other than showing that a man doesn't have to be rich or smart to be dignified."

While the *Gump* phenomenon is fairly recent, Groom's career as a writer reaches back considerably further, to the University of Alabama, where he edited the campus humor magazine, *The Mahout*. Though he originally planned to follow his father into the legal profession, upon graduating Groom went not to law school but to Vietnam, where he attained the rank of captain. On returning, Groom sought a position with *Esquire*, *Time*, or *Newsweek*, but instead found his way back to Mobile. He did find a job, though not one so glamorous as he had hoped. As he said to William Grimes, "Here, I'd been a captain leading 160 men around, and I ended up working in a paper box factory earning a dollar an hour." However, by coincidence, Groom met the managing editor of the *Washington Star*, who hired him as a reporter. During his eight years covering the courts and police beat, Groom became friends with the nephew of Irwin Shaw, a fellow reporter, and through him became acquainted with New York's literary life.

Groom's first novel dates from this period. *Better Times Than These* is the straightforward story of a company of the Seventh Cavalry in Vietnam. Nicholas Proffitt, writing in *The Washington Post*, described it as "one of the earlier, and better novels to come out of the war." With his second novel, *As Summers Die*, Groom turned toward the South, where his fiction has largely remained. As Proffitt observed, "Two landscapes loom large in the work of Winston Groom, both of them green, both of them hothouses for chicanery and violence: Vietnam and the American South." In this case the South is coastal Louisiana, where oil is discovered under land belonging to a black woman. The result is a struggle between her community and the two white brothers whose father had given her the land. Groom's small but respectful following during this period is reflected in a review by Larry McMurtry. Writing in the *New York Times Book Review*, McMurtry described *As Summers Die* as "what used to be called a rousing good yarn, with boat chases in the bayous, impassioned courtroom dramas and occasional fornication."

As Summers Die was followed by *Conversations with the Enemy*, an examination of Robert Garwood, an American private who was imprisoned by the Viet Cong and, on his return, dishonorably discharged from the Marines under accusations of desertion and collaboration. A detailed recreation of Private Garwood's 14 years of internment, noting, for example, that Garwood ended up speaking English with a Vietnamese accent, *Conversations* was nominated for the Pulitzer Prize. In the words of Webster Schott (*Washington Post Book World*), Garwood's life is "a tale conceived by Franz Kafka, invested with moral dilemma by William Shakespeare," and Groom's account is "as close to the truth as we will ever know about one of the most surreal events in American history." Thus, even though Groom attained popular atten-

tion when *Forrest Gump* made it big on the big screen, he had enjoyed a steady amount of respectful reviews throughout his career.

Since publishing *Forrest Gump* in 1986, Groom has written one other work of nonfiction, *Shrouds of Glory,* an account of Confederate General John Bell Hood's Tennessee campaign. Groom considers it one "of the greatest might-have-beens of the Civil War." Hood's plan was to seize Nashville, resupply his army from the Union warehouses there, and then march through the mountains to Richmond, which was under attack by General Grant, thus freeing General Lee to march on Washington, or pursue General Sherman. The campaign, of course, was a disaster. Groom's faithful representation of the campaign is rendered in language that becomes elegant, at times, as in this description of the moments before a cavalry charge: "There were tunes of glory, tunes of death, 20,000 bayonets gleaming on a lovely autumn afternoon, an army of veterans with the veteran's understanding of what they were about to face."

—Jason Mitchell

GURGANUS, Allan

Born: Rocky Mount, North Carolina, 11 June 1947. **Education:** Monterey Language School, Monterey, Mexico and the Radioman and Cryptography School San Diego, 1966; Pennsylvania Academy of Fine Arts, Philadelphia 1966-67; Harvard University, 1969-70; Sarah Lawrence College, Bronxville, New York, 1970-72. **Military Service:** U.S. Navy, 1966-70. **Career:** Desk clerk and salesperson of art reproductions, 1969-70; night watchman in a vitamin factory, 1970-72; professor of fiction writing, University of Iowa, 1972-74, Stanford University, 1974-76, Duke University, 1976-78, Sarah Lawrence College, 1978-86, and University of Iowa Writers' Workshop, 1989-90; artist, with paintings in many private and public collections; member of board, Corporation of Yaddo; cofounder, "Writers for Harvey Gantt," "Writers Against Jesse Helms." **Awards:** Jones lecturer, Stanford University; PEN prizes for fiction; National Endowment for the Arts grants; Ingram Merrill award; Wallace Stegner fellowship; Sue Kaufman prize for First Fiction, American Academy and Institute of Arts and Letters, for *Oldest Living Confederate Widow Tells All*; *Los Angeles Times* Book Prize for fiction and Southern Book Award for Fiction, Southern Book Critics Circle, both 1991, for *White People*. **Agent:** International Creative Management, 40 West 57th Street, New York, New York 10019.

PUBLICATIONS

Short Stories

Good Help, with illustrations by the author. Rocky Mount, North Carolina Wesleyan College Press, 1988.
Blessed Assurance: A Moral Tale (novella). Rocky Mount, North Carolina Wesleyan College Press, 1990.
White People: Stories and Novellas. New York, Knopf, 1991.
The Practical Heart. Rocky Mount, North Carolina Wesleyan College Press, 1993.

GURGANUS

Novels

Oldest Living Confederate Widow Tells All. New York, Knopf, 1989.
Plays Well with Others. New York, Knopf, 1997.

Uncollected or Short Fiction and Nonfiction

"Seven Details the Major Critic of the Show Felt to be Over-Explicit," in *The Atlantic*, February 1975.
"Communique," in *The Atlantic*, September 1976.
"Comfort," in *Mademoiselle*, June 1977.
"Storied Objects," in *House & Garden*, May 1989.
"The Ramada Inn at Shiloh," in *GRANTA 35*, Spring 1991.
"Forced Use." In *Faber Book of Gay Short Fiction* edited by Edmund White. London: Faber & Faber, 1991.
"Ode to Boy," in *The Yale Review*, October 1992.
"See Me in the Movies," in *Modern Maturity*, April/May 1994.
"How I Fought in the Civil War," in *TV Guide*, April/May 1994.
"Local Man Has Sex With Corpse," in *GRANTA 46*, Winter 1994.
"The Original-Sin School of Brussels Sprouts Cooking," in *The New York Times Magazine*, March 10, 1996.
"What AIDS Teaches Us," in *A & U*, February 1998.

*

Critical Studies: "Mouth of the South" by Tom Prince, *New York*, August 1989; "PW Interviews Allan Gurganus" by Sam Staggs, *Publishers Weekly*, August 1989; "Black & Blue & Gray: An Interview With Allan Gurganus" by Jeffrey Scheuer, *Poets and Writers*, November/December, 1990; "Interview With Allan Gurganus" by D. C. Denison, *The Writer*, October 1991; *Parting the Curtains: Interviews With Southern Writers* edited by Dannye R. Powell, et al., Winston-Salem, J. F. Blair, 1994. "

*   *   *

When North Carolina native Allan Gurganus burst onto the market-driven literary scene of the late 1980's with his over-sized first novel, *Oldest Living Confederate Widow Tells All*, he was 42 years old, an uncollected short-story writer and an itinerant professor of creative writing. Segments of the work, which Gurganus says he began in 1981, had been appearing in various forms since 1984, and its release by Knopf was recognized as a major publishing event; in a decade that had witnessed the debuts of Jill McCorkle, Kaye Gibbons, and Bob Shacochis, the unparalleled success of the novel brought its author a measure of celebrity, and in hindsight may have done more than any work of the period to rekindle interest in contemporary Southern fiction as a popular, marketable literature. Gurganus, once described by his friend and teacher John Cheever as "the most morally responsive and technically brilliant writer of his generation," went on to publish a novella, *Blessed Assurance* (1990), *White People* (1991)—a collection of short stories—and the novel *Plays Well with Others* (1997). "The Practical Heart," a family memoir, was published in *Harper's* in 1993 and later as a chapbook.

Confederate Widow is an intimate oral history as related by 99-year-old Lucy Marsden, a lifetime resident of Falls, North Carolina, who married a local Confederate veteran (thirty-seven years her senior) when she was fifteen years old. Interviewed in a rest home, Lucy talks with very little prompting. Although the gen-

eral trend of her story—Captain Marsden's youthful war experiences are followed by narratives of courtship, marriage, parenthood and death—makes an effort at linearity, the novel is structured around Lucy's conversational and mimetic styles, which are free-ranging. Grisly war episodes (such as the short life of Will Marsden's childhood friend, Ned Smythe, whose death in the Virginia backwoods obsesses Marsden for the rest of his life) alternate with rest home anecdotes; incidents from plantation life, which Lucy never knew, contrast with her memories of a stifling Reconstruction childhood.

In "The Tribe that Answers," Lucy appropriates the voice of Castalia—Marsden's ageless housekeeper and a former slave—to tell the story of her capture and transportation from Africa. "Castalia's" narrative, by significantly broadening the emotional and historical range of the text, commemorates the cross-cultural origins of what is thought to be a racially divided South. "Look at young Mr. Elvis," Lucy observes at one point. "At age nineteen, and after being born into the cracker race, that child got full credit for personally inventing a hundred and fifty years of black folks' blues." (To even the score, in the novel's final war memory a Confederate officer attributes a quote of Turgenev's to the sayings of "some wise old slave woman" from his childhood.) Reliable or unreliable, Lucy brings her personality to bear on the pleasurable task of playing history; a survivor, she is also an actor, whose multiple roles assert her capacity for a century of personal and social change.

With a collector's instincts, Gurganus has cultivated a versatile literary imagination composed of borrowed memories, voices, and idioms; he is a folklorist, but as *White People* was to demonstrate, primarily a folklorist of the Southern middle class. Cheever's presence, if not his influence, can be sensed here, particularly in the apprenticeship stories "Minor Heroism," "Condolences to Every One of Us," and "Art History." "Minor Heroism," a study in the estrangement of a father and son, was the first gay fiction published in *The New Yorker*, owing to Cheever's intervention. The collection documents two creative turning points in Gurganus' career. "A Hog Loves Its Life" (1986), set like *Confederate Widow* in the composite town of Falls, North Carolina, details stages in the relationship between a boy and his grandfather, a local wit and storyteller. This work represents Gurganus' earliest full treatment of oral tradition in Southern life, reflected in the phrase, "Language, like love, starts local." "Adult Art" (1986), also set in modern Falls, explores the homosexual double life of a school superintendent; despite the fact that the subject was not a new one for Gurganus, and although this story also uses spoken narrative and local color, it is unique in its maturity and candor, and marks Gurganus' simultanous emergence as a gay, and regional, writer.

Like those of Thomas Wolfe, Truman Capote, and several generations of Southern authors, Gurganus' finest work has been the product of an extended Northern self-exile. *Plays Well with Others*, which Gurganus wrote after settling in North Carolina indefinitely, is set in New York City in the final years of the sexual revolution and the early days of the AIDS epidemic. "We're all continually upstaged by the scale of our own times and tragedies. In the end, the name of the ship that took you down is better known than you will ever be," writes narrator Hartley Mims, Jr.

Mims (the great-grandson of a Confederate colonel, and gay), who comes to the city from Falls to make a living as a writer, meets Angie, a painter from Savannah, and Robert, a composer.

Written in the form of a memoir, *Plays Well with Others* takes a nostalgic cultural myth—New York as the patron goddess of struggling young artists—and dissolves it in a tragedy with metaphors (the *Titanic*, the Holocaust, Vietnam) that grow increasingly impersonal, as Mims loses not only his friends, but an era of his life, to AIDS. "My address book often seems to me the best book I've ever written," he reflects, having lived to see this symbol of his community transformed into a list of vital statistics. "Certainly it contains the most complicated characters. Surely it's the work in progress longest."

Louis Rubin has observed that the Southern writer's sense of—or sensitivity to—*community*, of one's presence within it and its presence within the writer, placed limitations on the creative art-ist in the Old South, which (to the extent that they were still in force in the New South) the region's modernists would escape by detaching themselves and turning inward. A postmodern Southerner, Gurganus has meaningfully chosen for the narrator of his second novel a gregarious artist who draws little distinction between his life and his work until a devastating mortality draws it for him. Though the folkloric qualities of his Falls stories suggest a writer both in and of a particular place and time, they conceal the dual nature of Gurganus' detachment—from his native soil by choice, and again from his chosen community (the beseiged gay community of 1980's Manhattan) by external forces. Having managed to preserve and utilize the pleasures of community life under the same circumstances in which an older South first lost them—in the wake of calamity—it remains for the amanuensis of Confederate widows to tell us why they are disappearing, and what they have to say about it.

—George deMan

H

HAGY, Alyson

Born: Alyson Carol Hagy in Springfield, Ohio, 1 August 1960.
Education: Williams College, B.A. with honors, 1982; University of Michigan, M.F.A. 1985. **Career:** Lecturer, University of Virginia and University of Michigan; assistant professor of English, University of Wyoming. **Awards:** Avery and Jule Hopwood Award for Short Fiction, University of Michigan, 1984; Roy W. Cowden Fellowships, University of Michigan, 1984 and 1985; Grant, Michigan Council for the Arts, 1989.

Publications

Madonna on Her Back. N.p., Stuart Wright, 1986.
Hardware River Stories. New York, Poseiden Press, 1991

*   *   *

Alyson Hagy emerged with her first collection of short stories in 1986 after having been widely published in journals. Referred to as one of a group of fine new American voices, Hagy writes stories that are indelibly imprinted by place, usually the rural South, where she spent much of her youth, or the Midwest, where she has spent most of her adulthood. Her characters are ordinary people, often in fairly ordinary, if conflicted situations. These characters often make decisions based on their desires, rather than on societal norms, and their means for surviving the results is frequently the hinge of Hagy's stories.

Her first collection, *Madonna on Her Back* (1986), introduced Hagy as an innovative voice, though several reviewers noted elements of the writer's workshops she had attended, particularly her use of stock characters through whom Hagy writes about issues, rather than telling stories. Primarily set in rural areas, the collection's eight stories are well-crafted. "No Kind of Name" tells the story of a woman who both wants and fears love. "Mister Makes" is the story of a welfare mother whose first baby is dead and who is now caring for a deformed— and soon to die— second child. Her tale is told to the background choruses of neighborhood gossip. In "Infrared Signature," a group of old hippies decide to take down a plane with a fishnet, and in "Stadia" we observe a young man becoming consumed with grief for his dead father.

Hagy's second collection, *Hardware River Stories* (1991), is similarly polished but offers a more unflinching, vivid perspective, moving from sentimentality into realism about the confusing relationship between violence and desire, set in rural America. In "The Field of Lost Shoes," the narrator tells of an afternoon spent with his lover and her child, while "The Grief Is Always Fresh" shows just how many ways grief can be negotiated in small town America. In "Ballad and Sadness," the sister of a pedophile has a rather distracted one night stand, and in "Kettle of Hawks," a son, his mother and a gay farmworker play out a story of love and deception.

Hagy is haunted by the things that plague other people and compels her readers by examining the how obsession begins. Her direct narrative and precision of language are as compelling as her stories and her characters. Not surprisingly, considering her interest in place, Hagy has recently been examining the relationship between landscape and character in America. She says that this may be why, after a childhood spent in the mountains of Virginia, she is now living in Wyoming, "a beautiful but isolated place. That sort of isolation," Hagy says, "feeds into my fiction." Hagy has completed but has yet to publish a novel about horseracing in Kentucky and a collection of short stories about North Carolina's Outer Banks.

—Virginia Watkins

HAINES, John

Born: John Meade Haines in Norfolk, Virginia, 29 June 1924.
Education: Attended National Art School, Washington, D.C., 1946-47; American University, 1948-49; Hans Hoffmann School of Fine Art, 1950-52; and University of Washington, 1974. **Family:** Married 1) Ella Hussey, 10 October 1960; 2) Jane McWhorter, 23 November 1970; 3) Leslie Sennett, October, 1978 (divorced); children: Blair, Anne, Karen, Peter (stepson). **Military Service:** U.S. Navy, 1943-46. **Career:** Since 1946 has worked as hunter, gardener, fisherman, trapper, housepainter, carpenter, and writer; homesteader in Alaska, 1954-69; freelance lecturer and writer, since 1969; employed briefly as a clerk in the U.S. Department of the Navy, Washington, D.C.; Alaska Humanities Forum program director, 1972-73; poet-in-resident, University of Alaska, 1972-73; writer-in-residence, Sheldon Jackson College, 1982-83, Ucross Foundation, 1987, Montalvo Center for the Arts, 1988, and Djerassi Foundation, 1988; guest writer, Midnight Sun Conference, University of Alaska, 1979-82 and 1986-87; panelist and guest writer, Moorhead College, University of New Mexico, University of Texas, and Center for Northern Studies, all 1980, Anchorage Community College and Juneau Museum of Art, both 1981; member of staff, Sitka Writers Symposium, 1986; visiting writer, Loft Mentor Series, 1987; visiting professor at numerous institutions. **Awards:** Sculpture prize, Corcoran Gallery, 1948; Jennie Tane Award for Poetry, *Massachusetts Review*, 1964; Guggenheim fellowship, 1965-66, 1984; National Endowment for the Arts grant, 1967-68; Amy Lowell Scholarship, 1976-77; Alaska State Council on the Arts grant, 1979, fellowship, 1987; Alaska Press Club Award, for contributions to Alaska newspapers, 1981; Governor's Award, for life contributions to the arts in Alaska, 1982; Ingram Merrill Foundation grant, 1987; L.D.: University of Alaska, 1983.

Publications

Poetry

Winter News. Wesleyan University Press, 1966, revised edition, 1983.

Suite for the Pied Piper. Ox Head Press, 1968.
The Legend of Paper Plates. Unicorn Press, 1970.
The Mirror. Unicorn Press, 1970.
The Stone Harp. Wesleyan University Press, 1971.
Twenty Poems. Unicorn Press, 1971
Leaves and Ashes. Kayak Press, 1975.
In Five Years Time. Smokeroot Press, 1976.
Cicada. Wesleyan University Press, 1977.
In a Dusty Light. Graywolf Press, 1977.
The Sun on Your Shoulder. Graywolf Press, 1977.
News from the Glacier: Selected Poems, 1960-1980. Wesleyan University Press, 1982.
New Poems, Story Line Press. 1990.
The Owl in the Mask of the Dreamer: Collected Poems. Wesleyan University Press, 1993.

Nonfiction

Living off the Country: Essays on Poetry and Place. University of Michigan Press, 1981.
Other Days. Graywolf Press, 1982.
Of Traps and Snares. Dragon Press, 1982.
Stories We Listened To. Bench Press, 1986.

Other

The River Is Wider Than It Seems (script for documentary film). Montana Committee for the Humanities, 1980.
You and I and the World (essays). University of Michigan Press, 1988.
The Stars, the Snow, the Fire. Graywolf Press, 1989.

Translator, *Miguel Hernandez*. El Amor Ascentia, Ox Head Press, 1967.

Contributor, *Minus Thirty-One and the Wind Blowing: Nine Reflections about Living on Land*. Alaska Pacific, 1980.
Contributor, *On Nature*. North Point Press, 1987.
Contributor, *Essays, Memoirs and Reflections*. Graywolf Press, 1987

Author of foreword, *John Muir, Travels to Alaska*. Sierra Books, 1987.

Author of preface, *Edwin Muir, The Story and the Fable*. Rowan Tree, 1987.

*   *   *

Born in Norfolk, Virginia, Haines's literary reputation is based mostly on the poetry he has written concerning his experiences in the Alaskan wilderness that expresses his spiritual and physical affinity to the landscape, which he frequently depicts in metaphysical terms. Haines draws comparisons between his work and those of Scandanavian writers and the Scottish poet Edwin Muir. Due to its consistent handling of nature themes, much of Haines's poetry is compared to the naturalist verse of American literary figures Henry David Thoreau and Robert Frost. However, Haines's work contains bleak assessments of encroaching commercialization, which he describes as "the accumulating ruin of the North American landscape." Haines's later work increasingly

relies on elements of sculpture and painting to explore themes of mortality.

The son of a naval officer, Haines developed an interest for the visual arts at an early age. After serving in the U.S. Navy from 1943-46 and having received several battle stars in World War II, Haines studied art at the National Art School, the American University, and at the Hans Hoffmann School of Fine Art in New York. Many critics observe that Haines's schooling is evident in much of his poetry, particularly in his detailed observations and colorful, often surreal depictions of natural forms.

Before homesteading in Alaska in 1954, Haines began hunting, fishing, trapping, gardening, and writing during the late 1940s. "Words began to fasten themselves to what I saw," he wrote. "I learned the names of the things to be found there, characteristics of the subarctic the world over . . . I learned to hunt, to watch, and to listen, to think like a moose, if need be, or a marten, or a lynx. I watched the river, and saw in its gray and swirling water, heavy with silt, the probable trace of salmon, and knew where to set my nets . . . It was an awakening, profound and disturbing. Everything was so new to me that it was like finding myself for the first time with my feet on the earth." Haines built his own home in Richardson, sixty miles outside Fairbanks, Alaska, and began writing poetry.

Haines received a Guggenheim Fellowship in 1965. The next year, he published his first volume of verse, *Winter News* (1966), which details Haines's Alaskan experiences, "born of the isolation in which I then lived—that remote, largely self-contained world of the forest, of snow and animal life, of hunting and gathering— and into which news of the outside world penetrated even so. What I wrote then emerged with difficulty from a kind of spell, one that I was reluctant to break, knowing that once I did, nothing would ever be quite the same." Many poems, such as "If the Owl Calls Again" and "The Mole," are meditations on the philosophical changes as well as the mental and physical acuity necessary for survival in the arctic wilderness.

Haines received a grant from the National Endowment for the Arts in 1967. His next verse collection, *The Stone Harp* (1971), was less enthusiastically received due to the more politically didactic and reactionary tone of the poems. In several poems, Haines abandons Alaskan subject matter to address American social and political concerns. "By the time I came to write the poems of *The Stone Harp*," Haines later wrote, "many things had changed, and the spell had been broken. The outside world of public events, of politics and history and, to an extent, of professional necessity, intruded more and more. I re-entered, reluctantly yet necessarily, the world I had left behind many years before."

The Stone Harp is divided into three sections: "In Nature," "America," and "Signs." The "In Nature" poems has Haines attempting to construct metaphors for human alienation and destructiveness from his observations of nature. "America" harshly condemns U.S. politicians and policies, particularly President Lyndon Johnson and American involvement in the Vietnam conflict. "Signs" depicts Haines's apocalyptic view of U.S. culture and the environment. The volume's concluding poem, "The Flight," wrote Haines, "reflects directly my reading of Mikhail Sholokov's novels of the turbulent Civil War period in Russia, with their images of deserted villages, of a people uprooted and driven on the roads."

Haines published several small volumes in the early 1970s, much of which is wistful and nostalgic and collected in *Cicada* (1977). Poems from *In a Dusty Light* (1977) are reprinted in Haines's next major volume, *News from the Glacier* (1982), where his work features more detailed depictions of historical and geologic topics and includes expansive use of color, an element evident throughout *New Poems, 1980-88* (1990). His visual arts background is evident in "Death and the Miser," which takes as its subject a painting by Hieronymous Bosch, and "Head of Sorrow, Head of Thought," which borrows its name from female portraits by Auguste Rodin. "The Owl in the Mask of the Dreamer" presents Haines's brief history of sculpture, with three stanzas referring to a piece by Alberto Giacometti. *The Owl in the Mask of the Dreamer: Collected Poems by John Haines* (1993) contains many new poems that continue Haines's exploration of paintings, sculpture and literature: "The Poem without Meaning" examines a stone sculpture of St. Luke, and "In the Sleep of Reason," "Stalled Colossus," and "The Fates" reference etchings and paintings by Goya. Haines returns to Rodin in "The Burghers of Calais" and "Age of Bronze," concerning two of Rodin's famous sculptures. The volume's final poem, "Night," is told from the point of view of a sculpted female figure by Michelangelo and examines Jungian themes of death, life, and consciousness.

—Bruce Walker

HALEY, Alex

Born: Alex Murray Palmer Haley in Ithaca, New York, 11 August 1921. **Education:** Alcorn Agricultural & Mechanical College (now Alcorn State University); Elizabeth City Teachers College, 1937-39. **Family:** Married Nannie Branch, 1941 (divorced, 1964); two children; married Juliette Collins, 1964 (divorced); one child. **Military Service:** U.S. Coast Guard, 1939-59, retiring as chief journalist. **Career:** Freelance writer, 1959-92; founder and president of Kinte Corporation, Los Angeles, 1972-92; board member of New College of California, 1974, and King Hassan's Royal Academy; film producer, *Palmerstown, USA,* 1980; advisor, African American Heritage Association, Detroit; general editor, Raintree Steck-Vaughn, Austin, Texas. **Awards:** *Roots: The Saga of an American Family* won over 250 awards, including special citations from the National Book award committee and Pulitzer Prize committee, 1977; Spingarn Medal from NAACP, 1977; nominated to Black Filmmakers Hall of Fame, 1981, for producing *Palmerstown, U.S.A.,* 1981; Litt.D. from Simpson College, 1971, Howard University, 1974, Williams College, 1975, and Capitol University, 1975; honorary doctorate from Seton Hall University, 1974. **Died:** 10 February 1992, in Seattle, Washington, of cardiac arrest.

PUBLICATIONS

Novels

Roots: The Saga of an American Family. New York, Doubleday, 1976.
A Different Kind of Christmas. New York, Doubleday, 1988.

Alex Haley's Queen: The Story of an American Family, with David Stevens. New York, W. Morrow, 1993.

Other

The Autobiography of Malcolm X As Told to Alex Haley, with Macolm X. New York, Grove, 1965.
The Playboy Interviews, edited by Murray Fisher, New York, Ballantine, 1993.

Uncollected Essays

"My Search for Roots," in *Reader's Digest*, May 1974.
"In Search of the African," in American History Illustrated, Fall 1974.
"Alex Haley on Kids in Search of Their Roots," in *Parents*, Spring 1977.
"What *Roots* Means to Me," in *Reader's Digest*, May 1977.
"Sea Islanders, Strong-Willed Survivors Face Their Uncertain Future Together," in *Smithsonian*, October 1982.

*

Media Adaptations and Features: Television—*Roots,* 1977, and *Roots: The Next Generations,* 1979, ABC; *Alex Haley: The Search for Roots*, WNET 13 Educational Broadcasting, Princeton, Films for the Humanities, 1977. **Film—***Malcolm X,* directed by Spike Lee and adapted from *The Autobiography of Malcolm X.*, 1992.

Critical Studies: *Alex Haley: Author of 'Roots'* by Doreen Gonzales, Hillside, New Jersey, Enslow Publishers, 1994; *Alex Haley* by David Shirley, New York, Chelsea House Publishers, 1994.

*   *   *

The writing career of the author of the blockbuster book of the 1970s had a modest beginning. During the twenty years Alex Haley served in the Coast Guard, he ghostwrote love letters for his shipmates, published an article in the syndicated *This Week*, a Sunday newspaper supplement, and achieved status as the Guard's only chief journalist. When he left the service, however, Haley knew he wanted to be a writer. Determined to be independent, he turned down government employment and lived a penurious life in New York City as a free-lance writer, subsisting on small sums from magazine assignments. His first break came with his 1962 interview with jazz trumpeter Miles Davis for *Playboy* magazine. The article led to a much-acclaimed feature on Malcolm X and to Haley's series, "Playboy Interview," which included sessions with Martin Luther King, Jr., Melvin Belli, and leader of the American Nazi Party, George Lincoln Rockwell. The series was later published in 1993 as *The Playboy Interviews.*

The Malcolm X article led to the thoughtful collaboration that became *The Autobiography of Malcolm X As Told to Alex Haley* (1965). As Haley relates in the book's introduction, he transcribed Malcolm X's conversations over a two year period, capturing the leader's voice as he related his transformation from Malcolm Little to Malcolm X and his espousal and then rejection of the Nation of Islam. Haley's unobtrusive editing and organization of Malcolm's story led to a powerful portrait of the complex leader.

With Malcolm X's assassination in 1965 and increasing interest in the activist's life and ideas, the book surged to huge sales and inclusion in many college courses. In 1992, director Spike Lee used the book as primary source material for his film, *Malcolm X*.

As a child raised in Henning, Tennessee, Haley often listened to his maternal grandmother, Cynthia Palmer, and his aunts reminiscence about their African ancestors brought to America on slave ships. He was especially curious about an African named "Kintay," who refused to acknowledge his slave name, "Toby." Inspired by the women's oral narratives, Haley devoted twelve years to reconstructing his genealogy; his research included a trip to Gambia and an interview with a griot (an oral historian). He recreated his findings into an international bestseller, *Roots: The Saga of an American Family* (1976). Spanning seven generations, *Roots* chronicles the Americanization of Kunta Kinte and his descendants.

Nearly the first quarter of the book concentrates on Kinte's life, beginning in the 1750s in Juffure Gambia in West Africa. Haley's splendid African setting of Mandinkan is complete with authentic myths, rituals and mores. Haley convincingly recounts Kinte's harrowing Middle Passage after he is sold into slavery in 1767. An *Ebony* magazine article described Haley's personal reconstruction of lying in a ship's hold in his attempt to authentically portray Kinte's emotional anguish as he crossed the ocean. Continued in what James Baldwin calls the "bleak, terrifying landscape" of the New World, the narrative tells of Kinte's fierce desire for freedom and his contempt for obedient slaves. Kinte recites stories to his daughter, Kizzy, continuing the African oral tradition and commences the family's story. Kizzy, in turn, passes the African sounds and stories on to her son, "Chicken" George, a gamecock trainer and a popular figure in Haley's family history. Amid violence and cruelty, the family saga and storytelling continues through George's son Tom, who marries Irene, a half Native American woman, in North Carolina. Their daughter Cynthia, a freed slave and Haley's storytelling grandmother, marries Will Palmer in Henning, Tennessee. Their daughter Bertha marries Simon Haley, and they have three sons, with Alex Murray Palmer Haley the eldest. These later generations are caught up in the events of world wars, the Depression, and the Civil Rights struggle for equality.

Listed as nonfiction, the book won well over 250 prizes, including the Pulitzer Prize. Its immense impact on all aspects of American culture led critic Ali A. Mazuri to list it, along with *Uncle Tom's Cabin* and the Harlem Renaissance, as literary milestones. In 1977 David Wolper produced the television mini-series *Roots;* broadcast over eight consecutive evenings, the overwhelmingly popular program drew one hundred thirty million viewers. Now regarded as a sociological phenomenon, the "literary-television" event put Haley on the interview and lecture circuits. With his new-found wealth, the modest Haley and his brothers founded the Kinte Corporation, dedicated to the preservation of African-American genealogies. For the corporation he recorded *Alex Haley Speaks*, offering tips on how to research a genealogy.

Needless to say, the book also drew criticism. Calling it "factional" and Haley a simultaneous investigative reporter and fiction writer, historians discussed the accuracy of the southern setting. Several praised his surefooted depiction of the pre-Civil War and post-Reconstruction periods; others pointed out factual errors and Haley's idealization of history. Literary critics placed the book within the tradition of late nineteenth century historical romances and, pointing to the heavy artificial dialect, discussed its similarities with works by Southern writers such as Joel Chandler Harris. Some found the book's sudden shift from omniscient narrator to Haley's personal narrative voice disappointing. In 1977, two charges of plagiarism were lodged against Haley. The first, citing copyright infringement, was dropped; the second, brought by novelist Harold Courlander for *The African* (1968), was settled out of court.

Haley's continued writing about the South and his family. In 1980, he and Norman Lear collaborated on the television series, *Palmerstown, U.S.A.*, which portrayed the friendship of a white youth and a black youth in the rural South during the Depression. In 1988, he published the novella *A Different Kind of Christmas*. Its protagonist, Fletcher Randall, while attending Princeton, experiences a moral conversion to the wrongness of slavery. He returns home to participate in the Underground Railroad, despite his upbringing as the son of slaveholders.

At the time of his death, Haley was working on a Alex Haley's *Queen* (1993) with David Stevens. This epic traces the Haley family from its Irish roots to the birth of Haley's paternal grandmother in Florence, Alabama. Daughter of a slave woman and a confederate colonel, Queen served as slave to her half sisters, but was freed after the Civil War. The Haley family saga also describes Ku Klux Klan activities and the Cherokee "Trail of Tears." Although not as popular as *Roots, Queen* also was developed for television.

A major influence on American culture, Haley inspired a generation to seek out its heritage. *Roots* objectively showed the finality of slavery and the sometimes subtle consequences of assimilation. Most importantly, Haley successfully challenged the existing mythology that African Americans are without a history by ennobling his family's own. As James Baldwin noted:

> *Roots* is a study of continuities, of consequences, of how a people perpetuate themselves, how each generation helps to doom, or helps to liberate, the coming one . . . . It suggests with great power, how each of us, however unconsciously, can't but be the vehicle of the history which has produced us.

—Judith C. Kohl

HALL, James Baker

Born: Lexington, Kentucky, 14 April 1935. **Education:** University of Kentucky, B.A. 1957; Stanford University, M.A. 1960. **Family:** Married Joan Joffe, June, 1960 (divorced); married Mary Ann Taylor (a writer), September 30, 1982; two children. **Career:** Lecturer in writing and photography, Massachusetts Institute of Technology, 1968-72; lecturer in photography, University of Connecticut, 1971-73; assistant professor, 1973-75, associate professor, 1975-83, professor of English, since 1983, director of creative writing, since 1973, University of Kentucky; part owner of Matrix Photographic Services, 1971-73; contributing editor of Aperture (publisher of photography books); advisory editor of *Callaloo*; contributing writer to several journals. **Awards:** Stegner Fellowship in fiction, Stanford University, 1960-61; first prize, New England "Photo-Vision 1973"; National Endowment for the Arts grant, 1980; Frank Stanford Memorial Prize, *Ironwood*, 1983, for "First Winter Snow." **Address:** Department of English, University of Kentucky, Lexington, Kentucky 40506.

PUBLICATIONS

Novels

Yates Paul: His Grand Flights, His Tootings. World Publishing, 1963.
Music for a Broken Piano. Boulder, Fiction Collective Two, 1983.

Poetry Collections

Getting It On Up to the Brag. Monterrey, Kentucky, Larkspur, 1975.
Her Name. Minneapolis, Pentagram, 1981.
Stopping On the Edge To Wave. Middletown, Connecticut, Wesleyan University Press, 1988.

Nonfiction

Orphan in the Attic, photographs by Hall and an essay by Roger Rawlings. Lexington, University of Kentucky Art Museum, 1995.

Editor and contributor, *Ralph Eugene Meatyard*. Millerton, New York, Aperture, Inc., 1974.

Contributor of a biographical essay, *Minor White: Rites & Passages: His Photographs Accompanied by Excerpts from His Diaries and Letters*. Millerton, New York, Aperture, 1978.

*

Critical Studies: "*Music for a Broken Piano*" by Larry McCaffery, *American Book Review*, January-February 1984; "James Baker Hall" interview with L. Elizabeth Beattie, *Conversations with Kentucky Writers*, Lexington, University Press of Kentucky, 1996.

James Baker Hall comments:

My public career as an artist has been complicated . . . by my devotion to several different media.

The preoccupation of my vision seems to be with transience, with time....

*   *   *

James Baker Hall has published fiction, nonfiction, poetry, and photography, and even today continues to expand genres, having worked with film over the past several years. While he began his career on a fiction writing fellowship at Stanford, it is perhaps as

a poet that he has done his best work. As a Wallace Stegner Fellow he wrote one novel, unpublished, then developed a story he had written at Stanford into his first published novel, *Yates Paul: His Grand Flights, His Tootings* (1963). One critic described it as "a comic novel about fear and loneliness, about several kinds of darkrooms and about the courage it takes to come out of them." The novel, not widely reviewed, soon went out of print and is chiefly noteworthy now for signaling the author's later interest in photography.

For the rest of the 1960s, Hall taught writing and photography at colleges in Massachusetts and Connecticut. After writing an article about the Magnum photographers for *Esquire*, he became a contributing editor for *Aperture*, the leading publisher of photography books. He published insightful, comprehensive monographs, *Ralph Eugene Meatyard* (1974) and *Minor White: Rites & Passages* (1978), on two important twentieth century photographers.

Two years after he moved back to his home town, Lexington, to teach at the University of Kentucky, he published a poetry chapbook, *Getting It On Up to the Brag* (1975) and, later, another chapbook, *Her Name* (1981). He then published his second novel, *Music for a Broken Piano* (1983), which, although kept in print for a longer time, has fared little better than the first novel, though it is an accomplished work. Set in the mountains of western Massachusetts in the late 1960s, the novel depicts the tensions that arise when forty people attempt to form a commune in which to live out the idealism of that era. This enterprise is spurred by the arrival of the sole black member of the group, a talented, brooding, brilliant man named Makar, a gadfly who challenges others to examine the sources of their interest in the commune and in each other. Other major characters are Makar's antagonist, Toni McKugh, a determined feminist, and Nathan, a liberal Jewish filmmaker who tries constantly to resolve the inevitable conflicts that occur between other characters' political ideals, practical loyalties, and personal affections.

Author Larry McMurtry called the novel "a trip to the dark side of the liberal imagination. It is a book about the longing for community, about the real world's refusal to be tempted by idealizations, about the destructiveness of certain forms of fantasy. The writing is wonderful, the characters compelling." Another author, Harold Jaffe, commented that, though the novel "is firmly grounded in the flower-child decade, it displays a contemporary awareness of the sources of failure for that decade's ideals." He added that the novel is not a comfortable reading experience: "it forces us to examine our lives and assumptions in ways that are painful, unnerving."

In speaking of his work, Hall has said: "My public career as an artist has been complicated ... by my devotion to several different media.... The preoccupation of my vision seems to be with transience, with time" He goes on to elucidate the connection between his early interest in photography and his maturation as a poet: "The nature poems are trying to achieve ... the meditative concentration on the subject that punches one through time into a kind of timelessness."

This urge to depict moments in which the timelessness and transience of nature, including human nature, is a vividly apparent in

Stopping On the Edge to Wave (1988), which Hall has said contains "most of my mature work." Praised by Richard Wilbur as "an excellent book [of] keen sightings which are also visions," it collects poems that first appeared in the *New Yorker, Poetry, Paris Review, Sewanee Review*, and elsewhere. In one poem, "To Get There," which introduces the theme of transcience, Hall writes of an evening spent looking out a window:

> There is no place to go,
> it takes a long time to get there . . . .
>
> I am watching
> the buildings become buildings
> again. They empty into the streets,
> the streets into cabs, the streets
> are full of empty cabs—always going somewhere.

If, at first glance, these poems suggest a futility, an aimlessness to the motions of daily life, closer reading shows that the poet finds not despair but rather a joy available to the act of seeing clearly. There is tranquil acceptance, as if he has chosen to bear authentic witness to the constancy of life's tendency toward loss. Further, on observing these losses through time—often symbolized in these poems through the passage of a ray of sunlight across objects in a room—the viewer moves into the places created by those passages, facing death. But from the shadows he is able even more accurately to describe what the light touches.

This perspective, offered early in the book, recurs without becoming tedious. Rather, the poet illuminates more facets with each poem. In another poem of childhood, he describes watching the sunlight move:

> I lived the whole time with my hands cupped to the open
>   eye,
> the light advancing . . . .
>
> If the shadow of the catalpa touched
> the sunwall of the house at 3:30
> I waited several minutes
> and entered behind it,
> branching out slowly,
> respectful of such a broad expanse of white, of silence . . .

The poem proceeds to summon fragmented images of the mother, bits from memory, as if the narrator, looking back, knows there is more to be seen but can't find it just yet.

But later poems in the collection pause longer in the light, accomplishing the poet's aim to capture both mortality and timelessness. In "The First Winter Light," Hall personifies light moving across the floor:

> it mounts the stove
> as though it knows it perfectly, from the beginning
> has been witnessing its shape . . . .
>
> I forget
> that I am afraid
> and then remember again
> that someday I will see this all for the last time....

> And any time now
> I will go into the other room.

"No moment is trapable," Hall has told an interviewer. "The essential experience is one of everything being taken away at the same time that it is given." This sentiment is brought to bear, artfully, on technique as well. A poem will start in the third person, narrating actions taken by an unnamed "he," then shift to the first, as if, in the act of imagining a story, the poet will not obstruct the resurgence of any memory that may suddenly insist on use of the "I." It is as if one cannot count on stability, even in the act of writing, of imagining a fictional character's actions.

The themes of much of Hall's writing are echoed in the final, title poem of the collection:

> The scene always takes place
> at the gate, outside the wall . . . .
>
> Our condition always is
> That I have the key
> That you have the key
> That we know what we are doing there
> or here or anywhere. There is no key.
> We stand atop whatever we can find
> to climb up on, arm in arm,
> peering over the wall . . . .
>
> The light falls
> from the buildings into the streets
> and keeps falling.
> What more could we have
> come all this way to know, hoping
> to find our way
> back to the room
> of flowers, the bed,
> the familiar stories? Everything
> on the edge is familiar
> where nothing is
> the last thing we see,
> like this light,
> before things get too swift for us . . .

In Hall's work—his fiction about the inevitable changes that befall even the most well-intentioned of human endeavors, his attention to photography, and his poetry—the author displays, perhaps ironically, a marked tranquillity which is itself instructive, suggesting as it does a complete appreciation of life, born of an acute attention to its impermanence.

—David Y. Todd

HANNAH, Barry

Born: Meridian, Mississippi, 23 April 1942. **Education:** Mississippi College, Clinton, B.A. 1964; University of Arkansas, Fayetteville, M.A. 1966, M.F.A. 1967. **Family:** Divorced; three children. **Career:** Member of the Department of English, Clemson University, South Carolina, 1967-73, University of Alabama, University, 1975-80; writer for the director Robert Altman, Hollywood, 1980; writer-in-residence, Middlebury College, Vermont, 1974-75, University of Iowa, 1981, University of Mississippi, 1982, 1984, since 1985, and University of Montana, Missoula, 1982-83; interim chairman, Iowa Writer's Workshop, 1998. **Awards:** Bellaman Foundation award in fiction, 1970; Atherton fellowship from Bread Loaf Writers Conference, 1971; Arnold Gingrich Award for short fiction from *Esquire* magazine, 1978, for *Airships*; special award, American Academy of Arts and Letters, 1978; Guggenheim Award, 1983; Mississippi Governor's Award in the Arts, 1986; Award in Fiction, Mississippi Institute of Arts and Letters, 1994.

PUBLICATIONS

Novels

Geronimo Rex. New York, Viking Press, 1972.
Nightwatchmen. New York, Viking Press, 1973.
Ray. New York, Knopf, 1980.
The Tennis Handsome. New York, Knopf, 1983.
Power and Light. Winston-Salem, Palaemon Press, 1983.
Hey Jack! New York, Dutton, 1987.
Boomerang. Boston, Houghton Mifflin, 1989.
Never Die. Boston, Houghton Mifflin, 1991.

Short Story Collections

Airships. New York, Knopf, 1978.
Two Stories. Jackson, Mississippi, Nouveau Press, 1982.
Black Butterfly. Winston-Salem, Palaemon Press, 1982.
Captain Maximus. New York, Knopf, 1985.
Bats Out of Hell. Boston, Houghton Mifflin/Seymour Lawrence, 1993.
High Lonesome. Boston, Atlantic Monthly Press, 1996.

Other

In Honor of Oxford at One Hundred and Fifty. Grenada, Mississippi, Salt-works, 1987.

Contributor, *Men Without Ties.* New York, Abbeville Press, 1997.

*

Critical Studies: *Barry Hannah* by Mark J. Charney, New York, Twayne, 1992; *Barry Hannah, Postmodern Romantic* by Ruth D. Weston, Baton Rouge, Louisiana State University Press, 1998.

*   *   *

Barry Hannah works in the venerable tradition of the Southern Grotesque, as even a casual reader will see. His fiction includes such shocking sights as decapitations, vivid car accidents, a corpse, ribs exposed, flesh eaten away, swirling in the eddies of the Mississippi River, and a women's rape by a love-starved walrus, among many others. Truman Capote considered him "the maddest writer in the U.S.A." The influence of Flannery O'Connor is readily apparent, as Hannah freely admits. Yet Hannah is no acolyte of O'Connor's—his work is decidedly rooted in his own time, his grotesques not drawn from the ranks of the backwoods fundamentalists but from the university towns and country clubs

of the contemporary South. His language, as well, is uniquely his own; as one critic observed, "Barry Hannah writes the most consistently interesting sentences of any writer in America today."

Hannah's first novel, *Geronimo Rex*, appeared in 1972 to great acclaim, including a National Book Award nomination. The novel is a paean to southern adolescence and discoveries of music, firearms, girls, and style. The story centers on Harry Monroe, a young Louisianan with literary aspirations. While the civil rights struggle of the 1960's rages around him, Harry abandons himself to the pleasures of liquor and sex, and then, at his lowest point, adopts Geronimo as a sort of spiritual father. As he remarks: "What I especially liked about was that he had cheated, lied, stolen, usurped, killed, burned, raped . . . . I thought I would like to get into that line of work." Instead, Harry becomes friends with Bobby Dove Fleece, a shy young man with domineering parents, and the two of them defeat a local bigot, Whitfield Peter, in the book's climactic shootout. Harry goes on to graduate school to appear in Hannah's next novel, *Nightwatchmen*, in which he and an eccentric detective attempt to catch a mysterious murderer plaguing Southern Mississippi University.

Airships is comprised both of new material and stories that had previously appeared in such magazines as *Esquire*. This collection served to confirm Hannah as a major writer of rare imagination. The subjects are wide-ranging, including a homosexual soldier deeply in love with Jeb Stuart, a time of economic collapse during which trespassers are shot and eaten, and, in the brilliant "Mother Rooney Unscrolls the Hurt," an elderly woman, alone, at the moment when she mistakenly thinks she is dying.

Ray, which is set in Tuscaloosa, Alabama, centers around a doctor who served as a pilot in the Vietnam war and has come to confuse those experiences with his reading of the Civil War, leading to some interesting parallels between the two conflicts. The doctor drinks heavily, then writes prescriptions for himself and for friends whose lives seem as directionless as his. The novel's emphasis on death and violence reflects the author's fascination with those themes; as Hannah explains it, he is most interested in those personalities and events which are at the limits of human experience.

Expanded from a story in *Airships* (leading one reviewer to label it "sequel as sideshow"), *The Tennis Handsome* follows the exploits of French Edward, a beautiful but brain-damaged tennis player, and his handler Baby Levaster, one of whose chief pleasures is to shoot people with a shotgun loaded with popcorn. At various stages in the novel, French is also a poet and a religious devotee. Many critics were put off by the book's hyperbolic violence (which includes the walrus rape scene, mentioned above, as well as deaths by fire and crossbow), but in general the reception was mixed, as others considered *The Tennis Handsome* to be an impressive novel, with novelist Tom McGuane asserting, "*The Tennis Handsome* is a miracle of invention, a fable of sport and lust, all written in a kind of moon-landing English."

1985 saw the publication of *Captain Maximus*, Hannah's second collection of short stories. Most prominent of the stories here are "Idaho," a reflection on the death of poet Richard Hugo, as well as the coming of middle-age, with its recognition of limits, and "Power and Light," a story of working women. One of these,

Polly Buck, works in Seattle's central power plant; of her Hannah writes: "This girl is chaining your breakfast together, citizen. She is hitching the light up for your asinine patio party, your old starlight teevee movies, your electric toothbrush, vibrator, Magic Fingers." Critical reaction to *Captain Maximus* was often quite hostile; Terrence Rafferty declared that "this collection has the feel of those grim, creepy miscellanies that appear after an artist's death, like all the albums assembled from unearthed, marginal Hendrix material, full of vagrant riffs and aimless jams, fragments which serve only as eerie reminders of the stilled voice." Though Rafferty could not have known it at the time, Hannah was battling alcoholism during the time of this book, as well as during the composition of *Boomerang and Never Die.*

Bats Out of Hell, then, marks a turning point for Hannah, because it was his first work made since hanging up his cup. Hannah refuses, however, to criticize drinking; as he said in a recent interview, "I'm not going to come down on booze, because it's done a great deal for me, frankly," he said then. "It's like scolding an old friend now that you don't need him."

Though Hannah admits to having had some reservations about writing without the comfort of alcohol, *Bats Out of Hell* is an unqualified success, reminiscent of the earlier *Airships* yet with an undertone of social criticism new to Hannah's work. *Bats* was quickly followed by *High Lonesome*, which was similarly well-received. In one review, Sven Birkerts says that Hannah's great gift, which shines through in this collection of thirteen stories, is "in writing the music of the unsettled, the disrupted, the damaged self in its encounters with the hard world" and that this gift is especially apparent in the stories "Drummer Down" and "Get Some Young." Both of these are complex stories, the former dealing with the reversal of fortunes in a friendship between a teacher and student, and the latter centered around what Birkerts calls "the tormented sexual ambiguities of husband, wife, and stranger." Currently, Hannah is nearing completion of a new novel, which is tentatively entitled "Yonder Stands Your Orphan With His Gun," which he describes as a tale about "zombies of the new South."

—Jason Mitchell

HARDWICK, Elizabeth

Born: Elizabeth Bruce Hardwick in Lexington, Kentucky, 27 July 1916. **Education:** University of Kentucky, Lexington, A.B. 1938, M.A. 1939; Columbia University, New York, 1939-41. **Family:** Married poet Robert Lowell in 1949 (divorced 1972); one daughter, Harriet Winslow Lowell. **Career:** Full time writer beginning 1940s; journalist and reviewer, beginning mid-1940s; adjunct associate professor, Barnard College, New York; founder and advisory editor, *New York Review of Books.* **Awards:** Guggenheim fellowship, 1948; George Jean Nathan award, for criticism, 1966; American Academy of Arts and Letters, award for literature, 1974, for Belles Lettres and criticism, 1992; Iva Sandrof Award for Lifetime Achievement in Publishing, National Book Critics Circle, 1995. **Member:** American Academy of Arts and Letters, 1977.

PUBLICATIONS

Novels

The Ghostly Lover. New York, Harcourt Brace, 1945.
The Simple Truth. New York, Harcourt Brace, 1955.
Sleepless Nights. New York, Random House, 1979.

Essay Collections

A View of My Own: Essays in Literature and Society. New York, Farrar Straus, 1962.
Seduction and Betrayal: Women and Literature. New York, Random House, 1974.
Bartleby in Manhattan and Other Essays. New York, Random House, 1983.
Sight Readings: Essays on Writers, Biographies About Them, and Public Happenings Here and There. New York, Random House, 1998.

Uncollected Short Stories

"People on the Roller Coaster," in *O. Henry Memorial Award Prize Stories of 1945.* New York, Doubleday, 1945.
"Saint Ursula and Her Eleven Thousand Virgins," in *Yale Review,* March 1945.
"The Mysteries of Eleusis," in *The Best American Short Stories 1946,* edited by Martha Foley. Boston, Houghton Mifflin, 1946.
"What We Have Missed," in *O. Henry Memorial Award Prize Stories of 1946.* New York, Doubleday, 1946.
"The Temptations of Dr. Hoffman," in *Partisan Review,* Fall 1946.
"The Golden Stallion," in *Sewanee Review,* Winter 1946, *The Best American Short Stories 1947,* edited by Martha Foley. Boston, Houghton Mifflin, 1947.
"Evenings at Home," in *The Best American Short Stories 1949,* edited by Martha Foley. Boston, Houghton Mifflin, 1949.
"The Friendly Witness," in *Partisan Review,* April 1950.
"A Florentine Conference," in *Partisan Review,* May-June 1951.
"A Season's Romance," in *New Yorker,* 10 March 1956.
"The Oak and the Axe," in *New Yorker,* 12 May 1956.
"The Classless Society," in *New Yorker,* 19 January 1957, *Stories from The New Yorker 1950-1960.* New York, Simon and Schuster, 1960.
"The Purchase," in *New Yorker,* 30 May 1959, *The Best American Short Stories 1960,* edited by Martha Foley and David Burnett. Boston, Houghton Mifflin, 1960.
"Two Recent Triumphs," in *Gallery of Modern Fiction,* edited by Robie Macauley. New York, Salem Press, 1966.
"The Faithful," in *New Yorker,* 19 February 1979, *The Best American Short Stories 1980,* edited by Stanley Elkin and Shannon Ravenel. Boston, Houghton Mifflin, 1980.
"The Bookseller," in *The Best American Short Stories 1981,* edited by Hortense Calisher and Shannon Ravenel. Boston, Houghton Mifflin, 1981.
"Back Issues," in *New York Review of Books,* 17 December 1981.
"On the Eve," in *New York Review of Books,* 20 December 1983.
"Shot!: A New York Story," in *The New Yorker,* September 1993.

Other

Editor, *Selected Letters* by William James. New York, Farrar Straus, 1961.

Editor, with Robert Atwan, *Best American Essays 1986.* New York, Ticknor and Fields, 1986.

Author of foreword, *Intellectual Memoirs: New York, 1936-1938* by Mary McCarthy. New York, Harcourt Brace, 1992.

*   *   *

The pieces in Elizabeth's Hardwick's 1998 collection, *Sight Readings: Essays on Writers, Biographies About Them, and Public Happenings Here and There*, display her graceful and insightful prose that has made her an important contributor to American letters of the latter half of the twentieth-century. From her emergence on the New York literary scene in the 1940s, to stays in Europe, the American Midwest, and New England with her husband, poet Robert Lowell, during the 1950s, to her helping found the *New York Review of Books* in the early 1960s and contributing regularly to that esteemed journal, Hardwick has been in the center of literary activity for more than fifty years.

An unstinting critical stance (in a 1959 article in *Harper's* she chastised American book reviewers—"sweet, bland commendations fall everywhere upon the scene") combined with wisdom from her studies and personal relationships with many writers inform her tough-minded and expansive essays. Pieces in *Sight Readings*, for example, address the works and milieus of Edith Warton and Henry James ("Old New York"), Gertrude Stein and Djuna Barnes ("Americans Abroad"), Richard Ford and Joan Didion (contemporary Americans). Her earlier collection, *Seduction and Betrayal: Women and Literature* (1974), is among the finest studies of women in literature, and *Bartleby in Manhattan and Other Essays* (1983) contains literary musings as well essays on social issues of the turbulent 1960s and 1970s. "Whatever her subject," wrote Anne Tyler in a *New Republic* review of *Bartleby in Manhattan,* Hardwick "has a gift for coming up with descriptions so thoughtfully selected, so exactly right, that they strike the reader as inevitable." Tyler added: "Mere aptitude of language, of course, is not sufficient. What makes *Bartleby in Manhattan* memorable is the sense of the author's firm character."

Hardwick's reputation as a novelist has been less certain, and her short stories, which appeared intermittently for nearly fifty years in leading journals, magazines, and anthologies, have yet to be collected and published as a group. Hardwick's first novel, *The Ghostly Lover,* published in 1945, was promising, but its early feminist slant was not rightly appreciated. The novel centers on Marian Coleman, who learns that she cannot settle for the comforts and security of a traditional marriage. Shifting between her maturing in a small Southern town and her adult life in New York, the novel offers telling glimpses into her listless and troubled family, of hot, lazy days in an unnamed Southern town and grubby days studying in New York, and the dreams of the ghostly men who pursue her. Marian knows the value of concealment, but through her experiences she tries to find that love is not "the hard, demanding surrender she had imagined." Marian suffers from a peculiar emptiness, one that comes from knowing that what men want from her is not in her, but is "tuned to a certain imaginary pitch in women" that men have invented. The novel closes with Marian's act of independence: she walks unseen away from her lover who has come to the station to meet her, away from a demanding surrender.

The novel roughly incorporates biographical elements. Born and raised in Lexington, Kentucky, Hardwick was one of eleven children. She attained a B.A. in 1938 and an M.A. in 1939 from the University of Kentucky, then moved to New York City and studied from 1939 to 1941 at Columbia University. The urban environment of New York appealed to her and she remained there for most of the rest of her life; she traveled and relocated with her husband, the famed poet Robert Lowell, for brief stays at the University of Iowa, the University of Indiana, and the University of Cincinnati in the early 1950s. The couple then spent six years in Boston, where Hardwick completed her second novel, *The Simple Truth*, before returning to New York. There, in 1963, she helped found the *New York Review of Books*, which soon became a leading literary journal and featured many of her essays. In 1969 she became the first woman to receive the George Jean Nathan Award, presented for her outstanding drama criticism.

The Simple Truth, a tightly plotted probing of the motives behind a frightful act, examines the death of a beautiful college girl, Betty Jane Henderson, in her boyfriend's rooming-house, after hours. The trial of the boyfriend, Rudy, dominates the book and offers numerous perspectives, most importantly of two curious onlookers, the affable Mr. Parks and the middle-aged Anita Mitchell, who is drawn to the case to investigate the working of the unconscious. The truth about the act, late at night, in a rooming-house where two lovers frolicked and struggled, ultimately emerges, but equally interesting are the psyches of the characters who become caught up in the trial.

These two early novels were competent—the writing was careful, the characters ordinary but well-developed. *Sleepless Nights* appeared in 1979 and daringly broke from the strictures of Hardwick's earlier narrative style, more openly confronting autobiographical elements and handling them effectively. Roaming among recollections, the book continually surprises us with its fleeting memories of rooms we have all known, feelings we have felt, losses we have never remedied. In retrospect, Hardwick's earlier novels show a niggling regret on the author's part that the story is not a little more important, that life for women is not a little more adventuresome. *Sleepless Nights* reflects a more mature sensibility—one that has learned that ordinary experience needs no apology.

Sleepless Nights offers a record of life's obscenities through the insomniac narrator, identified as "Elizabeth" in the novel and blending in autobiographical elements. Hardwick's decision to create a persona with her own name heightens our sense of how life informs fiction. The Elizabeth of this book is very nearly Elizabeth Hardwick, a career journalist, writer, reviewer for *Partisan Review* and the *New York Review of Books,* and ex-wife of an often anguished poet (Hardwick and Lowell divorced in 1972 and he quickly remarried). The memories and imaginings of the persona curl about the lives of deprived souls, of which Elizabeth is one. The deprived souls weaved into the story as fictional characters or as references to actual people include Josette, a Boston cleaning-lady, victim of "unfair diseases," with her "breasts hacked off by cancer," and Billie Holiday, self-destructive, haunting, pure style, who died in agony with police at her bedside, denied in her last hours the drugs her body craved (Elizabeth wonders at the "sheer enormity" of Holiday's vices). Alex A., Elizabeth's bachelor friend, is an intellectual and failed academic who reads and writes all day, drinks continuously, smokes cigarettes, and complains when she plays jazz records. He does not marry the woman who might have made his life different. Elizabeth's other half, the partner of the "we" she alludes to, complains in the narrative of Alex's tyranny by weak women. Other characters include Elizabeth's mother, bearer of nine children—childbearing is "what she was always doing, and in the end what she had done"— and a neighborhood prostitute, Juanita, who died of "prodigious pains and sores."

This is a bitter, troubling book of memories to keep us all awake. But if the dose is bitter, it is also Hardwick's most expansive portrait of life—her most intimate character study and strongest cast of characters. The laundress, the cleaning-lady, the Boston spinster, the middle-aged persona whose divorce has brought her back to her old territory, the mother troubled that her son cannot cope, and a couple too long married and endlessly complaining are all authentic. The style is often sparse; the details are selected with startling directness and simplicity, yet the whole is very full.

—Carol Simpson Stern and Mel Koler

HARRIS, Thomas

Born: Jackson, Mississippi, 1940. **Education:** Baylor University, B.A., 1964. **Family:** Wife Harriet (divorced, 1960s); one daughter. **Career:** Reporter, Waco *News-Tribune*, 1963-66; general assignment reporter and night editor, *Associated Press*, New York City, 1968-74; full-time writer since 1968; contributed stories to such magazines as *True* and *Argosy*, 1960s; full-time writer since 1975. **Address:** c/o St. Martin's Press, 175 Fifth Ave., New York, New York 10010.

PUBLICATIONS

Novels

Black Sunday. New York, Putnam, 1975.
Red Dragon. New York, Putnam, 1981.
Silence of the Lambs. New York, St. Martin's, 1988.

*

Film Adaptations: *Black Sunday* was filmed by John Frankenheimer for Paramount, 1977; *Red Dragon* was adapted for film as *Manhunter* by Michael Mann for De Laurentiis Entertainment Group, 1986; *Silence of the Lambs* was filmed by Jonathan Demme for Orion, 1991.

Critical Studies: *It's a Print!: Detective Fiction from Page to Screen*, edited by William Reynolds and Elizabeth A. Trembley, Bowling Green, Ohio, Popular Press, 1994; Thomas Harris Issue, *Notes on Contemporary Literature*, January 1995; "Consuming Cannibals: Psychopathic Killers as Archetypes and Cultural Icons" by Joseph Grixti, *Journal of American Culture*, Spring 1995; "Transmorgrified Gothic: The Novels of Thomas Harris" by Tony Magistrale, *A Dark Night's Dreaming: Contemporary American*

Horror Fiction, edited by Tony Magistrale and Michael A. Morrison, Columbia, University of South Carolina Press, 1996.

* * *

Crime-reporter turned novelist, Thomas Harris is perhaps most widely known for the Oscar-winning Jonathan Demme film based on his novel *Silence of the Lambs* (1988). Harris, however, needs no help from Hollywood to attract an audience; each of his three novels quickly became national bestsellers. All are crime-thrillers: fast-paced, intricately plotted, suspense-charged narratives fueled by the urgency of a countdown to catastrophe. While *Black Sunday* (1975) operates in the arena of international politics and terrorism, the terrain explored by *Red Dragon* (1981) and *Silence of the Lambs* is much more intimate. Here, Harris maps the inner landscapes of both detective and criminal, an investigation that suggests some disconcerting correspondences. It is in this area—the realm of human psychology—that Harris works at his chilling best.

Black Sunday establishes some key components of Harris's subsequent work in its examination of the links between violence and madness. A conventional thriller, the novel pits Black September, a Palestinian guerilla group planning a massacre during the Super Bowl, against David Kabakov, a wildcard major in the Israeli Secret Service dispatched to aid an incredulous American government. What distinguishes *Black Sunday* is Harris's imaginative introduction of the terrorists' doomsday weapon (an explosive-laden television blimp) and his careful characterization of the insane Vietnam veteran who pilots it. Indeed, much of the novel's interest lies in the delicate relationship established between the Black September operative and this haunted, volatile madman on whom the success or failure of their mission depends.

Harris's obvious interest in exploring psychological depths is given full fictional rein in his second novel, *Red Dragon*. Trading terrorism for spine-tingling horror, Harris presents the nightmarish exploits of Francis Dolarhyde, a serial killer convinced that the massacre of whole families will aid his transformation into the godlike Red Dragon of the Apocalypse. Intent on catching him before he can repeat his gruesome monthly ritual is Will Graham, an FBI agent with a special aptitude in the area of imaginative projection. This ability enabled him to capture Doctor Hannibal Lecter, a psychiatrist who killed and ate his patients. And it is the psychopathic Lecter to whom Will applies for help in solving the Dolarhyde case, a visit that also allows him to regain the mindset required to track the killer.

Meticulous in its forensic accuracy and terrifying in its detailed unfolding of the origins of Dolarhyde's obsession, *Red Dragon* is more disturbing in its emphasis on duality and the fine line between sanity and insanity. Harris gives the traditional detective-versus-criminal relationship a subtle edge by establishing an unnerving identification between investigator and psychopathic serial killer. Projecting himself into the mind of a madman, Graham is forced to acknowledge his own heart of darkness. Thus, Lecter's words echo throughout Graham's investigation of Red Dragon, Lecter's symbolic protégé: "The reason you caught me is that we're *just alike.*"

Lecter returns to play a major role in *Silence of the Lambs,* where his insight is sought by Clarice Starling, an FBI agent in pursuit of a serial killer. Like *Red Dragon,* the novel grips the reader with its psychological intensity and its elegant manipulation of suspense, building to a shattering climax. With serial-killer Jame Gumb, Harris creates an even more macabre madman than Francis Dolarhyde. Gumb, too, is obsessed with metamorphosis, flaying his victims in order to make himself "a girl suit out of real girls." Again, Harris presents an intimate portrait of derangement. Lecter brings to the novel an added psychoanalytic dimension. Feeding on pain and suffering, he refuses to cooperate with Starling unless she provides him with her formative primal scene: the haunting screams of lambs being taken to the slaughter. His analysis accurately pinpoints Starling's investment in the case and the empathetic link with Gumb's sacrificial victims that allows her to solve it. As with Will Graham, the self-recognition that Lecter promotes is disconcertingly enabling.

Starling represents something of an anomaly among the heroines of detective fiction because she is intelligent, competent, and highly likable. Nevertheless, it is Hannibal Lecter who has become immortalized in the popular imagination as the hero of Harris's novels. What sets Harris's work apart from most run-of-the-mill crime-thrillers is his exploration of the motivations behind criminal madness. His killers are human monsters whose psychoses can be mapped, but the brilliant Lecter remains frighteningly inexplicable. As a psychiatrist, Lecter is able to accurately plumb the inner depths of those he encounters, but he himself remains ultimately unreadable. What makes Lecter so chilling is his insistence on both detective and reader's confrontation with their own inner demons. Perhaps public fascination with Lecter is the fascination we feel with all serial killers, the attraction of the monster that we could become. Thus, it is fitting that Harris gives Lecter the final word in *The Silence of the Lambs*: "Some of our stars are the same, Clarice."

—Jackie Buxton

HEARON, Shelby

Born: Shelby Reed in Marion, Kentucky, 18 January 1931. **Education**: University of Texas, B.A. (with honors) 1953. **Family**: Married Robert J. Hearon, Jr. (an attorney), 15 June 1953 (divorced, 1977); married Billy Joe Lucas (a philosopher), 19 April 1981; two children (first marriage). **Career**: Freelance writer since 1966; visiting lecturer, University of Texas at Austin, 1978-80; instructor, Bennington College Summer Program fiction workshop, summer, 1980; visiting associate professor, University of Houston, spring, 1981, and University of California at Irvine, 1987; writer in residence, Wichita State University, spring, 1984, Clark University, spring, 1985, and Ohio Wesleyan University, spring, 1989; visiting professor, University of Illinois at Chicago, spring, 1993; visiting distinguished professor, Colgate University, fall, 1993, and University of Miami, Coral Gables, spring, 1994; Member of judging panel for numerous fiction and nonfiction awards. **Awards**: Jesse H. Jones fiction award, Texas Institute of Letters, 1973, for *The Second Dune,* and 1978, for *A Prince of a Fellow*; Guggenheim fellowship, 1982; National Endowment for the Arts fellowship, 1983; PEN Syndication fiction prize, 1983, for "Missing Kin," 1984, for "The Undertow of Friends," 1985, for "Vast

Distances," 1987, for "Growing Boys," and 1988, for "I've Seen It Twice"; Women in Communications award, 1984; Ingram Merrill grant, 1987; American Academy of Arts and Letters literature award, 1990; University of Texas distinguished alumnus, 1993. **Agents**: Literary—Wendy Weil, Weil Agency, 232 Madison Ave., #1300, New York, New York 10016; Lecture Agent—Bill Thompson, BWA, 61 Briarwood Circle, Needham Heights, Massachusetts 02194.

PUBLICATIONS

Novels

Armadillo in the Grass. New York, Knopf, 1968.
The Second Dune. New York, Knopf, 1973.
Hannah's House. New York, Doubleday, 1975.
Now and Another Time. New York, Doubleday, 1976.
A Prince of a Fellow. New York, Doubleday, 1978.
Painted Dresses. New York, Atheneum, 1981.
Afternoon of a Faun. New York, Atheneum, 1983.
Group Therapy. New York, Atheneum, 1984.
A Small Town. New York, Atheneum, 1985.
Five Hundred Scorpions. New York, Atheneum, 1987.
Owning Jolene. New York, Knopf, 1989.
Hug Dancing. New York, Knopf, 1991.
Life Estates. New York, Knopf, 1994.
Footprints. New York, Knopf, 1996.

Other

Barbara Jordan, with Barbara Jordan. New York, Doubleday, 1979.

Contributor, "Order," in *Her Work: Stories by Texas Women.* Bryan, Texas, Shearer, 1982.
Contributor, "Missing Kin," in *Available Stories.* New York, Ballantine, 1985.
Contributor, "The British Museum," in *New Growth.* San Antonio, Corona, 1989.
Contributor, "The Undertow of Friends," in *Common Bonds.* Dallas, Southern Methodist University Press, 1990.

*   *   *

Though Shelby Hearon's novels are firmly rooted in the South, she does not present it as a region populated by mad aristocrats, bestial poor whites, and downtrodden blacks. Though there are eccentrics in her fiction, they are not grotesques; though there is rage, it is more likely to result in a slammed door or a discreet adulterous episode than a shooting; and though her characters sometimes have to face tragedy, they also find numerous occasions to laugh at the situations in which they are placed and at each other. In other words, Hearon writes about the South as it is experienced by most of those who live there.

Hearon's Southern settings are not the only justification for describing her as a Southern writer, if not a Gothic one. She is preoccupied with place. *A Small Town,* for example, begins and ends with a reference to the fault line that caused the great earthquake of 1811, which changed the course of the Mississippi and destroyed a town. There is more to the geography of Venice, Missouri, however, than its placement on the fault line. The author provides a verbal map of the town, noting the names of streets, the location of the schools and the public library, and pointing out who lives in what house. Obviously she believes that the place where one lives both affects and reflects one's identity. In *Hannah's House*, a house is a stage setting, a suitable place for a marriageable daughter to receive her very conventional suitor.

In *Hug Dancing*, which like much of Hearon's work takes place in Texas, a change of dwelling symbolizes a real change of outlook and identity. Thus, Cile Tait's move from her husband's parsonage to a "fixer-upper" symbolizes her flight from a stifling marriage to a revision. Drew Williams, the man she loves, knows about property. By moving to her own home, he fears that Cile is rejecting him; ironically, he is later tempted to break off their relationship for fear a divorce will cost him grandfather's farm.

Although in *Hug Dancing* the New South is rapidly replacing the Old, not everyone approves of putting supercolliders in the place of dairy herds. Many characters in Hearon's novels still have Old South values, such as the belief that the past lives on in the present. Hearon's narrative structure emphasizes this point. A novel may begin in the present, but then it will move back and forth through time like a front-porch storyteller. Thus, *Life Estates* begins with a telephone call from Harriet Calhoun in East Texas to Sarah Rankin, her friend since boarding school, who now lives in the Blue Ridge area of South Carolina. Though the ostensible purpose of this call is to finalize arrangements for Sarah's annual visit to Texas, the conversation ranges over events of four decades. Similarly, on a drive into the mountains, Sarah contemplates the history of the area, thinks back on her marriage, recalls her sixteenth year and her first sexual experience, and finally relives an excursion with her parents when she was four.

In most of her novels, including *Life Estates*, Hearon uses a single narrator, speaking in the first person. Thus, she can keep the leaps through time from being confusing. One exception is *Five Hundred Scorpions*, where Hearon uses the third person in order to follow events in the lives of two protagonists, Paul Sinclair, who has gone to Mexico in pursuit of happiness, and his wife Peggy Sinclair, who is back home in Virginia, discovering that she is an exciting person, after all.

Like Peggy, most of Hearon's women more thoughtful women characters are actively seeking their own identities. Sometimes marriage has deprived them of a sense of self. Harriet Calhoun thinks that unless she is still a wife, she is no one; by contrast, Sarah, who has a business of her own, knows who she is whether or not she has a spouse. Interestingly, both women had stayed in their marriages, even though they had not shared their husbands' beds in years. The next generation is not so committed. Like Clara Blue in *Armadillo in the Grass*, they may only fantasize, but more often, like the indomitable protagonist in *Group Therapy*, they are willing to get divorced and move on.

As any Southerner knows, the only ties that cannot be dissolved or ignored are those of family. Hearon is fascinated with the way parents and children, grandparents and grandchildren, aunts, uncles, and cousins, move through each other's lives, expressing approval and disapproval, love and hate, but never indifference. Like the two brothers in *A Small Town*, they may not speak for decades,

but they are never unaware of each other's existence. Hearon's characters are often desperate to escape from their extended families, or at least from their closest relatives. However, in *Owning Jolene*, the story of a child whose divorced parents routinely snatch her away from each other, Hearon shows how denying family ties brings one to emptiness and despair.

Hearon has explained the genesis of her novels as arising from her curiosity about specific issues. *Five Hundred Scorpions* is about what happens when a man follows his dream, *Life Estates* about how women deal with widowhood, *Footprints* about the feelings of parents who have donated a dead child's organs. However, the pervasive theme of Hearon's works is the age-old question of free will versus determinism. Was it coincidence or fate, Cile asks in *Hug Dancing*, that caused her mother to be drowned in a flash flood, that directed Drew's family to move away immediately afterwards? *Footprints* poses similar questions, not only as to the accident, but also about why the elderly preacher who received the donated heart died in spite of it all. To the Scotch-Irish Calvinists who so influenced Southern culture, it was evident that history, geography, and family heritage, along with divine will, set the pattern for one's life. Shelby Hearon's women protagonists are intelligent enough to recognize that there is much they cannot control, but determined enough to win some impressive victories in their pursuit of freedom.

—Rosemary M. Canfield Reisman

HENLEY, Beth

Born: Elizabeth Becker Henley in Jackson, Mississippi, 8 May 1952. **Education**: Southern Methodist University, B.F.A. 1974; University of Illinois, Urbana, 1975-76. **Career**: Actress, Theatre Three, Dallas, 1972-73, Southern Methodist University Directors Colloquium, 1973, and the Great American People Show, New Salem, 1976; teacher, Dallas Minority Repertory Theatre, 1974-75, University of Illinois, Urbana, 1975-76. **Awards:** Pulitzer prize, 1981; New York Drama Critics Circle award, 1981; Guggenheim award, *Newsday*, 1981; Oppenheimer award, 1981. **Agent:** Gilbert Parker, William Morris Agency, 1350 Avenue of the Americas, New York, New York 10019.

PUBLICATIONS AND FIRST PRODUCTIONS

Plays

Am I Blue? (produced in Dallas, 1973). New York, Dramatists Play Service, 1982.
Crimes of the Heart (produced in Louisville, 1979, New York, 1980, London, 1983). New York, Viking Press, 1982.
The Miss Firecracker Contest (produced in Los Angeles, 1980, London, 1982, New York, 1984). New York, Dramatists Play Service, 1985.
The Wake of Jamey Foster (produced in Hartford, Connecticut, and New York, 1982). New York, Dramatists Play Service, 1983.
The Debutante Ball (produced in Costa Mesa, California, 1985, New York, 1988, London, 1989). Jackson, University of Mississippi Press, 1991.

The Lucky Spot (produced in New York, 1987, London, 1991). New York, Dramatists Play Service, 1987.

Abundance. Produced in Costa Mesa, California, 1989, New York, 1990.

Control Freaks (also director). Produced in Chicago, 1992, Hollywood, 1993.

Signatures. Produced in 1992.

L-Play. Produced in Louisville, 1997.

Screenplays: *The Moon Watcher*, 1983; *True Stories* with David Byrne and Stephen Tobolowsky, 1986; *Crimes of the Heart*, 1987; *Nobody's Fool*, 1987; *Miss Firecracker*, 1990.

Scripts for television pilots: *Morgan's Daughters*, 1979; *Survival Guides*, with Budge Threlkeld, 1985.

Other

Beth Henley: Monologues for Women. 1992.

*   *   *

Since the Pulitzer Prize awarded to *Crimes of the Heart* in 1981 was the first to a woman in 23 years, the play was heralded as a breakthrough and Beth Henley as a feminist flag-bearer. Pulitzers to Marsha Norman in 1983 and to Wendy Wasserstein in 1989 seemed to confirm this optimism, as the prior total for women since 1917 was only five. Yet female dramatists remain a minority in mainstream theatre and Henley's relationship to feminism remains problematical.

The prophecy of her Pulitzer thus unfulfilled, Henley's subsequent plays have not approached the success of her first Broadway effort despite similar themes and characters. Even those critics who concede feminist possibilities to the playwright's favored form of tragicomic realism are troubled by the recurrent pattern of female characters questing for an identity to be only partially and pathetically realized. Since these characters are primarily Southern, it is a pattern that, in veering toward stereotypes, may present as much difficulty for Southerners as for feminists.

Set in a kitchen in Hazelhurst, Mississippi, *Crimes of the Heart* typifies Henley's placement of women in a private and emotional sphere. The Magrath sisters are reunited under the roof of Old Granddaddy, a dominating patriarch who reared them after their father's desertion and mother's consequent suicide. The youngest, Babe, has shot her prominent husband, who has "brutalized" her and struck her teenaged black lover. Twice attempting suicide, Babe finds meaning in a badly played saxophone and a romantically inclined lawyer. The oldest child, Lenny, conquers the shame of a "shrunken ovary" to contact a former beau and thus becomes her "own woman." Meg, who left home only to fail as a singer, on the other hand, repudiates her errant sexuality and resists the temptation of a former, now married, lover. She instead focuses on family, urging her sisters toward a rebirth of identity through a female bonding reflected in the "magical, golden, sparkling glimmer" of Lenny's birthday celebration at play's end.

The seeming triumph of this image accounts for the play's reception as does the appeal of a Southern grotesque reminiscent of Flannery O'Connor in Babe's idiosyncratic behavior, Lenny's fe-

male disfigurement, and Meg's morbid obsessions. Yet the power of the comedy notwithstanding, these women remain unempowered, their identities still relegated to the private sphere. The South where women and blacks are beaten remains unchallenged, its offstage existence rendering the onstage conclusion more retreat than victory. Henley's other major Southern plays portray similarly desperate women on similarly desperate quests. In *The Miss Firecracker Contest*, Carnelle, another product of a dead mother and deserting father, sought affirmation in sex and obtained only a tainted reputation and venereal disease. Carnelle plans to tap-dance her way past her Miss Hot Tamale label to Miss Firecracker of Brookhaven, Mississippi, before escaping in a "blaze of glory." Former title-holder, Cousin Elain, had escaped, but returns to her husband and sons, while the semi-literate seamstress, Popeye, who hears voices in her protruding eyes, finds love in the fetishistic Cousin Delmount. As Elain sneaks off to meet Carnelle's syphilitic ex-lover, the finale of fireworks reflects the garishly dyed red hair of the contest loser, providing her only glorious blaze.

Equally limited and maudlin are the possibilities for Southern women presented in *The Wake of Jamey Foster* and *The Debutante Ball*, plays which were as ill-fated as their characters. Deserted for a "fat yellow-haired woman," Marshael Foster suffered disillusionment even before her husband's freakish death. No more fortunate are her sister, Collard, who has left home for a life of abortions and drinking, nor her sister-in-law, Katty, who mothers a philandering husband since she cannot carry a baby to term. The sole empowerment for these women consists of taking charge of the funeral and leaving Marshael to sleep, comforted by a song played on spoons by a smelly admirer. Only Pixrose, an arson-plagued orphan who recalls Popeye, appears strong by default. Even when wake gives way to ball, the women are doomed, as Teddy's disastrous debut thwarts social rehabilitation for a mother accused of her abusive husband's murder. Pregnant by a deformed stranger because she feared being impolite, Teddy, like Carnelle, parodies the Southern beauty-belle role, her ball gown—and her future—stained by the blood of her miscarried fetus.

Thus, the disarming colloquialisms and bizarre endings of these plays often obscure but fail to mitigate the powerlessness of women. Whether homebodies or escapees, infertile or promiscuous, battered or battering, they are reduced to freaks in a male-centered world. Nor is the grotesque restricted to the South or to the present, as evidenced by *Abundance*, which portrays the lives of two women over 25 years in the Wyoming territory. Bess and Macon, both mail-order brides, bond in the face of the former's psychologically disfigured and the latter's physically disfigured husbands. After five years as the kidnaped but contented bride of an Indian, Bess appropriates the adulterous Macon's independence. A tattooed freak reluctantly returned to her white husband, she commercializes her story and abandons her friend. She reunites with Macon, now disfigured as well by syphilis, as two freaks who can only weakly whistle and laugh.

Whether Henley's reunions and resolutions occur in homes or on frontiers, their off-beat, even dead-on, humor yields laughter in character and audience which celebrates transient, if not illusory, transformations. Although Henley claims that her female characters are "alive with burning poetic vision," it is a vision which seems to enflame and engulf only them. As they succumb to the pitfalls, such as lunacy, loneliness, lust, and love, which Henley dramatizes in *L-Play*, these questers emerge as grotesquely compromised survivors. Victimized by their sex and punished for their sexuality, Henley's women seek solace in each other while still yearning for men and abnegating their power to change the South, the West, or the world.

—Janet V. Haedicke

HIAASEN, Carl

Born: Fort Lauderdale, Florida, 12 March 1953. **Education:** Emory University, Atlanta, Georgia 1970-72; University of Florida, Gainesville, 1972-74, B.A. in journalism 1974. **Family:** Married Constance Lyford in 1970 (divorced 1996); one son. **Career:** Reporter, Cocoa *Today,* Florida, 1974-76; since 1976, journalist, *Miami Herald,* Florida. **Awards:** National Headliners Award, Distinguished Service Medallion from Sigma Delta Chi, Public Service First Place Award from Florida Society of Newspaper Editors, Clarion Award from Women in Communications, Heywood Broun Award from Newspaper Guild, all 1980 for an investigative newspaper series about dangerous doctors; Green Eyeshade Award from Sigma Delta Chi, first place award for in-depth reporting from Florida Society of Newspaper Editors, grand prize for investigative reporting from Investigative Reporters and Editors, all 1981 for a newspaper series on drug smuggling in Key West; Silver Gavel award, American Bar Association, 1982. **Agent:** Esther Newberg, International Creative Management, 40 West 57th Street, New York, New York 10019.

PUBLICATIONS

Novels

Powder Burn, with William D. Montalbano. New York, Atheneum, 1981.
Trap Line, with William D. Montalbano. New York, Atheneum, 1982.
A Death in China, with William D. Montalbano, New York, Atheneum, 1984.
Tourist Season. New York, Putnam, 1986.
Double Whammy. New York, Putnam, 1987.
Skin Tight. New York, Putnam, 1989.
Native Tongue. New York, Knopf, 1991
Strip Tease. New York, Knopf, 1993.
Stormy Weather. New York, Knopf, 1995.
Naked Came the Manatee, with other Florida authors. New York, Putnam, 1996.
Lucky You. New York, Alfred A. Knopf, 1997.

Others

Team Rodent: How Disney Devours the World. New York, Ballantine Publishing, 1998.

*

Interview: "Sun, Sand and Tirades: An Interview with Carl Hiaasen," *Armchair Detective,* Vol. 29, no.1, 1996.

Critical Studies: "Carl Hiaasen's Environmental Thrillers" by Peter Jordan, *Studies in Popular Culture,* Vol. 13, no.1, 1990; "Is Nature Necessary" by Dana Phillips, *The Ecocriticism Reader: Landmarks in Literary Ecology* edited by Cheryll Glotfelty and Harold Fromm. Athens, University of Georgia Press, 1996.

Manuscript Collection: Mugar Memorial Library, Boston University.

Carl Hiaasen comments:
  My novels are my own personal therapy for releasing a lot of the venom that I guess builds up naturally when you're a native Floridian and you watch the place [being] paved over. I can write happy endings, which I can't do in real life very often. I can kill off crooked politicians in the most diabolical ways I can conceive of. It gives me great satisfaction.

*   *   *

Carl Hiaasen writes novels that are a bizarre combination of social satire, broad slapstick comedy, black humor, romance, and environmental criticism. Like Elmore Leonard, he has taken the crime novel into the mainstream, subverting that genre's formulas and dealing throughout his works with matters of more overarching social and cultural importance than, say, who killed Roger Ackroyd. Since 1976 an award-winning reporter for the *Miami Herald* (and twice a Pulitzer Prize finalist) and a columnist for that paper since 1985, Hiaasen expresses outrage in his journalism and fiction at the despoiling of the Everglades, Florida's wetlands, and the state's natural beauty.

Hiaasen's career as a novelist began with the publication of three works jointly authored with the late William D. Montalbano. *Powder Burn,* their first effort, is a talky and unconvincing revenge story concerning Florida's drug trade. *Trap Line* is better plotted and more convincing; it too involves drug dealers and the protagonist's revenge against them. The third, *A Death in China,* disappoints as much by its labored plot as by its labored writing.

None of these journeyman works prepares us for Hiaasen's first solo effort, *Tourist Season,* a wonderfully funny novel full of surprising plot twists and with a sardonic narrative voice that Hiaasen has used in all his succeeding books. The story opens with twin murders—that of a Shriner tourist and that of the president of Miami's Chamber of Commerce—and concludes with the murders of 8 more and the kidnapping of the Orange Bowl Queen at halftime of that peculiar football spectacle. The perpetrators are led by a deranged newspaperman, Skip Wiley, who is motivated by his hatred of unrestrained development and particularly by plans to level Osprey Island to build condominiums. The novel's protagonist, Brian Keyes, a former newspaperman who is now a private investigator, is a wise-cracking, dogged, and law-abiding good man, the flip side of the Wiley coin. Doppelgangers, surreal plots, ironic and cynical protagonists, and ferocious authorial anger in this work become characteristic of Hiaasen's later books.

Double Whammy is perhaps Hiaasen's best and funniest, novel. Its protagonist, R. J. Decker, a former news photographer turned private detective, has been hired to investigate cheating on the bass-fishing circuit. He enlists a mad hermit, Skink, who is the former governor of the state, to help him, and they discover the dark and murderous connections between bass-fishing tournaments, bass-fishing TV shows, the Outdoor Christian Network, and a televangelist/real estate developer who has built his newest project, Lunker Lake and the town around it, on a polluted landfill which will not sustain aquatic life. The novel also includes one of Hiaasen's most inspired creations, a macabre and deranged murderer, Tom Curl, who spends much of the book with a severed and decaying pitbull's head locked onto his arm.

Skin Tight also features a disfigured villain, one who has lost his hand to a barracuda and who has had it replaced with a weedwacker. The story's protagonist, Mick Stranahan, a retired investigator for Florida's State Attorney's office, survives an attempted assassination and begins to consider which of his old cases might have prompted that attempt, eventually settling on an inept plastic surgeon who murders his dissatisfied customers. (As a journalist, Hiaasen's own 1980 investigation into dangerous doctors won him numerous awards.) The novel's plot is convulted and complex, its characters again bizarre and comic.

Hiaasen's protagonist in *Native Tongue* is again a burned out ex-reporter, Joe Winder, who has taken a public relations job shilling for the Amazing Kingdom of Thrills, a Disney-like theme park in the Florida Keys developed by Francis X. Kingsbury, aka Frankie King, a mobster now in the Witness Protection Program. Kingsbury wants to further develop Key Largo by bulldozing it, erecting condos and golf courses, but when two blue-tongued mango voles, perhaps the last two on earth, disappear from his park, his plans begin to come wildly apart, as Winder and Skink conspire to thwart his schemes. Hiaasen's ability to control amazingly convoluted plots is masterful here.

Strip Tease is a much better book than the Demi Moore/Burt Reynolds movie version might suggest: Erin Grant (the protagonist) is a very well-realized and sympathetic character, despite the cliche that she strips to make enough money to support her child. The villainous politicians and sugar industry magnates who own them are here less comic and consequently more frightening than in the previous novels. *Stormy Weather* takes the aftermath of Hurricane Andrew as its starting point and throughout various kinds of villains begin to prey on the victims of the disaster. Skink also appears here to help set things to right, but the novel recycles too many of Hiaasen's character types—maimed villains, for example—and resolves too few of its plot lines (except in a perfunctory epilogue) to be altogether successful. Still, Hiaasen's satiric anger at the riffraff despoiling his native state is impressively in evidence. Hiaasen provides an amusing chapter to *Naked Came the Manatee*, a novel written serially by a group of Florida writers over 13 weeks for the *Miami Herald*, while in *Team Rodent*, one of the volumes in the Ballantine Publishing's "Library of Contemporary Thought," he rails against virtually everything Disney, particularly the way that corporation's role in the overdevelopment of the state.

Lucky You, Hiaasen's most recent novel, takes as its protagonists Tom Krome, a down-on-his-luck reporter, and JoLayne Lucks, a veterinarian's assistant who has purchased one of two winning state lottery tickets and plans to use her $14,000,000 to buy a Edenic plot of land to preserve it from strip-mallers. The other winners, however, are two racist militiamen, Bodean and Chub, who steal her ticket in order to buy weaponry and recruits

for their fight against invading NATO troops and just about everyone. The novel is set in Grange, a town famous for its religious sightings, weeping Madonna, road-stain Jesus, and holy cooters. While the novel lacks the manic energy and anger of his earlier novels, this is one of Hiaasen's strongest books, well-plotted and funny.

In sum, Hiaasen has throughout his career so far used his novels to make important statements about Florida and the way the greed of its inhabitants has led to the trashing of that state. He has done so within one of the most formulaic of novelistic genres—the crime novel, which he has shown need not be formulaic at all. And he has managed, while venting an often ferocious anger, to remain hilariously funny.

—David K. Jeffrey

HOFFMAN, William

Born: Henry William Hoffman in Charleston, West Virginia, 16 May 1925. **Military Service:** U.S. Army during World War II, 1943-46; served with the medical corps at the Normandy invasion and the "Battle of the Bulge." **Education:** Kentucky Military Institute, 1943; Hampden-Sydney College, B.A. 1949; Washington and Lee University Law School, 1949-50; University of Iowa (Writers' Workshop), 1950-51. **Family:** Married Alice Sue Richardson, 17 April 1957; two daughters; three grandchildren. **Career:** Journalist, Washington *Evening Star*; worked with the Chase National Bank; professor and writer-in residence at Hampden-Sydney College, sporadically since 1952; frequently lectures on writing and reads from his works at colleges, universities, libraries, and book festivals; visiting scholar, *Sigma Tau Delta*, James Madison University, 1991 and 1995; invited participant, Virginia Festival of the Book, Charlottesville, and North Carolina Literary Festival, Chapel Hill, 1998. **Awards:** National Endowment for the Arts Creative Writing Fellowship, 1976; Virginia Cultural Laureate, inducted, 1986; *The Fictional World of William Hoffman: A Three-Evening Symposium,* Longwood College, 1988, sponsored by the Virginia Council for The Humanities, Longwood & Hampden-Sydney Colleges; Emily Clark Balch Prize, 1988, for "Sweet Armageddon," Virginia Quarterly Review); Andrew Lytle Prize, *Sewanee Review,* 1989, for "Dancer"; Jeanne Charplot Goodheart Prize, *Shenandoah*, 1989; John Dos Passos Prize for Literature, 1992; O. Henry Prize, 1996, for short story "Stones"; Fellowship of Southern Writers, elected 1998; The Hillsdale Prize, 1998; featured writer, North Carolina/Virginia College English Association, James Madison University, Fall, 1998; D. Litt., Hampden-Sydney College, 1980, Washington and Lee University, 1995.

PUBLICATIONS

Novels

The Trumpet Unblown. Garden City, Doubleday, 1955.
Days in the Yellow Leaf. Garden City, Doubleday, 1958.
A Place for My Head. Garden City, Doubleday, 1960.
The Dark Mountains. Garden City, Doubleday, 1963.
Yancey's War. Garden City, Doubleday, 1966.

A Walk to the River. Garden City: Doubleday, 1970.
A Death of Dreams. Garden City: Doubleday, 1973.
The Land That Drank the Rain. Baton Rouge, Louisiana State University Press, 1982.
Godfires. New York, Viking, 1985.
Furors Die. Baton Rouge, Louisiana State University Press, 1990.
Tidewater Blood. Chapel Hill, Algonquin, 1998.

Play

The Love Touch. Produced at the Barter Theatre, Abingdon, Virginia, 1967.

Short Story Collections

Virginia Reels. Urbana, University of Illinois Press, 1978.
By Land, By Sea. Baton Rouge, Louisiana State University Press, 1988.
Follow Me Home. Baton Rouge, Louisiana State University Press, 1994.

*

Critical Studies: "The Intolerable Wrestle" by Robert Buffington, in *Modern Age*, Winter 1972; "(Henry) William Hoffman" by Jeanne R. Nostrandt, in *Southern Writers: A Biographical Dictionary* edited by Robert Bain, Joseph M. Flora, and L. D. Rubin, Jr., Baton Rouge, Louisiana State University Press, 1979; "The Fugitive Hero In New Southern Fiction" by Gary Davenport, in *Sewanee Review*, Summer 1983; "About Any Kind of Meanness You Can Name" by Walter Sullivan, in *Sewanee Review*, Fall 1985; "Wonderful Geographies" by Greg Johnson, in *The Georgia Review*, Summer 1989; "The Fiction of William Hoffman: An Introduction" by William Frank, in *Hollins Critic*, February 1991; "Fiction and the Furniture of Consciousness" by William Frank, in *Sewanee Review,* Spring 1992; "(Henry) William Hoffman" by William Frank, in *Contemporary Fiction Writers of the South* edited by Joseph M. Flora and Robert Bain, Westport, Greenwood Press, 1993.

*   *   *

William Hoffman takes for the geography of his fiction the coal-mining mountains of West Virginia, the piedmont clay of Virginia, and the shell-encrusted beaches of the Chesapeake Bay. Reared in the West Virginia home of his great-grandfather, who owned a coal mine, Hoffman lives in a tobacco-growing area of Virginia, sharing his time on the Chesapeake Bay. His fictional themes search out the complexities of the basic human condition as revealed in life of the twentieth century: war and peace, mysteries and murders, loves and jealousies, institutions (sacred and secular), labor disputes and the American dream. His study of scene and character examines the Southern community—family, religion and language—and its inherent values. This sense of place translates into the larger scene, his geography into the world.

Hoffman's war experiences (in World War II he served with medical corps at the Normandy invasion and the "Battle of the Bulge") gave him a changed viewpoint on life; his characters, especially in the three war novels, reflect this change. *Days in the Yellow Leaf,* his first written but second published novel, is a an

apprentice work. The sensitive Tod Young sees his life, family, and friends differently after being in war, and finds that violence and death, hate and deceit, are as inevitable in life as in war. *The Trumpet Unblown* more directly reflects Hoffman's own war experiences. Tyree Shelby, the central figure, encounters primitive and evil actions among his fellow soldiers as well as with the enemy. The protagonists of both novels conclude that war, itself, is an outgrowth of human nature; fighting a declared war is merely doing battle with mankind's darker side.

The third work, *Yancey's War*, is a more distant perspective of Hoffman's point of view. Published two decades after World War II, the novel looks at the dehumanizing aspects of war realistically, but also with humor. Yancey is an inept officer (and an inept human) who does not survive the war *because* of that ineptitude, rather than from an encounter with the enemy. He is his own worst enemy: therein lies the irony and the humor. Charles Elgar, on whose life Yancey necessarily intrudes, finds his well-bred Southern values useless as he faces both war and the crude, mean-spirited Yancey. The relationship between these two in a private war contains humor and conflict, while the plot reveals the horror and dehumanization of the larger war. In fact, Hoffman's stories demonstrated the psychological ramifications of experiencing war years before the Vietnam "non-war" recognized and named "post-traumatic stress syndrome."

Everyday battles of life most interest Hoffman. *The Dark Mountains* concerns the coal mining operations of West Virginia, the men who build the industry and those who mine the product. James MacGlauglin, loosely based on Hoffman's great-grandfather James Kay, is a Scot immigrant as a young boy in America. Following the American Dream by using his innate wit, intelligence, fortitude and industriousness, he attains the Dream. His honorable character contributes to his success while, at the same time, blinding him to weaknesses in others. When base motives of those less industrious and more greedy impose on his success, and times change from striving to better one's self to surviving a world war, MacGlauglin cannot accommodate the shifting value system. He, like Hoffman's war protagonists, finds the old values useless in a self-centered, war-corrupted world, and his confused existence mimics that of the war-stressed soldier.

Confusion also characterizes Guy Dion in *A Death of Dreams* when he speaks from the mental hospital where he is confined. His fragile hold on reality brings him pain as he observes the scene outside his window; the mountain there seems to appear and disappear according to his shifting perception. In demonstrating the losses men suffer as they decline, Dion bemoans his greatest pain as "the death of dreams." Claytor Lewis Carson of *The Land That Drank the Rain* physically moves from a California dreamland to the Cumberland Mountains of eastern Kentucky. Ironically, his life in the dreamland was one of sham and dishonesty, and he seeks a renewal for his drought-ridden spirit in a hermit's mountain life. Only by his concern, however, for a lost and unloved youth does he find a spirit-replenishing "rain": the lessons of self-sacrifice and courage in human interaction teach him the redeeming quality of love.

A lack of caring for one's fellow man is at the crux of *A Place for My Head, A Walk to the River* and *Godfires.* Three protagonists from old Virginia families seem to be "dead men" in their lives. Two are lawyers with no real successes in their careers, and one is a businessman who chairs the officers' board of his church. Impelled into action at the behest of someone appealing to their sense of duty and *noblesse oblige*, each finds his redemption as a byproduct of that action. They emerge from lethargy and mediocrity as their lives move from self-absorption to becoming useful instruments for others. Billy Payne (*Godfires*), for instance, clarifies his vision as he is forced into soul-searching as a captive in an imprisonment similar to that experienced by captured Americans in Vietnam. In *A Place for My Head*, Angus McCloud's standards leave him vulnerable to the machinations of a new social structure, with no place to lay his head. Jackson LeJohn of *A Walk to the River* believes participation in war "killed" him, his marriage "revived" him, and his wife's death killed him again. "To grieve," he says, "a man had to be alive and to care about something." This theme—to be alive is to experience suffering—recurs throughout Hoffman's fiction.

Furors Die returns to a coal-mining West Virginia locale, tracing the lives of two boys from different backgrounds and lifestyles, the privileged Wylie Duval and the redneck Amos Cody. Cody, the quintessential entrepreneur, and Duval, the well-bred businessman, experience a reversal of fortunes, each uncovering the truth and values of his life. Ultimately, each acts on those beliefs and standards as he comes to better understand himself in a tragic, but hopeful finale. The suspense novel *Tidewater Blood* is a story involving an aristocratic Chesapeake Virginia family whose ancestral past contains a dark secret rooted in West Virginia. Hoffman's landscape covers his fictional geography in this one story. The reprobate son, Charles LeBlanc, sets out to prove himself innocent of a crime and to find the guilty person, a quest taking him from Tidewater, Virginia, to the West Virginia coal mines. As in the traditional quest journey, Charles uncovers finds different from what he expected. His search reveals the conflicting cultural values Hoffman explores in other novels; his unraveling of the mystery examines the motives and assumptions of human conduct. With the LeBlanc family saga, Hoffman fine-tunes his craft of mystery writing without abandoning his usual morality quest.

Using the interior monologue and narrative viewpoint, Hoffman delves into the psychological process of self-discovery in his characters. Through their conflicts he reveals the mysteries in life and the often unanswerable questions. The search, itself, becomes its own reward: Billy Payne, the lawyer/detective seeking the murderer of the town's leading citizen, and Charles LeBlanc, the detective searching for a criminal in order to save himself. Most of Hoffman's central characters are detectives, men searching the mysteries and finding themselves. Human survival and its sacrifices, maintaining values in a world of situation ethics, lifting oneself "by the bootstraps" to live the American dream, and learning redemption through love as necessary to life are Hoffman's major themes. The short story collections (*Virginia Reels; By Land, By Sea*; and *Follow Me Home*) reiterate these themes and fictional devices, but in a more intense and focused manner. Religion and its values, life and its searches, morality and its articulation are central to the fiction. His characters, encompassing the spectrum of mankind, find their humanness as the common denominator. The easy flow of Hoffman's storytelling belies the sharpness of his perspective, the craftsmanship of his art, and the keenness of his ear for language. Each story is a finely-wrought artifact where life is both tragic and courageous, but never without hope.

—Jeanne R. Nostrandt

HOOD, Mary

Born: Brunswick, Georgia, 16 September 1946. **Education:** Georgia State University, A.B. 1967. **Career:** Writer, since 1967; has held various jobs, 1967-80s. **Awards:** Flannery O'Connor award for short fiction, 1984, *Southern Review*/Louisiana State University Short Fiction award, 1984, both for *How Far She Went*; National Magazine award for fiction, 1986, for "Something Good for Ginnie"; Lillian Smith award, Dixie Council of Authors and Journalists Author-of-the-Year award, Townsend prize for fiction, Georgia State University, all in 1988 for *And Venus is Blue*. **Agent:** Eric Ashworth, Candida Donadio & Associates, 231 West 22nd St., New York, New York 10011.

<small>PUBLICATIONS</small>

How Far She Went. Athens, University of Georgia Press, 1984.
And Venus Is Blue. New York, Ticknor & Fields, 1986.
Familiar Heat. New York, Knopf, 1995.

*

Critical Studies: *Southern Writers at Century's End*, Jeffrey J. Folks and James A. Perkins, editors, Lexington, University Press of Kentucky, 1997.

Mary Hood comments:
   The world speaks. I listen and write what I hear.

*   *   *

Though she was born in the coastal Georgia town of Brunswick, Mary Hood has spent most of her life in Cherokee County, north of Atlanta. During the time since Hood graduated from Georgia State University in 1967 and began writing full-time, the area has gone from rural to suburban. The environment in which she has composed her work, including two books of short stories and a novel, is one rapidly losing its history and character.

Certainly this factor has had an impact on her writing, reflected in the dedication of her first book, *How Far She Went*: "For little Victoria, big enough." Victoria, to those in the know, is not a girl; it's a town that according to David Aiken in *Southern Writers at Century's End*, "once had a ferry, a mill, a small village, family cemeteries, and an agrarian way of life." But Victoria lies now at the bottom of Allatoona, a large man-made lake near where Hood lives. Aiken noted that Hood wrote the stories in *How Far She Went* while a subdivision grew practically outside her window: "As trees were being cut and bulldozers were moving closer, Hood recorded the turmoil and dislocation in a few stories that well-wishers thought would never find an audience."

But they did, and a look at the names of the publishers of Hood's three books—each of which is larger than the one before—suggests her growing stature as a writer. After nearly two decades of rejections, Hood published *How Far She Went* in 1984, and its nine haunting stories soon gained her an audience far beyond Georgia. *And Venus Is Blue*, another collection two years later, received considerably more attention. Particularly notable was the title story, vignettes that explore the thoughts of Delia Racing as she drives from Maryland to Pinedale, Georgia, to attend the funeral of her father, James, a suicide. Broken into nine sections, it portrays parts of Delia's life while depicting the single day on which she experiences these memories.

For nine years following the publication of *And Venus Is Blue*, Hood's output was limited to assorted short stories and other items in periodicals. Her next major work, *Familiar Heat* (1995), was a novel. Set in Sanavere, Florida, a fishing village, *Familiar Heat* centers on Faye Parry and her husband, Vic, who operates a fishing boat. Faye suffers amnesia after being assaulted by bank robbers, and she struggles to reclaim her memories and her life. Though the format is different, *Familiar Heat* shares elements with the two collections that preceded it. Principal among them is the theme of memory and recollection, central in so many of Mary Hood's stories, as well as the quest for truth behind the veil of falsehood. Though *Familiar Heat* is a single tale, it brings together stories of more than a dozen characters. The story begins with a wedding in one Catholic chapel and ends with the dedication of another such chapel.

Hood, who lists herself as a "humming" Quaker, had among her early literary influences a book about a missionary family, the Whitmans, traveling to Oregon in the 1830s who were killed by Indians. Haunted by the story, she told Aiken, "I asked all sorts of questions about truth, about books . . . about what has to be told, about justice, about God's care." The fact that she was dyslexic did not prevent her from absorbing an astonishing array of writers: "After college," she said, "I read. My education began. Balzac, Turgenev, Chekhov, Dickens (whom I'd read all along, as my best friend, comforter, and delight), I. B. Singer, Katherine Anne Porter, Katherine Mansfield, Willa Cather, Virginia Woolf, Flannery O'Connor, Eudora Welty, Ernest Hemingway. Stories, always the short thing, if possible." In the years when she was trying to get published, Hood worked in a variety of jobs—substitute school teacher, library assistant, and department store clerk among them. An accomplished visual artist, she made money with an enterprise that itself seems like something out of a Southern Gothic story—painting portraits of deceased pets, sometimes with a saintful radiance around their faces. In addition, she worked as a polling officer in the community around the former Victoria, which still bore that name, and her work is an affirmation that "little Victoria" was, indeed, "big enough."

—Judson Knight

HUDGINS, Andrew

Born: Andrew Leon Hudgins, Jr., in Killeen, Texas, 22 April 1951. **Education:** Huntingdon College, B.A. 1974; University of Alabama, M.A. 1976; Syracuse University, 1976-78; University of Iowa, M.F.A. 1983. **Career:** Elementary school teacher, Montgomery, Alabama, 1973-74; adjunct instructor in composition,

Auburn University, 1978-81; lecturer in composition, Baylor University, 1984-85; associate professor of English, University of Cincinnati, since 1985; Wallace Stegner fellow in poetry at Stanford University, 1983-84; fellow at Yaddo Writers' Colony, summers, 1983, 1985, 1987, and 1988; John Atherton fellow in poetry at Bread Loaf Writers' Conference, 1985; fellow at MacDowell Colony, summer, 1986; Alfred Hodder fellow at Princeton University, 1989-90. **Awards:** Academy of American Poets award, 1984; Society of Midland Authors and Texas Institute of Letters awards, 1986; New Writers Award in poetry from Great Lakes Colleges Association and Alabama Library Association award, both 1987, for *Saints and Strangers*; fellowships from National Endowment for the Arts, 1986, and Fine Arts Work Center, Provincetown, Massachusetts, 1986-87; grant from Ingram Merrill Foundation, 1987; Witter Bynner Foundation Prize for poetry from American Academy and Institute of Arts and Letters and Poets' Prize, both 1988 for *After the Lost War*. **Address:** Department of English, ML 69, University of Cincinnati, Cincinnati, Ohio 45221.

PUBLICATIONS

Poetry

Saints and Strangers. New York, Houghton, 1985.
After the Lost War: A Narrative. New York, Houghton, 1988.
The Never-Ending: New Poems. New York, Houghton, 1992.
The Glass Hammer: A Southern Childhood. New York, 1995.
Babylon in a Jar. New York, Houghton Mifflin, 1998.

Nonfiction

The Glass Anvil (Poets on Poetry). Ann Arbor, University of Michigan Press, 1997.

*   *   *

Anyone who has entertained Andrew Hudgins knows a thrill and unease as he gestures, taps time with foot and leg, or punctuates conversation with bourbon glass swinging. Deep within Hudgins wells a very human energy which fuels and ignites poems. Like many who grew up in the South of the 1960s, Hudgins never doubts language's life and death nature. In "The Social Order" (*Glass Hammer*, 1994) he portrays his Aunt Ruth, who after giving her yard man a mason jar of water

set the jar gently in the sink,
and after he'd gone back to work,
she shattered it with a claw hammer.
Maybe you know what to say.
I don't. I love some of these people.
Let Jesus love them all. Let Jesus
love every fucking one of them.

As his poems demonstrate, word and action marry for good and ill, to help and to hurt. The covenant between word and action cuts to the heart of who we are as human beings.

If he represents a direction in southern letters, Hudgins represents a generation that voices its uncertainty concerning what to say. Good words go bad and bad words sometimes thread their way toward the good. He is nowhere eager, however, for theoretical speculation; he traces the affective and effective faces of language, unwilling to bind language by system or description. Hence a poem like "Threats and Lamentations" (*Glass Hammer*) refuses editorial closure, content rather with the fracas of voices which mark our human family.

> Mom, Andrew spit in my Kool-Aid.
> You'll be the death of me. If you
> don't pull that pouty lip back in,
> I'll knock it back in place for you,
> young man. Just once I'd like to pee
> without somebody yelling "Mom!"
> Mom, Andrew's breathing on my pillow.
> Each night I pray for you. You hush now.

Where we first experience language and where we first learn its manifold features—in home and household—there that same language wraps itself about us to nurture, to murder, to name.

Hudgins cannot be placed, then, in that line of southern poet which carries forward a dialogue with predecessors or peers— Ammons, Dickey, Justice, or Prunty, for example; rather, he adopts strategies which allow exploration of language at its generative roots. His first collection, *Saints and Strangers* (1985), announced his abiding drive to explore the interstice of language with action, not language with language. Of poets exploring language for the sake of language, Peggy Rosenthal in a recent essay notes: "The isolated image, pulled from the wreckage of civilization's lost coherence, became modernism's characteristic literary unit." Rejecting this motif, Hudgins explores the enacted word.

Fixation on the image alone betrays a profound suspicion of both past and future—a potential denial of action itself. Hudgins contemplating "The Cestello Annunciation" (*The Never-Ending*, 1992) confronts that moment when each of us, like the Virgin herself, must accept or deny the future's gestation and birth.

> . . . her whole body pulls away.
> Only her head, already haloed, bows,
> acquiescing. And though she will, she's not yet said,
> Behold, I am the handmaid of the Lord,
> as Botticelli, in his great pity,
> lets her refuse, accept, refuse, and think again.

Language which trusts action, his poems seem to assert, transforms the cage of self with its dung-crusted bottom sheet and its upward-restraining metal bars into a womb of spectacular generation.

Because language and action transform one another, each has the power to desecrate or purify the other. Hence, like so many southern poets before him, Hudgins portrays language grounded in genuine action generating a genuine, though uncertain, future. Fixation on the image alone is fixation on mind alone, which ultimately denies action toward a future.

The pieces in *Poems After the Lost War: A Narrative* (1988) posit themselves as the voice of nineteenth-century poet Sidney Lanier. This narrative and poetic strategy liberated Hudgins at a crucial moment in his career. These poems license a space prior to and apart from contemporary linguistic and poetic gear and tackle as they slip into the character of one who bowed but did not break. Losing the war did not annul Lanier's ability to live and love. He does not fix an image of loss; he fixes on all those human actions which generate language and joy. Hence, even as death intrudes, this voice taps the wells of language at their source.

> . . . this afternoon
> she tilted my head back into her lap
> and spread my hair across the blue
> cloth of her dress. Slowly, with Job's
> long patience, she combed through my head,
> picking through each dark, separate strand,
> finding the lice and crushing them,
> one by one, beneath her fingernail.
> Such life that clings to me! Such death
> it takes to keep my body clean!
> This is the greatest gift: to know
> that someone loves you as you are
> and loves you anyway. . . .

This narrative turn privileges fundamental human acts, suspicious of all the higher-order thinking that provoked war in the first place. This voice that finds love even at grave's edge does so unashamedly, without Freud, Heidegger, Derrida, or the other trappings of our century.

"Dragonfly," a poem from *Babylon in a Jar*, displays Hudgins at his urgent best, demanding some accounting at the edges of language, action, and time.

> . . . Book says what I've always called
>   a dragonfly is really,
>   with its
>   long,
>   slender body, a
>   damselfly
>   that strafes the pond clabber, soars,
>   swoops,
>   hovers, sideslips, loops
>   and twists,
>   sunlight revealing a new glint
>   of iridescent
>   shimmer — purple, red,
>   green, turquoise, gold, gunmetal blue —
>   with every pass.
>   It's hunting: a whip
>   tip
>   cracking gnats
>   out of the air
>   so quick that I can't see it happen
>   and wouldn't know except I trust
>   Book, Book,
>   the goddamn book because
>   I cannot see the hunting. See
>   what looks like
>   exhilaration
>   (loop
>   and soar),
>   but isn't. Book insists on purpose.
>   Not even blood sport. Work.
>   But its purpose

                    is not
                              my purpose: pleasure
                                            (dive, jink, roll,
          then
                    stillness at great speed)
                              beside still water.

"Book," this poem contends, sees only utilitarian ends; hence, it cannot look beyond the present moment. Watching the flesh and blood Hudgins rock your porch chairs into an infinity of shrubbery, spilling fine bourbon among the ferns, you discover this man who derives blessedness and joy from words and deeds done together. As Howard Nemerov is the last, great celebrant of word and thing in twentieth-century American poetry, so Andrew Hudgins may be the last, best celebrant of word and act here at century's close.

—Don Keck DuPree

HUMMER, T. R.

Born: Terrence Randolph Hummer in Noxobee County, Mississippi, 7 August 1950. **Education:** University of Southern Mississippi, B.A., M.A. 1974; University of Utah, Ph.D. 1980. **Family:** One son. **Career:** Assistant professor of English, Oklahoma State University, Stillwater, 1980-84; assistant professor of English, Kenyon College, Gambier, Ohio, and Middlebury College, Vermont; visiting professor, Exeter College, England; writer-in-residence, University of California, Irvine; former senior editor of *Kenyon Review* and *New England Review*; professor and director of creative writing, University of Oregon, Eugene. **Awards:** National Endowment for the Arts fellowship, 1987, 1992-93; Guggenheim fellowship, 1992-93. **Address:** Department of English, College of Arts and Sciences, University of Oregon, Eugene, Oregon 97403-1286.

PUBLICATIONS

Poetry

Translation of Light. Stillwater, Oklahoma, Cedar Creek Press, 1976.
The Angelic Orders. Baton Rouge and London, Louisiana State University, 1982.
The Passion of the Right-Angled Man. Urbana, University of Illinois Press, 1984.
Lower-Class Heresy. Urbana, University of Illinois Press, 1987.
The 18,000-Ton Olympic Dream. New York, Quill/Morrow, 1990.
Walt Whitman in Hell. Baton Rouge, Louisiana State University Press, 1996.

Editor

The Imagination as Glory: Essays on the Poetry of James Dickey, with Bruce Weigl. Urbana, University of Illinois Press, 1984.
The Unfeigned Word: Fifteen Years of New England Review, with Devon Jersild. Hanover, New Hampshire, University Press of New England for Middlebury College Press, 1993.

*

Interview: "Poetry: Connecting with the World: An Interview with T.R. Hummer" by Phil Paradis, *Cimarron Review,* April 1985.

* * *

Southern writing in Faulkner's day could draw on the mythology of farming life, its rituals of male passage into manhood through hunting, the deflowering of girls white or black under the full moon, the death of grandparents, and the burial of family relations. All these were fresh in the age of nearly universal agriculture. By the time James Dickey came to write about these myths, they were at once remove from a Southerner's daily life. They were remembered, but at a distance, as places and events outside Atlanta and other cities, as a part of the disappearing past.

With T.R. Hummer and his generation Southern rural life and its folklore are now almost gone. Hummer makes good use of his own experience growing up on a Mississippi farm, but the act of reliving it is self-conscious, rhetorical. He is at his best when narrating an exciting moment in a boy's life, as in "Calf," from his book, *The Angelic Orders,* where his father pulls the shattered parts of a half-born calf from the mother cow. The details are frightening and vivid, and the boy's soul is shaped by the terrifying ordeal of death, birth, and a father's authority:

> The calf's back legs tear off
> Like rubber boots pulled out of mud.
> My brother turns away,
> But I can't take
> My eyes from the place
> Where the calf was, and now
> Is not, or cannot be seen.
> My father shakes his head.
> *We only got half.*
> Rolls up his sleeves.
> *It's going to be mean.*
> *Hold her head.*

Contemporary Southern poetry is influenced by the work of Dickey and Dave Smith. Hummer coedited a book of essays about the former, called *The Imagination as Glory,* and studied under Smith at the University of Utah. He carries the mark of both writers, who fashioned a lush, sonorous rhetorical style in which the labors of growing up male in the South are sung variously in laments, love songs, and dirges over lost innocence. The style was originally minted by Faulkner's prose, with its trademark inner voices set in italics, a technique imported into Hummer's dialogical meditations with the self. Throw in the musical narratives of James Wright and you have nearly the whole pantheon of giants marking the Southern style.

Hummer is more quintessentially Southern in his sense of poetry as the exploration of pain, suffering, and regret. The argument of his poetry is that we are shaped by our losses; what we lose becomes our emotional heritage:

> *the real*
> Boundary between hypothesis and truth
> *Is pain.*

In Hummer's psychology, memory is the imagination and pain is what we remember best. The poetry seems once removed from an older Christian reading of life as a pilgrim's journey toward redemption; Hummer's pilgrims suffer without religious consolation, but a form of religious faith appears in the beauty of the language, the lyric inspiration that rises from their sorrows. In "Inner Ear," from *Lower-Class Heresy,* the balance mechanism of the inner ear is ambiguously described as "*A small sealed chamber with a fine dust inside,*" a tomb, in other words, with the past inside it giving us our orientation in the world:

> The dust is always settling, always falling.
> *Your body knows. That's how it tells up from down.*

In the closing poem of *Lower-Class Heresy* we get this telling observation:

> The fact is, the world is the same as yesterday,
>
> Only colder, that's all, and what I want to see
> As a visionary difference is only a difference in vision,
> In light that makes me focus on the boundaries between
>   things,
> Their dark and believable presences in the air of almost-
>   night.

Hummer is more articulate and penetrating in *Lower-Class Heresy* about his methods than he is in earlier books. Solitude, he tells us in the poem "Cold," "is the laboratory of the heart." Consciousness is a result of growing up into adulthood; one wakes up into manhood to find oneself stranded in a difficult place, shorn of the usual supports of parents, grandparents, a usable past. In "The Moon and Constellations," the only place from which his language arises, Hummer says, is from the adamant principle of the body, which "appropriates everything." The hand he holds up to "whatever shatter of moon there is" confirms only "the one great law of the physical, / The body."

Hummer's capacities for lyric music and self-analysis are large. If his voice seems a little indistinct from his contemporaries, it is not for reasons of talent or skill but rather the region that raised him. The South demands that its body of myths be articulated according to certain laws of psychology and language. Although writers tend to lose something of their precise selves in the process, what they give us to read is a unique descent into the American psyche where the sexes are drawn in vivid opposing colors and the ceremonies of coming-of-age are written in high operatic registers.

—Paul Christensen

HUMPHREY, William

Born: Clarksville, Texas, 18 June 1924. **Education:** Attended Southern Methodist University and University of Texas. **Family:** Wife, Dorothy; stepdaughter Antonia Weidenbacher. **Career:** Teacher at Bard College, Annandale-on-Hudson, New York, 7 years, and briefly at Smith College, Northampton, Massachusetts, Yale University, New Haven, Connecticut, and Washington and Lee University in Lexington, Virginia. **Awards:** Best Book of Fiction for the Year, Texas Institute of Letters, 1958, for *Home from the*

Hill, 1965, for *The Ordways*; grant in Literature, National Institute of Arts and Letters, 1963; Lon Tinkle Award for lifetime achievement, Texas Institute of Letters, 1996. **Died:** Hudson, New York, 20 August, 1997

PUBLICATIONS

Novels

Home from the Hill. New York, Knopf, 1958.
The Ordways. New York, Knopf, 1965.
Proud Flesh. New York, Knopf, 1973.
Hostages to Fortune. New York, Delacorte Press, 1984.
No Resting Place. New York, Delacorte Press, 1989.
September Song. Boston, Houghton Mifflin/Seymour Lawrence, 1992.

Short Story Collections

The Last Husband and Other Stories. New York, Morrow, 1953.
A Time and a Place: Stories. New York, Knopf, 1968.
The Collected Stories of William Humphrey. New York, Delacorte Press, 1985.

Other

The Spawning Run: A Fable. New York, Knopf, 1970.
Ah, Wilderness! The Frontier in American Literature. El Paso, Texas Western Press, 1977.
Farther Off from Heaven. New York, Knopf, 1977.
My Moby Dick. New York, Doubleday, 1978 1979.
Open Season: Sporting Adventures. New York, Delacorte Press, 1986.

*

Media Adaptations: "The Last of the Caddoes: was adapted for film by Ken Harrison and released by Phoenix/BFA Films and Video in 1982.

Critical Studies: *William Humphrey* by James W. Lee, Austin, Steck Vaughn, 1967; *William Humphrey* by Mark Royden Winchell, Boise, Boise State University, 1992.

*   *   *

Born in East Texas, where (as he puts it in one of his novels) "the South draws up to a stop" and the West begins, Humphrey devoted much of his fiction and non-fiction to the exploration of this native terrain. Coming as a member of the "second generation" of the Southern Renaissance, he faced the problem of following distinguished literary ancestors and of

trying in spite of their influence to forge his own literary response to the region. Some readers of Humphrey have found him too derivative of the older generation of southern writers. But there are important differences between Humphrey and his elders, which link him more strongly with contemporaries like O'Connor and Percy.

Humphrey's first work was in short fiction, and the early stories now seem a record of his search for a subject. Those collected in his first book, *The Last Husband and Other Stories*, display a uniform polish, but many of them bear little resemblance to Humphrey's mature work. The skillfully-wrought title story, which concerns the adulterous habits of New York commuters, seems to have migrated from a John Cheever collection. But the book also contains some very characteristic work. "The Shell" concerns an East Texas boy whose revered father has died (as Humphrey's own father did when the author was in his thirteenth year). The boy's chief memento of his father, a skilled hunter, is an unfired twelve-gauge shotgun shell, and he has waited anxiously for the day when he is old enough to lift his father's weapon, chamber the shell, and bring down a quail with it, thus living up to the dead patriarch's high standard of manhood. The story ends when at the climactic moment the boy squeezes his trigger and discovers, with an irony whose meaning is hard to miss, that the fabled shell is a dud.

"The Shell" captures many of Humphrey's characteristic themes and topics: the importance of sporting rituals for men, the recurring theme of the son's relationship to a formidable father figure, and above all the ultimate uselessness of that father and his antique virtues in the present. The difficulty for Humphrey's protagonists is not that of living up to powerful fathers or even that of living without them, but rather of recognizing that those fathers have nothing to give their sons. If the classic writers of the Southern Renascence gave us, in Allen Tate's phrase, a literature conscious of the past in the present, then Humphrey gives us a present from which the past is utterly and painfully absent.

This theme governs Humphrey's first three novels, all of which focus on families in his own corner of East Texas. Taken together they amount to a kind of social history of the region, a history whose theme is the gradual alienation of the present from the past. *The Ordways* makes a beginning: it records the migration of a Tennessee family to Clarksville, Texas, during the waning days of the Civil War and follows their fortunes through the end of the nineteenth century (with an epilogue bringing the story up to the 1960s). These Southerners, led by their Confederate-veteran patriarch, bring not only all living kin but the bones of their ancestors as well, packed in barrels.

The determined traditionalism of the Ordways as they take up residence at the edge of the South is defensive, a way of warding off the rootless modern world represented by those prairies stretching westward from Clarksville. But as the novel proceeds that world threatens nonetheless: an Ordway child is kidnaped and taken west. His father—though determined to restore his family and exact the revenge which tradition demands, and though he scours west Texas for months, ancestral Confederate pistol in hand—finds the search futile and his own enthusiasm for it distressingly perishable; one day he simply gives up and returns home, acknowledging his failure to preserve the family against encroaching chaos.

Home from the Hill takes up the story of another East Texas family, during the 1930s. The Hunnicutts are the largest landowners in the county, and Captain Wade Hunnicutt is the community's unquestioned male ideal, his stature confirmed by his legendary skill as hunter. But the story is mostly about Wade's son Theron, one of nature's reactionaries who idolizes his father, takes more literally than the Captain himself does the aristocratic

code he seems to embody, and is devastated by his eventual discovery of his father's human weaknesses. The skillfully constructed plot propels itself, by a complex but seemingly inevitable system of causes and effects, toward an apocalypse: the murder of the Captain, the descent into madness of his wife Hannah, and Theron's self-destruction. By hopelessly trying to live his father's life, Theron loses his own, figuratively and then literally.

Proud Flesh concerns yet another troubled, aristocratic family attempting to live out its hyper-Faulknerian passions in the late 1960s. This work, which concerns the lingering death and long-delayed burial of the Renshaw family's matriarch Edwina, has been the most underrated of Humphrey's novels. Readers have failed to recognize that the mad Renshaws—who end up trying to preserve Edwina's corpse in the local icehouse—are the protagonists not of a tragedy but of a black comedy, a novel more akin to *The Loved One* than *The Sound and the Fury*. The intense traditionalism and family loyalty which were mythically heroic in *The Ordways* and genuinely tragic in *Home from the Hill* are here reduced, by their utter irrelevance to the world in which they are enacted, to the stuff of farce. The history recounted by these three novels is essentially the story of a traditional society losing the use of its traditions and coming to live, unwillingly but inescapably, in what one Humphrey character calls "these mean times I had been born into."

After *Proud Flesh* Humphrey turned his talents, for several years, primarily to non-fiction, winning a substantial new audience with his writing about hunting, fishing, and the outdoors. His most significant works in this vein are two short books, *The Spawning Run* and *My Moby Dick*, which display a lightness and humor which might surprise some readers of his often grim and violent Southern fiction. Humphrey's outdoor writing is collected in the volume *Open Season*. During these years he also composed a powerful memoir, *Farther Off From Heaven*, which primarily concerns the death of his father, the event which seems to have been the biographical inspiration of so much of his work.

In the mid-1980s, after a hiatus of more than ten years, Humphrey returned to fiction with *Hostages to Fortune*, a harrowing novel and a startling new departure for the author. Set in upstate New York rather than Texas, concerning not a large family but a single man who is, pointedly, both divorced and orphaned, the novel traces the effort of Ben Curtis to return to normal life after a series of personal tragedies. His help comes not from the resources of family and region but only from the comfort afforded by the rituals of sport as they are observed at an old fishing club. Humphrey's last novel, *No Resting Place*, returns to the South, but on a very different errand than before; here the protagonists are Cherokee Indians in the 1820s at the time of their forced removal from the Southeast to Oklahoma and Texas. But the theme of broken traditions, and of survivors left to carry on, links this novel with Humphrey's early work.

In 1992 Humphrey published his last book, *September Song*, a collection of stories. As the title implies and as might be expected from a writer nearly seventy, the main themes were advancing age, lost powers, encroaching death. But—as with so much of Humphrey's work—the grimness of his themes was balanced by both his craftsmanship and by the humor which has never been far from the surface in Humphrey's work. Though an uneven collection, *September Song* contains enough first-rate material to make a fitting last chapter of Humphrey's distinguished career.

—John Grammar

HUMPHREYS, Josephine

Born: Charleston, South Carolina, 2 February 1945. **Education:** Duke University, A.B. 1967; Yale University, M.A. 1968; doctoral study at University of Texas at Austin, 1968-71. **Family:** Married Thomas A. Hutcheson, 30 November 1968; two children. **Career:** Assistant professor of English, Baptist College at Charleston, 1971-78; writer since 1978. **Awards:** Danforth Foundation fellowship, 1968; Woodrow Wilson fellowship, 1968; Ernest Hemingway prize from P.E.N. American Center, 1985, for *Dreams of Sleep*; Guggenheim Foundation fellowship, 1985; Lyndhurst fellowship, 1986-1988; American Academy Literature prize in fiction. **Agent:** Harriet Wasserman Agency, 230 East 48th St., New York, New York 10017.

PUBLICATIONS

Novels

Dreams of Sleep. New York, Viking, 1984.
Rich in Love. New York, Viking, 1987.
The Fireman's Fair. New York, Viking, 1991.

Nonfiction

Contributor, *A World Unsuspected: Portraits of Southern Childhood*. Chapel Hill, University of North Carolina Press, 1987.
Contributor, *The Prevailing South: Life and Politics in a Changing Culture*. Atlanta, Longstreet Press, 1988.
Contributor, *Gal*. New York, Harcourt Brace, 1994.

*   *   *

Like many of her southern literary predecessors, Josephine Humphreys writes about place, family and history. In works by William Faulkner, Thomas Wolfe, Robert Penn Warren, or Walker Percy, often a white male intellectual character controls the narrative, theorizing about the South's tragic history and his own paralysis in the face of change. By contrast, in Humphrey's work, unlikely characters—e.g., adolescent girls, a black bartender and church sexton—emerge as the voices capable of changing the story. Her protagonists rely upon the imaginative possibilities that lie within the self, rather than in the external world, seeking to change their present circumstances rather than retreat stoically from what they cannot control.

In *Dreams of Sleep* (1984), which is set in Charleston, South Carolina, Humphreys writes out of the heads of three characters, Will and Alice Rees and their baby-sitter, Iris Moon, collapsing the boundaries between gender and class in order to explore familial breakdown and reconstruction. Obsessed with poetry and mournful over the fragmentation of society and the literal disintegration of the city's historical monuments, Will is a parodic recreation of the classic southern male narrator. In the midst of an

affair with his secretary, he becomes incapable of nurturing the other relationships in his life, perpetuating the animosity between himself and his mother, alienating his recently-separated best friend, Danny, and ignoring the depression that has overwhelmed his wife. Instead, it is Iris who deals with a dysfunctional family of her own, who awakens strength in Alice, once a Phi Beta Kappa and a mathematician.

Rather than be enthralled by home and history like her husband, Alice seeks a space that is conducive to wholeness of self. In her "dream of sleep," all of her selves—mother, wife, and mathematician—can co-exist, and she is not forced to sacrifice one for another. Will, Alice and Iris all must work through their memories, the failures of their families, and their own shortcomings during the course of the novel. The narrative does end with some reconciliation among its characters, but Humphreys makes it manifest that families are fragile without the diligence of those bound by love, and that love itself must transcend the language that we use to describe it.

In *Rich in Love* (1987), young Lucille Odom speculates about the "insides" of history, that which resists exposure or is kept invisible by those who don't want the true story revealed. She also wrestles with her own secret self, the self that, after her mother's abandonment, her father's subsequent breakdown, and her sister's sudden marriage and pregnancy, embarks on an affair with her sister's husband, himself an historian. Forced to keep the family functional in the midst of such crises, Lucille turns for solace to Rhody, her mother's black friend who becomes the only one to see Lucille's own struggle to sustain her sanity and identity. Narrated in the first person from Lucille's perspective, the novel documents Lucille's maturation and celebrates her ability to tell her story, to name it significant enough to merit some history of its own.

The Fireman's Fair (1991) marks a departure for Humphreys. In this novel, the central character is a white male lawyer from whose perspective the story is told in the third person. Like a Walker Percy character, Rob Wyatt suddenly quits his job, moves out of his nice home, and takes up residence in a beach bungalow, just as a hurricane is pummeling the South Carolina community in which he lives. Through Wyatt, Humphreys parodies the southern intellectual male, making him finally so absurd that the reader turns to Albert, Rob's black friend who is a church sexton and a bartender, for the truth. Albert's reactions to Rob confirm the reader's own, making Albert's voice the explanatory gloss for Rob's story. Having lost Louise, his one true love, to Hank, his former law partner, Rob fails to learn from his previous lack of action, falling for the younger Billie but losing her also, due to his own indecisiveness and failure to tell her the truth. Through a subversion of her main character's reliability, Humphreys pulls Albert from the margins to the center, extolling his honor of language even as she unflinchingly portrays Rob's shortcomings and carelessness with words. Like *Dreams of Sleep*, this novel ends happily, with Rob and Billie's reunion, even though it does not resolve all of the issues raised by their once-ruptured relationship.

Humphrey's lyrical prose and well-crafted narratives have garnered her more critical attention than most novelists who have published only three books. Also of interest is the fact that Humphreys made possible the publication of *Gal* in 1994. As the audience of a fellow Charlestonian, a young black woman for whom Ruthie Bolton is a pseudonym, Humphreys recorded the oral story and transcribed the tapes onto the pages that would become the non-fiction account of "Ruthie's" life. Humphreys' foreword is included in the book's published form. Clearly indebted to her community, Humphreys writes about South Carolina with an historian's accurate eye, but like her character, Lucille Odom, Humphreys' real target is that which cannot be easily seen, that which resists easy declaration in words, the story that sometimes struggles to be heard.

—Elinor Ann Walker

I-J

IVINS, Molly

Born: Monterey, California, 30 August 1944. **Education:** Smith College, BA; Columbia University, M.A.; Institute of Political Science, Paris. **Career:** Reporter, the *Houston Chronicle*, *Minneapolis Star Tribune*, and *Texas Observer*, 1970-76; *New York Times*, reporter, 1976-77, Rocky Mountain bureau chief, Denver, 1977-80; columnist, *Dallas Times Herald*, 1980-92, and *Forth Worth Star Telegram*, since 1992; contributor to *The Nation*, *Mother Jones*, *The Progressive*, *Ms.*, and other magazines. **Awards:** Three-time Pulitzer finalist; Outstanding Alumna, Columbia School of Journalism, 1976; Lifetime Achievement Award, The National Society of Newspaper Columnists, 1994.

PUBLICATIONS

Molly Ivins Can't Say That, Can She? New York, Random House, 1991.
Nothin' But Good Times Ahead. New York, Vintage Books, 1992.
You've Got to Dance With Them What Brung You: Politics in the Clinton Years. New York, Random House, 1998.

* * *

To Molly Ivins, the great pity of the opening of the Texas legislature is that "many a village is deprived of its idiot." 1996 presidential candidate Bob Dole is proof that "somewhere in Transylvania, there is an empty grave." Her appraisal of Texas congressman Dick Armey? "If ignorance ever goes to $40 a barrel, I want drillin' rights on that man's head." Pat Buchanan's famous "culture war" speech to the 1992 Republican National Convention "probably sounded better in the original German." Of an unfortunate legislator she once remarked, "if that man's IQ slips any lower, we'll have to water him twice a day," prompting a boycott of her then-employer, the *Dallas Times Herald*. And politics, according to Ivins, is "the greatest form of free entertainment ever invented."

Observations like these have won a broad and loyal following for this self-described "dripping fangs liberal," whose column appears in over 200 newspapers. Her first collection of essays was the best-selling *Molly Ivins Can't Say That, Can She?*, which Texas governor Ann Richards described as "more fun than riding a mechanical bull and almost as dangerous." The title of the collection is a legacy of the boycott: in response to the pressure to censor Ivins, the newspaper filled Dallas with billboards bearing that question. The collection was followed by two equally popular books, *Nothin' But Good Times Ahead* and *You Got to Dance with Them What Brung You.*

Ivins's chief subject matter is, of course, politics, and while the subject is commonplace, Ivins's approach is unusual. She takes on the issue of government from a decidedly progressive/populist angle, in language that is casual and folksy with an often scatalogical undertone. This has prompted the criticism that Ivins is a "professional Texan." In her defense, she argues that an ap-

preciation for metaphor is a matter of her Southern heritage. Further, Ivins belies the common (and generally true) observation that liberals, in their fear of being insensitive, do not make good humorists.

Ivins is merciless, sometimes bordering on mean, as in her statements on Bob Dole and Pat Buchanan, yet feels strongly that satire should only be directed against the powerful—the theme of her 1993 speech to a convention of editorial cartoonists. "Satire is by tradition and definition a weapon of the powerless," she observed. "When it is aimed against the powerless, it seems to me that it is not only cruel but profoundly vulgar." As examples of the abuse of satire she often employs Rush Limbaugh's attacks on Chelsea Clinton (the "White House Dog"), handicapped people, the poor, and others. Limbaugh also has attacked Ivins, an experience that she compares to "being gummed by a newt. It doesn't hurt but it does leave your ankle slimy."

Common political themes running through Ivins's work include the need to remove special-interest funding from the campaign process (a particularly prominent theme in *You Got to Dance with Them What Brung You*), the importance of democratic control of capital, the hypocrisy of many of the "family values" crowd, and the ever-increasing concentration of wealth at the top of the scale.

The title of Irvins's third collection, *You Got to Dance with Them What Brung You*, refers to one of the oldest sayings in politics, and she trains her eye in several pieces to analyze President Bill Clinton's job performance as well as Clinton bashing, offering sardonic and insightful views of well-financed attacks on the president's actions, but also taking issue with Clinton's decisions, particularly his support of welfare reform. Her arguments against the welfare reform bill Clinton signed into law is reflective of her larger social concerns, where Ivins expresses compassion for the poor, particularly children, attacks racism and homophobia, and laments the rise of terrorism on American soil. In fact, it is a mistake to assume that Ivins's interest is limited to politics. She is a very astute observer of Southern folkways, and much of her work, including tributes to friends and family, even political figures (Morris Udall and Barbara Jordan), are quite touching.

—Jason Mitchell

JAKES, John

Pseudonyms: William Ard, Alan Payne, Jay Scotland. **Born:** John William Gates in Chicago, Illinois, 31 March 1932. **Education:** DePauw University, A.B. 1953; Ohio State University, M.A. in American literature 1954. **Family:** Married Rachel Ann Payne in 1951; three daughters and one son. **Career:** Copywriter, then promotion manager, Abbott Laboratories, North Chicago, 1954-60; copywriter, Rumrill Company, Rochester, New York, 1960-61; freelance writer, 1961-65, since 1971; copywriter, Kircher Helton and Collett, Dayton, Ohio, 1965-68; copy chief, then vice-president, Oppenheim Herminghausen and Clarke, Dayton, 1968-70; creative director, Dancer Fitzgerald Sample, Dayton, 1970-71; Writer-in-Residence, DePauw University, Greencastle, Indiana, Fall 1979. **Awards:** LL.D.: Wright State University, 1976, Litt.D.: DePauw University, 1977, L.H.D.: Winthrop College, 1985. **Address:** c/o Rembar and Curtis, Attorneys, 19 West 44th Street, New York, New York 10036.

PUBLICATIONS

Novels

The Texans Ride North (for children). Philadelphia, Winston, 1952.
Wear a Fast Gun. New York, Arcadia House, 1956.
A Night for Treason. New York, Bouregy, 1956.
The Devil Has Four Faces. New York, Bouregy, 1958.
This'll Slay You (as Alan Payne). New York, Ace, 1958.
The Imposter. New York, Bouregy, 1959.
Johnny Havoc. New York, Belmont, 1960.
Johnny Havoc Meets Zelda. New York, Belmont, 1962; as *Havoc for Sale*, New York, Armchair Detective Library, 1990.
Johnny Havoc and the Doll Who Had "It." New York, Belmont, 1963; as *Holiday for Havoc*, New York, Armchair Detective Library, 1991.
G.I. Girls. Derby, Connecticut, Monarch, 1963.
When the Star Kings Die. New York, Ace, 1967.
Brak the Barbarian. New York, Avon, 1968.
Making It Big. New York, Belmont, 1968; as *Johnny Havoc and the Siren in Red*, New York, Armchair Detective Library, 1991.
The Asylum World. New York, Paperback Library, 1969.
The Hybrid. New York, Paperback Library, 1969.
The Planet Wizard. New York, Ace, 1969.
Secrets of Stardeep (for children). Philadelphia, Westminster Press, 1969.
Tonight We Steal the Stars. New York, Ace, 1969.
Brak the Barbarian Versus the Sorceress. New York, Paperback Library, 1969.
Brak Versus the Mark of the Demons. New York, Paperback Library, 1969.
The Last Magicians. New York, Signet, 1969.
Black in Time. New York, Paperback Library, 1970.
Mask of Chaos. New York, Ace, 1970.
Master of the Dark Gate. New York, Lancer, 1970.
Monte Cristo #99. New York, Curtis, 1970.
Six-Gun Planet. New York, Paperback Library, 1970.
Mention My Name in Atlantis—Being, at Last, the True Account of the Calamitous Destruction of the Great Island Kingdom, Together with a Narrative of Its Wondrous Intercourses with a Superior Race of Other-Worldlings, as Transcribed from the Manuscript of a Survivor, Hoptor the Vintner, for the Enlightenment of a Dubious Posterity. New York, DAW, 1972.
Time Gate (for children). Philadelphia, Westminster Press, 1972.
Witch of the Dark Gate. New York, Lancer, 1972.
On Wheels. New York, Warner, 1973.
Conquest of the Planet of the Apes (novelization of screenplay). New York, Award, 1974.
Brak: When the Idols Walked. New York, Pocket Books, 1978.
Excalibur!, with Gil Kane. New York, Dell, 1980.
California Gold. New York, Random House, 1989.

Kent Family Chronicles

The Bastard. New York, Pyramid, 1974.
The Rebels. New York, Pyramid, 1975.
The Seekers. New York, Pyramid, 1975.
The Furies. New York, Pyramid 1976.
The Titans. New York, Pyramid 1976.
The Warriors. New York, Pyramid, 1977.
The Lawless. New York, Jove, 1978.
The Americans. New York, Jove, 1980.

North and South Trilogy

North and South. New York, Harcourt Brace, 1982.
Love and War. New York, Harcourt Brace, 1984.
Heaven and Hell. New York, Harcourt Brace, 1987.

Novels as Jay Scotland

The Seventh Man. New York, Bouregy, 1958.
I, Barbarian. New York, Avon, 1959; as *John Jakes* (revised edition), New York, Pinnacle, 1976.
Strike the Black Flag. New York, Ace, 1961.
Sir Scoundrel. New York, Ace, 1962; as *King's Crusader* (revised edition), New York, Pinnacle 1977.
Veils of Salome. New York, Avon, 1962.
Arena. New York, Ace, 1963.
Traitors' Legion. New York, Ace, 1963; as *The Man from Cannae* (revised edition), New York, Pinnacle, 1977.

Novels as William Ard

Make Mine Mavis. Derby, Connecticut, Monarch, 1961.
And So to Bed. Derby, Connecticut, Monarch, 1962.
Give Me This Woman. Derby, Connecticut, Monarch, 1962.

Short Stories

The Best of John Jakes edited by Martin H. Greenberg and Joseph D. Olander. New York, DAW, 1977.
Fortunes of Brak. New York, Dell, 1980
The Best Western Stories of John Jakes edited by Martin H. Greenberg and Bill Pronzini. Athens, Ohio University Press, 1991; as *In the Big Country: The Best Western Stories of John Jakes*, Thorndike, Maine, Hall, 1993.

Plays

Dracula, Baby (lyrics only). Chicago, Dramatic Publishing Company, 1970.
Wind in the Willows. Elgin, Illinois, Performance, 1972.
A Spell of Evil. Chicago, Dramatic Publishing Company, 1972.
Violence. Elgin, Illinois, Performance, 1972.
Stranger with Roses, adaptation of his own story, Chicago, Dramatic Publishing Company, 1972.
For I Am a Jealous People, adaptation of the story by Lester del Rey, Elgin, Illinois, Performance, 1972.
Gaslight Girl. Chicago, Dramatic Publishing Company, 1973.
Pardon Me, Is This Planet Taken?. Chicago, Dramatic Publishing Company, 1973.

Doctor, Doctor! music by Gilbert M. Martin, adaptation of a play by Moliere. New York, McAfee Music, 1973.
Shepherd Song. New York, McAfee Music, 1974.

Other

Tiros: Weather Eye in Space. New York, Messner, 1966.
Famous Firsts in Sports. New York, Putnam, 1967.
Great War Correspondents. New York, Putnam, 1968.
Great Women Reporters. New York, Putnam, 1969.
The Bastard Photostory. New York, Jove, 1980.
Susanna at the Alamo: A True Story (for children). New York, Harcourt Brace, 1986.

Editor, with Martin H. Greenberg, *New Trails: Twenty-Three Original Stories of the West from Western Writers of America.* New York, Doubleday, 1994.

*

Bibliography: *In The Best Western Stories of John Jakes* edited by Martin H. Greenberg and Bill Pronzini, Athens, Ohio University Press, 1991.

Manuscript Collections: University of Wyoming, Laramie; DePauw University, Greencastle, Indiana.

Critical Study: *The Kent Family Chronicles Encyclopedia* edited by Robert Hawkins, New York, Bantam, 1979.

*   *   *

John Jakes began his writing career inauspiciously, publishing pulp fiction in the western and science fiction genres. It was not until the mid-1970s, when he began writing mass-market historical fiction, that he earned significant notice. In 1974 he published *The Bastard*, the first of eight books in his American Bicentennial series that became widely popular, followed by the equally well read *North and South* trilogy, another cycle of historical fiction. As in all of his writings, these series are distinguished by exhaustive research of historical incidents brought to dramatic life.

The 50 books written in the first 20 or so years of Jakes' career should not be overlooked. Though most are rightly categorized as pulp fiction, Jakes learned his craft writing science fiction, mystery and suspense novels, children's books, and westerns. Several critics find his *Brak the Barbarian* series and pieces found in *The Best of John Jakes* as noteworthy additions to the science fiction genre.

Jakes' breakthrough began when he was contracted to write several books to help commemorate the 1976 Bicentennial of the United States. The series, originally scheduled to be five books, became eight titles and made Jakes famous. The books, which are best known collectively as the Kent Family Chronicles, follow the Kent family through seven generations from the colonial era to end of the 19th century. Each volume focuses on a certain time in the history of the United States: *The Bastard* and its follow-up, *The Rebels* (1975), concern the American Revolution as experienced by Philip Kent. As the

series progresses, the Kent family takes part in major American events, including the War of 1812 and the Texas's fight for sovereignty.

Critics were generally positive in their reviews of the series, finding them similar in factual scope and dramatic depth to Alex Haley's *Roots*, a contemporary epic that traces the history of an African American family. All of the volumes in the Kent Family Chronicles were characterized by lively plotlines and memorable characters; each book sold at least 3.5 million copies, and the whole series sold over 40 million copies.

Jakes could have continued this series on through the 20th century, as his publisher wanted, but instead chose to write another saga, The North and South trilogy. These works focus on two families—the Hazards, Pennsylvania industrialists, and the Mains, slaveowning Southern aristocrats. Beginning with *North and South* (1982), the families' destinies become woven together: family patriarchs became friends while attending West Point, but the Civil War forces them to become enemies. The experiences of the families reflect social attitudes and events before, during and after the Civil War, then continue into the periods of Reconstruction and the conquering of the American frontier. The North and South books were praised for meticulous research of the Civil War era and fast-paced narratives.

Though Jakes takes some liberties mixing fiction and fact in his historical novels, the results are reader-friendly. Indeed, Jakes has said that his novels "may be the only shot some people have at history." Gay Andrews Dillin in the *Christian Science Monitor*, concurs: "Remember how easy it was to doze off in your American history class? Well, if John Jakes had been the teacher, you wouldn't have!"

—Annette Petrusso

JARMAN, Mark

Born: Mark Foster Jarman in Mount Sterling, Kentucky, 5 June 1952. **Education:** University of California, Santa Cruz, B.A. 1974; University of Iowa, Iowa City, 1974-76, M.F.A. 1976. **Family:** Married Amy Kane in 1974; two daughters. **Career:** Teacher and writing fellow, University of Iowa, Iowa City, 1974-76; instructor of English, Indiana State University, Evansville, 1976-78; visiting lecturer of English, University of California, Irvine, 1979-80; assistant professor of English, Murray State University, Kentucky, 1980-83; assistant professor, 1983-86, associate professor, 1986-92, and since 1992 professor of English, Vanderbilt University, Nashville; poetry editor, *Intro 13,* Associated Writing Programs, Norfolk, 1982; co-publisher, 1985-87, Story Line Press, and co-editor, 1981-89, *The Reaper,* both with Robert McDowell; advisory editor, Story Line Press, 1987-89. **Awards:** Academy of American Poets Prize, 1974; National Endowment for the Arts fellowships, 1977, 1983, 1992; Robert Frost Fellowship, Bread Loaf Writers Conference, 1985; Guggenheim fellowship, 1991; The Poets' Prize, 1991, for *The Black Riviera;* Lila Wallace-*Reader's Digest* grant, 1992.

PUBLICATIONS

Poetry

Tonight is the Night of the Prom. Pittsburgh, Three Rivers Press, 1974.

North Sea. Cleveland, Cleveland State Poetry Center, 1978.

The Rote Walker. Pittsburgh, Carnegie-Mellon University Press, 1981.

Far and Away. Pittsburgh, Carnegie-Mellon University Press, 1985.

The Black Riviera. Middletown, Connecticut, Wesleyan University Press, 1990.

Iris. Brownsville, Oregon, Story Line Press, 1992.

Questions for Ecclesiastes. Brownsville, Oregon, Story Line Press, 1997.

Nonfiction

The Reaper Essays, with Robert McDowell. Brownsville, Oregon, Story Line Press, 1996.

Editor

Rebel Angels: 25 Poets of the New Formalism, with David Mason. Brownsville, Oregon, Story Line Press, 1996.

* * *

Mark Jarman's poems, more than those of any other poet of his generation, effectively combine the difficult Audenesque virtues of versatility, precision, and lyric resonance. The key word behind Jarman's poetry is "recovery," reclaiming the past in a society intent on erasing the past as soon as its currency fades and in healing the wounds of painful experience. This double-edged pursuit must often lead to the exploration of elusive, private memory. In Jarman's poetry the search evokes a deftly balanced tension, a decision made over and over, from poem to poem, about what can and cannot be revealed and in what settings those revelations must truthfully appear.

Jarman, long a believer in the poet's responsibility to root poems in the landscape of a particular region, often returns to Scottish and Southern California settings, his personal landscapes of childhood and adolescence, and to Kentucky and Tennessee, where he has lived and taught for a number of years. In "The Supremes," from his 1985 collection *Far and Away,* Jarman brings back a long-ago morning of surfing as it ends in Ball's Market for sweet rolls. On the store's television set the boys watch the famous Motown group:

> Gloved up to their elbows, their hands raised
> toward us palm out, they sing,
> 'Stop! In the Name of Love' and don't stop . . .

"Every day of a summer," the poet realizes, "can turn, from one moment, into a single day." The poem moves on, recalling a scene in Diana Ross's first film and "the summer it brought back," its minute details carefully laid out, adding up to . . . what? Unexpectedly, the poem opens up to speculate on the singers' very different memories of that summer and then winds back to the boys in the market:

> But what could we know, tanned white boys,
> wiping sugar and salt from our mouths
> and leaning forward to feel their song?
> Not much, except to feel it
> ravel us up like a wave
> in the silk of white water,
> simply, sweetly, repeatedly,
> and just as quickly let go.

A moment passes, but memory's durable capacity for haunting, for staying with those who live and feel experience (rather than sleepwalking through life), can provoke a personal breakthrough, a revelation that may prove relevant to all. "The Supremes" leads us to the discovery that the remembered day and summer, the surfing boys, the local market that would not last, and the famous singing group combine in the poet's memory to form an experience the essence of which was "full of simple sweetness and repetition." Jarman's poems thrive on such breakthroughs, where ordinary vision, focusing intently, becomes something more penetrating, more revealing, in which key words, such as "sweetness" and "repetition," take on more than their usual weight, acting both as summaries of the past and as signposts indicating future experience.

In *Iris,* the seminal book-length narrative poem published in 1992, Jarman adapts the challenging double pentameter of Robinson Jeffers to tell the story of a lower-middle-class Kentucky woman's search for meaning. A single mother, running from an abusive marriage and drug-related violence in her home, Iris's most compelling constant in a twenty-year odyssey (aside from caring for her daughter and invalid mother) is the poetry of Jeffers. When a community college English teacher asks her why she reads such a poet, Iris gives him a thoughtful answer:

> She put her hand across her mouth and spoke through
> parted fingers. "I don't think I can tell you.
> I have to. I love the poetry. I think there's something
> else that he's not telling."

It is this conviction that ultimately leads her to California and then, years later, to a car trip north to see Jeffers's rugged home, Tor House, located on a windy precipice overlooking Monterey Bay. It is there, in the shadow of "The house where pain and pleasure had turned to poetry and stone, and a family had been happy" that the truth of Jeffers's experience and her own life click into place. Because the evidence of Jeffers's domestic life contradicts his stern philosophy, Iris taps into her own capacity to interpret life's complexity. She realizes at last that what we live and how we interpret complex experience may in fact amount to more than a seamless life. This is the key she has been searching for, and it unlocks the point of view that validates her many compromises and difficult decisions.

For Jarman poetry fails if it does not provide the key to such elusive discoveries. A minister's son, Jarman forever pushes against inherited faith, testing both its truthfulness and his own capacity to believe. This effort finds its most distilled expression in *Questions for Ecclesiastes,* published in 1997, and in a related series of sonnets. In "In Via Est Cisterna" the poet watches how his mother is able to recall only one phrase from a Latin class she took as a girl. Once again, the suggestive significance of the phrase transcends the literal and mundane:

> *A well is in the road.* It is profound,
> I'm sure, it is a phrase with many levels.
> And then, I see one: the woman with five husbands
> Met Jesus there. But my mother had only one—
> Unless now having lost him she understands
> That he was never who she thought, but someone
> *Who was different men with different women through the years.*
> In the road is a well. *It fills with tears.*

Making the leap from a fragment of ancient personal experience—the Latin phrase—to the ramifications of infidelity is typical of the territory one might expect to cover in Mark Jarman's poems. These brief, varied examples verify Jarman's technical virtuosity and his storytelling and lyric preeminence among his peers.

—Robert McDowell

JAUSS, David

Born: Windom, Minnesota, 25 February 1951. **Education:** Southwest Minnesota State College (now Southwest State University), B.A. 1972; Syracuse University, M.A. 1974; University of Iowa, Ph.D. 1980. **Family:** Married Judith Kuno, 21 August 1971; two children. **Career:** Instructor in English, Southwest State University, Marshall, Minnesota, 1974-77; assistant professor, 1980-83, associate professor, 1983-88, professor of English and creative writing, since 1988, director of creative writing, since 1980, University of Arkansas at Little Rock; fiction and managing editor, *Crazyhorse*, 1981-91. **Awards:** James A. Michener fiction fellowship from the University of Iowa, 1982-83; O. Henry Prize from Doubleday, 1983, for short story "Shards"; creative writing fellow of the Arkansas Arts Council, 1986; Pushcart Prize, 1989, for short story "Freeze," and 1991, for short story "Glossolalia"; *Best American Short Stories* selection for "Glossolalia," 1991; National Endowment for the Arts Creative Writing Fellowship, 1993; Associated Writing Programs Award for Short Fiction, 1995, for the collection *Black Maps*. **Address:** Department of English, University of Arkansas at Little Rock, Little Rock, Arkansas 72204-1099.

PUBLICATIONS

Short Story Collections

Crimes of Passion. Chicago, Story Press, 1984.
Black Maps. Amherst, University of Massachusetts Press, 1996.

Poetry Collection

Improvising Rivers. Cleveland, Cleveland State University Press, 1995.

Other

Editor, *Strong Measures: Contemporary American Poetry in Traditional Forms.* New York, Harper & Row, 1986.
Editor, *The Best of Crazyhorse.* Fayetteville, University of Arkansas Press, 1990.

Uncollected Short Stories

"The Post Office," in *New Writers*, 1975.
"October Reunion," in *Cimarron Review*, 1976.
"The Lifeguard," in *Maryland Review*, 1987.
"The Jury," in *Crosscurrents*, 1987.
"Misery," in *Denver Quarterly*, 1990.
"The Point," in *Pikeville Review*, 1994.
"Dear Husband, Wherever You Are," in *Arkansas Times*, 6 September 1996.

Uncollected Poems

"Here," in *Shenandoah*, 1989.
"Sunbathing, 1967" and "My Grandmother's Hands," in *Poem*, 1996.
"The Wandering Between Worlds," in *Black Warrior Review*, 1996.
"The Real Tortured," in *Sonora Review*, Spring/Summer 1997.
"The Only Language," *Denver Quarterly*, Winter 1997/1998.
"Mirror Light," in *Green Mountain Review,* Spring/Summer 1998.

Uncollected Essays

"Making It New: Contemporary American Experiments with Traditional Verse Forms," in *Verse*, 1988.
"The Age of Fatigue," in *The Literary Review,* 1990.
"Contemporary American Poetry and All That Jazz," in *Crazyhorse*, 1992.

*   *   *

As one of the few writers to have won the "big three" awards for American short fiction—the Pushcart Prize (twice), an O'Henry Award, and inclusion in *The Best American Short Stories* anthology—David Jauss has achieved high standing among contemporary short story writers. In addition, Jauss has made significant contributions as an editor and, increasingly, as a gifted poet. In all three areas Jauss's work is notable for its intelligence and an impeccable craftsmanship of the variety that does not call attention to itself, but instead directly and simply brings the reader face to face with what it means to live in post-World War II America.

Jauss's vision of contemporary life is not always reassuring. Indeed, he would no doubt agree with Yeats that "the center cannot hold." Jauss's characters are forever searching for a center, an anchor, some guiding principle to keep chaos at bay; that search, however, is rarely satisfactorily concluded.

The difficulty of coming to terms with one's own life is illustrated throughout the stories in Jauss's first collection, *Crimes of Passion* (1983). The protagonist of "Hook," for example, announces at the outset that "I've got some sort of problem. I don't know, my heart's rabid or something." A hard drinking, hard fighting Vietnam veteran from Arkansas, Hook seems cast from a familiar mold. But it is the way Hook varies from the stereotype that furnishes the story's conflict. That is, if Hook could only accommodate himself to what seems his "natural" place in society, he might not be so plagued with self-doubt. Rather than being the traditional unreflective "macho" tough guy, though, Hook hates what his temper has done to his relationships with people, especially women. In a further complication for this "redneck" southerner, Hook's girlfriend is a quadroon, technically of one-fourth Negro blood, but all-black in Hook's subculture. A Hollywood script would have Hook conquering his inner demons and defying racist society by skipping off into the sunset with his Carina, but such is not for Jauss. By the end Hook has not won the girl, has not conquered himself, has not in fact even achieved greater understanding of himself.

The remaining stories in Crimes of Passion vary greatly in setting (from the South to the Upper Midwest to Central America), voice (gently comic to coldly objective to unsettlingly paranoiac), and characterization (protagonists including a dying Catholic nun, a psychotic murderer, and a Spanish explorer). All to one degree or another, however, share in the general pattern established by "Hook" of burdening a character with an intelligence and sensitivity (yes, even Hook) too fine to allow that character to accommodate himself to life's absurdities.

In Jauss's next collection, *Black Maps* (1995), the tones, settings, and character types are just as varied as in the earlier collection; but the characterization is altogether more profound, the conflicts and themes more richly compelling, the author's vision more mature. Here, Jauss proves himself to be especially adept at dramatizing the lives of those marginalized in various ways in modern society: the Vietnam "grunt" on the verge of madness and murder ("Freeze"); the newspaper proofreader whose late-night existence reflects his "dark night of the soul" ("The Late Man"); and a Dominican baseball player torn by a desire to "make it" in two worlds, the United States and his native land, in both of which he is in one sense or another an alien ("The Bigs").

As interesting as these stories of the marginalized are, two other kinds of stories show Jauss at his most compelling. One type (see especially "Torque," "Beautiful Ohio," "Brutality," and "Rainier") dramatizes that most human and universal conflict between men and women. This also was a frequent theme in Jauss' first collection, but here Jauss is less condemning and ironic, more sympathetic and forgiving. His characters may blunder and fail one another, but the fault lies in emotions and conditions of life that are simply too powerful for them. By the end the reader judges less than he empathizes because the conflicts are so humanly true.

The other type of story Jauss might be best at is dramatizing the lives of children. "Firelight" is a beautiful, heartbreaking story of a boy wrenched by a welfare agency from a mother inadequate to the task of caring for him, but a mother whom, in spite of everything, he loves. In "Glossolalia," arguably Jauss's most memorable story, a young boy threatens to descend into the same suicidal madness that afflicts his father. The story is at least guardedly hopeful, however; the boy survives to adulthood and has a son of his own, and if he's plagued by fears for his son, these only springs from love.

Even during his most prolific period as a short story writer, Jauss was publishing poems, and since the mid-1990's he has focused almost exclusively on poetry. Just as with the stories, the poetry in his first collection, *Improvising Rivers* (1995), evinces a great variety of subject matter: poems about fishing, about baseball, about jazz, about literary figures. These subjects do not, however, serve as ends in themselves but are points of departure for speculations on the human condition. In addition to these, one finds poetry of a much more personal nature, especially concerning Jauss's wife and children. Although Jauss is at this time less well known as a poet than as a fiction writer, it is altogether possible that it is in poetry that he shows himself to be the most inventive, compassionate, and compelling.

Jauss's editorial achievements deserves at least a word. For over a decade through his singular efforts he kept afloat *Crazyhorse*, one of America's premier literary magazines, the sort of venue without which poets and short story writers would have virtually no forum for their works. Also, *Strong Measures: Contemporary American Poetry in Traditional Forms* (1986), the anthology Jauss co-edited with Philip Dacey, helped draw attention to and in some ways anticipated the vital "new formalism" movement in contemporary poetry.

In American culture, where success is equated with high sales and movie tie-ins, it is the novelist who reaps the lion's share of the rewards and fame, but Jauss's varied talents make him an interesting and important contemporary writer.

—Dennis Vannatta

JONES, Edward P.

Born: Arlington, Virginia, 5 October 1950. **Education:** Attended College of the Holy Cross, Worcester, Massachusetts, and the University of Virginia. **Career:** Writer for *Tax Notes*. **Awards:** Finalist for the National Book Award, 1992, for *Lost in the City*.

PUBLICATIONS

Short Story Collection

Lost in the City. New York, Morrow, 1992

*   *   *

A new voice in short fiction, Edward P. Jones tells stories of the Washington, D.C. of his childhood. His Washington is a city of working-class black families whose days are such a struggle that Jones cannot help thinking of them as heroes. It is those heroes who people the stories in his collection of short fiction, *Lost in the City* (1992), which was nominated for the National Book Award.

The fourteen stories in this collection are set during the 1950s, a time of transition for African-Americans, many of whom were moving up from the American South. Hoping to secure better lives for themselves by moving, these ordinary people had no idea what odds would meet them in the city. Place plays a huge part in their lives; they are lost within their own section of the capital, which is separated from the white bureaucratic downtown above Constitution Avenue.

Jones' primary characters are young people, learning hard truths about the uncertainties of life. They are consistently meeting with obstacles they don't yet understand, and are continually faced with personal and familial loss. Their frustration and despair are revealed in the photographs accompanying each story. However, that despair is neither debilitating, nor does it create characters who are to be pitied, either by themselves or by the reader, as a sense of pride and dignity ensure the reader's respect.

In "Young Lions," the protagonist becomes involved in criminal acts, even knowing that in doing so he will lose the love and trust of his girlfriend. "The Store" tells of the narrator's progression from alienation into legitimacy, which results in a feeling of community for those around him. In "The Girl Who Raised Pigeons," a father contemplates leaving his newborn daughter on the street and just walking away. In that crucial moment he cannot abandon her, and the incident helps him strive to be a competent father. These characters, including another a father who stabs his wife and then has to live with his children's questions, are presented in a straightforward manner with their faults and troubling thoughts and acts.

In other of Jones's stories, often delivered with irony, the theme of struggle and ultimate survival against adversity emerges. "His Mother's House," for example, depicts a woman who ignores the obvious existence of the drugs that her son sold to buy her a house. In "A New Man," a man drives his fifteen-year-old daughter away, then searches for her endlessly, and in "The Night Rhonda Ferguson Was Killed," the level of irony is almost too pronounced. A young girl plans on capitalizing on her friend's show business success, only to discover at the end of the day that her friend has been killed.

These stories are presented with a distinctive prose style, spiced by Jones's ear for dialogue and idioms of Washington, D.C. and displaying a strong narrative voice, where Jones exhibits his abilities with an impressive range of dramatic effects and insights. Jones's stories about the specific concerns and struggles of a community on the fringe of the heart of American politics are universal, an understanding born of the author's unsentimental approach to probing the environment and actions of his characters.

—Virginia Watkins

JONES, Gayl

Born: Lexington, Kentucky, 23 November 1949. **Education:** Connecticut College, New London, B.A. in English 1971; Brown University, Providence, Rhode Island, M.A. 1973, D.A. 1975. **Career:** Member of the Department of English, University of Michigan, Ann Arbor, 1975-83. **Awards:** Howard Foundation award, 1975; National Endowment for the Arts grant, 1976. **Address:** Lotus Press, P.O. Box 21607, Detroit, Michigan 48221.

PUBLICATIONS

Novels

Corregidora. New York, Random House, 1975.
Eva's Man. New York, Random House, 1976.
The Healing. Boston, Beacon Press, 1998.

Poetry

Song for Anninho. Detroit, Lotus Press, 1981.
The Hermit-Woman. Detroit, Lotus Press, 1983.
Xarque. Detroit, Lotus Press, 1985.

Short Stories

White Rat. New York, Random House, 1977.

Play

Chile Woman. New York, Shubert Foundation, 1975.

Other

Liberating Voices: Oral Tradition in African American Literature. Cambridge and London, Harvard University Press, 1991.

Uncollected Short Stories

"Almeyda," in *Massachusetts Review,* Winter 1977.
"Ensinança," in *Confirmation* edited by Amiri and Amina Baraka. New York, Morrow, 1983.

*

Critical Studies: *Engendering the Subject: Gender and Self-Representation in Contemporary Women's Fiction* by Sally Robinson, Albany, State University of New York Press, 1991; *Bridging the Americas: The Literature of Paula Marshall, Toni Morrison and Gayl Jones* by Stelamaris Coser, Philadelphia, Temple University Press, 1994.

*   *   *

Gayl Jones's first novel, *Corregidora,* focuses on the lingering effects of slavery in black America—specifically on its sexual and psychological manifestations in the life of Ursa Corregidora, a Kentucky blues singer. The great granddaughter of a Portuguese plantation owner who fathered not only her grandmother but also her mother, and who used his progeny both in the fields and in his own whorehouse, Ursa is unable to free herself of painful and obsessive family memories. In each personal relationship she finds yet again the sickness of the master-slave dynamic. Her short-lived first marriage is convulsive with desire, possessiveness, humiliation, and violence; her second, safer, marriage fails as she cannot forget the first.

In relating Ursa's story, Jones shows the difficulty of loving when abusive relationships have been naturalized by cultural continuity, when so much has been taken that one's only dignity is in withholding. Her taut and explicit idiom, sometimes plainly narrative, sometimes wildly stream-of-consciousness, captures the nuances of a tormented sexuality that is both specific to black experience and symptomatic of our troubled gender system. "I knew what I still felt. I knew that I still hated him. Not as bad as then, not with the first feeling, but an after feeling, an aftertaste, or like an odor still in a room when you come back to it, and it's your own." The book's ending, almost unbearably intense but strangely hopeful, suggests that we may begin to heal ourselves only as we confront the deep sexual hatred that pervades our lives.

Whereas *Corregidora* allows us to perceive the construction of personality as historical process, *Eva's Man* offers a very different kind of experience, one that many readers have found profoundly disturbing. Eva Canada, the main character of the novel, tells her tale from an institution for the criminally insane, where she has been imprisoned for a hideous sexual crime of murder and dental castration. Like Ursa, Eva has been damaged by abuse and by a legacy of violence; unlike the protagonist of *Corregidora,* she has no sense of how her past motivates her present. As she speaks her disjointed narrative, an ugly story disrupted by flashes of recalled nastiness, she remains alien to us, a personality beyond promise or repair.

> I put my hand on his hand. I kissed his hand, his neck. I put my fingers in the space above his eyes, but didn't close them. They'd come and put copper coins over them. That's why they told you not to suck pennies. I put my forehead under his chin. He was warm. The glass had spilled from his hand. I put my tongue between his parted lips. I kissed his teeth.

In *Eva's Man,* Jones takes us into the pathological mind, and we do not find ourselves there. As the tidy reader-protagonist identification is denied us, we are left with the horror of what we can't sympathetically imagine. Jones's unflinching violation of our strongest taboos—made all the more chilling by her starkly controlled prose—raises a number of questions about the roles of writers, readers, and cultural conventions. Beyond shock value, what does a writer achieve in presenting the truly sordid? Is our understanding necessarily dependent upon the protagonist's understanding? What do disturbing books demand of us that comforting ones do not? How must we see the world in order to change it?

The stories that make up *White Rat* suggest that Jones is intent on keeping those questions before us. The majority of these pieces ("Legend," "Asylum," "The Coke Factory," "The Return," "Version 2," "Your Poems Have Very Little Color in Them") are about madness or extreme psychic alienation. Some ("The Women," "Jevata") address the painful complications of desperate sexual arrangements. The most attractive, of course, are those few ("White Rat," "Persona," "The Roundhouse") that hint at successful human connection despite overwhelming odds. Like *Eva's Man,* most of the stories in *White Rat* challenge our notions of what fiction should do. What we make of Gayl Jones's work depends largely on what we are willing to perceive as the function of art—on how, as readers, we enter into the dialogue.

The Healing (1998) continues Jones' presentation of women struggling for identity amid violence and few opportunities. Harlan

Jane Eagleton is the primary narrator among a diverse group of women, which includes her female relatives and a musical star, Joan Savage, whose mood swings result in the kinds of turbulent events familiar to Jones' work—the larger forces within which her protagonists maneuver. In this work, a particularly violent act sets off a chain of events that leads Harlan, Savage's manager, to become a faith healer. Jones' skill with dialogue is vital: often rambling conversations lead to abrupt changes and repetitions, ultimately propelling the narrative forward while digressing with side issues, creating a kind of realism where more happens than one can immediately discern and order while also capturing the rich nuances of the particular idiom of her characters.

—Janis Butler Holm and Mel Koler

JONES, Madison

Born: Madison Percy Jones, Jr., in Nashville, Tennessee, 21 March 1925. **Education:** Vanderbilt University, A.B. 1949; University of Florida, 1950-53, A.M. 1951. **Military Service:** U.S. Army, Corps of Military Police, Korea, 1945-46. **Family:** Married Shailah McEvilley in 1951; two daughters and three sons. **Career:** Farmer in Cheatham County, Tennessee, 1940s; instructor in English, Miami University, Oxford, Ohio, 1953-54, and University of Tennessee, Knoxville, 1955-56; member of the Department of English from 1956 (now emeritus), writer-in-residence, 1967-87, and professor of English, 1968-87, Auburn University. **Member:** Alabama Academy of Distinguished Authors; Fellowship of Southern Writers. **Awards:** Fellowships, *Sewanee Review,* 1954, Rockefeller, 1968, Guggenheim, 1973; Alabama Library Association Book Award, 1968; Lytle Prize, for short fiction, 1992. **Agent:** Harold Matson Company, Inc., 276 Fifth Avenue, New York, New York 10001.

PUBLICATIONS

Novels

The Innocent. New York, Harcourt Brace, 1957.
Forest of the Night. New York, Harcourt Brace, 1960.
A Buried Land. New York, Viking Press, 1963.
An Exile. New York, Viking Press, 1967.
A Cry of Absence. New York, Crown, 1971.
Passage through Gehenna. Baton Rouge, Louisiana State University Press, 1978.
Season of the Strangler. New York, Doubleday, 1982.
Last Things. Baton Rouge, Louisiana State University Press, 1989.
To the Winds. Atlanta, Longstreet Press, 1996.
Nashville 1864: The Dying of the Light. Nashville, J.S. Sanders & Co., 1997.

Uncollected Short Stories

"The Homecoming," in *Perspective*, Spring 1952.
"Dog Days," in *Perspective*, Fall 1952.
"The Cave," in *Perspective*, Winter 1955.
"Home Is Where the Heart Is," in *Arlington Quarterly*, Spring 1968.

"A Modern Case," in *Delta Review*, August 1969.

"The Fugitives," in *Craft and Vision* edited by Andrew Lytle, New York, Delacorte Press, 1971.

"The Family That Prays Together Stays Together," in *Chattahoochee Review* (Dunwoody, Georgia), Winter 1983.

"A Beginning." In *Homewords* edited by Douglas Paschall, Knoxville, University of Tennessee Press, 1986.

"Zoo," in *Sewanee Review,* Summer 1992.

"Before the Winds Came," in *Oxford American*, Winter 1994.

Other

History of the Tennessee State Dental Association. Nashville, Tennessee Dental Association, 1958.

*

Film Adaptation: *I Walk the Line,* 1970, from the novel *An Exile.*

Manuscript Collections: Emory University, Atlanta; Auburn University, Alabama.

Interview: *Southern Quarterly*, Spring 1983.

Critical Studies: "Madison Jones" by Reed Whittemore, *New Republic,* July 1971; *Separate Country* by Paul Binding, New York, Paddington Press, 1979; *The History of Southern Literature* edited by Louis Rubin, Louisiana State University Press, 1986.

Madison Jones comments:

Generally, on a more obvious level, my fiction is concerned with the drama of collision between past and present, with emphasis upon the destructive elements involved. More deeply, it deals with the failure, or refusal, of individuals to recognize and submit themselves to inevitable limits of the human condition.

*   *   *

There is a homogeneity of theme that links together into a coherent body the published fiction of Madison Jones. The setting of these books is invariably Jones's native south. But whether their time is the late eighteenth-century settlement days or the region's more recent past, his unvarying song is abstraction, ideology, and its consequences. *The Innocent,* his first novel, set in rural Tennessee immediately after the coming of modernity, treats the attempts by a young southerner, Duncan Welsh, to repent of earlier impiety and reestablish himself upon inherited lands in inherited ways. The enterprise is a failure because of Duncan's deracinated preconception of it. Welsh "sets up a grave in his house." Soon, he and his hopes are buried in another.

A Cry of Absence again focuses on a fatal archaist, a middle-aged gentlewoman of the 1960s who is anything but innocent. Hester Glenn finds an excuse for her failures as wife, mother and person in a self-protective devotion to the tradition of her family. But when her example proves, in part, responsible for her son's sadistic murder of a black agitator, Hester is driven to know herself and, after confession, to pay for her sins with suicide.

A kind of Puritanism distorts Mrs. Glenn. In *The Innocent,* the error is a perversion of the Agrarianism of Jones's mentors (Lytle, Davidson). But in his other novels the informing abstractions are not so identifiably southern. Jones's best, *A Buried Land,* is set in the valley of the Tennessee River during the season of its transformation. Percy Youngblood, the heir of a stern hill farmer (and a central character who could be any young person of our century), embraces all of the nostrums we associate with the futurist dispensation. He attempts to bury the old world (represented by a girl who dies aborting his child) under the waters of the TVA; but its truths (and their symbol) rise to haunt him back into abandoned modes of thought and feeling. In *An Exile* Hank Tawes, a rural sheriff, is unmanned by a belated explosion of passion for a bootlegger's daughter. His error has no date or nationality, but almost acquires the force of ideology once Tawes recognizes that, because he followed an impulse to recover his youth, his "occupation's gone." *Forest of the Night* tests out an assumption almost as generic, the notion that man is inherently good. An interval in the Tennessee "outback" is sufficient to the disabusement of Jonathan Cannon. There is no more telling exposé of the New Eden mythology.

In all of Jones's fiction there operates an allusive envelope embodied in a concrete action and supported by an evocative texture. That action is as spare as it is archetypal; and in every case its objective is to render consciousness. Jones is among the most gifted of contemporary American novelists, a craftsman of tragedy in the great tradition of his art.

—M. E. Bradford

JONES, Patricia Spears

Born: Forest City, Arkansas, 11 February 1951. **Education:** Rhodes College, Memphis, B.A. 1973; Vermont College, Montpelier, M.F.A. in writing 1992. **Career:** Editor, *W.B.* magazine, 1975; grants program director, Coordinating Council of Literary Magazines, New York, 1977-81; administrator, *Heresies Collective*, New York, 1982-83; program coordinator, Poetry Project at St. Mark's Church, New York, 1984-86; program specialist, New Works Program, Massachusetts Council on the Arts and Humanities, Boston, 1987-89; program director, Film News Now Foundation, New York, 1990-91; grant writer, 1991-94; director of planning and development, 1994-96, New Museum of Contemporary Art, New York; consultant, since 1996. **Awards:** New York Foundation for the Arts award in poetry, 1986, fellowship, 1993; Goethe Institute travel grant, 1989; Divers Forms Artists Projects grant, 1991; National Endowment for the Arts Opera Music Theater Program award, 1993, fellowship, 1994; Bread Loaf Writers Conference fellowship, 1996; Foundation for Contemporary Performance Arts award, 1996.

PUBLICATIONS

Poetry

The Weather that Kills. Minneapolis, Coffee House Press, 1995.

Other

Editor with others, *Ordinary Women: An Anthology of New York City Women Poets*, New York, n.p., 1978.

*

Patricia Jones comments:

I am one of those people whose love of words began quite early. I love to read just about anything. I started writing in early adolescence. It was a way of getting beyond the small town's social and cultural parameters. Growing up black in America in the 1950s and early 1960s was difficult, full of complex social obligations, negotiations, family secrets, and enormous social changes giving rise to the Civil Rights Movement. Plus there was soul music and rock and roll and jazz and film from places like Rome, Paris, and London, as well as Hollywood.

From reading about the Living Theater to working with Mabou Mines; from listening to Jimmy Hendrix on the radio to hearing him live a few months before his death; from watching the Vietnam War on TV to protesting the war at college, I feel quite strongly the social dynamism of those early years tempered by my maturation as a person and a poet. I admire the willingness of my fellow artists to take risks, mess up, get up and try something else in an effort to communicate whatever it is that they (we) think is important. Words can kill or heal or merely disrupt the quotidian. I hope my work is in some way disruptive, delightful, different.

*   *   *

The 35 poems that make up Patricia Spears Jones first volume, *The Weather that Kills,* can be grouped into pieces concerned with the human condition, personal issues, love, music, and place. The poems are open in form and exhibit striking images, which are potent with surprise and insight: businessmen are "podium-headed" and "the oops of life like a stadium wave / wraps the planet" ("You Just Got the Call").

While Jones' poems often announce their origins in specific circumstances, seldom do they remain within those confines, for Jones allows the poem to associatively and imaginatively expand into unusual and epiphanic intersections. Nowhere is this more so than in "The Perfect Lipstick," where "black men in sequined dresses" emerge from the historical process that begins with

> Columbus in a toy ship.
> Off to discover the perfect route—
> the fastest way to China, the Indies, all that spice.

Jones locates the poetic of the human condition in the risks that must be taken "in the new world where the most dangerous of dreams / come true" ("The Perfect Lipstick"), for we live in "an era of dangerous greed and too easily satisfied lust" ("You Just Got the Call"). Though there is a place for human action—moral, empathetic, dissenting—we are also made aware of the "weather," forces that are beyond human intervention:

> We look across the lake. The mountains tremble
> at an immeasurable speed.
> And we have nothing to do with it.

("Measure")

Finally, there is nothing that outlasts the ravages of history but art: "And the print survives" ("Blumen").

"Halloween Weather," the suite that concludes the volume, is so various in what it touches and so rich in its collage of voice, image, and sound that the pulsations of global life are made tangible and cannot be refused: "we walk as if from one funeral to another . . . happy for the privilege." The everyday circumstances that we endure and do not comprehend is the starting places of Jones's exploration of the human condition: "The Perfect Lipstick" is generated by a historical reenactment ("When the life-sized replicas of the Nina, / the Pinta, and the Santa Maria / precariously sailed into New York harbor"); "Measure" commences "In the traffic jam on the way to the picnic"; and "You Just Got the Call"—a poem on Keith Haring's death—opens with cartoonish intimacy as the artist dresses ("Swish, you put on your underwear"). Jones's handling of autobiographical elements is informed by her awareness of the problems inherent in "mythic retelling": in "Glad All Over," for example, she states that it is exactly the seductions of "Mythic retelling" that she rejects, allowing her to confront a personalized history rather than expand her own life mythopoetically. Thus, though she refracts her own experience of the civil rights struggle through adolescent curiosity sparked by seeing Julian Bond at a 1965 SNCC rally, the poem's climax is reached at the text's halfway point, with her own mother's confrontation of police troopers, and from that vantage the poem expands to take in a score of "hard truths."

Similarly, in "The Birth of Rhythm and Blues" her own birth is related to the traumatic, wild, and pleading music that her parents were surrounded by in the years of "global nightmare"—encompassing the Korean conflict, Billie Holiday, Big Boy Crudup, Little Richard, and Ruth Brown: "so they cut my mother's belly and drag me out / wailing too." The music is a necessity because song is "where the hurting stops and healing begins." However, there is also a dialectic in music, for it contains men "bleeding and bleeding into / music's deep well." Music also figures largely in "In My Father's House," as the poet tries to connect to a distant parent: "I'd listen to the albums' bright music / wishing the swirling strings, their incessant backbeat, / would make me love my father." Music also makes possible protest and social change in "Healing Sheath" ("Someone intones platitudes, / but the beat breaks another back") and "Sly and the Family Stone Under the Big Tit" ("always loving the way we thought the world / should be").

Jones's handling of love is somewhat sentimental. However, the love theme in *Weather* is marked by maturity, acceptance, and wisdom. "Encounter and Farewell" frames an erotic interlude in New Orleans that begins with the "foreplay" of a "walk / through the French Quarter exploring souvenir shops." The details of lovemaking are explicitly presented but they do not occupy the entirety of the world. There is a context of past and present and of other cities: "We are / making love as we did before in Austin and Manhattan." "5:25 A.M." is also rife with tender specifics ("The weight of you / is traced on my sheets"), but there is an ironic reciprocity formulated by life's contingencies—"That's why the stereo's too loud," "That's why the buses are late." Love brings the world into focus, but it does not banish the irritations: the beautiful moments come out of "storms" and makes possible "a song so sweet it makes my teeth ache."

Jones's poems that address music and travel are never routine. Her sensibility is fresh, curious, and vital. San Francisco is plunged into the emergency of the AIDS epidemic: "Men here, lovers, friends, are / learning women's work." Likewise, music is chiefly present as a means to increase our awareness of the presence of frustrating liabilities that refuse to be ameliorated. Confronting Charlie Parker's death "of heartbreak," "Gossip" states that "What we love is the falling, the falling." Jones implies that because the mass of humans embrace destruction, it is the task of the poets to work towards the world's salvation:

It is what we do not speak of
when the radio plays
something memorable
and we lack the skill
to carry the tune.

—Jon Woodson

JONES, Rodney

Born: Falkville, Alabama, 11 February 1950. **Education:** University of Alabama, B.A. in English 1971; University of North Carolina, Greensboro, M.F.A. 1973. **Family:** Married Virginia Kremza in 1972 (divorced 1979); one daughter; married Gloria Nixon de Zepeda Jones in 1981; one son. **Career:** Writer-in-residence, Virginia Intermont College, Bristol, 1978-84; professor, Department of English, Southern Illinois University, Carbondale. **Awards:** Lavan Younger Poets award, Academy of American Poets, 1986, for *The Unborn;* National Endowment for the Arts fellowship; Guggenheim fellowship; General Electric Foundation Younger Writers award, 1986; Jean Stein prize, American Academy and Institute of Arts and Letters, 1989; National Book Critics Circle award, 1989, for *Transparent Gestures.* **Address:** Department of English, Southern Illinois University, Carbondale, Illinois 62901.

PUBLICATIONS

Poetry

Going Ahead, Looking Back. Knoxville, Southbound Books, 1977.
The Story They Told Us of Light. Birmingham, University of Alabama, 1980.
The Unborn. Boston, Atlantic Monthly Press, 1985.
Transparent Gestures. Boston, Houghton Mifflin, 1989.
Apocalyptic Narrative and Other Poems. Boston, Houghton Mifflin, 1993.
Things That Happen Once: New Poems. Boston, Houghton Mifflin, 1996.

* * *

It has been said that, when compared to other contemporary American poets, Southern poets alone still have the ability to appeal to a wide audience. If one accepts that as true, and that Southern poets still allow their readers insights into the specifics that create connections between the individual and the regional, the historical and the modern, then Rodney Jones might be said to be their ideal representative.

With his wide range in subject matter—from singing the praises of a mosquito and looking into the mind of an anarchic mechanic in *The Unborn* (1985) and *Transparent Gestures* (1989), to standing beside a disemboweled murder victim while friendly onlookers offer coffee in *Things That Happen Once: New Poems* 1996—Jones' poetry embraces both the abstractions of the intellect and spirit as well as the concreteness of the flesh. In "The Sorrow Pageant" (1996), for example, Jones presents the reader with a meditation on an overturned truckload of pigs in rural Mexico, and in spite of the poem's obvious physical comedy, the poem takes us, in the end, into the spiritual realm as Jones moves us to contemplate the pigs as gifts for the peasants observing the wreck:

I hoped they were the kind of men who saw the sweet
    humor, who still
believed in fate as perfect expression,
That before they ate, they would give thanks for the phe-
    nomenon, for the
miracle of those pigs.

This poem also exemplifies the well-developed sense of the absurd that runs through Jones' work, as in the poem "For My Sister" (1996), in which a whore's "seven brats" explain to the speaker, "In the mornings, when it's cold, we got to lay / Under the bed and push. We got to crank mama up." However, beneath the absurdities and the irony also lies a fine elegiac sensibility in keeping with Jones' characteristic acknowledgment of permanent uncertainties at which the reader only arrives by a circuitous route, as in the close of this poem:

. . . For, from the beginning we had been taught that part
of the difference is nurture, and another part silence, so
    as our
bodies
grew strange, there were no words.   And only today af-
    ter years it
came to me
        that the shack had burned and I thought you would
    want to know.

The absurdities of the physical world are often used as a relief (employing both definitions of the word) against which are set the eloquent leaps into the intellectual realm at the close of most of his poems.

Another example of Jones' play with opposing realms is "Mortal Sorrow" (1995), which begins, "The tortures of lumbago consumed Aunt Madge" and continues: "but I want someone to see / now that they lie safe in / graves Beyond the vacant stores, just that someone listened," followed by another leap back to the concrete—"I remember Mrs. Lyle who called it a thorn in the flesh, and Mr. / Appleton who had no roof in his mouth."

Jones ability to create and maintain a solid connection between the tangible and imaginative realms is similar to that of Philip Levine, although, unlike Levine, Jones does not cast off the trappings of reality as he ascends onto another plain. As he says at the end of "The troubles that women start are men" in *Things that Happen Once* (1996), "Whatever I'd dream, the world is not a lie." Also like Levine's poetry, in Jones' work one can find a clear class-consciousness, though it is inclusive and apolitical, for while allowing for the tension of juxtapositions, Jones does not offer any resolutions.

With its many variations in subject matter and form, and its consistencies in voice and tone, Jones' poetry establishes an order that enables the reader to be both amused and moved by the chaos that is (and was) human existence. And this does present a very broad appeal, because it feels like wisdom.

—Dawn Gilchrist Young

JUSTICE, Donald

Born: Donald Rodney Justice in Miami, Florida, 12 August 1925. **Education:** University of Miami, B.A. 1945; University of North Carolina, Chapel Hill, M.A. 1947; Stanford University, 1948-49; University of Iowa, Ph.D. 1954. **Family:** Married Jean Ross in 1947; one son. **Career:** Visiting assistant professor, University of Missouri, Columbia, 1955-56; assistant professor, Hamline University, St. Paul, Minnesota, 1956-57; lecturer, 1957-60, assistant professor, 1960-63, and associate professor, 1963-66, Reed College, Portland, Oregon, 1962; associate professor, 1966-67, and professor, 1967-70, Syracuse University; visiting professor, University of California, Irvine, 1970-71; professor of English, University of Iowa, 1971-82; since 1982 professor of English, University of Florida, Gainesville; Bain-Swiggett Lecturer, Princeton University, 1976; visiting professor, University of Virginia, 1980. **Awards:** Rockefeller grant, 1954; Lamont Poetry Selection award, 1959; Inez Boulton prize, 1960, and Harriet Monroe memorial prize (*Poetry,* Chicago), 1965; Ford fellowship, in theater, 1964; National Endowment for the Arts grant, 1967, 1973, 1980; American Academy award, 1974; Guggenheim fellowship, 1976; Pulitzer prize, 1980; Bollingen prize for poetry, 1991, award, 1991; Lannan Literary award for poetry, 1996. **Member:** American Academy of Arts and Sciences, 1992; National Institute of Arts and Letters, 1992.

PUBLICATIONS

Poetry

The Summer Anniversaries. Middletown, Connecticut, Wesleyan University Press, 1960.
A Local Storm. Iowa City, Stone Wall Press, 1963.
Night Light. Middletown, Connecticut, Wesleyan University Press, 1967.
Four Poets, with others. Pella, Iowa, C.U.I. Press, 1967.
Sixteen Poems. Iowa City, Stone Wall Press, 1970.
From a Notebook. Iowa City, Seamark Press, 1972.
Departures. New York, Atheneum, 1973.

Selected Poems. New York, Atheneum, 1979.
Tremayne. Iowa City, Windhover Press, 1984.
The Sunset Maker: Poems/Stories/A Memoir. New York, Atheneum, 1987.
A Donald Justice Reader. Hanover, New Hampshire, University Press of New England, 1991.
New and Selected Poems. New York, Knopf, 1995.

Recording: *Childhood and Other Poems.* Watershed, 1983.

Other

Platonic Scripts. Ann Arbor, University of Michigan Press, 1984.

Editor *The Collected Poems of Weldon Kees.* Iowa City, Stone Wall Press, 1960; revised edition, Lincoln, University of Nebraska Press, 1975.
Editor with Paul Engle and Henri Coulette, *Midland.* New York, Random House, 1961.
Editor with Alexander Aspel, *Contemporary French Poetry.* Ann Arbor, University of Michigan Press, 1965.
Editor *Syracuse Poems 1968.* New York, Syracuse University Department of English, 1968.
Editor with Betty Adcock, *Poems* (recorded on audio cassette). Washington, D.C., Archive of Recorded Poetry and Literature, 1989.
Editor with Robert Mezey, *The Collected Poems of Henri Coulette.* Fayetteville, University of Arkansas Press, 1990.
Editor *The Collected Poems of Weldon Kees.* Stone Wall Press, 1960; Lincoln, University of Nebraska Press, 1992.
Editor with Eavan Boland, *Poems* (recorded on audio cassette). Washington, D.C., Archive of Recorded Poetry and Literature, 1992.
Editor with Cooper R. Mackin and Richard D. Olson, *The Comma after Love: Selected Poems of Raeburn Miller.* Akron, University of Akron Press, 1994.

Translator, *L'Homme qui se ferme/The Man Closing Up* by Guillevic. Iowa City, Stone Wall Press, 1973.

*

Manuscript Collection: University of Delaware Library, Dover.

Critical Studies: *Alone with America* by Richard Howard, New York, Atheneum, 1969, revised edition, Atheneum, 1980; "On Donald Justice" by Greg Simon, in *American Poetry Review 5* (Philadelphia), No. 2, 1976; "Flaubert in Florida: On Donald Justice" by Michael Ryan, in *New England Review and Breadloaf Quarterly,* Vol. 7 No. 2, Winter 1984; "Donald Justice Special Issue" edited by Dana Gioia and William Logan, in *Verse,* Winter/Spring 1992; "The Progress of Donald Justice" by Lewis Turco, in *The Hollins Critic,* Vol. 29, No. 4, October 1992; *Certain Solitudes: Essays on the Poetry of Donald Justice* edited by Dana Gioia and William Logan, University of Arkansas Press, 1997.

*   *   *

Justice is admired for his austere handling of quotidian details and formal structures in his poetry. While his literary output is relatively small, each poem demonstrates Justice's mastery of traditional poetic forms while commenting on contemporary alienation, loss, and depression. Justice's early poems often take the form of a still life, containing little autobiographical detail and no elements of confessional poetry. Instead, he abstractly details common events to examine existential themes. For example, Justice's early poem "The Snowfall," displays his stylistic and thematic concerns: "The classic landscapes of dreams are not/More pathless, though footprints leading nowhere/Would seem to prove that a people once/Survived for a little even here."

In his later work, Justice displayed his perception of art's inherent inability to capture life's complexities, although it is made more bearable. He explained in his essay, "Meters and Memory": "The terror or beauty or, for that matter, the plain ordinariness of the original event, being transformed, is fixed and made more tolerable. That the event can recur only in its new context, the context of art, sheers it of some risks, the chief of which may anyhow have been its transitory character."

Justice's choice of style and subject matter in his first two volumes can be viewed as passive and lacking in variety, or better as muted and restrained detailing of contemporary life. In these poems, Justice presents characters with unrealized potential and little passion for living. In the pieces in Justice's first published volume, *The Summer Anniversaries* (1960; revised 1981), the poet uses restrained language and tone in expressing a bleak outlook on life. Justice himself commented in a later poem: "How fashionably sad those early poems are!/On their clipped lawns and hedges the snows fall." Justice's second volume, *Night Light* (1967), is marked by a looser, more relaxed style that still adheres to stylistic formality. Thematically, *Night Light* alternately details contemporary ennui and despair, which are underscored by Justice's rejection of overt drama in favor of minute details of day-to-day life.

Justice's next major work, *Departures* (1973), incorporates pieces from the earlier *Sixteen Poems* (1970) that experiment with traditional forms through random compositions and loose translations, which results in poems that create a chance structure of their own and display Justice's increased confidence and control over his verse forms. Details of the poems are layered in a seemingly uncoordinated fashion that resonate with the work's meaning rather than clearly delineating it. *Departures* was nominated for a National Book Award. Justice reworked many of his earlier pieces and added new works for his *Selected Poems* (1979), which displays his mastery of such traditional forms as ballads, sestinas and villanelles, as well as the freer verse of *Departures*. Many of the later pieces included in *Selected Poems* reflect Justice's conviction that art can never totally capture reality, and that reality is distorted by artistic endeavors. The achievement of his first three books of poems, *The Summer Anniversaries, Night Light,* and *Departures,* became clearer when gathered with later, uncollected work in *Selected Poems,* which was awarded the 1980 Pulitzer Prize in poetry.

While Justice's body of poetic work contains no works of considerable length, many of them contain elegiac qualities, reflecting Justice's belief that art is humankind's striving for immortality. This forms the basis for much of what he characterizes as "Mordancies of Armchair"—poems concerning suicide, lost friends and death—contained in *The Sunset Maker: Poems/Stories/A Memoir* (1987). In this work, Justice draws on his childhood piano lessons as a motif to explore themes of mortality and memory and art's ability to outlast them. These poems also display Justice's belief that music and the themes and sounds of poetry are closely related.

In his volume of essays, *Platonic Scripts* (1984), Justice wrote that a new tradition of poetry could be started "with not much more than this. Not forgetting rhythm; not forgetting truth." His work pays testament to that sentiment as a conscious attempt to mitigate mortality with tightly controlled stanzaic forms: "My mother's face all smiles, all wrinkles soon;/...All fixed into place now, all rhyming with each other." *A Donald Justice Reader: Selected Poetry and Prose* (1991), which was awarded the Bollingen Prize, and *New and Selected Poems* (1995) are good starting points for those yet to experience the music of this important literary figure and master poetic craftsman.

—Bruce Walker

K

KAY, Terry

Born: Terry Winter Kay in Hart County, Georgia, 10 February 1938. **Education:** West Georgia College; LaGrange College, A.B. 1959. **Family:** Married Tommie Duncan, August 1959; four children. **Career:** Columnist, *Decatur-De Kalb News*, 1959-62; sports writer, *Atlanta Journal*, 1962-65, film and theatre critic, 1965-73; creative director of Pace Corp., 1973-74; account executive with Walburn & Associates (public relations firm), 1975-77; public information manager and external affairs representative, Oglethorpe Power Corporation, Chamblee, Georgia, 1977-80; full-time writer and television scriptwriter (including regular contributions to the television series, *In the Heat of the Night*), beginning 1980s; regional theatre, including director (twice) of the Summer Creative Writing Program at Emory University; visiting lecturer in English and speaker at literary events. **Awards:** Georgia Author of the Year Award, 1981, for *After Eli*; Emmy Award, 1990, for script, *Run Down the Rabbit*, a television Christmas special aired in 1989.

PUBLICATIONS

Novels

The Year the Lights Came On. Boston, Houghton Mifflin, 1976.
After Eli. Boston, Houghton Mifflin, 1981.
Dark Thirty. New York, Poseidon Press, 1984.
To Dance with the White Dog. Atlanta, Peachtree Publishers, 1990.
To Whom the Angel Spoke: A Story of Christmas. Atlanta, Peachtree Publishers, 1991.
Shadow Song. New York, Pocket Books, 1994.
The Runaway. New York, W. Morrow, 1997.
The Kidnapping of Aaron Greene. New York, W. Morrow, 1999.

Other

Run Down the Rabbit (screenplay). Broadcast in 1989.

*

Media adaptations: *To Dance with the White Dog*, CBS-TV Hallmark Hall of Fame special, 1990.

*   *   *

Terry Kay writes the kind of Southern plain-folks stories in which no one is plain at all; some characters are a little peculiar, quite a few are funny—by their own design or not, and all the major players have lives that go way deeper than the bone. They are quintessentially Southern and universally human.

Kay came by these people, and the spare, hardscrabble setting a lot of them inhabit, by nature. He was born next to the last of twelve children on a Hart County, Georgia, farm near the Savannah River, in a rolling countryside just south of the Blue Ridge Mountains. His childhood spanned the waning years of the Great Depression and the whole of American involvement in World War II. During that time many in the rural upland South still read at night by kerosene lamps and got their water from a spring or hand-dug well. Kids were a necessity, to tend the chickens and hogs and hoe vast fields of cotton they would help pick in the fall. In such a household Terry Kay grew up. He played football at Royston High School and went to West Georgia College and on to LaGrange College, where he attained a degree in social science.

Full of confidence, he married his sweetheart, Tommie Duncan, and looked ahead to graduate school at Duke. He didn't get there. The only opening Terry could find was selling insurance, and Tommie was the first to notice that he wasn't all that good at it. As he would later tell an interviewer, one morning when she left him in bed as she headed out for work Tommie told him pointedly, "By the time I get home tonight you'd better have a job." He did. Following an ad offering a chance to learn an "interesting profession," Terry went to work at the *Decatur/Dekalb News* as a copy boy. He made $40 a week. Pretty soon he noticed that he could write about as well as the reporting staff, and three years later he was writing sports for the *Atlanta Journal*, where he would become a nationally-recognized theater critic.

As a critic Kay interviewed celebrities of film and stage; such associations led him into a job as a creative director for films and television. He and Tommie had a growing family, and following the money he went white-collar, into the offices of an area power company, where he rose to the top rung of executives. Meanwhile, pushed by friend Pat Conroy, Kay began writing fiction. Brought up on stories, he embellished what he had always known and found the tales that seemed just common to him would enchant editors, who would actually pay him for it.

Kay was totally unschooled as a writer. All that he knew of the craft he had learned on the job. The secret, one that comes very hard to a lot of people, he has said, is to "turn loose and do it," to open the gates, get out of the way and let the story flow. Among his early books were *The Year the Lights Came On* (1976), *After Eli* (1981), which earned him a Georgia Author of the Year award, and *Dark Thirty* (1984).

In 1990, *To Dance with the White Dog*, the book that would make him internationally famous, was published, and it was later made into a CBS-TV film starring Hume Cronyn and Jessica Tandy. *White Dog* is based on Kay's own family's experience with a bereaved old father, an elderly man whose beloved wife has died. Despite the fact that he is surrounded on the old farm place and in the community by his children who love him, there is ever a gap of understanding that cannot span the generations; the old man haunts the clean-swept family graveyard, grieving himself to death.

And then to his door comes the mysterious white dog. He tries to run it off. Patiently, it returns. He throws it a biscuit. which it gratefully accepts. He makes huge pans of biscuits, and the oddly graceful creature makes its way into his kitchen, and the man's heart. The incident strikes terror into the hearts of his loving daughters, who hear about the white dog but cannot see it. One of the novel's great comic moments occurs in the detective ploy of these middle-aged women, who black their faces like commandos and hide in a ditch by night, outside their father's door, to try to spy on the liaison between man and dog.

The phantom dog brings healing and joy, and ultimate acceptance. Its story brought Kay profound acclaim from readers as far away as South Africa's Bishop Desmond Tutu, who said of the novel, "I found it all such a moving experience, a lovely, enduring tribute to love. The book will be like a dear friend, an old friend, much cherished and held in high esteem."

In the same year of *White Dog*'s publication Kay won an Emmy for his screenplay for *Run Down the Rabbit*, a television Christmas special aired in 1989. He also did scriptwriting for the television series *In the Heat of the Night*. He and Tommie now live in a house with electricity and abundant running water in Lilburn, Georgia, where writing has turned out to be job enough.

Two of Kays' novels of the 1990s, *The Runaway* and *Shadow Song*, like *White Dog*, explore conflicts between times of enchantment and more mundane and cruel realities, continuing his brand of plain-folks stories in which no one is plain at all. *The Runaway* is set in the small town of Crossover after World War II, where a new sheriff, Frank, and postwar euphoria abate the racial polarization evidenced by the reign of the previous sheriff, whose actions came to be called Logan's Law—the "law of the way things are." Two precocious friends, similar in adventurousness to Tom Sawyer and Huck Finn, run away from home. Son Jesus, a serious and mathematically gifted black twelve-year old, and Tom, a mischievous white twelve-year old, flee downriver, like Huck and Jim in the *Adventures of Huckleberry Finn*. They are retrieved, but not before they discover human bones buried in an old sawmill. The bones are discovered to be those of Son Jesus' father, who had been missing for several years and presumed to have been one of three victims of racially motivated murders. Complications ensue as Frank's investigation increases racial tension and he begins wooing a young widow whose husband may have been involved in the crime. Violence escalates, and the friendship of Son Jesus and Tom is challenged.

Shadow Song focuses on Bobo Murphy, a somewhat successful middle-aged artist who has lived his whole life in Georgia. Haunted by a summer he spent in the Catskills waiting tables at a posh resort when he was 17, Bobo takes the opportunity to revisit his past when he learns of the death of Avrum Feldman, a cranky but insightful retiree he met at the resort. Feldman had worshiped a renowned opera singer—a devotion that inspired Bobo to pursue Amy, a lovely and wealthy girl vacationing at the resort. While the resort has lost its charm, much like Bobo's own life, Amy reappears and Bobo has the opportunity to transcend his own, self-imposed limitations, to act upon the mystical views he learned from Feldman.

—Dot Jackson

KENAN, Randall

Born: Brooklyn, New York, 12 March 1963. **Education:** University of North Carolina, B.A. 1985. **Career:** Editor, Alfred A. Knopf, New York City, 1985-89; lecturer, Sarah Lawrence College, since 1989, Vassar College, since 1989, and Columbia University, since 1990. **Awards:** New York Foundation of the Arts grant, 1989; MacDowell Colony fellowship, 1990. **Address:** Sarah Lawrence College, Bronxville, New York 10708.

PUBLICATIONS

A Visitation of Spirits. Grove Press, 1989.
Let the Dead Bury Their Dead and Other Stories. Harcourt, 1992.
James Baldwin (part of the series *Lives of Notable Gay Men and Lesbians*). Chelsea House, 1994.
A Time Not Here: The Mississippi Delta. Twin Palms Publishing, 1997.
Walking on Water, In press.

*   *   *

Randall Kenan's fiction is rife with appealing qualities, grounded in realism with fanciful flights that reflect confusion on the part of characters and evoke enriching cultural qualities. A dexterous writer, Kenan empoys rapid chronological shifts, multiple, interweaving narratives, and symbolic events, all of which blur distinctions between the fanciful and the everyday, the living and the deceased.

A Visitation of the Spirits (1989), his first novel, introduces readers to the fictional community of Tims Creek, North Carolina, which was founded by escaped slaves. The work's main narrative concerns Horace T. Cross, an intellectually gifted teenager who undergoes a midnight journey of self-discovery, learning much about his own life and the history of his family. Cross struggles with demons—from personal ones that include his unaccepted homosexuality, to forms that might be real or not: amid much discovery, much else remains ambiguous and shadowy in the world of Tims Creek. Intercut with Cross's tragic endeavor is the story of his elder cousin, the Reverend James Malachai, and his trip with an aunt and uncle to visit a dying relation. The threesome reflect on Cross and the history of Tims Creek during the course of their journey.

Kenan's narrative is complexly structured while efficiently and eloquently relaying underlying tension. He makes leaps through time: Cross's quest takes place in April 1984, while the sojourn of his relatives occurs in December of 1985; the narrative shifts between first and third person; characters enter and pass through clever discourses on everything from chicken plucking to current trends in music. Cross's internal battle between repression and desire is reflected in Kenan's repeated working of themes relating to possession, grieving, and memory.

Kenan compounds his multi-perspective narrative style in *Let the Dead Bury the Dead and Other Stories* (1992), a short story collection that delves further into Tims Creek. The stories are interconnected, further enriching the reader's knowledge of a community where it seems that every home has fascinating stories and skeletons. Like

A Visitation of the Spirits, many of Kenan's stories have the dead among the living and manifestations of evil and good, mixing elements of myth and folk stories with evocations of everyday reality. Kenan continues to experiment with narrative, showing a variety of storytelling skills. The title story, for example, is a history of the founding and subsequent development of Tims Creek presented in the form of an academic paper, complete with annotations, by a narrator, "RK." He gets a significant amount of his information from Reverend Green, who has compiled oral histories, diary entries, letters and other material into an unfinished chronicle discovered by RK. Within this opus, myth and fact are again intertwined, making Kenan's writing simultaneously specific about events and suggestive of larger forces at work.

Kenan's fictional interests are mirrored in his first non-fiction study, a biography of James Baldwin, the first in a series of books published by Chelsea House called Lives of Notable Gay Men and Lesbians. Like Kenan's character Horace T. Cross, Baldwin, too, struggled with repressed homosexuality, and like Kenan wrote works rich with symbolism and a reality that embraces fanciful elements. Kenan's biography encompasses both literary history and life story.

—Emma Cobb

KILGO, James

Born: James Patrick Kilgo in Darlington, South Carolina, 1941. **Education:** Wofford College, B.A.; Tulane University, M.A. and Ph.D in American literature. Career: Professor, University of Georgia, since 1967, and director of the English Department's creative writing program; columnist for local periodicals and essayist (contributing to the *Georgia Review, Sewanee Review, Gettysburg Review*, and *New England Review/Bread Loaf Quarterly*), beginning late 1970s; illustrator and wood carver.

PUBLICATIONS

Essay Collections

Deep Enough for Ivorybills. Chapel Hill, Algonquin Books, 1988.
Inheritance of Horses. Athens, University of Georgia Press, 1994.

Nonfiction

Pipe Creek to Matthews Bluff: A Short History of Groton Plantation. Burlington, Vermont, Groton Land Company/Vanguard Books, 1988.
The Blue Wall: Wilderness of the Carolinas and Georgia (photographs by Thomas Wyche, essay by James Kilgo). Sandlapper Publishing, 1996.

Novel

A Daughter of My People. Athens, University of Georgia Press, 1998.

*   *   *

James Patrick Kilgo began writing at a relatively late point in his career, some fifteen years after he began teaching American literature at the University of Georgia. Known among his friends as an entertaining storyteller, he was invited in the late 1970s by a weekly newspaper to write a series of columns on nature and hunting. The success of these weekly columns, and the pleasure he found in writing them, convinced him to try his hand at more serious forms of creative writing, especially nature writing. He began to write a series of essays based on his hunting experiences, and in 1988 these culminated in his first book, *Deep Enough for Ivorybills*. Within a decade, this book and later volumes, along with essays in the *Georgia Review, Sewanee Review, Gettysburg Review,* and *New England Review/Bread Loaf Quarterly*, garnered for Kilgo a reputation of considerable standing among writers of nonfiction in America, especially writers of the natural world.

Kilgo was born and grew up in Darlington, South Carolina, where his family had lived for several generations. One of his great-grandfathers founded Duke University. His maternal grandfather was a Methodist minister. He received his BA degree from Wofford College and his MA and PhD in American Literature from Tulane University, where he studied under Donald Pizer and wrote a dissertation on novels about World War II. In 1967 he began teaching at the University of Georgia, where he is now a professor in the English department, whose creative writing program he directed for several years.

Widely read in American literature, Kilgo has studied American nature writers in depth. An amateur artist, he drew the illustrations for his first book and has tried wood carving as well. Writers who have influenced him, he says, "in addition to the obvious influences of Faulkner and Hemingway, are Cormac McCarthy and Annie Dillard, the latter because of where I was when I first read her, Cormac because he reminded me of the power of stories of elemental things, that such stories have perennial appeal." One might add to this list the sketches of John James Audubon, the nineteenth-century Southern humorists, and the more recent writings of Frank Burroughs, Barry Lopez, Peter Matthiessen, and Wendell Berry.

Deep Enough for Ivorybills is a series of narratives loosely centered on Kilgo's experiences as he learns the skills of hunting. Although hunting and the outdoors are the apparent subjects of this book, and one of the reasons for its popularity, other concerns are the real points of focus. The essays are organized in a loosely chronological order and tend to concern specific individuals or incidents. Usually the ostensible subject becomes an opportunity for commentary on more abstract issues. In "Actual Field Conditions," for example, Kilgo discusses his fondness for birdwatching and describes an experience in a south Georgia rookery. The breeding birds he observes instruct him in the seething fecundity of the natural world and of his kinship with it. "Worthy Blood" describes Kilgo's killing of his first buck and his friendship with Billy Claypoole (a central character in the book), while in "Isaac's Blessing" Kilgo's description of his son's introduction to the hunt and associated rituals becomes a father's general expression of love and concern for his son as he grows towards manhood. Several essays center on Kilgo's family, most notably "Grandfather," in which Kilgo meditates at length on the tangled connections of the hunt with the land and with his family heritage.

Throughout these essays Kilgo maintains an always questioning, never self-satisfied attitude towards his subject. He is aware that his love of the natural world stands in paradoxical contrast to his love of the hunt, and the resultant tension invests many of the essays with a self-reflective irony. He is never confident of his own motives for enjoying the hunt, never certain that he has conducted himself appropriately, always seeking to understand the causes and consequences of his actions. The essays, therefore, become an extended consideration on how to live and conduct one's affairs in the world.

The title *Deep Enough for Ivorybills* refers to a species of woodpecker widely believed to be extinct, though some naturalists believe it may persist in remote swampy regions of the American southeast. Kilgo uses the ivorybill as a symbol of the qualities that he seeks in the woods and the hunt: an elemental knowledge of self, of kinship with fellow men, of oneness with the natural world. Running throughout these essays is a persistent sense of the author's disquietude–the fear that by having settled too deeply in to his domestic life as a father, husband, and college professor he has lost important connections to his past and the world. By returning to the hunt, accepting the tutelage and friendship of people like Billy Claypoole and Jack Bass, Kilgo seeks to restore these connections, but more importantly to gain assurances about his own identity. He discovers that the hunt itself is not that important, certainly not as a means of masculine self-expression, but serves as a vehicle towards affirmation of the importance of kinship with his family and his fellows. Thus, while the essays at first appear to trace Kilgo's growing appreciation for the hunt, they in fact record his discovery that the hunt is incidental and of his heightened appreciation for the meaning of personal relationships. This is clearly the theme of the final three essays of the book—"Bass Water," "Amazing Grace," and "Peace in the Valley"—which center on the death of Jack Bass and bring the volume to an end on notes of acceptance and valediction.

Inheritance of Horses is a collection of independent essays, rather than a series of closely related narratives centered on a specific subject. There is considerable unity among them, nonetheless, and the effect is that of a unified whole. Turning from the hunt and his sense of alienation from his domestic existence, Kilgo now focuses on concerns closer to home. Members of his immediate family figure significantly in these essays, and Kilgo himself is often the protagonist as he hunts for arrowheads, drinks moon shine with mountain men, or hurdles in a jeep with a friend at breakneck speed down a logging road on Brasstown Bald, the highest mountain in North Georgia. While Kilgo consistently seems to relish the telling of an event, he inevitably moves beyond the event to muse on such issues as time, mortality, friendship, and family. Kilgo is never maudlin or sentimental in his treatment of these issues, nor does he ever become didactic. Rather, his attitudes become evident through implication and context. Emphasis always remains on the experience the essay describes, the interaction between the author and his subject. The most powerful piece in this volume is the final, title essay, in which Kilgo writes about his two grandfathers and recounts his discovery through a cache of family letters of a deep and personal relationship between the men. He uses the discovery to meditate on the themes of friendship, family, heritage, and mortality that bind this collection together.

A Daughter of My People, a novel, relates the story of a love affair in South Carolina early in the twentieth century between a mixed-races woman named Jennie and a white man named Hart Bonner. Jennie herself is part white, the child of a union between Hart Bonner's grandfather and one of his slaves. When Hart's brother Tison becomes attracted to Jennie and attempts to seduce her, Hart kills him, and when Hart realizes that he will be arrested for murder and that Jennie will in one way or the other be punished, he kills himself to protect her. When the Klan gathers outside the Bonner house to "punish" Jennie, the family turns them away, claiming Jennie as one of its own. She is then sent away to work in another part of the state, and the Bonners never see her again.

Although the story contains all the lurid elements of a sensationalist Southern romance––incest, interracial love, murder, hunting, the Klan—Kilgo avoids exploiting them and instead focuses on how the characters bear up under the circumstances of their love affair, on how their families and the surrounding community react as well. Kilgo's prose style is spare and even minimalist, yet at the same time highly descriptive, and the novel's evocations of the swamp country in which the Bonner family lives are especially striking. Hemingway is a clear influence in this book, but Kilgo's prose is distinct and not derivative.

The basic theme of the novel grows out of its historical origins: Kilgo based the story on a series of events from his own family history, and most of the characters are based on his own ancestors. However, he fleshes out these names and events with a fictional context. His basic theme is that of family ties, responsibility, and identity. These govern both his portrayal of the Bonner family as well as to his treatment of race. For the most part, Kilgo avoids analyzing Jennie and Hart from a modern perspective. Hart does love Jennie, but he is also a product of his own times, and the paradox between his inherited racism and his genuine love for a black woman is often evident. Jennie loves Hart, but she is also resentful that their affair must remain clandestine and that to the outside community she is still a white man's black whore. Kilgo does not present the Bonner family as representative of Southern whites in the post-Reconstruction South, nor does he suggest that his story is a revisionist account of black-white race relations. Still, his implication is that the lives of white and black Southerners are complexly intertwined, and that racial problems in America must be resolved on the basis of these connections, rather than of differences.

In his nonfiction and his fiction Kilgo compulsively links his observations of the outer world with his own efforts to define and understand his place in his family and among his fellow men. His best work, especially his non-fiction, is distinguished by his rich narrative voice and his keen ability to record experiences and observations with a vigorous, compelling language. In essays about the hunt, the natural world, and his family Kilgo takes subjects well traveled by other writers and makes them fresh, new, and distinctly his own.

—Hugh Ruppersburg

KINCAID, Nanci

Born: Nanci Leigh Pierce Kincaid in Tallahassee, Florida, 5 September 1950. **Education:** Undergraduate studies at University of Wyoming and Virginia Tech; Athens State College, Athens, Alabama, 1986-87, B.A. in English; University of Alabama, Tuscaloosa, M.F.A. fiction writing 1991. **Family:** Married Dick Tomey; five children. **Career:** Instructor, University of Alabama, 1988-90, University of North Carolina, Charlotte, 1992-96, Carolina Writer's Workshop, Wingate University, 1998; panelist, including Southern Literacy Festival, Nashville, 1992, Writers Today Conference, Birmingham Southern, Alabama, 1992, and Southern Literacy Festival, 1997; keynote speaker, Eudora Welty Writer's Conference, Columbus, Mississippi, 1993; visiting writer, Meridian Community College, Meridian, Mississippi, 1994; presenter, North Carolina Writer's Network, 1995, Eudora Welty Writer's Conference, Mississippi University for Women, 1998, and Brandeis University National Women's Committee, Tucson Chapter, Book and Author, 1998. **Awards:** Herbert L. Hughes Fiction Award, *The Rectangle*, 1986-87; W. B. Yeats Writer's Award, Athens State College, 1987; Fiction Award, Southern Literary Festival, Oxford, Mississippi, 1987; Virginia Center for Creative Arts Fellowship, 1989; Teaching Writing Fellowship, University of Alabama, 1990; University of Alabama Graduate Council Fellowship, 1990-91; MacDowell Colony Fellowship, 1993; Yaddo Fellowship, 1989 and 1994; Mary Ingraham Bunting Fellow, Radcliffe College, 1994-95; Emerging Artist Award, Alabama Fine Arts Society, 1996.

PUBLICATIONS

Novels

Crossing Blood. New York, G.P. Putnam Sons, 1992.
Balls. Chapel Hill, Algonquin Books, 1998.

Short Story Collection

Pretending the Bed Is a Raft. Chapel Hill, Algonquin, 1997.

Uncollected Short Stories

"Like the Old Wolf In All Those Wolf Stories," in *St. Andrew's Review*, 1987.
"Head Walking," in *The Rectangle*, 1987.
"Past Useless," in *Missouri Review*, 1991.
"Any Crazy Body," in *Southern Exposure*, 1991.
"Above the Neck," in *New Letters*, 1991.
"For Colored Only," in *Emrys Journal*, 1991.
"Can't Speak For the Sky," in *Ontario Review*, 1991.
"A Sturdy Pair of Shoes That Fit Good," in *Crescent Review*, 1991.
"Heaven is No Use If You're Dead When You Get There," in *Shenandoah*, 1992.
"Snakes," in *Southern Exposure*, 1992.
"Won't Nobody Ever Love You Like Your Daddy Does," in "Walking on Water," *Southern Humanities Review*, 1994.
"This is Not the Picture Show," in *New Stories From the South*, Chapel Hill, Algonquin Books, 1996.

Uncollected Poems

"White Picket Fences," in *The Owen Wister Review*, 1985.
"Scraps That Fall" and "Looking for a Little Mild Trouble," in *Elk River Review*, 1991.
"Boiled Peanuts," in *The Rectangle*, 1987.
"Blue Eyes and Such," in *St. Andrew's Review*, 1987.

Uncollected Essays

"The Place Poe Knows," in *The Carolina Quarterly*, 1995.
"As Me and Addie Lay Dying," in *The Southern Review*, 1994.
"If They're So Smart Why Can't They Talk Right?," in *Novel and Short Stories Writer's Market*, 1991.

*

Nanci Kincaid comments:

My mother worried that I was an eavesdropper. She used to call me "radar ears." All my life I've been accused of hearing what was never said—of chronically over-hearing, you know. Like many basically shy people (some folks may want to dispute this claim), I'm more or less in a constant state of listening. I think that's why I write—because I'm so full of voices and phrases constantly echoing, cluttering up my mind. I have to write them out to clear my head, to clear some space for something else.

I come from a family of good people, the kind of people who are a little uneasy with fiction because after all it's technically a bunch of lies you're trying to make people believe. It's like lying on purpose or something. Maybe even getting paid to lie. I think my family might be happier if I'd just give up on fiction and try my hand at the factual truth or something. Write some uplifting stories that would make everybody feel good. Devotional, maybe. Of course, that's exactly what I'm doing in my own way.

I'm never sure whether it's the lies my family object to in fiction or all the truth those lies tell. That's the magic—that you can create a fictional character and put him/her in a fictional setting and circumstance and be totally surprised by the way this character manages things—by what he/she has to teach you about yourself and this all-too-real world we live in. The trouble is you can never count on a fictional character (or any real ones either) to teach you exactly what you want to learn. They don't promise to promote your fondly held beliefs, or your personal view of the world. Often, just the opposite. In the best fiction, I think, you can locate enough of yourself to relax and trust, but at the same time be challenged and stretched by the unfamiliar.

*   *   *

Though she no longer lives in the region, novelist and short story writer Nanci Kincaid considers herself a Southern writer and claims Alabama as her home state. She grew up, in the 1950s and 1960s, in Florida and Alabama, in "a dual culture. An either/or world." Everyone fell into categories: black or white, rich or poor, male or female, saved or unsaved, ignorant or educated, Southern or not. "In the sixties," she continued, "when the Civil Rights movement took hold of the South, it took hold of me too and to this day has never let go . . . I think of the black-white conflict as the most crucial issue in American life—because in my American life that was/is true."

Much of Kincaid's work is concerned with revealing how complicated this "either/or," "black-white" region actually is. In her fiction, she is often interested in apprehending it in as pure a state as possible and, like Harper Lee and Elise Sanguinetti, frequently employs the point of view of children, particularly adolescent girls, whose attention is wide-eyed but not naive. For instance, her first novel, *Crossing Blood*, set in Florida and Alabama, is the first-person narrative of a young girl, Lucy Conyers, who comes of age in the South of the 1960s. Through her pretty mother, Sarah, who practices the Christian values of tolerance and love, and her stepfather, Walter, a decent man who believes in the Southern "natural order," Lucy witnesses the blighting character of race hate on even the most private aspects of life. When Lucy and her family move out of their trailer and into a small house at the end of California Street in Tallahassee, Florida, they are "about as close to French Town as you can get and still be a white person." On the other side of the dividing line are their black neighbors, Melvina, Old Alfonso, and their brood of children. The families' parallel existence and the invisible but rigid boundary between them fascinate Lucy.

Lucy is attracted to Melvina's intelligent and wary son Skippy. For Kincaid, desire and love are most often positive values that attest to a natural yearning for the other. More mysterious and harder to explain are the complex categories that govern the interactions of black and white adults. Indeed, what Lucy grapples with, and what Kincaid is so good at representing, is the interaction of race, socialization, and personality. Ultimately, the people Lucy knows and loves defy categorization, but damage is done: tensions ignite between Lucy's family and Melvina's because of Old Alfonso's "niggerish ways." Violence flares, and blame and hate divide the families. Eventually, though, small gestures are made—a gift of money, a jar of soup—and though they signify neither forgiveness nor forgetting, they do point to a recognition that life, bigger than any individual or his or her actions, goes on. When Lucy and Skippy finally embrace, their connection is a hopeful sign.

In *Crossing Blood*, Kincaid so skillfully and tenderly delineates the love, need, and overlapping lives of Sarah and Melvina that their relationship is a central drama of the book. In this it anticipates her collection of short stories, *Pretending the Bed Is a Raft*, published in 1997. In its eight stories, Kincaid looks intensely, often from a young girl's or woman's point of view, at love, infidelity, friendship, children, death, and responsibility. For example, in "Like Your Daddy Does" young Tammy begins to see that love and betrayal are not clear cut. "When I was fourteen I had good and bad memories, too, but things change places, Tammy," her mother, Norma June, says to her, explaining how she can have continued a long-time affair with her next-door neighbor's husband. In "Just Because They've Got Papers Doesn't Mean They Aren't Still Dogs," the longest piece in the collection, one woman's grief over her husband's death precipitates in another a meditation on loss—of loved ones, football games, jobs, and dogs—and love. In the title story, a young wife and mother, poor, burdened, and dying of cancer, methodically and purposefully makes the most

of her last days and reveals what pleasure and happiness a short life can hold and share. Loss of innocence, growing pains, and the power of physical love to heal are among the themes dominating the collection, but a more fundamental concern is the impact of these experiences on the human spirit and its will to endure.

Kincaid's nonfiction mirrors many of her fictional concerns. In her essay, "As Me and Addie Lay Dying," Kincaid explores Southern womanhood, its limited expectations, radical contradictions, and crushing sacrifices. She delineates the influence of representations of the South and the cult of true womanhood in her own life and in contemporary fiction. In her contribution to *Daughters of Kings*, "Not a Jewish Woman," she expands her ideas of what it means to be a Southerner and a woman. More and more in these essays and, she hints, in her forthcoming novel, *Balls*, she looks at the South from the outside, from the perspective of non-Southerners and at a geographical remove: "To be of a culture, but without the culture, can be an eye-opening experience," she writes.

If *Pretending the Bed Is a Raft* is indicative, Kincaid is honing her focus on the interior lives of regular people—who live in trailer parks, coach football teams, and do secretarial work—and how they exercise desire, make love and find fulfillment, achieve understanding, and define themselves in the world. Her published work has established her willingness to question and explore the codes on which personal and social interaction are based. Her representations of Southern life and of women and children have authenticity and dimension, and they increasingly point toward new insights and fresh images. She explores how human potential can be crushed or limited by circumstances and discovers quite often that it nevertheless finds expression. Her vision is rooted in experience—"Expect the worst," says Belinda, the speaker in the short story "Total Recoil"—and she eschews nostalgia and sentimentality. But her vision is not bleak, and to "expect the worst" we must add "but believe the best can happen." The redemptive powers of love, forgiveness, and acceptance are a code for grace, which, her fiction affirms, is, in sometimes surprising forms, available to us.

—Jay Lamar

KING, Florence

Pseudonyms: Laura Buchanan, Cynthia, Veronica King, Emmett X. Reed, Niko Stavros, and Mike Winston. **Born:** Washington, D.C., 5 January 1936. **Education:** American University, B.A. 1957; University of Mississippi, 1958-59. **Career:** History teacher, Suitland, Maryland, mid-1950s; file clerk, National Association of Realtors, late 1950s; feature writer, *Raleigh News and Observer*, Raleigh, North Carolina, 1964-67; assistant editor, *Uncensored Confessions*, 1967-68; book reviewer, *Newsday*; novelist, essayist, and columnist since mid-1960s, including *National Review* ("The Misanthrope's Corner"); Member of usage panel, *American Heritage Dictionary*, 1986. **Awards:** North Carolina Press Women Award, 1965, for reporting.

PUBLICATIONS

Nonfiction

Southern Ladies and Gentlemen. New York, Stein & Day, 1976.
WASP, Where Is Thy Sting? New York, Stein & Day, 1976.
He: An Irreverent Look at the American Male. New York, Stein & Day, 1978.
When Sisterhood Was in Flower. New York, Viking, 1982.
Reflections in a Jaundiced Eye. New York, St. Martin's, 1990.
Lump It or Leave It. New York, St. Martin's, 1990.
With Charity Toward None: A Fond Look at Misanthropy. New York, St. Martin's, 1992.
The Florence King Reader. New York, St. Martin's, 1996.

Fiction

The Barbarian Princess, as Laura Buchanan. New York, Berkeley Publishing, 1977.
Confessions of a Failed Southern Lady. New York, St. Martin's, 1985.

*   *   *

An iconoclast by trade, Florence King is a bisexual, self-proclaimed "right wing Republican" and royalist who collects guns and is known for her sharp wit and caustic observations. She considers copy editors "brachycephalic, web-footed cretins who ought to be in an institution learning how to make brooms," for example, derides do-gooders as "Helpists," and declares that "trying to sell books to TV watchers is like selling chastity in a brothel."

King was born and raised in Washington, D.C., the child of a tomboy mother (who delighted in cursing and once hung a punching bag in the gazebo) and a gentle English father. After graduating from American University in 1957, King undertook a year of study at the University of Mississippi, where her literary career began, in a sense. While in Oxford she wrote over 100 stories for such magazines as *Uncensored Confessions*, beginning with "My God! I'm Too Passionate for My Own Good!." She moved on because, as she observed, "eventually there were no sins left and it hurt the confessions magazines." Following a three-year stint writing interviews and wedding announcements for the *Raleigh News and Observer*, King again turned her attention to erotic fiction, eventually writing thirty-seven novels (among them *Moby's Dick*) under a number of pseudonyms. King believes these experiences rendered valuable lessons in writing, particularly discipline, which she characterizes as learning "how to apply the seat of the pants to the seat of the chair."

It was during a decade spent in Seattle that King published her first book under her own name. *Southern Ladies and Gentlemen*, based on an article she published in *Harper's*, is a witty and often very shrewd discussion of Southern social phenomena, including "the gay confederation," the differences between rednecks and good ole boys, and the role of "female trouble" in perpetuating the Southern matriarchy. This book was soon followed by similar studies of repression and social behavior, *WASP, Where Is Thy Sting?, He: An Irreverent Look at the American Male,* and *When*

Sisterhood Was in Flower, a satire of feminism, then two fictional works, a bodice-ripper called *The Barbarian Princess* (published under the name Laura Buchanan) and the heavily autobiographical *Confessions of a Failed Southern Lady*. *Confessions of a Failed Southern Lady* is a fictional recounting of King's life story, with stereotypes replaced by more endearing, if still bizarre, characters.

Following *Confessions*, King encountered what she considers one of the most formative experiences of her career as a writer—menopause. As she noted: "I never liked being a woman, I never liked having to be feminine, although I could do a pretty good imitation of it. But once you go through the menopause, you get your true personality back." In *Reflections in a Jaundiced Eye*, her first book after this momentous event, King's work took the harsher tone that characterizes her later work, as readers of her *National Review* column, "The Misanthrope's Corner," know well. This collection contains King's popular satire on "Helpism," an American penchant for believing "expert" problem-solvers can improve the lives of individuals. She also identifies America's greatest social problem as an epidemic of "feminized" niceness that mires society in a helpless tolerance of everything. This affliction, King believes, is merely the repression of natural misanthropy and takes the form of political correctness ("nothing more than female touchiness writ large"), the anti-smoking crusade, environmental extremism, and the faux "friendliness" of American politics and advertising.

As King develops these themes in this collection and in *Lump It or Leave It* and *With Charity Toward None*, the ultimate source of cloying sweetness is democracy itself, for in a democratic society one's status is in large measure a matter of the opinions of others. Rather than carry the burden of constant sweetness and light, she proposes that all people should frankly admit true and natural feelings. More than an ideal therapy, misanthropy is also the source of genuine wit. As King noted, in order to be truly witty one "must have a dismal outlook on life and human nature. You have to be a misanthrope, a loner, an introvert—all the things Americans don't want to be and don't think people should be. Wit goes for the jugular; humor goes for the jocular."

With Charity Toward None specifically addresses King's views on democracy, which in her opinion forces a false charity upon the individual and is a chief enemy of excellence. Considering what she calls excessive niceness, such human characteristics as superior beauty, talent, and wit are not considered positive qualities in democratic societies, but instead an assault on the self-esteem of those less beautiful, talented, or witty.

The Florence King Reader, which collects her eight previously published works released since the mid-1970s, is not a conventional anthology. King remarks in her introduction, with her usual bluntness: "One of the values of an anthology is supposed to be the opportunity it gives readers to see how an author has grown over the years. Well, tough titty." Instead, King claims to "have cut, revised, edited and in general rewritten the excerpts. Polishing and tightening my prose is my idea of good, clean narcissistic fun." With a kind of common sense humor poking at absurdities in American life, King has indeed played the role of misanthrope. She summed herself up to

Alanna Nash in *Writer's Digest,* "I don't suffer fools, and I like to see fools suffer."

—Jason Mitchell

KINGSOLVER, Barbara

Born: Annapolis, Maryland, 8 April 1955. **Education:** DePauw University, B.A. (magna cum laude) 1977; University of Arizona, M.S. 1981, and additional graduate study. **Family:** Married Joseph Hoffmann, 1985; two daughters. **Career:** Various odd jobs, including archaeologist, x-ray technician, biological researcher, and technical editor; research assistant in department of physiology, 1977-79, technical writer in office of arid lands studies, 1981-85, University of Arizona, Tucson; free-lance journalist, 1985-87; full-time writer, since 1987; established the annual Bellwether Prize in 1997 for first-time novelist whose work reflects literary merit and social commitment. **Awards:** Feature-writing award, Arizona Press Club, 1986; American Library Association awards, 1988, for *The Bean Trees,* and 1990, for *Homeland;* citation of accomplishment from United Nations National Council of Women, 1989; PEN fiction prize and Edward Abbey Ecofiction Award, both 1991, for *Animal Dreams.* **Member:** International Women's Writing Guild, Amnesty International, Committee for Human Rights in Latin America, Phi Beta Kappa. **Agent:** Frances Goldin, 305 East Eleventh St., New York, New York 10003. **Website:** http://www.kingsolver.com.

PUBLICATIONS

Novels

The Bean Trees. New York, Harper, 1988.
Animal Dreams. New York, Harper, 1990.
Pigs in Heaven. New York, HarperCollins, 1994.

Short Story Collection

Homeland and Other Stories. New York, Harper, 1989.

Nonfiction

Holding the Line: Women in the Great Arizona Mine Strike of 1983. Tucson, ILR Press, 1989.
High Tide in Tucson: Essays from Now or Never. New York, HarperCollins, 1995.

Poetry

Another America/Otra America. New York, Seal Press, 1994.

Other

The Complete Fiction: The Bean Trees, Homeland and Other Stories, Animal Dreams, Pigs in Heaven. New York, HarperCollins, 1995.

*

Critical Studies: *A Reader's Guide to The Fiction of Barbara Kingsolver: The Bean Trees, Homeland and Other Stories, Animal Dreams, Pigs in Heaven,* edited by Jennifer Fleischner, New York, HarperPerennial, 1994.

*   *   *

Barbara Kingsolver's works stress the importance of involvement in family, community, and the natural world, of actively moving from an emphasis on self to participation with and caring for others and asserting oneself in social causes. Her protagonists are introduced as resourceful young women who feel detached and lack a sense of purpose beyond immediate needs until they take part in events that bring them into a more active role in family and community affairs. Similarly, her works begin as easy-going, engaging, amusing reads while gradually introducing compelling issues—abuse, illegal immigration and adoption, environmental hazards, the effects of encroaching commercialization. Metaphors and allusions—relating to the natural world, dreams, and Native American legends—are among devices that further enrich her stories of characters who come alive and find a sense of dignity by recognizing conflicts and hardships and taking an active role in helping to resolve them.

Kingsolver's own social activism came early. In second grade she wrote an essay, "Why We Need a New Elementary School," that was published in her local, rural Kentucky newspaper and helped encourage voters to pass a bond issue bringing more funds to the school district. Her 1995 collection of 25 essays, *High Tide in Tucson,* reflects her concern for family, community, and the natural world, ranging on such topics as her battle of wills with her two-year-old daughter to the significance of a wild pig in her garden. She also writes about her experiences in Africa (where she traveled as a child with her parents), Europe (where she lived after graduating from Depauw University), and the Southwest, where she settled while attaining an M.S. at the University of Arizona.

Kingsolver's biology background is evident in her loving recreation of natural settings apparent in all her work, and her continued social activism is reflected in her support of various causes that take precedence over author tours and celebrity-circuit rounds. In 1997, after having become established over the past decade as a respected and popular writer, Kingsolver instituted the Bellwether Prize, an annual award given to a first novel that represents outstanding literary quality and a commitment to serious fiction as a tool for social change.

Kingsolver's first novel, *The Bean Trees* (1988), exemplifies such merit and commitment. It begins as a spirited "on the road" journey across America, as Marietta Greer sets off in a 1955 Volkswagen to escape her small-town Kentucky life that, for her, holds no promise. She takes a new name, Taylor, based on the first town where she buys gasoline (having kept her "fingers crossed through Sidney, Sadorus, Cerro, Gordo, Decatur, and Blue Mound," Illinois). This kind of breezy style is maintained until the car breaks down in Oklahoma and Taylor is given an abused baby, whom she names Turtle, to care for. She presses on to Arizona, where another automotive problem leads to her discovery of illegal aliens and the existence of Guatemalan death squads. The two stops, then, become catalysts for her commitment to caring for another human being and becoming involved in political causes. Kingsolver's description of natural settings (including the Bean Tree metaphor) and urban environments (featuring such enterprises as Jesus Is Lord Used Tires) add depth and humor to the work.

Taylor and Turtle return in *Pigs in Heaven* (1994), living a calm and uneventful life until a freak accident brings media attention to Turtle and she is recognized by a member of her Native American community back in Oklahoma. Taylor runs off with Turtle, but their dire circumstances and a combination of events—some humorous, as when Taylor's mother arrives on the scene and offers a unique solution to complicated legal entanglements over Turtle's adoption, some touching, as when Taylor comes to realize that her reasons for wanting to keep the child may not be in the child's best interest—leads to their return to Oklahoma. Their progression from isolation to a larger sense of finding a home is underscored by descriptions of Native American community gatherings in Oklahoma.

Animal Dreams (1990), published between the Taylor/Turtle novels, is Kingsolver's most artistic work, drawing on dreams, natural imagery, and Native American legends for symbols and extended metaphors and employing dual narrators. The novel relates the search for identity of Codi Noline, who returns to her hometown (significantly called Grace, Arizona) to care for her ailing father. The father-daughter relationship had long been strained, and Codi had never felt a sense of community in Grace, both of which contribute to her lifelong feeling of alienation. Caring for her father and becoming involved in local environmental and social conflicts activates her sense of purpose, however. As in Kingsolver's other novels, the movement from self-concern to family and community involvement is presented subtly and in original ways, with different events and metaphors that make each of the works unique and non-formulaic. This development of rising social consciousness, expanded by Kingsolver's natural metaphors and imagery, were recognized by critics and resulted in such honors for *Animal Dreams* as the PEN fiction prize and the Edward Abbey Ecofiction Award.

Similar traits are evident in Kingsolver's other works. In addition to *High Tide in Tucson* and her three novels, Kingsolver has published a short story collection, *Homeland and Other Stories* (the title story announces the major theme of the stories—searching for home), *Another America/Otra America* (with poems in English and Spanish that address harrowing realities of war and abuse), and *Holding the Line: Women in the Great Arizona Mine Strike of 1983* (about the role of women in the Phelps Dodge Copper Company labor conflict). A political agenda is more apparent in Kingsolver's poetry and non-fiction work, but it seems a logical outcome for someone who has shown repeatedly in her fiction and her actions that involvement in community—from family to society—is inevitable and necessary to expand beyond self and into larger purposes.

—Perry Bear

KLAPPERT, Peter

Born: Rockville Center, New York, 14 November 1942. **Education**: Cornell University, B.A. 1964; University of Iowa, M.A.

1967, M.F.A. 1968. **Career:** Rollins College, Winter Park, Florida, instructor in English, 1968-71; Harvard University, Briggs-Copeland Lecturer in English and General Education, 1971-74; visiting lecturer, New College, Sarasota, Florida, 1972; writer-in-residence, 1976-77, assistant professor, 1977-78, College of William and Mary; since 1978, assistant professor of English, George Mason University. **Awards:** Yale Series of Younger Poets award, 1970, for *Lugging Vegetables to Nantucket*; resident fellowships at Yaddo, 1972, 1973, 1975, at MacDowell Colony, 1973, 1975, at Virginia Center for the Creative Arts, 1978, and at Millay Colony for the Arts, 1978; National Endowment for the Arts fellowship in creative writing, 1973; Lucille Medick Award, Poetry Society of America, 1977. **Address:** Department of English, George Mason University, 4400 University Dr., Fairfax, Virginia 22030.

PUBLICATIONS

Poetry Collections

Lugging Vegetables to Nantucket. New Haven, Yale University Press, 1971.
Circular Stairs, Distress in the Mirrors, Marlboro, Vermont, Griffin Press, 1975.
The Idiot Princess of the Last Dynasty. New York, Knopf, 1984.
52 Pick-up: Scenes from the Conspiracy. Orchises, 1984.

Other

On a Beach in Southern Connecticut (chapbook). Iowa City, Annual Increase, 1966.
After the Rhymer's Guild (essay and chapbook), Sarasota, New College Press, 1971.
Non Sequitur O'Connor (chapbook). Cleveland, Bits Press, 1977.

Contributor, *Language and Public Policy*. National Council of Teachers of English, Chicago, 1973.
Contributor, *Fifty Contemporary Poets: The Creative Process*, edited by Alberta T. Turner. New York, McKay, 1977.
Contributor, *The Young American Poets*. New York, Follett, 1972.
Contributor, *The American Poetry Anthology*. New York, Avon, 1976.
Contributor, *The Ardis Anthology of Contemporary American Poetry*, New York, Ardis, 1976.

*

Critical Studies: "Wit and Then Some" by X. J. Kennedy, *Counter/Measures*, Vol. 2, 1973; "An Interview with Peter Klappert" by Kathe Davis Finney and Michael Finney, *Falcon*, Spring 1977; "Loss of a Landscape" by Gary Q. Arpin, *Greenfield Review*, Spring-Summer 1979; "Peter Klappert Speaks Out" by Gabriele Glang, *Phoebe*, Summer 1979.

*   *   *

Peter Klappert's poetry features sophisticated interplay of philosophy, dark humor, and verbal wit, displaying a mastery of language in many verse forms, which combine to create an emotional and intellectual argument for the reconciliation of rationalism and compassion. Klappert's poetry constitutes a body of work that abjures religious and political affiliations, subjects that he frequently satirizes along with intellectual and moral absolutism. He has said, "I am drawn to the amoral quality of art, the way it stands outside moral codes or, more accurately, creates its own moralities. In any case, that's why I write; to locate myself in time and space, to discover what I truly believe and feel."

Many of Klappert's poems are thematically linked by his detailing of extreme contrasts between humanity's capability for kindness and its most violent and base behavior. Klappert's perception of humanity's failure to live according to civilized ideals is often tempered by his use of comedic examples of human frailty. Many poems catalogue modern methods of inhumanity, much of which is focused on World War II atrocities.

In style and form, Klappert's work resembles the verse of American poets Wallace Stevens and Theodore Roethke, though Klappert moved away from Stevens' concern with aesthetics ("Five years ago I was quite deliberately a disciple of Wallace Stevens, but I find, now, that I am much more interested in poems than in the theory of poetry," he stated in *The Young American Poets*, published in 1972). Stevens's attempt to synthesize form and function while addressing reality and the imagination, and the resonant nature of language employed by Roethke to examine psychological and emotional themes are important considerations when reading Klappert's verse. He has published only four full collections, all between 1971 and 1984, concentrating most of his attention on teaching. Klappert has been an instructor at George Mason University since 1978.

Klappert was born in Rockville Center, New York. His father was a film producer whose responsibilities included photographing World War II Nazi concentration camp atrocities for use by the prosecution at the Nuremberg Trials. Klappert attended Cornell University—originally as a preveterinary student, then as an English major with a minor in zoology —and the University of Iowa, where he earned both an M.A. in Renaissance literature and an M.F.A. in the Writers Workshop.

Klappert's won the prestigious Yale Series of Younger Poets competition in 1970 for verse published in his first major volume, *Lugging Vegetables to Nantucket* (1971). The poems are marked by verbal energy, even a sense of youthful swagger, displaying Klappert's use of puns and humor, his attention to sound and rhythms of language, and his adept handling of poetic forms. They reflect Klappert's assertion, a year later, that "Words are not simply a means: they are in themselves—in their heft, feel, plunge, resonance, shape, aerodynamics—part of the end." Thematically, many of the poems—including "The Babysitters," a long satirical poem about academia, and the shorter "Poem for L. C."—present language as the last defense against the extremes of academic sterility and cultural and behavioral socialization.

Klappert avows that imprecise use of language results in comic or tragic implications for individuals, social groups, and even nations, obscuring or abstracting real meaning. A facility with language by the personae in "The Babysitters" becomes a device to avoid immersion in human experience. It is the poet's responsibility, according to Klappert, to use language to breach alienation and to serve as arbiter of the language that binds humanity to more ideal behavior. Klappert stated that he felt his ideal reader, "Would

be one who loves language, who is attracted by the mystery—the unparaphrasability—of successful poems, and who believes in the basic, decent, high-minded (but not necessarily humorless) seriousness of art, even as he loathes the pomposity of saying so."

Klappert's concerns with the importance of language and alienation are expanded in his later work. *Circular Stairs, Distress in the Mirrors* (1975) concerns the shadow, or double, in a Jungian sense, reflected in poems that address relationships between the conscious and unconscious personality and limitations in experiencing reality solely through rational constructs. The poems are frequently peopled by individuals unable to connect rational and emotional aspects of their personality and are, therefore, unable to connect emotionally with others. The unconscious is probed further in *The Idiot Princess of the Last Dynasty* (1984), which included the first installments of Klappert's long sequence "Non Sequitur O'Conner."

Inspired by his reading of Djuna Barnes's 1936 novel *Nightwood*, Klappert began writing poems in the voice of one of the book's characters, Dr. Matthew O'Connor; that Europe was on the brink of World War II adds further resonance to O'Connor's commentary. In Barnes's novel, O'Connor—based on a real figure from the Paris streets of the 1930s—is a transvestite, an abortionist, and a disenfranchised Roman Catholic. Klappert uses O'Conner as an embodiment of moral impotency in the twentieth century: O'Connor witnesses the horrors of modern times without ever fully engaging in them and at the same time is ineffective in preventing them. "The Vietnam protest period is certainly related to my involvement in all this," Klappert said in a 1979 interview. He also credits the photo albums of Nazi crimes kept by his father after the Nuremberg Trials.

In another interview, Klappert elaborated on the connection he perceived between Nazi atrocities and Vietnam: "There was the Vietnam War and the question of collaboration with the enemy, which for many of us between 1965 and 1974 was our own elected government. That led to the question of what I would have done under the Nazi Occupation. Could I imaginatively get myself into it enough to get a sense of what I might have been capable of? Coming from a middle-class background, would I have done what the uptight middle class has always done—watch out for itself?... I decided to plunge into the ugliest side of human history. Going down and through instead of over." Klappert places his insightful, if dubious prophet at the sites of the century's most horrific actions as well as at such cultural landmarks as the literary and artistic salons of Paris during the 1920s.

—Bruce Walker

KOMUNYAKAA, Yusef

Born: Bogalusa, Louisiana, 29 April 1947. **Education:** University of Colorado, B.A. 1975; Colorado State University, M.A. 1978; University of California, Irvine, M.F.A. 1980. **Military Service**: Served in Vietnam as a correspondent and editor of *The Southern Cross*, 1969-70; recipient of Bronze Star. **Family:** Married Mandy Sayer. **Career:** Instructor of English composition,

Colorado State University, 1976-78; teaching assistant in poetry and writing instructor, University of California, Irvine, 1980; instructor in English composition and American literature, University of New Orleans, 1982-84; poet-in-the-schools, New Orleans, Louisiana, 1984-85; professor of English, Indiana University, 1985-97; visiting associate professor, 1991-92, and Holloway Lecturer, University of California, Berkeley, 1992-93; visiting professor, Washington University, St. Louis, 1995-96; professor of creative writing, Princeton University, 1997-present; editor, *Ploughshares* (journal), Spring 1997. **Awards:** San Francisco Poetry Center Award, 1986; Thomas Forcade Award, 1991; *Kenyon Review* Award for Literary Excellence, 1991; Kingsley Tufts Award, Pulitzer Prize, William Faulkner Prize, all 1994, for *Neon Vernacular: New and Selected Poems*; *Colorado Review* Literary Award, 1995; Furious Flowers Award, James Madison University, 1995; Hanes Poetry Prize, 1997.

PUBLICATIONS

Poetry Collections

Dedications & Other Darkhorses. Boulder, Rocky Mountain Creative Arts Journal, 1977.
Lost in the Bonewheel Factory. Amherst, Massachusetts, Lynx House Press, 1979.
Copacetic. Middletown, Connecticut, Wesleyan University Press, 1984.
I Apologize for the Eyes in My Head. Middletown, Connecticut, Wesleyan University Press, 1986.
Toys in a Field. N.p., Black River Press, 1986.
Dien Cai Dau. Middletown, Connecticut, Wesleyan University Press, 1988.
February in Sydney. N.p., Matchbooks, 1989.
Magic City. Middletown, Connecticut, Wesleyan University Press, 1992.
Neon Vernacular: New and Selected Poems. Middletown, Connecticut, Wesleyan University Press, 1993.
Thieves of Paradise. Middletown, Connecticut, Wesleyan University Press, 1998.

Other

Author of introduction, *Interrogations,* by Leroy Quintana. Tucson, Burning Cities Press, 1990.
Author of introduction, *Dragonfly,* by Vince Gotera. San Antonio, Pecan Grove Press, 1995.

Coeditor, with J.A.S. Feinstein, *The Jazz Poetry Anthology.* Bloomington, Indiana University Press, 1991.
Coeditor, with J.A.S. Feinstein, *The Second Set: The Jazz Poetry Anthology, II.* Bloomington, Indiana University Press, 1997.

Translator, with Martha Collins, *The Insomnia of Fire by Nguyen Quang Thieu.* Amherst, University of Massachusetts Press, 1995.

Contributor, *Southern California Anthology*, Vol. XIII, edited by X. J. Kennedy. Los Angeles, Scanthology-Professional Writing Program, 1996.

*

Interviews: "Lines of Tempered Steel: An Interview with Yusef Komunyakaa" with Vincente F. Gotera, *Callaloo: A Journal of African American and African Arts and Letters*, Spring 1990; with Muna Asali, *New England Review*, Winter 1994; *Swing Low: Black Men Writing* by Rebecca Carroll, New York, Carol Southern Books, 1995.

Critical Studies: "Depending on the Light: Yusef Komunyakaa's *Dien Cai Dau*" by Vincente F. Gotera, *America Rediscovered: Critical Essays on Literature and Film of the Vietnam War* edited by Owen W. Gilman, New York, Garland, 1990; "Folk Idiom in the Literary Expression of Two African American Authors: Rita Dove and Yusef Komunyakaa" by Kirkland C. Jones, *Language and Literature in the African American Imagination* edited by Carol Blackshire Belay, Westport, Connecticut, Greenwood Press, 1992; "Yusef Komunyakaa: The Unified Vision" by Alvin Aubert, *African-American Review*, Spring 1993; "Rejecting 'Sweet Geometry': Komunyakaa's 'Duende'" by Don Ringnalda, *Journal of American Culture*, Fall 1993; "On Yusef Komunyakaa" by Michael Faber, *The Southern Quarterly*, Winter 1996.

*   *   *

Yusef Komunyakaa often concludes his poems with a surprising turn of some kind. In "Facing It," for instance, the poet recalls viewing the Vietnam Veterans Memorial in Washington, D.C. Komunyakaa himself served as a reporter for a military newspaper in Vietnam, and he describes feelings of sorrow, sympathy, and alienation as he confronts the black granite wall. The poem ends as he looks away from his own dim reflection in the wall to watch another visitor:

In the black mirror
a woman's trying to erase names:
No, she's brushing a boy's hair.

With that gentle self-correction, the poet captures the power of the imagination that is animating the woman's visible actions. We are surprised not only by the abrupt shift in perspective from that of the poet to that of another mourner, but by the compensations of memory and the woman's poignant (if temporary) denial of present pain. In a 1994 interview, Komunyakaa confirms the value of the unexpected in poetry: "If I don't have surprises, poetry doesn't work for me. What gives my poetry its surprising element is that I have not systematically planned out in a directed way what I am going to say. It is a process of getting back to the unconscious." He tells his poetry students "to be ready for the surprises, and to take them as gifts," and Komunyakaa's poems are full of such reverence for the gifts of feeling, language, and experience.

Komunyakaa has taught at all levels of education and currently holds the position of professor of creative writing at Princeton University. He grew up in rural Louisiana, and memories of his childhood provide the subject for many of his poems, especially those in *Magic City* (1992). In one of the poems in that collection, "My Father's Love Letters," Komunyakaa speaks of both his disdain and respect for his father. The poet recalls writing letters to his absent mother at the dictation of his illiterate and abusive father. The poet acidly remarks, "Sometimes I was happy / She had gone, & sometimes wanted / To slip in a reminder, how

Mary Lou / Williams' Polka Dots & Moonbeams / Never made the swelling go down." But if Komunyakaa criticizes his father, he also seems to identify with him. The poet offers a final vision of his father as an artist figure who possesses an aesthetic sensibility and who struggles almost physically with language:

> This man,
> Who stole roses & hyacinth
> For his yard, would stand there
> With eyes closed & fists balled,
> Laboring over a simple word, almost
> Redeemed by what he tried to say.

Komunyakaa has said that Bogalusa "was a terrible place to grow up, really," due to poverty and racism, and also due to the vocational limitations for black men. Though his literary aspirations were not encouraged, he read enthusiastically and widely among the books available in the Negro library. And not all the recollections of his childhood are melancholy. In "Slam, Dunk, & Hook," the poet writes with fondness of playground basketball games. He writes in a measure at once athletic and delicate, and demonstrates that beauty and poetry were not absent in his early life:

> We had moves we didn't know
> We had.
> Our bodies spun
> On swivels of bone & faith,
> Through a lyric slipknot
> Of joy, & we knew we were
> Beautiful & dangerous.

There is a distinct musical quality—frequently modeled on jazz rhythms—evident in "Slam, Dunk, & Hook" and elsewhere in Komunyakaa's work. He explains that "Poetry is the primary medium I have chosen because of the conciseness, the precision, the imagery, and the music in the lines. I think of language as our first music." His poems are often composed of a single stanza of relatively short lines, and this formal unity symbolizes the kind of unbroken synthesis that is possible in music.

His service in Vietnam is another of Komunyakaa's important (if also "terrible") sources for poetic material. He tells that it was not until after he had returned from the war and written the poem "Instructions for Building Straw Huts" that he felt sure of his poetic calling. Like so many of his other pieces, Komunyakaa's Vietnam poems blend compassion and aggravation, and create vivid images with a minimum of detail. Watching some prisoners of war

> stumble-dance
> across the hot asphalt
> with crokersacks over their heads

the poet asks, of himself as much as of these men

> How can anyone anywhere love
> these half-broken figures
> bent under the sky's brightness"

Komunyakaa has published ten collections of poetry and has edited, translated, or contributed to many more books. He has translated the work of the Vietnamese poet Nguyen Quang Thieu, and Komunyakaa's own poetry has been translated into Czech, French, Italian, Korean, Russian, and Vietnamese. *Neon Vernacular: New and Selected Poems* (1993) won the Pulitzer Prize and contains selections from his first seven books. A *Collected Poems* is due to be published in 1999.

In his most recent publication, *Thieves of Paradise* (1998), Komunyakaa reflects on the virtues and the hazards of becoming an established and anthologized poet. In "What Counts," the poet thumbs through a volume of works by various poets:

> counting the dead faces
> I've known.
> Two Roberts—
> Hayden & Duncan.
> Dick
> Hugo.
> Bill Stafford &
> Nemerov.

He wonders,

> Do I want my name
> here, like x's in the eyes
> of ex-lovers?

For answer, the poet concludes,

> I'm thankful
> for the cities we drank
> wine & talked about swing
> bands from Kansas City
> into the after hours
> under green weather
> in this age of reason.

Again, Komunyakaa surprises. He swerves not to avoid the issue but because the proper response to such a question is no response at all. What counts for this poet has little to do with canonization or with anything else that comes after his poems. Instead, Komunyakaa privileges experience itself and the sensuous rhythms of music, poetry, and love.

—Jeannine Johnson

KURALT, Charles

Born: Charles Bishop Kuralt in Wilmington, North Carolina, 10 September 1934. **Education:** University of North Carolina, B.A. 1955. **Family:** Married Sory Guthery, 1957 (divorced); married Suzanna Folsom Baird, 1 June 1962; two children (first marriage). **Career:** Reporter and columnist, *Charlotte News*, 1955- 57; CBS News, Columbia Broadcasting System, writer, 1957-59, host of *Eyewitness to History*, 1959, correspondent for Latin American bureau, 1960-63, chief correspondent for U.S. West Coast, 1963, overseas correspondent until 1967, feature reporter for "On the Road" segments on *The CBS Evening News*, 1967-97, anchor of

CBS News Sunday Morning, 1979-97; contributor to periodicals, including *Saturday Review, Field and Stream, TV Guide,* and *Reader's Digest.* **Awards:** American Legion Writing Contest, (national; as a high school student); Ernie Pyle Memorial Award, Scripps-Howard Foundation, 1959; nine Emmy Awards, National Academy of Television Arts and Sciences, between 1969-92; George Foster Peabody Broadcasting Awards, University of Georgia, 1969, 1976, and 1979; Media Award, Odyssey Institute, 1979; Broadcaster of the Year, International Radio and Television Society, 1985. **Died:** 4 July 1997.

PUBLICATIONS

Nonfiction

To the Top of the World: The Adventures and Misadventures of the Plaisted Polar Expedition, March 28-May 4, 1967. New York, Holt, 1968.
Dateline America. New York. Harcourt, 1979.
On the Road with Charles Kuralt. New York, Putnam, 1985.
Southerners: Portrait of a People, with Irwin Glusker. Birmingham, Alabama, Oxmoor House, 1986.
North Carolina Is My Home, with Louis McGlohan (also a record album). Charlotte, East Woods, 1986.
A Life on the Road. Putnam, 1990.
Growing up in North Carolina by Charles Kuralt and The Uncommon Laureate: Sketches in the life of Charles Kuralt, by Wallace H. Kuralt, Jr. Chapel Hill, North Caroliniana Society, Inc. and North Carolina Collection, 1993.
Charles Kuralt's America. New York, G.P. Putnam's Sons, 1995.

*

Recordings: Audio—*A Life On the Road,* New York, Simon & Schuster Audioworks, 1990. **Microfilm**—*On the Road with Charles Kuralt,* produced by CBS News, Sanford, North Carolina, Microfilming Corp. of America, 1983. **Video**—*The Spirit of America with Charles Kuralt* (13 vols.; organized by states and regions), CBS News, Santa Monica, BFA Educational Media, 1976; *The Spirit of America with Charles Kuralt: The Declaration of Independence,* CBS News, Santa Monica, BFA Educational Media, 1976; *Satisfaction, A Job Well Done,* CBS News, Santa Monica, Salenger Educational Media, 1984; *20 Years On the Road with Charles Kuralt,* produced by Charles Kuralt and Bernard Birnbaum, director by Ken Sable, New York, Carousel Film & Video, 1988; *On the Road with Charles Kuralt: Unforgettable People,* CBS News, New York, CBS-TV, 1989; *On the Road with Charles Kuralt: The Seasons of America,* CBS News, New York, CBS-TV, 1989.

Charles Kuralt commented:
When I finally shook off the tempo of daily journalism and fell into the rhythms of the countryside, I didn't have to worry about finding stories any longer. They found me.

*   *   *

Jazz pianist Loonis McGlohon, who collaborated with Charles Kuralt on *North Carolina Is My Home,* remembers the time that Kuralt, America's best-known traveling journalist, went with a group of friends to a jazz concert at Carnegie Hall. At the end,

Kuralt, then host of the perennially popular *CBS Evening News* ongoing segment "On the Road," stood with his wife and friends in a stagedoor line of a hundred or so fans to get his program signed by the stars. There were quite a few well-knowns in the crowd; McGlohon remembers his own amusement as the autograph seekers furtively pointed out "Margaret Whiting! Or is that Peggy Lee?" Kuralt passed through unrecognized. "Until," says McGlohon, "we went to the bar after the show. When Charles ordered a drink, every head in the place turned and stared." That deep, ringing voice was unmistakable.

The incident tells much about Kuralt and the way he operated, rarely in the focus of his own limelight. He loved to visit people along the American byways, to find out about their lives and experiences and talents, to put them front and center in his interviews, and to share with the rest of the world the interesting things about them—and there always were interesting things. In the memory of a buddy, Kuralt was "just a big old rambling Southern Everyman," unfazed and certainly unspoiled by his own celebrity.

Charles Bishop Kuralt was born into an educated, middle-class family in Wilmington, North Carolina, on September 10, 1934. Wallace Kuralt, his father, was a social worker, and Ina, his mother, a teacher. The grandparents with whom he spent a lot of his childhood were tobacco farmers. The whole family read a great deal; Charles's brother, Wallace would later become one of the South's best-known booksellers with his Intimate Bookshops, headquartered in Chapel Hill.

While Kuralt was in high school he won an American Legion writing contest, a hint of things to come. His prize included an introduction to President Harry Truman and a radio broadcast of Edward R. Murrow reading the essay. Charles was drawn to broadcasting very early. Loonis McGlohon remembers their first meeting, in the late 1940s, when Loonis was playing jazz at WBT Radio in Charlotte. "Charles was just a kid, 15 years old. He'd come in and hang around. He loved music. But he was already such a good writer." The story was told that Kuralt's deep secret yearning was to sing, himself, on the stage at Carnegie Hall. He knew music and he had a splendid voice—but the twain would rarely meet, on pitch. He would have to stick with speaking.

After he earned his B.A. at the University of North Carolina, Kuralt went to work as a reporter at the *Charlotte News.* It was a paper that fostered fine writers; very shortly Kuralt was given a reserved space for his people stories, the colorful pieces at which he excelled. Says Dick Gorrell, an editor who was Kuralt's *Charlotte Newsy* contemporary, "Those little front-page stories, every day, they WERE Charles Kuralt. And he was those stories." About the time the public became addicted to those pieces, Charles moved on to write news for CBS Radio in New York. He was then 23. He won the Ernie Pyle Memorial Award for reporting in 1959. At that time television was the coming medium and a year into his job at CBS he was writing television news. As a correspondent he would soon cover the 1960 presidential election, then traveled the world, reporting from far corners. Such success is not won so early without cost. His young marriage to Sory Guthery, with whom he had two children, ended as his career soared. He then married Suzanne Folsom Baird, the wife who survives him, in 1962.

At the same time his ideas were shifting about what he wanted to be reporting. He told interviewers that flying at night he liked to gaze down at the twinkling towns and farmsteads, and the real world began to haunt him. The real news was not the ephemeral sorties of politics, the international hostilities that nothing remedies, the fads and fashions of the day. News was in the stories of these "ordinary" people, whose lives had depth and meaning and passion. In 1967, in the first of a series of cantankerous motor homes whose vagaries would continuously plague his crew, Kuralt and two co-workers set out to the heart of America. They were "On the Road."

Over the next three decades, his regular segment, "On the Road," broadcast on *The CBS Evening News* would win nine Emmy Awards and innumerable other prizes. Kuralt would write several highly-popular books on his travels, including *Dateline America* (1979), *On the Road with Charles Kuralt* (1985), *Southerners: Portrait of a People*, (1986) and, with Loonis McGlohon, *North Carolina Is My Home* (1986). McGlohon tells of an old couple who stopped Kuralt on the street and regaled him with a lengthy story about how they grew corn. "They told him how they grew their silver queen, how fine it was, how many bushels, on and on. And he listened. When they finally told him goodbye and walked on, he said to me, 'You know, that was really interesting. I didn't know all that about growing silver queen.' That was Charles. There's nobody I admired more. I think he knew more than anybody I've ever known, because he listened."

The collaborators, two Carolina boys, grew to be the closest of friends over many years of working together. When North Carolina celebrated its bicentennial, Governor Jim Hunt asked Kuralt and McGlohon to compile a work that would represent the state. They produced a record album of song and story called *North Carolina Is My Home*, which also became a book, and as Loonis says, a dog-and-pony show that eventually toured the U.S. and played in Canada and London. The Kuralt-McGlohon Carolina show was once booked for lupus benefit in New York City, for a dinner crowd of 700 who'd paid $1,000 a plate. McGlohon says, "I told the lady who called us, 'Nobody at your dinner is going to understand this show—it's about grits and collard greens and cornbread.' She said, 'Come on and see.' We went, and the people were wonderful." The last performance, a benefit for the Charlotte Symphony, was 10 days before Kuralt died on July 4, 1997, ironically, of lupus. "He wasn't feeling well but he wouldn't admit it," McGlohon says. "The doctor said he'd had lupus for probably five years, but it had not been diagnosed."

No matter what befell, Kuralt was always "up," and always gracious. "The last conversation I had with him," McGlohon says, "he'd been to the drugstore and a young woman had come up to him and introduced herself as the winner of a Kuralt scholarship, and thanked him. He kept saying to me, 'Wasn't that the nicest thing? Wasn't that nice?' He just always appreciated people."

—Dot Jackson

L

LEAR, Patricia

Born: Patricia Merritt in Memphis, Tennessee, 10 August 1944. **Education**: Bennett College, A.A. 1962-64; Hood College, B.A. 1964-66. **Family:** Married William Schureman Lear (divorced, 1995); two children. **Career**: Editorial assistant, *Vogue* magazine, 1971-73; homemaker; fiction and freelance magazine writer. **Awards:** Grants from Yaddo, 1989 and 1992, Bread Loaf, 1992, Virginia Center for the Creative Arts, 1993, Ucross Foundation, 1993, The MacDowell Colony, 1993 and 1996, and Illinois Art Council, 1994; O. Henry Award, 1991, for the short story "Powwow"; Walter E. Dakin fellowship, University of the South, 1992. **Agent:** Amanda Urban, International Creative Management, 40 West 57th St., New York, New York 10019.

PUBLICATIONS

Short Story Collection

Stardust, 7-Eleven, Route 57, A & W, and So Forth. New York, Knopf, 1992.

Uncollected Short Stories

"Summer Party," in *Triquarterly*, Spring/Summer 1999.

*

Patricia Lear comments:

I did not intend to become a "Southern" writer but too many people I respect say I am.

I left Memphis with my family at age 10 and moved to Kansas City. My Memphis relatives think of me as a total Yankee, especially since I married a New Yorker and only came back to Memphis for an occasional visit.

I think it is one of the greatest things that I have become this voice of the *new* South—as someone once said about me some place. My family in Tennessee just scratches their heads and wonders, "what is this world coming to?"

* * *

Patricia Lear enjoyed an auspicious literary debut, in her forties, with her short story collection, *Stardust, 7-Eleven, Route 57, A & W, and So Forth* (1992). The stories draw her on impressions from her early youth in Tennessee to reflect on the increasingly urbanized and commercialized landscape, speech patterns, and disconnected people attempting to establish a foothold in contemporary society. Her recreation of colloquial idioms is especially remarkable, achieving a staccato rhythm while her characters exaggerate, use colorful expressions, and occasionally make earthy insights. Small but significant revelations occur during life's routines in her fiction, as characters living detached lives struggle for a more secure existence and more meaningful relationships. In the O. Henry Award-winning story "Powwow," for example, such issues as suicide, aging, and single parenting are addressed in a simple, quiet story concerning a woman's visit to her ailing grandfather.

"Solace," the source of the title of her short story collection (based on the names of the protagonist's dogs), confronts the failure of a relationship and the lack of meaningful examples of behavior in a society dominated by popular culture. Newly separated C. W. identifies with happy manhood as depicted in a beer commercial and attempts to live his life accordingly, taking his teenaged son and two female companions to a resort where he envisions the women clinging lovingly to their men as they drink beer and have a good time. However, the son is disinterested in living this vision, the women prove to be more independent than unthinkingly admiring, and the whole trip is a failure. Still, C. W. continues to pursue the clearest form of happiness he can envision.

"After Memphis" is another portrait of a character without meaningful examples of maturity, as a woman recalls being uprooted from her home in the South as a girl and never achieving a firm sense of identity, family, or community, suggesting that popular culture often provides life models, subsuming the role of traditional family and social environments. "Angels" exhibits the sense of detachment and lively recreation of language present throughout the collection as well as its quiet moments of insight; a brief encounter between a woman who recently had a mastectomy and a handyman who is also an aspiring actor, becomes a humorous and poignant passing moment in life, the kind that is memorable, if not life transforming.

—Mel Koler

LEE, Harper

Born: Nelle Harper Lee in Monroeville, Alabama, 28 April 1926. **Education:** Huntington College, Indiana, 1944-45; University of Alabama, Tuscaloosa, 1945-49; Oxford University. **Career:** Airline reservation clerk with Eastern Air Lines and British Overseas Airways, New York, during the 1950s; left to devote full time to writing. **Awards:** Pulitzer prize for fiction, 1961; Alabama Library Association award, 1961, Brotherhood award of National Conference of Christians and Jews, 1961; Bestsellers' Paperback of the Year award, 1962 (all for *To Kill a Mockingbird*). **Member:** National Council on Arts, 1966-72. **Agent:** McIntosh & Otis, Inc., 18 East 41st St., New York, New York 10017.

PUBLICATIONS

Novel

To Kill a Mockingbird. Philadelphia, Lippincott, 1960.

Other

"Love—In Other Words," in *Vogue*, 15 April 1961.
"Christmas to Me," in *McCalls*, December 1961, 1963.

Adaptations

To Kill a Mockingbird (film), Universal Studios, 1962, screenplay by Horton Foote.
To Kill a Mockingbird (play), adapted by Christopher Sergel, 1987.

Critical Studies: "The Romantic Regionalism of Harper Lee" by Fred Erisman, in *Alabama Review*, 1973; "Atticus Finch—Right and Wrong" by Monroe Freedman, in *Alabama Law Review*, Winter 1994; *"To Kill a Mockingbird": Threatening Boundaries* by Claudia Durst Johnson, New York, Twayne, 1994; "Understanding *To Kill a Mockingbird*: A Student Casebook to Issues, Sources, and Historic Documents" by Claudia Durst Johnson, New York, Greenwood, 1994; "The Margins of Maycomb: A Rereading of To Kill a Mockingbird" by Teresa Godwin Phelps, in *Alabama Law Review*, Winter 1994; "The Law and the Code in Harper Lee's To Kill a Mockingbird" by Robert O. Stephens, in *Southern Cultures*, Winter 1995; "Blues for Atticus Finch: Scottsboro, Brown, and Harper Lee" by Eric J. Sundquist, in *The South as an American Problem*, Athens, University of Georgia Press, 1995.

*   *   *

Harper Lee has written only one novel, but that novel, *To Kill a Mockingbird*, has firmly established her reputation as one of the most influential Southern writers of her generation. Since its publication in 1960, *To Kill a Mockingbird* has sold nearly 20 million copies and has never been out of print, in either hardcover or paperback. It won the Pulitzer Prize for Fiction in 1961 and, thirty years later, in a 1991 "Survey of Lifetime Reading Habits" conducted jointly by the Book-of-the-Month-Club and the Library of Congress, *To Kill a Mockingbird* was second only to the *Bible* in books "most often cited as making a difference" in people's lives. With the exception perhaps of Ralph Ellison, no other one-time novelist has met with such lasting critical and popular success.

Lee's novel is narrated by Scout Finch, who, from the standpoint of the late 1950s, is looking back to events that occurred one summer in Maycomb, Alabama, in 1935. Of the many things that happened that summer, two stand out most clearly and have most influenced the kind of woman Scout has become. First, there is the story of the slow emergence of Boo Radley, a recluse who lives next door to the Finches and who during the course of the summer develops a quiet, peculiar, and ultimately live-saving friendship with Scout and her brother, Jem. Second, there is the story of Tom Robinson, a black man falsely accused of raping a poor white woman. This second story touches Scout's life because her father, Atticus, has been appointed by the court to defend Tom Robinson. From the moment she first hears her father called a "nigger-lover" to the moment when she stands with pride as her father walks out of court at the end of the trial, Scout learns much about courage and honor by watching her father confront Maycomb's racism and prove (albeit without an attendant acquittal) Tom's innocence.

Thematically, the novel can be summed up in Atticus's advice to Scout early in the novel: "You never really understand a person until you consider things from his point of view . . . until you climb into his skin and walk around in it." The stories of Boo Radley and Tom Robinson—along with other lesser stories, such as Jem's penitential service to Mrs. Dubose and Atticus's willingness to accept "entailment" payments from the Cunninghams—teach Scout about the power of sympathy and the need to overcome the artificial barriers that are used to separate people. Although citizens of Maycomb, Boo and Tom are both outsiders, or, to use more recent critical terminology, they are both "the Other": Boo because of his reclusiveness, Tom because of his color. Through her experience and Atticus's example, Scout learns not to fear the Other but to have compassion for him and his circumstances. Instead of wanting to exploit Boo for her own fun (as she does in the beginning of the novel by putting on gothic plays about his history), Scout comes to see him as a "mockingbird"—that is, as someone with an inner goodness that must be cherished. And while the story of Atticus's defense of Tom Robinson doesn't end as happily as Scout's relationship with Boo, there is a recognition that something positive—some slight empathy—has come out of the tragedy. As Atticus tells his children at the end of the novel, the fact that the jury took several hours to pass its "inevitable" verdict is perhaps the "shadow of a beginning."

Despite its secure place in southern and American letters, *To Kill a Mockingbird* has not, until very recently, been the focus of much literary explication. The critical scholarship on the novel is surprisingly thin. It was not until the 1994 publication of Claudia Durst Johnson's *"To Kill a Mockingbird": Threatening Boundaries* that a book-length study of the novel appeared. However, as Johnson points out in her work, "Some of the more interesting criticism of the novel, and certainly the largest volume of commentary on the novel, has been done by legal rather than literary scholars." For the most part, this legal scholarship has focused on Atticus as a man who—in the words of one writer—"taught a community and his two young children about justice, decency and tolerance, and who drove a generation of real-life Jems and Scouts to become lawyers themselves."

The legal scholarship on the novel took an interesting turn in 1992 when Hofstra University law professor Monroe Freedman, in a column in *Legal Times*, charged Atticus Finch with racism and warned young lawyers that Lee's hero should not serve as a role model because he was "a passive participant in [the] pervasive injustice" of segregation. The critical dissensus represented by Freedman's stand is beginning to work its way into literary readings of the novel. When *To Kill a Mockingbird* first appeared, the consensus was that Lee had written, as one reviewer put it, "a most pervasive plea for racial justice." Recent essays by Eric J. Sundquist and Teresa Godwin Phelps, however, highlight the more disturbing implications of Lee's narrative. For Sundquist, the novel's "narrative marginalization of black life functions as a form of segregation," and, according to Phelps, "While the novel depicts change in one facet of law and society, it reinforces the status quo in other troubling aspects," such as its disparaging treatment of poor whites and its casual attitude toward Mayella Ewell's sexual abuse.

For nearly forty years, *To Kill a Mockingbird* has been a permanent part of America's literary landscape. While new trends in scholarship suggest that the novel may be coming under attack from some quarters, the novel's status is secure. One can easily imagine forty years from now that *To Kill a Mockingbird*, despite its shortcomings, will remain one of those books that continues to make a difference in people's lives.

—Christopher Metress

LINNEY, Romulus

Born: Philadelphia, Pennsylvania, 21 September 1930. **Education:** Oberlin College, A.B. 1953; Yale School of Drama, M.F.A. 1958; New School of New York City, novel workshop, 1960. **Family:** Married Ann Leggett Sims, 14 April 1963 (divorced, 1966), one child; married Margaret Jane Andrews (an actress), 14 September 1967; one child. **Career:** Actors' Studio, New York City, stage manager, 1960; visiting associate professor of dramatic arts, University of North Carolina at Chapel Hill, 1961; director of fine arts, North Carolina State College, beginning 1962; faculty member, 1964-72, Manhattan School of Music, New York City; visiting professor at institutions, including Columbia University, 1972-74, Connecticut College, 1979, University of Pennsylvania, 1979-86, and Princeton University, 1982-85; writer and director; six summers of professional Equity stock as actor and director; instructor at Wake Forest and Columbia University, and playwriting professor with The Actors Studio, The New School, New York. **Awards:** National Endowment for the Arts grant, 1974; Guggenheim fellow, 1980; Obie Award, *Village Voice*, 1980, for *Tennessee*, 1992, for sustained excellence in playwriting; Mishma Prize, 1981, for *Jesus Tales*; Academy-Institute Award, American Academy and Institute of Arts and Letters, 1984, for literature; Rockefeller fellow, 1986; American Theatre Critics Award for distinguished playwriting, 1988, for *Heathen Valley*; Hollywood Drama-Logue Award (three occasions); honorary doctorate, Wake Forest University, 1998. **Agent:** Gilbert Parker, William Morris Agency, 1350 Avenue of the Americas, New York, New York 10019.

PUBLICATIONS

Novels

Heathen Valley. New York, Atheneum, 1962.
Slowly, by Thy Hand Unfurled. New York, Harcourt, 1965.
Jesus Tales. San Francisco, North Point Press, 1980.

Plays

The Sorrows of Frederick. New York, Harcourt, 1966.
The Love Suicide at Schofield Barracks:Democracy and Esther. New York, Harcourt, 1973.
The Sorrows of Frederick: Holy Ghosts. New York, Harcourt Brace Jovanovich, 1977.
Old Man Joseph and His Family. New York, Dramatists Play Service, 1978.

Tennessee. New York, Dramatists Play Service, 1980.
Childe Byron. New York, Dramatists Play Service, 1981.
El Hermano, Dramatists Play Service, 1981.
The Captivity of Pixie Shedman. New York, Dramatists Play Service, 1981.
The Death of King Philip. New York, Dramatists Play Service, 1984.
Laughing Stock (includes *Goodbye, Howard, F.M.*, and *Tennessee*). New York, Dramatists Play Service, 1984.
A Woman without a Name. New York, Dramatists Play Service, 1986.
Sand Mountain (includes *Sand Mountain Matchmaking* and *Why the Lord Come to Sand Mountain*). New York, Dramatists Play Service, 1985.
Pops (includes *Can Can, Clair de Lune, Ave Maria, Gold and Silver Waltz, Yankee Doodle, Songs of Love*). New York, Dramatists Play Service, 1987.
Heathen Valley. New York, Theatre Communications Group, 1988.
Three Plays (includes *Juliet, Yancey, April Snow*). New York, Dramatists Play Service, 1989.
Holy Ghosts. New York, Dramatists Play Service, 1989.
Three Poets (contains *Komachi, Hrosvitha, Akhmatova*). New York, Dramatists Play Service, 1990.
Unchanging Love. New York, Dramatists Play Service, 1991.
Romulus Linney: Seventeen Short Plays. Newbury, Vermont, Smith & Kraus, 1992.
Six Plays. New York, Theatre Communications Group, 1993.
Ambrosio. New York, Dramatists Play Service, 1993.
2. New York, Dramatists Play Service, 1993.
Spain. New York, Dramatists Play Service, 1994.
True Crimes. New York, Dramatists Play Service, 1996.
A Christmas Carol by Charles Dickens, adapted by Linney. New York, Dramatists Play Service, 1996.

Radio/Television Plays

Ten Plays For Radio, with Norman A. Bailey and Domenick Cascio. Burgess, 1954.
Radio Classics, with Bailey and Cascio. Burgess, 1956.
The Thirty-fourth Star. CBS, 1976.
Feelin' Good (series). PBS, 1976-77.

Other

Janet Fish: Recent Paintings & Watercolors. New York, Miller, Robert Gallery, 1989.

* * *

Romulus Linney is a prolific playwright whose works are most often produced at festival, university, and off-Broadway venues, with occasional turns on Broadway, all of which accounts for his strong reputation in theatre circles and modest popular renown. He addresses big topics—love, religion, politics, the influence of the past, particularly in the form of domineering parental figures—in full length dramas and in the one act plays of which he is acknowledged as a master.

While ranging wide in physical and temporal settings, from depicting Jesus at Nazareth to a creative writing class in contemporary Alabama, Linney's plays frequently focus on individuals in conflict over personal and social responsibilities, characters attempting to understand or defend their behavior, and individuals searching for identity within powerful religious, social, political, or cultural milieus. Folk culture and homespun wisdom tend to prevail in his comedies, while self-deception, overwhelming social forces, or dark histories overcome the protagonists of his tragedies.

One way to approach Linney's vast output is to divide his work into three broad categories—works set in the South, works that center on historical figures, and the remaining plays that fall outside of those divisions—while acknowledging that certain themes, including individuals in conflict with themselves or engaged in defending an ideal, recur throughout his work. Many of Linney's works are set in the South, where he spent part of his childhood, and reflect his fascination with revivalist religion and folk culture. His plays and novels set in the South are of two kinds: dark tragicomedies favoring an approach that can be called Southern Gothic, and light, folk comedies that draw humor from self-delusions of characters and in ordinary goings-on.

Linney's first two works were novels, *Heathen Valley* (1962; adapted for theatre in 1988) and *Slowly, by Thy Hand Unfurled* (1965; adapted for theatre as *A Woman without a Name* in 1986), set in Appalachian communities of the nineteenth century. *Heathen Valley* concerns the efforts of an Episcopalian bishop to establish a mission in western North Carolina, where superstition and bawdiness reign. While exploring good and evil, decadence, and communal influence, the story develops local color through the language of the characters and the influence of place and history.

Heathen Valley introduces a recurring trait in Linney's characters—individuals who make a sudden "about face" in their behavior. In this work, the bishop is overcome by his own dark past and suddenly converts his congregation to an obscure sect of Christian faith-healing as he descends into madness, while a base man who became an assistant to the bishop restores a sense of order in the community. *Slowly, by Thy Hand Unfurled* is related as the diary of a strong-willed woman who perseveres through tragedy and hardship in her family, her compassion tested by the blame and guilt directed at her by a son who holds her responsible for the family's miseries. In the adapted play the woman reads aloud from her journal as characters seated around her act out events. In these works and his later play *Holy Ghosts,* Linney explores the role of religion in the lives of insular communities beset by economic hardship, disorder, lack of education, and superstition.

In *Holy Ghosts,* a host of outcasts gather for a revival meeting of a sect where members handle snakes as a demonstration of faith. The characters include a woman recently escaped from an abusive husband, the husband who arrives to reclaim her, a preacher's son with whom the woman has fled, a man suffering a terminal illness, a woman with a promiscuous past and another who is extremely timid, a troubled couple with their newborn, and a man who imagines his dead dog is present. Reflecting on a strange form of religious devotion, particularly of a charismatic sect variety, the play presents character studies of outcasts and confused people searching for a sense of community: the eccentric takes on more universal significance in the characters' desire for meaning, companionship, and compassion.

Among Linney's other works set in the South are comic examinations of the influence of community, of characters engaged in self-deception, and of character-types, all of which are exhibited in the three one-act plays, *Goodbye, Howard, F.M.,* and *Tennessee,* collectively titled *Laughing Stock. Goodbye, Howard, F.M.* approaches farce in depicting three elderly women in a hospital awaiting the imminent death of their brother while attempting to conceal evidence of their own aging and fretting about how to break the news of their brother's death to their mother.

Goodbye, Howard, F.M. is set in a creative writing class at an Alabama college, where a failed but still idealistic novelist leads a small collection of aspiring writers that includes a Faulknerian character (or, perhaps, a caricature of Faulkner) who carries around a shoebox filled with a bottle of whiskey and a 1,000-plus page manuscript of shocking events and language. *Tennessee* is a comedy where folk wisdom and poetic language help color a love story, as a woman comes to a mountain home and relates to the family living there the tale of her courtship and marriage, which began as a misinterpreted sign of mutual love.

In these short plays and the best of his works set in the South, Linney is able to draw on local color and homespun language to create believable characters and types, some of whom change behavior and develop, while others remain brutish, simple-minded, vapid, or self-indulgent. Folk wisdom saves the day in *Sand Mountain,* which consists of two related one act comedies of life on the Tennessee frontier.

One of the plays, *Sand Mountain Matchmaking,* concerns the courting of a young, independent-thinking widow, and the other, *Why the Lord Came to Sand Mountain,* has the Lord and St. Peter visiting an impoverished and unwed mountain couple and their fourteen children. The widow of the first play is counseled by an old hills woman who suggests a test that will allow the widow to sort out her suitors and find the best among them, and the impoverished family of the second play win over the Lord and St. Peter with their simple ways, culminating with a round of folktale storytelling. A folk version of the lives of Joseph, Mary, and Jesus related in this play was the basis for an earlier work, *Old Man Joseph and His Family,* where Joseph broods over the immaculate conception issue (fearing he may have been cuckolded) and Jesus is treated by others as a confused and rebellious teenager. In this play, religious figures are humanized in the "Bible of the Folk" manner of Appalachia.

Historical figures appear in several other of Linney's plays, including *Childe Byron,* where Lord Byron appears as a ghost, relates many escapades where Linney draws on Byron's writings for poetic and graphic detail, and reconciles with his dying daughter. Linney's most powerful plays with historical figures are *The Sorrows of Frederick* and *2.* The former begins with King William Frederick II of Prussia rallying his soldiers in battle then abruptly departing them after receiving news that his favorite dog has died. During his ride home to bury the dog, numerous flashbacks reveal how Frederick compromised his idealism and love of culture to please his domineering father and to excel in political intrigues that fortified his power. *2* is set at the beginning of the Nuremburg War Trials, as Herman Goering, second in command in the Nazi Third Reich and the man responsible for concentration camps, prepares for his trial on crimes against humanity. Intelligent and benignly demonic, Goering refuses to take responsibility for his actions, arguing that individuals cannot be tried for the crimes of nations and that a World Court cannot act fairly against conquered people. Linney draws on Goering's actual testimony to reflect on a characteristic theme—how individuals blind themselves to ugly truths—and to show one of many facets of evil, in this case how monstrosities can be perpetrated by intelligent, charasmatic individuals.

The Sorrows of Frederick and *2* explore discrepancies between ideals and actions, as Frederick anguishes over his life choices and Goering rationalizes evil, and both characters compromise their humanity. *Three Poets,* a group of one act plays also based on historical figures, is among works by Linney in which larger forces, including political authority, overwhelm the individual. *Three Poets* shows sensitive and insightful female poets threatened because of jealousy (*Komachi,* based on the ninth-century Japanese poet brutalized by the prince she dared to challenge), for daring to celebrate physical manifestations of love (*Hrosvitha,* based on the tenth-century nun who wrote of emotional and physical pleasure), and for not submitting to authoritarian power (*Akhmatova,* based on the Russian poet of the twentieth century who defied Stalin by committing her verse to memory instead of having her writings confiscated).

Linney also explores American idealism in several plays, including *The Love Suicide at Schofield Barracks,* where the government's failure to end the war in Vietnam prompts a general and his wife to sacrifice themselves to bring attention to the carnage, and *Memory Mountain,* an allegory where an Appalachian family experiences 200 years of American history and repeated temptations to compromise their simple values, finally turning to the audience for help. These plays remind us of the difficulty of maintaining innocence and idealism in the face of temptation and overwhelming social forces (which appear as religious and political forces in other Linney works), complementing other plays where self-deception and compromised values lead to anguish and tragedy. Amid such complex waves of influence in Linney's comedies, simple values prevail, humor helps expose human foibles, and folk stories express age-old wisdom.

—Perry Bear

LOTT, Bret

Born: R. Bretley Lott in Los Angeles, California, 8 October 1958. **Education:** California State University, Long Beach, B.A. 1981; University of Massachusetts, Amherst, M.F.A. 1984. **Family:** Married Melanie Kai Swank, 28 June 1980; two sons. **Career:** Cook's trainer, Big Yellow House, Inc., Santa Barbara, California, 1977-79; salesman, RC Cola, Los Angeles, 1979-80; reporter, *Daily Commercial News,* Los Angeles, 1980-81; instructor in remedial English, Ohio State University, 1984-86; professor of English, College of Charleston, South Carolina, since 1986; fiction editor, *Writer's Forum,* University of Colorado, since 1986; director, Charleston Writer's Conference, 1989-94; member of faculty, M.F.A. Program, Vermont College of Norwich, since 1994; judge for AWP Award Series in short fiction, 1992; panelist for NEA fellowships in creative writing, 1993; judge for Illinois Arts Council

Fellowships in literature, 1995; book reviewer for periodicals, including *New York Times Book Review, Raleigh News & Observer, Southern Review, Los Angeles Times,* and *San Francisco Chronicle.* **Awards:** Three Syndicated Fiction Project awards from PEN/NEA, for "I Owned Vermont," 1985, "The Difference Between Men and Women," 1991, and "A Way Through This," 1993; Ohio Arts Council fellowship in literature, 1986; South Carolina Arts Commission fellowship in literature, 1987-88; Bread Loaf fellow in fiction, Bread Loaf Writers' Conference, 1991; Distinguished Research award, College of Charleston, 1995. **Member:** Associated Writing Programs; Poets and Writers, Inc. **Agent:** Marian Young, Young Agency, 812 West 181 St., New York, New York 10033.

PUBLICATIONS

Novels

The Man Who Owned Vermont. New York, Viking Press, 1987.
A Stranger's House. New York, Viking Press, 1988.
Jewel. New York, Pocket Hardcover, Simon and Schuster, 1991.
Reed's Beach. New York, Pocket Hardcover, Simon and Schuster, 1993.
The Hunt Club. New York, Villard Books of Random House, 1998

Short Story Collections

A Dream of Old Leaves. New York, Viking Press, 1989.
How to Get Home. Raleigh, John F. Blair, Publisher, 1996.

Nonfiction

Fathers, Sons, and Brothers: The Men in My Family. New York, Harcourt Brace, 1997.

Stories in Anthologies

20 Under 30, edited by Debra Spark. New York, Charles Scribners Sons, 1986.
Louder Than Words, Volume II edited by William Shore. New York, Vintage, 1991.
Flash Fiction, edited James Shapiro. New York, W. W. Norton, 1992.
Sudden Fiction, edited by James Shapiro. New York, W. W. Norton, 1996.
Brave New Fiction, 1990-1995, edited by Brian Christopher Hamilton and Renee Vogel. Portland, Helicon West, 1996.
The Sacred Place, edited by Scott Cairns and Scott Olsen. Salt Lake City, University of Utah Press, 1996.

*

Critical Studies: Review by Michiko Kakutani, in *New York Times,* 6 June 1987; review of *The Man Who Owned Vermont* by Carolyn See, in *New York Times,* 6 July 1987; review of *Jewel* by Carolyn See, in *Los Angeles Times,* 4 November 1991; interview in *Atlanta Journal-Constitution,* 10 November 1991.

* * *

"You got to have the stories to tell," Lonny the plumber tells Rick, the main character of *The Man Who Owned Vermont.* "You have to. You have to share the stories you got, or you'll die." This advice, the only advice that Lonny has to give about Rick's failing marriage in Bret Lott's first novel, focuses on an idea central not just to this novel but to all of Lott's writing. Each person's life, no matter how ordinary, contains stories, and the ability to communicate lies in sharing those stories. More than the power of stories to move or change listeners, Lott writes of the power of stories to free the teller.

With the exception of his most recent work, *The Hunt Club*, a mystery novel whose resolution depends upon surprising plot twists, the stories that Lott's characters have contain no fantastical happenings or roller coaster plot lines. The hardships of love appear in marriage, separation, infertility, and divorce. Family tragedies come in the form of heart attacks, car accidents, or children's deaths. The characters struggle with the difficulty of life, and in this ordinary struggle create interesting stories. As Carolyn See wrote in a *Los Angeles Times* review of *The Man Who Owned Vermont*, "What makes this narrative so engrossing is the pure familiarity of it."

In *The Man Who Owned Vermont*, Rick, an RC Cola salesman in Northampton, Massachusetts, cannot talk to his wife either about her miscarriage or their relationship. The book opens with Rick tagging along after a plumber sent to find a leak in his apartment; he hangs on each story the plumber tells as if busted toilets contain the answer to why his own wife moved out with all of their furniture ten days before. Through bits of flashback, Lott slowly reveals the facts behind Rick's separation, strategically illustrating his inability to come to terms with his own story. The story he cannot tell is of his wife's miscarriage. In the early stages of Paige's, his wife's, pregnancy, the couple was driving to the Jersey shore for a vacation when Paige asked Rick several times to pull into a rest stop. Out of stubbornness and anger over their late start, Rick kept driving. When he finally pulled off at an exit, she miscarried in the ladies room of a Mobil station, and Rick, when he found her, flushed the remains of their child down the toilet.

The novel focuses not on these past events but on Rick's coming to terms with himself. In a painstakingly slow process, Rick begins to talk to people he barely knows, to tell them stories about himself. "They were small stories," Rick explains, "irrelevant as far as I could see, but it was the telling of them that did something." All of these conversations seem like practice for the conversation he finally recognizes he needs to have with his wife. Michiko Kakutani wrote in the *New York Times* that this novel depicts "the redemptive powers of love," but the redemption comes from telling stories. Through stories, characters connect and communicate.

This idea of the power of stories pervades Lott's novels. In *A Stranger's House*, an infertile husband and wife resist talking about their own situation and only discuss other people. Throughout the novel, the husband tells anecdotes he hears while working for a local newspaper, but neither he nor his wife can talk about what happens in their own lives. Similarly, *Reed's Beach* charts the rocky path back to communication and intimacy that a couple faces after the death of a child. However, for the main character of *Jewel*, storytelling takes on a more epic scope. Through her stories, Jewel gives a part of herself to her children.

In telling stories about her childhood, her husband, and their children, Jewel holds her family and their past together. The story of Jewel comes from Lott's own family history. "The plot is true," he told the *Atlanta Journal-Constitution*, and is based on the life of Lott's grandmother. Jewel chronicles the two decades after World War II as experienced by a woman from rural Mississippi whose sixth child is born with Down's Syndrome. The plot follows the diagnosis of baby Brenda Ray and the doctor's assessment that since she will probably not live past the age of two, the family should send her to an institution and not worry about her. Jewel, who could no more forget one of her children than forget her own history, determines to love and raise this child, often at the expense of attention to her other children or her husband. When she learns in *Reader's Digest* about a place in Los Angeles that cares for and teaches mentally retarded children, Jewel decides she must uproot her family and move west to "the new Jerusalem" to save her child's life. By the end of the novel, Jewel discovers that through the stories she has told, her history will continue through the lives of her descendents. "My lives, the long string of them that started with the death of my daddy and went on from there, right up to and including this moment, that long string of lives wasn't over. My life would never be over, but would be carried on. . . ."

In striving to fill in the details of Jewel's lives, Lott chronicles the social environment of the rural South in the 1940s and 1950s. Leston, her husband, makes what money the family has by leading a crew to scour the pine forests for stumps, which they dynamite out of the ground and haul away to be turned into turpentine. It is Jewel's job in this business to fix the breakfast of eggs, bacon, grits, and biscuits to feed the men, a breakfast the white workers eat at the table while the black workers eat on the porch outside. Especially through the relationship between Jewel and an African American woman named Cathedral, Lott charts the racism inherent in Jewel's Mississippi society. It is Jewel who teaches Cathedral how to read, but it is Cathedral's son who is murdered for passing on that skill to other African Americans in the 1960s.

Only when Jewel moves her family to California does she begin to see herself and her background from a different perspective. She understands the look that people give her family when they try to get a loan for a house and when Leston looks for a job; in the strange world of Los Angeles, she feels she is "only a cracker from Mississippi." She recognizes almost instinctively that when she refers to Cathedral as a "niggerwoman," she has committed a grave error, so that when someone politely tells her that people no longer use this word, she consciously tries to adapt to and use the correct word, "colored." These details create the realism of Jewel's story, but also reveal how place can shape characters.

Through his attention to detail, Lott repeatedly creates concrete settings for his stories. The Quabbin Reservoir and the small towns that surround the Amherst/Northampton area of western Massachusetts provide the map for both *The Man Who Owned Vermont* and *The Stranger's House*; the piney woods of Mississippi and the urban sights of Los Angeles track Jewel's migration from a stagnating South to a developing West; the landscape and roads of Charleston and its environs dominate *The Hunt Club* and find their way into many of Lott's short stories. The details are not of the tourist variety, exotic and rare, but are the kind of ordinary facts and sights noticed only by the people who live there, details Lott uses to reveal to a passer-by—the reader—the importance of the ordinary to everyday living. If you were to drive down a road described in *The Hunt Club*, you would expect to find the Piggly Wiggly positioned exactly as the book claims.

Critics have noted this attention to details of the ordinary sort, citing this part of his craft as the basis for his particular place in contemporary literature. In her review of *Jewel*, Carolyn See argues that the power of Lott's artistic vision lies in his "eye for detail." His particular way of seeing incorporates an "uncanny ability to see into the lives of the American working class and to see the magic there as well." With the massive description of a character's environment, Lott brings his microscope to the individual. He centers his writing on human relationships, usually family relationships, and the stories people tell that help create bonds between them. Lott's are the kind of stories that have most to do with the human condition in a world where life is a struggle.

—C. E. Newell

LOWRY, Beverly

Born: Beverley Fey in Memphis, Tennessee, 10 August 1938. **Education:** Attended University of Mississippi, 1956-58; Memphis State University, B.A. 1960. **Family:** Married Glenn Lowry, 3 June 1960; two children (a son, Peter, died in the mid-1980s). **Career:** Associate professor of fiction writing, University of Houston, beginning 1976, and also worked as actress; member of humanities board of Cultural Arts Council of Houston and board of directors of Houston Festival. **Awards:** National Endowment for the Arts fellow, 1979-80. **Agent:** Maxine Groffsky, 2 Fifth Ave., New York, New York 10011. **Address:** Department of English, University of Houston, Houston, Texas 77004.

PUBLICATIONS

Novels

Come Back, Lolly Ray. New York, Doubleday, 1977.
Emma Blue. New York, Doubleday, 1978.
Daddy's Girl. New York, Viking, 1981.
The Perfect Sonya. New York, Viking, 1987.
Breaking Gentle. New York, Viking, 1988.
Crossed Over: A Murder, A Memoir. New York, Knopf, 1992.
The Track of Real Desires. New York, Knopf, 1994.

*   *   *

In *The Track of Real Desires*, Sissy Westerfield describes her friends as people who at fifty have no pension plans and are "still trying to figure out how to live in the world." Many of the characters in Beverly Lowry's novels are confused not only about where they are going, but about who they are. Their efforts to invent themselves are often hilarious, sometimes pathetic, occasionally even tragic.

In her first two novels, *Come Back, Lolly Ray* and *Emma Blue,* Lowry places her protagonists' problems on their society. Eunola, Mississippi, is a fictionalized version of Greenwood, Mississippi, where the Lowrys went to live when Beverly was six, only to find that without solid local contacts and an impressive pedigree they would never be accepted. *Come Home, Lolly Ray* is the story of Lolly Ray Lasswell, who naively believes that because she is so much admired as a champion baton twirler, she is exempt from Eunola's snobbery. When she comes home from college pregnant and unmarried, Lolly Ray finds out how wrong she was. After her baby is born, she entrusts the child to her family and departs. *Emma Blue* continues the story. Unlike her mother, Emma Blue Lasswell has no illusions about where she stands in Eunola. However, while this spunky heroine loathes the caste system that condemns her, she values tradition and is fascinated with stories from the past. In the local public library, Emma Blue conducts what she regards as an archaeological dig, reconstructing Eunola's history in order to understand her connection to the past and establish her own identity.

Sixteen years later, Lowry again set a novel in Eunola. However, in *The Track of Real Desires* she looks at the town through the eyes of the elite, brought together at a dinner party in honor of their old friend, Leland Standard, a local girl who has been gone for thirty-five years. Like a comedy of manners, the story exposes the difference between the characters' public pretensions and the underlying realities of their lives: drug addiction, alcoholism, sexual obsession, marital misery, adultery, financial desperation, and pervasive despair. None of the adults has realized the dreams of youth, except for the honored guest herself and a philosophical plumber, whose goal is, as he puts it simply, "the life well lived."

The setting of Lowry's third novel, *Daddy's Girl*, is Houston, where people are not to tied to propriety. Still, Sue Shannon Stovall Muffaletta does not want her suburban neighbors to find out that in addition to being a dedicated Little League mother and the cherished child of Big Jim Stovall, she is also M. M. Sue, a country music lyricist, and June Day, who sings at bars near the refineries and cavorts with the patrons. There are a number of interesting characters in *Daddy's Girl*, but it subject is really Sue's effort to integrate her various selves into a single entity.

In the middle 1980s, a series of personal losses, including the accidental death of her son, Peter, caused a marked change in the tone of Lowry's fiction. Gone is her unqualified faith in the future; present is a new preoccupation with fate or chance, even a hint that felicity may invite disaster. In the short story "Out of the Blue," for example, a young man has just sorted out his feelings about two women and is ready to commit himself to the mother of his unborn child when a couple of carjackers decide to kidnap and murder him. In *The Track of Real Desires*, death comes to Sissy Westerfield while she is driving along the levee road in her Mustang convertible, listening to opera on the radio and pleasuring herself at the same time. It is not just the inevitability of death that troubles Lowry, but the timing.

In Lowry's later works, isolation continues to be an important theme. However, in *The Perfect Sonya* the childhood experience that made Pauline Terry an emotional cripple was not social injustice but elemental evil. Pauline's memory of her father's sexual advances has become fused with another recollection, his insistence that despite her fear she approach a stuffed bear outside an Arkansas store. To Pauline, the bear symbolizes the violation of nature, which explains her inability to connect fully with any other human being. Such symbols appear throughout the novel. Back in Texas to see her dying father, Pauline has an affair with another older man, who lives on Snake Creek. Pauline is drawn toward the water, yet afraid of the snakes. She does imagine swimming among them unharmed, their companion, not their enemy. However, when the story ends it is not clear whether or not Pauline will ever commit herself to life.

Lowry's own search for meaning after her son's death took her to see Karla Faye Tucker, a Texas death-row inmate who had used a pickaxe to kill two people. Remembering how she once feared that Peter would end up in prison, Lowry felt that she could relate to Karla Faye. In *Crossed Over: A Murder, A Memoir*, Lowry used fictional techniques to tell the stories of both young people and to delve into her own memories. A troubled teenager also appears in *Breaking Gentle*, but Bethany Caldwell is just one of four major characters in this novel about an East Texas farm family. Again, the subject is alienation, but in this case the cause is inadequate communication, as the author demonstrates by switching from one point of view to another, often in mid-conversation. Not until the Caldwells learn to respect each other as they do their quarter horses can they feel free to break out of their isolation.

If there are two qualities that mark both Lowry's works and her life, they are honesty and courage. Though her books deal with such issues as social injustice, personal frustration, isolation, alienation, unqualified evil, and unjustified tragedy, Lowry finds much to laugh at in human behavior and a good deal to admire, in particular, Southern women who insist on becoming more than their society expects. In them seems to lie our best hope for a better world.

—Rosemary M. Canfield Reisman

LYON, George Ella

Born: George Ella Vernon in Harlan, Kentucky, 25 April 1949. **Education**: Centre College of Kentucky, B.A. 1971; University of Arkansas, M.A. 1972; Indiana University, Ph.D. 1978. **Family**: Married Stephen Lyon (a musician), 3 June 1972; two children. **Career**: Instructor in English and creative writing, University of Kentucky, Lexington, beginning 1977; member of executive committee of Women Writers Conference, 1979-84; visiting assistant professor, Centre College of Kentucky, 1979-80, writer in residence, 1985; lecturer, Transylvania University, 1984-86; visiting faculty, Radford University, 1986, University of Kentucky, 1991-92; coordinator of writers' residency program for Kentucky Arts Council, 1982-84; Member, Nuclear Freeze Group. **Member**: Modern Language Association of America, Virginia Woolf Society, Society of Children's Book Writers, Appalachian Writers Association, Phi Beta Kappa. **Awards**: Lamont Hall Award from Andrew Mountain Press, 1983, for *Mountain*; Golden Kite Award from the Society of Children's Book Writers, for *Borrowed Chil-*

dren; Kentucky Bluegrass Award, for *Basket*; Jesse Stuart Media Award, Kentucky School Media Association, for distinguished body of work. **Address**: 913 Maywick Dr., Lexington, Kentucky 40504.

Publications

Poetry

Mountain. Hartford, Connecticut, Andrew Mountain Press, 1983.
Growing Light. Mill Springs Press, 1987.
Catalpa. Lexington, Wind Publications, 1993.

Children's Books

Father Time and the Day Boxes. Scarsdale, New York, Bradbury, 1985.
A Regular Rolling Noah. Scarsdale, New York, Bradbury, 1986.
A B Cedar: An Alphabet of Trees. New York, Orchard Books, 1989.

Play

Braids. Produced at Transylvania University, Lexington, Kentucky, 1985.

Young Adult Novel

A Throne in Goose Rock, New York, Orchard Books/F. Watts, 1987.

Novels

Borrowed Children. New York, Orchard Books, 1988.
Red Rover, Red Rover, New York, Orchard Books, 1989.
Here and Then, New York, Orchard Books, 1994.
With a Hammer for My Heart. New York, Orchard, 1996.

Picture Books

Together. New York, Orchard Books, 1989.
Come a Tide. New York, Orchard Books, 1990.
Basket. New York, Orchard Books, 1990.
Cecil's Story. New York, Orchard Books, 1991.
The Outside Inn. New York, Orchard Books, 1991.
Who Came Down That Road. New York, Orchard Books, 1992.
Dreamplace. New York, Orchard Books, 1993.
Mama Is a Miner. New York, Orchard Books, 1994.
Five Live Bongos. New York, Scholastic Inc., 1995.
A Day at Damp Camp. New York, Orchard Books, 1996.
Ada's Pal. New York, Orchard Books, 1996.
A Wordful Child. Katonah, New York, Richard C. Owen Publishers, 1996.
A Sign. New York. Orchard Books, 1998.
Counting on the Woods: A Poem. DK Pub., 1998.
A Traveling Cat. New York, Orchard Books, 1998.

Other

Choices: Stories for Adult New Readers. Lexington, University Press of Kentucky, 1989.

Editor, with Bob Henry Baber and Gurney Norman, *Old Wounds, New Words: Poems from the Appalachian Poetry Project.* Ashland, Kentucky, Jesse Stuart Foundation, 1994.

*   *   *

George Ella Lyon writes children's picture books, young adult novels, and poetry. She is also the author of one play, *Braids,* and has been a contributor to numerous scholarly journals focusing on American literature, women's issues, and Appalachian literature and culture. Her numerous works focus on the concerns and the culture of Appalachian people, especially the inhabitants of her native Kentucky.

Generally, her adolescent novels deal with the typical concerns of the young as they attempt to mature into adults. These novels offer strong, adolescent, female characters who face and overcome seemingly insurmountable personal challenges. In similar fashion, Lyon's poetry offers powerful memories of her life while growing up in Appalachia. These poems include remembrances of religious experiences, recollections of family life and the loss of family members through death, as well as literary poems commemorating her favorite author, Virginia Woolf.

A number of Lyon's works are award winners. Her young adult novel *Borrowed Children,* which won the Golden Kite Award from the Society of Children's Book Writers, is a coming-of-age novel set in the Appalachian area of Kentucky. It examines the parallel experiences of a mother and a daughter who both care for their younger siblings because of their mother's incapacitation, one due to grief and the other due to sickness. The novel is rich in characterization with many diverse and fully developed characters that adequately relate the Appalachian culture of Kentucky after the Great War.

Another of her adolescent novels, *Basket,* which won the Kentucky Bluegrass Award, tells the story of a grandmother's basket as it becomes embedded in many family legends. *Red Rover, Red Rover* deals with a young girl's loss of her grandfather through death, her brother who goes away to boarding school, and her best friend whose family moves away to another town. The novel is set in the Appalachian mountains in 1962 as the main character, a young lady by the name of Sumi, finds herself facing adolescence without her three closest friends. In Sumi, Lyon offers young women a positive role model to follow as they too face the challenges that come with puberty and their changing roles in life.

Here and Then, a novel that combines historical events with time travel, does not really qualify as young adult and really should be read by younger readers. The novel is plagued by a series of weak characters who face unrealistic challenges and a plot that is at times very confusing and hard to follow. The main character, Abby, finds herself haunted by a Civil War nurse named Eliza Hoskins. When she writes in her diary, she opens a connection between herself and Eliza in the earlier time. Abby and her best friend Harper formulate an elaborate plan to raise money to buy medical supplies to carry back in time to Eliza who will need them to save many lives during an upcoming battle. Although this novel suffers from serious flaws, it is still an interesting and easy read for younger readers who enjoy historical fiction.

Lyon's numerous children's picture books deal with many different themes. Books like *Mama Is a Miner, Come a Tide, A Regular Rolling Noah,* and *Basket* deal with Appalachian themes. In *Mama Is a Miner,* Lyon describes the life of a female Kentucky coal miner through the eyes of her daughter. The visually stunning images from the illustrator Peter Catalanotto add to the modernity of this picture book. On the other hand, the picture book, *Come a Tide,* gives a light-hearted account of the spring floods in rural Appalachia. *A Regular Rolling Noah* is a tale of a young boy hired to shepherd a boxcar full of farm animals from Kentucky to Canada.

Lyon's *Father Time and the Day Boxes* and *A B Cedar,* on the other hand, have no particular ties to the Appalachian culture that Lyon writes so eloquently about. *Father Time,* illustrated by Robert Andrew Parker, offers beautiful imagery and tells a story of how each day comes to us as Father Time tosses down one of the 365 packets he keeps safe in his vault in the clouds. *A B Cedar* is an alphabet book that uses drawings of different trees to illustrate the alphabet. The novels, children's books, and poetry of George Ella Lyon offer interesting insights into rural Kentucky Applachian culture as seen through the experiences that the author had as she grew up in this culture.

Lyon has said that writing for her is a spiritual journey. This spiritual journey is quite clearly seen in her many works of fiction. Indeed, as she so eloquently says, "I believe all of us are given different gifts which require that we give up our ego selves in order to receive and pass the gift on. We do this imperfectly, of course, but in the labor we feel God's presence, and in the synthesis of song or poem, dance or painting, we share in the joy of the Maker." May we all share in the labor and synthesis that makes up the world of George Ella Lyon.

— Keith Stiles

LYTLE, Andrew

Born: Andrew Nelson Lytle in Murfreesboro, Tennessee, 26 December 1902. **Education:** Sewanee Military Academy, Sewanee, Tennessee (Validictorian, Class of 1920); New College, Oxford, Fall, 1920; Vanderbilt University, Nashville, B.A. 1925 (Phi Beta Kappa); Yale University School of Drama, New Haven, Connecticut, 1927-29. **Family:** Married Edna Langdon Barker, 1938 (died 1963); three daughters. **Career:** Professor of history, Southwestern College, Memphis, Tennessee, 1936; professor of history, University of the South, Sewanee, Tennessee, and managing editor, *Sewanee Review,* 1942-44; lecturer, 1946-48, and acting head, 1947-48, University of Iowa School of Writing, Iowa City; lecturer in creative writing, University of Florida, Gainesville, 1948-61; lecturer in English, 1961-67, professor of English, 1968-73, editor, *Sewanee Review,* 1961-73, University of the South; visiting professor of English, University of Kentucky, 1976, Vanderbilt University, 1978. **Awards:** Guggenheim fellowship, 1940, 1941, 1960; *Kenyon Review* fellowship, 1956; National Institute of Arts and Letters Fellowship, 1966-67; University of the South Brown fellowship, 1978, 1981; Lyndhurst Foundation Award, 1985; Ingersoll Foundation prize, 1986; Litt.D. from Kenyon College, Gambier, Ohio, 1965, University of Florida, 1970, and University of the South, 1973; D.H.L from Hillsdale College, Michigan, 1985. **Died:** In 1995.

PUBLICATIONS

Novels

The Long Night. Indianapolis, Bobbs Merrill, 1936.
At the Moon's Inn. Indianapolis, Bobbs Merrill, 1941.
A Name for Evil. Indianapolis, Bobbs Merrill, 1947.
The Velvet Horn. New York, McDowell Obolensky, 1957.

Short Stories

A Novel, A Novella and Four Stories. New York, McDowell Obolensky, 1958.
Alchemy. Winston-Salem, North Carolina, Palaemon Press, 1979.
Stories: Alchemy and Others. Sewanee, Tennessee, University of the South, 1984.

Uncollected Short Story

"Old Scratch in the Valley," in *Virginia Quarterly Review*, 1935.

Other

Bedford Forrest and His Critter Company (biography). New York, Minton Balch, 1931.
The Hero with the Private Parts: Essays. Baton Rouge, Louisiana State University Press, 1966.
A Wake for the Living: A Family Chronicle. New York, Crown, 1975.
The Lytle/Tate Letters, with Allen Tate, edited by Thomas Daniel Young and Elizabeth Sarcone). Jackson, University Press of Mississippi, 1987.
Southerners and Europeans: Essays in a Time of Disorder. Baton Rouge, Louisiana State University Press, 1988.
From Eden to Babylon: The Social and Political Essays of Andrew Nelson Lytle, edited by M.E. Bradford. Washington, D.C., Regnery, 1990.
Kristin: A Reading. Columbia, University of Missouri Press, 1992.

Editor, *Craft and Vision: The Best Fiction from The Sewanee Review.* New York, Delacorte Press, 1971.

*

Bibliographies: *Andrew Nelson Lytle: A Bibliography 1920-1982* by Stuart Wright, Sewanee, Tennessee, University of the South, 1982; *Andrew Lytle, Walker Percy, Peter Taylor: A Reference Guide* by Victor A. Kramer, Boston, Hall, 1983.

Manuscript Collections: Joint University Libraries (Vanderbilt University), Nashville, Tennessee; University of Florida Library, Gainesville.

Critical Studies: "Andrew Lytle Issue" of *Mississippi Quarterly,* State College, Fall 1970; *The Form Discovered: Essays on the Achievement of Andrew Lytle* edited by M. E. Bradford, Jackson, University and College Press of Mississippi, 1973; *The Southern*

Vision of Andrew Lytle by Mark Lucas, Baton Rouge, Louisiana State University Press, 1986; "Andrew Lytle Issue" of the *Chattahoochee Review,* DeKalb College, Summer 1988.

Video: *Andrew Lytle: The Steady Sense of Time* produced by Vernon S. Taylor, University of the South Press, Sewanee, Tennessee.

Andrew Lytle commented:
It is the writer's nature to discover for himself his meaning by matching his knowledge of experience against his imagination. This never comes in a burst of light, but out of a gradual exploration into the dark places of the mind and heart of man.

*   *   *

Described by Robert Penn Warren as "the perfect listener to tales because he was the perfect teller of tales," Andrew Lytle grew up in middle Tennessee hearing many of the family and community stories recorded in his cultural memoir, *A Wake for the Living*. A graduate of Vanderbilt University where he associated with the Fugitive poets, Lytle wrote his first essay, "The Hind Tit," for the Agrarian manifesto, *I'll Take My Stand* (1930). In the cogency of its argument against forces that threaten the family and community and in the beauty of its description of the daily life of a yeoman farmer, "The Hind Tit" reveals a literary promise that led to a novella, four short stories, four novels, a biography, and some of the most astute literary, social, and political criticism in Southern letters.

In his commentary on Andrew Lytle, Robert Weston argues that Lytle's subject is the myth of progress in reverse, a position confirmed in many of Lytle's essays but qualified in his fiction that dramatizes both the light and dark sides of tradition. Raised in the pre-modern South, "closer to the 12th century than to (the world of) my grandchildren," Lytle attacks the South's shift from an agrarian to an urban-industrial society in his social and political essays, but concedes in his fiction that the old agrarian order cannot be restored. Carefully guarding the distinction between the voice of the social critic and that of the artist, he asserts: "In 'The Hind Tit' I took a position. It was a real fight, but I knew when I began writing fiction that the life of the action would take precedence. An artist cannot take such a position. It was like closing a door."

Lytle's biography of Nathan Bedford Forrest, the Tennessee Civil War hero, attributes the defeat of the South less to Yankee invaders than to flaws within the Confederate high command, especially the inordinate focus on Virginia and the faulty leadership of General Braxton Bragg, the villain of the book. Forrest himself has many qualities of the epic hero, "a born god of battle" who knows that the way of the wilderness is "to kill or be killed." Forrest, strategically, is the man of the forest.

Pleasant McIvor, the protagonist of Lytle's first novel, *The Long Night*, is also a man of the forest. In his vendetta against the men who killed his father, Pleasant, even more than Forrest, reveals the ethics of total war—he takes no prisoners. While the biography of Forrest examines strategic blunders that weakened the South during the war, *The Long Night* explores internal reasons for Southern failure. Pride infects the McIvor clan, which seems dangerously isolated from its community. Driven by the voice of his father's ghost, Pleasant must choose to serve the living or the dead. Caught up in the larger violence of the Civil War, he finally chooses to serve the living—too late. With a need as compulsive as that of the ancient mariner, he confesses to his nephew after hiding nearly 40 years in the wilderness.

The most relentless exegesis of violence in American literature, *The Long Night* can be read as a critique of the antebellum South; however, Pleasant's family has been driven into exile from its traditional roots, and "to turn west in those days was to turn away forever." *At The Moon's Inn* also deals with the fatal movement West. Lytle's novella, "Alchemy," serves as a prologue which describes the shine of Inca gold that lured Hernando de Soto and his army into the American wilderness. Four years later a few half-naked men straggled out. The rest had found not gold but death. Here, as in *The Long Night*, the lure of the wilderness represents the chaos that lies beyond the boundaries of civilization and just beneath the surface of life. Both novels are tragic, describing a dying society within which characters turn away from the outer world of political, social, and religious restraints towards the darker realm of "the autonomous mind."

That autonomous ego becomes the subject of Lytle's third novel, *A Name for Evil*, in which Henry Brent, a failed writer and obsessed first-person narrator, sacrifices his art for an "idea," attempting to regenerate the agrarian past by restoring an ancestor's farm. Like Pleasant McIvor, he hears the voice of a family ghost out of a violent past, a voice that reflects his own dark desires. A labyrinthine garden of ice becomes the symbol of Henry's disordered psyche. The other labyrinth is the novel itself, a maze of suggestiveness that recalls its fictional model, Henry James's *The Turn of the Screw*.

Although Lytle's first essay, "The Hind Tit," suggests that a reconstitution of agrarian life is possible, *A Name for Evil* reveals that the moment has forever passed. What remains is the world that Lucius Cree enters at the end of Lytle's fictional masterpiece, *The Velvet Horn*. Vividly dramatizing the disintegration of the old order, *The Velvet Horn* also describes a society in the process of renewal, as Lucius, searching for the dark truth of his origins, is guided by his uncle, Jack Cropleigh, to marriage and the full responsibilities of manhood. Although Lytle stated that his original intention was to "do a long piece of fiction on a society that was dead," he was "saved by the creative act," and discovered that "out of death comes life." Nominated for The National Book Award, *The Velvet Horn* has been described as "the last indubitable masterpiece of literary modernism."

Fiction writer, critic, editor, historian, Lytle also taught Flannery O'Connor at the University of Iowa Writer's Workshop and established writing programs at the University of Florida and the University of the South, where many contemporary Southern authors were his students.

Witnessing most of the great changes of the twentieth century, including the decline of the society into which he was born and the triumph of the world he crusaded against in *I'll Take My Stand*, Lytle dedicated his art not to a narrow defense of the traditional South but to the truth of his imagination, wherever it led. "Life is melodrama. Only art is real."

—Thomas M. Carlson

M

MADDEN, (Jerry) David

Born: Knoxville, Tennessee, 25 July 1933. **Education:** Knox High School, Knoxville; Iowa State Teachers College (now University of Northern Iowa), Cedar Falls, 1956; University of Tennessee, Knoxville, B.S. 1957; San Francisco State College, M.A. 1958; Yale Drama School (John Golden fellow), New Haven, Connecticut, 1959-60. **Military Service:** U.S. Army, 1955-56. **Family:** Married Roberta Margaret Young in 1956; one son. **Career:** Instructor in English, Appalachian State Teachers College, Boone, North Carolina, 1958-59, and Centre College, Danville, Kentucky, 1960-62; lecturer in creative writing, University of Louisville, Kentucky, 1962-64; member of the Department of English, Kenyon College, Gambier, Ohio, and assistant editor, *Kenyon Review,* 1964-66; lecturer in creative writing, Ohio University, Athens, 1966-68; writer-in-residence, 1968-92, director, Creative Writing Program, 1992-94, and since 1994, director, United States Civil War Center, Louisiana State University, Baton Rouge. **Awards:** Rockefeller grant, 1969; National Endowment for the Arts prize, 1970; Bread Loaf Writers Conference William Raney fellowship, 1972. **Address:** 614 Park Boulevard, Baton Rouge, Louisiana 70806.

PUBLICATIONS

Novels

The Beautiful Greed. New York, Random House, 1961.
Cassandra Singing. New York, Crown, 1969.
Brothers in Confidence. New York, Avon, 1972.
Bijou. New York, Crown, 1974.
The Suicide's Wife. Indianapolis, Bobbs Merrill, 1978.
Pleasure-Dome. Indianapolis, Bobbs Merrill, 1979.
On the Big Wind. New York, Holt Rinehart, 1980.

Short Stories

The Shadow Knows. Baton Rouge, Louisiana State University Press, 1970.
The New Orleans of Possibilities. Baton Rouge, Louisiana State University Press, 1982.

Uncollected Short Stories

"My Name Is Not Antonio," in *Yale Literary Magazine* (New Haven, Connecticut), March 1960.
"Hair of the Dog," in *Adam* (Los Angeles), April-November 1967.
"The Master's Thesis," in *Fantasy and Science Fiction* (New York), July 1967.
"Nothing Dies But Something Mourns," in *Carleton Miscellany* (Northfield, Minnesota), Fall 1968.
"The Day the Flowers Came." In *The Best American Short Stories 1969,* edited by Martha Foley and David Burnett. Boston, Houghton Mifflin, 1969.

"A Voice in the Garden," in *English Record* (Oneonta, New York), October 1969.
"Traven." In *Short Stories from the Little Magazines,* edited by Jarvis Thurston and Curt Johnson. Chicago, Scott Foresman, 1970.
"Home Comfort," in *Jeopardy* (Bellingham, Washington), March 1970.
"No Trace." In *The Best American Short Stories 1971,* edited by Martha Foley and David Burnett. Boston, Houghton Mifflin, 1971.
"Night Shift." In *Playboy's Ribald Classics 3.* Chicago, Playboy Press, 1971.
"A Secondary Character," in *Cimarron Review* (Stillwater, Oklahoma), July 1972.
"The Spread-Legged Girl," as Jack Travis, in *Knight* (Los Angeles), October 1972.
"The Singer." In *Scenes from American Life: Contemporary Short Fiction,* edited by Joyce Carol Oates. New York, Vanguard Press, 1973.
"Here He Comes! There He Goes!," in *Contempora* (Atlanta, Georgia), Summer 1973.
"Wanted: Ghost Writer," in *Epoch* (Ithaca, New York), Fall 1973.
"The World's One Breathing," in *Appalachian Heritage* (Pippa Passes, Kentucky), Winter 1973.
"Hurry Up Please, It's Time." In *The Botteghe Oscure Reader,* edited by George Garrett and Katherine Garrison Biddle. Middletown, Connecticut, Wesleyan University Press, 1974.
"The Hero and the Witness," in *New Orleans Review,* vol. 4, no. 3, 1974.
"On the Big Wind." In *The Pushcart Prize 5,* edited by Bill Henderson. Yonkers, New York, Pushcart Press, 1980.
"Putting an Act Together," in *Southern Review* (Baton Rouge, Louisiana), Winter 1980.
"Code-a-Phone," in *Crescent Review* (Winston-Salem, North Carolina), vol. 1, no. 1, 1983.
"Lights," in *New Letters* (Kansas City), Winter 1984-85.
"Rosanna," in *South Dakota Review* (Vermillion), Summer 1985.
"Was Jesse James at Rising Fawn?," in *South Dakota Review* (Vermillion), Autumn 1985.
"Willis Carr at Bleak House." In *The Bread Loaf Anthology of Contemporary American Short Stories,* edited by Robert Pack and Jay Parini. Hanover, New Hampshire, University Press of New England, 1987.
"Gristle," in *Appalachian Heritage* (Berea, Kentucky), Spring-Summer 1988.
"Children of the Sun," in *New Letters* (Kansas City), Summer 1988.
"The Invisible Girl," in *The Southern California Anthology 7.* Los Angeles, University of Southern California Master of Professional Writing Program, 1989.
"The Demon in My View," in *Southern Review* (Baton Rouge, Louisiana), Spring 1989.
"Crossing the Lost and Found River," in *Chattahoochie Review* (Dunwoody, Georgia), Winter 1989.
"James Agee Never Lived in This House," in *Southern Review* (Baton Rouge, Louisiana), Spring 1990.

"A Forgotten Nightmare," in *The Southern Californian Anthology* (Los Angeles), 1991.

"The Last Bizarre Tale," in *Southern Short Stories.* Huntsville, Texas, Huntsville Texas Review Press, 1991.

A Survivor of the Sinking of the Sultana, in *Appalachian Heritage* (Berea, Kentucky), 1992.

"If the Ash Heap Begins to Glow Again . . . ," in *Louisiana English Journal* (Eunice, Louisiana), October 1993.

"Fragments Found on the Field," in *Gulf Coast Collection* (Montrose, Alabama), 1994.

"Hairtrigger Pencil Lines," in *Louisiana Cultural Vistas Magazine* (New Orleans), Spring 1994.

Plays

Call Herman in to Supper. Produced in Knoxville, Tennessee, 1949.

They Shall Endure. Produced in Knoxville, Tennessee, 1953.

Cassandra Singing (produced in Knoxville, Tennessee, 1955); published in *New Campus Writing 2,* edited by Nolan Miller, New York, Putnam, 1957; (expanded version, produced Albuquerque, New Mexico, 1964).

From Rome to Damascus. Produced in Chapel Hill, North Carolina, 1959.

Casina, music by Robert Rogers, lyrics by Joseph Matthewson. Produced New Haven, Connecticut, 1960.

In My Father's House, in *First Stage* (Lafayette, Indiana), Summer 1966.

Fugitive Masks. Produced Abingdon, Virginia, 1966.

The Day the Flowers Came (produced Baton Rouge, Louisiana, 1974); Chicago, Dramatic Publishing Company, 1975.

Other

Wright Morris. New York, Twayne, 1965.

The Poetic Image in Six Genres. Carbondale, Southern Illinois University Press, 1969.

James M. Cain. New York, Twayne, 1970.

Harlequin's Stick, Charlie's Cane: A Comparative Study of Commedia dell'Arte and Silent Slapstick Comedy. Bowling Green, Ohio, Popular Press, 1975.

A Primer of the Novel, For Readers and Writers. Metuchen, New Jersey, Scarecrow Press, 1980.

Writers' Revisions: An Annotated Bibliography of Articles and Books about Writers' Revisions and Their Comments on the Creative Process, with Richard Powers. Metuchen, New Jersey, Scarecrow Press, 1981.

Cain's Craft. Metuchen, New Jersey, Scarecrow Press, 1985.

Revising Fiction: A Handbook for Writers. New York, New American Library, 1988.

The Fiction Tutor. Fort Worth, Texas, Harcourt Brace, 1990.

Editor, *Tough Guy Writers of the Thirties.* Carbondale, Southern Illinois University Press, 1968.

Editor, *Proletarian Writers of the Thirties.* Carbondale, Southern Illinois University Press, 1968.

Editor, *American Dreams, American Nightmares.* Carbondale, Southern Illinois University Press, 1970.

Editor, *Rediscoveries: Informal Essays in Which Well-Known Novelists Rediscover Neglected Works of Fiction by One of Their Favorite Authors.* New York, Crown, 1971.

Editor with Ray B. Browne, *The Popular Cultural Explosion: Experiencing Mass Media.* Dubuque, Iowa, William Brown, 2 vols., 1972.

Editor, *Nathanael West: The Cheaters and the Cheated.* Deland, Florida, Everett Edwards, 1973.

Editor, *Remembering James Agee.* Baton Rouge, Louisiana State University Press, 1974.

Editor, *Creative Choices: A Spectrum of Quality and Technique in Fiction.* Chicago, Scott Foresman, 1975.

Editor with Virgil Scott, *Studies in the Short Story.* New York, Holt Rinehart, 1975; 6th edition, 1984.

Editor with Peggy Bach, *Rediscoveries II.* New York, Carroll and Graf, 1988.

Editor, *Eight Classic American Novels.* San Diego, Harcourt Brace, 1990.

Editor, *The World of Fiction* (short stories). Fort Worth, Texas, Holt Rinehart, 1990.

Editor with Peggy Bach, *Classics of Civil War Fiction.* Jackson, University of Mississippi, 1991.

Editor, *A Pocketful of Prose: Contemporary Short Fiction.* Fort Worth, Texas, Harcourt Brace, 1992.

Editor, *A Pocketful of Prose: Vintage Short Fiction.* Fort Worth, Texas, Harcourt Brace, 1992.

*

Bibliography: "A David Madden Bibliography 1952-1981" by Anna H. Perrault, in *Bulletin of Bibliography* (Westport, Connecticut), September 1982.

Manuscript Collection: University of Tennessee Library, Knoxville.

Critical Studies: "A Conversation with David Madden," and "The Mixed Chords of David Madden's *Cassandra Singing*" by Sanford Pinsker, in *Critique* (Atlanta), vol. 15, no. 2, 1973; "An Interview with David Madden," in *The Penny Dreadful* (Bowling Green, Ohio), vol. 3, no. 3, 1974; "The Story Teller as Benevolent Con Man" by Madden, in *Appalachian Heritage* (Pippa Passes, Kentucky), Summer 1974; interviews in *Southern Review* (Baton Rouge, Louisiana), vol. 11, no. 1, 1975, *New Orleans Review,* Spring 1982, and *Louisiana Literature* (Hammond), Fall 1984; by Jeffrey Richards in *Contemporary Poets, Dramatists, Essayists, and Novelists of the South,* edited by Robert Bain and Joseph M. Flora, Westport, Connecticut, Greenwood Press, 1994.

David Madden comments:

I've been trying all my life to pass the test F. Scott Fitzgerald set for himself. "The test of a first-rate intelligence is the ability to hold two opposed ideas in the mind at the same time and still retain the ability to function." Camus's concept of the absurd helped clarify Fitzgerald's: one's life should be a self-created contradiction of the fact that life is basically absurd. A similar polarity has given some form to my art as well as my life. It was not books but my grandmother's storytelling and the movies' charged images that inspired me to write. My first literary hero was the Dionysian Thomas Wolfe; then came the Apollonian James Joyce. In the tensions between those two extremes I have tried to shape my own work. I have practiced for a long time now the concept that it is between the limitations externally imposed by the form I'm working in and limitations I imposed on myself in the writing of a specific work that I experience genuine and productive freedom. Two metaphors of the artist (and the teacher) are useful for me: the magician and the con man. As with the magician's techniques of illusion, art works by a phantom circuit; and the relationship between writer and reader is like that between the con man and his mark, except that the climax (the sting) is beneficial for both. For me, the function of fiction is to create imaginary words; discipline and technique enable me to cause that to happen. And in that process I consider my reader as an active collaborator.

(1995) Because it is on the crest of a single great wave of creative energy that I enter up all the activities in my life and in my writing, I reject the perception that the fact that I have not published a novel in 15 years is evidence of diminished capacity. In all that time, I have researched and revised *Sharpshooter,* a Civil War novel, and published 14 chapters from it. I have also created the United States Civil War Center. I have the first draft of a book that provides a unique perspective on ancient London Bridge (1110 to 1828). I have always worked simultaneously on five major projects, while taking up dozens of other life and literary projects. Surfing on the one great, never-ending wave of creative force is the life-work for me.

*   *   *

Much of David Madden's fiction is autobiographical. Like Lucius Hutchfield in *Bijou,* Madden goes over his personal history again and again, remolding details. Incidents appear in more than one work; short stories are absorbed into novels; the short novel *Brothers in Confidence* becomes the first half of the longer novel *Pleasure-Dome,* as Madden works at perfecting the tale of his life. Arranged in chronological order Madden's fictional autobiography would begin with two stories from *The Shadow Knows,* "The Pale Horse of Fear" and the title story, then continue on through *Bijou, The Beautiful Greed, Pleasure-Dome,* to the elegiac story "The World's One Breathing."

Madden's goal is to transport his readers into "the Pleasure-Dome." As Lucius says in the novel of that name, "Everyday life is an effort to disentangle facts and illusions. There are rare moments in our lives when we transcend captivity in fact-and-illusion through pure imagination and dwell in the Pleasure-Dome, a luminous limbo between everyday experience and a work of art." Lucius knows well the value of a good story. He is an aspiring writer, and his older brother is a con man—which for Madden is nearly the same thing: "The relationship between the storyteller and the listener is like that between the con man and his mark," Madden has said. Madden himself is at his best when emulating the oral storytelling style he learned from his grandmother when he was growing up in the Tennessee hills, the setting of much of his fiction.

In the stories collected in *The Shadow Knows* the characters are caught between the knowledge that their old lives—in many cases rural or small town lives—are disappearing, and that the new lives available to them are spiritually unsatisfying. Madden's world here is primarily one of moonshiners and county fairs, motorcycles and coalmines, but a few of these stories are set outside the mountains. "Love Makes Nothing Happen," set in Alaska, is the best of these, while "The Day the Flowers Came," set in some

faceless suburb, is maudlin and unbelievable. Two of the mountain stories here turn up as Lucius's memories in *Bijou.*

Bijou picks up Lucius's story in early adolescence, when he becomes an usher in a movie theater. Lucius tries to reinvent his life in the image of the films he sees. The Bijou itself is a symbol of the exotic mysteries of adulthood: ". . . the Bijou . . . seemed foreign, beyond his life, as if he were entering a special Bijou experience prematurely. The Bijou was somehow for other people, people who were superior to him because they'd had Bijou experiences he hadn't had." The promising framework of the theater as Lucius's doorway into adulthood is unfortunately overloaded with page after page of movie synopses, and undercut by the repetitive nature of his experiences with the other characters. We last see Lucius lurking about Thomas Wolfe's house, ready to give up films for the idea of the writer's life.

The Beautiful Greed relates the adventures of a young man named Alvin (who is just a little older than Lucius at the end of *Bijou*) on a merchant marine voyage to South America. This novel was Madden's first, and it seems thin in almost all regards when compared to his later works, though the plot here is unusually straight for Madden.

Pleasure-Dome is perhaps Madden's finest novel to date, despite a structure of two clumsily hinged together story lines. Lucius Hutchfield is once again the main character. He has been in the merchant marine and has become a writer since the events of *Bijou.* Lucius spends the first half of the novel trying to free his younger brother from jail by using his storytelling gifts. But it is the eldest brother, the con man, who succeeds in this—by telling taller tales than those Lucius tells. The second half is a cautionary tale about the responsibilities of being a storyteller. A boy's outlaw side lies dormant until Lucius awakens it with a story about Jesse James. The boy tries to emulate the outlaw's success with a young woman, with disastrous results. Though the boy goes to prison he is happy: he has on some small scale entered the world of legendary figures.

Cassandra Singing, the story of a wild boy and his invalid sister, is generally considered one of Madden's least autobiographical works, but it would be more accurate to say that Madden's character is here split between Lone and his sister Cassie. Lone is the motorcycle rider, the one with the need to escape the small world of the hills, while bedridden Cassie's life is in touch with the country's oral tradition, through the songs and stories she knows. That these two lie down together as the novel's end may be more of a self-portrait than a suggestion of incest. *On the Big Wind* is a loose string of satiric sketches with obvious targets, tied together by the voice of Big Bob Travis, nomadic radio announcer. The most telling thing here is "The World's One Breathing," spliced in from *The Shadow Knows.*

The Suicide's Wife stands apart from the rest of Madden's work. It is the story of a woman, and a story of the city. The language and plot are very spare and straightforward. Ann Harrington's husband kills himself, leaving "a vacuum into which *things* rushed." The novel is the story of Ann's struggle to gain a command over these "things," which is also the struggle to open herself to possibilities: "Before, I had never really imagined possibilities. Since she never caused events, they just happened, and she took them as they came." Ann's triumph over the foreboding world of "things" is symbolized by her successful quest to earn a driver's license, an official recognition of her right to take herself where she wants to go.

—William C. Bamberger

MADHUBUTI, Haki R.

Born: Don L. Lee in Little Rock, Arkansas, 23 February 1942. **Education:** Wilson Junior College; University of Illinois, Chicago Circle; Chicago City College, A.A. 1966; Roosevelt University, Chicago, 1966-67; University of Iowa, Iowa City, M.F.A. 1984. **Military Service:** United States Army, 1960-63. **Family:** Married Johari Amini; two children. **Career:** Apprentice curator, DuSable Museum of African American History, Chicago, 1963-67; stock department clerk, Montgomery Ward, Chicago, 1963-64; post office clerk, Chicago, 1964-65; junior executive, Spiegels, Chicago, 1965-66; taught at Columbia College, Chicago, 1968; writer-in-residence, Cornell University, 1968-69, Morgan State College, Baltimore, 1972-73, Howard University, 1970-75, and Central State University, Wilberforce, Ohio, 1979-80; poet-in-residence, Northeastern Illinois State College, Chicago, 1969-70; lecturer, University of Illinois, Chicago, 1969-71; since 1967, editor and publisher, Third World Press, Chicago; since 1969, director, Institute of Positive Education, Chicago; since 1972 editor, *Black Books Bulletin,* Chicago; since 1984, associate professor of English, Chicago State University; founding member, Organization of Black American Culture Writers Workshop, 1967-75. **Awards:** National Endowment for the Arts grant, 1969, 1982; Kuumba Workshop Black Liberation award, 1973. **Address:** Third World Press, 7524 South Cottage Grove Avenue, Chicago, Illinois 60619.

PUBLICATIONS (EARLY WORKS THROUGH 1971 AS DON L. LEE)

Poetry

Think Black. Detroit, Broadside Press, 1967; revised edition, 1968, 1969.
Black Pride. Detroit, Broadside Press, 1968.
Back Again, Home. Detroit, Broadside Press, 1968.
One Sided Shoot-Out. Detroit, Broadside Press, 1968.
For Black People (And Negroes Too). Chicago, Third World Press, 1968.
Don't Cry, Scream. Detroit, Broadside Press, 1969.
We Walk the Way of the New World. Detroit, Broadside Press, 1970.
Directionscore: Selected and New Poems. Detroit, Broadside Press, 1971.
Book of Life. Detroit, Broadside Press, 1973.
Earthquakes and Sunrise Missions: Poetry and Essays of Black Renewal 1973-1983. Chicago, Third World Press, 1984.
Killing Memory, Seeking Ancestors. Detroit, Lotus, 1987.
GroundWork: Selected Poems of Haki R. Madhubuti/Don L. Lee (1966-1996). Chicago, Third World Press, 1996.
Heartlove: Wedding, Love, and Extended Family Poems. Chicago, Third World Press, 1998.

Other

Dynamite Voices: Black Poets of the 1960s. Detroit, Broadside Press, 1971.
Kwanzaa: A Progressive and Uplifting African American Holiday. Chicago, Third World Press, 1972.
From Plan to Planet: Life Studies: The Need for Afrikan Minds and Institutions. Detroit, Broadside Press, 1973.
(Introduction) *Horizons East,* by Jube Shiver, Jr. Syracuse, Group Alternative Media Associates in the 3rd World, 1974.
A Capsule Course in Black Poetry Writing, with others. Detroit, Broadside Press, 1975.
Enemies: The Clash of Races. Chicago, Third World Press, 1978.
Say That the River Turns: The Impact of Gwendolyn Brooks. Chicago, Third World Press, 1987.
Black Men: Obsolete, Single, Dangerous? Afrikan American Families in Transition: Essays in Discovery, Solution, and Hope. Chicago, Third World Press, 1990.
Claiming Earth: Race, Rage, Rape, Redemption: Blacks Seeking a Culture of Enlightened Empowerment. Chicago, Third World Press, 1994.
Africa-Centered Education: Its Value, Importance, and Necessity in the Development of Black Children. Chicago, Third World Press, 1994.

Author of introduction, *So Far, So Good,* by Gil Scott-Heron. Chicago, Third World Press, 1990.

Editor, with Patricia L. Brown and Francis Ward, *To Gwen with Love.* Chicago. Johnson, 1971.
Editor, *Children of Africa.* Chicago, Third World Press, 1993.

*

Recording: *Rappin' and Readin','* Detroit, Broadside Press, 1971.

Critical Studies: "The Relevancy of Don L. Lee as a Contemporary Black Poet" by Annette Sands, *Black World* (Chicago), June 1972; "Some Black Thoughts on Don L. Lee's *Think Black:* Thanks by a Frustrated White Academic Thinker" by Eugene E. Miller, *College English* (Champaign, Illinois), May 1973; *New Directions from Don L. Lee* by Marlene Mosher, Hicksville, New York, Exposition, 1975; *Part of Nature, Part of Us*, by Helen Vendler, Cambridge, Harvard University Press, 1980.

*   *   *

Looking at the continuum of his writing, one is impressed by Haki R. Madhubuti's matured technical independence, worldview, awareness of the social implications of technology, and abiding love for his people. The result is poetry that successfully conveys spontaneity and emotional compulsion as well as thoughtful ideological commitment. Beginning as one of the young African-American poets who emerged during the Black Arts movement in the late 1960s, Madhubuti (known at the start of his career as Don L. Lee) proved to be one of the most powerful in content and one of the most creative and influential in technique. Some earlier perceptions of him as brash, irreverent, or almost fanatical served to divert attention from certain qualities and habits that underlie his revolutionary stance—intellectual thirst, broad and intense reading and study, high seriousness, thoughtful reflection, and a predilection for both analysis and synthesis.

His artistic outlook has always been consciously utilitarian and informed by sociopolitical concerns centering in black people's self-definition, self-determination, self-help through collective and institutional efforts, and humanness. Examples include "In the Interest of Black Salvation," which shows disillusionment with orthodox Euro-American religion; "Back Home Again," an account of an excursion into an alien (white) "establishment" world and a subsequent return to blackness; "But He Was Cool," a satire on vapid, faddish, and showy lifestyles affected by some African-Americans; and "Re-Act for Action," a cry for aggression against racism.

While his focus is socioethnic, Madhubuti's thematic concerns may be considered universally relevant. A people's needs, he asserts, are food, clothing, shelter, and education. In the context of this worldview, he believes that the miseducation of African-Americans has conditioned them to "do what / they / have been taught to do." Thus, because African-American men find themselves "walking the borders / between / smiles and outrage," they must see clearly and act responsibly and morally. He writes that "conscious men do not make excuses / do not expect their women to carry their water, / harvest the food and prepare it too. / World over it is known that / breast sucking is only guaranteed for babies." As a corollary he points out the inherent power of women: "if black women do not love, / there is no love." Of their inherent beauty, he writes that "dark women are music / some complicated well worked / rhythms / others simple melodies." To both men and women, he advises, "be what you want your children to be."

An example of Madhubuti particular interest in the African diaspora is shown by the dedication of the title poem in his collection *Killing Memory, Seeking Ancestors* to Nelson and Winnie Mandela. Thinking in international terms, he foresees "The End of White World Supremacy" as "The day, hour, minute / and / second that the / chinese / and / japanese / sign / a / joint / industrial / and / military / pact."

Madhubuti prefers the speech of the African-American urban masses, much of it well suited for oral delivery, and, in fact, he is in demand for public appearances. Particularly in his earlier poetry, he frequently achieves desired aural effects through extra vowels or consonants, phonetic spellings, and elisions. In his earlier work he is partial to spatial arrangements, broken words, unconventional syntax and punctuation, and the ampersand and diagonal. Throughout his corpus he is fond of playing with words, particularly syntactic reversals and the breaking of words into components—for irony, purposeful double meaning, emphasis of discreet components of meaning, aural effects, and other reasons. His imagery is strong, concrete, and specific. Occasionally his late poetry, most noticeable in *Killing Memory, Seeking Ancestors,* moves toward prose poetry, as in "Poet: Whatever Happened to Luther." Frequently he builds a poem's tension incrementally, withholding its point or resolution until the end, at which time the poem's logic or impact is made manifest.

Madhubuti illustrates the office of poet as shaman, griot, priest, prophet, and seer.

—Theodore R. Hudson

MAJOR, Clarence

Born: Atlanta, Georgia, 31 December 1936. **Education:** The Art Institute, Chicago (James Nelson Raymond scholar), 1952-54; Armed Forces Institute, 1955-56; New School for Social Research, New York, 1972; Norwalk College, Connecticut; State University of New York, Albany, B.S. 1976; Union Graduate School, Yellow Springs and Cincinnati, Ohio, Ph.D. 1978. **Military Service:** U.S. Air Force, 1955-57. **Family:** Married 1) Joyce Sparrow in 1958 (divorced 1964); 2) Pamela Ritter in 1980. **Career:** Research analyst, Simulmatics, New York, 1966-67; director of creative writing program, Harlem Education Program, New Lincoln School, New York, 1967-68; writer-in-residence, Center for Urban Education, 1967-68, and Teachers and Writers Collaborative, Columbia University Teachers College, 1967-71, both New York; lecturer, Brooklyn College, City University of New York, 1968-69, spring 1973, 1974-75, Cazenovia College, New York, summer 1969, Wisconsin State University, Eau Claire, fall 1969, Queens College, City University of New York, springs 1972, 1973, and 1975, and fall 1973, Sarah Lawrence College, Bronxville, New York, 1972-75, and School for Continuing Education, New York University, spring 1975; writer-in-residence, Aurora College, Illinois, spring 1974; assistant professor, Howard University, Washington, D.C., 1974-76, and University of Washington, Seattle, 1976-77; visiting assistant professor, University of Maryland, College Park, spring 1976, and State University of New York, Buffalo, summer 1976; associate professor, 1977-81, and professor, 1981-89, University of Colorado, Boulder; director of creative writing, 1991-93, and since 1989 professor, University of California, Davis; visiting professor, University of Nice, France, 1981-82, fall 1983, University of California, San Diego, spring 1984, and State University of New York, Binghamton, spring 1988; writer-in-residence, Albany State College, Georgia, 1984, and Clayton College, Denver, Colorado, 1986, 1987; distinguished visiting writer, Temple University, Philadelphia, fall 1988; guest writer, Warren Wilson College, 1988. Editor, *Coercion Review,* Chicago, 1958-66; staff writer, *Proof* and *Anagogic and Paideumic Review,* Chicago, 1960-61; associate editor, *Caw,* New York, 1967-70, and *Journal of Black Poetry,* San Francisco, 1967-70; reviewer, *Essence* magazine, 1970-73; columnist, 1973-76, and contributing editor, 1976-86, *American Poetry Review,* Philadelphia; editor, 1977-78, and since 1978 associate editor, *American Book Review,* New York; associate editor, *Bopp,* Providence, Rhode Island, 1977-78, *Gumbo,* 1978, *Departures,* 1979, and *par rapport,* 1979-82; member of the editorial board, *Umojo,* Boulder, Colorado, 1979-80; editorial consultant, Wesleyan University Press, Middletown, Connecticut, 1984, and University of Georgia Press, Athens, 1987; since 1986 fiction editor, *High Plains Literary Review,* Denver. Also artist: individual shows—Sarah Lawrence College, 1974; First National Bank Gallery, Boulder, Colorado, 1986. **Awards:** National Council on the Arts award, 1970; National Endowment for the Arts grant, 1970, 1975, 1979; Creative Artists Public Service grant, 1971; Fulbright-Hays Exchange award, 1981; Western States Book award, for fiction, 1986; Pushcart prize, for short story, 1989. **Agent:** Susan Bergholtz, 340 West 72nd Street, New York, New York 10023. **Address:** Department of English, Sproul Hall, University of California, Davis, California 95616.

PUBLICATIONS

Poetry

The Fires that Burn in Heaven. Privately printed, 1954.
Love Poems of a Black Man. Omaha, Nebraska, Coercion Press, 1965.
Human Juices. Omaha, Nebraska, Coercion Press, 1965.
Swallow and Lake. Middletown, Connecticut, Wesleyan University Press, 1970.
Symptoms and Madness. New York, Corinth, 1971.
Private Line. London, Paul Breman, 1971.
The Cotton Club: New Poems. Detroit, Broadside Press, 1972.
The Syncopated Cakewalk. New York, Barlenmir House, 1974.
Inside Diameter: The France Poems. Sag Harbor, New York, and London, Permanent Press, 1985.
Surfaces and Masks. Minneapolis, Coffee House Press, 1988.
Some Observations of a Stranger at Zuni in the Latter Part of the Century. Los Angeles, Sun and Moon Press, 1989.
Parking Lots. Mount Horeb, Wisconsin, Perishable Press, 1992.

Novels

All-Night Visitors. New York, Olympia Press, 1969.
NO. New York, Emerson Hall, 1973.
Reflex and Bone Structure. New York, Fiction Collective, 1975.
Emergency Exit. New York, Fiction Collective, 1979.
My Amputations. New York, Fiction Collective, 1986.
Such Was the Season. San Francisco, Mercury House, 1987.
Painted Turtle: Woman with Guitar. Los Angeles, Sun and Moon Press, 1988.
Dirty Bird Blues. N.p., 1996.

Short Stories

Fun and Games. Duluth, Minnesota, Holy Cow! Press, 1990.

Uncollected Short Stories

"Church Girl," in *Human Voices 3* (Homestead, Florida), Summer-Fall 1967.
"An Area in the Cerebral Hemisphere." In *Statements,* edited by Jonathan Baumbach, New York, Braziller, 1975.
"Dossy O." In *Writing under Fire,* edited by Jerome Klinkowitz and John Somer, New York, Dell, 1978.
"Tattoo." In *American Made,* edited by Mark Leyner, Curtis White, and Thomas Glynn, New York, Fiction Collective, 1987.

Other

Dictionary of Afro-American Slang. New York, International, 1970; as *Black Slang: A Dictionary of Afro-American Talk,* London, Routledge, 1971.
The Dark and Feeling: Black American Writers and Their Work. New York, Third Press, 1974.
Juba to Jive: A Dictionary of African-American Slang. New York, Viking, 1994.

Editor, *Writers Workshop Anthology.* New York, Harlem Education Project, 1967.

Editor, *Man Is Like a Child: An Anthology of Creative Writing by Students.* New York, Macomb's Junior High School, 1968.
Editor, *The New Black Poetry.* New York, International, 1969.
Editor, *Calling the Wind: Twentieth Century African-American Short Stories.* New York, Harper Collins, 1993.
Editor, *The Garden Thrives: Twentieth Century African-American Poetry.* New York, Harper Collins, 1995.

*

Bibliographies: "Clarence Major: A Checklist of Criticism" by Joe Weixlmann, in *Obsidian* (Fredonia, New York), vol. 4, no. 2, 1978; "Toward a Primary Bibliography of Clarence Major" by Joe Weixlmann and Clarence Major, in *Black American Lierature Forum* (Terre Haute, Indiana), Summer 1979.

Critical Studies: In *New York Times,* 7 April 1969; *Quarterly Journal of Speech* (New York), April 1971; *Saturday Review* (New York), 3 April 1971; *Chicago Sun-Times,* 28 April 1971; *Poetry* (Chicago), August 1971; *Virginia Quarterly Review* (Charlottesville), Winter 1971; *New York Times Book Review,* 1 July 1973; *Interviews with Black Writers* edited by John O'Brien, New York, Liveright, 1973; "Five Black Poets: History, Consciousness, Love and Harshness," in *Parnassus* (New York), 3, Spring-Summer 1975; and *Drumvoices: The Mission of Afro-American Poetry—A Critical History, New York,* Doubleday, 1976, both by Eugene B. Redmond; *The Life: The Lore and Folk Poetry of the Black Hustler* by Dennis Wepman, Ronald B. Newman, and Murray B. Binderman, Philadelphia, University of Pennsylvania Press, 1976; "Clarence Major: Persephone in Fragments," in *Open Form and the Feminine Imagination,* by Stephen-Paul Martin, Washington, D.C., Maisonneuve Press, 1988.

Clarence Major comments:
I am trying to break through the artificial effects of language. I'm also trying to break down the artificial distinctions between poetry and fiction.

* * *

"In a novel, the only thing you have is words," Clarence Major told interviewer John O'Brien. "You begin with words and you end with words. The content exists in our minds. I don't think it has to be a reflection of anything. It is a reality that has been created inside of a book." Major's fiction exists as a rebellion against the stereotype of mimetic fiction—that telling a story, one of the things fiction can do, is the only thing fiction can do.

His first novel, *All-Night Visitors,* is an exercise in the imaginative powers of male sexuality. Major takes the most physical theme—the pleasure of the orgasm—and lyricizes it, working his imagination upon the bedrock and world of sense not customarily indulged by poetry. The pre-eminence of the imagination is shown by blending Chicago street scenes with fighting in Vietnam—in terms of the writing itself, Major claims that there is no difference. His second novel, *NO,* alternates narrative scenes of rural Georgia life with a more disembodied voice of fiction, and the action advances as it is passed back and forth, almost conversationally, between these two fictive voices. In both books, language itself is the true locus of action, as even the most random and routine development is seized as the occasion for raptures of prose (a fellatio scene, for example, soon outstrips itself as pornography and turns into an excuse for twelve pages of exuberant prose).

Major's best work is represented in his third and fourth novels, *Reflex and Bone Structure* and *Emergency Exit*. In the former, he describes an action which takes place legitimately within the characters' minds, as formed by images from television and film. "We're in bed watching the late movie. It's 1938. *A Slight Case of Murder.* Edward G. Robinson and Jane Bryan. I go into the bathroom to pee. Finished, I look at my aging face. Little Caesar. I wink at him in the mirror. He winks back. I'm back in bed. The late show comes on. It's 1923. *The Bright Shawl.* Dorothy Gish. Mary Astor. I'm taking Mary Astor home in a yellow taxi. Dorothy Gish is jealous."

Throughout *Reflex and Bone Structure,* which treats stimuli from social life and the output of a television set as equally informative, Major insists that the realm of all these happenings is in language itself. "I am standing behind Cora," he writes. "She is wearing a thin black nightgown. The backs of her legs are lovely. I love her. The word standing allows me to watch like this. The word nightgown is what she is wearing. The nightgown itself is in her drawer with her panties. The word Cora is wearing the word nightgown. I watch the sentence: the backs of her legs are lovely."

As a result, the action of this novel takes place not simply in the characters' behavior but in the arrangements of words on the page. Here Major makes a significant advance over the techniques of his innovative fiction contemporaries. Many of them, including Ronald Sukenick (in *Up*) and John Barth (in the stories of *Lost in the Funhouse*), took a metafictive approach, establishing fiction's self-apparency and anti-illusionism by self-consciously portraying the writer writing his story. In *Reflex and Bone Structure,* however, Major accomplishes the task of making the words function not as references to things in the outside world but as entities themselves; the action is syntactic rather than dramatic, although once that syntactic function is served the action, as in the paragraph cited, can return for full human relevance. Indeed, because the activity is first located within the act of composition itself, the reader can empathize even more with the intensity of feeling behind it.

Emergency Exit is Major's most emphatic gesture toward pure writing, accomplished by making the words of his story refer inward to his own creative act, rather than outward toward the panoramic landscape of the socially real. The novel's structure makes this strategy possible. *Emergency Exit* consists of elementary units of discourse; words, sentences, paragraphs, vignettes, and serial narratives. The novel is composed of equal blocks of each, spread out and mixed with the others. At first, simple sentences are presented to the reader. Then elements from these same sentences (which have stood in reference-free isolation) recur in paragraphs, but still free of narrative meaning. The plan is to fix a word, as word, in the reader's mind, apart from any personal conceptual reference—just as an abstract expressionist painter will present a line, or a swirl of color, without any reference to figure. Then come a number of narratives, coalescing into a story of lovers and family. When enough sections of the serial narrative have accumulated to form a recognizable story, we find that the independent and fragmentary scenes of the sentences and paragraphs have been animated by characters with whom we can now empathize. Fore-

stalling any attempt to rush off the page into incidental gossip is the memory and further repetition of these words—whether they be of black mythology, snatches of popular song, or simply brilliant writing—all within Major's arresting sentences and paragraphs. A word, an image, or scene which occurs within the narrative leads the reader directly back to the substance of Major's writing. All attention is confined within the pages of the book.

Silent as a writer for the better part of a decade, though actively engaged in teaching, speaking, and world travel, Major takes the occasion of his fifth novel, *My Amputations,* to comment on his own identity as a writer and person. His protagonist, named Mason Ellis, has a biography which matches Major's own, and his responsiveness to black music and folklore recalls the techniques of *Emergency Exit.* Mason's writing is like a closet he steps into in a recurring dream: a "door to darkness, closed-off mystery" through which his muse leads him in search of his personal and literary identities, both of which have been assumed by an "Impostor" nearly a decade ago (when Major's last novel was written). Mason's personal struggle has been with "the unmistakable separation of Church and State," which for him produces an unbearable polarity between spirit and body, mentality and sexuality, and eventually a contradiction between "clean" and "dirty" which he refuses to accept. His muse must guide him away from this middle ground of separation where he languishes; imprisoned in various forms of life (which correspond to Major's background growing up in Chicago and serving in the Air Force), he must literally "write his way out" by constructing a different paradigm for God's interests and Caesar's. Falsely jailed while "the Impostor" continues his career, Mason joins a group of urban terrorists who rob a bank to finance their dreams—in his case, the recovery of his role as novelist. To do this, Mason adopts the pose of the black American writer abroad, living in Nice and speaking at various universities across Europe. But at every stage the concerns of State intervene, as each country's particular style of political insurgency disrupts his visit. Even his idealistic goal of Africa is torn by conflicts of body and spirit, and he finds himself either caught in the crossfire of terrorists or imprisoned as a political suspect. These circumstances, while being complications in the narrative, prompt some of the novel's finest writing, as Major couches Mason's behavior in a linguistic responsiveness to the terroristic nature of our times.

The achievement of *My Amputations* is its conception of Mason Ellis as a creature of the world's signs and symbols. He moves in a world of poetic constructions, where even crossing the street is an artistic adventure: "Mason Ellis sang 'Diddie Wa Diddie' like Blind Blake, crossed the street at Fifth Avenue and Forty-Second like the Beatles on the cover of *Abbey Road* and reaching the curb leaped into the air and coming down did a couple of steps of the Flat Foot Floogie." Not surprisingly, Major points his character toward a tribal sense of unity in Africa, pre-colonial and hence pre-political, where the separations of "Church" and "State" do not exist.

With his novels *Such Was the Season* and *Painted Turtle: Woman with Guitar* Major makes his closest approach to narrative realism, yet in each case the mimesis is simply a technical device that serves an equally abstract purpose. *Such Was the Season* is ostensibly a gesture toward that most commercially conventional of formats, the family saga, as a nephew from Chicago returns to the

Atlanta home of an old aunt who helped raise him. His visit, however, entails not just the usual thematics of family history and a touch of matriarchy but rather a spectrum study of African-American culture in its many forms, from bourgeois society to political power-playing. Because the narrator is Aunt Eliza herself, the novel becomes much more a study in language than social action, however, for the emphasis remains not on the events themselves but upon her blending them into an interpretive narrative. That Major is ultimately interested in these aesthetic dimensions rather than in the simply social is evident from *Painted Turtle,* in which the story of a native American folksinger's career is told only superficially by the episodic adventures surrounding her work; at the heart of her story is the nature of her poetic expression, passages of which are reproduced as transcriptions of her songs—which are unlike any folksongs the reader may have heard, but much like the linguistic constructions Aunt Eliza fashions in the previous novel as a way of making the emerging reality of her family meaningful to her.

—Jerome Klinkowitz

MASON, Bobbie Ann

Born: Mayfield, Kentucky, 1 May 1940. **Education:** University of Kentucky, Lexington, 1958-62, B.A. 1962; State University of New York, Binghamton, M.A. 1966; University of Connecticut, 1972. **Family:** Married Roger B. Rawlings in 1969. **Career:** Writer, *Mayfield Messenger,* 1960, and Ideal Publishers, New York; contributor to numerous magazines, including *Movie Star, Movie Life,* and *T.V. Star Parade,* 1962-63; assistant professor of English, Mansfield State College, Pennsylvania, 1972-79; frequent contributor to magazines, including the *New Yorker,* which has first reading rights to her stories. **Awards:** Hemingway award, 1983, for *Shiloh and Other Stories;* National Endowment award, 1983; Pennsylvania Arts Council grant, 1983, 1989; Guggenheim fellowship, 1984; American Academy and Institute of Arts and Letters award, 1984; Southern Book award, 1994, for *Feather Crowns.* **Agent:** Amanda Urban, International Creative Management, 40 West 57th Street, New York, New York 10019.

PUBLICATIONS

Short Story Collections

Shiloh and Other Stories. New York, Harper, 1982.
Love Life. New York, Harper, 1989.
Midnight Magic: Selected Short Stories of Bobbie Ann Mason. New York, Harper, 1998.

Novels

In Country. New York, Harper, 1985.
Spence + Lila. New York, Harper, 1988.
Feather Crowns: A Novel. New York, Harper, 1993.

Other

The Girl Sleuth: A Feminist Guide to the Bobbsey Twins, Nancy Drew, and Their Sisters. New York, Feminist Press, 1975.

Nabokov's Garden: A Nature Guide to Ada. Ann Arbor, Michigan, Ardis, 1976.

*

Manuscript Collection: University of Kentucky, Lexington.

Critical Studies: "Making Over or Making Off: The Problem of Identity in Bobbie Ann Mason's Short Fiction," in *Southern Literary Journal* (Chapel Hill, North Carolina), Spring 1986, and "Private Rituals: Coping with Changes in the Fiction of Bobbie Ann Mason," in *Midwest Quarterly* (Pittsburg, Kansas), Winter 1987, both by Albert E. Wilhelm; "Finding One's History: Bobbie Ann Mason and Contemporary Southern Literature," in *Southern Literary Journal* (Chapel Hill, North Carolina), Spring 1987, and "Never Stop Rocking: Bobbie Ann Mason and Rock-and-Roll," in *Mississippi Quarterly* (Jackson), Winter 1988-89, both by Robert H. Brinkmeyer, Jr.; "The Function of Popular Culture in Bobbie Ann Mason's *Shiloh and Other Stories* and *In Country*" by Leslie White, in *Southern Quarterly* (Hattiesburg), Summer 1988; "Bobbie Ann Mason: Artist and Rebel" by Michael Smith, in *Kentucky Review* (Lexington), Autumn 1988; "Downhome Feminists in *Shiloh and Other Stories*" by G. O. Morphew, in *Southern Literary Journal* (Chapel Hill, North Carolina), Spring 1989; "An Interview with Bobbie Ann Mason," by Bonnie Lyons and Bill Oliver, in *Contemporary Literature,* Winter 1991; "An Interview with Bobbie Ann Mason" by Dorothy Combs Hill, in *Southern Quarterly,* Fall 1992; "New Roles, New History and New Patriotism: Bobbie Ann Mason's *In Country*" by June Dwyer, in *Modern Language Studies,* Spring 1992.

*   *   *

A native of Kentucky, Bobbie Ann Mason draws from her regional background to tell the stories of lower middle class and impoverished people caught in the cusp between traditionalism and fast-changing contemporary culture. Her characters often live in Hopewell, her fictional version of her own hometown, Mayfield. As small town and rural life are impacted by the spread of commercial culture—fast food chains, malls, department stores—and popular culture transmitted via television, radio, and print media, her characters struggle with their need for individual expression and their obligations to family, and with feelings of isolation and transience—struggles reflected in relationships that are often emotionally and intellectually fragile.

Along with giving voice to characters in language that reflects their backgrounds, Mason's work is important as a chronicle of the changing physical landscape of the contemporary South. Brand names and popular culture references infiltrate her characters' vocabularies as strip-malling, chain-store spreading, and convenience-promising change sweeps into previously isolated regions. Characters try to make their way amid the changes—some with faith that the transformations bring improvements, others experiencing a deeper alienation—while losing a sense of traditional roles and opportunities, often unsure of how to proceed and struggling to articulate their feelings.

Mason came to national attention with her first short story collection, *Shiloh and Other Stories* (1982). In these pieces and later ones collected in *Love Life* (1989) and *Midnight Magic: Selected*

Short Stories of Bobbie Ann Mason (1998), characters are often presented at a point of transition in their lives. Earlier pieces are usually set in the present with characters mired in an impasse but about to move forward, while later stories frequently mix past and present. "Shiloh" presents the strained relationship of Norma Moffitt and her husband, Leroy, a truck driver on medical leave not sure what to do next with his life or his job. Being together for an extended period for the first time, the couple grows further apart, and a trip to Shiloh, which Leroy hopes will revive their marriage, ends up being the catalyst for revealing their differences. Similarly, the couple in "The Rookers," Mack and Mary Lou, have problems being alone together after their last child leaves home.

Other recurring themes in Mason's short stories include the role of tradition in people's lives—whether they learn to live without it, like Carolyn in "Drawing Names," or find it meaningful, like Joe McClain in "Graveyard Day"—and people faced with the choice of remaining in their native area or pursuing dreams and happiness elsewhere. In "Residents and Transients" from *Shiloh and Other Stories,* for example, the narrator, Mary, returns to rural Kentucky and settles with her husband in the farmhouse that her parents left to move to Florida, but her affair with her dentist, feelings of renewal in the landscape of her youth, and indecision about moving with her husband to a better location for his practice all represent the theme announced in the title.

"Piano Fingers," from *Love Life*, is an example of Mason's increasing blend of past and present in her stories. This piece concerns a twenty-six year-old man suspended between childhood and old age facing job and marriage troubles. While waiting in his car for his daughter to complete her piano lesson, the narrator experiences a sense of melancholy. Such sudden moments of reflection, often triggered by noticing a sight that one might have previously been indifferent to, become potentially insightful, as characters face the possibilities and limitations of their disquieted lives.

The protagonist of Mason's first novel, *In Country* (1985), is one of many Mason characters facing difficult choices. Samantha "Sam" Hughes is a teenager just graduating from high school: her remarried mother lives in Lexington and wants her daughter to enroll at the University of Kentucky, but Sam, leery of her mother and new stepfather, stays with her Uncle Emmett, a disabled Vietnam veteran, and enrolls at Murray State as a commuter student. Through Emmett, Sam hopes to understand her own past, especially her father who died in Vietnam before her birth. After failing to reach insight through Emmett and his other Vietnam veteran friends, Sam has a telling visit to the Vietnam Memorial in Washington, D.C. Among Sam's resources for personal reflection are elements of popular culture: for example, some of her impressions of war come from watching the television show *M*A*S*H*, which hardly prepares her for understanding dislocations the Vietnam War brought to the working-class people around her.

The title of Mason's next novel, *Spence + Lila*, suggests enchanting love, such as that which leads people to announce their love by carving their names onto trees or school desks. However, this work explores the threatened relationship of the title characters, an older married couple, and the manner in which they meet the challenge. Lila faces life-threatening mastectomy and obstructions from hardened arteries in her neck. Her husband, Spence,

and their family, face the prospect of life without her. The couple's relationship and sometimes awkward ways of communicating their love is central to this work about two aging people, while relationships with family members and the physical surroundings enrich the story. Their farm was once isolated, but encroaching urbanization has challenged their ability to retain their livelihood. Spence's impassioned belief in the farm ("This is all there is in the world—it contains everything there is to know or possess, yet everywhere people are knocking their brains out trying to find something different, something better") and his observations on commercial culture, including an exasperating trip to the local Wal-Mart, underscore the effects of change on traditional lifestyles.

In many ways, *Spence + Lila* neatly sums up Mason's recurring themes, and it is not surprising that she turned to the past for her next work, *Feather Crowns: A Novel,* which is dedicated to the memory of her father, who died in 1990 at around the time Mason moved to Lexington for an extended period. Set in Kentucky at the beginning of the 20th century, the story concerns the Wheelers, Christie and James, and the birth of their quintuplets, the first set recorded in North America. Their birth inspires a kind of media frenzy common in America, and after all five babies eventually die the couple is compelled by economic circumstances to go on an exploitative lecture tour with the five bodies of their babies on display. Eventually, the bodies of the quints end up in a scientific institute for research.

After their marriage in 1890 and the birth of their third child a few years later, the Wheelers moved to his family farm in Hopewell, which James viewed as a kind of paradise, but proves too small for the growing family, which the arrival of quintuplets strains further. The Hopewell Quintuplets become media darlings, drawing attention from all quarters—showered with gifts, victimized by greedy businessmen seeking good advertisement potential, scorned by the religiously superstitious—and the Wheelers' lives become a media carnival of questionable motivations within and outside the family. The media tour nearly destroys the relationship between James and Christie, and their struggle to maintain their love amid the turbulence of the larger world and economic hardships are the stuff that makes Mason's work so vital.

—Emma Cobb

McCARTHY, Cormac

Born: Charles McCarthy in Providence, Rhode Island, 20 July 1933. **Education:** University of Tennessee. **Military Service:** U.S. Air Force, 1953-56. **Family:** Married Lee Holman in 1961 (divorced), one child; married Anne de Lisle, 1967 (divorced). **Awards:** Ingram-Merrill Foundation grant for creative writing, 1960; William Faulkner Foundation award, 1965, for *The Orchard Keeper*; American Academy of Arts and Letters traveling fellowship to Europe, 1965-66; Rockefeller Foundation grant, 1966; Guggenheim fellowship, 1976; MacArthur Foundation grant, 1981; National Book award, 1992, for *All the Pretty Horses*; Lyndhurst Foundation grant; Institute of Arts and Letters award. **Agent:** Amanda Urban, International Creative Management, 40 West 57th Street, New York, New York 10019.

PUBLICATIONS

Novels

The Orchard Keeper. New York, Random House, 1965.
Outer Dark. New York, Random House, 1968.
Child of God. New York, Random House, 1974.
Suttree. New York, Random House, 1979.
Blood Meridian; or, The Evening Redness in the West. New York, Random House, 1985.
All the Pretty Horses. New York, Knopf, 1992.
The Crossing. New York, Knopf, 1994.
Cities of the Plain. New York, Knopf, 1998.

Plays

The Gardener's Son (teleplay). Broadcast on PBS, 1977.
The Stonemason: A Play in Five Acts. Hopewell, New Jersey, Ecco Press, 1994.

*

Critical Studies: *The Achievement of Cormac McCarthy* by Vereen M. Bell, Baton Rouge, Louisiana State University Press, 1988; *Perspectives on Cormac McCarthy* edited by Edwin T. Arnold and Dianne C. Luce, Jackson, University Press of Mississippi, 1993; *Notes on Blood Meridian* by John Sepich, Louisville, Kentucky, Bellarmine College Press, 1993; *Sacred Violence: A Reader's Companion to Cormac McCarthy*, edited by Wade Hall and Rick Wallach, El Paso, Texas Western Press, 1995; *Cormac McCarthy* by Robert L. Jarrett, New York, Twayne Publishers, 1997.

*   *   *

Once an obscure "writer's writer" whose books sold few copies and who lived, very modestly, from grant to grant, Cormac McCarthy has recently emerged as an unlikely superstar of American fiction. His sudden rise to fame owes nothing to self-promotion, for he still adheres to his lifelong habit of reclusiveness: he gives no readings, blurbs no books, and is that rare writer who has never taught in college (or even graduated from one). But with the publication of *All the Pretty Horses*, an appealing highbrow western which won the National Book Award in 1992 and went into more than twenty hardcover printings, McCarthy emerged triumphantly from obscurity; today he is probably as well-known as any serious writer in America.

His old obscurity is easier to understand than his new fame, for his work, even in his most popular book, is difficult in several senses. Most obviously, his situations are always violent, sometimes nauseatingly so. "There's no such thing as life without bloodshed," McCarthy has said, and indeed the timeless human will to violence is one of his major preoccupations. And the author seems to make no moral judgments about this violence: his evil characters are seldom punished or even explained. The difficulty of inferring moral judgments from the books is really an aspect of a broader characteristic, which is their stubborn resistance to interpretation of any sort.

Though the novels are crowded with literary and biblical allusions and with what look to be symbols, their effect is often hieroglyphic—one has the feeling of confronting a code whose meanings, though tantalizingly present, remain encrypted and hidden. In place of obvious clues to meaning, McCarthy offers an almost exaggeratedly realistic rendering of the world in all its specificity. He is an astonishingly acute observer whose vast learning embraces everything from fur-trapping to Mexican history, and a lyrical and exact prose stylist able make these matters vivid and compelling. Much of the time McCarthy seems content to lay the world before us in all its mystery and let it, as it were, speak for itself.

McCarthy's work consists of two now equal major portions—a group of four novels set in the south in the nineteenth and twentieth centuries, and another group of four set in the southwest and Mexico during the same periods. The southern books are *The Orchard Keeper, Outer Dark, Child of God*, and *Suttree*. They are related to one another not only in setting but in theme: all of them take place in towns or cities of East Tennessee, and all of them concern the ephemeralness of those communities, and of the civil human impulses they represent, when confronted by wildness in nature or in the human heart.

Of these books *The Orchard Keeper* offers the most in the way of affirmation. To be sure, the events of the novel all revolve around the violent death of a murderous drifter, Kenneth Rattner, whose decomposing corpse forms an almost literal centerpiece for the book. But the major characters—his son John Wesley, the bootlegger who killed him in self-defense, and the old man who faithfully tends his makeshift grave in the woods—form relationships with one another which bring some good out of the event. Such affirmation is altogether missing from the next two novels, which descend much further into human depravity.

Outer Dark concerns the incestuous relationship between Culla Holme and his sister Rinthy, the birth and abandonment of their child, and the horrifying consequences that ensue from these events. *Child of God* is even darker: its protagonist Lester Ballard is a dispossessed farmer who, for reasons McCarthy declines to specify, becomes a serial killer and necrophilic; his crimes are accounted for, with whatever irony the title may contain, only as the will of the Almighty.

Suttree, the last of McCarthy's "southern" books and by most reckonings the best, makes something of a departure. The setting is urban, a dangerous slum neighborhood of Knoxville, and the protagonist Cornelius Suttree, unlike his predecessors, is reflective, articulate, and well-educated, though willingly living among the poor, ignorant, and desperate. But thematically *Suttree* is closely related to the earlier work. Suttree has abandoned wealth and privilege in order to confront life in all its violent mystery, aiming to extract a truth therefrom; but he comes away with only a negative illumination: he learns that life is ceaseless flux—a truth symbolized by the Tennessee River along whose banks the action takes place—and the effort to locate stable truths in that flux is delusive and even destructive.

In 1976, even before *Suttree* was published, McCarthy moved to El Paso, Texas, where he has lived ever since. The move signaled his discovery of a new fictional venue; since *Blood Meridian* appeared in 1985, he has been writing westerns, though highly sophisticated ones which refract the familiar frontier myths through a bewildering array of ironic lenses. That first western novel, set in Texas and Mexico in the 1840s and based on real historical events, may offer the darkest view ever taken of frontier settlement. The white settlers and the Indians they displace seem equally depraved and murderous, and their confrontations result, said one reviewer, in a level of violence unequaled in literature since *The Iliad*.

All the Pretty Horses came next and seemed a new beginning; here the violence is much more restrained and the hero, John Grady Cole, is by far the most admirable of McCarthy's protagonists. His horseback adventure in Mexico, where he travels because his native Texas in 1949 is no longer a frontier, brings him his share of horror and heartbreak, but he returns from it with his idealism and romanticism intact, ready for further adventures.

Seasoned McCarthy readers knew to wait until the other shoe dropped, which it did in *The Crossing*, the next installment of what McCarthy calls his *Border Trilogy*. This novel seems a dark parody of *All the Pretty Horses*; another young man, Billy Parham, crosses the border on an idealistic mission, the return of a captured wolf to its home in the mountains of northern Mexico. But by the time his adventure is over he has lost the wolf, which dies horribly, his loved younger brother Boyd, who dies heroically, and every shred of his faith in God or man.

The trilogy was completed with the publication of *Cities of the Plain*, which brought together the two protagonists of the earlier books. In 1952 John Grady and Billy are cowboys on a New Mexico ranch near El Paso and Juarez, the "cities" alluded to in the title. John Grady, known to his friends as "the all-American cowboy," is the same impossibly idealistic soul who passed untainted through *All the Pretty Horses*; here he is intent upon one more heroic border-crossing, hoping to rescue the beautiful girl he loves from captivity in a Juarez brothel. In this venture Billy is his reluctant accomplice; their adversary is the theatrically evil pimp Eduardo, whom John Grady inevitably meets in violent conflict at the novel's end.

McCarthy knowingly invokes the tropes of Hollywood and fairy tale here, but he undermines them with the horrible events of his ending: the beautiful Magdalena is killed while trying to escape, and though John Grady takes lethal revenge on her pimp, he does so at the cost of his own life. Billy is again a survivor, left even more hopeless and bereft than at the end of *The Crossing*.

As a whole McCarthy's *Border Trilogy* both rejects and perversely affirms the romantic myths of the west: "the all-American cowboy" lives in a world of illusions, believing himself the hero of a fairy tale; but in his stubborn refusal to acknowledge his error, he achieves a heroism which McCarthy permits to stand.

Apart from the novels, McCarthy's work includes a stage play, *The Stonemasons*, and a screenplay, *The Gardener's Son* (which was filmed and broadcast on PBS). Though serious students of the author must take account of these, neither achieves the power of his novels, in part because the dramatic form offers no outlet for the astonishing powers of description which makes the novels so vivid. As a whole McCarthy's work is limited in theme—his is a masculine world in which domestic life, family, and even erotic

love have minor places—but within the limits he has set for himself enormously powerful and compelling; he surely warrants the attention which has lately come his way.

—John Grammar

McCLANAHAN, Ed

Born: In Kentucky. **Family:** Married, wife Hilda. **Career:** Worked as a school bus driver and farmhand; educator, Free University, University of Kentucky, and Northern Kentucky University; co-editor *The Free You*, a literary journal; contributor to magazines, including *Esquire, Playboy*, and *Rolling Stone.*

PUBLICATIONS

Novels

The Natural Man. New York, Farrar, Straus, and Giroux, 1983.
A Congress of Wonders. Washington, D.C. , Counterpoint, 1996.

Other

Famous People I Have Known (memoir). New York, Farrar, Straus, Giroux, 1985; with "Furthermore," a new afterword, Frankfort, Kentucky, Gnomon Press, 1997.
My Vita, If You Will: The Uncollected Ed McClanahan. Washington, D.C., Counterpoint, 1998.

*

Ed McClanahan comments:

Writing is like performing brain surgery on yourself—it's not something you want to hurry with. For me, it's a painstaking, intricate process because the language itself—I mean the sound of it, the internal cadences, the way the voices play off contrapuntally against each other—sometimes becomes the engine that drives the narrative, instead of the other way around. Anyhow, I'd like to think it takes so long to write this book (*A Congress of Wonders*) because, as the saying goes, my mill grinds slow but exceeding fine. Which still beats the hell out of "My mill hardly grinds at all."

—from an interview with Amy Firis, *City Beat* (Cincinnatti), issue 226, http://www.citybeat.com

*   *   *

In speaking about his work, Ed McClanahan says: "For me, where the act of writing really goes on is in the interplay between the written voice and the speaking voice. I like for there to be a counterpoint between those two things . . . to write in a deliberately overblown literary voice which plays off against those really earth voices of my characters. And, to some extent, I like to amalgamate the two voices, so that sometimes I can get both of them going at once in a kind of weird harmony." As the comment may suggest, McClanahan's writing displays an exuberant humor and elegant style, reminiscent of Mark Twain as well as of Sterne and Dickens.

His first novel, *The Natural Man* (1983) is set in a small Kentucky town during the 1940s. It is the story of 15-year-old Harry Eastep, "a slouching, shambling, gangling tangle of ganglia . . . bespectacled and modestly precocious," and his adventures with Monk McHorning, a hulking, swaggering orphan who has been recruited by the high school principal to play for the basketball team. Monk stands 6'5", weighs 238 pounds, and seems to have an endless supply of raunchy jokes to tell. He also plays basketball "with violent abandon, felling friend and foe alike," and the town looks eagerly to him to break the high school team's losing streak.

To Harry, Monk is "the most accomplished personage" he's ever met, and he soon becomes Monk's most devoted follower. Harry does Monk's homework to keep him eligible for the team. After hours, he hangs out with his hero at the local pool hall. Soon, though, Harry finds himself in competition with Oodles Ockerman, the dim-witted, corpulent daughter of Newton Ockerman, who runs the town movie theater, where Harry works. Along with the rest of the town, Harry eagerly awaits one of the theater's coming attractions, a purported sex-education film. Meanwhile, as Monk's success on the basketball court begins to add up, the pool hall proprietor starts trying to bribe Monk to cheat in some upcoming games.

These complications add suspense to the story, but, as one reviewer noted, "It's McClanahan's treatment of it that makes it a thing to marvel at. Hardly a sentence lacks comic effect." But while the novel is comic, McClanahan portrays the small town Needmore with sensitivity and depth. Characters one might have predicted would end badly reveal unexpected strengths. The novel concludes on a note of faith, in wry acceptance of the inevitable change in human fortune.

After the novel's enthusiastic reception, McClanahan published a memoir, *Famous People I Have Known* (1985). Starting with an incident from his freshman year in college, when he met a famous singer one evening, McClanahan tells stories of the 1960s culture at Stanford University, of the changes he observed in the country and in himself during those years, and of his decisions to move back to Kentucky in the mid-1970s.

McClanahan's 1972 essay on musician Little Enis, whom he calls "a personal favorite of mine," appears as a chapter of the memoir. McClanahan has suggested Enis was for him a perfect subject to write about, since profiling Enis afforded him a chance to contrast his unique style of elaborate description with humorous country talk. At one point, for example, he describes Enis as "this pugnacious-looking little banty rooster with a skin-tight gold-sateen cowboy shirt and an underslung lower jaw and a great sleek black-patent-leather Elvis Presley pompadour," then quotes Enis: "People sometimes asks me what I think of these people like you, which has got the long hair and all. And . . . actually, see I've had long hair my own self."

In 1996, McClanahan's third book, *A Congress of Wonders*, appeared, to strong reviews in *Newsweek* and elsewhere. Composed of three long stories, the book revives the setting of *The Natural Man*, McClanahan's mythical Burdock County, and several of its minor characters. The stories further cement the author's reputation as "Kentucky's King of the Small-Town Baroque," in the

words of one critic, and they are profoundly, if often darkly, comic. In each, a character undergoes mystical, if not patently supernatural, transformation. The stories also explore, further perhaps than the author's previous work, the more shadowy regions of the human heart, often through the depiction of near-freakish characters reminiscent of Flannery O'Connor. The first, "Juanita and the Frog Prince," tells of a ghoulish, evil young man, born with two noses, who is jailed for manufacturing a bomb that killed a man who dared to insult him. The second story, "The Congress of Wonders," first published in *Esquire* magazine in 1988, is set in a carnival in 1944. A young teenage boy, Wade, tags along with his older brother Sonny, who is leaving soon to fight in World War II. McClanahan's distinctive mix of exuberant language, comic exaggeration, and genuine pathos is abundantly evident in this poignant story of a younger brother's yearning to keep his older brother from harm.

The third, novella-length work, "Finch's Song: A Schoolbus Tragedy," depicts the "irresolute" Finch Fronk, a constant target of jokes in town, "a sick old man of thirty-three, and getting sicker every day." Fearful that he might suffer heart attack at the slightest cause, he is nonetheless compelled to take employment as a schoolbus driver. While the tribulations he undergoes on the job and in town, as an object of ridicule, supply much of the novella's comedy, the narrative also concludes with an image of sacrifice and redemption as subtle as any in O'Connor's work, and rendered perhaps, with a gentler touch.

McClanahan has cited Twain, O'Connor, and Faulkner as influences. As he told one interviewer, "I'm a very slow writer," acknowledging that "writing is a kind of singing to me, literally like composing . . . I like to get every word right." He has been praised by Ken Kesey, Robert Stone, and others. Reviewing *The Natural Man* in the *New York Times Book Review*, author Ivan Gold wrote: "I predict it will eventually find its place beside great coming-of-age books like *The Adventures of Huckleberry Finn* and *Catcher in the Rye*." McClanahan has, by an inventive mingling of the Southern vernacular with the archaic, and by precise and comic descriptions of small-town life, achieved a revered body of work that is recognizably his in every page.

—David Y. Todd

McCORKLE, Jill

Born: Jill Collins in Lumberton, North Carolina, 7 July 1958. **Education:** University of North Carolina at Chapel Hill, B.A. (with highest honors) 1980; Hollins College, M.A. 1981. **Family:** Married; two children. **Career:** Teacher at public schools in Brevard Country, Florida, 1982-83; acquisitions librarian, Florida Institute of Technology Library, Melbourne, 1983-84; secretary at medical school, University of North Carolina at Chapel Hill, since 1984, lecturer in creative writing, since 1986; instructor in creative writing, University of North Carolina, Chapel Hill, 1985-87, 1989-91, and Duke University, since 1986; instructor, Tufts University, 1987-89; Briggs Copeland Lecturer in Fiction, Harvard University, 1991-96; member of fiction faculty, Bennington College, since 1993. **Awards:** New England Booksellers.award for *Crash Diet*, 1993; University of North Carolina-Chapel Hill Young

Alumni award, 1994. **Agent**: Liz Darhansoff, 1220 Park Ave., New York, New York 10128.

PUBLICATIONS

Novels

The Cheer Leader. Chapel Hill, Algonquin Books, 1984.
July 7th. Chapel Hill, Algonquin Books, 1984.
Tending to Virginia. Chapel Hill, Algonquin Books, 1987.
Ferris Beach. Chapel Hill, Algonquin Books, 1990.
Carolina Moon. Chapel Hill, Algonquin Books, 1996.

Short Fiction

Crash Diet. Chapel Hill, Algonquin Books, 1992.

*   *   *

Jill McCorkle writes about the New South and the terrors and strengths inherent in southern community. The product of a small town in North Carolina, McCorkle displays great sensitivity to voice and characterization in her fiction, writing easily from the perspectives of the old and the young, the black and the white. Her fictional landscapes—dotted with malls and burger joints— are familiar to the contemporary reader, as are the complexities of family life. Like many southern women writers, McCorkle targets family and community as her subjects, but rather than praise these institutions unequivocally, McCorkle raises questions about the sanctity of such forces in women's worlds. The family or community can confine as easily as it can protect, causing its inhabitants to live double lives, nurture separate selves, and McCorkle's fiction often addresses the stories that develop along the gaps between the exterior and the interior.

The Cheer Leader (1984) is a classic example of such an exploration. A novel of education and development, McCorkle's first work is a bildungsroman that recounts the maturation of its main character, Jo Spencer. It also simultaneously records her descent into, and fragmentation as a result of, anorexia. Divided into four sections, the book opens with Jo's narration of her childhood via a series of photographs. In the second section, Jo delivers a straightforward, first person narrative in which she describes the pressures of adolescent girlhood. Her narration switches from first person to third in the next section, symbolic of her own disappearing identity as she succumbs to anorexia. The fourth section suggests that the process of healing has begun, though the novel's open ending realistically implies that creating a strong and centered female self is a perilous process in a society that bombards a woman with mixed messages about strength and sexuality.

July 7th (1984) satirizes a New South where prestige and respect are based upon how much money a family possesses. Fittingly, society's marginal members emerge as the trustworthy voices here. A comic novel, this book celebrates and ridicules its subjects, weaving together several plot lines and incorporating many characters. Ostensibly the story of Charles Husky's murder and Granner Weeks's birthday celebration—two disparate occasions, to be sure—the novel probes the small community of Marshboro, North Carolina, and exposes the virtues and faults of its inhabitants.

Tending to Virginia (1987) celebrates the female community— on the surface. Embedded in stories that span generational boundaries are horrific tales of incest and abuse, versions of history that are exposed only when the female characters gather to support the pregnant Virginia, who in confusion and frustration has recently left her husband. Storytelling becomes at once a healing process and a way to continue to hide family secrets, for the women agree to keep the most disturbing aspects of their shared lives shielded from the rest of the world only after exposing them to each other. A multi-voiced narrative, the novel extols oral discourse and suggests that every history is prey to the gaps in its telling.

Ferris Beach (1990) is another novel that targets a young, female protagonist and her struggles to create an independent self. Kate Burns, affectionately called Kitty, actively seeks a viable female role model, rejecting her mother's cold practicality for the more glamorous lives of her cousin Angela and her best friend's mother, Mo Rhodes. Angela and Mo, however, finally prove unsatisfactory, each revealing a kind of immaturity that leaves Kitty disappointed. Kitty and her mother Cleva struggle to accept each other over the novel's course. Despite its festive title, which is apt to conjure images of ferris wheels and beach balls, the novel in fact addresses difficult subjects: death, rape, the fragility of mother/daughter relationships, the perils of growing up female.

Crash Diet (1992) is a collection of stories told from the perspectives of all kinds of women, old and young, fat and thin, black and white, rich and poor. More often abandoned by a community than embraced by one, these female characters struggle to articulate their stories in an unheeding society, just as they struggle to make their lives meaningful. Often marginalized by race, occupation or social status, the voices McCorkle creates here usually succeed in seizing upon their own worthiness. With humor and a gift for creating realistic fictional voices, in *Crash Diet* McCorkle deals relentlessly with the social concerns that much of her fiction targets.

Carolina Moon (1996) is a refreshingly funny novel set in the small fictional town of Fulton, North Carolina. In its present, the book centers around Quee Purdy, the irrepressible entrepreneur, whose secret life is recorded in letters she's written her former lover (not her husband), now dead, and which end up in the dead letter pile at the Post Office, where they are read by a postal worker nearing retirement. The narrative switches in this way between past and present, finally uniting the two as Quee reconciles her disparate existences.

In her fiction, Jill McCorkle addresses serious contemporary issues even as she writes with humor. Her works are specific explorations into the daily lives of human beings, always grounded in careful evocations of place and character.

—Elinor Ann Walker

McCRUMB, Sharyn

Born: Sharyn Elaine Arwood in Wilmington, North Carolina, 26 February 1948. **Education:** University of North Carolina at Chapel

Hill, B.A. in communications and Spanish 1970; Wake Forest University, graduate study in speech and theater, 1977; Virginia Technological Institute, M.A. in English 1985. **Family:** Married David Kenneth McCrumb, 9 January 1982; three children. **Career:** Teacher and assistant director, Adult Basic Education Department, Forsythe Technical Institute; reporter, *Smoky Mountain Times,* Bryson City, North Carolina; writer, since 1976; Virginia Polytechnic Institute and State University, assistant film librarian, 1981-82, university film librarian 1982-88, member of Appalachian studies faculty, since 1983, and adjunct professor of communications and journalism, 1986-88; guest fictions editor, *East Tennessee State University Literary Magazine,* 1991, *Artemus Literary Magazine,* 1998; Oxford University Fulbright Scholarship judge, 1991 and 1993; editor, Reprint Appalachian Fiction Series, University of Tennessee Press, since 1997; professional writer, since 1976. **Awards:** Macavity award for best book, *If Ever I Return, Pretty Peggy-O,* 1990; Best Appalachian Novel award, *The Hangman's Beautiful Daughter* (1992); Anthony award, Agatha award, Macavity award, and Nero award, all for *She Walks These Hills,* 1994; Outstanding Contribution to Appalachian Literature, *The Rosewood Casket,* 1996.

PUBLICATIONS

Elizabeth MacPherson Mysteries

Sick of Shadows. New York, Avon Original Paperback, 1984.
Lovely in Her Bones. New York, Avon Original Paperback, 1985.
Highland Laddie Gone. New York, Avon Original Paperback, 1986.
Paying the Piper. New York, Ballantine Original Paperback, 1988.
The Windsor Knot. New York, Ballantine, 1990.
Missing Susan. New York, Ballantine, 1991.
MacPherson's Lament. New York, Ballantine, 1992.
If I'd Killed Him When I Met Him. New York, Ballantine, 1995.

Jay Omega Mysteries

Bimbos of the Death Sun. TSR Original Paperback, 1987.
Zombies of the Gene Pool. New York, Simon & Schuster, 1992.

Ballad Series

If Ever I Return, Pretty Peggy-O. New York, Scribner's, 1990.
The Hangman's Beautiful Daughter. New York, Scribner's, 1992.
She Walks These Hills. New York, Scribner's, 1994.
The Rosewood Casket. New York, Dutton, 1996.
The Ballad of Frankie Silver. New York, Dutton, 1998.

Short Stories

Foggy Mountain Breakdown and Other Stories. New York, Ballantine, 1997.

*

Sharyn McCrumb comments:

My books are like Appalachian quilts. I take brightly colored scraps of legends, ballads, fragments of rural life, and local tragedy, and I piece them together into a complex whole that tells not only a story, but also a deeper truth about the culture of the mountain South.

*   *   *

Because Southern writers seem consistently compelled to help their audience understand the region, Southern fiction repeatedly portrays the whole web of Southern culture, with emphasis upon blood ties/family, sense of community, and attachment to place. Like McCrumb herself, Southern culture blends the "flatland South" of her mother's family with the "Appalachian South" of her father's people. Emphasizing both the origin of her fiction's "two voices" and the role of music in her creative processes, she characterizes the result as "a cultural mix of Ernest Tubb meets Debussy." McCrumb further comments: "The duality of my childhood, a sense of having a foot in both cultures, gave me that sense of *otherness* that one often finds in writers; the feeling of being an outsider, observing one's surroundings, and looking even at personal events as once removed." The result is literary realism: her fiction has increasingly moved from domestic mysteries with a Southern/Appalachian background to portrayal of mountain culture jarred by contact with contemporary issues and problems.

McCrumb rejects minimalism, explaining that "coming from a race of storytellers, I could not figure out how to write a book in which nothing much happens to people you don't care about anyway." For McCrumb, storytelling is an art form: "I grew up seeing the world as a wild and exciting place; the quiet tales of suburban angst so popular in modern fiction are Martian to me."

McCrumb's fiction is usually classified according to either sleuth or setting: eight Elizabeth MacPherson mysteries, two Jay Omega mysteries, five Ballad Novels, and a collection of short stories through 1998. With the publication of *The Rosewood Casket* and *The Ballad of Frankie Silver,* however, McCrumb has turned her attention primarily to her Ballad series.

Sick of Shadows, the first MacPherson novel, is primarily a domestic mystery. The second, *Lovely in Her Bones*—with its dedication to her father "for my roots in Appalachia"—marks McCrumb's move toward serious regional fiction, as local history, customs, and social issues become key elements. These novels set a pattern that recurs with shifts in emphasis throughout all three series: 1) generally Southern, frequently Appalachian, settings and characters; 2) plots involving a mystery, usually with serious implications, though the perpetrator may be portrayed sympathetically; 3) comic relief with humor sometimes closely linked to pathos; 4) emphasis upon tradition and blood ties, with serious examination of the family; 5) isolated characters whose eccentricity borders on madness; and 6) exploration of topical issues such as cultural identity, dysfunctional families, or destruction of the natural environment.

The Southern settings are obvious. Elizabeth's sleuthing generally takes place in Georgia, North Carolina, Tennessee, and Virginia. The locales of the Omega mysteries are a Southern university town and Wall Hollow, Tennessee. The Ballad Novels are set in and around Hamelin, Tennessee. Likewise McCrumb's characters constitute a cross-section of Southern society: local aristocrats, college professors, red-neck bullies, Pentecostal preachers, escaped convicts, transplanted Northerners, middle class Southerners, lifelong mountain residents, comic and serious pseudo-frontiersmen, lawmen, ghostly figures from the past, and—as a recurring character—Nora Bonesteel, whom McCrumb describes as "the keeper of the legends. The woman who knew the quilt patterns. She has all the treasure of our past in store. Nora has the sight. She is all that is native and fun."

Unlike the Ballad novels, where McCrumb began with a theme, in the MacPherson and Omega novels she began with a traditional mystery plot, though sometimes the murderers seem unusually likeable. For example, Elizabeth MacPherson admires Amelanchier Stecoah, whom McCrumb describes as "Nora Bonesteel with training wheels." More sympathetic still are the emotionally abused husband killers in *If I'd Killed Him When I Met Him*.

Murder figures prominently in the Ballad Novels, too; even *The Rosewood Casket*, though not primarily about murder, teases the reader with old mysteries. Often, the crime has its roots in desperation or cruelty, or both; the past broods over the present, and contemporary characters seem destined to repeat the mistakes of their ancestors. Katie Wyler's murder of her baby while trying to escape Indians is echoed a century later as Sabrina Harkryder kills her child to escape an equally oppressive captivity, and Rab Greer's killing of Katie parallels Euell Pentland's murder of his wife (*She Walks These Hills*).

The Ballad of Frankie Silver juxtaposes Spencer Arrowood's interest in the first female murderer executed in North Carolina with an impending execution in Tennessee, and the long-ago murder of Fayre Stargill as revealed in *The Rosewood Casket*. Moreover, murderers in these novels are portrayed as especially complex. Dovey Stallard seems partially redeemed by her love of the land; Josh Underhill (*The Hangman's Beautiful Daughter*) kills his parents and youngest brother only to end the family's cycle of cruelty and violence, but lingers in spirit form to protect his sister.

Since most McCrumb novels contain at least two episodes of murderous violence, comic relief is welcome. Usually, though, the humor is deeply tinged with irony and sometimes with pathos. Much of the humor in the MacPherson novels lies either in word play between Elizabeth and her brother or in the ironic commentary of her cousin Geoffrey. With a deft comic touch, McCrumb also creates incongruous situations such as the reproduction of an 18th-century Bavarian castle in 20th-century Georgia, an Indian herbalist who dries her medicinal herbs in a microwave and prefers pizza to traditional mountain fare, the disastrous results when Geoffrey shoves a cougar into a pen of ducks, an amateur contract killer whose would-be victim seems to lead a charmed life, a literature professor who wields no power in her department until she announces that she is a political lesbian, and—most delightful—the larcenous ladies of the Home for Confederate Widows, who not only sell an antebellum mansion the county actually owns, but make off with Union gold originally stolen by their Confederate ancestors 127 years before.

In the Ballad Novels humor only briefly lightens the mood. Hank the Yank amuses himself and his radio audience with facetious reports concerning the manhunt for a senile prison escapee, and novice hiker Jeremy Cobb sets out to retrace a frontierswoman's escape, carrying only the necessities: portable

stove, water-purification equipment, freeze-dried chili mac, cooking utensils, and portable shower—which he discards piece by piece along the trail (*She Walks These Hills*). Again, the gloom of Tavy Annis' impending death (*The Hangman's Beautiful Daughter*) is tempered somewhat when he and his friend con their way into the executive offices of Titan Paper Company and force its president to drink water from their heavily polluted river.

Typically, McCrumb uses deaths—sometimes violent—to reveal complex relationships within families. Elizabeth's relationship with her own family is a significant element throughout that series, but the "great war between men and women" is explored most fully in the failed marriages of *If I'd Killed Him When I Met Him*: Eleanor Royden shoots the ex-husband who dumped her and then used the legal system to harass her; and, generations earlier, Lucy Todhunter confounded the legal and medical establishment by somehow poisoning her cruel husband. In contrast, Donna Jean Morgan uses the law, suing for criminal conversion when her husband announces that God has told him to take a second wife. Elizabeth's mother, Margaret, gains revenge on her ex-husband by announcing that she is a lesbian; Miri Malone concludes that all males lack sensitivity.

Family relationships are central in the Ballad Series, too. Among the issues in *If Ever I Return, Pretty Peggy-O* are Tyndall Johnson Garner's ambivalence toward her terminally ill mother, Spencer Arrowood's sibling rivalry with his dead brother, and the resulting tension between Spencer and his mother, Jane. *The Hangman's Beautiful Daughter* examines mothers' treatment of children. Janet Underhill not only fails to protect her children from her husband's abuse, but sometimes even participates in their torment. In contrast, Tammy Robsart dies saving her son, and Laura Bruce carries to term a baby she knows is dead. *She Walks These Hills* likewise deals with parents' protectiveness; Spencer Arrowood concludes that both Harm and Rita Sorley in a sense have sacrificed their lives for their daughter.

The fullest exploration of complex family interrelationships, though, occurs in *The Rosewood Casket*. A dying Randall Stargill requests that his sons build his casket. Besides the physical difficulties involved, each son must reappraise his relationship with his father and his brothers, including the almost legendary wild brother who died many years earlier. Randall's secretiveness has rendered intimacy and commitment impossible. Now, each must examine himself, reflect upon his ongoing role in the family, determine the direction of his future, and decide how he feels about the family land.

Tradition, which consistently plays a significant role in McCrumb's novels, is almost always linked to family history and attitude toward the land. Elizabeth's pride in her Scottish heritage closely resembles Amerlanchier Stecoah's obsession with the oral traditions of the Cullowhees. Philip Todhunter's threat to sell Lucy's family farm may have been a cause of his murder. The spirit of Katie Wyler still haunts the wilderness that was her home, and in fighting to keep her land Dovey Stallard considers herself the true descendant of Cherokee chief Nancy Ward.

McCrumb's characters frequently are eccentric, sometimes mad. Typical is the Chandler family; all of them are eccentric, but Alban truly believes he is Ludwig of Bavaria. Also questionable is Miri

Malone's sanity: she wants to legally marry a porpoise. Similarly detached from reality, Eleanor Royden cheerfully acknowledges shooting her ex-husband and his new wife; she revels in her celebrity, giving countless interviews and speculating about a possible television movie.

Eccentricity and madness figure prominently in the Ballad Novels. Vernon Woolwine is Hamelin's resident eccentric, dressing in various costumes according to his identity on any particular day, but Pix-Kyle Weaver is truly mad, acting out his Vietnam fantasies by killing animals and a person. Likewise, Spencer Arrowood is convinced that only madness can explain Josh Underhill's slaughter of his family, but the tragedy of madness is seen most completely in Harm Sorley, imprisoned for killing the man who had made his land a toxic waste dump. After twenty-seven years' separation from his family and the mountains—his short-term memory destroyed by Korsakoff's syndrome—Harm breaks out of prison and for several weeks wanders through the mountains, looking for his home. Eventually madness leads directly to his death and indirectly to his wife's murder.

As McCrumb's primary focus has shifted toward regional fiction, topical issues have increased in significance; contemporary conflicts illuminate timeless concerns. In *Lovely in Her Bones*, the issue of strip mining serves primarily as the motive for murder, but destruction of the natural environment figures prominently on several levels in *The Hangman's Beautiful Daughter*, where large corporations poison the rivers, killing the fish and the people.

With similarly increasing seriousness, McCrumb addresses a variety of contemporary social issues, from dysfunctional families to the aftermath of the Vietnam war. In *MacPhearson's Lament*, physical abuse results in second-degree murder, but abuse takes more subtle forms in the legal and psychological harassment of *If I'd Killed Him When I Met Him*. Obviously, child abuse is central to *The Hangman's Beautiful Daughter*, where it is shown to be as poisonous as the run-off from the paper mill. Lack of communication has virtually destroyed the Stargill family, and the pattern seems destined to continue. In contrast, Joe LeDonne still relives the Vietnam war in his nightmares, but he reaches out to help Spencer Arrowood understand how a tour there could change soldiers like his brother. In fact, *If Ever I Return, Pretty Peggy-O* portrays the varied effects of Vietnam upon not only the generation whose lives it blighted, but also the revisionists who have begun to romanticize the horrors they never experienced.

Clearly Sharyn McCrumb is more than a writer of domestic mysteries; she is a significant contemporary writer. She best summarizes her work: "So much conflict; so much drama; and two sides to everything. Stories I learned, involved character, and drama, and they always centered around irrevocable events that mattered."

—Charmaine Allmon Mosby

McLAURIN, Tim

Born: Fayetteville, North Carolia, 14 December 1953. **Education:** University of North Carolina. **Military Service:** Served in the U.S. Marines. **Family:** Married Janelle Clark (divorced); married Katie Earlie (divorced); two children. **Career:** Peace Corps volunteer; carnival snake handler, truck driver, house construction worker; instructor at University of North Carolina and Duke University; since 1991, professor of creative writing, North Carolina State University. **Agent:** Rhoda Weyr, 151 Bergen Street, New York, New York 14416.

PUBLICATIONS

Novels

The Acorn Plan. New York, W. W. Norton, 1988.
Woodrow's Trumpet. New York, W. W. Norton, 1989.
Cured by Fire. G. P. Putnam's Sons, 1994.
The Last Great Snake Show. G. P. Putnam's Sons, 1997.

Nonfiction

Keeper of the Moon. New York, W. W. Norton, 1990.

Poetry Collection

Lola. Asheboro, North Carolina, Down Home Press, 1997.

*

Video recording: *Life and Death on the Farm*, with Gary Hawkins, University of North Carolina Center for Public Television, 1990.

Warned by one of his college professors that people do not want to read about drunks and street people, Tim McLaurin took heart when he read books by William Kennedy about the low life of Albany, New York. He set out to describe the low life he knew, which was that of rural North Carolina. Of his first novel, *The Acorn Plan* (1988), McLaurin has said it "was about coming home from the service and having to establish myself as a young man, deciding whether I was going to be one of the tough guys or go off to school."

The characters in *The Acorn Plany* are gritty, hard-working men trying not to self-destruct. Billy Riley works in a petshop while he is on parole for having almost killed a Fort Bragg soldier in a drunken brawl. He falls in love with Cassie, a Fayetteville stripper, and they double-date on a fishing trip picnic with Billy's Uncle Bubble and his once-homeless friend Wilma. Worried about Billy's excessive drinking, Uncle Bubble quits his job in the cotton mill to devote himself to consuming all the wine in the world as a lesson to Billy. The title of the book comes from Billy, who argues that nature is not fair. Many acorns fall, and only one in a million grows into a big tree. He worries about the ones that do not make it.

Woodrow's Trumpet (1989) is about the changing South and McLaurin's rage at its urbanization and homogenization. Woodrow is a country fellow who is seen as eccentric by his family and neighbors, tries to maintain his individuality and his roots while surrounded by liberal hypocrites. When their mother dies, Woodrow, Porter, and Benson inherit the lovely, rolling land of their family farm. Woodrow's share is a five-acre plot surrounded by a subdivision because Benson has sold the land around it. Nadean Tucker, a recovering addict back home from nWashigton, D.C., and an eighteen-year-old orphan, Ellis, live with him. Woodrow and his coon dogs hunt near the Haw River, and his hunting horn is the mournful trumpet for which the book is named. The "liberal" young moderns of the Whispering Pines subdivision at first lionize Woodrow and Nadean, inviting them to their fashionable dinner parties, and the couple reciprocate with a "down home" barbecue. But when Nadean wants a beach of her own, and Woodrow gives it to her by importing sand for the front yard, building a pool, planting an enormous palm tree, and surrounding it with pink, plastic flamingoes, their neighbors are shocked at their tackiness and have the building code changed to eliminate the beach. Bulldozers prepare the ground for a new subdivision instead of Nadean's beach, which had been her heart's desire. The horn Ellis blows at novel's end is both an affirmation of hope and a symbol of a wish for peace and for a place that can bring happiness.

In *Keeper of the Moon* (1990), a memoir of the author's boyhood near Fayetteville, North Carolina, we read about LJ, the boyhood friend whom young Tim pursuaded to mow the scrubby McLaurin lawn in return for a sandwich of Merita white bread, baloney, and a dab of mayonnaise, and the two Lumbee Indian boys who competed with Tim and LJ in a race, only to end up in a pit, covered with bushes. Tim and LJ pretended they were jungle natives in their pine woods, cutting spears from reeds and painting their faces like those they found in *National Geographic*. They canoed and camped, listened to long sermons in the Primitive Baptist Church, rented out Tim's telescope, and read everything to be found on snakes. One of his grandmothers was a storyteller in East Fayetteville, and Tim, as he grew up listening to her, realized the importance of landand the rural life and recognized that his family and their friends were a rich source of characters, tales, and dialects.

Cured by Fire (1994) is about a successful Southerner, Lewis, who fails to find real meaning in his life until he has lost everything. He and the migrant worker Elbridge have had their lives changed forever by the fires that destroyed their families. McLaurin has said that one of the themes is sudden loss, "the potential that there is a sword always hanging over your head, and it could fall." Another theme is how middle class White America looks at the ugliness in the world, admiing the physically attractive and disdaining the maimed and the weak. A third theme is spiritual: Lewis, an agnostic who had looks, family, and money, thought he had a kind of agreement with God that he would be all right if he did not hurt anyone. Elbridge had nothing but his faith in God. When calamity hits them, the hideously maimed Lewis wants to live to punish himself and God. Elbridge simply wants to understand and begins to realize that he needs to minister to others. Both men finally achieve a kind of transcendent peace.

The Last Great Snake Show (1997) begins with a private party at The House of Joy, a brothel, juke joint, and carnival sideshow in Wilmington, North Carolina. Miss Darlene runs the place, but she is dying because a tornado has left her with an "inoperable splinter of glass embedded in her brain." Her three employees set off to take her to see the land in Oregon she has bought but never

seen. Their van, the Jubilee Express, actually a converted school bus, takes them on the journey, which they finance by performing a hootchie-kootchie show along the way. Kitty, a rich coed running from an arranged marriage, joins the original group of Darlene, Cappy (the show manager and a former Army Airborne Seargeant, the snake handler Jubal, and Glory, a black stripper and prostitute. Jubal, who is clearly a McLaurin alter-ego, grabs rattlesnakes before they strike and milks them, drinking their venom. He had planned to major in marine biology in college, but gave up the idea after his brother died in a marlin-fishing accident. The North Carolinians are swindled, beaten up, chased out of town, and jailed. Kitty saves them each time, usually with her secret cache of money.

In *Lola* (1997), one of the six voices who tell the five-part story is a serpent, a fitting character for cLaurin, who was a carnival snake handler. Other voices are John Wesley Stewart, a farmer who is going to be buried on his own three-hundred acre farm; his son David; his daughters Julia and Lola; and Fenner, the hired man. As in *Woodrow's Trumpet,* one of the themes is the distress caused by developers who build on despoil the countryside. After the death of the patriarch, the other members of his family sever their ties to the land, and lot-maker flags, symbolic of the insidious invasion of the farm, spring up. David, an intellectual whose talent lies in writing, loves the land but prefers books; he admits that his farmer-father was "a good man I hardly knew." Julia has spent a lonely life caring for her sister Lola, who is dim-witted but pure in spirit, a child-woman who weaves clover bracelets. Fenner, who is deeded the twelve acres on which his house is located, loves bourbon, fried corn bread, butterbeans, and ham biscuits, and celebrates rural living, as does McLaurin himself.

—Sue Laslie Kimball

McMURTRY, Larry

Born: Wichita Falls, Texas, 3 June 1936. **Education:** North Texas State College, B.A. 1958; Rice University, M.A. 1960; Stanford University, California (Stegner fellow), 1960-61. **Family:** Married Josephine Scott in 1959 (divorced 1966); one son. **Career:** Taught at Texas Christian University, 1961-62, Rice University, 1963-64, 1965, George Mason College, 1970, and American University, Washington, D.C., 1970-71; since 1971 owner, Booked Up, Inc., antiquarian booksellers, Washington, D.C., Archer City, Texas, and Tucson, Arizona; regular reviewer, *Houston Post,* 1960s, and *Washington Post,* 1970s; contributing editor, *American Film,* New York, 1975; president, PEN American Center, 1989. **Awards:** Guggenheim grant, 1964; Pulitzer Prize for *Lonesome Dove,* 1986. **Address:** Booked Up Inc., 2509 North Campbell Avenue, No. 95, Tucson, Arizona 85719.

Publications

Novels

Horseman, Pass By. New York, Harper, 1961; published as *Hud,* New York, Popular Library, 1963.
Leaving Cheyenne. New York, Harper, 1963.
The Last Picture Show. New York, Dial Press, 1966.

Moving On. New York, Simon and Schuster, 1970.
All My Friends Are Going to Be Strangers. New York, Simon and Schuster, 1972.
Terms of Endearment. New York, Simon and Schuster, 1975.
Somebody's Darling. New York, Simon and Schuster, 1978.
Cadillac Jack. New York, Simon and Schuster, 1982.
The Desert Rose. New York, Simon and Schuster, 1983.
Lonesome Dove. New York, Simon and Schuster, 1985.
Texasville. New York, Simon and Schuster, 1987.
Anything for Billy. New York, Simon and Schuster, 1988.
Some Can Whistle. New York, Simon and Schuster, 1989.
Buffalo Girls. New York, Simon and Schuster, 1990.
The Evening Star. New York, Simon and Schuster, 1992.
Streets of Laredo. Simon and Schuster, 1993,
Pretty Boy Floyd, with Diana Ossana. New York, Simon and Schuster, 1994.
The Late Child. New York, Simon and Schuster, 1995.
Dead Man's Walk. Simon and Schuster, 1995.
Comanche Moon. New York, Simon and Schuster, 1997.
Zeke and Ned, with Diana Ossana. New York, Simon and Schuster, 1997.

Uncollected Short Stories

"The Best Day Since," in *Avesta*, Fall 1956.
"Cowman," in *Avesta*, Spring 1957.
"Roll, Jordan, Roll," in *Avesta*, Fall 1957.
"A Fragment from Scarlet Ribbons," in *Coexistence Review,* vol. 1, no. 2, 1958.
"There Will Be Peace in Korea," in *Texas Quarterly*, Winter 1964.
"Dunlop Crashes In," in *Playboy*, July 1975.

Other

In a Narrow Grave: Essays on Texas. Austin, Texas, Encino Press, 1968.
It's Always We Rambled: An Essay on Rodeo. New York, Hallman, 1974.
Larry McMurtry: Unredeemed Dreams, edited by Dorey Schmidt. Edinburg, Texas, Pan American University, 1980.
Film Flam: Essays on Hollywood. New York, Simon and Schuster, 1987.

Screenplays: With Peter Bogdanovich, *The Last Picture Show*, produced by Columbia Pictures, 1971, B.B.S. Productions, 1970; *Texasville*, Columbia Pictures, 1990; *Montana* (teleplay), Turner Network Television (TNT), 1990; *Falling from Grace*, Columbia Pictures, 1992; With Cybill Shepherd, *Memphis* (teleplay; based on a novel by Shelby Foote), Turner Home Entertainment, 1992.

*

Media Adaptations: *Hud*, based on *Horseman, Pass By*, was produced by Paramount in 1962, and won two Academy awards from the Academy of Motion Picture Arts and Sciences; *Lovin' Molly*, based on *Leaving Cheyenne*, was produced by Columbia Pictures in 1974; *Terms of Endearment*, based on the novel of the same title, was produced by Paramount in 1983, and won four Golden Globe awards, the "best picture" award from the New York Film Critics Circle, and five Academy awards from the Academy of Motion Picture Arts and Sciences, including "best picture of the year"; *Lonesome Dove*, based on the novel of the same title, was produced as a television miniseries for Columbia Broadcasting System (CBS) in 1989; *Return to Lonesome Dove*, based on characters from *Lonesome Dove,* was produced as a television miniseries for CBS in 1993.

Manuscript Collection: University of Houston Library.

Critical Studies: *Larry McMurtry* by Thomas Landess, Austin, Texas, Steck Vaughn, 1969; *The Ghost Country: A Study of the Novels of Larry McMurtry* by Raymond L. Neinstein, Berkeley, California, Creative Arts, 1976; *Larry McMurtry* by Charles D. Peavy, Boston, Twayne, 1977; *Larry McMurtry's Texas: Evolution of a Myth* by Lera Patrick Tyler Lich, Austin, Texas, Eakin Press, 1987; *Taking Stock: A Larry McMurtry Casebook* edited by Clay Reynolds, Dallas, Southern Methodist University Press, 1989.

*   *   *

Larry McMurtry enjoys the distinction of being a popular and respected writer while essentially unmasking myths, sentimentalism, and romantic visions of the wild west, small town life, and urban prosperity. Still, the frontier spirit and a sense of adventure are indispensable to his work and appeal. Vitality and its converse expression of decadence and absurdity mark his characters, as they struggle against or succumb to questionable values and lifestyles; those who achieve some measure of triumph enact a code or understanding through which they retain a sense of humanity and dignity in the face of tragedy or absurdity.

McMurtry can be considered a regional writer of the Southwest, since so much of his work is set there, but his novels range widely—from small town Thalia, Texas, to Montana, to the Pacific, to Washington, D.C. In a grand sense, then, his work represents a large, sprawling exploration of historical and contemporary approaches to the question of what it means to be an American. It is fitting, too, that an author concerned with the influence of popular culture (the mytholigized Wild West, for example) has succeeded critically in several popular media: in addition to being a best-selling author, McMurtry has had novels adapted into award-winning films and television productions. *Hud, The Last Picture Show,* and *Terms of Endearment*—three markedly different stories—all won major film awards, and *Lonesome Dove* is generally considered one television's finest miniseries.

The son and grandson of cattle ranchers, McMurtry was raised in sparsely populated Archer County in north central Texas. The ranching life was becoming modernized as he grew up, but stories told within his family of adventures and hardships on the frontier influenced him, even as he became more interested in books and writing than in life on the range. In Archer City, where he attended high school, McMurtry found little inspiration for his imagination, but the area is recreated repeatedly in his work. Experiences of growing up in a post-heroic period, feeling a sense of disconnectedness, and attempting to transfer the life of action into daring and independence of imagination are prominent in his fiction.

McMurtry's large body of work can be herded into a few groupings that share similarities of subject, approach, or style. His first three novels: *Horseman, Pass By*; *Leaving Cheyenne;* and *The Last Picture Show*, published from 1961 to 1966, are set in an area much like Archer County and introduce the town of Thalia. His next three, *Moving On, All My Friends Are Going to Be Strangers,* and *Terms of Endearment*, published from 1970 to 1975, have modern Houston as their principal setting.

McMurtry's next three novels, *Somebody's Darling, Cadillac Jack,* and *The Desert Rose*, published from 1978 to 1983, move away from Texas to examine characters in bastions of American culture—Hollywood, Las Vegas, Washington, D.C. Since the mid-1980s McMurtry's works can be divided into historical westerns—*Lonesome Dove, Anything for Billy,* and *Buffalo Girls*—and sequels or prequels to earlier published works—*Texasville, Some Can Whistle, The Evening Star, Streets of Laredo, The Late Child,* and *Dead Man's Walk*. The *Lonesome Dove* Series (which includes *Streets of Laredo, Dead Man's Walk,* and *Comanche Moon*) overlaps the last two groupings.

Horseman, Pass By, his first novel, concerns Lonnie Bannon, a young narrator who witnesses tragic events on his grandfather's ranch. Lonnie observes examples of adult males—Hud, his ruthless step-uncle, Jesse, a hired-hand and storytelling drifter, and Homer, his grandfather, a rugged pioneer—in the process of establishing his own identity. *Leaving Cheyenne* is generally similar in setting and in the thematic exploration of young people facing different values and lives than their elders. In this story of Molly Taylor and the two men she loves through her life—the rancher Gid and the cowboy Johnny—each of the three characters narrates portions, offering different perspectives while developing the conflicts, disappointments, and small triumphs in their lives. Both novels had scenes in the fictional town of Thalia, the main setting for McMurtry's third book, *The Last Picture Show*, where a group of teenagers are struggling toward adulthood in the debilitating monotony of small town life. Narrated in the third-person, unlike the immediacy of experience in the two previous books that had first-person narrators, *The Last Picture Show* features a lively cast of characters—roughnecks, fervently religious people, football stars, and young women anxious for love, among them—who are alternately bored, sexually obsessed, reckless, earnestly searching, and self-righteous, as McMurtry satirizes hypocrisy and addresses ways in which individuals create limited opportunities in small town life.

The next three novels, *Moving On, All My Friends Are Going to Be Strangers*, and *Terms of Endearment,* which some have called his "urban trilogy," depart in setting to Houston, and the characters are more aimless than those in Thalia. They have more security and potential but spend energy in meaningless pursuits, sharing in the burgeoning prosperity of Houston while being beset by inner feelings ranging from turmoil to ennui. Comic touches offer a satiric edge that lightens the bleakness of their dispassionate lives. In *Terms of Endearment*, subtle humor comes in the form of several hapless suitors seeking the hand of Aurora Greenway, an emotionally-hardened New England-born widow living in Houston. The relationship between Aurora and her daughter, Emma, who longs for something more than the proper life her mother expects, has several dramatic turns, particularly late in the novel as Emma suffers through a deteriorating marriage and becomes terminally ill

from cancer. The characters seem to learn and love only during crises.

Following *Terms of Endearment*, McMurtry published three novels with primary settings outside of Texas—Hollywood in *Somebody's Darling*, which follows the career of a young female film director, cross-country rambling in *Cadillac Jack*, played for more ribald humor in detailing the capers of an aging antiques dealer, and Las Vegas in *The Desert Rose*, where a showgirl with a heart of gold struggles to live with dignity. The main characters attempt to find some means of fulfillment amid crass surroundings, participating in and perhaps trapped by recognizable forms of American popular culture. The settings of these novels have changed, but themes remain common in narratives delineating individuals attempting to transcend limitations of their surroundings and to discover something beyond materialistic values.

With the help of award-winning cinema adaptations of *The Last Picture Show* and, especially, *Terms of Endearment*, McMurtry had by the mid-1980s established a solid literary reputation and popular recognition, but *Lonesome Dove,* his eight-hundred-page, Pulitzer Prize-winning, 1985 novel, clearly made him a major contemporary writer. A powerful indictment of the romantic mystique of the American Western, revealing tedium, difficult struggles for survival, dangerous outlaws, Indians savagely defending their territory, and a hostile environment, *Lonesome Dove* also celebrates the frontier spirit in depicting people who live amid those hardships and strive to persevere without sacrificing their humanity. An extraordinary epic of the days when the range was still wide open, *Lonesome Dove* develops many memorable characters, particularly the former Texas Rangers Gus McCrae and Woodrow Call. The novel begins with Gus and Woodrow living out their days on a bare ranch near the Mexican border before undertaking one last great adventure—a cattle drive to help settle the frontier of Montana. The idea for the novel, McMurtry told the *New York Times Book Review,* was inspired by recountings of cattle drives by his uncles. In *Lonesome Dove* the drive is an epic ordeal, fraught with dangers, death, and losses and illuminated by an excellent cast of well-drawn characters, from the crusty former rangers to young adults like Newt, the unacknowledged son of Woodrow Call, undergoing a rite of passage.

Even with its unromanticized portrait of the West, *Lonesome Dove* is majestic in its sweep and its drama of heroic and flawed characters. *Anything for Billy* and *Buffalo Girls*, on the other hand, are more straightforward debunkings of the mythology of the West, with heroes portrayed as sad inhabitants of a dying era. *Anything for Billy* casts as narrator Benjamin Sippy, a depressed Easterner and would-be writer fascinated by cowboy adventures. Leaving behind his mundane life for the adventure he expects in the west from having read dime novels, Sippy meets a hapless coward with a reputation as a gunfighter, whom he helps transform through writing and deception as Billy the Kid. McMurtry's version of Billy the Kid removes all the heroism as well as the famed partnerships that turn adversarial (John Chisum, Pat Garrett), leaving a wholly unsympathetic character far from the kind of larger-than-life gunslinger perpetuated by the likes of Sippy, a writer and reader of pulp fiction. *Buffalo Girls* presents such historical characters as Calamity Jane, Wild Bill Hickok, Buffalo Bill Cody, and Sitting Bull as weary old drunks, traveling together in Buffalo Bill's Wild West Show and recreating their legendary skills and adventures, but fading as rapidly as the frontier—the myths replaced by the hard realities of settlement, which included killing off the buffalo and rounding up Indians.

During this period McMurtry also began writing sequels to his past works: *Texasville*, generally considered the best of works that haven't been as a well received as their predecessors, is set thirty years after the events of *The Last Picture Show*, the residents now middle-aged and facing rough economic times after prospering during the oil boom of the 1970s and '80s. Stripped of all ideals and wallowing in violence and decadence, the characters in decline are presented with a coldly cynical humor, powerful in observations of how opportunities for realizing simple values—security, family, love—become lost and changed. Absurd humor, sudden tragedies, and static lives dominate the other sequels: *Some Can Whistle* (continuing the story of *All My Friends are Going to be Stranger)* and *The Evening Star* (continuing *Terms of Endearment)* contain characters attempting to reconcile with their friends and families and overcome their own disappointments as they move towards old age, while *The Late Child* picks up the story of Harmony, from *The Desert Rose*, through her journey with her sisters and her young son, who proves a catalyst for the weary adults to improve their lives.

Another set of sequels and prequels expands the *Lonesome Dove* saga. These works are immensely popular among a devoted group of readers but have received mixed reviews. McMurtry's storytelling skills, historical realism, and non-romanticized heroism is displayed even as the adventures become more larger-than-life, of a type he easily satirized in earlier works. *The Streets of Laredo* is a sequel to *Lonesome Dove*, while *Dead Man's Walk* and *Comanche Moon* are prequels that follow the adventures of Gus and Woodrow as young Texas Rangers. These expansions on *Lonesome Dove* engender an exciting critical question, of whether the saga has been enriched or whether the singular achievement of *Lonesome Dove* is being lessened. In the least they represent McMurtry's notable accomplishment of re-mythologizing the west, invoking the frontier spirit and sense of adventure replete with realistic depictions of hardships, danger, and unrelenting tragedy.

—Perry Bear

McPHERSON, James Alan

Born: Savannah, Georgia, 16 September 1943. **Education:** Morris Brown College, Atlanta, 1961-63, 1965, B.A. 1965; Morgan State College, Baltimore, 1963-64; Harvard University, Cambridge, Massachusetts, LL.B. 1968; University of Iowa, Iowa City, M.F.A. 1971. **Family:** Married in 1973 (divorced); one daughter. **Career:** Instructor, University of Iowa Law School, 1968-69; lecturer in English, University of California, Santa Cruz, 1969-70; assistant professor of English, Morgan State University, 1975-76; associate professor of English, University of Virginia, Charlottesville, 1976-81; professor of English, University of Iowa, beginning 1981; guest editor of fiction issues of *Iowa Review,* 1984, and *Ploughshares,* 1985, 1990; since 1969, contributing editor, *Atlantic Monthly,* and since 1994, staff writer, *Double-Take.* **Awards:** First prize, *Atlantic* short story contest, 1965, for "Gold Coast";

grant from Atlantic Monthly Press and Little, Brown, 1969; award in literature, National Institute of Arts and Letters, 1970; Guggenheim fellow, 1972-73; Pulitzer Prize, 1978, for *Elbow Room*; MacArthur fellowship, 1981; Excellence in Teaching Award, University of Iowa, 1991. **Agent:** Brandt and Brandt, 1501 Broadway, New York, New York 10036.

PUBLICATIONS

Short Story Collections

Hue and Cry. Boston, Little Brown, 1969.
Elbow Room. Boston, Little Brown, 1977.

Nonfiction

Crabcakes. New York, Simon & Schuster, 1998.

Editor and Contributor

Editor with Miller Williams, *Railroad: Trains and Train People in American Culture.* New York, Random House, 1976.
Editor with DeWitt Henry, *Fathering Daughters: Reflections by Men.* Boston, Beacon Press, 1998.

*

Interview: "Interview with James Alan McPherson" by Bob Shacochis, *Iowa Journal of Literary Studies,* 1983.

Critical Studies: "Some Other Hue and Cry" by Hoyt Fuller, *Negro Digest,* October 1969; "Attention, American Folklore; Doc Craft Comes Marching In" by Rosemary M. Laughlin, *Studies in American Fiction,* Autumn 1973; "The Image of Women in Selected Short Stories by James Alan McPherson" by Edith Blicksilver, *CLA Journal,* June 1979; *The Politics of Style: Language as Theme in the Fiction of Berger, McGuane, and McPherson* by Jon Wallace, Durango, Colorado, Hollowbrook, 1992; *Wrestling Angels into Song: The Fictions of Ernest J. Gaines and James Alan McPherson* by Herman Beavers, Philadelphia, University of Pennsylvania Press, 1995.

*   *   *

In his two collections of brilliant short fiction, *Hue and Cry* and *Elbow Room,* James Alan McPherson has surveyed and defined a sensibility of contemporary black American culture. His work, sharply realistic and dramatic, focuses on the connections and abrasions of black and white individuals in our time. The insights accumulated in the stories form a comprehensive mosaic of life in the United States as viewed by black citizens.

Hue and Cry, McPherson's first collection, revolves around the world of work and black positions in it. The stories deal with "traditional" black occupations—waiter, Pullman porter, stockboy, janitor—from the inside, where each position is a window on the white world. McPherson's controlled, incisive style offers shrewdly defined character-types almost mythic in proportion. Stories like "A Solo Song: for Doc," which describes the end of a man's lifelong career as a railroad waiter, offer important illuminations on daily life. "Gold Coast" and "Hue and Cry," two of the best-known stories of the book, deal directly with the tensions and tragic ironies of black-white sexual relationships.

The stories in *Elbow Room* are more complex extensions of McPherson's concerns. His narrative style is often dense and subtle, but his focus is still on archetypal characters and situations. "The Story of a Dead Man," for example, is a kind of bad-man ballad contrasting a near-mythic "bad nigger" with his educated, upwardly mobile nephew. This "Railroad Bill" character is a fighting, lying wanderer whose existence embarrasses blacks aspiring to gentility in white middle-class terms. The same theme emerges in "Elbow Room," which describes the marriage of a young white draft resister to a sharp, urbane African-American woman, narrated by a black consciousness tormented with problems of definition. The young white man is obsessed with the question, "What is a nigger?" He finally bursts out:

"At *least* I tried! At *least* I'm *fighting!* And I know what a *nigger* is, too. It's what you are when you begin thinking of yourself as a work of art!" I did not turn to answer, although I heard him clearly. I am certain there was no arrogance at all left in his voice.

McPherson's stories are carefully crafted, subtle and penetrating observations of the range and variety of the contemporary experience. His characters are vivid storytellers, too, and he captures their inflections and idioms precisely. His people—black and white—struggle to know themselves and each other, to penetrate the barriers of appearances to the central mysteries of being. As the narrator of "Just Enough for the City" expresses it:

I think love must be the ability to suspend one's intelligence for the sake of something. At the basis of love therefore must be imagination. Instead of thinking always "*I am I,*" to love one must be able to feelingly conjugate the verb *to be.* Intuition must be part of the circuitous pathway leading ultimately to love.

This seeking for love and identity, love for self and others, the world itself, is at the center of McPherson's stories. His people become visible to others because they learn to see themselves.

A long absence from publishing, save for essays he has contributed to various periodicals, ended with *Crabcakes,* McPherson's first book since the Pulitzer Prize-winning *Elbow Room.* Comprised of meditations and recollections, the pieces range from nostalgia—reminiscences about his fellow waiter on the Great Northern Railway, who went on to become a respected lawyer—to everyday scenes in Baltimore, to the author's difficult decision to sell a Baltimore house he purchased impulsively twenty years before. This piece explores his relationship with an elderly tenant whose life of self-reliance and religious values (she always enclosed a small, upbeat note with her rent check) contrast with the author's mulling over missed opportunities. Other pieces find delights in Baltimore (roaming the fish markets, eating crabcakes), Iowa, where he has taught since the early 1980s, and Japan.

McPherson's letter to a friend in Japan gradually acknowledges a crossroads he has reached, and earlier melancholy sentiments are tempered with simple delights he has experienced: "If nothing in the future of the present seems permanent," he writes, "one can always focus on . . . the future enjoyment of a Maryland crabcake. Such exercises of the imagination keep hope alive."

—William J. Schafer and Mel Koler

MILLER, Vassar

Born: Vassar Morrison Miller in Houston, Texas, 19 July 1924. **Education:** University of Houston, B.S. 1947, M.A. 1952. **Career:** Full-time writer since the early 1950s; instructor in creative writing, St. John's School, 1975-76. **Awards:** Texas Institute of Letters Poetry Award, for *Adam's Footprint,* 1956, *Wage War on Silence,* 1960, and *My Bones Being Wiser,* 1963; appointed alternate poet laureate of Texas, 1982. **Address:** 1615 Vassar Street, Houston, Texas 77006.

falsePUBLICATIONS

Poetry

Adam's Footprint. New Orleans, New Orleans Poetry Journal, 1956.
Wage War on Silence: A Book of Poems. Middletown, Connecticut, Wesleyan University Press, 1960.
My Bones Being Wiser. Middletown, Connecticut, Wesleyan University Press, 1963.
Onions and Roses. Middletown, Connecticut, Wesleyan University Press, 1968.
If I Could Sleep Deeply Enough. New York, Liveright, 1974.
Small Change. Houston, Wings Press, 1977.
Approaching Nada. Houston, Wings Press, 1977.
Selected and New Poems, 1950-1980. Austin, Texas, Latitudes Press, 1982.
Struggling to Swim on Concrete. New Orleans, New Orleans Poetry Press. 1984.
If I Had Wheels or Love: Collected Poems of Vassar Miller. Dallas, Southern Methodist University, 1991.

Other

"What Is a Poet?," in *Poets on Poetry* edited by Howard Nemerov, New York, Basic Books, 1966.

Editor, *Despite This Flesh: The Disabled in Stories and Poems.* Austin, University of Texas Press, 1985.

*

Manuscript Collection: The Vassar Miller Papers, University of Houston Special Collections.

Critical Studies: *Poets Laureate of Texas: 1932-1966* by Margaret Royalty Edwards, San Antonio, Naylor, 1966; "A Dark Texas of the Soul" by Paul Christensen, *Pawn Review* 8, 1984; *Heart's Invention: On the Poetry of Vassar Miller* edited by Steven Ford Brown, Houston, Ford-Brown, 1988; "Ever a Bridegroom: Reflections on the Failure of Texas Literature" by Larry McMurtry, *Range Wars: Heated Debates, Sober Reflections, and Other As-*

sessments of Texas Writing edited by Craig Clifford and Tom Pilkington, Dallas, Southern Methodist University Press, 1989.

Video: *A Tribute to Vassar Miller,* Friends of the University of Houston Libraries, Houston, University of Houston, 1983.

Vassar Miller comments:
Poetry, like all art, has a trinitarian function: creative, redemptive, and sanctifying. It is creative because it takes the raw materials of fact and feeling and makes them into that which is neither fact nor feeling. It is redemptive because it can transform the pain and ugliness of life into joy and beauty. It is sanctifying because it thus gives the transitory at least a relative form and meaning.

*   *   *

Vassar Miller has stated that she believes poetry serves three functions: creative, redemptive, and sanctifying. "Poetry is creative," she said, "in that it makes an artifact where none was before, only a mass of thoughts and emotions and sensations; it is redemptive, since it makes art out of non-art, something of beauty and value; it is sanctifying in that it confers order upon chaos."

The religious and physical yearning in Miller's body of work has invited comparisons to the poetry of mystical poet Henry Vaughan and the Jesuit poet Gerard Manley Hopkins (she has acknowledged the influence of Hopkins' "sprung rhythm" technique, and her first published poem appeared in the *Hopkins Review*). Her use of traditional verse forms—the sonnet, a form for which Hopkins is particularly noted, villanelles, blank verse and monologues—reflects affinities to the poetry of Emily Dickinson, Walt Whitman, Sylvia Plath, and Robert Lowell. Miller writes lyric verse that addresses her religious and metaphysical concerns, her womanhood, and her affliction with cerebral palsy. Much of her work refers to struggle—believing in the concept of a supreme being in light of her physical disability, affirming that doubt is critical for a total comprehension of Divinity.

Many of Miller's poems use her chronic ailment as a metaphor for human suffering and loneliness. Miller often balances her verse's somber subject matter with humor as well as erotic and emotional images. The religious nature of her work is tempered by her refusal to advance any specific, organized theological views or biblical interpretations.

Miller was born in Houston, Texas, to a prominent real-estate developer and his wife, also named Vassar, who died when Miller was one-year-old. Afflicted with cerebral palsy since birth, Miller received her first typewriter at the age of eight, which assisted in her efforts to communicate through writing. Although she was raised Presbyterian, the family maid took her to evangelistic meetings when she was a young woman. Since then, Miller has been associated with the Episcopal faith, the Roman Catholic Church, and the Covenant Baptist Church, the latter of which adheres to the Catholic Church's seasons of Lent, Easter, Pentecost, and Advent.

Miller claimed her choice of organized worship is for personal not theological reasons and has not diminished her sympathy with the Episcopal and Roman Catholic observance of the sacraments.

Many of her poems cull imagery from her experiences with various Christian religions. "Accepting," for example, was written following her attendance at a Roman Catholic Ash Wednesday observance. Following high school, Miller earned a B.S. and M.A. from the University of Houston, where she wrote her master's thesis on the mysticism in the poetry of Edward Arlington Robinson.

Miller's first volume of verse, *Adam's Footprint* (1956), collects forty-three lyric poems arranged in alphabetical order. Evidence of Miller's religious concerns prevail throughout the poems, as well as humanity's relationship with God and with each other. The successful composition of the poems from this inaugural volume were critically validated by their inclusion in Donald Hall's *New Poets of England and America*. Her next volume, *Wage War on Silence* (1960), displays her mastery of traditional forms and Miller's belief that poetry often unsuccessfully attempts to express rationally the irrational and emotional aspects of human life.

My Bones Being Wiser (1963) marked Miller's increasingly confessional approach, leading to comparisons to Lowell and Plath, and was interpreted by many critics as feminist in content. Miller responded that, due to her physical challenges, she felt equally alienated from men and women. *Onions and Roses* (1968) attracted more comparisons with confessional poets. "On Approaching My Birthday," for example, includes stark references to the death of her mother and Miller's cerebral palsy. The tragic realism of the "Onion" poems, however, are mediated by the inclusion of "Rose" poems pertaining to grace and perfection found in the corporeal world.

If I Could Sleep Deeply Enough (1974) addresses the mental anguish that is incumbent with her physical malady. Miller portrays sleep as both a restorative state of being and a harbinger of death. One poem, "Spastics," bitterly attacks healthy individuals who demean the physically challenged with ill-advised sympathy. In contrast to her earlier volumes, *If I Could Sleep Deeply Enough* contains very few poems adhering to traditional forms. Instead, Miller employs more experimental free-verse forms, including unrhymed poems and three-lined stanzas.

Miller wrote the poems collected in *Approaching Nada* (1977) while living briefly in Phoenix, Arizona. The pieces work together as one extended poem that refers to God as "Nada," an inherently unknowable force. Miller's spiritual autobiography, *Approaching Nada* affirms her status as a major religious/mystical poet in its assertions of the sustenance to be found in God's love. Miller's embrace of religious beliefs also incorporates an acceptance of death as a spiritual consummation with God. *Small Change* (1977) continues Miller's meditations on death, exemplified in "Memento Mori," written to the memory of poet Anne Sexton.

The more recent works in *Selected and New Poems, 1950-1980* include many poems that confront social attitudes toward the physically challenged, a theme that Miller expanded on in editing *Despite This Flesh: The Disabled in Stories and Poems* (1985). In the book's Introduction, Miller wrote that well-meaning individuals often do more to further the plight of the handicapped, leaving them "killed with kindness, stifled by over protection, choked by subtle if sometimes unconscious snubs by genuinely good people." In turn, she identifies "too many handicapped folk [who] linger, bound by depression, self-pity, or fear in the back bedrooms of their own minds" and states the volume's purpose "is to prevent such pointless dying that his anthology has come into being."

Struggling to Swim on Concrete (1984) associates religious meditation with spiritual quest, again linking the physical and inner worlds, of ailments, desire, and triumphs, confessional about the hidden self, exultant in exertion, exploring the dark and light. "Love's Bitten Tongue," a twenty-two sonnet sequence concluding the volume, demonstrates Miller's technical brilliance, as each concluding line becomes the initial line of the succeeding sonnet and subtle syntactical and rhythmic transformations reflect her tonal control and masterful evocation of varying moods.

If I Had Wheels or Love: Collected Poems of Vassar Miller (1991) collects the best of Miller's poetry, including "Affinity," which explores darkness and pain in the manner of Flannery O'Connor, the "Approaching Nada" series, her insightful explorations of writers ("Emily Dickinson Comes To The Dinner Party"), religious figures, and musicians, and elegies, love songs, and meditations—a rich body of work that affirms Larry McMurtry's declaration in a 1981 speech at the Fort Worth Art Museum where he called Miller perhaps the greatest author Texas had produced. Indeed, McMurtry's national reputation has been of considerable assistance to Miller. In the preface to *Heart's Invention*, which collects critical essays on Miller's work, McMurtry noted five characteristics that define both the poetry and the person of Vassar Miller: clarity, precision, intelligence, honesty, and tenacity, and these are certainly in evidence in *If I Had Wheels or Love*.

—Bruce Walker

MITCHELL, Joseph

Born: Joseph Quincy Mitchell in Fairmont, North Carolina, 27 July 1908. **Education:** University of North Carolina, Chapel Hill, 1925-29. **Family:** Married Therese Dagny Engelsted Jacobsen, 27 February 1931; two daughters. **Career:** Reporter, New York *World,* 1929-30, New York *Herald Tribune,* 1929-31, and New York *World Telegram* 1931-38; staff writer, the *New Yorker* magazine, beginning in 1938; commissioner, New York City Landmarks Preservation Commission, 1982-87. **Awards:** National Institute of Arts and Letters, 1965; State of North Carolina gold medal for literature, 1983. **Member:** Vice-president, 1971, and secretary, 1972-74, National Institute of Arts and Letters; Historians, Society for Industrial Archeology, James Joyce Society, Friends of Cast-Iron Architecture, Gypsy Lore Society (England), Century Association. **Died:** In 1996.

PUBLICATIONS

Nonfiction

My Ears Are Bent (collection of newspaper articles). New York, Sheridan House, 1938.

Apologies to the Iroquois With A Study of the Mohawks (the former by Edmund Wilson, the latter by Mitchell). New York, Farrar, Straus, 1960.

Short Story Collections

McSorley's Wonderful Saloon. New York, Duell, 1943.
Old Mr. Flood. New York, Duell, 1948.
The Bottom of the Harbor. Boston, Little Brown, 1959.
Joe Gould's Secret. New York, Viking Press, 1965.
Up in the Old Hotel, and Other Stories. New York City, Vintage Books, 1993.

*

Critical Studies: "The Grammar of Facts" by Malcolm Cowley, in *New Republic* (New York), 26 July 1943; "The Art of Joseph Mitchell" by Stanley Edgar Hyman, in *New Leader* (New York), 6 December 1965; *Here at the New Yorker* by Brendan Gill, New York, Random House, 1975; "Paragon of Reporters: Joseph Mitchell" by Noel Perrin, in *Sewanee Review* (Sewanee, Tennessee), Spring 1983.

*   *   *

Throughout his works Joseph Mitchell places himself in the tradition of the tall tale in America and reveals why he can say in *McSorley's Wonderful Saloon* to the "Gifted Child" that Mark Twain's *Life on the Mississippi* is the one book he likes above all others. He walks in wonder and records what he sees. All of his central figures emerge as larger-than-life people, yet there is almost always a quality of reflection and tone-setting that makes them believable as well as memorable.

In an author's note to *McSorley's Wonderful Saloon,* Mitchell concludes: "There are no little people in this book. They are as big as you are, whoever you are." And he then works with a fine eye, ear, and hand to give profile to such "little" people as John McSorley, president of "an organization of gluttons called the Honorable John McSorley Pickle, Beefsteak, Baseball Nine and Chowder Club"; Mazie P. Gordon, owner of, ticket seller, and bouncer at the Venice theater in the Bowery; King Cockeye Johnny Nikanov, a Russian and King of the Gypsies in New York; Lady Olga Jane Bardwell, a freak show lady with a 14-and-a-half-inch beard, mustache, and her fourth husband; and various others. His favorite setting is lower Manhattan, and his stories become urban pastorals, strongest when he focuses with care on his people: Mr. Hugh G. Flood, in *Old Mr. Flood,* and Joe Gould, in *Joe Gould's Secret,* exemplify best Mitchell's role as profilist-storyteller.

Mr. Flood, age 93 to 95 and wants to live to be 115, is a "seafoodetarian" who can eat bushels of clams and consume large quantities of whiskey. From the many scenes and wild anecdotes of "Old Mr. Flood," "The Black Clams," and "Mr. Flood's Party" comes a man whom the narrator obviously loves, one who, as Mr. Mitchell says, is not one man but "several old men, who work or hang out in Fulton Fish Market." He's too big to exist, but he is nonetheless there, and the *I* of the story penetrates his moods—from extreme loneliness to convivial joy—with touching sensitivity. One feels that Mr. Flood will indeed live to age 115.

Joe Gould, on the other hand, is, as the author says in a note, "a lost soul." As Professor Sea Gull in *McSorley's Wonderful Saloon,* he is a tall-tale character too—a blithe and emaciated little man who has been a notable in the cafeterias, diners, barrooms, and dumps of Greenwich Village for a quarter of a century. A Harvard alumnus, class of 1911, he sometimes brags that he is the last of the bohemians. Of chief interest to Mitchell is Gould's *An Oral History of Our Time*—a document 11 times as long as the Bible, over 9,000,000 words in longhand and still unfinished. As a solitary nocturnal wanderer he talks much of his *Oral History* and of his ability, among other things, to translate Longfellow's "Hiawatha" into sea gull. Here he shouts to a Village waitress: "I'm Joe Gould, the poet; I'm Joe Gould, the historian; I'm Joe Gould, the wild Chippewa Indian dancer; and I'm Joe Gould, the greatest authority in the world on the language of the sea gull."

Joe Gould's secret, however, discovered by Mitchell years later, is that there is no *Oral History.* Gould has not only duped Mitchell and the people but has duped himself. He can recite it but cannot put it down. Mitchell keeps the secret until he writes it down in his story, stepping out of, as he says, "the role I had stepped into the afternoon I discovered that the *Oral History* did not exist."

My Ears Are Bent and *The Bottom of the Harbor* show Mitchell's consistency throughout his career in reporting on but also building on the people and places of his world, from Sloppy Louie's, the old Fulton Ferry Hotel, and the "Baymen" to the rats on the waterfront. When he writes of his home country in rural North Carolina he uses his same profilist's eye and feeling for his "people" to bring to life such characters as Mrs. Copenhagen Calhoun in "I Blame It All on Mama," Uncle Dockery in "Uncle Dockery and the Independent Bull," and Mr. Catfish Giddy in "The Downfall of Fascism in Black Ankle County." Mitchell is the country boy who went to the city to find his way—and found it in the *New Yorker,* where he perfected the urban tall-tale pastoral.

—Frank T. Phipps

MONTGOMERY, Marion

Born: Marion Hoyt Montgomery, Jr. in Thomaston, Georgia, 16 April 1925. **Military Service:** U.S. Army, 1943-46; became sergeant. **Education**: University of Georgia, 1947-53, A.B., M.A. **Family:** Married Dorothy Carlisle, 20 January 1951; five children. **Career:** Assistant director of university press, 1950-52, business manager of *Georgia Review,* 1951-53, instructor, 1954-60, assistant professor, 1960-67, associate professor, 1967-70, professor of English, since 1970, University of Georgia, Athens; instructor, Darlington School for Boys, 1953-54; writer-in-residence, Converse College, 1963. **Awards:** Eugene Saxton Memorial Award, 1960; Georgia Writers Association Award for Fiction, 1964, for *Darrell,* and for poetry, 1970, for *The Gull and Other Georgia Scenes;* award for poetry, *Carlton Miscellany,* 1967; Earhart Foundation grant for critical work. **Address:** Department of English, University of Georgia, Athens, Georgia 30602.

PUBLICATIONS

Poetry

Dry Lightening. Lincoln, University of Nebraska Press, 1960.
Stones from the Rubble. Memphis, Argus Books, 1965.
The Gull and Other Georgia Scenes. Athens, University of Georgia Press, 1969.

Novels

The Wandering of Desire. New York, Harper, 1962.
Darrell. New York, Doubleday, 1964.
Ye Olde Bluebird (novella). Sarasota, New College Press, 1967.
Fugitive. New York, Harper, 1974.

Criticism

Ezra Pound: A Critical Essay. Grand Rapids, Eerdmans, 1970.
T. S. Eliot: An Essay on the American Magus. Athens, University of Georgia Press, 1970.
The Reflective Journey toward Order: Essays on Dante, Wordsworth, Eliot, and Others. Athens, University of Georgia Press, 1973.
Eliot's Reflective Journey to the Garden. Troy, New York, Whitston Publishing, 1978.
The Prophetic Poet and the Spirit of the Age. La Salle, Illinois, Sherwood Sugden; *Volume I: Why Flannery O'Connor Stayed Home,* 1980, *Volume II: Why Poe Drank Liquor,* 1983, *Volume III: Why Hawthorne Was Melancholy,* 1984.
Poets, and the Reflective Poet. La Salle, Illinois, Sherwood Sugden, 1980.
Virtue and Modern Shadows of Turning: Preliminary Agitations. Lanham, Maryland, Intercollegiate Studies Institute, University Press of America, 1990.

Nonfiction

Possum, and Other Receipts for the Recovery of "Southern" Being. Athens, University of Georgia Press, 1987.
The Trouble with You Innerleckchuls. Front Royal, Virginia, Christendom College Press, 1988.
The Men I Have Chosen for Fathers: Literary and Philosophical Passages. Columbia, University of Missouri Press, 1990.
Liberal Arts and Community: The Feeding of the Larger Body. Baton Rouge, Louisiana State University Press, 1990.

*   *   *

Marion Montgomery's fiction and criticism are ambitious in their scope and experimental approaches. Generally eschewing linear development, Montgomery favors thematic approaches that accommodate extended digressions, liberal use of anecdotes, and tangential forays into subject areas that at times seem unrelated to the main body of a story or critical discourse. Careful and patient (occasionally diligent) reading, however, is gradually rewarded with treasures from such forays, as the author patterns forms that expand on the implications of content.

Much of Montgomery's fiction addresses transitions between the Old and New South as distinctions emerged during such eras as the Depression, the post-World War II years, and contemporary times. Montgomery's works labor for authentic perspectives, drawing on such elements as history, lore, colloquial speech, and careful evocation of setting. As his novels relate tragicomic consequences that result from characters attempting to live out ambitious ideas based on dubious values, readers are informed about regional history, observe vanities of the times, and learn about characteristics of landscapes in Georgia wire-grass country, rural Tennessee, or modern Atlanta suburbs. Montgomery's concern for accuracy is addressed in his 1967 novella, *Ye Olde Bluebird,* which centers on friends, one from the north, the other from the south, and their conflict over a play that presents a laudable social message through stereotypical views of the Southern society.

Montgomery has published numerous critical texts exploring ways in which authors approached the theme of modernity, a prominent concern in his own work. Like his fiction, Montgomery's criticism is based in sound historical roots and details while pursuing discursive courses and digressions, rambling over a wide range of topics and drawing on a wealth of allusions and anecdotes. He has published texts on Ezra Pound, Dante, and Wordsworth, among others, including several on T. S. Eliot. Montgomery's nonlinear approach yields insights informed by scholarship, presenting writers and their works with specificity on their intellectual, social, and physical development and milieus. His three-part series *The Prophetic Poet and the Spirit of the Age* is a prime example of his pursuit and elaboration of particular themes within an expansive framework, with enticing titles announcing his major concerns—*Volume I: Why Flannery O'Connor Stayed Home, Volume II: Why Poe Drank Liquor, Volume III: Why Hawthorne Was Melancholy.*

Montgomery's approach is best illustrated in his fiction, which is ambitious, knowledgeable, and complexly structured (or rambling free-form, some might argue). Differences among rural and urban lifestyles and values, change, historical patterns, and characters obsessed with realizing a vision are central to his three novels, *The Wandering of Desire* (1962), *Darrell* (1964), and *Fugitive* (1974).

The Wandering of Desire is the most ambitious of these in scope, narrative approach, and implications. The novel relates the efforts of two men to tame the hard, wire-grass country of Georgia for prosperous farming. Wash Mullis is a self-made man who cleared a swamp and established profitable cotton fields and a huge farm, growing more vain and materialistic with each new success and fueling his insatiable appetite for money and sex. Natural disasters, including pestilence and fire, coupled with human deceit and his monomaniacal passion for power, sap his fortune, and he is eventually forced to forfeit his land to a bank. Veterinarian "Doc" Blalock buys the land to experiment with scientifically-progressive ranching techniques, but his efforts end in death, tragedy and financial ruin.

This summary presents events as they happen chronologically, but the narrative unfolds nonsequentially through thematic patterns, rather than through chronological development. Anecdotes and digressions are interspersed prodigiously, relating events to the larger history of the region and reinforcing a cycle of human vanity and natural disasters, which power over Mullis' common

man energy and Doc's faith in science. The times at which events take place in the novel matter little: historical references underscore the difficulties confronting simple survival in the region, let alone the large-scale undertakings of Mullis and Doc to control nature. Their tragedies are Biblical in proportion (epigraphs from Ecclesiastes help frame the story), arising from the unpredictability of nature, violence, duplicity, and unforeseen events (Doc's prized bull kills Mullis' son and has to be destroyed).

Faithful attention to landscape, careful recreation of dialect (including a bardic, rural narrative voice), characters whose outlooks and actions reflect the tough lives they lead, and skillful use of irony and symbolism are elements of this novel's ambitious scope, amplified by discursive digressions. An arresting final image has the two aged men sitting broken and humbled as the landscape they thought they could conquer begins to return to its original form.

Darrell, Montgomery's second novel, is a much more conventionally-structured work, most significant for reflecting the author's thematic interest in vanity, the changing nature of the South, and idyllic visions of rural life among urbanized Southerners. The title character convinces his aged grandmother to move with him to Atlanta, away from their small town life. They settle in an Atlanta suburb, and Darrell immediately gets into the spirit of things by placing a pink flamingo on his front lawn, one of many garish aspects of popular culture he wants to embrace to reflect his new life. He instead experiences indifference, crass commercial culture, and tedium as a way of life, with a constant need for new thrills to make life interesting. Darrell befriends a dying girl who has become the center of a media circus playing the human interest angle, an all-too common phenomenon wickedly satirized by Montgomery. Darrell, partly manipulated by the girl and partly out of love, takes her away to fulfill her desire to visit a zoo, an act that leads to tragic consequences. With his simple delusions—a romanticized view of urban life further propagated by various forms of popular culture—Darrell is significant as a recurring character-type in Montgomery's work—a person deluded in a grand vision and the dire consequences that result from his pursuit.

While Darrell leaves the country for the city, Walt Mason in *Fugitive*, Montgomery's third novel, seeks a better life in the country. The title of this work references the group of Southern writers who championed traditional agrarian values. *Fugitive* offers a contemporary approach to pursuing such values, as Mason quits his successful country music songwriting career in Nashville for a life of rural simplicity in the small town of Weaverton, Tennessee. There he encounters a host of local characters, ranging from a murderous, backwoods moonshiner to a wise simple man who becomes a kind of historical guide. Mason ardently pursues his agrarian values: he restores a house (a deeply symbolic act suggesting the reclamation of agrarian traditions) and falls in love with a modest woman. However, discrepancies abound between his vision and contemporary realities. For example, he discovers that technology can be as vital to rural life as it is to the modern city, and that television and other forms of popular culture are just as prominent in rural life as they were in Nashville. Continuing to pursue his bucolic vision even as commercial culture continues to encroach (including a much-anticipated country music festival) and some forms of modernity improve country life, Mason is a kind of Everyman of the contemporary South. Montgomery's discursiveness—through digressions, shifting points of view, anecdotes, interruptions, and philosophical musings—place Mason's contemporary problems within a larger history; the complexity of the novel's form itself is an ironic counterpointing of Mason's pursuit of a plain, good life he associates with the past.

—Perry Bear

MORGAN, Elizabeth Seydel

Born: Atlanta, Georgia, 1939. **Education:** Hollins College, Roanoke, Virginia, B.A. 1960; Virginia Commonwealth University, Richmond, M.F.A. 1986. **Career:** Started the creative writing course at St. Catherine's School in Richmond, Virginia; full-time writer. **Awards:** National Endowment for the Humanities fellowship, Harvard University; Virginia Film Festival's Governor's Screenwriting Competition Award, 1993.

PUBLICATIONS

Poetry Collections

Parties. Baton Rouge, Louisiana State University Press, 1986.
The Governor of Desire. Baton Rouge, Louisiana State University Press, 1993.
On Long Mountain. Baton Rouge, Louisiana State University Press, 1998.

Other

Translator, *Electra*, in *Euripides 2*, edited by David R. Slavitt and Palmer Bovie. Philadelphia, University of Pennsylvania Press, 1997.

*   *   *

For Elizabeth Seydel Morgan, poetry is an invitation, a loving gesture extended to someone else to share in an ordinary moment. Morgan might well be speaking of herself when she evaluates the work of another artist in "Swing, Boat, Table," a poem from *On Long Mountain* (1998):

> What Hanno has made of wood this year:
> a swing, a boat, a table.
>
> He doesn't believe he's made art this year;
> the swing, the boat, the table
>
> are objects he made to invite those he loves
> to sit down.

For this artist, the aesthetic value of his creations is less important than its capacity to provide a common ground for profound human connections.

Morgan suggests that poetry enables intimacy, and at times it even performs a remedial or therapeutic service. But if art can join us, it can also reinforce our fundamental isolation from each other. In "Poetry Reading," another poem from *On Long Mountain*, Morgan teases her audience:

> This is my last poem:
> pay attention.
> I know there were minutes—
> whole poems back there—
> when I lost you.
> I know your mind tried, for a while,
> to stay behind your eyes
> but at times, it just had to be excused . . .

The poet is aware that her words are the direct cause of her audience's inattention, and she imagines that her poem has inspired bittersweet memories of lost loves and lost opportunities. These daydreams eventually restore Morgan's listeners to her performance, but the distances between and among those present at the poetry reading are only imperfectly overcome.

Morgan has published three volumes of poems, the strongest of which is *On Long Mountain.* *The Governor of Desire* (1993) is an uneven collection, but contains many accomplished poems. Morgan derives her title from Shakespeare's Sonnet 113, two lines of which serve as her book's epigraph: "And that which governs me to go about / Doth part his function and is partly blind." The sonnet ends, "Incapable of more, replete with you, / My most true mind thus maketh mine eye untrue." And Morgan is at her best when her eye remains true to the physical world of the present—or to memories of the past—without falsely idealizing them. For instance, in "Sunset on Eastern Beaches," the poet compares sundown at Tuscany and Key West to sundown at the Outer Banks: "But the last light on eastern beaches / does not command response. Here on Nag's Head / the air is washed. The sand turns gold. / The whitecaps flap like sunbleached flags / and clean cottons we wear down now / from the cottages after our showers." While the last lights of Italy and Florida are imbued with the glorified adornments of poetic tradition, the unaffected landscape of North Carolina resists such romanticizing. The brilliance of the sunset on western shores pales when experienced from the eas,: "Our faces glow with sun / we cannot see." The effusions and ornaments of the extraordinary are inappropriate here, and Morgan quietly valorizes what is simple and common and dear.

In addition to poetry, Morgan writes screenplays and has published a translation of Euripides' *Electra* in the Penn Greek Drama Series. She has recently been included in the Library of Virginia's Special Collection of Virginia Authors.

—Jeannine Johnson

MORGAN, Robert

Born: Hendersonville, North Carolina, 3 October 1944. **Education:** Emory College, Oxford, 1961-62; North Carolina State University, Raleigh, 1962-63; University of North Carolina, Chapel Hill, 1963-66, B.A. 1965; University of North Carolina, Greensboro, 1967-68, M.F.A. 1968. **Family:** Married Nancy K. Bullock in 1965; one son and two daughters. **Career:** Teaching assistant, University of North Carolina, Greensboro, 1967-68; instructor, Salem College, Winston-Salem, North Carolina, 1968-69; lecturer, 1971-73, assistant professor, 1973-78, associate professor, 1978-84, professor, 1982-92, and since 1992 Kappa Alpha Professor of English, Cornell University, Ithaca, New York. **Awards:** National Endowment for the Arts fellowships, 1968, 1974, 1981, 1987; Southern Poetry Review prize, 1975; Eunice Tietjens award, 1979; Jacaranda Review fiction prize, 1988; Guggenheim fellowship, 1988-89; Amon Liner prize, 1989; James G. Hanes Poetry prize, 1991; North Carolina award in literature, 1991. **Address:** Department of English, Goldwin Smith Hall, Cornell University, Ithaca, New York 14853.

PUBLICATIONS

Poetry

Zirconia Poems. Northwood Narrows, New Hampshire, Lillabulero Press, 1969.
The Voice in the Crosshairs. Ithaca, New York, Angelfish Press, 1971.
Red Owl. New York, Norton, 1972.
Land Diving. Baton Rouge, Louisiana State University Press, 1976.
Trunk and Thicket. Fort Collins, Colorado, L'Epervier Press, 1978.
Groundwork. Frankfort, Kentucky, Gnomon Press, 1979.
Bronze Age. Emory, Virginia, Iron Mountain Press, 1981.
At the Edge of the Orchard Country. Middletown, Connecticut, Wesleyan University Press, 1987.
Sigodlin. Middletown, Connecticut, Wesleyan University Press, 1990.
Green River: New and Selected Poems. Hanover, New Hampshire, University Press of New England, 1991.

Short Stories

The Blue Valleys: A Collection of Stories. Atlanta, Georgia, Peachtree, 1989.
The Mountains Won't Remember Us and Other Stories. Atlanta, Georgia, Peachtree, 1992.
The Hinterlands: A Mountain Tale in Three Parts. Chapel Hill, North Carolina, Algonquin Books, 1994.
The Truest Pleasure. N.P., 1995.

Other

Good Measure: Essays, Interviews and Notes on Poetry. Baton Rouge, Louisiana State University Press, 1993.

*

Bibliography: "Robert Morgan: A Bibliographical Chronicle, 1963-1981" by Stuart Wright, in *Bulletin of Bibliography* (Westport, Connecticut), 39(3).

Manuscript Collections: Emory University, Atlanta, Georgia; University of North Carolina, Chapel Hill.

Critical Studies: *"Land Diving"* by William Matthews, in *Meridian* (New York), 1980; "Robert Morgan's Pellagian Georgics: Twelve Essays" by William Harmon, in *Parnassus*

(New York), Fall/Winter 1981; "A Conversation with Robert Morgan" by Suzanne Booker, in *Carolina Quarterly* (Chapel Hill, North Carolina), Spring 1985; "Recovering Pieces of the Morgenland" by Robert Schultz, in *Virginia Quarterly Review* (Charlottesville), Winter 1988; *"At the Edge of the Orchard Country"* by Ted Kooser, in *Prairie Schooner* (Lincoln, Nebraska), Summer 1989; chapter in *Looking for Native Ground: Contemporary Appalachian Poetry* by Rita Sims Quillen, Boone, North Carolina, Appalachian Consortium Press, 1989; "Pieces of the Morgenland: The Recent Achievements in Robert Morgan's Poetry" by P. H. Liotta, in *Southern Literary Journal* (Chapel Hill, North Carolina), Spring 1990; Robert Morgan issue of *The Iron Mountain Review,* Summer 1990; "Coming Out from under Calvinism: Religious Motifs in Robert Morgan's Poetry" by John Lang, in *Shenandoah* (Lexington, Virginia), Summer 1992.

Robert Morgan comments:

Since I was in college I have been writing both poetry and fiction, but all my first seven books were volumes of poetry. Like many of the poets of the 1960's I began writing in open forms and only started experimenting with rhyme and traditional form in the mid 1970's. Many of my poems have been concerned with the Blue Ridge Mountains of North Carolina where I grew up, but I have also written about American history, Upstate New York where I have lived since 1971, the sciences, and about family stories and characters. I especially like to write about machines and gadgets.

No one has yet discovered a culture without poetry. Language itself was probably a discovery of the poetic imagination, and only later put to use for practical ends, as pure mathematics can be used for physical description and problem solving. And while it is true poetry is a medium of the gut as well as the mind, it is also true poetry is rarely just a secular art. Materialistic cultures will always prefer prose fiction. The subject of many novels is money, while the subject of most poems is rediscovery of spiritual desire. Poems work by stirring memory, by unexpected connections, accuracy of naming, delight in wordplay. And the music of poetry comes as much from the quickness of what is said as from the pattern of syllables.

When I was about 15 I wanted to write some epic work, poem, or musical composition, as grand as the Cicero Mountain across the river from our house. But later, as I actually began writing verse, I became more interested in compression, indirection, in the use of simple language to embody complex experience. My ideal was to write poetry accessible to everyone, but tough enough, and rich enough, to reveal something on each successive reading. That is an ideal I am still working toward.

*   *   *

In a period when disconnection, disaffection, and disaffiliation seem the coin of the poetry realm, it is a pleasure to read a poet as connected as Robert Morgan. His poetry is connected to a particular place, the Blue Ridge Mountains of his native North Carolina, and it explores his ties to the people of that region, to generations of family, to the earth and natural process, to animals, plants, and things, to the historic, prehistoric, and geological past.

His poems, as well as his stories, reflect the strengths of these deep connections, this rootedness. Together with his fine sense of craft, his allegiance to his native area gives his writing a quiet power and universality.

The titles of Morgan's collections, along with several luminous lines and images, signal his allegiances. *At the Edge of the Orchard Country* reveals a regional tie but implies a universe beyond; *Groundwork* suggests the native soil that he works, even mines; the title poem of *Land Diving* dramatizes an important Morgan principle, "The meaning is the closeness"; the concrete *Trunk & Thicket* includes a telling prose memoir titled "Homecoming"; and *Red Owl* contains the short poem "New-plowed Ground" that features an apt metaphor for Morgan's poetics: "You can't navigate without/getting dirt in your shoes."

In the essay "The Cubist of Memory," Morgan claims that as a Southern poet he decided to reject Faulknerian rhetoric and "go off in an unknown direction ... toward plainness, compactness, simplicity.... To help free myself from myself—from ego, ambition, self-consciousness—to get on with the work, I tried to be true to objects, and to the verbal objects that measured and enacted world and thought." In many of his poems, especially those collected in *At the Edge of the Orchard Country* and *Sigodlin,* he does indeed achieve a Southern lushness of detail tempered by what one might ordinarily consider a Midwestern reserve and plainness of language. In these poems there is a balance between the concrete and the abstract, the romantic and the classical, the scientific and the literary, the head and the heart. His poem about a treaty with the Cherokees, "Ninety-Six Line," ends with an image of Morgan's poised standing in different worlds: "I grew up," he says, "with one foot in the English/country, one in the high dark/hunting ranges, and felt a chill/when stepping across to either/imaginary dominion."

It is hard to think of a contemporary American poet with a deeper sense of family ties, customs, and lore than Morgan. The ordinary, everyday rural objects he looks upon constantly reveal traces and residues of former lives. He loves to tell the stories, some eccentric, that open up the lives of parents, cousins, aunts and uncles, grandparents, great-grandparents. He is haunted by the uncle, after whom he was named, who died in England in World War II. One of his best poems, "White Autumn," a classic "portrait" poem, celebrates the life and world of his matriarchal great-grandmother. Morgan's loving detail brings to life not only the individual woman but also several generations of family, the history of a region, and layers of the collective past. We see the matriarch rocking in her chair on her mountain porch: "The cats passed through her lap and legs/and through the rungs of her seat" as "She rode that upright cradle to sleep/and through many long visits with tiers of family,/kissing the babies like different kinds of fruit." We can see the independent, strong-hearted leader of the clan "bath[ing]/in a warm river of books and black coffee." Like any fine poet, Morgan makes us enter into many lives by taking us within one individual life deeply lived: "On that creaking throne she ruled a tiny kingdom/through war, death of kin." Kinship is Morgan's major theme and deepest metaphor.

—Norbert Krapf

MORRIS, Willie

Born: William Weaks Morris in Jackson, Mississippi, 29 November 1934. **Education:** University of Texas, B.A. 1956; Oxford University, B.A. 1959, M.A. 1963. **Family:** Married Celia Ann Buchan, 30 August 1958 (divorced 1970); one child; married JoAnne Prichard (an editor), 1990. **Career:** Reporter and editor, *Daily Texan*, University of Texas student newspaper, 1955-56; editor-in-chief, *Texas Observer*, Austin, 1960-62; editor, 1963-65, executive editor, 1966-67, editor-in-chief, 1967-71, *Harper's*; writer in residence, University of Mississippi; consultant on the Rob Reiner motion picture *Ghosts of Mississippi*, 1996. **Awards**: Rhodes Scholarship, 1956; Houghton-Mifflin Company Literary fellowship, 1967, for *North Toward Home*; Carr P. Collins Award, 1967, and Francis Parkman Prize, Texas Institute of Letters, 1968, all for *North Toward Home*; Steck-Vaughn Award, Texas Institute of Letters, 1972, for *Good Old Boy: A Delta Boyhood*; Richard Wright Medal for Literary Excellence, Natchez Literary Festival, 1996.

PUBLICATIONS

Autobiographies

North Toward Home. New York, Houghton, 1967.
New York Days. Boston, Little, Brown and Co., 1993.

General Nonfiction

Yazoo: Integration in a Deep-Southern Town. New York, Harper, 1971.
A Southern Album: Recollections of Some People and Places and Times Gone By, with Irwin Glusker. Birmingham, Oxmoor, 1975.
James Jones: A Friendship. New York, Doubleday, 1978.
The Courting of Marcus Dupree. New York, Doubleday, 1983.
Faulkner's Mississippi, text by Willie Morris, photographs by William Eggleston. Birmingham, Oxmoor House, 1990.
After All, It's Only a Game, with art by Lynn Green Root. Jackson, University Press of Mississippi, 1992.
My Dog Skip. New York, Random House, 1995.
The Ghosts of Medgar Evers: A Tale of Race, Murder, Mississippi, and Hollywood. New York, Random House, 1998.

Children's Books

Good Old Boy: A Delta Boyhood. New York, Harper, 1971.
Good Old Boy and the Witch of Yazoo. Oxford, Mississippi, Yoknapatawpha Press, 1989.
Prayer for the Opening of the Little League Season, illustrated by Barry Moser. San Diego, Harcourt Brace, 1995.

Novel

The Last of the Southern Girls. New York, Knopf, 1973.

Essay Collections

Terrains of the Heart and Other Essays on Home. Oxford, Mississippi, Yoknapatawpka Press, 1981.

Always Stand in Against the Curve and Other Sports Stories. Oxford, Mississippi, Yoknapatawpka Press, 1983.
Homecomings, with the art of William Dunlap. Jackson, University Press of Mississippi, 1989.
My Two Oxfords, with wood engravings by John DePol. Council Bluffs, Iowa, Yellow Barn Press, 1992.

Editor

The South Today: 100 Years after Appomattox. New York, Harper, 1965.

*

Manuscript Collection: University of Mississippi.

*   *   *

Willie Morris draws upon personal experience to evoke local color and to connect significant events in his native Mississippi with larger issues in contemporary America. Whether recalling boyhood mischief-making and such friends as Slit McGee, Rivers Applewhite, and Pinkey Posey, or examining race relations from his experiences with desegregation and violence, or exploring more general topics, Morris' observations are infused with his Southern sensibility and, therefore, celebrate the region's culture and history. In *Terrains of the Heart and Other Essays on Home,* he explains, "I go back to the South, physically and in my memories, to remind myself who I am, for the South keeps me going."

North Toward Home (1967) initiated his blending of personal history and larger events through engaging narratives. This autobiographical work relates incidents from his childhood in the delta's edge town of Yazoo City, where his parents moved when he was six months old. The *London Sunday Times* praised the memoir as "the finest evocation of an American boyhood since Mark Twain"; like Twain's works, the playful adventures of a group of children are set against the background of turbulent social conflicts, as Morris's development into a young man is intricately connected with social strife and change from the 1940s and 1950s that culminated with civil rights struggles and desegregation in the 1960s as well as a more modernized local environment.

By 1960, Morris had graduated from the University of Texas and had studied at Oxford University as a Rhodes Scholar. He returned to Austin from England to be active in social issues as editor of the liberal *Texas Observer* from 1960 to 1962. In 1963 he became the youngest-ever editor of the nation's oldest magazine—*Harper's,* resuscitating the failing journal and leading it back into respectability by seeking out and publishing pieces by high-profile authors, including William Styron, David Halberstam, Robert Penn Warren, and Norman Mailer. Morris resigned from his Editor-in-Chief position (followed by most of the magazine's contributing editors) in 1971 during a dispute with ownership over editorial policy.

Good Old Boy (1971), dedicated to his son, continued Morris' reminiscences on his adventurous childhood, including an episode where he helped concoct an elaborate plan to infiltrate a local haunted house; the incident was expanded on later in *Good Old Boy and the Witch of Yazoo* (1989). A more sober view of growing up is related in *Yazoo: Integration in a Deep-Southern Town* (1971), which recounts the effects on local residents of forced integration of public schools. Other works with themes related to Morris' heritage include the essays collected in *Homecomings* (1989) and his feature *Faulkner's Mississippi* (1990), expanded into a book from a *National Geographic* cover story (March 1989) on Faulkner and the physical and social landscape so crucial to the Nobel Prize-winner's work. Morris' love of sports is reflected in *Always Stand in Against the Curve and Other Sports Stories* (1983) and *A Prayer for the Opening of the Little League Season* (1995), the latter of which celebrates children's baseball. The excitement and flavor of football is captured in *The Courting of Marcus Dupree* (1983), which centers on the talents and feats of the University of Oklahoma running back. By focusing on a much sought-after athlete, Morris exposes the tremendous pressure and intrigue of big-time college recruiting, compares the easy adulation across racial lines for athletic feats with the more painfully slow progress in civil rights, and, as in his autobiographical pieces, connects one person's experiences with larger social events.

In the early 1990s, Morris published another sports-themed title, *After All, It's Only a Game* (1992), a loving tribute to his dog and canines in general, *My Dog Skip* (1995), and a second autobiography, *New York Days* (1993), which picks up his life after he left the South to head *Harper's. New York Days* recounts his struggles to successfully transform *Harper's* into an influential journal and the conflicts that led him to resign, interspersed with anecdotes involving the many people he encountered and detailing the literary and social scene of New York during the 1960s.

About the time Morris started at *Harper's,* Medgar Evers, a civil rights activist, was murdered in Jackson, Mississippi. Morris followed two trials of the alleged killer, Byron de la Beckwith, both of which ended in hung juries. Beckwith was later convicted in a third trial thirty years later, in 1994, which Morris covered as a freelance reporter. Disappointed by the lack of public and media interest in the third trial, Morris helped convince filmmaker Rob Reiner to explore the incident and the trials in a major motion picture and served as consultant on the eventual film, *Mississippi Burning* (1996). The film also failed to generate much public or critical praise. Morris followed up the film with his own work, *The Ghosts of Medgar Evers: A Tale of Race, Murder, Mississippi, and Hollywood* (1998), which interweaves incidents in Evers' life with the author's experiences, muses on violence and progress in race relations, discusses the making of the film, and considers reasons why the movie failed to stir the public. Continuing to explore the area of Mississippi he knows so well as a microcosm for America, Morris evokes the local color and is especially insightful about the difficulties of adequately recreating history, particularly in film, as sites familiar to him are transformed into movie sets, changing a reality that is by itself a complicated maze of the mysterious and the ordinary—a land "full of ghosts," as Morris describes it. "To me there is no more haunted, complex terrain in America than the countryside between Port Gibson, Mississippi, and the river," he writes in *The Ghosts of Medgar Evers.* Probing the mysteries of that terrain and discovering that it teems with universal significance and meaning has been his fruitful endeavor for over three decades, from being raised in a family that valued the art of storytelling, through lived experiences, and through his return to the region, after great success elsewhere.

—Perry Bear

MURRAY, Albert

Born: Nokomis, Alabama, 12 June 1916. **Education:** Tuskegee Institute, B.S. 1939; postgraduate work, University of Michigan, 1940, Northwestern University, 1941; New York University, M.A. 1948; University of Paris, postgraduate work, 1950. **Military Service:** U.S. Air Force, 1943-62, retired as major. **Family:** Married Mozelle Menefee, 31 May 1941; one child. **Career:** Instructor, 1940-43, director of College Little Theatre, 1946-51, Tuskegee Institute; lecturer, Graduate School of Journalism, Columbia University, 1968; O'Connor Professor of Literature, 1970, O'Connor Lecturer, 1973, professor of humanities, 1982, Colgate University; visiting professor of literature, University of Massachusetts, Boston, 1971; Paul Anthony Brick lecturer, University of Missouri, 1972; writer in residence, Emory University, 1978; adjunct associate professor of creative writing, Barnard College, 1981-83; lecturer and participant in symposia. **Member:** PEN International, Authors League of America, Authors Guild, Alpha Phi Alpha. **Awards:** Lillian Smith Award for fiction, 1974, for *Train Whistle Guitar*; Deems Taylor Award, ASCAP, for music criticism, 1976, for *Stomping the Blues*; Lincoln Center Directors Emeriti Award, 1991; Litt.D., Colgate University, 1975.

PUBLICATIONS

Nonfiction

The Omni-Americans: New Perspectives on Black Experience and American Culture. New York, Outerbridge & Dientsfrey, 1970; as *The Omni-Americans: Some Alternatives to the Folklore of White Supremacy.* St. Paul, Minnesota, Vintage Book, 1983.
South to a Very Old Place. New York, McGraw, 1972.
The Hero and the Blues. Columbia, University of Missouri Press, 1973.
Stomping the Blues. New York, McGraw, 1976.
Good Morning Blues: The Autobiography of Count Basie, with Count Basie. New York, Random House, 1985.
Reflections on Logic, Politics, and Reality: A Challenge to the Sacred Consensus of Contemporary American Thinking. Riverdale, New York, Braimanna, 1989.
The Blue Devils of Nada: A Contemporary American Approach to Aesthetic Statement. New York, Pantheon, 1996.

Novels

Train Whistle Guitar. New York, McGraw, 1974.
The Spyglass Tree. New York, Pantheon, 1991.
The Seven League Books. New York, Pantheon, 1996.

*

Interview: *Conversations with Albert Murray* edited by Roberta S. Maguire, Jackson, University Press of Mississippi, 1997.

Critical Studies: "Human Nature is Finer" by Robert Coles, *New Yorker*, October 17, 1970; "The View from the Chinaberry Tree" by James Alan McPherson, *Atlantic,* December 1974; "Stomping the Blues: Ritual in Black Music and Speech," John Wideman, *American Poetry Review*, Fall 1978.

*   *   *

Albert Murray's works celebrate the vitality of African-American culture, showing a legacy of richness and complexity, courage and endurance. Murray contends that African-Americans have thrived in the face of diversity and change. This was an especially salient perspective when he began publishing in the 1960s and 1970s, as sociological studies and economic data routinely described a beleaguered people burdened by a history of suffering, antagonism, and economic deprivation. Perseverance, improvisation (through which a negative situation is confronted and made the best of), and artistic expression are among the attributes Murray presents from within the community in representative forms—through prose that draws on the style of blues and jazz music and is infused with black vernacular. In his works, historical facts, observations on contemporary experience, and examples from music and literature continually emphasize an experience of triumph in the face of hardship, and pride in cultural diversity, expressed in culture—music, religion, language, food, fashions—and communal rituals.

Murray's "meandertale," *South to a Very Old Place,* is a metaphorical and occasionally literal retracing of his path from Alabama to a distinguished career in several areas. Commissioned by Willie Morris, editor of *Harper's,* who underwent his own meandering journey that led from Mississippi to New York, Murray's adventure begins in his Harlem area residence (where the activities remind him of his origins) and goes back through New England, south to the Carolinas and Georgia, to Alabama, and up to Memphis, where he concludes by reveling in the blues. Murray was born in Nokomis, Alabama, which figures prominently in his trilogy of novels, *Train Whistle Guitar, The Spyglass Tree*, and *The Seven League Books.* He was educated at Tuskegee Institute, where in *South to a Very Old Place* he stops to reminisce and to take a contemporary view of the institution, and performed postgraduate work at the University of Michigan and Northwestern University (he later earned an M.A. from New York University and studied at the University of Paris) before joining the U.S. Air Force in 1943; he served as a training officer until 1962, when he retired as a major. During his period in the service, Murray taught at Tuskegee and after retiring he taught at Columbia and Colgate universities, among others. In *South to a Very Old Place,* his academic background is in evidence in stops to meet with such notable writers as C. Vann Woodward, Robert Penn Warren, and Walker Percy. He also explores his downhome roots, through which he makes a compelling contrast between peoples' lives and reports of their downtrodden existence appearing in studies and magazine articles. Writing about their lives Murray evokes a lively "downhome sensibility" and intersperses monologues by plain people with his own ruminations on race relations. *South to a Very Old Place,* then, blends local color, oral rhythms, and journalistic reporting.

Two of Murray's enduring themes—reflections on African-American experiences and the blues as a metaphor for those experiences—are examined in *South to a Very Old Place* in the context of place and language. This style mixes with more theoretical musings in his other nonfiction works: historical background and theoretical frameworks are developed most lucidly in *The Omni-Americans: New Perspectives on Black Experience and American Culture,* Murray's first book, and the blues as metaphor for experience is explored in several works, including *The Hero and the Blues, Stomping the Blues,* and *The Blue Devils of Nada: A Contemporary American Approach to Aesthetic Statement. The Omni-Americans* is ambitious in style (coordinate phrases are among the grammatical elements Murray uses to effect a kind of bluesy style) and content, arguing his concept that American culture is comprised of myriad influences and that ethnic differences among Americans are exaggerated: culture defines people, not race.

As examples of a composite culture that unites all citizens as Omni-Americans, Murray cites the infusion of African-American music and dance as examples of the types of influence imbedded in the larger culture. A kind of heroic person that emerges who can conceptualize life out of chaos and against hostile forces, using the varieties of culture to learn how to cooperate, the way a musician might improvise, using whatever means necessary to synthesize disparate elements into a more harmonic whole. In this and his Blues titles, Murray cites the blues as representative of culture, where the hero excels at improvisation on recurring themes to confront conflicts and threats and make the best of a situation. Murray terms this as "antagonistic cooperation"—enduring strains through the talent of improvising, which has a profound social usefulness requiring wit and resourcefulness to deal with ever-shifting complexities.

Murray's trilogy of novels dramatizes his type of hero and the celebration of African-American life apparent in his nonfiction; in form, his prose style that links passages and phrases within stream-of-consciousness narratives resembles a blues composition. *Train Whistle Guitar* depicts the coming-of-age of Scooter in Gasoline Point, Alabama, during the 1920s. Through his experiences, listening to elders in such settings as barbershops and front porches, reading books, and taking many opportunities to explore life and his surroundings, Scooter acquires a talent for improvising in confronting conflict, including encounters with sex, violence, and death. As he discovers his true origins, he begins to understand his community as well, which he often observes from a tall "spyglass" tree; what he finds, beyond hardships, is the inspiration needed to persevere.

The Spyglass Tree finds Scooter as a student at a small, black college, where his experiences provide further insight and unite his childhood self in a small town with his present self as a student about to embark on adulthood. *The Seven League Boots* has Scooter graduating from college and playing brass with a Swing Orchestra led by the Bossman, who resembles pianist and composer Duke Ellington. As Scooter pursues fame and is challenged by temptations, the question of how well he uses his hard-earned talents in life situations hangs in the balance. The journey motif is worked by Murray in the form of road trips, and a history of American music is encountered along the way to the denouement in a smoky nightclub.

—Perry Bear

N-O

NORDAN, Lewis

Born: In Mississippi, 23 August 1939. **Education:** Millsaps College, B.A. 1963; Mississippi State University, M.A. 1966; Auburn University, Ph.D. 1973. **Military Service:** U.S. Navy, 1958-60. **Family:** Married Alicia Blessing; children: Russell Ammon (deceased), Lewis Eric, John Robert (deceased). **Career:** Teacher at public schools in Titusville, Florida, 1963-65; instructor in English, Auburn University, 1966-71, and University of Georgia, 1971-74; worked variously as an orderly, nightwatchman, and clerk, 1975-81; assistant professor of English, University of Arkansas, 1981-83, and University of Pittsburgh, since 1983. **Awards:** John Gould Fletcher Award for fiction, University of Arkansas, 1977, for short story "Rat Song"; National Endowment for the Arts grant, 1978-79; Porter Fund Prize, 1987; Notable Book Award, American Library Association and Best Fiction Award, Mississippi Institute of Arts and Letters, both 1992 for *Music of the Swamp*. **Address:** Department of English, University of Pittsburgh, Pittsburgh, Pennsylvania 15260.

PUBLICATIONS

Short Story Collections

Welcome to the Arrow-Catcher Fair. Baton Rouge, Louisiana State University Press, 1983.
The All-Girl Football Team. Baton Rouge, Louisiana State University Press, 1986.
Music of the Swamp. Chapel Hill, Algonquin Books, 1991.
Sugar Among the Freaks: Selected Stories. Chapel Hill, Algonquin Books, 1996.

Novels

Wolf Whistle. Chapel Hill, Algonquin Books of Chapel Hill, 1993.
The Sharpshooter Blues. Chapel Hill, Algonquin Books, 1995.
Lightning Song. Chapel Hill, Algonquin Books, 1997.

*

Lewis Nordan comments:

I was a storyteller a long time before I became a writer. Everyone in my family is a storyteller, though none of the others are writers. For a long time I thought I was somehow defective for not being able to tell the truth—the 'truth,' I should say—without changing it, amplifying it, or romanticizing it. This seemed to be a flaw in my character. Now I think that it may be a flaw, but it is also a gift for which I am grateful.

* * *

Lewis Nordan's fiction, set in the Mississippi Delta, mingles the familiar tone of the Southern tall tale with innovative techniques of such modern writers as Beckett and Garcia Marquez. As in Beckett's existentialist plots—*Molloy, Malone Dies*, and others—Nordan's narrators often will assert a fact only to question it, doubting even their ability to speak a truth, or to know memory from imagination. And, as in Garcia Marquez's magic-realist stories, a character's death does not always end his participation in the drama. Nordan is as funny as Beckett, as steeped in setting as Garcia Marquez. His comic stories invoke unusual pity, even as he exaggerates, occasionally, for the sake of satire, well beyond plausibility. In his landscape we not only find the familiar figures—the village idiot and the opium-addicted pharmacist—but also singing llamas and "rats the size of collies" barking from the tupelos.

Nordan introduced his mythical community of Arrow Catcher, Mississippi, in *Welcome to the Arrow-Catcher Fair* (1983), a collection of stories, the last of which features the young hero Sugar Mecklin and his family, who also figure in the second collection, *The All-Girl Football Team* (1986). Most of these stories were republished in *Sugar Among the Freaks* (1996). In one story, the fourteen-year-old Sugar describes his mother making up tales about the models in Sears and Roebuck catalogs, including a "suicide among the inhabitants of Sporting Goods. I loved and was terrified by the unpredictable drama and pain." Later in the story, Sugar witnesses an accidental drowning in the local swimming pool, and that evening at home, wary that his mother will "milk it for . . . effect," reluctantly answers her summons to her bedroom where, seated in her nightgown, she asks, "If I asked you to, well, *kill* me . . . honey, would you?" In a manner reminiscent of Tennessee Williams's Amanda Wingfield (*The Glass Menagerie*), she begins to enthrall the boy with another fantastic, morbid story, and Sugar concludes: "I wanted to call out to my father [in the next room], but I knew he was too drunk to wake up. I knew I could not call out anyway, because it would say the truth to her ...: 'You are insane, you are ruining my life.' I wanted to protect her from that embarrassment."

Nordan consistently acknowledges, beneath the surface absurdities, the emotional truths of his characters' lives. The deeper reality he acknowledges sharpens the comedy of their tendency to act out the stereotypes they believe about themselves. Sugar, for example, ridicules a "white trash neighbor," then laments his father's dissolutions, his mother's "terrible cooking," and his a "white trash" family. A critic praises the stories as "boisterous" and notes they prefigured a style made more apparent in later books—Nordan's "back-porch-and-grits kind of magic realism."

This surreal quality appears in *Music of the Swamp* (1991), a novel-in-stories about Sugar Mecklin's colorful, painful eleventh year, and it establishes an ambivalence toward the Mississippi Delta, a place "filled with death" as well as with love and the "boogie-woogie beat" of blues. In one section, Sugar sees a girl, Dixie Dawn McNeer, who aspires to opera, singing beautifully in her cabbage patch until her father comes out and beats her. The mother then prepares to give a huge party for the girl, "the most elaborate single event in white-trash history," and Sugar describes it in a passage at once so specific and grandiose it becomes apparent he is fantasizing: On the tables were "smoked oysters, raw vegetables with mustard dip, smoked bluefish and trout and salmon . . . liver pate . . . large cakes . . . . All across the lawn, there were areas arranged for various games [blindfold games, running games, croquet, badminton]." Party favors and "Ice cream for a hundred" are included as well.

Later, after another one of his father's drinking bouts, Sugar digs holes under his family's house and, for a moment, believes he's discovered a beautiful, dead woman buried beneath a thick glass in the earth. "It is impossible that I saw . . . this," he says. "And yet I know that I did . . . . Still I am not sure what was real and what my mind invented." But whether it was real or imagined, he decides, "in the dead woman's face I had seen my mother's beauty, the warm blood of her passion, as my father had once known her and had forgotten." When he accompanies his parents on their attempt at a second honeymoon, they wind up in a cottage on the Gulf Coast, rented for cheap just after a hurricane, and dead fish are strewn on the beach. And yet, in his father's hope to see porpoises in the ocean, Sugar understands the man's desire for a "metaphor for romance," as if "the love he and Mama had once shared . . . would have swum back to them, alive and renewed in its gentleness."

In the epilogue, Sugar, a grown man, discovers that he indeed cannot distinguish what he has invented and what recalled. But he sees that his love for his home and hopes for his life feed his imagination. He concludes "There is great pain in all love, but we don't care, it's worth it." In so precisely addressing the way hope colors memory, and how love persists, Nordan invests the novel's grotesque and comic events with a wistful, honest longing.

Although set in rural Mississippi, these first books pay sparing attention to race, including "racial violence," Nordan observed once. "I didn't know I was avoiding it, which I was." He added, "I also didn't know how to write about sex, either, though I'd had plenty of experience with both." The title of his novel, *Wolf Whistle* (1993), refers to a historical incident, the lynching of Emmett Till, which occurred in Mississippi in 1955 near Nordan's home town. The novel depicts what happens to Bobo, a black teenage boy visiting Arrow Catcher, who, after making a similar gesture toward a woman as Emmett Till was alleged to have made, is brutally murdered.

Here, as elsewhere in Nordan's writing, his subtle as well comical overt allusions to English literature—here to Blake and Coleridge—enrich its symbols. The author also reveals a complex compassion in entering the point of view not only of Bobo but of the murderers and other townspeople. These last include a fourth-grade schoolteacher, Alice, who takes her pupils on field trips: the first, to the bedside of Glenn, a classmate injured while trying to set fire to his father, Solon, who helped kill Bobo. Alice's understanding of the "dark and magical and evil world in which he had been killed" deepens as the novel progresses. The last field trip is to the courthouse, for the trial of the murderers. In a passage more brutal than his usual work, but exemplifying Nordan's spooky, vivid poetry, he describes the murdered boy's perspective: "From the eye that Solon's bullet had knocked from its socket and that hung now upon the child's moon-dark cheek in the insistent rain, the dead boy saw the world as if his seeing were accompanied by an eternal music, as living boys, still sleeping, unaware, in their safe beds, might hear singing from unexpected throats one morning when they wake up, the wind in a willow shade, bream bedding in the shallows of a lake, a cottonmouth hissing on a limb,

the hymning of beehives . . . the cry of herons or mermaids in the swamp, and rain across wide water. In this music the demon eye saw what Bobo could not see in life, transformations, angels and devils, worlds invisible to him before death." The passage goes on to describe, in mournful lyric, his murderer's labors at sinking the body in a lake, and "the ghosts of lovers," and the mourning mother of the dead boy, and, eventually, the dreams of Sugar Mecklin the morning he will wake to discover Bobo's body, floated to the surface, and thus bring this evidence of the murder to light.

Violence to some degree returns in Nordan's next novel, *The Sharpshooter Blues* (1995), though this book also offers images of rebirth and of healing, at least for some of the characters. The novel opens with Mr. Raney, a fishcamp proprietor, taking Hydro, his twenty-year-old son, a kind-hearted, hydrocephalic boy, on a boatride home across a swamp. Earlier that evening, Hydro has shot, in self-defense, a malevolent young man and woman who were trying to rob the general store. Hydro tries to claim his responsibility for the killing but is not listened to. A young boy, Louis, who witnessed the event, initially says nothing while the town attempts to learn who shot "these two beautiful children."

The novel explores characters' struggles to understand the shooting, and the mysterious longings of Morgan the Sharpshooter, whom they soon blame. The characters include a memorable one new to Nordan's oeuvre, the inimitable Prince of Darkness, "a skinny baldheaded man . . . raised from the dead when he was just a boy," who, when not plying his trade of undertaker, recites from Shakespeare and Tennessee Williams. Later, Morgan is revealed to be having an affair with Louis's mother, and Louis and his younger sister suffer from their parents' neglect. Louis, tempted to falsely accuse Morgan of the killings, ultimately lets go his vindictive urge. This plot may suggest the novel is grim, but one critic described it as "lush and tragicomic," a story fueled by love "between father and son, between brother and sister—a love that can pull the town back from the brink of disaster."

If, in *Wolf Whistle*, Nordan explicitly addresses race, he as directly confronts the power of sex in *Lightning Song* (1997), his first novel not set in Arrow Catcher, though still in the Delta. Novelist Valerie Sayers observes that, "in plot summary, it might sound like one of those depressingly perky and eccentric white Southern stories, but it isn't: it's deeper and richer and more complex." Leroy Dearman, twelve, enjoys a life on his family's llama farm, which is, mostly, idyllic. The idyll is disrupted by the arrival of Uncle Harris, the brother of Leroy's father, Swami Don, a one-armed character from a previous novel. Harris, recently separated, arrives in a red sportscar and takes up residence in the attic with a tassled lamp and, as Leroy later discovers privately, a stack of girlie magazines.

Simultaneous with his own awakening to sex—or more accurately, near-derangement over it—Leroy is disturbed to see his mother's sexual attraction to Harris, and his father's apparent indifference. The charging of the sexual atmosphere around them is comically reflected by the frequency of lightning strikes near the house. Llamas sing in the pastures at night while Leroy lies awake, tormented by thoughts of love, yearning to know more. Eventually, his dreams are answered when he falls in love with his instructor at baton twirling camp, and she initiates him into the mysteries of twirling and of lovemaking. As in the previous novels, but perhaps even more masterfully here, Nordan's compassion and comic gifts yield powerful images and surprising revelations.

Most of Nordan's books are, as Malcolm Cowley said of Faulkner's Yoknapatawpha novels, as planks "cut from the still living tree." Characters recur, and their histories evolve from one book to the next. They undergo transformations both funny and profound, as Nordan's writing blends comedy and satire without being limited by these methods, invoking instead a full range of emotion and insight. As Sayers put it, "juxtaposing the ordinary and the . . . surreal, he evokes pity and sadness and affection and hope."

—David Y. Todd

NORMAN, Marsha

Born: Marsha Williams in Louisville, Kentucky, 21 September 1947. **Education:** Durrett High School, Louisville; Agnes Scott College, Decatur, Georgia, B.A. in philosophy 1969; University of Louisville, 1969-71, M.A. 1971. **Family:** Married Michael Norman, 1969 (divorced 1974); Dann C. Byck, Jr., in 1978 (divorced 1986); Tim Dykma, 1987; two children. **Career:** Worked with disturbed children at Kentucky Central State Hospital, 1969-71; teacher, Brown School, Louisville, from 1973; book reviewer and editor of children's supplement (*Jelly Bean Journal*), Louisville *Times*, mid-1970s; playwright-in-residence, Actors Theatre, Louisville, 1977-78, and Mark Taper Forum, Los Angeles, 1979; since 1988, treasurer, the Dramatists Guild. **Awards:** American Theater Critics Association, award for best play produced in regional theatre during 1977-78, for *Getting Out*; National Endowment for the Arts grant, 1978; Rockefeller grant, 1979; John Gassner New Playwrights Medallion, Outer Critics Circle, and George Oppenheimer-*Newsday* Award, both 1979 for *Getting Out*; Rockefeller playwright-in-residence grant, 1979-80, at the Mark Taper Forum; Susan Smith Blackburn Prize, Antoinette Perry (Tony) Award nomination for best play, Pulitzer Prize for drama, Columbia University Graduate School of Journalism, and Elizabeth Hull-Kate Warriner Award, Dramatists Guild, all 1983 for *'Night, Mother*; Literary Lion Award, New York Public Library, and American Academy of Arts and Letters grant, both 1986; Antoinette Perry (Tony) Award for best book of a musical and Drama Desk Award for best book of a musical, 1991 for *The Secret Garden*. **Agent:** Jack Tantleff, The Tantleff Agency, 375 Greenwich Street, New York, New York 10013.

PUBLICATIONS AND FIRST PRODUCTIONS

Plays

Getting Out (produced in Louisville, 1977). New York, Avon, 1980.
Third and Oak: The Laundromat (produced in Louisville, 1978). New York, Dramatists Play Service, 1980.
Third and Oak: The Pool Hall (produced in Louisville, 1978). New York, Dramatists Play Service, 1985.
Circus Valentine. Produced in Louisville, 1979.
Merry Christmas. Produced in Louisville, 1979.

'Night, Mother (produced in Cambridge, Massachusetts, 1982). New York, Hill and Wang, 1983.
The Holdup (produced in San Francisco, 1983). New York, Dramatists Play Service, 1987.
Traveler in the Dark. Produced in Cambridge, Massachusetts, 1984; revised versions produced Los Angeles, 1985, New York, 1990.
Four Plays (includes *Getting Out*, *Third and Oak*, *The Holdup*, *Traveler in the Dark*). New York, Theatre Communications Group, 1988.
Sarah and Abraham. Produced in Louisville, 1988.
D. Boone. Produced in Louisville, 1992.
Collected Plays (includes *Loving Daniel Boone*, *Sarah and Abraham*, *Getting Out*, *Third and Oak*, *Travelers in the Dark*, *Circus Valentine*, and *The Hold Up*). Lyme, New Hampshire, Smith and Kraus, 1997.

Author of book and lyrics, *The Secret Garden*. Produced by Virginia Stage Company, Norfolk, 1989.
Author of book and lyrics, *The Red Shoes*. Produced at the Gershwin Theater, New York City, 1993.

Novel

The Fortune Teller. New York, Random House, 1987.

*

Television Plays: *It's the Willingness,* Public Broadcasting Service (PBS), 1978; *In Trouble at Fifteen,* NBC television program *Skag*, Lorimar Productions, 1980; *The Laundromat,* HBO, 1985; *Third and Oak: The Pool Hall*, American Playwrights Theatre: The One Acts, Arts and Entertainment, 1989; *Face of a Stranger*, CBS, 1991.

Screenplays: *'Night, Mother*, Universal, 1986.

Theatrical Activities: Director, *Semi-Precious Things* by Terri Wagener, Louisville, 1980.

*   *   *

"I know now, all these years and plays later, that I always write about solitary confinement." If this realisation only came to Marsha Norman with the anthologizing of *Getting Out* in 1988, it also eluded critics who generalized on her early successes and tended to find a playwright grasping at various fragments of social significance and dissecting them within a broad spectrum of dramaturgic experimentation. Yet the focalizing drive towards the character locked within herself certainly is a recurrent motif, and relates suggestively to another of Norman's statements quoted in *The Feminist Companion to Literature in English*: "What you cannot escape seeing is that we are all disturbed kids."

Norman's perception derives from her early experience working with disturbed children, partly at the Kentucky Central State Hospital, and is most obviously illustrated in *Getting Out*. But most of her plays take place at the intersection of the confined and the disturbed. *Third and Oak: The Laundromat* parodies the idea of "standing by your man" in its portrait of two women accidentally meeting in the middle of the night carrying shirts that are the relics of relationships they want to think still survive; but it ends with an assertion of the strength of solitude. If *The Holdup* presents itself as a parody of the frontier myth, it is also a study of a very naive young man's detachment from a suffocating mother to a point of self-sufficient isolation. *Traveler in the Dark* is more complex in its structuring of relationships, but the same dynamics recur in the central character of Sam, the famous surgeon trying to place himself as father, husband, and son, fleeing back to his (now absent) mother when his professional skills leave him stranded and helpless beside a dying friend. But it is Norman's two full-length plays with female protagonists that most amply illustrate her skills at feminising and contemporising the problem play.

If the material of *Getting Out* sounds in synopsis rather like a case study with obvious elements of social didacticism, its technique is reminiscent of O'Neill's *Strange Interlude* in its schizoid presentation of the main character: the whole action follows the first day of notional freedom for Arlene, just released on parole after serving a murder sentence, but unable to detach from her "criminal" self, Angie, played by another actor. Detachment, however, is just the obverse of the integration she seeks into society, into a straight career, and into her fragmented family, but the quest for some kind of bonding is thwarted by the people she meets: her former pimp and her prison guard, both with an agenda of brutal exploitation, her mother who in effect rejects her, and her new neighbor, another ex-con who still carries the ambience of the prison with her. Instead, integration comes with the self she has tried to exorcize, and the play's ending has Arlie and Arlene laughing playfully together.

Jessie Cates, whose suicide is the entire action of *'Night, Mother*, is a restatement and development of this integration. As the often-quoted introductory statement emphasizes, she has only just got herself together: only in the last year has she "gained control of her own mind and body," and the choice of suicide is the triumphant result of that control. But in the period before that control, there is a quest for identity as daughter, wife, and mother, a search through pockets of silence most graphically illustrated by her epileptic fits. This abnormality, read as a biological deviance parallel to Arlie's anti-social propensities, means that Jessie too has constantly been generating her own state of solitary confinement.

Because they have both in different senses been "inside," Jessie and Arlene are both highly receptive to "reports" of the personal history that they have been out of touch with. The murder for which Angie was locked up is relayed back to her by people who saw it covered on television. Jessie wants to know what she, her other self, looks like during fits, and this is directly related to the search for control that is central to all of Norman's protagonists. Arlene's hunt for normal work will bring her to meet strangers who nevertheless know the television image of Arlie, a gaze as brutal, as impersonal, and as invasive as the thought of the two-way mirrors in the prison washrooms. The reductiveness of this is severe, a total denial of adult dignity, like Jessie regressing to a condition of infantile dependence when she wets herself during fits—and only knowing it has happened because others told her that they cleaned her up.

Such a crisis of identity reflects the blur of societal positioning that both women face. An absent father confronts them with an Oedipal/Electral ambiguity. Society tells both of them that they have failed as mothers of the sons who are having their own problems of integration. And both are threatened by the blackmail of dependence from one of Jane Gallop's "phallic mothers," through whom, in Luce Irigaray's terms, there is the prospect of "femininity" being "effaced to leave room for maternity"—especially as these mothers do not hesitate to hit them with evidence of their own incompetence as mothers. But in their ultimate refusal to disavow themselves in the face of such pressures, or to annihilate the "disturbed kid" in themselves and now in society at large, there is the defiant insistence that the dismantling of structures may not just be anarchic but may bring a more integrated sense of self—if, necessarily, in confinement. Jessie's final wish for her son may serve as Norman's final gloss on the anxieties of modern mothercraft: if he spends his inheritance on dope, she hopes it is at least good dope.

—Howard McNaughton

NORRIS, Helen

Born: Miami, Florida, 22 June 1916. **Education:** University of Alabama, A.B. 1938, M.A. 1940; graduate work in English at Duke University, 1965. **Family:** Married Thomas Reuben Bell, Jr. (divorced). **Career:** Homemaker and teacher, including Huntingdon College, 1966-69; attended Yaddo and the MacDowell writers' colony.

PUBLICATIONS

Novels

Something More than Earth. Boston, Little, Brown and Company, 1940.
For the Glory of God. New York, Macmillan, 1958.
More Than Seven Watchmen. Grand Rapids, Michigan, Zondervan, 1985.
Walk with the Sickle Moon. New York, Carol Pub. Group, 1989.

Short Story Collections

The Christmas Wife. Urbana, University of Illinois Press, 1985.
Water into Wine. Urbana, University of Illinois Press, 1988.
The Burning Glass. Baton Rouge, Louisiana State University Press, 1992.

*

Interview: With Emma Coburn Norris, *Alabama Review,* Spring, 1988.

*　　*　　*

The title of Helen Norris's third collection of short stories, *The Burning Glass,* would be just as appropriate for any of her other fictional works, for a "burning glass," or magnifying glass, can indeed start a fire. Norris not only reveals the inner lives of her characters but often she shows those lives illuminated and transformed by divine grace.

This pattern is already evident in Norris's first novel, written while she was studying with the famous Hudson Strode at the University of Alabama. *Something More than Earth* is set on a cotton plantation much like the one near Montgomery, Alabama, where Norris was reared. Though conceived as a study of the cotton planter's problems in the changing South, the novel is also the story of an unhappy woman attempting to win the love of the man she persuaded to marry her by offering him her land. The protagonist of Norris's second novel, *For the Glory of God*, is an equally troubled young man, a seminary student assigned for a summer to a church that no attends. Both books end in reconciliations, which, it is implied, are effected through divine grace.

Although there was a gap of eighteen years between the publication of Norris's first and second novels, then twenty-seven years more before two more books appeared in print, over the course of time Norris does not change markedly in tone, theme, or technique. She writes very seriously about how out of loss and loneliness can come new understanding, acceptance, an enhanced existence. Habitually, she uses the third person point of view, so that even while exploring the inner lives of her characters she maintains a certain distance from them, as if she wished them to reach their own conclusions without authorial interference. One reason for this consistency may be that the breaks are more apparent than real, for Norris continued to write even when she was not submitting works for publication. Moreover, over time she never wavered in her religious beliefs, and specifically, in her commitment to traditional Anglicanism. With its emphasis on self-discipline, self-examination, and the quiet operation of grace, Norris's faith is a constant presence in her works.

Thus, though the subject of Norris's third and probably her best novel, *More Than Seven Watchmen*, is again the difference between the church as an earthly institution and the church as a divine entity, the work is primarily concerned with how human beings see God reflected in the world he made. Again her protagonist is a priest, but in this case it is he who has rejected the community. In a sense, Thomas Beckett died when his young wife died. Even though he keeps producing sermons, celebrating mass, and tending to the business and the buildings of the church, Beckett backs off from closer contacts with his parishioners, unable to relate to their earthly concerns because he no longer sees any value in life. Then, Beckett is presented with problems he cannot assign to his curate: a young runaway who has taken refuge in the church tower; the boy's cat, whom he is hiding for fear the kittens she is about to deliver will not be allowed to live; and the boy's aunt, a young widow, who is overburdened and nearly destitute. Norris is no religious sentimentalist: she does not have Beckett change in an instant. Instead, she shows his movement toward a new orientation as a step-by-step process, culminating on Christmas Eve, when, having relinquished his role as celebrant to his long-suffering curate, Beckett finds the familiar words of the liturgy and of his beloved John Donne flaming into a new meaning.

Walk with the Sickle Moon also begins with loss and loneliness and moves toward revelation and redemption. The story is told from the perspective of Laura Kendall, an American widow who has gone to France to search for her dead son's illegitimate child and, if possible, to take him back to the States with her. However, not only does she find herself happily involved with the boy's grandfather, a widower, but, more important, she comes to a new understanding of the difference between possessing someone and loving him.

Norris's short fiction is also preoccupied with loss and loneliness. For example, among the stories in her collection *Water into Wine* are "The Cormorant," about a war veteran who has withdrawn from society; "Mrs. Moonlight," in which an elderly woman, who feels that she has lost her children dwells on her memories; and "White Hyacinths," about a desperate young musician who cannot seem to break out of his solitude. The best-known of Norris's short stories, the title work of *The Christmas Wife*, is a poignant account of a widower's attempt to relive Christmas as it used to be by employing a stranger to be his "wife" for the holiday. Isolation and alienation are also important themes in *The Burning Glass*. In "Mirror Image," a young woman rejects the father who long ago abandoned her; in "Bread upon the Waters," an orphan is once again deprived of a home and family; and in "Raisin Faces," an old woman must choose between her greedy children and the black maid who has stolen her silver but offers her some kindness.

If there is a flaw in Norris's fiction, it is that sometimes her plots seem contrived. Stories such as "A Bee in Amber" and "The Healing," for example, demand more suspension of disbelief than the reader may be willing to offer, while the unlikely happy ending of *Walk with the Sickle Moon* mars a convincing account of personal illumination. "Inside the Silence," where a woman is so changed by her visit to a death camp that she cannot contemplate a possible romantic involvement, is more convincing. In a revealing interview with her friend Emma Coburn Norris, published in *Alabama Review* (Spring, 1988), Helen Norris speaks of a true artist as operating on the "razor's edge between divinity and folly." The fact that occasionally the author does lose her balance by no means detracts from her real achievements. Few other writers have her insight into loss and loneliness or her understanding of humanity's need for the divine.

—Rosemary M. Canfield Reisman

NYE, Naomi Shihab

Born: Naomi Shihab in St. Louis, Missouri, 12 March 1952. **Education:** Trinity University, B.A., 1974. **Family:** Married Michael Nye, 2 September 1978; one son. **Career:** Since 1974, freelance visiting writer at all levels; University of Texas at Austin, visiting writer, spring, 1995. **Member:** Poets and Writers, Texas Institute of Letters, RAWI (Association of Arab American writers). **Awards:** Voertman Poetry Award, Texas Institute of Letters, 1980, for *Different Ways to Pray*, and 1982, for *Hugging the Jukebox*; National Poetry Series, winner, 1982, for *Hugging the Jukebox*; Lavan Award, Academy of American Poets, 1988; Charity Randall Prize for Spoken Poetry, with Galway Kinnell, International Poetry Forum, 1988; *Sitti's Secrets* named a best book of 1994 by *School Library Journal*.

PUBLICATIONS

Poetry

Tattooed Feet (chapbook). Texas City, Texas Portfolio, 1977.
Eye-to-Eye (chapbook). Texas City, Texas Portfolio, 1978.
Different Ways to Pray. Portland, Oregon, Breitenbush, 1980.
On the Edge of the Sky (chapbook). Madison, Wisconsin, Iguana, 1981.
Hugging the Jukebox. New York, Dutton, 1982.
Yellow Glove. Portland, Breitenbush, 1986.
Invisible. Denton, Texas, Trilobite, 1987.
Red Suitcase: Poems. Brockport, New York, BOA Editions, Ltd., 1994.
Words under the Words: Selected Poems. Portland, Oregon, Eighth Mountain Press, 1995.

Children's Books

Sitti's Secrets. New York, Four Winds Press, 1994.
Benito's Dream Bottle. New York, Simon & Schuster Books for Young Readers, 1995.
Lullaby Raft. New York, Simon & Schuster Books for Young Readers, 1996.

Nonfiction

Never in a Hurry: Essays on People and Places. Columbia, University of South Carolina Press, 1996.

Other

Modifying editor for poetry translations with Salma Khadra Jayyusi, *Fadwa Tuqan, A Mountainous Journey: An Autobiography.* St. Paul, Graywolf, 1990.
Modifying editor with translator May Jayyusi, *Muhammad al-Maghut, The*
Fan of Swords: Poems. Washington, D.C., Three Continents, 1991.

Editor, *This Same Sky: A Collection of Poems from around the World.* New York, Four Winds, 1992.
Editor, *This Same Sky: A Collection of Poems from around the World.* New York, Four Winds Press, 1992.
Editor, *The Tree Is Older than You Are: A Bilingual Gathering of Poems and Stories from Mexico with Paintings by Mexican Artists.* New York, Four Winds Press, 1995.
Editor, *I Feel a Little Jumpy Around You: A Book of Her Poems & His Poems Collected in Pairs.* New York, Simon & Schuster Books for Young Readers, 1996.

*

Recordings: *Rutabaga-Roo* (songs), Flying Cat, San Antonio, 1979; *Lullaby Raft* (songs), Flying Cat, San Antonio, 1981; *The Spoken Page* (poetry reading), International Poetry Forum, Pittsburgh, 1988.

*   *   *

A resident of San Antonio, Texas, since she was a high school student, Nye has drawn increasing public and critical recognition for her poetry as well as for editing collections of Mexican and Middle Eastern verse. In her poems, Nye often adopts an incantatory and didactive voice to capture and comment on the metaphysical and ethical essence of such diverse subject matter as Texas landscapes, elderly people, and popular culture. The result is poetry that is playfully and imaginatively instructive, borrows from Eastern and Middle Eastern and Native American religions, and resembles the meditative poetry of William Stafford, Wallace Stevens, and Gary Snyder.

"Poetry is a conversation with the world; poetry is a conversation with the words on the page in which you allow those words to speak back to you; and poetry is a conversation with yourself," Nye told Bill Moyers (*The Language of Life with Bill Moyers*). "The mother speaking to a child is also a poem," she added. "I am loyal to those domestic impulses that want to acknowledge all the little parts of our lives."

In "For Lost and Found Brothers," the opening poem of her award-winning collection *Hugging the Jukebox* (1982), Nye relates her initiation into the family of poets. Identifying her affinities with the nineteenth-century French Symbolists and twentieth-century American Beat poets, Nye writes "You lived in France at the foot of the mountains / with paper, with creamy white days. / You hiked railroad tracks dreaming of mirrors, / how one life reflects another" and adopts Zen Buddhist imagery to trace her lineage:

> Thank you, a stone thrown in, a stone quietly sinking.
> Thank you, a ripple returned.
> So today when you bend to sign the first page of your book
> there are other things to thank too,
> the days folded behind you, in your wake, this day connected, more mirrors, more birds.

The daughter of a Palestinian immigrant and a American mother of German descent, Nye lived with her family in St. Louis, Missouri, Ramallah, Jordan, and Old City, Jerusalem, before moving to San Antonio, where she attended high school and continues to reside. Nye's father was a journalist and her mother an artist; both encouraged their daughter's interest in writing.

Nye wrote her first poems at age six and published several in a children's magazine one year later. "I can never understand it when teachers claim they are 'uncomfortable with poetry,'" Nye wrote in her essay "Lights in the Windows," "as if poetry demands they be anything other than responsive, curious human beings. If poetry comes out of the deepest places in the human soul and experience, shouldn't it be as important to learn about one another's poetry, country to country, as one another's weather or gross national product? It seems critical to me. It's another way to study geography!" In 1995, Nye was one of the featured poets in Bill Moyer's PBS series, *The Language of Life with Bill Moyers*. Her thoughts and selections of her poems from this appearance are collected in the Moyers's book of the same name.

Nye's first collection, *Different Ways to Pray* (1980), introduced her method of imbuing the commonplace with intellectual, emotional, and metaphysical importance. The title poem, for example, lists a variety of ways individuals connect to their God, ending with "Fowzi the fool, / who beat everyone at dominoes, / insisted he spoke with God as he spoke with goats, / and was famous for his laugh."

Her next volume, *Hugging the Jukebox*, which was selected by Josephine Miles as a winner of the 1982 National Poetry Series, is divided into three sections. The first details the author's home life in Texas, the second serves as a travelogue through Central and South America, and the third grapples with interpersonal communication. In "At the Seven-Mile Ranch, Comstock, Texas," Nye imbues the landscape with anthropomorphic qualities: "Out here it's impossible to be lonely. / The land walking beside you is your oldest friend, / pleasantly silent, like already you've told the best stories and each of you knows how much the other made up." In "Rebellion against the North Side," Nye indicts contemporary American society's obsession with designer fashion and materialism: "There will be no monograms on our skulls. / You who are training your daughters to check for the words / 'Calvin Klein' before they look to see if there are pockets / are giving them no hands to put in those pockets." Later, Nye adds: "Since when do children sketch dreams with price tags attached? / Don't tell me they were born this way. / We were born like empty fields. / What we are now shows what has been planted." Nye concludes that the two words comprising the designer's name "are temporary as clouds. / Clouds? Tell your children to look up. / The sky is the only store worth shopping in / for anything as long as a life."

Many of the poems in Nye's next major collection, *Yellow Glove* (1986), pertain to her life as a teacher away from San Antonio and display an air of wistfulness and longing for her home, while others show a degree of impatience and anger at the social injustices she witnesses first-hand throughout the world. Many of the poems document her travels to Calcutta, India, Jerusalem, and Pakistan. *Words Under the Words: Selected Poems* (1995) contains verse from her first three volumes. *Red Suitcase* (1994) returns Nye to Palestine to examine the political issues of the Middle East, a topic she metaphorically uses to consider issues of personal exile.

—Bruce Walker

OFFUTT, Chris

Born: Christopher John Offutt in Haldeman, Kentucky, 24 August 1958. **Education:** Morehead State University, B.A. in theatre; Iowa Writers Workshop. **Family:** Wife Rita; two children. **Career:** Odd jobs, including house painter, circus performer, slaughterhouse worker, restaurant worker, and photographer; freelance writer. **Awards:** James Michener Grant, Kentucky Art Council; Whiting Foundation Award; included in *Granta* magazine's selection of the twenty Best Young American Fiction, 1996. **Address:** c/o Simon and Schuster, 1230 Avenue of the Americas, New York, New York 10020.

PUBLICATIONS

Short Story Collection

Kentucky Straight. New York, Vintage Books, 1992.

Memoir

The Same River Twice. New York, Simon & Schuster, 1993.

Novel

The Good Brother. New York, Simon & Schuster, 1997.

*

Critical Study: *Conversations with Kentucky Writers* edited by L. Elizabeth Beattie, Lexington, University Press of Kentucky, 1996.

Chris Offutt comments:
I think that a lot of stories . . . of the South, if they're about rural characters, there's an implicit agreement between the writer and the reader that we're talking about 'them,' . . . 'those people.' . . . I don't make any deals that way with the reader. These are my people.

My attempt in [*Kentucky Straight*] was to destroy the stereotypes . . . . The people in Eastern Kentucky have incredibly complicated lives, very rich lives . . . . It's a really hard world.

*   *   *

Chris Offutt writes with a terse elegance that conveys the wit, anger, and intelligence of his characters. After the publication of his first two books, he received a prestigious Whiting Foundation Award and, in 1996, *Granta* magazine included him in its selection of the twenty Best Young American Fiction Writers. His narratives are marked by a tough honesty, detailed knowledge of the woods, trenchant dialogue, and conclusions of profound understatement. But in his style and tone, he also bears distinct resemblance to three older masters of Appalachian fiction: James Still, whose novel *River of Earth* (1940) Lee Smith cites as an enduring, primary text of the region; Gurney Norman, whose story collection *Kinfolks* (1972) has won praise in the *New Yorker*, *Nation* and elsewhere; and the early Cormac McCarthy macabre novels of Appalachia, *The Orchard Keeper, Child of God,* and *Outer Dark,* that began appearing in the mid-1960s.

The first story in *Kentucky Straight* begins, "Not a one on this hillside finished high school. Around here a man is judged by how he acts, not how smart he's supposed to be . . . . I don't hunt, fish or work. Neighbors say . . . I'm like my father and Mom worries that maybe they're right." The narrator, Junior, tells of his father's insane behavior: the man shot a dog under the porch, stood during a church sermon and declared his intention to faith-heal another dog's broken leg, then eventually committed suicide. Later Junior, simply to prove himself, goes to the town VISTA office to sign up for the high school diploma equivalency test. In Junior's dialogue with the administrator, who offers to waive the test fee because Junior is unemployed and living with his mother, Offutt depicts how a number of his characters survive:

> "Do you receive welfare assistance?" the administrator asks. "No, ma'am." "Then how do you and your mother get along?" "We don't talk much," Junior quips. The VISTA worker persists: "What do you . . . do for money?" "Never had much need for it," he says. "What about food?" "We grow it."

Junior passes the test and declines her offer of employment in town, intending instead to pay the test fee by collecting deposits on bottles he finds in creeks, walking in the hills. Dumbfounded, she laments, "Sometimes I don't know what I'm doing here." He answers, "None of us do . . . . Most people around here are just waiting to die . . . . What's funny is, everybody gets up awful early anyhow."

In keeping to the hills, Junior, like other characters in these stories, hews to nature. After he'd quit school he "took to the woods hunting mushrooms, ginseng and mayapple root." His brother quit to work in town, proudly spending his earnings on consumer goods and a trailer home. When neighbors joke that Junior's pursuit of the diploma but not work recalls their father's insanity, Warren fights them to defend the family's honor.

In this story, Offutt presents most of the book's themes. The people in the hills maintain their own peculiar form of integrity and a fierce loyalty to family, and they live with a deep understanding and knowledge of nature. They are tough people, intelligent if not intellectual, modest but alert. They see the point of any exchange and get to it quickly. They hunt, build houses, play poker, grow marijuana for cash, find their way at night by the stars, discipline their children. The jokes come sharply and fast. Some of the stories are mythical—as in "The Leaving One," where an old woodsman teaches his grandson the proper way to depart this life—but Offutt's style is free of affectation. Most of his characters live in material poverty with its attendant problems. He does not romanticize their lives.

Offutt's memoir, *The Same River Twice* (1993), narrates the travels he made around the U.S. in his twenties. These chapters alternate with the chronicle of his later settling with his wife on the bank of a river in Iowa, awaiting the birth of their son. Offutt first leaves home for New York, where he begins to learn of the world outside the hills. His humility, sense of humor, and strong survival instincts carry him through the ensuing years—he works in a slaughterhouse, for a circus, in restaurants—drifting from New York to Minnesota and the plains, from California to Boston. All the while, he reads widely and keeps a journal, writing poetry. Eventually he finds himself a mosquito-bitten "naturalist" in the Everglades, "I'd left Kentucky and set into motion a pattern of repetitive exile that had ended by dropping me into a rapidly sinking swamp." After barely escaping a hurricane, he notes, "In the sudden rain I realized I was crying, utterly frustrated by my desire to be defeated."

Returning to Boston, he meets a psychologist named Rita. After reading his poems, she encourages him to begin writing prose. They marry. "I taught her to drive a car, play poker, and shoot pool. Rita returned me to the species with a careful formula of protection and guidance." In a lyrical final chapter, their son is born. A nurse hands him the swaddled infant: "We stared at each other . . . . I cried and sang to him. Nine months of fear spiraled away. His birth was my rebirth."

The Good Brother (1997), a novel, starts out in the Kentucky hills. Virgil Caudill, a laconic, moral young man, becomes caught in a terrible conflict after his wild brother Boyd is murdered. The neighbors, his family, and even the sheriff expect Virgil to kill the man suspected of the crime. Perhaps more even than *Kentucky Straight*, this section of the book draws "the dark side of Appalachia," as one critic noted, "in a stark, cutting way," displaying "the poverty, simple joys, and the hopelessness of a culture that has been transformed from being based on pride to being based on welfare."

After giving in to the community's pressure, Virgil flees westward, changing his name to Joe Tiller. He stops in the woods of Montana, trying to sort out a new identity and decide how he will live. The plot complicates when, through another violent act, he falls in with a group of people who, calling themselves "patriots," embrace their own forms of violence in opposition to the U.S. government. Virgil, ambivalent and scared, is drawn to an independent sister of one of the men. He observes the vigilantes' determination to live by a moral code.

The novel depicts the tragedy of Virgil's failure to escape the way of life he had tried to leave in Kentucky. It also suggests that the urge toward violent revenge arises not just from isolated pockets of wilderness but from the larger American culture. One critic termed it "a fine first novel from a fierce writer," while another called it a "sensitive picture of a proud people." A third found the ending particularly "sad and convincing," noting, "As a portrait of a good man's life shattered by violence, Offutt's novel is persuasive, original, and disturbing." In pointed, sharp sentences—a style enhanced, no doubt, by a good ear for the dialect of his native mountains as well as by his apprenticeship to poetry—Offutt has produced an already impressive body of work that explores, without gloss or innocence, the ironic, often tragic struggles of Americans to understand, and live up to, their complex heritage.

—David Y. Todd

P

PASTAN, Linda

Born: Linda Olenik in New York City, 27 May 1932. **Education**: Fieldston School, New York; Radcliffe College, Cambridge, Massachusetts, B.A. 1954; Simmons College, Boston, M.L.S. 1955; Brandeis University, Waltham, Massachusetts, M.A. 1957. **Family**: Married Ira Pastan in 1953; two sons and one daughter. **Awards**: Dylan Thomas award, 1955; Swallow Press New Poetry Series award, 1972; National Endowment for the Arts grant, 1972; Bread Loaf Writers Conference John Atherton fellowship, 1974; Alice Fay di Castagnola award, 1977; Maryland Arts Council grant, 1978; Bess Hokin prize (*Poetry*, Chicago), 1985; Maurice English award, 1986; poet laureate of Maryland, 1991-94; International Poetry Forum Charity Randall citation, 1995. **Agent**: Jean V. Naggar Literary Agency, 336 East 73rd Street, New York, New York 10021.

PUBLICATIONS

Poetry

A Perfect Circle of Sun. Chicago, Swallow Press, 1971.
On the Way to the Zoo. Washington, D.C., Dryad Press, 1975.
Aspects of Eve. New York, Liveright, 1975.
The Five Stages of Grief. New York, Norton, 1978.
Selected Poems. London, Murray, 1979.
Setting the Table. Washington, D.C., Dryad Press, 1980.
Waiting for My Life. New York, Norton, 1981.
PM / AM: New and Selected Poems. New York, Norton, 1982.
A Fraction of Darkness. New York, Norton, 1985.
The Imperfect Paradise. New York, Norton, 1988.
Heroes in Disguise. New York, Norton, 1991.
An Early Afterlife. New York, Norton, 1995.
Carnival Evening: New and Selected Poems. New York, Norton, 1998.

Recording: *Mosaic*, Watershed, 1988.

*　　*　　*

"Pictures and writings are portraits of their authors," Linda Pastan quotes the painter Gauguin in her essay, "Writing about Writing." That being so, the portrait of Pastan is one of domesticity fueled by her decision to dedicate herself to raising a family before embarking on her literary career. Pastan, born in New York City, attended Radcliffe College, where she won the *Mademoiselle* magazine poetry contest during her senior year. Sylvia Plath was the runner-up. Pastan's promising career was suspended when she married Ira Pastan just after graduation. She did not take up the pen seriously again until her children were in school, a fact spelled out in the title of her collection, *Waiting for My Life* (1981). Her first collection of poems had been published a decade earlier, when she was nearly forty. Meanwhile, her family had settled in Maryland, where Pastan was later honored as the state's poet laureate, a position she held from 1991 to 1994.

Pastan's ability to infuse the mundane with imagery, metaphor and larger meaning has been compared to Emily Dickinson. Dickinson, wrote Dave Smith in *American Poetry Review*, "took her dailiness to the heights of metaphysical vision. . . . It may be, Dickinson is Pastan's ghost, though less perhaps in sound than in what to look at and how to show it." This is exhibited in "Letter to a Son at Exam Time" from *Waiting for My Life*: "You woke up/on the wrong side/of my life./For years I counted myself to sleep/on all the ways I might lose you:/death in its many-colored coat lounged/at the schoolhouse door/delivered/the milk, drove the carpool."

This focus on events of everyday life has earned Pastan both praise for accessibility and criticism for simplicity. Some critics, such as Peter Stitt, determined that Pastan had found a happy medium. In the *Georgia Review* he wrote that Pastan "does not cause brain strain, like the early Mark Strand, and she does not leave us breathless, sweating, far from civilization, like Galway Kinell—but she is a wonderful writer nevertheless and works in a rich, human vein." The *San Francisco Review of Books* concurred: "In her work there is a return to the role of the poet as it served the human race for centuries: to fuel our thinking, show us our world in new ways, and to get us to feel more intensely."

Children figure heavily in Pastan's work—she has three and writes of them often, whether in a personal address or a more detached observation. An example of the latter occurs in "AM," among the new works in *PM/AM*: "The child gets up/on the wrong side of the bed./There are splinters of cold light/on the floor,/and when she frowns/the frown freezes on her face/as her mother has warned her it would." The a.m. hours are crucial to Pastan, as she begins to write as soon as she awakens, which accounts for the prominence of dreams in her work.

While later poems stray from the theme of domesticity, they remained rooted in universal experiences. *The Imperfect Paradise* has poems addressing mortality, death, grief, marital crisis and love. In *An Early Afterlife* Pastan moves outside to marvel at the wonders of the natural world and links them to human conditions. In "At Indian River Inlet," for example, she writes: "Long before there was light, water/existed as if chaos itself/had been a kind of rainstorm./Maybe that's why this landscape seems/so elemental, a place/where blues and greens leak/into each other, where water/and land are married/with all the binding ties of salt." Pastan also addresses the fears and realities of the maturing self. In "Sometimes," she imagines herself sitting at the periphery of a family gathering: "I seem to leave/my body—/plump effigy/of a woman, upright/on a chair—/and as I float/willingly away/toward the chill/silence of my own future,/their voices break/into the syllables/of strangers, to whom/with this real hand/I wave good-bye." Or, in "Mercy": "Perhaps our aging eyesight fails/simply because it's easier not to see/what has become of our faces/in the mirrors or in the dark windows/of early winter where we gaze through/our reflections into the cold."

As with all Pastan's work, *An Early Afterlife* celebrates the joys of life, all the while recognizing they are intertwined with pain.

This realization is exemplified in "The Way Things Are": "I wake this morning/to the heaviness of flesh/to the throb of a mourning dove/and the wood thrush/with its premonitions/of beauty, to the sun/which is no color/and every color."

—Kristin Palm

PAYNE, David

Born: William David Payne in Henderson, North Carolina, 13 April 1955. **Family**: Married. **Career**: Writer. **Awards**: Houghton Mifflin fellowship, 1984. **Agent**: Ned Leavitt, The Ned Leavitt Agency, 70 Wooster St., Suite 4F, New York, New York 10012.

PUBLICATIONS

Novels

Confessions of a Taoist on Wall Street: A Chinese American Romance. Boston, Houghton Mifflin, 1984.
Early from the Dance. New York, Doubleday, 1989.
Ruin Creek. New York, Doubleday, 1993.

*   *   *

David Payne's literary career did not start as one would expect, with a semi-autobiographical novel set in his native North Carolina. *Confessions of a Taoist on Wall Street* begins in a Taoist monastery in Szechwan, China, and ends on Wall Street in New York City. The fact that the protagonist, Sun I, is a Taoist, rather than a Buddhist or a Hindu, undoubtedly has more to do with the similarity in sound between the two words "Tao" and "Dow" than with theology or philosophy. However, to do the author justice, his novel is much more than a seven-hundred-word explication of a pun. The words that seem so nearly identical are used to symbolize opposite ways of looking at the world. Taoism advocates selflessness and respect for nature; in Wall Street, where the Dow reigns supreme, nothing matters but self-interest. What Sun I finally learns is that life according to the principles of Lao-Tse is rich and meaningful, while the Dow, which seemed to promise fulfillment and happiness, is ultimately empty and sterile.

Though *Confessions of a Taoist on Wall Street* won its author a Houghton Mifflin Literary fellowship award, it was not universally praised. Even critics who marveled that one book could contain such a wealth of characters and incidents and found much to admire in Payne's pyrotechnical style complained that the book was simply too long. *Early from the Dance* and *Ruin Creek* are considerably shorter than Payne's first novel and also very different.

Both *Early from the Dance* and *Rain Creek* are set in the fictional town of Killdeer, North Carolina, which like Payne's birthplace of Henderson, North Carolina, is in the hilly tobacco country northeast of Raleigh, and also in the coastal area known as the Outer Banks. Both are retrospective novels, beginning in the present and then moving into a past the protagonist has never fully comprehended. Thus, they incorporate two articles of a

Southerner's creed, that one cannot escape either from the place where one was reared or from the people with whom one's formative years were spent. The novels also reflect the traditional Christian principle, with which the Taoists would concur, that there is a difference between repenting of one's sins and avoiding the consequences of one's actions.

In all three books there are characters who have to decide whether to stay in familiar territory or to strike out into the unknown. In *Confessions of a Taoist on Wall Street*, until the arrival of his uncle, Hsaio, Sun I never considered leaving his monastery or abandoning his vocation as a Taoist priest. Hsaio had promised Sun I's American father, Eddie Love, that when the boy was old enough, he would be told about his ancestry. As Hsaio wisely points out, this knowledge may not bring him happiness, but Sun I says that since Hsaio's arrival has already cost him his peace of mind, he may as well hear the whole story. After telling him that the Loves had been immensely wealthy, Hsaio gives Sun I a purse with a cryptic message from his father, urging him to "Unlock the Great Cathedral of the Dow." Finding the portents favorable, Sun I sets out on what seems to be as much a quest for his father as for mastery of the Dow or at least some comprehension of its significance.

Early from the Dance begins with the protagonist's mission seemingly accomplished. Thirteen years before, Adam Jenrette, or "A.," ventured forth in search of success; now he is a famous artist. A. goes back to Killdeer to attend a funeral, perhaps to claim a legacy, never having recognized the fact that his present discontent is the result of his never having dealt with the past. A. had left Killdeer convinced that he was responsible for his best friend's suicide. His quest, then, is for forgiveness.

Ruin Creek also begins in the present. However, in this novel the protagonist is not a tormented soul like A., but simply an adult puzzled by his childhood memories, especially those of the summer his parents' marriage broke up. Joey Madden's quest is for understanding.

There are several themes common to all three of Payne's novels. One of them is a search for a lost father. Though everyone seems to think that Eddie Love is dead, Sun I cannot help looking for him. Ironically, Sun I does not meet him, or someone he believes to be his father, until after he first conquered Wall Street and then lost everything he had gained. In *Early from the Dance*, A. rejects his father after finding him in bed with a mistress, substituting as his mentor another older man, Cleanth Faison, who turns out to be the embodiment of evil. In *Ruin Creek*, Joey seeks his father's true identity. The basketball hero in the photographs does not seem to bear any resemblance to the sad, defeated man Joey sees every night.

In these novels, the protagonist sees his father's involvement with another woman as a betrayal. In *Early from the Dance*, A. sees it as denying "Everything my father had given me, every sacredness implies in the world *gentleman*." However, though A. cannot recapture his lost innocence, when he realizes that he has betrayed his friend, he can forgive his father and eventually himself. There is no better tutor than loss, especially the loss of one's own elevated opinion of oneself. At his most arrogant, Sun I discards his only trustworthy advisor, and the consequence is disaster. Though he cannot recoup his financial losses, he has gained a new humility, which is the beginning of wisdom.

Confessions of a Taoist on Wall Street does have some notable defects. Except for some interpolated stories, it is a first-person narrative, but there is no consistency in voice. At one point, Sun I is businesslike and terse; at another, he piles analogy onto analogy, prepositional phrase onto prepositional phrase, like a college freshman who has not yet learned to edit. *Early from the Dance* and *Ruin Creek* are much more highly polished. Although in both novels he uses a number of different narrators, Payne has the characters so clearly fixed in his own mind that there is never a false note. Both voice and style are handled with the seeming ease of an Olympic champion.

Though the later books may not be as original in conception or as ambitious in execution as the first one was, they are not so easily put aside. In them, Payne displays the skills so evident in the finest Southern writers, an ear for colloquial speech, an appreciation of the relationship between character and place, and a willingness to look for moral realities within the confusion of contemporary life.

—Rosemary M. Canfield Reisman

PEARSON, T. R.

Born: Thomas Reid Pearson in Winston-Salem, North Carolina, 27 March 1956. **Education:** North Carolina State University, B.A. 1977, M.A. 1980; Ph. D. coursework, Pennsylvania State University, 1981. **Family**: Married to Marian Young. **Career:** Instructor, Peace College, Raleigh, North Carolina, 1980-81; painter and carpenter; screenwriter. **Address:** Marian Young, The Young Agency, 156 Fifth Avenue, #608, New York, New York 10010.

PUBLICATIONS

Novels

A Short History of a Small Place. New York, Linden Press, 1985.
Off for the Sweet Hereafter. New York, Linden Press, 1986.
The Last of How It Was. New York, Linden Press, 1987.
Call and Response. New York, Linden Press, 1989.
Gospel Hour. New York, William Morrow, 1991.
Cry Me a River. New York, Henry Holt, 1993.

Screenplays (Uncredited)

The Rainmaker, 1997.
The Runaway Jury. 1998.

*   *   *

Some critics have called the novels of T. R. Pearson rambling and frustrating; others have labeled him a genius, comparing him to Mark Twain, William Faulkner, J. D. Salinger, Eudora Welty, and Ring Lardner. Although he does not shape his work for easy popular consumption—he cheerfully admits that his style is "clearly self-indulgent" and his sentences routinely reach

Faulknerian length—Pearson has garnered cult status and tremendous critical acclaim since 1985 when his highly-regarded first novel, *A Short History of a Small Place,* announced him as a unique Southern voice. Since that time he has continued to work steadily, publishing six novels and gradually refining his style so that his most recent book, *Cry Me a River*, displays a relatively restrained if still loquacious storyteller.

The most identifiable element of Pearson's work is his style, drawn from the Southern oral tradition and the syntax of the Old Testament, marked by lengthy sentences and verbose narrative personae who never choose one word or phrase when two will do. The construction of his narratives is likewise marked by excess, for his novels diverge from the plot at any excuse. This prolixity initially made it very difficult for Pearson to find a publisher, and a literary agent described *A Short History of a Small Place* as "too slow and indirect and oblique" to ever see print. But Pearson's unusual style sets him apart from his peers and—if occasionally maddening—is generally cited by critics as his most important contribution to contemporary letters.

Pearson's humor—partly drawn from his meandering syntax, partly from the outlandish situations, slapstick, and endearing characters he creates—is another significant feature of his style. Like Twain and the Southwest local colorists, he is a master of the tall-tale. The sledding great-grandmother in *The Last of How It Was,* the micturating monkey of *A Short History of a Small Place*, and the lightning-struck logger of *Gospel Hour* are only a few examples of his penchant for spinning astounding yarns. Pearson's astute use of language—circumlocution, repetition, and a mastery of dialect—adds verbal humor to the physical.

The small town of Neely, North Carolina—a fictional stand-in for Reidsville, in north-central North Carolina—is the setting for many of Pearson's books, and critics have compared his consistent and loving attention to this locale with William Faulkner's fictional creation Yoknapatawpha County. By recreating a small Southern town and examining it from different angles, Pearson has been able to assess the changing nature of the South and address a number of central issues related to those changes. While his novels are tremendously entertaining, they are also thematically rich. *A Short History of a Small Place*, for example, in its chronicle of the fall of Neely's aristocratic Pettigrew family, resembles Faulkner's *Absalom, Absalom!* in its depiction of the movement from the Old to the New South. *The Last of How It Was* tackles racial and social prejudice, *Gospel Hour* reveals the pervasive nature of religion in the South, and *Cry Me a River* concerns itself with the uneasy undercurrent of violence in Southern culture.

Pearson's work as a whole may be considered to deal with the considerable problem of forging identity, community, and meaning in a South that no longer has useful myths and rigid social structures to order it. Pearson's is a world of stark contrasts, uproarious humor and dark impulses, a world strongly related to the Southern Gothic tales of Flannery O'Connor; Pearson himself has acknowledged his tremendous debt to O'Connor, and the similarities between the two—once one puts aside Pearson's idiosyncratic style—are startling. Many of Pearson's characters are true grotesques, often distinguished by a bizarre physical characteristic (such as "the bald Jeeter," a hairless woman who appears in *A Short History of a Small Place* and *Off for the Sweet Hereafter*, and Louis Benfield's grandmother, a woman so immensely fat that upon falling down in *The Last of How It Was* she can only be hoisted from the floor with the assistance of a strategically-applied shovel. Violence also pervades the novels, particularly in *Cry Me A River,* where several major characters die cruel deaths, and *The Last of How It Was,* where the two central stories recounted in the book are the murder of a mule-stealing Indian by two of Louis Benfield's ancestors and the murder of a black man by Louis' grandfather.

Although Pearson postulates a dark and mystifying world, he also presents moments of grace, particularly in the form of human connection and in the passing of stories. Storytelling, in fact, becomes a way in which the characters in many of Pearson's books order their existence. As Louis Benfield, the narrator of the first Neely books, listens to the stories told by his father, mother, and other adults, he learns to synthesize his own version of reality from those presented him. We are likewise invited to create meaning in Pearson's world—and to enjoy the ride while we listen to his stories.

—Greg Garrett

PERCY, Walker

Born: 28 May 1916, in Birmingham, Alabama. **Education:** University of North Carolina, B.A. 1937; Columbia University, M.D. 1941. **Family:** Married Mary Bernice Townsend in 1946; children: Ann Boyd, Mary Pratt. **Career:** Intern, Bellevue Hospital, New York City, 1942; full-time writer, 1943-90. **Awards:** National Book Award for fiction, 1962, for *The Moviegoer;* National Institute of Arts and Letters grant, 1967; National Catholic Book Award, 1971, for *Love in the Ruins; Los Angeles Times* Book prize, 1980, National Book Critics Circle citation, 1980, American Book Award nomination, 1981, notable book citation from American Library Association, 1981, all for *The Second Coming; Los Angeles Times* Book Prize for current interest, 1983, for *Lost in the Cosmos: The Last Self-Help Book;* St. Louis Literary award, 1986; Ingersoll prize from Ingersoll Foundation, 1988. **Member:** American Academy and Institute of Arts and Letters (fellow). **Died:** 10 May 1990, of cancer, in Covington, Louisiana.

PUBLICATIONS

Novels

The Moviegoer. New York, Knopf, 1961.
The Last Gentleman. New York, Farrar, Straus, 1966.
Love in the Ruins: The Adventures of a Bad Catholic at a Time near the End of the World. New York, Farrar, Straus, 1971.
Lancelot. New York, Farrar, Straus, 1977.
The Second Coming. New York, Farrar, Straus, 1980.
The Thanatos Syndrome. New York, Farrar, Straus, 1987.

Nonfiction

The Message in the Bottle: How Queer Man Is, How Queer Language Is, and What One Has to Do with the Other. New York, Farrar, Straus, 1975.

Lost in the Cosmos: The Last Self-Help Book. New York, Farrar, Straus, 1983.
Novel-Writing in an Apocalyptic Time. New Orleans, Faust Publishing Company, 1986.
State of the Novel: Dying Art or New Science. New Orleans, Faust Publishing Company, 1988.
Signposts in a Strange Land edited by Patrick Samway. New York, Farrar, Straus,
1991.

Correspondence

A Thief of Peirce: The Letters of Kenneth Laine Ketner and Walker Percy edited by Patrick H. Samway. Jackson, University Press of Mississippi, 1995.
The Correspondence of Shelby Foote and Walker Percy edited by Jay Tolson. New York, Center for Documentary Studies, 1996.

*

Bibliographies: *Walker Percy: A Bibliography: 1930-1984* by Stuart Wright, New York, Meckler, 1986; *Walker Percy: A Comprehensive Descriptive Bibliography* by Linda Whitney Hobson, New Orleans, Faust, 1988.

Interviews: *Conversations with Walker Percy* edited by Lewis Lawson and Victor A. Kramer, Jackson, University Press of Mississippi, 1985; *More Conversations with Walker Percy* edited by Lewis Lawson and Victor A. Kramer, Jackson, University Press of Mississippi, 1993.

Biographies: *Pilgrim in the Ruins: A Life of Walker Percy* by Jay Tolson, Chapel Hill, University of North Carolina Press, 1994; *Walker Percy: A Life* by Patrick H. Samway, New York, Farrar, Straus and Giroux, 1997.

Critical Studies: *Walker Percy's The Last Gentleman: Introduction and Commentary* by Ellen Douglas, New York, Seabury, 1969; *The Sovereign Wayfarer: Walker Percy's Diagnosis of the Malaise* by Martin Luschei, Baton Rouge, Louisiana State University Press, 1972; *Walker Percy: An American Search* by Robert Coles, New York, Little, Brown, 1978; *The Art of Walker Percy: Stratagems for Being* edited by Panthea Reid Broughton, Baton Rouge, Louisiana State University Press, 1979; *Walker Percy: Art and Ethics* edited by Jac Tharpe, Jackson, University Press of Mississippi, 1980; *Walker Percy* by Jac Tharpe, New York, Twayne, 1983; *Percy and the Old Modern Age,* by Patricia Lewis Poteat, Baton Rouge, Louisiana State University Press, 1985; *In Search of Self: Life, Death, and Walker Percy* by Jerome L. Taylor, New York, Cowley, 1986; *Walker Percy: A Southern Wayfarer* by William Rodney Allen, Jackson, University Press of Mississippi, 1986; *The Fiction of Walker Percy* by John Edward Hardy, Urbana, University of Illinois Press, 1987; *Understanding Walker Percy* by Linda Whitney Hobson, Columbia, University of South Carolina Press, 1988; *Walker Percy: Critical Essays* edited by Donald J. and Sue Mitchell Crowley, New York, G. K. Hall, 1989; *Walker Percy: The Making of an American Moralist,* 1990, and *Pilgrim in the Ruins,* 1992 by Jay Tolson, New York, Simon & Schuster; *Walker Percy: Novelist and Philosopher* edited by Jan Nordby Gretlund and Karl-Heinz Westarp, Jackson, University Press of Mississippi, 1991; *Walker Percy: Books of Revelations* by Gary M. Ciuba, Athens, University of Georgia Press, 1992; *The Myth of the Fall & Walker Percy's Last Gentleman* by Bernadette Prochaska, New York, Peter Lang, 1993; *The Signs of Christianity in the Work of Walker Percy* by Ann M. Futrell, Catholic Scholarly Press, 1994; *Autobiography in Walker Percy: Repetition, Recovery, and Redemption* by Edward J. Dupuy, Baton Rouge, Louisiana State University Press, 1996; *Walker Percy: The Last Catholic Novelist* by Kieran Quinlan, Baton Rouge, Louisiana State University Press, 1996; *Walker Percy: Prophetic, Existentialist, Catholic Storyteller* by Robert E. Lauder, New York, Peter Lang, 1996; *At the Crossroads: Ethical and Religious Themes in the Writings of Walker Percy* by John F. Desmond, Troy, New York, The Whitson Publishing Company, 1997.

Walker Percy commented:

"[We live] in the century of the love of death ... a death in life, of people who seem to be living lives which are good by all sociological standards and yet who somehow seem to be more dead than alive. Whenever you have a hundred thousand psychotherapists talking

about being life-affirming and a million books about life-enrichment, you can be sure there is a lot of death around."

*   *   *

Walker Percy published his first novel, *The Moviegoer,* in 1961, at the relatively advanced age, for a first-time novelist, of forty-four, and for the next three decades edified, delighted, and intellectually and spiritually informed an enormously appreciative audience of American and European readers, with five more novels, two collections of essays and *jeux d'esprit,* and numerous interviews, including one "self-interview." Percy was a philosopher as well as a novelist; he told his old friend Shelby Foote that he thought he would be remembered for his philosophical work in language and semiotics more than for his novels. But first, before either novelist or philosopher, he was a pilgrim, a searcher, what he often called a "wayfarer." He was on what he called The Search, and all the protagonists of his novels are on it, too. The Search is, as Binx Bolling puts it quite simply in *The Moviegoer,* "what anyone would undertake if he were not sunk in the everydayness of his own life. To become aware of the possibility of the search is to be onto something. Not to be onto something is to be in despair."

It is a search for transcendent order and purpose, one could say, or, with Marion Montgomery, it is the attempt to solve a problem "older than Descartes and Pascal, ... older than Aquinas and Plato," the attempt to encounter "the timeless under the burden of time." Percy and his characters refuse the secular culture's attempt to objectify the human, to reduce the person to mere self, to machine or animal, to angel or beast rather than incarnate mystery. What Percy's main characters seek, beyond identity, purpose, meaning, and love-all the secularly-approved goals-is God. As Dr. Thomas More exclaims in *Love in the Ruins,* "Dear God, I can see it now, why can't I see it other times, that it is you I love in the beauty of the world and in all the lovely girls and dear good friends, and it is pilgrims we are, wayfarers on a journey, and not pigs, or angels."

The novels are about our greatest drama, about life and death matters. The question, "How can human beings live in the twen-

tieth century?" expresses not just an abstract concern, for Percy or for us. Theoretically the problem is finding what Percy terms a coherent "anthropology" or theory of what it means to be human, but practically the problem is how to keep from blowing one's brains out on an ordinary Wednesday afternoon. Percy's main characters seek self-understanding in order to combat the urge to self-destruction. Percy's many essays about language, semiotics, God, Roman Catholicism, the South, and racial relations help provide the intellectual and social context of the novels, but it is in those novels that Percy most effectively uses his philosophy and theology. His seriousness about life's mystery, along with his incisive perceptions of quotidian details and his humor, are what make his novels so appealing to so many. One encounters a sense of exile, of not belonging in the contemporary world, that one recognizes immediately and sharply. There is both an "outsiderness" presented accurately and vividly and an inwardness of the soul that seems perfectly realized on the page. What is joyful about life is also dazzlingly rendered-along with a hint, neither forced nor phony, that we exiles may somehow indeed find a belonging.

Percy was genuinely an intellectual and unabashedly a Roman Catholic: his novels, his philosophical essays, and his essays about the South and America were all the products of a stern and thoughtful orthodox Christianity. But it was an othodoxy that was broad, built on the Protestant Sren Kierkegaard and the secularists Wittgenstein, Heidegger, Sartre, and Camus, as well as religious thinkers Gabriel Marcel, Jacques Maritain, Martin Buber, and Eric Voegelin. And his characteristic humor, brilliant and explosive, always accompanies and is very much a part of the serious theological ground of his work.

He was not sentimental or romantic about his religion. It supported his serious themes of community, intersubjectivity, and reconciliation. His was a philosophical, critical, yet sacramental sensibility encountering the mystery of being human. The "coherent anthropology" he thought the modern age was lacking was built on the church's doctrine of the fallen nature of man ("Our lapses are not due to synapses," as Allison Huger rhymingly says to Will Barrett toward the end of *The Second Coming*) and the redemptive acts of God. Such ideas about the nature of the human imply a wholeness of the person, as opposed to "the dread chasm that has rent the soul of Western man ever since the famous philosopher Decartes ripped body from mind and turned the very soul into a ghost that haunts its own house," as Dr. Thomas More remarks in *Love in the Ruins.*

The protagonists' search, especially in the first two novels, involves the difficult rejection of the ancestors' southern Stoicism and the easier rejection of the contemporary culture's shallow secularism. Each character tries some of the culture's inadequate, gnostic ideas, represented by physical symbols such as the movies, a telescope, a "lapsometer," a computer, but settles to more solid ground before the novel's end. The characteristic Percy protagonist—Binx Bolling, Will Barrett, Thomas More, Allison Huger-turns to the middle, between the shallow wishful thinking of the secular humanists and the raw despair of the Stoics and nihilists. Lancelot Lamar, of *Lancelot,* is an exception, but the novel uses the religious sensibility implied in his silent listener, his friend "Percival," to balance Lancelot's metastatic anger. Each novel ends with a minimal hope gleaming through the despair: Binx puts Kate on a bus and then, in attending to his Smith stepbrothers and stepsisters on the last day of Lonnie Smith's life, confirms Lonnie's Christian sense of the worthiness of sacrificial living; Will Barrett pursues the nihilist Sutter Vaught at the end of *The Last Gentleman*; Thomas More joins SOUP ("Southerners and Others United to Preserve the Union, In Repayment of an Old Debt to the Yankees, Who Saved It Once Before and Are Destroying It Now"); Percival says "Yes" to Lancelot's last question; Will and Allison begin a small and local but plausible attempt to build the kingdom at the end of *The Second Coming*; and at the end of The Thanatos Syndrome Father Smith advises Thomas More, "if you keep hope and have a loving heart and do not wish secretly for the death of others, the Great Prince Satan will not succeed in destroying the world."

Percy was very much a Southern writer but for good reasons, shared by many other Southern writers, wished not be limited as "Southern." As Lewis Simpson has noted, however, he was like Faulkner a writer who used the local to speak to the global: "the context of Percy's stories is the history of the South, past and present, as an integral representation of the modern world; like Faulkner his deep, underlying motive is a sense of the novelist's responsibility for dramatizing and interpreting the modern crisis of self in its relation to human nature and human history."

Now he is considered to be one of the greatest twentieth-century Southern writers, along with Faulkner, Welty, and O'Connor. The eminent author Robert Coles, speaking to parents at The Lovett School in Atlanta, said that his "three pieces of advice to Southerners" were to "read Walker Percy, read Walker Percy, and read Walker Percy." There are weaknesses in Percy's fiction. In *Love in the Ruins* there is a bit of Southern chauvinism. There is an overabundance of characters and incident in *Love in the Ruins*, *Lancelot*, and *The Thanatos Syndrome,y* and for some readers' tastes, in all of his novels except *The Moviegoer*. Until Allison Huger in *The Second Coming* there are no women characters of great depth, except possibly for Kate Cutrer in *The Moviegoer*. Some readers may find too much cruelty in his assaults on flabby twentieth-century secular and religious fads. But overwhelming these defects are the truthful details of the inner life and of the life of the contemporary South, the wit, the delightful minor characters—and, finally, the seriousness of his themes.

Walker Percy died 10 May 1990, eighteen days before his seventy-fourth birthday. His impact is attested to by the profound and respectful critical attention his works have received from Lewis Simpson, Alfred Kazin, Cleanth Brooks, Robert Coles, Bertram Wyatt-Brown, Lewis Lawson, and many others, and by the two very helpful biographies that have already appeared. His was "a powerful and searching criticism of the modern world," Brooks wrote. Assessing his influence, Fred C. Hobson wrote that "If Southern writers of the 1940s, 1950s and even the 1960s wrote under the shadow of Faulkner, many of the best Southern writers today write with Percy in their minds and veins."

In *The Second Coming,* the most generous of his novels, Percy wrote, "Home is a place, any place, any building, where one sinks into one's self and finds company waiting." For many readers in the last four decades, Percy's novels are themselves a kind of home one sinks into to find company.

—Michael M. Cass

PHILLIPS, Dale Ray

Born: Burlington, North Carolina, 30 April 1955. **Education:** University of North Carolina, Chapel Hill, B.A. 1977; Hollins College, M.A. 1985; University of Arkansas, M.F.A. 1990. **Career:** Writer in residence, Arkansas Writers in the Schools Program, 1985-89, South Carolina Governor's School of the Arts, 1998; teaching assistant in English, 1985-88, visiting assistant professor, 1988-89, University of Arkansas; adjunct lecturer, University of Houston, 1990-91; visiting instructor, Clemson University, 1993-97. **Agent:** Armanda Urban and Sloan Harris, International Creative Management, 40 West 57th Street, New York, New York 10019.

PUBLICATIONS

Short Story Collection

My People's Waltz. New York, W. W. Norton, 1999.

Short Stories, First Publications

"His Grandfather's Pecker," in *Greensboro Review,* Summer 1978.
"The Motion of Falling Bodies," in *Greensboro Sun,* December 1979.
"What Men Love For," in *Atlantic,* April 1988; reprinted in *Best American Short Stories,* New York, Houghton Mifflin, 1989.
"What We Are Up Against," in *Story,* Autumn 1990.
"My Southern Gothic Story Called 'The Honeymooners.'" In *New Stories and Poems from the Hollins Writing Program,* Charlottesville, University Press of Virginia, 1992.
"When Love Gets Worn," in *GQ,* September 1993.
"Everything Quiet Like Church," in *Story,* Spring 1994; reprinted in *New Stories from the South: The Year's Best, 1995,* Chapel Hill, Algonquin Books, 1995.
"At the Edge of the New World," in *Ploughshares,* Fall 1996.
"Corporeal Love," in *Story,* Spring 1996; reprinted in *New Stories from the South: The Year's Best, 1997,* Chapel Hill, Algonquin Books, 1997.
"Why I'm Talking," in *Atlantic,* March 1996.
"Notes on the Nature of Love," in *Intro 16,* Winter 1998.

*

Dale Ray Phillips comments:

What I try to do is get at something essential that I know—that love hurts sometimes, but it is very important to keep struggling with its crooked nature; that people can be very big heroes in the small gestures we make when things matter; that a little sex in a story is generally a good idea; and that we all become the stories we tell each other.

*   *   *

Dale Ray Phillips is one of the most gifted writers on the southern literary landscape of the present time. To read one of his short stories is to experience the joy of discovering a new voice in a region that is renowned for its excellence in fiction. While his stories echo the graceful prose of Peter Taylor, the true idiom of Eudora Welty, and the zany humor of Barry Hannah, they are something new under the southern sun in their unique combination of poignancy, wisdom, and sorrow.

Southern writers of fiction delight in telling stories in which one person talks to another one, either to a reader or to another character in the story. In William Faulkner's masterpiece *Absalom! Absalom* (1936), Quentin Compson hears Thomas Sutpen's story from his family and friends and he, in turn, tells the story to his Harvard roommate. Eudora Welty's "Why I Live at the P.O." (1941) presents the talkative Sister recounting her family's troubles to a passerby at the post office. And, Jack Burden explains to the reader the political tragedy of Willie Stark in Robert Penn Warren's *All the King's Men* (1946), a novel in which the narrator tells about events that have already happened.

This technique, known as the "retrospective narrative," is one especially favored by Phillips and one that contributes much to the tone and impact of his stories. In "What Men Love For" (1988), for example, Richard, the narrator of this as well as several stories, begins his narrative, "When I was twelve, my father called on weeknights to convince my mother that he would return safely that weekend and to assure himself that his house was still in order." The episode that follows traces the course of the failing marriage of Richard's parents. As a child of twelve, the narrator could not grasp the subtleties of this declining love relationship, nor understand the major sign of his mother's debilitating depression—"cutting her face out of old pictures of herself." As a child, he could only conclude that he was "afraid that my father would guess that nervousness had returned, and that they would take her away again." Later, as an adult, he can articulate a meaningful judgement about her condition, "she was extremely melancholy."

In this same story, Richard and his father take a midnight ride on a motorcycle his father has restored as a hobby. To the young boy, the motorcycle ride is a wonderful adventure, but to the grown man who tells the story in retrospect, the ride has become laced with meaning. The passage of time allows him to select his childhood memory and to voice its meaning with the wisdom that comes with maturity. Thus, in the final scene, father and son race down a mountain road on the Harley-Davidson, and Richard concludes: "We were blood-full of the moment wherein, against all possibilities, you lean into the curve and take your chances of making it.... This moment is what men love for. You are the father and son caught in a homeward motion."

A child could not normally be this articulate and poetic, but from the double-vision of the adult Richard, the concept is plausible and the reader accepts its relevance as a learning experience. Phillips uses this technique especially well in order to reflect on the changes that time brings to the human condition.

From the origins of Southern literature in the nineteenth century, Southern writers have been fascinated with the notion that time is humankind's great destroyer, and so it is in the fiction of Phillips. In story after story, Phillips creates a world filled with the longing for happiness that can never last for more than a few moments and a need for love made even more poignant through the realization that it will soon be gone with the wind. For example, an especially well-wrought story, "Corporal

Love" (1988), examines the tension between the moment of love's perfection and its inevitable diminishment. Here, Richard, the narrator, reviews his love affairs leading up to his marriage and divorce from Lisa. Now divorced, Richard and Lisa reunite briefly for a camping trip with their young daughter. After an evening filled with the joy of family life, one of several such scenes of deep felicity in Phillips's fiction, Richard stares at his sleeping daughter and his ex-wife and reflects, "I knew that to doze would be to break the spell of what I was feeling . . . I would have to muster my stiff bones soon, but for awhile I lingered, adoring them, in love with these women, and the grace of this borrowed moment, for the imperfections of things which pass." The story ends with Richard struggling to maintain the joy and wonder of the miracle of human love.

In such outstanding novels as William Faulkner's *The Sound and the Fury* (1929), Thomas Wolfe's *Look Homeward, Angel* (1929), and Pat Conroy's *The Prince of Tides* (1986), family provides Southern authors with an important arena in which individuals conduct the search of discovering what it means to be human. An especially fine examination of family dynamics is found in "Why I'm Talking" (1996), perhaps Phillips's finest story to date. In this piece, Richard's mother has been hospitalized after a suicide attempt, his father is on a business trip, and Richard has gone to live with his grandfather and his mistress, an African American named Miss Minnie, by whom the old man has fathered a daughter. The eight-year-old narrator has decided to stop talking, "My reasoning seemed sound enough," he explains, "whatever had abducted my mother might steal me if I let out too many words." The grandfather dies of a stroke, during which he bites off part of his tongue, Miss Minnie flees to parts unknown, and Richard's mother and father are reunited briefly but with only a fond hope for a permanent bond.

Richard's father dreams of a new beginning: "He was full of the contagious hopefulness people adopt when disaster forces them to start over." Richard himself, knowing that even though the future holds little promise, remarks, "we had somehow become a family, caught in the awkwardness of shaping our first reunion as we reinvented the story of the rest of our lives together." And, on what does he depend to give his life a semblance of stability? Invention and imagination—the ability of the human mind to make up stories to make life bearable. In the end, Richard decides to break his silence but not to reveal the secrets of that summer with his grandfather to his mother. "Some chimeras would have to be constructed to keep this good feeling alive, and so I answered her with this voice, which love had taught to deceive."

Like Thomas Wolfe, Phillips knows that you can't go home again, that the idyllic moments of innocence and happiness may exist for only a brief span of time, but that these moments are so precious the artist must try to render them immortal on the written page. If anyone recently has entertained the idea that the traditional markers of Southern fiction have faded at the close of the twentieth century, then he or she may need only read the short stories of Dale Ray Phillips to see how vibrant and powerful old themes and concerns can still be.

—Harold Woodell

PHILLIPS, Jayne Anne

Born: Buckhannon, West Virginia, 19 July 1952. **Education:** West Virginia University, Morgantown, B.A. 1974; University of Iowa, Iowa City, M.F.A. 1978. **Family:** Married Mark Brian Stockman in 1985; one son and two stepsons. **Career:** Taught at Humboldt State University, Arcata, California, Williams College, Williamstown, Massachusetts, Boston University, and Brandeis University, Waltham, Massachusetts. **Awards:** Pushcart prize, 1977, for *Sweethearts*, 1979, for short stories "Home" and "Lechery," 1983, for short story "How Mickey Made It"; National Endowment for the Arts grant, 1977, 1984; Coordinating Council of Literary Magazines Fels award, 1978, for *Sweethearts*; St. Lawrence award, 1978, for *Counting*; American Academy Kaufman award, 1980, for *Black Tickets*; O. Henry award, 1980, for "Snow"; Bunting Institute fellowship, Radcliffe College, 1981. **Agent:** International Creative Management, 40 West 57th Street, New York, New York 10019.

PUBLICATIONS

Novels

Machine Dreams. New York, Dutton, 1984.
Shelter. Boston, Houghton Mifflin, 1994.

Short Story Collections

Sweethearts. Carrboro, North Carolina, Truck Press, 1976.
Counting. New York, Vehicle, 1978.
Black Tickets. New York, Delacorte Press, 1979.
How Mickey Made It. St. Paul, Bookslinger Press, 1981.
Fast Lanes. New York, Vehicle, 1984.

Uncollected Short Stories

"Something that Happened," in *The Best American Short Stories 1979* edited by Joyce Carol Oates and Shannon Ravenel, Boston, Houghton Mifflin, 1979.
"Bess," in *Esquire* (New York), August 1984.

Other

The Last Day of Summer: Photographs (photographs by Jock Sturges). New York, 1992.

*   *   *

Jayne Anne Phillips first garnered attention for *Black Tickets* (1979), a collection of short stories that, like all her fiction, pierce to the core of human experience in a keen, unsentimental manner. There are three types of stories in *Black Tickets*: brief and technical character studies, inner soliloquies, and family dramas. The first two types of stories give voice to subjects and feelings usually left untold. The characters in these sketches—prostitutes, drug addicts, and destitute people—live on the outskirts of society. They tell stories, however brief, and sometimes only a few paragraphs, about their street-centered world, loves, and sexual alienation.

Sometimes Phillips's sketches are highly stylized: "Stripper," "Cheers," and "Happy," are extraordinarily forged. The other type of story found in *Black Tickets* is a longer, usually family-centered middle-class drama, like "Souvenir" and "The Heavenly Animal," concerned with problems lurking just below consciousness. "Home," a centerpiece of *Black Tickets*, concerns the relationship between a mother and her daughter. Phillips delineates the struggles of relationships across generations through carefully formed observations.

Unlike the brief moments captured in her short stories, Phillips' first novel, the sprawling *Machine Dreams* (1984), presents a family drama in depth. Using different narrators and mixing passages of letters, third person narration, and autobiography, Phillips describes the saga of the Hampsons, a lower middle class family living in a small town in West Virginia. Spanning two generations in the time period from about 1930-70, Phillips chronicles the lives of Jean and Mitch, a couple just getting by financially and emotionally, and their children—daughter Danner, and son Billy—through the family's collapse. Their story is familiar, but it is Phillips' judicious use of nuance and detail that add up to an intensely disquieting summary of the woes of an American experience.

Machines are Phillips' central motif in the novel, subtlety used throughout the narrative. Each character's life is most affected by machines—automobiles, airplanes, trucks, trains, TVs and radios. They represent potential for fulfillment, now and in the future, beyond the problems of everyday life. Both Danner and Billy, for example, use cars as a means for finding human bonds in sexual experiences. Their father takes his interests in technological promise and mechanics to the point of founding his own concrete plant. The enterprise is doomed, however, because it does not fit the needs of the local market. His wife, Jean, is forced to continue her education because of the plant's failure and her need to help support her family. While returning to study was already a goal of her's, the circumstances make the activity relatively depressing. The impending doom in this story lies in the inability of the Hampsons to comprehend or command what is happening in their lives. *Machine Dreams* is a compelling elucidation on American cultural mythology, most particularly a great faith in machines and technology, and a commentary on the dissolution of dreams on a national and personal scale.

In 1984, Phillips published *Fast Lanes*, a short story collection that explores many of the same themes as *Machine Dreams*. Again highlighting the problems of disjunction, especially from the past, Phillips' characters in *Fast Lanes* are wafted along by life, forming relationships haphazardly. The strongest stories are those concerning America in the late 1960s and early 1970s, an era in which Phillips' themes of displacement were common.

Phillips' second novel, *Shelter*, is an intense and focused book that continues to explore loss, in this case the loss of childhood innocence. Phillips employs many different voices in telling the story of four lonely, clumsy, adolescent campers attending a summer camp for girls in West Virginia in 1963. Each chapter has an interior monologue belonging to a different consciousness. Ostensibly, the narrative focuses on 15-year-old Lenny Swenson, her friend Cap Briarley, Lenny's 11-year-old sister Alma, and her friend, Delia Campbell, but it is in secondary characters like Buddy, the small son of the camp cook, Carmody, the ex-con stepfather of Buddy, and Parson, a holier-than-thou crazy man who lives near the camp that Phillips facets her deeper mysteries. Parson took a job laying pipe with a nearby road crew to follow Carmody, a man he knew in prison.

"I wanted to think about evil," Phillips told Andrew Delbanco in the *New Republic*, explaining her motivation for writing *Shelter*, "about whether evil really exists or if it is just a function of damage, the fact that when people are damaged, they damage others." Larger family concerns among the four girls, including an affair among two of the parents, one of whom committed suicide, and their own awkward adolescent struggles trying to make sense of the world are presented in the interior monologues, but larger evils loom, including child molestation and incest. Ann Hulbert summarized *Shelter* in the *New York Times Book Review*: "To be sure, Ms. Phillips plays skillfully with the rich metaphoric implications of violated children—the religious overtones of creatures being cast out, the mythic dimensions of generational rivalry and decay."

—Annette Petrusso

PICKERING, Sam

Born: Samuel Francis Pickering, Jr., in Nashville, Tennessee, 30 September 1941. **Education:** University of the South, B. A. 1963; Cambridge University, B. A. 1965, M. A. 1970; Princeton University, Ph.D. 1970. **Career:** Instructor, Montgomery Bell Academy, Nashville, 1965-66; assistant professor, Dartmouth College, 1970-78; associate professor, University of Connecticut, 1978-84, professor, since 1984, and coordinator of Graduate Studies, 1984-86; affiliated with the Institute in Children's Literature (NEH-sponsored), University of Connecticut, 1983, 1985 and the Rare Book School, Columbia University, summer 1985; research associate, University of Western Australia, 1993-94 and American Antiquarian Society, 1994; book reviewer. **Awards:** National Endowment for the Humanities fellowship, 1974; American Council of Learned Societies grant, 1976.

PUBLICATIONS

Essay Collections

A Continuing Education. Hanover, New Hampshire, University Press of New England, 1985.
The Right Distance. Athens, University of Georgia Press, 1987.
May Days. Iowa City, University of Iowa Press, 1988.
Still Life. Hanover, University Press of New England, 1990.
Let it Ride. Columbia, University of Missouri Press, 1991.
Trespassing. Hanover, New Hampshire, University Press of New England, 1994.
The Blue Caterpillar and Other Essays. Gainesville, University Press of Florida, 1997.
Deprived of Unhappiness. Athens, Ohio University Press, 1998.

Literary Scholarship

The Moral Tradition in English Fiction, 1785-1850. Hanover, New Hampshire, University Press of New England, 1976.

John Locke and Children's Books in Eighteenth-century England. N.p., Knoxville, 1981.
Moral Instruction and Fiction for Children. Athens, University of Georgia Press, 1993.

Other

Walkabout Year: Twelve Months in Australia. Columbia, University of Missouri Press, 1995.

Co-editor, *Children's Literature,* 8 volumes. New Haven, Yale University Press, 1979-81.

*   *   *

Sam Pickering counts among the handful of contemporary writers who practice, with aplomb, the art of the essay. The word essay, of course, derives from a French term: *essai*. It represents, in its roots, an "attempt," an exploration, a form of verbal wandering. The genre has its roots in the essays of Montaigne, the sixteenth-century French essayist who might well be considered the great ancestor of Pickering himself: the learned man who lets his mind range freely over deeply human topics, such as the nature of nature or the nature of human relations.

Pickering, who grew up in Tennessee and was educated at the University of the South, is a Southerner to the core, and his core values are those one associates with that group of Southern writers who are called the Fugitives. That is, Pickering is fiercely traditional, almost radically so, and his work reflects this bias. Like Robert Penn Warren and John Crowe Ransom—two of the original Fugitives—he admires the countryside, taking immense pleasure in the natural world; he is instinctively against industrialization and its discontents. The whole project of literary Modernism, with its emphasis on Freud, on dislocation, on obliquity, goes against his grain. Pickering also has something in common with Wendell Berry, the Kentucky regionalist (another master of the essay), although Pickering does not himself, like Berry, practice the agrarian life.

Though a perpetual Southerner in his persona, Pickering left the Deep South for the east at a youngish age, taking his Ph.D. in English from Princeton University. He also spent time at Cambridge University, in England, where he took a second bachelor's degree in 1965. His first teaching job was at Dartmouth College, where he began his writing career as an essayist. From Dartmouth in 1978 he moved to the University of Connecticut, where he has remained, publishing nine books of essays through 1998, one book-length autobiographical volume, and three books of literary scholarship. In addition to this primary work, Pickering has been a prolific book reviewer, writing countless essays for the *Sewanee Review, The Virginia Quarterly,* and other periodicals.

In the essay format, which he has perfected, Pickering adopts the persona of the congenial, wise, bemused southern gentleman who is perpetually astonished by what he discovers in his peregrinations. He is the bright amateur, at home in the world of books and children, academics and the natural world. Indeed, in the more recent essays, the natural world comes to play an increasingly important part in his life as he wanders the woods of

Connecticut, or Nova Scotia, or (as in *Walkabout Year*, his account of twelve months spent in Australia) the Antipodes.

A typical Pickering essay begins with a peculiar, eye-catching sentence: "Pod Malone was the worst stutterer in Smith County, Tennessee," or "Reading occasionally influences life." One can expect almost anything to follow from such an observation as the writer's mind roves. Pickering has a kind of wildness in him that is reflected in the forms the essays take. As the narrative proceeds, way always leads on to way, and the reader knows that one will never get back to the original starting point. But one does not regret this lack of traditional unity: Pickering is the quintessential essayist-as-wanderer, and it would be churlish to expect a neat package, a return ticket to the point of embarkation.

A classic example of the Pickering form is "Particulars" (from *The Right Distance*). The essay opens conversationally with the sort of thing one might hear around a Southern dinner table: "Nobody in Carthage, Tennessee, believed Cousin James Ligon would marry." As one might expect, Cousin James did marry, although he "did not introduce her [his wife] around Carthage, and naturally people wondered what she was like. The possibilities range crazily. Indeed, there are "a couple of particulars" about the woman that do emerge, and these are strangely defining.

Pickering muses, "Often particulars are not simply greater than wholes but remarkably different, and the person who strides along contemplating grand designs is certain to tumble over small details." This said, the author has *carte blanche* to roam the world of particular, odd things that define character and create a sense of place. "In life," says Pickering, "a person has got to keep a weather eye cocked for particulars." This leads him to a range of particulars that even the most imaginative reader would have a hard time foreseeing.

For instance, Pickering recalls a time when a particular former colleague complimented him and his work to his face but wrote horrible things about him behind his back. Pickering resolved to get his own back, and the opportunity to do so arrived several years later. He was lecturing at a "western university" when he discovered from the Chair of the department that his former colleague and his wife had applied for positions there. Pickering lavished praise on both of them, then added, *sotto voce*: "There is one particular about her, but I hate to mention it." The Chair teased the particular from the "reluctant" Pickering, and it was damning, "She is a little contentious and if thwarted in any way is liable to accuse the department of sexism and sue the university." Revenge was sweet.

In one of his finest essays, "The Blue Caterpillar"—the title of his 1997 collection—Pickering writes about a time when he was asked to play a part in an elementary school production of *Alice in Wonderland* in which his daughter, Eliza, had a part. "Sixty-seven girls and one adult danced in *Alice*," he writes. "Eliza was the Queen of Hearts, and I was the Blue Caterpillar. I was excited. Never had I been in a ballet. Fifty-two years is a long time to be a chrysalis, and I was eager to split the pupal shell, pump my wings, and flutter through an auditorium." Caterpillars, of course, have only the slightest knowledge of the changes happening around and within them. Pickering, too, seems only dimly aware of these changes in himself: that is, anyway, the stance

adopted by his typical persona. The reader (cued in by Pickering) sees more of what is happening to Pickering than his blinkered narrator—a technique akin to dramatic irony in the theater.

Most crucially, Pickering is a close observer—as any essayist must be. He attends to everything from the minutia of a flower to the demented politics of a university to the endlessly shifting roles of partners in marriage. He uses himself (as in "The Blue Caterpillar") as an example; he becomes, in effect, a wry version of Ralph Waldo Emerson's "transparent eyeball" who sees everything and is nothing himself, as "when a man hides behind a oak at the edge of a baseball field and watches his son bat." That, too, says the author, "is Wonderland."

Pickering's first collection, *A Continuing Education*, appeared in 1985. His most recent, *Deprived of Unhappiness*, came out in 1998. Although the content of his essays shifts as Pickering moves through life and his circumstances vary, the form of the essays has changed little: something strikes the narrator, the well-crafted persona; beginning with personal observation, the speaker (often literally) takes a walk through the world, collecting anecdotes, waltzing with ideas, piecing things together, making sense of a senseless world. The tone is always light-hearted, often extremely funny, although dark undertones can be heard if one listens closely. In the end, one feels one knows Sam Pickering, although even this is part of the fiction. More importantly, one has learned something about the world itself as reading translated into knowledge.

—Jay Parini

PINKWATER, Daniel Manus

Pseudonym: Manus Pinkwater. **Born:** Memphis, Tennessee, 15 November 1941. **Education:** Bard College, Annandale-on-Hudson, New York, B.A. 1964. **Family:** Married Jill Schutz in 1969. **Career:** Art instructor, Children's Aid Society, 1967-69, Lower West Side Visual Arts Center, 1969, and Henry Street Settlement, 1969, New York, and Bonnie Brae Farm for Boys, Millington, New Jersey, 1969; assistant project director, Inner City Summer Arts Program, Hoboken, New Jersey, 1970; regular commentator, *All Things Considered,* National Public Radio, since 1987; exhibiting artist. **Awards:** New Jersey Institute of Technology Award, 1975, for *Fat Elliot and the Gorilla;* American Library Association Notable Book Award, 1976, for *Lizard Music;* Junior Literary Guild Selection, 1977, for *Fat Men from Space; New York Times* Outstanding Book, 1978, for *The Last Guru;* Children's Choice Book Award, International Reading Association and the Children's Book Council, 1981, for *The Wuggie Norple Story;* Parents' Choice Award (literature), 1982, for *Roger's Umbrella*. **Agent:** Susan Cohen, Writers House Inc., 21 West 26th Street, New York, New York 10010.

PUBLICATIONS

Science Fiction Novels for Children

Wizard Crystal. New York, Dodd Mead, 1973.
Magic Camera. New York, Dodd Mead, 1974.

Blue Moose (as Manus Pinkwater). New York, Dodd Mead, 1975.

Wingman (as Manus Pinkwater). New York, Dodd Mead, 1975.

Lizard Music (as D. Manus Pinkwater). New York, Dodd Mead, 1976.

Fat Men from Space. New York, Dodd Mead, 1976.

The Big Orange Splot. New York, Hastings House, 1977.

The Blue Thing. Englewood Cliffs, New Jersey, Prentice Hall, 1977.

Alan Mendelsohn: The Boy from Mars. New York, Dutton, 1979.

Pickle Creature. New York, Four Winds Press, 1979.

Return of the Moose. New York, Dodd Mead, 1979.

Yobgorble, Mystery Monster of Lake Ontario. Boston, Houghton Mifflin, 1979.

The Magic Moscow. New York, Four Winds Press, 1980.

Attila the Pun. New York, Four Winds Press, 1981.

Tooth-Gnasher Superflash. New York, Four Winds Press, 1981.

The Worms of Kukumlima. New York, Dutton, 1981.

Slaves of Spiegel. New York, Four Winds Press, 1982.

The Snarkout Boys and the Avocado of Death. New York, Lothrop, 1982.

I Was a Second Grade Werewolf. New York, Dutton, 1983.

Devil in the Drain. New York, Dutton, 1984.

The Snarkout Boys and the Baconburg Horror. New York, Lothrop, 1984.

The Frankenbagel Monster. New York, Dutton, 1986.

The Moosepire. Boston, Little Brown, 1986.

The Muffin Fiend. New York, Lothrop, 1986.

Guys from Space. New York, Macmillan, 1989.

Borgel. New York, Macmillan, 1990.

Wempires. New York, Macmillan, 1991.

The Phantom of the Lunch Wagon. New York, Macmillan, 1992.

Spaceburger: A Kevin Spoon and Mason Mitz Story. New York, Macmillan, 1993.

Ned Feldman, Space Pirate. New York, Macmillan, 1994.

Mush, a Dog from Space. New York, Macmillan, 1995.

Wallpaper from Space. New York, Atheneum Books for Young Readers, 1996.

General Fiction for Children

The Hoboken Chicken Emergency. Englewood Cliffs, New Jersey, Prentice Hall, 1977.

The Last Guru. New York, Dodd Mead, 1978.

Java Jack, with Luqman Keele. New York, Crowell, 1980.

The Wuggie Norple Story, illustrated by Tomie de Paola. New York, Four Winds Press, 1980.

Roger's Umbrella, illustrated by James Marshall. New York, Dutton, 1982.

Young Adult Novel. New York, Crowell, 1982; as *Young Adults,* New York, Tor, 1985.

Ducks! Boston, Little Brown, 1984.

Aunt Lulu. New York, Macmillan, 1988.

Uncle Melvin. New York, Macmillan, 1989.

Doodle Flute. New York, Macmillan, 1991.

NORB, with Tony Author. Seattle, MU Press, 1991.

Author's Day. New York, Macmillan, 1993.

Second Grade Ape, illustrated by Jill Pinkwater. New York, Scholastic, 1997.

Young Larry, illustrated by Jill Pinkwater. New York, Marshall Cavendish, 1998.

At the Hotel Larry, illustrated by Jill Pinkwater. New York, Marshall Cavendish, 1998.

Rainy Morning, illustrated by Jill Pinkwater. New York, Atheneum Books for Young Readers, 1998.

Wolf Christmas, illustrations by Jill Pinkwater. New York, Marshall Cavendish, 1998.

Big Bob and the Thanksgiving Potato, illustrated by Jill Pinkwater. New York, Scholastic, 1998.

Ice-cream Larry, illustrated by Jill Pinkwater. New York : Marshall Cavendish, 1999.

General Fiction for Children as Manus Pinkwater

The Terrible Roar. New York, Knopf, 1970.

Bear's Picture. New York, Holt Rinehart, 1972.

Fat Elliot and the Gorilla. New York, Four Winds Press, 1974.

Three Big Hogs. New York, Seabury Press, 1975.

Around Fred's Bed, illustrated by Robert Mertens. Englewood Cliffs, New Jersey, Prentice Hall, 1976.

Novel for Adults

The Afterlife Diet. New York, Random House, 1995.

Other

Superpuppy: How to Choose, Raise, and Train the Best Possible Dog for You, with Jill Pinkwater. New York, Seabury Press, 1977.

Fish Whistle: Commentaries, Uncommentaries, and Vulgar Excesses. Reading, Massachusetts, Addison-Wesley, 1989.

Chicago Days/Hoboken Nights. Reading, Massachusetts, Addison-Wesley, 1991.

The Education of Robert Nifkin. New York, Farrar, Straus, & Giroux, 1998.

*

Media Adaptations: Video—*Lizard Music,* Children's Television International, Lincoln, Nebraska, Great Plains National Instructional Television Library, 1980; *Blue Moose,* Positive Images, 1982; *The Hoboken Chicken Emergency* (television movie), Public Broadcasting System (PBS), 1984.

*   *   *

One of the few genuine heirs of dada and surrealism in contemporary fantastic literature, Daniel Manus Pinkwater is also unusual in that he has attained a considerable reputation among adult readers even though virtually all of his fiction has been published for children and young adults. Writers as diverse as Samuel R. Delany, Harlan Ellison, and Vonda McIntyre have counted themselves among his fans, and it seems reasonable to suspect that Pinkwater's adult constituency may be nearly as large as that of his younger readership. Pinkwater tacitly acknowledges this by sprinkling his work liberally with arcane literary and cultural allusions likely to be lost on younger readers—such as a version of The Shadow named "Lamont Penumbra" in *Attila the Pun,* or references to dadaism and pataphysics in *Young Adult Novel.*

Pinkwater's world is a bizarre and endlessly inventive place where licensed realtors are controlled by aliens, where aliens all wear identical plaid sport coats and lust after junk food, where time-traveling moose detectives haunt the Canadian wilderness, where W. A. Mozart is a comic-book superhero, where planets bear names like Ziegler and Spiegel and cities names like Lenny, and where outer space is dotted with root beer stands. On a more serious level, it is a world in which outsiders can be heroes—overweight kids with thick glasses, mental patients, eccentric uncles, and—most often—kids whose interests and hobbies set them apart from their peers. For example, *Alan Mendelsohn: The Boy from Mars* draws a sensitive portrait of what it is like to be an outcast in school—and what it might be like to get revenge.

These themes are apparent in Pinkwater's most widely known novel, *Lizard Music.* Victor, who is considered "a freak" at school because he is a fan of Walter Cronkite rather than of rock stars, finds himself alone in the house during his parents' vacation. Staying up late, he catches a TV program of lizards playing music. Lizards begin to appear to him everywhere, and he wonders if he is hallucinating until a mysterious figure called the Chicken Man (who always introduces himself with the name of a different Northern Renaissance painter— Grunewald, Van Eyck, Cranach, etc.) reveals that a society of lizards is indeed living on an invisible island in the lake next to Hogboro (Pinkwater's name for Chicago, apparently) and is broadcasting TV programs. The Chicken Man takes Victor to the island, where he witnesses the wonders of the lizard society in a kind of crazed parody of Renaissance utopias. Earlier, Victor had watched a film called *The Invasion of the Pod People* on television and had begun to worry that people might actually be replaced by emotionless replicas from outer space; now he learns that "lizards and pods are natural enemies," and the lizards come to represent individuality and freedom of thought.

Conformity seems to be one of Pinkwater's main targets. Another film Victor sees on television describes an invasion of aliens in plaid sport coats who strip the Earth of its junk food. This is the plot of Pinkwater's own *Fat Men from Space,* and one of many cross-allusions to other Pinkwater books. The fat men, it turns out, are from the planet Spiegel, ruled over by the evil Sargon, who wants to steal all the junk food in the universe. In *Slaves of Spiegel* (itself the third book in the "Magic Moscow" trilogy), a Hoboken ice-cream parlor, its owner, and his assistant are kidnapped whole to participate in an intergalactic junk-food cookoff.

Pinkwater's most successful series characters appear in *The Snarkout Boys and the Avocado of Death* and *The Snarkout Boys and the Baconburg Horror.* Walter Galt and Winston Bongo, both outsiders at Genghis Khan High School, make a habit of sneaking out to late movies at the Snark Theatre after their parents are asleep. This leads them into a series of adventures involving a girl named Rat, the Chicken Man (from Lizard Music), the great detective Osgood Sigerson (a version of Sherlock Holmes), and his arch-enemy Wallace Nussbaum (a version of Moriarty). In the first of these adventures, Rat's uncle, a brilliant avocado scientist, disappears—kidnapped by Nussbaum to prevent his completing work on a giant telepathic avocado computer that can release the minds of real estate agents from alien control. In the second novel, a werewolf seems to be terrorizing the town of Baconburg.

Even Pinkwater's picture books for younger readers offer surrealistic twists on conventional fantasy images. *The Moosepire*

(the third book in a trilogy that began with *Blue Moose* and *Return of the Moose*) offers what appears to be a moose vampire but becomes a time travel story. *I Was a Second Grade Werewolf* concerns a boy who thinks he has turned into a werewolf, but can't get anyone to notice. *Guys from Space* are friendly aliens who invite a young boy to join them in visiting different planets, "just looking around," and stopping off for a root beer on the way home. *The Frankenbagel Monster* recasts Frankenstein as a mad bagel maker whose giant "Bagelunculus" threatens to destroy earth—until it goes stale. The devil himself appears as a tiny but grouchy inhabitant of a kitchen sink drain in *Devil in the Drain.*

In recent years, Pinkwater has been a popular commentator on public radio, and his commentaries (collected as *Fish Whistle*) may offer some clues to autobiographical elements in his writing. The title character of *Borgel,* for example, is a mysterious older relative of indeterminate nationality whose nostalgia for the "Old Country" and questionable "gift" for languages recalls Pinkwater's accounts of his father and uncles. But Borgel also turns out to be an intergalactic adventurer who takes his young nephew on a wild quest in space and time for "the great Popsicle." As with other Pinkwater books, the juxtaposition of sharply observed, recognizable characters with an epic sense of silliness worthy of the Marx Brothers seems to suggest that eccentricity alone can be a key to salvation.

Given the ubiquitous references to food and eating in nearly all his books, it hardly came as a surprise when Pinkwater's first adult novel, *The Afterlife Diet* (1995), should turn out to be a paean to food and to fat people (whom Pinkwater calls the "circumferentially challenged"). Opening in a heaven exclusively populated by the overweight and resembling a tacky Catskills resort—where God appears onstage telling lame jokes—the novel traces the before-and-after death adventures of a heartless book editor named Milton Cramer and a failed writer named Milo Levi-Nathan. Nearly every aspect of the book concerns eating; even Levi-Nathan's psychotherapist operates out of a delicatessen and punctuates his sessions with orders for muffins and pastrami sandwiches.

Structurally a bit chaotic, *The Afterlife Diet* consists largely of set-pieces, including lengthy excerpts from Levi-Nathan's attempts at science fiction and horror novels and a catalog of bizarre and always unsuccessful weight-loss programs ranging from abusive group sessions to a concentration camp in upstate New York run by an ex-Nazi doctor. With its huge cast of characters, its broad range of satirical targets, and its resolutely politically incorrect tone, the novel is perhaps best taken in small doses, but it does reveal that Pinkwater's inventiveness is no less manic when directed to older readers.

—Gary K. Wolfe

POWELL, Padgett

Born: Gainesville, Florida, 25 April 1952. **Education:** College of Charleston, B.S in chemistry, 1975; University of Houston, M.A. in creative writing 1982. **Family:** Married Sidney Wade;

two children. **Career:** Professor of English and creative writing, University of Florida in Gainesville; reviewer, contributing to such periodicals as *Florida Historical Quarterly*, *New York Times Book Review*, and *Georgia Review*. **Awards:** American Book Award Nominee, 1984, for *Edisto*; Whiting Writers' Award, 1986; Rome fellowship from the American Academy of Arts and Letters, 1987; Fulbright Award, 1989; Pushcart Prize XIV: Best of the Small Presses, for "Typical," 1990; O. Henry Award, 1995, for "Trick or Treat."

PUBLICATIONS

Novels

Edisto. New York, Holt, 1984.
A Woman Named Drown. New York, Farrar Straus, 1987.
Edisto Revisited. New York, Henry Holt, 1996.

Short Story Collections

Typical. New York, Farrar Straus Giroux, 1991.
Aliens of Affection. New York, Henry Holt, 1998.

Uncollected Fiction

"Voice from the Grave," in *Esquire,* January 1987.
"Circus," in *Southwest Review,* Spring/Summer 1994.
"Life of the Party," *in Southwest Review,* Spring/Summer 1994.
"In Love with Me," *in Harper's,* August 1994.
"Louisiana," in *Harper's,* March 1996.

Nonfiction

"Hitting Back." In *A World Unsuspected: Portraits of Southern Childhood,* edited by Alex Harris. Chapel Hill, University of North Carolina Press, 1987.
"Learning to Hit Back," in *Harper's,* August 1987.
"Our Southern Words and Pictures," in *Southern Living,* January 1990.
"The Allure of Southern Women," in *GQ: Gentlemen's Quarterly,* March 1990.
"Nashville, N. C., Biltmore Estate, Mr. Vanderbilt's French Renaissance Chateau in the Woods," in *New York Times Magazine,* 20 October 1991.
"Lore of the Low Country," in *House and Garden,* June 1992.
"Eccentric, Authentic New Orleans," in *New York Times Magazine,* 18 October 1992.
"Tales of the Low Country," in *Travel and Leisure,* May 1994.
"Grappling with a Giant," in *Harper's,* July 1996.
"My Favorite Store: Randall Made Knives," in *New York Times Magazine,* 6 April 1997.

*

Audio Recordings: "Typical," read by Padgett Powell, and "The Story: Sources and Resources" in *A Night of Literary Feasts, Chapter II,* also under title, *Jacksonville Public Libraries Foundation's Day of Lectures: Perspiration and Inspiration—the Craft and Vision of Writing,"* Jacksonville, Jacksonville Public Libraries Foundation, 1990; "The Winnowing of Mrs. Schuping," read by Christina Pickles in *Selected Shorts: A Celebration of the Short Story,*

Vol 10, New York, Symphony Space, 1996; speech given by Padgett Powell as part of the *Exhibition and Events,* School of the Art Institute of Chicago, Visiting Artists Program, Chicago, February 27, 1997.

Manuscript Collection: Unprocessed collection of 8000 items housed at Duke University Library.

Bibliographies: "Padgett Powell: A Bibliography" by Mary O'Neill and John S. Spencer, in *Bulletin of Bibliography,* December 1992; "Padgett Powell" by Thomas M. Carlson, in *Contemporary Fiction Writers of the South: A Bio-bibliographical Sourcebook,* edited by Joseph M. Flora and Robert Bain, Westport, Connecticut, Greenwood Press, 1993; "Padgett Powell," in *Contemporary Southern Men Fiction Writers: An Annotated Bibliography* by Rosemary M. Canfield Reisman and Suzanne Booker-Canfield, Pasadena, Salem Press, 1998.

Critical Studies: "Where the Boys Are" by William H. Pritchard, *New Republic,* 30 April 1984; "The Eden of *Edisto*: The Fall into the Then-Next" by Sybil Estess, in *Southern Review,* Autumn 1984; "*A Woman Named Drown*" by T. Coraghessan Boyle, in *New York Times Book Review,* 7 June 1987; "A Potpouri of Characters and Their Stories" by Michiki Kakutani, in *New York Times,* 16 August 1991; "Padgett Powell" by Thomas M. Carlson, in *Contemporary Fiction Writers of the South: A Bio-Bibliographical Sourcebook,* edited by Joseph M. Flora and Robert Bain, Westport, Connecticut, Greenwood Press, 1993; "Carolina Slacker" by Scott Spencer, in *New York Times Book Review,* 31 March 1996.

Padgett Powell comments:
I discovered Faulkner at a late age—thank God.

*   *   *

Described by Saul Bellow as "the best American writer of the younger generation" after the publication of his first novel, *Edisto,* Padgett Powell writes about the decline of Southern tradition and the alienated victims of what he calls the "latest reconstruction in the South." Facing severely diminished family and community expectations, Powell's Southerners ask Faulknerian questions without the exalted rhetoric or passion. Faulkner's Quentin Compson exclaims: "I don't hate [the South]! I don't hate it!" Powell's Mrs. Hollingsworth in a recent story, "Trick or Treat," recites: "'I love it. I love it not.' . . . indicating with her arm the trees and air and houses and suspiring history and ennui" and feeling nothing but vague discontent. Married with children, anticipating an affair with a 12-year-old boy, Mrs. Hollingsworth does "not entertain highfalutin notions of decadence. Just boredom." Like her pumpkin-headed "Lolito," most of Powell's characters are "a little visionary if you [take] the long charitable view of them." Powell's novels afford the reader that leisure. Many of his short stories do not.

Powell's first novel, *Edisto,* dramatizes a traditional Southern family in trouble while it satirizes sentimental Southern themes. The adolescent narrator, Simons Manigault, describes home on Edisto Island as a "Southern barony" with "deerfly for stock and scrub oak for crop." The "planter's wife" has been abandoned by "the planter," the loyal black servant has left town, and the new generation is left to seek identity in a post-war South littered with "veterans." The "war," however, took place in Vietnam. As "the old order" is replaced by "new business," Simons's family reunites on an "Arab-financed, model railroader's plot of Paradise" called Hilton Head. Through a language as hyperactive as Simons himself, this picaresque narrative recalls earlier experiments in the genre by Twain and Salinger, especially *The Adventures of Huckleberry Finn*, which also reduces the verities of Southern tradition to farce.

The narrator of Powell's second novel, *A Woman Named Drown*, sounds like an older Simons who drops out of a Ph.D. program in chemistry to hit the road with a middle-aged actress whose last leading role was in a play called *A Woman Named Drown*. A parody of the deliquescent Southern literary heroine, she takes Al on a "little downside sabbatical" through seedy, abandoned tourist strips in Florida where he meets characters who "have at their center no center, no towardness." Both narrators are the children of Southern gentry; both abandon what Simons calls a "then-next" life to discover the "now" through the help of an older companion. Both are writers who take "notes on life" and develop a language that matches their experiences. Al calls it "new utterance," Simons calls it "jive," like "James Brown guitar riffs of five notes that run twenty minutes, and then one of the five notes goes sharp and a statement is made." Tumbling syntax, run-on sentences, and elliptical constructions heavily laced with puns and double-entendres constitute language play, which can be dazzling in Powell's fiction but can also cloy. Although Simons and Al discover in the lab of life that "chemistry never changes, chemical "titration" unfortunately becomes tit rating" at the end of *Drown*.

Edisto Revisited revisits themes, characters, and locations found in the first novel. Although he now has an architectural degree, Simons continues to retreat from educational and family expectations, taking to the road like Al in *Drown* where the traditional code of honor and duty is replaced by appetite and impulse. Described by Scott Spencer as "a man more annoyed than haunted by the past and looking not so much for a place to stand as a place to hide," Simons becomes "a visionless architect shacked up with his cousin." Another satirical treatment of the older South and the burden of Southern history ("The Wawer! The Wawer!"), the novel concludes with Simons "AWOL, following his mother, not his father—absent with opprobrious love. He deigned not the Wawer, in all its aspects. He surrendered early."

The conventional narrative structure of *Edisto* and *Edisto Revisited* is rejected in most of the pieces collected in *Typical*, which reflects the post-modern influence of Donald Barthelme, Powell's teacher at the University of Houston, "my literary uncle, my coach." Allegorical sketches such as "Mr. Irony," Dr. Ordinary," and "Mr. Desultory" reduce characters to ideas and perception to style. However, a few stories, such as "The Modern Italian" and "The Winnowing of Mrs. Schuping," reject allegory and stream-of-consciousness monologues in favor of grotesque but sympathetically developing characters and more conventional third-person narrative structures. Mrs. Schuping provides a lively spoof of Faulkner's lonely spinsters by reeling in a three hundred pound "big creaking booger" of a sheriff and bedding him without either one of them ending up in the morgue.

In Powell's most recent collection, *Aliens of Affection*, the literary tradition of the Southern grotesque is burlesqued, as eccentrics and outcasts—a brain-damaged cyclist, a peeping Tom, a strip-club addict—inhabit a vaguely depicted landscape, rather than the more physically located South described in the novels. Powell's South, in these stories, often resembles a Halloween freak show where "mechanical intelligence" is measured "in inverse proportion to dental health." But when the costumes are put aside, real human beings begin to emerge, rendered through Powell's distinctly Southern blend of colloquial diction and baroque lyricism. His South, however, has become increasingly arid, banal, and absurd. "The thing about the South," Mrs. Hollingsworth lugubriously declaims, "is that it's a vale of tears that were shed a long time ago. It's a vale of dry tears"—not a garden but a wasteland—or, in one story, a dump.

—Thomas M. Carlson

PRATT, Minnie Bruce

Born: Selma, Alabama, 12 September 1946. **Education**: University of Alabama, B.A. (with honors) 1968; University of North Carolina at Chapel Hill, Ph.D. in Renaissance English literature 1979. **Family**: Married Marvin E. Weaver, 1966 (divorced 1976); companion of Leslie Feinberg, since 1992; two children. **Career**: Instructor, Fayetteville State University, Fayetteville, North Carolina, 1975-80; assistant professor of English, Shaw University, Raleigh, North Carolina, 1980-82; member of graduate faculty of women's studies program, George Washington University, Washington, D.C., 1984-88; faculty member of women's studies program, University of Maryland, College Park, 1984-91; writer-in-residence, Community Writer's Project, Syracuse, New York, 1988; member of graduate faculty, Union Institute, Cincinnati, Ohio, since 1990; member of editorial collective, *Feminary: A Feminist Journal for the South, Emphasizing Lesbian Visions*, 1978-83. **Awards**: Woodrow Wilson fellowship, 1968; Fulbright fellowship, 1968; National Endowment of the Arts fellowship, 1968, creative writing fellowship, 1990; Academy of American Poets, Lamont Poetry Selection, 1989, for *Crime against Nature*; *American Voice* Harriet Simpson Arnow Prize, 1990, for "I Am Ready to Tell All I Know"; American Library Association Gay/Lesbian Book Award for *Crime against Nature*, 1991; Fund for Free Expression, Lillian Hallman/Dashiell Hammett award, 1991; Gustavus Myers Center, Outstanding Book Award, 1992. for *Rebellion: Essays 1980-1991*. **Agent**: Charlotte Sheedy, 65 Bleecker Street, 12th Floor, New York, New York 10012. **Address**: P.O. Box 8212, Jersey City, New Jersey 07308.

PUBLICATIONS

Poetry

The Sound of One Fork (chapbook). Durham, Night Heron Press, 1981.
We Say We Love Each Other. San Francisco, Spinsters Ink, 1985; Ithaca, New York, Firebrand Books, 1992.
Crime against Nature. Ithaca, New York, Firebrand Books, 1990.

Short Story Collection

S/HE. Ithaca, New York, Firebrand Books, 1995.

Other

Yours in Struggle: Three Feminist Perspectives on Anti-Semitism and Racism, with Elly Bulkin and Barbara Smith. N.p., Long Haul Press, 1984.
Rebellion: Essays 1980-1991. Ithaca, New York, Firebrand Books, 1991.

Critical Studies: "Poets Live the Questions: Jewelle Gomez and Minnie Bruce Pratt Discuss Politics and Imagination," in *Out/ Look,* Spring 1992; interview with Elaine Auerbach, in *Belles Lettres,* vol. 8, no. 1, Fall 1992.

*

Minnie Bruce Pratt comments:

I grow up and read Shelly who says of another nightsinging bird: "A poet is a nightingale, who sits in darkness and sings to cheer its own solitude with sweet sounds."

But I ask myself, "What if the singer—the poet, the writer, the person who moves through the world—has been taught to fear the darkness? How do I sing in a language imbued with the most grotesque images of darkness? A language in which solitude exists only in relation to a damaged damned other?"

In the place I grew up, my saw-mill county-seat town in Alabama, the people who ran its economic/sexual system, the racist state, were determined to regulate mind, body, and imagination.

But there was always the danger that folks might decide to go back to raw data, to our sensual and sensory experiences, to the immediate history and shared memory of our lives. We might begin to make our own comparisons, draw our own conclusions, act individually and collectively, write poems and stories about what was not allowed.

So judgements were erected as partitions between us. And the authorities put up signs, everywhere. These were the public words, relentless repetitive reminders. Words that were an attempt to convince us of the inevitability of white racial superiority, of the impossibility of escape from the fact that some were bosses and others servants, of the immovability of a whole system of category and metaphor.

Of course, almost every Southern child, white or black, stopped at least once at water labeled Black or White, and sneaked a sip. We said "This is just like *my* water. What's the difference between us?"

But this was a hidden, secret making of a bond between us. This was a private unspoken metaphor. Any public speech or action that crossed the arbitrary divisions of "race" was discouraged by the authorities, to say the least. To say the most, people often died when, with their lives, they sought to imagine, and then make, a way out of the categories that had been imposed on them.

Public transgression was violently punished, while those who made the laws did their best to control what Trotsky has called "the physical power of thought"—the way an account of the ideas and deeds arising from one struggle for freedom might fire the imagination, and then the actions, of people in other circumstances. For instance, at one time the state I lived in had a "literature ordinance." This law made it a crime to possess one or more pieces of "radical" literature—defined as anti-fascist or labor publications, and as liberal magazines like *The Nation* and *The New Republic.*

For anything might happen if we began to question the words *Black* and *White.* What if we began to question the weight those words carried? If we saw the way some folks' backs bent under the weight, and other folks walked free, and that the reasons given in the words *Black* and *White* made no sense.

Anything might happen if we went underneath the words, back to our bodies, and asked them to speak. Anything might happen if we listened to the other one speaking of her and his life. Our pleasure and pain might not seem so different. Things that we'd been taught were opposite might seem to agree. We'd been kept apart by a rule called "law," called "right reason." Together, we might become creators of a new humanity, a new commonality.

Anything might happen if we took the horrors and wonders of our lives, and claimed ourselves with words that refused to abide in the opposition, the ranking of white and black, or, for that matter, male and female, normal and queer.

Queerness was not marked officially with any sign. But anyone who crossed *White* and *Black* was assumed to be queer. Any lover across guarded borders, and challenger to the necessity of rich and poor, anyone who brought together contradictions that had been separated into good and evil—that person was called *queer.*

Art was queer, and so were artists. And so was the innate human ability to create—the ability from which language itself arises. The power to see correspondence between two things and make a word from that. The power to make metaphor, to lead people with words to a new connection between disparate realities. The power to find similarities between dissimilars and create language for what is shared.

The gift of carrying life back and forth, back and forth, the work like breath between two distinctly different others. That gift was the queerest gift of all.

*   *   *

On the dustjacket of her volume of poetry, *Crime against Nature,* Minnie Bruce Pratt is described as a "lesbian poet, essayist, and teacher." But Pratt's work seems to transcend such categories. She combines her work as a poet, an essayist, and a teacher with her work as a grass-roots activist. That is not to say that her poetry is didactic. Far from it, she puts the aesthetic to work in the service of the political without surrendering her sense of beauty or compromising her vision of human equality.

Pratt's career as a poet began with the publication of her chapbook, *The Sound of One Fork,* which deals directly with the poet's process of coming to know and understand herself as a lesbian and as a white woman. These themes are developed in her first volume of poems, *We Say We Love Each Other*, in which a community of women emerges as a vital force in the poet's journey towards self-discovery.

Her second book of poetry, *Crime against Nature*, is dedicated to Pratt's two sons, Ranson and Ben, who were taken from her when her ex-husband discovered she was a lesbian. In "Poem for My Sons," Pratt prays for her sons to remember her "as a woman making slowly toward / an unknown place." She asks her children's forgiveness for having let their father take them, but she also asks for justice. In "No Place," we are privy to the thoughts of a woman who feels alienated, even among women:

> Groups of women pass by, talking, as if we are not
> there. Who can I ask for help? I am awkward, at a loss.
> We are together, we have come across. We have no place
> to go.

The book registers the anguish and uncertainty of a mother who is ready to give up her shame. Indeed, the self-doubt of the early poems gives way to a righteous anger in the six-part, title poem at the end of the book. In "Crime against Nature" Pratt points to the irony of a system that regards her love for women as a "Crime against nature" but refuses to see the concept of child "custody" as the "prison term" it seems to be.

Pratt makes particularly interesting use of punctuation in these poems; they are full of caesuras and pregnant pauses that refuse to let the reader hurry through. In an interview with Elaine Auerbach, Pratt explains that *Crime against Nature* "is in fact a long poem, but I didn't think of having to make a very coherent narrative out of it." The pieces of the book are designed to allow the reader "to pace themselves through this very difficult material."

Pratt is not, if she ever was, simply a lesbian's poet. She identifies as a lesbian, but in *S/HE*, her 1995 book of stories, she interrogates those categories of identity such as gender, sex, race, sexuality, and class, that have been assigned to her by other people. In the autobiographical essay "Gender Quiz" that begins the book, she explains:

> I have lived my life at the intersection of great waves
> of social change in the United States in the twentieth
> century: the Black civil rights and liberation movements,
> the women's liberation movement, the lesbian/gay/bisexual
> liberation movement, the transgender liberation movement.
> The theory developed by each has complicated our
> questions about the categories of race, sex, gender,
> sexuality, and class. And these theories have advanced
> our ability to struggle against oppressions that are
> imposed and justified using these categories.

According to Pratt, questions such as "male or female?" or "white, black, other?" that are ubiquitous and seemingly innocuous, need to be rephrased in order to include those who fall between such categories. Pratt wants us to ask ourselves, "how many ways are there to have the *sex* of girl, boy, man, woman?," and to ask each other, "What is your dream of who you want to be?"

Written in the first person, these episodic stories are autobiographical and speak of both sexual passion and harassment in a language that is refined enough to be called poetry. The one paragraph-long story, "Ashes," could easily be a prose poem. Note the extensive use of rhyme and assonance in the following passage: "You told me you began to cry when you read the word *ashes* in one of my poems, you didn't know why." Like the poems in her earlier volumes, these stories are infused with a revolutionary spirit, even at the level of language. The pieces are narrative, yet Pratt suggests that they "give theory flesh and breath."

While it is generically innovative, Pratt's work is thematically coherent. In her 1984 essay, "Identity: Skin Blood Heart," reprinted in *Rebellion*, she makes clear that identity can be based on notions of skin and blood that divide people; she implies that it takes heart to overcome our cultural differences. Since her early work has been reprinted by Firebrand Books, it reaches an ever widening audience and in its wake forms the community that Pratt finds a continuing source of inspiration.

—Catherine D. Halley

PRICE, Eugenia

Born: 22 June 1916, in Charleston, West Virginia. **Education:** Attended Ohio University, 1932-35; Northwestern University, dental student, 1935-37. **Career:** Serial writer for "In Care of Aggie Horn" radio show, National Broadcasting Co., Chicago, 1939-42, for "Joyce Jordan, M.D.," Proctor and Gamble, Cincinnati, Ohio, 1944-46; owner, Eugenia Price Productions (radio), 1945-49; writer, producer, and director of "Unshackled," 1950-56, WGN, Chicago; free-lance writer; lecturer in the United States and Canada, 1949-63. **Awards:** Coastal Georgia Historical Society, 1968, for the *St. Simons Trilogy*; St. Simons Island held a "Eugenia Price Day" in 1971; distinguished service award in literature, Georgia College, and Belles-lettres citation, St. Augustine Historical Society, 1974; Matson Award, Chicago Friends of Literature, 1978, for *Maria*; Governor's Award in the Arts for literature, 1978; Litt.D., Alderson-Broaddus College, 1967. **Died:** Of congestive heart failure, 28 May 1996.

PUBLICATIONS

Spiritual Nonfiction

Discoveries Made from Living My New Life. Grand Rapids, Michigan, Zondervan, 1953.
Never a Dull Moment: Honest Questions by Teen Agers, with Honest Answers by Eugenia Price. Grand Rapids, Michigan, Zondervan, 1956.
The Burden Is Light: The Autobiography of a Transformed Pagan Who Took God at His Word. New York, Revell, 1955; revised edition, Pillar Books, 1975.
Early Will I Seek Thee: Journal of a Heart that Longed and Found. New York, Revell, 1957.
Share My Pleasant Stones Every Day for a Year. Grand Rapids, Michigan, Zondervan, 1958.
Woman to Woman. Grand Rapids, Michigan, Zondervan, 1959.

Strictly Personal: The Adventure of Discovering What God Is Really Like. Grand Rapids, Michigan, Zondervan, 1960; as *What Is God Like?,* Oliphants, 1965.

Beloved World: The Story of God and People as Told from the Bible. Grand Rapids, Michigan, Zondervan, 1961.

A Woman's Choice: Living through Your Problems. Grand Rapids, Michigan, Zondervan, 1962.

God Speaks to Women Today. Grand Rapids, Michigan, Zondervan, 1964.

The Wider Place: Where God Offers Freedom from Anything That Limits Our Growth. Grand Rapids, Michigan, Zondervan, 1966; as *Where God Offers Freedom,* Oliphants, 1966.

Make Love Your Aim. Grand Rapids, Michigan, Zondervan, 1967.

Just as I Am. Grand Rapids, Michigan, Zondervan, 1968.

Learning to Live from the Gospels. New York, Lippincott, 1968.

The Unique World of Women in Bible Times and Now. Grand Rapids, Michigan, Zondervan, 1969.

Learning to Live from the Acts. New York, Lippincott, 1970.

No Pat Answers. Grand Rapids, Michigan, Zondervan, 1972.

Leave Your Self Alone. Grand Rapids, Michigan, Zondervan, 1979.

At Home on St. Simons. Atlanta, Peachtree Publishers, 1981.

Getting through the Night. New York, Doubleday, 1982.

What Really Matters. New York, Doubleday, 1983.

Another Day. New York, Doubleday, 1984.

Inside One Author's Heart: A Deeply Personal Sharing with My Readers. New York, Doubleday, 1992.

Novels

The Beloved Invader. New York, Lippincott, 1965.

New Moon Rising. New York, Lippincott, 1969.

Lighthouse. New York, Lippincott, 1971.

Don Juan McQueen. New York, Lippincott, 1974.

Maria. New York, Lippincott, 1977.

Margaret's Story. New York, Lippincott, 1980.

Savannah. New York, Doubleday, 1983.

To See Your Face Again. New York, Doubleday, 1985.

Before the Darkness Falls. New York, Doubleday, 1987.

Stranger in Savannah. New York, Doubleday, 1989.

Bright Captivity. New York, Doubleday, 1991.

Where Shadows Go. New York, Doubleday, 1993.

Beauty from Ashes. New York, Doubleday, 1995.

Other

St. Simons Memoir: The Personal Story of Finding the Island and Writing the St. Simons Trilogy of Novels. New York, Lippincott, 1978.

Diary of a Novel. New York, Lippincott, 1980.

*

Manuscript Collection: Boston University.

Critical Studies: *Eugenia Price's South: A Guide to the People and Places of Her Beloved Region* by Mary B. Wheeler, Atlanta, Longstreet Press, 1993.

*   *   *

Eugenia Price had essentially three careers, as the originator and force behind radio soap opera in the 1940s, as a popular dispenser of spiritual advice during the 1950s through the 1970s, and as the author of hugely successful romance novels set in the American South from the 1970s until the time of her death in 1996.

After attending Ohio University and studying dentistry at Northwestern University, Price decided to try her hand at writing, and she began her career at the National Broadcasting Company in Chicago as a serial writer for "In Care of Aggie Horn." Her keen sense of what would appeal to daytime radio listeners ensured her success, and she subsequently developed a number of radio serials for Procter & Gamble.

In the late 1940s, Price experienced an intense religious conversion, and in 1953 she published her first book, *Discoveries Made from Living My New Life* (1953) to chronicle her experiences and explain her faith. She followed it with a string of mostly successful and insightful nonfiction books. Like *Discoveries Made from Living My New Life, The Burden Is Light: The Autobiography of a Transformed Pagan Who Took God at His Word* (1955), *Early Will I Seek Thee: Journal of a Heart that Longed and Found* (1957), and *Strictly Personal: The Adventure of Discovering What God Is Really Like* (1960) recounted her personal discovery and fulfillment.

Additional titles addressed issues of particular importance to children or women, including *Never a Dull Moment: Honest Questions by Teen Agers, with Honest Answers by Eugenia Price* (1956), *Woman to Woman* (1959), and *A Woman's Choice: Living through Your Problems* (1962), and celebrated womanhood, including *God Speaks to Women Today* (1964) and *The Unique World of Women in Bible Times and Now* (1969). Still others were of the inspirational and self-help variety, including *Share My Pleasant Stones Every Day for a Year* (1958), *Make Love Your Aim* (1967), and *Just as I Am* (1968). Another group of works urged readers toward a life based on Biblical tenets and eschewing advances in psychology and analysis that arose during the twentieth century; *Learning to Live from the Gospels* (1968), *Learning to Live from the Acts* (1970), and, especially, *Leave Your Self Alone* (1979) are most prominent among these. That most of these books have been republished several times indicates that early readers are passing the texts onto their children as they mature. During Price's lifetime, the books earned her a reputation as a leading religious writer.

However, Price became even better known for her sweeping historical romance novels in the picturesque backdrop of the American South. Her novels create compelling sagas that blend personal stories of love and tragedy (as in her earlier radio serials) with the dramatic events of the region's history. Her first series of novels was inspired by a trip to St. Simon's Island, off the coast of Georgia, where she later settled. Price's great love for and sympathy with the area were manifest in her lyrical, detailed descriptions, while her understanding of the region's history gave the books an authenticity that immediately appealed to readers. The St. Simon's books (*The Beloved Invader,* 1965; *New Moon Rising,* 1969; and *Lighthouse,* 1971) were a huge success, and Price followed them with a Florida trilogy (*Don Juan McQueen,* 1974; *Maria,* 1977; and *Margaret's Story,* 1980) and a Savannah quartet

(*Savannah*, 1983; *To See Your Face Again*, 1985; *Before the Darkness Falls*, 1987; and *Stranger in Savannah*, 1989). A final St. Simon's trilogy (*Bright Captivity*, 1991; *Where Shadows Go*, 1993; and *Beauty from Ashes*, 1995) was completed just before her death.

—Tammy J. Bronson

PRICE, Reynolds

Born: Edward Reynolds Price in Macon, North Carolina, 1 February 1933. **Education:** Duke University, Durham, North Carolina, 1951-55 (Angier Duke scholar), A.B. (summa cum laude) 1955 (Phi Beta Kappa); Merton College, Oxford, 1955-58 (Rhodes scholar), B.Litt. 1958. **Career:** Member of the faculty since 1958, assistant professor, 1961-68, associate professor, 1968-72, professor of English, 1972-77, and since 1977, James B. Duke Professor, Duke University; Writer-in-residence, University of North Carolina, Chapel Hill, 1965, UNC Greensboro, 1971, and University of Kansas, Lawrence, 1967, 1969, 1980; Glasgow Professor, Washington and Lee University, Lexington, Virginia, 1971; member of the faculty, Salzburg Seminar on American Studies, 1977; editor, *Archive*, Durham, 1954-55; advisory editor, *Shenandoah*, Lexington, Virginia, since 1964; chair, National Endowment for the Arts Literature Advisory Panel, 1976. **Awards:** Faulkner Foundation prize, 1962; Sir Walter Raleigh Awards, 1962, 1976, 1981, 1984, 1986; Guggenheim fellowship, 1964; National Association of Independent Schools award, 1964; National Endowment for the Arts fellowship, 1967; National Institute of Arts and Letters Award, 1971; Bellamann Foundation award, 1976; Lillian Smith award, 1976; North Carolina Award, 1977; Roanoke-Chowan Award for Poetry, 1983; National Book Critics Circle award, 1987; Bobst award, 1988; Fund for New American Plays grant, 1989, for *New Music*; R. Hunt Parker Award, NC Literary & Historical Society, 1991; Pulitzer Prize fiction finalist for *The Collected Stories*, 1994; Litt.D.: St. Andrews Presbyterian College, North Carolina, 1978; Wake Forest University, 1979; Davidson College, 1992. **Agent:** Harriet Wasserman Literary Agency, 137 East 36th Street, New York, New York 10016. **Address:** 4813 Duke Station, Durham, North Carolina 27706.

PUBLICATIONS

Novels

A Long and Happy Life. New York, Atheneum, 1962.
A Generous Man. New York, Atheneum, 1966.
Love and Work. New York, Atheneum, 1968.
The Surface of Earth. New York, Atheneum, 1975.
The Source of Light. New York, Atheneum, 1981.
Mustian (2 novels and a story). New York, Atheneum, 1983.
Kate Vaiden. New York, Atheneum, 1986.
Good Hearts. New York, Atheneum, 1988.
The Tongues of Angels. New York, Atheneum, 1990.
Blue Calhoun. New York, Atheneum, 1992.
The Promise of Rest. New York, Scribner, 1995.
Roxanna Slade. New York, Scribner, 1998

Short Story Collections

The Names and Faces of Heroes. New York, Atheneum, 1963.
Permanent Errors. New York, Atheneum, 1970.
Home Made. Rocky Mount, North Carolina Wesleyan College Press, 1990.
The Foreseeable Future: Three Long Stories. New York, Atheneum, 1991.
An Early Christmas. Rocky Mount, North Carolina Wesleyan College Press, 1992.
The Collected Stories. New York, Atheneum, 1993.

Uncollected Short Stories

"Night and Day at Panacea," in *Harper's*, August 1974.
"Commencing," in *Virginia Quarterly Review*, Spring 1975.
"His Final Mother," in *New Yorker,* 21 May 1990.
"Two Useful Visits," in *Virginia Quarterly Review*, Summer 1990.
"Serious Need," in *Esquire*, November 1990.
"Full Day," in *Harper's*, January 1991.

Plays

Early Dark (produced New York, 1978). New York, Atheneum, 1977.
Private Contentment. New York, Atheneum, 1984.
New Music: A Trilogy. New York, Theatre Communications, 1990.
Full Moon and Other Plays. New York, Theatre Communications, 1993.

Poetry Collections

Late Warning: Four Poems. New York, Albondocani Press, 1968.
Torso of an Archaic Apollo—After Rilke. New York, Albondocani Press, 1969.
Lessons Learned: Seven Poems. New York, Albondocani Press, 1977.
Christ Child's Song at the End of the Night. Privately printed, 1978.
Nine Mysteries (*Four Joyful, Four Sorrowful, One Glorious*). Winston-Salem, North Carolina, Palaemon Press, 1979.
Vital Provisions. New York, Atheneum, 1982.
House Snake. Northridge, California, 1986
The Laws of Ice. New York, Atheneum, 1986.
The Use of Fire. New York, Atheneum, 1990.

Other

The Thing Itself (address). Durham, North Carolina, Duke University Library, 1966.
Two Theophanies: Genesis 32 and John 21. Privately printed, 1971.
Things Themselves: Essays and Scenes. New York, Atheneum, 1972.
The Fourth Eclogue of Vergil. Privately printed, 1972.
An Apocryphal Hymn of Jesus. Privately printed, 1973.
Presence and Absence: Versions from the Bible. Bloomfield Hills, Michigan, Bruccoli Clark, 1973.
A Nativity from the Apocryphal Book of James. Privately printed, 1974.
Annuciation. Privately printed, 1975.

Conversations, with William Ray. Memphis, Memphis State University, 1976.

The Good News According to Mark. Privately printed, 1976.

Oracles: Six Versions from the Bible. Durham, North Carolina, Friends of the Duke University Library, 1977.

A Palpable God: Thirty Stories Translated from the Bible with an Essay on the Origins and Life of Narrative. New York, Atheneum, 1978.

Christ Child's Song at the End of the Night. Privately printed, 1978.

Question and Answer. Privately printed, 1979.

The Annual Heron. New York, Albondocani Press, 1980.

Country Mouse, City Mouse (essay). Rocky Mount, North Carolina, Friends of the Wesleyan College Library, 1981.

A Start (miscellany of early work). Winston-Salem, North Carolina, Palaemon Press, 1981.

A Common Room: Essays 1954-1987. New York, Atheneum, 1987.

Real Copies: Will Price, Crichton Davis, Phyllis Peacock, and More. Rocky Mount, North Carolina Wesleyan College Press, 1988.

Back Before Day. Rocky Mount, North Carolina Wesleyan College Press, 1989.

Clear Pictures: First Loves, First Guides. New York, Atheneum, 1989.

Michael Egerton (for children). Mankato, Minnesota, Creative Education, 1993.

A Whole New Life. New York, Atheneum, 1994.

The Honest Account of a Memorable Life: An Apocryphal Gospel. North Carolina Wesleyan College Press, 1994.

Contributor, *Writers Dreaming,* edited by Naomi Epel. New York, Carol Southern Bks., 1995.

Contributor, *The Store of Joys: Writers Celebrate the North Carolina Museum of Art's Fiftieth Anniversary.* Raleigh, North Carolina Museum of Art, 1997.

Editor and contributor, *The Three Gospels: The Good News According of Mark, the Good News According the John, and Honest Account of a Memorable Life.* New York, Scribner, 1996.

*

Song: "Copperline," with James Taylor. 1991.

Bibliography: *Reynolds Price: A Bibliography 1949-1984* by Stuart Wright and James L.W. West III, Charlottesville, University Press of Virginia, 1986.

Interviews: "A Conversation with Reynolds Price" by Wallace Kaufman, *Shenandoah,* Summer 1966; "Reynolds Price," audio recording, with Lynn Ballard, Columbia, Missouri, American Audio Library, 1982; "Reynolds Price: The Art of Fiction LXXVII," with Frederick Busch, *Paris Review* 121, Winter 1991; *Conversations with Reynolds Price* edited by Jefferson Humphries, Jackson, University Press of Mississippi, 1991; "Reynolds Price," with Dannye Romine Powell, *Parting the Curtains,* New York, Doubleday, 1995.

Critical Studies: "The Reynolds Price Who Outgrew the Southern Pastoral" by Theodore Solotaroff, in *Saturday Review* , 26 September 1970; *Reynolds Price* by Constance Rooke, Boston, Twayne, 1983; "Reynolds Price" by David Marion Holman, *Fifty*

Southern Writers After 1900, Joseph M. Flora and Robert Bain, editors, New York, Greenwood Press, 1987; "Reynolds Price and Religion: The 'Almost Blindingly Lucid' Palpable World" by Lynn Veach Sadler, *Southern Quarterly,* Winter 1988; *Reynolds Price: From 'A Long and Happy Life' To 'Good Hearts'* edited by Sue Laslie Kimball and Lynn Veach Sadler, Fayetteville, North Carolina, Methodist College Press, 1989; "Reading as a Woman: Reynolds Price and Creative Androgyny in *Kate Vaiden*" by Edith T. Hartin, *Southern Quarterly,* Spring 1991.

*   *   *

Reynolds Price is the most prolific of contemporary American literary writers still publishing in 1998. From his first novel in 1962, *A Long and Happy Life,* beginning the Mustian family story, through the sagas of the Kendal-Mayfields in *The Surface of Earth, The Source of Light,* and *The Promise of Rest,* up to *Roxanna Slade* in 1998, Price's fiction has evolved from revealing the thoughts and visions of a simple country girl to exploring the limits of reality in the artist's vision. Rosacoke Mustian wants a conventional life with a family that she believes makes for "a long and happy life." By the time Price presents her again in *Good Hearts,* she has moved into middle age and into an understanding of the reality of loving relationships. In the intervening quarter century, Price contrasts her mature growth with that of the simple girl of rural North Carolina, a move from his depiction of a romantic girl's aspirations to a realistic woman's wisdom.

The larger novels of the Kendal-Mayfields cover the first half of the twentieth century. As he develops narrative technique, Price involves more realistic details to this saga—correspondence, dialogue in conversational diction, internal monologues in poetic imagery. He explores generations of the family through its life cycles, examining inherited traits and tendencies, family, and relationships as confining or supportive. These families, more sophisticated than the Mustians, reveal a comprehension of the continuity of generations, their virtues and vices. The structure is more mythic and the theme more intensive in questioning the mystery in life, an idea Price first introduced in *A Generous Man* (1966) and examined further in *Love and Work* (1968). He deepens his psychological and theological interests as his works develops, translating religious texts and retelling the Gospels. This interest underlies his fiction as well as his non-fiction—a belief in God and prayer, the existence and presence of forms of reality not usually encountered in everyday life. Ironically, as his fiction moves from pastoral, rural yearnings of the heart to the realistic, detailed explorations of the mind, his characters learn their need for transcendency.

Price's microcosm of family sagas depicts humanity's need for this transcendence. His increasing interest in theology takes more direct form in his writings after he came through his own dark night of the soul with spinal cancer in 1984. Afterward, his investigation into philosophical questions increased, his faith in things unseen strengthened. Many of his non-fiction works attest to this interest, such as the biblical and religious examinations and essay collections. *A Whole New Life* metaphorically relates his illness as a death and a descent into hell, his healing as a rebirth.

His memoir *Clear Pictures* (1989) is a result of his learning meditation and being hypnotized to relieve chronic pain from his surgeries. The later novels reflect the meditative influence in the monologues and conversations of characters who come to know and to attain peace with themselves: Wade Mayfield of *The Promise of Rest,* or the title character of *Roxanna Slade,* for instance.

From his earliest writings, Price explored confusions of the heart and mind, the visions of youth and its conflicts with tradition. As his work evolves, he examines more deeply the mind in conflict with itself, family roots and relationships, the failure of the body, the availability of an unseen power, and the disguises of love. His agrarian scenes and provincial characters give way to sophisticated inquirers in middle-class situations. He has called himself the chronicler of his own time and place; he is also the historian of his family and experiences. Personal experience he translates into his writing, reworks into imaginative fiction, shapes into drama, and concentrates into poetry. His raw material for structure, language, scene and characters stems from the eastern North Carolina of his childhood and the Piedmont North Carolina in which he lives.

The language of his fiction reflects the expressions and nuances of his native South, its speech patterns taking a conscious and deliberate shape. "The voice of the story is the vision of the story," he told interviewer Wallace Kaufman. The complexity of his rhetoric matches the complexity of his theme, and he often uses irony for comic effect. For example, Rosacoke Mustian plays the Virgin Mary in a Christmas pageant when she is surely no virgin, nor is she *the Virgin.* The irony turns back on itself as Price implies the innate comedy in human affairs.

Reconciliation is key to Price's characters finding themselves and coming to terms with their lives. In *Good Hearts,* Rosacoke's maturity and compromise with her husband, Wesley, who deserted her in his mid-life crisis, brings about a reconciliation, the "happy" ending she longed for in *A Long and Happy Life.* Rob Mayfield in the longer sagas recognizes he must reconcile with his father's memory in order to have a sense of himself. Wade Mayfield, in *The Promise of Rest,* understands, probably more analytically than do most characters, that he must tie up the loose ends of his life so that he can die peacefully. The journey of life, often begun in quest of some envisioned reward—a long and happy life, a successful career, a care-free existence—takes a new importance in his characters' minds. They mature through understanding that the journey itself is the most important part of life, rather than the attained reward. Then reconciliation takes place, recognition of self and contentment with life are the by-products.

Reynolds Price's structure in his writing develops from an external one in which his landscape impinges on the characters' lives, to an internal one in which the landscape reflects the characters' lives—visions, dreams, philosophical musings. Their internal journeys prepare them for life in the real world, and Price shows this preparation as the process of maturing. They learn to change the things they can and to profit from those they cannot change; they learn reconciliation.

In his latest novel, *Roxanna Slade,* Price uses the voice of a ninety-four-year-old protagonist in a retrospective narrative. Her life covers the entire century and is a history in itself. The author, through Roxanna, takes stock of life and of the time and place, and he finds a will to live—to dance and to sing even if it is

only a hum and a sway—in the aged voice. Her life comes full circle, like a hoop, as the century closes toward the millennium; she shows no fear of death or of the hereafter. Price believes a writer's success is dependent on his opening direct lines to his inner self, the material deposited in his mind. In the final paragraphs of *Clear Pictures,* he says: "If I have an aim to whatever time is left to my faculties, it may be the oldest aim of all, to go on being a picture maker. . . . I concentrate on offering scenes, people in rooms or God in hearts."

—Jeanne R. Nostrandt

PRUNTY, Wyatt

Born: Eugene Wyatt Prunty in Humbolt, Tennessee, 15 May 1947. **Education:** University of the South, B.A. (with honors) 1969; Johns Hopkins University, M.A. 1973; Louisiana State University, Ph.D. 1979. **Military Service:** U. S. Navy, 1969-72; deck and gunnery commissioned officer. **Family:** Married Barbara Heather Svell, 14 August 1973; two children. **Career:** Instructor in English, Louisiana State University, 1978-79; assistant, associate, and full professor of English, Virginia Polytechnic Institute and State University, Blacksburg, 1979-89; visiting associate and professor (Coleman Chair), Johns Hopkins University, 1987-89; Carlton Professor of English and director of the Sewanee Writers' Conference, University of the South, since 1989; taught at various times at Washington and Lee University, Bread Loaf School of English, and Bread Loaf Writers' Conference; poetry editor, *Sewanee Theological Review*; founding editor, Sewanee Writers Series, 1997.

Publications

Poetry Collections

Domestic of the Outer Banks. Inland Boat Press, 1980.
The Times Between. Baltimore, Johns Hopkins University Press, 1982.
What Women Know What Men Believe. Baltimore, Johns Hopkins University Press, 1986.
Balance as Belief. Baltimore, Johns Hopkins University Press, 1989.
The Run of the House. Baltimore, Johns Hopkins University Press, 1993.
Since the Noon Mail Stopped. Baltimore, Johns Hopkins University Press, 1997.

Criticism

Fallen from the Symboled World. New York, Oxford University Press, 1990.

*   *   *

Wyatt Prunty's first published poem appeared in the Autumn 1968 issue of the *Sewanee Review* while the poet was still a student at the University of the South. He was taught and encouraged by Allen Tate and Andrew Lytle, who was then editor of the *Review.* Since graduation from the college, he has published poems singly and in groups in well over a hundred periodical numbers, in an early chapbook called *Domestic of the Outer Banks*, (1980), and in five collections published by the Johns Hopkins University Press: *The Times Between* (1982), *What Women Know What Men Believe* (1986), *Balance as Belief* (1989), *The Run of the House* (1993), and *Since the Noon Mail Stopped* (1997).

After naval service, graduate study, and ten years teaching at Virginia Tech and Johns Hopkins, Prunty returned to Sewanee as Carlton Professor of English in 1989. In that fall, funds received from the estate of Tennessee Williams were deemed sufficient to put into action plans for the Sewanee Writers' conference, and Prunty was named director. He gathered for the summer of 1990 a distinguished group of poets and fiction writers for the faculty and brought in additional writers, editors, publishers, and agents. The achievement of that first summer set a standard that has made the Conference an important gathering place in American letters. In 1991, Prunty became poetry editor of the *Sewanee Theological Review* (formerly *Saint Luke's Journal*), which has since published work by Anthony Hecht, Howard Nemerov, Mona Van Duyn, Richard Wilbur, and many younger poets. In 1997 he became founding editor of a poetry and fiction book project, the Sewanee Writers Series, and brought into print its first volume, John Bricuth's *Just Let Me Say This About That* (1998). Prunty's criticism has appeared in literary quarterlies over the years, and his critical survey of the conditions of contemporary poetry, *Fallen from the Symboled World*, was published by Oxford University Press in 1990.

Prunty's place as a southern writer depends, of course, not on his organizing, editing, or criticism, however distinguished, but on the poems. Much of his work deals with the family and the relationships between generations. He has the natural poetic interest in childhood and an equally pronounced interest in the aging, finding courage and wisdom but also humor and despair in physical and mental decline. Memorable passages bring youth and age together. In the powerful narrative poem "Haying," a boy pursued by yellow jackets falls to the bed of a truck and cannot move. The older men gather, put tobacco juice on the stings but, knowing their limits, wait patiently for the doctor, not knowing if the boy's future is play time or paralysis: "The men talk on, as calmly as before— / Complain about the heat, swat flies, light up." In "A Winter's Tale," the birth of a son and death of a father collide mysteriously: "Ian, your birth was my close land / Turned green, the stone rolled back for leaving, / My father dead and you returned." Seldom is the poet so personal and, though often serious, somber. He can also move to humor with Nemerovian wit. In "The Actuarial Wife," the title character says about her children, "We should have waited until / They were older to have them." Faced with a husband who smokes, she "clarifies their options for retirement: 'Darling, if one of us dies, / I'm going to live in Paris.'"

One also finds a number of writerly poems tied through dedication, dramatization, or echo to Stevens, Frost, Auden, Thomas, Graves, Roethke, Nemerov, Wilbur, Lowell, Justice, and others. Another fertile strategy for Prunty, an American strategy that looks back to Jonathan Edwards as much as to Emerson, is to seize on a small event or object and pay attention until an emblematic power emerges. The behavior of birds or dogs, a box of leaves, or music on a stand, even a Zamboni at the rink will serve this pur-

pose. The results can be disturbing, even shocking, or humorous, but they always surprise in the way the commonplace can do when it ceases to be common.

Prunty is often associated with the new formalism which, in view of his critical book (subtitled *Precedents for the New Formalism*), his verse, and the preferences he has declared seems fair enough. Fair if one bears in mind that the term covers a vast and complex range of purpose and practice. Prunty has expressed his own frustrations with the label, but admits that it "seems the best we can do-for now." His verse is in fact formal, though it is not a collection of ornate historical or nonce forms. Some handful of poems in *Since the Noon Mail Stopped* have fourteen lines, for example, but only one is in the strict sense a sonnet. Most of the verse is blank with frequent variation between four and five beat lines and a loose iambic base; some lines are so loose as to seem extra-metrical. He uses rhyme with skill but sparely, and while some poems are tightly rhymed from start to finish, others begin in blank verse and introduce distant and slant rhyme so subtly that only at the close does the rhymed environment assert itself. Such verse is formal, to be sure, but hardly the stuff to justify, if they are ever justified, cries of repressive and elitist tactics.

On the contrary, Prunty's forms are consonant with his own claims that the issue is not so much form as it is the poet's "modes of thought, the means for figuration." Among the many "figurative modes of thought" that interest Prunty, he has special praise for the "New Critical staples of irony, paradox, and ambiguity." Not surprisingly, perhaps, these are staples of his own poetry. In "The Kite," a poem first published in 1975, "the private craft of kites" serves as a figure for poetry. "Flying by the force of being held," kite and formal poem survive through the skill of one who understands "This craft of putting fragile things aloft, / Of letting go and holding on at once."

A similar paradox is at the heart of Prunty's justly celebrated and most frequently appropriated poem, "Learning the Bicycle," which opens the 1989 collection, *Balance as Belief*. Here the speaker thinks back on his daughter's failed attempts to ride but knows that on some tomorrow she will balance on her bike and ride away, far from

> the place I stop and know
> That to teach her I had to follow
> And when she learned I had to let her go.

Prunty's epigrammatic force reminds us of Donne's formulations of Christian paradox: "That I may rise and stand, o'erthrow me," or "Therefore that he may raise the Lord throws down."

In the remarkable poem "Good-bye," Prunty uncovers the tensions between the reassuring warmth of the title's etymology— God be with you—and the cold pain of love's separations: "This is good-bye, this breaks the heart." The poem's understanding of the battered heart and the fallen world would be wholly familiar to Donne. In the world of Prunty's poem, "the root takes hold, . . . and burrows out of sight":

> Like our Fall again, self-separating
> And hungry as our nakedness.
> Whatever leaf we took to cover that

Turned into sickness and to death—
A mother's pain, and food by sweat
Out of a grudging field whose furrows
Approximate the way we end.

Paradox gives way to rich and painful paradox pointing, in terrifying language, to a familiar resolution:

We eat and drink
Good-bye collectively, and call
It love by a raveling tale.

. . . .

We arrive out of our terrible freedom
Which kills and loves us like a starving mother.

The poem's exploration of the passages of life, the ritual beginnings and endings, is difficult, almost surreal, but finds its form
and psychological depth in the poet's secure handling of the familiar counters of our poetic tradition, the symbols of belief.

—William E. Clarkson

R

REED, Ishmael

Born: Emmett Coleman, took his surname from his stepfather, Bennie Stephen Reed, in Chattanooga, Tennessee, 22 February 1938. **Education:** Attended State University of New York at Buffalo, 1956-60. **Family:** Married Priscilla Rose, 1960 (divorced 1970); one son and one daughter; married Carla Blank (a modern dancer); one daughter. **Career:** Teacher in prose workshop, St. Mark's in the Bowery, New York City, 1966; co-founder and director, Yardbird Publishing Company, Berkeley, California, 1971-75; co-founder, Reed, Cannon & Johnson Communications, Berkeley, 1973, Before Columbus Foundation, Berkeley, 1976, and *Quilt* magazine, Berkeley, 1980; guest lecturer, University of California at Berkeley, University of Washington, State University of New York at Buffalo, Yale University, Dartmouth College, Sitka Community Association, Columbia University, University of Arkansas at Fayetteville, and Harvard University; Regent's Lecturer at the University of California, Santa Barbara, 1988. **Awards:** National Endowment for the Arts writing fellowship, 1974; Guggenheim award, 1974; National Institute of Arts and Letters award, 1975; Lewis Michaux award, 1978; American Civil Liberties Union award, 1978; Pushcart Prize, 1979; three New York State publishing grants for merit; three National Endowment for the Arts publishing grants for merit; California Arts Council grant.

PUBLICATIONS

Novels

The Free-Lance Pallbearers. Garden City, New York, Doubleday, 1967.
Yellow Back Radio Broke-Down. Garden City, New York, 1969.
Mumbo Jumbo. Garden City, New York, Doubleday, 1972.
The Last Days of Louisiana Red. New York, Random House, 1974.
Flight to Canada. New York, Random House, 1976.
The Terrible Twos. New York, St. Martin's Press, 1982.
Reckless Eyeballing. New York, St. Martin's Press, 1986.
The Terrible Threes. New York, Atheneum, 1989.
Japanese by Spring. New York, Atheneum, 1993.

Poetry Collections

catechism of d neoamerican hoodoo church. London, Paul Breman, 1970.
Conjure: Selected Poems, 1963-70. Amherst, University of Massachusetts Press, 1972.
Chattanooga: Poems. New York, Random House, 1973.
A Secretary to the Spirits. New York, NOK, 1978.
New and Collected Poems. New York, Atheneum, 1988.

Essay Collections

Shrovetide in Old New Orleans. Garden City, New York, Doubleday, 1978.
God Made Alaska for the Indians: Selected Essays. New York, Garland, 1982.

Writin' is Fightin': Thirty-Seven Years of Boxing on Paper. New York, Atheneum, 1988.
Airing Dirty Laundry. Reading, Massachussetts, Addison-Wesley, 1993.

Other

Cab Calloway Stands In for the Moon. Flint, Michigan, Bamberger Books, 1986.

Editor, *The Rise, Fall, and . . . ? of Adam Clayton Powell.* New York. Bee-Line, 1967.
Editor, *19 Necromancers from Now.* Garden City, New York, Doubleday, 1970.
Editor, *Yardbird Lives!* New York, Grove, 1978.
Editor, *Calafia: The California Poetry.* Berkeley, Y'bird Books, 1979.
Editor, with Kathryn Trueblood and Shawn Wong, *The Before Columbus Foundation Fiction Anthology: Selections from the American Book Awards, 1980-1990.* New York, W. W. Norton, 1992.
Editor, with Kathryn Trueblood and Shawn Wong, *The Before Columbus Foundation Poetry Anthology.* New York, Norton, 1992.
Editor, *Multi America: Essays on Cultural Wars and Cultural Peace.* New York, Viking Books, 1997.

Play

The Lost State of Franklin, with Carla Blank and Suzushi Hanayagi. 1976.

*

Recordings: *Ishmael Reed Reading His Poetry,* 1976; *Ishmael Reed and Michael Harper Reading in the UCSD New Poetry Series,* 1977.

Bibliography: *Ishmael Reed: A Primary and Secondary Bibliography* by Elizabeth A. Settle and Thomas A. Settle, Boston, G. K. Hall, 1982.

Interviews: With Robert Gover, *Black American Literature Forum,* Spring 1978; with Kevin Bezner, *Mississippi Review,* Vol. 20, nos. 1-2, 1991; *Ishmael Reed: An Interview* by Cameron Northouse, Dallas, Contemporary Research Press, 1993; *Conversations with Ishmael Reed* edited by Amritjit Singh and Bruce Dick, Mississippi, University of Mississippi Press, 1995.

Critical Studies: "Ishmael Reed and the Politics of Aesthetics, or Shake Hands and Come Out Conjuring" by Chester J. Fontenot, *Black American Literature Forum,* Spring 1978; *Ishmael Reed and the New Black Aesthetic Critics* by Reginald Martin, 1987; "Ishmael Reed's Syncretic Use of Language: Bathos as Popular Discourse" by Reginald Martin, *Modern Language Studies,* Spring 1990; "Chango, el gran putas as Liberation Literature" by Ian I. Smart, *College Language Association Journal,* September 1991; "Postmodernism, Ethnicity and Underground Revisionism in Ishmael Reed" by David Mikics, *Postmodern Culture,* May 1991; "The Limbs of Osiris: Reed's *Mumbo Jumbo* and Hollywood's

The Mummy" by Carol Siri Johnson, *MELUS,* Winter 1991-92; "Babaluaiye: Searching for the Text of a Pandemic" by Barbara Browning, *AIDS: The Literary Response* edited by Emmanuel S. Nelson, 1992; *Ishmael Reed,* by Jay Boyer, Boise, Boise State University, 1993; *Ishmael Reed and the Ends of Race* by Patrick McGee, New York, St. Martin's Press, 1997.

* * *

An interview with Malcolm X cost Ishmael Reed his job as cohost on the liberal Buffalo, New York, Community Roundtable radio show and set the controversial tone for much of the critical reception to the work of this, until recently, highly underrated novelist, poet and essayist. In "serious play," Reed's work challenges literary and cultural conventions through parody and satire. His imaginative fusion of beliefs and "dialects" of folk culture with such diverse genres as science fiction, film, Westerns, and detective novels parodies the received form of the novel and resonates in the assertion of his character, the Loop Garoo Kid, that, "No one says a novel has to be one thing. It can be anything it wants."

Reed's first novel *The Free-Lance Pallbearers* (1967) reveals his concern over his own relationship to the Afro-American literary tradition and its relationship to the Western tradition. An inversion of the confessional African American narrative, this novel, told by Bukka Doopeyduk, parodies the narrative voices used in works by Wright, Baldwin, Hurston and Ellison. At the same time, Reed's good versus evil dichotomy blames individuals from all strata and races for betraying and exploiting poor African Americans. Actualizing his call for complete artistic freedom and expression, Reed includes negative black characters and also individualizes his writing style through non-standard spellings, oddly placed capitalizations and radio broadcast techniques. In *Yellow Back Radio Broke-Down* (1969), Reed adds Hoodoo (vaudou or, popularly, voodoo) to his signature characteristics, which he explains in the essay "Shrovetide in Old New Orleans." This metaphysical system of signs syncretizes aspects of African, Caribbean and South American religions and emphasizes the African concept of time, where past and present events overlap, thus appearing to occur simultaneously. This overlap moves throughout *Yellow Back Radio Broke-Down* beginning with the Homeric dactyl hexameter meter of the novel's title. Here, Reed merges his knowledge of classical mythology with his play with group dialects—in street-talk, "broke down" means to explain. Set in the nineteenth century but embraced by the 1960s counter-culture, this send up of the western novel sets the Loop Garu Kid, a divine HooDoo jester in disguise, as a circus lariat and whipsnake artist against the wealthy rancher Drag Gibson, to whom the desperate adults have turned after their children take over the town of Yellow Back Radio. Reed intends The Kid's predicament to parallel that of the modern black in white Christian society.

Reed uses radio techniques to outline the complicated symbolic narrative of *Mumbo Jumbo* (1972), a novel about writing camouflaged as a detective story. In 1920s New Orleans traditional conditioned behavior breaks down because of the electrifying anti-plague "Jes Grew," a HooDoo counterattack to the modern wasteland. Detective Papa LeBas searches for the only written text of the black Osiris, which represents the critic searching and decoding a text, just as the reader must decode the doubling and redou-

bling signification in this postmodern novel. Amid murder, jazz, mythology and HooDoo, Reed attacks Christianity, parodies intertextuality, and mimics scholarly apparatus as he develops his theme of the origins of the true Afro-American aesthetic.

In *The Last Days of Louisiana Red*, Papa LeBas reappears to solve the murder of restauranteur Ed Yellings, whose gumbo cures certain cancers. The ensuing family struggle parodies Antigone, complete with Chorus, as a sister sets brother against brother. Pointing to the novel's matriarchy and finding unpalatable the characters Minnie, co-opted by white consumerism, and Nanny Lisa, a black mammy gone bad, some critics accused Reed of misogyny; others pointed to the larger issue of what these women lose through assimilation.

Flight to Canada (1976), a slave narrative/historical novel, focuses on the divisiveness of assimilation and the obligation of the artist as mediator between the past and the future. Reed presents the stories of three fugitive slaves against that of their immensely wealthy, depraved master, Arthur Swille III, whose vision is to became king after the North and the South destroy each other. While two slaves, representative "types," hold values reminiscent of Reed's earlier characters, the third, writer Raven Quickskill, seeks his freedom in Canada, where he learns that freedom is a state of mind as much as a place. Using his HooDoo, Quickskill becomes a distinguished poet and returns as the appropriate biographer of Swille's heir, Uncle Robin, the "faithful" slave, a disguised HooDoo priest. Robin symbolizes the past while Quickskill the writer (Reed?) points toward the future.

The futuristic *The Terrible Twos* (1982) and its sequel *The Terrible Threes* (1989) satirize Reaganomics and its consequences. In an all too familiar fictional America, a former model is President, a television executive runs the country, the CIA fakes wars for conservative purposes, and Santa Claus intercedes to save New York City from a bombing that will be blamed on Third World countries. Santa Claus finally reconciles with Black Peter, his estranged blackamoor partner, and the two vainly try to surmount the ills of a self interested America caught in its childlike "terrible" stages.

Reed breaks new ground in *Reckless Eyeballing* (1986) as he looks at the consequences of assimilation for all hyphenated-Americans. In the novel the seductive American Dream lures black characters in search of success, like playwright Ian Ball, into self betrayal. Reed shows blacks following the same pattern of earlier ethnic groups. *Japanese by Spring* (1993) features the sudden rise to power of humanities professor Chappie Puttputt at Jack London College, and includes one Ishmael Reed as commentator on such events as the aftermath of the Rodney King trial. The novel takes aim at academics, feminists, Anita Hill, political correctness and Japanese baiting.

In addition to novels, Reed has also published collections of poetry and essays that focus on his concern with the freedom, or lack thereof, of the black in American society. This concern corresponds with his early cofounding of Yardbird Publishing Company in 1971, Reed, Cannon, and Johnson Communications Company in 1973, and the Before Columbus Foundation in 1976, all intended to assist and encourage minority writers and develop a more accurate American literature. For Yardbird Publishing, Reed edited *The Yardbird Readers*; he also edited *Multi America: Essays on Cultural Wars and Cultural Peace* (1997), which continues the discussion of assimilation and racial conflict. Its contributors include Morrison and Baraka, but more importantly, artists and students representing multi-ethnic America. They are Reed's American literary gumbo, which is multicolored, multivocal and multicultural.

—Judith C. Kohl

REED, John Shelton

Born: 8 January 1942. **Education:** Massachusetts Institute of Technology, B.S. 1964; Columbia University, Ph.D. 1970. **Family:** Married Dale Volberg, 1964; two children. **Career:** William Rand Kenan, Jr., Professor of Sociology, adjunct professor of American Studies, and director of the Institute for Research in Social Science, University of North Carolina at Chapel Hill; Fulbright-Hays senior lecturer in American studies and sociology, Hebrew University of Jerusalem, 1973-74; senior associate member, St. Antony's College, Oxford University, 1977-78. **Award:** Guggenheim fellow, St Antony's College, Oxford University, 1977-78. **Member:** American Sociological Association, American Association for Public Opinion Research, Southern Sociological Society, Southern Historical Association. **Address:** c/o Social Forces, Hamilton Hall, University of North Carolina, Chapel Hill, North Carolina 27514.

PUBLICATIONS

The Enduring Effects of Education, with Herbert H. Hyman and Charles R. Wright.
The Enduring South. Washington, D.C., Heath 1972.
One South. Baton Rouge, Louisiana State University Press, 1982.
Southerners. Chapel Hill, University of North Carolina Press, 1983.
Perspectives on the American South, with Merle Black. New York, Gordon and Breach, 1984.
Southern Folk, Plain and Fancy. Athens, University of Georgia Press, 1986.
Whistling Dixie: Dispatches from the South. New York, Harcourt Brace, 1990.
Surveying the South. Columbia, University of Missouri Press, 1993.
My Tears Spoiled My Aim and Other Reflections on Southern Culture. New York, Harcourt Brace, 1993.
Kicking Back. Columbia, University of Missouri Press, 1995.
Southern Humor. Durham, Duke University Press, 1995.
Glorious Battle. Nashville, Vanderbilt University Press, 1996.
1001 Things Everyone Should Know About the South, with Dale V. Reed. New York, Doubleday, 1997.
Sports in the South. Chapel Hill, University of North Carolina Press, 1997.

*   *   *

For almost as long as there has been a South there have been confident predictions of its cultural demise. To elegant Virginians, the settlement of the crude Mississippi and Alabama fron-

tier signaled the end of Southern civilization. In William Faulkner's "The Tall Men" we find that estimable Mississippian's fear that New Deal price supports would destroy the self-reliance of the Southern small farmer, and in our own time many point to the emergence of the mall culture as yet another sign of "the end of the South as we know it."

Against this conventional wisdom, John Shelton Reed has built a distinguished career by exploring the ways in which the South remains distinctive, beginning with his first book, *The Enduring South*, which revealed the findings of a number of surveys on Southern attitudes. For example, Southerners watch less television than others and consider spending time with friends a very important leisure activity. Support for capital punishment and traditional Protestant Christianity remains much higher in the South than in the country at large. Most important, though, Southerners claim a stronger allegiance to region than other Americans, which Reed considers compelling evidence of a persistent Southern identity.

Reed came to his awareness of Southern distinctiveness as many others have—by living in the north. Growing up in east Tennessee, he had little reason to reflect on the matter, but after moving on to the Massachusetts Institute of Technology he learned that "when a young man or woman from the South goes to school in the North, you are reminded where you came from. You are called upon to defend it." Reed's response to this challenge is a long string of books written for both academic and popular audiences and his work as a columnist in a number of conservative journals.

A recent work directed toward readers outside academe is *1001 Things Everyone Should Know About the South*. As its title promises, *1001 Things* is an extensive collection of short essays on almost every imaginable aspect of Southern culture, from "Grit Lit" to foodways to the greater significance of Elvis. In a similar vein, *Whistling Dixie* collects a number of pieces written for such publications as the *Daily Tarheel* and the *Georgia Historical Review*. Both of these books highlight one of the most notable characteristics of Reed's work: its willingness to delve into issues of popular culture, something still fairly unusual in academic circles. Reed seems to revel in what many refer to as "low culture" and even shares with his readers such gems of the lower orders as a recipe for vienna sausage sandwiches. Regarding a recent North Carolina controversy over a city ordinance forbidding upholstered furniture on porches, Reed commented on the law's hidden class agenda, given how the poor tend to move their worn living room furniture onto the porch, and remarked, "they can have my La-Z-Boy when they pry it from my cold, dead hands."

Reed's willingness to take ordinary Southerners quite seriously is at the center of an earlier and very highly regarded book, *Southern Folk, Plain and Fancy*. As other writers have before him, as varied as Daniel Hundley and William Faulkner, Reed creates a social typology of Southerners, but unlike these predecessors he views the "plain people" with a strong measure of sympathy. Long predating the current (and sudden) academic interest in poor whites, this book examines the longtime scapegoating of the plain people, who have been blamed for everything from the South's poverty to its history of racial conflict, and proposes, as an alternative to the traditional cracker, a people with a distinctive culture worthy of serious study and preservation.

The other chief strain running through Reed's work, one that at first seems to contradict his interest in popular culture, is a conservatism that has much more in common with I'll Take My Stand than with the "Contract with America." Reed praises the South's adherence to what Faulkner called "the old verities" and laments such "trendy foolishness" as political correctness. He defends the rebel flag, arguing that although some have flown it for objectionable reasons, in the end it is not a symbol of racism but of Southern bravery. In one of his frequent contributions to *Reason*, a conservative journal, Reed suggests that modern students read the Agrarians, who "disliked alienated labor and automobiles, ecological degradation and total war, all fashionable complaints on modern campuses" yet offered solutions that were "very old- fashioned: The family farm. Revealed religion. Good manners."

That Reed's combination of genuine delight in the culture of the plain people and social conservatism seems contradictory says more about what passes for conservatism today than it does about Reed. Those who have grown used to the modern right's disdain for the poor might be surprised to find that there is a tradition of conservatism that values common people, even the lowest among them, and that Reed, along with the Agrarians, Richard M. Weaver, and even the antebellum pro-slavery theorists, stands in this strain of Southern thought.

—Jason Mitchell

REYNOLDS, Sheri

Born: Conway, South Carolina, 19 August 1967. **Education:** Davidson College, A.B. 1989; Virginia Commonwealth University, M.F.A. 1992. **Career:** Instructor in creative writing, Old Dominion University, Norfolk, Virginia. **Email address:** SReynolds@odu.edu

PUBLICATIONS

Novels

Bitterroot Landing. New York, Putnam, 1994.
The Rapture of Canaan. New York, Putnam 1995.
A Gracious Plenty. New York, Harmony Books, 1997.

* * *

Like Mary Lee Settle, who often refers to the voices of her past, Sheri Reynolds is a novelist for whom voices—past and present, those of author and character—inform every aspect of her work. She follows the themes of innocence and miracles into the sacred realm of nature. She creates heroines alienated from their surroundings, yet strong and terrible enough to transcend the mundane and survive in the small towns of the American South.

In 1994, Reynolds published the first of her three novels, *Bitterroot Landing*, which tells the story of Jael, who is sold for sex by her grandmother, then adopted by a deacon. After running away from his river boat only to be seduced and abandoned by a virtual stranger, she hides out in the woods and begins matter-of-

factly to mutilate her body. During this time, in the shelter of an enormous oak, she begins to be healed by nature's divine power. Later, she is rescued and taken to a small city. After beginning work as a church janitor, she receives the same healing from spirit figures that actually grow from within her own soul and speak with her voice.

In 1995, *The Rapture of Canaan* was published to very little initial response. However, when Reynolds' second book became an Oprah Winfrey recommended read sales skyrocketed and reviews poured in. Referred to as her second coming-of-age novel, *Rapture* was praised for its real characters and its devastating portrayal of organized religion. Reynolds uses lyrical and graceful language to tell a staggering tale. Nynah Huff is Reynolds' fifteen year old narrator and the granddaughter of the founder of the Church of Fire and Brimstone and God's Almighty Baptizing Wind.

Life is harsh and isolated for this group in rural Carolina, and Nynah has questions about how to live within the theology of her grandfather's church while being tempted by her prayer partner James. Nynah finds herself listening to the voices of her family and friends, asking Jesus for some guidance, and finally listening to what comes from within herself. The result of her independence is catastrophic to the congregation and her grandfather, but liberating for both Nynah and those she feels responsible for.

A Gracious Plenty (1997) emerged to praise for the lyric quality of its prose and much criticism of the plot, which some critics referred to as unbelievable. Other critics called her story charming and inventive, finding her story, voice, and characters nothing less than authentic. Finch Noble is a woman who, at the age of four, was scarred by boiling water and has been isolated ever since. She owns and cares for the cemetery that sits beside her house, and as the story begins, learns to speak to the spirits who rest there. With the communion between the living and the dead, the theme of voices that emerged in Reynolds' earlier books grows to a fever pitch here. In a chorus reminiscent of Greek drama, the spirits reveal their regrets and teach Finch about her rural Southern town. With their help, Finch solves two town mysteries and challenges the hypocrisy of her hometown. In the end, though, it is Finch's own voice that she must listen to.

Throughout her writings, Reynolds creates characters who follow the voices they hear. Her compassion for those characters and her desire to get them out of the dire circumstances in which they find themselves have earned the ultimate respect of a readership eager to listen to what she has to say next, in the voice they've come to recognize as hers.

—Virginia Watkins

RICE, Anne

Pseudonyms: Anne Rampling; A. N. Roquelaure. **Born:** Howard Allen O'Brien in New Orleans, Louisiana, 4 October 1941; name changed to Anne c. 1947. **Education:** Texas Women's University, Denton, Texas, 1959-60; San Francisco State College (now University), B.A. 1964, M.A. 1971; University of California, Berkeley, 1969-70. **Family:** Married Stan Rice, 1961; one daughter,

Michele (deceased), and one son, Christopher. **Career:** Has held a variety of jobs, including waitress, cook, theater usherette, and insurance claims examiner; full-time writer since the 1970s. **Awards:** Joseph Henry Jackson Award (honorable mention), 1970. **Agent:** Jacklyn Nesbit Associates, 598 Madison Ave., New York, New York 10022.

PUBLICATIONS

Novels

The Feast of All Saints. New York, Simon and Schuster, 1980.
Cry to Heaven. New York, Knopf, 1982.
The Mummy; or, Ramses the Damned. New York, Ballantine, 1989.
Vampire Chronicles.
   Interview with the Vampire. New York, Knopf, 1976.
   The Vampire Lestat. New York, Ballantine, 1985.
   The Queen of the Damned. New York, Knopf, 1988.
   The Tale of the Body Thief. New York, Knopf, 1992.
   Memnoch the Devil. New York, Knopf, 1995.
Lives of the Mayfair Witches.
   The Witching Hour. New York, Knopf, 1990.
   Lasher. New York, Knopf, 1993.
   Taltos: Lives of the Mayfair Witches. New York, Knopf, 1994.
The Servant of the Bones. New York, Knopf, Random House Large Print, 1996.
Violin. New York, Knopf, 1997.
Pandora : New Tales of the Vampires. New York, Knopf, 1998.

Novels as Anne Rampling

Exit to Eden. New York, Arbor House, 1985.
Belinda. New York, Arbor House, 1986.

Novels as A. N. Roquelaure

The Claiming of Sleeping Beauty. New York, Dutton, 1983.
Beauty's Punishment. New York, Dutton, 1984.
Beauty's Release: The Continued Erotic Adventures of Sleeping Beauty. New York, Dutton, 1985.
The Sleeping Beauty Novels: The Claiming of Sleeping Beauty, Beauty's Punishment, and Beauty's Release. New York, Dutton, 1991.

*

Film Adaptations: *Interview with the Vampire*, 1994; *Exit to Eden*, 1994.

Critical Studies: *Prism of the Night: A Biography of Anne Rice* by Katherine M. Ramsland, New York, Dutton, 1991; *Anne Rice* by Bette B. Roberts, New York, Twayne, 1994; *Conversations With Anne Rice* by Michael Riley and Anne Rice, New York, Fawcett Books, 1996; *The Gothic World of Anne Rice*, edited by Gary Hoppenstand and Ray B. Browne. Bowling Green, Bowling Green State University Press, 1996.

Video: *A Visit with Anne Rice*, VHS Tape, New Orleans, Corbitt Design, Inc., 1997.

*   *   *

"[I am] a divided person with different voices, like an actor playing different roles," commented Anne Rice in an interview with the *New York Times*. Author of nearly twenty novels under as many as three pseudonyms, Anne Rice (born Howard Allen O'Brien) has produced a rich and increasingly diverse oeuvre, each area of which has proven quite successful, both among popular audiences and, to a lesser extent, among critics. The fragmentation of Rice's own corpus into three thematic rubrics, as well as three distinct, corresponding authorial voices, has yielded over the span of her prolific career a surprisingly unified and cohesive body of work—one which, perhaps by virtue of that very fragmented character, has appealed so profoundly to an increasingly motley postmodern readership.

Under her own name, Anne Rice portrays a variety of supernatural phenomena and agents of the occult, each of which she endows with her trademark human sensitivity and integrates into the relevant fabric of contemporary (usually Southern) American society; of these, Rice's most enduringly successful effort remains her first novel, *Interview with the Vampire* (1976), which acquired considerable critical acclaim and accrued a readership of cult proportions.

Under the pseudonym Anne Rampling, meanwhile, she produced a pair of novels—*Exit to Eden* (1985) and *Belinda* (1986)—which, while decidedly more mainstream in content than her occult fiction, nonetheless retain a moderate measure of sexuality, an aspect which she has explored consistently and aggressively until it has since become a dominating and oft-celebrated feature of her corpus at large. This articulation of sexuality is pushed to more shrill level in the *Sleeping Beauty* trilogy, a series written under the pen name A. N. Roquelaure that explores through the narrative agency of the fairy-tale princess, Sleeping Beauty, a realm of sadomasochistic fantasy and erotic congress. Clearly delineated along the author's three noms de plum, these three genres indicate a variety of disparate themes, styles, and of course, subject matter. Governing her work entire, however, is the undeniable presence of Rice's own singular literary imagination, a voice which synthesizes these divergent thematic strands into a unified, if multifarious, whole.

Rice's first offering, *Interview with the Vampire*, is generally considered her flagship novel, predicating both a creative and stylistic standard against which the successive texts of the *Vampire Chronicles* may be measured. Organized as a flashback, the narrative features Louis, a brooding, world-weary, Byronic protagonist who is converted unwillingly to vampirism, and, as such, is forced into an eternal, unnatural existence comprised of alternating violence and solitude.

In *Interview with the Vampire*, Rice not only chronicles the unfortunate events of Louis's life from the moment of his conversion in 1791 to the date of the eponymous interview in the mid-1970s, but also establishes a particular setting, at once historic and atmospheric, that underscores the profoundly sensual, cathartic character of the novel at large: the story's lavish setting in belle epoque New Orleans proves just as crucial to Rice's construction of the decadent narrative as does her careful development of Louis, his mentor Lestat, and their protégé, Claudia. Moreover, many critics have commented on the emphatically erotic undertones that color both the potent relationship between Louis and Lestat, as well as traditional vampire lore in general, and have cited counter-culture audiences in particular as the original source of Rice's readership.

From its counterculture genesis, *Interview with the Vampire* has garnered greater and greater popular (if not always critical) appeal, perhaps because the basic themes with which Rice is concerned—good and evil, love and loss, sex and death—remain so profoundly universal to the human experience. As Susan Ferraro commented in *New York Times Magazine:* "Rice's vampires are loquacious philosophers who spend much of eternity debating the nature of good and evil. Trapped in immortality, they suffer human regret. They are lonely, prisoners of circumstance, compulsive sinners, full of self-loathing and doubt. They are, in short, Everyman Eternal."

Second in the *Vampire Chronicles* series is *The Vampire Lestat* (1985), in which Rice relegates her former protagonist, Louis, to a marginal role, instead tracing the convoluted history of Lestat's vampiric experience from his initial conversion to his stint as a leather-clad, Harley-riding rock star in the mid-1980s. Presented as Lestat's autobiography, in an elaborate publicity campaign to inaugurate his new music career, *The Vampire Lestat* not only chronicles the history of vampirism and vampire discourse from its origins in ancient Egypt, but also investigates more explicitly and extensively than *Interview with the Vampire* the ontological implications of vampirism in general.

The Vampire Lestat was met with only lukewarm reviews, as was the third installment in the series, *The Queen of the Damned* (1988), which features a matriarchal tyrant, Akasha, whom Lestat has awakened from a long dormancy. Mother to all vampires, Akasha intends to repair the miseries of the world by obliterating all but ten percent of human males and by organizing a peaceful matriarchy in their stead. While Rice has, to a large extent, marginalized the role of Lestat in *The Queen of the Damned*, and has instead handed over narrative duties to an entire collection of vampires, Lestat once again seizes the limelight in *The Tale of the Body Thief* (1992).

The fourth installment of the *Vampire Chronicles* recounts Lestat's increasing exhaustion and frustration with immortality, as well as his fruitless suicide attempt. Approached by a mortal who agrees to exchange bodies with Lestat for several days, he may once again encounter his world through the limited and flawed vision of a mortal, and only begins to (re)adjust to some of the more ignominious functions and exigencies of human existence before his partner absconds with Lestat's previous, immortal body. Lestat, now saddled with an awkward human form, makes a final appearance in *Memnoch the Devil* (1995), reportedly the last of the *Vampire Chronicles*. Like Dante, Lestat embarks on a guided tour of heaven, hell, and purgatory at the behest of Satan himself, who attempts to recruit Lestat as his assistant. In this final (and, according to many critics, exceedingly ambitious) offering, Rice refuses to cap neatly the vast catalogue of vampires she has posited in the four preceding texts, allowing them instead to spill forth in a perverse and encyclopedic parade—to be apotheosized or anathematized as the reader alone sees fit.

Although the literary life of Lestat (supposedly) ended with *Memnoch the Devil* in 1995, Rice's long-standing preoccupa-tion with the supernatural has hardly abated. Throughout the two decades that spanned her production of the *Vampire Chronicles*, Rice released to dismal reviews *The Mummy: or, Ramses the Damned* (1989), in which a British Egyptologist resuscitates the mummy of the ancient Egyptian ruler, Ramses the Great, with a restorative elixir. Shortly thereafter, Rice published *The Witching Hour* (1990), the first in the *Lives of the Mayfair Witches* trilogy, all of which were set in Rice's own antebellum New Orleans mansion. In the first novel of three, Rice introduces Rowan Mayfair, the thirteenth of the many generations of Mayfair witches, who must protect herself from the malevolent Lasher.

The sequel, *Lasher* (1993), features the reincarnation of the titular character as the son of Rowan Mayfair, while the third and final installment, *Taltos* (1994), introduces a beneficent giant, Ashlar, who also becomes closely involved with the Mayfair witches. Predictably, reviewers and audiences alike found the *Mayfair Witches* series considerably less convincing and less compelling than the *Vampire Chronicles*, in part because the rather byzantine narratives of the Mayfairs remain highly self-referential and, as such, esoteric, requiring that the reader be familiar with a dense litany of characters and locales.

Abandoning for the moment her status as purveyor of the supernatural, Rice turned her attentions to more terrestrial (though hardly banal) subject matter in her historical novels, *The Feast of All Saints* (1980) and *Cry to Heaven* (1982). The former explores the difficulties and anxieties of a fair-skinned mulatto boy, Marcel Ferronaire, and his sister, Marie, who, like some 18,000 free people of color in antebellum Louisiana, lived with and among the contradictory forces of freedom and discrimination. Thematically speaking, *The Feast of All Saints* is not so much of a departure from the *Vampire Chronicles* and the *Mayfair Witches* series as it might initially appear; like her occult novels, her historical fiction concentrates on the perspective of an outside observer, a pariah who may participate in the hegemonic society only peripherally. In *Cry to Heaven*, meanwhile, Rice makes this theme almost physically explicit: her narrative foray into the arena of eighteenth-century Italian castrati yields the tale of Tonio Treschi, a Venetian soprano whose brother has him kidnaped and castrated. The androgynous figure of Tonio appears wholly concomitant with Rice's earlier representations of homoerotics in the *Vampire Chronicles*. *Violin* (1997) reappropriates the musical sensuality of *Cry to Heaven* in a narrative that weds both her supernatural and her historical traditions. In none of her historical novels, however, does Rice allow that latent sexuality free reign.

If *Violin* represents Rice's fusion of history and the occult, *Exit to Eden* and *Belinda*, both written under the pseudonym Anne Rampling, offer a synthesis of erotic and romantic narratives. Both novels assume the form not of erotica proper, but rather of conventional romances tempered with a heaping dose of sadomasochistic sexuality. Only in her self-described erotic novels, written under the pseudonym A. N. Roquelaure, does Rice allow that sexual impulse to exist in a wholly unfettered form. *The Claiming of Sleeping Beauty* (1983), *Beauty's Punishment* (1984), and *Beauty's Release: The Continued Erotic Adventures of Sleeping Beauty* (1985) all represent considerable variations on the Sleeping Beauty fairy-tale and trace the journey of Beauty's sexual initiation within a fantastic arena that Rice herself has termed in an interview with *People*, "the Disneyland of S&M."

—L. Michelle Wallace

RICH, Adrienne

Born: Adrienne Cecile Rich in Baltimore, Maryland, 16 May 1929. **Education**: Roland Park Country School, Baltimore, 1938-47; Radcliffe College, Cambridge, Massachusetts, A.B. (cum laude) 1951 (Phi Beta Kappa). **Family**: Married Alfred H. Conrad, 1953 (died 1970); three children. **Career**: Lived in the Netherlands, 1961-62; taught at YM-YWHA Poetry Center Workshop, New York, 1966-67; visiting poet, Swarthmore College, Pennsylvania, 1966-68; adjunct professor, Graduate Writing Division, Columbia University, New York, 1967-69; lecturer, 1968-70, instructor, 1970-71, assistant professor of English, 1971-72, and professor, 1974-75, City College of New York; Fannie Hurst Visiting Professor, Brandeis University, Waltham, Massachusetts, 1972-73; professor of English, Douglass College, New Brunswick, New Jersey, 1976-78; A.D. White Professor-at-Large, Cornell University, Ithaca, New York, 1981-85; visiting professor, San José State University, California, 1985-86; professor of English and feminist studies, Stanford University, California, since 1986; Clark Lecturer and distinguished visiting professor, Scripps College, Claremont, California, 1983; Burgess Lecturer, Pacific Oaks College, Pasadena, California, 1986; columnist, *American Poetry Review*, Philadelphia, 1972-73; co-editor, *Sinister Wisdom*, 1980-84. **Awards**: Yale Series of Younger Poets Award, 1951; Guggenheim fellowship, 1952, 1961; Ridgely Torrence memorial award, 1955; American Academy and Institute of Arts and Letters Award, 1961; Amy Lowell traveling scholarship, 1962; Bollingen Foundation grant, for translation, 1962; Bess Hokin prize, 1963, and Eunice Tietjens memorial prize for *Poetry*, Chicago, 1968; National Translation Center grant, 1968; National Endowment for the Arts grant, 1970; Shelley memorial award, 1971; Ingram Merrill Foundation grant, 1973; National Book Award, 1974; Donnelly fellowship, Bryn Mawr College, Pennsylvania, 1975; Fund for Human Dignity award, 1981; Ruth Lilly Prize, 1986; Brandeis University Creative Arts Medal, 1987; Elmer Holmes Bobst Award, 1989; Commonwealth Award in Literature, 1991; Frost Silver Medal of the Poetry Society of America, 1992; *Los Angeles Times* Book Award in poetry, 1992; Lenore Marshall/*Nation* award, 1992; William Whitehead award, 1992; Lambda Book award, 1992; Academy of American Poets fellowship, 1992; The Poets' Prize, 1993; Fred Cody Award, 1994; Harriet Monroe Prize, 1994; MacArthur fellowship, 1994; D.Litt. from Wheaton College, Norton, Massachusetts, 1979, Brandeis University, 1987, City College of New York, 1990, and Harvard University, 1990. **Address**: c/o W.W. Norton, 500 Fifth Avenue, New York, New York 10110.

Publications

Plays

Ariadne. privately printed, 1939.
Not I, But Death. privately printed, 1941.

Poetry

A Change of World. New Haven, Yale University Press, 1951.
Poems. Oxford, Fantasy Press, 1952.
The Diamond Cutters and Other Poems. New York, Harper, 1955.
Snapshots of a Daughter-in-Law: Poems 1954-1962. New York, Harper, 1963.
Necessities of Life: Poems 1962-1965. New York, Norton, 1966.
Selected Poems. London, Chatto & Windus, 1967.
Leaflets: Poems 1965-1968. New York, Norton, 1969.
The Will to Change: Poems 1968-1970. New York, Norton, 1971.
Diving into the Wreck: Poems 1971-1972. New York, Norton, 1973.
Poems Selected and New 1950-1974. New York, Norton, 1975.
Twenty-One Love Poems. Emeryville, California, Effie's Press, 1976.
The Dream of a Common Language: Poems 1974-1977. New York, Norton, 1978.
A Wild Patience Has Taken Me This Far: Poems 1978-1981. New York, Norton, 1981.
Sources. Woodside, California, Heyeck Press, 1983.
The Fact of a Doorframe: Poems Selected and New 1950-1984. New York, Norton, 1984.
Your Native Land, Your Life. New York, Norton, 1986.
Time's Power: Poems 1985-1988. New York, Norton, 1989.
An Atlas of the Difficult World: Poems 1988-1991. New York, Norton, 1991.
Collected Early Poems, 1950-1970. New York, Norton, 1993.
Dark Fields of the Republic: Poems 1991-1995. New York, Norton, 1995.
Selected Poems, 1950-1995. Knockeven, Ireland, Salmon Publishers, 1996.

Other

Of Woman Born: Motherhood as Experience and Institution. New York, Norton, 1976.
Women and Honor: Some Notes on Lying. Pittsburgh, Motheroot, 1977; London, Onlywomen Press, 1979.
On Lies, Secrets, and Silence: Selected Prose 1966-1978. New York, Norton, 1979.
Compulsory Heterosexuality and Lesbian Existence. Denver, Antelope Press, 1980.
Blood, Bread, and Poetry: Selected Prose 1979-1985. New York, Norton, 1986.
What Is Found There: Notebooks on Poetry and Politics. New York, Norton, 1993.

Translator with William Stafford and Aijaz Ahmad, *Poems by Ghalib*. New York, Hudson Review, 1969.
Translator, *Reflections*. New York, Red Dust, 1973.

Editor, *The Best American Poetry 1996*. New York, Scribner, 1996.

*

Poetry Recordings: *Today's Poets 4*, with others, Folkways; *Adrienne Rich Reading at Stanford*, Stanford, 1973; *A Sign I Was Not Alone*, with others, Out & Out, 1978; *Planetarium: A Retrospective*. Watershed, 1986; *Tracking the Contradictions: Poems 1981-1985*. Watershed, 1987.

Manuscript Collection: Schlesinger Library, Radcliffe College, Cambridge, Massachusetts.

Critical Studies: *Adrienne Rich's Poetry,* edited by Barbara Charlesworth Gelpi and Albert Gelpi, New York, Norton, 1975, revised edition, 1993; *American Triptych: Anne Bradstreet, Emily Dickinson, Adrienne Rich* by Wendy Martin, Chapel Hill, University of North Carolina Press, 1984; *The Transforming Power of Language: The Poetry of Adrienne Rich* by Myriam Diaz-Diocaretz, Utrecht, HES, 1984; *Reading Adrienne Rich: Reviews and Re-visions 1951-1981* edited by Jane Roberta Cooper, Ann Arbor, University of Michigan Press, 1984; *Translating Poetic Discourse: Questions on Feminist Strategies in Adrienne Rich* by Diaz-Diocaretz, Amsterdam, Benjamins, 1985; *A New Tradition? The Poetry of Sylvia Plath, Anne Sexton, and Adrienne Rich* by Janice Markey, Frankfurt, P. Lang, 1985; *The Aesthetics of Power: The Poetry of Adrienne Rich* by Claire Keyes, Athens, University of Georgia Press, 1986; "Adrienne Rich: North America East," in *Praises and Dispraises* by Terrence DesPres, New York, Viking, 1988; "'Driving to the Limits of the City of Words': The Poetry of Adrienne Rich," in *The Didactic Muse* by William Spiegelman, Princeton, New Jersey, Princeton University Press, 1989; *Skirting the Subject: Pursuing Language in the Works of Adrienne Rich, Susan Griffin, and Beverly Dahlen* by Alan Shima, Uppsala, Uppsala University Press, 1993; *The Dream and the Dialogue: Adrienne Rich's Feminist Poetics* by Alice Templeton, Knoxville, University of Tennessee Press, 1994.

*   *   *

Adrienne Rich's earliest volume, *A Change of World,* introduces two themes that have persisted throughout her career: the pyrrhic victories of human accomplishment in the battle against time and the plight of being a woman. Many poems describe the patience and accommodation every woman must learn if she is to remain in a relationship with a man, who by nature is distant and detached, in an "estranged intensity / Where his mind forages alone" ("An Unsaid Word"). *The Diamond Cutters and Other Poems* reiterates how patience, resignation, and isolation are a woman's fate, "We had to take the world as it was given," she writes, for "[we] live in other people's houses" ("The Middle-Aged"). The title poem in *Snapshots of a Daughter-in-Law* treats the woman's "blight" in a mythic, historical, and literary context. In fact, Rich insists, the traditional and proper roles of good wife and housekeeper are a woman's funeral preparations: "soon we'll be off. I'll pack us into parcels / stuff us in barrels, shroud us in newspapers" ("Passing On"). The perverse dependency upon men for sustenance, and the isolation from other women that accompanies it, lead women to self-hatred. The only real alternatives are depression or suicide, "A thinking woman sleeps with monsters / The beak that grabs her, she becomes."

Necessities of Life concentrates primarily upon erotic experience. The poet is in search of both a comfortable relationship with her own body and a relationship with a woman that will give her the childlike (and even womblike) security she has lost. To her lover she says, "Sometimes at night / you are my mother / ... and I crawl against you, fighting / for shelter, making you / my cave" ("Like This Together"). In *Leaflets,* her political rage sur-

faces. As poet and woman, she calls for sisterhood, a new politics, and a new language. Her resistance is active,

> I'd rather
> taste blood, yours or mine, flowing
> from a sudden slash, than cut all day
> with blunt scissors on dotted lines
> like the teacher told."

The Will to Change deals with the problems of retaining the "oppressor's language" ("The Burning of Paper Instead of Children"). It is essential to return to feeling, she argues, and she connects erotic sexuality, poetry, and political action: "When will we lie clear headed in our flesh again?" she asks, for whenever "a feeling enters the body / [it] is political." Finally, admitting that "we have come to an edge of history when men . . . have become dangerous to children and other living things, themselves included," she commits herself to total sexual-political warfare.

Driving into the Wreck admits her total antipathy toward men: "I hate you," she says to her male adversary, and continues, "The only real love I have ever felt / was for children and other women." "Phenomenology of Anger" is a militantly feminist poem that rages against repressed human energy, which men handle in war and murder, but which women escape only in "Madness, Suicide, Death." "The Stranger" goes beyond sexual warfare, as Rich, the poet who is a prisoner of language, becomes androgynous; perhaps love and nurturing will be restorative: "I am the androgyne / I am the living mind you fail to describe / in your dead language," she writes, and as "mermaid" and "merman," she concludes, "We circle silently / about the wreck / we dive into the hold."

In *Your Native Land, Your Life,* Rich raises a confident and elegant political voice. She accepts her "verbal privilege" as a poet to incite her audience to action against the injustices endured by every minority—from American Indian and black to Jew and lesbian. As the title suggests, she reflects on her own experiences in order to raise larger moral issues. Many poems are intimate revelations of her experiences as a Jew, woman, and daughter ("the eldest daughter raised as a son, taught to study but not to pray"). "Sources" raises key questions about identity, choices, and helplessness: *"With whom do you believe your lot is cast? / From where does your strength come? / I think somehow, somewhere / every poem of mine must raise those questions / ... There is a whom, a where / that is not chosen that is given and sometimes falsely given / in the beginning we grasp whatever we can to survive."* At times she worries that she is becoming self-consciously political and wonders if "Everything we write / will be used against us / or against those we love." Ultimately, however, through the common pain of human relationships and survival in time, there may be a transcendent "purification." She would connect herself with the world's pain, even though "the body's pain and the pain on the streets / are not the same but you can learn / from the edges that blur / you who love clear edges / more than anything watch the edges that blur."

In *Time's Power* Rich again recalls her childhood loneliness and a life mixed "with laughter / raucousing the grief" and suggests that in the end "all we read is life. Death is invisible / . . . Only the living decide death's color" ("Living Memory"). She has been like a visitor to a foreign land, in an alien universe: "So why am I out here, trying / to read your name in the illegible air? / —vowel washed from a stone, / solitude of no absence, / forbidden face-to-face / . . . / trying to hang these wraiths / of syllables, breath / without echo, why?" Other poems recall the wounds of a painful mother-daughter relationship and Rich's special sensitivity to women's, especially lesbians,' experiences—as victims of a hostile, punitive culture. Several historical poems are particularly interesting, including "Letters in the Family" and "Harper's Ferry."

Rich shoulders the burdens of the world in *An Atlas of the Difficult World*. In many poems she clearly transcends the role of feminist poet, now deeply concerned with how, in any number of disenfranchised groups, various elements—history, culture, and individuals—create and impose evil upon the innocent. Her subjects range from the victims of the concentration camp to a woman beaten by her husband in a trailer to two lesbians brutally attacked while vacationing. Gays and lesbians become emblematic of the many in society scarred by injustice and indignity. The title poem, in 13 parts, is a devastating image of the individual lost in the American "Sea of Indifference, glazed with salt." She says of this society, "I don't want to know / wreckage, dreck and waste," but as she admits, "these are the materials" of "our fissured, cracked terrain." America is "a cemetery of the poor / who died for democracy." Among her heroes—always the more modest members of society—are Leo Frank, hung in 1915 solely because he was a Jew; the father of Anne Sullivan (Helen Keller's teacher), forced to come to America during the Irish potato famine; Latino migrant workers in California; the imprisoned George Jackson.

The volume also returns to familiar themes of feminist rage: "You were a woman walked on a leash. / And they dropped you in the end" ("Olivia"), the difficulties of childhood ("That Mouth") and age ("She"), Jewish female identity ("Eastern War Time"), and death ("Final Notations"). Some of her descriptive passages, particularly of nature, are unusually beautiful. She writes of the black-eyed Susan, that flower which, during "Late summers, early autumns / . . . binds / the map of this country together," that here is "the girasol, orange gold- / petalled / with her black eye / [which] laces the / roadsides from Vermont to / California / . . . her tubers the / jerusalem artichoke / that has fed the Indians, fed the hobos, could feed us all." The poet asks, "Is there anything in the soil . . . that makes for / a plant so generous?" It is what is called "humanity"—politically, socially, and ecologically—that is responsible for natural and individual "waste": "The watcher's eye put out, hands of the / builder severed, brain of the maker starved / those who could bind, join, reweave, cohere, replenish / now at risk in this segregate republic." The concept of "waste" haunts the volume.

—Lois Gordon

RICHARD, Mark

Surname pronounced rih-SHARD. **Born**: Lake Charles, Louisiana, 9 November 1955. **Education**: Washington and Lee University, B.A. in journalism 1980. **Family**: Wife, Jennifer Allen; one child, Roman. **Career**: Worked variously as a radio announcer, aerial photographer, naval correspondent, and for three years as a com-

mercial fisherman; member of faculty, 1989, 1990, 1991, and writer-in-residence, fall 1992, Writers' Voice, West Side Y, New York City; member of faculty, Sewanee Writers' Conference, 1992-94, 1997; Tennessee Williams fellow, University of the South, spring 1994; Southern writer-in-residence, University of Mississippi, fall 1994-fall 1995; visiting writer, Arizona State University, Tempe, Arizona, 1997-98. **Awards**: Virginia Prize for fiction, 1985; Hemingway Short Story Contest, 1987; Jeanne Goodheart Shapriot fiction prize, 1988; New York Foundation for the Arts fellowship, 1989; National Magazine Award finalist for fiction, Pen/Ernest Hemingway Foundation Award, and Whiting Foundation Writers' Award, 1990; National Endowment for the Arts fellowship, 1990; Mary Francis Hobson Medal for Arts and Letters, 1996.

PUBLICATIONS

Novel

Fishboy: A Ghost's Story. New York, Doubleday/Nan A. Talese, 1993.

Short Story Collections

The Ice at the Bottom of the World. New York, Alfred A. Knopf, 1989.
Charity. New York, Doubleday/Nan A. Talese, Fall, 1998.

Uncollected Fiction

"Twenty-one Days Back," in *Shenandoah*, Fall, 1980.
"Just Name Some Place," in *The Quarterly*, Spring, 1989.

Uncollected Nonfiction

"Profile, Tom Waits," in *Spin*, June, 1994.
"Ten Commandments of Childhood," in *New York Times Magazine,* October 1995.
"Home for the Holidays," in *Oxford American*, Winter, 1996.
"Inside the Christian Coalition," in *Spin*, January 1996.
"Inside the Christian Coalition," in *George* magazine, August 1996.

*

Audio/Video Documentaries: "Disappearing Guineamen of the Chesapeake Bay," British Broadcasting Corporation (BBC-3), December 1993; "The Tennessee Valley Authority Legacy," British Broadcasting Corporation (BBC-3), September 1994; Profile, "Carson McCullers," British Broadcasting Corporation (BBC-3), September 1995; "Emerging Irish Writers," British Broadcasting Corporation (BBC-3), October 1995.

Critical Studies: "A Book in Search of a Buzz: The Marketing of a First Novel" by Michael Norman, *New York Times Book Review*, January 30, 1994; "Reader by Reader and Town by Town: A New Novelist Builds a Following" by Michael Norman, *New York Times Book Review*, February 6, 1994.

Mark Richard comments:
We have a culture that is pretty apocalyptic and has a short attention span.

When my life is in turmoil, I gravitate toward the coast. You can't go any farther unless you want to grow fins or drown yourself.

*   *   *

Mark Richard began his writing career in 1986 after working as a radio announcer, aerial photographer, naval correspondent, and for three years as a commercial fisherman. His first collection of short stories, *The Ice at the Bottom of the World*, received the Pen/ Ernest Hemingway Foundation Award in 1990 for best first book of fiction. His novel *Fishboy* provoked a two-part profile in the *New York Times Book Review* on the marketing of a first novel and the beginning of a successful career.

Like the early Cormac McCarthy, Richard writes about isolated, often psychologically or physically maimed characters who search for community as it disintegrates around them. Some fear the earth itself may be facing destruction. Charles believes in "The Theory of Man" that "the planet has entered an orbit too near the sun," and the burning "orange and red ravine" in "Gentleman's Agreement" indicates "where the world [is] coming to an end." All creatures seem to be living on the cusp of apocalypse—the end of life as we know it and perhaps the return of the Messiah in some strange form. That is the subject of *Fishboy,* which the stories collected in *Ice at the Bottom of the World* anticipate.

How do creatures withstand the threat of fire or ice, the two poles of feeling in these stories? Not through isolation, although the chances for human contact are very limited and nearly always exist outside the context of family. Living like Thoreau, alone and close to nature, provides no answer. "On the Rope" and "Her Favorite Story," respectively, describe nature's capacity to destroy by flood and fire. As they seek companionship, these creatures tell stories that transcend the category of the Southern Gothic through incongruous humor that laughs at a harsh and unpredictable world. "Happiness of the Garden Variety," the tale of a bloated horse named Buster who deflates after devouring a vegetable garden, recalls Faulkner's use of frontier humor in "Spotted Horses."

Love remains a possibility in Richard's fiction but can appear grotesque from a normal perspective. In "Feast of the Earth, Ransom of the Clay," a dirt-eating man who lives in mud caves behind a graveyard grieves at the funeral of the one woman who befriended him. A humanized grim reaper, he presides over a garden of death but sings like a bird at the very lip of the grave.

Like Faulkner, Welty, and O'Connor, Richard employs two dominant styles—one spare, one ornate. The voice of his first person narrators is elliptically terse and colloquial with little use of figurative language. However, when describing non-human nature, the language often becomes elevated and metaphorically lyrical—especially when nature is in turmoil—fire or flood. In the aftermath of natural and human catastrophe, Richard's shell-shocked narrators try to find meaning through contact with other survivors.

The imagery of catastrophe suggests biblical antecedents—the ruined garden in "Her Favorite Story" and "Happiness of the Garden Variety," the flood in "On the Rope." In most of Richard's fiction, water is always near—threatening and beckoning. Seven stories in "Ice" have snakes—most have birds and dogs. All are

handled with more sympathy than many of the human beings. If we live in a fallen world, don't blame the snakes! They also are trying to survive. If we fail in our escape flights from earth (one airplane is about to crash; another is shot down), don't blame the birds. They also must return to earth. One gets crushed by an idiot in the novel *Fishboy.*

Many of the stories sympathetically portray the dilemma of children in precarious circumstances. Although they seldom play or seek comfort and safety, they rarely complain. A surrealistic novel, *Fishboy* is narrated by a victim of child-abuse, a thrown-away child who struggles for life in a depraved world surrounding a cratered lake into which "a speck of heaven [has] fallen so heavily it sent a wave against the tide." Half fable, half myth, this novel becomes a sea journey in search of a refuge from fire and flood. Undergoing a shocking metamorphosis from "human-being boy" to fish, and "sentenced to cook" in a boiling pot, Fishboy's body is sacrificed to the world's appetite while his spirit, like sweet-scented steam, whispers to us in our dreams insisting that "I, too, began as a boy." A grotesque and hopeful transformation myth, *Fishboy*, in richly alliterative almost baroque prose, explores the realm of the holy ghost.

Richard's second collection of short stories, *Charity,* continues to experiment with language and narrative structure, reflecting the influence of Donald Barthelme as much as Welty and O'Connor. Still developing apocalyptic themes of natural disaster and loss, these stories range in style from the semi-realistic to the darkly comic grotesque. The title story describes the futile efforts of a "broken child" to make friends with "a boy with a tail." In "Gentleman's Agreement" a lonely child waits for the return of his fire-fighting father from a burning forest in which a bear hugs a man and cries. In the gothic tale "Fun at the Beach," a shrinking man with animal teeth hangs upside down like a bat and sucks the blood of his all-too-willing victims. "Where Blue is Blue," a detective story in dialect about the murder of a carnival contortionist, describes a drunken Sherlock Holmes-type named Cecil who paints pictures of the crime and offers them to the suspects.

Mark Richard demonstrates in his own fiction "that fictional power is best derived from finding the extraordinary in the ordinary." In bleak but often recognizably Southern landscapes, spiritually and socially disenfranchised characters learn to endure emotional and natural disaster. Described by Vince Aletti (*Voice Literary Supplement*, July, 1989) as an author who "reaches past his mall-crawling Southern contemporaries to roots in rich Faulknerian darkness and comic confusion, a place where the horrific and the hilarious converge," Mark Richard's fiction remains cautiously optimistic. "It's been said that I write about fringe characters who have no hope," he says. "But you have to bring the lights down so that the point of light is apparent. Only in the dark do we see the hope."

—Thomas M. Carlson

ROBBINS, Tom

Born: Thomas Eugene Robbins in Blowing Rock, North Carolina, 22 July 1936. **Education:** Hargarve Military Academy, Virginia;

Washington and Lee University, Lexington, Virginia; Richmond Professional Institute (now Virginia Commonwealth University), graduated 1960. **Military Service:** Served in the U.S. Air Force in Korea. **Family:** Married Terrie Robbins (second marriage; divorced); one child. **Career:** Copy editor, Richmond *Times-Dispatch,* 1960-62, and Seattle *Times* and *Post-Intelligencer,* 1962-63; reviewer and art columnist, *Seattle Magazine,* and radio host, 1964-68; full-time writer since the late 1960s. **Agent:** Phoebe Larmore, 228 Main Street, Venice, California 90291.

Publications

Novels

Another Roadside Attraction. New York, Doubleday, 1971.
Even Cowgirls Get the Blues. Boston, Houghton Mifflin, 1976.
Still Life with Woodpecker. New York, Bantam, 1980.
Jitterbug Perfume. New York, Bantam, 1984.
Skinny Legs and All. New York, Bantam, 1990.
Half Asleep in Frog Pajamas. New York, Bantam, 1994.

Uncollected Short Story

"The Chink and the Clock People." In *The Best American Short Stories 1977* edited by Martha Foley, Boston, Houghton Mifflin, 1977.

Other

Guy Anderson (biography). Seattle, Gear Works Press, 1965.
Guy Anderson, with William Ivey and Wallace S. Baldinger (exhibition catalogue). Seattle, Seattle Art Museum, 1977.

*

Film Adaptation: *Even Cowgirls Get the Blues* adapted for film by Gus Van Sant and released by Fine Line Features, 1994.

Critical Studies: "Avant-garde and After," *The Practice of Fiction in America: Writers from Hawthorne to the Present* by Jerome Klinkowitz, Iowa State University Press, 1980; *Tom Robbins* by Mark Siegel, Boise, Idaho, Boise State University, 1980; *Readings from the New Book on Nature: Physics and Metaphysics in the Modern Novel* by Robert Nadeau, University of Massachusetts Press, 1981; "Unlikely Heroes: The Central Figures in *The World According to Garp, Even Cowgirls Get the Blues, and A Confederacy of Dunces*" by William Nelson, *The Hero in Transition* edited by Ray B. Browne and Marshall W. Fishwick, Bowling Green University Popular Press, 1983; *Tom Robbins: A Critical Companion* by Catherine E. Hoyser and Lorena Laura Stookey, Westport, Connecticut, Greenwood Press, 1997.

*   *   *

Tom Robbins has made a name for himself by writing novels that defy the ordinary in terms of plot, language, characterization, and theme, and by cultivating a following of countercultural groupies (who have receded in number since the 1970s). His novels display such trademarks as an episodic, nonlinear structure that Robbins has called "psychedelic," based on his early LSD experiences; a cast of bizarre characters with names like Bonanza

Jellybean and Marx Marvelous, who search for the meaning of life; a style characterized by outrageous metaphors and absurd images; and an optimistic philosophy based on Eastern mysticism, quantum physics, antimaterialism, feminism, and above all, playfulness.

But Robbins' style that stands out most, at times stealing the show from his quirky plots and characters and usually delighting the reader with flamboyant images, such as one from *Skinny Legs and All* (1990) in which the sound of a quarter being dropped into a pay phone is described as "a hollow yet musical clink, like a robot passing a kidney stone."

Robbins's first book, *Another Roadside Attraction* (1971), became a cult classic with its 1973 paperback edition that was marketed largely by word-of-mouth among college students. In this work, a group of eccentrics discover Christ's mummified body. They bring it to a hot dog stand called Capt. Kendrick Memorial Hot Dog Wildlife Preserve, where they try to disprove Christianity. "The point of *Another Roadside Attraction,*" according to Jerome Klinkowitz in *The Practice of Fiction in America,* "is the reinvention (through perception) of reality, a revitalization of life which logic and authority have dulled beyond appreciation." The book repudiates the authority of Christianity, reflecting Robbins's belief, as he once said, that "religion is spirituality in which the spiritual has been killed. . . . Spirituality doesn't lend itself to organization."

His second and most popular book, *Even Cowgirls Get the Blues* (1976), is about a beautiful woman, Sissy Hankshaw, who learns to live with her socially unacceptable, oversized thumbs by becoming the best hitchhiker in the country. When she arrives at the Rubber Rose Ranch, a former cosmetic farm for women that has been taken over by cowgirl feminists, she discovers the path to wisdom with the help of Chink, a Japanese hermit. Chink teaches Sissy that Americans must learn to reach back to their spiritual roots in Pantheism, which is characterized by feminine receptivity rather than masculine aggression. Mark Siegel has written in his study of Tom Robbins that the novel "posits the abandonment of out-worn mainstream social roles that are destructive in their rigidity."

Robbins's first two novels were received enthusiastically by most critics. But by the time his next novel, *Still Life with Woodpecker* (1980), was published, reviewers were tiring of his flamboyant style. Julie B. Peters wrote in the *Saturday Review* that Robbins's writing "is marbled with limping puns heavily splattered with recurrent motifs and a boyish zeal for the scatological." Another reviewer criticized the novel for being too "cute." In addition, some critics disliked the fact that, instead of the larger social messages of his previous works, the novel centered on the personal relationship between a princess and a "good-hearted terrorist."

The publication of his next three novels, *Jitterbug Perfume, Skinny Legs and All,* and *Half Asleep in Frog Pajamas,* brought Robbins relatively little critical praise. It appears that his style and message have largely lost their appeal for a generation of critics who have outgrown their attraction to playfulness and countercultural ethics. In his review of *Skinny Legs and All* for the *New York Times Book Review,* Joe Queenan wrote, "Mr.

Robbins is still a very funny guy, but he—and we—are getting a bit old for comic books." Others find that the old philosophical enlightenment of his first books had turned into didacticism. Karen Karbo of the *New York Times Book Review* argued that "unless his work was imprinted on you when you were 19 and stoned, you'll find him forever unreadable. A sober 21-year-old is already too steely-eyed and seasoned to frolic in Mr. Robbins's trademark cuckoo plots, woo-woo philosophizing, overwrought metaphors and cheerful misogyny."

Nevertheless, Robbins continues to craft his quirky and ultimately optimistic novels of the search for the meaning of life, convinced that our culture remains as materialistic, conformist, and confused as ever. He once wrote, "social action on the political/economic level is wee potatoes. Our great human adventure is the evolution of consciousness. We are in this life to enlarge the soul and light up the brain." This is what Robbins tries to achieve with his writing.

—Anne Boyd

RUBIN, Louis D., Jr.

Born: Louis Decimus Rubin, Jr., in Charleston, South Carolina, 19 November 1923. **Education:** Attended College of Charleston, 1940-42; Yale University, 1943-44; University of Richmond, B.A. 1946; Johns Hopkins University, M.A. 1949, Ph.D. 1954. **Military Service:** U.S. Army, World War II, Specialized Training Division, 1943-46. **Family:** Married Eva M. Redfield (a political science professor), 2 June 1951; two sons. **Career:** Reporter, *Bergen Evening Record*, Hackensack, New Jersey, 1946-47; city editor, *News Leader,* Staunton, Virginia, 1947-48; Associated Press staff writer, 1948; instructor in English, Johns Hopkins University, 1948-54; assistant telegraph editor, *Morning News,* Wilmington, Delaware, 1949; assistant professor of American Civilization, executive secretary of the American Studies Association, University of Pennsylvania, Philadelphia, 1954-55; associate editor, *News Leader,* Richmond, Virginia, 1956-57; associate professor, 1957-59, professor, 1960-67, chairman of English department, 1959-67, Hollins College; visiting professor at Louisiana State University, summer, 1957, University of North Carolina, spring, 1965, University of California, Santa Barbara, summer, 1966, and Harvard University, summer, 1969; Fulbright professor, University of Aix-Marseilles, Nice, France, summer, 1960; professor of English, 1967-72, university distinguished professor of English, 1972-89; professor of English, 1967-72, university distinguished professor of English, 1972-89, University of North Carolina at Chapel Hill; lecturer, American studies summer seminars, Kyoto, Japan, 1980; lecturer under the auspices of U.S. State Department in Austria and Germany, 1981; president and founder, Algonquin Books of Chapel Hill, 1982-88, editorial director, 1989-91; editor of *Hopkins Review,* 1949-53, *Provincial,* 1956-57, *Hollins Critic,* 1963-69, Southern Literary Studies series, Louisiana State University Press, 1964-73, 1975-93, and *Southern Literary Journal,* 1969-89; advisory editor, University of North Carolina Press; member of editorial advisory board, *Mississippi Quarterly,* 1973-75; coordinator, U.S. Information Agency Forums, 1973-74, 1976-78. **Member:** South Atlantic Modern Language Association, Society for the Study of Southern Literature (member of executive council, 1968-76; president, 1974-76), Fellowship of Southern Writers (chancellor, 1991-93), Phi Beta Kappa. **Awards:** *Sewanee Review* fellowship, 1953; Guggenheim fellowship, 1956; American Council of Learned Societies fellowship, 1964; Distinguished Virginian Award, 1972; Mayflower Society award, 1978; Jules F. Landry Award, Louisiana State University Press, 1978; South Carolina Academy of Authors, 1987; O Max Gardner Medal, 1989; North Carolina Award, 1992; R. Hunt Parker Award, lifetime contributions to literary heritage of North Carolina, 1996; North Carolina Literary Hall of Fame, Southern Pines, North Carolina, inducted 17 May 1997; the North Carolina Literary Festival in April, 1998, honored Rubin for his untiring efforts on behalf of writers and scholars, and for his willingness to assist them with his inspiring mind and endless generosity and support; Litt D. from University of Richmond, 1974; D.Litt. from Clemson University, 1986, College of Charleston, 1989, University of The South, Sewanee, 1992, and University of North Carolina at Asheville, 1993.

PUBLICATIONS

Nonfiction

Thomas Wolfe: The Weather of His Youth. Baton Rouge, Louisiana State University Press, 1955.

No Place on Earth: Ellen Glasgow, James Branch Cabell, and Richmond-in-Virginia. Austin, University of Texas Press, 1959.

The Faraway Country: Writers of the Modern South. Seattle, University of Washington Press, 1963; published as *Writers of the Modern South: The Faraway Country,* 1966.

The Curious Death of the Novel: Essays in American Literature. Baton Rouge, Louisiana State University Press, 1967.

The Teller in the Tale, Seattle, University of Washington Press, 1967.

George W. Cable: The Life and Times of a Southern Heretic. Indianapolis, Pegasus, 1969.

The Writer in the South. Athens, University of Georgia Press, 1972.

Black Poetry in America: Two Essays in Interpretation, with Blyden Jackson. Baton Rouge, Louisiana State University Press, 1974.

William Elliott Shoots a Bear: Essays on the Southern Literary Imagination. Baton Rouge, Louisiana State University Press, 1976.

Virginia, A Bicentennial History. New York, Norton, 1977.

The Wary Fugitives: Four Poets and the South. Baton Rouge, Louisiana State University Press, 1978.

A Gallery of Southerners. Baton Rouge, Louisiana State University Press, 1982.

A Southern Renascence Man, with Thomas L. Connelly. Ann Arbor, Books on Demand, 1984.

Uneeda Review, with William Harmon (a literary spoof using pseudonym J. Parkhurst Schimmelpfennig). New York, Nick Lyons Books, 1985.

Before the Game, with photographs by Scott Mylin. Dallas, Taylor Publishing, 1988.

The Edge of the Swamp: A Study in the Literature and Society of the Old South. Baton Rouge, Louisiana State University Press, 1989.

Small Craft Advisory: A Book About the Building of a Boat. New York, Grove/Atlantic, 1991.

The Mockingbird in the Gum Tree: A Literary Gallimaufry. Baton Rouge, Louisiana State University Press, 1991.
Babe Ruth's Ghost and Other Historical & Literary Speculation. Seattle, University of Washington Press, 1996.

Editor

Southern Renascence: The Literature of the Modern South, with R. D. Jacobs). Baltimore, Johns Hopkins Press, 1953.
The Lasting South, with J. J. Kilpatrick. Baltimore, Regnery, 1957.
Teach the Freeman: Correspondence of Rutherford B. Hayes and the Slater Fund for Negro Education, 1881-1893, two volumes. Baton Rouge, Louisiana State University Press, 1959.
South: Modern Southern Literature in Its Cultural Settings, with R. D. Jacobs. New York, Doubleday, 1961.
The Idea of an American Novel, with J. R. Moore. New York, Crowell, 1961.
The Hollins Poets. Charlottesville, University Press of Virginia, 1967.
A Biographical Guide to the Study of Southern Literature. Baton Rouge, Louisiana State University Press, 1969.
The Yemassee Lands: The Poems of Beatrice Ravenel. Chapel Hill, University of North Carolina Press, 1969.
Southern Writing, 1585-1920, with R. B. Davis and C. H. Holman. Chapel Hill, Odyssey, 1970.
Thomas Wolfe: A Collection of Critical Essays. Upper Saddle River, New Jersey, Prentice-Hall, 1973.
The Comic Imagination in American Literature. New Brunswick, New Jersey, Rutgers University Press, 1973.
Southern Literary Study: Prospects and Possibilities, with C. Hugh Holman. Chapel Hill, University of North Carolina Press, 1975.
The Literary South. New York, Wiley, 1979; Baton Rouge, Louisiana State University Press, 1986.
Southern Writers: A Biographical Dictionary, with Robert Bain and Joseph N. Flora. Baton Rouge, Louisiana State University Press, 1979.
The American South: Portrait of a Culture. New York, Voice of America, 1979, revised edition, 1993.
The History of Southern Literature, with Blyden Jackson, Rayburn S. Moore, Lewis P. Simpson, and Thomas Daniel Young. Baton Rouge, Louisiana State University Press, 1985.
Thomas Wolf, Mannerhouse: A Play with a Prologue and Four Acts, with J. L. Idol, Jr. Baton Rouge, Louisiana State University Press, 1985.
An Apple for My Teacher: Twelve Authors Tell about Teachers Who Made the Difference. Chapel Hill, Algonquin Books, 1987.
The Algonquin Library Quiz Book. Chapel Hill, Algonquin Books, 1990.
Vanderbilt Tradition: a festschrift in honor of Thomas Daniel Young. Baton Rouge, Louisiana State University Press, 1991.
A Writer's Companion, in association with Jerry Leath Mills. Baton Rouge, Louisiana State University Press, 1995; New York, HarperCollins, 1997.
Cleanth Brooks and Allan Tate: Collected Letters, 1933-1976, with Alphonse Vinh. Columbia, University of Missouri P, 1998.

Novels

The Golden Weather. New York, Atheneum, 1961.
The Boll Weevil and the Triple Play, illustrated by Robert Alden Rubin. Charleston, Tradd Street P, 1979.

Surfaces of a Diamond. Baton Rouge, Louisiana State University Press, 1981.
Heat of the Sun. Atlanta, Longstreet Press, 1995.

*

Critical Studies: "Louis D. Rubin, Jr., *Virginia*" by John B. Boles, *American Historical Review,* June 1980; "Louis Rubin and the Making of Maps" by Eudora Welty, *Sewanee Review,* Spring 1989; "The Edge of the Swamp: A Study of the Literature and Society of the Old South" by George R. Bodmer, *The Filson Club History Quarterly,* April 1990; "Of Canons and Cultural Wars: Southern Literature and Literary Scholarship after Midcentury" by Fred Hobson, and ". . . And Ladies of the Club" by Jim Wayne Miller, *The Future of Southern Letters* edited by Jefferson Humphries and John Lowe, New York: Oxford University Press, 1996.

*   *   *

Louis D. Rubin's prodigious output of books and articles speaks to the importance of Southern Letters in the twentieth century. Recognized as the authority on Southern Literature, Rubin spends his career studying, defining, and promoting this body of work as essential to any evaluation of American Literature. H. L. Mencken, the spirit behind the fellow journalist and former Baltimore resident, called for such a scholar and writer early in the century. Rubin began his career in journalism, both as an editor with *The Hopkins Review* and as reporter and editor for the Associated Press and a number of newspapers. This experience impressed on him the importance of speed in writing without neglecting supporting details, and through journalism he developed the conversational tone in his style that brings students to his scholarship.

Rubin is primarily a teacher of literature and writing, both in the classroom and in his books, to which his essays and criticism attest. His approach to the study of Southern American Literature is historical, analytical, technical, and literary. His lectures and writings set up the study of Southern American Literature in a two-fold method: 1) a general overview in which the South and its writers, along with their literary concerns over several hundred years, give the study structure; 2) analysis of literary genres as they develop throughout that historical period and represent the present. Rubin's introduction to *The History of Southern Literature* reminds readers:

> The facts are that there existed in the past, and there continues to exist today, an entity within American society known as the South, and that for better or for worse the habit of viewing one's experience in terms of one's relationship to that entity is still a meaningful characteristic of both writers and readers who are or have been part of it.

Rubin's theory of literary study and criticism involves "the teller in the tale," bringing an awareness of the storyteller back into critical evaluation of fiction. He does not mean by this idea a biographical criticism, but rather one in which the scholar recognizes the personality of the writer who created the narrator. Understanding the mind-set of the writer and his individual circumstances gives the scholar a deeper insight into the artifact, itself; the work must still satisfy the criteria of objective, formalist criticism.

He maintains that the writer is a personal presence in his work, imagining the possibilities characters might explore in a time and place he adopts, but whose language and actions speak in a universal voice. *The Literary South*, for instance, is a textbook anthology divided into five chronological sections for which Rubin provides an introduction with historical, biographical and critical discussion. The literary selections that follow illustrate the introduction and elicit informed discussion.

The Curious Death of the Novel is a collection of Rubin's essays in which he critically evaluates specific American writers—Mark Twain, Henry James, Karl Shapiro, H. L. Mencken, Ellen Glasgow, Flannery O'Connor, and others. Rubin's subtitle for the collection says more about the book's theme than does the title: "Or, What to Do About Tired Literary Critics." By thorough analysis in the discussions, he demonstrates effective critical evaluation, bringing up-to-date the methods introduced in the 1920s and 1930s by the Fugitive-Agrarian literary movement.

A later book, *The Mockingbird in the Gum Tree*, treats American literary figures and examines the methods by which American writers found their voice, their language. Especially noteworthy are the discussions of community and other characteristics that give Southern American Literature its distinctiveness. His essays on William Faulkner, Eudora Welty and Robert Penn Warren are thorough illustrations of his theories. In his essays and critical writings as in his lectures, Rubin's sense of humor and sometimes acerbic wit filter through the otherwise serious tone. He sees criticism as ordering and finding meaning, coherence and significance, but believes the language need not be dry, jargon-ridden or abstruse. These chapters illustrate a humorous, common sense approach and a conversational tone that make for clarity.

Rubin's fiction is almost an afterthought to his teaching and critical essays. Three novels use the Charleston, South Carolina, setting of his boyhood with vivid detail and poetic imagery. His memories provide him with the scene and its ambience, the characterization and language, but the stories are fiction—reworkings of Rubin's retrospection and introspection. The earliest novel, *The Golden Weather* (1961) examines, with care, humor and nostalgia, a thirteen-year-old boy's passage from childhood to adolescence in the 1936 rendition of a golden time and place. *Surfaces of a*

Diamond (1981) follows the same boy in 1939 as he experiences growing pains and search for self. Community and family play a large part in his finding identity and in cushioning the pains of becoming adult. If the books seem more memoir than fiction, so much the better for readers' suspension of disbelief. Rubin's last novel, *Heat of the Sun* (1995), returns to the Charleston of 1940 and similar detailed images of a time and place. The story is a mystery: a young reporter (outsider) comes to Charleston, his fiancé's home, and uncovers hidden facts about she and her family. The perspective is an outsider's viewpoint rather than the retrospective narration of a Charlestonian, giving the story a distance necessary for mystery.

If form follows function, Rubin's nonfiction books and essays demonstrate the theories and methods he seeks to instill about American Literature, especially Southern Literature. He teaches and supports students in their endeavors to write by encouraging efforts, evaluating manuscripts, seeking criticism from other well-known writers, and identifying publishing sources. He founded (with protégé Shannon Ravenel) the Algonquin Books press in 1982 in a shed in his backyard to further the publishing of Southern writers who met obstacles with New York publishers. That small press is now a major publishing house, still catering to Southern writers. During his career, he advanced such writers as Lee Smith, Kaye Gibbons, Clyde Edgerton, John Barth, Jill McCorkle and Annie Dillard; few would be as successful if not for his interest and assistance. He once wrote, "The primary reason for teaching creative writing is to help a young person give shape and form to his or her imagination in language."

Louis D. Rubin, Jr. is the quintessential mentor; he teaches, supports and furthers the prospects of future writers, teachers and critics; then he withdraws to the background out of the spotlight he abhors. In Chapel Hill, the North Carolina Literary Festival in April, 1998, honored Rubin for his untiring efforts on behalf of writers and scholars, and for his willingness to assist them with his inspiring mind and endless generosity and support. In retirement, he continues to broaden his interests, taking up the artist's paint brush with the same exuberance he types the computer keys or builds a boat. His restless intelligence and talents drive him to investigate many outlets without neglecting those he has perfected. His latest book is in progress—a nonfiction account of seaports around the South.

—Jeanne R. Nostrandt

S

SALLIS, James

Born: Helena, Arkansas, 21 December 1944. **Education:** Tulane University, New Orleans, Tulane scholar and fellow, 1961-63; University of Texas, Arlington, advanced study in Russian and French, 1983-84. **Family:** Married Jane Rose in 1964 (divorced), one child; married Karyn. **Career:** Poetry editor, *Riverside Quarterly,* Canada, 1964-66; editor, *New Worlds,* London, 1966-68; reviewer, *Boston After Dark* and *Fusion,* Boston, 1970-71; features writer, reviewer, and columnist, *Texas Jazz,* 1980-83; guest lecturer; teacher of writing workshops, Clarion College, Pennsylvania, University of Washington, Tulane University. **Agent:** Vicky Bijur, 333 West End Avenue #5-B, New York, New York 10023.

Publications

Short Story Collections

A Few Last Words. New York, Macmillan, 1970.
Limits of the Sensible World. Austin, Host, 1995.

Music Nonfiction

Down Home: Country-Western. New York, Macmillan, 1971.
The Guitar Players: One Instrument and Its Masters in American Music. New York, Morrow, 1982.
The Guitar in Jazz. Lincoln, University of Nebraska Press, 1996.

Novels (Lew Griffin Series)

The Long-Legged Fly. New York, Carroll & Graf, 1992.
Moth. New York, Carroll & Graf, 1993.
Black Hornet. New York, Carroll & Graf, 1994.
Eye of the Cricket. New York, Walker and Co., 1997.
Bluebottle. New York, Walker and Co., 1998.

Criticism

Difficult Lives: Jim Thompson-David Goodis-Chester Himes. Brooklyn, Gryphon, 1993.

Editor, *Ash of Stars: On the Writing of Samuel R. Delany.* Jackson, University Press of Mississippi, 1996.

Novels

Renderings. Seattle, Black Heron Press, 1995.
Death Will Have Your Eyes. New York, St. Martin's Press, 1997.

Other

Editor, *The War Book.* New York, Dell, 1971.
Editor, *The Shores Beneath.* New York, Avon, 1970.
Editor, *Jazz Guitars: An Anthology.* New York, Morrow, 1984.

Translator, *Saint Ginglin,* by Raymond Queneau. Dalkey Archive, 1993.

*

James Sallis comments:

When I first began writing, science fiction was like a huge trunk that had dropped out of the sky and broken open, and everyone could make of its riches what he might. Mike Moorcock had assumed editorship of *New Worlds.* Damon Knight was starting up his *Orbit* series. Early work of people like Tom Disch, Ursula le Guin, Chip Delany, Joanna Russ, and Roger Zelazny was everywhere. Today, I think, the mystery genre offers a similar latitude for highly personal expression within an established readership. This is why you have writers like Stephen Greenleaf, K. C. Constantine, James Lee Burke, or Neal Barrett, excellent writers who could make it on any ground, gravitating towards the mystery. There are still traditional whodunits, still standard-fare P.I. stories, but there's also room for a lot more. Writers like David Lindsay have pushed the genre to the very edge.

Feet firmly in both camps, I work towards the day when "literary" writers will come to realize what energy they forego in setting themselves apart and when "genre" writers will stop retreating defensively behind fictive walls. Literature is not some imposing sideboard with discrete drawers labeled poetry, mystery, serious novel, science fiction—but a long buffet table laid out with all manner of fine, diverse foods. You can go back and forth, take whatever you want or need.

Everyone interests me. Scratch half an inch into anyone's life and that person becomes as intriguing, mysterious and inexhaustible as the sea. In fact, I often think that in making use of such marginal characters I may simply be taking the easy way out. But I myself have lived a marginal life, largely among people like those you encounter in the books, and my own values are certainly not standard-issue middle class.

One of the many joys I've had in writing the Griffin books is in refusing to let these people be clichés—or more precisely, in first setting them up as clichés, then ransoming them. Special cases, right? Griffin himself, who starts out as the prototype hard-boiled dick and turns himself inside out in the novel's course. Or LaVerne, the prostitute with a heart of gold—who starts working at a rape crisis center and goes on to an M.A. in psychology. Or tough, pragmatic homicide cop Don Walsh, whom Lew keeps from eating his gun.

* * *

James Sallis has come late in his career to crime fiction, though his interest in the field traces back to his earliest days as a writer, and he has written an excellent study of three prominent hard-boiled writers in *Difficult Lives: Jim Thompson-David Goodis-Chester Himes.* He began writing in the field of speculative fiction in the 1960s as a member of a diverse and eclectic group of authors that included J. G. Ballard, Thomas Disch, Samuel Delany, and Harlan Ellison, among many others, who were categorized as the "New Wave" because of their radical departure from the traditional ideas of fictive structure and content. He has continued to publish short fiction in that field sporadically, but his most important fiction is the series featuring the New Orleans African-American thug *cum* private investigator *cum* professor, Lew Griffin.

The volumes that began with *The Long-Legged Fly* and continued with *Moth, Black Hornet, Eye of the Cricket,* and *Bluebottle,* comprise one of the most interesting and worthwhile departures from "standard" crime fiction—some have described them as literary noir—to have appeared in these latter times. Sallis is a translator and enthusiast of French literature, and his approach is at most only partially that of a genre writer. In interviews he has described *The Long-Legged Fly* as "what might have happened if Raymond Chandler and Samuel Beckett had collaborated on a detective novel," and while by his own admission the description was semi-fanciful he feels that in many ways it was a fair one.

Sallis disdains the conventional picture of literature as a huge sideboard with discreet drawers labeled "mystery," "serious novel," science fiction," etc., preferring to view it instead as "a long buffet table filled with fine, diverse foods. You can go back and forth and take whatever you want or need." His novels reflect his views, with passages at times worthy of the best of the terse, clipped hard-boiled style, and others of a thoroughly (some critics have said overly at times) literary nature, with quotes as likely to come from Camus as Chandler.

In Griffin he has created an existential man alienated from his world, one who has time and again hit bottom and lost all connections. He chronicles his life not in a straightforward manner, but by slipping back and forth from the present to various times in the past, slowly over the course of the series filling in the portrait of a man who has gone from little more than an alcoholic street thug to a sober teacher of French literature still seeking to redeem and understand what he has done and been.

Sallis's novels are not as easily read as most "genre" fiction; certainly not on the level they deserve. They are non-linear in narration and filled with literary allusions and symbolism, perhaps at times too much so. Sallis has lived at various times in New Orleans, and the ambiance of the town permeates the books in marvelous fashion. Over the course of the series the portrait of Griffin is magnificent if tortuously drawn, and supporting players fully characterized as well. At its best, which makes up a not inconsiderable portion of his work, his prose will stand most comparisons and not be found wanting.

In their own way these books stretch the boundaries of crime fiction, the private detective novel in particular, much as the best of the New Wave did science fiction. To use a phrase so overworked that Sallis would probably disdain it despite its appropriateness, they are a breath of fresh air.

—Barry W. Gardner

SAMS, Ferrol

Born: Fayetteville, Georgia, 26 September 1922. **Education:** Attended Mercer University, Macon, Georgia; Emory University, Atlanta, M.D. 1949. **Family:** Married Helen Fletcher on 18 July 1948; four children. **Military Service:** U.S. Army, 1943-47. **Career:** Physician, Fayetteville, GA, since 1951; Emory University, Atlanta, creative writing instructor, since 1991. **Awards:** Townsend prize for fiction, Georgia State University, 1991, for *When All the World Was Young*; D.Lit., Mercer University, 1987, Emory University, 1992, Medical University of South Carolina, 1993, Rhodes College, 1994.

PUBLICATIONS

Novels

Run with the Horsemen. Atlanta, Peachtree Publishers, 1982.
The Whisper of the River. Atlanta, Peachtree Publishers, 1984.
When All the World Was Young. Atlanta, Longstreet Press, 1991.

Short Fiction

The Widow's Mite and Other Stories. Atlanta, Peachtree Publishers, 1987.
Epiphany (three novellas). Atlanta, Longstreet Press, 1994.

Nonfiction

The Passing: Perspectives of Rural America, Paintings by Jim Harrison. Atlanta, Longstreet Press, 1988.
Christmas Gift!. Atlanta, Longstreet Press, 1989.

*

Critical Studies: *Contemporary Fiction Writers of the South*, edited by Joseph M. Flora and Robert Bain, Westport, Connecticut, Greenwood Press, 1993; *Speak So I Shall Know Thee: Interviews with Southern Writers* by William J. Walsh, Jefferson, North Carolina, McFarland & Co., 1993.

Ferrol Sams comments:
I had this idea of writing a novel that would describe events and procedures that are gone.

I wanted my grandchildren to know what life was like when I was younger. As I got into it, I said, "Hey, this is working, I'm enjoying this." I'd start over, tear it up, start over. Finally I got into the full swing of it. I think I sort of taught myself how to write a book. Then about halfway through I learned that I didn't have to stick to the facts. I said, "Hell, I can make this up and I can change names and I can have a good time with this." So I did. Then I got the fever.

*　　*　　*

Ferrol Sams has won praise for the novels of his Porter Osborne trilogy, two books of short fiction, and two nonfiction works. Yet writing is not Sams's primary profession: since 1951, he has practiced medicine alongside his wife, Helen, in the town of

Fayetteville, south of Atlanta. He was born there into a family with a rich oral storytelling tradition that centered around the house built by his great-grandfather, Porter Sams, near present-day Fayetteville in 1848. He was close to his father, Ferrol, Sr., who gave him the lasting nickname of "Sambo," and his mother, Mildred, a strong spiritual and literary influence.

Sams went to college at Mercer University in Macon, where an English professor named Fred Jones had a significant influence on his writing, then entered medical school at Emory University in Atlanta. The United States entered World War II and Sams left school after two quarters to join the army. After serving in France, Sams returned to medical school and in 1946 met his future wife, Helen, "over a cadaver," as Linda Welden reports in *Contemporary Fiction Writers of the South*. They eventually had four children, two of whom became physicians and joined them in establishing a medical clinic. Sams continues to practice medicine at the clinic, where he and his wife are known respectively as "Sambo" and "Doctor Helen." He is also heavily involved in community and charitable activities and taught Sunday school at his local church for many years.

For many people, those activities would have been plenty, but at the age of fifty-eight, Sams began writing a novel, which would become *Run with the Horsemen* (1982), the first of three Porter Osborne novels. In this work Porter is a young farm boy growing up in Georgia during the interwar years. Like Sams, Porter wants to become a doctor, but loves pranks as much as he does medicine. *Run with the Horsemen* received very strong reviews nationally, as did the followup novel, *The Whisper of the River* (1984), in which Porter has gone off to a college much like Mercer and, again, his attention is divided between the serious business of his studies and the serious business of making mischief. The trilogy was completed with *When All the World Was Young* in 1991. Porter is now in medical school, and the coming-of-age tale tells of his leaving school to serve his country. In between the second and third books of the Osborne series, Sams published a collection of short stories, *The Widow's Mite and Other Stories* (1987), and two nonfiction works.

The world of Sams's stories is heavily influenced by tradition, and he has said that his interest in writing came from a desire to record the passing of old ways before they were gone. Much of his work is informed by an awareness of the changing of the guard in the South and the world at large. He neither bemoans the changes or exults in them; his work is simply a record of what has been, and what is coming to be.

—Judson Knight

SANCHEZ, Sonia

Born: Wilsonia Benita Driver in Birmingham, Alabama, 9 September 1934. **Education**: Hunter College, New York, B.A. in political science 1955; New York University, 1959-60; Wilberforce University, Ohio, Ph.D. in fine arts 1972. **Family**: Married Albert Sanchez (divorced), Etheridge Knight (divorced); one daughter and two sons. **Career**: Staff member, Downtown Community School,

1965-67, and Mission Rebels in Action, San Francisco, 1968-69; instructor, San Francisco State College, 1967-69; lecturer in black literature, University of Pittsburgh, 1969-70, Rutgers University, New Brunswick, New Jersey, 1970-71, Manhattan Community College, New York, 1971-73, and City University of New York, 1972; associate professor, Amherst College, Massachusetts, 1972-73, and University of Pennsylvania, Philadelphia, 1976-77; associate professor of English, 1977-79, professor of English, since 1979, Faculty Fellow, Provost's Office, 1986-87, Presidential Fellow, 1987-88, and Laura Carnell Chair in English, Temple University, Philadelphia; columnist, *American Poetry Review,* 1977-78, and *Philadelphia Daily News,* 1982-83. **Awards:** P.E.N. award, 1969; American Academy grant, 1970; National Endowment for the Arts award, 1978; Smith College Tribute to Black Women award, 1982; Lucretia Mott award, 1984; Before Columbus Foundation award, 1985; Oni Award from International Black Women's Congress, 1992; PEN fellow, 1993. **Address:** Department of English, Temple University, Broad and Montgomery, Philadelphia, Pennsylvania 19041.

PUBLICATIONS

Poetry

Homecoming. Detroit, Broadside Press, 1969.
WE a BaddDDD People. Detroit, Broadside Press, 1970.
Liberation Poem. Detroit, Broadside Press, 1970.
It's a New Day: Poems for Young Brothas and Sistuhs. Detroit, Broadside Press, 1971.
Ima Talken bout The Nation of Islam. Astoria, New York, Truth Del., c.1971.
Love Poems. New York, Third Press, 1973.
A Blues Book for Blue Black Magical Women. Detroit, Broadside Press, 1974.
I've Been a Woman: New and Selected Poems. Sausalito, California, Black Scholar Press, 1978; revised edition, Chicago, Third World Press, 1985.
Homegirls and Handgrenades. New York, Thunder's Mouth Press, 1984.
Under a Soprano Sky. Trenton, New Jersey, Africa World Press, 1987.
Wounded in the House of a Friend. Boston, Beacon Press, 1995.
Does Your House Have Lions?. Boston, Beacon Press, 1997.

Recordings: *Homecoming*, Broadside Voices, 1969; *We a BaddDDD People*, Broadside Voices, 1969; *A Sun Woman for All Seasons*, Folkways, 1971; *Sonia Sanchez and Robert Bly*, Black Box, 1971; *Sonia Sanchez: Selected Poems, 1974*, Watershed, 1975; *IDKT: Captivating Facts about the Heritage of Black Americans*, Ujima, 1982.

Plays

The Bronx Is Next (produced New York, 1970). Published in *Drama Review* (New York), Summer 1968.
Sister Son/ji (produced Evanston, Illinois, 1971, New York, 1972). Published in *New Plays from the Black Theatre*, edited by Ed Bullins, New York, Bantam, 1969.
Dirty Hearts '72, in *Break Out! In Search of New Theatrical Environments*, edited by James Schevill, Chicago, Swallow Press, 1973.

Uh, Uh: But How Do It Free Us? (produced Evanston, Illinois, 1975). Published in *New Lafayette Theatre Presents*, edited by Ed Bullins, New York, Doubleday, 1974.
Malcolm Man/Don't Live Here No Mo' (produced Philadelphia, 1979.)
I'm Black When I'm Singing, I'm Blue When I Ain't (produced Atlanta, 1982.)

Short Stories

A Sound Investment, Chicago, Third World Press, 1980.

Other

The Adventures of Fathead, Smallhead, and Squarehead (for children). New York, Third Press, 1973.
Crisis in Culture. Black Librarian Press, 1983.

Editor, *Three Hundred Sixty Degrees of Blackness Comin' at You*. New York, 5X, 1972.
Editor, *We Be Word Sorcerers: 25 Stories by Black Americans*. New York, Bantam. 1973.

*

Critical Studies: "Sonia Sanchez and Her Work" by S. Clarke, in *Black World* (Chicago), June 1971; "The Poetry of Three Revolutionists: Don L. Lee, Sonia Sanchez, and Nikki Giovanni" by R. Roderick Palmer, in *CLA Journal* (Baltimore), September 1971; "Sonia Sanchez Creates Poetry for the Stage" by Barbara Walker, in *Black Creation* (New York), Fall 1973; "Notes on the 1974 Black Literary Scene" by George Kent, in *Phylon* (Atlanta), June 1974; *Black Women Writers at Work,* edited by Claudia Tate, New York, Continuum, 1983; *Black Women Writers (1950-1980)*, edited by Mari Evans, New York, Doubleday, 1984.

*   *   *

"Sonia Sanchez is a lion in literature's forest," stated Maya Angelou upon the paperback release of Sanchez' *Does Your House Have Lions?*. "When she writes she roars, and when she sleeps other creatures walk gingerly." This high praise from one of the most important poets of the 20th century is well earned. Sanchez has been a key figure in African American literature since releasing her first volume of verse, *Homecoming*, in 1969. In this collection, Sanchez set forth a political and cultural agenda that has remained central to her work throughout her career. Her early writing was published by Broadside Press, an African American-owned small press operating in Detroit.

Politically, Sanchez' early work is rooted in black nationalism—a cultural movement that reached its height in the 1960s and promoted an African American identity that was clearly distinguished from the white establishment. Nation of Islam leader Malcolm X figures heavily in her work, and she has credited him with influencing her style as well as her politics. "A lot of our words and language came from Malcolm," she stated. "He was always messing with the language and messing with people, and sometimes in a very sly kind of way demanding things of people and also cursing people out." While later work is not born of any specific ideology, Sanchez continues to focus on all aspects of the African

American experience, as well as the joys and tribulations of womanhood.

These aspects range from addressing racism to drug abuse and AIDS to celebrating and incorporating African American culture, especially jazz and blues music. Her staccatoed, rhythmic early verse has been compared with the music of jazz innovator John Coltrane and noted by critics as being distinctly born out of African American oral traditions. "The distinguishing characteristic of her work is a language which catches the nuance of the spoken word, the rhythms of the street, and of a music which is partly jazz and partly a lyricism which underlies ordinary conversation," commented C. W. E. Bigsby in *The Second Black Renaissance: Essays in Black Literature*. Sanchez is also known for her plays, short stories and children's books.

Sanchez was born Wilsonia Benita Driver in Birmingham, Alabama, and was raised for a time by her paternal grandmother. Her mother died when Sanchez was only a year old, her grandmother when Sanchez was five. After several tumultuous years, marked by frequent moves to various relatives and abuse by her stepmother, in 1943 Sanchez moved with her father and his third wife to New York City. She began writing out of a sense of isolation and a desire to express herself without the hindrance of the stutter she had developed during childhood.

Sanchez studied political science and poetry at Hunter College in New York and after graduation studied creative writing at New York University. One of her teachers was acclaimed poet Louise Bogan, who encouraged Sanchez to pursue a literary career. Sanchez formed a writers' workshop in Greenwich Village, attended by such seminal poets as Ameri Baraka (LeRoi Jones), Haki R. Madhubuti (Don L. Lee) and Larry Neal. She married Puerto Rican immigrant Albert Sanchez, but the two later divorced.

Sanchez' poetry has explored a variety of styles, techniques and subjects over time. *Homecoming* addresses the difficult realities of the urban, African-American world, as seen through the eyes of an educated woman viewing the place she grew up through new eyes. "I returned tourist/style to watch all/the niggers killing/ themselves with/three-for-oners . . . I have learned it/ain't like they say/in the newspapers," she writes in the title poem. *We a BaddDDD People* treads similar territory, although Sanchez addresses personal demons here as well, such as in "A Poem for my Father." *Love Poems* is more imagistic and here Sanchez experiments with new forms, including haiku.

The autobiographical *A Blues Book for Blue Black Magical Women*, dedicated to "Queens of the Universe" and divided into the sections "Past," "Present," "Rebirth," and "Future," has been labeled "a spiritual autobiography." The volume traces the development of one woman's personal and social consciousness as she evolves in the black Muslim community. By 1978, Sanchez was revered enough to release a volume of collected works. *I've Been a Woman* features celebrated past works as well as new poems. *Homegirls and Handgrenades* and *Under a Soprano Sky* were noted for the maturity they revealed. Critics commended Sanchez for maintaining her political fervor even as she evolved as a writer.

Sanchez did not publish *Wounded in the House of a Friend* until eight years after *Under a Soprano Sky*, but it was eight years well spent. At turns compassionate, prideful, angry, and determined, she writes about betrayals, hardships, and triumphs, exhorting readers to "Catch the fire . . . and live/live/livelivelivelive." Sanchez followed up that volume with the poignant *Does Your House Have Lions?*, a painful and honest exploration of her brother's death from AIDS. Each poem in the series was composed in difficult terza rima form. "Sonia Sanchez is a brave an loving sister," wrote Haki R. Madhubuti. "This powerful and riveting work chronicles her brother's death from AIDS, yet this is not an AIDS book. It is a poet's complex and insightful telling of her family's confrontation with itself, their brother-son, their history and a fatal illness. Truly, this is a work of love and art that confirms Ms. Sanchez as one of the nation's finest poets."

—Kristin Palm

SANDERS, Dori

Born: York County, South Carolina, c. 1930. **Education:** Attended community colleges in Maryland. **Career:** Farmer and storyteller; lecturer. **Awards:** Honorary doctorate, Newberry College, Newberry, South Carolina.

PUBLICATIONS

Novels

Clover. Chapel Hill, Algonquin Books, 1990.
Her Own Place. Chapel Hill, Algonquin Books, 1993.

Nonfiction

Dori Sanders' Country Cooking: Recipes and Stories from the Family Farm Stand. Chapel Hill, Algonquin Books, 1995.

* * *

Dori Sanders' South is an unusual one—that of a privileged African American. Sanders grew up on a large (now almost 300 acres) peach farm. Similar to her best-known character, Clover, Dori was the daughter of a school principal, a prudent man. He purchased 81 acres in 1915 because he thought the sandy soil of the Filbert, South Carolina, area would be wonderful for Elberta peaches and sweet potatoes. He was right. The Sanders farm has prospered and is known for its quality vegetables and peaches. Today, visitors from all over the world visit the Sanders Farm Stand on Highway 321, not just to buy produce but hoping to buy peaches (and perhaps a book) from Dori Sanders herself. Usually they're successful because Dori still works on the farm and goes away only in the winter months to write or to undertake short lecture tours.

The deceptively fragile-seeming novelist boasts that her Massey-Ferguson tractor is bigger than the one her older brother Orestus drives and that she handles her share of the chores easily. Her typical workday begins at 4:30 a.m. and ends at sunset. She tries to maintain that schedule year-around, on and off the farm. Dori finds beauty in everything, rocks included. Farm visitors are offered rocks she lovingly gathers from the fields. Lucky folk get

to visit the grandest rock of all—her storytelling rock. There, as a child some 60 years ago, she began telling stories. The tremendous outcropping, as tall as the trees, must be seen to be believed. *People* magazine photographer Thomas England captured its size and coral-like texture in a photo published July 19, 1993. Jack Daniel Davis, writing in the July, 1996, issue of *IdioM,* gave his impression after having been driven there in Dori's yellow truck: "'That is THE most FANTASTIC rock in the world!' I shouted, jumping out before the truck stopped . . . . The Gods put that rock there for the storytellers to find. That rock would seem more at home in Monument Valley than at the top of a hill on a peach farm in Filbert, S.C. . . . Dori showed me the hole in the rock where her child tales were born. She showed me the ledge where she sits now. As a child she could slip her whole body into the tiny cleft."

One of a houseful of children of Marion Sylvester and Cazetta Sylvia Patton Sanders, Dori was graduated from Roosevelt High School in Clover, South Carolina and attended community colleges in Maryland. Throughout her life Dori has told stories and been a keen observer of the world around her. She writes her observations on bits of paper, which usually find their way into her books. She is also blessed with a photographic memory and says that since childhood her mind has been like a sponge.

These qualities help her to "play-act," which rids her of nervousness before cameras or on stage. She told Dannye Romine Powell of the *Charlotte Observer,*

> I have to play-act to go on this tour.... There is nothing that has prepared me for the things that I've been exposed to ... I pretend I'm not Dori Sanders. I usually will pick a character, and usually they're all faded movie stars. They had a manner.... I'm Lena Horne ... or I'm Joan Crawford ... Oh, yes. The way she just held her body straight, held her head high. That's where I get the courage to go on the stage. If I didn't play-act, I couldn't do it.

The thousands who have seen her on stage or on television would find this revelation hard to believe. Dori grabs an audience the minute she opens her mouth and keeps it mesmerized through her last word. She is a natural humorist; many think she is as good a comedienne as she is a writer.

Sanders began her writing career while she was living with her sister, a university dean, and working winters as a motel banquet manager in Maryland. Her boss came upon some napkins she'd scribbled on, noticed a flair for writing and encouraged her to do more. She completed a manuscript and submitted it to Algonquin, but the editors pronounced it a little too melodramatic; however, they recognized the talent, and a certain freshness of style. Sanders then decided to write about what she knew best—farm life, and the editors were delighted.

The idea for *Clover* (1990) came while she was watching traffic pass in front of the peach shed. First a black funeral procession crept by and a very sad little girl waved timidly to Dori. Sometime later a white funeral passed, and a very sad young woman made eye contact with her. Dori's imagination ran rampant. What if . . .: The white woman became stepmother to the black child, whose widowed father was killed on the day of his second wedding. "They dressed me in white for my daddy's funeral," symbolically opens the novel of subtle conflict. The conflict is cultural and culinary rather than color; Clover's main worry is whether white Sara Kate knows how to cook grits well.

Although written as an adult novel, *Clover* quickly became popular as a young adult book and is on the required reading lists at schools throughout the nation. Thus, Sanders has been drawn into hundreds of schools for workshops and readings. *Clover* remained on the *Washington Post*'s best-seller list 10 weeks; it was made into a movie for television and has been translated into six languages. *Publisher's Weekly* praised it, "Infusing her first novel with black vernacular as convincing as Alice Walker's, imaginative metaphors that rival Maya Angelou's and humor as delicious as Zora Neale Hurston's, Sanders has created a fresh new voice."

That new voice followed with another best-seller in 1993, *Her Own Place*. This novel has a mature woman narrator: Mae Lee Barnes is a survivor who raises five children on land that she buys. In her retirement she becomes the first black hospital auxiliary member. As did 10-year-old Clover, Mae Lee quickly endears herself to readers.

Food is important in both novels, so it follows that *Dori Sanders' Country Cooking: Recipes and Stories from the Family Farm Stand* (1995) is her third publication, a cookbook with stories that entertain while they instruct. A major source for the recipes was her Aunt Vestula, a fine plantation cook from near Charleston. It was in her mother's kitchen that Dori learned to cook, as a child. But it was her father's world that formed the writer. "He loved words," she says. He wrote and he always made sure that his children had plenty to read, between chores. Her father is the subject of her current work in progress.

—Gayle Edwards

SAYERS, Valerie

Born: Beaufort, South Carolina, 8 August 1952. **Family:** Married Christian Jara, 29 June 1974, 2 children. **Education:** Fordham University, B.A. (cum laude) 1973; Columbia University, M.F.A. 1976. **Career:** Worked variously as a waitress, free-lance consultant and scriptwriter, and associate editor at an anarchist publishing house; part-time instructor at Polytechnic Institute of New York and City University of New York; instructor and director of the creative writing program, University of Notre Dame; editor, *Notre Dame Review*; reviewer, including *New York Times Book Review*. **Agent:** Esther Newberg, International Creative Management, 40 West 57th St., New York, New York 10019.

PUBLICATIONS

Novels

Due East. New York, Doubleday, 1987.
How I Got Him Back; or, Under the Cold Moon's Shine. New York, Doubleday, 1989.
Who Do You Love? New York, Doubleday, 1991.

The Distance Between Us. New York, Doubleday, 1994.
Brain Fever. New York, Doubleday, 1996

*   *   *

Due East, South Carolina, is a fictional coastal town peopled by well-intentioned and often comically hapless characters with strong family ties and feelings of love who are trying to do their best in an uncertain world. With affection and poignant satire, Valerie Sayers has developed this rich setting and a colorful assembly of characters, several of whom appear in more than one of her books. In the finest sense of regional literature—where an author cultivates universal themes and significance as well as idiosyncracies of characters in a local setting over several works—Sayers has created a quirky, contemporary realm in which such concerns as love, communication, death, and relationships are addressed as individuals are comically thwarted and surprised in their attempts to gain order and happiness in their lives. In her creation of a distinctly Southern setting that broadens with each work and features recurring characters, Sayers's work can be likened in an instructive, if superficial, sense to Faulkner's stories of Yoknapatawpha County. She shares as well with Faulkner an interest in experimentations with narrative, including use of multiple viewpoints.

Sayers developed Due East and its people based on her experiences in Beaufort, South Carolina, where she was raised and lived until she was 17. Then she set off for New York, not quite in the manner of Professor Tim "Looney" Rooney, who appears in Sayers's second novel, *How I Got Him Back; or, Under the Cold Moon's Shine* (where he falls in love with the heroine of her first novel, *Due East*) and is the focus of her fifth novel, *Brain Fever*. Rooney sets off to New York as a professor attempting to rediscover his emotional, psychological, and spiritual bearings; Sayers went off to school, graduating from Fordham University, attaining an MFA from Columbia, then teaching at Polytechnic Institute of New York and City University of New York. She subsequently settled in at Notre Dame as director of the university's creative writing program. ,That Southern landscape of Beaufort, however, has proven to be a setting of endless riches for the writer whom Pat Conroy called "the most authentic new fiction voice since Mary Gordon."

Due East, Sayers's first novel, introduces the town and relates the story of fifteen-year-old Mary Faith Rapple and her father, Jesse. Mary Faith is bright and seemingly self-sufficient (her mother died three years earlier), but she is desperately lonely, while Jesse is gentle and withdrawn into grief and alcohol after the loss of his wife. Their tenuous relationship is threatened by a lapse in communication, and when Mary Faith intentionally gets pregnant, Jesse renews his attention to their relationship, which draws him out of his desolate state. The comical, even farcical elements that recur in Sayers's work are reflected here in Jesse's attempt to deal with the pregnancy: he tries to confront the man he thinks is the baby's father, but instead becomes romantically involved with and impregnates the young man's mother.

Sayers's penchant for experimenting with narrative occurs in this work through her use of separate voices—Mary Faith's first-person narration and a third-person narrator reporting Jesse's point of view. This disjunction presented in alternating chapters reveals a growing communication gap until the novel's conclusion, when the two voices are brought together for the first time and a tentative, but by no means definitive recovery is revealed.

Mary Faith reappears in Sayers's second novel, *How I Got Him Back*, as one of three women struggling to hang on to their man. Mary Faith has had a four-year affair with Stephen Dugan and wants to marry him; Marygail, Stephen's wife, intends to win back his love and fortify their marriage; and Becky Perdue, one of the primary narrators of the novel, wants to win back her husband, Jack, who has left her for another woman. Tim Rooney, who is in love with Mary Faith and recovering from a nervous breakdown, is also featured in this novel, as is Father Berkeley, an alcoholic priest who reflects the yearning of all the characters in his pursuit of spiritual peace and sanity in a mixed-up world. *Who Do You Love?* and *The Distance Between Us* continues to probe the heartfelt miseries as well as the redeeming qualities of love and relationships. The latter presents a romance between Steward, a staid young man from a wealthy background, and Franny, a wild, fun-loving girl. Their relationship survives years of separation, her marriage, and his continuing success and opportunities.

Brain Fever, her fifth novel in ten years, features the loves and travails of Tim "Looney" Rooney, a fifty-something part-time philosophy professor. Quitting his medication and security, Rooney leaves his intended bride in Due East and heads for New York City with $15,000. His adventures include teaming with a hitchhiker and boarding with her friends in Manhattan, where he begins searching for his ex-wife. The story gradually turns from a light, picaresque comedy to more serious issues, as Professor Tim slides into madness and becomes a street person. A chance meeting with a former student helps lift Rooney out of misery, but the novel's dark turns are more inexorably painful than those presented in Sayers's earlier work, adding yet more breadth of human drama to her natives of Due East.

—Aaron Badushe

SEAY, James

Born: Panola County, Mississippi, 1 January 1939. **Education:** University of Mississippi, B.A. 1964; University of Virginia, M.A. 1966. **Family:** Married Lee Smith, June 17, 1967 (divorced 1982); two children. **Career:** Instructor in English, Virginia Military Institute, 1966-68; assistant professor of English, University of Alabama, 1968-71, Vanderbilt University, 1971-74; lecturer in English, University of North Carolina, Chapel Hill, since 1974. **Awards:** Southern Literary Festival Prize, 1964; Academy of American Poets Poetry Prize, 1966; Emily Clark Balch Prize, 1968. **Address:** Department of English, University of North Carolina, Chapel Hill, North Carolina 27514.

PUBLICATIONS

Let Not Your Hart. Middletown, Connecticut, Wesleyan University Press, 1970.
Water Tables. Middletown, Connecticut, Wesleyan University Press, 1974.

The Light as They Found It. New York, Quill, 1990.
Open Field, Understory: New and Selected Poems. Baton Rouge, Louisiana State University Press, 1997.

* * *

Admired by fellow Southern poets such as James Dickey and Fred Chappell, James Seay has created a substantial body of work since his début in 1970 with his first published collection of poems, *Let Not Your Hart*. Born in 1939 in Mississippi, Seay grew up in his native state and attended the University of Mississippi, where he received his bachelor's degree. Later Seay obtained a Master's in English from the University of Virginia before teaching at various Southern schools. He has always lived in his native South and his poetry reflects that deep attachment.

The story-telling heritage of the South is in rich evidence in *Let Not Your Hart*. In "The Barber With California Tan," Seay relates the story of a barber, one of the many small-town characters he knew from Southern life, whose razor "trembles" at Seay's neck "claims an eternal California tan, / says he went there once to harvest citrus fruit." The California excursion was most likely the highlight of the barber's life—his one big adventure as a young man before going home to Mississippi to trim mustaches and cut hair. Seay's compassion for the barber is evident in the concluding lines of the poem:

> For proof he rolls the sleeve of his nylon barber suit
> And bares the hairless white arm of an aging man.
> When he is done and I have paid, I rise
> And walk through winter sunlight fragile as glass.

The ending lines of Seay's poem suggest the fragility of human self-esteem, and the poet is unwilling to shatter the barber's self-delusion.

The elegiac "One Last Cheer for Punk Kincaid" from his first book illustrates Seay's narrative strength. The poem concerns an ex-high school football star who goes to prison for cattle rustling. Ironically, Punk Kincaid drowns in an effort to retrieve the body of a drowning victim. Punk's body is not recovered and Seay imagines that "the drowned are running interference / for Punk Kincaid / As he returns a punt / From deep inside his own territory. Unlike his surviving teammates, including the narrator of the poem, Punk Kincaid dies young and his death probably saves him from a bitter life that peaked early in high school and was already on the skids.

There is evinced in Seay's poems, however, an appreciation for the mundane life of the ordinary man. Seay's style of quiet, nonjudgmental observation of the stringent limitations of ordinary lives is the focus of one poem (with the ironic title, "Big Money Comes to My Hometown") about his hometown where the workers who once made ice buckets and camp stoves are retrained to make bomb fins for the Federal Government. Some 100 to 200 workers taking Seay's old graveyard shift in the factory will enjoy the privilege of making bomb fins "for minimum wage / and learn to watch / the small, grave hours / of the dark." There is no way out for Seay's townsmen. They will live all their lives in this small town and pray that the U.S. Government doesn't pull out and take their repetitious jobs away.

Seay's second book, *Water Tables*, shows his growth as a poet. The imprint of family ties, a common subject for Southern writers, is portrayed in a poem Seay wrote for his oldest son, "For Joshua, At His Great-Grandfather's Grave." Seay describes a visit to a family cemetery in a Virginia valley where coal miners "with black lung / drop into the shafts each morning, / knowing no other way." The poet volunteers his willingness to accept on behalf of his young son both the heritage and the history of their family ties that the son can now only dimly understand:

> I accept
> that all is marked for this wall, this valley,
> that this is what the numbers add up to,
> I accept, I accept,
> all but what has been marked against
> your green assembly.

Forseeing his own eventual death, Seay affirms for his son that "there is only one faith / and it is written in these leaves."

Seay's early style was marked by a brash directness which now begins mellowing into a softer, more reflective indirectness honed by a lean, spare lyricism. The geography of Seay's Southern terrain and waters, the patterns of family history, and the presence of friends appear frequently in his poetry. An example of his celebration of friendship is the pixish "The Ballet of Happiness." A former student writes Seay asking him if he is happy. Unable to answer, the poet remembers his student's one time response to the same question. What had made her happy were:

> Friends calling in the moonlight
> to her balcony, saying they had to come
> to dance for the Ballet of Happiness.
> Which they did, their bright mescaline eyes
> smiling up at her, and when it was over
> they bowed like children in a play and left—just walked
> across the grass,
> leaving her dazzled and happy
> with the funny shapes of their footwork fading in the dew.

The imagery of the student's friends dancing for her under the moonlight evokes for us a sense of stepping into a live fairy tale, and in this way Seay transforms the commonplace of private events by suggesting deeper mysteries within reach of our understanding. And yet Seay shares with many Southern poets a wariness with overdone surrealism and symbolism. Seay's late poems may often be obliquely subtle; however, they never lose their accessibility and remain concretely rooted in human existence and the natural world.

The Light as They Found It (1990) is a literary triumph. Seay acquires in this work a rich mastery of his craft which is now at full service to his recurring themes of family, community, and nature. A key poem in this collection that beautifully weds all three themes together is "Where Our Voices Broke Off." Seay's sense of wonderment over the natural world and man's place within it is displayed in these following lines: "Last night from its porch I looked up / With my wife and friends to our share of the galaxy, whorled pure and free of mainland lights." Seay's urbanized Southern Everyman may still enter into a deeper communion with his own community and environment, but it requires his full alert attention. In the following brilliant passage Seay unites into a beautiful whole, man, community, and nature in faultless lines:

> I felt our voices drawn out into the dark
> and it seemed to me the round island was a stone
> turning beneath us, grinding our voices with the shells of
> shrimps in the kitchen pail,
> the quilts by the door,
> the hyphens in the names of boats at anchor—all of it
> drawn
> and turning under the stone—the drums of paint
> for the lighthouse diamonds, the bright water that breaks
> on shoals and jetties, whatever yields to silence, ground
> with our voices and spread like gust across the spaces.

The voice of the older poet is quiet, mellowing like fine aged bourbon, more appreciative and accepting of what life has to offer as gifts which one receives by not demanding them in the first place. In "Gifts Divided" Seay's words glide smoothly like a spring breeze:

> This morning the light lay across the table
> in a way that lifted
> from the shallow of a favored bowl the tincture
> of petals I floated there
> half without a plan over the course of a year
> I had hoped long lost.
> A simple fingerbreadth of water
> would have buoyed—for what while longer?

The "failure of early happiness" and sorting out its "obsessively sad riddle" is now accepted calmly in middle age as one accepts the sweetness of the light and beauty to be found in life's "ongoing patter and patterning."

In Seay's newest poems, some of which are printed in *Open Field, Understory* (1997), a selection of his entire *oeuvre*, he continues to give us pleasure with poems written in various styles, using rhyme, assonance, couplets, open forms, and even haiku. There are some beautiful elegies for dead friends, family members, and admired persons. In "Gift List," Seay writes about a long-dead distant cousin, Mrs. D. G. Hay, who at age 83 made a list in her birthday book of who had attended an old party and what they gave her as presents. Long-deceased matrons with old-fashioned names like Ola Swango, Alma Lemaster, Sadie Page, and Boothe Wilkes come back to life through Seay's act of imagination. As the poet comes across this list he reads with amusement, Mrs D. G. Hay's meticulous itemization of her friends's presents that transform "into joy and longing" when Seay sees his mother's face:

> In her name there, and the listed gift,
> Lucy Belle Seay—cake
> her given name miscast in Mrs Hay's crabbed hand,
> but wholly light in all that came
> off the page, Lucie, the cake in her hands
> offered, the bread
> of every day she had folded with light
> and brought as a gift."

The tender concluding lines of the poem summarizes James Seay's mature poetic vision with its respect for the continuity in human life of family, memory, and the nurturing bread of every day life with its gift of insight and wonder.

— Alphonse Vinh

SETTLE, Mary Lee

Born: Charleston, West Virginia, 29 July 1918. **Education:** Sweet Briar College, 1936-38. **Family:** Married Rodney Weathersbee, 1939 (divorced); one son; married Douglas Newton, 1946 (divorced); married William Littleton Tazewell, 1978. **Career:** Model and actress, New York, New York, 1938-39; served in the British Women's Auxiliary Air Force and as a writer for the Office of War Information in London during World War II; assistant editor at *Harper's* magazine, 1946; freelance journalist in London, including etiquette expert for *Woman's Day* (as Mrs. Charles Palmer) in 1949 and English correspondent to *Flair*, 1950-51; associate professor, Bard College, New York, 1956-76; visiting lecturer, University of Virginia, 1978. **Awards:** Guggenheim fellow, 1958, 1960; Merrill Foundation award, 1975; National Book Award, 1978, for *Blood Tie*; Janet Heidinger Kafka Prize, 1983, for fiction. **Address:** c/o Farrar Straus & Giroux, 19 Union Square West, New York, New York 10003-3304.

PUBLICATIONS

Novels

The Love Eaters. New York, Harper, 1954.
The Kiss of Kin. New York, Harper, 1955.
Beulah Quintet:
  O Beulah Land. New York, Viking, 1956.
  Know Nothing. New York, Viking, 1960.
  Prisons. New York, Putnam, 1973.
  The Scapegoat. New York, Random House, 1980.
  The Killing Ground. New York, Farrar Straus, 1982.
Fight Night on a Sweet Saturday (originally part of the Beulah Series). New York, Viking, 1964.
The Clam Shell. New York, Delacorte Press, 1971.
Blood Tie. Boston, Houghton Mifflin, 1977.
Celebration, illustrated by John Collier. New York, Farrar Straus, 1986.
Charley Bland. Franklin Center, Pennsylania, Franklin Library, 1989.
Choices. New York, Talese/Doubleday, 1995.

Uncollected Short Stories

"Congress Burney," in *Paris Review,* 7, 1954-55.
"The Old Wives' Tale," in *Harper's Magazine,* September 1955.
"Paragraph Eleven," in *The Girl in the Black Raincoat* edited by George Garrett. New York, Duell, 1966.
"Coalburg, Virginia: One of the Lucky Ones," in *While Someone Else Is Eating* edited by Earl Shorris. Garden City, Doubleday, 1984.

Other

All the Brave Promises: The Memories of Aircraft Woman 2nd Class 2146391. New York, Delacorte, 1966.
The Story of Flight (for children), illustrated by George Evans. New York, Random House, 1967.
The Scopes Trial: The State of Tennessee v. John Thomas Scopes. New York, Watts, 1972.
Water World (for children). New York, Dutton, 1984.
Turkish Reflections: A Biography of a Place. New York, Prentice Hall, 1991.

*

Critical Studies: "The Searching Voice and Vision of Mary Lee Settle" by Peggy Bach, in the *Southern Review,* October 1984; "Mary Lee Settle and the Tradition of Historical Fiction," *South Atlantic Quarterly,* Summer 1987, and "Mary Lee Settle and the Critics" in *Virginia Quarterly Review,* Summer 1989, both by Brian Rosenberg; *Understanding Mary Lee Settle* by George Garrett, Columbia, University of South Carolina Press, 1988; "Mary Lee Settle: 'Ambiguity of Steel'" by Jane Gentry Vance, in *American Women Writing Fiction: Memory, Identity, Family, Space* edited by Mickey Pearlman, The University Press of Kentucky, 1989; *Mary Lee Settle's Beulah Quintet: The Price of Freedom* by Brian Rosenberg, Baton Rouge, Louisiana State University Press, 1991.

*   *   *

Mary Lee Settle is most famous for her five novels known collectively as The Beulah Quintet, but she has also written important works of non-fiction as well as several other distinctive novels, including *Blood Tie*, which won the National Book Award in 1978. By the time she won that honor Settle had clearly established her reputation, yet some journalists reporting the award referred to her as a previously unknown author, a circumstance reflective of Settle's career until the 1980s, when the completion of the Beulah Quintet assured that her body of work could rightly be called a major literary accomplishment of the second half of the twentieth century.

Her fiction reveals exhaustive research blended well with her journalistic training and powers of observation. In The Beulah Quintet, for example, she dramatized factual incidents, recreated historical communities based on the kinds of people who actually settled there, and wrote seamless, flowing narratives where, as George Garrett noted, "technique is used to disguise itself." In exploring the past, particularly a distinctive moment in time, Settle reveals its affects on the present—the influence of memory, sense of place, and relationships as well as the power of the historical moment.

Born in Charleston, West Virginia, Settle moved with her family when she was an enfant to Harlan County, Kentucky, where her father owned a coal mine. After other stops in Kentucky, West Virginia, and Florida (her father was an engineer), the family returned to Charleston, where Settle lived until she was 18. She attended Sweet Briar College for two years, then left for New York City, where she worked as a model and actress from 1938 until her marriage in 1939. When her English husband was called into military service at the beginning of World War II, Settle went to England and served in the British Women's Auxiliary Air Force for a year before transferring to the Office of War Information in London as a writer. After the war she returned divorced to New York City, where she worked briefly as an assistant editor at *Harper's* before quitting to devote herself to writing. Settle remarried and returned to England, where she wrote prolifically.

Unable to interest publishers in her fiction, Settle wrote journalistic pieces as a means for financial support. Settle told *Contemporary Authors* that journalism was "the best training in the world. During that time I learned how to meet deadlines; I grew up as a get-it-on-the-page journalist who could research enough to write 5,000 lively words about anything in a few days." For a year she wrote as Mrs. Charles Palmer, etiquette expert for *Woman's Day*, and in 1949 she was English correspondent for *Flair* magazine. Her first two novels, *The Love Eaters* and *The Kiss of Kin,* and were published in 1954 and 1955, respectively, but neither has received serious attention. Settle had also begun work on what would become her greatest achievement, The Beulah Quintet.

In The Beulah Quintet, written over 28 years, Settle delineates 300 years of American and American-related history by telling the story of three West Virginia families, the Laceys, the Catletts, and the McKarkles. Beginning in Oliver Cromwell's England, when a common ancestor to the families refuses to recognize Cromwell's power and is summarily executed (*Prisons*, 1973), Settle leads the families through the American Revolution (*O Beulah Land*, 1956), the American Civil War (*Know Nothing*, 1960), the West Virginia coalminer's strike of 1912 (*The Scapegoat*, 1980), and finally to the present day when in the concluding book, *The Killing Ground* (1982).

Settle connected her experience in West Virginia—what she observed of its people, history, and landscape—with extensive historical research. In her quest to investigate the social and political motivations that led to the formation of the United States, Settle succeeded in writing compelling historical fiction through well-researched prose, development of characters and dialogue, and eye for detail. Her realistic evocation of the hardships of settling in the New World and the variety of people who came is most noteworthy. Settle's research had revealed that over three-quarters of settlers who came to Virginia from 1675 to 1775 were probably felons. *O Beulah Land* describes the founding of the fictional West Virginia community of Beulah by Hannah Bridewell, a transported London prostitute, and Jeremiah Catlett, a fugitive bondsman, in the years before the American Revolution.

The first two books published in The Beulah Quintet were released in 1956 and 1960. Neither attracted great attention, and Settle focused on teaching during much of the 1960s: she was an associate professor at Bard College in New York beginning in 1956 and retiring in 1976, interrupted by stays in England from 1969 to 1971 and in Turkey from 1972 to 1974.

Settle had written *Fight Night on a Sweet Saturday* (1964) with the intention of making it the concluding volume (of what was then The Beulah Trilogy), but the book was a commercial and critical failure, though even in this disappointment there are eloquent moments. Settle later reworked some of the ideas central to *Fight Night* in what became the final Beulah book, *The Killing Ground*, published in 1982. After the failure of *Fight Night*, Settle published a memoir, *All the Brave Promises* (1966), of her experi-

ences in the British Women's Auxiliary Air Force during World War II. Settle dispels romantic myths that had sprung up about the war years, describing instead the exhausting sense of loss, boredom, and depravation.

Settle wrote *Prisons*, the first book chronologically in the Beulah Quintet and the third to be published, during her time in Turkey. In that novel she turned to England of the seventeenth century in her search for the seeds of American democracy. *The Scapegoat*, published in 1980 and forming the fourth novel of the Beulah Quintet, revolves around a West Virginia coal miners' strike that occurred in 1912, with characters that include the historical figure Mother Jones, the United Mine Workers organizer. In the concluding book, *The Killing Ground,* Settle reveals that the narrator, Hannah McKarkle, a descendant of all three families, wrote the books to understand her family's history. She is compelled to do so because her brother, Johnny, dies a violent death in jail and she is trying to understand the forces that precipitated the event.

Blood Tie was written after Settle returned to West Virginia from Turkey. This work concerns a group of expatriates who have dropped out of American society of the 1970s to live in Turkey. Using multiple narrators, Settle captures expatriates disillusioned with what America has become and trying to a survive in a place strange to them. Settle later wrote a non-fiction book, *Turkish Reflections* (1991), about Turkey and her experiences in that country. More than a travel book or personal memoir, *Turkish Reflections* is a combination of history, a description of the current state of that nation, a bit of travelogue, and Settle's own experiences there. She, too, had despaired at the state of American society and politics while also becoming enchanted with the landscape and climate of Turkey.

After completing the Beulah series in 1982, Settle's next novel was distinctly different. Like *Blood Tie, Celebration* (1986) concerns a group of expatriates, this time in London and living relatively joyful lives. A minor character in *The Killing Ground* was the focus of her next novel, *Charley Bland* (1989), where the female narrator has known the title character since childhood and relates the story of his life and their affair together. Set in a small community in the 1960s, Settle probes the inner tickings of America at a specific time and place by delving into the emotions and psychology of the main characters. Similarly, the heroine of Settle's 1995 novel *Choices*, Melinda Kregg Dunston, escapes her life as a Virginia debutante in 1930 after her father's suicide and lives an extraordinary life of activism and service to others in the Kentucky coal mines, in Spain of the late 1930s, in London during and after World War II, and in Mississippi during the 1960s battle for civil rights. Here, again, as in all her work, history is dramatized and made real, with actual events recreated and experienced by well-drawn characters—with the details and vivid writing that makes her prose so powerful.

—Emma Cobb

SHELNUTT, Eve

Born: Eve Brown Waldrop in Spartanburg, South Carolina, 29 August 1941. **Education:** University of Cincinnati, B.A. in English, 1972; University of North Carolina at Greensboro, M.F.A. in creative writing, fiction and poetry, 1973. **Family:** Married William Shelnutt, 1961 (divorced 1968); one child; one grrandchild; married Mark Logan Shelton, 1981 (divorced 1988). **Career:** Assistant professor, Western Michigan University, 1975-80; professor, Goddard College, 1980-81; associate professor, University of Pittsburgh, 1980-88; professor, Ohio University, 1988-94, and The College of The Holy Cross, 1994; since readings and workshops at numerous colleges, universities, and institutes; director of Balfour Foundation for enhancement of writing in the Worcester, Massachusetts and public schools.

PUBLICATIONS

Short Fiction Collections

Sparrow 62 (chapbook). Santa Barbara, Black Sparrow, 1977.
The Love Child. Santa Barbara, Black Sparrow Press, 1979.
The Formal Voice. Santa Barbara, Black Sparrow Press, 1982.
Descant (chapbook). Raleigh, The Palaemon Press, 1982.
The Musician. Santa Rosa, California, Black Sparrow Press, 1987.
The Girl, Painted. Pittsburgh, Carnegie Mellon University Press, 1996.

Poetry Collections

Air and Salt. Pittsburgh, Carnegie-Mellon University Press, 1983.
First a Long Hesitation. Pittsburgh, Carnegie Mellon University Press, 1992.
Recital in a Private Home. Pittsburgh, Carnegie Mellon University Press, 1988.

Other

The Magic Pencil: Teaching Children Creative Writing. Atlanta, Peachtree Publishers, Ltd., 1988.
The Writing Room: Keys To the Craft of Fiction and Poetry. Atlanta, Longstreet Press, 1989.

Editor, *Writing: The Translation of Memory.* New York, Macmillan Publishers, 1990.
Editor, *The Confidence Woman: 26 Women Writers at Work.* Atlanta, Longstreet Press, 1991.

*

Eve Shelnutt comments:

I write not only in order to ask questions about human relationships but also in order to live through my characters more fully than the discipline required to write demands. In terms of form, what interests me is balancing all fictional elements within the story's compression so precisely that its unity cannot be reduced to its parts. My fiction will not be taken up by book-discussion groups, and that is as it should be: my stories require a solitary reader's surrender to intimacy, in an era of endless talk as its displacement.

*   *   *

Since 1994, Eve Shelnutt has been permanent writer-in-residence at the College of the Holy Cross in Worcester, Massachusetts,

where she is also director of the Balfour Foundation for the enhancement of writing in the Worcester public schools. She is author or editor of fourteen books, including three collections of short fiction, three collections of poetry, and several writing texts for adults and children and volumes of collected essays.

The middle of three sisters, Shelnutt was born in Spartanburg, South Carolina, in 1941 and spent most of her early life in transit. Her father, a broadcast journalist, and her mother, a gifted musician, moved regularly in search of better paying jobs, and Shelnutt spent childhood years on Long Island Sound, in Venice, California, and in many points in between. She has written that she "was born into my parents' restlessness, bred of my father's need and ambition and of my mother's grudging allegiance, if not to motion, then to him, or maybe to her idea of Family that resolved itself into a configuration hard to bear for its difference from her aristocratic background."

The circumstances of Shelnutt's childhood, including her eclectic educational experiences and her parents' two marriages and divorces, and particularly the rootlessness that characterized her early life, have been powerful influences in her writing and career. She married her first husband, an air force officer and engineer, in 1961, and after the birth of her son, Gregory William Shelnutt, began to take writing classes at Wright State University in Dayton, Ohio.

After her first story won the *Mademoiselle* Fiction Award, Shelnutt began teaching in a federally funded local arts program. When her marriage ended in divorce in 1968, Shelnutt began to write nonfiction for local papers, attended Bread Loaf Writers Conference, and earned a BA in English from the University of Cincinnati. Supported by a Randall Jarrell fellowship, she went on to earn an M.F.A. in 1973 at the University of North Carolina at Greensboro, where she worked with Fred Chappell. She credits Chappell for imparting "some kind of permission" to her to "break out of the tedium of the prose I had been writing so that I could begin to suffuse it with the music that had been the constant attendant to my reading as a child."

Shelnutt is adamant that this experience and Chappell's "presence as a person and the shocking affirmation of my hopes for myself that studying with him represented" was crucial to her work. It was here that she began to have access to her past and to explore her "lifelong fury at language" from which her first work sprang and with which all her work engages. Believing that as a writer "all you have to use is language and yourself," Shelnutt has focused on the inner, reflective lives of characters interacting with others and with their circumstances. Her fictional world is not narrow; indeed, through emphasis on detail and the use of multiple perspectives, particularly, her work opens up large territories. Among the inquiries she forges in those discovered places are questions of moral character and development, of our relation to language and representation, the point and potential of literature. She feels strongly that good readers must make a commitment to pursue these questions with the writer through form and content, "Fiction is the locale of a democratic enterprise which asks the reader continually what his or her responsibilities to the writing are."

From her first volume, *The Love Child* (1979), through *The Girl, Painted* (1996), she has produced work noted for its dense yet economical style, its reliance on images, and its daring in form and content. Shelnutt has said that the "politics" of her fiction "reside in the focus of the stories, which is on small acts between people," and that her "characters' conflicts arise from their interactions. What each character effects and is affected by sums up the characters for the reader." She sees her focus as quite distinct from most contemporary fiction which "suggests an anomie afflicts contemporary man." This affliction may indeed be contemporary, but it is not one that she is particularly interested in.

Although a Southerner by birth, Shelnutt does not see herself as a particularly "Southern" writer. In fact, she resists casual assignation to the category of Southern writing at all and has written that the "young Southern writer's predicament . . . is to find herself pulled contradictorily by a Southern culture that, despite allowances for differences, defines Southern writing proscriptively enough to clash with the realities of a broader world culture, a culture that does not bind change so loosely to continuity." Once more, the issue is the trustworthiness of language, which, Shelnutt suggests, is used too glibly in the South to be faithful to experience. Instead, her focus is to "replicate in form a state of flux that seem[s] to constitute both my life and my passion for it." The celebrated sense of place in Southern literature is refocused: "Place for me is language and form . . . . In writing, how to capture what cannot be said in any language sounds elusively in the ear, an echo like music from an imagined source of wholeness that by its persistence as desire earns respect and endless labor."

After earning her M.F.A. at UNC-Greensboro, Shelnutt took a teaching position at Western Michigan University, where she completed her first collection of stories, *The Love Child.* Since then she has taught at Goddard College and held tenured positions at University of Pittsburgh and Ohio University, in addition to Western Michigan University and the College of the Holy Cross. Her works continues to appear in respected journals, including *Crazy Horse, Poet & Critic, Ploughshares, Shenandoah, Black Warrior Review,* and *America,* and she is at work on a book of criticism and is under contract with Carnegie Mellon Press for a collection of novellas, *The Three Fates of Anna Bersai.* She travels extensively, giving readings, finding that her "true place is on the road."

—Jay Lamar

SIDDONS, Anne Rivers

Born: Sybil Anne Rivers in Atlanta, Georgia, 9 January 1936. **Education:** Auburn University, B.A.A. 1958; attended Atlanta School of Art, c. 1958. **Family:** Married Heyward L. Siddons in 1966; 4 stepsons. **Career:** Worked in advertising with Retail Credit Co., c. 1959, Citizens & Southern National Bank, 1961-63, Burke-Dowling Adams, 1967-69, and Burton Campbell Advertising, 1969-74; full-time writer since 1974; senior editor, *Atlanta* magazine; member of governing board, Woodward Academy, and member of publications board and arts and sciences honorary council, Auburn University, 1978-83. **Awards:** Alumna achievement award in arts and humanities, Auburn University, 1985; Georgia Author of the Year, 1988.

PUBLICATIONS

Novels

Heartbreak Hotel. New York, Simon & Schuster, 1976.
The House Next Door. New York, Simon & Schuster, 1978.
Fox's Earth. New York, Simon & Schuster, 1980.
Homeplace. New York, Harper, 1987.
Peachtree Road. New York, Harper, 1988.
King's Oak. New York, HarperCollins, 1990.
Outer Banks. New York, HarperCollins, 1991.
Colony. New York, HarperCollins, 1992.
Hill Towns. New York, HarperCollins, 1993.
Downtown. New York, HarperCollins, 1994.
Fault Lines. New York, HarperCollins, 1995.
Up Island. New York, HarperCollins, 1997.
Low Country. New York, HarperCollins, 1998.

Film Adaptation: *Heart of Dixie,* adapted from her novel *Heartbreak Hotel,* 1989.

Nonfiction

John Chancellor Makes Me Cry. New York, Doubleday, 1975.
Go Straight on Peachtree. Dolphin Books, 1978.

*   *   *

In *John Chancellor Makes Me Cry* (1975), Anne Rivers Siddons relates the every day choices of her life in Atlanta, a southern setting she knows intimately and recreates often in her fiction. The memoir's humor is often compared to that of Erma Bombeck, who called Siddons "unique" and "original in her essays." Chancellor's name in the title points to Siddons's liberal use of popular culture references.

These popular references continue in the title of her first novel *Heartbreak Hotel* (1976); throughout, lyrics from Elvis Presley's hit song establish the 1956 time period, as do civil rights activities in Montgomery and references to Martin Luther King. Maggie Deloach, a protected Alabama college girl, defies convention and chooses a liberal journalist over her Delta-raised fraternity gentleman. Critics admired the novel's "anything but nostalgic" detail.

Over the past two decades Siddons's writings have become more complex and ambitious as signature techniques and motifs develop related to her women characters—who must make choices between two ways of life—and her superb evocation of time and place.

After the poorly received horror novel *The House Next Door* (1978), Siddons wrote *Fox's Earth* (1980), which introduced a signature theme: an out-of-her-element woman, usually working class, either conquers or is defeated by the wealthy society into which she marries. *Homeplace* (1987) introduces another Siddons's motif. New York journalist Mike Winship returns to Georgia after 20 years to confront and make peace with her past. Both themes will recur in Siddons's bestsellers.

In the mesmerizing *Peachtree Road* (1988), the names say it all: Sheppard Gibbs Bondurant III tells of his obsession with, and the South's destruction of, Lucy Bondurant Chastain Venable, his passionate, emotion-ridden cousin. Prefaced by James Dickey's "Looking for the Buckhead Boys," this book authentically recreates 1960s Atlanta and the Buckhead wealthy who strove to build the leading city of the new South, sometimes at their own peril. The highly praised novel launched Siddons onto the bestseller list and earned her awards, as well as comparisons to Pat Conroy, Truman Capote, and Tennessee Williams.

Named Georgia Author of the Year in 1988, Siddons also has been awarded the American Psychological Association's first media award, which cites her "insightful, intelligent, and compassionate" depiction of "people with emotional illnesses of personal crises." This award-winning talent is also reflected in later novels.

Horses, nuclear waste, sacred woodlands and a traumatized daughter tangle up the new life of recently divorced Andy Calhoun, another Siddons woman who must choose between men and contrasting lifestyles in *King's Oak* (1990), named for the huge tree that dominates the wooded tract adjacent to the Big Silver bomb plant in Pemberton, Georgia. The more popular *Outer Banks* (1991) finds cancer sufferer Kate Abrams rejuvenated after a confrontational reunion with three sorority sisters in North Carolina when the truth comes out about their college vacations. Her depictions of the power of old friendships are right on target.

The absorbing multigenerational saga bestseller *Colony* (1992) captivates readers as it follows South Carolinian Maude Gascoigne from bride of Princeton man Peter Chambliss through 70 summers to a time when she is matriarch of his family's Maine camp. The breathtaking descriptions of Maine attest to Siddons's eye for authentically rendered settings. Rome and Tuscany are described in *Hill Towns* (1993), another bestseller, which looks at the nature of love and leads an emotionally scarred woman to independence. With the crises and triumphs of Catherine Gaillard, Siddons is at the height of her storytelling powers.

Through poems, song lyrics, and political events, Siddons's novels resonate with recognizable events from her era, but *Downtown* (1994) is her most autobiographical novel. The innocent Smoky O'Donnell leaves Savannah to assume her position on *Downtown*, a hot Atlanta magazine patterned after *Atlanta* magazine, where Siddons served as senior editor. Through career, moral, and political choices, Smoky's innocence disappears with that of America's.

In *Fault Lines* (1995), Merritt Fowler, living in wealthy Atlanta, is about to crack like the California earthquake at novel's end, but through flight and a bittersweet adulterous affair she rescues herself from the role of perpetual caretaker of her younger sister, dictatorial husband, anorexic daughter, and Alzheimer-debilitated mother-in-law for the benefit of them all. In *Fault Lines*, Siddons avoids fluff fiction with her excellent landscapes and characters, who are believable and for whom we care. *Up Island* (1997) is similarly satisfying, from its collection of odd characters—"a six-foot Southern Betrayed Wife and her widowed father and a senile old Portuguese lesbian and a one-legged schoolteacher and a mongrel dog and two aberrant swans" among them—and Siddon's skillful evocation of the haunts of Martha's Vineyard. There, newly divorced Molly Redwine remains behind after a vacation to heal, emotionally and physically, from losses and pain, dark family secrets and troubled dreams. From her privileged upbringing, a happy marriage, and family life in suburban Atlanta, to discovering deception by her husband and nasty family secrets, Molly's placid, uneventful life is thrown into disarray. As she begins to live on her own accord and care for others, a surprising series of events leads to self-discovery for a woman who had led a safe and dutiful life.

—Judith C. Kohl/Mel Koler

SKINNER, Margaret

Born: Memphis, Tennessee, 3 April 1942. **Education**: University of Memphis, B.A. 1985, M.A. 1987. **Career**: Instructor, University of Memphis, 1988, 1992, and 1993, and since 1993 assistant professor of creative writing; member of Literary Arts Panel, Tennessee Arts Commission, board of directors, Tennessee Writers Alliance, board of advisers, West Tennessee Historical Society. **Address**: Department of English, University of Memphis, Memphis, Tennessee 38152.

PUBLICATIONS

Novels

Old Jim Canaan. Chapel Hill, Algonquin Books, 1990.
Molly Flanagan and the Holy Ghost. Chapel Hill, Algonquin Books, 1995.

*   *   *

Margaret Skinner is a typical Southern novelist in that she has a special fondness for the familiar. Born, reared, and educated in Memphis, Tennessee, where she continues to live and work, Skinner has already found enough material there for two very different novels. That achievement is especially impressive because the action in these two books is limited to just two areas within Memphis, the Irish Catholic Pinch district and the black neighborhoods near the famous Beale Street, while all of the characters are in some way connected with a single large Irish family.

However, if the author has staked a rather small claim as far as geography is concerned, she ranges at will through history. In *Old Jim Canaan*, though most of the chapters are dated either 1914 or 1921, one of them describes the yellow fever outbreak of 1878, and others are set at the turn of the century. Merlin Mahon's comments at the beginning of the chapter titled "Mr. Crump" reach back to an even more distant time, presenting a truly panoramic view of Memphis's eventful history.

Molly Flanagan and the Holy Ghost is more limited, as it takes place in the mid-1950s, when the twelve-year-old protagonist is almost the same age her father was at the beginning of *Old Jim Canaan*. Though there are no formal flashbacks in the later novel, people like Molly's Catholic godmother, Byrd Maclaurin, consider it their duty to keep the dead alive. Molly likes to commune with her paternal grandparents, whose photographs are displayed on a table in the living room, and her father often takes her to visit his family members in Calvary Cemetery nearby. In fact, though her grandfather Nate Flanagan died before she was born,

Molly feels so close to him that she can hardly bear it when she discovers he committed suicide and therefore must be in Hell.

There is such a zest for life in Skinner's characters and such exuberance in her narrative style that even the most minor incidents become high drama and often high comedy as well. The ordinary Saturday with which *Old Jim Canaan* begins is a good example. After Jim Flanagan and his cousin, George Mahon, have their new long trousers fitted for "the Confirmation," the real action begins. The title character, who is the vice lord of Memphis and the terror of his family, comes down to breakfast to find that his sister Jo is cutting back on his prunes and responds with a diatribe on women for Jim's benefit. The boys are sent to return a borrowed goat. The goat bolts, Jim gets into a fight, the boys move on to Beale Street and then to a carnival strip show before they go home and face the music, since all of their activities have been reported by Old Jim's informants.

Even the grimmer episodes in *Old Jim Canaan* have their share of comedy. Though the war between rival factions for control of the city involves arson, bloodshed, and murder, it has its funny moments, as when the Italian grocery-store proprietor attacks Jim's enemies with flour, or when Merlin Mahon introduces himself to Old Jim and offers his legal services keeping tally of the dead. When he sees that even with bullets whizzing around his head Mahon never spills his drink, Old Jim decides not just to hire him but to marry him off to one of his nieces.

Skinner's flair for comedy is also evident throughout *Molly Flanagan and the Holy Ghost*. The book would be worth reading if only for the account of the neighborhood picnic. Convinced that pigeons are a health hazard, Molly's mother Elizabeth invites her neighbors to a picnic in the Flanagan front yard and, with the evangelical fervor of her Protestant forebears, exhorts them to turn from their evil ways and stop putting out pigeon food. Unfortunately, her audience has been enjoying Jim's Southern Comfort, a mixture of yeast, sugar, honey, a bushel of ripe peaches, and six quarts of bourbon, which has been aging for several weeks in George Mahon's basement. However, Skinner exhibits a skill in building individual episodes that she has not yet mastered where an entire novel is concerned.

Neither of the books is driven by a single, compelling issue. In *Old Jim Canaan*, we are asked to worry about the vice war, about Old Jim's blighted romance, about a swimming competition, and about a number of problems within the family, including Rosie Mahon's alcoholism. Had the author told the entire story from young Jim Flanagan's point of view, these matters could all have been related to his coming of age. However, the shifts in point of view, along with movements back and forth through time, make the novel as a whole less effective than it could have been.

Molly Flanagan and the Holy Ghost also has a number of plot lines, including two pregnancies, physical and sexual abuse in a neighbor's family, an ongoing feud between Catholics and Protestants, and the question of what should be done about Molly's defective vision. Though the Holy Ghost made it into the title, he/she has largely vanished from the novel. However, the fact that *Molly Flanagan and the Holy Ghost* is told from a single point of view gives it a unity that its predecessor does not have.

Nevertheless, *Old Jim Canaan* is a delight to read, and it has considerable thematic depth. One is asked to consider, for example, the Catholic church's definition of good and evil as it applies to Jim Canaan, whose dirty money not only contributes to the economic health of Memphis but also, funnelled through pious women like his sister Jo, supports charitable works and even the church that considers him a damned soul.

The question of what constitutes true religion is also one of the major themes in *Molly Flanagan and the Holy Ghost*. The defect in Molly's vision, which causes her to look in two directions at the same time, symbolizes the way she pulled between the Catholics and the Protestants in her family. However, faced with real tragedies in her neighborhood and even in her own family, Molly sees that there are more important things in life than theological differences. An operation restores her vision, but it is life that teaches her about courage, honor, tolerance, and compassion, the qualities Margaret Skinner defines so well in her two memorable novels.

—Rosemary M. Canfield Reisman

SMITH, Dave

Born: David Jeddie Smith in Portsmouth, Virginia, 19 December 1942. **Education:** University of Virginia, 1961-65, B.A. in English 1965; College of William and Mary, Williamsburg, Virginia, 1966; Southern Illinois University, M.A. 1969; Ohio University, Ph.D. in English 1976. **Military Service:** U.S. Air Force, 1969-72; staff sergeant. **Family:** Married Deloras Mae Weaver in 1966; one son and two daughters. **Career:** Teacher of English and French, and football coach, Poquoson High School, Virginia, 1965-67; part-time instructor, Christopher Newport College, Newport News, Virginia, 1970-72, Thomas Nelson, Community College, Hampton, Virginia, 1970-72, and College of William and Mary, 1971; instructor, Western Michigan University, Kalamazoo, 1974-75; assistant professor, Cottey College, Nevada, Missouri, 1975-76; assistant professor, 1976-79, director of the creative writing program, 1976-80, and associate professor of English, 1979-81, University of Utah, Salt Lake City; associate professor of English, University of Florida, Gainesville, 1981; professor of English, Virginia Commonwealth University, Richmond, 1981-90; since 1990 professor of English, Louisiana State University, Baton Rouge; visiting professor of English, State University of New York, Binghamton, 1980; editor, *Sou'wester* magazine, Edwardsville, Illinois, 1967-68; founding editor, *Back Door* magazine, Poquoson, Virginia and Athens, Ohio, 1969-79; poetry editor, *Rocky Mountain Review*, Temple, Arizona, 1978-80; columnist, *American Poetry Review*, Philadelphia, 1978-82; since 1990 co-editor, *Southern Review*, Baton Rouge. **Awards:** *Kansas Quarterly* prize, 1975; Breadloaf Writers Conference John Atherton fellowship, 1975; Borestone Mountain award, 1976; National Endowment for the Arts fellowship, 1976, 1981; *Southern Poetry Review* prize, 1977; American Academy of Arts and Letters award, 1979; *Portland Review* prize, 1979; Guggenheim fellowship, 1982; Lyndhurst fellowship, 1987-89; Virginia prize in poetry, 1989. **Agent:** Timothy Seldes, Russell and Volkening Inc., 50 West 29th Street, New York, New York 10001. **Address:** Department of English, Louisiana State University, Baton Rouge, Louisiana 70803.

PUBLICATIONS

Poetry

Bull Island. Poquoson, Virginia, Back Door Press, 1970.
Mean Rufus Throw Down. Fredonia, New York, Basilisk Press, 1973.
The Fisherman's Whore. Athens, Ohio University Press, 1974.
Drunks. Edwardsville, Illinois, Sou'wester, 1974.
Cumberland Station. Urbana, University of Illinois Press, 1976.
In Dark, Sudden with Light. Athens, Ohio, Croissant, 1977.
Goshawk, Antelope. Urbana, University of Illinois Press, 1979.
Dream Flights. Urbana, University of Illinois Press, 1981.
Blue Spruce. Syracuse, Tamarack, 1981.
Homage to Edgar Allan Poe. Baton Rouge, Louisiana State University Press, 1981.
In the House of the Judge. New York, Harper, 1983.
Gray Soldiers. Winston-Salem, North Carolina, Stuart Wright, 1983.
The Roundhouse Voices: Selected and New Poems. New York, Harper, 1985.
Three Poems. Child Okeford, Dorset, Words Press, 1988.
Cuba Night. New York, Morrow, 1990.
Night Pleasures: New and Selected Poems. Newcastle upon Tyne, Bloodaxe Books, 1992.
Floating on Solitude: Three Volumes of Poetry (Illinois Poetry Series). Urbana, University of Illinois Press, 1996.
Fate's Kite: Poems, 1991-1995. Baton Rouge, Louisiana State University Press, 1996.

Novel

Onliness. Baton Rouge, Louisiana State University Press, 1981.

Short Stories

Southern Delights. Athens, Ohio, Croissant, 1984.

Other

Local Assays: On Contemporary American Poetry. Urbana, University of Illinois Press, 1985.
Pharaoh, Pharaoh: Poems, with Claudia Emerson Andrews. Baton Rouge, Louisiana State University Press, 1997.

Editor, *The Pure Clear Word: Essays on the Poetry of James Wright.* Urbana, University of Illinois Press, 1982.
Editor, with David Bottoms, *The Morrow Anthology of Younger American Poets.* New York, Morrow, 1985.
Editor, *The Essential Poe.* New York, Ecco Press, 1990.

*

Recording: *The Colors of Our Age,* Watershed, 1988.

Manuscript Collection: Ohio University Rare Books Library, Athens, Ohio.

Critical Studies: "The Mind's Assertive Flow," in *New Yorker,* July 1980, and *Part of Nature, Part of Us,* Cambridge, Massachusetts, Harvard University Press, 1981, both by Helen Vendler;

The Giver of Morning: On the Poetry of Dave Smith (includes bibliography) edited by Bruce Weigl, Birmingham, Alabama, Thunder City Press, 1982; "Unfold the Fullness: Dave Smith's Poetry and Fiction" by Thom Swiss, in *Sewanee Review,* Summer 1983; "Southern Weather" by Helen Vendler, in *New Yorker,* 1 April 1990.

Dave Smith comments:

The poems I have written are attempts to conflate the lyric and the narrative. I believe we make meaning by telling a tale, and poetry without meaning does not exist. But poetry is also song. I have wanted to find meaning and song in the prosaic and ordinary moments of our lives, in the local place and in the colorfully immediate. I began by wanting a language in the poem that was neither excessively and artificially poetic nor slack and crude as most talk, in most circumstances, usually is. I wanted a rough, measured music swelling out of and defining a narrative occasion in the way a particular man's talk, once heard, carries the full weight and shape of idiosyncratic character. All this rests on my assumption that poetry emerges from the individual spirit in crisis, that poetry matters because it is the death-wrestler, the courage-giver. Poetry is an entertainment, but it exists to give us pleasure in all the ways enumerated by Dr. Samuel Johnson: the pleasures of memory, of landscape, of diversion, of identity, of event, and of knowledge. Such pleasures arrive only from the struggle with words to know what can be known, to reveal and reinforce the human bond, the human responsibility in this world. I would be pleased to think my poems had such an effect on readers.

*   *   *

Although many parts of his career and canon reflect his life outside the South, Dave Smith is very clearly identified as a contemporary Southern poet, both by himself and by other poets and critics. Certainly his personal origins in eastern Virginia and western Maryland seem Southern enough, as does his present professional situation at Louisiana State University, where he is poetry editor of the *Southern Review.* Between these parts of his life, Smith lived in and wrote about several places outside the South, ranging from the West to Europe, but he has always returned to variations of his Southern identity in both personal, professional, and poetic terms. In his persistent exploration of both the Southern cultural heritage and the contemporary poetic situation, Smith recalls his most important literary progenitors, Robert Penn Warren and James Dickey. In fact, Smith's recent poetry reconsiders the major conflicts and contradictions of Southern culture in confronting the elusive other of race, gender, and class through innovations of genre, mode, and form. For all these reasons, Dave Smith is one of our most important contemporary Southern poets.

In his first important collection of poetry, *The Fisherman's Whore* (1974), Smith drew on his early life in the coastal low country around Portsmouth, Virginia, to discover a balance between the harsh beauty of the coastal estuaries and the hard life of Chesapeake watermen. For example, his title poem represents both the major matter and the typical form of his early work; tough, terse diction and packed, yet concise lines working within orderly, if dense stanzas and long, often periodic sentences to realize the controlling metaphor of fishing craft as the watermen's real loves. Some poetic forebears extend back through other American contemporaries, like Theodore Roethke and James Wright, to earlier figures as different as Edgar Allan Poe and Walt Whitman, as far as the traditional Anglo-Saxon bards of "The Seafarer" and "The Wanderer." Almost too insistent in staking out his poetic place, this collection certainly marked Dave Smith as a young poet worth watching.

Cumberland Station (1976) presents the other part of the poet's Southern roots in the Allegheny mountain country around Cumberland, Maryland, where he enjoyed long visits with grandparents, uncles, and cousins. The poems represent other masculine traditions of nature and sport, as well as of work and wandering, here in terms of railroads. With this new matter Smith's poetic form evolved in different directions, in particular toward more extended personal narratives in looser verse structures. Again, the title piece proves a good example by using the symbolic center of the railroad to represent not just regional history, but national and personal developments as well. The mature persona returns to an important scene of his youth, the small city's railroad depot; once the heart of a thriving railroad town, Cumberland's station is now a decaying monument to post-industrial decline, and to the loss of the poet's personal connections as well. Diction and rhythm are still taut, but open to more variation and diversification in terms of lines, sentences, and stanzas. The central narrative thrust of the poet's return home is hedged with sidebars of other lives, alternative experiences, and different meanings. Literary influences seem to include not just the earlier examples, but Lewis Simpson, Robert Lowell, Richard Hugo, and other contemporary American writers trying to make sense of the 1970s.

This trend toward variety and diversity continued in Smith's next collection, *Goshawk, Antelope* (1979), a book shaped to a great extent by his Western experience, living in Salt Lake City and teaching at the University of Utah. His response to a new environment, just as beautiful and demanding in its own terms as his earlier sea and landscapes, drew him toward more abstraction and expressionism. In this way, the title text provides a pattern for the whole volume by juxtaposing two totemic creatures within the context of the West, as well as the poet's earlier development. Deeper echoes of past encounters with animal vitality and human nature appear as recollections of archetypal family experiences, including avatars of father and mother figures, realized in dreamlike narratives marked by precision of diction and syntax, of structure and sound.

Such modes were developed in Smith's two succeeding collections, *Dream Flights* (1981) and *Homage To Edgar Allan Poe* (1981), which extend themselves toward narratives like the nightmares discovered both in the human psyche and in the alienation of contemporary America. The best of the 1981 dream sequences include the title selection, as well as "Artificial Niggers," with its allusion to Flannery O'Connor, and "The Pornography Box," a disturbing fantasia on his dead father's memorial collection of the pornographic arts. The long title piece of the extended literary homage also proves particularly effective; in six discrete sections its central narrative conflates Poe's personal and poetic personae with Smith's in recognition of the dark side of creativity. Smith's style moves both toward tighter, more traditional forms in the manner of Poe, and toward looser, more diverse forms in Whitman's mode as well.

New balances and accommodations are discerned in succeeding volumes, *In the House of the Judge* (1983) and *The Roundhouse Voices* (1985), especially as the latter is also a selected poems demonstrating Smith's development through the earlier volumes. The new work in both books presents a mature balance of disparate elements, at once more abstracted and more real, more accepting and more confrontational, more formal and more relaxed. After an introductory section developing the symbolism of houses, the three parts of the 1983 volume consider the poet's youth in his two parts of the South and then his maturity in a rented house in northern Pennsylvania. In the title poem, and in others, like "Toy Trains in the Landlord's House," the persona realizes how we must accept the worlds that others have built for themselves and for us, even as we inherit them.

"The Roundhouse Voices" serves as an introduction for the 1985 selection, extending the metaphor of houses, in this case with a dialogue of ancestral voices prophesying the inexorable movement of time that defines how we emerge out of the past of others into our own identity. Smith did well to choose this long effort as the title piece of his first selected poems, as it represents the several narratives, themes, and styles that had emerged as his poetic possibilities by his maturation as a poet. The subject matter of railroads also proves appropriate, as some of Smith's best poetry centers on imagery that probes the ambivalence of contemporary technology in images of railroads and automobiles, photographs and films.

In the late 1980s and the early 1990s, Smith experienced a number of personal and professional transitions, especially a greater engagement with criticism and editing. His more recent volumes of poetry—*Cuba Nights* (1990) and *Night Pleasures* (1992), the latter another selected poems—seem deliberate attempts to delimit his poetic territory, as even the new settings, stories, and styles recall earlier efforts—the long poem "Southern Crescent" from the 1992 collection, for example. At the same time, Smith continues to develop as a poet: his most recent book, *Fate's Kite* (1996), is a collection of uneasy sonnets—all of 13 lines of 11 syllables—with most elliptical, enigmatic, and intriguing. Again, Smith seems much like his major mentor, Robert Penn Warren, near the same stage in his career, with a history of diverse achievements and varied possibilities for the future. At this century's end, Dave Smith remains, perhaps, our most important contemporary Southern poet.

—Joseph R. Millichap

SMITH, Julie

Born: Annapolis, Maryland, 25 November 1944. **Education:** University of Mississippi, B.A. 1965. **Family:** Married Lee Poyor. **Career:** Clerk, reporter, feature writer, *New Orleans Times-Picayune*, 1965-66; copy editor, *San Francisco Chronicle*, 1966-69, reporter, 1969-79; full time writer since 1979. **Awards:** Edgar Allan Poe Award for best novel, 1991, for *New Orleans Mourning*. **Agents:** Charlotte Sheedy, 65 Blecker Street, 12th Floor, New York, New York 10012; Vicki Bijier, 333 West End Avenue, New York, New York 10012.

PUBLICATIONS

Novels

Death Turns a Trick. New York, Walker, 1982.
Sourdough Wars. New York, Walker, 1984.
True-Life Adventure. New York, Mysterious Press, 1985.
Tourist Trap. New York, Mysterious Press, 1986.
Huckleberry Fiend. New York, Mysterious Press, 1987.
New Orleans Mourning. New York, St. Martin's Press, 1990.
The Axeman's Jazz. New York, St. Martin's Press, 1991.
Dead in the Water. New York, Ivy Books, 1992.
Jazz Funeral. New York, Fawcett Columbine, 1993.
New Orleans Beat. New York, Fawcett Columbine, 1994.
Other People's Skeleton. New York, Ivy Books, 1994.
House of Blues. New York, Fawcett Columbine, 1995.
The Kindness of Strangers. New York, Fawcett Columbine, 1996.
Crescent City Kill. New York, Fawcett Columbine, 1997.
82 Desire. New York, Ballantine Publishing Group, 1998.

Short Stories

"Grief Counselor," in *Mike Shayne Mystery Magazine*, 1978; *Miniature Mysteries: 100 Malicious Little Mystery Stories* edited by Isaac Asimov, et. al., Taplinger, 1981; *Last Laughs: The 1986 Mystery Writers of America Anthology* edited by Gregory Macdonald, Mysterious Press, 1986.
"The Wrong Number," in *Mike Shayne Mystery Magazine*, 1979.
"Crime Wave in Pinhole," in *Alfred Hitchcock's Mystery Magazine*, 1980; *The Arbor House Treasury of Mystery and Suspense* edited by Bill Pronzini, et. al., Arbor House, 1981.
"Project Mushroom," in *Ellery Queen's Mystery Magazine*, 1983; *101 Mystery Stories* edited by Bill Pronzini, et. al., Avenel, 1986.
"Red Rock." In *Raymond Chandler's Phillip Marlowe: A Centennial Celebration* edited by Byron Preiss, Knopf, 1988.
"Blood Types." In *Sisters in Crime* edited by Marilyn Wallace, Berkeley, 1989.
"Cul-de-Sac." In *Sisters in Crime II*, edited by Marilyn Wallace, Berkeley, 1990.
"Montezuma's Other Revenge." In *Justice for Hire* edited by Robert Randisi, Mysterious Press, 1990.
"A Marriage Made in Hell." In *Eye of a Woman* edited by Sara Paretsky, Delacourt Press, 1991.
"Silk Strands." In *Deadly Allies* edited by Marilyn Wallace and Robert J. Randisi, Bantam, 1992.
"Strangers on a Plane." In *Unusual Suspects* edited by James Grady, Black Lizard Press, 1996.
"The End of the Earth." In *Detective Duos* edited by Marcia Miller and Bill Pronzini, Oxford University Press, 1997.
"Where the Boys Are." In *Mary Higgins Clark Mystery Magazine,* September 1998.
"Too Mean to Die." In *Blue Lightning* edited by John Harvey, Slow Dancer Press, 1998.
"Fresh Paint." In *Irreconcilable Differences* edited by Lia Matera, HarperCollins, 1999.

Nonfiction

"Spendor in the Mildew." In *A Place Called Home* edited by Mickey Perlman, St. Martin's Press, 1996.

* * *

The British writer P. D. James differentiates between mysteries that are merely entertaining and "detective novels," serious works whose plot happens to involve a crime. Most of Julie Smith's works fall into the second category. Smith's primary interest has always been one which is almost universal among Southern writers, the sense of place. To her, place is more than where one happens to live; it is also who one is. Smith's first subject was the San Francisco Bay Area, which she had come to know well while working as a reporter for the *San Francisco Chronicle*. In *Death Turns a Trick*, Smith began a series in which her sleuth was the lawyer Rebecca Schwartz, while *True-Life Adventure* and *Huckleberry Fiend* had a male detective, Paul MacDonald, a mystery writer.

In her San Francisco novels, Smith writes as a long-time resident, not as a prejudiced, polyester-clad "Know-nothing easterner," as Schwartz describes the city's visitors in *Tourist Trap*. Although these books mention such tourist attractions as cable cars, gay bars, Union Square, and Telegraph Hill, there are also real insights into how San Franciscans think—for example, their passion for movie gossip—that feeds their own long-standing prejudices against Los Angeles. Schwartz undoubtedly reflects the feelings of most San Franciscans when she deplores what has happened to Pier 39. Its transformation during the space of just ten years from a real pier to a "ticky-tacky" tourist heaven of tasteless T-shirts and terrible food shows how greed is demolishing the city and its history.

Though the subject of these novels is San Francisco, they contain some hints of the author's continuing interest in her native South. Schwartz often quotes her law partner Chris Nicholson, a Virginian who brought with her to California a taste for bourbon, a store of colloquialisms, and some useful notions—like the idea that nothing a lady does when she is drunk really counts. Smith's first detective novel set in the South was *New Orleans Mourning*, which won the 1991 Edgar Allan Poe Award for best novel, the first time since 1956 that coveted prize had been given to an American woman. While Smith returned to Rebecca Schwartz and San Francisco for *Dead in the Water* and *Other People's Skeletons*, most of her novels written during the 1990's were continuations of the series that began with *New Orleans Mourning*.

Though both of the cities in which these novels are set seem to have everything the author needs, a heady atmosphere, eccentric characters, and a culinary tradition, the New Orleans books are more profound than those set in San Francisco. One reason for this difference may be a technical one. By abandoning a first person narrator in favor of authorial omniscience, Smith can report what various characters are thinking, thus broadening the scope of her work and often intensifying the suspense. Another reason may be that her protagonist, Skip Langdon, is much more complex than Rebecca Schwartz. Born into one of New Orleans's old families, Skip shares the memories of other children of privilege, who lived in the same neighborhood, played together, and attended the same private schools. Skip broke the pattern, choosing an unconventional career and associating with people very unlike her friends from earlier days. Even the man in her life is an outsider; while Steve Steinman, a Los Angeles filmmaker, loves New Orleans, Skip has to explain it to him. Ironically, one reason Steve is so attracted to Skip is her insider's knowledge. Skip's Uptown connections can also be useful in police work. A telephone call to her Kappa sister Allison Gaillard will elicit all the information she needs about almost everyone, or at least, everyone who matters in New Orleans. However, Skip's upper-class background can also hamper her. Even those of her fellow detectives who are capable of ignoring her gender and of admiring her courage, like Jim Hodges, her partner in *House of Blues*, will never accept her as one of them.

Because of Skip's background and her job, the author of these novels can examine all of the smaller groups that make up New Orleans. *New Orleans Mourning* is set among the city's elite, *Jazz Funeral* among those with new money, *The Kindness of Strangers* and *Crescent City Kill* among the dispossessed. In *The Axeman's Jazz*, Skip moves among people obsessed with twelve-step programs, in *New Orleans Beat* among those who live in their computers.

Despite their differences, Smith's characters are all bound to the same place, which Smith sees as rapidly deteriorating. One of her themes is the growth of crime, now so widespread that ladies carry hand guns in the Garden District. Smith is also concerned about widespread corruption, which enables evil people like the preacher Errol Jacomine to consolidate their power. Smith also emphasizes the pervasiveness of evil when, as in *House of Blues*, she finds the solution to a crime in the secrets of seemingly irreproachable families. Clearly, any social system that encourages pride in class or family is doomed. At some point, as in *House of Blues*, the Carnival masks will be removed and everyone will see the corruption beneath.

Another of Smith's themes is the need for tolerance. Skip Langdon tends to be judgmental, especially where her family is concerned. However, in *New Orleans Beat*, when she overhears what she considers an ideal family quarreling just like her own, she has to revise her opinions. There is also an ongoing plot line about Skip's attempts to mother the orphaned niece and nephew of her landlord and friend Jimmy Lee Scoggin. Parenting, they both discover, is not as easy as they thought.

Despite its flaws, Skip still prefers New Orleans to San Francisco. In *New Orleans Beat*, she explains why: though Southern society can be stifling, Southerners do care about each other, as proven by their very interest in family history. Though Skip's assessment of place is not necessarily that of her creator, it should be noted that not long after she settled on New Orleans as the subject of her detective novels, Julie Smith made it her permanent home.

—Rosemary M. Canfield Reisman

SMITH, Lee

Born: Grundy, Virginia, 1 November 1944. **Education:** Hollins College, Roanoke, Virginia, 1963-67 (Sorbonne in Paris for junior year, 1965-66), B.A. **Family:** Married poet James E. Seay, 1967 (divorced 1982), two sons; married columnist Harold (Hal) B. Crowther, Jr., 1985. **Career:** Internship with James J. Kilpatrick, *Richmond News Leader*, 1968: journalist, *Tuscaloosa News*, 1968-70; teacher, Harpeth Hall School, Nashville, 1971-74, Carolina

Friends School, Durham, 1975; writer-in-residence, Hollins College, spring 1976; instructor, Duke University, 1977; lecturer in writing fiction, University of North Carolina, Chapel Hill, 1978-81; director, Summer Writing Workshop, University of Virginia, Abingdon, 1979-80; instructor in writing fiction, Cumberland Valley Writers Conference Summer Workshop, Nashville, 1981; member of faculty, North Carolina State University, Raleigh, since 1981; advisory board member, North Carolina Writers Network, and visiting professor, Virginia Commonwealth University, 1989; fellow at Center for Documentary Studies, Duke University, 1991-93. **Awards:** Book of the Month Club Award, 1967, for *The Last Day the Dogbushes Bloomed* (College English Writing Contest); O. Henry Award, 1979, for "Mrs. Darcy Meets the Blue-eyed Stranger at the Beach," 1981, for "Between the Lines"; Sir Walter Raleigh Award, 1983, for *Oral History*, 1989, for *Fair and Tender Ladies*; North Carolina Award for Fiction, 1984; John Dos Passos Award for Literature, 1987; Weatherford Award for Appalachian Literature (Berea College, Kentucky) and Appalachian Writers Award, 1987; Lyndhurst Prize, 1990-92; Robert Penn Warren Award (1st recipient), PEN/Faulkner Award, elected to Fellowship of Southern Writers, 1991; Lila Wallace/Reader's Digest Award, 1995-97; Elizabeth Kirkpatrick Doenges Artist/Scholar Award (Mary Baldwin College, Virginia), 1997-98. **Website:** http://www.beca.org/fotl/leesmith/herwords.html.

PUBLICATIONS

Novels

The Last Day the Dogbushes Bloomed. New York, Harper & Rowe, 1968.
Something in the Wind. New York, Harper & Rowe, 1971.
Fancy Strut. New York, Harper & Rowe, 1973.
Black Mountain Breakdown. New York, Putnam, 1980.
Cakewalk. New York, Putnam, 1981.
Oral History. New York, Putnam, 1983.
Family Linen. New York, Putnam, 1985.
Fair and Tender Ladies. New York, Putnam, 1988.
Me and My Baby View the Eclipse. New York, Putnam, 1990.
The Devil's Dream. New York, Putnam, 1992.
Saving Grace. New York, Putnam, 1995.
Pete & Shirley: The Greatest Tar Heel Novel, with Clyde Edgerton and Fred Chappel. Asheboro, North Carolina, Down Home Press, 1995.
News of the Spirit. New York, Putnam, 1997.

Nonfiction

"The Voice Behind the Story" in *Voicelust: Eight Contemporary Fiction Writers on Style,* edited by Allen Wier & Don Hendrie, Jr. Lincoln, University of Nebraska Press, 1985.
"A Stubborn Sense of Place: Writers and Writings on the South," in *Harper's*, August 1986.
The Official Travel Guide to Nashville—Music City, U. S. A. Nashville, Southern Media Ventures, 1993.
Lee Smith (videocassette). Annenberg/CPB Collection, 1997.

Other

Cardinal: A Contemporary Anthology from North Carolina, with Reynolds Price and Fred Chappel. Raleigh, Jacar Press, 1986.

Bob, a Dog. Chapel Hill, The Mud Puppy Press, 1988. (Edition limited to 374 copies)

Appalachian Portraits, photos by Shelby L. Adams. Jackson, University Press of Mississippi, 1993.

We Don't Love With Our Teeth. Portland, Oregon, Chinook P., 1994.

Love, Santa. New York, McClanahan, 1995.

The Christmas Letters. Chapel Hill, Algonquin Books, 1996.

Good Ol'Girls, musical collaboration with Jill McCorkle; songs by Marshall Chapman & Matraca Berg; director, Paul Ferguson. Scheduled debut in Chapel Hill, Durham, Raleigh area, Winter 1998-99.

*

Interviews: With Edwin T. Arnold, *Appalachian Journal,* Spring 1984; with Pat Arnow, *Now and Then,* Summer 1989; with Nancy C. Parrish, *Appalachian Journal,* Summer 1992; with Claudia Loewenstein, *Southwest Review,* Autumn 1993; with Elizabeth Herion-Sarafidis, *The Southern Quarterly,* Winter 1994; with Dannye Romine Powell, *Parting the Curtains: Voices of Great Southern Writers,* New York, Doubleday, 1994; with Wayne Johnson Pond, *Lee Smith* (sound recording), Research Triangle Park, National Humanities Center, 1995; with Linda Byrd, *Shenandoah* Summer 1997; with Jeanne McDonald, *Poets & Writers,* November 1997.

Critical Studies: "Artists and Beauticians: Balance in Lee Smith's Fiction" by Lucinda H. MacKethan, *Southern Literary Journal,* Fall 1982; "The World of Lee Smith" by Anne Goodwyn Jones, in *Southern Quarterly,* Fall 1983 (reprinted in *Women Writers of the Contemporary South* edited by Peggy Whitman Prenshaw, Jackson, University Press of Mississippi, 1984; "Southern Women Writing About Southern Women—Jill McCorkle, Lisa Alther, Ellen Gilchrist, Lee Smith" by D. K. Darden, *Sociological Spectrum,* Vol. 6, 1986; "Lee Smith's Smoking Pistol: *Family Linen* and William Faulkner's *As I Lay Dying*" by Susie Paul Johnson, *Postscript,* Vol. 7, 1989; "The Power of Language in Lee Smith's Oral History" byCorinne Dale, *Southern Quarterly,* Winter 1990; "Postscript: Writing Letters Home" by Susie Paul Johnson, in *Daughters of Time: Creating Woman's Voice in Southern Story,* Athens, University of Georgia Press, 1990; "Lee Smith: The Storyteller's Voice" by Harriette C. Buchanan, in *Southern Women Writers: The New Generation* edited by Tonette Bond Inge, Tuscaloosa, University of Alabama Press, 1990; "From Shadow to Substance: The Empowerment of the Artist Figure in Lee Smith's Fiction" by Katherine Kearns, in *Writing the Woman Artist* edited by Suzanne W. Jones, Philadelphia, University of Pennsylvania Press, 1991; "A Question of Culture—and History: Bobbie Ann Mason, Lee Smith and Barry Hannah" by Fred Hobson, *The Southern Writer in the Postmodern World,* Athens, University of Georgia Press, 1991; "Lee Smith" by Elizabeth Pell Broadwell, in *Contemporary Fiction Writers of the South* Joseph M. Flora and Robert Bain, editors, Westport, Greenwood Press, 1993; "Let Us Now Praise the Other—Women In Lee Smith Short Fiction" by William Teem, *Studies in the Literary Imagination,* Fall 1994; "The Southern Voices of Lee Smith: An Annotated Bibliography" by Michelle Manning, *Bulletin of Bibliography,* June 1996.

*   *   *

Three decades of Lee Smith's publishing career (1968-98) began with her first novel written while she was a student at Hollins College. She tells of learning the importance of using one's own experience by reading in Louis Rubin's class the stories of Eudora Welty. *The Last Day the Dogbushes Bloomed,* using the perspective of a nine-year-old girl, stems from Smith's childhood. Using her college experience as material for the second novel, *Something in the Wind,* she feared she "had used up" her life. Her journalistic experience in the years following college sharpened her already keen perception and vivid imagination, and she recognized the wealth of fictional material available in her current experience and in material reworked from her early life.

Grundy, the southwestern Virginia town in which she was reared—its sounds and expressions, its people and their lives—influences Smith's fictional world. Its rhetoric rings with a musical language—sometimes harmonious, sometimes cacophonous—to reveal nuances of place and character. The sense of family and community, religion and superstition in Appalachia define her fiction as innately American and Southern; this sense of place, however, also strikes a chord of universal recognition.

Especially significant are the strong female characters Smith creates: Ivy Rowe of *Fair and Tender Ladies;* Granny Younger, Pricey Jane and Dory Cantrell of *Oral History;* and Grace Shepherd of *Saving Grace,* for instance. Like their Appalachian forebears, these characters face almost unbearable odds with a grace and long-sufferance that brings them through crisis after crisis. Perhaps because they expect so little of life even as they dream, the people of Smith's fiction face their lives and their deaths with an indomitable spirit and a fierce determination. They hold a healthy respect for fate or the uncontrollable, but they work with all the means available to them to better their lot. Sometimes those odds include the environment in which they live, its people and its culture; other times the characters struggle with the outside world for understanding.

Smith's vision is dark, at times, as in *Black Mountain Breakdown;* other times it is comic, as in *Fancy Strut.* In either case, her central characters display an independence and pride in determining their own lives; they are bright and industrious, but ordinary people. That they are honest and open may be their unique quality; becoming closed with hidden motives or secrets brings trouble, as in *Family Linen.* The plots evolve out of the conflicts and crises of these characters as they learn to understand themselves in a more complex way. Smith tells a good story, just as the Appalachian tale-spinners of her home tell good stories. Readers hear their voices telling the tales, hear the variations in tone and pitch, when reading the fiction.

From her own childhood, Smith, who lived among a number of storytellers, always had the impulse to write, "I grew up in the midst of people just talking and talking and talking and telling these stories" (quoted from her web page, http://www.beca.org/fotl/leesmith/herwords). Her fiction gives the impressions of being *heard* rather than being *read.* Her fictional language blends poetry and music, language not unlike that she heard when, as a child, she peeped from behind doors in her father's dime store to observe and listened to his customers. Her fascination with narration and point of view stems from this ear for rhetoric, and her most memorable people are those created from Smith's focus on language to reveal character. "I ended up becoming a writer and a professor," she says. "By then, I'd realized that some of the best stories I had to tell were those I'd heard so long ago in Buchanan County spoken in the most picturesque and precise language I would ever hear: Appalachian English."

Smith's themes involve women who seek their own identities and their own voices. While such themes seem characteristic of contemporary American fiction, Smith is not a part of the 1970's irresponsible "drop out" faction; nor is she presenting characters who flounder in an existential drift toward identity. Her characters evolve into searchers as a natural progression of their development, never forgetting (if not always relishing) where their selfhood is rooted. They find themselves both a part of their community and distant from it; their visions are more artistic or creative than those of a community seeking only survival. The crises often come from their being trapped in a dualistic world, and often from internal family or community conflicts. Some of them, Ivy Rowe of *Fair and Tender Ladies*, for instance, return to the place of their roots at the culmination of their lives, "You will find me back up on Sugar Fork where I belong."

The narrative structures of Smith's fiction encompass traditional forms in innovative ways. She uses the epistolary form in *Fair and Tender Ladies* and *The Christmas Letters;* the first-person narrative for *The Last Day the Dogbushes Bloomed* and *Something in the Wind* (books using her adolescent experience); and an omniscient narrator for *Black Mountain Breakdown* (illustrating the psychological fragmenting of the protagonist who is both a character in the story and an observer outside the self). Smith chooses the mystery or detective story formula for *Family Linen*, but frames the secrets and unsolved murder in several generations of family (rather than individual) fragmentation.

In *Fancy Strut*, a satire, Smith uses multiple perspectives to focus on a small town and its festival preparations for its sesquicentennial. In *Oral History*, her multiple points of view follow five generations of the Cantrell family as it evolves (or disintegrates) into the modern world. The frame structure is also part of this story structure, a means by which Smith layers time and generations. Within the frame of present time, the reader hears (as though on tape) ancient voices tell the tale of the first Almarine Cantrell, who inherited all the hills and hollers he could see from his front porch, down to the present "Al" Cantrell, who lost the land, then "made a killing in AmWay" and repurchased it, only to make it into a tourist attraction—"Ghostland." Family and community values get lost in the loss of land; ghosts from the past have their say (on tape) to those in the twentieth century—family, community, and, finally, readers.

Smith's themes and structures revolve around family and community through their rituals and events: weddings, births, deaths, seasonal change, illnesses, festivals, and burials postponed until ground thaw. These events bring scattered family and community together to settle unresolved crises or solve long-unanswered mysteries. They also serve to elicit self-searching in her characters. In the larger sense, each protagonist is on a quest for self-discovery with the end result a mystery until reconciliation of the past with the present. The fragmented pieces, layered by time, rework into a completed whole; the past, which is never readily accessible to the seeker, does, nonetheless, impinge on the present.

Voices from that past instruct the present in her fiction. Ivy Rowe (*Fair and Tender Ladies),* in her dying, hears the long-ago voice of her father teaching his children to recognize seasons: "Slow down now, slow down now Ivy. This is the taste of spring." The old rituals, reworked and modernized, have meaning for the people of Smith's stories, while they also speak to the readers of her fiction. They serve Smith as both unifying devices and fictional vehicles. Her concerns involve a consciousness of the past and its ramifications: "If we have anything different, we should try to preserve it, because we are becoming such a plastic race" (McGehee). Lee Smith's fiction preserves an important aspect of that past as it leads readers through their present to recognition and self-discovery.

—Jeanne R. Nostrandt

SMITH, William Jay

Born: Winnfield, Louisiana, 22 April 1918. **Education:** Washington University, B.A. 1939, M.A. 1941; attended Institut de Touraine, Universite de Poitiers, diplome d'etudes francaises; graduate study at Columbia University, 1946-47, at Oxford University as a Rhodes Scholar, 1947-48, and at University of Florence, 1948-50. **Family:** Married Barbara Howes (a poet), 1 October 1947 (divorced, June 1965), two children; married Sonja Haussmann, 3 September 1966. **Military Service:** U.S. Naval Reserve, 1941-45; became lieutenant; awarded commendation by French Admiralty. **Career:** Assistant in French, Washington University, 1939-41; instructor in English and French, Columbia University, 1946-47, visiting professor of writing and acting chair of writing division, 1973, 1974-75; lecturer in English, Williams College, 1951, poet in residence and lecturer in English, 1956-64, 1966-67; staff member, University of Connecticut Writers Conference, 1951; freelance writer, 1951-59; writer in residence, Arena Stage, Washington, D.C., 1964-65, writer in residence, 1965- 66, professor of English, 1970-80, professor emeritus, since 1980, Hollins College; lecturer at Salzburg Seminar in American Studies, 1974; Fulbright lecturer, Moscow State University, 1981; poet in residence, Cathedral of St. John the Divine, 1985-88; lecturer at colleges, clubs, writers' conferences (including Suffield Writer-Reader Conference, 1959-62, and University of Indiana Writers Conference, 1961), and book fairs, and has presented television programs on poetry for children; democratic member, Vermont House of Representatives, 1960-62; poetry reviewer, *Harper's*, 1961-64; editorial consultant, Grove Press, 1968-70; consultant in poetry, Library of Congress, 1968-70, honorary consultant, 1970-76; jury member, National Book Award, 1962, 1970, 1975, Neustadt International Prize for Literature, 1978, and Pegasus Prize for Literature, 1979; chairman of board of directors, Translation Center, Columbia University. **Member:** American Academy of Arts and Letters (vice president for literature, 1986-89), Association of American Rhodes Scholars, Authors Guild (member of council), PEN, Authors League of America, Century Association. **Awards:** Young Poets Prize, *Poetry* magazine, 1945; alumni citation, Washington University, 1963; Ford fellowship for drama, 1964; Union League Civic and Arts Foundation prize, *Poetry* magazine, 1964; Henry Bellamann Major Award, 1970; Russell Loines Award, American Academy and Institute of Arts and Letters, 1972; National Endowment for the Arts fellowship, 1972, 1975 and 1979; Gold Medal of Labor, Hungary, 1978; New England Poetry Club Golden Rose, 1980; Ingram Merrill Foundation grant, 1982; California Children's Book and Video Awards recognition for excellence (preschool and toddlers category), 1990, for *Ho for a Hat!*; medal (medaille de vermeil) for service to the French language, French Academy, 1991; Pro Cultura Hungarice medal, 1993; D.Litt., New England College, 1973. **Agent:** Harriet Wasserman, 137 East 36th St., No. 19D, New York, New York 10061.

PUBLICATIONS

Poetry

Poems. Pawlet, Vermont, Banyan Press, 1947.
Celebration at Dark. New York, Farrar, Straus, 1950.
Snow. New York, Schlosser Paper, 1953.
The Stork: A Poem Announcing the Safe Arrival of Gregory Smith. New York, Caliban Press, 1954.
Typewriter Birds. New York, Caliban Press, 1954.
Poems 1947-57. Boston, Little, Brown, 1957.
Two Poems. Mason Hill Press, 1959.
Prince Souvanna Phouma: An Exchange between Richard Wilbur and William Jay Smith, with Richard Wilbur. Boston, Chapel Press, 1963.
The Tin Can, and Other Poems. New York, Delacorte, 1966.
New and Selected Poems. New York, Delacorte, 1970.
A Rose for Katherine Anne Porter. New York, Albondocani Press, 1970.
At Delphi: For Allen Tate on His Seventy-Fifth Birthday, 19 November 1974. Boston, Chapel Press, 1974.
Venice in the Fog. New York, Unicorn Press, 1975.
Verses on the Times, with Richard Wilbur. New York, Gutenberg Press, 1978.
Journey to the Dead Sea. New York, Abbatoir, 1979.
The Tall Poets. New York, Palaemon Press, 1979.
Mr. Smith. New York, Delacorte, 1980.
The Traveler's Tree, New and Selected Poems. New York, Persea Books, 1980.
Plain Talk: Epigrams, Epitaphs, Satires, Nonsense, Occasional, Concrete and Quotidian Poems. New York, Center for Book Arts, 1988.
Journey to the Interior. Roslyn, New York, Stone House Press, 1988.
Collected Poems, 1939-1989. New York, Macmillan, 1990.
The World Below the Window: Poems, 1937-1997. Baltimore, Johns Hopkins University Press, 1998.

Children's Poetry

Laughing Time. Boston, Little, Brown, 1955.
Boy Blue's Book of Beasts. Boston, Little, Brown, 1957.
Puptents and Pebbles: A Nonsense ABC. Boston, Little, Brown, 1959.
Typewriter Town, illustrated by Smith. New York, Dutton, 1960.
What Did I See? New York, Crowell-Collier, 1962.
My Little Book of Big and Little (Little Dimity, Big Gumbo, Big and Little), three volumes. New York, Macmillan, 1963.
Ho for a Hat! Boston, Little, Brown, 1964; revised, Joy Street Books, 1989.
If I Had a Boat. New York, Macmillan, 1966.
Mr. Smith, and Other Nonsense. New York, Delacorte, 1968.

Around My Room and Other Poems. New York, Lancelot, 1969.
Grandmother Ostrich and Other Poems. New York, Lancelot, 1969.
Laughing Time and Other Poems. New York, Lancelot, 1969.
Laughing Time: Nonsense Poems. New York, Delacorte, 1980.
The Key. New York, Children's Book Council, 1982.
Birds and Beasts. New York, Godine, 1990.
Laughing Time: Collected Nonsense. New York, Farrar, Straus, 1990.

Compiler with Louise Bogan, *The Golden Journey* (anthology). New York, Reilly & Lee, 1965.
Compiler, *Poems from France.* New York, Crowell, 1967.
Compiler, *Poems from Italy.* St. Paul, New Rivers Press, 1973.
Compiled with Carol Ra, *The Sun Is Up: A Child's Year of Poems.* Honesdale, Pennsylvania, Wordsong/Boyds Mills Press, 1996.

Editor with Carol Ra, *Behind the King's Kitchen.* New York, Boyds Mills Press, 1992.

Criticism

The Spectra Hoax. Middleton, Connecticut, Wesleyan University Press, 1961.
Herrick. New York, Dell, 1962.
The Streaks of the Tulip: Selected Criticism. New York, Delacorte, 1972.
Green. St. Louis, Washington University Libraries, 1980.

Drama

The Straw Market. Produced at Arena Stage, Washington, D.C., 1965.
Army Brat: A Dramatic Narrative for Three Voices. First produced in New York City, 1980.

Editor

Light Verse and Satires of Witter Bynner. New York, Farrar, Straus, 1976.
Brazilian Poetry, with Emanuel Brasil. New York, Harper, 1984.
Dutch Interior: Postwar Poetry of the Netherlands and Flanders, with James S. Holmes. New York, Columbia University Press, 1984.
Life Sentence: Selected Poems, by Nina Cassian. New York, W.W. Norton, 1990.

Translations

Scirocco by Romualdo Romano. New York, Farrar, Straus, 1951.
Poems of a Mulitmillionaire by Valery Larbaud. New York, Bonacio & Saul/Grove, 1955.
(And editor) *Selected Writings of Jules Laforgue.* New York, Grove, 1956.
The Children of the Forest by Elsa Beskow. New York, Delacorte, 1970.
Two Plays by Charles Bertin: Christopher Columbus and Don Juan. Minneapolis, Minnesota University Press, 1970.
The Pirate Book by Lennart Hellsing. New York, Delacorte, 1972.

(With Max Hayward) *The Telephone* by Kornei Chukovsky. New York, Delacorte, 1977.

(With Leif Sjoeberg) *Agadir* by Artur Lundkvist. Columbus, Ohio State University Press, 1980.

(With Ingvar Schousboe) *The Pact: My Friendship with Isak Dinesen* by Thorkild Bjoernvig. Baton Rouge, Louisiana State University Press, 1983.

Moral Tales by Jules Laforgue. New York, New Directions, 1985.

(With Leif Sjoeberg) *Wild Bouquet: Nature Poems* by Henry Martinson. New York, Bookmark Press, 1985.

Collected Translations: Italian, French, Spanish, Portuguese. St. Paul, New Rivers Press, 1985.

(With Edwin Morgan and others) *Eternal Moment: Selected Poems* by Sandor Weoeres. St. Paul, New Rivers Press, 1988.

(With wife, Sonja Haussmann Smith) *The Madman and the Medusa* by Tchicaya U Tam'Si. Charlottesville, University Press of Virginia, 1989.

Christopher Columbus by Charles Bertin. Roslyn, New York, Stone House Press, 1992.

Other

Children and Poetry: A Selective, Annotated Bibliography, with Virginia Haviland. Washington, D.C., Library of Congress, 1969; revised, 1979.

Compiler, *A Green Place: Modern Poems.* New York, Delacort Press/Seymour Lawrence, 1982.

Compiler, *Here is My Heart: Love Poems.* Boston, Little, Brown, 1999.

Memoir

Army Brat, A Memoir. New York, Persea Books, 1980.

*

Manuscript Collection: A collection of Smith's manuscripts is housed at Washington University, St. Louis, Missouri.

Audio Recording: *William Jay Smith,* Kansas City, New Letters, 1982.

Interview: "An Interview with William Jay Smith," Elisavietta Ritchie, *Voyages,* Winter 1970.

Critical Studies: "*The Tin Can, and Other Poems*" by John Malcolm Brinnin, *Partisan Review,* Winter 1967; "*The Tin Can, and Other Poems*" by James Dickey, New York, Farrar, Straus & Giroux, 1968; "William Jay Smith and the Art of Lightness" by Dorothy Judd Hall, *Southern Humanities Review,* Winter 1968; "New Urns For Old" by Thomas H. Landess, *Sewanee Review,* Winter 1973; "The Dark Train and the Green Place: The Poetry of William Jay Smith" by Josephine Jacobsen, *Hollins Critic,* February 1975.

William Jay Smith commented:

I am a lyric poet, alert, I hope, as my friend Stanley Kunitz has pointed out, "to the changing weathers of a landscape, the motions of the mind, the complications and surprises of the human comedy." I believe that poetry should communicate: it is, by its very nature, complex, but its complexity should not prevent its making an immediate impact on the reader. Great poetry must have its own distinctive music; it must resound with the music of the human psyche.

*   *   *

William Jay Smith has been a vital force on several fronts in American literature since World War II—as a writer, promoter, translator, editor, compiler, and advisor. His own poetry reflects the diversity of his achievement as a man of letters, revealing a resourceful, lyric poet talented in a range of styles, from classic forms to more contemporary, experimental methods. His insatiable thirst for learning makes his large body of verse continually refreshing and spills over into his other endeavors, which include a memoir, *Army Brat,* he adapted into a play, his large original and translated collection of children's verse, and his service the cause of literature in various capacities.

Smith was born in Louisiana to a career military man. Much of his youth was spent as an army brat living in the St. Louis area. He earned his B.A. and M.A. from Washington University in St. Louis; his facility with languages, particularly French (he attended the Institut de Touraine, Universite de Poitiers, and received a diploma in French studies), landed him a position as liaison officer on French navy vessels during World War II.

Following the war, Smith began graduate study and teaching at Columbia University, then went to Oxford University as a Rhodes Scholar and later attended the University of Florence. He had contributed verse to several journals and had two collections, *Poems* (1947) and *Celebration at Dark* (1950), published during this period. During the 1950s, Smith's reputation as a poet and translator grew steadily, as did his family: they settled in Pownal, Vermont, and Smith was later elected to represent his district in the Vermont House of Representatives in 1960. Smith served literature in an official capacity as consultant to the Library of Congress from 1968 to 1970 and in an honorary position through 1976, and taught at several institutions, including Hollins College from 1970 to 1980, when he became professor emeritus. In addition to being a prolific poet, Smith was busy as a translator, editor, and writer of children's verse—all in all a remarkable range of service to literature.

Smith's early verse favors traditional lyric forms, with strict adherence to metrical and rhyme patterns. Carefully detailed images predominate and connect through metaphor and symbol with ruminations on a particular subject. Conventional Romantic topics—love, nature, myth—are addressed in a variety of approaches, from light verse to pointed satire. As Smith developed his style after gaining initial recognition for *Poems* and especially for *Celebration at Dark*, a more pervasive sensuousness became evident in his verse, and succeeding poems show more daring in evoking emotion and elaborating descriptions. An interest in poetry as a craft is present—not surprising for a poet developing his voice and becoming a particularly active public figure promoting the art form. The influence of Wallace Stevens is evident in such poems. Although Smith is not as daring as Stevens, the earlier poet's example is apparent in such poems as "In Memoriam, Wallace Stevens," where Smith adopts Stevens' penchant for metaphorical flourishes while retaining tight control of the lyric form.

The Tin Can, and Other Poems (1966) introduces a clear change in Smith's verse, as he adopts free verse forms to undertake more expansive and varied approaches and opens new possibilities of expression. "The Tin Can" addresses this change, as the speaker announces his intention to retreat for secluded meditation and to explore the totality of existence, including darker aspects of life, which Smith had explored more occasionally in his earlier verse. Surrealistic images become more predominant as symbols and metaphors, drawn in this volume from a desolate, wintry, New England landscape, as Smith explores his subconscious and probes beyond external surface details. The title of "The Tin Can" refers to a Japanese expression for undertaking a meditative seclusion, as in "going to the Tin Can." Smith's later verse continues the looser forms introduced with this volume. "My recent poems," he said at the time, "have been written in long unrhymed lines because the material with which I am dealing seems to lend itself to this form, which is often close to but always different from prose." Social issues, degradation of culture, despoliation of nature, desire and loss are more prominent themes in Smith's later work, while characteristic celebrations of nature and community remain; in fishing trips, walks in nature, and human relationships come affirmations and meaning that connect patterns in nature with experiences in life.

Smith's memoir, *Army Brat* (1980), provides a clear portrait of the artist as a young man, showing his impressions, eye for detail in even the most mundane scenes, and tension between emotion and desire, formal discipline (the military life around him) and imagination and discovery. Art, in the forms of music and literature, inspire the young man to a larger sense of purpose—of wanting to learn more, experience more, know more. These are the qualities that mark Smith's development as a poet, learning to master forms and then experimenting more freely as a mature artist. Along the way, Smith has been much sought after and obliging to publishers, academia, prize- and grant-awarding institutions, and other institutions promoting the art of poetry, while serving the cause himself in voluminous and continually refreshing verses, as a mature craftsman and playful children's poet, for readers of all ages.

—Mel Koler

SPENCER, Elizabeth

Born: Carrollton, Mississippi, 19 July 1921. **Education:** Belhaven College, Jackson, Mississippi, 1938-42, A.B. 1942; Vanderbilt University, Nashville, 1942-43, M.A. 1943. **Family:** Married John Rusher in 1956. **Career:** Instructor, Northwest Mississippi Junior College, Senatobia, 1943-44, and Ward-Belmont College, Nashville, 1944-45; reporter, Nashville *Tennessean*, 1945-46; instructor, 1948-49, and instructor in creative writing, 1949-51, 1952-53, University of Mississippi, Oxford; Donnelly fellow, Bryn Mawr College, Pennsylvania, 1962; creative writing fellow, University of North Carolina, Chapel Hill, 1969; writer-in-residence, Hollins College, Virginia, 1973; member of the creative writing faculty, 1976-81, adjunct professor, 1981-86, Concordia University, Montreal; visiting professor, University of North Carolina, Chapel Hill, 1986-92; charter member, 1987, vice-chancellor,

1993, Fellowship of Southern Writers. **Awards:** American Academy Recognition award, 1952, Rosenthal award, 1957, and Award of Merit Medal, 1983; Guggenheim fellowship, 1953; *Kenyon Review* fellowship, 1957; McGraw-Hill fiction award, 1960; Bellaman award, 1968; National Endowment for the Arts grant, 1982, and award, 1988; Salem award, 1992, for literature; Dos Passos award, 1992, for fiction; North Carolina Governor's award, 1994, for literature; D.L., Southwestern (now Rhodes) University, Memphis, 1968; LL.D., Concordia University, Montreal, 1988; Litt.D., University of the South, Sewanee, Tennessee. **Member:** American Academy of Arts and Letters, 1985. **Agent:** Virginia Barber, 353 West 21st Street, New York, New York 10011.

PUBLICATIONS

Novels

Fire in the Morning. New York, Dodd Mead, 1948.
This Crooked Way. New York, Dodd Mead, 1952.
The Voice at the Back Door. New York, McGraw Hill, 1956.
The Light in the Piazza. New York, McGraw Hill, 1960.
Knights and Dragons. New York, McGraw Hill, 1965.
No Place for an Angel. New York, McGraw Hill, 1967.
The Snare. New York, McGraw Hill, 1972.
The Salt Line. New York, Doubleday, 1984.
The Night Travellers. New York, Viking, 1991.
The Snare. Jackson, Mississippi, Banner Books, 1993.

Short Story Collections

Ship Island and Other Stories. New York, McGraw Hill, 1968.
The Stories of Elizabeth Spencer. New York, Doubleday, 1981.
Marilee: Three Stories. Jackson, University Press of Mississippi, 1981.
The Mules. Winston-Salem, Palaemon Press, 1982.
Jack of Diamonds and Other Stories. New York, Viking, 1988.
On the Gulf. Jackson, University Press of Mississippi, 1991.

Uncollected Short Stories

"To the Watchers While Walking Home," in *Ontario Review*, 1982.
"Madonna" and "Puzzle Poem," in *Hudson Review*, Summer 1983.
"Up the Gatineau," in *Boulevard*, Spring 1989.
"The Weekend Travellers," in *Story*, Winter 1994.
"The Runaways," in *Antaeus*, Spring 1994.
"The Master of Shongalo," in *Southern Review*, Winter 1995.

Play

For Lease or Sale. In *Mississippi Writers 4: Reflection of Childhood and Youth* edited by Dorothy Abbott. Jackson, University Press of Mississippi, 1991.

Other

Conversations with Elizabeth Spencer edited by Peggy Whitman Prenshaw. Jackson, University Press of Mississippi, 1991.
Landscapes of the Heart: A Memoir. New York, Random House, 1997.

*

Bibliographies: By Laura Barge, 1976, and by C.E. Lewis, 1994, both in *Mississippi Quarterly*.

Manuscript Collections: National Library of Canada, Ottawa; University of Kentucky, Lexington.

Critical Studies: *Elizabeth Spencer* by Peggy Whitman Prenshaw, Boston, Twayne, 1985; *Self and Community in the Fiction of Elizabeth Spencer* by Terry Roberts, Baton Rouge, Louisiana State University Press, 1994.

Elizabeth Spencer comments:

I began writing down stories as soon as I learned how to write; that is, at about age six; before that, I made them up anyway and told them to anybody who was handy and would listen. Being a rural Southerner, a Mississippian, had a lot to do with it, I have been told, with this impulse and with the peculiar mystique, importance, which attached itself naturally thereto and enhanced it. We had been brought up on stories, those about local people, living and dead, and Bible narratives, believed also to be literally true, so that other stories read aloud—the Greek myths, for instance—while indicated as "just" stories, were only one slight remove from the "real" stories of the local scene and the Bible. So it was with history, for local event spilled into the history of the textbooks; my grandfather could remember the close of the Civil War, and my elder brother's nurse had been a slave. The whole world, then, was either entirely in the nature of stories or partook so deeply of stories as to be at every point inseparable from them. Even the novels we came later to read were mainly English 19th-century works which dealt with a culture similar to our own—we learned with no surprise that we had sprung from it.

Though I left the South in 1953, I still see the world and its primal motions as story, since story charts in time the heart's assertions and gives central place to the great human relationships. My first three novels, written or projected before I left the South, deal with people in that society who must as the true measure of themselves either alter it or come to terms with it. Years I spent in Italy and more recently in Canada have made me see the world in other than this fixed geography. The challenge to wring its stories from it became to me more difficult at the same time that it became more urgent that I and other writers should do so. A story may not be the only wrench one can hurl into the giant machine that seems bent on devouring us all, but is one of them. A story which has been tooled, shaped, and slicked up is neither real nor true—we know its nature and its straw insides. Only the real creature can satisfy, the one that is touchy and alive, dangerous to fool with. The search for such as these goes on with me continually, and I think for all real writers as well.

I returned to the South in 1986 and have found a not altogether different world, for the South can maintain its continuity better perhaps than most other areas. But the media and the electronic age are doing their work of restructuring, and enduring as a separate, recognizable region of the United States tests and will continue to test the considerable talents of southern writers. We remain, however, what we have always been—storytellers, some of the world's best.

*   *   *

In a list of the second generation of Southern Renaissance writers, Elizabeth Spencer's name often appears along with those of Walker Percy, Flannery O'Connor, and Eudora Welty, a friend since they met in Jackson while Spencer was at Belhaven College. By having Donald Davidson as her mentor at Vanderbilt, Spencer is also linked to the Fugitive Movement. Though she published her first novel in 1948, five decades later Spencer is still writing fine prose. As her experience of life became broader, Spencer ventured into different settings and dealt with new issues, yet she still explores the same timeless themes: the conflict between individual freedom and the pressure to conform; the need for a sense of place, family, community, and history; and the eternal battle between good and evil.

In Spencer's first two novels, *Fire in the Morning* and *This Crooked Way*, both set in rural Mississippi, critics saw the influence of Faulkner and the Southern Gothic tradition. Her third book, *The Voice at the Back Door*, broke new ground. Prompted by a childhood memory of a black woman who arrived at her parents' back door badly beaten by a white man and having to be sent out of town for her own protection, the novel dealt with the plight of the Southern black, still subservient, but raising a voice that must be heard.

A sojourn in Italy in the 1950s prompted a change of setting for Spencer's next publications, the novellas *The Light in the Piazza* and *Knights and Dragons*, both of which involve Americans in Italy. In the second of these, Spencer demonstrates her interest in another issue, a woman's quest for identity. Initially Martha Ingram, the heroine of *Knights and Dragons*, reacts her former husband's harassment by seeking a knight to slay her dragon. Eventually, however, she realizes that such dependence will only result in still another loss of identity and of freedom.

The identity theme is also important in the novel *The Night Travellers*, set in Canada, where the focus is not on the male Vietnam War protesters but on the women whom they use and abandon in the name of their cause. *The Snare* is another example of Spencer's interest in contemporary issues. Set in New Orleans, it attempts to explain why the drug-ridden counter-culture is so appealing to young people. The protagonist is Julia Garrett, a victim of childhood sexual abuse, who is so anxious to escape the past that she is easily enticed into a way of life which in fact offers only another enslavement in a different form.

The Snare also demonstrates Spencer's mastery of her craft. She moves easily between the past and the present and between one point of view and another, for instance, first telling the story through the eyes of a reporter who finds Julia appealing, then having Julia write her own story. In *This Crooked Way*, Spencer uses five different points of view to present a rounded picture of her subject, a religious fundamentalist. On the other hand, the Marilee Summerall stories are all told by Marilee, who even as a young girl is a perceptive observer. In "A Southern Landscape," an older Marilee explains why the memory of Windsor, a ruined antebellum mansion, and of Foster Hamilton, whom she sometimes dated, are both so important to her. Foster was so thoroughly a Southern gentleman that when a lady like Marilee's mother appeared he could change in an instant from being drunk to total sobriety. Like Windsor, like the hand on top of the Presbyterian church that points eternally toward heaven, Foster will never change. He is part of the "sure terrain," the "permanent landscape of the heart," that is perhaps even more essential to free spirits like Marilee and Spencer herself.

That passage from "A Southern Landscape" much later provided the title for a Spencer's memoir, *Landscapes of the Heart*. In one section of that volume, Spencer considers her feelings about the Mississippi Gulf Coast, the setting for a number of her short stories, as well as one novel. In one sense, the area was an extension of Mississippi society, for year after year the same people would return to the same hotels, eat at the same restaurants, amuse themselves in the same way. Because she belonged to that society, Spencer has happy memories of summers at the Gulf. However, she can empathize with an outsider like Nancy Lewis in "Ship Island," who is so involved in a futile attempt to be accepted that she very nearly loses her own identity in the process. Ironically, the Gulf Coast did not turn out to be a "sure terrain" after all, for in August, 1969, Hurricane Camille struck, transforming the area forever. In *The Salt Line*, Spencer expresses her own shocked reaction to the loss of what seemed so permanent. She also shows how, though after the hurricane some people revealed the greed and evil in their hearts, others reflected the best in human nature, accepting what they must, rebuilding where they could.

As Spencer explains in *Landscape of the Heart*, soon after her books began appearing she was made to feel so ill at ease whenever she went home for a visit that she knew she could not live in the South. However, during the twenty-eight years that she and her husband spent in Montreal, Spencer often turned to the South she remembered for subjects and characters. In *The Stories of Elizabeth Spencer*, for example, six of the eight stories in the final section, written between 1972 and 1977, had Southern settings. When in 1986 Spencer and her husband moved to Chapel Hill, North Carolina, she was indeed coming home. However much she deplored snobbery and racism, Spencer had always clung to her faith in the basic goodness of her own people and to a belief that some adherence to tradition is essential for a civilized and stable society. As her narrator says in "The Cousins," "Whatever Southerners are, there are ways they don't change, the same manners to count on, the same tone of voice, never lost." There is something to be said for abiding grace, whether it is found in conduct on the tennis court, or in prose like that of Elizabeth Spencer.

—Rosemary M. Canfield Reisman

STEELE, Max

Born: Henry Maxwell Steel in Greenville, South Carolina, 30 March 1922. **Education:** Furman University, 1939-41; University of North Carolina, 1942; Vanderbilt University, 1943-44, and University of California, Los Angeles, 1944, as meteorology cadet; University of North Carolina, B.A. 1946; graduate study in painting at the Academie Julienne, 1951, and in French literature and language, Sorbonne, University of Paris, 1952-54. **Military Service:** U. S. Air Force, Weather Wing, 1942-46. **Family:** Married Diana Whittinghill, 31 December 1960; two sons. **Career:** First published story appeared in *Harper's*, August 1944; advisory editor, *Paris Review*, 1952-54; lecturer, University of North

Carolina, 1956-58, Breadloaf Writers Conference, 1956, University of California, San Francisco, 1962-64; University of North Carolina, Chapel Hill, writer-in-residence, 1966-67, lecturer, 1967-68, associate professor, 1968-72, professor, 1972-88, director of creative writing program, 1968-88, and professor emeritus, 1988-present; director at Squaw Valley Writers Conference, 1970 and 1972, and Rollins Writers Conference, 1972. **Awards:** Harper Prize for *Debby*, 1950, Eugene F. Saxton Memorial Trust Award, 1950, Mayflower Cup Award, 1950; O. Henry Prize, 1955 and 1969; National Endowment for the Arts and Humanities grants, 1967 and 1970; D. Litt., Belmont Abbey, 1970; Standard Oil Award for Excellence in Undergraduate Teaching, 1971; Distinguished Alumna Award, Furman University, 1971; North Carolina Literary Festival (invited participant), April 1998.

PUBLICATIONS

Novels

Debby. New York, Harper, 1950.
The Goblins Must Go Barefoot (*Debby* retitled). New York, Perennial Library, 1966.

Children's Fiction

The Cat and the Coffee Drinkers. New York, Harper & Row, 1969.
Where She Brushed Her Hair, and Other Short Stories. New York, Harper & Row, 1968.
The Hat of My Mother. Chapel Hill, Algonquin Books, 1988.

Uncollected Short Stories

"English 23a: A Paper Long Overdue." In *An Apple for My Teacher*, edited by Louis D. Rubin, Jr., Chapel Hill, Algonquin Books, 1987.
"Speak, Painting, Speak." In *The Store of Joys*, edited by Huston Paschal, Winston-Salem, John F. Blair, 1997.

*

Critical Studies: "More Misses Than Hits" by James Degnan, *Kenyon Review*, 30, 1968; "Explosion of Talent" interview with Marjorie Hudson, *Carolina Alumni Review*, Summer 1988; "Max Steele" by Jeanne R. Nostrandt, *Southern Writers: A Biographical Dictionary* edited by Robert Bain, Joseph M. Flora, and Louis D. Rubin, Jr., Baton Rouge, Louisiana State University Press, 1979.

*   *   *

Max Steele is essentially a short story writer and teacher of creative writers. His only novel, *Debby*, was well-received and a prize-winner in 1950, but his published fiction since that time has been in the short story form. Probably the most obvious characteristic of Steele's writing is his humor and wry wit. This does not mean he is less than serious in his fiction; in fact, his perceptions into the potential of the human spirit to survive and grow rivals that of the poet. It does mean that Steele presents the human comedy with such twists and turns that readers must re-examine values and take an inward look at themselves. Steele's readers observe the ordinary human being—children, adults, and elderly—with an indulgent smile and a recognition or remembrance of themselves. In a *Harpers'* review, Katherine Jackson called this "the lunatic logic that illuminates everything" in Steele's writing.

At the core of his stories is a single moment when the narrator reaches understanding, much as Henry James uses an instant of recognition as pivotal in his fiction. Steele's point of view, however, is from innocence—the perception of a child or the adult's remembered childhood. He asks his readers to recover their childlike perception when they were in possession of a sensibility they since may have lost. An example is the narrator of "The Cat and the Coffee Drinkers" (a story published as a book ostensibly for children). The boy narrator learns more than just how to drink coffee and how to kill a cat, as one review misreads the story. While he learns the love of reading, he learns about discipline, work, manners, respect, courage, and, most importantly, dignity. To Steele, these values define civilization, and the child learns them by observation rather than by lessons.

Steele's artistic eye transforms the scenes into language, freezing the crucial moment into a vivid and unforgettable one. Miss Effie, the boy's teacher, has shown the children how to kill a cat by chloroform, which she must do after her aging pet has been hit by a car and then mauled by dogs. The children at once understand both the cruelty of life and the necessity in life for courage and mercy. At the same time, they observe Miss Effie carry out the difficult task with the same expression and dignity with which she taught them to drink coffee—black for the pure pleasure of it and without sugar or cream to disguise it as nourishment. The honesty of her character comes across to the children without overly dramatic action or emotional expression as she sends them home early to say to their parents: "the only thing Miss Effie had to teach you today was how to kill a cat." The narrator's final sentence is his permanent image of Miss Effie, "of her coming through the garden from the toolshed and standing in the doorway a moment to say that she had nothing more to teach us."

Steele shows the defining experience of life to be a mixture of cruelty and death, analysis and understanding, caring and mercy. The young narrator learns life lessons from his observation of adults—their manner and expressions more than their actions and words. The story is a retrospective narrative in which a boy tells of his experiences as a pre-schooler in a selective kindergarten. Steele often uses the "unreliable" narrator, letting his protagonist reveal more than he realizes, while the reader, through dramatic irony, understands more than is said. Steele, however, goes further by implying that the narrator, himself, comprehends more than he is capable of articulating. His children's point of view is only surface to the deeper understanding the child has but cannot express. The adult reader (the audience Steele expects) understands not only because his language is refined, but because he recognizes his own inner child. This is the "A-ha!" of Steele's fiction.

In his essay "Speak, Painting, Speak," Steele reacts to a painting in the North Carolina Museum of Art. Noting that "we've learned from physics that the observer changes the thing observed," he suggests that maybe the work is "not a surface painting," that painting, like fiction, must be more than what really happened: "to have worth they must also tell in what way the creating of

the scene informs or transforms the soul of the artist or writer." Elizabeth Easton, in a *Saturday Review* article, finds that his "stories are like scenes glimpsed from a moving train: situations that may lead to something, but one is never around to find out what. It isn't necessary; there is an odd sort of completeness to the fragment." The completeness in Steele's fiction is when memorable moments (fragments) work into a whole story for readers, evolving as they experience life.

The innocent who knows more than he can articulate is central to Steele's stories. If his plots and images sometimes seem surreal, as in "Hear the Wind Blow" with its woman producing an eight-pound blue egg, the reader has only to remember the child's acceptance of a goose laying a golden egg. Children's demarcation between reality and fantasy is blurred, and that blurred vision is essential to seeing clearly in Steele's work. He questions the realness of reality and the emptiness of life without imagination that strains the reality: the "observer changes the thing observed," according to physics, he reminds readers. His "Promiscuous Unbound," with its six-year-old protagonist's affair with his thirty-two-year-old neighbor, a lady of considerable charms named Mrs. Ludie Shaggs, is a play on the myth of Prometheus. A Titan bound by chains to a rock in punishment for bringing fire from the gods to mankind, Prometheus achieves freedom (is unbound) from Hercules. In Steele's story, the fire is of a different kind, but is, nonetheless, forbidden to the child. The tone is tongue-in-cheek, an extravagant comedy played out with Steele's humorous examination of the boundaries of life. He often pairs unlikely characters in his stories, juxtaposing their differing qualities so that the ensuing relationship may be examined, the eccentricities reevaluated. Steele's microscope focuses on the spaces between action and scene.

"A Caracole in Paris" and "The Wanton Troopers," his two stories about an American veteran of World War II living in Paris as an artist, reflect Steele's own experience living and studying art in Paris for five years after his war experiences. In the first story, two Americans from the South meet at a Paris cafe and become friends, but not in a definable relationship—lovers or siblings. One is tempted to believe that this story's seed is in Steele's experience in Paris described in "Speak, Painting, Speak," in which he says, "I spent hundreds of rainy afternoons . . . [by] Notre Dame near where lived a wise old woman analyst who was trying to help me make sense out of a deep sorrow and disorder. (A good enough definition of art itself.)" Here, again, the line between reality and fantasy is blurred; Steele asks readers to observe the quality of the relationship without articulating a definition.

His fictional style presents stories by skillful construction in vivid images and with little drama; the substance of the stories lies in the nebulous area of innocence meeting experience. The humor—sometimes wry, sometimes ribald, and often ironic—asks readers to reexamine their own definitions of life, to reevaluate from a child's perspective, observing life and learning from expression and manner.

Finally, Steele's fiction is imaginative, like the poet; focused, colorful (and sometimes surreal), like the artist; meditative, like the philosopher; and respectful of sacred values, like the theologian. His protagonists are like Alice in her Wonderland; they fall through the rabbit hole into a world of adults with absurd actions.

Like Alice, his readers must step through the looking glass to find the inner child. From his own childhood during the Depression, Steele remembers an image of his mother standing in the doorway holding a silver pitcher of water with real ice, "to assure us that the Depression will soon be over, that soon there will be iced tea again." Steele's own memory blooms with these moments of "A-has!" that he carries over into his fiction, exhorting his readers to remember their own such moments.

—Jeanne R. Nostrandt

STILL, James

Born: LaFayette, Alabama, 16 July 1906. **Education:** Lincoln Memorial University, A.B. 1929; Vanderbilt University, M.A. 1930; University of Illinois, B.S. 1931. **Career:** Librarian, Hindman Settlement School, Hindman, Kentucky, 1932-39, 1952-62; free-lance writer, 1939-41, 1945-52; associate professor of English, Morehead State University, 1962-71; free-lance writer, since 1971; visiting professor, Ohio University, 1970, and Berea College, 1972; speaker, Lilyan Cohen Lecture Series, Clinch Valley College, 1987; member of board of directors, Kentucky Humanities Council, since 1980; commentator for radio show, *All Things Considered*, National Public Radio. **Awards:** MacDowell Colony fellowship, 1938; O. Henry Memorial Prize, 1939, for short story "Bat Flight"; Southern Authors Award from Southern Women's National Democratic Organization, 1940, for *River of Earth*; Guggenheim fellowships, 1941-42, 1946-47; fiction award from American Academy of Arts and Letters, 1947; Weatherford Award, 1978, for Appalachian writing; Marjorie Peabody Waite Award, American Academy and Institute of Arts and Letters, 1979; Milne Award for service to the arts, Kentucky Arts Council, 1981; Book of the Year citation, Appalachian Writers Association, 1987; The James Still Room at Johnson-Camden Library, Morehead State University, was dedicated in 1961; James Still fellowships for advanced studies for the humanities, social science, and Appalachian studies were established at the University of Kentucky in 1980; Litt.D. from Berea College, 1973, and University of Kentucky, 1979; L.H.D. from Lincoln Memorial University, 1974. **Agent**: Mitch Douglas, International Creative Management, 40 West 57th St., New York, New York 10019.

PUBLICATIONS

Poetry Collections

Hounds on the Mountain, New York, Viking, 1937.
River of Earth: A Poem and Other Poems. New York, King Press, 1983.
The Wolfpen Poems, Berea, Kansas, Berea College Press, 1986.

Novels

River of Earth. New York, Viking, 1940, reissued, University of Kentucky Press, 1970.
On Troublesome Creek. New York, Viking, 1941.
Sporty Creek. New York, Putnam, 1977.

Short Story Collections

Pattern of a Man and Other Stories. Lexington, Kentucky, Gnomon, 1976.

Children's Books

Jack and the Wonder Beans. New York, Putnam, 1976.
The Velveteen Rabbitt, from the Story by Margery Williams. New Orleans, Anchorage Press, 1980.
An Appalachian Mother Goose. Lexington, University of Kentucky Press, 1998.

Other

Way Down Yonder on Troublesome Creek: Appalachian Riddles and Rusties. New York, Putnam, 1974.
The Wolfpen Rusties: Appalachian Riddles and Gee-Haw Whimmy-Diddles. New York, Putnam, 1975.
The Run for the Elbertas. Lexington, University Press of Kentucky, 1983.
The Man in the Bushes: The Notebooks of James Still, 1935-1987. Lexington, University Press of Kentucky, 1988.
Rusties and Riddles and Gee-Haw Whimmy Diddles. Lexington, University Press of Kentucky, 1989.
The Wolfpen Notebooks: A Record of Appalachian Life. Lexington, University Press of Kentucky, 1991.
The Secret History of the Future. New York, S. French, 1992.

Contributor, *The World of Psychoanalysis.* New York, Braziller, 1966.
Contributor, *From the Mountain.* Memphis, Memphis State University Press, 1972.

*

Sound recordings: *Appalachian Writers,* Washington, D.C., National Public Radio, 1980.

*   *   *

James Still is a beloved figure among writers and readers of Appalachian literature, a field that has suffered considerable neglect despite the quality of such writings as the novels of Harriette Simpson Arnow, Lee Smith, John Ehle and Still, himself. Still's masterpiece *River of Earth*, published in New York by Viking in 1940 and re-issued by the University of Kentucky Press in 1977, has maintained a healthy following largely in the region, in part due to a swell of academic interest in Appalachian literature But only the unprecedented success of Charles Frazier's *Cold Mountain* has broken a long-standing barrier that has somehow relegated books dealing with the Appalachian region to a side-channel of the publishing and marketing mainstream.

Still was born on July 16, 1906 in Lafayette, Alabama, just below Talladega Mountain and the northeasterly sweep of the Blue Ridge. His parents, Lonie Lindsey and J. Alex Still, were on their way to a big family; Still likes to tell that he was very shortly kicked out of the cradle by a younger brother. He said that once the baby could stand alone, in that household it was considered adult.

"Aside from the *Holy Bible*, we had three books at home," Still wrote in an autobiographical sketch. These were *The Anatomy of the Horse, The Palaces of Sin, or the Devil in Society*, and a hefty volume with a missing back, *Cyclopedia of Universal Knowledge*. "I learned from *The Palaces of Sin* of drinking gin and playing at cards. The author, one Colonel Dick Maple, 'spent his fortune with lavish hand, but awoke from his hypnotic debauch at Society's Shame.' *The Anatomy* was beyond my comprehension. The *Cyclopedia* was my introduction to a wider world. Subjects covered were eclectic—philosophy, physics, rhetoric, growing of fruit trees, rules for games, social and business correspondence ... a selection of poems, including Shakespeare, Byron, Shelley and Keats. I memorized the haunting 'Ozymandias,' and Cleopatra's swan song, 'I am dying, Egypt dying.' The *Cyclopedia* was my first stab at a liberal education."

J. Alex Still, a veterinarian who knew and raised his cap and spoke to every horse in the region, had sorely wanted to go back to Texas, where the young family had once lived before James was born. The elder Still wore cowboy boots and a big cowboy hat and considered himself a displaced Texan. But there had been a little girl who died in Alabama. And the mother would not leave that grave. James heard so much about Texas as a little child that he said he thought of himself as Texan, if only by proxy.

But that was not the part of the world that would ultimately claim him. Or make his name. When James Still was about to finish high school, he came across a catalog for a school called Lincoln Memorial University in Harrogate, Tennessee, established by a Union general in honor of the common mountain sympathy for the Union cause. A student could work for tuition. "In the fall I set off with $60 earned as an office boy at the factory and door-to-door delivery of the *Atlanta Constitution*." At school he would work in the quarry, digging up limestone from a pasture and running the rock crusher. When Christmas came he had but one nickel left of his savings and spent the holidays shoveling gravel, only to find, later, a silver dollar in his pocket. "An 'angel' had put it there," he says.

There was not enough to eat at school, and Still remembers most having no money to buy extra food. "My overriding memory of those years was of being hungry. We ate everything.... Walnut trees were plentiful on the hills of Harrogate and we cracked bushels. We raked our hands through snow under apple trees for overlooked fruit. The president of Lincoln Memorial spirited me into his house to try on a suit he could spare. It fitted perfectly. I broke into tears when he presented it to me. Not from joy . . . from humiliation. I never wore it."

He finished college in 1929, in the class with Jesse Stuart. He invited a wealthy Northern mentor to come to the commencement, and the man came, in his long chauffeured limousine, arranging, while there, to get Still into Vanderbilt, where he earned an M.A. in literature in one year. The following year Still earned his library science degree at the University of Illinois. His first job was at Hindman Settlement School in Knott County, Kentucky. Still had come home to roost. Except for his years in service in World War II, Hindman has been his principal home and writing base. At 92, Still remains in the Wolfpen vicinity, setting for his finest poems. Though he now lives in more modern quarters, nearby he maintains his old log cabin on Dead Mare Branch, near Hindman.

It was in that cabin that he wrote *River of Earth*, which tied with Thomas Wolfe's *You Can't Go Home Again* for the 1940 Southern Authors Award. Though he never quit writing, for many years Still made no attempt to get his work published in book form because he felt it would not get much attention. Nonetheless, his stories and poems appeared in such outlets as the *Atlantic Monthly* and in several years his short work won a place in Best American Short Stories.

The language of his novels, *River of Earth* and the similar *Sporty Creek*, is a hallmark for the effective use of dialect. "When I came to be writing about Kentucky, dialect was both a problem and a challenge," Still wrote. "Edward Weeks, editor of the *Atlantic*, warned me early on, 'Dialect is out of fashion.' My intentions are to evoke speech. Dialect too strictly adhered to makes a character appear ignorant when he is only unlettered."

Still evokes speech that is real and true. How else would one accurately paint an exchange between two little school boys as this, in *River of Earth*?:

> "Yonder comes the teacher," Leth said. "But there's a spell yet before books. Jonce Weathers has got to clean up after the bats. The floor gets ruint every night."
> "Where, now, do them bat-birds stay of a day?"
> "Yon side the ceiling, hanging amongst the rafters. . . ."

Still has been working on material he's gathered in Central America. A few years ago, he and Appalachian poet Jim Wayne Miller met and took a journey to Yucatan for each other's company and the research. Not long ago, Miller died in his middle age. He would have loved to see James Still work on, and publish, and publish.

—Dot Jackson

STOKESBURY, Leon

Born: Oklahoma City, Oklahoma, 5 December 1945. **Education:** Lamar State College of Technology, B.A. 1968; University of Arkansas, M.A. 1972, M.F.A. 1972; Florida State University, Ph.D. 1984. **Family:** Married Susan Thurman in 1980, daughter, Erin Elizabeth, born in 1985. **Career:** Published his first poems in *Pulse*, the Lamar University student magazine, and edited the magazine during his senior year; attended the Bread Loaf Writers Conference on scholarship, 1969, as a fellow, 1990; worked in the North Slope oil fields, Alaska, summer 1970; instructor in English, Lamar University, 1972-75; poet in residence, North Texas State University (now the University of North Texas), Hollins College, 1980-81, and University of Southwestern Louisiana, 1984; professor, McNeese State University, 1985-87; professor and director, creative writing program, Georgia State University, since 1987. **Member:** Texas Institute of Letters. **Awards:** First prize, Collegiate Poetry Contest, *Southern Poetry Review*, 1971, for "To Laura Phelan"; co-winner, Associated Writing Program's poetry competition, 1975; the co-winner (with Sydney Lea), Poets' Prize, 1997, for *Autumn Rhythm*.

PUBLICATIONS

Poetry Collections

Often in Different Landscapes. Austin, University of Texas Press, 1976.
The Drifting Away. Fayetteville, University of Arkansas Press, 1986.
Autumn Rhythm: New and Selected Poems. Fayetteville, University of Arkansas Press, 1996.

Editor

The Made Thing: An Anthology of Contemporary Southern Poetry. Fayetteville, University of Arkansas Press, 1987.
Articles of War: A Collection of American Poetry about World War II. Fayetteville, University of Arkansas Press, 1990.
The Light the Dead See: Selected Poems of Frank Stanford. Fayetteville, University of Arkansas Press, 1991.

*

Critical Studies: "Second Gear" by R. S. Gwynn, *New England Review and Bread Loaf Quarterly,* Autumn 1986; "Two Young Poets" by David Baker, *Crazy Horse,* Winter 1988; "Fwame Wesistent Suits" by R. S. Gwynn, *Hudson Review,* Spring 1998.

*   *   *

Leon Stokesbury's poems show the careful craftsmanship of a writer subtly adapting and refreshing traditional forms through contemporary idioms and cadences. Having published only three volumes over a period of twenty years and known to frequently revise his compositions, Stokesbury is a meticulous artist of polished verse remarkable for its range of topics—landscapes, family, art, and popular culture among them.

Within these larger concerns, Stokesbury deftly balances variations in tone and approach: his descriptive landscape poems with finely realized metaphors span the icy, open terrain of Alaska to more lush areas of California or the Ozarks, to various locales in Eastern Texas—urban enclaves, flatlands, and pine forests; family life can be meaningful at times, with members genuinely caring for each other, while at other times it can be constricting with pressures and expectations; heavy symbolism can weigh in occasional surrealist sallies, while ordinary adolescent experiences prove instructive in others; and intrusive elements of popular culture are critically examined in some poems, while frequent allusions to art celebrate higher ideals and probe themes of individual responsibility. This diversity is especially well-rendered through the ongoing tension between playfulness and responsibility, humor and pathos, clowning and seriousness, throughout Stokesbury's work.

Stokesbury began receiving attention for his poetry as early as his undergraduate years at Lamar State College of Technology (now University), where he published his first poems in *Pulse*, the Lamar student magazine, and edited the magazine during his senior year. Encouraged by poet Alistair Reid, Stokesbury submitted a poem, "The Lamar Tech Football Team Has Won Its Game," to the *New Yorker*, which published it in a 1967 issue.

After graduating from Lamar, Stokesbury attended the Bread Loaf Writers Conference on scholarship in 1969, and in 1971 he won first prize in the Collegiate Poetry Contest sponsored by the *Southern Poetry Review* for "To Laura Phelan." During this period he had briefly joined his parents in Alaska—his father held various positions in the petroleum industry— where he worked a summer in North Slope oil fields in 1970; he returned to the South to attain his M.A. and M.F.A. at the University of Arkansas, where he studied under James Whitehead and Miller Williams and became friends with fellow poet Frank Stanford, then Stokesbury began an academic career as an instructor in English at Lamar.

The title of Stokesbury's first collection, *Often in Different Landscapes* (1976), speaks to his varied concerns and approaches. "To Laura Phelan: 1880-1906" reflects his verse's characteristic creative tension between playfulness and responsibility. Beginning as a blackly humorous approach to a student escapade, where drunken young men pilfer a tombstone and then eventually return it, but not to its proper place in the cemetery, the tone gradually shifts to meditations on temporality and death and on the person whose grave the speaker has disturbed. Other poems are set in various landscapes, where descriptions capture a particular sense of place and evoke metaphors for a time in the writer's life or offer more general observations.

Some of the poems in *Often in Different Landscapes* recall sights and experiences from Stokesbury's East Texas boyhood, others of rugged beauty and a sense of foreboding in California, of the Ozarks both wild and tamed (small mountains with trees sticking up seem like "the white hairy bellies of fat old men / who have lain down there"), and of Alaska, where the poet adjusts to endless summer days. In the fine Alaskan poem "The North Slope," the bleak, white landscape symbolizes the speaker's own feeling of barrenness. The power of the large, indifferent whiteness gains further resonance through the poet's allusions to Herman Melville's *Moby Dick*. Stokesbury's landscape poems often extend metaphors through allusions to art. Though not overtly imitative, they reference a tradition of landscape writing, recalling formal and thematic approaches of T. S. Eliot, Robert Frost, Gerard Manley Hopkins, and others while being fresh and individually specific to a place and time.

The Drifting Away contains several poems about things passing or loss, with Stokesbury balancing seriousness and lightness. Poems on elements of popular culture can be poignantly satirical, as when shopping malls are compared with cathedrals and consumers form an unholy congregation. The easy and idealistic celebration of family life dominating popular media is contrasted with pressures that lead to strained relations; difficult situations—a stroke, or a family member's depression—lead to contemplations on familial relations, realistically presenting hardships and a humbling humanity. Several poems suggest that serious and committed attention to craft offers a sense of salvation, with art and the artist repeatedly as a focus. As in the family poems, however, the life of the artist is presented with balance, as in Stokesbury's elegy, "A Few Words for Frank Stanford: 1948-1978," for his friend, a fellow poet who committed suicide. The elegy celebrates Stanford's gift and also cautions about being overly consumed with the power of art.

A similar approach is evident in "The Royal Nonesuch," from *Autumn Rhythm: New and Selected Poems*. In this elegy to New Orleans poet Everette Maddox, artistic gifts are celebrated while the poem cautions against indulgences that can become self-destructive. Such is the creative tension that informs Stokesbury's own verse, reflected in his balance of tones and his careful craftsmanship that accommodates occasional rough edges of phrasing while maintaining lyrical qualities. Art in many forms, from high culture to pop culture (the book's title references a Jackson Pollock painting) in its most liberating craftsmanship and artificial senses—from the accomplishment of craft to the environment-controlled shopping mall. Another elegy, "Senor Wences and the Man in the Box," is a serious exploration of the poet's relationship with his father through connections with a comedy skit that appeared frequently on the old *Ed Sullivan* television show.

"Stokesbury is deeply immersed in popular culture," noted R.S. Gwynn, "and he likes to remind readers that Shakespeare and Twain were popular artists." The pervasiveness of pop culture in Stokesbury's work reflects its overwhelming presence in our lives, and whether played for fun, or satire, or criticism, the references help us understand our surroundings as Stokesbury endeavors to explore them within his craft.

—Mel Koler

STONE, Ruth

Born: Roanoke, Virginia, 8 June 1915. **Education:** University of Illinois, Urbana; Harvard University, Cambridge, Massachusetts; Radcliffe Institute (now Bunting Institute), Cambridge, Massachusetts, 1963-65. **Family:** Married Walter B. Stone (died 1959); three daughters. **Career:** Seminar teacher, Radcliffe College, 1963-65, and Wellesley College, 1965; member of the department of English, Brandeis University, 1965-66; poet-in-residence, University of Wisconsin, 1967-69; artist-in-residence, University of Illinois, 1971-73; visiting professor, Indiana University, 1973-74; creative writing chair, Center College, Danville, Kentucky, winter 1975; Hurst Visiting Professor, Brandeis University, 1975; visiting professor, University of Virginia, 1977-78; Regents Lecturer, spring 1978, and visiting lecturer, fall 1978, spring 1981, University of California, Davis; poet-in-residence, fall 1984, and visiting professor, fall 1985, spring 1986, New York University; adjunct professor, Cooper Union, New York, 1986; visiting professor, fall 1989, spring 1990, Old Dominion University; since 1990 professor of English and creative writing, State University of New York, Binghamton. **Awards:** Bess Hokin prize, *Poetry,* 1954; *Kenyon Review* fellowship, 1956; Robert Frost Fellow at Breadloaf Writers' Conference, summer, 1963; Radcliffe Institute fellowship, Harvard University, 1963-65; Shelley Memorial Award, Poetry Society of America, 1964; grant from American Academy of Arts and Letters, 1970; Guggenheim fellowships, 1972, 1975-76; Delmore Schwartz Award, 1983-84; Whiting Award, 1986; Paterson Prize, 1988. **Address:** Department of English, State University of New York, Binghamton, New York 13901.

PUBLICATIONS

Poetry

In an Iridescent Time. New York, Harcourt Brace, 1959.
Topography and Other Poems. New York, Harcourt Brace, 1971.
Unknown Messages. Hindsboro, Illinois, Nemesis Press, 1973.
Cheap: New Poems and Ballads. New York, Harcourt Brace, 1975.
American Milk. Fanwood, New Jersey, From Here Press, 1986.
Second-Hand Coat: Poems New and Selected. Boston, Godine, 1987.
The Solution. Towson, Maryland, Alembic Press, 1989.
Who Is the Widow's Muse. Cambridge, Massachusetts, Yellow Moon Press, 1991.
Simplicity. Northampton, Massachusetts, Paris Press, 1995.

*

Recordings: *Ways of Survival,* Watershed, 1986; *A Movable Feast,* National Public Radio, 1987.

Critical Studies: "On the Poetry of Ruth Stone: Selections and Commentary" by Harvey Gross, *Iowa Review,* Spring 1972; "Interview: Ruth Stone," with Sandra M. Gilbert, *California Quarterly,* Autumn 1975, and "Sex Wars: Not the Fun Kind" by Gilbert and Susan Gubar, *New York Times Book Review,* 27, December 1987; "On Ruth Stone" by various authors, *Extended Outlooks: The Iowa Review Collection of Contemporary Women Writers* edited by Jane Cooper, Gwen Head, Adelaide Morris, and Marcia Southwick, New York, Collier, 1982; "Six Women Poets," *Easy Pieces* by Geoffrey H. Hartman, New York, Columbia University Press, 1985; "Entire Histories" by Donald Hall, *Hungry Mind Review,* Spring 1988; "Art in Obscurity" by Julie Fay, *Women's Review of Books,* 6, July 1989; *The House Is Made of Poetry: The Art of Ruth Stone* edited by Wendy Barker and Sandra M. Gilbert, Carbondale, Southern Illinois University Press, 1996.

Ruth Stone comments:

I think my work is a natural response to my life—what I see and feel changes like a prism, moment to moment—a poem holds and illuminates. It is a small drama—I think, too, my poems are a release, a laughing at the ridiculous, and songs of mourning, celebrating marriage and loss, all the sad baggage of our lives—it is so overwhelming, so complex. Outside the window here is teeming with life from far down in the soil to far up in the sky. Poems are a way of seeking patterns within this complexity.

*   *   *

Although at age forty-four she was no beginner when she published her first book, *In an Iridescent Time,* in 1959, Ruth Stone was working largely within the elegant, formal conventions of that era, showing her respect for the likes of Ransom and Stevens. Thus, along with many other women poets of the 1950s—for example, Sylvia Plath and Adrienne Rich—she began her career by expressing a female vision through a male medium. Nevertheless, within the largely regular forms of these early poems there is heard a complex woman's voice compounded of the artful naivete of fable and tale and the deceptive simplicity of a sophisticated artist. The voice is as responsive to marriage, family, and human solitude as to animals, landscapes, and seasons. Given to gorgeous diction, eloquent syntax, and powerful statement, along with occasional colloquialisms, *In an Iridescent Time* contains nothing callow or unformed, although today it appears marked by a somewhat overdone artfulness. This impression is confirmed by Stone's own changes as she has developed and explored the various possibilities of her special voice.

There was a conspicuous silence of twelve years before Stone's next book, *Topography and Other Poems,* appeared, and the single most determinative cause of that hiatus—as well as of its fruit—must have been her poet-scholar husband's unexpected suicide in 1959 when they were in England, leaving Stone and her three daughters to fend for themselves. She returns repeatedly here and in subsequent volumes to this devastating experience, and without either over- or underplaying it she somehow manages to survive and grow strong, as Hemingway's Frederic Henry says, in the "broken places." Thus, there is a deepening of her emotional range, accompanied as we would expect by a corresponding roughening of rhythm and diction. The more general poetic and political rebellions of the 1960s were no doubt operative as well, but Stone never becomes programmatic. A Keatsian poet "of Sensations rather than of Thoughts"—although like Keats she is certainly not without thought—so busy is she with her responses to the pressures of the lived life that she cannot afford time for philosophizing or moralizing.

Stone's second volume, *Topography and Other Poems,* deals with her first attempts to absorb her husband's death, her reactions to the people around her, her return with her daughters to the seasons of Vermont, her subsequent travels, and her continuing growth as a poet, mother, and person. She begins using more direct speech and unrhymed free verse lines of variable length—not, however, without her characteristic touches of elegance. In "Changing (For Marcia)" she writes to her eldest child, noticing the changes in her, and reflects that "Love cannot be still; / Listen. It's folly and wisdom; / Come and share."

That Stone had regained her voice and creative will at this time was shown four years later by the publication of *Cheap: New Poems and Ballads.* Here we find her risking relationships with others while still trying to deal with her husband's death and the loss of their life together, and she mines an iron vein of mordant wit to make bearable that bitterness. Some of her lines strike a late Plathian note of barely contained hysteria: "I hid sometimes in the closet among my own clothes" ("Loss"). But near a barn young bulls are bellowing ("Communion"), and solace is found in the germinative force of nature. "Cocks and Mares" concludes with a marvelous evocation of female power in wild mares.

Second-Hand Coat: Poems New and Selected, which came out in 1987, contains forty-six new poems. Along with exploring her evolving feelings about her lost husband, Stone probes more deeply into her childhood years and early family memories. Once again she balances between "fertility/futility" ("Pine Cones"), and in addition she reaches a new level of outrageous fantasy and satire. In "Some Things You'll Need To Know . . . " a "poetry factory" is described in which "The antiwar and human rights poems / are processed in the white room. / Everyone there wears sterile gauze."

The Solution, a chapbook of eighteen poems which came out in 1989, adds yet another new note—the emergence of Stone's other self, her doppelgänger, as, for instance, in "The Rotten Sample." "Bird in the Gilbert's Tree" is truly remarkable, beginning with the question "What is that bird saying?" and continuing on to give in verbal form what is strictly nonverbal, a tour de force worthy of Lewis Carroll:

> And you, my consort, my basket,
> my broody decibels,
> my lover in the lesser scales;
> this is our tree, our vista,
> our bagworms.

Who Is the Widow's Muse? makes of the doppelgänger a dramatic and structural device in a sequence of fifty-two relatively short lyrics (perhaps for a year's cycle), plus a prefatory poem as introduction. Here the muse, a realistic—not to say caustic—voice, serves to limit and control the operatic tendency of the widow's voice in her endless quest for ways to come to terms with her husband's death. As a result the tone is a miraculous blend of desolation and laughter, a unique achievement. At the end, when the widow wants to write "one more" poem about her loss, the muse "shakes her head" and, in an almost unbearably compassionate gesture, "took the widow in her arms"; the poem concludes

> 'Now say it with me,' the muse said.
> 'Once and for all ... he is forever dead.'

Thus is Stone solving, in her own particular way, the problem of expressing a female vision through a female idiom.

Stone's 1995 volume *Simplicity* contains the poems of *The Solution* as well as a hundred pages of later work. Some still deal with her husband, but the rest derive from an independent inspiration—although it is of a rather somber mood, for at the age of eighty Stone has grown into a deep knowledge of suffering and survival. Her range is broad as well, shifting from the common to the cosmic in a moment, from the ordinary to the surreal. Riding a train or bus, she notes the passage of weathers and seasons, the isolation of those beside her, and the small towns and shops sliding by. She is the poet of hope in the midst of doom, of love as it encounters death, and of the apocalypse forthcoming in the mundane. "The Artist" is revelatory, showing the painter in his own painting—an old Oriental scroll—climbing a mountain to reach a temple. Although he has been walking all day, he will not get there before dark, "And yet there is no way to stop him. He is / still going up and he is still only half way."

—Norman Friedman

STUART, Dabney

Born: Richmond, Virginia, 4 November 1937. **Education:** Davidson College, North Carolina, 1956-60, A.B. 1960; Harvard University, Cambridge, Massachusetts (Summer Poetry Prize, 1962), A.M. 1962. **Family:** Married Sandra Westcott (third marriage) in 1983; one daughter and two sons. **Career:** Instructor in English, College of William and Mary, Williamsburg, Virginia, 1961-65; instructor, 1965-66, assistant professor, 1966-69, associate professor, 1969-74, professor, 1974-91, and since 1991, S. Blount Mason Professor of English, Washington and Lee University, Lexington, Virginia. Visiting professor, Middlebury College, Vermont, 1968-69, and Ohio University, Athens, Spring 1975; resident poet, Trinity College, Hartford, Connecticut, 1978; visiting poet, University of Virginia, Charlottesville, 1981, 1982-83. Poetry editor, *Shenandoah,* Lexington, 1966-76, and editor-in-chief, 1988-95; member of the editorial board, Poets in the South, 1974-82; poetry editor, *New Virginia Review,* 1983. **Awards:** Poetry Society of America Dylan Thomas prize, 1965; National Endowment for the Arts grant, 1969, fellowship 1974, 1982; Borestone Mountain award, 1969, 1974, 1977; Virginia Governor's award, 1979; Guggenheim fellowship, 1987-88. **Address:** Department of English, Washington and Lee University, Lexington, Virginia 24450.

PUBLICATIONS

Poetry

The Diving Bell. New York, Knopf, 1966.
A Particular Place. New York, Knopf, 1969.
Corgi Modern Poets in Focus 3, with others, edited by Dannie Abse. London, Corgi, 1971.
The Other Hand. Baton Rouge, Louisiana State University Press, 1974.
Friends of Yours, Friends of Mine. Richmond, Virginia, Rainmaker Press, 1974.
Round and Round: A Triptych. Baton Rouge, Louisiana State University Press, 1977.
Rockbridge Poems. Emory, Virginia, Iron Mountain Press, 1981.
Common Ground. Baton Rouge, Louisiana State University Press, 1982.
Don't Look Back. Baton Rouge, Louisiana State University Press, 1987.
Narcissus Dreaming. Baton Rouge, Louisiana State University Press, 1990.
Light Years: New and Selected Poems. Baton Rouge, Louisiana State University Press, 1994.
Second Sight: Poems for Paintings by Carroll Cloar. N.p., 1996.
Long Gone. N.p., 1996.

Short Stories

Sweet Lucy Wine: Stories. Baton Rouge, Louisiana State University Press, 1992.

Other

Nabokov: The Dimensions of Parody. Baton Rouge, Louisiana State University Press, 1978.

*

Manuscript Collection: Virginia Commonwealth University, Richmond.

Critical Studies: By X.J. Kennedy, in *Shenandoah* (Lexington, Virginia), Autumn 1966; John Unterecker, in *Shenandoah* (Lex-

ington, Virginia), Autumn 1969; Dannie Abse, in *Corgi Modern Poets in Focus 3,* 1971; by the author, in *Contemporary Poetry in America,* edited by Miller Williams, New York, Random House, 1973; D. E. Richardson, in *Southern Review* (Baton Rouge, Louisiana), Autumn 1976; Stephen Dobyns, in *Washington Post Book World,* 7 November 1982; Fred Chappell, in Roanoke *Times* (Virginia), 27 March 1983, and 30 August 1987; "Ghostlier Demarcations, Keener Sounds" by Barbara Fialkowski, in *Poets in the South* (Tampa, Florida), Fall 1984; Robert Gingher, in Greensboro *News and Record* (North Carolina), 7 June 1987; Paul Ramsey, in *Chronicles* (Rockford, Illinois), March 1989; "Every Poet in His Humor" by Fred Chappell, in *The Georgia Review* (Athens), Winter 1990; "A Dream Not of Wholeness, but of Endless Dreaming" by Gilbert Allen and "The Long Mirror: Dabney Stuart's Film Allusion" by Fred Chappell in The Dabney Stuart issue of *Kentucky Poetry Review,* 27(1), Spring 1991; by Warren Werner in *The Chatahoochee Review* (Dunwoody), Winter 1991; by Greg Johnson in *The Georgia Review* (Athens), Winter 1992-93; by Haines Sprunt in *The Hollins Critic* (Roanoke), June 1993; "Six Davidson Poets: The Consolation of Some memorable Language" by Barbara Mayer, in *The Davidson Journal* (Davidson, North Carolina), Fall 1993.

Dabney Stuart comments:

My work ranges formally from traditional English patterns to associative, non-metrical verse. My more recent poems (since and including *Common Ground*) have been characterized by a combination of aspects of both strains in individual poems, including the use of irregularly patterned half-rhymes, acrostic structures, and *nonce* forms. I have been consistently involved with certain themes and subject matter: family relationships, particularly those involving parents and children, levels of consciousness mirrored in language, the unforeseen and ubiquitous past, shifting perspective, cultural icons, isolation, dreams, the hidden self. The work of Alice Miller (*Prisoners of Childhood, Thou Shalt Not Be Aware*), Margaret Mahler, certain 17th century poets, and others have significantly aided me in developing an understanding of the sources of my work, and the ways of its maturation. See my autobiographical statement, "Knots into Webs," in volume 105 of the *Dictionary of Literary Biography.*

*   *   *

In his first book, *The Diving Bell,* Dabney Stuart revealed himself as a skillful and intelligent poet. His command of language and his confident handling of relatively traditional forms are combined with a gentle candor that enables many of the poems in the volume to transcend the category of Lowellesque confessional verse into which they run the risk of falling. There is nothing trite about his contribution to this genre, however. For example, in a poem for the small daughter whom he seldom sees he speaks of her as a conjurer, "Your voice a wand, you called the olive grapes," but he later adds,

> Yet, deserting your role,
> You called me by my name—
> I'd rather
> have been that metaphor, your father.

Here language is both image and instrument.

Stuart's second book, *A Particular Place,* advances into more adventurous territory. In fact, it includes a number of poems about place, contemplative in tone and dwelling on stone and water, air and stillness. But it also explores deeper regions of symbol and myth and psychic landscapes in poetry that owes little to traditional forms. For instance, consider these lines from "The Charles River":

On summer evenings here
Lovers may kiss to Stravinsky:
Le sacre du printemps.
If they lie close enough
To the bank, the music and the river
Lapping the stones
Become one sound ....

Although some of the poems are more successful than others, the ones that do succeed achieve a haunting resonance.

Stuart's later books *The Other Hand* and *Round and Round* continue to work within the formal and thematic boundaries set by his first two books. That is, most of the poems are written in free verse and tend toward fairly short lines; thematically, the poems are still immersed in the contemplative, second-generation Deep Image poetry Stuart used in *A Particular Place.* The changes that occur in the work of these two books primarily involve tone. Stuart begins to exhibit a wider range of tonal expression—from the caustic to the contemplative. These lines from the poem "Mystic" offer an example of Stuart's manipulation of tone: I have seen God O Yes/Don't fondle me with doubt/or any lower case vanity." *Songs for Champagne Saturday* also does not offer any major deviation from the work of his earlier volumes. The poems here are competent and interesting but not particularly memorable.

Common Ground, however, shows Stuart moving beyond the earlier books and charting new terrain in which to work. The poems now usually have a longer, more sonically interesting line. The exploration in *Round and Round* begins to have an effect on his tone. For instance, Stuart begins to occasionally use a very authoritative tone, as in the end to "Turntables," where he writes about a newborn: "His small body, new in the air,/filling it;/The human music. The awful human music." He is also capable, however, of successfully returning to a more meditative voice, as in "Snorkeling in the Caribbean." Filled by numerous fine poems, *Common Ground* is work that fulfills the promise his first book offered and is thus a turning point in his career.

The poems that have followed—in *Don't Look Back* and *Narcissus Dreaming* and the newer work in his selected poems, *Light Years*—all profit from what Stuart apparently learned while writing *Common Ground. Don't Look Back* has several very strong poems, including "Casting," "Taking the Wheel," and the title poem. Ranging over primarily personal terrain, the poems are emotional, yet they are still shaped by the precision that guided Stuart's early work. Many of the poems of *Narcissus Dreaming* are also powerful. Consider, for instance, the closing lines of the title poem; Narcissus, fishing in a place where the surface ripples wrinkle his reflection, finally gets a bite, and so he reels in his line and pulls in his reflection, "a laid out suit/of clothes lifted/by its center," which he "lowers" into "the boat" and "takes...upon himself,"

drenched, obscene,
a perfectly imperfect fit,
leaving the water
imageless, opaque,
other.

Firm control of tone and a staccato rhythm fueled by disjointed, surprising line breaks create several memorable poems in this book.

If the new poems in *Light Years* indicate where Stuart may be headed, the emphasis on control of tone remains important. Such control allows Stuart to adapt the short-lined poem he's so frequently written on a variety of subjects. That he succeeds with such adaptation and maintains interesting rhythmic effects—something that was lacking in the earlier work of Deep Image lineage—speaks to the flexibility of Stuart's voice. His subjects here include an executive discovering poetry, time-share condos, funerals, a fence, and sleepwalking. *Light Years* is a fine and comprehensive collection that spans thirty years of Stuart's work and reveals the enduring strength and appeal of his poetry.

—Fleur Adcock and Tod Marshall

STYRON, William

Born: William Clark Styron, Jr., in Newport News, Virginia, 11 June 1925. **Education:** Christchurch School, Virginia; Davidson College, North Carolina, 1942-43; Duke University, Durham, North Carolina, 1943-44, 1946-47, B.A. 1947 (Phi Beta Kappa). **Military Service:** Served in the United States Marine Corps, 1944-45, 1951: 1st Lieutenant. **Family:** Married Rose Burgunder (a poet) in 1953; three daughters and one son. **Career:** Associate editor, Whittlesey House (division of McGraw-Hill), 1947; since 1952 advisory editor, *Paris Review*; since 1964 fellow, Silliman College, Yale University, New Haven, Connecticut; member of the editorial board, *American Scholar,* Washington, D.C., 1970-76; frequently writes for such publications as *Sewanee Review, Life, Esquire, Harper's* and *New York Review of Books*; Duke University mounted an exhibition of his manuscripts, editions and other materials for "William Styron in Mid-Career," 1976. **Awards:** American Academy Prix de Rome, 1952, for *Lie Down in Darkness*; Pulitzer Prize, 1968, for *The Confessions of Nat Turner*; Howells Medal, American Academy of Arts and Letters, 1970, for *The Confessions of Nat Turner*; American Book Award and National Book Award, 1980, for *Sophie's Choice*; Styron Scholarship established, Christopher Newport College (Newport News, Virginia), 1980; Connecticut Arts Award, 1984; Cino del Duca Prize, 1985; commandeur, Ordre des Arts et des Lettres (France), 1987; MacDowell Medal, 1988; Bobst award, 1989; National Magazine award, 1990; National Medal of Arts, 1993; National Arts Club Medal of Honor, 1995; Commonwealth Award, 1995; Litt.D.: Duke University, 1968, Davidson College, Davidson, North Carolina, 1986. **Member:** American Academy of Arts and Sciences and American Academy of Arts and Letters; commander, Legion of Honor (France).

PUBLICATIONS

Novels

Lie Down in Darkness. Indianapolis, Bobbs Merrill, 1951.
The Long March. New York, Random House, 1956.
Set This House on Fire. New York, Random House, 1960.
The Confessions of Nat Turner. New York, Random House, 1967.
Sophie's Choice. New York, Random House, 1979.

Short Story Collections

Shadrach. Los Angeles, Sylvester and Orphanos, 1979.

Uncollected Short Stories

"Autumn," and "Long Dark Road." In *One and Twenty,* edited by W.M. Blackburn. Durham, North Carolina, Duke University Press, 1945.
"Moments in Trieste." In *American Vanguard, 1948,* edited by Charles I. Glicksburg. New York, Cambridge, 1948.
"The Enormous Window." In *American Vanguard, 1950,* edited by Charles I. Glicksburg, New York, Cambridge, 1950.
"The McCabes," in *Paris Review,* Autumn-Winter 1959-60.
"Pie in the Sky." In *The Vintage Anthology of Science Fantasy,* edited by Christopher Cerf. New York, Random House, 1966.

Play

In the Clap Shack (produced New Haven, Connecticut, 1972). New York, Random House, 1973.

Other

The Four Seasons, illustrated by Harold Altman. University Park, Pennsylvania State University Press, 1965.
Admiral Robert Penn Warren and the Snows of Winter: A Tribute. Winston-Salem, North Carolina, Palaemon Press, 1978.
The Message of Auschwitz. Blacksburg, Virginia, Press de la Warr, 1979.
Against Fear. Winston-Salem, North Carolina, Palaemon Press, 1981.
As He Lay Dead, A Bitter Grief. New York, Albondocani Press, 1981; originally published as a report of William Faulkner's funeral in *Life,* 20 July 1962.
This Quiet Dust and Other Writings. New York, Random House, 1982.
Darkness Visible (memoirs). New York, Random House, 1990.
A Tidewater Morning (Three Tales from Youth). Helsinki, Eurographica, 1991; New York, Random House, 1993.
Inheritance of Night: Early Drafts of Lie Down in Darkness. Durham, Duke University Press, 1993.

Author of introduction, *No Beast So Fierce: A Novel,* by Edward Bunker. New York, Vintage, 1993.
Author of introduction, *Fathers and Daughters: In Their Own Words,* by Mariana Cook. San Francisco, Chronicle Books, 1994.

Author of prologue, *The Face of Mercy: A Photographic History of Medicine at War.* New York, Random House, 1993.

Editor, *Best Short Stories from the Paris Review.* New York, Dutton, 1959.

*

Adaptations: *Shadrach,* screenplay by Susanna Styron, film, 1998.

Video recording: *William Styron: The Way of the Writer,* American Masters, PBS, WNET, 22 January 1997.

Manuscript Collections: Duke University and Library of Congress.

Bibliographies: *William Styron: A Descriptive Bibliography* by James L.W. West III, Boston, Hall, 1977; *William Styron: A Reference Guide* by Jackson R. Bryer and Mary B. Hatem, Boston, Hall, 1978; *William Styron: An Annotated Bibliography of Criticism* by Philip W. Leon, Westport, Connecticut, Greenwood Press, 1978.

Interviews: *Conversations with William Styron,* edited by James L.W. West III, Jackson, University Press of Mississippi, 1985; "William Styron," with Naomi Epel, *Writers Dreaming,* New York, Carol Southern Books, 1993.

Critical Studies: "William Styron: Notes on a Southern Writer in Our Time" by Louis D. Rubin, Jr., *The Faraway Country: Writers of the Modern South,* Seattle, University of Washington Press, 1963; *William Styron* by Robert H. Fossum, Grand Rapids, Michigan, Eerdmans, 1968; William Styron by Cooper R. Mackin, Austin, Texas, Steck Vaughn, 1969; *William Styron* by Richard Pearce, Minneapolis, University of Minnesota Press, 1971; *William Styron* by Marc L. Ratner, New York, Twayne, 1972; *William Styron* by Melvin J. Friedman, Bowling Green, Ohio, Popular Press, 1974; The Achievement of William Styron edited by Irving Malin and Robert K. Morris, Athens, University of Georgia Press, 1975, revised edition, 1981; *Critical Essays on William Styron* edited by Arthur D. Casciato and James L.W. West III, Boston, Hall, 1982; *The Root of All Evil: The Thematic Unity of William Styron's Fiction* by John K. Crane, Columbia, University of South Carolina Press, 1985; *William Styron* by Judith Ruderman, New York, Ungar, 1989; special issue on William Styron, *Southern Literary Journal,* Fall 1995; *The Novels of William Styrony* by Gavin Cologne-Brookes, Baton Rouge, Louisiana State University Press, 1995; "The Confessions of William Styron" by Joan Crowder, 6 June 1998, website http://news.newspress.com/archive/styron.htm; *William Styron: A Life* by James L. W. West, III, New York, Random House, 1998.

*   *   *

Lie Down in Darkness, William Styron's first novel, won much acclaim when it appeared in 1951. After his own descent into and emergence from darkness, Styron recognized its autobiographical elements. He is a Southern writer whose sensibilities lie with family and community, cultural values, and language. His creation of protagonist Peyton Loftis comes out of his innate melancholia; she embodies his viewpoint on the effects of modern family and social ills. His native Tidewater, Virginia, is the setting in which he explores his concern that a disintegration of cultural and family values brings devastating results. He remembers Newport News as being "a strangely soulless community. . . but [in *Lie Down in Darkness*] it was difficult to establish a spiritual connection with such a city, basically callow and without a past to supply it with the unaesthetic, those necessities of southern life—myth and tradition," he noted in the *Sewanee Review*.

The episode of Peyton's funeral cortege, akin to Faulkner's funeral journey of Addie Bundren, uses images out of his memory—a real Daddy Grace and mass baptisms in Hampton Roads. In *Lie Down in Darkness,* his focus is on a single character who suffers a modern tragedy as victim of family, community and society. Also her own victim, she struggles in all the wrong ways for survival in a loveless, ego-driven world. Ultimately, she chooses to "lie down in darkness." In recent years, Styron speaks of his abuse of alcohol to anesthetize his sense of sadness and tendency to suicide. He told interviewer Naomi Epel, "I know for sure . . . that I had inserted this depressive mood into the characters of my fiction throughout my career. From Peyton Loftis to Sophie."

Melvin Friedman noted that Styron deals with large themes and demanding subjects through allusion; he draws attention to Greek culture and myths as he does to Biblical references. He also alludes to such masters of literary achievement as Shakespeare, Faulkner, Conrad and Fitzgerald. He sees modern society battling the same human problems his predecessors envisioned. In *The Long March,* intelligent marines grapple with a military machine that would turn them into robots—marching figures rather than thinking humans. Forced on an extraordinary march, two marine reservists struggle to retain their dignity against the inhumaneness of a process denying them individuality. Admittedly autobiographical, Styron wrote this novella with an urgency unlike that he usually feels, having returned from such a march himself. Still, he reports such advantages in his military service as comradeship, endurance, pride and self-discipline.

In *Set This House on Fire,* Styron explores the theme of a naive American in Europe. His narrator is a Virginian, supported by a scenic South, while the crux of the novel takes place abroad. Styron creates American characters from a modern arena—boisterous, irresponsible, drunk on life, but they are heirs to the same innocence Mark Twain and Henry James explored, ill-prepared for and ignorant of an established culture. This *tour de force* was not as well-received as was his first novel, probably because American readers were not ready for less than complimentary images of themselves.

Along with extensive praise and literary prizes, William Styron has often been at the center of controversy because of his writing. *The Confessions of Nat Turner* brought about one of the most heated and irrational criticisms of all. Styron calls it "a meditation on history." His story of Nat Turner's humanity in spite of history's depiction of him as the mad leader of a monstrous revolt and the probable cause of Virginia's Legislature failing to free slaves misses the mark with a segment of readers. Claiming a proprietorship of Nat's thought process because he and they are Black, they ignore the fact that literary writers speak to the basic human condition rather than as propagandistic speakers for any isolated group.

Equally irrational was a similar reaction on a smaller scale by some Jewish groups to his 1980 prize-winning novel *Sophie's Choice.* Sophie, who is not a Jew, is, nonetheless, a victim of Hitler's insane genocide. Styron recognizes that the Holocaust involved not only the six million Jews exterminated, tragic as it was, but also extermination of nearly seven million non-Jews, often forgotten or ignored. Sophie's is the voice that speaks for all humanity victimized by the horror; her choice is the most difficult any human must make. The forcing of that choice crippled her for the remainder of her life, and another choice cut short that life. Sophie is an "improvisation" on a real person Styron once knew for a brief time, but the story sprang from a dream or a waking vision merging into a conscious creation. Styron uses the universality of Nazi crimes against humanity as a frame in which he focuses on tragedy at the individual level. His theme projects disintegrating values at the individual level into reverberation at the human level, examining the presence of evil in the modern world. Such evils as genocide and robot-like humans as killing machines are evidence of the disintegration and degradation in twentieth century society in his novels. He also implies, however, that man's salvation is his responsibility and lies in self-redemption.

This Quiet Dust and Other Writings is a collection of essays written over three decades in which Styron shares his thoughts on writing, other writers, and the process of writing. Often Styron comments that his own work is a long, laborious and painful outpouring of creativity. He remarked in an interview with Phillip Caputo in 1985, "I am solaced by the belief that if my work has any quality at all, it has this quality because of its long germination time." His use of the word "solace" implies an innate sadness, presaging his own descent into the dark world of his illness described in *Darkness Visible: A Memoir of Madness.* For those afflicted with the disease of clinical depression, the book offers hope to the hopelessness they feel. For the literary scholar, the book offers a deeper insight into Styron's fictional works since 1951.

Many characters since Peyton Loftis of *Lie Down in Darkness* have been suicidal, a reflection of Styron's own melancholia and suicidal thoughts before hospitalization. In *A Tidewater Morning*, he fictionally reworks the day of his mother's death. At the core of his illness, he believes, is his inability to deal with the grief of that time. His characters search for methods of overcoming their depression, usually to no avail. The novels illustrate that healing and regeneration are impossible without a loving environment in which to find the courage and strength to take responsibility for one's self.

Styron is a Southern writer; he sees language, family and community, and clear-cut values as inextricably bound one to the other in characterization. His sense of place uses a Southern landscape for definition: *Lie Down in Darkness, Set This House on Fire,* and *A Tidewater Morning,* specifically. The three stories comprising *A Tidewater Morning* illustrate Styron's post-illness return to his native locale as he plumbs his early memory. The title story about a mother's death is therapeutic; he faces a long-buried grief. "Shadrach," the second story, is Styron dealing with slavery issues from a boy's viewpoint. The opening story, "Love Day," concerns a marine about to go into war who thinks of his father's part in building the ships. The stories are first-person narrations from the same person; they are important landmarks in the narrator's life and represent themes indicative of Styron's fiction.

In other stories, Styron alludes to Southern imagery, as for example in *Sophie's Choice,* "Poland is a beautiful, heart-wrenching, soul-split country which in many ways . . . resembles or conjures up images of the American South." The moral authority in his fictional voice and eloquence in its language stem from his roots in the religious values and expressions of his native Virginia. Remembering his grandmother's admonition, Styron says, "I've never forgotten that I am a Southerner. . . the remembrance of those hands is alone enough for me to forge a lasting bond with our unfathomable past, and to prevent me from being anything but a southerner, wherever I live" (*Sewanee Review*).

—Jeanne R. Nostrandt

T

TAYLOR, Henry

Born: Henry Splawn Taylor in Loudoun County, Virginia, 21 June 1942. **Education:** University of Virginia, 1960-65, B.A. in English 1965; Hollins College, Roanoke, Virginia, 1965-66, M.A. in English and creative writing 1966. **Family:** Married Sarah Spencer Bean, 1965 (divorced 1967); Frances Carney, 1968 (divorced 1995); two sons; Sarah Spencer, 1995. **Career:** Instructor, Roanoke College, 1966-68; assistant professor, University of Utah, Salt Lake City, 1968-71; associate professor, 1971-75, and since 1975 professor, American University, Washington, D.C; writer-in-residence, Hollins College, spring 1978; distinguished poet-in-residence, Wichita State University, Kansas, spring 1994. **Awards:** National Endowment for the Arts fellowship, 1978, 1986; Witter Bynner Poetry award, 1984; Pulitzer Prize, 1986, for *The Flying Change.* **Member:** Academy of American Poets.

PUBLICATIONS

Poetry

The Horse Show at Midnight: Poems. Baton Rouge, Louisiana State University Press, 1966.
Breakings. San Luis Obispo, California, The Solo Press, 1971.
An Afternoon of Pocket Billiards. Salt Lake City, University of Utah, 1975; with *The Horse Show at Midnight,* Baton Rouge, Louisiana State University Press, 1992.
The Flying Change. Baton Rouge, Louisiana State University Press, 1985.
Understanding Fiction: Poems, 1986-1996. Baton Rouge, Louisiana State University Press, 1996.

Other

Compulsory Figures: Essays on Recent American Poets. Baton Rouge, Louisiana State University Press, 1992.

Editor, with Frank N. Magill, *Magill's (Masterplots) Literary Annual 1972, 1973, 1974.* Englewood Cliffs, Salem Press, 1972, 1974, 1975.
Editor, *The Water of Light: A Miscellany in Honor of Brewster Ghiselin.* Salt Lake City, University of Utah Press, 1976.

Translator with Robert A. Brooks, *The Children of Herakles* by Euripides. New York, Oxford University Press, 1981.

*

Bibliography: *Henry Taylor: A Bibliographic Chronicle, 1961-87* by Stuart Wright, in *Bulletin of Bibliography* 45(2), June 1988.

Interviews: *The Writer's Voice: Conversations with Contemporary Writers* edited by George Garrett, New York, Morrow, 1973; "An Interview with Henry Taylor" by Dan Johnson, *Window,* Spring 1976.

Henry Taylor comments:

The landscape of rural northern Virginia, and the equestrian sports that thrive there, have both been central to my life and my writing. Though it has been years since I rode competitively, the images and sensations of those days, and the recollection that I have communicated deeply with other creatures without using any words, have given me my own sense of the place of language in human experience. Possibly under the additional influence of my Quaker faith and upbringing, I try to encourage the poem's tendency to drift from speech toward a more nearly silent existence. But my belief in what I am doing always meets a severe test in any statement of mine about what I have done or am doing.

However, there can be no doubt of the importance to my work of various writers and mentors, including but certainly not limited to Fred Bornhauser, R.H.W. Dillard, Fred Chappell, Kelly Cherry, George Garrett, May Sarton, David Slavitt, Carolyn Kizer, William Jay Smith, Robert Watson, Richard Bausch, Robert Bausch, Maxine Kumin, and others whose work, example, and friendship have helped me toward better work and better commitment to it.

*   *   *

Over the years the poetry of Henry Taylor has revealed itself to be very much of a piece. Although he first became known for witty parodies of other poets, which Robert Bly published in *The Sixties,* and has continued to write poems that arise from an essentially classical sense of satire and humor, his is a poetry that draws its real strength not so much from his formal skills, his intelligence, and his wit, all of which are considerable, but rather from an inescapable moral and metaphysical tension that informs it line by line. The characters and speakers of Taylor's poems are always pulling away from something and being drawn back to it, seeking something lost or never found while accepting a life without it, or being perpetually wounded by the inexorable movement of time but forcing themselves to examine and reexamine its wearing away of their lives.

The title poem of his Pulitzer prizewinning third book, *The Flying Change* (1985), brings this tension sharply into focus as it describes a riding maneuver in which a horse can change leads during a moment of suspension in the air, a maneuver made more difficult by the weight of the rider. "The aim of teaching a horse to move beneath you is to remind him how he moved when he was free," the poems says, but it goes on to extend that perception into a meditation about time and loss and freedom:

> A single leaf turns sideways in the wind
> in time to save a remnant of the day;
> I am lifted like a whipcrack to the moves
> I studied on that barbered stretch of ground,
> before I schooled myself to drift away
>
> from skills I still possess, but must outlive.
> Sometimes when I cup water in my hands
> and watch it slip away and disappear,

I see that age will make my hands a sieve;
but for a moment the shifting world suspends

its flight and leans toward the sun once more,
as if to interrupt its mindless plunge
through works and days that will not come again.
I hold myself immobile in bright air,
sustained in time astride the flying change.

Even in the poems of his precocious first collection, *The Horse Show at Midnight* (1966), which was published before his twenty-fourth birthday, Taylor wrote of characters (often much older than himself) who are striding the flying change, learning their limitations, understanding what they can do and charting the boundaries of what they cannot, living, as he puts it in "A Blind Man Locking His House," in "the weather of despair" without giving in to despair. In his book, *An Afternoon of Pocket Billiards* (1975), he continued his exploration of the tension between freedom and restraint in a more directly personal vein. Early in the collection, for example, he writes in "Goodbye to the Old Friends" of his turning away from the traditions and Quaker beliefs of his family, but later in the book, in "Return to the Old Friends," he finds himself back among the Friends, trying to recall "the force I was opposing / in my father's calm eyes as I fled rejoicing," even as he takes up again the burden of the past and the healing fact of his belief.

Time and again in his poems Taylor returns to the image of home as the place where one's wild freedom is painfully broken but also as the place toward which one blindly makes one's way through the dangerous dark. No wonder that so many of the central metaphors of his most personal work are drawn from the schooling of horses, the art of restraining wildness without losing its beauty and power. It also is not surprising that his is a poetry which, even though it is often violent and nakedly realistic, is usually written in traditional forms. Not since Edwin Arlington Robinson has an American poet consistently written narratives of such unrestrained emotional force in such disciplined and formal verse.

Taylor's later poems of lost and recovered love, which have appeared in journals, make it clear that he is continuing to explore and develop the central themes of his work. The title of his most recent collection, *Understanding Fiction: Poems, 1986-1996*, shows that he has lost none of his sense of humor and daring. The art of restraining wildness without losing its beauty and power—the subtlest "adjustment of voice or detail" makes all the difference, he writes in one poem—continues to be explored in form and content, as displayed in the title poem about telling a story. The stories here are of recognizable people—building contractors, insurance executives—their tragedies, the sense of purpose found as work becomes craft.

Together, Taylor's books should make clear what the Pulitzer revealed to many readers who were unfamiliar with his work—that Henry Taylor is a poet whose deeply felt, superbly crafted poems form a body of work which cannot be ignored in any serious assessment of contemporary American poetry.

—R. H. W. Dillard and Mel Koler

TAYLOR, Mildred

Born: Jackson, Mississippi, 13 September 1943. **Education:** University of Toledo, B.Ed. 1965; University of Colorado, M.A. 1969. **Career:** U.S. Peace Corps, teacher of English and history in Tuba City, Arizona, 1965, and in Yirgalem, Ethiopia, 1965-67, recruiter, 1967-68, instructor in Maine, 1968; study skills coordinator at University of Colorado, 1969-71, and member of the Black Student Alliance, working with students and university officials to structure a Black Studies Program at the University; temporary office worker in Los Angeles, Calif., 1971-73; writer, since 1973. **Awards:** First prize in African-American category, Council on Interracial Books for Children, 1973, for *Song of the Trees*; *New York Times'* Outstanding Book of the Year citation, 1975, for *Song of the Trees*; American Library Association Notable Book citation for *Roll of Thunder, Hear My Cry*, 1976; *Boston Globe-Horn Book* Honor Book citation and Newbery Medal, 1977, for *Roll of Thunder, Hear My Cry*; Buxtehuder Bulle Award, 1985, for *Roll of Thunder, Hear My Cry*; Coretta Scott King Award and *New York Times'* Outstanding Book of the Year citation, 1982, for *Let the Circle Be Unbroken*; Coretta Scott King Award, 1988, for *The Friendship*; Christopher Award, 1988, for *The Gold Cadillac*; ALAN (Assembly on Literature for Adolescents of NCTE-National Council of English) honors for contributions to Young Adult literature, 1997. **Address:** c/o Dial Books, 2 Park Avenue, New York, New York 10016.

PUBLICATIONS

Children's Books

Song of the Trees. New York, Dial, 1975.
Roll of Thunder, Hear My Cry. New York, Dial, 1976.
Let the Circle Be Unbroken. New York, Dial, 1981.
The Friendship. New York, Dial, 1987.
The Gold Cadillac. New York, Dial, 1987.
The Road to Memphis. New York, Dial, 1990.
Mississippi Bridge. New York, Dial, 1990.
The Well: David's Story. New York, Dial, 1995.

Other

"Newbery Award Acceptance Speech," in *Horn Book*, August 1977.

*

Critical Studies: "Mildred D. Taylor" by Phyllis J. Fogelman, *Horn Book*, August 1977; "The Color of Skin: Mildred Taylor" by David Rees, *The Marble in the Water: Essays on Contemporary Writers of Fiction for Children and Young Adults*, Boston, Horn Book, 1980; "Profile: Mildred D. Taylor" by Sharon L. Dussell, *Language Arts*, May 1981.

*   *   *

Throughout her childhood, Mildred Taylor had traveled every summer to visit relatives in Mississippi. As she describes in her Newbery Medal Acceptance Speech in 1976, for *Roll of Thunder,*

Hear My Cry, "it was a magical time" rich with night times of hearing the storytellers, her relatives, share tales of their days in racially-segegrated Mississippi. Taylor relates as well that at some point she realized the stories were not magic; she understood trips to the South were not fun, given that the baskets of food her mother prepared were actually brought along because many restaurants served "Whites only." She learned the harsh reality that they had to take water on the trips, that they would need to sleep in the car, and trips were longer since the South she visited restricted "Colored folks" from drinking fountains, restrooms, and motels. She learned to fear police sirens, having seen her father more than once subjected to searches and hearing of relatives jailed for driving a car "too good" for a colored person to be driving. Taylor records this story in *The Gold Cadillac* (1987).

Offsetting the tragedy of assaults on human dignity that so clearly marked the experience of her family and others in the pre-Civil Rights years of the 20th century, Taylor emphasizes the role or her father, who impressed on his chidren that they were "somebody,"and that they had self-respect. He offered them principles on which to build their lives; primarily, that anger was futile in the fight against bias. Taylor recounts that her father told her she needed a "much stronger weapon." That weapon is Taylor's power as a writer to put into novels and stories for children and young adults real stories of human pride and dignity in a clearly racist society. Taylor offers a real, true sense of Black history and of Black people, which she discovered repeatedly lacking in history books in her own education.

The second force dominating Taylor's life was a strong family experience. Her roots in family that bore oppression and humiliation and bonded despite many attempts at destruction inspired the Logan family, who appear in nearly all her novels. Again in her own words from the Newbery Award Acceptance Speech, Taylor explains, "I will continue the Logans' story with the same life guides that have always been mine, for it is my hope that these books, one of the first chronicles to mirror a black child's hopes and fears from childhood innocence to awareness to bitterness and disillusionment, will one day be instrumental in teaching children of all colors the tremendous influence that Cassie's generation—my father's generation—had in bringing about the great Civil Rights Movement of the fifties and sixties. Without understanding that generation and what it and the generations before it endured, children of today and of the future cannot understand or cherish the precious rights of equality which they now possess . . . . If they can identify with the Logans, who are representative not only of my family but of the many black families who faced adversity andsurvived, understand the principles by which they lived, then perhaps they can better understand and respect themselves and others."

Taylor's books are as vital as those about the Holocaust. Every child and every teacher needs to learn through Taylor's poignant, tragic retellings about the human potential for inhumanity, injustice and hatred. Though she hates violence and hates to write of it, Taylor knew the stories of lynchings, night riders, verbal abuse, false accusation, and cruelty were her weapon for addressing prejudice. Her books, particularly the trilogy, *Roll of Thunder, Hear My Cry, Let the Circle Be Unbroken,* and *The Road to Memphis,* portray as well the richness of family,the love of the land, and the dignity of those who can endure despite incredible oppression.

—Mary Warner

TAYLOR, Peter

Born: Peter Hillsman Taylor in Trenton, Tennessee, 8 January 1917. **Education:** Vanderbilt University, 1936-37; Southwestern University, 1937-38; Kenyon College, 1940. **Military Career:** U.S. Army, 1941-45. **Career:** Professor of English, University of North Carolina at Greensboro, 1946-47; professor of English, University of Virginia, 1967-94; visiting lecturer, Indiana University, 1949, University of Chicago, 1951, Kenyon College, 1952-57, Oxford University, 1955, Ohio State University, 1957-63, Harvard University 1964 and 1972-73, and University of Georgia, 1985. **Awards:** Guggenheim Fellowship in fiction, 1950; National Institute for Arts and Letters grant in literature, 1952; Fulbright fellowship, 1955; first prize, O. Henry Memorial Awards, 1959, for the short story "Venus, Cupid, Folly and Time"; Ohioana Book Award, 1960, for *Happy Families Are All Alike*; Ford Foundation fellowship, 1961; Rockefeller Foundation grant, 1964; National Academy and Institute of Arts and Letters, gold medal for literature, 1979; Ritz Paris Hemingway Ward and PEN/Faulkner Award, 1986, and Pulitzer Prize for fiction, 1987, all for *A Summons to Memphis*. **Died**: In 1996.

PUBLICATIONS

Novels

A Woman of Means. New York, Harcourt, 1950.
A Summons to Memphis. New York, Knopf, 1986.
In the Tennessee Country. New York, Knopf, 1994.

Short Story Collections

A Long Fourth and Other Stories. New York, Harcourt, 1948.
The Widows of Thornton. New York, Harcourt, 1954.
Happy Families Are All Alike. New York, McDowell, 1959.
Miss Leonora When Last Seen and Fifteen Other Stories. New York, Obolensky, 1963.
The Collected Stories of Peter Taylor. New York, Farrar, Straus, 1969.
In the Miro District and Other Stories. New York, Knopf, 1977.
The Old Forest and Other Stories. Garden City, NY, Dial, 1985.
The Oracle at Stoneleigh Court. New York, Knopf, 1993.

Plays

The Death of a Kinsman: A Play. Collected in *The Widows of Thornton.* New York, Harcourt, 1954.
Tennessee Day in St. Louis: A Comedy. New York, Random House, 1957.
A Stand in the Mountains, in *Kenyon Review,* March 1968; hardcover, New York, Beil, 1986.
Presences: Seven Dramatic Pieces. Houghton, 1973.

Uncollected Fiction

"The Party," in *River*, March 1937.

"The Lady Is Civilized," in *River*, April 1937.

"The School Girl," in *American Prefaces*, Spring 1942.

"Attendant Evils, in *Vanderbilt Miscellany, 1919-1944*, Nashville, Vanderbilt University Press, 1944.

"Uncles," in *New Yorker*, 17 December 1949.

"A Cheerful Disposition," in *Sewanee Review*, Spring 1967.

"The Megalopolitans," in *Ploughshares*, Vol. 2, no. 4, 1975.

"Peach Trees Gone Wild in the Lane," in *Ploughshares*, Vol. 2, no. 4, 1975.

"His Other Life," in *Ploughshares*, Vol. 2, no. 4, 1975; also in *Agenda*, Winter/Spring 1976.

"Knowing," in *Agenda*, Winter/Spring, 1976.

"Five Miles from Home," in *Ploughshares*, Vol. 5, no. 2, 1979.

Nonfiction

"Tribute at Yale." In *Alumni News* (UNC-Greensboro), Spring 1966; earlier versions: "That Cloistered Jazz," *Michigan Quarterly Review*, Fall 1966; "Randall Jarrell," in *Randall Jarrell, 1914-1916*, New York, Farrar, 1967.

Literature, Sewanee, and the World: Founders' Day Address 1972. Sewanee, University of the South, 1972.

"Robert Traill Spence Lowell: 1917-1977," in *Proceedings, American Academy and Institute of Arts and Letters*, no. 28, 1978.

"Acceptance by Peter Taylor," in *Proceedings, American Academy and Institute of Arts and Letters*, no. 29, 1979.

"A Commemorative Tribute to Jean Stafford," in *Shenandoah*, Spring 1979, and *Proceedings, American Academy and Institute of Arts and Letters*, no. 30, 1980.

"Eudora Welty." In *Eudora Welty: A Tribute*. Winston-Salem, North Carolina, Stuart Wright, 1984.

"Reminiscences." In *In The Fugitives, the Agrarians, and Other Twentieth Century Southern Writers*. Charlottesville, The Alderman Library, The University Press of Virginia, 1985.

"Tennessee Caravan, 1920-1940." In *Tennessee: A Homecoming*, Nashville, Third National Corp., 1985.

Audio Recordings: *Peter Taylor Reading and Commenting on His Fiction* Archive of Recorded Poetry and Literature, 1987; *"Three Heroines" and "The Instruction of a Mistress," Read by Peter Taylor*. Produced by New Letters on the Air. American Audio Prose Library, NL17.

*

Manuscript Collections: Jean and Alexander Heard Library Special Collections, Vanderbilt University; Alderman Library, University of Virginia.

Media Adaptations: "Interrupted Honeymoon," *U.S. Steel Hour Television*, adaptation of "Reservations," 6 September 1961; "The Old Forest," Pyramid Films, 1984.

Bibliographies: *Andrew Lytle, Walker Percy, Peter Taylor: A Reference Guide* by Victor A. Kramer, Boston, G.K. Hall, 1983; *Peter Taylor: A Descriptive Bibliography, 1934-87* by Stuart Wright, Charlottesville, University Press of Virginia, 1988.

Critical Studies: *Southern Accents: The Fiction of Peter Taylor* by Catherine Clark Graham, New York, Lang, 1993; *Peter Taylor* by Albert Griffith, Boston, Twayne, 1970, revised, 1990; *Conversations with Peter Taylor*, by Hubert H. McAlexander, Jackson, University Press of Mississippi, 1987; *Critical Essays on Peter Taylor* by Hubert H. McAlexander, Boston, G.K. Hall, 1993; *Peter Taylor: A Study of the Short Fiction*, James Curry Robison, Boston, Twayne, 1988; *The Craft of Peter Taylor* by C. Ralph Stevens, Tuscaloosa, University of Alabama, 1995.

*   *   *

In his 1948 introduction to *A Long Fourth and Other Stories*, Robert Penn Warren noted that Peter Taylor's stories "are officially about the contemporary, urban, middle class world of the upper South, and he is the only writer who has taken this as his province." By the time Taylor published his last work in 1994, the second part of Warren's statement no longer held true. Other writers, foremost among them Anne Tyler, had learned to follow Taylor's lead and to mine the rich ambiguities of life in the urban South. Taylor himself never turned from this material. In his three novels and more than sixty short stories, he wrote again and again about the middle-class worlds of Memphis and Nashville, often focusing on the pivotal transition years of the 1930s and 1940s. For some critics, especially in the 1960s, Taylor's fiction, both in subject and technique, seemed to grow old-fashioned. However, for most other critics, especially his fellow writers, Taylor was, as Anne Tyler dubbed him, "the undisputed master of the short story form," a writer's writer whose lucid prose and commitment to compression and suggestion were unparalleled in contemporary American fiction.

Perhaps because of his long association with many of the Nashville Agrarians—Taylor studied under Allen Tate at Southwestern, followed John Crowe Ransom to Kenyon, and remained lifelong friends with Andrew Lytle—Taylor is often misread as having, if not agrarian sympathies, then at the least a sentimental longing for the values of a pre-urban southern past. Nothing could be further from the truth. Certainly, the urban South Taylor writes of is a grim place. As Warren noted in his *Long Fourth* introduction, Taylor's South "is a world vastly uncertain of itself and the ground of its values, caught in a tangle of modern commercialism and traditions and conventions gone to seed." But we search in vain if we believe we can find in Taylor's fiction a place, either in the country or in the past, where such uncertainties and entanglements do not or did not exist.

In the preface to his 1968 play *A Stand in the Mountains*, Taylor describes the principal characters of that play in terms that would apply to almost all of the men and women of whom he has written: "They are for the most part those whose forebears left the land a generation or so ago, and with their good names and their connections and their natural endowments went to the new Southern cities and towns to make a place for themselves."

The key phrase here is "to make a place for themselves." Most of Taylor's Southerners have their roots in families and towns where one's place was, for better or worse, predetermined. But now, having moved to the urban centers, these Southerners are forced to find their way in a world where the rules of the old order clash with those of the new. Many of Taylor's characters fail to that way. Like Harriet Wilson in "A Long Fourth" (1946), Helen Ruth Lovell in "A Wife of Nashville" (1949), or the self-destructive families in "The Captain's Son" (1976), too many of Taylor's characters cannot make the necessary adjustments, and they remain locked into the old ways and old gestures, all of which prove impotent in the face of change. The frustration these characters feel is best articulated by Edmund Harper at the end of "Guests" (1959): "Our trouble was . . . we were lost without our old realities. We couldn't discover what it is people keep alive for without them."

Most of Taylor's characters do make changes and learn to play by, and take advantage of, the new realities. Unfortunately, such changes can exact a high cost and, more often than not, rely heavily upon self-deception. In *A Woman of Means* (1950), the narrator's father, Gerald Dudley, has adapted well to city life. Having little nostalgia for the old ways—he tells his son, "You learn a lot of things in the country . . . but a mighty lot of good it did me when I went into hardware"—Dudley becomes a successful businessman. Although adjusting well to the new demands of business—where one's place is tied to one's prosperity—Dudley fares less well in his family life. Accused of marrying his second wife in order to gain her wealth, and suspecting in turn that she married him in order to get the son she never had, Dudley can never say for certain what his, or his wife's, motives are. He may have learned a lot of new realities in the hardware business, but, to paraphrase the novel, a mighty lot of good it does him when he tries to understand himself. While Dudley admits his own confusion and limited success at finding a place in the new order, many of Taylor's other characters seem more comfortably adjusted. Very often, however, this adjustment is founded upon self-deception.

In "The Dean of Men" (1969), for instance, the narrator applauds himself for the choices he has made and the quieter life he has settled for by proclaiming that, whatever his shortcomings, he is at least not, like his own father, "tyrannizing over old women and small children." What he doesn't realize, and what Taylor's story makes all too clear, is that his lack of tyranny has less to do with his rejecting the old ways of his father than it does with his succumbing to new ways that tell him he needn't care about his family or make any significant sacrifices for them. A similar kind of comfortable self-deception is at the heart of Taylor's most celebrated work, his 1986 Pulitzer Prize-winning novel *A Summons to Memphis*, which ends with Phillip Carver boasting of his "serenity." What Phillip doesn't seem to recognize is that his serenity is nothing more than the "peace and quiet" that comes to a man when he decides that his family and his past "mean nothing" to him in the present moment.

Is this to say that Taylor's fiction is without its admirable characters? Not exactly. Miss Leonora of "Miss Leonora When Last Seen" and Cousin Aubrey of *In the Tennessee Country* are among those characters who acknowledge the new order of things and seem to make their adjustments while retaining their independence and achieving self-understanding. However, because of Taylor's tantalizing irony and his masterful use of unreliable narration, it is indeed difficult to say to what extent any of his characters truly come to terms with the new realities of the urban, middle-class South. That Peter Taylor was one of our greatest short story writers is, to remember Anne Tyler's phrasing, undisputable. But there will always remain about his work an aspect of "disputabil-ity," a haunting sense that we, like the characters we are reading about, have entered a world where the old certainties no longer exist and the new certainties come with too great a price, if they indeed come at all.

—Christopher Metress

THOMPSON, Hunter S.

Born: Hunter Stockton Thompson in Louisville, Kentucky, 18 July 1939 . **Education:** Attended public schools in Louisville; studied journalism at Columbia University. **Military Service:** U.S. Air Force, 1956-58. **Family:** Married Sandra Dawn in 1963 (divorced); children: one son. **Career:** Sports writer in Florida; Caribbean correspondent, *Time,* 1959; *New York Herald Tribune,* 1959-60; South American correspondent, *National Observer,* 1961-63; West Coast correspondent, *Nation,* 1964-66; columnist, *Ramparts,* 1967-68, *Scanlan's Monthly,* 1969-70; national affairs editor, *Rolling Stone,* 1970-84; global affairs correspondent, *High Times,* 1977-82; media critic, *San Francisco Examiner,* 1985-90; editor at large, *Smart,* beginning 1988; political analyst for various European magazines (including *London Observer, Tempo, Time Out, Das Magazine, Nieuwe Revu,* and *Die Woche*), beginning 1988; candidate for sheriff, Pitkin County, Colorado, 1968; member, Sheriff's Advisory Committee, Pitkin County, 1976-81; executive director, Woody Creek Rod and Gun Club. **Member:** Overseas Press Club, National Press Club, American Civil Liberties Union, Fourth Amendment Foundation (founder), National Rifle Association, U.S. Naval Institute, Air Force Association, National Organization for the Reform of Marijuana Laws (NORML; member of national advisory board, beginning 1976), Hong Kong Foreign Correspondents Club. **Agent:** Janklow & Nesbit, 598 Madison Ave., New York, New York 10022.

PUBLICATIONS

Nonfiction

Hell's Angels: A Strange and Terrible Saga. New York, Random House, 1966.
Fear and Loathing in Las Vegas: A Savage Journey to the Heart of the American Dream, illustrated by Ralph Steadman. New York, Random House, 1972.
Fear and Loathing on the Campaign Trail '72, illustrated by Ralph Steadman. Straight Arrow Books, 1973.
The Great Shark Hunt: Strange Tales from a Strange Time; Gonzo Papers, Volume One. New York, Summit Books, 1979.
The Curse of Lono, illustrated by Ralph Steadman. New York, Bantam, 1983.
Generation of Swine: Tales of Shame and Degradation in the '80s; Gonzo Papers, Volume Two. New York, Summit Books, 1988.
Songs of the Doomed: More Notes on the Death of the American Dream; Gonzo Papers, Volume Three. New York, Summit Books, 1990.
Silk Road: Thirty-Three Years in the Passing Lane. New York, Simon & Schuster, 1990.
Better than Sex: Fear and Loathing on the Campaign Trail, 1992. New York, Random House, 1993.

Better Than Sex: Confessions of a Political Junkie. New York, Random House, 1994.
The Proud Highway: Saga of a Desperate Southern Gentleman, 1955-1967. New York, Villard, 1997.

Novels

Untitled Novel. David McKay, 1992.
The Rum Diary: The Long Lost Novel. New York, Simon & Schuster, 1998.

*

Sound Recordings: *Songs of the Doomed,* New York, Simon & Schuster Audio, 1990; *Sound Bites from the Counter Culture,* New York, Atlantic, 1990.

Film Adaptations: *Where the Buffalo Roam,* 1980 (from several works, including *Fear and Loathing in Las Vegas* and *Fear and Loathing on the Campaign Trail '72; Fear and Loathing in Las Vegas,* produced and directed by Terry Gilliam, 1998.

Critical Studies: *Wampeters Foma & Granfalloons* by Kurt Vonnegut, Jr., New York, Delacorte, 1974; *Gates of Eden: American Culture in the Sixties* by Morris Dickstein, New York, Basic Books, 1977; *The Life of Fiction* by Jerome Klinkowitz, Urbana, University of Illinois Press, 1977; *Fables of Fact: The New Journalism as New Fiction* by John Hellman, Urbana, University of Illinois Press, 1981; *Hunter S. Thompson* by William McKeen, Boston, Twayne Publishers, 1991; *Fear and Loathing: The Strange and Terrible Saga of Hunter S. Thompson* by Paul Perry, New York, Thunder's Mouth Press, 1992; *When the Going Gets Weird: The Twisted Life and Times of Hunter S. Thompson: A Very Unauthorized Biography* by Peter O. Whitmer, New York, Hyperion, 1993; *Hunter: The Strange and Savage life of Hunter S. Thompson* by E. Jean Carroll, New York, Dutton, 1993.

*   *   *

As a participatory journalist (one who covers a news story by becoming part of it), Hunter S. Thompson has gained a following as much for his hilarious antics as for his sharp observations of U.S. culture and politics. After years of struggling as a conventional journalist, Thompson's breakthrough came in an assignment on the Hell's Angels, a California motorcycle gang depicted as savage rapists and thugs by the mainstream press. Thompson gained the trust of several gang members, then rode with the Hell's Angels for a year to research an article for *Nation* magazine that became the basis for his book, *Hell's Angels: A Strange and Terrible Saga* (1966). As a piece of journalism, the portrait is more conventional than Thompson's later works. Elmer Bendiner wrote of the book in the *Nation:* "Thompson's point of view remains eminently sane and honest. He does not weep for the Angels or romanticize them or glorify them. Neither does he despise them." In riding with this notorious gang, Thompson's reputation as a daredevil was sealed.

Thompson unveiled his brand of participatory journalism, which he labeled "gonzo journalism," in "The Kentucky Derby Is Decadent and Depraved" (1970), an article for *Scanlan's Monthly.* In covering this remnant of Southern gentility, replete with the sa-

voring of mint juelps and the singing of "My Old Kentucky Home," Thompson had collected a number of vivid impressions, but when deadline came, Thompson froze. "I'd blown my mind, couldn't work," he recalled in a *Playboy* interview. "So finally I just started jerking pages out of my notebook and numbering them and sending them to the printer. I was sure it was the last article I was ever going to do for anybody." Instead, many praised the article as a breakthrough in journalism. Thompson continued: "And I thought . . . if I can write like this and get away with it, why should I keep trying to write like the *New York Times?*"

Thompson later produced his gonzo classic, *Fear and Loathing in Las Vegas: A Savage Journey to the Heart of the American Dream* (1972). Sent to Las Vegas to cover a desert motorcycle race and a district attorney's conference on drugs, Thompson managed to do neither. Instead, as he recounts in first person adventures, Raoul Duke (Thompson's guise) and his "300-pound Samoan attorney," Dr. Gonzo (actually, a Chicano lawyer named Oscar Zeta Acosta), spend the time ingesting heavy quantities of alcohol and drugs, sit in at law-and-order conventions, and otherwise run amok in the desert glitter city. The surreal visions induced by drugs and alcohol encompass the odd people, events, and pop culture setting, leading Duke and Dr. Gonzo to find truths about 1970s America following the counterculture rebellion of the 1960s. *National Observer* contributor Michael Putney called the book "a trip, literally and figuratively, all the way to bad craziness and back again. It is . . . an acid, wrenchingly funny portrait of straight America's most celebrated and mean-spirited pleasuredome, Las Vegas."

In proposed jacket copy for *Fear and Loathing in Las Vegas,* later published in *The Great Shark Hunt: Strange Tales from a Strange Time; Gonzo Papers, Volume One* (1979), Thompson described "gonzo journalism": "My idea was to buy a fat notebook and record the whole thing as it happened, then send in the notebook for publication—without editing. That way, I felt the eye and the mind of the journalist would be functioning as a camera . . . True Gonzo reporting needs the talents of a master journalist, the eye of an artist/photographer, and the heavy balls of an actor. Because the writer must be a participant in the scene, while he's writing it—or at least taping it, or even sketching it. Or all three."

Thompson took the gonzo approach to covering the 1972 Presidential election campaign in *Fear and Loathing on the Campaign Trail '72* (1973). As a press outsider for *Rolling Stone* magazine, Thompson had the freedom to produce a straight coverage of a political campaign, though *Campaign Trail* contains his usual fine-tunings of the truth. Still, Thompson "recorded the nuts and bolts of a presidential campaign with all the contempt and incredulity that other reporters must feel but censor out," noted Morris Dickstein in *Gates of Eden: American Culture in the Sixties.* After *Fear and Loathing on the Campaign Trail,* Thompson's output dropped off. With the *Curse of Lono* (1983), he returned to gonzo journalism after a decade hiatus. Here, Thompson's coverage of the Honolulu Marathon takes back seat to the narrator's delusion that he has become a Hawaiian god. Critics found the book hilarious, though not as well written as his 1970s work. Reviews have been more mixed for his hodgepodge compendiums of previously published material, among them *The Great Shark Hunt.*

With his fondness for firearms and his legendary capacity for alcohol and drug use, Thompson may be better remembered for his renegade behavior than for his talent as a writer. Nevertheless, "for all of the charges against him, Hunter S. Thompson is an amazingly insightful writer," wrote Jerome Klinkowitz in *The Life of Fiction.* "His 'journalism' is not in the least irresponsible. On the contrary, in each of his books he's pointed out the lies and gross distortions of conventional journalism . . . Moreover, his books are richly intelligent."

—Eric Patterson

TILGHMAN, Christopher

Born: Boston, Massachusetts, 5 September 1946. **Education:** Yale University, B.A. in French 1968. **Family:** Married Caroline Preston (author of the novel *Jackie by Josie,* 1997); three children. **Military Service:** U. S. Navy, 1968-71. **Career:** Freelance editor and writer, 1971-89; lecturer in creative writing, Emerson College, 1990-92; member of faculty, Aspen Writers' Conference, 1992, University of Virginia, 1993, Napa Valley Writers' Conference, 1994, 1995, and 1997, Yale Summer School, 1995, St. Mary's College, 1996, Fine Arts Writing Center, 1997; Rea Visiting Fellow in Fiction, University of Virginia, 1996; writer in residence, Emerson College, since 1996; coeditor, *Ploughshares* (Vol. 18, no. 4, 1993), book reviewer; juror, National Endowment of the Arts literary fellowships, 1994; reviewer, Fine Art Work Center Writing Committee, since 1995. **Awards:** Massachusetts Artists Foundation Fellowship in fiction, 1987; Emily Clark Balch Award, *Virginia Quarterly Review,* 1989; Denise and Mel Cohen Award, *Ploughshares,* 1989; Whiting Writers Award, 1990; Guggenheim Fellowship, 1992; Ingram Merrill Foundation Award for Fiction, 1993.

PUBLICATIONS

Short Story Collections

In a Father's Place. New York, Farrar, Straus & Giroux, 1990.
The Way People Run. New York, Random House, 1999.

Novel

Mason's Retreat. New York, Random House, 1996.

*   *   *

Characterized by a focus on family and place, Tilghman's narratives usually begin with a strong visual image evoking locales he knows intimately, especially New England, Montana and Maryland's Eastern Shore. Perhaps because he is the scion of an Eastern Shore family dating back to the seventeenth century, Tilghman's stories are usually set in rural areas, but during the mid-twentieth century; some critics have seen his well-plotted stories as old fashioned as the rural landscapes and lives they chronicle.

Often his characters grapple with the residue of their family's past, which looms over them; frequently, they only come to understand particular events years later. The Chester River setting of "On the Rivershore," the first of seven stories in his prize-winning debut volume, *In A Father's Place* (1990), captures the social tensions of the Chesapeake Bay region as the old way of life slowly erodes like the land undermined by the water. Cecil, a tenant farmer's son, inadvertently witnesses his father murdering a trouble making waterman. Desperate, Cecil runs to Mr. McHugh of the Big House, who aids the tenant farmers by sinking the body in the river, but not before a confrontation with the local watermen. Common sense and a desire for "what's best for the water" break their code of "No one kills a waterman," and the opposing forces of land and water conspire in the river burial. Thirty years later, Cecil returns for his father's funeral to a region and people much altered by events such as the Vietnam War.

In "Loose Reins," Hal returns to his family's Montana ranch ostensibly to check out his mother's marriage to Roy, a now sober, longtime family ranchhand. In reminiscences, Hal recalls for the reader his family's history—of his Yale educated father's prosperous ranch, his debutante mother's transformation, and his rivalry with his brother. In the story's climactic scene, after Roy reveals his hatred for the father who looked "right through" his family, Hal must reevaluate his memories of Roy's earlier attention and affection.

Although there are hints of family history elsewhere, the closest Tilghman comes to autobiography is in "Norfolk, 1969"; he served in the Navy upon graduation from Yale University. Charlie Martin looks back at his forlorn arrival in Norfolk with Julie, his bride. Their marriage seems doomed as they burst into tears at the prospects of his three-year tour of duty. At first ambivalent about the Navy, Charlie experiences an epiphany at sea and comes to esteem his ship. On land, Julie assumes leadership in the counterculture anti-Vietnam movement, which Charlie cannot fully enter. They divorce and, years later, only the mystery of the sea is left for Charlie.

Often anthologized, the volume's title story returns to Maryland's Eastern Shore and the Big House. Here, as elsewhere, Tilghman characteristically describes details of landscape and household. Events swirl around Dan, a widowed lawyer, residing in his large waterfront mansion filled with antiques. His daughter Rachel has come home to announce her move to Seattle; his son Nick, a writer, arrives with girlfriend, Patty Keith, who positions herself in Dan's chair reading Deconstructionist theory. Dan soon comes to view Patty as a soul-sucking witch and a struggle ensues between them over Nick, the antiques, the house, the family, and a tradition-laden way of life. "I think you're all in a fantasy," Patty flings at Dan, who, as if gathering strength from the hurricane winds blowing off the water, demands she leave the house. Later, waiting for Rachel and Nick to return from the sail they couldn't resist despite the stormy water, a joyful Dan, swept clean by the wind, sits at the water's edge and, with astonishment, reflects upon himself at the center of a full life.

Many of Tilghman's stories have appeared in magazines and reviews. "Things Left Undone" (*Southern Review*) stems from a difficult episode in Tilghman's personal life when his oldest son was nearly diagnosed with cystic fibrosis. The story, its title from

The Book of Common Prayer's Public Confession, festered for years. It, too, opens on the banks of a Chesapeake Bay farm. At dawn, Denny McCready, a dairy farmer, turns his back on the "first yellow light dappling the water" with a foreboding sense that his love for his newborn son is inadequate. Hours later, doctors tell he and his wife that Charlie, named for Denny's taciturn father, will soon die of cystic fibrosis. After Susan's grief stricken breakdown and subsequent move into town, Denny hibernates in his old machine workshop. Eventually, the Bay rescues him. Much to his father's consternation ("What in hell is this?"), Denny rehabs a boat and, gradually, his relationship with his father. Meanwhile, Susan, seeking a sign of absolution and end to her mourning, waits on the shore for Denny. The manner of his hand's clasp will predict their marriage's future.

The opening paragraph of the title piece of Tilghman's second volume of stories, *The Way People Run*, reveals Tilghman's dense writing technique as we learn that a tired Barry, father of two daughters, after driving for days is approaching a Western town he knows something about. The town is where his Grandfather, affectionately remembered by townspeople as "an old parry dog" but detested by Barry's mother for his desertion, found contentment, leaving behind a junkyard of cars as a monument. Barry came west on job interviews after his Wall Street firm closed; he, too, seeks contentment and permanence, which he tries to find at the town's Virginian Cafe and with May, its waitress. Barry uses his earlier rescue of a child during an accident as an excuse to stay in town rather than push on. After his liaison with May, he admits to himself that he has left his wife and daughters behind; again on the road he wonders if this experience is the way things happen, "the way people run."

In his first novel, *Mason's Retreat* (1996), Tilghman gathers many of his earlier themes—family dynamics, tradition and its consequences, social and racial hierarchies, fathers and sons, revitalized women, sibling rivalry, infidelity, water and locale. In 1936, the expatriate Edward Mason, owner of a collapsed machine tools business in England, returns accompanied by his wife Edith and sons, fourteen-year old Sebastien and six-year old Simon, to claim his heritage, the Retreat, a dilapidated mansion on Maryland's isolated Eastern Shore. As if to pass the family history on to the next generation, Simon's grandson, Harry, introduces the Mason's Faulkneresque tragedy, but the point of view soon passes to the watchful Sebastien who intuitively understands Edward's inadequacies as a farmer and a father. Unable to focus reality and his self image, Edward fails to connect with McCready, the tenant farmer (perhaps related to Denny in "Things Left Undone"), Robert the black farmhand, or Edith and his children. Sebastien thrives in the fields, learning the ways of farming at Robert's side, while Edith, aided by the local black women, reclaims the Retreat and herself. When Edward's business revives with the coming of the war, Edith refuses to return to England with him. Her subsequent infidelity prompts Edward's intervention and sets in motion Sebastien's grievous plan to thwart the family's removal to England. Simon's son, Harry, ends the novel by recognizing that we must retell family stories as testament to earlier truths, honor to earlier pain and forgiveness for earlier mistakes, but that each generation, each person, begins anew. Like Dan in "In A Father's Place," Harry understands "One life, one's own, is plenty." No doubt these recurring themes of family and tradition nurtured by

conviction will reappear in Tilghman's forthcoming novel, *A Few Necessities*.

—Judith Kohl

TILLINGHAST, Richard

Born: Richard Williford Tillinghast in Memphis, Tennessee, 25 November 1940. **Education**: University of the South, Sewanee, Tennessee, A.B. 1962; Harvard University; Cambridge, Massachusetts (Woodrow Wilson fellow), A.M. 1963, Ph.D. 1970. **Family**: Married 1) Nancy Walton Pringle in 1965 (divorced 1970); 2) Mary Graves in 1973; three sons and one daughter. **Career**: Assistant editor, *Sewanee Review*, University of the South, Sewanee, Tennessee; professor of English, University of California, Berkeley, 1968-73; instructor, San Quentin Prison College Program, 1975-78; visiting assistant professor, University of the South, 1979-80; Briggs-Copeland Lecturer, Harvard University, 1980-83; since 1983 professor of English, University of Michigan, Ann Arbor; faculty associate, Michigan Institute for the Humanities, 1988-89 and 1993-94. **Awards**: Sinclair-Kennedy travel grant, 1966-67; Creative Arts Institute grant, 1970; National Endowment for the Humanities grant, 1980; Breadloaf Conference fellowship, 1982; Michigan Arts Council grant, 1985; Millay Colony residency, 1985; Yaddo Writers' Retreat residency, 1986; Michigan Council for the Arts grant, 1986; American Research Institute fellowship, 1990; Amy Lowell travel grant, 1990-91; travel grants to Northern Ireland from the British Council, 1992-94; Ann Stanford prize for poetry, 1992.

PUBLICATIONS

Poetry

The Keeper. Cambridge, Massachusetts, Pym Randall Press, 1968.
Sleep Watch. Middletown, Connecticut, Wesleyan University Press, 1969.
The Knife and Other Poems. Middletown, Connecticut, Wesleyan University Press, 1980.
Sewanee in Ruins. Sewanee, Tennessee, University Press, 1981.
Fossils, Metal, and the Blue Limit. Bennington, Vermont, White Creek Press, 1982.
Our Flag Was Still There. Middletown, Connecticut, Wesleyan University Press, 1984.
The Stonecutter's Hand. Boston, David R. Godine, 1995.

Other

Robert Lowell: Damaged Grandeur. Ann Arbor, University of Michigan Press, 1995.

*

Critical Studies: "Five Sleepers" by Robert Watson, in *Poetry* (Chicago), March 1970; "The Future of Confession" by Alan Williams, in *Shenandoah* (Lexington, Virginia), Summer 1970; Bruce Bennett, in *New York Times Book Review*, 10 May 1981; Alan Williamson, in *Parnassus* (New York), Winter 1981; "Reflections on *The Knife*" by Andrea Blaugrund, in *Harvard Advocate* (Cambridge, Massachusetts), December 1981; Paul Breslin, in *New York Times Book Review,* 22 July 1982; Wyatt Prunty, in *Southern Review* (Baton Rouge, Louisiana), Fall 1984.

Richard Tillinghast comments:

I see poetry as a kind of invocation of the spiritual realities inherent in things—the hidden and mysterious significance of colors, sounds, smells, textures. It is something like the speech of animals and plants, if they could speak. As an early, oral, nonrational art, unashamedly archaic in its origins, poetry still carries some of the magic of the early days of the human race. At its best it is consistent with the grace, naturalness, solidity, charm, thrill, and sense of necessity that are found in the earliest human accomplishments: hunting, fire-building, cooking, cultivation of the soil, fishing, and weaving. To mention poetry in the same breath with these things must also remind one of the practice, skill, and expertise that are necessary for the accomplishment of good writing.

*   *   *

Memphis-born Richard Tillinghast writes poetry concerned with history and place and how the two are often intertwined. Employing such images as contemporary humans engaged in basic activities—building fires, fishing, weaving, and agriculture—Tillinghast's poetry connects his personae with the evolutionary, geological, and historical natures of the poems's landscapes. The result is a body of work that connects modern readers with the essence of the human origins, as well as defining poetry as an act of primal human instinct with mystical qualities.

Similarly, Tillinghast's poetry on contemporary life is marked by references to an almost prehistoric awakening of consciousness. In "Waking on a Train," for example, from Tillinghast's first volume of verse, *Sleep Watch* (1969), the poet refers to the physiological instincts of the human body that connect it with prehistoric origins: "Your body begins to know it hasn't slept/It thinks of all the parts of itself/that would touch a bed." The deliberate nature of Tillinghast's poetry, which includes irregular spacing and frequent lists of descriptive phrases, are among elements that evoke mystical qualities.

Tillinghast studied at the Memphis Academy of Art, the University of the South at Sewanee, and Harvard University. At Harvard he was a writing student of Robert Lowell, who became the subject of Tillinghast's critical study, *Robert Lowell: Damaged Grandeur* (1995). *Sleep Watch* features his deft interpretation of human states of sleeping, dreaming and near-waking. In these poems Tillinghast borrowed images freely from surrealist paintings and film. Critical response was mostly favorable, including the claim by James Dickey that Tillinghast was "the best poet of the younger generation: that is mine and the one beyond it." Following the publication of *Sleep Watch*, Tillinghast published *The Knife and Other Poems* (1980).

In the volume's title poem, Tillinghast conjures the memory of his brother while driving in California and recounts losing a knife once belonging to a grandfather in a river. The poem addresses Tillinghast's concerns with historic and intuitive knowledge: "My one brother,/who saw more in the river than water/who understood what the fathers knew . . . /seeing with opened eyes." Later

in the poem, the brother dives to recover the knife while "the long-jawed predatory fish/the alligator gar/watched out of prehistory/schooled in the current, watching unwondering." Tillinghast concludes the poem by observing the knife:

> I see in its steel
> the worn gold on my father's hand
> the light in those trees
> the look on my son's face   a moment old
> like the river   old like rain
> older than anything that dies can be.

Tillinghast's next major work, *Our Flag Was Still There* (1984), includes the sequence "Sewanee in Ruins" and other poems that address his historical concerns. In "Sewanee in Ruins," he examines the past and future of the University of the South by utilizing epistolary sources, diaries and personal experience. The campus's destruction during the United States Civil War is presented alongside Tillinghast's vision of the present campus destroyed by nuclear attack. The verse included in *The Stonecutter's Hand* (1994) is also historical, but in a more personal manner. Tillinghast explores historical concepts in architecture, landscapes and human memory.

—Bruce Walker

TYLER, Anne

Born: Minneapolis, Minnesota, 25 October 1941. **Education:** Duke University, Durham, North Carolina, 1958-61, B.A. 1961; Columbia University, New York, 1961-62. **Family:** Married Taghi Modarressi (a psychiatrist and writer), 3 May 1963; two children. **Career:** Russian bibliographer, Duke University Library, 1962-63; assistant to the librarian, McGill University Law Library, Montreal, 1964-65; full-time writer, reviewer, and editor since 1965. **Awards:** American Academy of Arts and Letters award, 1977, for *Searching for Caleb*; Janet Kafka prize, 1981, for *Morgan's Passing*; PEN Faulkner award, 1983, for *Dinner at the Homesick Restaurant*; National Book Critics Circle Award, 1986, for *The Accidental Tourist*; Pulitzer Prize, 1989, for *Breathing Lessons*. **Agent:** Russell and Volkening Inc., 50 West 29th Street, New York, New York 10001.

PUBLICATIONS

Novels

If Morning Ever Comes. New York, Knopf, 1964.
The Tin Can Tree. New York, Knopf, 1965.
A Slipping-Down Life. New York, Knopf, 1970.
The Clock Winder. New York, Knopf, 1972.
Celestial Navigation. New York, Knopf, 1974.
Searching for Caleb. New York, Knopf, 1976.
Earthly Possessions. New York, Knopf, 1977.
Morgan's Passing. New York, Knopf, 1980.
Dinner at the Homesick Restaurant. New York, Knopf, 1982.
The Accidental Tourist. New York, Knopf, 1985.
Breathing Lessons. New York, Knopf, 1988.

Saint Maybe. New York, Knopf, 1991.
Ladder of Years. New York, Knopf, 1995.
A Patchwork Planet. New York, Knopf, 1998.

Children's Books

Tumble Tower. New York, Orchard Press, 1993.

Uncollected Short Stories

"Laura," in *Archive*, March 1959.
"The Lights on the River," in *Archive*, October 1959.
"The Bridge," in *Archive*, March 1960.
"I Never Saw Morning," in *Archive*, April 1961.
"The Saints in Caesar's Household," in *Archive*, April 1961.
"The Baltimore Birth Certificate," in *Critic: A Catholic Review of Books and the Arts*, February 1963.
"I Play Kings," in *Seventeen*, August 1963.
"Street of Bugles," in *Saturday Evening Post*, 30 November 1963.
"Nobody Answers the Door," in *Antioch Review*, Fall 1964.
"Dry Water," in *Southern Review*, Spring 1965.
"I'm Not Going to Ask You Again," in *Harper's*, September 1965.
"Everything But Roses," in *Reporter*, 23 September 1965.
"As the Earth Gets Old," in *New Yorker,* 29 October 1966.
"Two People and a Clock on the Wall," in *New Yorker*, 19 November 1966.
"The Genuine Fur Eyelashes," in *Mademoiselle*, January 1967.
"The Tea Machine," in *Southern Review*, Winter 1967.
"The Feather Behind the Rock," in *New Yorker,* 12 August 1967.
"A Flaw in the Crust of the Earth," in *Reporter*, 2 November 1967.
"Who Would Want a Little Boy?" in *Ladies Home Journal*, May 1968.
"The Common Courtesies," in *McCall's*, June 1968.
"With All Flags Flying," in *Redbook*, June 1971.
"Outside," in *Southern Review*, Autumn 1971.
"The Bride in the Boatyard," in *McCall's*, June 1972.
"Respect," in *Mademoiselle*, June 1972.
"A Misstep of the Mind," in *Seventeen*, October 1972.
"Spending," in *Shenandoah*, Winter 1973.
"The Base-Metal Egg," in *Southern Review*, Summer 1973.
"Neutral Ground," in *Family Circle*, November 1974.
"Half-Truths and Semi-Miracles," in *Cosmopolitan*, December 1974.
"A Knack for Languages," in *New Yorker,* 13 January 1975.
"The Artificial Family," in *Southern Review*, Summer 1975.
"The Geologist's Maid," in *New Yorker*, 28 July 1975.
"Some Sign That I Ever Made You Happy," in *McCall's*, October 1975.
"Your Place Is Empty," in *New Yorker,* 22 November 1976.
"Holding Things Together," in *New Yorker,* 24 January 1977.
"Average Waves in Unprotected Waters," in *New Yorker,* 28 February 1977.
"Under the Bosom Tree," in *Archive*, Spring 1977.
"Foot-Footing On," in *Mademoiselle*, November 1977.
"Uncle Ahmad," in *Quest*, November/December 1977.
"Linguistics," in *Washington Post Magazine*, 12 November 1978.
"The Geologist's Maid" In *Stories of the Modern South,* edited by Ben Forkner and Patrick Samway. New York, Penguin, 1981.
"Laps," in *Parents*, August 1981.
"The Country Cook," in *Harper's*, March 1982.

"Teenage Wasteland," in *Seventeen*, November 1983; in *Editors' Choice 1,* edited by George E. Murphy, Jr. New York, Bantam, 1985.
"Rerun," in *New Yorker,* 4 July 1988.
"A Street of Bugles," in *Saturday Evening Post*, July-August 1989.
"A Woman Like a Fieldstone House" In *Louder than Words,* edited by William Shore. New York, Vintage, 1989.
"People Who Don't Know the Answers," in *New Yorker*, 26 August 1991.

Nonfiction

"Youth Talks about Youth: 'Will This Seem Ridiculous?,'" in *Vogue*, February 1965.
"Olives Out of a Bottle," in *Archive*, Spring 1975; in *Critical Essays on Anne Tyler*, 1992.
"Because I Want More than One Life," in *Washington Post*, 15 August 1976.
"Trouble in the Boys' Club: The Trials of Marvin Mandel," in *New Republic*, 30 July 1977.
"Chocolates in the Afternoon and Other Temptations of a Novelist," in *Washington Post Book World*, 4 December 1977.
"Writers' Writers," in *New York Times Book Review*, 4 December 1977.
"My Summer," in *New York Times Book Review*, 4 June 1978.
"The Books of Christmas One," in *Washington Post Book World*, 3 December 1978.
"Please Don't Call It Persia," in *New York Times Book Review*, 18 February 1979.
"Still Just Writing," in *The Writer on Her Work: Contemporary Women Writers Reflect on Their Art and Situation*, 1980.
"A Visit with Eudora Welty," in *New York Times Book Review*, 2 November 1980.
"Reynolds Price: Duke of Writers," in *Vanity Fair*, July 1986.
"Why I Still Treasure 'The Little House,'" in *New York Times Book Review*, 9 November 1986.
"Books Past, Present and to Come," in *Washington Post Book World*, 6 December 1992.

Other

Editor with Shannon Ravenel, *The Best American Short Stories 1983.* Boston, Houghton Mifflin, 1983.

Manuscript Collection: William R. Perkins Library, Duke University, Durham, North Carolina.

*

Critical Studies: *Art and the Accidental in Anne Tyler* by Joseph C. Voelker, Jackson, University Press of Mississippi, 1989; *The Temporal Horizon: A Study of the Theme of Time in Anne Tyler's Major Novels* by Karin Linton, Uppsala, Sweden, Studia Anglistica, 1989; *The Fiction of Anne Tyler* edited by C. Ralph Stephens, Jackson, University Press of Mississippi, 1990; *Understanding Anne Tyler* by Alice Hall Petry, Columbia, University of South Carolina Press, 1990; *Critical Essays on Anne Tyler* edited by Alice Hall Petry, New York, G.K. Hall, 1992; *Anne Tyler* by Elizabeth Evans, New York, Twayne, 1993; *Anne Tyler as Novelist* edited by Dale Salwak, Iowa City, University of Iowa Press,

1994; *Anne Tyler. A Bio-Bibliography* by Robert W. Croft, Westport, Connecticut, Greenwood Press, 1995; *Anne Tyler: A Critical Companion* by Paul Bail, Westport, Connecticut, Greenwood Press, 1998; *An Anne Tyler Companion* by Robert W. Croft, Westport, Connecticut, Greenwood Press, 1998.

*   *   *

When Anne Tyler published her ninth novel, *Dinner at the Homesick Restaurant,* in 1982, the immediate book sales for the first time were impressive, as they have remained for her subsequent novels. Such popular acclaim prompted paperback reissues of earlier titles, which, as Robert W. Croft recently pointed out, have all sold astonishingly well: *The Accidental Tourist* paperback sold over 1,500,000 copies, spurred in part by the award-winning movie starring William Hurt and Geena Davis. But Tyler has always had confident supporters in Phyllis Peacock, her high school English teacher, Reynolds Price, her Duke University mentor, and Eudora Welty, as well as a loyal and ever-growing public who since *If Morning Ever Comes* (1964) eagerly await every new Tyler novel. Tyler discounts her earliest work and certainly her fiction of the 1980s and 1990s involves more intricate plots, skillful manipulation of time, and memorable characters who are lovable, eccentric, curious, hesitant, hopeful, resilient, and occasionally zany.

For most readers, Baltimore equals "place" in Tyler's fiction; however, other locales have had their influence. Born in Minneapolis, Tyler spent her earliest years in Minnesota, Illinois, and Pennsylvania; childhood in Celo, a North Carolina land trust community; adolescence in Raleigh; and young married life in Montreal with her Iranian-born husband, the late Dr. Taghi Modarressi. Southern traits that reviewers and critics note in her fiction stem from early years in the South and from inheritance—her paternal grandfather, Charles Shirley Tyler, was born in Beaufort, South Carolina. A man with varied occupations (a paper broker, banker, and later an egg farmer), Charles Tyler studiously avoided honors, a trait his son and his novelist granddaughter have assiduously emulated. Her other grandparents were born in Michigan, Nebraska, and Minnesota; all attended college. Stanley Almont Mahon, Tyler's maternal grandfather (a mining engineer), wrote wonderful letters to his children; he also wrote poetry, surreptitiously. These grandparents, along with her remarkable parents, set an intellectual tone for the family.

The too familiar opening line of Tolstoy's *Anna Karenina* (a novel Tyler rereads every summer) lies at the heart of Anne Tyler's fiction, "All happy families resemble one another, but each unhappy family is unhappy in its own way." Tyler's fictional families, from the Hawkes clan in *If Morning Ever Comes* (1964) to the Gaitlins in *A Patchwork Planet* (1998), reflect her abiding interest in the infinite details of a family's life from the delight in marriage, births of children, and successful careers to the grief brought by failures, illnesses, and deaths.

Tyler values characters for what her fellow writer and admirer Doris Betts calls their "down-the-street courage," the ability of ordinary people to survive disappointments and, given their circumstances, to act heroically. Jeremy Pauling (*Celestial Navigation*), Tyler's most complete artist and her most withdrawn character, briefly conquers his agoraphobia to venture alone beyond the confines of his house to find his "wife" and children. That he

fails to win them back is inevitable, and the novel ends with the main characters left to confront either a lonely life (Jeremy) or an anxious and financially insecure existence (his "wife" Mary with the six children). Ezra Tull (*Dinner at the Homesick Restaurant*), a born caretaker turned restaurateur, loses his only love, a spiky tomboy named Ruth Spivey, who succumbs to the misguided courtship of Cody, Ezra's handsome brother. Ezra never fully recovers from his loss, but he goes on living, looks after his nearly blind mother and gives comfort to strangers through the ambience of his Homesick Restaurant. Macon Leary (*The Accidental Tourist*), nearly immobilized by his young son's murder and his wife's abandoning him, escapes from the eccentric and cloistered home of his sister and two divorced brothers when he assumes the complex responsibility of life with Muriel Pritchett (a character with a comic spirit as well as common sense) and her allergy-ridden son, Alexander. Ian Bedloe (*Saint Maybe*) literally atones for the guilt of his brother Danny's suicide and his sister-in-law's death when he abandons his plans for college and accepts the responsibility of raising Danny's stepchildren. These male characters and a *host* of female characters in Tyler's novels exist within families that have tell-tale signs of a dysfunctional malaise, but most, as Doris Betts has observed, survive breaks and disasters. These families mend and endure.

Tyler's keen eye and ear for detail results in characters who seem as real as neighbors down the street, and her ready gift for humor helps readers sympathize with her characters' foibles, misguided decisions, and failures. If she has chosen to avoid experimentation in fiction and usually to avoid confronting contentious political and social issues, Tyler succeeds in reminding readers that the family has not disappeared from the pages of fiction, but is alive, struggling, and surviving. She knows that in the midst of local and national tragedies, ordinary daily life continues and requires its own measure of courage. The quotidian remains at the core of her fiction: Family life with its repetitive daily routine and with problems that, like a recurring fever, seldom completely go away.

Although Tyler's reputation rests upon her accomplishments as a novelist, she has published many short stories, beginning in 1959 when "Laura" and "The Lights on the River" appeared in *Archive* at Duke University. Later stories appeared in national publications, including *Harpers*, the *Saturday Evening Post*, and the *New Yorker*. Considering them generally inferior work, Tyler will not allow these stories to be collected (some have been anthologized), even though several, especially "Average Waves in Unprotected Waters" and "Your Place Is Empty," are outstanding. Tyler has frequently reviewed books in the *New York Times Book Review, Washington Post Book World, Chicago Tribune,* and other major newspapers, an activity that reflects her prodigious reading.

Generous in answering inquiries from serious scholars, Tyler does not participate in the visiting-author-lecturer circuit, declines to attend awards ceremonies, and gives interviews sparingly. She means what she said many years ago: any activity besides family life and writing simply fritters her away. With fourteen novels published, as well as short stories, essays, and book reviews, Tyler has earned a prominent place in American letters.

—Elizabeth Evans

U-V

UHRY, Alfred

Born: Atlanta, Georgia, 1936. **Education:** Brown University, B.A. 1958. **Family:** Married Joanna Kellogg, 13 June 1959; four children. **Career:** Worked with composer Frank Loesser, 1960-63; instructor in English and drama, Calhoun High School, New York City, until 1980; instructor in lyric writing, New York University, 1985-88; affiliated with Goodspeed Opera House, 1980-84; comedy writer for television scripts. **Awards**: Pulitzer Prize for drama, 1988, and Academy Awards for best film and best screenplay adaptation, 1990, for *Driving Miss Daisy*; Tony Award for best play, 1997, for *The Last Night of Ballyhoo*. **Agent**: Flora Roberts Agency, 157 West 57th St., Penthouse A, New York, New York 10019. **Address**: Playwrights Horizons, 416 West 42nd St., New York, New York 10036.

PRODUCTIONS

Plays

Chapeau. Produced at Saratoga Performing Arts Center, 1977.
Driving Miss Daisy (produced Off-Broadway, 1987). New York, Theatre Communications Group, 1988.
The Last Night of Ballyhoo (produced New York, Helen Hayes Theater, 1996). New York, Theatre Communications Group, 1997.

Screenplays

Mystic Pizza, with Amy Jones, Perry Howze, and Randy Howze. Metro-Goldwyn-Mayer, 1988.
Driving Miss Daisy. Warner Bros., 1989.
Rich in Love. Metro-Goldwyn-Mayer, 1993.

Other

Lyricist, *Here's Where I Belong* (musical based on John Steinbeck's novel *East of Eden*; book by Terrence McNally, music by Robert Waldman). Produced in New York City, 1968.
Lyricist and librettist, *The Robber Bridegroom* (musical based on Eudora Welty's novella of the same title; music by Robert Waldman). Produced Off-Off Broadway, 1975; produced on Broadway, 1975; published, New York, Drama Book Specialists, 1978.
Lyricist, *Swing* (book by Conn Fleming; music by Robert Waldman). Produced in Wilmington, Delaware, 1980; produced at John F. Kennedy Center for the Performing Arts, 1980.
Lyricist and librettist, *America's Sweetheart*. Produced in Hartford, Connecticut, 1985.

Adaptor, *Little Johnny Jones*. Produced on Broadway, 1982.

*

Alfred Uhry comments:

"Sentiment was never going to get her way" (speaking of his grandmother on whom the character Miss Daisy is based). "When I was a little boy and wrote her letters, she would send them back to me—corrected."

*   *   *

Alfred Uhry's two major prizewinning works, *Driving Miss Daisy* (Pulitzer Prize for Drama, Academy Awards for best film and best adaptation from another medium) and *The Last Night of Ballyhoo* (Tony Award for best play), are set in Atlanta and draw on his family experiences for scenarios in which interactions among small groups of characters reveal individual fears, assumptions, prejudices, shortcomings, and strengths. Subtlety is the key to Uhry's work, as seemingly small incidents become catalysts for insights. Through uneasy relationships within families and between people from different backgrounds, Uhry explores such themes as aging and social expectations. Allusions to topical events—the Civil Rights movement of the 1960s in *Driving Miss Daisy,* the advent of World War II in *The Last Night of Ballyhoo*—expand the scope of those particular concerns into more universal significance.

Driving Miss Daisy focuses on the relationship between a cantankerous, elderly Jewish woman and her chauffeur, an African-American man, over a period spanning nearly three decades. The play begins as seventy-two-year-old Miss Daisy wrecks her new car, prompting her son, Boolie, to hire a driver for her. Boolie hires Hoke, a man several years younger than Miss Daisy, and while she grudgingly consents to his services she repeatedly finds fault with Hoke. Through this basic premise of bringing together characters from different backgrounds and classes, Uhry develops a subtle exploration of individuals confronting their aging and individual assumptions. Larger social issues are deftly maneuvered into the work through references to topical events of the 1950s-70s period, including the rise of the 1960s Civil Rights movement, as the self-styled non-discriminating Miss Daisy discovers her own biases and the unassuming Hoke becomes more assertive. The formality maintained by the characters helps the author avoid sentimentalism and easy resolutions, as well as being a source of humor, suggesting divisions that are difficult to transverse even as the two characters gradually find friendship and mutual respect.

The different backgrounds and attitudes of Miss Daisy and Hoke are uncovered during routine trips to a store, a synagogue, and other daily activities. During a visit to a cemetery Miss Daisy discovers that Hoke is illiterate when he fails to locate the headstone where she had asked him to place flowers. Miss Daisy's underlying prejudice surfaces when she accuses Hoke of stealing a can of salmon missing from her pantry. Such incidents further their discomfort with each other but also become opportunities for drawing closer. For example, the cemetery incident leads Miss Daisy to help teach Hoke to read, and the false theft accusation reveals to her racial preconceptions she had insisted she was above. In subtle ways, the two begin to support each other even as their differences remain apparent.

Driving Miss Daisy is based on an actual relationship and is the culmination of an on-again, off-again theatrical career Uhry had begun nearly twenty-years before the play was first produced. Miss Daisy is based on Uhry's grandmother, a crusty former schoolteacher whose obstreperous behavior showed in her insistence on driving after her eyesight and reflexes had begun to noticeably decline. As in the play, she was forced to give up driving and took the services of a black chauffeur. Uhry's childhood experience of racism in the South was of the kind of discretion masked in genteel and polite surface behavior, rather than more overt forms of aggression and violence. In small and telling incidents, *Driving Miss Daisy* reflects this kind of discrete racism, as dangerous and certainly as pervasive as more conspicuous forms of prejudice.

Uhry was born and raised in Atlanta. His father was a furniture designer and artist, his mother a social worker. After graduating from Brown University in 1958, Uhry moved to New York City, where he worked with composer Frank Loesser from 1960 to 1963. For the next two decades he worked as an instructor in English and drama at Calhoun High School in New York City and as a lyricist, contributing to such musicals as *Here's Where I Belong* (based on John Steinbeck's novel *East of Eden*), *The Robber Bridegroom* (based on Eudora Welty's novella of the same title), and *Swing*. He received a Tony Award nomination for his work on *The Robber Bridegroom*, a rustic musical about a gentlemanly thief of money and love in backwoods Mississippi. The play was a hit on New York's Off-Broadway circuit in 1975 and ran on Broadway for nearly one hundred fifty performances during the 1976-1977 season. Other projects failed, including a revival of George M. Cohan's *Little Johnny Jones* starring teen idol Donny Osmond and a musical about gangster Al Capone (*America's Sweetheart*). Uhry was working as an instructor in lyric writing at New York University, was affiliated with Goodspeed Opera House, and was contemplating retiring from theatre work when he began writing *Driving Miss Daisy*.

After the theatrical success of *Driving Miss Daisy,* Uhry turned to writing screenplays. Before adapting the play into an Academy Award winning film (the cinema version of *Driving Miss Daisy* won four Oscars, including best film and, for Uhry, best screenplay adaptation), Uhry helped finish the script for the 1988 film *Mystic Pizza*, which became a cult favorite. The film concerns three young women working in a pizza parlor in Mystic, Connecticut. Already credited to three screenwriters, the script came to the playwright with some problems and a story that interested him as the father of four daughters. The three working-class Portuguese-American girls face emotional crises: Jojo is in love but is not ready for marriage, Daisy is involved with a rich young man with questionable motives, and Kat, set on attending Yale, falls in love with a married man. Uhry helped rework the resolution and injected some humor into the script, an element evident in his plays as well: *Driving Miss Daisy* has droll moments appropriate to the formal behavior of the characters, and *The Last Night of Ballyhoo* is sprinkled with one-liners. Uhry later teamed with film director Bruce Beresford, with whom he had worked on the cinema version of *Driving Miss Daisy*, to adapt Josephine Humphries' novel *Rich in Love*. Centering on a family in South Carolina abandoned by the mother, the film focuses on Lucille, the youngest daughter, who comes of age during her family's crisis.

The Last Night of Ballyhoo was commissioned for the 1996 Cultural Olympiad in Atlanta, which accompanied the Summer Olympic Games. Set in 1939 at the time when the film *Gone with the Wind* was having its world premiere ("the last time Atlanta was in the international spotlight" previous to the Olympics, according to Uhry), the play draws on his parents' love story and blends elements of social charm and bigotry during a period about to change with the advent of World War II. Ballyhoo was a custom for young Jewish Southern belles, similar to a Coming Out Ball. The young debutante in this play is Lala Levy, humorously neurotic and tragically dateless. Her mother, Boo, is distressed by this situation, as is an aunt whose beautiful daughter returns home for a stay from college; other characters include an older brother intensely serious in his role as family leader, and the girls' ballyhooed dates—a tactless scion of an established Southern Jewish family and an obnoxious northerner from Brooklyn. Preparations for and attendance at the gala ball parallel the gala Atlanta premier of *Gone with the Wind* as well as the gala events that occur in the film prior to the outbreak of the Civil War. Small and quirky complications among family members are developed alongside weightier issues—cultural identity among Southern Jews, for example—as people prepare for and react variously to Ballyhoo social functions and other, general cultural practices, such as Christmas, as the play explores assumptions of class and issues of cultural assimilation.

—Mel Koler

VOIGT, Ellen Bryant

Born: Ellen Bryant in Danville, Virginia, 9 May 1943. **Education**: Converse College, B.A. 1964; University of Iowa, M.F.A. 1966. **Family**: Married Francis George Wilhelm Voigt, 5 September 1965; two children. **Career**: Instructor in English, Iowa Wesleyan College, 1966-69; teacher of literature and writing, 1970-78, director of writing program, 1975-78, Goddard College, Plainfield, Vermont; associate professor of creative writing, Massachusetts Institute of Technology, 1979-82; M.F.A. program for writers, visiting faculty member, Warren Wilson College, Swannanoa, North Carolina, since 1981; professional pianist; member of board of directors of Associated Writing Programs; served as judge of poetry contests, taught at writers' conferences, including Bread Loaf, Ropewalk, Aspen, Napa Valley, and Sandhills. **Awards**: Grants from Vermont Council on the Arts, 1974-75, National Endowment for the Arts, 1976-77, and Guggenheim Foundation, 1978-79; Pushcart Prize, 1983, 1991; Emily Clark Balch Award, *Virginia Quarterly Review*, 1987; Hanes Poetry Award, 1994; nominee, National Book Critics Circle poetry award, 1995.

PUBLICATIONS

Poetry Collections

Claiming Kin. Middletown, Connecticut, Wesleyan University Press, 1976.
The Forces of Plenty. New York, Norton, 1983; Pittsburgh, Carnegie-Mellon, 1995.
The Lotus Flowers. New York, Norton, 1987.

Two Trees. New York, Norton, 1992.
Kyrie: Poems. New York, Norton, 1995.

Other

Mercy, with Kathleen Pierce. Pittsburgh, University of Pittsburgh Press, 1991.

Contributor, *Poetry in Public Places.* New York, American International Sculptors Symposium, 1977.
Contributor, *Ardis Anthology of New American Poetry.* Ann Arbor, Ardis, 1977.
Contributor, *The Norton Anthology of Poetry.* New York, Norton, 1983.
Contributor, *The Bread Loaf Anthology of Contemporary Poetry.* Hanover, New Hampshire, University Press of New England, 1983.
Contributor, *The Morrow Anthology of Younger American Poets.* New York, Morrow, 1985.
Contributor, *The Antaeus Anthology.* New York, Bantam, 1987.

Editor with Gregory Orr. *Poets Teaching Poets: Self and the World* (essays). Ann Arbor, University of Michigan Press, 1996.

*   *   *

Ellen Bryant Voigt's poems concern separation and connection. She is a careful observer of nature and human behavior, and her vision is clear and compassionate. Her first book, *Claiming Kin,* seeks parallels everywhere between human life and nature. It is nature, for example, that gives us a model for hope. Perhaps we, like the snake, may "rise up in new skins / a full confusion of green" ("Snakeskin"). On the other hand, nature's more ominous lessons are acknowledged as well. The black widow spider, for example, ties sensuality and fertility to death. Voigt's nature poems complement others where she attempts to claim and come to terms with her human kin. Many of her poems concern the family, which she characterizes as "the circle of fire." In the long poem "Sister," the speaker returns to her family to deal with her mother's illness and finds herself reexamining the tangle of feelings that comprise her relationship with her sister:

When we were little
I used to wish you dead;
then hold my breath and sweat
to hear yours
release, intake, relax into sleep.

In *The Forces of Plenty,* her second volume, Voigt examines many of the same themes, but whereas her writing has become more confident, her stance has, perhaps wisely, become less so. She moves away from the exuberant lushness of *Claiming Kin,* with its "thick pythons / slack and drowsy, who droop down / like untied sashes / from the trees" ("Tropics") and its emphasis on what joins, to look more closely at what separates. Ironically, as the speaker remarks in "January," it is our very ability to reflect on nature that separates us from it:

If I think I am apart from this, I am a fool.
And if I think the black engine of the stove
can raise in me the same luminous waking,

I am still a fool,
since I am the one who keeps the fire.

A sense of mortality pervades this book, which includes several elegies, making life and happiness more precious and more fragile. In "Year's End" two parents' relief at their own child's recovery from illness is tempered by the knowledge that a friend's child has just died, and they listen to their own child's breath "like refugees who listen to the sea, / unable to fully rejoice, or fully grieve."

The Lotus Flowers incorporates and finds salvation in some of the hard truths first observed in *The Forces of Plenty.* In "The Farmer," for example, a man stung by a swarm of bees is saved by "the years of smaller doses— / like minor disappointments, / instructive poison, something he could use." These poems, however, are even more deeply rooted in personal experience and in her rural Southern background. There is a tinge of melancholy in her poems about the past, a lament for the loss of innocence, as in "Nightshade," in which the daughter cannot forgive her father for accidentally poisoning the dog and says that "without pure evil in the world, / there was no east or west, no polestar / and no ratifying dove." In its concern with place and pattern, the title poem is a culmination of this book's themes. The shape made by the girls on their pallets—"spokes in a wheel"—echoes the shapes of the constellations they study, and the stars in these constellations mirror the lotus flowers, no "folder / into candles," through which the girls had earlier rowed. In this poem the opposition between nature and humanity, innocence and knowledge, individual and community seems temporarily resolved.

This resolution shifts, however, in *Two Trees,* the most austere and foreboding of her books. Although it contains poems of family and nature, like her previous volumes, *Two Trees* is most concerned with the spiritual aspects of these subjects, and music and myth provide its major subjects and metaphors. The emphasis here is on what separates—the music that "keeps the girl apart / as she prefers..." ("Variations: At the Piano") or "beauty that divides us" ("First Song")—and on the loss of innocence. The title poem retells the expulsion from paradise and the eternal longing that results: "while the mind cried out / for that addictive tree it had tasted, / and for that other crown still visible over the wall." A sense of resignation pervades the book. What makes us human is not an ability to control our fate, but our need to struggle and reach out to one another: "The one who can sings to the one who can't / who waits in the pit, like Procne among the slaves, as the gods decide how all such stories end" ("Song and Story"). Her innovative adaptation of musical variations, in which three sets of poems called "variations" expand aspects of a titled poem, skillfully merges theme and technique and makes of this collection a haunting whole.

Voigt's style has grown more flexible with each book in order to accommodate her increasingly complex vision. Her subjects range from the intimacies of daily life to the exploration of our place in the universe. We can only look forward to more work from a poet who dares to say that "Nothing is learned / by turning away" ("Talking the Fire Out" from *The Forces of Plenty*).

In *Kyrie,* her fifth collection of poetry, Voigt explores people confronting the influenza pandemic of 1918-1919, which killed an estimated twenty-five million people around the world, about a half a million in the United States. While giving voice to myriad people offering numerous perspectives on human suffering, with metaphoric parallels to the contemporary AIDS epidemic, the poems in this collection continue Voigt's exploration of the possibilities of poetic form, in this case, the sonnet. Some of her sonnets adhere to traditional rhyme and metrical patters, while other challenge with near rhymes, accentual pentameter, and variations approaching free verse. The sonnets, without titles or numbers, form a poignant narrative that extend her concern for separation and connection, expressing a compassionate collection of voices engaged in braving human misery.

—Kathleen Aguero and Mel Koler

WALDROP, Howard

Born: Houston, Mississippi, 15 September 1946. **Education:** University of Texas, Arlington, 1965-70, 1972-74. **Military Service:** Served as an information specialist in the U.S. Army, 1970-72. **Career:** Linotype operator, *Arlington Daily News,* 1965-68; advertising copywriter, Lindell-Keyes, Dallas, 1972; auditory research subject, Dynastat Inc., Austin, 1975-80; fulltime writer since 1980. **Awards:** Nebula Award, 1980; World Fantasy Award, 1981. **Agent:** Joseph Elder Agency, P.O. Box 298, Warwick, New York 10990.

PUBLICATIONS

Novels

The Texas-Israeli War: 1999, with Jake Saunders. New York, Ballantine, 1974.
Them Bones. New York, Ace, 1984.
A Dozen Tough Jobs. Willimantic, Connecticut, Zeising, 1989.

Short Stories

Howard Who?: Twelve Outstanding Stories of Speculative Fiction. Garden City, New York, Doubleday, 1986.
All about Strange Monsters of the Recent Past: Neat Stories. Kansas City, Missouri, Ursus, 1987; expanded as *Strange Monsters of the Recent Past,* New York, Ace, 1991.
Strange Things in Close-up: The Nearly Complete Howard Waldrop. London, Legend, 1989.
Night of the Cooters: More Neat Stories. Kansas City, Missouri, Ursus, 1990.
You Could Go Home Again. New Castle, Virginia, Cheap Street, 1993.
Going Home Again. New York, St. Martin's Press, 1998.

* * *

Howard Waldrop is one of science fiction's most distinctive stylists, one of the very few who might truly be called unique. Working predominantly in the shorter forms Waldrop has amassed an acclaimed body of work which consistently surprises, enlightens, and entertains. It isn't possible to define a typical Waldrop story in terms more precise than "odd": take "Fin-de-Cycle," in which the Dreyfus Affair that racked France in 1895 is viewed by characters including painter Henri Rousseau, dramatist Alfred Jarry, and film pioneer Georges Melies, as everyone cycles around Paris; or "Flying Saucer Rock 'n' Roll," the partially true story of a Doo-wop singing contest between rival gangs that is interrupted by a UFO and causes a massive power failure along the whole East Coast of the U.S; or the last of the Dodos, in Depression-era Mississippi, "The Ugly Chickens."

Waldrop's hallmarks are multiple, not least being his eclecticism: Dinosaurs, jazz, UFOs, rock 'n' roll, cowboys, comics, the movies. A second characteristic must be the phenomenal research

involved in these stories, which reveals itself in Waldrop's apparent belief that if it has been researched, use it, don't waste it. "Thirty Minutes over Broadway," runs 37 pages and is followed up with annotations covering a further 12 pages and detailing everything from the aircraft specs used in the story to the comic book and B-movie allusions of character names.

It is this depth that makes even a weaker Waldrop story, such as the novella "A Dozen Tough Jobs," entertaining. Some of the allusions are clumsy in this retelling of the labours of Hercules—here a paroled convict called Houlka Lee, narrated by the young black servant I. O. Lace—but others are more subtle. Waldrop avoids a direct retelling of the labours, preferring instead to focus on the social interactions of 1920s Mississippi so that in typical Waldrop fashion the story eventually says more about I. O. than about Houlka. What makes this charming but apparently lightweight story important is the revelation it casts upon Howard Waldrop as a Southern writer. His blend of savagery and romance is tied strongly to a sense of place, so that after "A Dozen Tough Jobs," for all its weaknesses, it becomes hard to conceive of Hercules' labours taking place anywhere but Spunt County, Mississippi in 1927.

Waldrop's solo novel, *Them Bones,* is also set in the South, albeit an alternative Louisiana where the Arabs and Aztecs rule and neither Christianity nor the Roman Empire ever happened. Ostensibly a time-travel novel, this is a detailed picture of Amerindian culture as it might have been. As in "The Ugly Chickens," the reader feels a sense of loss at this.

The games Waldrop plays with history make his stories amusing and entertaining in themselves, as in "Ike at the Mike," in which young Senator E. Aaron Presley watches the jazz performance of legendary musicians Ike Eisenhower and Louis Armstrong. The story moves along from this, however, via little asides about President Kennedy (and without ever saying so, directly hints that this might be Robert Kennedy) being the "first two-term president since Huey "Kingfish" Long to an analysis of the importance of this music to people, of its power and its resonance. And when, at the end, you discover that the story doesn't actually have a plot of any sort, the absence has been made superfluous by the emotional intensity of Waldrop's exposition.

Music of one form or another, along with most other forms of popular culture, is a significant element in Waldrop's fiction. One of the many stories to deal directly with music is "Do Ya, Do Ya Wanna, Wanna Dance," a romance about youthful idealism and dreams from the viewpoint of 20 years on. The first paragraph is in typical Waldrop voice:

The light was so bad in the bar that everyone there looked like they had been painted by Thomas Hart Benton, or carved from dirty bars of soap with rusty spoons.

Later, the narrator joins his friends and notes pithily, "I seemed *not* to have interrupted a conversation."

This easy, conversational style and the historical games belie the dark heart of Waldrop. By denying the accepted significance of historical events, Waldrop might be seen to offer a new innocence that penetrates to objective truth. His stories frequently begin in light, but quickly threaten some ultimate catastrophe. Occasionally, the general foreboding is built on real evidence, such as one particularly nasty scene in "Do Ya, Do Ya Wanna, Wanna Dance," but in most of Waldrop's stories it is the character's fears that the reader feels, and it may never be clear on what basis these are founded. Ultimately, for the Waldropian character one finds a transition from the aesthetic to the religious and, frequently, a sense of self-recognition, which is the essence of the Southern grotesque, and Howard Waldrop's unique contribution to science fiction. Other writers, outlaw fantasists such as Leigh Kennedy, Steven Utley, George R. R. Martin, etc., and non-genre authors such as T. Corraghessan Boyle may have done it intermittently, but only Waldrop has done it to such extent.

—Kev P. McVeigh

WALKER, Alice

Born: Alice Malsenior Walker in Eatonton, Georgia, 9 February 1944. **Education:** Spelman College, Atlanta, 1961-63; Sarah Lawrence College, Bronxville, New York, 1963-65, B.A. 1965. **Family:** Married Melvyn R. Leventhal in 1967 (divorced 1976); one daughter. **Career:** Voter registration and Head Start program worker, Mississippi, and with New York City Department of Welfare, mid-1960s; teacher, Jackson State College, 1968-69, and Tougaloo College, 1970-71, both Mississippi; lecturer, Wellesley College, Cambridge, Massachusetts, 1972-73, and University of Massachusetts, Boston, 1972-73; associate professor of English, Yale University, after 1977; Distinguished Writer, University of California, Berkeley, Spring 1982; Fannie Hurst Professor, Brandeis University, Waltham, Massachusetts, Fall 1982; co-founder and publisher, Wild Trees Press, Navarro, California, 1984-88. **Awards:** Bread Loaf Writers Conference scholarship, 1966; *American Scholar* prize, for essay, 1967; Merrill fellowship, 1967; MacDowell fellowship, 1967, 1977; Radcliffe Institute fellowship, 1971; Lillian Smith award, for poetry, 1973; Rosenthal Award, American Academy of Art and Letters, 1974; National Endowment for the Arts grant, 1977; Guggenheim grant, 1978; American Book Award and Pulitzer Prize, 1983; for *The Color Purple*; O. Henry award, 1986; Ph.D., Russell Sage College, Troy, New York, 1972; D.H.L., University of Massachusetts, Amherst, 1983. **Address:** c/o Harcourt Brace Jovanovich Inc., 1250 Sixth Avenue, San Diego, California 92101.

PUBLICATIONS

Poetry

Once. New York, Harcourt Brace, 1968.
Five Poems. Detroit, Broadside Press, 1972.
Revolutionary Petunias and Other Poems. New York, Harcourt Brace, 1973.
Good Night, Willie Lee, I'll See You in the Morning. New York, Dial Press, 1979.

Horses Make a Landscape Look More Beautiful. New York, Harcourt Brace, 1984.
Her Blue Body Everything We Know: Earthling Poems 1965-1990. San Diego, Harcourt Brace, 1991.

Novels

The Third Life of Grange Copeland. New York, Harcourt Brace, 1970.
Meridian. New York, Harcourt Brace, 1976.
The Color Purple. New York, Harcourt Brace, 1982.
The Temple of My Familiar. San Diego, Harcourt Brace, 1989.
Possessing the Secret of Joy. New York, Harcourt Brace, 1992.
By the Light of My Father's Smile. New York, Random House, 1998.

Short Stories

In Love and Trouble: Stories of Black Women. New York, Harcourt Brace, 1973.
You Can't Keep a Good Woman Down. New York, Harcourt Brace, 1981.
Everyday Use, edited by Barbara T. Christian. New Brunswick, Rutgers University Press, 1994.

Children's Books

Langston Hughes, American Poet (biography). New York, Crowell, 1974.
To Hell with Dying. San Diego, Harcourt Brace, 1988.
Finding the Green Stone. San Diego, Harcourt Brace, 1991.

Nonfiction

In Search of Our Mothers' Gardens: Womanist Prose. New York, Harcourt Brace, 1983.
Living by the Word: Selected Writings 1973-1987. San Diego, Harcourt Brace, 1988.
Warrior Marks: Female Genital Mutilation and the Sexual Blinding of Women, with Pratibha Parmar. New York, Harcourt Brace, 1993.
The Same River Twice: Honoring the Difficult—A Meditation on the Making of the Film 'The Color Purple' Ten Years Later. New York, Scribner, 1996
Alice Walker Banned. San Francisco, Aunt Lute Books, 1996.
Anything We Love Can be Saved: A Writer's Activism. New York, Random House, 1997.

Other

Editor, *I Love Myself When I Am Laughing . . . and Then Again When I Am Looking Mean and Impressive: A Zora Neale Hurston Reader.* Old Westbury, New York, Feminist Press, 1979.

*

Recordings: Film—*Alice Walker, Author*, a production of Schlessinger Video Productions, a division of Library Video Co., 1994.

Bibliographies: *Alice Malsenior Walker: An Annotated Bibliography, 1968-1986* by Louis H. Pratt and Darnell D. Pratt, Westport, Connecticut, Meckler, 1988; *Alice Walker: An Annotated Bibliography 1968-1986* by Erma Davis Banks and Keith Byerman, London, Garland, 1989.

Interview: "A Wind Through The Heart: A Conversation With Alice Walker and Sharon Salzberg on Loving Kindness In A Painful World," *Shambhala Sun,* January 1997.

Critical Studies: *Brodie's Notes on Alice Walker's "The Color Purple,"* by Marion Picton, London, Pan, 1991; *Alice Walker,* by Conna Histy Winchell, New York, Twayne, 1992; *Alice Walker,* by Tony Gentry, New York, Chelsea, 1993; *Alice Walker and Zora Neale Hurston: The Common Bond* edited by Lillie P. Howard, Westport, Connecticut, 1993; *Alice Walker: Critical Perspectives Past and Present* edited by Henry Louis Gates and K.A. Appiah, New York, Amistad, 1993; *Everyday Use/Alice Walker* edited and with an introduction by Barbara T. Christian, New Brunswick, Rutgers University Press, 1994; *The Voices of African American Women: The Use of Narrative and Authorial Voice in the Works of Harriet Jacobs, Zora Neale Hurston, and Alice Walker* by Yvonne Johnson, New York, P. Lang, 1996.

Alice Walker comments:

My activism—cultural, political, spiritual—is rooted in my love of nature and my delight in human beings.

*   *   *

Believing that activism is a force to follow, Walker has focused on painful, sometimes hopeful, themes from the beginning of her career. Using her art, she often transmutes personal or family events into poetry or fiction. In her first poetry collection, *Once* (1968), her topics include the beauty as well as the dangers of Africa, love, suicide, and the civil rights movement. In *Revolutionary Petunias and Other Poems* (1973) she introduces the theme of "incorrectness"—self realization by refusing to capitulate to others' expected behavior. For instance, in the collection's title poem, murderer Sammy Lou, about to be executed, urges her children to water her colorful petunias, not ever realizing that others expected her to succumb to her house's gray ugliness and not plant cheerful flowers.

The short stories of *In Love and Trouble* (1973) enunciate Walker's preoccupation with "the spiritual survival, the survival whole of my people," particularly of black woman who endure oppressive, frustrating lives. "The Revenge of Hannah Kemhuff" narrates events similar to those experienced by Walker's mother. During the Depression, a white woman judges Hannah's hand-me-down clothes too fine and, thus, denies her food donations. Years later, after a difficult life, Hannah seeks help from Tante Rosie, the rootworker. Terrified of Hannah's suggested revenge through voodoo, the white woman dies imprisoned in her own befouled house. In "Roselily," Roselily relinquishes her freedom, despite its burdens, by marrying a black Muslim in order to secure her children's future. In *Alice Walker Banned* (1996), Walker recounts how this story and "Am I Blue," labeled "anti-religious" and "anti-meat eating" respectively, were removed from a 1994 California examination. While researching voodoo, Walker discovered validation of her own artistic goals in the "complete, complex, undi-

minished" black characters of Zora Neale Hurston. With the anthology *I Love Myself When I Am Laughing . . . and Then Again When I Am Looking Mean and Impressive* (19792), Walker led the positive reassessment of Hurston's work.

Drawing upon her youth in Georgia and civil rights work in Mississippi, Walker's first two novels lay bare the economic, racial and political realities of the rural south. Violence ravages three generations of sharecroppers in *The Third Life of Grange Copeland* (1970), which introduces the negative black male portrait for which Walker is continually criticized. Trapped and frustrated, Grange and his son Brownfield, both alcoholic wife abusers, commit desperate acts. Grange's abandonment of his family leads to his wife's suicide and the irredeemable dissolution of Brownfield, who murders his wife but, blaming "white crackers," refuses to acknowledge his guilt for the family's destruction. Only after accepting his responsibility can Grange rescue his granddaughter, Ruth; in an ultimate sacrifice, he murders Brownfield to secure Ruth's "survival whole." In *Meridian* (1976), a committed civil rights worker not unlike Walker herself wrestles with personal questions about violence for the revolution and the myth of motherhood.

The poems in *Good Night, Willie Lee, I'll See You In The Morning,* (1979)—the phrase is Walker's mother's farewell to her dead husband—emphasize love, but also mourn children sold into slavery (the wrenching "Early Losses: A Requiem"). Walker's subsequent poetry collections continue with the same topics and intensities as do her short stories. In *You Can't Keep A Good Woman Down* (1981) Walker experiments with narrative form in stories about violence, interracial rape and pornography. Finally, her writing experiments and passions coalesced in the novel *The Color Purple* (1982), for which Walker became the first African American woman to win the Pulitzer Prize. In this epistolary novel fourteen year old, barely literate, Celie confides in her letters to God and her sister Nettie, banished by their abusive step-father, her struggles with rape, incest, childbirth and spousal abuse as the servant-wife of Mr._____ , a character based on Walker's grandfather. Finally, Celie is rescued through her reciprocated lesbian love for the flamboyant singer Shug Avery, Mr.____'s live-in mistress. Shug helps Celie first discover Nettie's letters, hidden by Mr.____, and, then slowly, her own self worth. After thirty years, the novel ends as Celie is reunited with Nettie, now a missionary in Africa.

Unprepared for the stinging controversy that swirled around the novel and its acclaimed movie by Steven Spielberg, Walker eventually published *The Same River Twice: Honoring the Difficult—A Meditation on the Making of the Film 'The Color Purple' Ten Years Later* (1996). Bold and angry, the memoir includes her rejected movie script, journal entries, and letters to movie participants; it exorcises Walker's pain to the public's protests to her negative images of black men.

The title essay of *In Search of Our Mothers' Gardens: Womanist Prose* (1983) metaphorically urges black women to find strength for their autonomy and creativity, their "wholeness," within their foremothers' gardens and quilts, an image used again in the republished title story of *Everyday Use* (1994). Abridging a black folk expression, Walker coined "womanist" to summarize the concerns of black feminists about the devastation of racism, classism and sexism on black families and communities. The volume also includes the important "Beyond the Peacock: The Reconstruction of Flannery O'Connor." Typical of Walker's writing, reminiscences of a visit to a former Walker house just down the road from O'Connor's house lead to a discussion of O'Connor's refreshing, unsentimental, white southern writing.

In *Living By The Word* (1988), Walker continues her political activism with essays about homosexuality, vegetarianism, animal rights, and the self validation achieved when people, even characters such as uneducated Celie, speak in their own idiom and tell their own stories.

Walker stresses that "storytelling is how we survive . . . . Stories . . . they're culture. That's how we learn from each other." Walker carries this idea into *The Temple of My Familiar* (1989), an international patchwork quilt of geography and people that transcends time. Old, black Miss Lissie weaves stories of her reincarnated lives and guides Fanny, Celie's granddaughter from *The Color Purple,* and others towards an understanding of their ancestors and, thus, themselves. The novel's magic realism allows Walker to recreate 500,000 years of history and offer a creation myth centered on women in Africa.

A more successful novel, certainly more controversial, is *Possessing The Secret of Joy* (1992), which focuses on female genital mutilation, to Walker an extreme form of child abuse. Tashi, a minor character in *The Color Purple*, and other voices narrate the horrifying consequences of Tashi's decision to undergo this female initiation ritual. The critical uproar over the novel labeled Walker a Western meddler in African women's sexuality and rights. Persistent in this civil rights issue, because "the world is one," Walker donated a portion of the book's royalties to educating everyone on the debilitating emotional and physical effects of clitoridectomy. She assisted in its documentation in *Warrior Marks: Female Genital Mutilation and the Sexual Blinding of Women* (1993). Surprisingly personal, the emotional essays in *Anything We Love Can Be Saved: A Writer's Activism* (1997) include topics ranging from a defense of Winnie Mandela to the joy of dreadlocks, to Walker's characteristic pilgrimages to places such as Jung's house in Switzerland and Hurston's grave in Florida, to affectionate tributes to Audre Lorde, her mother and daughter.

—Judith C. Kohl

WALKER, Margaret

Born: Birmingham, Alabama, 7 July 1915. **Education**: Northwestern University, Evanston, Illinois, B.A. 1935; University of Iowa, Iowa City, M.A. 1940, Ph.D. 1965. **Family**: Married Firnist James Alexander in 1943 (died 1980); two daughters and two sons. **Career**: Social worker, newspaper reporter, and magazine editor; writer, Works Progress Administration, 1936-39; instructor, Livingstone College, Salisbury, North Carolina, 1941-42 and 1945-46, West Virginia State College, 1942-43; professor of English, 1949-79, professor emerita of English, 1979-present, and director of the Institute for the Study of the History, Life, and Culture of Black Peoples, 1968-1979, Jackson State University, Mississippi. **Awards**: Yale Series of Younger Poets award, 1942; inducted into

Alpha Kappa Alpha sorority, West Virginia State College, 1942; Rosenwald fellowship, 1944; Yale University Ford Fellowship, 1954; Houghton Mifflin Literary fellowship, 1966; Fulbright fellowship, 1971; National Endowment for the Arts grant, 1972; D.Litt., Northwestern University, 1974, and Rust College, Holly Springs, Mississippi, 1974; D.F.A., Denison University, Granville, Ohio, 1974; D.H.L., Morgan State University, Baltimore, Maryland, 1976; National Endowment for the Arts Senior Fellowship, 1991; College Language Association Lifetime Achievement Award, 1992; Governor of Mississippi Lifetime Achievement Award, 1992.

PUBLICATIONS

Poetry Collections

For My People. New Haven, Connecticut, Yale University Press, 1942.
Ballad of the Free. Detroit, Broadside Press, 1966.
Prophets for a New Day. Detroit, Broadside Press, 1970.
October Journey. Detroit, Broadside Press, 1973.
For Farish Street Green. Jackson, n.p., 1986.
This is My Century: New and Collected Poems. Athens, University of Georgia Press, 1989.

Novels

Come Down from Yonder Mountain. Toronto, Longman, 1962.
Jubilee. Boston, Houghton Mifflin, 1966.

Others

How I Wrote Jubilee. Chicago, Third World Press, 1972.
A Poetic Equation: Conversations Between Margaret Walker and Nikki Giovanni. Washington, D.C., Howard University Press, 1974.
The Daemonic Genius of Richard Wright. Washington, D.C., Howard University Press, 1982; as *Richard Wright: Daemonic Genius,* New York, Warner, 1988.
How I Wrote Jubilee and Other Essays on Life and Literature, edited by Maryemma Graham. New York, Feminist Press, 1990.
For My People, with photographs by Ronald L. Freeman. Jackson, University Press of Mississippi, 1992.
On Being Female, Black, and Free: Essays by Margaret Walker, 1932-1992, edited by Maryemma Graham. Knoxville, University of Tennessee Press, 1997.

*

Recording: The Poetry of Margaret Walker, Folkways, 1975.

Critical Studies: "The 'Etched Flame' of Margaret Walker: Biblical and Literary Re-Creation in Southern History" by R. Baxter Miller, *Tennessee Studies in Literature,* 1981; "Fields Watered with Blood: Myth and Ritual in the Poetry of Margaret Walker" by Eugenia Collier, *Black Women Writers (1950-1980): A Critical Evaluation* edited by Mari Evans, Garden City, New York, Anchor-Doubleday, 1984; *Black and White Women of the Old South: The Peculiar Sisterhood in American Literature* by Minrose Gwin, Knoxville, University of Tennessee Press, 1985; "Black Women's

Literature and the Task of Feminist Theology" by Delores Williams, *Immaculate and Powerful: The Female in Sacred Image and Social Reality* edited by Clarissa Atkinson, Boston, Beacon Press, 1985; "Jubilee: The Black Woman's Celebration of Human Community" by Minrose Gwin, Conjuring: Black Women, Fiction, and Literary Tradition edited by Marjorie Pryse and Hortense Spillers, Bloomington, Indiana University Press, 1985; "The Black Woman as Artist and Critic: Four Versions" by Margaret McDowell, *Kentucky Review*, Spring 1987; "'Bolder Measures Crashing Through': MargaretWalker's Poem of the Century" by Eleanor Traylor, *Callaloo*, Fall 1987; "Margaret Walker's Richard Wright: A Wrong Righted or a Wright Wronged?" by Michel Fabre, *Mississippi Quarterly*, Fall 1989; "Margaret Walker: Black Woman Writer of the South" by Joyce Pettis, *Southern Women Writers: The New Generation* edited by Tonette Bond Inge, Tuscaloosa, University of Alabama Press, 1990; "From *Uncle Tom's Cabin* to Vyry's Kitchen: The Black Female Folk Tradition in Margaret Walker's *Jubilee*" by Charlotte Goodman, *Tradition and the Talents of Women* edited by Florence Howe, Urbana, University of Illinois Press, 1991; "The South in Margaret Walker's Poetry: Harbor and Sorrow Home" by Ekaterini Georgoudaki, *Cross-Roads*, Spring-Summer 1994.

*   *   *

In 1942, Margaret Walker's collection *For My People* won the prestigious Yale Series of Younger Poets competition. Walker's achievement marked the first time an African-American woman had been awarded a national literary prize. As she tells in a 1992 interview, the path between submission and success was not a straightforward one. Walker submitted her manuscript—which included her now-famous title poem and over two dozen others—to the competition for the first time in the late 1930s. That first year, it was sent back immediately. The next year, she sent it directly to Stephen Vincent Benet, the judge of the competition. Benet wrote back to applaud and encourage her poetry, but he did not choose her as the winner. Walker sent it in a third time, and again Benet wrote to her, expressing his regret at having to deny it the prize. The year that she won the Yale award she had not officially entered the competition. Instead, Benet wrote to Walker, requesting that she once more submit the manuscript, which he then crowned as winner.

The poem "For My People" has had the rare good fortune of not only receiving widespread critical praise but of proving a great commercial success as well. This has also been the case for Walker's historical novel, *Jubilee*, which has been translated into seven languages and has never been out of print. Walker has declared, "My books have been popular—that is, they have been successful with the people—and that is all I could wish."

Her signature poem has had a profound and lasting effect on generations of readers, a longevity contrasted by the powerful but brief burst of time in which the poem was composed. Walker recalls that she wrote much of it "in fifteen minutes on a typewriter. I think it was just after my twenty-second birthday and I felt it was my whole life gushing out." The poem exhibits a kind of refined spontaneity of feeling throughout, as these lines reveal:

For the cramped bewildered years we went to school to
    learn

to know the reasons why and the answers to and the
people who and the places where and the days when, in
memory of the bitter hours when we discovered we
were black and poor and small and different and nobody
cared and nobody wondered and nobody understood.

The lines tumble forward, accumulating force and speed until they slow at the end of the stanza. The object of the verbs "cared" and "wondered" and "understood" is implied, and this grammatical deficiency further accelerates the lines. The syntax also underscores the feelings of insignificance and indignation of these young, black children: they are simultaneously present and absent in the line, as they feel they are expected, by white culture and traditions, to be in life.

Benet, in his foreword to *For My People*, describes the character of Walker's poetry: "Straightforwardness, directness, reality are good things to find in a young poet. It is rarer to find them combined with a controlled intensity of emotion and a language that, at times, even when it is most modern, has something of the surge of biblical poetry." Indeed, Walker recognizes the Bible as one of her first and most important literary influences, and she taught a course in bible as literature at Jackson State University for over twenty-five years. In 1949 Walker began her long teaching career at Jackson State. She retired in 1979 and is now professor emerita of English at the University. She also helped establish the Margaret Walker Alexander National Research Center there. The center is an extension of the Institute for the Study of the History, Life, and Culture of Black Peoples and, according to its mission statement, it is "a national resource for collecting, preserving, and interpreting twentieth-century African American history through living memories, archival records, material culture, and the built environment."

Literature, intellectual examination, and social activism are intimately bound for Walker, as is indicated by the aim of the research center that bears her name and by the epitaph she has written for herself: "Here lies Margaret Walker / Poet and Dreamer / She tried to make her life / a Poem."

Walker has a deep personal stake in her writing, and her work derives from experience. Much of *Jubilee* was inspired by and relies on stories told to her by her grandmother. Walker says of her famous civil war novel: "Long before *Jubilee* had a name, I was living with it and imagining its reality. Its genesis coincides with my childhood, its development grows out of a welter of raw experiences and careful research, and its final form emerged exactly one hundred years after its major events took place."

Personal experience also informs much of Walker's poetry. Her verse style is often declamatory, sometimes celebrating or consecrating life, at other times incriminating or challenging it. Behind her work is an indefatigable impulse to humanize and value black experience. Walker is compelled to reveal racism and decry sexism, to chronicle the lives and emotions of nearly invisible persons, and to record unjust conditions that are all too visible in African-American communities, especially those in the South. At various times in her life Walker has studied, worked, and traveled in the North. However, spiritually and psychologically she has never left the South and has lived the majority of her life there. Walker observes: "The South is my home, and my adjustment or accommodation to this South—whether real or imagined (mythic and legendary), violent or nonviolent—is the subject and source of all my poetry. It is also my life." In one of her early poems, "Southern Song," Walker very simply sanctifies her relationship to the South and to her art, "I want my careless song to strike no minor key; no fiend to / stand between my body's southern song— the fusion of / the South, my body's song and me."

—Jeannine Johnson

WATSON, Brad

Born: In Mississippi. **Education:** Mississippi State University, B.A. in English, 1978; University of Alabama, M.F.A. in creative writing/American literature, 1985. **Career:** Odd jobs, including garbage collection, acting, and newspaper reporting; lecturer, University of Alabama, 1988-95; Briggs-Copeland Lecturer in English and American Literature and Language, Harvard University, 1996-present. **Award:** Sue Kaufman Prize for First Fiction, American Academy of Arts and Letters, 1997.

PUBLICATIONS

Last Days of the Dog-Men. New York, W.W. Norton, 1996.

*

The stories in *Last Days of the Dog-Men* are diverse in setting, characters, and focus, but they are linked by each having significant canine presences, which illuminate, often subtly, the human spirit and experience. "Ultimately, the dog, . . . its constant presence in human experience coupled with its nearness to the feral world, is the alter ego of man himself"—a quote from David Gordon White's *Myths of the Dog-Man*—serves as the epigraph to the volume. Actually, the dog shares relatively few of humankind's qualities, but its capacity to be anthropomorphized into a mirror for ourselves gives it a compelling hold on our hearts and imaginations, which Watson uses to great effect. Watson's dogs have distinct personalities and traits, but they are not Wegman drag creations, and he never mocks the animals—or their human relationships.

In addition to dogs, the stories in *Last Days of the Dog-Men* share some common thematic obsessions, notably how we get along in the world alone and collectively and where we find purpose and meaning in life. Watson's characters often are stuck at questions of the primary quandary: Who am I?; What is my human potential and how is it to be fulfilled?; What does it mean to live with dignity?; and In what can I have faith? The drive to discover identity, articulate it in a way that connects one to life, and acknowledge the authenticity of self inform all of the stories.

Besides the riddles of existence, Watson's characters address the conundrums of love and its complicated network of need, dependency, commitment, and trust. In the title story, a married couple discovers how easily simple carelessness can lead to betrayals so deep and irredeemable that hope of connection is as remote as the moon. The lunar landscape of romance is full of craters of unfilled need, failure, and suspicion. In such a bleak

place, the constancy and accepting nature of dog love looks positively divine. When it happens, as in "Agnes of Bob" and "Bill," it frees the individual to be his or her best self, to love without reservation or expectation, or perhaps to discover himself or herself.

These stories, all set in the South, are marked by precise, nuanced writing that captures the texture and heft of its subjects. Objects have weight, houses have liveable dimensions, and front porches address vistas of genuine scope. The prose is detailed and vivid and never squeamish:

> The grizzled bitch lay on her side in the fading sunlight in Sam's front yard, her black wrinkled teats lumped beside her like stillborn pups. It had been a sunny late-October day but now cool evening crept along the edge of the sky and Sam could see the dog's sides shiver as she labored to breathe. Her dark coat was patchy with mange and her eyes looked bad. When Sam walked closer they went to slits and a low growl came from her throat. He could smell her from ten feet away: a ripe, sweet rotten smell." ("The Wake")

Watson is attentive to the rustling sound and motion of the out-of-doors and the natural world is frequently exquisitely evoked:

> I could hear the last shot echo over field after field, and then a great silence. A strange ecstasy sang in my veins like a drug. I raised the gun and fired the last shell into the air, the flame from the barrel against the darkening sky, and the chamber locked open, empty. Then silence. Not even a sifting of wind in the leaves. Not a single wheezy note from a blackbird, or any other kind of bird. I wanted the moment to last forever." ("The Retreat")

These stories are contemporary: they describe the lacks, stresses, and small gifts that characterize modern lives. Alienation, loneliness, betrayal, pointlessness are certainly part of Watson's fictional world, but as often as not there are also pinpricks of hope and humor. The heavens often offer signs of a vaster scheme, glimpsed only at the edges of the horizon sometimes but nevertheless a potent and genuine comfort if it can be accepted. A surprising number of Watson's characters know astronomy, and connections with ancient myths and heroes are interwoven throughout all the stories. Such an overarching vision raises his stories from the merely momentary and gives his characters a sense of belonging over time that is relatively rare in modern fiction. His male characters, especially, are complex and well drawn, but all are, in the words of one reviewer, "alive with honest, thrumming energy."

—Jay Lamar

WELTY, Eudora

Born: Eudora Alice Welty in Jackson, Mississippi, 13 April 1909. **Education:** Mississippi State College for Women, 1925-27; University of Wisconsin, B.A. 1929; Columbia Graduate School of Business, 1930-31. **Career:** Free-lance correspondent and publicist, Jackson radio station and local newspapers, 1931-33; publicity agent with Mississippi Works Projects Administration (WPA), 1933-36; wrote reviews of World War II reports under pseudonym Michael Ravenna, *New York Times Book Review,* 1942-44; William Allan Neilson Professor, Smith College, 1962; honorary consultant in American letters, Library of Congress, 1958-61; appointed to the National Council of the Arts, 1972; lectured and conducted writing workshops at Duke University and Millsaps College. **Awards:** O'Henry Award, 1941, for "A Worn Path"; Guggenheim Fellowship, 1942, 1949; American Academy of Arts and Letters Award, 1944; National Institute of Arts and Letters election, 1952; William Dean Howells Medal, 1955, for *The Ponder Heart*; Creative Arts Medal, Brandeis University, 1966; Edward McDowell Medal, 1970; named to American Academy of Arts and Letters, 1971; National Institute of Arts and Letters Gold Medal, 1972, and Pulitzer Prize, 1973, for *The Optimist's Daughter*; National Medal of Literature and Presidential Medal of Freedom Awards, 1981; American Book Award, 1981, 1984; Commonwealth Award, Modern Language Association, 1984; National Medal of Arts, 1986; Jackson Public Library named to honor Eudora Welty, 1986; *Chevalier de L'ordre d'Arts et Lettres* (France), 1987; National Book Foundation Medal, 1991, Helmerich Distinguished Author Award, and Cleanth Brooks Medal in Southern Letters, 1991; Eudora Welty Society organized, 1991; Frankel Prize, National Endowment for the Humanities, 1992; PEN/Malamud Award for excellence in the short story, 1993; Eudora Welty Writers' Center established by Mississippi legislature at her childhood home, 741 N. Congress St. in Jackson, 1995, dedicated May 1, 1996; Legion of Honor (France), 1996; D. Litt. from University of North Carolina at Chapel Hill, University of the South, Washington University at St. Louis, Smith College, University of Wisconsin, Western College for Women, Millsaps College, Yale University, Harvard University, and University of Dijon (France).

PUBLICATIONS

Novels

The Robber Bridegroom. New York, Doubleday, Doran, 1942.
Delta Wedding. New York, Harcourt, Brace, 1946.
The Ponder Heart. New York, Harcourt, Brace, 1953.
Losing Battles. New York, Random House, 1970.
The Optimist's Daughter. New York, Random House, 1972.

Short Story Collections

A Curtain of Green. New York, Doubleday, Doran, 1941.
The Wide Net and Other Stories. New York, Harcourt, Brace, 1943.
The Golden Apples. New York, Harcourt, Brace, 1949.
Selected Stories. New York, Modern Library, 1953.
The Bride of the Innisfallen. New York, Harcourt, Brace, 1955.
Thirteen Stories. New York, Harcourt, Brace and World, 1965.
The Collected Stories of Eudora Welty. New York, Harcourt, Brace, Jovanovich, 1980.
Morgana: Two Stories from 'The Golden Apples.' Jackson, University Press of Mississippi, 1988.

Nonfiction

Short Stories. New York, Harcourt, Brace, 1949.
Place in Fiction. London, House of Books, 1957.
Three Papers on Fiction. Northampton, Massachusetts, Smith College, 1962.
A Sweet Devouring. New York, Albondocani Publishers, 1969.
One Time, One Place: Mississippi in the Depression: A Snapshot Album. New York, Random House, 1971.
A Pageant of Birds. New York: Albondocani Publishers, 1974.
Fairy Tale of the Natchez Trace. Jackson, The Mississippi Historical Society, 1975.
Welty. Jackson, Mississippi Dept. of Archives and History, 1977.
The Eye of the Story: Selected Essays and Reviews. New York: Random House, 1978.
Conversations with Eudora Welty. Jackson University Press of Mississippi, 1984.
One Writer's Beginnings. Cambridge, Harvard University Press, 1984.
Photographs. Jackson, University Press of Mississippi, 1989.
A Writer's Eye: Collected Book Reviews. Jackson, University Press of Mississippi, 1994.
More Conversations with Eudora Welty. Jackson, University Press of Mississippi, 1996.

Children's Literature

The Shoe Bird. New York, Harcourt, Brace and World, 1964.

Plays

The Ponder Heart. Produced at The Music Box, New York, 1956.
Eudora Welty's 'The Hitch-Hikers.' New York, Dramatists Play Service, 1990.

*

Adaptations: Opera—*The Ponder Heart* adapted by Alice Parker and first performed in Jackson, New Stage Theatre, 1982. **Plays**—*A Season of Dreams* adapted by Frank Hains and first performed in Jackson, New Stage Theatre, 1968; *The Robber Bridegroom* adapted by Alfred Uhry (book & lyrics) and Robert Waldman (music), first performed in New York, 1976; *Sister and Miss Lexie* (scripts based on "June Recital," *Losing Battles,* and "Why I Live at the P. O.") adapted by David Kaplan and Brenda Currin, first performed in New York, Chelsea Theatre Center, 1981; *The Wide Net* script by Anthony Herrera, *American Playhouse,* PBS Television, 1987.

Manuscript Collection: Mississippi Department of Archives and History, Jackson.

Bibliography: *Eudora Welty: A Bibliography of Her Work* by Noel Polk, Jackson, University Press of Mississippi, 1994.

Interviews: "Fiction as Event: An Interview with Eudora Welty" by Jeanne Rolfe Nostrandt, *New Orleans Review,* 1979; "Eudora Welty" (interview), *Parting the Curtains* by Dannye Romine, New York, Doubleday, 1994.

Critical Studies: *The Faraway Country: Writers of the Modern South* by Louis D. Rubin, Jr., Seattle, University of Washington

Press, 1963; *A Season of Dreams: The Fiction of Eudora Welty* by Alfred Appel, Jr., Baton Rouge, Louisiana State University Press, 1965; "A Tribute to Eudora Welty," special issue of *Shenandoah*, Spring 1969; *Mississippi Quarterly*, Special Issue: Eudora Welty, Fall 1973 and Fall 1986; "Eudora Welty and the Children's Hour" by Jeanne Rolfe Nostrandt, *Mississippi Quarterly*, Winter 1975-1976; *Eudora Welty: A Reference Guide* by Victor H. Thompson, Boston, G. K. Hall, 1976; "Eudora Welty" by J. A. Bryant, *Seven American Women Writers of the Twentieth Century: An Introduction* edited by Maureen Howard, Minneapolis, University of Minnesota Press, 1977; *Eudora Welty: Critical Essays* edited by Peggy Whitman Prenshaw, Jackson, University Press of Mississippi, 1979; *Eudora Welty's Achievement of Order* by Michael Kreyling, Baton Rouge, Louisiana State University Press, 1980; *Eudora Welty* by Elizabeth Evans, New York, Ungar, 1981; *The Heart of the Story: Eudora Welty's Short Fiction* by Peter Schmidt, Jackson, University Press of Mississippi, 1991; "The Oldest Root Sometimes Blooms Most: Eudora Welty," *Fiction of the Home Place* by Helen Fiddyment Levy, Jackson, University Press of Mississippi, 1992; "Special Feature: Eudora Welty," *Southern Quarterly*, Summer 1982, and "The World of Eudora Welty," special issue, Fall 1993; *Eudora Welty's Aesthetics of Place* by Jan Nordby Gretlund, Columbia, University of South Carolina Press, 1994; "Katherine Anne Porter and Eudora Welty," *A Common Life: Four Generations of American Literary Friendship and Influence* by David Laskin, New York, Simon & Schuster, 1994; "Ellen Glasgow and Eudora Welty: Writing the Sheltered Life," *Feminine Sense in Southern Memoir* by Will Brantley, Jackson, University Press of Mississippi, 1995; *The Late Novels of Eudora Welty* Jan Nordby Gretlund and Karl-Heinz Westarp, editors, Columbia, University of South Carolina Press, 1998; *Eudora Welty Newsletter* edited by Pearl A. McHaney, Department of English, Georgia State University, Atlanta; "Welty, Eudora," *Eudora: How a Southern Writer Came to Lend Her Name to a Computer Program*. Online, 19 May 1998, http://www4.torget.se/artbin/artor_weltypreface.html

*   *   *

Eudora Welty is among the best American writers of fiction and, arguably, the finest short story writer of the twentieth century. The same piercing intellect that enables her creativity also drives her impulse to evaluate others' work. *The Eye of the Story* and *A Writer's Eye* collect her essays and reviews from the *New York Times Book Review* and other periodicals. These non-fiction books indicate Welty's acumen as literary critic.

As writer of fiction, however, her place in posterity's literary canon is assured. While most of Welty's stories use Mississippi as their locale, her sense of place extends to the basic human condition in any geography. From her travels over much of Mississippi with the Works Projects Administration during the Depression, Welty developed a sensibility for many kinds of people, places and language, but she saw their humanity as common denominator. Carrying a small camera, she snapped photos of everyday scenes that seemed to mark human elements of a particular time and place. The expressions captured in photographic images and in her memory became material for her fiction. The penetrating vision directing her photography and permeating her nonfiction is part of her creative imagination, and her dramatic instinct reveals her love of storytelling through her narrators.

Welty's introduction to the reading public was a story, "Death of a Traveling Salesman," first published in *Manuscript* in 1936. Her first collection of stories, *A Curtain of Green* (1941) set the pace, tone and landscape out of which most of her fiction would emerge. In these stories and those that followed in 1943's *The Wide Net*, she examined family and community life in Mississippi, exploring the dreams and imaginations of her central characters. Extrapolated to the human condition, dreams become a way of projecting one's being out of current circumstances. In "A Piece of News," for instance, a young woman living in backwoods' poverty imagines herself into the life of a person with her name whose obituary she reads in a newspaper; in "First Love," a boy who is deaf and mute imagines heroic qualities in the person of Aaron Burr, whom he sees but cannot hear about. The irony implicit in these stories and the humor in which Welty couches their actions disguise the underlying kinship to the human race of dreamers. Her use of multiple perspectives gives her stories shape and her characters many dimensions.

The jewel in Welty's crown of stories is "A Worn Path," the final piece in *A Curtain of Green*. The narrator, Phoenix Jackson, is just what her name implies—an eternal figure. She is no less real, however, in Welty's creative use of the mythological phoenix symbol and her modern depiction of the medieval quest journey. The story personifies in this figure the power of and capacity for love, endurance and courage in humanity; it is the most concentrated presentation of Welty's interest in the mysteries of the human heart. The humor, revealed in dramatic irony, adds to the character's reality and demonstrates Welty's perception of the comic in human endeavor.

Humor, one of the most important qualities of her fiction, is Welty's device to alleviate underlying pathos or tragedy, thereby avoiding sentimentality. Her crafting of comedy into stories covers the spectrum of wit and humor. No funnier scene exists than the slap-stick depiction of the two drunken fishermen staggering down the street and into the burning house, then fumbling at putting out the fire ("June Recital" in *The Golden Apples)*. This collection of seven interrelated stories work together as a novel, covering forty years in the small town of Morgana, Mississippi. Though she did not invent this structure, Welty mastered it by using the same characters and place in a non-chronological time line. Each story is from the viewpoint of a different character and an omniscient narrator who reveal information about other characters in the community. Underlying the plot are allusions to mythology, especially Irish legend, and to such writers as Yeats and Joyce. Some critics have found vestiges of Chekhov in her contrived disorder, but her combining of realistic and modern characteristics is uniquely her own.

Use of many cultural legends is another characteristic of Welty's work. An avid reader of fairy tales and mythology since childhood, Welty incorporates them into her fiction as they represent human traits in a modern world. The allusions speak to the heroic and the shortcomings of human potential; love is not only a redeeming virtue, but the salvation of many of her characters. At the core of her characters, however, is the need for a sense of identity. Her people move forward or grow in proportion to their understanding of place as part of selfhood. Their roots reach into the depths of family and cultural heritage; their sense of place results from the values, language and community identity of that heritage. Loch Morrison, Virgie Rainey and the orphaned "Easter," in *The Golden Apples,* are outstanding examples. They *might* all be offspring of King MacLain (the mostly unseen but legendary figure Welty uses to tie the stories together) in that they inherit at least a kinship to his spiritual and restless self.

Place and character names also invoke characteristics of a person or locale before revealing a likeness to the legendary counterpart. The stories depict modern people re-enacting the age-old drama of the human struggle and comedy. Words, especially written words, hold magical and mystical possibilities for Welty; in the poetic sense of mutliple connotations, they depict image and reveal passion in her fiction. She *sees* her stories objectively, she says, only when she *reads* them aloud. *The Robber Bridegroom,* Welty's first novel or novella, is a Natchez Trace fairytale. It capitalizes on the oral history emerging from the wooded overgrowth of the nineteenth century Natchez Trace, combining it with an American frontier reworking of Irish folktale brought by Irish immigrants. Echoes of the Grimm brothers' work also resound in the story.

Delta Wedding and *The Optimist's Daughter* examine family and community values as they relate to characters' understanding of selfhood, using two protagonists who reach this recognition at different stages of their lives. In these novels, as with most of her work, Welty uses events and their rituals as impetus to thrust her characters into action, to instigate their search for identity—deaths and funerals, marriages and weddings, homecomings and reunions. In *The Ponder Heart,* she uses a possible murder and its subsequent trial for comic purposes in revealing an underlying pathos in the isolation or alienation of the narrator and the protagonist. Often her stories examine the difference between isolation and solitude; Robert Penn Warren named this aspect of her work "love and separateness."

Welty uses rituals as ideal fictional events for drawing together members of family and community, bringing stories to their climax or characters to their crises. Wanderers in her fiction, those who reach a sense of identity and move forward in their lives, represent Welty's idea of personal growth and cultural continuity: Laurel McKelva of *The Optimist's Daughter,* Virgie Rainey and Loch Morrison of *The Golden Apples,* are examples. The stories in *The Bride of the Innisfallen* use a different geography—Europe and the rootless foundation of a ship—but the characters reflect values as do Welty's Mississippi people, inheritors of the human condition. The exceptional story concerns the mythological Circe; having a god's foreknowledge, she regrets the loss of humanity's mystery and passion. *The Shoe Bird,* a modern fairy tale, is her only book for children.

With mythology, legend, folktale and oral history, Welty ties her Mississippi stories to world literature. In the title essay to *Place in Fiction,* among her several acclaimed writings on literature, she states, "every writer needs to stand somewhere." Welty stands in her place, the South, and her work springs from the reflected sense of family, community, values and language. Her naming patterns and her allusions connect her fictional world to a human scene. Her vision encompasses life with a sense of the comic and the tragic, the noble and the absurd, as no other writer of this century has done.

Writing has to come from inside, she believes, and the writer must have a passion to write. Her passion is evident on every page of her fiction. Her ear for and love of language gives her stories a soft, subtle lyricism, but her rhetorical choices direct a penetrating thrust to the heart of the matter. Her artistic eye, like the lens of a camera, focuses on detail and the essential in human endeavor played out in tragedy, pathos or comedy. A scrim of the mystical and magical is the overlay of her stories, giving them an atmosphere "in a season of dreams."

—Jeanne R. Nostrandt

WEST, Michael Lee

Born: Lake Providence, Louisiana, 1953. **Family:** Married; two children. **Career:** Worked as a registered nurse before turning to fiction fulltime in the 1990s.

PUBLICATIONS

Novels

Crazy Ladies. Atlanta, Longstreet Press, 1990.
She Flew the Coop: A Novel Concerning Life, Death, Sex, and Recipes in Limoges, Louisiana. New York, HarperCollins Publishers, 1994.
American Pie. New York, HarperCollins, 1996.

*   *   *

Michael Lee West's novels, full of wry humor and humanity, cut to the heart of small-town life in the South. Her precise understanding of regional idioms and idiosyncrasies renders the distinctive voices of her characters, no matter the race or class. If there is a philosophical thread to her works, perhaps it is a hardball version of Murphy's Law: everything that can go wrong will go terribly wrong. Her incisive comedic techniques remind one of Mark Twain and the yarn-spinners of the Old South.

With an offbeat sense of humor, she exposes her characters' deepest urges as well as their most inane thoughts. She probes their bittersweet sibling rivalries, sexual drives and repressions, mind-numbing griefs, and itches of sudden wanderlust. There may be a hint of sophistication in her choice of town names: Limoges, Louisiana, and Tallulah, Tennessee, but there is no condescension in her treatment of the peccadilloes of small-town eccentrics. When a few of her characters escape to New Orleans, Mexico, or California, the new milieu is realistically portrayed. With a sure knowledge of popular culture, she also evokes other eras, such as the Great Depression and the watershed decades of the 1950s and 1960s.

West's debut novel, *Crazy Ladies* (1990), employs a sophisticated narrative technique used by the mature Faulkner in *As I Lay Dying.* Her story is told by six characters in first-person monologues, each an intimate journal with unconventional insights into human nature. The book opens with the words of Miss Gussie, married to a bank teller in 1932, when banks were desperate to remain solvent. The little town of Crystal Falls is troubled by the murders of several women, and four pages into the book a young man bursts into Gussie's house and tries to rape her at knife point. Gussie grabs her loaded shotgun and manages to shoot him. When her husband comes home, he identifies the young man as the son of the president of the bank where he works. That night they dig a hole in the garden and bury the body, convinced that a plea of self defense would not work in court against such a powerful local family.

The awful secret has its grim effect on the generations that follow. It is the inevitability of the novel—the steady grinding of the mills of the gods—that energizes it. Miss Gussie's daughters, the love-starved Dorothy and the lovable Clancy Jane and their daughters—Bitsy (who entraps and marries the son of the town's banker) and Violet (strong, perceptive, and bent on a Ph.D.)—also relate illuminating chapters. The book ends in 1971 with Queenie, a superbly drawn black character, narrating the misty, beautiful finale. A remarkable footnote to her high level of achievement is the fact that the bulk of West's first novel was written in about a year while she worked as a registered nurse and cared for a husband and two sons.

Her second novel, *She Flew the Coop: A Novel Concerning Life, Death, Sex and Recipes in Limoges, Louisiana* (1994), is also a mixture of catastrophe and comedy. It begins with a striking sentence: "On the first warm Saturday in March, while geese flew north and crawfish filled the bayous, Olive Nepper turned against Jesus." A few sentences later, the 16-year-old girl, pregnant by the local preacher, swallows a bottle of rose poison mixed with a Nehi orange drink. In her resulting prolonged coma, Olive becomes the catalyst for the many voices of Limoges residents, who gossip about her condition and the history of the little town, occasionally swapping recipes and menus for diversion. As Olive's mother says, "Cooking is soothing and predictable, the way life isn't."

For the most part, the Limoges men are a salacious and sorry lot, including the pseudo Reverend T.C. Kirby, seducer of teenage girls; Olive's father, the pharmacist Henry Nepper, who has frequent trysts in the stockroom with DeeDee Robichaux; and Burr Donnell, who loves rough sex and abuses his wife Sophie, the Neppers' maid. Much of the plot of *She Flew the Coop* revolves on these men getting their "just desserts," as Limogians might say. In *Crazy Ladies* the male characters are treated more as incidental background objects, and most have the decency to die young and get out of the way of the main story line. DeeDee Robichaux dismisses both males and females in Limoges as "snotty, backward, or religious—sometimes all three."

American Pie (1996) has fewer principal characters and a tighter plot than *She Flew the Coop*, but the humorous probing into the nature of the residents of Tallulah, Tennessee, is no less hilarious. Three vastly different sisters and a lovably eccentric grandmother provide West with all the mouthpieces she needs for comments on small-town culture. Freddie, the smart sister, was expelled from medical school for "stealing organs" and now lives in California and Mexico with her marine biologist husband, who is studying grey whales. Freddie no longer considers herself "from" the South, "that realm of fantastic cooks, ancestor worshippers, prejudiced fools, and eccentric ladies who took to their beds for decades."

The wild sister, Jo-Nell, who aspires to be a salty-talking, hard-loving, honkey-tonk angel, has most of the funny lines. Married three times, and going out with a variety of men in between, she learned that bankers were "cheapskates," doctors "too tired to make good lovers," and politicians "too political and paranoid." As she drives home from her favorite bar, her Volkswagen is struck by a train. Her prolonged stay in the hospital reunites the family, bringing Freddie back to town, where she is drawn moth-like to an old flame.

The gawky plain sister, Eleanor, wears mismatched outfits and is so afraid of being attacked by a rapist that she cannot go shopping alone at the Winn-Dixie. Minerva Pray, the grandmother, has a long litany of tragic deaths in her life, but her great mission is to take complete dinners to the bereaved in a town that always seems to be burying somebody. When she dies, the whole town reciprocates, and the funeral, as described by Jo-Nell, was like a "big party where the guest of honor is put on display like a honey-baked ham."

Many young southern novelists turn for subject matter to the bizarre and the Gothic, but Michael Lee West achieves her effects with genuine people whose localized conflicts reflect the universal in all of us.

—Benjamin Griffith

WHITE, Bailey

Born: Thomasville, Georgia, 31 May 1950. **Education:** Florida State University, B.A. **Career:** Elementary school teacher (first grade), Thomasville City School System, Thomasville, Georgia; National Public Radio, periodic commentator on *All Things Considered* (radio news program). **Agent**: Jonathon Lazear, Lazear Agency, Inc., 430 First Ave. N., Suite 416, Minneapolis, Minnesota 55401.

PUBLICATIONS

Nonfiction

Mama Makes up Her Mind, and Other Dangers of Southern Living. New York, Vintage Books, 1994.
Sleeping at the Starlite Motel, and other Adventures on the Way Back Home. Reading, Massachussetts, Addison-Wesley, 1995.

Novel

Quite a Year for Plums. New York, Random House, 1998.

*   *   *

To Bailey White, a first-grade teacher in south Georgia, there truly is no place like home. Home is hope. Home is grace. Home is time, memory, and who we are, and who we should be. Both of her nonfiction books, *Mama Makes Up Her Mind, and Other Dangers of Southern Living* (1994) and *Sleeping at the Starlite Motel, and Other Adventures on the Way Back Home* (1995), embrace the sense of place, that tried-and-true theme in Southern literature. "Civilized Friends," the first essay in her second collection, beautifully encapsulates this theme when a friend who lives in Paris urges her to visit. White declines:

> I'm afraid I will find myself abandoned in the middle of a busy intersection, and I will stand there and stand there, trying to find the courage to cross the street, and cars will whizz by in five or six directions, and their drivers will blow their horns and shout at me in a language I do not speak. And eventually I will wither up and be blown away like a piece of ash and lost in the gray shadows of a great city far from home.

Well aware of her circumstance, a genteel, shy, middle-aged woman who has lived almost her whole life in the house in which she was reared (much as Eudora Welty, the mother of contemporary Southern literature, has), White sees the world amazingly clearly by, ironically, excavating the idea of home.

Home is also love, a reverence for family and tradition, however odd. *Mama Makes Up Her Mind*'s "Good Housekeeping" begins with White's mother's announcement that she has invited the family of a cousin's bride for Thanksgiving dinner. "My mother," White observes, "was sitting in the kitchen, dammed in by stacks of old *Natural History* magazines. Behind her a bowl of giant worms, night crawlers, was suspended from the ceiling." White reports that she, who was watching the worms, and her sister, who "was eyeing the jars of fleas on the kitchen counter, part of an ongoing experiment with lethal herbs," were left speechless by the announcement while the worms—their "castings" used as part of Mama's garden compost and kept in the kitchen so they could be fed table scraps—"would come to the edge of the bowl, loop [themselves] out, swag down—where [they] would hang for an instant, [their] coating of iridescent slime gleaming—and then drop down like an arrow into another bowl on the floor." In classic White style, she cinches the scene:

> My mother had an idea that the worms missed the excitement of a life in the wild, and she provided this skydiving opportunity as an antidote for boredom . . . . Those worms, or their ancestors, had been there my whole life, but somehow, until this moment, it had not seemed odd to have a bowl of night crawlers getting their thrills in the kitchen.

White's sense of humor runs rampant through her essays, including this one, which goes on to redefine the phrase "good housekeeping" and to solidify the idea of place as metaphor.

Home is also people, and a metaphor for unfaltering hope, as illustrated in "Produce Stand," from *Sleeping at the Starlite Motel*. The essay begins with the message on the flashing arrow sign for Mr. Grange's roadside stand:

> FOR DUST THOU ART
> AND UNTO DUST SHALT THOU RETURN
> *plums   peaches   watermelon*

Mr. Grange adjusts his advertisement to reflect the season, but through it all, he "is looking for someone from Idaho. On the back wall of the produce shed hangs a schoolroom map of the continental United States. Every time new customers come in, Mr. Grange finds out where they are from. Then he sticks a tack in the map of that state. Tacks cover the states of Georgia, Alabama, South Carolina, and Florida like the scales of a reptile. There are two tacks in the state of Maine, four in California. But so far there is not a single tack in the state of Idaho." He also adorns his shed with home-made decorations: in the spring, Mr. Grange cuts bunnies out of freezer paper "folded accordion-style," and then, in his "slow, workmanlike way, he takes a pink crayon and colors a nose on every bunny."

Unless she includes herself, White presents her subjects objectively, and the fact that she does not glorify (or for that matter, condemn) them encourages her readers trust her. In this manner, lovingly without sentimentalizing, she concludes her portrait of Mr. Grange:

> A gentle breeze blows out of the west. In the field behind the produce stand the corn is up. The first peaches will soon be in. Mr. Grange gets out his map and wipes off the dust. He gets out his box of tacks. He sets his aluminum chair out in the sun. And way across the land, across fields and woods and towns and rivers and lakes, in Idaho, the travelers begin to stir.

Through a well-balanced blend of humor and poignancy, this essay illustrates perfectly why White is such an appealing writer—clear, direct, and honest, with a poet's eye for observation and a poet's sense of rhythm and timing.

White is, in an era of escalating phoniness, very, very real. She is a Voice of the People, a voice that has, literally, been heard across America for eight years on National Public Radio's *All Things Considered*. Because her commentaries are composed for radio, they are also easily devoured in one quick sitting, well able, in a matter of seconds, to transport any reader to a front-porch swing and a sip from a glass of sweet iced tea. In 1998, her fans can expect a new book—*Quite a Year for Plums*—and, although her publisher classifies it a novel, White prefers to think of it as "connected stories," stories, no doubt, about Thomasville, Georgia. About home.

—Jennifer Hubbard

WILCOX, James

Born: Hammond, Louisiana, 4 April 1949. **Education:** Yale University, B.A. (magna cum laude), 1971. **Career:** Editorial assistant, 1971-72, assistant editor, 1973-76, associate editor, 1976-77, Random House, New York, New York; associate editor, 1977-78, Doubleday, New York, New York; full-time writer since 1978. **Awards:** Guggenheim fellowship. **Agent:** Amanda Urban, International Creative Management, 40 West 57th St., New York, New York 10019.

PUBLICATIONS

Novels

Modern Baptists. New York, Dial, 1983.
North Gladiola. New York, Harper & Row, 1985.

Miss Undine's Living Room. New York, Harper & Row, 1986.
Sort of Rich. New York, Harper & Row, 1989.
Polite Sex. New York, HarperCollins, 1991.
Guest of a Sinner. New York, HarperCollins, 1993.
Plain and Normal. New York, Little Brown & Co., 1998.

*   *   *

Perhaps the most original voice in Southern humor to emerge during the last few decades has been that of James Wilcox. His satiric novels fuse farce and psychological melodrama to examine the dilemmas of modern life and the modern individual. Beginning with *Modern Baptists* in 1983, he casts an eye of humane humor, wit, and moral reprobation on first the Southern and then the New York City landscape, both of which he presents as representative of contemporary America. Although his first four novels are set in the rural South, his fiction cannot accurately be described as regional, or at the least it is not marked by the usual limitations of regional literature. The small town where his first four novels take place provides a setting and a cultural context, but Wilcox's themes are not regional in nature.

Wilcox was born in Hammond, Louisiana, in 1949. His father was a music professor, and his mother played the oboe; music figures significantly in his novels, and several of his main characters are musicians. Wilcox himself is an amateur pianist and once played the cello. After graduating from Yale in 1971 with a B.A. in English (he studied creative writing with Robert Penn Warren), Wilcox held a series of editing positions with Random House and with Doubleday, where he was an associate editor. He became a full-time writer in 1978. Wilcox is well known among readers and critics of contemporary American fiction. Unfortunately, he has not had popular success with his novels, and only the first of them sold really well. A 1994 article in *The New Yorker* ("Moby Dick in Manhattan," by James B. Stewart, 27 June 1994) chronicled his difficulties and more or less made him out to be much like the hapless protagonist in one of his novels. His novel, *Guest of a Sinner*, appeared in 1993, and he has published only book reviews since then. A new novel, *Plain and Normal*, is slated for publication by Little Brown & Co. in the fall of 1998.

Wilcox's early novels are drawn with broadly comic strokes that have grown more subtle and muted as his career has advanced. They inevitably concern characters who struggle to free themselves from difficult, often ridiculous situations in which they have become entangled. *Modern Baptists* (1983) focuses on Carl Bobbie Pickens, a middle-aged, overweight assistant manager of the Sonny Boy Bargain Store in Tula Springs, Louisiana. A series of mishaps that include a misdiagnosed mole, the loss of his job, the sudden appearance of his ex-convict half-brother FX (an aspiring actor), and his love for Toinette Quaid, a Hollywood wannabe, propel him into depression and despair, and almost to suicide. The events in the book are so intensely comic that the seriousness of Bobbie's crisis is not at first clear. He is the prototype of all Wilcox protagonists. His good intentions and essentially moral nature are equaled only by his basic ineptitude and his penchant for bad decisions that mire him in difficult situations beyond his control.

A large retinue of vividly drawn minor characters populate *Modern Baptists*, and Wilcox frequently orchestrates scenes in which many of these come together to surround the major figures. The penultimate scene in the first novel is a Christmas party organized for poverty-stricken residents of Tula Springs by Donna Mae Keeley, a neurotic young lawyer who pretends that she remains in Tula Springs to be of service to the downtrodden when in fact she lacks the courage to go elsewhere. She holds the party in an abandoned community recreation center that turns out to have been built on a toxic waste dump. Wilcox's main strength as a novelist lies in his portrayal of characters: often with only a few words he evokes a fully imagined individual. He engages in gentle lampooning rather than in caricature, and even his least appealing characters are three-dimensionally human.

Wilcox sets his first four novels in a fictional town called Tula Springs, a small backwater of a Southern town well off the interstate. Wilcox very deliberately writes about a dead South in these novels. A few decades in the past, the citizens of Tula Springs would not have cared about their isolation from the world. Their own sense of community would have sustained them. But now the rest of the world, through television, radio, and other media, has intruded into Tula Springs, and misery results for the characters who feel isolated on the margins of society.

Rather than exploiting the local color aspects of his Southern setting, Wilcox uses it as a wellspring of community and interconnectedness. Many of the same characters appear in each of the first four novels. Wilcox explains that "I've always been fascinated by the idea of novels that are not really series but have interconnected characters. . . . Different characters are emphasized in different books, giving a multiple perspective on the same self-contained county." He carries this interconnectedness into his fifth novel, *Guest of a Sinner* (1993), where Bobbie's half-brother F. X. appears as a character, even though the setting is New York City.

In *North Gladiola* (1985), *Miss Undine's Living Room* (1986), and *Sort of Rich* (1989), Wilcox improvises on the formula of *Modern Baptists*: neurotic and inept middle-aged characters trying to extricate themselves from difficult situations, surrounded by a cast of eccentric and peculiar minor characters. In one form or another the main characters experience a major life crisis that manifests itself in both moral and existential form. Wilcox's protagonists, often seriously flawed in their basic moral character, try hard to live decent lives, and the novels devote much attention to their struggles towards this end. At the same time, they are searching for meaning and value, trying to convince themselves that existence means something. In this sense Wilcox's fiction is linked to that of such writers as Walker Percy, John Updike, Saul Bellow, and Anne Tyler, all of whom often focus on individuals seeking to understand their place in the modern world.

The protagonist of *North Gladiola*, Ethyl Mae Coco, is the middle-class equivalent of Bobbie. Beset with pretensions to the upper class and an aspiring performer as the organizing member of the Tula Springs Pro Arts Quartet, Mrs. Coco is the mother of six children, all but one of whom have moved out of town, probably, the novel implies, to be as far from her as possible. Her increasingly complicated life reaches a crisis when she learns that a fifty-year old Korean graduate student, Duk Soo, who plays cello in the Pro Arts quartet, has fallen in love with her and that she is suspected of killing her next door neighbor's pet Chihuahua. More clearly than in *Modern Baptists*, this crisis involves spiritual as well as moral issues, which she is helped to resolve through her confession to a Samoan Catholic priest. Such buffoonery becomes gradually more muted in the third and fourth novels, which continue to follow the basic pattern established in *Modern Baptists*.

In *Miss Undine's Living Room,* the main character Olive Mackie, another middle-aged woman, seeks to unravel the mystery of the death of her elderly uncle's attendant, whose body was found beneath the window of his room. The protagonist of *Sort of Rich* is Gretchen Peabody Aiken-Lewes, a former inhabitant of New York who has moved to Tula Springs as a result of her marriage to Frank Dunbar. Gretchen's New York sensibility comes often into conflict with the small-town values of Tula Springs, which are made doubly evident in the eccentric cast of characters whom her husband has gathered around him. His sudden death produces a major crisis in Gretchen's life, and she must decide how to put her affairs back in order.

All of Wilcox's novels concern spiritual and psychological crises in the lives of his characters. Certainly in *Sort of Rich* Wilcox begins to regard psychological and spiritual conflict as so closely related that they seem undistinguishable. For example, while Mrs. Coco in *North Gladiola* sought counsel for her troubles from a Samoan priest, Gretchen consults a psychiatrist. This novel also suggests the beginnings of a transition to the second major phase of Wilcox's career. Gretchen is a former resident of New York City, and her Northern perspective plays a major role in the novel, thus anticipating Wilcox's last two novels, which move from Tula Springs to New York City, where Wilcox himself has lived since the early 1970s.

Polite Sex (1991) focuses on a young woman named Emily Brix and her friend Clara Tilman, both of whom have moved from Tula Springs to New York to seek careers in acting. Emily is a talented actor and writer, while Clara is beautiful but not especially intelligent. While Clara has a successful career as an actress and is happily married, Emily is fortunate in neither her personal nor her professional lives. Her husband, for example, leaves her to becomes priest, and she has a love affair of sorts with F. X. Pickens, the ex-convict and minor actor from *Modern Baptists*. This novel is subdued, ironic, and mildly comic in tone, and there is little of the antic farce that characterizes the earlier works. Although several characters are from Tula Springs, Wilcox makes little of their origins and focuses instead on the vagaries of their lives in the city, how circumstances may drive the deserving to dissatisfaction and the less deserving to happiness, the necessity of struggling to accept the lot that life deals.

Wilcox's sixth and most recent novel, *Guest of a Sinner* (1993) focuses on a modestly talented pianist, Eric Thorsen, who lives alone in New York. No one in the novel has any connections to Tula Springs, but the characteristic trappings of a Wilcox novel are still in evidence: a memorable group of supporting and often eccentric characters, difficult situations (an unwelcome and unending visit from Eric's father, a downstairs neighbor whose cat-ridden apartment emits a horrible stench, a best friend who announces that he is gay, the disastrous collapse of a sister's love affair, and the unwelcome attentions of a woman who is having an affair with an ex-priest), and a protagonist who is trying to adjust to his lot in life. This novel ends on a more forthrightly optimistic note than most of Wilcox's novels. Thorsen accepts that he cannot change many of the things in his life that perturb him, and he ultimately finds happiness in a relationship with Wanda.

As a novelist Wilcox has advanced significantly in style and technique in *Guest of a Sinner* over *Modern Baptists*, yet both these novels, through their concern with middle-aged characters seeking order and meaning in their personal and professional lives show that for Wilcox the discovery of some sort of sustaining meaning in life is a basic theme. In his best books—*Modern Baptists*, *North Gladiola*, and *Guest of a Sinner*—Wilcox evokes both wild comedy and deep pathos from his characters and their difficult lives. He views the world through a distinctive lens of satire, compassion, and hilarity that is the hallmark of the most accomplished of comic novelists in American fiction.

—Hugh Ruppersburg

WILKINSON, Sylvia

Born: Durham, North Carolina, 3 April 1940. **Education:** University of North Carolina at Greensboro, B.A. 1962; Hollins College, M.S. 1963; graduate study at Stanford University, 1965-66. **Career:** Novelist and writer of children's fiction and nonfiction since early 1960s; instructor in English, art, and drama, Asheville-Biltmore College (now University of North Carolina at Asheville), 1963-65; instructor in English, College of William and Mary, 1966-67; lecturer in creative writing, University of North Carolina at Chapel Hill, 1967-70; visiting writer, Creative Writing Learning Institute of North Carolina, 1968-69, Washington College, 1974-75 and 1984, and University of Wisconsin, Milwaukee, 1985; writer-in-residence at Hollins College, 1969 and 1975, Richmond Humanities Center, 1972-80, Sweet Briar College, 1973-75, 1977; participant in Poetry in the Schools program, 1972, and in various writers' workshops; National Humanities Faculty, since 1975; worked in stock-car and sprintcar racing crews, as a timer and scorer of auto races, played competitive tennis (eastern North Carolina women's tennis champion in 1959 and Durham champion for two years), and painter with several one-artist shows. **Member:** Authors League of America, Authors Guild, PEN, International Motor Sports Association, Sports Car Club of America, Sierra Club, Animal Protection Society. **Awards:** Creative writing fellowship, Hollins College, 1963; Eugene Saxton Memorial Trust Grant, 1964, for *Moss on the North Side*; Wallace Stegner Creative Writing fellowship, Stanford University, 1965-66; Merit Award for literature, *Mademoiselle*, 1966; Sir Walter Raleigh Awards for North Carolina fiction, 1968, for *A Killing Frost*, and 1977, for *Shadow of the Mountain*; Feature Story Award, *Sports Car* magazine, 1972, for article "Chimney Rock Hillclimb"; creative writing fellowship, National Endowment for the Arts, 1973-74; Guggenheim fellowship, 1977-78; service award, University of North Carolina at Greensboro, 1978; honorable mention, Kafka Award, American Women Fiction Writers, 1978, for *Shadow of the Mountain*. **Agent:** Liz Darhansoff, L. D. Literary Agency, 70 E. 91st St., New York, New York 10028.

PUBLICATIONS

Novels

Moss on the North Side. Houghton Mifflin, 1966.
A Killing Frost. Boston, Houghton Mifflin, 1967.
Shadow of the Mountain. Boston, Houghton Mifflin, 1977.
Cale. Boston, Houghton Mifflin, 1970.
Bone of My Bones. New York, Putnam, 1982.
On the 7th Day God Created the Chevrolet. Chapel Hill, Algonquin Books, 1993.

Nonfiction

The Stainless Steel Carrot: An Auto Racing Odyssey. Boston, Houghton Mifflin, 1973.
Dirt Tracks to Glory: The Early Days of Stock Car Racing as told by the Participants. Chapel Hill, Algonquin Books, 1983.

Children's Books

Endurance Racing. Chicago, Childrens Press, 1981.
Can-Am. Chicago, Childrens Press, 1981.
Stock Cars. Chicago, Childrens Press, 1981.
Super Vee. Chicago, Childrens Press, 1981.
Sprint Cars. Chicago, Childrens Press, 1981.
Formula Atlantic. Chicago, Childrens Press, 1981.
Formula One. Chicago, Childrens Press, 1981.
Automobiles. Chicago, Childrens Press, 1982.
Trans-Am. Chicago, Childrens Press, 1983.
Kart Racing. Chicago, Childrens Press, 1985.
I Can Be a Race Car Driver. Chicago, Childrens Press, 1986.

*

Sylvia Wilkinson comments:

The largest density of Ph.D.'s in the U.S. now sits in front of computers beside the fields where my grandparents chopped out weeds 40 years ago. And I'd rather chop weeds.

*   *   *

For most of her life, Sylvia Wilkinson has nurtured two major passions—writing and the world of auto racing. The Durham, North Carolina, native has often combined the two in both fiction and nonfiction books she produced primarily during the 1970s and 1980s. But she made her literary mark 20 years earlier with her first two books, both coming-of-age novels, *Moss on the North Side* (1966) and *A Killing Frost* (1967). Many in the literary world recognized that a fresh, new talent had arrived. The late teacher and poet Randall Jarrell called her "The best writer of prose fiction that I've ever taught . . . at her best, she's really an inspired writer (and) has a detailed personal knowledge of the world she writes about." Wallace Stegner, another respected writer, agreed. A quote from him on the cover of *Moss* says the novel "has what not one first novel in fifty has: whole pages and chapters that show great natural talent under complete control." The honors and accolades and awards poured in. Wilkinson received *Mademoiselle* magazine's Merit Award for literature in 1966 and received a Wallace Stegner Creative Writing fellowship to Stanford University in 1965-66.

After her third novel, *Cale*, was published in 1970, Wilkinson won an NEA grant and a Guggenheim, along with encouraging recognition from her peers. In 1986, Louis D. Rubin Jr., her former teacher and mentor from Hollins College, where she attained her master's degree in English and writing, published a revision of *Cale* through Algonquin Books of Chapel Hill. Strongly believing that Wilkinson had not received the critical acclaim she deserved for that book, Rubin called her "one of the more remarkable writers who have been publishing fiction during the last several decades."

Bone of My Bones, published in 1982, drew mixed reviews. Lisa Mitchell of the *Los Angeles Times*, and Fred Chappell, of UNC Greensboro and Poet Laureate of North Carolina, applauded the book and Wilkinson's talent. "Sylvia Wilkinson is a marvel of subtle skill," Mitchell wrote in the *Times* 1982 review. Of the book, she wrote, "Not a word is false." Chappell added: "She deals with poverty better than she has ever done before, never pointing at it, making it a part of the weather; not merely a social condition, but a total psychological demeanor." He continued: "I have never read a page by Ms. Wilkinson that was not alive with creative movement and creature feeling. *Bone of My Bones* surely has plenty of both."

Ten years later, in 1993, Algonquin published Wilkinson's novel *On the 7th Day, God Created the Chevrolet*, the story of two brothers, Zack and Tom Pate, growing up in the rural South. Actor and race car driver Paul Newman, who got to know Wilkinson through the racing circuit and has used her timing skills on the track, said the book "brings back the old days of stock cars in vivid style. Wilkinson knows her stuff." This represented a new and somewhat strange phase, during which Wilkinson received lavish praise from the racing press but was virtually ignored by the literary press. *Auto Week* publisher Leon Mandell wrote, "This is the best racing novel I've ever read; in fact, it's probably the first fine novel about racing ever written."

Wilkinson also produced eleven nonfiction works in her "World of Racing" series for young adults between 1981 and 1986. During this same period, she wrote *Dirt Tracks to Glory: The Early Days of Stock Car Racing as Told by the Participants*, published in 1983. "Non-fiction is an exercise for me," she says. "It's like a racing mechanic who works on VW's during the weekend. I know I can do it. It uses the same skills, but not the same emotions."

Between books, Wilkinson patches together a living by occasionally working as a timer for various race teams, financial investing and living on the cheap. She makes her home in a brown-shingled cottage in El Segundo, California., with race driver John Morton and four cats, an aquarium and the occasional orphaned opossum. Their home, with its lavender shutters and mass of purple bougainvillea spilling over the roof in front, is comfortable but contains few modern conveniences.

Although she travels widely with Morton for races, she prefers a simple life. "I think you've got to create your own oasis," she said. And this she has done, with a rampant English garden in their back yard, where a Western jay often pays a visit to the small, long-haired person who rescued and raised him.

Wilkinson doesn't dash off books. She takes the Hemingway approach—writing hundreds of pages that usually get discarded.

Her books are organic, filled with detail and description that take years to craft. She began writing *Moss On the North Side* when she was in the seventh grade. She finished it when she was 25. "There were lots of drafts, lots of thrown-away pages," she says. "I spent five years on the *7th Day*. I made it a lot more difficult than it should have been. Louis Rubin says maybe I'm destined to write this way, but it's a difficult thing to do, when you look on the cutting floor, and there's a year of your life."

Although rural life in North Carolina is her heritage, she says she has mined that territory for the last time. "It's been done. Lots of times by other people. It is not something I'm going to churn anymore. Now, I'm to the point that I don't know the difference between what happened to me and what happened to my characters. The South I wrote about doesn't exist anymore." "The largest density of Ph.D.'s in the U.S. now sits in front of computers beside the fields where my grandparents chopped out weeds 40 years ago," she says. "And I'd rather chop weeds."

—Pat Borden Gubbins

WILLIAMS, Joan

Born: Memphis, Tennessee, 26 September 1928. **Education:** Attended Southwestern College, Memphis, Chevy Chase Junior College; Bard College, B.A. 1950; Fairfield University, M.A. 1985. **Family:** Married Ezra Drinker Bowen, 1954 (divorced, 1970); two children; married John Faragason, 1970. **Career:** First published story, "Rain Later," published in *Mademoiselle* magazine, 1949; clerk at a Doubleday bookshop, New Orleans, and editorial assistant, *Look* magazine, early 1950s. **Member:** PEN, Authors Guild. **Awards**: National Institute of Arts and Letters, grant in literature, 1962; John P. Marquand First Novel Award, 1962, for *The Morning and the Evening*; Guggenheim fellow, 1986.

PUBLICATIONS

Novels

The Morning and the Evening. New York, Atheneum, 1961.
Old Powder Man. New York, Harcourt, 1966.
The Wintering. New York, Harcourt, 1971.
County Woman. Little, Brown, Boston, 1982.
Pay the Piper. Dutton, New York, 1988.

Short Story Collection

Pariah and Other Stories. Little, Brown, 1983.

*

Teleplay: *The Graduation Dress* cowritten with William Faulkner, produced on *General Electric Theater* for Columbia Broadcasting System, October 30, 1960.

Uncollected Letters: *Selected Letters of William Faulkner* edited by Joseph Blotner, New York, Random House, 1977.

*   *   *

Like her early mentor and close friend William Faulkner, Joan Williams has carved out her own respectable literary niche from her "little postage stamp" of territory situated in the hill country of Northwest Mississippi. Williams began her literary career with the publication of a short story, "Rain Later," which appeared in the August 1949 issue of *Mademoiselle*. The author was then an undergraduate student at Bard College in New York. A fateful meeting in that same month with Faulkner later prompted a letter correspondence between Williams and the celebrated author. Faulkner had read "Rain Later" and was impressed enough with the young Williams's potential that he wrote her an enthusiastic letter offering his service as her mentor. Their friendship would deepen in time and Williams and Faulkner became lovers, briefly; however, their friendship endured following this short romantic interlude.

Despite Faulkner's efforts to mentor Williams, his voice was different from hers, and in later years Williams would declare that her greatest literary inspirations were derived from the works of Eudora Welty and Katherine Anne Porter.

But Williams is only partially correct in this late estimation. The ghost of Faulkner will always haunt Williams and perhaps Faulkner's greatest contribution to Williams's growth as an artist were through his personal example and encouragement, as well as introducing her to his New York literary agent, Howard Ober, whose agency still represents Williams to this day.

Williams's first novel, *The Morning and the Evening* (1961), shows echoes of Faulkner with its richly sensitive treatment of Jake Darby, a Benjy-like retarded mute. Written in a taut narrative style that fully evokes small-town Mississippi life of five decades ago, Williams tells the story of Jake Darby's painful relationship to his well-meaning but incomprehending community, which tries to help Jake cope after the death of his mother. A few townswomen extend to Jake individual acts of charity and kindness; however, the community fails to help Jake acquire self-sufficiency. To assuage its collective guilt, the community consigns Jake to an institution. Ironically, Jake is dismissed by the authorities who deem him sane. Rejected and cast off from both his community and the institution, Jake has no place to go and lives out the remainder of his short existence on the margins of his world. An incidental fire releases Jake from his suffering and isolation when he perishes in its flames. In Williams's first novel, she establishes the recurring themes of her later works: the loneliness and isolation of individuals pitted against the narrowness and unforgiving social conventions of Southern life. For this first novel, Williams won the $10,000 John P. Marquand Award as well as the praise of fellow Southern writers William Faulkner, Robert Penn Warren, and William Styron.

Always a slow writer, Williams did not publish her second novel, *Old Powder Man* (1966), until five years following the release of *The Morning and the Evening*. Her second novel is an autobiographical work depicting the difficult relationship between Frank "Son" Wynn and his daughter Laurel. The two main protagonists of this novel are derived from Williams's father and herself. *Old Powder Man* portrays the life of an ambitious dynamite salesman. Son grows up in poverty and vows to make something of himself in the lucrative dynamite business. The novel spans thirty years of Son Wynn's life and chronicles his rise to worldly fortune followed by the demise of his personal life. Wynn sacrifices two wives and a strained relationship with his daughter to his monomaniacal ambition. Too late does Son discover at the end of his life when he is dying from emphysema what life was truly about. Son Wynn finally sees the emptiness of his worldly ambitions and what it has cost him as a man. Robert Penn Warren has called this novel the Southern version of *Death of a Salesman*. And yet there is mercy in Williams's often harsh world. Son's daughter, Laurel, emerges as a strong character near the end of the novel and obtains a modest reconciliation with her dying father. A sense of profound regret and loss permeates the ending of *Old Powder Man*.

In 1971, Williams published her third and most intimate novel, *The Wintering*. The book remains of abiding interest to readers of William Faulkner since in this heavily autobiographical roman a clef, Williams recounts the story of budding young writer, Amy Howard, and her love affair with a world-famous Southern writer, Jeffrey Almoner. Indeed, it was William Faulkner no less who had at one point suggested to his protegé that she write a novel about their relationship. Faulkner even suggested the name of Almoner for his own fictional persona. As a matter of fact, Amy Howard is Williams at age twenty, and Jeff Almoner is Faulkner at fifty-one, when he had already passed his peak as a creative artist.

Much of *The Wintering* is heavily autobiographical right on down to the letters and conversations taken down verbatim between Williams and Faulkner. Of course, there are clearly fictitious inventions, such as Amy's life and romance in Greenwich Village with a failed artist and Almoner's sympathetic Swiss-born wife, Inga. Normally a writer of straightforward fiction, Williams is at her most experimental in this novel with her frequent use of letters (Faulkner had recommended that Williams write an epistolary novel), juxtaposition of time and space, and her use of the interior monologue to describe the inner states of her characters. Nonetheless, it remains true that the novel's most realized and believable character is not Jeff Almoner/William Faulkner but Amy Howard/Williams. Following several unsatisfactory love affairs with young men her own age, Amy returns to Jeff Almoner's warm love only to find him dead from a heart attack. In dying, Almoner gives Amy a final parting gift, since her grief for him releases her pent-up emotions and inhibitions that prevent her from writing. As we leave Amy at the conclusion of *The Wintering*, we see her sitting by a window completing her first novel, which Jeff Almoner's New York literary agent plans to have published.

In her fourth novel, *Country Woman*, Williams tackles the theme of a middle-class, middle-aged Southern woman's self-awakening during the turbulent civil rights movement era when Mississippi was forcibly integrated by the Federal government. The author intends a close parallel between black student James Meredith's efforts to break through the racial barriers of the University of Mississippi and those of Allie McCall's struggle to achieve an authentic personhood. Allie is led by her creator to question all the received ideas about class, race, and traditional female roles under which she was raised in the Old South. Stagnating in a dreary marriage to her husband Tate and constantly at the beck and call of her selfish elderly father, Allie finds renewed purpose in life by championing the cause of Elgie Hale, an escaped black convict unjustly accused of murdering Allie's rebellious mother

when Allie was a little girl. Allie achieves self-liberation by standing up for Elgie and by exposing a sadistic young killer who is the spoiled scion of a feared and wealthy local family. Despite some plot implausibilities, *Country Woman* is a fine achievement and shows Williams's continued skill in handling the inner psychology of her Southern women characters.

It is evident from her most recent novel, *Pay the Piper* (1988), that Williams's long-term expatriation from her Southern homeland has cost her dearly. The author has publicly admitted that she might have written far more if she had remained in the South, which alone stimulates her creative imagination. Despite its gripping psychological intensity, the novel fails to engage the reader wholly. *Pay the Piper* is the frightening story of expatriate Southerner Laurel Perry's disastrous marriage to Hal MacDonald, a psychopathic former convict and scion of an old Mississippi family, following Laurel's abandonment of her Northern husband in a vain attempt to recover her Southernness.

Williams's other existing book, *Pariah*, a collection of her short stories, reveal her close ties to the art of Eudora Welty. In some important ways, Williams's gifts as a writer is best suited to the short story form and it is to be regretted that she has not decided to pursue more seriously this genre so close to poetry. In this collection of stories, one sees Williams at her best with her evocative imagery of hot, languid summers in Mississippi, the drawling speech of country people so well-remembered, and her natural sympathy for the loneliness of human beings, whether male or female, black or white.

Novelist Anne Tyler especially admired the story "Jesse," which is the first-person narrative of a black sharecropper. Tyler regarded this work as a poetic masterpiece. In another remarkably sensitive short story, "No Love for the Lonely," an old maid and an old bachelor who have known each other all their lives attempt one last desperate time to reach out with love only to fail in loneliness and isolation.

Although seldom read today, Williams is a writer of genuine talent and possessor of a distinctive voice. She has the ability to conjure the sights, smells, and sounds of the world in which she grew up—that is Memphis and the hard scrabbled area around Arkabutla where her mother's people come from. Williams looks upon her flawed Mississippi world with a dispassionate eye. And yet her authorial gaze is never without deep empathy for her lonely, haunted characters hemmed in by the narrow constraints of their lives and who still hunger for love and community.

—Alphonse Vinh

WILLIAMS, John A.

Pseudonym: J. Dennis Gregory. **Born:** John Alfred Williams in Jackson, Mississippi, 5 December 1925. **Education:** Syracuse University, A.B. 1950. **Military Service:** Served in U.S. Navy,

1943-46. **Family:** Married Carolyn Clopton in 1947 (divorced); two sons; married Lorrain Isaac in 1965, one son. **Career:** Case worker for Onondaga County Welfare department, Syracuse, 1950-52; public relations department, Doug Johnson Associates, Syracuse, 1952-54, and Arthur P. Jacobs Company; staff member, CBS, Hollywood and New York, 1954-55; publicity director, Comet Press Books, New York, 1955-56; publisher and editor, *Negro Market Newsletter,* New York, 1956-57; assistant to the publisher, Abelard-Schuman, publishers, New York, 1957-58; director of information, American Committee on Africa, New York, 1958; European correspondent, *Ebony* and *Jet* magazines, 1958-59; announcer, WOV Radio, New York, 1959; contributing editor, *Herald Tribune Book Week,* 1963-65; Africa correspondent, *Newsweek,* New York, 1964-65; columnist, stringer, special assignment, and/or staff, various black newspapers, periodicals and news agencies, including the *National Leader, Progressive Herald, Age, Defender, Post-Standard, Tribune, Courier,* and the Associated Negro Press, 1965-66; narrator and co-producer of programs, National Education Television, 1965-66; interviewer for *Newsfront* program, 1968; lecturer in Afro-American literature, College of the Virgin Islands, summer 1968; lecturer in creative writing, City College of the City University of New York, 1968-69; guest writer, Sarah Lawrence College, Bronxville, New York, 1972-73; contributing editor, *American Journal,* 1972-74; regents lecturer, University of California, Santa Barbara, 1972; distinguished professor of English, LaGuardia Community College, City University of New York, 1973-75; contributing editor, *Politicks,* 1977; visiting professor, Boston University, Massachusetts, 1978-79; visiting professor of English, New York University, New York City, 1986-87; professor of English, 1979-1990, Paul Robeson Professor of English, 1990-93, Rutgers University; Member of editorial board, *Audience,* 1970-72; member of board of directors, *Journal of African Civilizations,* since 1980; member of board of directors, New York State Council on the Arts; member of board of directors, Rabinowitz Foundation; member of Coordinating Council of Literary Magazines, 1983-85, chair, 1984. **Awards:** American Academy grant, 1962; Syracuse University Outstanding Achievement award, 1970; National Endowment for the Arts grant, 1977; Before Columbus Foundation award, 1983. Litt.D.: Southeastern Massachusetts University, North Dartmouth, 1978. **Address:** 693 Forest Avenue, Teaneck, New Jersey 07666.

PUBLICATIONS

Novels

The Angry Ones. New York, Ace, 1960; as *One for New York,* Chatham, New Jersey, Chatham Bookseller, 1975.
Night Song. New York, Farrar Straus, 1961.
Sissie. New York, Farrar Straus, 1963; as *Journey out of Anger,* London, Eyre and Spottiswoode, 1968.
The Man Who Cried I Am. Boston, Little Brown, 1967.
sons of darkness, sons of light: A Novel of Some Probability. Boston, Little Brown, 1969.
Captain Blackman: A Novel. Garden City, New York, Doubleday, 1972.
Mothersill and the Foxes. New York, Doubleday, 1975.
The Junior Bachelor Society. New York, Doubleday, 1976.
!Click Song. Boston, Houghton Mifflin, 1982.
The Berhama Account. New York, New Horizon Press, 1985.
Jacob's Ladder. New York, Thunder's Mouth Press, 1987.

Other

Africa: Her History, Lands, and People. New York, Cooper Square, 1962.
The Protectors (on narcotics agents; as J. Dennis Gregory) with Harry J. Anslinger. New York, Farrar Straus, 1964.
This Is My Country, Too. New York, New American Library, 1964.
The Most Native of Sons: A Bibliography of Richard Wright. New York, Doubleday, 1970.
The King God Didn't Save: Reflections on the Life and Death of Martin Luther King, Jr. New York, Coward McCann, 1970.
Flashbacks: A Twenty-Year Diary of Article Writing. New York, Doubleday, 1973.
Minorities in the City. New York, Harper, 1975.
If I Stop I'll Die: The Comedy and Tragedy of Richard Pryor, with Dennis A. Williams. New York, Thunder's Mouth Press, 1991.
Ways In: Approaches to Reading and Writing about Literature, with Gilbert H. Muller. New York, McGraw-Hill, 1994.

Editor, *The Angry Black.* New York, Lancer, 1962.
Editor, *Beyond the Angry Black.* New York, Cooper Square, 1967.
Editor, with Charles F. Harris, *Amistad I and II,* 2 volumes. New York, Knopf, 1970-71.
Editor, with Gilbert H. Muller, *Introduction to Literature.* New York, McGraw-Hill, 1985; revised as *The McGraw-Hill Introduction to Literature,* 1995.
Editor, with Gilbert H. Muller, *Bridges: Literature across Cultures,* New York, McGraw-Hill, 1994.

*

Manuscript Collection: Syracuse University, New York; University of Rochester, New York.

Critical Studies: *The Evolution of a Black Writer: John A. Williams* by Earl Cash, New York, Third Press, 1974; "John A. Williams' *Sissie*" by Ralph Beckley, Sr., *MAWA Review,* June 1990.

Media Adaptations: *Sweet Love, Bitter,* adapted from the novel *Night Song,* 1967.

*   *   *

John A. Williams, one of the most prolific African American writers of the twentieth century, remains best known for the ten novels so vibrantly and indelibly imprinted by his life experiences, including *The Man Who Cried I Am, Captain Blackman,* and *!Click Song.* This frequently autobiographical fiction often alludes to or thematically incorporates issues linked to the impact of twentieth-century publishers' biases on African American writers. And though African American writers and professors populate Williams's fiction, they represent only one of several autobiographical components in his work.

In settings closely resembling the Syracuse of his childhood, Willaims recreates racist incidents that too often circumscribed his Navy, college and professional careers, details African American contributions to the U.S. military, interweaves political conspiracies, and depicts the adventures of African American expatriates in Europe and Africa in his novels in much the same way that they have punctuated Williams's life.

Williams has excelled as a chronicler of the dreams, pathos and frustrations of his peers, displayed in his ability to simultaneously reveal both the heterogeneity of the African American community and the universality of oppression's pain.

Though born in his parents' home in Jackson, Mississippi, the oldest of John Henry and Ola Williams's two girls and two boys, Williams was reared and educated in the northern city of Syracuse, New York. In 1943, during the course of World War II, Williams interrupted his high school education to join the Navy. Following an honorable discharge in 1946, Williams returned to his hometown, married, and enrolled at Syracuse University. Upon graduating in 1950, he pursued his studies in the graduate school at Syracuse. By now the father of two sons, he held jobs that ran the gamut from foundry work to clerking in a supermarket.

In this regard, Williams was typical of his college-educated peers, whose career aspirations were often constrained by segregation and discrimination. In his book entitled *John A. Williams,* Earl Cash recalls an interview in which Williams observed that "Loblaw's Supermarket on Adams Street . . . must have had the most intellectual group of clerks in the city. They were trying to do something, I suppose, democratic. But all of the black people there had at least a bachelor's degree and some had master's." Subsequent jobs included social work and insurance sales. Then, in 1954, after his marriage fell apart, Williams moved to Los Angeles. A year of job hunting resulted in a dead-end insurance sales position, and a disillusioned Williams departed for home.

His return to New York marked the beginning of a haphazard, often frustrating, and frequently impoverished career as a writer. Free-lance articles, magazine assignments, stints on Madison Avenue, and other writing jobs provided an erratic income during the early years. In the *Flashbacks* essay "Career by Accident," Williams recalls that when *The Angry Ones* was accepted for publication, he had vowed to quit writing if he couldn't sell that third draft. By the time the book was published, his advance had long since been spent. Then, in the space of a week, he contracted for three books, two novels, and a nonfiction work. These events marked the advent of his since uninterrupted commercial success.

By 1961, in addition to numerous articles and short stories, Williams had published two novels, and his first nonfiction volume, *Africa: Her History, Lands, and People,* was nearing completion. For the rest of the decade, while juggling a schedule that included extensive traveling, lecturing, and writing in several genres, Williams managed to average at least one major book per year.

It was during this period that Williams became embroiled in an unforgettable controversy. After he was named 1961 recipient of the prestigious American Academy of Arts and Letters fellowship to Rome, Williams's award was mysteriously withdrawn. His suspicion that racial discrimination was the culprit was confirmed when Alan Dugan, the poet who eventually received the award, made a courageous public disclosure affirming Williams's hunch. In the wake of the ensuing scandal, the American Academy prize for literature was discontinued for a time. Although this was a painful and disheartening experience, Williams used the incident in *The Man Who Cried I Am.* Like many other indignities, this became grist for the novelist's mill.

This autobiographical element of Williams's fiction is quite evident in his first novel, which opens as thirty-year-old publicist Stephen Hill, a World War II veteran who was the first in his family to attend college, relocates from Los Angeles to New York. The insensitivity and pandering to stereotypes exhibited by the unethical vanity press editor for whom Hill works are based upon Williams's firsthand experience. Published in 1960, and originally titled *One for New York,* the book was released as *The Angry Ones* when the publisher insisted that "anger" would sell more books. Williams, eager to have a novel published, reluctantly agreed to the change.

Night Song probes the elusive world of the black jazz musicians whose lives and songs are both in and of the night. The narrative evolves around three virtually co-equal protagonists. David Hillary, an unemployed alcoholic professor, is haunted by his possible responsibility for the auto accident that killed his wife. As the book opens, Hillary meets Eagle, a drug-addicted musical genius whose life is loosely patterned after that of Charlie "Yardbird" Parker, in a pawnshop. In pawning a wedding band and saxophone, respectively, each has metaphorically "sold himself to the devil." They head downtown—seeking oblivion in the "night" of New York's jazz scene—on a journey akin to Dante's. Whereas Eagle ultimately rescues Hillary, it is Keel Robinson, the Harvard seminary-trained former preacher, who acts as Eagle's "guardian angel." As owner of a coffee house catering to jazz musicians, this dropout from both Christianity and Islam serves as foil to both Hillary and Eagle.

Sissie, Big Ralph, Ralph, Jr., and Iris Joplin, the primary characters of *Sissie,* are survivors. It is through their survival strategies that Williams deconstructs the era's popular myths regarding black families. The kinship, strength, hope and love evidenced in this story are Williams's tribute to his own family. Based in part upon the Williamses of Syracuse, these characters reappear (individually and/or collectively) in *The Man Who Cried I Am, The Junior Bachelor Society,* and *!Click Song.* For Williams, the Joplins become an archetypal domestic grouping.

Between 1960 and 1963, Williams published the trilogy of *The Angry Ones, Night Song,* and *Sissie.* Each traced the problems faced by blacks in a white society. The world of publishing explored in *The Angry Ones,* the New York jazz scene of *Night Song,* and the pain and celebration of *Sissie*'s Joplin family were initially considered part of a canon of protest writing framed by moral outcry and reformist solutions. However, many later critics noted that Williams's educated, middle-class characters embraced the same post-war expectations as the African American populace of the time, who had faith in the promises of both integration and assimilation. Although each book highlights ways that institutionalized racism limits the characters' educational, employment, and housing prospects, those setbacks are repeatedly contrasted to an inner fortitude that seemingly strengthens them. With this referent, Stephen Hill's sense of hope after quitting the vanity press job can be interpreted as in accord with the early 1960s spirit of optimism. Nonetheless, the fact remains that the nonviolent, apolitical, often ahistorical characters of Williams's early novels share dreams of success and fulfillment that are repeatedly thwarted. In this regard, their aspirations and experiences mirror those of the working and middle-class blacks of Williams's world.

Not surprisingly, as the apocalyptic events of the late 1960s radically altered the worldview and politics of many African Americans, the themes of Williams's fiction also changed. The militancy and black nationalism of the era, refracted by Williams's military service and travels in the American South, Europe, and Africa, end up shaping Williams's second trilogy, *The Man Who Cried I Am*, *sons of darkness, sons of light,* and *Captain Blackman,* in much the same way that the "meism" of the late 1970s and early 1980s would place its imprint upon *Mothersill and the Foxes, The Junior Bachelor Society,* and *!Click Song.*

Williams's second trilogy has been referred to as the "Armageddon" novels. The disenchantment with racial progress, the political overtones, and the apocalyptic conclusions of these works brought Williams unprecedented international fame and commercial success. The adventures of expatriate writers Max and Harry, their discovery of the U.S. government's genocidal "King Alfred Plan," *sons of darkness, sons of light*'s conspirators, and Abraham Blackman's dreamed participation in every U.S. military initiative exemplify the shift in tone and narrative that Bernard Bell, in *The Afro-American Novel and Its Tradition,* refers to as "a shift from an appeal to white conscience to black consciousness."

Mothersill and the Foxes, with its search for rural peace, marks the beginning of a third phase, in which Williams rejects the political urgency of his 1960s and 1970s novels for more introspective themes. In *The Junior Bachelor Society,* we discover a group of nine men in their late forties returning to Central City for the seventieth birthday of their high school coach. Among this group of troubled men seeking reaffirmation is Ralph Joplin, Jr., now a successful playwright.

Ultimately, *The Junior Bachelor Society* becomes one of celebration, as the bachelors discover that in spite of the hardships they've endured, there's still reason to hope. In *!Click Song,* Williams reverts to a plot involving the careers of two writers, as he had in *The Man Who Cried I Am.* Cato Douglass is the black writer whose experiences the author contrasts to those of his Jewish classmate Paul Cummings. In a highly autobiographical work, Williams uses Cato Douglass as the prism through which the lives of all black artists can be seen. Douglass, unable to overcome the racism of the publishing industry, is in many ways Williams's reminder to his readers that in the thirty years since his portrayal of Stephen Hill, little had changed.

In *Jacob's Ladder,* Williams returns to two favorite topics—Africa and politics. Set in the pre-Vietnam era, this novel of international intrigue finds Chuma Fasseke, president of a small fictitious African nation, trying to block U.S. intervention while he finishes a nuclear reactor. The ensuing diplomatic negotiations are led by the newly appointed U.S. ambassador, a childhood friend of Fasseke's named Jake Henry, who ultimately realizes that the CIA has lied to him and plans to destroy the nuclear reactor and assassinate his friend. By returning to the political thriller format that brought him such success during the 1970s, Williams, perpetual chronicler of his times, also affirms both the mainstream American 1980s shift in focus from "me" to "we" and the renewed black American interest in Africa.

Williams's writings, in addition to their notable artistic and literary merit, perhaps offer the clearest window into the lives of highly educated twentieth-century African Americans. Williams ultimately shows that for this group, as for the African American community as a whole, the "American Dream" has remained elusive.

—Gloria H. Dickinson

WILLIAMS, Miller

Born: Hoxie, Arkansas, 8 April 1930. **Education:** Arkansas State College, Conway, B.S. in biology 1951; University of Arkansas, Fayetteville, M.S. in zoology 1952. **Family:** Married Lucille Day in 1951 (divorced); married Rebecca Jordan Hall in 1969, two daughters and one son. **Career:** Biology instructor, McNeese State College, Lake Charles, Louisiana, and Millsaps College, Jackson, Mississippi; instructor, 1962-63, and assistant professor of English, 1964-66, Louisiana State University; associate professor of English, Loyola University, New Orleans, 1966-70; Fulbright professor of American studies, National University of Mexico, 1970; co-director, graduate program in creative writing, 1970-84, associate professor, 1971-73, since 1973 professor of English and since 1978 chair of the comparative literature program, University of Arkansas; visiting professor, University of Chile, Santiago, 1963-64; poetry editor, Louisiana State University Press, 1966-68; editor, *New Orleans Review,* 1968-69; since 1978, contributing editor, *Translation Review,* Richardson, Texas; since 1980, director, University of Arkansas Press; president, American Literary Translators Association, 1979-81. **Awards:** Henry Bellaman award, 1957; Breadloaf Writers Conference fellowship, 1961; Amy Lowell traveling scholarship, 1963; Arts Fund award, 1973; American Academy in Rome fellowship 1976; H.H.D., Lander College, Greenwood, South Carolina 1983; Poets' Prize, 1991, for *Living on the Surface*; Charity Randall citation for contribution to poetry as a spoken art; John William Corrington award for literary excellence. **Address:** Department of English, University of Arkansas, Fayetteville, Arkansas 72701.

PUBLICATIONS

Poetry Collections

A Circle of Stone. Baton Rouge, Louisiana State University Press, 1964.
Recital (bilingual edition). Valparaiso, Chile, Ediciones Océano, 1964.
So Long at the Fair. New York, Dutton, 1968.
The Only World There Is. New York, Dutton, 1971.
Halfway From Hoxie: New and Selected Poems. New York, Dutton, 1973.
Why God Permits Evil: New Poems. Baton Rouge, Louisiana State University Press, 1977.
Distractions. Baton Rouge, Louisiana State University Press, 1981.
The Boys on Their Bony Mules. Baton Rouge, Louisiana State University Press, 1983.
Imperfect Love. Baton Rouge, Louisiana State University Press, 1986.
Living on the Surface: New and Selected Poems. Baton Rouge, Louisiana State University Press, 1989.

Adjusting to the Light. Columbia, University of Missouri Press, 1992.

Points of Departure. Champaign, University of Illinois Press, 1995.

The Ways We Touch. Champaign, University of Illinois Press, 1997.

Other

The Poetry of John Crowe Ransom. New Brunswick, New Jersey, Rutgers University Press, 1972.

Railroad: Trains and Train People in American Culture, with James A. McPherson. New York, Random House, 1976.

Patterns of Poetry: An Encyclopedia of Forms. Baton Rouge, Louisiana State University Press, 1986.

Editor, with John William Corrington, *Southern Writing in the Sixties: Fiction and Poetry.* Baton Rouge, Louisiana State University Press, 2 vols., 1966-67.

Editor, *Chile: An Anthology of New Writing.* Kent, Ohio, Kent State University Press, 1968.

Editor, *The Achievement of John Ciardi: A Comprehensive Selection of His Poems with a Critical Introduction.* Chicago, Scott Foresman, 1969.

Editor, *Contemporary Poetry in America.* New York, Random House, 1973.

Editor, with John Ciardi. *How Does a Poem Mean?,* revised edition. Boston, Houghton Mifflin, 1975.

Editor, *A Roman Collection: Stories, Poems, and Other Good Pieces by the Writing Residents of the American Academy in Rome.* Columbia, University of Missouri Press, 1980.

Editor, *Ozark, Ozark: A Hillside Reader.* Columbia, University of Missouri Press, 1981.

Translator, *Poems and Antipoems,* by Nicanor Parra. New York, New Directions, 1967.

Translator, *Emergency Poems,* by Nicanor Parra. New York, New Directions, 1972.

Translator, *Sonnets of Giuseppe Belli.* Baton Rouge, Louisiana State University Press, 1981.

*

Manuscript Collection: Special Collections, University of Arkansas Library, Fayetteville.

Critical Studies: "About Miller Williams" by James Whitehead, in *Dickinson Review* (North Dakota), Spring 1973; "Translating the Dialect: Miller Williams' Romanesco" by John DuVal, in *Translation Review* (Richardson, Texas), 1990; *Miller Williams and the Poetry of the Particular* edited by Michael Burns, Columbia, University of Missouri Press, 1991.

Miller Williams comments:

I'm not sure that one ought to discuss one's poetry in public; it seems somehow not quite decent, and besides, almost anyone will have a better perspective on a body of poems than the poet. It may mean something if I say that I distrust the Romantic Vision and dislike the Classical. Beyond this, the poems are there to be read, for what they have to say and how they say it.

*   *   *

Miller Williams is a poet of the American small town, its streets and neighborhoods, its bus stations and shabby factories. Simple logic reveals, however, that a town ultimately takes its character from the character of its people. Williams has learned this lesson early and learned it well, for a strength throughout his career has been his adeptness at portraiture. In the introduction to Williams's first book of poems, *A Circle of Stone,* Howard Nemerov links him to the character-portrait tradition of Edgar Lee Masters, and one may as well add to that tradition those of Edwin Arlington Robinson and John Crowe Ransom. Where Williams is most successful at these portraits, he achieves a balance between the subtle irony of Masters or Ransom and the more blatant irony of Robinson. "On the Death of a Middle Aged Man," perhaps Williams's best-known early poem, strikes such a balance.

A reader learns quickly of the character's unambiguous feeling toward his unambiguous name:

> Beverly
> who wished his mother wanting a girl again
> had called him something at best ambiguous
> like Francis or Marion

Williams achieves subtle irony, though, in giving ambiguity a large role in the poem, in the question, for example, of whether the sexual encounters of Beverly's sweetheart, Helen, really "counted" since they were with her older brother and her minister. Ambiguity enriches the poem, too, in Williams's statement that Beverly "went for eleven years to the Packard plant/and bent to Helen who punched the proper holes/how many bodies." This bending to connotes both a romantic gesture, bowing, and a sexual one, bending toward or bending over someone in the act of lovemaking. Williams retains this ambiguity, in his *Halfway from Hoxie: New and Selected Poems,* when he changes "bent to" to "turn for," the act of turning suggestive again both of a romantic gesture and a sexual one, as in "turning a trick."

Williams's work calls to mind—in addition to Masters, Robinson, and Ransom—such Latin American surrealists as Nicanor Parra, whose poems Williams translated and published as *Emergency Poems.* Taking ideas and images to their zany extremes seems a surrealist method for which Williams has a flair. "I Got Out of the House for the First Time," "Toast to Floyd Collins," and "And Then," all new poems in *Halfway from Hoxie,* use repetition to create a sense of lost equilibrium and absurdity, with "And Then" conveying a more serious tone than the first two:

> Your toothbrush won't remember your mouth
> Your shoes won't remember your feet
>
> Your wife one good morning
> will remember your weight
> will feel unfaithful
> throwing the toothbrush away
> dropping the shoes in the Salvation Army box
> will set your picture in the living room
>
> someone wearing a coat you would not have worn
> will ask was that your husband
> she will say yes

Williams's stylistic range encompasses an ornate but energetic formalism, a flat, prosaic free verse and a more sharply hewn free verse. In "Leaving New York in the Penn Central to Metuchen" (*Halfway from Hoxie*), Williams uses alliteration in his rhymed couplets to such a degree that it might be called overused if the lines did not evoke so well the motion of a subway train: "Go buck, go hiss and the bright balled works/tremble and turn. Go clank and the car jerks."

More than a handful of poems, however, leave behind rhythm when they leave behind rhyme. "Lying," from *Distractions,* lacks a vitality which a stronger sense of music would give it. The casualness of the lines does approach the mood of someone passing time, but one cannot help but feel that the language itself lacks energy:

> Standing beside a library in Brooklyn
> I wait for my ride to come. I turn some pages.
> A man puts his foot on a fire hydrant
> and bends to tie his shoe. I see a gun.

Yet Williams can, as "And Then" illustrated above, shape his free verse to musical ends, avoiding the prosaic and giving that free verse an almost incantatory power.

Two of Williams's finest poems, both from *Distractions,* depart from his typical sardonic tone. In "Rebecca, for Whom Nothing Has Been Written Page after Page," Williams addresses a granddaughter and tries to explain that, despite his esteem for language, language cannot do justice to a description of her. This theme is not new, yet Williams's tone succeeds in establishing an intimacy rare in his own work and a degree of intimacy rare in the work of many other poets. After acknowledging the serviceability of language, Williams writes elegiacally of its limitations:

> What phrase explains, what simile can guess
> a daughter's daughter? We half know who you are,
> moment by moment, remembering what you were
> as you grow past, becoming by quick revisions
> an image in the door.

The sardonic tone is gone, too, in "Evening: A Studio in Rome," and while it would be hard to prove a cause-and-effect relationship, this change in tone seems to allow Williams to write movingly of a city just as he can write movingly of small towns. This meditative poem, in contrast to some of his others, is more luxurious, more willing to take its time in fleshing out the moment:

> The window here is hung in the west wall.
> It lays on the opposite wall a square of light.
> Sliced by the lopsided slats of the broken blind,
> the light hangs like a painting. Now, and now,
> the shadow of a swallow shoots across it.

One recognizes Williams's deftness with alliteration, here the "sw" in "swallow" breaking up nicely the "sh" in "shadow" and in "shoots." What is new, however, is the acute perception of the swallow's shadow on the wall: "Now, and now." Such a patience also provides the poet with his final passage, a passage which seems to indicate that Williams's good poems have gotten better:

> This minute Rome is dark
> as only Rome is dark, as if somebody
> could go out reaching toward it, and find no Rome.

—Martin McGovern

WILLIAMSON, Greg

Born: Greg Wesley Williamson in Columbus, Ohio, 26 June 1964. **Education:** Vanderbilt University, Nashville, Tennessee, B.A. 1986; University of Wisconsin—Madison, M.A. 1987; Johns Hopkins University, Baltimore, Maryland, M.A. 1989. **Family:** Married Karen Allyson Bane in 1998. **Career:** Teaching fellow, 1988, lecturer, 1989-98, visiting professor, 1998, Johns Hopkins University. **Awards:** Nathan Haskell Dole Prize for poetry, *The Lyric*, 1991; Nicholas Roerich Poetry Prize, Story Line Press, 1994; John Atherton Fellowship in Poetry, Breadloaf Writers' Conference, 1996.

PUBLICATIONS

Poetry Collection

The Silent Partner. Brownsville, Story Line Press, 1995

Uncollected Poems

"Ozymandias," "The Doorman at the End of the Couch," "Quick Stop Lickety Split Mart," in *Poultry: A Magazine of Voice.*
"Myopia," in *Parnassus Literary Journal*, Spring, 1991.
"Club Charon," "Art and Politics at the Museum of Public Figures," The State of the Art," "On the Death of a Most Impressive Fellow Graduate Student," "On a Poem that Almost Came," "Centerfold Calendars," in *The Epigrammatist.*
"For Immediate Release," in *The Vanderbilt Review*, Spring, 1991.
"Taking Time Apart," in *Nebo: A Literary Journal.*
"Below the Bridge," in *Southern Poetry Review*, Spring, 1991.
"Home for a Day," in *The Lyric,* Summer, 1991.
"Teaching the Common Causes," in *Sou'wester*, Summer, 1991.
"Piano Lessons," in *America.*
"An Economic Proposal," in *New Republic*, October 5, 1992.
"To His Love," in *Sparrow*, Fall, 1994.
"A Form of Fulfillment," in *The New Criterion*, May, 1993.
"A Dream Song," in *Partisan Review*, Spring, 1995.
"Up in the Air," in *Paris Review*, Spring, 1995.
"The Top Priority," in *Story*, Summer, 1996
"A Photograph I Saw of a Father and Son," in *Agni,* 1996.
"Nervous Systems," in *Southwest Review*, Winter, 1998.
"The Dark Days," in *Yale Review*, Winter, 1998.

Anthologized Poems

"Walter Parmer," "The Counterfeiter," Waterfall," "Annual Returns." In *Rebel Angel: 25 Poets of the New Formalism* edited by Mark Jarman and David Mason. Brownsville, Story Line Press, 1996.

"The Dark Days." In *The Best American Poetry, 1998* edited by John Hollander. New York, Scribner, 1998.

* * *

Writing about Greg Williamson's first book in the *Yale Review*, critic Willard Spiegelman celebrates him as heir to the legacy of Howard Nemerov. In his praise for *The Silent Partner*, Spiegelman remarks that Williamson, like Nemerov, has "a charming, unpretentious bookishness, a wit that is always gentle, never arch, an interest in 'reading' the various alphabets of the world . . . ."

A native of Nashville, Williamson attended Vanderbilt University where he graduated with honors in 1986. As an undergraduate he studied with the poets Donald Davie and Mark Jarman. He took an M.A. in English from The University of Wisconsin in 1987, then ultimately landed, in the fall of 1988, in the Writing Seminars at Johns Hopkins University, where he pursued a second M.A., and studied, along the way, with Hugh Kenner, John Irwin, Wyatt Prunty and Peter Sacks. It was during that year, in fact, that Willamson first met Howard Nemerov and John Hollander, too.

Given the list of poets and critics in Greg Williamson's past—arguably some of the most profound minds of the late twentieth century in American letters—it should be no surprise that his poetry mirrors the intelligence and complexities of those with whom he studied. Consider the formal and thematic dexterity of the companion pieces, "Narcissus . . . And Echo." On facing pages in the book, "Narcissus . . ." on the left-hand side, ". . . And Echo" on the right, the poems are of equal length, (four four-line stanzas), rhymed abba. The poet has appropriately rhymed the end words of Narcissus with the corresponding end words of Echo.

Narcissus, who was never very wise,
Observed a water-spirit in the pond
And grew enamored of the comely blonde
Who matched his gaze and filled his shallow eyes.
("Narcissus . . .")

Echo, who tricked a queen with her replies,
Received a sentence only to respond
And gradually became a vagabond,
A voice, unable to extemporize.
(". . . And Echo")

Both poems end with the same question posed. "Who are you?" Narcissus asks his lovely self; "Who are you?" Echo asks Narcissus.

It is this notion of repetition and replication that captivates Greg Williamson's poetry. Narcissus and Echo serve his purpose well, to question, as he does frequently in his poems, the relationship between art and the world it strives to recreate. While both characters suffer their individual plights—Narcissus, his self-obsession, Echo, her arrogance—both are also trapped in mimetic life sentences, and serve as figures in tandem, for the very struggles and limitations of the artist. In an age when poetry is so often wrought with the singular and private themes of the individual poet, Williamson reminds us that the wonderful (and artful) thing about poetry is that it has the capacity, perhaps even the responsibility, to work with that which is both layered and illusive.

Many of Williamson's poems explore the multiple ways which we see or, to borrow Willard Spiegleman's phrase, "read" the world in which we live. In "Eye Strain," a man visits the eye doctor only to discover his need for prescription glasses. "How long, / he asked himself, had he been seeing wrong / the world?" Williamson writes. In "Outbound," a poem about riding backwards on a train, the speaker states, "Whatever comes to view / Corrects the view." Heraclitus haunts this poetry, which so often concerns itself with the tantalizing pursuit of knowledge and definition, particularly "Waterfall":

In still transparency, the water pools
High in a mountain stream, then spills
Over the lip and in a sheet cascades
Across the shoal obeying hidden rules . . .

The poem ultimately turns the figure of the waterfall to words:

So too with language, so even with this verse.
From a pool of syllables, words hover
With rich potential, then spill across the lip
And riffle down the page, for better or worse
Making their chancy trip . . .

In his letter to John Taylor, Keats wrote his famous (and often misappropriated) declaration that "if Poetry comes not as naturally as the Leaves to a tree it had better not come at all." Keats was not suggesting, as some contemporary poets might presume, that the writing of poetry should be effortless and breezy, but rather that it should appear to be so—to seem unforced and organic. In his poem "The Counterfeiter," Williamson examines the paradox the truly gifted counterfeiter faces, and uses him as a figure for the poet as well. Both must make their works of art without calling attention to themselves; both "must account for every tiny line." And if each has done his job well, his hand will remain unnoticed in the end, as larcenist and poet alike must

profit by anonymity,
But deep regret competes with honest pride:
To labor toward complete obscurity
And treasure a craft that will efface [their] will,
Render his name unknown and all [their] skill
Unrecognized, long after [they have] died.

In the era of the New Formalism, Williamson distinguishes himself as one of the premier practitioners of rhyme and meter. He calls to mind that statement of Keats, and reminds us that one must often sweat and struggle to give the appearance of effortlessness.

—Daniel Anderson

WILLINGHAM, Calder

Born: Calder Baynard Willingham, Jr. in Atlanta, Georgia, 23 December 1922. **Education:** The Citadel, 1940-41; University of

Virginia, 1941-43. **Family:** Married Helene Rothenberg, 1945; one child; married Jane Marie Bennett, 1953; five children. **Award:** British Film Academy Award, best screenplay, 1969, for *The Graduate*. **Died:** In 1995.

PUBLICATIONS

Novels

End as a Man. New York, Vanguard, 1947.
Geraldine Bradshaw. New York, Vanguard, 1950.
Reach to the Stars. New York, Vanguard, 1951.
The Gates of Hell. New York, Vanguard, 1951.
Natural Child. New York, Dial, 1952.
To Eat a Peach. New York, Dial, 1955.
Eternal Fire. New York, Vanguard, 1963.
Providence Island. New York, Vanguard, 1969.
Rambling Rose. New York, Delacorte, 1972.
The Big Nickel. New York, Dial, 1975.

Screenplays

The Strange One (based on his novel *End as a Man*). Columbia, 1957.
Paths of Glory (based on the novel of the same title by Humphrey Cobb), with Stanley Kubrick and Tim Thompson. United Artists, 1957.
The Vikings. United Artists, 1958.
One-Eyed Jacks. Paramount, 1961.
The Graduate (based on the novel of the same title by Charles Webb), with Buck Henry. Embassy Pictures, 1967.
Little Big Man (based on the novel of the same title by Thomas Berger). CBS Films, 1970.
Thieves Like Us. United Artists, 1973.
Rambling Rose (adapted from his novel). Carolco Pictures, 1991.

*   *   *

Atlanta-born Calder Willingham wrote novels, which alternated between autobiographic examinations of Southern life and satires of literary and social customs, as well as screenplays for several critically acclaimed films, including *The Graduate, Paths of Glory, One-Eyed Jacks*, and *Little Big Man*. Three of his novels feature the protagonist Dick Davenport, a fictional rendering of Willingham himself, who recounts many of the author's autobiographical experiences. Two of his other novels, *End As a Man* and *Rambling Rose*, also integrate Willingham's personal experiences in, respectively, their depiction of life in a military academy and as a young boy's sexual awakening.

While most of his film work was adapted from other mediums or written as collaborative efforts, Willingham won critical respect for his dialogue and social commentary, particularly for his screenplays for Stanley Kubrick's *Paths of Glory*, Mike Nichol's *The Graduate,* and Arthur Penn's *Little Big Man*.

Willingham was educated at The Citadel (1940-41), which is a model for the Academy in *End As a Man* (1947). Championed by bestselling author James T. Farrell as a permanent contribution to American literature, the novel gained public and critical notoriety, as well as two overturned obscenity charges, for its de-

piction of such adolescent preoccupations as bodily functions, sex, and the use of profanity, as well as a prominent character's homosexuality. The attention assisted the novel's advancement to bestseller status, while Willingham's adeptness at capturing Southern dialects, dialogue and setting won an even larger audience.

Willingham adapted *End As a Many* as a stage play, and again for the film *The Strange One*. The novel's title derives from the Academy's credo that its cadets live and die honorably as soldiers, but is used ironically by Willingham to illustrate that military training is dehumanizing. For example, the commanding officer's goal of his young charges becoming gentlemen is undermined by the Academy's encouragement of sadistic behavior. In such an environment, honor exists insofar as cadets guard their own self-interests by betraying one another to gain their superiors's approval.

The autobiographical aspect of Willingham's writing is also evident in his next two novels, *Geraldine Bradshaw* (1950) and *Reach to the Stars* (1951). Willingham's father was a hotel manager, an occupation that gave his son had ample material to draw from in creating characters. Featuring a well-read, aspiring writer and slightly pretentious bellhop named Dick Davenport, the two novels develop and challenge Davenport's preconceived notions that people are as they appear. In *Geraldine Bradshaw*, for example, Davenport attempts to seduce the title character whose notion of reality is distorted by romance and true-confession magazines. In *Reach to the Stars*, Davenport moves from the Chicago setting of *Geraldine Bradshaw* to California, where he works in a hotel populated by celebrities in the film industry. Willingham returned to his Dick Davenport protagonist for his last novel, *The Big Nickel* (1975): the title infers the vast success enjoyed by Davenport upon the publication of his own inaugural novel. *The Big Nickel* includes many characters with such real-life inspirations as Farrell and Norman Mailer.

Rambling Rose (1972) is another Willingham novel in the autobiographical mode. Set during the Great Depression in the rural South, the novel concerns the title character's influence on the middle-class family with whom she comes to stay. Narrated by a grown man reminiscing about his first sexual experiences at the age of thirteen, the novel recounts Rose's personal history of abuse and sexual promiscuity and her ability to remain unhardened by her experiences. The novel was adapted into a successful film 1991 film.

Willingham's talents with satire and parody are evident in *Natural Child* (1952), *To Eat a Peach* (1955), and *Eternal Fire* (1963). *Natural Child* concerns two male New York intellectuals and their respective relationships with two young women who have more provincial backgrounds. Willingham uses the novel to lampoon bohemians whose views on art and literature are naive, ill-informed, and pretentious. The title of *To Eat a Peach* is taken from T. S. Eliot's "Love Song of J. Alfred Prufrock" and relates to Prufrock's intellectual and emotional paralysis. The novel's protagonists are similiarly paralyzed by their tenuous grasp of human nature while working at a posh summer camp during World War II.

In *Eternal Fire*, Willingham satirizes the bizarre and fanciful elements as well as the overwrought prose style of many novels classified as Southern Gothic. Containing an abundance of sex, incest, murder, miscegenation, suicide, and voyeurism, *Eternal Fire* concerns a judge's efforts to thwart the romance and marriage of a young man and an unworldy, virginal schoolteacher. The judge employs a mulatto to seduce the schoolteacher, which triggers an unlikely chain of events. Hypocrisy is also evident in *Providence Island* (1969), where Willingham's protanonist is a television executive who takes a personal stand against advertisers while engaging in abundant sexual experiences and use of illicit substances.

Among Willingham's several well-known and highly regarded screenplays is *The Graduate*, which he co-wrote with Buck Henry. The film depicts the upper-class wealthy as immoral, manipulative, and unethical. By contrast, the protagonist, Benjamin Braddock, is a symbol of hope for the younger generation when he abandons the superfical life of the wealthy to pursue true love with the beautiful daughter of an alcoholic older woman who pursues him. Willingham again blended comic elements with social consciousness in his screenplay for *Little Big Man*, a film tracing the historical treatment of American Indians from the perspective of a white centenarian raised by Indians who killed his parents in an attack on their wagon train. Willingham adapted Humphrey Cobb's World War I novel *Paths of Glory* for Stanley Kubrick's classic anti-war film of the same title, and he later worked with Kubrick on *One-Eyed Jacks*, a film eventually completed by the film's star, Marlon Brando, when Kubrick abandoned the project.

Willingham had periods of notoriety and obscurity during his career and was occasionally lambasted by critics who condemned his fiction's candid, irreverent, and sometimes graphic language and depictions of sex. He defended himself on one occasion by writing, "The charge made by some that I am 'a verbose smut writer' and that my work is 'pornographic' amazes me. I see in my writing virtually none of the sadism of pornography or the nasty and jejune neuroticism of smut. On the contrary, the erotic power of my writing seems to me to derive from love and respect for humanity's better half. My best characters by no coincidence are girls and women. This is a cheap, cowardly, and lying criticism. These people fear the erotic for reasons of their own. Beyond such disgusting cowardice, they reflect and express the spiritual sickness of our time." Such defenses, though worth recalling when reading or watching Willingham's work, are not required of a writer so greatly praised by James M. Cain in the 1940s and Jack Kroll in the 1970s. Kroll, writing in *Newsweek,* called Willingham, "perhaps the outstanding talent of that generation" (of authors that included Norman Mailer, William Styron, and James Jones), and praised him as "the most original, the real, although perhaps subtlest, innovator, and the one writer who has achieved what used to be called mastery over the craft of his art."

—Bruce Walker

WILSON, Charles Reagan

Born: Nashville, Tennessee, 2 February 1948. **Education:** University of Texas, El Paso, B.A. 1970, M.A. 1972; University of Texas, Austin, Ph.D. 1977. **Family:** Married Marie Antoon. **Career:** Professor of history and Southern Studies, co-founder of Center for the Study of Southern Culture, University of Mississippi, 1981-present; director, Center for the Study of Southern

Culture, since 1998; also taught at the University of Wurtzberg, Wurtzberg, Germany, Texas Tech University, and University of Texas, El Paso.

PUBLICATIONS

Nonfiction

Baptized in Blood: The Religion of the Lost Cause, 1885-1920. Athens, University of Georgia Press, 1980.
Judgment and Grace in Dixie: Southern Faiths from Faulkner to Elvis. Athens, University of Georgia Press, 1995.

Others

Editor, *Religion in the South: Essays.* Jackson, University Press of Mississippi, 1985.
Editor with William Ferris, *The Encyclopedia of Southern Culture.* Chapel Hill, University of North Carolina Press, 1989.
Editor with Clyde H. Smith, *Mississippi: The State.* Jackson, Fort Church Publishers, 1991.
Editor, *The New Regionalism: Essays and Commentaries.* Jackson, University Press of Mississippi, 1998.

Author of foreword, *Sacred Space: Photographs from the Mississippi Delta* by Tom Rankin. Jackson, University Press of Mississippi, 1993.
Author of foreword, *Smile Pretty and Say Jesus: The Last Great Days of PTL* by James Hunter. Athens, University of Georgia Press, 1993.
Author of introduction, *Witness to Injustice* by David Frost, Jr., edited by Louise Westling. Jackson, University Press of Mississippi, 1995.

*   *   *

Upon stepping inside Charles Reagan Wilson's office at the University of Mississippi's Center for the Study of Southern Culture, one learns right away that the man is no stereotypical academic. In this high-ceilinged room in an antebellum observatory, the visitor finds a staggering collection of Southern kitsch. A Royal Crown Cola thermometer keeps Wilson apprised of the temperature. Nearby is an American Turpentine Association calendar, adorned with the vivacious Miss Gum Spirits posed in a grove of tapped pine trees. The chief glory of the collection, however, is a vial of what purports to be nothing less than the sweat of Elvis. As the package proclaims, "Elvis poured out his soul for you. Now you can let his perspiration be your inspiration." Wilson has never opened the vial, "I'm afraid it might be too powerful," he says.

Wilson's interest in what he calls "Southern tacky" reveals much about his more "serious" scholarly work. A specialist in Southern religious and cultural history, Wilson finds that fading Southern paraphernalia, the church fan, for example, are a valuable means of studying the region's popular religious iconography. His wide-ranging interest in subjects spanning serious academic attention to popular kitsch is particularly evidenced in *The Encyclopedia of Southern Culture*, which he coedited with William Ferris, now the chairman of the National Endowment for the Humanities. At over 1,600 pages, this monumental volume includes 1,260 essays from over 800 contributors, covering the whole range of the Southern experience, from such weighty matters as race and religion to the story of the Goo-Goo Cluster and country ham.

Wilson's first full-length work was *Baptized in Blood*, which examines the Southern civil religion of the Lost Cause, which came into being in the aftermath of the Civil War. All societies create myths, of course, and being that the South is the only culture in the world where evangelical Protestantism dominates, it is not surprising that its myths would take on a strongly religious dimension. In the catechism of the Lost Cause, Southerners are a chosen but tragic people whose defeat was sanctified by the blood of the brave. Such men as Jefferson Davis and Robert E. Lee took on the status of saints, as we see in the chapel at Washington and Lee University: where the altar would normally be one finds instead Valentine's famed statue of the dead Lee. Lee's body, one assumes, was broken for us.

Wilson's exploration of Southern civil religions continues in his most recent full-length work, *Judgment and Grace in Dixie*. In the early twentieth century, Wilson argues, other, more modern myths came to challenge that of the Lost Cause. Chief among these competing myths was one underlying the civil rights movement, in which Southern blacks were akin to the children of Israel, searching for the Promised Land. Sports and, of course, Elvis, provided other, sometimes complementary myths for the people of the South. What is particularly interesting is that many of these later myths provide for a sort of racial reconciliation. Elvis, as is commonly observed, merged black blues and white gospel into something all his own, making previously disfavored black music acceptable to a white audience.

Another of the unifying myths Wilson cites is the case of Bear Bryant, the highly successful football coach who brought a national championship to the University of Alabama and was borne to his grave by black pallbearers in one of the largest funerals in American history—over 500,000 mourners lined Interstate 59 to pay their respects for the man who made a cult of winning. The effect of these unifying myths, in the words of one anonymous Southerner cited by Wilson, is that the chief difference between blacks and whites in the South is that "blacks have pictures of Jesus and Martin Luther King Jr. in their houses and whites have pictures of Jesus and Elvis."

—Jason Mitchell

WILTZ, Chris

Born: Christine Wiltz in New Orleans, Louisiana, 3 January 1948. **Education:** University of Southwestern Louisiana, 1965, Loyola University, New Orleans, 1966-67, and University of New Orleans, 1967; San Francisco State College, B.A. 1969. **Family:** Married Kenneth McElroy, 25 November 1970 (divorced, 1976); married Joseph Pecot (a communications company president), 13 February 1976; one child, Marigny Katherine. **Career:** Bowes Co. (advertising firm), Los Angeles, proofreader, 1969; Tulane University, New Orleans, secretary in School of Medicine, 1969-70; Maple Street Bookshop, New Orleans, sales and orders, 1970-

71; Tulane University, grant researcher in School of Medicine, 1971-72; staff writer, Dealerscope (home electronics trade journals), 1978, Waltham, Massachusetts; focused on writing since late 1970s. **Agent:** Barney Karpfinger, The Karpfinger Agency, 500 Fifth Ave., Suite 2800, New York, New York 10010.

PUBLICATIONS

Novels

The Killing Circle. New York, Macmillan, 1981.
A Diamond Before You Die. Mysterious Press, 1987.
The Emerald Lizard. Mysterious Press, 1988.
Glass House. Baton Rouge, Louisiana State University Press, 1994

*   *   *

When the first detective novel by Chris Wiltz appeared, some reviewers assumed that the author was male. It was, after all, a work in the hard-boiled private eye tradition established by Dashiell Hammett, Raymond Chandler, and Mickey Spillane, considered a male domain until writers like Sue Grafton and Sara Paretsky introduced their tough, female private investigators.

Wiltz's Neal Rafferty is like the private eyes of those early novels. He is an ex-cop, reared in the working-class "Irish Channel" section of New Orleans. His speech is terse, but he can disarm anyone with a wisecrack. He has an eye for good-looking woman, and even the most sophisticated of them, like Catherine Garber in *The Killing Circle* and Lee Diamond in *A Diamond before You Die*, usually find him irresistible. However, Rafferty has bad luck with women. *The Killing Circle* begins with his mourning the death of one girl friend and ends with his discovering that another is a murderess. In *The Emerald Lizard*, a woman from Neal's past is killed, and his new love turns out to be addicted to violence. The novel concludes with a perky young legal secretary sitting by the fire with him, a sign, Rafferty hopes, that at last things will "get better."

Though Rafferty's character is based on this familiar formula, Wiltz gives him enough dimension to make him interesting. In his role as narrator, Rafferty reveals an impressive capacity for contemplation and analysis. In *The Killing Circle*, for example, he muses on his attachment to "home," by which he means the house where his parents live and his troubled relationship with his father, who seems unable to forgive Neal's being forced out of police work because he would not turn a blind eye to a politician's misdeeds. Ironically, it is this experience of rejection by his father that enables Neal to unriddle the various parent-child relationships in *The Killing Circle*.

Rafferty is also given to sociological analysis. He sees New Orleans as made up of a number of small societies, including not only the French Quarter and the Garden District, but also the Irish Channel and West Bank communities like Westwego, where most of the action of *The Emerald Lizard* takes place. Often Wiltz defines these places by describing those who live there. In *The Emerald Lizard*, Westwego is not just an area of shipyards, convenience stores, and seedy lounges like Jackie Silva's; it is where the urban cowboy Clem Winkler hangs out when he isn't bootlegging redfish and where Bubba Brevna runs a criminal empire from his headquarters in the Marrero Trailer Court.

Novels of the hard-boiled private-eye variety have always been marked by violence. *The Glass House* is filled with dead bodies, but in this case, violence is not incidental, rather it is the subject of the book. Here there are not just a few crimes for a private investigator to solve; in this case, it is a entire society that has gone wrong, and there is no obvious solution.

The protagonist of *The Glass House* is Thea Tamborella, who after ten years in the North has returned to her native New Orleans to dispose of her aunt's house. When Thea was a child, her parents were murdered in a grocery story holdup, and she went to live with her mother's sister in a large, impressive home on Convent Street and to be reared by her aunt's black housekeeper, Delzora Monroe. Thea became so fond of Delzora and her young son Burgess that, even though she knew that her parents' killers were blacks, Thea never succumbed to racism. In Amherst, Massachusetts, that was easier; in the New Orleans to which she has returned, Thea finds it more difficult than she would have believed.

Convent Street itself symbolizes what has happened to the city that Thea finds she still loves. Poor blacks live at one end, crowded into the Convent Street Housing Project, wealthy whites at the other, maintaining their huge old homes with the help of poorly-paid black housekeepers and yardmen. Crime used to be confined to the area where the blacks lived. Now, however, no one is safe. Black criminals have made the Project a place where the lives of other blacks have no value and have invaded the white areas as well. Wiltz shows how violence begets violence through characters like Lyle Hindermann, a white banker turned vigilante, and Burgess Monroe, a bright young man turned drug lord. Neither man intended to do harm, but both of them are responsible for the deaths of innocent people, and eventually both are killed. Wiltz's even-handed approach is also illustrated by her portrayal of policemen. She sees their brutality as the product of frustration. They are under constant pressure to perform an impossible task: to keep order in a society that is in the process of disintegrating.

No matter how much violence there is in Chris Wiltz's detective novels, one can read on, enjoying the scenery, the colorful characters, and the wisecracks along the way, certain that at the end of the book most of the appealing people, including the private eye himself, will still be alive. *The Glass House* does not offer any such reassurance. Wiltz can show how people are driven to embrace evil and can even insist that most people of both races have much good in them, but she does not have a solution for the problems that are convulsing her city and, we assume, many others throughout the nation. However, the very fact that Wiltz does not suggest easy answers makes *Glass House* a much more profound book than many others dealing with the same subject. When the glass windows in Thea's house are shattered by the very blacks who had always thought of it as a place of refuge, it is difficult to know where to begin. With a new girl friend beside him, Neal Rafferty can hope things will get better. Even though she is expecting the child of a man who loves her, Thea is not so confident about the future. *The Glass House* concludes with

Delzora, now childless, weeding her garden and wondering why "nothing changes," including our habit of being so cruel to each other.

—Rosemary M. Canfield Reisman

WOLFE, Tom

Born: Thomas Kennerly Wolfe, Jr., in Richmond, Virginia, 2 March 1930. **Education:** Washington and Lee University, Lexington, Virginia, A.B. (cum laude) 1951; Yale University, New Haven, Connecticut, Ph.D. 1957. **Family:** Married Sheila Berger (art director of *Harper's* magazine), 1978; one daughter and one son. **Career:** Reporter, *Springfield Union,* Massachusetts, 1956-59; reporter and Latin American correspondent, *Washington Post,* 1959-62; reporter and writer, *New York Sunday Magazine, New York Herald Tribune,* 1962-66; writer, *New York World Journal Tribune,* 1966-67; contributing editor, *New York* magazine, 1968-76, *Esquire* magazine, since 1977; contributing artist, *Harper's* magazine, 1978-81; exhibiting artist (drawings) and illustrator. **Awards:** Washington Newspaper Guild Awards for foreign news reporting and for humor, both 1961; award for excellence, Society of Magazine Writers 1970; Frank Luther Mott Research Award, 1973; named Virginia Laureate for literature, 1977; American Book Award and National Book Critics Circle Award, both 1980, for *The Right Stuff* ; Harold D. Vursell Memorial Award for excellence in literature, American Institute of Arts and Letters, 1980; Columbia Journalism Award, 1980; citation for art history, National Sculpture Society, 1980; John Dos Passos Award, 1984; Gari Melchers Medal, 1986; Benjamin Pierce Cheney Medal, Eastern Washington University, 1986; Washington Irving Medal for literary excellence, Nicholas Society, 1986; St. Louis Literary Award, Quinnipiac College, 1990; D.F.A., Minneapolis College of Art, 1971, and School of Visual Arts, 1987, L.H.D, Virginia Commonwealth University, 1983, Southampton College, 1984, Randolph-Macon College and Manhattanville College, 1988, and Longwood College, 1989, D.Litt, Washington and Lee University, 1974, St. Andrews Presbyterian College and John Hopkins University, 1990, and University of Richmond, 1993. **Agent:** Lynn Nesbit, Janklow and Nesbit, 598 Madison Avenue, New York, New York 10022.

PUBLICATIONS

Nonfiction

The Kandy-Kolored Tangerine Flake Streamline Baby (essays). New York, Farrar Straus, 1965.
The Electric Kool-Aid Acid Test. New York, Farrar Straus, 1968.
The Pump House Gang (essays). New York, Farrar Straus, 1968.
Radical Chic and Mau-Mauing the Flak Catchers. New York, Farrar Straus, 1970.
The Painted Word. New York, Farrar Straus, 1975.
Mauve Gloves and Madmen, Clutter and Vine, and Other Stories (essays). New York, Farrar Straus, 1976.
The Right Stuff. New York, Farrar Straus, 1979.
In Our Time (essays). New York, Farrar Straus, 1980.
From Bauhaus to Our House. New York, Farrar Straus, 1981.
Underneath the I-Beam: Sequel to The Painted Word. New York, Farrar, Straus, and Giroux, 1981.

The Purple Decades: A Reader. New York, Farrar, Straus & Giroux, 1982.
Frederick Hart: Sculptor. New York, Hudson Hills Press, 1994.

Editor, with E.W. Johnson, *The New Journalism.* New York, Harper, 1973.

Novels

The Bonfire of the Vanities. New York, Farrar Straus, 1987.
A Man in Full. New York, Farrar, Straus and Giroux, 1998.

Uncollected Short Stories

"The Commercial," in *Esquire* (New York), October 1975.
"2020 A.D.," in *Esquire* (New York), January 1985.

*

Interview: *Conversations with Tom Wolfe* edited by Dorothy M. Scura, Jackson, University Press of Mississippi, 1990.

Video: "Tom Wolfe," *Writer's Workshop,* a joint production of the University of South Carolina and the South Carolina ETV network, PBS, 1982; "Tom Wolfe, Part I," and "Tom Wolfe, Part I," *A World of Ideas with Bill Moyers,* a production of Public Affairs Television, Inc., 1988.

Critical Studies: "Reporting the Fabulous: Representation and Response in the Work of Tom Wolfe" by John Hellmann, *Fables of Fact: The New Journalism as New Fiction,* Urbana, University of Illinois Press, 1981; "Tom Wolfe: Pushing the Outside of the Envelope" by Chris Anderson, *Style as Argument: Contemporary American Nonfiction,* Carbondale, Southern Illinois University Press, 1987; "Tom Wolfe's Vanities" by Joseph Epstein, *New Criterion,* February 1988; "The Flap over Tom Wolfe: How Real Is the Retreat from Realism?" by Robert Towers, *New York Times Book Review,* 28 January 1990; "'The Masque of the Red Death' in Wolfe's The Bonfire of the Vanities" by Myles Raymond Hurd, *Notes on Contemporary Literature,* May 1990; "Tom Wolfe's American Jeremiad" by Barbara Lounsberry, *The Art of Fact: Contemporary Artists of Nonfiction,* Westport, Connecticut, Greenwood Press, 1990; Tom Wolfe Special Issue, *Journal of American Culture,* Fall 1991; *The Critical Response to Tom Wolfe,* edited by Doug Shomette, Westport, Connecticut, Greenwood Press, 1992; *Tom Wolfe* by William McKeen, New York, Twayne Publishers, 1995.

*　　*　　*

"The Hell with it . . . let chaos reign . . . louder music, more wine . . . . All the old traditions are exhausted, and no new one is yet established"—wrote Tom Wolfe in typically demonstrative fashion at the close of his 1973 introductory essay to *The New Journalism,* the anthology he co-edited with E.W. Johnson. In so forcibly reacting to the critical response to the bastard literary genre with which he has ever since been associated, Wolfe also directly challenged the eminence in America's prosaic culture of "The Novel."

Fourteen years later, Wolfe made his own debut on the "big fiction" circuit with *The Bonfire of the Vanities,* a work every bit as wide in scope and weighty in content as some of the heavy-wrought productions against which he had once railed. *The Bonfire of the Vanities* though, represents more an exploitation of the novel form than a homage to it, and—in its hurtling Technicolor progress through a world in which the horrible maxim is "All for one and one for all and lots for oneself!"—settled a few unanswered questions about the nature of Wolfe's output.

The Electric Kool-Aid Acid Test, upon which his original reputation rested, was not so much reportage as mutant, mind-lab biographical improvisation. While it relied more heavily on historical fact than most novels, and was every jumpy inch as distorted and disjointed as the hallucinogenically-induced experiences it sought to describe, ultimately, Wolfe's first novel-length outing was utterly dependent on his own imaginative vibrancy. Valuable not only as an insight into the addled consciousness of fellow experimentalist Ken Kesey, Wolfe's tract remains, in all its fragmentary, speeding glory, the outstanding document of 1960s counterculture; an exploration not only of the wild lifestyle of Kesey's Merry Pranksters, but a catalogue of the pressures that caused the embryonic hippie movement to self-combust.

This thick, rich stew of style and content followed one collection of pieces drawn from his journalistic career and emerged simultaneously with another. Through 37 articles, essays and musings, the reader is invited to trace the growth of Wolfe's technique and the development of a highly intuitive perceptive gift: catch him eyeing California's junior surf bums as they chill out on the extra-good vibe of being independent at 14 and living in low-rent garages ("they have this life all of their own; it's like a glass-bottom boat and it floats over the 'real' world"); journey through America's car-customizing shops and small-town racetracks; crest the adrenal wave of being very young and hip in swinging London; meet Phil Spector, Cassius Clay, Marshall McLuhan . . . the list goes on.

During the 1970s, Wolfe's inquisitive ardor seemed to have diminished somewhat. Fixing his attention on other areas of criticism, Wolfe turned in some surprisingly flat period pieces. In *Mauve Gloves and Madmen, Clutter and Vine,* however, he enjoyed a renaissance. Kicking off with a ritual dismemberment of a major author, and ending with a prophetic tale about the selfishness and ruthlessness of Manhattan cab-hailers, Wolfe roamed, among other things, through a dissertation on one woman's hemorrhoids, the story of a Navy pilot risking his life on a daily basis over North Vietnam, and a genuinely funny piece of short fiction concerning one black athlete's efforts to make a conscienable perfume commercial.

In 1979, entering yet another brain-warping space, Wolfe produced an effortless and enthralling, warts and all history of America's launch into astronautical flight. *The Right Stuff,* borne out of Wolfe's "ordinary curiosity," remains his best-written and most complete book, consummately encapsulating, in all seriousness, the adventurous spirit of the age, while, as in previous works, functioning on the intimate level of fraternity tale: Tom, the clever brother, spectates, while the rest of the gang go off running and jumping into all manner of colorful and phenomenal dangers—in this case, sitting atop a huge stick of dynamite, waiting "for someone to light the fuse." A must for vicarious thrill seekers everywhere (although not as appealing, probably to animal rights activists), *The Right Stuff* is Wolfe's second absolutely indispensable book—as vital to the social historian as the reader with only the most limited interest in space flight.

The Bonfire of the Vanities, like everything Wolfe has done, seeks to hold up a mirror to contemporary life and shout, "There! That's what its' like." Sherman McCoy's noisy descent from a fulgent cloud of privilege and wealth into the purgatorial nether-world of New York's criminal justice system is fitting reward for his participation in "the greed storm" of the consumerist 1980s.

Wolfe's incisive political awareness, his desire to penetrate the "thickening democratic facade," is equally as urgent as in his earlier denunciation of White liberal angst *Radical Chic* (further, his understanding of what makes the underclasses tick is as piercing as in its accompanying piece, *Mau-Mauing The Flak Catchers*). McCoy, a cartoon-like central character, is pitched on a spiraling express-ride into the deepest, most decrepit tunnels of urban deprivation, becoming the victim of the startling contrast between what he is capable of possessing and what others cannot hope to touch. McCoy's culpability matters little: it is significant only that he is suitably placed to become a totemic sacrifice in a political game—for this fact alone, Wolfe finally offers him a ragged salvation whilst damning almost everyone else.

Wolfe has held tenure as amanuensis, arbiter of style, master of the idiom, observer and interpreter of signs, symbols, and portents for quarter of a century. That he always wanted somehow to be a novelist, albeit of a unique kind, is self-evident. That whatever he next presents will be as innovative and stirring as what has gone before is equally so. What the subject will be, no one is likely to guess, for Wolfe has a magpie's approach and is capable of alighting on any glittering thing. Certainly, no-one will be bored.

—Ian McMechan

WOLFF, Tobias

Born: Tobias Jonathaln Ansell Wolff in Birmingham, Alabama, 19 June 1945. **Education:** Oxford University, B.A. 1972, M.A. 1975; Stanford University, M.A. 1977. **Military Service:** U.S. Army, 1964-68: lieutenant. **Family:** Married Catherine Dolores Spohn, 1975; two sons and one daughter. **Career:** Jones Lecturer in creative writing, Stanford University (Stegner fellow), 1975-78; beginning 1980 Peck Professor of English, Syracuse University, New York. **Awards:** National Endowment fellowship, 1978, 1985; Rinehart grant, 1979; O. Henry award, for short story, 1980, 1981, 1985; St. Lawrence award, 1981; Guggenheim fellowship, 1982; PEN/Faulkner award, 1985; Rea award for short story, 1989; Whiting Foundation award, 1990; Lila Wallace-Reader's Digest award, 1994; Lyndhurst Foundation award, 1994; Esquire-Volvo-Waterstone's award, 1994.

PUBLICATIONS

Short Stories

In the Garden of the North American Martyrs. New York, Ecco Press, 1981; as *Hunters in the Snow,* London, Cape, 1982.

Back in the World. Boston, Houghton Mifflin, 1985.
The Night in Question: Stories. N.p., 1996.

Novel

The Barracks Thief. New York, Ecco Press, 1984; London, Cape, 1987.

Uncollected Short Stories

"The Other Miller." In *The Best American Short Stories 1987,* edited by Ann Beattie and Shannon Ravenel, Boston, Houghton Mifflin, 1987.
"Smorgasbord." In *The Best American Short Stories 1988,* edited by Mark Helprin and Shannon Ravenel, Boston, Houghton Mifflin, 1988.
"Migraine," in *Antaeus* (New York), Spring-Autumn, 1990.
"Sanity," in *Atlantic* (Boston), December 1990.

Other

Ugly Rumours. London, Allen and Unwin, 1975.
This Boy's Life: A Memoir. New York, Atlantic Monthly Press, and London, Bloomsbury, 1989.
In Pharaoh's Army: Memories of the Lost War. New York, Knopf, and London, Bloomsbury, 1994.
Two Boys and a Girl (for children). N.p., 1996.

Editor, *Matters of Life and Death: New American Short Stories.* Green Harbor, Massachusetts, Wampeter Press, 1983.
Editor, *The Short Stories of Anton Chekhov.* New York, Bantam, 1987.
Editor, *Best American Short Stories, 1994.* New York, Houghton Mifflin, 1994.
Editor, *The Vintage Book of Contemporary American Short Stories.* New York, Vintage, 1994.

*

Critical Study: *Tobias Wolff: A Study of the Short Fiction* by James Hannah, 1996.

Tobias Wolff comments:

Writers are the worst interpreters of their own work. If their fiction is any good, it should be saying things they weren't aware of.

*   *   *

Tobias Wolff writes with a sparsity and clarity typical of the voices of the best writers of his generation, realists of the ilk of Raymond Carver, Richard Ford, William Kittredge, Jayne Anne Phillips, Mary Robison, and Stephanie Vaughan, all of whom are represented in *Matters of Life and Death,* an anthology of contemporary American short stories which Wolff put together in the early 1980s. In explaining his choices, Wolff wrote that in the stories "I heard something that I couldn't ignore, some notes of menace or hope or warning or appeal or awe; and in the matter of the stories themselves, the people who inhabit them and what they do, I saw something that I couldn't look away from."

The same should be said of Wolff's work. Every story, the novella *The Barracks Thief,* and the memoir *This Boy's Life* go right to the heart. Nowhere is there a slack page; Wolff writes as if each work were the only one he will every publish. He has admitted in interviews to being a relentless reviser. *The Barracks Thief,* scarcely a novella, was once a manuscript of several hundred pages. In the stories collected in *In the Garden of the North American Martyrs* and *Back in the World,* character development is quick and vivid, background material rare, as if Wolff has always kept clear in his mind Hemingway's axiom that stories get their energy from what is left unsaid. The result is a rather modest output. After 15 years of publishing, all of Wolff's work could easily be contained in a single volume of 600 pages. But this hypothetical volume would say as much if not more than any other conceivable work about the generation of American men born in the decade after World War II.

The men in Wolff's stories have fathers and uncles who fought and won in the good war; their own war is a squalid and ambiguous affair that went on and on in a very hot place, and the themes of these fictions are deceit, betrayal, failure, and self-loathing, and the queer persistence of fellow-feeling in spite of all of these. Wolff was himself a member of the Special Forces and had a tour of duty in Vietnam. Yet nowhere has he written—not yet, anyway—of combat or his service in Southeast Asia. Instead the war is insinuated, providing the future with menace, or the past with ambivalence and depth. In other words, unconfronted, unobtruded, the Vietnam war remains in Wolff's fiction what it is for most men of his age, non-combatants as well as soldiers, the great shaping force that can never quite be understood, much less expunged. Consequently, many of Wolff's characters seemed surprised who they have become, survivors of a catastrophe who have become dependent on safety. As the narrator of *The Barracks Thief* puts it:

> I didn't set out to be what I am . . . I'm a conscientious man, a responsible man, maybe even what you'd call a good man—I hope so. But I'm also a careful man, addicted to comfort, with an eye for the safe course. My neighbors appreciate me because they know I will never give my lawn over to the cultivation of marijuana, or send my wife weeping to their doorsteps at three o'clock in the morning, or expect them to be my friends. I am content with my life most of the time.

Comfort, however, scarcely describes the experience of reading Wolff's fiction. Instead, the reader is made uneasy by characters whose actions, often for the best of motives, lead them into error and excess. In "Hunters in the Snow" Tub and Frank rediscover their friendship while Kenny, bleeding or freezing to death, lies neglected in the back of the pick-up truck. In "Coming Attractions," a sister risks her life trying to get a bicycle out of the deep end of a swimming pool. In "Dessert Breakdown, 1968" a man nearly abandons his wife and children on a whim. And in "The Rich Brother," a man leaves his ineffectual younger brother by the side of a highway in the cold and an almost absolute darkness. Driving all of Wolff's fiction is the dynamism derived from the irreconcilable difference between who we might like to be and who our actions reveal us to be.

In *This Boy's Life,* an autobiography of his adolescence, Wolff writes "It takes a childish or corrupt imagination to make symbols of other people," and the comment affords an important insight into Wolff's aesthetic and ethical aims. For all of their economy, Wolff's works are never glib or shallow. They are never didactic, and the characters who inhabit them speak and act on their own in settings that are precisely and efficiently conceived. The plots move quickly, and since characters are never arrested and made to stand for something, reading Wolff is a headlong sort of business, wholly free of the artificial and emphatic closures of more ponderous writing. Invariably Wolff leaves the fate of his characters open. This can be exhilarating; however oblique the strike, we feel that we have made contact with the honest sufferings and joys of real people.

—Mark A. R. Facknitz

WOODWARD, C. Vann

Born: Comer Vann Woodward in Vanndale, Arkansas, 13 November 1908. **Education:** Henderson Brown, Arkansas, 1926-28; Emory University, A.B. 1930; Columbia University, M.A. 1932; University of North Carolina, Ph.D. 1937. **Military Service:** U.S. Naval Reserve, 1943-46; became lieutenant. **Family:** Married Glenn Boyd MacLeod, December 21, 1937 (died, 1982); one child, Peter (died). **Career:** Instructor in English, Georgia School of Technology (now Georgia Institute of Technology), Atlanta, 1930-31, 1932-33; Works Progress Administration, 1933-34; assistant professor of history, University of Florida, Gainesville, 1937-39; associate professor of history, Scripps College, Claremont, California, 1940-43; professor of history, Johns Hopkins University, Baltimore, 1946-61; Sterling Professor of History, Yale University, New Haven, 1961-77, professor emeritus since 1977; visiting assistant professor of history, 1939, James W. Richard Lecturer in History, 1954, University of Virginia; Commonwealth Lecturer, University of London, 1954; Harold Vyvyan Harmsworth Professor of American History, Oxford University, 1954-55; editor, "Forum Lectures on American History" series, Voice of America (radio); contributor to numerous scholarly journals, and contributor of essays and reviews to periodicals. **Member:** American Academy of Arts and Letters, American Philosophical Society, American Historical Association (president, 1969), Organization of American Historians (president, 1968-69), American Academy of Arts and Sciences (vice-president, 1988-89), Royal Historical Society, British Academy, Southern Historical Association (president, 1952). **Awards:** Bancroft Prize in American history, 1952, for *Origins of the New South: 1877-1913;* award in literature, National Institute of Arts and Letters, 1954; award from American Council of Learned Societies, 1962; creative arts award, Brandeis University, 1982; Pulitzer Prize in History, 1982, for *Mary Chestnut's Civil War;* Life Work Award, American Historical Society, 1986; Gold Medal for history, American Academy of Arts and Letters, 1990; LLD., University of Arkansas, University of North Carolina, and University of Michigan, 1971; LittD., Princeton University, 1971, and Cambridge University, 1975; LH.D., Columbia University, 1972, Northwestern University, 1977, and Johns Hopkins University, 1991; additional honorary doctoral degrees from universities of Brandeis, Cambridge, Colgate, Dartmouth, Emory, Henderson, Michigan, North Carolina, Pennsylvania, Princeton, Rutgers, Tulane, Washington and Lee, William and Mary, and Rhodes College.

PUBLICATIONS

History

Tom Watson, Agrarian Rebel. New York, Macmillan, 1938.
The Battle for Leyte Gulf. New York, Macmillan, 1947.
Reunion and Reaction: The Compromise of 1877 and the End of Reconstruction. Boston, Little, Brown, 1951.
Origins of the New South, 1877-1913, Volume 9 of *A History of the South* edited by W. H. Stephenson and E. M. Coulter. Baton Rouge, Louisiana State University Press, 1951.
The Strange Career of Jim Crow. New York Oxford University Press, 1955.
The Burden of Southern History. Baton Rouge, Louisiana State University Press, 1960.
The National Experience, with John M. Blum, Edmund S. Morgan, Willie Lee Rose, Arthur Schlesinger, Jr., and Kenneth M. Stampp. New York, Harcourt, Brace & World, 1963.
American Counterpoint: Slavery and Racism in the North-South Dialogue. Boston, Little, Brown, 1971.
Thinking Back: The Perils of Writing History. Baton Rouge, Louisiana State University Press, 1986.
The Future of the Past. New York, Oxford University Press, 1988.
The Old World's New World. New York, Oxford University Press, 1991.

Editor

Cannibals All! or, Slaves Without Masters by George Fitzhugh, 1857. Cambridge, Harvard University Press, 1960.
A Southern Prophecy: The Prosperity of the South Dependent upon the Elevation of the Negro by Lewis H. Blair, 1889. Boston, Little, Brown, 1964.
After the War: A Tour of the Southern States, 1865-1866 by Whitelaw Reid, 1866. New York, Harper & Row, 1965.
The Comparative Approach to American History, with two essays by Woodward. New York, Basic Books, 1968.
Responses of the Presidents to Charges of Misconduct. Washington, D.C., Delacorte, 1974.
Mary Chesnut's Civil War. New Haven, Yale University Press, 1981.
The Private Mary Chestnut: The Unpublished Civil War Diaries, with Elisabeth Muhlenfeld. New York, Oxford University Press, 1984.

General editor, *Oxford History of the United States,* eleven volumes. New York, Oxford University Press, 1982—.

Essays

"The Case of the Louisiana Traveler: *Plessy v. Ferguson,* 163 U. S. 537," in *Quarrels that Have Shaped the Constitution* edited by John A. Garraty. New York, Harper & Row, 1962.
"The Future of Southern History," in *The Future of History, Essays in the Vanderbilt University Centennial Symposium* edited by Charles F. Delzell. Nashville, Vanderbilt University Press, 1977.

*

Bibliographies: "The Published Writings of C. Vann Woodward: A Bibliography" by Louis P. Masur, *Region, Race, and Recon-*

struction: Essays in Honor of C. Vann Woodward edited by J. Morgan Kousser and James M. McPherson, New York, Oxford University Press, 1982.

Interviews: *Interpreting American History: Conversations with Historians* by John A. Garraty, New York, MacMillan, 1978.

Critical Studies: "Potter and Woodward on the South" by Eugene D. Genovese, *In Red and Black*, New York, Pantheon, 1968; "C. Vann Woodward" by David M. Potter, *Pastmasters: Some Essays on American Historians* edited by Marcus Cunliffe and Robin W. Winks, New York, Harper, 1969; "In Black and White" by Robert Coles, *New Yorker,* April 15, 1972; "C. Vann Woodward and the Burden of Southern Liberalism" by Michael O'Brien, *American Historical Review*, June 1973; "C. Vann Woodward: The Southerner as Liberal Realist" by Robert B. Westbrook, *South Atlantic Quarterly,* Winter 1978; *Region, Race, and Reconstruction: Essays in Honor of C. Vann Woodward* edited by J. Morgan Kausser and James M. McPherson, New York, Oxford University Press, 1982; *C. Vann Woodward, Southerner* by John H. Roper, Athens, University of Georgia Press, 1987; *Rethinking the South: Essays in Intellectual History* by Michael O'Brien, Annapolis, Johns Hopkins University Press, 1988; *C. Vann Woodward: A Southern Historian and His Critics* edited by John H. Roper, Athens, University of Georgia Press, 1997.

*   *   *

The eccentric essayist, social critic, and savant of sexual mores Florence King says that she alleviated the boredom of graduate school classes by reciting passages from works by C. Vann Woodward. And Albert Murray, the Alabama-born African American essayist, jazzist, and fiction writer, spends a chapter of his experimental "word-riffs" on the same man. Historians are not usually interesting to such personalities, and especially not a Yale emeritus professor and past president of the Southern Historical Association, the Organization of American Historians, and the American Historical Association. Such attention to the self-effacing scholar, whose friends and admirers admit is a mumbling "throwaway lecturer," is only one of the many ironies in the life of the historian who restored a sense of tragedy to American history by demonstrating the ironic "counterpoints" of its southern past.

Woodward was born 13 November 1908 in Vanndale, a town in the Arkansas delta founded by his mother Bess's people, the Vanns. His father, Hugh Allison (Jack) Woodward, and his uncle, Comer McDonald Woodward (for whom the boy was named), were Methodist college administrators and liberal reformists during a time in southern history when the most extreme acts of racial violence were being ameliorated and when conservative rules about class and caste were being challenged. Yet the worst was not completely gone by any means, and young Vann Woodward in the 1920s saw a lynch mob and also saw the Ku Klux Klan in full regalia enter his family church during a service to make a donation, one accepted readily, even smilingly, by the pastor. From his two families he took legacies of higher education, landed wealth, and a complex tradition of reform-from-above. In his own college days, he rejected the earnest pietism of the Vanns and the Woodwards and self-consciously adopted atheism, a breach that may explain the only real gap in his otherwise very full history of the modern South, for he has never granted much influence or authority among the Protestant churches in this "Christ-haunted land."

Teaching at a number of schools, but longest at Johns Hopkins University (1947-60) and Yale University (1960-78), Woodward has directed forty-two dissertations, and his students include university deans, one Ivy League president, a director of the National Endowment for the Humanities, three winners of the Pulitzer Prize, and a number of prominent scholars.

Woodward's career can be divided into thirds: 1926-38, youthful dissidence and leftist radical activism in Atlanta and Chapel Hill, culminating in his masterful biography of Georgia reformist-gone-sour Thomas E. Watson; 1938-55, a research mole and producer of provocative monographs that sent the entire profession in new scholarly directions, capped by his most controversial and most commercially successful work *The Strange Career of Jim Crow*, a book proclaimed by no less than Martin Luther King, Jr. to be "the Bible of the Civil Rights Movement"; 1955-today, an extremely long, and continuing, period of essay writing after the style of Montaigne, and these essays, grounded in previous research, themselves have provoked important research monographs by the friendliest of "critics" who disagree vigorously with him but always cite Woodward for sending them down a new path.

Woodward changed the study of southern history with six major new interpretations. First, he said that the once little-noted decade of the 1880s was a significant one, especially because of the complex interplay between economic forces, racial mores, and political fluidity. The year 1889 he marked as the "turn year" when race relations became more violently negrophobic and when choices about racial politics were significantly and tragically narrowed. Second, he has described the irony of southern identity, insisting that the fact of undeniable evil in slavery, the fact of undeniable defeat in the Civil War, and the fact of undeniable regional poverty in the period 1866-1960 in combination make the South a "counterpoint" to an American national identity that proclaims and celebrates innocence in social mores, invincibility in war, and affluence in material things. Third, Woodward noted the discontinuity in southern history, borrowing from Charles Austin Beard the concept of the Civil War as a "Second American Revolution" that changed American society more thoroughly than did the Revolutionary War of 1776.

For the South, Woodward described an antebellum class structure of landed gentry with great wealth and great influence on the national scene—and without many identifiable bourgeois values or practices. The postbellum South, he says, is dominated by "new men" with bourgeois values and practices, and this new elite measures its wealth in capital rather than land, and also enjoys a reduced level of power and influence on the national scenes.

The Strange Career of Jim Crow is his fourth contribution, and with it Woodward tries to show that the formal and legal institutions of segregation are put into place between 1898 and 1908 in response to political crises and economic distresses associated with the worldwide Panic (or recession) of 1893 and the collapse of the biracial Populist party in the region. The ideological direction of his interpretation is significant, because a generation of southern white integrationists were told by him that they could be southern without being segrationists. Fifth, and particularly re-

lated to his interpretation of the origins of segregation, Woodward attempted to develop a "usable past," not one marked by the historian's fallacy of presentism, but still a sense of the useful and usable interrelationship between concerns of the present and their roots in the past. An entire generation of college history students thus found Woodward to be in their words "relevant" in a way that other historians were not.

Finally, Woodward throughout his career has treated modernism, that is, a sense of confused identity, alienated and frustrated personal relations, and conflicted values bound up in the obvious loss of an antebellum nineteenth-century worldview and a dissatisfaction with its postbellum and twentieth-century replacement.

A close student of William Faulkner and Allen Tate and personal friends with Robert Penn Warren and Cleanth Brooks, Woodward publicized and celebrated the Southern Literary Renaissance and also participated in it, since his essays, especially those gathered in *The Burden of Southern History* and in *American Counterpoint*, are themselves part of the literary criticism and cultural values of that movement. Woodward, in all of his many works but especially in his magisterial *Origins of the New South*, employs a heightened sense of irony—both situational and in the structure of his language—and a deepened and broadened sense of stoic determination that the individual endure with dignity and courage a human condition that is finally tragic.

—John Herbert Roper

WRIGHT, C. D.

Born: Carolyn D. Wright in Mountain Home, Arkansas, 6 January 1949. **Education**: Memphis State University, B.A. 1971; University of Arkansas, Fayetteville, M.F.A. 1976. **Family**: Married Forrest Gander (a writer and teacher), 3 April 1983; one child. **Career**: Graduate teaching assistant, University of Arkansas, Fayetteville, 1973-76; poet-in-the-schools, Office of Arkansas Arts and Humanities, 1976-78; office manager, Poetry Center, San Francisco State University, 1980-82; visiting professor, Iowa Writer's Workshop, 1996; professor, Brown University, Providence, Rhode Island, since 1983; established Lost Roads Publishers, a small, nonprofit literary press, with her husband; contributor to periodicals, including *American Poetry Review, New Yorker, Paris Review, Epoch, Poetry East*, and *Sulfur*. **Awards**: National Endowment for the Arts fellowship, 1982, 1988; Witter Bynner poetry prize, 1986; Guggenheim fellowship, 1987; Bunting Institute fellowship, 1987; General Electric Award for younger writers, 1988; Whiting Foundation award, 1989; Rhode Island Governor's award for the Arts, 1990; Poetry Center Book award, 1992; Lila Wallace Writers' award, 1992; State Poet of Rhode Island, 1994. **Address**: English Department, Brown University, Providence, Rhode Island 02912.

PUBLICATIONS

Poetry Collections

Alla Breve Loving. Spokane, Mill Mountain Press, 1976.
Room Rented by a Single Woman. Fayetteville, Lost Roads Publishers, 1977.

Terrorism. Fayetteville, Lost Roads Publishers, 1978.

Translation of the Gospel Back into Tongues. Albany, State University of New York Press, 1981.

Further Adventures with You. Pittsburgh, Carnegie-Mellon Press, 1986.

String Light. Athens, University of Georgia Press, 1992.

Just Whistle. Berkeley, Kelsey Street Press, 1993.

Tremble. New York, Ecco Press, 1996.

Other

The Reader's Map of Arkansas. Fayetteville, University of Arkansas Press, 1995.

Editor, *The Lost Roads Project: A Walk-in Book of Arkansas.* Fayetteville, University of Arkansas Press, 1995.

*

Poetry Recordings: *C.D. Wright* (videotape), Poetry Center, San Francisco State University, 1992.

Critical Studies: "Politics and the Personal Lyric in the Poetry of Joy Harjo and C. D. Wright" by Jenny Goodman, *Melus: Theory, Culture, and Criticism,* Summer 1994.

C. D. Wright comments:

Poetry is my central station. All that can converge in a given individual intersects there for me, under the big clock. Many of my influences are extra-literary—friends, tress. Others answer to other arts—music, photography. Other disciplines—folklore, recent history. Still others, to temperament—leftist. And of course, a lifetime of reading helter skelter through the layers of time and translation only gaining consistency and some pattern, from rural to urban, with contemporary American poetry. I still try to sustain a certain tolerance toward the whole field even as my own writing seems to be shifting allegiances. I try not to forfeit what can never be recovered—my hardheaded, idiomatic bedrock. I try not to remain ignorant of the ever-changing present tense of poetry. Some say the genre is anachronistic. I say, these people, their lives have become too prosaic.

*   *   *

In the prose text "hills," which introduces her 1986 collection *Further Adventures with You,* C. D. Wright explains that her poems "are about desire, conflict, the dearth of justice for all. About persons of small means. They are succinct but otherwise orthodox novels in which the necessary characters are brought out, made intimate . . . , engage in dramatic action and leave the scene forever with or without a resolution in hand or sight. Each on the space of a page or less." This statement captures several qualities common to all the work of this Arkansas-born poet, whose earliest writing was dialect-based and regional in focus: its storytelling impulse, its focus on everyday things and events, its backdrop of melancholia and brooding violence, its necessarily elliptical brevity. Yet, in a crucial respect, Wright's later work has superseded the *ars poetica* she offers in "hills," for the relation between poetry and prose in her writing has become more complex and her lineated stories veer demonstratively towards less orthodox forms.

Typical of Wright's earlier "orthodox novels" is the poem "Vanish," from *Translations of the Gospel Back into Tongues* (1981). This is a poem of memory, loss, and desire—all states of absence that Wright's poem comes to occupy, offering its lineaments of story to mark the place the vanishing experience had occupied and now leaves bare. The poem offers fragmentary recollections of an encounter between a girl and a sailor, perhaps before the funeral of the girl's brother. The encounter ended long ago without issue, and the sailor and girl have separated. The poem's first-person voice shifts over the course of the poem's 31 lines from the aged sailor to the now mature girl. "Vanish" begins

> Because I did not die
> I sit in the captain's chair
> Going deaf in one ear, blind in the other.
> I live because the sea does.

By the end, however, the girl's fading memories swallow up the sailor's voice, consigning it to the near oblivion of the sea swell:

> Because I did not marry
> I wash by the light of the body.
> Soap floats out of my mind.
> I have almost forgotten
> The sailor whose name I did not catch,
> His salty tongue on my ear,
> A wave on a shell.

Only between these two drifting buoys of consciousness may the broken pieces of their common story surface, traces of the shipwrecked possibilities of love.

Wright's stories are often mediated through a wounded interiority or a dreaming mind, as in the title poem of her 1986 book, "Further Adventures with You":

> We are on a primeval river in a reptilian den.
>
> There are birds you don't want to tangle with, trees you cannot identify . . .
>
> Somehow we spend the evening with Mingus in a White Castle. Or somewhere. Nearly drunk. He says he would like to play for the gang.

The dream, with its expression of unspoken wishes, its mobilization of childhood memories and ephemera of the day, its enigmatic yoking of distant scenes, serves as an apt model for the lyric consciousness implicit in Wright's poetry generally and not only in her "dream poems." For dreams, despite their apparent incoherence, are ways of revisiting what in our waking lives is irrecoverable, whether because of passing time or by our failure to attend to it as it was lived. Poetry, too, may be such a mode of dreamlike remembrance. As Wright suggests: "The box this comes in," an allegorical "deviation on poetry," a meditation on poetry via the image of an antique box, "within the limits of this diminutive wooden world, I have made do with the cracks of light and tokens of loss and recovery that came my way."

Both *Further Adventures with You* and *String Light,* however, exhibit Wright's discovery of nonverse forms, which in turn seem to shift the center of gravity of her poetry from states of desire towards the experiential richness of language forms as such. Thus, in her sequence "The Ozark Odes," the section titled "Arkansas Towns" is dedicated purely to the delightful and strange placenames of Wright's home state—

    Acorn
    Back Gate
    Bald Knob
    Ben Hur
    Biggers
    Blue Ball

—all the way up to "Whisp," "Yellville," and "Zent."

Similarly, the prose poems subjoined to "What No One Could Have Told Them" isolate a single detail (a toddler urinating, the child yawning) and repeat it in new word contexts until the detail takes on luminosity as language, independent of its humble content. Wright's numerous prose poems, and above all the Kerouac-like "sketching" of "The Night I Met Little Floyd" and "The Next Time I Crossed the Line into Oklahoma" (both in *String Light*), bear out the distinction she drew in "hills"—whereas her poems are based on narrative, she says, her prose "is about language if it is about any one thing."

—Tyrus Miller

YOUNGBLOOD, Shay

Born: Columbus, Georgia. **Education**: Clark-Atlanta University, B.A. in mass communications 1981; Brown University, M.F.A. in creative writing 1993. **Career**: Peace Corps volunteer in the Dominican Republic; public information assistant, WETV, Atlanta; creative writing instructor, Syracuse Community Writer's Project, and theater writing instructor, Brown University and Rhode Island Adult Correctional Institution for Women. **Awards**: Hollywood NAACP Theatre Awards, best playwright, 1991, for *Talking Bones*; Kennedy Center's Lorraine Hansberry Playwrighting award, 1993, for *Square Blues*; 21st Century Playwrights Festival, Edward Albee Honoree, 1993; National Theatre Award from Paul Green Foundation, 1995.

Publications

Fiction

The Big Mama Stories. Ithaca, New York, Firebrand Books, 1989.
Soul Kiss. New York, Riverhead Books, 1997.

Plays

Shakin' the Mess Outta Misery (premiered at the Horizon Theatre, Atlanta, 1988). Woodstock, Illinois, Dramatic Publishing Company, 1994.
Communism Killed My Dog. Workshopped at Seven Stages Theatre, Atlanta, 1991).

Black Power Barbie in Hotel de Dream. First produced at Seven Stages Theatre, Atlanta, 1992.
Square Blues. Workshopped at the Bay Area Playwrights' Festival, 1993.
Talking Bones. Produced at Penumbra Theatre Company, St. Paul, Minnesota, 1994. Woodstock, Illinois, Dramatic Publishing Company, 1994.
Amazing Grace. Produced at the Children's Theatre Company, Minneapolis, 1995.

Critical Studies: *500 Great Books by Women* by Erica Bauermeister, Firebrand Books, 1989; interview in *Creative Loafing*, 1995, reprinted at URL: www.cc.emory.edu/CL/031895/voices.html.

*

Shay Youngblood comments:
I write to discover things about myself and about the world around me. . . . Most of my stories, poems, plays and novels come out of a passion to tell it like it is and like I want it to be. Stories that won't let me sleep I put to rest on the page.

*   *   *

In her novels and plays Shay Youngblood is concerned with giving voice to females attempting to assert their identity. As they strive to persevere in difficult circumstances, surreal and magical events—voices, visions, sounds—form part of a larger reality that can help transform their lives. In the play *Talking Bones*, for example, women from three generations struggle as owners and caretakers of Ancestor's Books and Breakfast, a peculiar Southern cafe where otherworldly elements lull individuals into dreamlike states and visions of the future.

Poetry, humor, and music help distinguish the enchantments, which serve as a kind of extraordinary creativity that characters can tap into for insights. A variety of character types in the play suggest different roles and approaches women assume to express their individuality and to persevere in tough conditions: the matriarch, Ruth, has a broken hearing aid but never fails to hear otherworldly voices, and her fierce determination to maintain the family legacy is comic at times but ultimately admirable; her daughter, Baybay, wants to sell the shop and pursue romantic dreams she has fashioned from romance novels and films.

Shakin' the Mess Outta Misery, another of Youngblood's plays, has a female cast and is also set in a small southern town. As in *Talking Bones*, elements of fantasy mingle freely with more recognizably realistic sets, effecting a place where past and present, memories and dreams, storytelling, music, and dance, interchange. The play revolves around Daughter, who returns home after the death of Big Mama, the grandmother who raised her. Comprised of a series of flashbacks to Daughter's childhood, spanning a period from the 1920s to the present, the play blends realism and fantasy to show a reality where magic, superstition, and larger spiritual forces are routinely accepted and respected as part of life. The mixture is evident in Daughter's memories:

    Daughter: Colored folks as you know are the most
    amazing people on this earth. Big Mama raised me in the

company of wise old black women like herself who managed to survive some dangerous and terrible times and live to tell about them. Their only admitted vice, aside from exchanging a little bit of no-harm-done gossip now and then, was dipping snuff. They were always sending me to Mr. Joe's grocery store to buy silver tins of the fine brown powder wrapped in bright colored labels with names like Bruton's Sweet Snuff, Georgia Peach and Three Brown Monkies. One time, my mean old cousin Dee Dee told me that snuff was really ground up monkey dust, a delicacy in the royal palaces of Africa.

In addition to Daughter and Big Mama, the circle of women include Aunt Mae (Big Mama's sister), Miss Corine (a hairdresser and professional maid), Maggie (a con woman), Miss Mary (a maid with unearthly powers), Miss Tom (a carpenter), Miss Lamama (a maid with an African husband and "African ways"), Dee Dee (Daughter's fast cousin and a know-it-all), and Fannie Mae (Daughter's mother and a dancing ghost).

Youngblood mined much of this same material to create a fictional work while she was writing the play. *The Big Mama Stories,* published in 1989 (the play premiered in 1988), is set in "the projects," a residential area set aside for blacks. As recounted through a loose connection of episodes, the narrator, like Daughter, is raised by a character named Big Mama and several other people who watch out for her: indeed, the novel's best moments occur when the circle of women gather to help heal the ill, celebrate a rite of passage, or participate in other forms of communal support. The narrative is disjointed, reading much like a series of scenes with rough transitions in between, smoothed by rich interplay among characters and Youngblood's excellent recreation of speech.

Soul Kiss, on the other hand, is more easily identifiable as a novel. A young girl's complex and erotic journey into adult-

hood, *Soul Kiss,* in the author's words, is about "the ways in which children and parents eroticize each other, and the consequences of such behavior." Protagonist Mariah Santos, seven-years old when the book begins in the 1960s, finds herself removed from the home in Kansas where she has lived with her mother, Coral. Her aunts, Merleen and Faith, who live in Georgia, take her under their care and provide her with a stable and conservative upbringing. But Mariah is confused, not surprising given the tumult of her early years and her refusal to acknowledge that she was abandoned.

As she matures Mariah becomes headstrong, finds comfort in music and poetry, becomes involved with drugs, and is sexually curious and romantically drawn to women. A drifter at the age of fifteen, she seeks out her father, Matisse, whom she has never met. An artist living in Los Angeles, he is ill-equipped to take on the role of fatherhood and has fantasized for years about Mariah's mother, whom Mariah closely resembles. Tension is heightened by the fact that Mariah herself has only a dim understanding of the difference between appropriate and inappropriate relationships. Through Mariah's confused perspective, Youngblood creates a fabulistic narrative that subverts conventions of the coming-of-age novel. As in her other work, language is vital to *Soul Kiss,* not only for recreating the nuances of her characters' speech, but also as a source of power, which makes Mariah's attraction to poetry all the more important: writing poems in a notebook becomes a means for her to order her thoughts and feelings, her world, in fact, and through these exercises she gains power, an ability to express herself—her psychic wounds, her dreams and desires—as she grows from a wayward girl to a young woman surer of her identity and more confident in making her way in the world.

—Judson Knight

TITLE INDEX

The following index lists the titles of separately published works of fiction, poetry, plays, and selected nonfiction and other publications included in the "Publications" sections of the entries in *Contemporary Southern Writers*. The name in parentheses is meant to direct the user to the appropriate entry, where full publication information is given. The term "series" indicates a recurring distinctive word, phrase, or name, in the titles of the entrant's book.

Morning for Flamingoes (Burke), 1990
Morrow Anthology of Younger American (Smith, D.), 1985
Moss on the North Side (Wilkinson), 1966
Most Native of Sons (Williams, J.), 1970
Moth (Sallis), 1993
Mother and Two Daughters (Godwin), 1982
Mother Love (Dove), 1995
Mothersill and the Foxes (Williams, J.), 1975
Mountain (Lyon), 1983
Mountains of Gilead (Ford, J. H.), 1961
Mountains Won't Remember Us and Other Stories (Morgan, R.), 1992
Move Over, Mountain (Ehle), 1957
Moviegoer (Percy), 1961
Moving On (McMurtry), 1970
Mr. Bedford and the Muses (Godwin), 1983
Mr. Field's Daughter (Bausch), 1989
Mr. Smith (Smith, W. J.), 1980
Mr. Smith, and Other Nonsense (Smith, W. J.), 1968
Mr. Universe (Grimsley), 1988
Mrs. Flowers (Angelou), 1986
Mrs. Whaley and Her Charleston Garden (Baldwin), 1998
Muffin Fiend (Pinkwater), 1986
Mulching of America (Crews), 1995
Mule Trader (Ferris), 1998
Mulebone (Gates), 1991
Mules (Spencer), 1982
Mules and Men (Gates), 1990
Multi America (Reed, I.), 1997
Mumbo Jumbo (Reed, I.), 1972
Mummy; or, Ramses the Damned (Rice), 1989
Murder at Monticello; or, Old Sins (Brown, R. M.), 1994
Murder She Meowed (Brown, R. M.), 1997
Museum (Dove), 1983
Mush, a Dog from Space (Pinkwater), 1995
Music for a Broken Piano (Hall), 1983
Music of the Swamp (Nordan), 1991
Musician (Shelnutt), 1987
Mustian (Price, R.), 1983
My Amputations (Major), 1986
My Bones Being Wiser (Miller), 1963
My Brother Fine with Me (Clifton), 1975
My Daddy Was a Pistol, and I'm a Son of a Gun (Grizzard), 1986
My Dog Skip (Morris), 1995
My Drowning (Grimsley), 1997
My Ears Are Bent (Mitchell), 1938
My Friend Jacob (Clifton), 1980
My House (Giovanni), 1972
My Life and an Era (Franklin), 1997
My Little Book of Big and Little (Little Dimity, Big Gumbo, Big and Little) (Smith, W. J.), 1963
My Moby Dick (Humphrey), 1978 1979
My Painted House, My Friendly Chicken, and Me (Angelou), 1994
My People's Waltz
My Silk Purse and Yours (Garrett), 1992
My Tears Spoiled My Aim and Other Reflections on Southern Culture (Reed, J. S.), 1993
My Two Oxfords (Morris), 1992
My Vita, If You Will (McClanahan), 1998
Mystic Pizza (Uhry), 1988

"N" Is for Noose (Grafton), 1998
Nabokov (Stuart), 1978
Nabokov's Garden (Mason), 1976
Naked Came the Manatee (DuFresne), 1996
Naked Came the Manatee (Hiaasen), 1996
Naked in Garden Hills (Crews), 1969
Name for Evil (Lytle), 1947
Names and Faces of Heroes (Price, R.), 1963
Narcissus Dreaming (Stuart), 1990
Nashville 1864 (Jones, M.), 1997
Nathan Coulter (Berry), 1960
Nathanael West (Madden), 1973
National Experience (Woodward), 1963
Native Dancer (Cofer), 1981
Native Tongue (Hiaasen), 1991
Nativity (Berry), 1981
Nativity from the Apocryphal Book of James (Price, R.), 1974
Natural Child (Willingham), 1952
Natural Man (McClanahan), 1983
Natural Selection (Barthelme, F.), 1990
Necessary Lies (Daugharty), 1995
Necessities of Life (Rich), 1966
Ned Feldman, Space Pirate (Pinkwater), 1994
Negro American Biographies and Autobiographies (Franklin), 1969
Negro in Twentieth Century America (Franklin), 1967
Negro Mood, and Other Essays (Bennett), 1964
Neon Rain (Burke), 1987
Neon Vernacular (Komunyakaa), 1993
Net of Jewels (Gilchrist), 1992
Nettles (Adcock), 1983
Never a Dull Moment (Price, E.), 1956
Never Die (Hannah), 1991
Never-Ending (Hudgins), 1992
Never in a Hurry (Nye), 1996
New and Collected Poems (Reed, I.), 1988
New and Selected Poems (Justice), 1995
New and Selected Poems (Smith, W. J.), 1970
New and Selected Poems 1942-1987 (Eaton), 1987
New and Selected Stories 1959-1989 (Eaton), 1989
New Black Poetry (Major), 1969
New Moon Rising (Price, E.), 1969
New Music (Price, R.), 1990
New Orleans Beat (Smith, J.), 1994
New Orleans Mourning (Smith, J.), 1990
New Orleans of Possibilities (Madden), 1982
New Poems (Haines), 1990
New Regionalism (Wilson), 1998
New Writers of the South (East), 1987
New Writing from Virginia (Garrett), 1963
New Writing in South Carolina (Garrett), 1971
New York Days (Morris), 1993
News from the Glacier (Haines), 1982
News of the Nile (Dillard), 1971
News of the Spirit (Smith, L.), 1997
Next (Clifton), 1987
Next Step in the Dance (Gautreaux), 1998
Night Comes Softly (Giovanni), 1970
Night for Treason (Jakes), 1956
Night Hurdling (Dickey), 1983
Night in Question (Wolff), 1996
Night Light (Justice), 1967

NOTES ON
ADVISERS AND CONTRIBUTORS

ADCOCK, Fleur. Temporary assistant lecturer in classics, University of Otago, Dunedin, 1958; has held library posts at University of Otago, 1959-61, and Turnbull Library, Wellington, 1962; assistant librarian, Foreign and Commonwealth Office Library, London, 1963-79. Arts Council creative writing fellow, Charlotte Mason College of Education, Ambleside, Cumbria, 1977-78; Northern Arts fellow, universities of Newcastle upon Tyne and Durham, 1979-81; Eastern Arts fellow, University of East Anglia, Norwich, 1984. Editor, with Anthony Thwaite, *New Poetry 4,* 1978; *The Oxford Book of Contemporary New Zealand Poetry,* 1982; and *The Faber Book of Twentieth Century Women's Poetry,* 1987. Editor and translator of *Hugh Primas and the Archpoet,* 1994; translator of *The Virgin and the Nightingale: Medieval Latin Poems,* 1983; *Orient Express,* by Grete Tartler; and *Letters from Darkness,* by Daniela Crasnaru, 1994. **Essay:** Dabney Stuart.

AGUERO, Kathleen. Assistant professor, Pine Manor College, Chestnut Hill, Massachusetts. Author of *Thirsty Day,* 1977, and *The Real Weather,* 1987. Editor of *Critical Challenges in Contemporary American Poetry* (with Marie Harris), 1987; *Ear to the Ground: An Anthology of Contemporary American Poetry* (with Harris), 1989; and *Daily Fare: Essays from the Multicultural Experience,* 1993. **Essay:** Ellen Bryant Voigt.

ANDERSON, Daniel. Currently Tennessee Williams fellow in poetry and visiting instructor at the University of the South in Sewanee, Tennessee. Poems have appeared in the *New Republic, Southern Review, Poetry, Raritan,* and *Southwest Review,* among other places, and his first collection of poetry, *January Rain,* was published in 1997 by Story Line Press. **Essay:** Greg Williamson.

AUBERT, Alvin. See his own entry. **Essay:** Ernest J. Gaines.

BADGETT, Frances E. Received B.A. from Hollins College in 1993. Has worked in Germany for writer and filmmaker Doris Dorrie and produced film, *Olanda's Wish.* Lives in Carrboro, North Carolina and is working on her first novel. **Essays:** James Applewhite; Charles Frazier; Tim Gautreaux.

BAKERMAN, Jane S. Professor of English, Indiana State University, Terre Haute. Author of numerous critical essays, interviews, and reviews; adviser and contributor, *American Women Writers, Vols. 1-4,* and *Twentieth-Century Crime and Mystery Writers* 1991. Editor of *Adolescent Female Portraits in the American Novel 1961-1981* (with Mary Jean DeMarr), 1983, and *And Then There Were Nine: More Women of Mystery* 1984. **Essay:** Lisa Alther.

BAMBERGER, William C. Editor and publisher of Bamberger Books, Flint, Michigan. Author of *A Jealousy for Aesop,* 1988, and *William Eastlake: High Desert Interlocutor;* criticism in *Review of Contemporary Fiction;* and fiction in *CoEvolution, Ascent,* and other periodicals. **Essay:** David Madden.

BEAR, Perry. Freelance writer and editor for arts, history, and travel publications. Also author of upcoming *That Landscape Is Your Soul.* **Essays:** Guy Davenport; Margaret Ellen Gibson; Melissa Greene; Barbara Kingsolver; Romulus Linney; Larry McMurtry; Marion Montgomery; Willie Morris; Albert Murray.

BERRY, K. Wesley. Completing doctorate in English at University of Mississippi; teaches writing and literature and is working on an environmental justice initiative for the Association for the Study of Literature and Environment (ASLE). **Essay:** Wendell Berry.

BETTS, Doris. Adviser. See her own entry.

BOYD, Anne. Doctoral candidate in American studies at Purdue University; dissertation covers popular American women writers of the nineteenth century. **Essay:** Tim Robbins.

BRADFORD, M. E. Professor of English and American studies, University of Dallas; member of the editorial board of *Modern Age;* author of *Rumors of Mortality: An Introduction to Allen Tate,* 1967; *A Better Guide Than Reason,* 1980; *Generations of the Faithful Heart: On the Literature of the South,* 1982; *A Worthy Company: Brief Lives of the Framers of the Constitution,* 1982; *Remembering Who We Are: Observations of a Southern Conservative,* 1985; and *The Reactionary Imperative: Essays Literary and Political,* 1989. Contributor of articles to *Bear, Man, and God,* 1971; *Allen Tate and His Work,* 1971; and editor of *The Form Discovered: Essays on the Achievement of Andrew Lytle,* 1973. **Essay:** Madison Jones.

BRONSON, Tammy J. Graduate assistant at SUNY Potsdam, New York, working toward M.A. in English. Published the poem "To Mary" in the *American Poetry Annual.* **Essay:** Eugenia Price.

BUXTON, Jackie. Doctoral candidate, York University, Toronto. Author of an article about postmodernism in *English Studies in Canada.* **Essay:** Thomas Harris.

CARLSON, Thomas M. Adviser. Author of guest preface, and essayist. Professor of English at the University of the South, where he teaches literature of the American south. His essays on southern writers have appeared in many publications, including the *Sewanee Review, Southern Review, Southern Magazine, Contemporary Fiction Writers of the South,* and *Encyclopedia of Southern Culture.* **Essays:** Andrew Lytle; Padgett Powell; Mark Richard.

CASS, Michael M. Professor of English at Mercer University in Macon, Georgia, where he is head of the Lamar Lectures Committee. Has published poetry and reviews in *The Southern Review,* and other journals. **Essay:** Walker Percy.

CHRISTENSEN, Paul. Professor of modern literature, Texas A&M University. Author of several books of poetry, as well as *Charles Olson: Call Him Ishmael,* 1979. Editor of *In Love, In Sorrow: The Complete Correspondence of Charles Olson and Edward Dahlberg,* 1990, and *Minding the Underworld: Clayton Eshleman and Late Postmodernism,* 1991. **Essay:** T. R. Hummer.

CLARKSON, William E. Professor of English and American literature at the University of the South. Formerly chair of department of English; former associate director of the Sewanee Writers' Conference; currently director of Sewanee's Interdisciplinary Humanities Program. **Essay:** Wyatt Prunty.

COBB, Emma. Graduate of Texas A&M and University of Georgia; a freelance writer who has done extensive research on the role of women writers in the early 20th-century South. **Essays:** William Baldwin; Richard Bausch; Patricia Cornwell; Shirley Ann Grau; Randall Kenan; Bobbie Ann Mason.

COLLEY, Rae M. Carlton. Currently serves as visiting assistant professor of English at State University of West Georgia. Has published essays on Katherine Anne Porter, Caroline Hentz, and D. H. Lawrence. Received Ph.D. from Emory University, and dissertation examines representations of Native Americans by 19th-century Southern and Northern women writers. **Essay:** Judith Ortiz Cofer.

COMAN, Jennifer. Pursuing M.A. in English at Texas A&M University; focus on creative writing. Assistant editor for Creative Publishing Company, College Station, Texas. **Essay:** Stephen Coonts.

CORE, George. See entry. **Essay:** Walter Sullivan.

DAMASHEK, Richard. Member of the Communications Division, Richland Community College, Decatur, Illinois. Author of articles on Randall Jarrell and Ingmar Bergman; contributor of reviews to *World Literature Today,* and other periodicals. **Essay:** R. H. W. Dillard.

DeMAN, George. Independent scholar and writer based in Atlanta. His essays and reviews have appeared in *Agni Review, Boston Book Review,* and *Creative Loafing.* **Essay:** Allan Gurganus.

DILLARD, R. H. W. See his own entry. **Essay:** Henry Taylor.

DOYLE, Paul A. Professor of English, Nassau Community College, State University of New York, Garden City. Editor, *Evelyn Waugh Newsletter and Studies* and *Nassau Review.* Author of *Sean O'Faolain,* 1968; *Introduction to Paul Vincent Carroll,* 1971; *Liam O'Flaherty,* 1971; *Guide to Basic Information Sources in English Literature,* 1976; *Pearl S. Buck,* 1980; and *A Reader's Companion to the Novels and Short Stories of Evelyn Waugh,* 1988; also author of bibliographies of O'Flaherty and Waugh, and *A Concordance to the Collected Poems of James Joyce,* 1966. Co-author of *Early American Trains,* 1993. Editor of *Alexander Pope's Iliad: An Examination,* 1960. **Essay:** John Ed Bradley.

DuPREE, Don Keck. Visiting Centenary Professor of Liberal Arts, Centenary College of Louisiana. His study of Henry Vaughn, *Labor at the Furnace,* will be published in early 1999. **Essay:** Andrew Hudgins.

EDWARDS, Gayle. Freelance writer and consultant on Southern literature. Lives in South Carolina. **Essays:** James Dickey; Dori Sanders.

EVANS, Elizabeth. Has published books on Eudora Welty (1981), Thomas Wolfe (1984), Anne Tyler (1993), and Doris Betts (1997), among others. **Essay:** Anne Tyler.

FRIEDMAN, Norman. Professor emeritus, Queens College, City University of New York. Author of *Poetry: An Introduction to Its Form and Art* (with C.A. McLaughlin), 1961; *Logic, Rhetoric, Style* (with McLaughlin), 1963; *Form and Meaning in Fiction,* 1975; *The Magic Badge* (poems), 1985; and *The Intrusions of Love* (poems), 1992. **Essay:** Ruth Stone.

GARDNER, Barry W. Retired after 31 years in the Fire Service; currently a freelance writer and reviewer for various mystery-related periodicals; crime fiction essayist for St. James Press's annual librarian's reference book *What Do I Read Next?* **Essay:** James Sallis.

GARRETT, Greg. Associate professor of English, Baylor University. Received Ph.D. from Oklahoma State University. Winner of the William Faulkner Prize for fiction. Has published thirty short stories in books, magazines, and journals in the U.S., Canada, and New Zealand, as well as articles in the U.S., England, and Australia on narrative, film, popular culture, and African culture. **Essay:** T. R. Pearson.

GORDON, Lois. Professor of English and comparative literature, Fairleigh Dickinson University, Teaneck, New Jersey. Author of *Stratagems to Uncover Nakedness: The Dramas of Harold Pinter,* 1969; *Donald Barthelme,* 1981; *Robert Coover: The Universal Fictionmaking Process,* 1983; *American Chronicle: Six Decades in American Life 1920-1980,* 1987; *American Chronicle: Seven Decades in American Life, 1920-1989,* 1990; also contributor of numerous articles on contemporary authors and American culture. **Essay:** Adrienne Rich.

GRAMMAR, John. Received his degrees from Vanderbilt University and University of Virginia; teaches English and American literature at the University of the South. Author of *Pastoral and Politics in the Old South;* also author of essays and reviews. **Essays:** Tony Earley; Horton Foote; William Humphrey; Cormac McCarthy.

GRIFFITH, Benjamin. Past professor of English and chairman of department, Tift College, Forsyth, Georgia, and West Georgia College, Carrollton, Georgia. Author and editor of books on authors, writing, and grammar, as wells as criticism and plays. **Essays:** David Bottoms; Michael Lee West.

GUBBINS, Pat Borden. Feature writer for the *Charlotte Observer;* has known Sylvia Wilkinson, on whom she essayed, since their student days in Greensboro. **Essay:** Sylvia Wilkinson.

HAEDICKE, Janet V. Assistant professor, Northeast Louisiana University, Monroe, Louisiana. Author of articles about feminism and modern American drama in such journals as *Modern Drama, Journal of Dramatic Theory and Criticism,* and *Illinois English Bulletin.* **Essay:** Beth Henley.

HALLEY, Catherine D. Instructor, University of Iowa. Author of articles about lesbian humorists and poets to various journals. **Essay:** Minnie Bruce Pratt.

HART, Kristin. Writer and editor specializing in biographical and critical reference sources in literature. In-house project editor for *Reference Guide to Short Fiction* and *Contemporary Women Poets,* as well as contributor to various other works. **Essay:** Fannie Flagg.

HESS, Mary. Ph.D. student in American history, Michigan State University, East Lansing. Formerly on Cultural Heritage staff of the Turner House, East Lansing. **Essay:** Angela Davis.

HOLLADAY, Hillary. Assistant professor of English, University of Massachussetts, Lowell; B.A., University of Virginia. Received M.A. from College of William and Mary, and Ph.D. from University of North Carolina at Chapel Hill. **Essay:** Lucille Clifton. **Essay:** Lucille Clifton.

HOLM, Janis Butler. Associate professor of English, Ohio University, Athens. Author of articles on cultural theory and Tudor conduct books. Editor of *The Mirror of Modesty* by Giovanni Bruto, 1987. **Essay:** Gayl Jones.

HUBBARD, Jennifer. Received B.A. from Meredith College; M.A. from James Madison University. Member of the English faculty, Woodberry Forest School, Virginia. **Essays:** Betty Adcock; Claudia Emerson Andrews; Bailey White.

HUDSON, Theodore R. Editorial consultant and former graduate professor of English, Howard University, Washington, D.C. Author of *From LeRoi Jones to Amiri Baraka: The Literary Works*, 1973; contributor of numerous articles. **Essay:** Haki Madhubuti.

HUGHES, Elaine W. Professor of English at University of Montevallo, where she teaches contemporary American and British literature. Currently co-editing reference work on Alabama authors, *A Biographical Guide to Alabama Literature.* **Essays:** John Barth; Larry Brown; Vicki Covington.

JACKSON, Dot. Writer and editor living in South Carolina. **Essays:** Jerry Bledsoe; Will Campbell; George Core; George Garrett; Terry Kay; Charles Kuralt; James Still.

JEFFREY, David K. Adviser and essayist. Professor and head of the English Department, James Madison University; formerly co-editor of *Southern Humanities Review.* Editor of *Grit's Triumph: Essays on the Works of Harry Crews,* 1983; also author of numerous articles on Crews, Edgar Allan Poe, Tobias Smollett, Alexander Pope, Herman Melville, and contemporary mystery writers. **Essays:** James Lee Burke; Harry Crews; Ellen Douglas; John Dufresne; Carl Hiassen.

JOHNSON, Jeanine. Received B.A. from Haverford College and Ph.D. from Yale University. Currently visiting assistant professor of English at Wake Forest University. **Essays:** A. R. Ammons; Yusef Komunyakaa; Elizabeth Seydel Morgan; Margaret Walker.

JONES, Paul Christian. Doctoral candidate at University of Tennessee, Knoxville, finishing a dissertation on antebellum southern literature. Author of articles on William Gilmore Simms and Evelyn Scott. **Essay:** Ellen Gilchrist.

KIMBALL, Sue Laslie. Founded the Southern Writers' Symposium at Methodist College. Co-editor of books about Reynolds Price, Doris Betts, and Paul Green; editor of *Robert Penn Warren Newsletter.* **Essays:** Fred Chappell; John Ehle; Tim McLaurin.

KLINKOWITZ, Jerome. Professor of English, University of Northern Iowa, Cedar Falls. Author of *Kurt Vonnegut Jr.: A Descriptive Bibliography* (with Asa B. Pieratt, Jr.), 1974; *Literary Disruptions,* 1975 (revised 1980); *Donald Barthelme: A Comprehensive Bibliography* (with others), 1977; *The Life of Fiction,* 1977;

Kurt Vonnegut, 1980; *The Practice of Fiction in America,* 1980; *The American 1960s,* 1980; *Peter Handke and the Postmodern Transformation* (with James Knowlton), 1983; *The Self-Apparent Word,* 1984; *Literary Subversions,* 1985; *The New American Novel of Manners,* 1986; *Kurt Vonnegut: A Comprehensive Bibliography* (with Judie Huffman-Klinkowitz), 1987; *A Short Season and Other Stories* (as Jerry Klinkowitz), 1988; *Rosenberg, Barthes, Hassan: The Postmodern Habit of Thought,* 1988; *Their Finest Hours: Narratives of the RAF and Lufiwaffe in World War II,* 1989; *Slaughterhouse-Five: Reforming the Novel and the World,* 1990; *Listen, Gerry Mulligan: An Aural Narrative in Jazz,* 1991; *Donald Barthelme: An Exhibition,* 1991; *Structuring the Voice,* 1992; and *Basepaths* (as Jerry Klinkowitz), 1995. Editor of *Innovative Fiction,* 1972; *The Vonnegut Statement,* 1973; and *Writing under Fire: Stories of the Vietnam War,* 1978 (all with John Somers); *Vonnegut in America* (with Donald L. Lawler), 1977; *The Diaries of Willard Motley,* 1979; *Nathaniel Hawthorne,* 1984; and *Writing Baseball,* 1991. **Essay:** Clarence Major.

KNIGHT, Judson. Founded The Knight Agency, Atlanta; freelance editor, including *The Last Olympics* (by A. Russell Chandler, 1996). Writer, including contributions to *Don't Fence Me In: An Anecdotal Biography of Lewis Grizzard By Those Who Knew Him Best,* 1995. **Essays:** Jim Grimsley; Lewis Grizzard; Mary Hood; Ferrol Sams; Shay Youngblood.

KOHL, Judith C. Professor emeritus of English and humanities, Dutchess Community College, and visiting professor, Vassar College. Has taught contemporary drama, recent American literature, contemporary international literature, and autobiographies of marginalized Americans. Reviewer for library journals and contributor to many biographical encyclopedias. **Essays:** Pam Durban; John Hope Franklin; Nikki Giovanni; Alex Haley; Ishmael Reed; Anne Rivers Siddons; Christopher Tilghman; Alice Walker.

KOLER, Mel. Freelance arts, history, and travel writer, editor, consultant, and reviewer on Internet sites. **Essays:** Roy Blount; Turner Cassity; Pat Conroy; Henry Louis Gates, Jr.; John Grisham; Patricia Lear; William Jay Smith; Leon Stokesbury; Alfred Uhry.

KRAPF, Norbert. Professor of English and director of Poetry Center, C. W. Post College, Long Island University, Greenvale, New York. Author of several collections of poetry, including *A Dream of Plum Blossoms,* 1985; *East of New York City,* 1986; and *Somewhere in Southern Indiana: Poems of Midwest Origins,* 1993; also author of fiction, translations, and articles in journals. Editor of *Under Open Sky: Poets on William Cullen Bryant,* 1986; editor and translator of *Beneath the Cherry Sapling: Legends from Franconia,* 1988, and *Shadows on the Sundial: Selected Early Poems of Rainer Maria Rilke,* 1990. **Essay:** Robert Morgan.

LAMAR, Jay. Assistant director of the Auburn University Center for the Arts & Humanities. **Essays:** Nanci Kincaid; Eve Shellnut; Brad Watson.

LaPRADE, Candis. Assistant professor of English and director of women's studies at Longwood College. Has published essays in *Notable Black American Women, Notable Black American Men,* and *The Oxford Companion to African American Literature;* is presently working on a book-length manuscript that explores how the concept of "voice" has shaped African American women's writing. **Essay:** Rita Dove.

LASSETER, Janice Milner. Professor of English and chair of Department of English, Samford University, Birmingham, Alabama. **Essay:** Elizabeth Dewberry.

LEIGH, Chris. Freelance writer. Author of numerous articles about American literature, Henry James, and Robert Penn Warren. **Essay:** William Cobb.

LYSTAD, Mary. Former research sociologist, National Institute of Mental Health, Washington, D.C. Author of *A Child's World,* 1974; *From Dr. Mather to Dr. Seuss: 200 Years of American Books for Children,* 1980; and *At Home in America,* 1982; also author of several books for children. **Essay:** Clyde Edgerton.

MACK, Tom. Author of numerous articles and conference presentations on American literature, academic assessment, and pedagogical issues; chair of the Department of English, University of South Carolina, Aiken. Co-editor of the *Oswald Review,* a national undergraduate journal of criticism and research in the discipline of English. **Essay:** Percival Everett.

MARSHALL, Tod. Member of the English Department, University of Kansas, Topeka. Author of poetry and criticism in various journals, including *Denver Quarterly, The Georgia Review, High Plains Literary Review,* and *Southern Review.* **Essays:** R. H. W. Dillard; Dabney Stuart.

McDOWELL, Robert. Publisher and editor, Story Line Press, Brownsville, Oregon. Author of *Quiet Money* (poetry), 1987; *The Diviners* (poetry), 1995; and *Sound and Form in Modern Poetry* (with Harvey Gross), 1995. Editor of *Poetry after Modernism,* 1990. **Essay:** Mark Jarman.

McGOVERN, Martin. Poet and critic, with work represented in *Sewanee Review, Poetry Review*, and *North American Review.* **Essay:** Miller Williams.

McMECHAN, Ian. Freelance writer. Author of articles on contemporary crime fiction. **Essays:** Madison Smartt Bell; Tom Wolfe.

McNAUGHTON, Howard. Reader in English, University of Canterbury, Christchurch, New Zealand. Author of *Bruce Mason,* 1976; *New Zealand Drama,* 1981; and the section on the novel in *The Oxford History of New Zealand Literature.* Editor of *Contemporary New Zealand Plays,* 1976, and *James K. Baxter: Collected Plays,* 1982. **Essay:** Marsha Norman.

McVEIGH, Kev P. Coordinator, British Science Fiction Association. Editor, *Vector,* since 1989. **Essay:** Howard Waldrop.

MEEM, Deborah T. Professor of English and women's studies, University of Cincinnati, Ohio. Co-editor of *Variant.* Author of articles on lesbian studies, feminist pedagogy, 19th-century literature, and composition in various journals. **Essay:** Dorothy Allison.

MERCHANT, Preston. Graduated from the University of the South in 1990; received M.F.A from University of Florida in 1996. Lives in New York. Has published poems and reviews in *Antioch Review, New England Review, Sewanee Review,* and *Verse.* **Essays:** Diann Blakely; Frank Burroughs.

METRESS, Christopher. Received Ph.D. in English from Vanderbilt University. Teaches freshman English and American literature, with a concentration in literature of the South and an emphasis on the Civil Rights movement of the United States at Samford University. **Essays:** Harper Lee; Peter Taylor.

MIDDLETON, David. Writer and editor based in Texas; recently edited *Mind and Blood: The Collected Poems of John Finlay* and *Hermetic Light: Essays on the Gnostic Spirit in Modern Literature and Thought.* **Essay:** John Finlay.

MILLER, Tyrus. Assistant professor, Department of Comparative Literature and English, Yale University, New Haven, Connecticut. Author of *Earthworks* (poems); contributor of articles to *Textual Practice, Hambone,* and *Paideuma*; and essays on Mina Loy, C. Day Lewis, and Walter Benjamin in edited volumes. **Essay:** C. D. Wright.

MILLICHAP, Joseph R. Has taught at University of North Carolina—Greensboro, University of Montana, University of Tulsa, and Western Kentucky University, where he was head of the department from 1984-94. Research interests, which include Southern Renaissance, railroads, and American literature, have been reflected in publications that include four books, a monograph, and over fifty articles. Recent project is a cultural reading of railroads in American literature. **Essays:** Ralph Ellison; Dave Smith.

MIOLA, Robert. Professor of English, Loyola College, Baltimore. **Essay:** Charles Edward Eaton.

MITCHELL, Jason P. Graduate of University of Montevallo and University of Alabama; currently doctoral candidate at University of Mississippi. **Essays:** Cleanth Brooks; William R. Ferris; Winston Groom; Barry Hannah; Molly Ivins; Florence King; John Reed.

MOSBY, Charmaine Allmon. Professor and undergraduate advisor at Western Kentucky University. B.A. from David Lipscomb University in Nashville, Tennessee; M.A. from Tulane University in New Orleans, Lousiana; Ph.D. in English from University of North Carolina at Chapel Hill. Teaching specialties are American literature with a Southern literature emphasis and intermediate composition. **Essays:** Tina McElroy Ansa; Sallie Bingham; Jesse Hill Ford; Sharyn McCrumb.

MULLIGAN, Elizabeth. Freelance writer. M.A. in teaching from Oakland University. **Essay:** Sue Grafton.

NOBLE, Donald R. Adviser. Professor of English at University of Alabama. Host and producer of television documentaries. Writer; editor, including *The Rising South: Changes and Issues, Vol. 1,* 1976.

NOSTRANDT, Jeanne R. Professor of English, James Madison University; earned M.Ed. in English from University of North

Carolina at Greensboro and Ph.D. from University of North Carolina at Chapel Hill. **Essays:** Doris Betts; Kaye Gibbons; Gail Godwin; William Hoffman; Reynolds Price; Louis D. Rubin; Jr.; Lee Smith; Max Steele; William Styron; Eudora Welty.

PALM, Kristin. Poet, editor, and journalist living in Michigan. **Essays:** Linda Pastan; Sonia Sanchez.

PARINI, Jay. Poet and novelist; professor of English at Middlebury College. **Essay:** Sam Pickering.

PARTINGTON, Leigh Tillman. Essay: Rick Bass.

PATTERSON, Eric. Freelance writer in Colorado; contributor to numerous magazines and books, including *Contemporary Popular Writers.* **Essays:** Lerone Bennett, Jr.; Charles East; Connie May Fowler; Hunter S. Thompson.

PETRUSSO, Annette. Graduate of University of Michigan and University of Texas; currently works as a freelance writer specializing in the areas of literature and biography. **Essays:** Alice Adams; Dave Barry; Frederick Barthelme; Stephen Barthelme; Rita Mae Brown; Moira Crone; Ossie Davis; John Jakes; Jayne Anne Phillips.

PHIPPS, Frank T. Former chairman, Department of English, University of Akron. **Essay:** William Mitchell.

RAVENEL, Shannon. Adviser. Series editor of the annual *Best American Short Stories* and *Best Short Stories from the South;* born and raised in the Carolinas, lives and works in Chapel Hill, North Carolina, where she serves as editorial director, Algonquin Books.

REILLY, John M. Professor of English, State University of New York, Albany. Author of many articles on Afro-American literature, popular crime writing, and social fiction; also author of bibliographical essays in *Black American Writers* and *American Literary Scholarship.* Editor of *Richard Wright: The Critical Reception,* 1978 and the reference book *Twentieth-Century Crime and Mystery Writers,* 1980 (2nd edition 1985). **Essay:** Alvin Aubert.

REISMAN, Rosemary M. Canfield. Former professor and chairperson of English Department, Troy State University, Alabama; currently adjunct professor at Charleston Southern University. Coauthor of *Contemporary Southern Women Fiction Writers,* 1994, and *Contemporary Southern Men Fiction Writers,* 1998, both published by Scarecrow Press. **Essays:** Shelia Bosworth; Linda Beatrice Brown; Alfred Corn; Janice Daugherty; Shelby Hearon; Beverly Lowry; Helen Norris; David Payne; Margaret Skinner; Julie Smith; Elizabeth Spencer; Christine Wiltz.

ROPER, John Herbert. Has taught at St. Andrews Presbyterian College, Laurinburg, North Carolina, University of North Carolina at Chapel Hill, and Emory College; served as general editor, "Minds of the New South" series, University of Virginia Press; publications include *C. Vann Woodward, Southerner,* 1987; editor of *C. Vann Woodward: A Southern Historian and His Critics,* 1997. **Essay:** C. Vann Woodward.

RUPPERSBURG, Hugh. Associate dean of Arts and Sciences and professor of English at University of Georgia. Author of *Voice*

and Eye in Faulkner's Fiction, 1983; *Robert Penn Warren and the American Imagination,* 1990; and *Reading Faulkner: Light in August,* 1994; edited two collections of Georgia writing—*Georgia Voices: Fiction,* 1992, and *Georgia Voices: Non-Fiction,* 1994, and is at work on a third collection of work by Georgia poets and a collection of critical essays about Don DeLillo. **Essays:** Jim Kilgo; James Wilcox.

SCHAFFER, William J. Professor of English, Berea College, Kentucky. Criticism represented in *Critique* and *Satire Newsletter.* Editor, *The William Nelson Reader.* **Essay:** James Allan McPherson.

SOLOMON, Andy. Professor of English, University of Tampa; fiction editor of *The Tampa Review;* regular book critic for *New York Times, Washington Post, Chicago Tribune, Boston Globe, Los Angeles Times, San Francisco Chronicle, Miami Herald,* and *St. Petersburg Times;* book commentator and essayist on National Public Radio. Author of fiction, poetry, and articles in *Atlantic, Boulevard,* and *New Orleans Review.* **Essay:** Madison Smartt Bell.

STERN, Carol Simpson. Professor and chairman of Department of Performance Studies, Northwestern University, Evanston, Illinois; member of advisory board, *Literature in Performance;* research consultant, *English Literature in Transition.* Author of *Text and Contexts* (with Bruce Henderson), 1991; contributor of articles and theatre and book reviews to *Victorian Studies* and Chicago *Sun-Times.* **Essay:** Elizabeth Hardwick.

STILES, Keith. Social research associate in Office of University Planning at Western Carolina University; B.A. in English literature as well as B.S.B.A. and M.B.A. Currently pursuing an M.A. in literature. **Essay:** George Ella Lyon.

SWANN, Christopher C. Candidate for M.A. in English, with an emphasis in creative writing, at University of Missouri, Columbia. Awarded Jean Amory Wornom Award for Distinguished Critical Writing and George A. Mahan Award for Creative Writing. Taught high school English for three years in the Atlanta public school system. Short fiction has appeared in the *Crescent Review.* **Essay:** Robert Fulghum.

TODD, David Y. Practiced law in Boston before earning M.F.A. in writing from University of Florida, where his fiction won a Henfield Transatlantic Review Award. Teaches at Florida State University. Contributor to *Boston Sunday Globe, Christian Science Monitor, New Woman, Sewanee Review, Witness, Yale Review,* and other periodicals. **Essays:** James Baker Hall; Ed McClanahan; Lewis Nordan; Chris Offutt.

VANNATTA, Dennis. Teaches English at University of Arkansas, Little Rock. Has published books on Nathanael West, H. E. Bates, Tennessee Williams, and the contemporary English short story as well as two collections of short stories, *This Time, This Place,* 1991, and *Prayers for the Dead,* 1994. **Essay:** David Jauss.

VINH, Alphonse. Educated at Yale College, Boston University, and Simmons College. Essayist, poet, short-story writer, and religious philosopher who has published in numerous journals, including *Crisis Magazine, Southern Quarterly Review, Choice,*

Southern Cultures, and *South Carolina Review.* Editor of *Cleanth Brooks and Allen Tate: The Collected Letters 1933-1976,* published in 1998 by University of Missouri Press. **Essays:** James Seay; Joan Williams.

WALKER, Bruce. Freelance writer and editor. **Essays:** Jack Butler; Mark Childress; John Haines; Shelby Foote; Donald Justice; Peter Klappert; Vassar Miller; Naomi Shahib Nye; Richard Tillinghast; Calder Willingham.

WALKER, Elinor Ann. Ph.D. in English from University of North Carolina at Chapel Hill; taught at the University of the South, Rockford College, and University of North Carolina. Her book on Richard Ford, part of United States Authors Series, is due from Twayne Publishers in 1999. **Essays:** Richard Ford; Josephine Humphreys; Jill McCorkle.

WALLACE, Michelle L. Currently pursuing her doctorate in English at Emory University, and is specializing in twentieth century Southern literature and popular culture. **Essays:** Maya Angelou; Anne Rice.

WARNER, Mary. Assistant professor of English and director of English Education, Western Carolina University, Cullowhee, North Carolina. **Essay:** Mildred Taylor.

WATKINS, Virginia. Feelance writer and editor living in Austin, Texas. Author of numerous articles about place and women and children in Southern fiction. After studying under George Longest, focus was retrained on race and gender association in contemporary Southern writing. **Essays:** Robert Olen Butler; Andre Dubus; Allison Hagy; Edward P. Jones; Sheri Reynolds.

WILOCH, Denise. Freelance writer and editor. **Essay:** Gloria Anzaldua.

WILSON, J. J. Professor of English, Sonoma State University, Rohnert Park, California. Co-editor, *Virginia Woolf Miscellany*; author of numerous articles on Woolf. Co-author, with Karen Peterson, of *Women Artists: Recognition and Reappraisal,* 1976. **Essay:** Marilou Awiatka.

WOLFE, Gary K. Professor of humanities, Roosevelt University, Chicago. Author of *The Known and the Unknown: The Iconography of Science Fiction,* 1979; *Elements of Research,* 1979; *David Lindsay,* 1982; *Critical Terms for Science Fiction and Fantasy,* 1986; contributor of articles and reviews for books and periodicals. Pilgrim Award recipient, 1987. **Essays:** Gregory Benford; Daniel Pinkwater.

WOODELL, Harold. Professor of English at Clemson University where he teaches southern literature. Publications include *The Shattered Dream: A Southern Bride at the Turn of the Century* and *All the King's Men: The Search for a Usable Past.* **Essays:** William Price Fox, Jr.; Dale Ray Phillips.

WOODSON, Jon. Associate professor of English, Howard University. Contributor to *African American Review, The Oxford Companion to Women's Literature, Conversations and Essays on Contemporary African American Poetry.* **Essay:** Patricia Spears Jones.

YOUNG, Dawn Gilchrist. Earned an M.A. from Columbia University, an M.F.A. from Warren Wilson College, and teaches at Swain County High School. **Essay:** Rodney Jones.